Creative Activities for Young Children

Creative Activities for Young Children

TENTH EDITION

MARY MAYESKY, PH.D.

WADSWORTH
CENGAGE Learning™

Australia • Brazil • Japan • Korea • Mexico • Singapore • Spain • United Kingdom • United States

Creative Activities for Young Children, Tenth Edition
Mary Mayesky

Executive Editor: Linda Schreiber-Ganster

Acquisitions Editor: Mark Kerr

Development Editor: Lisa Kalner Williams

Assistant Editor: Caitlin Cox

Marketing Manager: Kara Kindstrom Parsons

Marketing Communications Manager: Martha Pfeiffer

Content Project Management: PreMediaGlobal

Art Director: Maria Epes

Senior Print Buyer: Mary Beth Hennebury

Rights Acquisitions Specialist: Don Schlotman

Production House/Compositor: PreMediaGlobal

Cover Image: © Casper Holroyd

Cover Designer: Natalie Hill

International Edition:

ISBN-13: 978-1-111-52097-7

ISBN-10: 1-111-52097-6

Cengage Learning International Offices

Asia
www.cengageasia.com
tel: (65) 6410 1200

Australia/New Zealand
www.cengage.com.au
tel: (61) 3 9685 4111

Brazil
www.cengage.com.br
tel: (55) 11 3665 9900

India
www.cengage.co.in
tel: (91) 11 4364 1111

Latin America
www.cengage.com.mx
tel: (52) 55 1500 6000

UK/Europe/Middle East/Africa
www.cengage.co.uk
tel: (44) 0 1264 332 424

Represented in Canada by Nelson Education, Ltd.
tel: (416) 752 9100 / (800) 668 0671
www.nelson.com

Cengage Learning is a leading provider of customized learning solutions with office locations around the globe, including Singapore, the United Kingdom, Australia, Mexico, Brazil, and Japan. Locate your local office at: **www.cengage.com/global**

For product information: **www.cengage.com/international**
Visit your local office: **www.cengage.com/global**
Visit our corporate website: **www.cengage.com**

AVAILABILITY OF RESOURCES MAY DIFFER BY REGION. Check with your local Cengage Learning representative for details.

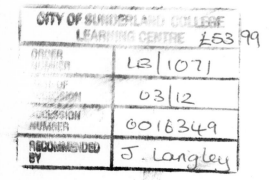
Printed in the United States of America
1 2 3 4 5 6 7 15 14 13 12 11 10

DEDICATION

To my granddaughter, Betty Ann, to whom I pass on the torch—

May the joy of learning you have found in young
children's eyes guide you as you begin your journey
in the early childhood profession.

Contents

Section 3

Section 4

Preface

The book you are holding in your hands is special for many reasons. As an author, it is special to me because it is the tenth edition of my text—an accomplishment that is rare in today's ever-changing publishing world—the same author for 10 editions! It is the tenth time that I—as a child developmentalist and nonart major—share with my readers my firm belief (and proof) that you don't have to be an artist to be creative. But one of the most outstanding reasons this book is special for me is that my granddaughter, Betty Ann, who was in photos in the fourth edition as a kindergarten child, is in this edition an early childhood student teacher! This makes my mission even more personal than ever in this edition.

I wish for her what I wish for you: that you keep children at the center of your practice. I hope the joy of working with young children that brought you to this profession will continue to sustain you through all the ups and downs the world throws your way. I sincerely hope that in all the trends that come and go, you rely on your own professional judgment to guide you in all your work with young children. Let this knowledge be your "inner teacher" to guide your journey through the latest challenge to our profession.

While working on these many editions, I have learned some important facts about early childhood professionals, and among them are these: We in the profession have lasted through the standards "invasion" and are making sense of it all to the benefit of young children. We are learning and finding developmentally appropriate uses for technology in our classrooms. We are using technology to continue our own professional education, connecting early childhood teachers around the world to the betterment of our profession. We are facing serious budget shortfalls, but this is not a new challenge, since early childhood teachers have long known how to stretch the dollar. And as I traveled with my photographer to five different Wake County public schools in Raleigh, North Carolina, to shoot photographs for this text, I observed firsthand all of these facts in the early childhood classrooms I visited. After all of these visits, I am happy to say dedication to the education of our youngest citizens is alive and well.

It is my sincere hope for Betty Ann and for each of my readers that this tenth edition assists you in your teaching journey in today's challenging world...that you find in these pages concrete, usable ideas to help you in your work with young children.

As in all of the previous nine editions, this edition is designed for the person who is dedicated to helping children reach their full potential. It is written for people who want to know more about creativity, creative children, creative teaching, and creative curriculum and activities. It has always been my intent to provide my readers in the pages of this text sound developmental theory, yet I have always tried to present practical application of these theories that you can use in actual classroom settings.

I have updated and revised this tenth edition to reflect an ever-increasing emphasis on creativity in all curriculum areas. In our world of rapidly changing technology, it is ever more crucial to encourage and cherish the creativity inherent in each and every child.

It is not enough for our students to know how to use technology. It is not enough for them to know facts or how to test well. In a world where the only constant appears to be change, young children need to know how to ask questions and to search for their own answers. They need to know how to look at things in many different ways and how to create their own sense of beauty and meaning in life.

New Features

Some specific features new to the tenth edition follow.

- New *Think About It* and *This One's for You* features in each chapter
- New lists of Additional Readings at the end of each chapter
- New and updated Helpful Web Sites in each chapter in addition to updated Web Sites referenced in the Online Companion
- New and updated Software for Children references in each chapter and updated information on software companies with contact information in Appendix H

- New activities for preschool, kindergarten to grade 3, and grades 4 to 5 in every chapter and more infant and toddler information and activities throughout.
- New activities for specific learning styles in chapter-end activities where applicable
- Additional information on right and left brain learning and brain research
- Expanded discussion on multiple intelligences
- New information on kid culture and its application in the early childhood program
- Expanded section on aesthetics as an art movement, as well as added discussion on art elements and principles of design, including an Art Talk Summary
- Updated information on standards and testing, information on the new edition of Developmentally Appropriate Curriculum (DAP), and a chart comparing previous DAP editions and the 2009 version
- Addition of up-to-date information on play research, group games and information on examples of play at different ages
- Expanded information on the use of technology in the early childhood program, including information on Web 2.0, activities using interactive white (smart) boards, and personal learning networks
- Additional information on human brain development and expanded discussion on Piaget's theories of mental development
- Discussion on Erickson's psychosocial theory of development and on Carl Rogers' psychosocially safe environment
- Information on state and national art standards, discussion on "creative fakes," models, and talking with children about their art
- Expanded discussion on musical concepts and the elements of music
- Additional information on digital storytelling, reading to children, working with parents on children's language arts development skills, and the use of computers in language arts
- Discussion on the National Early Literary Project and digital storytelling
- Information on introducing basic concepts of government and voting to young children
- Discussion on artists who made social commentaries and new section on social studies and art
- Added information on hazards on the playground

Creative Activities for Young Children is written for anyone who is interested in children, but because it is written especially for busy people who work with children in early childhood settings, the following points are emphasized.

- The approach to creativity is a practical one. A wide variety of activities is included in each chapter. All activities have been classroom tested.
- Information on why activities should be carried out as well as how to carry them out is presented. Theory is provided where it is needed.
- Learning activities are included to help readers experience their own creativity.
- References for additional reading are given at the end of each chapter so students can explore each subject in more depth as desired.
- Each chapter begins with carefully worded, easy-to-understand objectives and ends with a summary. Review questions are in each chapter where appropriate.
- Each section starts with reflective questions linking together the chapters in the section.

Part 1 presents a general discussion of various child development theories. Included in Part 1 are chapters on creativity, aesthetic experiences, and social–emotional and physical–mental growth, as reflected in art development theories. Part 1 sets an appropriate theoretical stage for application of these theories in specific curriculum areas presented in Part 2.

Part 2 covers the early childhood curriculum in Section 5 and Section 6. Section 5 covers creativity in curriculum areas. Section 6 addresses creativity in the multicultural, antibias curriculum.

The author and Delmar affirm that the Web site URLs referenced herein were accurate at the time of printing. However, because of the fluid nature of the Internet, we cannot guarantee their accuracy for the life of the edition.

Acknowledgments

The author gratefully acknowledges the contributions of the many people who helped bring this tenth edition into existence: Casper Holroyd for his understanding and patience with yet another edition taking over our lives, as well as for the cover photo and the many wonderful photos of children; my daughter, Claire M. Holroyd, who gave constant encouragement and the "good for you's" that helped me move along in the process; my stepdaughter, Jane H. Holding, who was always interested in a project that seemed endless to everyone; Gretchen M. Shaffer, director, and the children and staff at Highland Children's Center; Dr. Marcia Alford, principal, Dawn Wade, visual art teacher, and the children at Lacy Elementary School, Raleigh, NC; Dr. Maureen A. Hartford, past president of Meredith College; Laura Davidson, Dean of Library Information Services, and Gerry Sargent, administrative assistant to the Dean of Library Information Services, Meredith College; Gary W. Baird, principal, Lisa Coster, teacher and the children in Mrs. Coster's kindergarten class at Lead Mine Elementary School, Raleigh, NC; Gregory D. Ford, principal, and the teachers, staff, and children at Hilburn Elementary School, Raleigh, NC; and Jacqueline Jordan, principal, and the teachers and staff at Underwood Gifted and Talented Elementary School, Raleigh, NC.

Sincere thanks to my developmental and project editors from for their constant assistance and support during the process of publication.

Special thanks to Jane Barrett, my superb yoga instructor, who twice a week listened patiently when I needed to share my latest writing challenges and, more importantly, gave me in yoga the release and separation from writing that helped me survive another edition.

A Note of Caution

In all of the activity suggestions in this text, knowledge of the child's developmental level is the most basic guideline for use of any activity. However, in the interest of preventing any undue accidents and spread of infections, a few extra cautions follow.

An important note of caution is necessary regarding the use of egg cartons in any and all activities with young children. Because of the risk of the spread of salmonella, it is important that all egg cartons be washed with warm, soapy water and allowed to dry completely before use. For a similar reason, the same washing and drying procedure is required before using all Styrofoam trays that have held meat, fish, or poultry. Another important note is regarding the use of balloons with children under the age of three. Use of balloons with this age group is not recommended due to the danger of accidental aspiration. And finally, the use of any small objects that could fit into a child's mouth must be avoided for children under the age of three.

Instructor's Manual With Test Bank

A key supplement to the tenth edition of *Creative Activities for Young Children* is the Instructor's Manual. The Instructor's Manual includes answers to review questions, and discussion topics for every chapter of the text. In an effort to make teaching of the ideas in the text even more exciting and interesting for

the student, the Instructor's Manual also includes Observation Sheets, Student Activity Sheets, Small-Group Activity Sheets, and masters for overhead transparencies or projection. These additional teaching aids are provided for each chapter of the text and are tied into the main ideas of the chapter. In addition to these teaching aids, each chapter of the Instructor's Manual provides many supplemental teaching ideas to expand on and enrich teaching of each unit. These teaching strategies range from the traditional (such as activities using two- and three-dimensional media) to the innovative (activities such as an outdoor scavenger hunt for textures).

Instructor's PowerLecture CD-ROM

The new PowerLecture component provides instructors with all the tools they need in one convenient CD-ROM. Instructors will find that this resource provides them with a turnkey solution to help them teach by making available PowerPoint® slides for each chapter, a Computerized Test Bank, and an electronic version of the Instructor's Manual.

Professional Enhancement Booklet

The Professional Enhancement booklet for students, which is part of Delmar Cengage Learning's Early Childhood Education Professional Enhancement series, focuses on key topics of interest to future early childhood teachers and caregivers. Topics of interest include the No Child Left Behind Act and its impact on the creative arts; reflective practices; differentiated instruction; special topics in language arts and additional language arts activities; special topics in mathematics, social studies, and nutrition; information on appropriate art centers for different ages of children with examples of guidelines for use; and ideas for storing and maintaining art materials and equipment. Students will keep this informational supplement and use it for years to come in their early childhood practices.

CourseMate

The CourseMate Web site to accompany the tenth edition of *Creative Activities for Young Children* is your link to early childhood education on the Internet. The CourseMate contains many features to enhance and enrich your understanding of creative activities for the young child.

- Critical Thinking Forum—In this section, you have the opportunity to respond to "This One's for You" and "Think About It" concepts. Various creative activity scenarios and thought-provoking questions test your understanding of the text's content. You can share your ideas with classmates and interact informally with your instructor online.
- Web Activities—These activities direct you to a Web site(s) and allow you to conduct further research and apply content related to creative activities for young children.
- Web Links—For each chapter, a summarized list of Web links is provided for your reference.
- Sample Quizzes—Questions are provided online to test your knowledge of the material presented.
- Online Early Education Survey—This survey gives you the opportunity to respond to what features you like and what features you want to see improved on the Online Companion.
- Observation Sheets—These may be printed out and used for further observation of specific concepts in actual classroom settings.
- PowerPoint Presentations—These presentations cover the main points of each chapter and can serve as either an introduction to each chapter or a good tool for reviewing the chapter.

The CourseMate icon appears at the end of each chapter to prompt you to go online and take advantage of the many features provided. You can find the CourseMate at *www.cengage.com/login*.

WebTutor

Jumpstart your course with customizable, text-specific content for use within your Course Management System. Whether you want to Web-enable your class or put an entire course online, WebTutor™ delivers. WebTutor™ offers a wide array of resources including videos, quizzes, Web links, and more. Visit http://webtutor.cengage.com to learn more.

Reviewers

The author and editors at Cengage Learning wish to thank the following reviewers for their time, effort, and thoughtful contributions, which helped to shape the final text.

Jane Andrews, University of Missouri Kansas City
Cynthia Benton, SUNY College at Cortland
Pamela Bower-Basso, Rhode Island School of Design
Allen Caucutt, University of Wisconsin-Milwaukee
Irene Cook, California State University Bakersfield
Claude Endfield, Northland Pioneer College
John Funk, University of Utah
Leah Korth, Eastern Michigan University
Anita Kumar, Passaic County Community College

About the Author

Mary Mayesky, Ph.D., author of this tenth edition, is a certified preschool, elementary, and secondary teacher. She is a former professor in the Program in Education at Duke University, former director of the Early Childhood Certification Program, and supervisor of student teachers. She has served as assistant director for programs in the Office of Day Services, Department of Human Resources, State of North Carolina. She is also the former principal of the Mary E. Phillips Magnet School in Raleigh, North Carolina, the first licensed extended day magnet in the Southeast. She has served several terms on the North Carolina Day Care Commission and on the Wake County School Board.

Dr. Mayesky has worked in Head Start, child care, kindergarten, and YWCA early childhood programs and has taught kindergarten through grade 8 in the public schools. She has written extensively for professional journals and for general-circulation magazines in the areas of child development and curriculum design. She is a member of Phi Beta Kappa and was named Woman of the Year in Education by the North Carolina Academy of the YWCA. Her other honors include being named Outstanding Young Educator by the Duke University Research Council, receiving the American Association of School Administrators Research Award, and being nominated for the Duke University Alumni Distinguished Undergraduate Teaching Award. Her first nontextbook work, *Remembering Mrs. O'Donald: Growing, Learning, and Teaching*, a collection of personal stories about her educational experiences, has recently been published.

A marathon runner, Dr. Mayesky has completed 19 marathons and received many awards in road races and senior games. She is an active member of the Raleigh Host Lions Club, having served as its first woman president. Her passions are sewing, biking, running, reading on the radio for the blind, and yoga.

Part 1 presents a general discussion of various theories relating to child development. Beginning with the concept of creativity, theories, techniques, and basic program components and their relationship to the growth of creativity in young children are presented. Within this theoretical context of creativity, Part 1 provides basic information on planning and implementing creative activities for young children. Also included is a section on art and how it is related to the physical, mental, and social–emotional development of young children.

Practical information is included on how to set up an early childhood art program that encourages creativity, with chapters for both two- and three-dimensional activities. The concept of play and its relationship to a child's overall development as well as development of creativity in play is covered in Section 1. Technology and its place in the early childhood program within the context of creativity is also covered in Part 1.

At the end of each chapter in Part 1 are many suggested activities designed to reinforce the concepts covered. A wide variety of field-tested activities for young children up to grade 5 are also included in each chapter.

The review questions and references for further reading provided at the end of each chapter further reinforce the main concepts. Also included at the end of each chapter are suggestions for appropriate software to use with children as well as a listing of websites related to the chapter's topic. In essence, Part 1 sets the theoretical stage for application of these theories in the more specific subject and classroom areas presented in Part 2.

PART 1

Theories Relating to Child Development

SECTION 1
Fostering Creativity and Aesthetics in Young Children

SECTION 2
Planning and Implementing Creative Activities

SECTION 3
Art and the Development of the Young Child

SECTION 4
The Early Childhood Art Program

Fostering Creativity and Aesthetics in Young Children

REFLECTIVE QUESTIONS

After studying this section, you should be able to answer the following questions.

1. How could I change my current teaching strategies in order to better encourage the development of creativity in young children?

2. How do I encourage the development of a child's aesthetic sense in my classroom environment, lessons, and activities?

3. Are my teaching strategies based on the principles of creative development? How many of them encourage convergent thinking? How many encourage divergent thinking?

4. What thinking styles do my children have? Do I adapt my teaching to fit these individual differences?

5. Using the information about creativity and aesthetics, how will I now question my students about concepts and ideas?

6. As I plan classroom methods and management systems, am I keeping in mind the importance of cultivating creativity and the aesthetic sense in children?

7. What am I doing to help young children recognize their own uniqueness, creativity, and aesthetic sense?

8. What instructional strategies are best for the development of creativity and the aesthetic sense in young children?

9. What role will creativity have in my planning of curriculum for young children?

10. How will I talk with young children about their art and what they feel is beautiful?

11. How will I share with parents the importance of nurturing a child's creativity and sense of beauty?

12. How have I changed as a result of my learning about creativity and aesthetics?

The Concept of Creativity

OBJECTIVES

After studying this chapter, you should be able to:

1. Define creativity. Compare and contrast the kinds of creativity.

2. List three ways in which children benefit from an environment in which creativity is encouraged using three specific examples.

3. Discuss at least two ways teachers benefit from encouraging creativity in the classroom and possible positive outcomes for each.

4. Name five things a teacher can do to help children develop a willingness to express creativity. Rank these in order of importance and give an explanation for your ranking.

5. List several characteristics of creative children including positive and negative aspects of each characteristic.

Take a few minutes to watch a four-year-old child in action. At one moment he is building a tower out of blocks. Suddenly he spots one of his friends playing with a homemade finger puppet. He wants to make one, too. A bit later he is playing with a guinea pig, stroking its fur and tickling its chin. Next, he is placing long, wide strokes of color on a piece of paper and getting spots of paint on everything in sight.

What is this? Now he is at the sand table building a sand castle with a high sand tower that keeps falling over. He seems to have discovered something. It is easier to build a tower out of blocks than out of sand; so he is back building with wooden blocks. It looks as though he is back where he started, except that the new block tower does not look anything like the one he started earlier.

It is exciting to watch active young children studying the world around them. A couple of things become clear almost immediately. First of all, children are full of curiosity. They seem to enjoy investigating and finding out things. Second, they seem quite capable of doing this successfully. They are very creative in finding answers to problems that arise from their curiosity. A child can figure out how to reach a needed block that somehow got thrown behind the piano. Another child selects interesting materials in order to make a finger puppet that is different from all the others. Young children seem to have a natural ability to come up with creative answers, creative approaches, and creative uses of materials.

People who work with young children need to understand creativity and have the skills to help and encourage children to express their creative natures. They must realize the importance of creativity for both children and teachers. They need to be able to identify creativity in children and be able to help them develop a willingness to express this creativity.

What Is Creativity?

Perhaps the most important thing to realize about creativity is that everyone possesses a certain amount of it. Some people are a little more creative, and some a little less. No one is totally lacking in creativity.

Preschoolers often ask parents 100 questions in a single day (Hoefferth, 1998). This behavior reflects the enormous power curiosity has on children's creativity and motivation to learn in early childhood (Strom & Strom, 2002; Taylor, 2000). Young children tend to be highly open, curious, and creative. Unfortunately, many adults want children to conform. As outside pressures from adults grow, the children's environment closes in on them. They find it less and less rewarding to express interest in things, to be curious, and to be creative in investigating their world. To avoid this, it is important to know ways of encouraging a child's creativity. To begin with, one should understand the meaning of the term *creativity*.

There are many meanings for this word.

- A definition by one writer on the subject, May (1975, p. 39), describes creativity as the "process of bringing something new into being."
- Paul Torrance (1970), a pioneer in the study of the creative process, suggests that creativity is the ability to produce something novel, something with the stamp of uniqueness upon it.
- More recently, creativity has been defined as a combination of abilities, skills, motivations, and attitudes (Honig, 2006).

Much like athletic ability, creativity is really a combination of many different abilities. It is more useful to think of many types of creativities (Ripple, 1999, p. 629). There are many different interpretations of the term *creativity*. One researcher separates the types of creativity:

- **"Capital C" creativity** involves bringing into existence something genuinely new that receives social validation enough to be added to the culture. An example of Capital C creativity is the invention of the light bulb.
- **"Small c" creativity** involves ideas or products that are new to the person, but only to the person. An example of small c creativity is a child's new use of blending finger-paint colors (Ripple, 1999).

The following definition may help the student understand the concept of creativity better. Creativity is a way of thinking and acting or making something that is original for the individual and valued by that person or others. A person does not have to be the first one in the world to produce something in order for it to be considered a creative act. Creativity can be found anywhere, at home or school as easily as in art or science. As Paul Torrance, considered "the father of modern creativity," puts it, "Creativity is an infinite phenomenon. A person can be creative in an endless number of ways" (1971).

The Creative Process

When someone is creating something, there are usually two parts to that person's activity. The first part has to do with originality—the discovery of an idea, plan, or answer. The second part has to do with working out,

Take a moment to assess your own creativity by reading the two lists below. See if you can find yourself in either (or maybe both!) of these lists.

Passive Approach to Life—Do I . . . ?
- Get bored frequently
- Have few deep challenges in my life
- Have mostly temporary enjoyment, with little or no lasting product
- Have lots of prestructured activities
- Have little control over events in my life
- Observe rather than act
- Have few self-sufficiency interests
- Kill time
- Have few distinguished accomplishments
- Feel mentally "old"
- Have set opinions and attitudes

Creative Approach to Life—Do I . . . ?
- Have challenging interests
- Enjoy self-enriching activities
- Experience continuous satisfaction and tangible results
- Have a youthful spirit
- Aspire to more as I achieve new goals
- Enjoy the essence of a culture
- Stay mentally flexible through new insights
- Pursue creative interests
- Enjoy selected planned participation in activities
- Find my own self-enriching activities
- Experience personal achievement and involvement
- Feel at home in many conditions
- Use my time to develop self
- Get involved in life

FIGURE 1-1 • Creativity checklist.

THIS ONE'S for YOU!   This One's for You! Sir Ken Robinson: Creativity for Our World

Sir Ken Robinson is an internationally recognized leader in the development of creativity (www.sirkenrobinson.com). He believes that many of our schools are based on ideas from the 18th and 19th centuries. Back then, schools were designed to meet the needs of an industrial economy, and in many ways, they're based on the principle of industrialism. This means that like a production line, the focus is on conformity. As Robinson (2001) says, "It's about educating people in batches."

According to Robinson, two things inherent in creativity are **habits** and **habitats**. *Habit* means the routine that we follow during the course of our daily life. The more we do the same thing every day, the more we think the same way. So one of the ways of unleashing your creativity (and that of children) is to do different things, stimulate your imagination, do things you wouldn't normally do. For example, if you never go to a ballet, go to one. If there are some types of books you never read, go and read them. If there are people in your building you have never spoken to, go and speak to them. If you go to school the same way every day, go another way.

Robinson feels that to be creative, you must open your mind to new possibilities and new experiences and do things you haven't done before, because often, being creative is finding a new medium of expression for yourself. Open yourself to new experiences and question the things you take for granted.

Secondly, *habitats* are part of creativity. The environment we live in, the environment we work in, the way we arrange the desks, the buildings—all have a huge effect on not only how we think but also on how well we think. Redesigning your classroom or redesigning physical relationships between yourself and other people can have a huge liberating effect on your whole creative capacity.

According to Robinson, our approaches to education are "stifling some of the most important capacities that young people now need to make their way in the increasingly demanding world of the 21st century—the powers of creative thinking" (Robinson, 2009). All children start their careers with sparkling imaginations, fertile minds and a willingness to take risks with what they think. Too often in our schools, most students never get to explore the full range of their abilities and interests. Education is the system that's supposed to develop our natural abilities and enable us to make our way in the world. Instead, it too often stifles individual talents and abilities of too many children and kills their motivation to learn (Robinson, 2009).

Robinson blames not the teachers but the system. Our educational system is too linear. Schools are obsessed with time. "If you live in a world where every lesson is 40 minutes, you immediately interrupt the flow of creativity" (Robinson, 2009). He suggests that we need to eliminate the existing hierarchy of subjects. Elevating some over others only reinforces outmoded factory-like learning systems. This also offends the principle of diversity. The arts, sciences, humanities, physical education, languages, and math all have equal and central contributions to make to a child's education (Robinson, 2009).

---

proving, and making certain that the idea or answer works or is possible. The first part—discovering—involves using the imagination, playing with ideas, and exploring. The second part—process—involves using learned skills, evaluating, and testing.

Thought Processes and Creativity

There are two kinds of thinking that produce solutions to problems. One of these types is called **convergent thinking**. The other type is called **divergent thinking**. Convergent thinking usually results in a single answer or solution to a question or problem.

Divergent thinking opens things up and results in many answers to a single problem.

For example, if a child is asked to count the number of fish in an aquarium, there is only one correct answer. This is a question that leads children to convergent thinking. On the other hand, if a child is asked to tell as many things as possible about the aquarium, there are obviously many correct statements that can be made. Questions such as this encourage divergent rather than convergent thinking. Creativity requires both divergent and convergent thinking. Both types of thinking are important to creativity. Consequently, the teacher's challenge is to avoid replacing one with

FIGURE 1-2 • Young children find joy in exploring and being creative.

FIGURE 1-3 • A child's sense of wonder and delight is evident when she is allowed to be creative.

the other. Another way to think about this is that children must learn the "way things are done" (convergent thinking) before truly experiencing the creative process. For example, a child needs to learn how to hold and use a paintbrush (convergent learning) before she can experience the process of painting. An older child must learn the rules (e.g., what the parts of a book report are) before she can begin to break or change the rules to be creative (e.g., giving a book report as a board game).

In dealing with young children, the focus should be on the process—that is, developing and generating original ideas. This focus on the process encourages the development of creativity across the curriculum instead of being confined to art and music activities.

Creativity and Older Children

With older children, creativity involves greater emphasis on the criterion of high-quality, original products or solutions. The development of creative products emerges later in the child's development. An example of this is seen in fourth- and fifth-grade

science fair projects. It becomes very apparent that some projects are more creative than others. For example, a student who created and tested a new chair design may seem to have an idea of a different quality than another student who investigated which commercial cleaning product worked best on stains.

At this level with older children, creativity is perceived as original products or original solutions. Creativity with older children is more than the generation of ideas: It involves the creation of products. Original products are one of the characteristics of creativity with older children.

Creativity goes beyond possession and use of artistic or musical talent. Creativity is evidenced not only in music, art, and writing, but also throughout the curriculum, in science, social studies, and other areas.

It is vitally important to encourage older children's creativity. Many times at the middle elementary level, teachers identify their main instructional goals as helping children build cognitive and social skills. But the great engine that drives innovation and invention in society comes from people whose flame

Creativity isn't always recognized by teachers and peers. Actually, history is full of examples of people whose creativity wasn't recognized in their school or work experience.

Did you know that . . .

- . . . Albert Einstein was 4 years old before he could speak and 7 before he could read?
- . . . Beethoven's music teacher once said of him, "As a composer, he is hopeless"?
- . . . F. W. Woolworth got a job in a dry goods store at age 21, but his employers would not let him wait on customers because he "didn't have enough sense"?
- . . . Leo Tolstoy flunked out of college?
- . . . A newspaper editor fired Walt Disney because he had "no good ideas"?
- . . . Louisa May Alcott was told by an editor that she would never write anything that had popular appeal?
- . . . Winston Churchill failed the sixth grade?
- . . . Thomas Edison's teachers told him that he was too stupid to learn anything?
- . . . Admiral Richard Byrd had been retired from the Navy, declared "unfit for service," when he flew over both poles?
- Vincent Van Gogh began painting in 1880 and that he sold only one painting before his death in 1890?
- Paul McCartney wasn't particularly excited by school and didn't like music at his school?
- Mick Fleetwood had a really bad time at school, which he left at 16, and found his way into a London band that morphed into Fleetwood Mac?

FIGURE 1-4 • Identifying creativity.

On the long days in the library doing research for this 10th edition, I found that reading quotes about creativity often gave me a "jolt" of inspiration. I would like to share some of my favorite quotes in the hope that they may inspire you, too, in your creative endeavors as teachers of young children.

- "I am always doing that which I cannot do, in order that I may learn how to do it." Pablo Picasso
- "There are two ways of being creative. One can sing and dance. Or one can create an environment in which singers and dancers flourish." Warren G. Bennis
- "I'm always thinking about creating. My future starts when I wake up every morning. Every day I find something creative to do with my life." Miles Davis
- "It's a miracle that curiosity survives formal education." Albert Einstein
- "The problem is never how to get new, innovative thoughts into your mind, but how to get old ones out. Every mind is a building filled with archaic furniture. Clean out a corner of your mind and creativity will instantly fill it." Dee Hock
- "Creativity is a type of learning process where the teacher and pupil are located in the same individual." Arthur Koestler
- "If I had influence with the good fairy who is supposed to preside over the christening of all children, I should ask that her gift to each child in the world would be a sense of wonder so indestructible that it would last throughout life." Rachel Carson
- "My mother said to me, 'If you become a soldier you'll be a general; if you become a monk, you'll end up as the Pope.' Instead, I became a painter and wound up Picasso." Pablo Picasso

FIGURE 1-5 • Creativity quotes.

of creativity was kept alive in childhood. Research shows that, if not nurtured, creativity takes a nose-dive by fourth grade. Young children who were awesome artists in preschool no longer color the sky orange and pink just because they love the glowing colors (Honig, 2006).

Variety and Creativity

There is a kind of creativity that allows people to express themselves in a way that makes others listen and appreciate what they hear. There are creative abilities that enable human beings to discover meaning in nature—meaning that others had not understood before.

Creativity changes at different levels of development. Most people have ideas about what creativity is in adulthood, but what might we look for in a young child? It is crucial that early childhood teachers see creativity as part of the developmental process. For young children, a critical criterion for creative potential is originality (Tegano, Moran, & Sawyers, 1991). Thus, teachers of young children must understand the process that leads to original thinking.

Originality

Originality can be seen in a kindergarten classroom where children are making collages from pieces of torn tissue paper. Mary's experimenting with the material leads to her discovery of a way to make three-dimensional bumps in the collage. Her discovery of the three-dimensional aspect is a form of originality. Though making three-dimensional collages is certainly not a new idea in a kindergarten classroom, it is an *original* idea for Mary at that particular time. Consider another kindergarten classroom where the children are embellishing full-size outlines of their bodies. Most children are adding hair, faces, and clothes to their outlines, while Luis is making an internal drawing of his skeleton. Luis's drawing of his skeleton is an original idea for him at that particular time.

Process over Product

Let's return to Mary and her three-dimensional collage. Teachers of young children need to be grounded in the **process over product** philosophy. The teacher's observation of the *process* that leads to originality (exploration and experimentation with the materials) is more valuable than any *judgment of the product* (the three-dimensional bump may have been imperfect and collapsed in the end). Remember that young children do not always have the skills to make a creative product (an elaborate painting or a workable invention), and so the process that leads to originality is the focus of creative potential.

Early childhood classrooms are full of examples of the process of original thinking. We see complex dramas unfold as children act out scenes of their own design, discover clever block building solutions, and demonstrate unique interpersonal problem solving (Tegano et al., 1991).

Importance of Creativity

Creativity is the mainspring of our civilization: from the concept of the wheel, through the steamboat, the telephone, the automobile, the airplane, radio and television, computers, automation, the electronics industry, nuclear power, and space travel. Great inventions, scientific discoveries, the pushing back of frontiers, and all forms of artistic expression—painting, literature, music, drama—have depended on creative thinking of the highest order. Thus, the progress of civilization and humanity's present evolutionary stature are essentially the result of creative thinking and innovation. Our inherent creativity contributes to the very quality of our lives.

The rapid changes of our present age require that problems be tackled creatively. It is difficult to foretell

---

THIS ONE'S for YOU! Free Yourself—To Be Creative

One of the pioneers of research into children's creativity, Paul Torrance (1962), felt that we had to free ourselves to be creative before we can ever really be creative teachers. Here are some of his suggestions to free yourself to be creative.

- Don't be afraid to fall in love with something and to pursue it with intensity.
- Know, understand, take pride in, practice, develop, exploit, and enjoy your greatest strengths.
- Learn to free yourself from the expectations of others and to walk away from the games they impose on you. Free yourself to play your own game.
- Find a great teacher or mentor who will help you.

- Don't waste energy trying to be well rounded.
- Do what you love and can do well.
- Learn the skills of independence.
- Continue to be a student of life; allow yourself to explore new ideas, people and places.
- Participate in joyful exercise or movement activities on a regular basis—skating, dancing, running, playing on the playground with neighborhood kids.

How many of these apply to you? Are you free to be a creative teacher? Pick one or two of the suggestions that you most want to work on and then go!

FIGURE 1-6 • Creativity involves questioning and exploring.

exactly what knowledge we will need to solve future problems creatively. What the young are learning now will surely become obsolete. Everyone can and must continue to learn throughout life, but knowledge alone is no guarantee that we will meet future problems effectively. Only a strong creative ability will provide the means for coping with the future.

Children want to express themselves openly. They want to bring out new ideas and have new experiences. They enjoy creativity and benefit from it in many ways, including:

- learning to feel good about themselves.
- learning to seek many answers to a problem.
- developing their potential to think.
- developing their individuality.
- developing new skills.
- experiencing the joy of being different.

Teachers also benefit from encouraging creativity, in such ways as:

- being able to provide for more and greater variety in the program.
- learning to recognize children for their unique skills.
- being able to develop closer relationships with children.

- having fewer behavior problems.
- using a minimum of standardized curricula and external evaluation.

Characteristics of Creativity

Paul Torrance, a noted expert on creativity in children, has frequently emphasized that the kind of behavior teachers identify as desirable in children does not always coincide with characteristics associated with the creative personality. For example, teachers who think they value uniqueness may find that, when a child has spilled her milk because she tried an original method of holding the cup with her teeth, they don't like creative exploration as much as they thought they did!

This lack of conformity can be inconvenient, but teachers should realize that some creative individuals possess character traits that aren't always easy to appreciate. Some of these less attractive qualities include stubbornness, fault-finding tendencies, the appearance of haughtiness and self-satisfaction, and apparent discontent (Torrance, 1962). Yet it is easy to see that stubbornness might be a valuable quality when carrying through a new idea or that finding fault and being discontented could result in questioning and analyzing a situation before coming up with suggestions for improving it.

In all fairness, we must admit that we do not know at present if these less attractive attitudes lie at the root of creativity or if some of them are the result of mishandling by teachers, peers, and families as the child matures. On the other hand, Torrance also found that creative children possess many likable qualities, such as determination, curiosity, intuition, a willingness to take risks, a preference for complex ideas, and a sense of humor.

We point out these possible problems of encouraging creativity in children not to discourage teachers from fostering such behavior, but to enlighten them so that they will not subtly reject or discourage creative responses out of failure to recognize the positive side of such behavior. Ideally, understanding creativity will result in increased acceptance and valuing of creativity in young children. Acceptance is vitally important because it will encourage children to develop their creativity further. Let us now summarize the ways to encourage creativity in all young children.

FIGURE 1-7 • Young children are naturally curious and creative.

FIGURE 1-8 • Children benefit from creativity as they experience the joy of accepting their individuality.

Helping Children Express Creativity

There are at least eight things that can be done for children to help them express natural creative tendencies.

FIGURE 1-9 • With young children, the creative **process** is more important than the product.

Help children accept change. A child who becomes overly worried or upset in new situations is unlikely to express creative potential.

Help children realize that some problems have no easy answers. This may help prevent children from becoming anxious when they cannot find an immediate answer to a question or problem.

Help children recognize that many problems have a number of possible answers. Encourage them to search for more than one answer. Then they can evaluate all the different answers to see which ones fit the situation best.

Help children learn to judge and accept their own feelings. Children should not feel guilty for having feelings about things. Create an environment where judgment is deferred and all ideas are respected, where discussion and debate are a means of trying out ideas in a nonthreatening atmosphere.

Reward children for being creative. Let children know that their creative ideas are valued. In fact, the more creative the ideas or products, the more greatly they should be rewarded. It is also useful to help children realize that good work is sometimes its own reward.

Help children feel joy in their creative productions and in working through problems. Children should find that doing things and finding answers for themselves is fun. The adult should establish the conditions that allow this to take place.

THINK ABOUT IT   The Power of Imagination

"Imagination is more important than knowledge."
Albert Einstein

The power of imagination is the ultimate creative power. One dramatic example of the power of vivid imagination is that of Air Force Colonel George Hall. He was a POW locked in the dark box of a North Vietnamese prison for 7 years. Every day he played a full game of golf in his imagination. One week after he was released from his POW camp, he entered the Greater New Orleans Open and shot a 76 (Read, 2009).

Another incredible example is that of Vera Fryling, M.D. She was a Jewish teenager on the run from the Gestapo in World War II and lived undercover in Berlin during the Holocaust. During this time she imagined that she was a doctor, a psychiatrist in a free country. Overcoming the Nazis, Soviet Army, and a bout with cancer, she ended up on the faculty of the San Francisco Medical Society. "Imagination," she said, "can help one transcend the insults life has dealt us" (Read, 2009).

The real key to turning imagination into reality is acting as if the imagined scene were real and already accomplished. Instead of pretending it is a scene from the future, imagine it is as though you are truly experiencing it in the present. It is a real event in the now. The great masters of antiquity have told us through the ages that whatever you wish to be, then reality must conform. The problem most of us have is that we look at our lives through eyes of lack, seeing only what we don't have, and dwell on that. That is also active imagination. In this way you are imagining and actively taking this lack into your future by dwelling on it as your reality.

Arnold Schwarzenegger, five-time Mr. Universe, four-time Mr. Olympia, states about his training, "As long as the mind can envision the fact that you can do something, you can. . . . I visualized myself being there already—having achieved the goal already. It's mind over matter" (Leamer, 2005).

The epitome of using visualization to create and invent was Nikola Tesla. At an early age, Tesla trained his powers of visualization. In his autobiography, *My Inventions*, he describes,

> "Every night (and sometimes during the day), when alone, I would start out on my journeys—see new places, cities and countries—live there, meet people and make friendships and acquaintances and, however unbelievable, it is a fact that they were just as dear to me as those in actual life and not a bit less intense in their manifestations. This I did constantly until I was about seventeen when my thoughts turned seriously to invention. Then I observed to my delight that I could visualize with the greatest facility. I needed no models, drawing or experiments. I could picture them all as real in my mind." (Tesla, 1982)

Tesla was a prolific and unparalleled genius, giving us AC electricity and the electric car as well as many other devices, some which have not seen the light of day because they would revolutionize civilization's approach to energy.

This knowledge that the power to imagine is more powerful than physical practice is being used from medicine to the arts. Many famous musicians practice as often in their minds as they do with their instruments. Pablo Casals, a world-famous cellist, was one of them.

This power cannot be underestimated. You can prove it to yourself by taking one thing that is very important to you and imagining it as real in your life. You have nothing to lose by applying this technique and everything to gain. Your creative abilities will blossom and flourish the more you apply it to your life (Read, 2009).

Help children appreciate themselves for being different. There is a tendency to reward children for conforming. This discourages creativity. Children should learn to like themselves because they are unique.

Help children develop perseverance—"stick-to-itiveness." Help children by encouraging them to follow through. Provide chances for them to stick with an activity even if everyone else has moved on to something different.

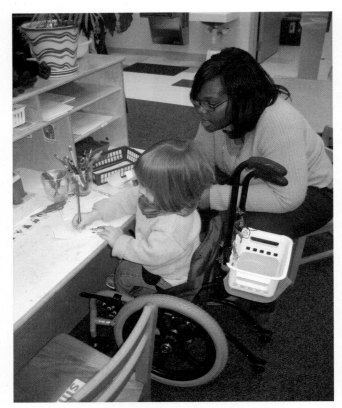

FIGURE 1-10 • Help children develop perseverance—"stick-to-itiveness."

FIGURE 1-11 • Effective teachers help children feel joy in their creative productions.

FIGURE 1-12 • A child who meets with unquestioning acceptance of her unique approach to the world feels safe expressing her creativity.

Summary

Creativity is a way of thinking and acting or making something that is original for the individual and valued by that person or others. Young children are naturally creative. This means they behave in ways and do things that are unique and valued by themselves or others. Creativity in preschool children is stimulated when they are allowed to think divergently. In many ways, both the child and teacher benefit from activities that encourage creativity. With older children, the focus of creativity is on the generation of original products or solutions.

Some kinds of creative behavior are not seen by adults as desirable in children. The inconvenience and possible frustration caused by the constantly questioning and exploring child may lead even well-meaning adults to discourage this behavior. Understanding and accepting these behavior traits can go

THIS ONE'S for YOU! Websites Relating to Creativity

For more information on the concept of creativity, check out some of the following websites.

Art in Action. http://www.artinaction.org
A nonprofit organization dedicated since 1982 to bringing visual arts education to the classroom. This site offers a newsletter and ideas for teachers.

Art Junction. http://www.artjunction.org/index.php
The University of Florida art education site shares project ideas that include self-expression. It also includes exercises to help children think more creatively and exercises to look at things from multiple points of view.

Broken Crayons. http://www.cre8ng.com
Broken Crayons is the website of Robert Alan Black, speaker and author on creativity and innovation. This site hosts weekly Creativity Challenges posted to several creativity discussion lists. This site exhibits great use of color and the crayon motif. Make sure you read the "Cre8v Thoughts" newsletter and view the four quadrants of the M.I.N.D. design questionnaire. (You even get to break the crayons as you move the mouse over the graphics.)

Creativity Pool. http://www.creativitypool.com
This is an inspiring knowledge base full of original ideas. It's the home of future innovation and tomorrow's most (in)famous inventions.

CreativityforLife.com. http://www.creativityforlife.com
This site is devoted to exploring creativity in our everyday lives. It features articles, newsletters, and personal creative activities.

Enchanted Mind. http://www.enchantedmind.com
Enchanted Mind is a well-designed site with a great deal of information on creativity techniques, inspiring articles, and puzzles, including some interactive Java puzzles. The site's use of color, graphics, and background images create the effect of a magazine.

Explore Creativity. http://www.pbs.org/parents/creativity
This site is filled with motivating, interactive activities that challenge the creativity and problem-solving skills of elementary students.

The Imagine Project, Inc. http://imagineproject.org
The Imagine Project, Inc. is founded on the principle that there exists within each child a creative energy. The sole purpose of this site is to encourage and guide children to nurture, develop, and recapture their innate creativity with the focus on creative arts.

Odyssey of the Mind. http://www.odysseyofthemind.org
Odyssey of the Mind promotes creative, team-based problem solving in a school program for students from kindergarten through college. The program helps students learn divergent thinking and problem solving.

a long way in encouraging creativity in children. Original thinking and the process that leads to it are also important criteria in understanding creativity in young children.

Children are being creative when they are solving problems, redefining situations, demonstrating flexibility, and being adventurous. Adults can help children develop a willingness to express creativity in many ways, such as by teaching them that change is natural in life and that many problems do not have easy answers. When children can go at their own pace and figure out

their own way of doing things in a relaxed learning situation, they are likely to become more creative.

Key Terms

"capital C" Creativity 4
convergent thinking 5
creativity 4
divergent thinking 5
process over product 8
"small c" creativity 4

Learning Activities

Changing the Known

Although creative thinking can be hard thinking, that does not mean it cannot be fun. This activity is designed to prove it. Try it alone or with a few classmates. When the activity is completed, it may be enjoyable to compare lists with those of others.

A. Materials needed: paper, pencil, wristwatch (or clock).

B. Time allowed: 2 minutes.

C. Task: List as many uses as you can (not related to building or construction) for a standard brick. Do not worry if some of them seem silly. The important thing is to think of using something in a new and different way.

It might be fun to try this exercise with a number of different objects: a nail, powder puff, paper clip, key, belt, cup, book, or other objects.

Just Suppose

Creative thinking occurs when one imagines what might be. It is a way of "playing" with the mind. Here is an exercise that allows you to experience this type of creative process. It can be done alone or with a few classmates.

A. Materials needed: paper, pencil.

B. Time allowed: unlimited.

C. Task: From the following 17 possibilities, choose any number of tasks.

1. "Just suppose" there is nothing made of wood in the room. What would change? What would things look like? What dangers might exist? What would you be unable to do?

2. "Just suppose" (try this with other people) you cannot use words, either written or spoken, for an hour. How can you communicate? What is frustrating about it? What is pleasing about it? What would it mean if it continued for days?

3. "Just suppose" you receive a million dollars and must spend it within 2 minutes. Make a list of ways to spend the money and compare lists with others in the class.

4. "Just suppose" you were the first person to meet a man from Mars and could ask him only three questions. What would they be? Compare your questions with those of others in the class.

5. "Just suppose" you were with Julius Caesar when he met Cleopatra for the first time. If you could say only one sentence, what would it be?

6. "Just suppose" you could be any person in the world for one hour. Who would it be? What would you do? Compare responses with classmates.

7. What would happen if all people awakened tomorrow morning to find themselves twice as large?

8. IMAGINE! Create seven sentences for which the seven-letter word *imagine* would be the acronym. All sentences should reflect in some way your thoughts about creative thinking, imagination, and ingenuity based on what you have learned by reading this unit.

Example: **I**deas should not be hoarded or hidden.
Many small solutions are necessary to solve big problems.
All people are created creative.
Good ideas drive out bad ideas.
Innovative ideas are resisted by "spectators."
Never mind what others think—use your own judgment.
Enjoy your fantasies—that's what they are for!

Now it's your turn!

9. Pick one or two characteristics associated with creativity that you would like to increase in your own life. For example, you might want to become more open to experience or more persistent. For a month, try to exercise that characteristic whenever you can. Record your efforts and see if you find that the characteristics can be changed.

10. Creativity is not always expressed in school-appropriate ways. For one week, pay careful attention to students causing disturbances in your room. Do you see evidence of creativity in their behavior? Propose and explain ways you could channel that originality in other ways. Get input from your fellow students on your ideas.

11. Begin collecting books and stories about individuals who display the characteristics associated with creativity in positive ways. Go to the website for suggested sources for these books. Share these books with your students. Consider the kinds of models that are being presented in your language arts, science, or social studies curricula. Would students be able to tell from them that you value originality, independence, or persistence?

12. Read two biographies of the same creative person—one written for adults and the other for children (see references for suggested books in the Online Companion). Keep track of the emphases and information that are different. Do both books accurately describe the successes and failures in the person's life, her or his triumphs and setbacks? How might these differences affect your students?

13. Divide a large piece of paper into squares and list one characteristic associated with creativity in each square. Leave the paper on your desk for two weeks. Each time a student does something to demonstrate a listed characteristic, put his or her name in that square. After the first time, just use tally marks. Be sure to mark the characteristic, even if it is displayed in a negative way. At the end of two weeks, see which names are listed most often. Are they the names of students you consider creative?

14. Next week, plan one class activity that you believe is truly unusual or novel, something no student in your class would have experienced before. Observe how your students respond. What does this tell you about your teaching?

15. If you had to define yourself in terms of the discipline in which you exhibit most of your creativity, what would you call yourself? A writer/teacher? A scientist/teacher? Pick an area in which you would like to develop your own creativity and begin keeping an idea book. After a month, read over your ideas and see whether there are any you would like to pursue further.

16. **What-ifs**

    Choose a "what if?" from the following list and then draw a picture or create a photo montage showing how life would be changed by this new condition.

    What if . . .

    it rained sneakers everyday?

    animals had people for pets?

    you had a dragon for a next-door neighbor?

    cows could fly?

    people were magnetic?

    Picasso had painted *American Gothic*?

    everyone lived on his or her own island?

    the oceans were made of chocolate pudding?

    every day at 2:00 p.m. gravity went away for 20 minutes?

    works of art came to life?

    nothing could be thrown away?

    all the art in the world was stolen by aliens?

    Write a short story to go along with your picture.

17. **Creative Challenge**

    Here is the best for last. What if you are trapped inside a box? This box is made of planks of wood all nailed together on the outside very tightly. All you have with you is a bow and one arrow, a piece of cardboard, a crayon and everything you are currently wearing. You can include whatever is in your pockets, too. (No cell phones!) Now, think of as many ways as possible for getting out of that box with only those items. How are you going to "step out of the box"?

Chapter Review

1. Compare and contrast the following terms and give at least one example for each term:
   a. Creativity
   b. Convergent thinking
   c. Divergent thinking

2. List five things a teacher can do to help children develop a willingness to express creativity and give a rationale for each.

3. Explain why children must engage in creative activities and give three examples of how to engage them in such activities.

4. List several characteristics of creativity and discuss the positive and negative aspects of each.

5. Discuss the concepts of original thinking and process over product and give several examples of their use in the early childhood program.

6. Explain the differences in criteria for older children and creativity and give examples of their application in your work with young children.

7. Why are both convergent and divergent thinking important to creativity? Use examples in your answer.

References

Hoefferth, S. (1998). *Children at work and play.* Ann Arbor, MI: University of Michigan Institute of Social Research.

Honig, A. S. (2006). Supporting creativity in the classroom. *Scholastic Early Childhood Today, 20*(5), 13–14.

Leamer, L. (2005). *Fantastic: The life of Arnold Schwarzenegger.* New York, NY: St. Martin's.

May, R. (1975). *The courage to create.* New York, NY: W. W. Norton.

Read, J. L. (2009). *The power of imagination.* Retrieved August 17, 2009, from http:www.enchantedmind.com/html/creativity/techniques/power_of_imagination.html

Ripple, R. (1999). Teaching creativity. In M. A. Runco & S. R. Pritzker (Eds.), *Encyclopedia of creativity* (Vol. 2). San Diego, CA: Academic Press.

Robinson, Sir K. (2001). *Out of your minds—Learning to be creative.* Oxford, GB: Capstone.

Robinson, Sir K. (2009). *The element: How finding your passion changes everything.* New York, NY: Penguin.

Strom, P., & Strom, R. (2002, March). Too busy to play. *Parenting for High Potential,* 18–22.

Taylor, M. (2000). *Imaginary companions and the children who create them.* New York, NY: Oxford University Press.

Tegano, D. W., Moran, J. D., III, & Sawyers, J. K. (1991). *Creativity in early childhood classrooms.* Washington, DC: National Association for the Education of Young Children (NAEYC).

Tesla, N. (1982). *My inventions: The autobiography of Nikola Tesla.* New York, NY: Hart Brothers.

Torrance, E. P. (1962). *Rewarding creative behavior: Experiments in classroom creativity.* Englewood Cliffs, NJ: Prentice Hall.

Torrance, E. P. (1970). *Encouraging creativity in the classroom.* Dubuque, IA: William C. Brown.

Torrance, E. P. (1971). Creativity and infinity. *Journal of Research and Development in Education, 4*(3), 35–41.

Additional Readings

Baer, J. (2008). Gender differences in creativity. *Journal of Creative Behavior, 42*(2), 75–105.

Carter, D. E. (2009). *Creativity 38.* New York, NY: HarperCollins.

Chua, R. Y., & Iyengar, S. S. (2008). Creativity as a matter of choice: Prior experience and task instruction as boundary conditions for the positive effect of choice on creativity. *Journal of Creative Behavior, 42*(3), 164–180.

Davis, J. H. (2008). *Why our schools need the arts.* New York, NY: Teachers College Press.

Dischler, P. A. (2009). *Teaching the three C's: Creativity, curiosity and courtesy. Activities that build a foundation to success.* Thousand Oaks, CA: Sage.

Downs, P., & Patton-McFarren, E. (2009). Masterpieces in the hallways. *Principal, 88*(3), 22–25.

Dutcher, A. J. (2009). Bibliography of recently published books on creativity and problem solving. *Journal of Creative Behavior, 42*(4), 283–284.

Eckhoff, A., & Urbach, J. (2008). Understanding imaginative thinking during childhood: Sociocultural conceptions of creativity and imaginative thought. *Early Childhood Education Journal, 36*(2), 179–185.

Edwards, D. (2009). *Artscience: Creativity in the post-Google generation.* Cambridge, MA: Harvard University Press.

Gardner, H., Claxton, G., & Craft, A. (Eds.). (2007). *Creativity, wisdom and trusteeship: Exploring the role of education.* Thousand Oaks, CA: Sage.

Katter, E. (2009). Why kids need art. *School Arts, 108*(8), 64–70.

Kharkhurin, A. V. (2009). The role of bilingualism in creative performance on divergent thinking and invented alien creature tests. *Journal of Creative Behavior, 43*(1), 59–71.

Lee, M., Um, J.-H., & Choe, I.-S. (2008). The relationship among creativity, motivation, and well-being of children. *International Journal of Psychology, 43*(4), 501–503.

Lubawy, J. (2009). *Visions of creativity in early childhood: Connecting theory, practice and reflection.* Castle Hall, NSW, Australia: Pademelon.

Nelson, H. (2009). Arts education and the whole child. *Principal, 88*(3), 14–17.

Ragsdale, S., & Saylor, A. (2009). *Building character from the start: 201 activities to foster creativity, literacy and play in K–3.* Minneapolis, MN: Search Institute Press.

Reese, S. (2009). Gazing into the future. *Techniques, 84*(5), 14–19.

Roskos-Ewoldsen, G., Black, S. R., & McCown, S. M. (2008). Age-related changes in creative thinking. *Journal of Creative Behavior, 42*(1), 33–60.

Ruggiero, V. R. (2008). *The art of thinking: A guide to critical and creative thought.* Essex, UK: Longman.

Runco, M. A. (2009). Creativity and education. *New Horizons in Education, 56*(1), 8–10.

Silva, P. J. (2008). Creativity and intelligence revisited: A latent variable analysis of Wallch and Kogan (1965). *Creativity Research Journal, 20*(1), 34–41.

Sternberg, R. J. (2009). Wisdom, intelligence and creativity synthesized. *School Administration, 66*(2), 10–11.

Stokes, P. D. (2008). Creativity from constraints: What can we learn from Motherwell? From Mondrain? From Klee? *Journal of Creative Behavior, 42*(4), 223–236.

Tarr, P. (2008). New visions: Art for early childhood. *Art Education, 61*(4), 19–24.

Yeh, Y.-C. (2008). Age, emotion regulation strategies, temperament, creative drama and preschooler's creativity. *Journal of Creative Behavior, 42*(2), 131–147.

Software for Children

Amazing Brain Train

Reinforces: *creative thinking, logic.* This is a collection of "brain training" puzzle games that include math, memory, and logic exercises. Players travel along a railroad track and earn fuel for the "brain train" as they play the games.

The Boohbah Zone

Reinforces: *creativity, language, color, shape.* A total of nine games and a vinyl dance pad are included. Child easily controls attributes of color, speed, and shape.

Click and Create With Mia

Reinforces: *creativity, art.* This software allows children to express their creative sides by offering several art tools that can be used separately or together to let their imagination run wild.

Crayola Art Studio

Reinforces: *creativity, art media.* This software includes 12 realistic art tools including tempera paint, acrylic paint, watercolor, chalk, crayon, oil pastel, markers and more. It is an easy-to-use draw-and-paint program for ages 4 and up.

Disney's Magic Artist Studio

Reinforces: *creativity, art techniques.* This software includes three different art studios: Skillboard Studio, the Gallery, and the Lesson Area. For ages 4 and up.

Foster's Home for Imaginary Friends: Imagination Invaders

Reinforces: *imagination, creativity.* This software is based on the Cartoon Network hit show *Foster's Home for Imaginary Friends.* Ages 6 and up.

Holly in Magic Land

Reinforces: *Imagination, creativity.* This is a seek-and-find puzzle game in which players search for hidden items on a screen full of jumbled objects. Players follow the story of a girl named Holly as she enters a magical town to find her lost daughter. Ages 6 and up.

ItzaBitza

Reinforces: *creativity, reading.* An award-winning magical drawing game that ignites imaginations and sparks a love of reading.

Kidspiration Version 3.0

Reinforces: *creativity, drawing, and painting.* Children draw and write directly on interactive whiteboards and tablet PCs. Ages 4 and up.

Kid Pix Deluxe 4

Reinforces: *creativity, drawing, and painting.* This classic draw-and-paint program is easy for preschoolers to use and offers endless possibilities for creativity. Children can explore line, color, and texture, and their artwork can be made into slideshow presentations. Ages 4 and up.

Smart Boy's Toys Club

Reinforces: *creativity, imagination.* A compilation of 18 preschool-level mini games that spark the imagination.

Helpful Websites

These websites are related to children's creativity and creative activities.

Animalia, http://pbskids.org/animalia

Art Scope, http://www.sfmoma.org/projects/artscope/index.html

Brain Connection, http://brainconnection.positscience.com

The Childhood Affirmations Program, http://www.childhoodaffirmations.com/general/us.html

Creativity Café, http://www.creativity.net

The Imagination Factory, http://www.kid-at-art.com/

National Foundation for Educational Research, http://www.nfer.ac.uk

National Network for Child Care, http://www.nncc.org/Curriculum/create.play.grow.html

Princeton Online, http://www.princetonol.com/groups/iad/lessons/early/early.html

Tikatok, http://www.tikatok.com

Young Artist Workshop, http://artistworkshop.blogspot.com/

Young Children on the Web, www.journal.naeyc.org/btj

For additional creative activity resources, visit our website at www.Cengage.com/login.

Promoting Creativity

OBJECTIVES

After studying this chapter, you should be able to:

1. Describe the relationship between creativity and the curriculum.

2. Describe the role of play and exploration in promoting creativity.

3. Demonstrate four questioning strategies to encourage creative thinking in young children.

4. List three questions to consider when modifying the curriculum to encourage creative thinking.

5. List four beliefs associated with the philosophy of differentiated instruction in the early childhood curriculum.

Creative thinking is not a station one arrives at, but a means of traveling. Creativity is fun. Being creative, feeling creative, and experiencing creativity is fun. Learning is more fun for children in settings where teachers and children recognize and understand the process of creative thinking. Incorporating creative thinking into all areas of the curriculum contributes to a young child's positive attitude toward learning. As one student teacher commented, "I used to think that if children were having too much fun, they couldn't be learning. Now I understand how they are learning in a more effective way." This unit addresses the relationship of creativity and the classroom environment, providing guidelines for encouraging creative thinking in the early childhood program throughout the day. In subsequent units, the same emphasis on creativity is applied to specific curriculum areas.

Creativity is an integral part of each day: It is part of circle time, reading time, and lunchtime—it is not limited to art, music, creative movement, or dramatic play. Creativity needs to be a natural part of the curriculum and the learning environment. Yet children need knowledge and skills to be creative—the curriculum outlines what they need to learn, and this unit will help you understand how to attain these goals. Throughout this unit, keep in mind that creative thinking is contagious— from teacher to child, from child to teacher, and also from child to child and teacher to teacher.

Promoting Creativity in the Curriculum

To express their creative potential, young children need knowledge and skills. Both knowledge and skills are necessary before creative potential can have true meaning (Amabile, 1996). Children cannot develop

FIGURE 2-1 • Young children express themselves openly and freely.

FIGURE 2-2 • Creativity is part of each day and is not limited to art activities.

high-level creative thinking skills without the basic knowledge and skills of a particular area, in the same way that a great chef must develop basic culinary skills before creating a gourmet recipe. The curriculum is the teacher's choice of what knowledge and skills are important and also developmentally appropriate for a particular group of children (Bredekamp, 2009).

An example of the need for a knowledge base emerged in the early pilot testing of a measure of creative potential for young children. The researchers were trying to adapt the classic "uses" task for preschool children. In this task, the children are asked to name all the uses they can think of for a common item. The number of original (i.e., unusual) answers serves as one measure of creativity (Torrance, 1962; Wallach & Kogan, 1965). The researchers were puzzled when a group of preschool children could think of only a few uses for common objects such as a clothes hanger and a table knife. The researchers realized that the reason for the limited response was that the children had little or no knowledge and skill in the use of clothes hangers and table knives. In fact, most preschool children are not allowed to use these items. Knowledge and skills, then,

are a prerequisite for creativity. Later research came up with better results when the children were asked to think of all the ways to use a box and paper, items about which the children had a working knowledge (Moran, Milgram, Sawyers, & Fu, 1985; Rushton & Larkin, 2007). Creativity evolves from a knowledge base—without knowledge, there is no creation. A child must understand in order to invent.

Thus, one important goal for the early childhood teacher is to provide an adequate base of knowledge and skills for children, while at the same time providing an environment that encourages creative thinking in the use of the knowledge and skills. The curriculum is the guide by which teachers determine *what* will be presented to children. Creativity is fostered according to *how* the curriculum is presented to the child (Runco, 2008).

> If you want to be creative, stay in part a child, with the creativity and invention that characterizes children before they are deformed by society.
>
> Jean Piaget

THIS ONE'S for YOU!

Curiosity . . . A Direct Link to Creativity

Children are curious by nature. From the moment of birth, they are drawn to new things. When children are curious about something new, they want to explore it. And exploration is a crucial part of the creative process. So curiosity is directly linked to creativity.

To ensure that curiosity doesn't fade with the young child you are working with, the following are some tips to encourage curiosity in young children.

- Recognize individual differences in children's style of curiosity. Some children may want to explore with only their minds, others in more physical ways—touching, smelling, tasting, and climbing.
- Realize that to some degree, these differences are related to temperament differences in the exploratory drive.

- Recognize that some children are more timid; others are more comfortable with novelty and physical exploration.
- Understand that even the timid child will be very curious; he may require more encouragement and reinforcement to leave safe and familiar situations.
- Try to redefine "failure." In real life, curiosity often leads to more mess than mastery, but it is how we handle the mess that helps encourage further exploration and thereby creativity.
- Use your attention and approval to reinforce the exploring, curious child.
- When exploration in the classroom is disruptive, contain it by teaching the child when and where to do that particular kind of exploration. For example, "Claire, let's play with water outside" (Perry, 2009).

Promoting Creativity Through Play and Exploration

Let's take a look at a preschool classroom where computers are available and observe the process of exploration as it leads into play. At first the computer is novel and children engage in random punching of keys—exploring what the keys can do. This leads to the eventual realization that specific keys have specific uses. This process of exploring the computer to discover what it can do may take several months, depending on the frequency of the child's exposure to the computer. When the child has gained an understanding of what the computer can do, she may move on to another question: "What can I do with the computer?" Equipped with the skills gained through exploration (using a mouse, for example), the child truly begins to play with the computer.

Here again, it is important for the child to have basic knowledge of what a computer can do and the skills to operate it. But young children also need to explore the computer before any more formal experiences take place. Then, after they have acquired knowledge and skills, they can use the computer creatively.

As children explore and play with materials in their environments, they are also in a sense shaping the brain (Catania, 2008). Those who research the human brain contend that experience, particularly in childhood, sculpts the brain (Fischer, Immordino-Yang, & Weber, 2007). The brain changes physiologically as a result of experience. New connections are formed every day in active interaction with the environment. Hands-on activities stimulate various regions of the brain, and active participation helps young children form stronger mental association with their existing understandings (Hinton, Miyamoto, & Della-Chiesa, 2008; Rushton & Larkin, 2007). Therefore, the opportunities to learn actively in an environment provided throughout life and particularly in the early years help to create us as unique individuals. Other researchers put it this way: "Throughout life, we are both shaped by and shaping our environment" (Fischer, Immordino-Yang, & Weber, 2007). Passive observation in the early childhood program is never enough. As the ancient Chinese proverb states, "Tell me and I forget. Show me and I remember. Let me do and I understand." Thus, the role of exploration and play is central to the development of creativity—at all ages.

Modifying Curriculum to Promote Creativity

Curriculum may be viewed as an outline of knowledge and skills to be learned rather than as a recipe for how they must be taught. The term *learn* implies that exploration and play are part of the process; the term *recipe* denotes a careful following of steps in a specific order and amount to come up with one precise product. As we know, young children are not all the same, so differing amounts and various combinations of ingredients are necessary for each child. Each child learns the same knowledge and skills in a unique way; therefore, the recipe is continually modified. Keep in mind that developmental needs serve as a guide to the sequence in which all concepts are introduced.

Creativity and curriculum complement each other. The curriculum is a guide to the knowledge and abilities that are necessary to develop creative thinking skills. The curriculum provides the content around which creativity may develop. How the content is presented to the child is the means to creative development. When modifying curriculum to encourage creative thinking, consider the following points:

- The curriculum must be developmentally appropriate for young children. This means it will allow children to be both physically and mentally active, engaging them in active rather than passive activities.
- Be alert and aware of children's interests. Choose materials and activities that are meaningful to children in your group. Children, like you, are drawn to materials and activities that interest them. Be sure to involve them in choosing materials and activities for the curriculum.
- Provide a variety of materials that encourage children's creative exploration. Allow children ample time not only to physically explore but also to mentally explore—think about—what they are doing.
- In planning curriculum, consider all the types of learning styles and multiple intelligences (ways of learning) of children in your group. (More information about learning styles and multiple intelligences is found in Chapter 5.) Plan activities that meet the different needs of all learners.

- Encourage children's divergent thinking and curiosity. Let them ask questions and search for solutions to their problems.
- Encourage older children's curiosity by giving credit in your grading system for questioning. In this strategy, students are concretely rewarded for curiosity.
- Be sure to provide opportunities for children to interact and communicate with other children and adults in an atmosphere of acceptance.

Enhancing Children's Creativity in the Curriculum

A note of caution is needed here in our discussion, especially about choosing creative activities for young children. Remember that a teaching activity that produces an enjoyable or creative outcome does not necessarily enhance creativity unless the *students* have the opportunity for creative thinking. There is a difference between creative teaching (the *teacher* is creative) and teaching to *develop children's creativity*. For example, when you examine books of so-called creative activities, you may find adorable illustrations and unusual activities, but the input from students is fairly routine. A color-by-number dragon filled with addition problems may have been an original creation for the illustrator, but completing the addition problems and coloring as directed provide no opportunities for originality on the part of students. A crossword puzzle in the shape of a spiral was an original idea for its creator, but it still requires students only to give accurate (convergent) responses to clues and fill in the correct spaces. In both of these examples, those who created the materials had the opportunity to be creative. The students did not. In other instances, classroom teachers may use enormous personal creativity in developing activities that allow few opportunities for students to be original.

Teaching to enhance creativity has a different focus: the essential creativity is on the part of the students. If the students developed a new form of crossword puzzle, they would have the opportunity to exercise creative thinking. Creativity can also be developed as students devise their own science experiments, discuss a fairy tale from the viewpoint of a character in it, or rewrite *Snow White* as it might be told by the stepmother. When we teach to enhance creativity, we may well be creative as teachers, but we also provide students the knowledge, skills, and surroundings necessary for their own creativity to emerge. The results may not be as flashy as the activities book, but they include real problem finding, problem solving, and communication by students.

It is also important to remember that challenges are not just for our students. We can also challenge ourselves as teachers. One way to do this is to reflect on the ways we are providing challenges in our program. We need to ask ourselves questions like the following:

- Do I take time to observe children in action before stepping in to "teach"?
- Do I provide opportunities for children to use new understandings and skills in many different situations before moving to the next skill?
- Do I provide open-ended activities for children each day?
- Do I add or modify the materials in learning centers or stations as I perceive children are ready for change?
- Do I feel comfortable being challenged? How can I challenge myself to grow as a learner and teacher?

Integrated Curriculum and Creativity

The curriculum that encourages creativity the most in young children is an integrated, whole curriculum. In an **integrated curriculum**, the artificial divisions among content areas are reduced. Although many teachers find it convenient to think about what the child will learn as separate categories of information, the integrated curriculum is not designed in that way.

Most often, an integrated curriculum is designed around a unit of study centered on a specific theme or project. The unit of study contains a coordinated series of learning activities planned around a broad topic that will involve the whole group. A unit in an integrated curriculum will involve all of the content areas (reading, math, art, music, social studies, etc.). Integrated curriculum units provide the topics and framework for planning activities for children. The length of time for the unit may vary, taking weeks or months. The amount of time depends on the topic and the interests of the children.

In an integrated curriculum, children are able to experience learning as a whole. For example, they can explore the idea of neighborhood and community by reading books, hearing stories, drawing and painting a community mural, and planning and preparing foods from their neighborhood and community. In this broad approach to learning, they are able to express themselves creatively in many areas and not just in the area of the arts. Section 5 presents many areas of the curriculum and creative approaches to each of these areas.

Creative Early Childhood Curriculum and Differentiated Instruction

Another term associated with effective curriculum for learners is **differentiated instruction**. Differentiated instruction is a way of thinking about teaching and learning. It is a philosophy. As such, it is based on a set of beliefs that relate to encouraging creativity in your children. The beliefs of differentiated instruction are as follows:

- Children who are the same age are different in their readiness to learn, their interests, their styles of learning, their experiences, and their life circumstances.
- These differences in children affect what they need to learn, the pace at which they need to learn it, and the support they need from teachers and others to learn it well.
- Children will learn best when they can make a connection between the curriculum and their interests and life experiences.
- Children will learn best when learning opportunities are natural.
- Children are more effective learners when classrooms and schools create a sense of community in which children feel significant and respected.
- The central job of teachers and schools is to maximize the capacity of each student (Tomlinson, 2000).

Differentiated instruction is a refinement of, not a substitute for, high-quality early childhood curriculum and instruction. Differentiated instruction is present in the early childhood classroom when the curriculum and instruction fit each child and children have choices about what to learn and how. Also, children taking part in setting learning goals is further evidence of differentiated instruction. Finally, in the early childhood classroom, with differentiated instruction, the

FIGURE 2-3 • With open-ended materials, children are free to be creative.

curriculum connects with the experiences and interests of individual children.

Differentiated instruction is not a new phenomenon in early childhood education. The one-room schoolhouses of the past offered teachers the challenge of finding ways to work with students with wide-ranging needs. The contemporary approach to differentiating has been shaped by the growing research on learning—drawing from the best practices in special education, gifted education, and multi-age classrooms; recent research on the brain and multiple intelligences; and developments in authentic assessment.

In summary, the aim of differentiating instruction is to maximize each child's growth by meeting each child where he or she is and helping the child to progress from there. In practice, it involves offering several different learning experiences in response to children's varied needs. More specific information about activities for different learning styles and multiple intelligences is presented in Chapter 5.

Creative Early Childhood Curriculum and Learning Styles

One of the components of differentiated instruction is the understanding of the different ways children learn. Children think and learn in different ways. In any group of children, there will always be a variety of different learning characteristics.

An important factor in understanding learning styles is understanding brain functioning. Both sides of the brain can reason, but by very different ways, and one side of the brain may be dominant. When we talk about a person who is **right-brained** or **left-brained**, we are referring to learning preferences based on functional differences between the hemispheres (sides) of the brain.

The left brain is considered **analytic** in approach. This means that a left-brain (**successive processor**) prefers to learn in a step-by-step sequential format, beginning with details leading up to understanding a concept or acquiring a skill.

The right brain is described as **holistic** or **global.** This means that a right brain (**simultaneous processor**) prefers to learn beginning with the general concept and then go on to specifics.

Children who are right-brained are those whose right hemisphere of the brain is dominant in their learning process. This is in contrast to the majority of children, whose left hemisphere is dominant in their learning style. Each hemisphere of the brain has distinctly different strengths and behavioral characteristics.

All of us use both hemispheres of the brain, but we may use one side more than the other. For instance, you might have a dominant right hemisphere, which simply means that it is your preferred or stronger hemisphere. It is the one in which you tend to first process most of the information you receive. That does not mean you don't use your left hemisphere. You may use your right hemisphere 60% of the time and your left hemisphere 40%. Similarly, when we talk about children who are right brained or left brained, we do not mean they use only one hemisphere but simply that they use one hemisphere to a greater extent than the other.

The right and left brain hemispheres have specialized thinking characteristics. They do not approach life in the same way. The left-hemisphere approach to life is part-to-whole. It sequences, puts things in order, and is logical. The right hemisphere learns whole-to-part. It does not sequence or put things in order. Rather, it looks at things in an overall way or **holistically**. Let's consider specific skills and in which hemisphere that skill is best developed.

Left hemisphere. The skills best developed in this side of the brain are handwriting, understanding symbols, language, reading, and phonics. Other general skills best developed here are locating details and facts, talking and reciting, following directions, and listening and auditory association. All of these are skills children must exercise on a day-to-day basis in school. We give children symbols; we stress reading, language, and phonics. We ask for details; we insist upon directions being followed, and mostly, we talk at children. In short, most of our school curriculum is left-brained. We teach to the child who has a dominant left brain.

Right hemisphere. The right hemisphere is associated with an entirely different set of skills. The right hemisphere has the ability to recognize and process nonverbal sounds. It also governs our ability to communicate using body language.

Although the motor cortex is in both hemispheres, the ability to make judgments based on the relationship of our bodies to space (needed in sports, creative movement, and dance, for instance) is basically centered in the right hemisphere.

The ability to recognize, draw, and deal with shapes and patterns as well as geometric figures lies in the right hemisphere. This involves the ability to distinguish between different colors and hues and the ability to visualize in color.

Singing and music are right-hemisphere activities. Creative art is also in debt to the right hemisphere. While many children who are left-brained are quite good in art, the "art" they make is structured; it must come out a certain way. They are most comfortable with models and a predictable outcome. Their pictures, or the things they create, are drawings made for Mother's Day or turkeys drawn for Thanksgiving. Children who are left-hemisphere dominant are good at other-directed art.

Children who are right-hemisphere dominant create "mystery" pictures. They show the pictures to you, but they aren't quite sure what you are looking at until they start talking about it. For example, they may show raindrops falling and the sun shining at the same time.

FIGURE 2-4 • Each child approaches creative activities in her or his own unique way.

After listening to a story, children who are right-brained can retell the story in their own words without any difficulty. However, they are so creative that they usually add their own details and ending. From an adult's perspective, it may seem they are exaggerating or embellishing. But in their terms, they are simply being what they are. They change stories, add details, and alter endings to meet their emotional needs. Feelings and emotions appear to be most dominant in the right hemisphere.

Now, armed with all of this information on children who are right or left brained, you need to reflect on your own work with children and ask yourself if your curriculum is directed toward only one type of learner. Are you in tune with the right-brained learners? You may find it helpful to go to the library and take out books with specific curricular ideas for children who are right-brained. At the very least, you need to be aware of yet another way in which each young child is unique. And finally, you may want to find out what kind of learner you are by using the checklist in the This One's for You! box on page 25.

THIS ONE'S for YOU! Which Type of Learner are You?

As we learned in this chapter, both sides of the brain can reason, but by very different ways, and one side of the brain may be dominant. Find out which type of learner you are by checking off which of the following characteristics best describes how you learn. While you probably will have checks in both lists, you most likely will have a majority of checks in one list, which generally indicates that particular style as your dominant learning style.

Check off the characteristics that are **most** like you in both of the lists below

Left (Analytic)

Successive Hemisphere Style

1. Verbal
2. Responds to word meaning
3. Sequential
4. Processes information linearly
5. Responds to logic
6. Plans ahead
7. Recalls people's names
8. Speaks with few gestures
9. Punctual
10. Prefers formal study
11. Prefers bright lights while studying

Right (Global)

Simultaneous Hemisphere Style

1. Visual
2. Responds to tone of voice
3. Random
4. Processes information in varied order
5. Responds to emotion
6. Impulsive
7. Recalls people's faces
8. Gestures when speaking
9. Less punctual
10. Prefers sound/music background while studying
11. Prefers frequent mobility while studying

Promoting Creativity Through Positive Acceptance

Adults who work with young children are in an especially crucial position to foster each child's creativity. In the day-to-day experiences in early childhood settings, as young children actively explore their world, adults' attitudes clearly transmit their feelings to the child. A child who meets with unquestionable acceptance of her unique approach to the world will feel safe in expressing her creativity, whatever the activity or situation.

The following are guidelines on how to help transmit this positive acceptance to children, which in turn fosters creativity in any situation.

- Openly demonstrate to young children that there is value in their curiosity, exploration, and original behavior.
- Allow children to go at their own pace when they are carrying out an activity that excites and interests them.
- Let children stay with what they are making until they feel it's finished.
- Let children figure out their own ways of doing things if they prefer to do so.
- Keep the atmosphere relaxed.
- Encourage guessing, especially when the answers make good sense.

Working with Older Children

In the upper elementary grades, teachers have an even greater challenge to promote creativity because the curriculum often dominates the program. There are often state-level guidelines for what to teach, at what level, with specific books and materials. Even in this situation, you can encourage creativity in your classroom. Here are some suggestions to help you get started.

To encourage creativity with older children:

- Use tangible rewards (stickers, prizes) as seldom as possible; instead, encourage children's own pride in the work they have done.
- Avoid setting up competitive situations for children.
- Downplay your evaluation of children's work. Instead, lead them to become more proficient at recognizing their own strengths and weaknesses.
- Encourage children to monitor their own work rather than rely on your surveillance of them.
- Whenever possible, give children choices about what activities they do and about how to do those activities.
- Make intrinsic (internal) motivation a conscious factor in your discussions with children. Encourage them to become aware of their own special interests and to take their focus off the extrinsic (external rewards).
- To build children's intrinsic (internal) motivation, help them build their self-esteem by focusing on and appreciating their unique talents and strengths.
- As much as possible, encourage children to become active, independent learners rather than to rely on you for constant direction. Encourage them to take confident control of their own learning process.
- Give children ample opportunities for free play with various materials, and allow them to engage in fantasy whenever possible.
- In any way you can, show children that you value creativity—that not only do you allow it, but you also engage in it yourself.
- Whenever you can, show your students that you are an intrinsically motivated adult who enjoys thinking creatively.

It may help to also consider these additional points on working with older students.

Time. Give students extended, unhurried time to explore and do their best work. Stand aside when students are productively engaged and motivated to complete an interesting and creative task.

Space. Provide students with an area to leave unfinished work to be completed later. Create an inviting workspace that has natural light, harmonious colors, and stimulating resources.

Materials. Provide an abundant supply of interesting and useful materials, including writing and art materials that students can use freely to invent, experiment, and demonstrate ideas and products.

Climate. Create a classroom atmosphere where students understand that mistakes are acceptable and it is appropriate to take risks. Allow a reasonable amount of noise, mess, and freedom.

Enrichment. Introduce students to out-of-class experiences so they encounter ideas to use in classroom learning. Help students reflect on their experiences and what they mean to them.

Even when you feel burdened by state standards and high-stakes testing, it's worth the effort to create a classroom environment that is both visually and mentally stimulating. Students need to be certain that a spark of learning—that electricity—is present in their daily lessons. Otherwise, you might as well turn out the lights and send the kids home.

FIGURE 2-5 • The curriculum must allow children to be both physically and mentally active.

THINK ABOUT IT

How Much Does Creative Teaching Enhance Elementary Students' Achievement?

Researchers with the Creative Education Foundation in Hadley, Massachusetts, examined the relationship between creative teaching and elementary students' achievement gains. Their study measured 48 third-, fourth-, fifth-, and sixth-grade teachers' creative teaching behaviors and the impact of these behaviors on students' reading, language, and mathematics achievement. All 48 teachers were observed on eight different occasions throughout the course of the academic year. Classroom observations lasted for an entire lesson plan, ranging from 31 minutes to 1 hour and 25 minutes (Schacter, Thum, & Zifkin, 2006).

For each teacher, during each observed lesson, both a creative teaching frequency score and a quality score were calculated. These scores were then used as predictor variables in a structural equation model to determine the magnitude of the relationship between creative teaching and classroom achievement gains in reading, language, and mathematics.

The results of the study demonstrated that (a) the majority of the teachers did not implement any teaching strategies that fostered students' creativity; (b) teachers who elicited students' creativity turned out students who made substantial gains; and (c) classrooms with high proportions of minority and low-performing students received significantly less creative teaching (Schacter et al., 2006, p. 61).

The researchers found these results disturbing because the benefits of being creative are well established. Creative people tend to be happier, achieve more, and receive more awards. They are more likely than their peers to make patentable inventions, publish articles, develop successful businesses, attain leadership positions later in life, and are in great demand by businesses worldwide (Csikszentmihalyi, 1996; Dacey & Lennon, 1998;

Mumford & Simonton, 1997; Torrance, 1995; U.S. Department of Labor, 1991).

After over 400 hours of observation, Schacter et al. found that the average teacher implemented very few teaching behaviors that increased student creativity. On average, each of the creative teaching behaviors assessed occurred less than once over the course of eight different lessons. Furthermore, in those rare instances when a teacher did elicit student creativity, the teaching strategy was not aligned with the lesson objective, was not explained or elaborated, and the purpose was not made clear to students.

Given the limitations of the study (sample size and frequency of observation), results demonstrate that creative teaching substantially improves student achievement. This finding runs counter to the way educators have responded to the standards and assessment movement. Many teachers have claimed that high-stakes accountability has limited their capacity to teach creatively because standards and state assessments dictate what and how to teach. The majority of teachers, therefore, feel that to increase student achievement, they must focus exclusively on the tested standards and devote little to no time to subjects and teaching strategies that do not appear on the state assessment. As the data from this study demonstrate, this reasoning is flawed. Instead of seeing accountability and teaching creatively as two different issues, this study suggests that the two are complementary. Based on the results, it would seem that the best approach for teachers is to focus on the standards and expand on their instructional strategy repertoire to include creative teaching techniques.

Consider the findings of this study and reflect on what you have observed in elementary classrooms today. Are your observations consistent with the findings of this study?

Creative Questioning for Children

Just the way a question is phrased or asked sets the stage for creative replies. For example, the request, "Describe (or tell me about) the sky . . ." would certainly elicit different responses than, "What color is the sky?" In the first, more open-ended (divergent) request, children are encouraged to share their personal feelings and experiences about the sky. This might be color or cloud shapes or even how jets, birds, and helicopters

can fill it at times. The second question is phrased in such a way that a one-word (convergent) reply would do. Or even worse, it may seem to children that there is one and only one correct answer!

In asking questions, then, a teacher can foster children's creativity. Let us now consider more specific examples of activities that focus on creative questioning. These activities suggest various ways of asking questions and are designed to draw out the creative

FIGURE 2-6 • Children are drawn to materials that interest them.

potential in young children. Activities that deal directly with specific art forms and media are found in later sections of this book.

1. Making things better with your imagination.

One way to help children think more creatively is to get them to "make things better with their imagination." Ask children to change things to make them the way they would like them to be. Here are some examples of questions of this type.

- What would taste better if it were sweeter?
- What would be nicer if it were smaller?
- What would be more fun if it were faster?
- What would be better if it were quieter?
- What would be more exciting if it went backwards?
- What would be happier if it were bigger?

2. Using other senses.

Young children can stretch their creative talents by using their senses in unusual ways. For example, children may be asked to close their eyes and guess what has been placed in their hands. (Use a piece of foam rubber, a small rock, a grape, a piece of sandpaper, etc.) Another approach is to have children close their eyes and guess what they hear. (Use sounds like shuffling cards, jingling coins, rubbing sandpaper, or ripping paper.)

When doing this exercise, the children should be asked for reasons for their guesses. Doing so makes the activity more fun and a better learning experience.

3. Divergent-thinking questions.

Any time you ask children a question requiring a variety of answers, you are encouraging their creative thinking skills. Here are some examples using the concept of water.

- How can you use water?
- What floats in water?
- How does water help us?
- Why is cold water cold? Why is hot water hot?
- What are the different colors that water can be? Why?
- What makes water rain? What makes it stop?
- What always stays underwater?

Divergent thinking questions using concepts such as sand, ice, smoke, cars, and similar topics are fun for children. They also encourage openness and flexibility of thinking.

4. What-would-happen-if?

The "What-would-happen-if?" technique has been used successfully by many teachers of young children to spark good thinking-and-doing sessions designed to ignite imaginations. Some of the following questions may be used.

- What would happen if all the trees in the world were blue?
- What would happen if everyone looked alike?
- What would happen if all the cars were gone?
- What would happen if everybody wore the same clothes?
- What would happen if every vegetable tasted like chocolate?
- What would happen if there were no more clocks or watches?
- What would happen if you could fly?

5. In how many different ways?

Another type of question that extends a child's creative thinking is one that begins, "In how many different ways . . .?" A few examples are provided here.

- In how many different ways could a spoon be used?
- In how many different ways could a button be used?

- In how many different ways could a string be used?
- In what new ways could we use this? How could it be modified to fit a new use?

All of these questioning strategies are intended to help an adult encourage creativity in young children. Children may also generate these types of questions once they have been modeled for them. Often, the use of these strategies is enough to begin a long-running and positive creative experience for the child as well as the teacher. They are limited only by the user's imagination.

Motivating Skills for Teachers

Some children need help in getting started. The fact that the activity is labeled "creative" does not necessarily make the child "ready to go." A child may be feeling restless or tired or may feel like doing something else. All teachers, even those with good ideas, face this problem. There are several ways to help children become motivated for the creative process.

Physical needs. Make sure children are rested and physically fit. Sleepy, hungry, or sick children cannot care about creativity. Their physical needs must be met before such learning can be appealing.

Interests. Try to find out, and then use, what naturally interests the child. Children not only want to do things they like to do, they want to be successful at them. Whenever children feel that they will succeed in a task, they are generally much more willing to get involved. Parents may be good resources for determining the child's interests.

Friends. Permit children to work with their friends. This does not mean all the time. However, some teachers avoid putting children who are friends together in working situations. They worry that these children will only fool around or disturb others. When this does happen, one should question the task at hand because it is obviously not holding the children's interest.

Activities for fun. Allow the activity to be fun for the child. Notice the use of the word *allow*. Children know how to have their own fun. They do not need anyone to make it for them. Encourage child-initiated activities and self-selection of creative materials, and emphasize voluntary participation of the children in the activities presented. Teachers are giving children opportunities for fun if they honestly can answer "yes" to these questions:

- Is the activity exciting?
- Is the activity in a free setting?
- Can the children imagine in it?
- Can the children play at it?
- Is there a gamelike quality to it?
- Are judgments avoided?
- Is competition deemphasized?
- Will there be something to laugh about?

Goals. Permit children to set and reach goals. Most of the excitement in achieving a goal is in reaching for it. Children should be given opportunities to plan projects. They should be allowed to get involved in activities that have something at the end for which they can strive. If the completion of an activity is not rewarding to a child, then the value of that activity is questionable.

Variety. Vary the content and style of what the children can do. It is wise to consider not only what will be next, but how it will be done, too. For example, the teacher has the children sit and watch a movie, then they sit and draw, and then they sit and listen to a story. These are three different activities, but in each of them, the children are sitting. The content of the activity has changed, but not the style. This can, and does, become boring. Boring is definitely not creative.

Habit is one of the worst enemies of creativity. Teachers who set the standard for valuing creativity by taking a chance on a "crazy" idea may positively influence the expression of creative potential by many children.

Challenge. Challenge children. This means letting them know that what they are about to do is something that will be exciting to try. An example of this is letting the children know that their next activity may be tricky, adventurous, or mysterious. It is the "bet-you-can't-do-this" approach with the odds in favor of the children.

Reinforcement. Reinforce the creative behavior of children. The basic need here is for something to come at the end of the activity that lets the children feel they would like to do it again. It could be the teacher's smile, a compliment, reaching the goal, hanging up the creation, sharing with a friend, or just finishing the activity. The main thing is that the children feel rewarded for and satisfied with their efforts.

The children's feelings. Try to make certain children feel good about what they are doing. Some teachers believe that if a child is working intensely or learning, that is enough. This may not be so. The most important thing is not what children are doing but how they *feel about* what they are doing. If children feel bad about themselves or an activity while doing it, this is a warning. The teacher must be continually in touch with how the children are feeling. This is the result of listening, watching, and being with the children in a manner that is open and caring.

Summary

Creativity is fun. Incorporating creativity into all areas of the curriculum contributes to a young child's positive attitude toward learning. Teachers who encourage children to work at their own pace and to be self-directed in a relaxed, nonjudgmental atmosphere are fostering creative development.

Young children need knowledge and skills to express their creative potential. The curriculum is the guide by which early childhood teachers determine *what* will be presented to children. Creativity is fostered according to *how* the curriculum is presented to the child. Differentiated instruction is a way of thinking about teaching and learning. Its aim is to maximize each child's growth by meeting each child where he or she is and helping him or her to progress.

Questioning strategies encourage creativity in young children. Even with creative activities, there may be motivational difficulties with some children. Appealing to natural interests, giving expectancies of success, reinforcing, and challenging are a few of the many ways to help children get started and keep going.

The learning environment needs to be a welcoming place. It must encourage exploration by its lack of strict time limits and stressful situations. It must be an environment that encourages children's self-expression and sharing of ideas.

FIGURE 2-7 • Young children explore their world in many ways.

FIGURE 2-8 • Allow children ample time not only to physically explore but also to mentally explore—think about—what they are doing.

Key Terms

Learning Activities

- Examine today's newspaper. What evidence of creative thought do you see in the stories or advertisements? Look for original ideas that are appropriate to the situation. Are all creative ideas socially appropriate?

- One of the most interesting and effective ways to explore creativity is to undertake a creative project of your own. Identify a problem and invent something to address it. For example, an invention might be an enormous version of a dentist's mirror that allows the user to check for leaves in the gutters without climbing a ladder, or a device that signals forgetful teenagers to retrieve their wet laundry. Look around for everyday annoyances or dilemmas that you might solve. What things around you might be improved, simplified, or made more elaborate? Alternatively, you might want to undertake a creative writing project, artistic endeavor, or other creative task. Whatever you choose, record your thoughts, feelings, and activities. How do you feel about creativity as you contemplate such a project?

- This is a small-group activity designed to help you focus on seeing "creatively." The object is to create something artistic out of lots of curved and straight lines. Each student has a piece of paper and a marker. Then, each student draws squiggles and swirls all over their paper. Then, switch papers with a neighbor. Each student then must create something out of the squiggles and swirls drawn by their partner. Or if a student so chooses, they may even just fill in the areas with different colors of designs. This is a great activity to get you thinking outside the box and create something out of nothing.

- Sketch your ideas for illustrating this quote by Alice Walker: "In search of my mother's garden, I found my own."

- With this quote in mind—"A house is a machine for living in" (LeCorbusier)—describe the kind of house you see yourself living in some day. Focus on visual images in your description.

- List three personal experiences that were challenging to you. Consider each and get in touch with the feelings experienced on those occasions.

  1. Was there any chance of failure during these experiences?

  2. What was your motivation?
  3. How did it feel to succeed?
  4. What does this mean for working with young children?
  5. How does it relate to creativity?
  6. List some of your reactions.

- Think about the influence of culture on your conception of creativity. Do you consider some forms of expression or activity more creative than others? Why? What forms of creative expression are most valued by the cultures of students in your group? Are they the same as those you value?

- "Become" one of the following objects and dramatize its characteristics in class:

bicycle	tire pump
wheelbarrow	hose
rake	beach ball

  Describe how you felt. Would children's dramatizations of these be similar? Different? Explain.

- Tape 10 to 15 minutes of classroom interactions in which you play an instructional role. Analyze your interaction in terms of the kinds of questions you used, the amount of time you waited for children to respond after asking a question, and the way you responded to children's talk.

- Observe a classroom and note the creative experiences available to children. To what extent do the experiences offered seem to contribute to the development of creativity? Describe your impressions and suggestions for improvement for the curriculum in creative expression.

- Observe a teacher and describe the kinds of questions used, the amount of time allowed for children to answer, and the kinds of responses made to children. Do you think the communication you observed is effective in encouraging divergent thinking? Why or why not?

- Practice your own divergent thinking by playing the activity "In how many different ways?" described in this chapter. Use a variety of objects: a key, a Lego® block, a paper clip, a spatula, a Dixie cup. Compare your responses to those of several children.

- Also play the "Making things better" game described in this chapter, comparing your responses to those of several children. Whose responses—yours or theirs—best meet the criteria for being creative?

- Observe a preschool child and a fifth-grade student in drawing activities. Do their approaches to art indicate any differences in their apparent levels of creativity? Is one age more creative than the other?
- Observe in several upper-level elementary non-art classes. Notice differences in the ways teachers reward creative behavior, such as when a student asks probing questions, comes up with different ways of doing things, enjoys experimenting, isn't satisfied with easy answers, and questions the teacher. Which teacher responses are most in keeping with the guidelines presented in this chapter?
- With a classmate, examine the same set of student papers or products. Do you agree on which are the most creative or original? Why or why not?
- Compile a creativity portfolio for at least one student. Include evidence of creative activities in at least three areas of the curriculum. You may want to share the information with the student's parents.
- How are creativity killers like evaluation, reward, competition, and lack of choice operating in your classroom? Investigate whether students are evaluated for creativity in your school district. If they are, examine the assessment procedure. Based on what you learned in this chapter, would you make any recommendations that might improve it?
- From your own peer group of students, select the most creative individuals. Is there general agreement on who these creative persons are? What were the criteria on which selections were made? How do these criteria align with those presented in this book?
- **Looking for Shadows.** People usually don't pay much attention to things they see every day. A key to being creative, however, is noticing things that other people often miss. Take shadows. Most people don't bother to look at shadows. But, once you start looking for shadows, you'll discover them everywhere. Looking at shadows is a good way to focus your vision and reacquaint yourself with the world around you.

For this exercise you'll need a flashlight, and a camera.

1. Begin by studying the shadows of things in your room. Take a strong flashlight and shine it on an object.

Notice how the position of the light determines the size and shapes of the shadow.

2. Go outside on a sunny day and concentrate on shadows. Watch the shadows of things moving around you. Notice how much detail you can see in shadows. If it's late afternoon, note how the shadows stretch out on the ground. For fun, play with your own shadow for a while.

3. Take a camera and shoot pictures of the shadows you see in your surroundings. Look for both familiar and unfamiliar shadows to record. Select your "best" shadow picture to hang on the class bulletin board.

Activities for Children

Water Play Activities for Creative Thinking

Water play lends itself to the development of creative thinking in young children. A creative teacher can extend the play of young children by asking thought-provoking, divergent-thinking questions, posing simple problems to solve with water and play objects. Some of these divergent-thinking questions follow.

- Can you make the water in your squeeze bottle shoot out like water from a hose?
- Can you make a water shower for the plants?
- Can you catch one drop of water on something? How many drops of water can you put on a jar lid?
- Can we think of some words to talk about what we do with water or that tell what water can do? (*sprinkle, pour, drip, trickle, drizzle, shower, splash, stir, ripple*, etc.)
- Could we collect some rainwater? How?
- How far can you make the water spray?
- Can you make something look different by putting it in water?
- Can you find some things that float (or sink) in the water?
- Can you make a noise in the water?

Divergent Questions About Water

Ask children some of the following questions to encourage their creative thinking.

- What are some uses of water?
- What floats in water?
- How does water help us?
- What always stays underwater?
- What are the different colors that water can be?

Follow up children's responses by encouraging them to draw, paint, or model in clay or play dough the ideas about water they experienced during this activity. Generate divergent questions about other topics such as fire, sand, smoke, and ice.

Space Explorers

When children need a "stretch," try one of these for fun.

- Have children pretend they are on a planet in space where they are much heavier than they are on earth. Have them lift their arms as though they weighed twice as much as they do.
- Have children pretend they are on the moon. Have them lift their arms as though they were very light—

almost weightless. Also have children "float" across the floor.

- Have children select a familiar activity such as dancing or moving to rhythms and carry out that activity on a strange planet, using slow motion because of increased weight.

Balloon Moves

Caution: Never use balloons with children younger than three years old.

Blow up a balloon for each child. If possible, use extra-thick balloons and blow them up only part way. Have extras on hand in case some balloons burst. Tie one end of a 3-foot piece of string or ribbon to each child's balloon. Tie the other end of the string/ribbon to the child's waist, if the child wishes.

Go outdoors with the children. Talk about the wind and how it makes the balloon move in different ways. Encourage children to use their bodies to nudge the balloon and make it move. Model new movements and make fun suggestions to extend children's movement exploration. Older children might work in pairs or in small groups to keep a balloon in the air on a calm day.

Indoors, allow children to move in creative ways with the balloon. Challenge children to devise movements different from those of their classmates in keeping their balloon in motion.

More Balloon Moves

Go outdoors and have children pretend to be carrying a balloon. When you say, "Go!" children pretend to let their balloons float off into the sky. Direct children to move as if they were these imaginary balloons, floating through space.

Falling Leaves

In this activity, children explore nature's cycles as they recreate the path of a leaf. Use music with a slow, floating quality. ("The Autumn" from *The Four Seasons* by Antonio Vivaldi or "Canon in D" by Pachelbel are two good choices). You will also need real or construction paper autumn leaves and a photograph or picture of an autumn tree.

Talk with children about how autumn affects leaves— how they change colors and then fall. Encourage children to move like a leaf as it twists and floats to the ground. Invite a few children to demonstrate some of these motions with their hands—for instance, reaching up high and slowly swaying down using both hands as if they were floating to the floor.

- Create a "woods in fall" atmosphere by bringing in colorful leaves (or cutting them out of paper). Hold each one up, then let it drop while children brainstorm words to describe its path. Write their words on a large piece of chart paper.
- Ask children to lift up their hands and copy the path of a floating, tumbling, twirling leaf. You may want to use some of their words from the previously mentioned chart. Then choose a space for them to recreate the path of a leaf with their bodies. Indicate the path by posting or drawing a picture of a tree at one end of the room and placing a leaf (for the leaf pile) at the other end.
- Group children at the "tree" end of the room. Tell them that in their playing falling leaves they should start with their hands reaching up high into the tree branches to show they are still attached to the tree, and then spin, sway, and float all the way to the designated leaf pile. Suggest that they start on tiptoe and gradually get lower and lower, crouching as they drift and twirl, until they are gently rolling along the floor toward the leaf pile.
- Put on the music and send the leaves on their way, one by one, with a tap for each. When all children have reached the leaf pile, ask them to relax and listen to the music. Repeat the activity, tapping each resting leaf when it's time to walk slowly back to the tree area and attach to the branches to begin again.
- Children also learn by watching each other. Have half the group watch the other half travel the leaf pathway. Add interest by asking the leaves to freeze their positions. Then ask the audience to notice and comment on the leaf shapes and places in their fall. Switch groups and repeat. Encourage children to try out any new movements they observed.

Circle Creations

- Have children find circle shapes in the room. Then have them draw circles of different sizes on their paper, doing at least five variations.
- Next, have the children find five different ways to make circular shapes with their bodies. Tell them to hold each shape still as if they were having a photo taken. Ask them to try to repeat their five ideas.
- Then, have them discover with a partner five different ways to make circle shapes together. They might change the level from high to low, face different directions, or use different parts of their bodies.
- Then, have them do the same thing in a small group.
- After you are done, ask the children to describe the ways they formed circles. How did they create circular shapes with a partner or a group? How was making circles with a partner or group different from making circles alone?

Creative Games

Have children create with their bodies a "machine" piece by piece. Some players become parts that move and make noise while others operate the machine. Others can guess what it is. Try making a lawnmower with people as wheels, body, and handle and have another player push it. Everyone can join in the sound effects as it cuts the lawn. More good objects to play: CD or MP3 player, garbage disposal, toaster, pencil sharpener, and water fountain.

Imagination Game

Divide the children into pairs. Have partners stretch out on their stomachs. One child in each pair holds the ankles of the other to form a snake. Then partners slither around the room and connect to each other to make a bigger and bigger snake. If snakes aren't your thing, then children could be caterpillars or earthworms.

Guess What I Am!

Without saying a word, a child acts out the movement of some object. Suggestions for the game include an airplane making a landing, a cement truck dumping its load, a clock telling the time of day. The child may think up things to do, or the teacher may whisper suggestions.

Scarves

Give each child in the group a colorful lightweight scarf. Encourage them to dance with their scarf in response to music. Use a record or tape of instrumental music, or turn the radio to a station that plays music. Encourage children to express their thoughts aloud as they dance.

Drawing for Creative Expression

Encourage children to use imagination in expressing their observations, ideas and feelings through drawing. Have them try some of the following:
- Draw a picture showing how you would improve human beings.
- Design a special machine or device to help the President.
- Draw a picture that shows how you would weigh an elephant.
- Design a machine that makes peanut butter.
- Draw a picture of a jellybean factory.
- Design an underground city.
- Design a dog-exercising machine.
- Draw a picture that shows how you would make your school a better place.
- Draw as many animals as you can on one page, some real, some imaginary.
- Draw a map for a brain surgeon. A heart surgeon.
- Draw a picture of something that can't be seen.
- Draw a picture of an angry sea or a noisy city. The lines you make should help to express the mood of your picture.
- Complete and then illustrate one of the following statements: "If only I could . . . " "Wouldn't it be strange if . . . " "Can you believe I saw . . . "

Becoming an Object

The teacher names inanimate objects. Children show with their bodies the shapes of the various objects. If the object is moved by an external force, they show with their bodies how the object would move. For instance, they may move like:
- An orange being peeled.
- A standing lamp being carried across the room.
- A wall with a vine growing over it.
- A paperclip being inserted onto paper.
- An ice cube melting.
- A balloon losing its air.
- A cloud drifting through the sky, slowly changing shapes.
- Smoke coming out of a chimney.
- A twisted pin being thrust into paper.
- A rubber ball bouncing along the ground.
- A boat being tossed by the waves.
- An arrow being shot through the air.
- A steel bar being hammered into different shapes.

Activities for Older Children (Grades 4–5)

Telling Tableaus

Tableaus are "frozen pictures" in which groups of students freeze or pose to act out a scene, a saying, a book title, etc. Before starting tableaus, discuss the skills necessary to be a good "freezer" (i.e., eyes staring blankly, no movement, frozen expression). Have students work in groups and give each group a caption (or better yet, have the students choose their own). Give students 5 to 10 minutes (more, if needed) to develop their scene and practice their frozen poses. Don't allow any props.

To begin the performances, have the first group come to the front of the room. Turn off the lights and have the other students close their eyes as the first group sets up their scene. When the scene is set, turn on the lights and have the students open their eyes. Then read the caption or have the class guess the title, whichever you feel is appropriate. Continue through the tableau scenes until all groups have had a chance to perform.

Television Drama

Record a part of a television show that will interest your students. Students will be able to tell you which are their favorite shows if you aren't sure. Show students a couple of minutes of the recording and then turn it off. Discuss the creativity the characters are using. Show more of the program and stop it at a critical point in the story. Have students work in pairs to brainstorm decisions the characters could make. Then turn the show back on to see what decision the character actually made and what happened as a result of that decision. Have students determine whether the characters came up with creative decisions and then defend their position.

Fairy Tales—Not Just Fancy

Fairy tales are naturally creative and full of fantasy. Use fairy tales for these activities for older children's creative exercises.

Creative fairy tale puppet show. Create a puppet show to retell your favorite fairy tale to the class. Change one thing about the story and see if the class can guess the change.

Fairy tale rating. Read four fairy tales of your choice. Rate them in order of your most to least favorite and explain why you rated them as you did. Write a short review of your favorite fairy tale explaining why everyone should read it.

Fairy tale journal. Pretend you have been put into a fairy tale, and in journal form discuss the events and characters you meet. Discuss what you like and dislike about the characters. Include at least eight entries.

Fairy tale logic. Choose a song that you think tells a story similar to one of the fairy tales you've read, and then write a short essay explaining why you chose this song and why it relates to your fairy tale.

Fairy tale music. Compose a song that tells the story of one of the fairy tales. Perform it for a group of students, and have them guess which fairy tale your song represents.

Fairy tale picture book. Create a picture book for your favorite fairy tale. Read it to another class.

Fairy tale day. Plan a Fairy Tale Day for the class, including activities for the entire day. This may include dressing up as your favorite character, eating fairy tale foods, playing games, and reading fairy tales.

Fairy tale rewrite. Rewrite a fairy tale from the perspective of one of the minor characters in the story. Read your story to the class.

Fairy tale game. Create a board game with a fairy tale theme. Include all of the main parts of the story in the game. Let students play the game and give you feedback. Make any changes that would make it more fun to play.

Five Whole Minutes—A Brainstorming Idea

Brainstorm with children a list of different things they think they can do in 5 minutes. Put the list aside. Have children do various things in 5-minute intervals (e.g., read, exercise, color, do math, walk, sit perfectly still, etc). Discuss their reactions. Talk about time management and how 5 minutes can be used most effectively.

Looking at Things in New Ways

Artists develop their visual abilities by continuous practice and use. They practice by looking at things closely, drawing them, and recording them in their mind's eye. Have your students (and you, too!) try some of these visual exercises to develop their and your own visual abilities.

- Draw a picture of something (like a bicycle or a shoe) showing it from different views on the same page.
- Fill a page full of drawings of bugs, seashells, or something you collect.
- Examine an object for 1 minute. Put the object away. Then draw a picture of what you remember about it. When you've finished, look at the object again and see how much you remembered about it.
- Use a magnifying glass to draw enlarged views of water drops, hair, plant leaves, and other small items.
- Go through a magazine and cut out a picture of something you like or find interesting to look at. Draw a picture of this image—only turn it upside down. This will make you look closely at what you're drawing.
- Draw a family member or friend from memory.
- Sit under a tree and draw the tree from your point of view. Draw other things around your backyard (or school yard) from unusual points of view. Or take pictures instead of drawing in this exercise.
- Take off your shoe and examine it closely. Feel its contours, look inside, turn it upside down. Once you've done this, draw a picture of it. Try this with other common objects around you.

Take a Drawing Break

When you find you have five to ten minutes to fill, have your students take a "drawing break" by drawing some of the following: Draw your lunch. Draw the teacher. Draw a friend. Draw your hand holding something. Draw a small object big. Draw a car. Draw a dream. Draw a nightmare. Draw a leaf. Draw yourself.

Creative Problem Solving—No Hands Allowed!

The objective of this activity is for students to use creative thinking and problem-solving skills to figure out ways to carry a variety of items without using their hands. In advance, gather together an assortment of large and small objects, such as cardboard boxes and stuffed animals. Set out the items for children to choose for the game.

- Meet as a group and invite children to talk about different ways people carry large and small objects. Ask children to demonstrate how they would hold and carry a box. Then, challenge them to think of other ways they might hold and carry the same box.
- Help children pair off and explain that each pair will work together to carry a cardboard box across the room. The only rule: No hands allowed!
- Give a box to each set of partners and invite them to figure out different ways to lift and hold the box without using their hands.
- After partners have had time to experiment, gather everyone together, along with the boxes, in an area with a lot of floor space. Ask partners to take turns carrying their boxes all the way across the room and back.
- Invite partners to choose an object of a different size from among the assorted items you had set out earlier. Encourage children to work together to find an original way to transport the new item across the

room and back. Encourage children to experiment with a variety of objects.

- Now combine sets of partners so that children are working in groups of four. Challenge them to move an object or two, making sure that everyone touches the object—without, of course, using their hands.

Experience Journal

Have children explore their environment. Pick a nearby location—a mall, a park, any area they enjoy exploring. Ask children to visit that location as an artist, writer, scientist, historian, or mathematician. They should observe their surroundings carefully and record their observations. Have children reflect on how their point of view affected their experience.

Historical Research

Have children go to the library and locate a newspaper from the day they were born. Have them examine the headlines, the advertisements, the sports pages, and the classified ads. Encourage children to ask relatives what they remember about that day. Arrange for children to listen to music or watch a movie that was popular then. Try to be aware of what children are learning and how they feel as the project progresses. Did history come alive? Have children record their feelings and think about what their experiences as an authentic historian were like.

Animal Artwork

The "scratch art" of a Jack Russell terrier named Tillamook Cheddar was featured on CNN. His owner gave him pieces of carbon paper wrapped around cardboard, which the little dog loved to dig at and scratch designs on. Go to his website, http://en.wikipedia.org/wiki/Tillamook_Cheddar_(dog) and decide if you think that his work is art or not. Should a dog have an exhibit in art galleries?

Chapter Review

1. Describe the relationship between creativity and the curriculum.
2. Describe the role of play and exploration in promoting creativity.
3. Demonstrate four questioning strategies that encourage creative thinking in the young child.
4. List three questions to consider when modifying curricula to encourage creative thinking.
5. Describe at least four characteristics of differentiated instruction.

References

Amabile, T. M. (1996). *Creativity in context.* Boulder, CO: Westview Press.

Bredekamp, S. (Ed.). (2009). *Developmentally appropriate practice in early childhood programs serving birth through age 8* (3rd ed.). Washington, DC: National Association for the Education of Young Children.

Catania, A. C. (2008). Brain and behavior: Which way does the shaping go? *Behavioral and Brain Sciences, 31*(5), 516–517.

Csikszentmihalyi, M. (1996). *Creativity: Flow and the psychology of discovery and invention.* New York: HarperCollins.

Dacey, J. S., & Lennon, K. H. (1998). *Understanding creativity: The interplay of biological, psychological, and social factors.* San Francisco, CA: Jossey-Bass.

Fischer, K. W., Immordino-Yang, M. H., & Weber, D. (2007). Toward a grounded synthesis of mind, brain, and education for reading disorders: An introduction to the field and this book. In K. W. Fischer, J. H. Bernstein, & M. H. Immordino-Yang (Eds.), *Mind, brain and education in learning disorders* (pp. 1–20). Cambridge, NY: Cambridge University Press.

Hinton, C., Miyamoto, K., & Della-Chiesa, B. (2008). Brain research, learning and emotions: Implications for education research, policy and practice. *European Journal of Education, 43*(1), 87–103.

Mumford, M. D., & Simonton, D. K. (1997). Creativity in the workplace: People, problems and structures. *Journal of Creative Behavior, 31,* 1–6.

Moran, J. D., III, Milgram, R., Sawyers, J. K., & Fu, V. R. (1985). Original thinking in preschool children. *Child Development, 54,* 921–26.

Perry, B. D. (2009). Emotional development: Curiosity—the fuel of development. *Scholastic Early Childhood Today.* Retrieved from http:www2.scholastic.com/browse/article.jsp?id=4043

Runco, M. (2008). Creativity and education. *New Horizons in Education, 56*(1), 18–23.

Rushton, S., & Larkin, E. (2007). Shaping the learning environment: Connecting developmentally appropriate practices to brain research. *Early Childhood Education Journal, 29*(1), 25–33.

Schacter, J., Thum, Y. M., & Zifkin, D. (2006). How much does creative teaching enhance elementary school students' achievement? *The Journal of Creative Behavior, 40*(1), 47–65.

Tomlinson, C. A. (2000). Reconcilable differences: Standards-based teaching and differentiation. *Educational Leadership, 57*(8), 7–11.

Torrance, E. P. (1962). *Guiding creative talent.* Englewood Cliffs, NJ: Prentice Hall.

Torrance, E. P. (1995). *Why fly? A philosophy of creativity.* Westport, CT: Ablex Publishing.

United States Department of Labor. (1991). *What work requires of schools.* Washington, DC: Author.

Wallach, M., & Kogan, N. (1965). *Modes of thinking in young children: A study of creativity-intelligence distinction.* New York, NY: Holt, Rinehart, & Winston.

Additional Readings

Amabile, T. M., Barsade, S. G., Mueller, J. S., & Straw, B. M. (2005). Affect and creativity at work. *Administrative Science Quarterly, 50*(3), 367–403.

Amabile, T. M., Constance, N. H., & Steven, J. K. (2002). Creativity under the gun. *Harvard Business Review, 80*(8), 52–61.

Bowkett, W., & Bowkett, S. (2008). *100 ideas for teaching creative development.* London, UK: Continuum International.

Church, E. B. (2002, March). When to challenge children. *Scholastic Early Childhood Today, 2,* 34.

Colker, L. (2008). Twelve characteristics of effective early childhood teachers. *Young Children, 63*(2), 68–73.

Davis, J. H. (2008). *Why our schools need the arts.* Reston, VA: National Association of Art Educators.

Diamond, A., & Amso, D. (2008). Contributions of neurosciences to our understanding of cognitive development. *Current Directions in Psychological Sciences, 4*(1), 136–149.

Fisher, C., & Amabile, T. (2009). Creativity, improvisation, and organizations. In T. Rickards, M. A. Runco, & S. Moger (Eds.), *The Routledge companion to creativity.* Oxford, UK: Routledge.

Freeman-Zachery, R. (2009). *Creative time and space: Making room for making art.* Cincinnati, OH: F & W Media.

Guning, S. (2009). *Audacious creativity: 30 ways to liberate your soulful creative energy—and how it can transform your life.* Cincinnati, OH: Creative Blast Press.

Hawley, R. (2008). *Beyond the Icarus factor: Releasing the free spirit of boys.* Rochester, VT: Inner Traditions/Bear & Co.

Holliday, T. K. (2008). My inner conflict between logic and creativity. *School Administrator, 65*(2), 48–51.

Jeffrey, G., & Woods, P. (2009). *Creative learning in primary school.* Oxford, UK: Routledge.

Justo, C. F. (2008). Creative relaxation, motor creativity, self-concept in a sample of children from early childhood education. *Electronic Journal of Research in Educational Psychology, 6*(1), 29–50.

Lynch, R. L. (2008). Creating a brighter workforce with the arts. *School Administrator, 65*(30), 26–28.

Moore, M., & Russ, S. W. (2008). Follow-up of a pretend play intervention: Effects on play, creativity, and emotional processes in children. *Creativity Research Journal, 20*(4), 427–436.

Patterson, B. (2008). *Kaleidoscope: Projects and ideas to spark your creativity.* Cincinnati, OH: North Light Books.

Ragsdale, S., & Saylor, A. (2009). *Building character from the start: 210 activities to foster creativity, literacy, and play in K–3.* Minneapolis, MN: Search Institute Press.

Ruggiero, V. R. (2008). *The art of thinking.* Upper Saddle River, NJ: Longman Publishing Group/Pearson.

Wilson, H. D. (2009). The Picasso in your classroom: How to meet the needs of talented artists in elementary school. *Gifted Child Today, 32*(1), 36–41.

Software for Children

Blue's Clues Art Time Activity, ages 3–6
Crayola Paint 'n Play Pony, ages 5–10
Curious George Paint & Print Studio, ages 3–8
Dream Chronicles, ages 8 and up
Freaky Creatures, ages 8 and up
Freddi Fish and the Case of the Missing Kelp Seeds, ages 3–8

Milo and the Magic Stone, ages 4–8
Professor Fizzwizzle, ages 6 and up
Rainbow Fish and the Most Beautiful Fish, ages 3–8
Rainbow Islands: Towering Adventure, ages 6 and up
Taki Mojo Mistake, ages 8 and up
World of Goo, ages 6 and up

Helpful Websites

These websites are related to children's creativity and creative activities.

**Arts Edge—Kennedy Center, http://artsedge
.kennedy-center.org/**
Block Corner, www.blockcorner.com
**Creative Teaching, Teaching, http://www
.creativeteachingsite.com**
Invention at Play, http://www.inventionatplay.org
Museum of Modern Art, http://www.moma.org

National Gallery's Art Zone, www.nga.gov/kids
PBS website, http://www.pbs.org
**Smithsonian's Lemelson Center, http://www
.invention.smithsonian.org/home**
Teaching Pre K–8, http://www.TeachingK-8.com

For additional creative activity resources, visit our website at www.Cengage.com/login.

CHAPTER
3

The Concept of Aesthetics

OBJECTIVES

After studying this chapter, you should be able to:

1. Define aesthetics.

2. List three things a teacher can do to help children develop their aesthetic sensitivity.

3. List five benefits of aesthetic sensitivity in children.

4. List at least three art elements to discuss with children.

The term **aesthetics** refers to an appreciation for beauty and a feeling of wonder. Aesthetic experience begins with and depends on the senses. It is seeing beauty in a sunset, hearing rhythm in a rainfall, and loving the expression on a person's face. Each person has an individual, personal sense of what is or is not pleasing.

The **Aesthetics Movement** in the art world began in early 1800 and lasted the decade. In the art world, the term *aesthetics* was invented or adapted from Greek by the German philosopher Baumgarten, whose work *Aesthetica* was published in 1750. In this particular work, the word was defined to mean the "science of the beautiful" or the "philosophy of taste." The word was used with its opposite, "Philistine," which in this context meant "one lacking culture" whose interests were bound by material and commonplace things as opposed to the high-minded spiritual and artistic values of the aesthetes. By 1880, the aesthetic movement in the arts was a well-established fact and the name itself became a part of everyday speech.

In the center of the movement was a close-knit group of self-appointed "experts" who passed on to their followers standards of color, ornament, and form for all aspects of art. These standards were in direct opposition to the ornate Victorian style. The aesthetic movement preferred the simple and sensible over the ornate. One of the most influential figures of the whole movement was Oscar Wilde, who lectured and spread the word of the aesthetic movement. The famous painter, Whistler, was another supporter of the aesthetic movement.

Aesthetic experiences emphasize doing things for the pure joy of it. Although there can be, there does not have to be any practical purpose or reason for doing. The goal of aesthetic experiences is a full, rich life for the child. You may take a ride in a car to feel its power and enjoy the scenery rather than to visit someone or run an errand. In the same way, a child plays with blocks to feel their shapes and see them tumble rather than to build something.

FIGURE 3-1 • Children grow in their aesthetic appreciation as they are actively involved in creative learning experiences.

FIGURE 3-2 • It is a common occurrence in early childhood programs to find young children moving rhythmically with their bodies.

Young children benefit from aesthetic experiences. Children are fascinated by beauty. They love nature and enjoy creating, looking at, and talking about art. They express their feelings and ideas through language, song, expressive movement, music, and dance far more openly than adults. They are not yet hampered by the conventional labels used by adults to separate each art expression into pigeonholes. Young children experience the arts as a whole. They are creative, inquisitive, and delighted by art.

It is interesting to note that creative adults involved in the arts are finally catching up with young children. On the contemporary arts scene, there is a movement toward **multimedia artwork**. Examples of this multimedia movement are walk-in sculpture environments; a mix of live dance and films; and a mix of art exhibitions with drama, where actors move into the audience to engage it in the drama. All of these are new ways adults are integrating the arts.

This exciting development may be new for sophisticated adult artists, but it is a familiar approach for young children. For instance, in early childhood programs, it is a common occurrence to find young children singing original songs while they paint or moving their bodies rhythmically while playing with clay. Young children naturally and unself-consciously integrate the arts—weaving together graphic arts, movement, dance, drama, music, and poetry in their expressive activities.

The capacity for aesthetics is a fundamental human characteristic. Infants sense with their whole bodies. They are open to all feelings; experience is not separated from thinking. A child's aesthetic sense comes long before the ability to create. All of an infant's experiences have an aesthetic component—preferring a soft satin-edged blanket, studying a bright mobile, or choosing a colorful toy. These choices are all statements of personal taste. As infants grow into toddlers, the desire to learn through taste, touch, and smell as well as through sight and sound grows, too. The ability to make aesthetic choices continues to grow through preschool. Preschoolers' ability to perceive, respond, and be sensitive becomes more obvious and more refined. This is obvious in their spontaneous creations using a wide variety of materials.

To develop an aesthetic sense in children, one must help them continuously find beauty and wonder in their world. This is any child's potential. In fact, it is the potential of every human being. To create, invent, be joyful, sing, dance, love, and be amazed are possible for everyone.

Children sometimes see and say things to please adults; teachers must realize this and the power it implies. Teachers who prefer that children see beauty as they themselves do are not encouraging a sense of aesthetics in children. They are fostering uniformity and obedience. Only children who choose and evaluate for themselves can truly develop their own aesthetic taste. Just as becoming literate is a basic goal of education, one of the key goals of all creative early childhood programs is to help young children develop the ability to speak freely about their own attitudes, feelings, and ideas about art. Each child has a right to a personal choice of beauty, joy, and wonder.

Children gain an aesthetic sense by doing. This means sensing, feeling, and responding to things. It can be rolling a ball, smelling a flower, petting an animal, or hearing a story. Aesthetic development takes place in secure settings free of competition and adult judgment.

Aesthetics and the Quality of Learning

Aesthetic learning means joining what one thinks with what one feels. Through art, ideas and feelings are expressed. People draw and sculpt to show their feelings about life. Art is important because it can deepen and enlarge understanding. All children cannot be great artists, but children can develop an aesthetic sense, an appreciation for art.

Teachers can encourage the aesthetic sense in children in a variety of ways. For example, science activities lend themselves very well to beauty and artistic expression. Because children use their senses in learning, science exhibits with things like rocks, wood, and leaves can be placed in attractive displays for children to touch, smell, and explore with all of their senses. They can experience with their senses artistic elements such as line, shape, pattern, color, and texture in these natural objects.

Sensory awareness is nourished by teachers who help young children focus on the variations and contrasts in the environment: the feel and look of smooth bark and rippling rough bark, the heaviness of rock

FIGURE 3-3 • The capacity to make aesthetic choices continues to grow through preschool.

and the lightness of pumice stone, the feathery leaf and the leathery leaf, the slippery marble and the sticky tar. All these are opportunities for expression in the arts, poetry, sound, movement, and many other art forms.

The arts are developed best as a whole. After hearing a story, some children may want to act it out. Some may prefer to paint a picture about it. Others may wish to create a dance about it, and some may want to make the music for the dance. These activities can lead to others. There should be a constant exchange, not only among all the art activities but among all subject areas. This prevents children from creating a false separation between work and play, art and learning, and thought and feeling.

There are three basic ways to provide young children developmentally appropriate aesthetic experiences in the early childhood program (Althouse, Johnson, & Mitchell, 2003):

1. Provide many opportunities to create art.
2. Provide many opportunities to look at and talk about art.
3. Help children become aware of art in their everyday lives.

Of these three, the most often overlooked is the second. Many teachers mistakenly believe that if they are not artists themselves, they are not able to adequately discuss art with young children. Yet, most young children enjoy talking about art if they are given the opportunity, as evidenced in the following scenario.

A small, bright-eyed child named Risa arrived at my first preschool art class in the arms of her mother. She participated enthusiastically in the looking, talking, and making activities, and she especially liked our visits to the art museum. Risa clearly loved art, and I looked forward to our time together.

One Sunday afternoon, I was presenting an adult program in the museum. It was a tough crowd, and I sweated as I looked from one to another, waiting for someone to answer my question about a painting. Suddenly Risa appeared from nowhere, making her way to me through all those adult legs. Her mother said she heard my voice during their family outing and insisted on coming over for "class." Risa stared raptly at the artwork and then, in her baby voice, answered my question. We had a good conversation about the painting, its colors, shapes, and subject matter. Risa, at three years of age, was able to describe a work of art and have a conversation about it. She was also the highlight of my presentation that afternoon (Villeneuve, 2003).

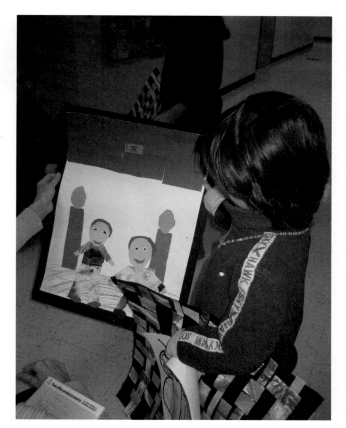

FIGURE 3-4 • Provide children with many opportunities to look at and talk about art.

The early childhood environment can be set up in such a way as to encourage this type of aesthetic discussion by implementing the following suggestions.

- In addition to the typical art center, include books about artists in the reading area (see the website for references).
- Include "real" art books in the reading and quiet areas of the room. These do not necessarily have to be children's books; young children will enjoy looking at artwork in any book.
- Display fine-art prints on bulletin boards and walls so that children can easily see them. Be sure to change them regularly. If they are up too long, they will quickly fade into the background.
- Include art objects on the science table, where appropriate. Geodes, shards of pottery, and crystals are all good starting points.
- Invite guest art educators into the classroom to show children art objects to look at, touch, and talk about.
- Give children an opportunity to choose their favorites from a selection of fine-art prints.
- Display fine-art prints near the writing and art centers.

Suggestions for Aesthetic Experiences with Older Children

Children experience a developmental shift around ages 7 to 8 that allows them to deal with more abstract ideas (more information about this shift is in Chapter 10). At this point, older children not only are able to experience the arts aesthetically but also begin discussing their own opinions, aesthetic tastes, and experiences. Thus, the teacher can engage children in grades 4 to 5 in discussions about what is art and why they consider something to be art or not. The following is an example of a combination 4th- to 5th-grade class involved in this type of aesthetics discussion.

This example demonstrates the type of environment for older children in which questioning is valued. In such an environment, students will feel comfortable raising questions about art and expressing their reactions to it. Teachers of older children need to encourage rather than suppress discussion of aesthetic questions as they emerge. This is done by providing students the time and environment for art-related experiences and inquiry.

THINK ABOUT IT   The Effects of Art on Inner-City Students' Self-Confidence, Creativity, and Self-Efficacy

Researchers at the University of California–Los Angeles conducted a study involving 103 inner-city nine-year-olds in public school classrooms in Los Angeles, California, and St. Louis, Missouri. Both schools were located in areas surrounded by poverty, crime, drug traffic and economic hardship.

The students in the study received regular instruction from highly skilled artists at Inner City Arts (ICA) in Los Angeles and through the Center of Contemporary Arts (COCA) in St. Louis. These institutions stand out as oases in their neighborhoods and city cultures. By public acclaim, both ICA and COCA present vivid symbols of the importance and the joy of the arts in attractive physical settings adorned with children's artwork, high-quality facilities and equipment, skilled, enthusiastic teachers who understand children, and an atmosphere of creativity and purpose. The researchers questioned what, apart from joy, industry, and a profusion of artwork, these programs could bring to the children participating in them (Catterall & Peppler, 2007).

To study the exact effects of these two programs, the study enlisted a treatment–comparison group design in which learning measures for arts participants were compared to learning measured for comparison students (those not in the arts programs). They also used pre- and post surveys that were completed by all of the subjects. In addition, they used regular structured observations of the classrooms to measure how the ICA and COCA programs operated.

The researchers chose third-grade classrooms, children in the nine- to ten-year range, because these children would be able to follow a simple written survey and because their self-beliefs were considered more malleable than those of older, more world-hardened children. They were able to use three entire classrooms of students and not volunteers of staff nominations for choosing participants in the arts program. This way, they were able to see the effects of the program on entire classrooms of students and determine the significance by comparing their scores with classrooms from the control group.

The researchers administered a survey instrument to both the arts and non-arts students prior to the start-up programs, and again within 2 weeks after the program ended. Because the children had generally below-average achievement levels, the survey items were worded with appropriate-level language. Also, because many of the third graders were still struggling to read, the surveys were given with research assistants and the principal investigator reading the items in front of the classroom while students followed along with rulers to guide their attention to the questions at hand.

The survey items were designed to measure self-concept, self-efficacy (the ability to achieve goals), and internal versus external attribution for success. The 13-item self-concept scale included statements such as "I am able to do things as well as most other people." The 7-item self-efficacy scale included statements such as "When I make plans, I think I can make them work" and "I have control over my future." The 2-item attribution scale contained this item "Good luck is more important than hard work." The survey also contained scales for elements of creativity based on the Torrance Test of Creativity, designed for elementary-age students (Abedi, 2002; Auzmendi, Villa, & Abedi, 1996).

The researchers reported two main findings in their study. The primary finding was that participation in a sustained program of high-quality visual arts instruction was associated significantly with growth in the children's beliefs of self-efficacy. They suggest this reflects the children's feelings of accomplishment in the visual arts. The children in the arts group believed they could be agents in creating their own futures. They were more optimistic about what the world has in store for them.

The second main finding was that the arts program had effects not only on self-efficacy beliefs, but also on children's originality as measured on the children's version of the Torrance Test of Creative Thinking (Abedi, 2002; Auzmendi, Villa, & Abedi, 1996).

In conclusion, the researchers argue that original thinking and self-efficacy may go hand in hand, and tendencies toward original thinking spawned by the arts may transfer to original thinking in general. They also argue that high-quality visual arts education encourages a sense of self-efficacy as well as creative, original thinking. Such outcomes benefit all children. But, as the researchers state, "They are particularly important when considering the lives of underprivileged children for whom educational and social advantages are scarce" (Catterall & Peppler, 2007, p. 559).

THIS ONE'S for YOU! | Very Special Arts (VSA)

Very Special Arts (VSA) is an international nonprofit organization founded in 1974 by Ambassador Jean Kennedy Smith. For more than 30 years, VSA has worked to create a society where people with disabilities can learn through, participate in, and enjoy the arts. Currently, more than 5 million people participate in VSA programs through a network of affiliates nationwide and in more than 60 countries.

Mission. The scope of the organization's work is immense, reaching people of all ages and abilities across the globe. Yet their mission remains simple: to use the arts to include people with disabilities in all aspect of society.

About VSA. Designated by the United States Congress as the coordinating organization for arts programming for persons with disabilities, VSA is supported by its affiliate network in offering diverse programs and events and innovative lifelong learning opportunities at all levels from local through international.

Learning Through the Arts. Programming and initiatives of VSA arts are guided by four essential principles:

- Every young person with a disability deserves access to appropriate arts learning experiences.
- All artists in schools and art educators should be adequately prepared to include students with disabilities in their instruction.
- All children, youth, and adults with disabilities should have complete access to community cultural facilities and activities.
- All individuals with disabilities who aspire to careers in the arts should have the opportunity to develop necessary skills.

Working for Change. VSA is committed to driving change—changing perceptions and practice, classroom by classroom, community by community, and ultimately society. There is still a long way to go to achieve inclusive arts access and equal opportunity of expression for all. But VSA, found at www.vsarts.org, is a wonderful starting point.

In their unit on art and history, prints of the work of Civil War photographer Matthew Brady were displayed and discussed. The fact was brought up by the teacher that Brady frequently repositioned and rearranged bodies of dead soldiers and other objects in composing war scenes to be photographed. The teacher used this fact to encourage the students' responses to her initial question: "Is there anything about Brady's practice that should disturb us?"

The discussion led the students in many directions involving such issues as differences between "real" photographic art and "staged" art and which was art in the truest sense. They also questioned the worth of Brady's work in general, with students evaluating each in their own way. Some saw the work as "political" and of little artistic worth. Others saw it as an artist using his "props" just like any other artist does. One student compared it to a still life painting the class had seen earlier.

Needless to say, this discussion led to a lot of research into Matthew Brady's life and work. But more importantly, the discussion helped students learn how to reflect upon and present their own opinions of art and to consider the views of others.

Benefits of Aesthetic Sensitivity

An **aesthetic sense** does not mean "I see" or "I hear"; It means "I enjoy what I see" or "I like what I hear." It means that the child is using taste or preference. Aesthetic sensitivity is important for children because it improves the quality of learning and encourages the creative process. Aesthetic sensibility in children has many other benefits, too.

- Children are more sensitive to problems because they have more insight into their world. This means they can be more helpful to other children and to adults.

Each language has its own system of words and rules of grammar. To learn a new language, you need to learn new words and a new set of rules for putting the words together. The language of visual art has its own system. The words of the language are the *elements* of art. They are the basic visual symbols in the language of art. Just as there are basic kinds of words in a spoken language such as nouns, verbs, adjectives, and adverbs, there are basic kinds of **art elements**. These elements are *line, shape/form, color, space, pattern and texture*. These six elements are the visual building blocks that the artist puts together to create a work of art. No matter what materials are used, the artwork will contain one or more of these visual elements. Sometimes one element will be more important than the others. Listed below are definitions for each of these elements with examples of using them in discussing art with young children.

Line is a continuous mark on a surface. Lines have a direction: horizontal, vertical, and diagonal. Lines may be straight or curved, fat or thin, long or short.

Example: "I notice you made your house with vertical and horizontal lines."

Shape/Form are two terms to describe the contours of enclosed spaces in art. *Shape* is used to refer to two-dimensional works such as drawings and paintings that can be measured by height and width. *Form* is used for three-dimensional pieces such as sculpture and architecture that can be measured by height, width, and depth. Shapes and forms may be described as *geometric, organic,* or *free-form*.

Geometric forms are mathematically precise forms based on geometric shapes. These refer to square, rectangle, triangle, circle, oval, and diamond shapes.

Organic forms are those that are natural.

Free-form shapes are images made of straight or curved lines or a combination of both.

Examples: "Look at that big yellow circle in the center of your drawing!" (geometric)

"Did you see how Mark made an organic-shaped design with his printing tool?" (organic)

"Watch how Eric uses his crayons to make a free-form design for a border." (free-form)

Color. There are three characteristics of color: *hue, value,* and *intensity.*

Hue is the color name, such as blue-green. There are *primary, secondary* and *tertiary*. The **primary colors** are red, blue, and yellow. The **secondary colors** are orange, violet (purple), and green. The **tertiary colors** are red-violet, red-orange, blue-violet, blue-green, yellow-orange, and yellow-green.

Example: "You used so many nice primary colors in your collage—red and blue especially."

Value refers to the relative lightness or darkness of a hue. Tints and shades are made when white (tint) or black (shade) is added to a hue.

Example: "I see you have made a lovely green tint for the leaves on your tree."

Intensity is varied by adding a hue's complementary color, the color opposite it on the color wheel, to the hue. For example, red becomes duller, less intense, when its opposite color, green, is added to it.

Example: "The intensity of your red flowers is great!"

Space refers to the areas above, below, between, within, and around an object. Space is created as an illusion in two-dimensional artwork. A three-dimensional art form—a sculpture, for example—has actual space such as width, height, and depth. Young children learn to create space by several means: overlapping, scale (size), and placement of shapes.

Example: "Scott, I can see in your picture how big your house is in your neighborhood."

Texture refers to the way something feels or looks like it would feel. It can be rough (like a sandpaper alphabet letter) or soft (like a chalk drawing); it can be furry (as in a piece of fabric) or slick (as in manipulating fingerpaint). It can be real like a piece of tree bark glued in a collage or visual, like the implied bark of a tree trunk drawn with crayons.

Example: "I see you used that piece of velvet to give the puppet's face a soft, smooth texture."

Some Other Art Terms

Foreground, middle, and background. The areas in a piece of art that appear closer to the viewer, next closest, and farthest away.

Contrast. This is created by putting lighter colors next to darker ones.

Light. The illusion created with lighter colors like white.

Design Concepts. Three design concepts in art are *pattern (repetition and rhythm), balance,* and *unity.*

Pattern (repetition and rhythm) is created when a particular shape, color, or motif (design) is repeated in a rhythmic way. Patterns provide harmonious or decorative effects in works of art.

Example: "Tell me how you made that pattern around the edge of your picture."

Balance is the principle of design that deals with visual weight in a work of art. Balance may be *symmetrical, radial,* or *overall*.

Example: "Adding flowers on both sides of your house gives your picture balance, Sally."

Unity is the feeling of wholeness or oneness in an artwork that is accomplished by using the elements and principles of art. A unified artwork seems harmonious; nothing should be added or removed.

Example: "Rose, that round grouping of flowers gives your painting a sense of unity, bringing it all together."

- Children are more likely to be self-learners because they are more sensitive to gaps in their knowledge.
- Life is more exciting for children because they have the capacity to be curious and to be surprised.
- Children are more tolerant because they learn that there are many possible ways of doing things.

FIGURE 3-7 • Example of balance. When a child adds windows to each open space in her drawing, she is creating balance.

FIGURE 3-5 • Example of space. Space is created as an illusion in two-dimensional artwork.

FIGURE 3-6 • Example of unity. A unified artwork seems harmonious. Nothing needs to be added or removed.

FIGURE 3-8 • Tints and shades are made when white (tint) or black (shade) is added to a hue (color).

- Children are more independent because they are more open to their own thoughts. They are good questioners for the same reason.
- Children can deal better with complexity because they do not expect to find one best answer.

Aesthetic Experiences

Aesthetic experiences for young children can take many forms. They can involve an appreciation of the beauty of nature, the rhythm and imagery of music or poetry, or the qualities of works of art. Far from being

THIS ONE'S for YOU!

The Aesthetic Environment: Art Elements in Action

The classroom environment itself can help young children develop their aesthetic sense. The elements in the early childhood room, just like those in a painting, all work together to produce a unified, aesthetically pleasing environment for young children. Simply visualize the early childhood room as a canvas, and each part of this canvas (room) is important to the entire composition (program). Next, consider the basic art elements listed below and how they are applicable to an aesthetically appealing early childhood environment.

Color/Hue. Just like in a piece of artwork, the use of color can create very different effects. Lots of blue in a painting gives the viewer a calm, quiet feeling. Bright reds and oranges create the opposite effect. Just as bright colors can dominate a painting, the same applies to color in the classroom. Too many bright colors may detract from art and natural beauty. If you have a choice, it is best to choose soft, light, neutral colors for walls and ceilings. This neural background allows children's artwork to stand out.

Just as color can be used to create unity and balance in a painting, it can also be used to create an aesthetically balanced early childhood classroom. For example, you can use color to coordinate learning centers so that children begin to see them as wholes rather than as parts. For the same reason, avoid having many different kinds of patterns in one place, as they disturb the balance in the room and can be distracting and overstimulating for young children.

Space. The way the artist creates space in a painting either gives the viewer a definite sense of "openness" or "closeness" or maybe a feeling in between the two. In the classroom, the sense of space is created by placement of the furniture and equipment.

Group similar furniture together to enhance the spacious feel of the room. Keep colors of furniture, such as shelving, as natural and neutral as possible. This helps focus children's attention on learning materials on the shelves. When choosing furnishings, select natural wood, which is more aesthetically appealing than metal or plastic. If furniture must be repainted, use one neutral color for everything so that there is greater flexibility in moving it from space to space. Instead of a mismatched collection that breaks up the space in the room, one color of

furniture creates a sense of spaciousness because all things "fit together."

Balance. When a child adds flowers to both sides of her house, she is creating balance in her art. In the same way, a teacher can create balance in the early childhood classroom by arranging materials in an orderly, aesthetically pleasing manner. For example, rotate materials on shelves rather than crowding them together. Crowded shelves are unbalanced as well as unattractive. They are also hard for children to use and maintain. Aesthetically pleasing containers for holding materials are natural wicker baskets and storage tubs. If storage tubs are used, put all of the same kind together on one shelf to maintain a sense of balance. For the same reason, if cardboard boxes are used for storage, cover them with a neutral color paper or paint them.

Composition. Just as this art element refers to the arrangement of the objects and spaces in a piece of art, it can also apply to the various arrangements in the classroom. To create an aesthetically pleasing environment, be conscious of the fact that everything in the room has an aesthetic effect. For this reason, decorate your classroom with care. Mount and display children's artwork rather than simply taping it to the wall. Provide artwork by fine artists from many cultures and avoid garish, stereotyped posters. Make sure that most artwork is displayed at the children's eye level. Be careful to avoid too many visual stimuli when displaying materials in the classroom. Consistently use one pattern or color combination on all display areas throughout the room. Display work by every child, but not every child's work in every display. Allow children to choose what they want displayed. Encourage children to help you create and change displays. They will take pride in seeing their work go on display.

Use shelf tops to display sculpture, plants, and items of natural beauty like shells, stones, and fish tanks. Avoid storing teachers' materials on the tops of shelves. If there is no other choice, create a teacher "cubby" using a covered box or storage tub.

Finally, see Appendix I for a checklist to assess your own classroom environment for its aesthetic appropriateness for young children. This appendix and the information in this section can help you create a "masterpiece" environment for the young children in your care.

a specialized talent, the recognition of aesthetic qualities comes quite naturally to children.

For instance, let us consider **art appreciation**. What adults have come to regard as strictly a "museum-type" experience—seeing and appreciating good artwork—is an enjoyable experience for young children whose fear of the "intellectual" is not yet developed. Art appreciation can occur in the early childhood program through the combined experiences of learning to look at and learning to create visual arts. Introducing young children to art appreciation should be a series of pleasurable experiences with time to look, enjoy, comment, and raise questions. It is a time when children learn to "see" with their minds, as well as their eyes. They begin to feel with the painter, the sculptor, or the architect and to explore their ideas and techniques.

As early childhood teachers, we don't ask ourselves whether language appreciation should be emphasized in our programs. We automatically encourage children to express themselves verbally and reflect on the words used by others. We want children to have fun with language, to appreciate its variety and its shades of meaning. Why should we not do the same for visual imagery—that is, encourage children to go beyond art's functional aspects and find satisfaction in its aesthetic possibilities (Epstein, 2001)?

Early childhood teachers have a responsibility to provide the very best our culture has to offer by introducing young children to a range of fine art by recognized artists, not merely what is easiest or most familiar.

Most children have plenty of exposure to cartoon characters, advertising art, and stereotyped, simplistic posters. These do not foster aesthetic development and are sometimes demeaning to children. Teachers often say, "Children like them," but the fact that children like something—for example, candy and staying up late at night—does not necessarily mean it is good for them. Children might never have seen a Van Gogh sunflower, a mother and child by Mary Cassatt, or a sculpture by Henry Moore. Yet, young children can learn to appreciate such fine art as these, as well as arts and crafts from many cultures, if introduced to them in the early years. From such experiences, children also gradually learn the concepts of design.

FIGURE 3-9 • Children gain an aesthetic sense by using many kinds of art materials.

FIGURE 3-10 • Aesthetic sensitivity means that the child is using his or her own taste or preference.

Language for Talking About Art

During group discussions, children should be encouraged to talk about the design qualities of a specific color, the movement of lines, the contrast of sizes and shapes, and the variety of textures. They should be helped to think and feel, as individuals, about a certain art object or piece of music. Their understanding of aesthetics, and their willingness and ability to discuss its concepts, will increase with experience.

As you talk about art with young children, start to introduce the language of art. For example, the teacher may say, "You made a secondary color here," or in another, "I see you drew straight lines, zigzag lines and diagonal lines in your drawing of our school." Talking about art in this way strengthens language development at an age when children are quickly developing a language system and vocabulary (Althouse, Johnson, & Mitchell, 2003).

The **language of art** is an expansion of the language of preschool. Both use terms like *color*, *shape*, *line*, and *size*. Descriptive words such as *empty* and *full* and comparison words such as *lighter* and *darker* are used by children and art critics alike. In encouraging art appreciation, teachers can help children expand the ways in which these common terms are used. Instead of focusing only on terms' *functional* aspects, such as clarifying that one wants the red cup, make observations about how features such as color evoke aesthetic responses: "The bright red dresses in that painting give the dancers a lively look." (See This One's for You! Speaking With Children About Art: Using Basic Art Elements and Design Concepts on page 44 and Appendix C, Art Talk Checklist, for more in-depth information on the language of art.)

Teachers can make children's art experiences meaningful through thoughtful dialogue. For example:

- Use descriptive rather than judgmental terms when talking about art. Say "I see . . ." or "It makes me think of . . ." rather than "I like it" or "It's pretty." Praise such as "Good work!" sets the teacher above the child–artist, in a superior judgmental position. It may leave the child artist anxious about whether you will at some later time announce that you do not like the child's efforts. And if you inadvertently pass over one child, does this overlooked child then worry that he or she is not "a good artist"? Respond to the child's efforts not from your head, but from your heart. Rather than pronounce a judgment, try describing your heartfelt response to the art. Use, "In your art, I feel (an emotion)" statements. For example, "I feel happiness, sadness, fear, love, power." You will create a better connection with the child by saying "I feel an emotion" rather than "I feel THAT YOU are showing (an emotion)." The "that you" makes a presumptuous assumption. Thus, avoid phrases, "I feel . . . that, like, as if . . . you are showing . . ." Using your OWN emotions, no one can argue about what you yourself feel.

After a small-group art activity, encourage children to look at one another's work and ask them, "Why do you think they look so different from one another even though you all made them out of the same paper and markers?"

- Introduce language to talk about the affect and aesthetics of the artwork. For example, "These colors look sad" or "All these little dots look busy on the page" or "This big, bright circle makes my eye keep coming back to it."
- Ask children to reflect on artistic intentions and feelings. "Why do you think this artist makes little pictures but that one makes big pictures?" is a question that young children can ponder.

Aesthetic experiences for young children should be chosen according to their interests and level of understanding. For young children ages 2 to 4, use artwork that is colorful and reflects a subject matter that is familiar to them, such as children, families, and animals. Older children can explore more abstract imagery, although research suggests that young children, while preferring both abstract and realistic art, tend to gravitate more toward abstract art (Danko-McGhee, 2006). Such details as dates and the social–political implications of a piece of art or music have no relevance for young children. Instead, a painting may appeal to them because of its bold colors as well as familiar subject.

Art appreciation also includes the development of an awareness of the aesthetic qualities of everyday manmade objects. Children are surrounded daily by an endless number of objects such as furniture, clothing, toys, buildings, and machines and countless images in films, television, newspapers, books, magazines, advertisements, and exhibits. Examples of good and bad design can be found in all areas of the environment. With guidance and experience, children will become more sensitive to their environment and eventually will develop more selective, even discriminating, taste.

THINK ABOUT IT

Aesthetic Awareness in Young Children—Theorists' Views

Many theorists study and write about young children and aesthetics. As teachers of young children, it is important to be aware of this area of early childhood education and its relation to classroom practice. The following summary of some of their ideas provides more ideas about young children's **aesthetic development** and how to enhance it.

Teaching young children ways to appreciate art is not the daunting task that it appears to be. At a very young age, children are quite capable of having an aesthetic experience on their own, whether it be the delight of mixing different-textured foods on the high chair tray or becoming visually engaged with a mobile suspended over the crib (Danko-McGhee, 2006).

When children express preferences for colors, shapes, sounds, tastes, and textures, they are actually making aesthetic choices. Long before young children can speak, their responses to shapes, colors, and other stimuli around them help to form their own special style of interacting with the world (Schirrmacher, 2005).

As young children grow, they continue to exercise their aesthetic senses while observing lines, textures, shapes, colors, and designs found in their environment. This includes images in picture books and artwork found in museums and in the popular media. These aesthetic experiences provide a starting point for understanding that there is a "language of art" (Anderson & Milbrandt, 2005, 4). Knowledgeable teachers can facilitate this learning process by pointing out to the child what is to be found in the beauty of an object or work of art.

Developmentally appropriate ways of engaging young children in appreciating works of art include *play, conversations,* and *authenticating the experience* (Danko-McGhee, 2006). *Play* involves finding connections between an artwork and the child by using tangible objects. *Conversations* engage the child in talking about the artwork with a focus on language details. When viewing art, adults can serve as role models for young children by using rich language to describe aesthetic qualities found in nature and in works of art. And finally, *authenticating the experience* guides children into related art activities. During this "appreciating"

process, children develop their perceptual discernment. "Looking at, reflecting upon, creating, and experiencing art teaches, guides, and refines perception. True perception requires thought" (Anderson & Milbrandt, 2005,16).

Having an aesthetic experience is the result of being deeply affected by sensory perception. Having an aesthetic experience increases our cognitive (mental) abilities. Through sensory perception, we are prompted to reflect and think (Csikszentmihalyi, 1996; Eisner, 2002; Goodman, 1984; Parsons & Blocker, 1993; Siegesmund, 2000; Smith, 2002).

Aesthetic education need not be exclusive to art activities. Eisner (2002, 43) suggests: "Aesthetic experience is in no way restricted to what we refer to as the fine arts. . . . Aesthetic experience, therefore, is potentially in any encounter an individual has with the world."

Maxine Greene (2001) suggests that teachers follow the thoughts of Herbert Read and instruct students to experience what it "feels like to live in music, move over and about a painting, travel round and in between the masses of sculpture, dwell in a poem (p. 302). We should teach our students to pay heed to and use their senses and feelings to understand the qualities of what is perceived in everything. In so doing, we should create more chances for students to find those "a-ha" moments by simply asking questions or calling attention to the elegance of uncomplicated tasks and everyday situations (Flannery, 1977).

Teachers can help their students to slow down, to smell the bread baking in the school kitchen, to listen to morning sounds, to catch and taste a raindrop, and to feel the stippling on the cinder block hall walls. Teachers can extend these lessons by allowing time for students to talk to their peers and write about their feelings and responses to their aesthetic experiences. Students begin to embrace authentic and meaningful learning as they come to realize that they are the agents that create these experiences, and they do not need to have something that an artist delivers to the classroom for passive appreciation (Heid, 2005).

FIGURE 3-11 • Children develop their aesthetic senses by doing, sensing, and responding.

Summary

Aesthetics is an appreciation for beauty and a feeling of wonder. The purpose of aesthetic experiences for children is to help them develop full and rich lives.

Children gain an aesthetic sense by doing, sensing, feeling, and responding to things. As children learn and grow in the early childhood years, a sense of aesthetics can be developed as they learn to join what they think with what they feel. Such aesthetic experiences allow children to express their feelings about what they are learning and experiencing. In this way, there is no false separation between work and play, art and learning, and thought and feeling. After the ages 7 to 8, children are able to mentally deal with more abstract ideas. At this time, children can engage in aesthetic discussions about their artistic opinions and ideas about what art is. Children with improved aesthetic sensitivity have a greater chance to be creative and have a more enjoyable learning experience.

Teachers can help develop children's aesthetic senses by involving them in the arts; introducing them to famous works of art, music, dance, or literature; allowing them to explore their environment; using the language of art in discussing children's work and that of other artists; and avoiding single solutions to complex problems.

Children benefit from their aesthetic sensitivity because it generates more excitement in their lives as well as more insight. The ability to use one's taste or to know one's preference, which is basic to an aesthetic sense, can improve the quality of learning. Aesthetic sensibility in children also helps them develop their feelings of sensitivity, independence, and tolerance.

Key Terms

aesthetic development 49
aesthetic experience 38
aesthetic learning 40
aesthetic movement 38
Aesthetics 38
aesthetic sense 43
art appreciation 47
art elements 44
balance 44
color 44
hue 44
intensity 44
language of art 48
line 44
multimedia artwork 39
primary colors 44
secondary colors 44
sensory awareness 40
shape/form 44
tertiary colors 44
unity 44
value 44

Learning Activities

Being Aware

To use one's aesthetic sense, one must pay close attention to that which is personally interesting. This means being aware of oneself and one's surroundings.

A. Try to think a new thought or make a discovery by paying closer attention to yourself.

B. Begin by going to a place that is quiet and relaxing. Sit down and take a minute to rest. Then say, "Now I am aware of . . ." and finish this statement with what you are in touch with at the moment. Notice whether this is something inside or outside yourself.

C. Make the statement again and see what happens.

1. Has your awareness changed?
2. Are fantasies, thoughts, or images part of your awareness?

D. Make the statement again, but this time think of a person.

1. Who comes to mind?
2. What does it mean?

E. Try the same sentence, but change your awareness by thinking of different things such as a flower, a picture, someone from the past, a child, your favorite place, and so on.

F. Notice that when thinking of something outside, one cannot think of something inside at the same time.

G. What does this mean for working with children? Compare your answers with classmates, and find out how they feel about this activity.

Moody Colors

- For this activity you will need a 9 × 13-inch piece of drawing paper and colored markers or colored pencils. Think about how artists such as Vincent van Gogh used color to express moods and emotions. Think about how color can affect your emotions.
- Fold the paper into eight sections.
- Think of eight different moods or emotions and write them lightly on the back of each section of the paper.
- Then draw each mood on the other side. What colors, shapes, and lines best show your mood? The drawings may be realistic, abstract, or somewhere in between.
- Now you have eight mini drawing or "thumbnail sketches."
- Show the drawings to a fellow student or friend without telling them what you wrote on the back. See if they can guess what mood or emotion you drew. If you like one a lot, you can make it into a full-size drawing.

Fruit

This is an activity to make new discoveries by paying closer attention to everyday things.

A. Take three different types of fruit. Close your eyes and pick each one up. Feel them with your fingers from top to bottom.

1. How are they different?
2. How are they the same?

B. Place the fruits against your face.

1. Do they feel different?
2. What about the temperature of the fruit?

C. Smell the fruits, being sure to keep your eyes closed.

1. How different are the aromas?
2. Which is your favorite?

D. Open your eyes and look at the fruits.

1. Hold them up to the light.
2. See if you can see anything new about each fruit.

E. What have you discovered from this activity? (Notice you did not taste or eat the fruit.)

1. Could you still receive pleasure from the fruit without eating it?
2. What does this mean for working with children?

F. Compare your answers with those of classmates, and find out their reactions to this activity.

Museum Explorations

Plan a trip to a local museum for a group of young children. Help the children to focus in the gallery with activities such as the following.

- Search for a particularly interesting picture. For example, in a room filled with paintings, ask children, "Can you find the painting where there is a bear, a house, a mother, and a baby?"
- Ask, "What would it feel like to be in the painting? Where would you like to go? What would you like to do if you were there?"
- Ask children to find two pictures that are the same in some way—the same colors, the same subject, the same feeling.
- Explore your own environment. Pick a nearby location—a mall, a park, any area you enjoy exploring. Visit that location as an artist, writer, scientist, historian, or mathematician. Look carefully and jot down as many interesting ideas, problems, and questions as you can. Reflect on how your point of view affected your experience.

Activities for Children

Art Talk

Display a print of Van Gogh's famous painting Starry Night. Ask young children the following questions about the painting.

- What do you see in the painting?
- What do you notice about the colors and lines?
- Show me the most important thing in the painting. Why do you think it is the most important thing?
- How does this picture make you feel?
- What do you think the artist was feeling when he was painting this picture?

Another kind of questioning about *Starry Night* might be related to having children imagine they are in the scene.

- If you were in the painting, where would you want to be?
- How would that feel?
- What kind of things do you think you would smell?
- What kind of animals might live there?

These questions could be used for any other painting of your choice.

Art in Nature

The beauty of nature is a continuing source of inspiration for young children. It is through nature that many children acquire some of their earliest ideas and concepts of design. A variety of experiences can be planned to help children observe and discover color, line, form, pattern, and texture in natural objects.

- Make a bulletin board arrangement of natural objects and materials.
- Begin a collection of natural objects such as flowers, weeds, twigs, stones, shells, seed pods, moss, and feathers for a touch-and-see display.
- Take a walking trip to observe color, shape, and texture in the immediate environment. Share individual discoveries with others during class discussion.
- Show films, conduct dramatizations, or read stories and poems to develop these concepts.
- Arrange a shelf or corner table for things of beauty children can admire. Contributions can be made by parents, some of whom may have objects that represent art of their own heritage. Keep changing the collection! Variety and contrast encourage young children's interest.
- Give children an opportunity to arrange objects in an aesthetically pleasing manner: flower bouquets; fruit and vegetable centerpieces; and collections of dried plants, leaves, and seed pods placed in a ball of clay or block of Styrofoam.

- Offer equipment such as magnifying glasses, kaleidoscopes, prisms, and safety mirrors to help sharpen children's visual sensitivity.
- In describing the children's artwork to them, use terms that relate to the color, form, texture, patterns, and arrangement of space.
- Be enthusiastic about your own sensory awareness and share your perceptions with children.

What ideas can you add to this list?

Magical Mixing Colors on Ice

Preschoolers are fascinated by how colors can be mixed together to form new ones. This activity combines color mixing with the concept of melting. The children will enjoy making colorful designs on the magic ice, but because food coloring may stain, be sure to wear old clothes and protect your table with newspaper.

For this activity you will need:

Eyedropper
Several cubes of ice
Shallow dish or pan
3 plastic bowls
Yellow, red, and blue food coloring

- Pour ½ cup of water in each of the bowls.
- Put a few drops of each color of food coloring into each bowl until the coloring is the desired intensity.
- Place the ice cubes in the shallow dish or pan.
- Discuss primary colors and how these three colors can be used to make all of the other colors.
- Show the children how to use the eyedropper to pick up some of the red color water and dribble it on the ice cube. Watch how the water reacts to the ice cube.
- Have the children dribble blue water on the same ice cube. Talk about how the blue water combined with the red water to make purple, and discuss the designs the colored water makes on the ice.
- When the children are done experimenting with red and blue, give them another ice cube and let them use yellow and blue to make green. Be sure to also experiment with the red and yellow color to make orange, too.
- After the children have experimented with all the color combinations, let them mix all of the different colors on the ice to see what happens. You can also show them how to pick up some of the new colors that they made with the dropper and put them on another piece of ice.
- As they play with the ice, the ice will begin to melt. Ask them why they think the ice is melting and explain that ice melts when the air temperature

goes below 32 degrees, because that is the temperature at which freezing occurs.

- When you are finished with the activity, have the children help you clean up. Although the children may have very colorful hands, they will be sure to remember the lessons learned about making new colors and the cool effect of colored water on ice.

Primary and Secondary Colors Pantomime

Elementary-age children can work on color recognition and affective response to color through pantomime sentences. Have children perform the following actions and then tell how each of the colors made them feel.

- You are the bright yellow sun shining in the summer sky.
- You are a blue bird flying across the blue sky.
- You are a violet opening your petals.
- You are an orange flame flickering atop a candle.
- You are a green leaf floating gently to the ground.
- You are a yellow jacket buzzing around a flower.
- You are a green bug crawling along the ground.
- You are a red fire engine speeding to the scene of a fire.
- You are an African violet growing in a pot.

Children will enjoy creating and playing their own pantomime sentences that incorporate primary and secondary colors. At the close of the activity, invite the children to tell how the colors in these new sentences made them feel.

Lucy's Science Project—Body Sculptures

Science projects and school science fairs give children hands-on opportunities to examine, test, and operate technical devices. These experiences can be applied to the more fanciful invention in the following activity.

Children working in small groups create Lucy's new invention using their bodies and machine-like sounds after hearing the following scenario. They may adapt a device currently in use, such as a computer, or create a futuristic contraption with a real or fantastic purpose.

Lucy is a second grader in the year 2090. She has been assigned the creation of a new technologic device as her science project. As a group, you are to become Lucy's invention. Your task is to create the device, name it, show how it works, and tell the rest of the class what it does.

Aesthetic Experiences in Autumn

The fall is a great time for children to explore the outdoors, learn about seasonal transitions, and develop their aesthetic skills. Nature-related experiences can foster a child's emerging sense of wonder, and the early years of life are the best time to begin providing direct, ongoing interactions with the natural world. Young children learn best when they are in an environment that is familiar and comfortable. Focus on the foliage, animals, and insects in your own backyard, the playground, or local park before venturing into heavily wooded areas. Keeping safety concerns in mind, adults should allow children to touch, feel, and smell while they explore the environment.

The young child is naturally sensitive to the wonders and beauty of nature: the colors and rhythm of leaves whirled by autumn winds, the texture of dried seeds and weeds, the form and color in the harvest. There are a number of things a teacher can do to enlarge children's understanding of their world and to encourage them to learn to look, feel, and think.

- Begin a collection of objects from nature for classroom use. Encourage closer observation of design in nature.
- Take children on walking trips to discover and observe the colors, shapes, and textures in trees, plants, clouds, buildings, and vehicles. Individual observation can be shared with others at group time.
- Have children draw and paint the beauty of nature as they see it, using their own feelings and ideas. Their growing visual awareness is gradually reflected in picture making as they mature in the ability to interpret their environment.
- Children can be encouraged to be more aware of their environment in only a few minutes. Discuss the fact that leaves will change color and watch together to see when this change happens. Make a game of finding the largest, smallest, and most unusually colored leaf. Focus on an evergreen or pine and talk about the needles and pinecones and the fact that they stay green and don't drop off. Talk about people needing jackets and animals growing winter coats.
- Collect leaves of different sizes and shapes. Show the children that one side is smooth and one side is rough. Have them put a piece of paper over the rough side of a leaf and rub a crayon on its side over the paper. The outline of the leaf will show through. It's fun to change colors. This technique can be used with any object that has texture.
- Fall is the time when apples are harvested. Tell children that there are almost 10,000 varieties of apples grown in the world! Buy one each of several kinds in the grocery store. Have children point out the many ways these apples are alike and different. Have children say each apple's name and taste a piece of each. If you cut two pieces from each one, can the children find the ones that taste the same or different?

Activities for Older Children (Grades 4–5)

Birthday Parties for Artists

Ask the children, "If you were planning a birthday party for a famous artist, what would you want the design, based on the style of that artist, to look like? How would you design a cup, plate, napkin, placemat, treat bag, party hat, and balloon to look as if they belonged together?"

Divide the class into teams of four. Have each team vote for the artist for whom they would plan a party. Have children review the artists they have learned about. List the names of those artists on the board. Display examples of their work, and provide folders with examples of each artist's work for children's review. Discuss the characteristic styles of these artists and how elements of those styles could be incorporated into the design of the party decorations.

Have student teams decide what their overall design should look like to reflect the style of their artist. Also have each group decide which art materials would best represent their artist.

Provide white napkins, balloons, paper plates, cups, treat bags, white paper, colored markers, tempera paint, and watercolors for children to make their party accessories.

Look Closely—Pantomime

Older children can be introduced to art history and gain insight into art criticism through this activity. By studying famous paintings, reproductions, or prints, children sharpen critical observation skills while analyzing artistic process and intent.

As an introduction to critical observation, have children study prints of famous paintings and identify people or objects in each print that can be interpreted through pantomime. Several prints (or similar materials) should be selected for study, and children should be given ample time to view each. Prompt thinking with questions such as, "What was the artist trying to say in this work?" or "What does the artist want you to think or feel when you see this?" or "What do you think is the most important image in this picture?" The class can then generate a list of people or objects in the prints that appear significant to them. After an appropriate list has been developed, call out the subjects and ask children to pantomime them.

Web Activities

Graphic artist M. C. Escher is known for his detailed drawings using patterns and optical illusions. View his work at the following websites:

- http://www.mcescher.com/

- http://www.worldofescher.com/gallery/
- http://www.cs.unc.edu/. Click on "Projects."

What is a metamorphosis? How does this artist organize line and shape to create his art? Describe the work you find most interesting. What is unique about it? How was he able to create such technical details? Besides artists and art viewers, who else might appreciate Escher's drawings?

Henri Matisse often used cut paper that he had painted to create collages. Look at reproductions of these collages in these websites:

- http://www.artloft.com/. Click on "Artist Directory."
- http://www.museum.cornell.edu. Click on "Collections."

Why would the artist choose collage instead of painting, drawing, or another medium? Which artwork appeals to you the most? Describe the composition. What colors, shapes, and patterns do you see? How does your eye move through the image? What do you see first, and then which way do you proceed? Did you find balance and unity in the collage?

Artistic Opinions

Aesthetic experiences for older children involve their opinions of art and their ability to express these opinions and to appreciate those of others. The following "art problems" are designed to capitalize on older children's ability to grasp more complex ideas and should encourage discussion about art and aesthetic appreciation.

A. The Problem of the Pile of Bricks
   This problem involves the nature of art and such questions as "What is art?" and "Is it representation?" and "Is it the expression and communication of emotion?" Consider the following possibility, based on an exhibit at the Tate Gallery (London) in 1976. A famous artist, known to be a "minimalist" sculptor, buys 120 bricks and, on the floor of a well-known art museum, arranges them in a rectangular pile, 2 bricks high, 6 across, and 10 lengthwise. He labels it *Pile of Bricks*. Across town, a bricklayer's assistant at a building site takes 120 bricks of the very same kind and arranges them in the very same way, wholly unaware of what has happened in the museum—he is just a tidy bricklayer's assistant. Can the first pile of bricks be a work of art while the second pile is not, even though the two piles are seemingly identical in all observable respects? Why or why not?

B. The Problem of the Fire in the Louvre

   The Louvre is on fire. You can save either the Mona Lisa or the injured guard who had been standing next to it—but not both. What should you do?

C. Is Shakespeare a Real Writer?
Lord Byron criticized Shakespeare as follows: "Shakespeare's name, you may depend on it, stands absurdly too high and will go down . . . He took all his plots from old novels, and threw their stories into dramatic shape, at as little expense of thought, as you or I could do" (Henderson, 1986). Is Shakespeare's use of familiar stories an aesthetic defect? Is Byron a good critic of Shakespeare?

Aesthetic Experiences in Autumn for Older Children

An appreciation of the fall season is probably even more important for middle and upper elementary-age students than for younger children because they are further removed from the early years' sense of wonder. In addition to carrying out the activities already covered, you may wish to approach this changing season with more complex artistic activities. Here are a few suggestions.

Textures

Provide students with a variety of leaves, long grasses, and other natural objects. You might want them to bring in similar natural objects as well. Have them make rubbings using white crayon or oil pastel and black paper. Suggest that students do a repeated rubbing of the item until the entire paper is covered. Discuss the results as a record of textures that can be viewed as artwork as well as a display for science. Students might want to research the types of grass and leaves they used in this activity.

Fall Textures

Have students make and illustrate vocabulary cards for words that describe fall textures. Have them arrange the items by tactile characteristics (e.g., rough, soft, smooth). Encourage them to use these terms appropriately in storytelling and in other activities.

Mystery Textures

Tell students they will make a mystery texture bag. Provide small paper bags for each student. Have them secretly collect items that have varied textures of fall or any season. These are the mystery items whose identities others will be guessing. Have students work with a partner: Partners exchange bags and try to guess what the mystery objects are by feeling the textures.

Lines, Patterns, Textures

Have students bring in large leaves. Place a magnifying glass over one part of the leaf and observe lines, patterns, and textures. Have students create large drawings of the small section of the leaf seen in the magnifying glass.

Varieties of Colors

Have students look selectively for gradations of the color red in leaves and bring their leaves to class. Have them describe the differences in color using descriptors such as *light, dark, shiny,* or *dull.* Focus on other visual elements in the same way. For example, ask students who are wearing rough textures to stand and point them out. Develop an awareness of terms that describe textures, such as *bumpy, prickly,* and *silky.*

Weather Diaries

Have students keep a weather diary with drawings that portray the weather as it occurs at the same time each day for 5 days. The time might be lunch or recess. At the end of 5 days, have students work in small groups to compare and contrast the different interpretations. The total group can choose drawings that best represent the weather for each day. The drawings might be put into a booklet titled "The Weather Diary of Grade Four." Present the booklet to the school library.

New Colors

Ask students to think about colors they have never seen in fall flowers or leaves. Have them create fall drawings or painting using these colors. Discuss the mood or feeling of these artworks with each student.

Photographers' Vision

Bring in books with fall photographs by Ansel Adams, Paul Weston, Alfred Steiglitz, Margaret Bourke-White, and other well-known photographers. Have students discuss the subject matter portrayed by these photographers. Discuss why each may have chosen his or her subject and how the images were planned. Does it look like the fall where you live? What are the similarities? The differences?

Fall Memory Book

Children in the primary grades can create a "fall memory book" with pressed leaves, pictures, and writings about fall activities and specific events they have enjoyed. Wrap the book in paper and put it away until it's almost spring. When they open it again and look at the leaves and read their writings, they will be able to remember fall and can compare the differences in seasonal colors.

Chapter Review

1. Define aesthetics.
2. List three things a teacher can do to help children develop their aesthetic sensitivity.
3. List five benefits of aesthetic sensitivity in children.
4. List at least two specific ways to introduce young children to the work of an artist and to involve them in art appreciation in general.
5. List at least three art elements to discuss with children.
6. What aesthetic experiences are appropriate for older children (grades 4 to 5) and why?
7. What are some art assignments and activities for children of various ages that will build sensitivity and values related to aesthetics?
8. What could be brought into a classroom to help children develop their aesthetic sensibilities?
9. What are the elements of art? Give examples of their use in talking with young children and their art.

References

Abedi, J. (2002). A latent-variable modeling approach to assessing reliability and validity of a creativity instrument. *Creativity Research Journal, 14*(2), 267–276.

Althouse, R., Johnson, M. H., Mitchell, S. T. (2003). *The colors of learning: Integrating the visual arts into the early childhood curriculum.* New York, NY: Teachers College Press.

Anderson, T., & Milbrandt, M. (2005). *Art for life.* Boston, MA: McGraw-Hill.

Auzmendi, E., Villa, A., & Abedi, J. (1996). Reliability and validity of a newly constructed multiple-choice creativity instrument. *Creativity Research Journal, 9*(1), 89–95.

Baumgarten, A. G. (1750). Aesthetica. Frankfurt: Oder Publishers.

Catterall & Peppler. (2007). Learning in the visual arts and the worldviews of young children. *Cambridge Journal of Education, 37*(4), 543–560.

Csikszentmihalyi, M. (1996). *Creativity.* New York, NY: Harper Perennial.

Danko-McGhee, K. (2006). Nurturing aesthetic awareness in young children: Developmentally appropriate art viewing experiences. *Art Education, 12*(9), 21–32.

Eisner, E. W. (2002). *The arts and the creativity of mind.* New Haven, CT: Yale University Press.

Epstein, A. A. (2001). Thinking about art: Encouraging art appreciation in early childhood settings. *Young Children, 56*(3), 38–43.

Flannery, M. (1977). The aesthetic behavior of young children. *Art Education, 30*(1), 18–23.

Goodman, S. (1984). *Of mind and other matters.* Cambridge, MA: Harvard University Press.

Greene, M. (2001). *Variations on a blue guitar.* New York, NY: Teachers College Press

Heid, K. (2005). Aesthetic development: A cognitive experience. *Art Education, 58*(5), 48–53.

Henderson, D. E. (1986). *Shakespeare.* New York, NY: Vintage.

Parsons, J. J., & Blocker, H. G. (1993). *Aesthetics and education.* Urbana, IL: University of Illinois Press.

Schirrmacher, R. (2005). *Art and creative development for young children.* Clifton Park, NY: Delmar Cengage Learning.

Siegesmund, J. (2000). *Reasoned perception: Art education at the end of art.* Unpublished dissertation, Stanford University, Palo Alto, CA.

Smith, R. A. (2002). *Aesthetics and criticism in art education: Problems in defining, explaining, and evaluating art.* Chicago, IL: Rand McNally.

Villeneuve, P. (2003). A child named Risa. *Art Education, 56*(4), 4.

Additional Readings

Amorino, J. S. (2008). An occurrence at Glen Rock: Classroom educators learn more about teaching and learning from the arts. *Phi Delta Kappan, 90*(3), 190–195.

Bundi, J. (2009). The talking art museum. *School Arts, 108*(9), 21–23.

Burke, E. (2008). *A philosophical enquiry into the sublime and beautiful.* Oxford, UK: Routledge.

Cameron, J. (2009). *The artist's way every day: A year of creative living.* New York, NY: Penguin Group.

Costello, D., & Willdson, D. (Eds.). (2008). The life and death of images. Ithaca, NY: Cornell Press.

Davies, S., Hopkins, R., Cooper, D. E., Stecker, R., & Higgins, K. M. (Eds.). (2009). *A companion to aesthetics.* Hoboken, NJ: John Wiley & Sons.

Davis, J. H. (2008). *Why our schools need the arts.* New York, NY: Teachers College Press.

Degarmo, C. (2009). *Aesthetic education.* Aurora, CO: BiblioLife.

Eagleton, T. (2009). *The ideology of the aesthetic.* New York, NY: John Wiley & Sons.

Hasio, C. (2008). *Color is everything.* Richmond, VA: Oaklea Press.

Henry, M. (2009). *Seeing the invisible.* London, UK: Continuum International.

Kearney, R., & Rasmussen, D. (Eds.). (2008). *Continental aesthetics.* New York, NY: John Wiley & Sons.

Lipsey, S. (2009). *Affinity of form.* Brooklyn, NY: Powerhouse Books.

Malone, M. (2009). *Chance aesthetics.* St. Louis, MO: Mildred Lane Kemper Art Museum.

May, M. E. (2009). *In pursuit of elegance: Why the best ideas have something missing.* Ashland, OR: Blackstone Audio.

McNulty, T. (2009). *The art of nature: Reflections on the Grand Design.* Fall River, MA: Fall River Press.

Morgan, R. C. (2008). *The end of the art world.* New York, NY: Allworth Press.

Margolis, J. (2008). *On aesthetics.* Clifton Park, NY: Cengage Learning.

Margolis, J. (2009). *What, after all, is a work of art? Lectures in the philosophy of art.* University Park, PA: Penn State University Press.

Nathan, L. (2008). *Why the arts make sense in education.* Phi Delta Kappan, 90(3), 177–181.

Ranciere, J. (2009). *Aesthetics and its discontents,* Hoboken, NJ: John Wiley & Sons.

Richmond, S. (2009). Art's educational value. *The Journal of Aesthetic Education, 43*(1), 92–105.

Rutgers, M. H. (2009). *Aesthetic Principles.* Aurora, CO: BiblioLife.

Saito, Y. (2008). *Everyday aesthetics.* New York, NY: Oxford University Press.

Santayana, G. (2009). *The sense of beauty (being): The outlines of aesthetic theory.* McLean, VA: IndyPublish.com.

Scruton, R. (2009). *Beauty.* New York, NY: Oxford University Press.

Snyder, G. (2008). *Place in space: Ethics, aesthetics, and watersheds.* New York, NY: Basic Books.

Sporre, D. J. (2008). *Perceiving the arts: An introduction to the humanities* (9th ed.). New York, NY: Prentice Hall.

Van DenBraembussche, A. (2009). *Thinking art.* New York, NY: Springer-Verlag.

VanVliet, R. (2009). *The art of abstract painting: A guide to creativity and free expression.* Kent, UK: Search Press.

Software for Children

Artsonia, ages 5 and up
Art Range 2.5, ages 3 and up
Clicker Paint, ages 5 and up
Creativity Express: Let's Start with Art! ages 7 and up
Emma at the Farm, ages 6 and up

Emma in the Mountains, ages 6 and up
Flip Boom, ages 5 and up
Noggin, ages 3–6
Wacom Bamboo Fun, ages 8 and up
Zoo Tycoon 2: African Adventure, ages 10 and up

Helpful Websites

Albright-Knox Art Games, http://www.albright-knox.org/artgames/index_launched.html

Arts Connected, http://www.artsconnected.org

The Art Institute of Chicago, http://www.artic.edu

Art Junction, http://www.artjunction.org

Cincinnati Art Museum, http://www.museumvideo-classroom.org

The Imagination Factory, http://www.kid-at-art.com

Inside Art, http://www.eduweb.com

J. Paul Getty Museum, http://www.getty.edu

Metropolitan Museum of Art, New York, http://www.metmuseum.org

The Museum of Modern Art, http://www.moma.org/

A. Pintura, Art Detective, http://www.eduweb.com/pintura

School Arts online http://www.davisart.com/Portal/SchoolArts/SAdefaykt.aspx

Young Tate Project Gallery, http://www.tate.org.uk/youngtate/projectgallery.htm

Virtual Museum of Japanese Arts, http://web-japan.org/museum

Whitney Museum of American Art, http://www.whitney.org

World Wide Arts Resources, http://wwar.com/

 For additional creative activity resources, visit our website at www.Cengage.com/login

Promoting Aesthetic Experiences

OBJECTIVES

After studying this chapter, you should be able to:

1. Describe three types of sensing and feeling.

2. Choose materials that have good aesthetic potential.

3. List four guidelines to help children work with aesthetic materials.

4. List six guidelines to use in talking with children about their artwork.

People search their world for what is important to them. They look for what they need. They see what they want. This is as true of preschool children as it is of adults.

Imagine that a group of people is taken into a room and are asked to look at a table. On the table are some food, a glass of water, and a small amount of money. Those who are hungry are most likely to look at the food. Those who are thirsty will probably look at the water. Those who are in debt are apt to look at the money. Those who need furniture will probably take a closer look at the table.

Children also look for things they need and want. A tired child looks for a place to rest. A lonely child looks for a friend. The point here is that only when children are physically well, feel safe, and sense that they belong can they be ready to develop an aesthetic sense.

Looking and Seeing

Children look in many different ways. Touching, patting, poking, picking, and even tasting are ways of looking for young children. Children look for what they need, but they also see what they find to be stimulating. Something can be stimulating to a child for many different reasons. It can be because it is colorful, exciting, different, interesting, changing, moving, weird, and so on. The list of stimulating things is seemingly endless. However, there are some basic guidelines for preparing a stimulating activity or object.

Can children experience it with more than one sense? Children enjoy what they can touch, see, and hear more than something they can only see or hear.

Can children interact with it? Children tend to enjoy what they can participate in. For children, the picture of a guinea pig will never replace a live

FIGURE 4-1 • A child expresses his aesthetic sense while playing creatively with different materials.

FIGURE 4-2 • Sensing and feeling are basic to an aesthetic sense.

guinea pig. For the same reason, an interactive computer game can never replace the fun and real-life learning experience of playing a game with friends.

Are the children interested in it? Children relate to what is familiar to them and part of their life. Talking about a food that children have never eaten cannot produce the kind of discussion that comes when they talk about their favorite food.

Is the activity well paced? Something that moves too quickly or too slowly eventually becomes boring. Watch how many children begin to fidget when the story is too long. Notice how children lose interest in toys that may appeal to adults but are too complex for children to use and enjoy.

Does it promise to be rewarding? Is the activity fun, adventurous, or exciting? Does it have something worthwhile at the end? If not, why should the children stick with it? Searching for a piece of a puzzle or looking for a hidden treasure is only fun if the children believe they can find it.

Sensing, Feeling, and Imagining

There are basically three types of sensing and feeling. The first is contact with the world outside of the person—actual sensory contact with things and events. It is seeing, hearing, smelling, tasting, and touching. The second is what people feel within themselves. This includes what they experience under their skin. Itches, tensions, muscular movements, discomfort, and emotions are all a part of this type of sensing. The third type of sensing and feeling goes beyond the present and reality. It is usually called *fantasy* and includes dreams, memories, images, and guesses.

For a child, each of these types of sensing and feeling is very important. All three can take place during the same activity. Any one can become more important than the other two, depending on what the child needs or wants at the moment. Most teachers are concerned about the child's sensory contact with the outside world. Children do many things that involve touching, seeing, and hearing; yet, what they feel inside and what they fantasize about are also important. The teacher must give attention to these two processes

FIGURE 4-3 • Children enjoy what they can touch and see.

as well. They are part of **aesthetic sensitivity**. Teachers should ask themselves two questions each day when working with preschool children. Both should be answered "yes," followed by the question, "How?"

The first question has to do with the inside feelings of the children: *Have the children done something today that has helped them feel good about themselves?* The second has to do with the fantasies of the children: *Have the children done something today that has helped them use their imagination in either the past, present, or future?*

Lesson plans, activities, and trips should be planned and evaluated with these two questions in mind. If teachers are sincere about answering yes to the two questions, their teaching will relate to all the ways children sense and feel.

Finding and Organizing Aesthetic Materials

Every teacher has many ideas about what materials are best for children. Sometimes the desired materials are too expensive or difficult to find. Schools have limited budgets, and even ordinary items can seem impossible to obtain. There are three resources with great potential: salvage material, commonly known as "junk"; the hardware store; and things the children bring in.

Before describing the organization of these materials, it is helpful to have some guidelines for choosing materials with good aesthetic potential.

* Choose materials that children can explore with their senses (touch, sight, smell).
* Choose materials that children can manipulate (twist, bend, cut, color, mark).
* Choose materials that can be used in different ways (thrown, bounced, built with, fastened, shaped).

The teacher isn't the only source of aesthetic materials. Children themselves enjoy finding materials because it involves exploration and discovery. Sometimes children's search for materials can be focused on something particular, such as objects for painting or building. The search for aesthetic materials also includes seeking new uses for familiar materials. For example, children might explore ways of modifying paint by mixing sawdust, sand, rice, or confetti with it. A natural follow-up to their experimentation in creating a new substance is to have them brainstorm ways in which the paint can be used. As they find that their discovered materials make their day-to-day work more interesting, they become alert to new possibilities. For both teacher and children, this can mean a constant supply of materials and new aesthetic experiences.

Older children will also enjoy collecting materials, but they can go further into associating materials with the elements of art. For example, the materials can

FIGURE 4-4 • Children tend to enjoy what they can actively participate in.

THINK ABOUT IT   Your Own Art Reproduction Collection!

Throughout this and other chapters, you will see many references to famous artists' work both in the chapter and in the activities at the end of each chapter. Although you can buy high-quality reproductions from many sources, there are other ways to collect prints. Out-of-date calendars are a good and inexpensive way to view artwork. Oversized art books borrowed from local libraries provide variety. The important idea is to have a rich, varied collection from different time periods and different cultures. Try to make selections from beyond the artists or kinds of artwork you like (Mulcahay, 2009).

The Internet has a multitude of sources for artwork that can be used in your work with young children. There are several good websites for images: http://

www.barewalls.com allows you to search by artist or style. In searching by style, you get a good overview of movements and periods in art history. The images are somewhat small, but they can be used with a small group of children. Art Resource, at http://www.artres.com/c/htm/Home.aspx, has more than 250,000 keyword-searchable fine-art images. Also see http://www.artnet.com and http://www.museumsyndicate.com/index.php for other fine-art imagery. And at http://www.artcyclopedia.com, you will find more than 8,000 famous artists and discover their works at art museum websites and image archives worldwide. This site was named one of the 25 Best Free Reference Sites by the American Library Association.

be selected and collected according to their design possibilities. Objects can be classified into art categories, such as those to be used for line, shape, texture, size, and color elements. The number and types of classifications will vary by the age level and interest of the children.

Aesthetic Use of Materials

The uses of materials collected by the teacher and children are limited only by the collectors' interests and imaginations. Of course, storage space and time to search can sometimes set boundaries on the exploration for aesthetic materials. However, what is most important is that the materials and what is done with them become personal statements of the children and teacher. This is not done by *what* is made but by *how* it is made—whether it is an art project, a building project, or another activity. The process of making and the child's personal involvement in it are the keys here—not the finished product.

Children must have the opportunity not only to find materials but also to try them out. This means much experimenting with the materials to determine what children believe they need. A question such as, "What would you like to say with these things?" might help both children and teacher get started. Assessing children's moods may be helpful, too. Do they seem to

feel happy, dreamy, sad, gentle, aggressive? Such questioning can help children reach their own purpose based on their experience and interests.

Another important consideration in the creative process is the number of materials. It is important to remember not to give children too many materials too often. Too much to choose from can overwhelm a child. The qualities of one material can be lost in the midst of so many others. An example of this would be to work with a certain color or a single material, such as clay or paper. In this way, the children can learn more about making their own aesthetic choices, as well as mastering specific skills.

While the process of exploring materials is the primary focus of aesthetic experiences, with older children (grades 4 to 5), the process usually involves the creation of more complex works of art. Children at this level pay greater attention to expressing specific ideas in their work. They are more intentional in their approach to using materials. Because they are not distracted by quantity of materials as younger children are, a variety of interesting materials needs to be available for their aesthetic experiences.

A man who has no imagination has no wings.

Muhammad Ali

FIGURE 4-5 • Children enjoy materials that require them to use their imagination.

Guidance in Using Aesthetic Materials

When children are exploring new materials of any kind, the teacher needs to provide guidance. With aesthetic materials, the guidance needs to be very gentle, supportive, and sensitive. This lets the child know that it is acceptable to take chances and be different. The following are some suggestions on how to give young children guidance when using aesthetic materials.

Ask questions aimed at helping children reach out for and get the "payoff" they are seeking. A question teachers can ask themselves that will help them ask the right question of children is, "What can I ask the children that would help them better understand what they want?" When the children are working with paints, this question may be something about color. When they are working with paper, it may be something about form, such as "What shape would you like it to be?" Even better, ask how paper feels because just seeing a shape is only one way of sensing paper.

Avoid always doing things the same way. Teaching children over and over to do something in only one way may ruin their aesthetic sense. Repetition tells them to stop thinking. For example, why always start to draw in the middle of a piece of paper? Why not sometimes draw from the edges or bottom? Or why not change the shape of the paper on which

children draw, using paper in the shape of a triangle, parallelogram, or circle?

Be positive and creative when using models or examples. Occasional use of models and examples of other childrens work is not uncommon in many classrooms today. Their use need not be a negative experience for children if they are used positively—as a springboard to unlocking each child's own creative approach to a shared, common theme (or object). Many times, a brief look at one or two other children's examples (which should not then be displayed for "copying" during the activity) can help motivate children to get started on making one of their own. Also, using a model produced by another child of the same age can encourage children in that it is something possible for them to do, too. Teacher comments throughout activities and the use of examples can help encourage each child to be creative in his or her approach. Statements like, "Claire, I notice that you are using so many bright primary colors," or "Jawan, you used that paper in a very different way to make your own design," clearly communicate the positive acceptance of different approaches.

Help children select the materials they prefer. This may mean asking children which materials they plan to use first, which materials they may not use at all, and which materials they may possibly use. Be patient with children and choices. Remember: The simplest choices for teachers become major decision-making opportunities for young children. What color paper, what color crayons or paint, what shape and size of paper, and which way to hold the paper are all options children should have. Children may require more time to work if many decisions must be made, but it's time well spent aesthetically and creatively.

Help children "hunt" for aesthetic qualities. Help children get in touch with what they feel about differences. For example, ask children to show what they like or think is better. Ask what is brighter, darker, happier, sadder. Encourage older children to identify and analyze more subtle and complex visual relationships such as how light affects our perception of colors, textures, and forms.

Help children use other senses when only one sense seems necessary. Children can be asked to hear what they see in a drawing or to draw what they hear in music. Colors can be related to feelings, music, and body movements, as well as to seeing. Older children can be encouraged to explore such ideas as how we perceive space and distance in art. They also need to be encouraged to continue to express in their art what they see, know, feel, and imagine.

Help children experience basic elements of art such as line, rhythm, and contrast in many art forms. Creative movements (or dance) display a strong relationship to the basic art element of line. For example, when children are moving in a wiggly or a twisting way, they can be given a signal to freeze or hold by striking a gong or stopping the music. The teacher might then appreciatively point out the different lines the body makes while it is held or frozen— the continuous curve from back toe through the body to the reaching, stretched fingers. Children can also make similar observations about each other's interesting body line designs in space. It is natural then to circle back from one's understanding of the body line to reaching, curving, or twisting lines in clay, crayon, or paint.

The element of **rhythm** is most frequently associated with music, dance, and poetry, but it can be just as much a quality in art. We find it in repeated shapes, colors, and textures that flow in a directional path, such as in children's nature print designs. We also sense rhythm in their block structures of repeated patterns. We know rhythm unmistakably in the pulse of movement and music. Good examples of rhythm in design can be found in the stylized geometric rhythmic patterns of traditional Native Americans in their

FIGURE 4-6 • Children must have the opportunity not only to find materials but also to try them out.

weaving, pottery, beadwork, and sand painting, which often tell stories about mountains, rivers, sun, and lightning.

The element of **contrast** provides one of the most exciting characteristics in all the arts. Sensitive teachers frequently help children become more aware of the power of contrast by pointing out how two colors next to each other make the shapes stand out. They comment on the roughly textured bark of a tree in contrast to its smooth leaves. Children appreciate the exaggerated features of "evil creature" puppets in contrast to the more subtle features of the heroes and heroines.

The concept of contrast for older children can be expanded from that presented to younger children. Contrast can involve the introduction of the color wheel. They can see on the color wheel how colors that are opposite one another are called *complementary* colors. These complementary colors provide more contrast than colors next to each other on the color wheel, called *analogous* colors. The idea of warm colors (reds, oranges, yellows) and cool colors (blues, greens, purples) is another concept appropriate for older children as they learn about creating contrast in their work. Figure 4–7 features additional suggestions about talking with children about their artwork. (See Chapter 3 for additional information on art elements.)

Kid Culture

A kindergarten teacher noticed that similar superheroes Lava Girl and Shark Boy kept popping up in the children's artwork. And when she noticed that multiple drawings about these characters emerged in other classrooms, she decided it was time to take notice. *Shark Boy and Lava Girl* was a popular children's movie. This is an obvious example of how visual culture reaches all ages, including our youngest students.

Looking at children's self-directed artwork is a window into children's visual culture. The term **kid culture** encompasses a broad range of media including television, computer games, movies, books, comic books, advertising, entertainment, toys, games, and trading cards. Fashion, industrial design and man-made environments, particularly playgrounds, shopping malls, stadiums, and skate parks are also a part of this culture. Attracted by powerful imagery and opportunities for play, children recreate their visual

How teachers use art talk with children and how they encourage them to share art talk determines in large part how well children express themselves with art media. The following suggestions are helpful for teachers in facilitating children's art expression.

- *Use correct art terms.* The teacher may say, "You made a secondary color." "How did you make that tint?" "I see you drew straight lines, zigzag lines, and diagonal lines." "Can you point out some free-form shapes in your collage?" Some elements to comment on: line, shape, form, texture, value, space, and color. Some design principles are: balance, movement, repetition, emphasis, and contrast. (See Chapter 3 for a complete discussion of art terms.)

- *Encourage children to reflect on their art experiences.* Keep art portfolios and ask questions about children's work. "Which picture do you like best?" "Which one did you work on the hardest?" When a child spends several days on a painting, talk to the child about the changes you observe each day.

- *Ask convergent questions.* "What color did you make?" "What geometric shape is this?" "What artist did you say the painting reminded you of?"

- *Ask divergent questions.* "What are some materials you could use in your farm picture?" "What ideas do you have about Monet's painting?"

- *Focus children's attention on the way they use art media.* "I see you are drawing circles with the blue marker." "How did you make the sides so high on your clay cup?" "You are making a shade with the black paint."

- *Label the child's actions.* "You are putting blue paint into red paint. What color did you make?" "You are making a shade with the black paint."

- *Introduce new art concepts with actions.* Model an art process as you present a concept. Do this by speaking as you work: "I want a lighter tint of blue for my sky. I think I'll add more white to my blue paint."

- *Verbalize a problem and help children find a solution.* A child becomes frustrated using a white crayon on white paper, and the teacher asks, "Could we see your drawing better if you use a different color crayon? What other colors could you use to help you see the lines?"

- *Encourage children to discuss and arrive at solutions to art problems.* "We need windows for our cardboard school bus. Is there anything in this box that we could use?" "Could we use this piece of plastic?" "Is there anything else we need?"

- *Encourage children to talk about their artwork.* The teacher says, "Tell me about this part of your picture." A child answers, "I drew pets—a cat, a gerbil, and a dog." The teacher says, "Tell me more about what is around your picture." The child answers, "I made a border of stars."

- *Share art experiences.* Listen to what children say to each other about their artwork. Encourage children to describe the processes they used to create a product.

- *Encourage children to talk together about their art.* Jaime watched Lin drawing a picture of the gerbils. The teacher said, "Lin, tell Jaime about your picture. How did you make brown paint?"

- *Talk with children about artists from various cultures and countries.* The teacher might show children artworks of several well-known artists, such as Monet, Bearden, and O'Keeffe. In this manner the teacher introduces children to a French impressionist, an African-American artist, and a female American artist.

- *Give children time to think about art.* Pose questions about art processes and wait for children to respond. "How did you paint your picture?" "What did you do first?" "How did you make that color?" Reflection is an important part of art process. All artists reflect on their work.

FIGURE 4-7 • Suggestions for talking with children about their art.

world through drawings, paintings, sculpture, and mixed media. In art, children are encouraged to pursue their interests, which are frequently influenced by this visual culture.

While adults may find some aspects of kid culture to be aesthetically unappealing, it is important to remember that children are independent thinkers who develop their own tastes based on exposure. One has to first become familiar with kid culture in order to discuss it without bias with children in the classroom.

Encourage children to talk about their ideas with each other and you, their teacher. This is how you

FIGURE 4-8 • Encourage children to talk together about their art.

can learn about current trends in kid culture and their strong impact on students' thinking. If you limit students' artwork to topics of your choosing, there will be no opportunity in school for children to fully explore that which intrigues them: their worlds, real and imagined. When the teacher steps back, permitting children to take ownership of their artistic and creative learning, the content will reflect topics most compelling to each artist. Within that list of student-originated topics, kid culture will always surface (Marshall & Vashe, 2008).

Displaying Children's Work

An important part of the teacher's role in developing children's aesthetic sensitivity is showing their work to parents and others. A good rule is that if children feel good about their work, let them show it. The work does not have to be complete. It should be displayed at children's eye level so that they, as well as adults, may enjoy it. Not every child in the group has to have his or her work displayed. Consider some of these suggestions when planning displays of children's art:

Wall Displays Much of what we want to display ends up on the wall—hung, taped, tacked, stapled, placed on a shelf, or otherwise fastened. Ideally, every last piece is thoughtfully and tastefully placed. Rare as that is, it is something to aspire to in early childhood classrooms. Much of common space wall area and classroom walls should be thought of as gallery space and should be arranged to engage the audience—either with necessary information on works of art or

documentation that expressed the values of the classroom/program and the children's efforts.

Paint or Vinyl Surfaces Neither paint nor vinyl wall surface is a perfect direct surface for display, although they are by far the most widely used with various kinds of tape. Vinyl tends to handle tape without damage, but often taped materials do not stay up on the wall long. Semigloss or eggshell painted surfaces allow for careful taping but sooner or later will require touching up or repainting.

Bulletin boards are useful in administration and teacher areas but are less attractive as display vehicles for children's artwork.

Map rails: Map rails are one-inch strips of cork for tacking or stapling and can be purchased with movable clips or hooks to attach paper. These offer flexibility and an economical solution in areas where taping to the wall is likely.

Three-dimensional displays Shelves and cabinets built in or surface mounted allow the display of three-dimensional artwork.

Hanging displays Artwork can be hung from the ceiling with strong nylon fishing line or fine wire (Greenman, 2005).

Set up displays to show the different ways children have used a medium, such as painting, collage, clay, and so on. Let the room reflect the children's diversity, their likes, their interests—much the way a well-decorated home reflects the interests and skills of the people who live in it. Children aren't clones, so we certainly don't expect to see 25 identical works of art with different names on them displayed in the room. How does this reflect children's diversity?

Take time at the end of the day to show artwork to the children, letting them talk about each other's work. Model for them how to make a positive comment.

Be sure to send all artwork home in a way that shows your respect for the artist and the art. Take care with children's work. Rolling dry paintings to take home shows you respect the work and the artist. Folding a wet painting does just the opposite. (More specific suggestions on displaying children's work are covered in Appendix D.)

Interpreting Children's Creative Work for Parents

Parents should be helped to see what the child liked about the creative work. All people have their own ideas of what creative talent is, parents being no

THIS ONE'S for YOU!   Create a Classroom Museum

Provide children (of all ages) a year-round aesthetic experience by incorporating a classroom museum into your program. It's "show and tell" in a more meaningful, aesthetic sense. This project will provide many creative opportunities for children to document their progress in many ways throughout the year. Here are the basics to get you started.

What Is a Classroom Museum? A **classroom museum** is a collection of items and artifacts related to a specific theme. Items and artifacts are brought in by the children for display. Using this approach for show and tell, the theme or topic is motivating and the exhibit grows gradually and joyfully. Decision making, problem solving, and communicating are skills practiced as children share/add their special selections. Treasures from home, a family-crafted item, or an occasional purchase—each contribution is worthy. The sharing is educational and enjoyable. Museum topics change each month, with teacher/child interest sparking the choice.

Essentials for Success

- Make a high-quality choice for the first museum of the year.

- Determine a clear purpose and definite goals for the museum as a curriculum tool appropriate for children's development.

- Invite family participation via an informative, friendly August newsletter, a September Parents' Night, and a special museum notice.

- Plan a simple but attractive museum area in the classroom. A suitable physical setup includes a backdrop for hanging pictures and a display table.

- Highlight the children's artifacts and show-and-tell experience.

- Select a child as a curator to encourage responsibility.

- Guide children's selection for show-and-tell artifacts to help foster respect for all contributions and ensure their survival in the classroom (especially fragile or sentimental items).

A good place to start in the beginning of the program year is with a "Me Museum." This is a good topic to start with because it encourages a feeling of community as teacher, and children learn more about each other.

Steps to Setting Up the Me Museum

- Awareness (with children)—Explore the concept of museum. Discuss possible items for a Me Museum. Plan ways that families can help. Frame a family museum notice. Establish routines for sharing.

- Contributions (from children)—Me Museum artifacts are always surprises. Descriptions delight. Personal histories in bits and pieces come alive. Students have shared stuffed animals, baby journals, family photos, toys, travel souvenirs, books or stories, ballet slippers, and other such objects.

- Integration (with children)—Growth in vocabulary occurs. Expressive language expands. Thinking and problem-solving skills are nurtured.

- Outcomes (for children)—Child by child, with each contribution, child-centered showing and sharing creates a caring community in which each child is important and friendships emerge.

To Continue the Museum. To create the next month's museum, brainstorm with the children some possible topics and themes. What do they want to learn about? What provokes their curiosity? What special interest do they want to share/explore with classmates? Inspired and motivated, many ideas are listed and voting follows (integrating math skills such as counting, graphing, predicting, and comparing).

First choice becomes the next museum, with second place a strong possibility for a future museum. The teacher also selects topics to coincide with curriculum or timely topics. Topics may vary from year to year. The steps of awareness, contributions, integration, and outcome all facilitate museum planning.

FIGURE 4-9 • Be positive when discussing the child's work.

exception. It is important, however, that they understand and know that what their children enjoy and feel about what they are doing is much more important than the finished product.

Parents should also know why some materials are used by their children and others are not. More importantly, parents should learn to approach their child's making of gifts, art exhibits, and displays as demonstrations of the child's aesthetic sense. With these displays, the child is saying, "This is how it is with me."

Parents want to know their children; children's creative work can help parents know more about their children. Teachers can assist parents by showing these visual examples of the creative process and pointing out that they are valuable for the process alone. Teachers can assist parents of older children to see and appreciate the progression of images that are growing more subtle and complex in their child's art.

Very few children will become professional artists, but given encouragement and experience, they can learn to work with many media, enjoy beauty, and discriminate with aesthetic understanding. A person naturally responds to a lovely sunrise, painting, or piece of music. These aesthetic experiences help us live fully in the moment. Such responses do not

THINK ABOUT IT   Encouraging Aesthetic Development by Listening to Children

Really *listening* to children and encouraging their dreams and fantasies are basic to their developing aesthetic senses. In this excerpt, a young teacher and mother shares what she learned about children's questions, adult answers, and listening.

Several years ago a friend offered me a bit of simple advice that has contributed significantly to how I regard children and learning. When young children are inquisitive, my friend said, ask them what they think, rather than provide the all-knowing adult answer.

Soon afterward, on a spring day, five-year-old Yara and I sat on the couch watching huge, lacy snowflakes falling outside. "Mom, did you ever wonder where those snowflakes come from?" she asked.

I started to remind her about the water cycle and what happens when the water freezes, but

I remembered my friend's advice and instead asked her what she thought.

"Did you ever think," she asked, "that those snowflakes are pieces of angels' wings floating down from heaven?"

As soon as Yara spoke, I understood that those special spring snowflakes had inspired her to think metaphorically rather than scientifically. She already knew something about the water cycle but at this moment wanted to go beyond scientific knowledge.

Young children are curious and often ask us to explain how complicated things work. But most of the time they don't really want to know what we think. Instead, they want to share with us the ideas they are mulling over. A careful listener often learns more about the child than facts reveal (White, 2002).

need to be taught, but a child might need assistance and exposure to appreciate them fully. Aesthetic enjoyment provides an avenue through which people can find focus and achieve balance and tranquility in an increasingly fast-paced world. Moreover, children who learn to love beauty in nature and in the arts are likely to want to support and protect these valuable resources.

Developing Your Sense of Aesthetics

Early childhood teachers need to protect the spirit, imagination, curiosity, and love of life and learning in young children as fiercely as we protect our environment. In a similar manner, early childhood teachers need to develop and protect their own aesthetic senses.

As you read through this book you will most likely find some activities that catch your attention, appeal to your spirit, and reflect your personality and philosophy. Indeed, it must be your personality and philosophy

that determine how you use any activity. All of the ideas and activities in this book are to be shaped and modified to suit your own needs with a particular group of children. Any idea will only be successful if you like it and are excited to use it with young children. You must mix a lot of yourself into all of your work with young children. Do not hesitate to mix in your philosophy and personality along with those of the children. Add a good portion of energy (yours and the children's), stir in a large measure of imagination, and you are on your way to a truly creative environment for young children.

The World Wide Web and Older Children's Aesthetic Experiences

In the activity sections of this book, you will find many activities for older children that involve references to virtual art museums. These virtual art museums tend to fall into two broad categories: those that are extensions of brick-and-mortar institutions, such as the Metropolitan Museum website (http://www.metmuseum.org) and those that exist only online, such as the Virtual Diego Rivera Web Museum (http://www.diegorivera.com). Some virtual art museums like the State Hermitage Museum (http://www.hermitagemuseum.org) function with corporate support, whereas others, like the American Museum of Photography (http://www.photography-museum.com), are the work of individuals with a special interest or expertise in art. One goal that all virtual art museums have in common is collecting, preserving, and sharing objects of aesthetic, cultural, or historical value with a viewing public dispersed around the world.

Effective use of these digital resources to support student learning depends on a good research question or task that challenges students to apply what they find online in meaningful ways. Internet-based assignments should encourage students to explore, gather information, think critically, and construct their own understandings of the curriculum topic at hand.

For example, the J. Paul Getty Museum website (http://www.getty.edu) offers a wealth of art images, thematic exhibitions, video clips, and accompanying text. Depending on your students' grade level, you might ask them to choose works of art from two different time periods that appear on the site to write a

FIGURE 4-10 • Help children select the materials they prefer.

THIS ONE'S for YOU!

This One's for You! The Story of "American Gothic"

"American Gothic" by Grant Wood is one of the most widely recognized paintings in America. This painting of the farmer standing in front of a wooden house, holding a pitchfork with his unsmiling daughter next to him, has an interesting creation story.

In August 1930, Grant Wood was visiting the town of Eldo, Iowa, when he came upon a house that would eventually make him famous. This five-room structure was built in the 1880s in a style known as Carpenter Gothic. Wood was impressed with its compactness and design, particularly the Gothic window in its gable.

Wood imagined a farmer and his daughter standing in front of the house. He immediately sketched his idea and had someone take a photograph of the house so that he could work out his idea when he returned home.

Back in his studio, Wood used old Victorian photographs and 19th-century portrait paintings to plan the scene he was to paint. His sister, Nan, and his dentist, Dr. Byron McKeeby, served as models and were dressed in the period clothes they are seen wearing. Even though they are seen standing together in the painting, each was painted during separate sittings.

The man was given a pitchfork to hold because Wood wanted him to be associated with haying in the 19th century rather than the more common farming practice of gardening in the 20th century. The pitchfork also symbolized masculinity, the devil, and farming and served as a compositional device to echo the ovalness of the people's faces and the repeated lines of the Gothic window. Wood worked on the painting for 2 months and finished it in time to enter it in a juried exhibition at the Art Institute of Chicago.

Although the jurors were at first divided over whether to accept the painting, it eventually got into the show and even received a bronze medal and a $300 price. At the time, it aroused great controversy and was called by one art critic "an insulting caricature of plain country people." But "American Gothic" gradually gained acceptance and has since become one of the most iconic paintings in America. The original "American Gothic" hangs today in the Art Institute of Chicago.

comparative analysis. Have students share their comparisons and collectively discuss the larger question of "How has art changed over time?"

Another classroom activity involves students becoming virtual art critics. Students choose an exhibition currently showing on a virtual art museum site for critical review. The Smithsonian American Art Museum (http://www.americanart.si.edu), for example, features more than 30 virtual art exhibitions among the main resources available on its website. The teacher is able to introduce the role of the art critic by providing samples of critical reviews to read and discussing what might be included in students' reviews.

A third virtual art museum activity is to have students use artworks that they study online as springboards for their own artistic compositions. Ask students to select a work from an online exhibit that relates to your current unit of instruction. Have students write a one-page analysis of the work they've chosen, using questions that you provide to guide their analysis. Following the writing activity, have students create their own interpretations of a landscape based on an idea or theme that the artists they studied used in their work.

A great place to find museum sites and special online collections is the Museum of Online Museums (http://www.coudal.com/moom/), which includes listings of links to hundreds of museum websites organized by topic.

Summary

Children look for things they need and want. They are stimulated by things they find interesting and rewarding.

There are three types of sensing and feeling. The first is contact through the five basic senses; the second is what the person feels inside; and the third is fantasy.

Many materials with aesthetic potential can be found. Anything children can explore, manipulate, and use in different ways has aesthetic potential. What is most important is that these materials (and what is done with them) become personal statements of the children.

Teachers and parents can help children explore this aesthetic potential by concentrating on the importance of the *process* and not the product in young children's creative work. With older children (grades 4 to 5), the process usually involves the creation of a more complex work. With all ages of children, the teacher can give supportive and gentle guidance by asking helpful questions, avoiding models, and helping children "hunt" for aesthetic qualities. How well teachers use art talk with children and how they encourage them to share art talk determines how well the children express themselves with art.

Displaying children's work at their eye level is yet another way to show appreciation for their involvement in the creative process. Parents' appreciation for these displays must also concentrate on the importance of the child's creative process and not on the finished product. The teacher's role is to help interpret children's work for parents. Effective use of Internet resources can support older students' aesthetic development.

Key Terms

aesthetic sensitivity 60
classroom museum 66
contrast 63
kid culture 63
rhythm 63

Learning Activities

Beautiful Things

Everyone has had some experience with beauty and has a special idea about what is beautiful. It can be a very interesting experience to examine this concept with each of the five senses.

A. Write down the three most beautiful things (living or nonliving) that you have ever experienced with each of your five senses.

B. As you write your list, try as much as possible to relive the sensations.

C. Answer the following questions.

1. Were most of your things living or nonliving?
2. How many involved people?
3. Did any of your answers surprise you?
4. How often do you encounter beautiful things?
5. Which sense seems to find the most beauty?
6. How much does finding beauty in life depend on the viewer?
7. What does this mean for working with children?

D. Compare your responses with those of fellow students.

Amazing Journey

A. Find a quiet place and relax. Close your eyes and think of something that amazes you or produces wonder in you.

B. Think of yourself as that something. (Take some time to get the feel of being it.)

C. Write a description of yourself as this something. (Use plenty of adjectives.)

D. As a result of this experience:

1. What emotions do you feel?
2. How are you like what really amazes you?
3. How are you unlike it?
4. Would you like to change in any way?

E. Compare your answers with those of your classmates.

F. Do you think children would enjoy using their imaginations like this?

Cyberspace Aesthetics

Visit the Internet for some aesthetic experiences.

A. Visit one or more of these Web pages featuring paintings by Vincent van Gogh:

- http://www.vangoghgallery.com/
- http://www.ibiblio.org/. Click on "Arts and Recreation."
- http://www.artchive.com/. Click on "The Archive," then on "Post-Impressionism."

Look at several works by this artist. Select the artwork that interests you most. What moods do you think the artist is trying to express in this painting? What features in the artwork made you think that? How was the artist able to convey these moods to the viewer?

B. Some artworks are not as easy to analyze because they are nonobjective—that is, they don't show any people, places, or things. Many modern artists work nonobjectively to express their unique ideas and feelings. How does an artist communicate this way? Can you explain how these artworks express ideas and feelings?

- http://www.ibiblio.org/. Click on "Arts and Recreation."
- http://www.artchive.com/. Click on "The Archive," then on "Abstract Expressionism."
- http://www.abstractart.20m.com/. Click on "Jackson Pollock."

C. Visit the Andy Warhol Museum at http://www.warhol.org/. Examine how art is used to commemorate famous people and important events in different cultures around the world. Then, see "Washington Crossing the Delaware" by Emanuel Gottlieb Leutze in 1851 at http://www.metmuseum.org/explore/gw/el_gw.htm. Create a work of art that commemorates a famous person or event in history. Then check out the Wall of Fame at Art Junction, http://www.artjunction.org/gal_fame.php to see how children have pictured their important events.

Aesthetics in the Animal World

Two famous Russian artists started the Asian Elephant Art and Conservation Project to help improve the welfare of domesticated elephants. The nonprofit organization raises funds through donations and the sale of artwork created by elephants that the AAEACP has trained to paint. The work is primarily abstract expressionist, but the elephants are also now being instructed on how to create realistic works.

- Go to the website http://www.elephantart.com and choose a work that you would like to purchase.

- Tell why you would like to have the artwork.
- Would you like to really own a painting by an elephant?
- Do you think that the elephants are the artists or are the people who train and help the animals with their paintings the true artists?

Making Cross-Curricular Connections

Here are some suggestions for cross-curricular connections using famous artists' work.

Math. Prompt students to recognize repeated geometric shapes in Grant Wood's "American Gothic" and mosaic patterns in M.C. Escher's "Relativity." Andy Warhol's "One Hundred Cans" is another good example to use to see geometric shapes.

History. Introduce artists in their historical context. For example, ask older students to consider how Mary Cassatt and Berthe Morisot illustrate the limitations placed on 19th-century women in society and as artists, and to note that Jasper Johns' "Three Flags" only has 38 stars because Hawaii and Alaska weren't admitted to the Union until 1959.

Science. Explain how George Seurat's method of using small dots to demonstrate how our eyes see color.

Literature. Students connect Michelangelo Caravaggio's realistic style and Henri Matisse's "Icarus" to figures from Greek mythology.

Pop culture. Ask students to reflect on Jasper Johns, who was one of the first artists to think about the design of everyday objects around us. Ask students to recognize how Caravaggio's lifestyle and Warhol's celebration of the celebrity have much in common with our contemporary culture.

Activities for Children

Aesthetic Thinking Through Art

Help the child to think of new ideas in responding to the following prompts.

A. Say to the child, "If you could invent a new means of transportation, what would it be? Draw or construct how it would look."

B. Ask the child, "If you had a funny-shaped piece of paper, what could you make it into?"

C. Ask, "How do you think the world would look to a giant? Draw a picture (or make a model) of it."

D. Ask, "What could you do with this empty box, this stick, this cardboard (beautiful junk)? How could you place it or arrange it to make something that's your very own idea?"

Sensory Experiences

Seeing

A. *Colors.* Have children look for colors in the room: "How many red things can you see?" Or play a guessing game: "I am thinking of something green in this room. What is it?" Colors sometimes tell us important things: Traffic lights tell us when to go or stop, red flags on a road mean danger, red lights in a building mean an exit. We must obey these signals. We can make different colors by mixing them. (Allow children to experiment with mixing colors.) Show a prism to see the colors. Blow soap bubbles, and look for the rainbow colors in them.

B. *Shapes.* Show blocks or other objects that are circles, squares, rectangles, and triangles. Have children find things in the room that are these shapes. We can see color and shape at the same time. Find a red square, a blue circle, an orange pyramid.

C. *Sizes*. Compare sizes of children and objects. Develop concepts of big, bigger, biggest, large, small, tall, short, thick, thin, wide, narrow, etc. Play riddles: "I am thinking of something that is white and round (clock)."

Listening

A. *Tape Recorder*. Children can listen to their own voices, to the voices of others, and to classroom sounds. Take the recorder on field trips and record sounds in animals' environments. Replay to review the trip and to help children remember the sequence of events. Record sounds in the environment: cars passing; steps in the corridor or on the street; children skipping, hopping, running. Ask questions like, "Do any of the animals sound alike? Which of the sounds was loudest? How would you describe that sound? Can you draw that sound?"

B. *Street Corner*. Listen to sounds. Identify them: car turning corner, wind blowing past sign, click as light changes, dog barking, rain dripping, wheels on wet pavement, animal footsteps, high heels on pavement, sneakers on pavement, noises from buildings.

C. *Classroom Sounds*. Listen to sounds of different toys, clock ticking, blocks falling. Have children cover their eyes and ask, "Where does the sound come from? What is the sound?" Have a volunteer walk (skip, run) across the back, the front, or along the side of the room.

D. *Stethoscope*. Listen to heartbeats of children, adults, and animals. Listen to someone's stomach after a snack. Scratch different objects on a tabletop (floor, rug, pipe) and listen to the sound through the stethoscope.

E. *Rhythms*. Beat out simple and then more complex rhythms with clapping hands. Ask children to repeat them. Then have them lead with their own sound rhythms.

Taste and Smell

Be sure to teach children proper precautions in tasting or smelling strange substances.

A. *Cooking*. Make puddings, candy, cakes. Smell before, after, and during cooking. Identify what's cooking by smell. Taste brown sugar, white sugar, molasses, corn syrup, maple syrup. Make lemonade with and without sugar. Squeeze tomatoes, apples, and oranges for juice. Question children about which smells they like and what smells they don't like. Draw a picture about smells.

B. *Snack or Lunch*. Talk about differences in taste between hamburgers and bologna, between peanuts and peanut butter, between potato chips and mashed potatoes. (These discussions may also get into sense of touch as well as smell and taste.) Have children guess what they will have for lunch from smells coming from the kitchen.

Touching (Tactile Awareness)

A. *Rough or Smooth?* Discuss tactile sensitivity with children. Make available objects of varying textures, such as silk, burlap, feathers, rope, seashells, mirrors, balls, driftwood, beads, furry slippers, and so on. Have children form small groups; give each group an object. Have each child in the group show how the object makes him or her feel. For example, a feather may stand in a straight line with arms and legs extended, and then move "softly," with arms waving gently from side to side.

B. *A Collage Made for Touching*. A texture collage is a bulletin board that all students can contribute to and use later for future projects. Have children bring in materials of different textures—sandpaper, flannel, velvet, burlap, plastic, bottle caps, pebbles, and paper clips—to glue on the board. Once the collage is complete, the children can make "rubbings" using charcoal sticks on newsprint. This board should encourage use of vocabulary-expanding words like "coarse," "smooth," etc.

C. *Creative Movement*. Discriminate between various textures through movements. Have children feel a texture such as that of silk and interpret it by moving the way it feels. Use a variety of textures that exhibit characteristics: bumpy, smooth, coarse, prickly.

D. *Outdoor Textures*.

1. Words to use: *rough, smooth, bumpy, soft, hard, sharp, cold, warm, wet, dry, same, different*.
2. At the beginning of the walk, ask children, "How do things feel?" Say, "Let's feel this building," or "Let's feel the back of this tree."
3. If a child does not know the meaning of the word *rough*, say to her while she feels the tree, "The tree bark feels rough. Let's see if we can find something else that feels rough."
4. If the child is familiar with the word *rough* and its meaning, say, "Can you find something that feels different from this rough tree?" (Example: a smooth leaf.) Or, "Can you find something that feels the same as this rough tree?"
5. As you continue your walk, find new objects to touch, and name their textures. Note: For very young children, begin with two simple words that express opposites, such as *rough* and *smooth, soft* and *hard*, or *wet* and *dry*.

E. *Hidden Objects in Boxes*. Hide objects inside boxes and have children feel and describe them without seeing them. Have them match a given object with its mate by hunting for the mate in the box without seeing it. Have children match objects by size and shape, or only by shape, by pulling them out of the boxes. (Some children may be able to do this only if they have felt both objects with the same hand.) Put several objects in the boxes to make the task harder; more similar objects also make the task harder.

F. *Hidden Multisensory Objects.* A multisensory feely bag game is perfect for the development of aesthetic senses and descriptive vocabulary. Place an interesting object in a bag and invite children to use as many different words as they can to describe it as they feel it. Write their words down in rows like a poem—*big, squishy, soft, round . . .* Pillow!

G. *Sandpaper Letter Game—Early Elementary.* Provide children with letters cut from sandpaper. Have them work in pairs. Blindfold one child and have the other child give a letter to the blindfolded one to feel and guess its identity. Award one point for each correct identification. Then have the partners switch places.

H. *Touch the Alphabet—Early Elementary.* Make a collection of tactile objects for the various letters of the alphabet. Use cotton balls for "c," denim for "d," a brick for "b," etc. Children will experience the tactile relationship as well as the letter/symbol relationship.

Colorful Bubbles

This activity will enhance children's visual perception and aesthetic skills by observing a variety of subtle color variations. They will also see how light can change these colors. Fine motor skills are also developed in this activity as children use eyedroppers.

Materials: Bubble wrap, clear packaging tape, medicine droppers, food coloring, mixing cups, water, and scissors.

Procedure:

1. Cut a piece of bubble wrap to a desired size. Use wrap that has at least 5/16-inch-height bubbles.
2. Using clear packaging tape, place bubble wrap onto the surface of a glass window that is at a level reachable for young children.
3. Cut tiny slits into the tops of bubbles. Let the child decide which bubbles to cut.
4. Have children fill medicine droppers with food coloring and squeeze a bit of the liquid into each bubble, filling about 3/4 of the bubble.
5. Add water in varying amounts to the food coloring to make a variety of shades.
6. The child can decide on the color choices and the arrangement of these colors on the bubble wrap. One color can be used and varying amounts of water can be added to investigate the subtle differences in color depending on the concentration of food coloring.
7. Encourage children to mix colors to make new ones.
8. When the project is complete, secure each bubble with a small piece of clear tape.

My Feelings

1. Distribute large pieces of drawing paper and watercolor markers to children.
2. Have children close their eyes and listen. Clearly and slowly say words that evoke emotion: *love, hate, cold, soft, fun, laugh.*
3. With their eyes still closed, children move their marker across their paper to reflect the emotion/ emotions they feel as you present each word.
4. Have students talk about how each word made them feel. Older children can write their responses on the back of their drawing.

My Imagination—Kindergarten and Up

Materials: String or yarn, scissors, paper, glue, washable markers or crayons

1. Have children glue a 6- to 8-inch-long piece of string or yarn on a piece of paper.
2. Direct children to pass their paper to the person sitting to their left.
3. Have children take this piece of paper and imagine what the visual represents.
4. Have students use markers or crayons to create something from the original string art.
5. Have children discuss what they saw and why it became what it did.

Famous Art Work Fun

Famous works of art are a great venue for talking about word choice. For instance, when examining Van Gogh's *Starry Night,* have children describe the swirling blue skies and bright orange stars. Write down the adjectives they use in large letters on an index card. Put all of the cards into a bag of adjectives and have each child pick one. The child then draws or paints three things that might be described by that adjective. For example, *prickly* could describe a cactus, a pinecone, and a porcupine. Children will enjoy looking at each other's pictures and guessing which adjective they picked.

Rainbow Reflections

Hang a crystal or prism outside in bright sunlight. If possible, place it in front of a light-colored surface, such as a white wall. On a bright, sunny day, take children outdoors where they'll discover the prism or crystal that you've hung up to catch the sunlight. Talk about the rainbow of colors made by the prism. What colors do they see? Have they ever seen a rainbow in the sky?

Take down the prism and let the children hold it. What happens when the sun catches it from behind? From the front? What happens when they walk with it? Ask children to carry it to a shady place. Does the rainbow disappear? Explain how the prism bends the sunlight to create colors.

There is another way to make a rainbow in the classroom. All that is needed is a glass of water and a sunny day. (Be sure to use a clear glass. The wider the mouth, the better.) When the glass is placed in sunlight, there should be a rainbow where the shadow would fall. What is made is a simple prism, which can be used in lessons about the color spectrum. Point out to children that a rainbow forms outdoors when drops of water in the air act as prisms.

Provide markers or paint and large sheets of white construction paper that children can use to create their own rainbows. If possible, provide prisms of different shapes and sizes that children can use to further their rainbow explorations.

Wind Words

Read the first stanza of "The Wind" by Robert Louis Stevenson.

"The wind blew shrill and smart
And the wind awoke my heart
Again to go a-sailing o'er the sea
To hear the cordage moan
And the straining timbers groan,
And to see the flying pennon lie a-lee."

Take children outside on a windy day or create a windy day indoors with an electric fan. Have children close their eyes and feel the wind in their faces and at their backs. Hold up a strip of tissue and watch its movements. Encourage children to call out words that describe how the wind feels to them and how it moves.

Mondrian Can Be Elementary

For this activity, you will need 9 × ½-inch or 9 × 1-inch strips of black paper, construction paper in primary colors, scissors, glue, and 9 × 9-inch white construction paper.

Piet Mondrian's work is interesting and fun to study for even the youngest student because of his simple shapes and primary colors. To get the children started on this Mondrian exercise, show several examples of reproductions by Mondrian's work (see Think About It: Your Own Art Reproduction Collection" box on page 61 for websites that contain examples of Mondrian's work), pointing out shapes he used, and introducing red, yellow, and blue as primary colors. Then encourage students to create their own versions.

Have students cut out primary-color construction paper squares and rectangles and glue them onto the white construction paper. Next, use the precut black strips of construction paper to create vertical or horizontal lines on the same page. The black strips can outline the edges of the primary color shapes.

To extend the activity, you could discuss the concepts of vertical, horizontal, and intersecting (crossing) lines, as well as the concepts of length and width. Another extension could be a musical one. Use the tune of "Three Blind Mice" and replace the words with "red, yellow, and blue." "Red, yellow, and blue. Oh, they are the primary colors, oh yes. We mix them together to get all the rest. Red, yellow, and blue. Red, yellow, and blue."

Fence Designs

For this activity, all you need is access to a chain link fence and colored paper cups. Push the cups into the diamond spaces in the fence. Cups need to be large enough to stick by pressure within the openings without collapsing the cup.

Form the pattern by placing cups in the links. You can make a colored flag, or even present a word, such as "GO TEAM," "WELCOME," or "USA."

Nature Murals

After a walk in the rain, a dance in the wind, or another outdoor experience, plan a group mural. After coming inside, discuss what was seen, heard, tasted, and felt. Discuss with the children things that can be included in a group mural. Allow each child to decide what she or he will make for the mural. Have children create individual works representing their personal experiences. These pictures and designs can be glued onto one large sheet of paper, creating the mural.

Art Walk

Discuss with the children the artworks they have created and the patterns and textures they created in their work. Then invite all of them on a walk around the school looking for patterns and textures.

Remind the children that art can be made by people when they draw, paint, or sculpt. People also can make useful things more beautiful, such as when they put patterns on clothing, make patterns with floor or wall tiles, or decorate a bulletin board. Have children bring their sketchbooks to sketch patterns they like or do quick rubbings of interesting patterns they find on the art walk.

Remind children that art is also found in nature. Have children look for and sketch examples of art in nature as well as in the design and decorative elements of the school building and playground.

After the walk, ask children to draw pictures of both human-made and natural art they found during their walk. Then ask them to write or dictate sentences that tell about their pictures. Display children's work to add to the art in your room.

As a follow-up to the art walk, invite local interior designers or landscape designers to visit the class to talk about how they use what they know about art to make rooms or yards more beautiful. Ask the visitor to bring along sketches or other visuals to share with the children. With the visitor's help, plan a simple design activity for children.

Fun with Shadows and Clouds

Capitalize on sunny summer days. Help children make and play with shadows cast by their hands, objects, and moving things. Look at clouds long and often. Find shapes that look like the beginning of a story, then tell the story. Look for another cloud figure that gives you an idea for how to continue the story.

Activities for Older Children (Grades 4–5)

Color Optics

The following are some color optics phenomena older children will enjoy exploring individually.

- **Afterimage.** This is probably the best-known illustration of how our eyes react to color. Have students stare at a page of solid color for about 30 seconds, then look at a dot on a page of white or gray. They will see color on the blank page—usually the complement or near complement of the color of the paper they had stared at. For example, they will see red if they had stared at a green piece of paper, or blue if they had stared at a yellow piece of paper.
- **Juxtaposition.** Color pigments placed side by side in small repeated strokes are altered by our vision to appear to combine, thus forming a different hue. This new optical effect is more vibrant than if the same pigments were blended together. This technique has been used historically by mosaic and stained glass artists, but most effectively by the 19th-century postimpressionists such as Georges Seurat. Use a print of his painting, *A Sunday Afternoon on the Island of Le Grand Jette,* to explore this concept. Then challenge students to try their hand at this visual mixing of colors.
- **Color Relativity.** The color gray appears much lighter when placed on a black background than it does against a white one. This dark/light effect holds true for many other colors as well. Yellow on a green background will appear to contain more red than it does on a white background.

Using pairs of colored sheets of paper, let students make their own discoveries of color optics by placing two samples of the same color on a variety of different backgrounds. Then have them compare results.

Activities Related to the Concept of Line

Lines are basic to art. Lines can convey different moods. Before drawing and painting experiences, you might want to discuss the variety of lines that we encounter in our daily lives. Ask students to think about telephone lines, clothes lines, lines of people, lines of music, the line of scrimmage. Then ask some of these questions to get them thinking: What do we associate with lines on a face? Where do you see long pairs of parallel lines? Where do you see more straight lines, in nature or in man-made objects? (Ask them to look around.) Where do you see more curves? Which conveys more movement: a straight line or a curvy one?

To encourage creative use of line in their work and to explore line and mood with students, ask questions like the following.

A. Verticals

1. What do you see in our environment that is made up of vertical lines? (skyscrapers, trees, telephone poles, rain, Gothic cathedrals, soldiers standing at attention)
2. What moods or feelings does a series of verticals convey? (Heavenward, of the sky, strong, straight, dignified)
3. Have you ever leaned against a vertical? (yes—a wall, a tree, a lamppost)
4. When is your body vertical? (when standing)

B. Horizontals

1. What in the environment is predominantly horizontal? (the horizon, the floor, a bed, a table, a still lake or pond)
2. What moods do these horizontals convey? (grounded, of the earth, relaxed, at rest, calm, serene, expansive)
3. When is your body horizontal? (when lying down, asleep)
4. Can you stand or sit on a horizontal? (yes—a sofa, the floor)

C. Diagonals

1. Where do you see diagonals? (a slide, a plane taking off, a ramp)
2. What feeling is conveyed by diagonals? (action, movement)

3. When is your body at a diagonal? (when you are running, walking fast, leaning into the wind)

D. Wavy lines

1. Where do you see wavy lines in the environment? (a wavy ocean, lake, river, snake, rolling hills)
2. What feelings do they convey? (undulating movement, relaxed, rhythmic, fluid)

E. Zigzag lines

1. Where do you see zigzag lines in the environment? (lightning, a jagged tear, the earth after an earthquake, crimped hair)
2. What moods do they convey? (tense, anxious, frenzied)
3. When does your body form a zigzag? (while jumping on a pogo stick)

F. Spirals

1. What do you see that is shaped in a spiral? (a spring, a slide, water going down a drain, a tornado, a coiled snake)
2. What feelings do spirals convey? (spinning, swirling, energy)
3. When is your body in a spiral? (while twirling on the dance floor or doing a pirouette)

Cyberspace Aesthetics

Have students use the Internet for the following aesthetic experiences.

- Kcho (pronounced KA-cho) is a well-known artist from the island of Cuba. Check out some of his large three-dimensional works, which are displayed around the world, at http://www.artnews.com/home/. Click on "Back Issues," go to the June 2000 issue, and search for "Kcho" or click on "Making Waves." Alternatively, go to http://www.walkerart.org/education/. Click on "Collections and Resources." Type "Kcho" in the "Search" box.
- What did you learn about the artist's background? How would you describe Kcho's work? What subjects and themes do you see in most of Kcho's art? What messages do you think the artist is communicating about his culture? How does he use different materials to express himself?
- Ramona Sakiestewa is a Hopi Indian fabric artist. Learn about the artist and her work at the following sites: http://www.lewallencontemporary.com. Click on "Browse by Artist" or go to http://www.dsg-art.com/s/sakiestewa/.
- Describe the design of Sakiestewa's art. What colors, lines, shapes, and textures can be seen? How do you think the work would be different if you saw it in person? Why do you think she uses this medium? What could she want viewers of her tapestries to know about her?

Is This Art?

Present this problem to your students to get them talking about what they consider to be "art."

One day your teacher says she wants to draw a picture of you. She takes a sheet of paper and covers the whole thing with chartreuse crayon (you know, that yellow-green color), and then she tacks it up on the board. Under it she writes, "This is a picture of my student." Would you be mad? Is this art? These questions will be interesting ones to answer. They will give you insight into how your students think about art.

Artists Like Us

Exposing children to the work of famous artists can help them find their artist within.

Materials: White drawing paper, markers, colored pencils, crayons, books or prints of art by famous artists such as Picasso, Cezanne, Seurat

1. Present the work of a great master such as Picasso for children to observe and discuss.
2. Invite children to notice specific qualities of the works and techniques used. For example, children might notice the unusual Cubist portraits of Picasso. You might ask, "How are these different from other portraits you have seen or even drawn?"
3. Provide art materials for children to create their own portraits in a particular artist's style.
4. Encourage children to give a title to their works and create a famous-artist-inspired art show or class art book.

Variation: Present the Pointillism style of George Seurat. Show how he preferred not to make brushstrokes but to paint by applying small dots of unmixed colors. Provide cotton swabs as painting tools and watercolors for children to paint their own Pointillism painting.

Water Designs Using an Overhead Projector

This is a wonderful way for children to explore the different aesthetic properties of materials—transparent, opaque, and semitransparent. It also encourages experimentation with a variety of materials.

Materials: Overhead projector, glass tray or glass baking dish filled with water, string, yarn, lace, food coloring, cooking oil, eye/medicine droppers, netting, pipe cleaners, feathers, and any other transparent or semitransparent materials.

1. Place the glass tray filled with water on top of the overhead projector.
2. Turn on the projector to project light onto a screen or wall.
3. Invite children to experiment with different materials by placing them into the water tray and watching the image projected onto the screen.
4. Encourage children to use drops of color and oil to see and document interesting results.
5. Small pieces of string and yarn can be added along with pipe cleaners twisted into interesting shapes to

further manipulate the image and see the aesthetic nature of the art materials.

6. Add other materials for further explorations of transparent properties, semitransparent properties, opaqueness, and color mixing.

Variation: More than one projector can be used. Images can be projected as large as the wall to create interesting environments for children. These environments could change on a daily basis depending on the project theme (underwater, forest, sunsets, storms). Musical selections accompanying these themes can be played while imagery is projected.

Nature Sketches

Have students take a sketchbook home and draw five to ten small patches of different textures they find in nature. Under each patch, have students write down the name of the material from which the sketch was made (a tree, a rock, a piece of a leaf). Have students use their sketches to create a colored and enlarged version of these textures on a suitably sized piece of paper. Display and discuss the drawings.

Patterns in Nature

Discuss regular and irregular patterns seen in plants, animals, and other natural forms in the spring. Some irregular patterns are found in the camouflage of animals. Structural patterns tend to be regular, as seen in shells, leaf veins, and many plants.

Forms of Letters

Have students create letter forms by printing them with objects. Almost all letters of the alphabet can be created from straight lines (edge of tongue depressor or cardboard), circles (bottle caps or spools), and half circles (rubber washers cut in half). Students can also use this printing technique to illustrate an original poem.

Group Objects

Have four or five students work in a group, using the objects from the preceding activity (cardboard, bottle caps, spools, and rubber washers cut in half). Have them share their printing objects to make a picture. Brainstorm creative ways to use the objects they have (e.g., repeated circles become animal shapes, edges of cardboard become repeated blades of grass, etc.) Display these pictorial prints in the classroom.

Georgia O'Keeffe's "The Mountain, New Mexico"

Obtain an art print of this work. It is an excellent example of a landscape and varieties of warm and cool colors. If this print is not available, any other landscape with warm and cool colors will suffice.

Briefly review the concept that colors are an important way to express moods and feelings in art. Point out that many color words help people to tell about feelings. Examples include "feeling blue," "green with envy," or "red with rage."

Explain that artists often refer to these color qualities as *warm* or *cool.* These terms can mean that a color is used to show warm things (a fire) or cool things (a lake). More often, the artist also remembers that colors help to express feelings.

Explain that the warm colors in O'Keeffe's painting show the red earth of mountains in New Mexico, but they also help to express the artist's warm feelings about the land: O'Keeffe thought that the forms and colors of the desert and nearby mountains were beautiful. Guide students to see the delicate shading and rhythmic curves that fill the whole painting. Discuss how the painting makes them feel about the place depicted.

As a follow-up activity, have students create a picture of a landscape on a planet no one has seen. Have them use warm or cool colors to express the feelings they want to convey about this place.

Chapter Review

1. List three types of sensing and feeling.
2. Give three guidelines to use in choosing materials that have aesthetic potential.
3. List four suggestions to help children work with aesthetic materials.
4. Discuss how to involve parents in their children's aesthetic experiences.
5. List some points to cover when discussing with parents how to interpret their children's creative works.
6. List some points to consider when displaying children's creative works.
7. List six guidelines to use in talking with children about their artwork.
8. What are some differences to expect in the aesthetic experiences of older children?
9. Give some examples of good questions to use with young children in discussing their art.
10. How can the World Wide Web be used to develop older children's aesthetic senses?

References

Greenman, J. (2005). *Caring spaces, learning places: Children's environments that work.* Redmond, WA: Exchange Press.

Marshall, J., & Vashe, M. (2008). Mining, bridging, and making: Developing and conveying concepts in art. *Art Education, 61*(1), 6–12.

Mulcahay, C. (2009). Providing rich art and activities for young children. *Young Children, 64*(4), 107–112.

Additional Readings

Barter, J. A. (Ed.). (2009). *Apostles of beauty: Arts and crafts from Britain to Chicago.* New Haven, CT: Yale University Press.

Caouette, R. (2008). How to think like Leonardo da Vinci. *Scholastic, 108*(2), 58–59.

Child, T. (2008). *The desire of beauty: Being indication for aesthetic culture.* London, UK: Biblio Bazaar.

Eckhoff, A., & Guberman, St. (2008). Daddy Daycard, Daffy Duck, and Salvador Dali: Popular culture and children's art viewing experiences. *Art Education, 59*(5), 19–24.

Johnson, N. (2008). Developing verbal and visual literacy through experiences in the visual arts: 25 tips for teachers. *Young Children, 63*(1), 74–79.

Lorimer, M. R. (2009). Using interdisciplinary arts education to enhance learning. *Principal, 88*(3), 8–13.

Tankersley, L. M. (2009). *Found art: Discovering beauty in foreign places.* Danvers, MA: Zondervan.

Unrath, K., & Leuhrman, M. (2009). Bringing children to art—Bringing art to children. *Art Education, 62*(1), 41–47.

Williams, T. T. (2009). *Finding beauty in a broken world.* Louisville, CO: Sounds True.

White, R. (2002). *Young Children's relationship with nature. Its importance to children's development.* Kansas City, MO: White Hutchison Leisure & Learning Group.

Software for Children

Backyard Bugs, ages 5–11
Blue's Clues Treasure Hunt, ages 3–6
Bust-A-Move Plus! ages 6 and up
ColorZ, ages 6 and up
Dino Master, ages 5 and up
Endless Ocean, ages 6 and up
Fishdom, ages 6 and up
Hot Wheel Custom Car Designer, ages 5 and up
Kidspiration Version 3, ages 4 and up
Krazy Art Room, ages 4 and up

My SKY, ages 8 and up
Ollo and the Sunny Valley Fair, ages 3–6
Perception Zone, ages 3–8
Play With Pictures, ages 5 and up
Starry Night Elementary, ages 5–9
The Legendary Starfy, ages 5 and up
The Senses, ages 5–12
Up! ages 5 and up
Zenses—Zen Garden, ages 6 and up

Helpful Websites

A Lifetime of Color, http://www.alifetimeofcolor.com

Archives of American Art, http://www.aaa.si.edu

Art Education 2.0, http://www.arted20.ning.com

Art Interactive—Hirshhorn Museum, http://hirshhorn.si.edu/

Ask Joan of Art—Smithsonian American Art Museum, http://americanart.si.edu/research/tools/ask

Curator's Corner, http://www.davisart.com

Enchanted Learning, http://www.EnchantedLearning.com/Home.html

Museums Index at World Wide Arts Resources, http://wwar.com/museums.html

National Gallery of Art Classroom for Teachers and Students, http://www.nga.gov/education/classroom

Seattle Art Museum, http://www.seattleartmuseum.org

The Baltimore Museum of Art, http://www.artbma.org/

 For additional creative activity resources, visit our website at www.Cengage.com/login.

REFLECTIVE QUESTIONS

After studying this section, you should be able to answer the following questions.

1. What do I know about the attention span and activity levels of the young children in my group? How will I include this information in my lesson planning?

2. What can I do to improve the classroom environment for young children in my care by focusing on developmental levels and individual needs and interests of young children?

3. Am I aware of the importance of developmentally appropriate practice (DAP) and how to implement it in my classroom?

4. Is my classroom reflective of the individual differences present in the group of children using it?

5. In planning lessons, do I include activities that address the learning styles (multiple intelligences) of children in my group?

6. Do I use methods of differentiated instruction in my classroom that are designed to meet the children's individual learning styles?

7. Do I plan lessons that encourage children's higher-level thinking using Bloom's taxonomy of learning?

8. Have I created a positive and safe physical environment for the young children in my care? What strengths and weaknesses are evident in my classroom arrangement and management practices?

9. Have I included all of the media I can that are developmentally appropriate for young children in my classroom? What changes do I need to make to improve my use of media with young children?

10. Does my classroom reflect all of the ethnic and cultural groups appropriate for my group of children?

11. How do I encourage independent learning and exploration in the arrangement of my room? In my lesson planning? In my choice and use of media?

12. Do I enjoy being in and teaching in my classroom the way it is currently arranged? Do the children enjoy being there? How can I rearrange it to make it more enjoyable for both myself and the children?

13. Are my room arrangement, choice of media, interest centers, and presentation of lessons enticing to the children's interests? Do they encourage convergent or divergent thinking?

14. How will the needs of children from varying backgrounds be addressed in planning a creative and safe environment?

15. Am I aware of the national standards in the content areas and the approach my state has taken to meet the No Child Left Behind Act?

16. Am I working to develop my teaching skills to become as accomplished a teacher as I can be?

17. Does the environment I create for young children provide space, time, and opportunities for all types of play?

18. What role does play have in the total development of young children?

19. How can I plan and arrange the classroom environment so young children are encouraged to play in a way that emphasizes problem solving and exploration?

20. Have I included enough dramatic play materials for all the developmental levels and multicultural backgrounds of my children?

Children, Teachers, and Creative Activities

OBJECTIVES

After studying this chapter, you should be able to:

1. Discuss the terms *differentiated instruction, process learning, multiple intelligences, and developmentally appropriate practice.*

2. Explain Bloom's taxonomy and its place in the early childhood environment.

3. Ask a series of questions to better understand and work with young children's developmental levels.

4. Discuss attention span and activity patterns as they relate to young children.

5. Discuss three aspects of the teacher's attitude that have an impact on children's creativity.

6. Explain the teacher's role as facilitator in children's creative activities.

7. List the general planning guidelines for creative activities.

8. Discuss strategies for handling transition times.

9. Discuss national standards for teachers and both elementary- and preschool-level curriculum content.

Planning creative activities always begins with the child. Each child is unique; each has his or her own way of being and his or her own way of responding to the world. The teacher should be aware of each child's level of development, strengths, abilities, and special personality. With this knowledge, teachers can relate their own personalities and unique skills to those of each young child. Thus, an atmosphere is created in which both adult and child remain themselves in order to help and respect each other.

Watching a child at play helps an adult understand this young person. A teacher is able to see how the child uses materials and relates to other children. In many educational experiences, and especially in creative activities, the teacher is a facilitator. To **facilitate** means to help along, to guide, to provide opportunities, and to be sensitive and caring without interfering. The meaning as used here is that the teacher allows the young child to deal directly with the materials, with the teacher acting as an aide rather than a leader or judge. Because the emphasis is on divergent thinking and not on right answers in creative activities, judging is not necessary. Guidance and feedback, however, are helpful. Because creative activities are open-ended, there are no simple standards for evaluating them. The teacher's role, then, is one of encouraging, questioning, and experimenting.

> I never teach my pupils; I only attempt to provide the conditions in which they can learn.
>
> Albert Einstein, 1879–1955,
> German physicist

Consider the Child

Developmental Level

In many early childhood books and journals, we often see the phrase **developmental level**. Generally, when we speak of a child's development, we are referring to four major areas of growth: physical, social, emotional, and intellectual. These areas serve as a framework on which we organize our knowledge and observations of children. These four areas combined make up the individual child. When the needs of a child are met in each of these areas in any particular activity, we can be fairly well assured that the overall growth of that child is being encouraged.

Another aspect of a child's development refers to **individual differences**. For example, two children may be exactly the same age but they may be performing at different levels in one or more areas of development. Both children may be within the normal range of development. Therefore, a teacher must not only have a knowledge of developmental levels but must also tune in to the different levels of each child's progress in the four major areas.

A child's ability is closely related to his or her level of development. If a teacher understands this, failure and frustration can be avoided when planning creative activities. Answers to the following questions can help adults better understand and work with a young child.

- What is special about the child?
- What are the child's interests?
- What are the child's strengths?
- What abilities and skills are already developed?
- What is the child's home life like?
- How does the child relate to adults?
- How does the child respond to other children?
- What are the motor skills (large- and small-muscle) of the child?
- How does the child express himself or herself?
- How does the child speak?
- How does the child solve problems?
- With what materials does the child enjoy working?
- How does the child learn?

When you have answers to these questions, you are able to plan creative activities that meet the specific needs of young children.

Developmentally Appropriate Practice

Developmental level and individual differences, discussed earlier, are two of the basic components of **developmentally appropriate practice (DAP)**. This term captures a set of core ideas that are the basis of early childhood education contained in a statement adopted by the National Association for the Education of Young Children (NAEYC) Governing Board in the early 1990s and later published as part of the book *Developmentally Appropriate Practice in Early Childhood Programs* (Bredekamp & Copple, 1997). The third and most recent edition of *Developmentally Appropriate Practice* was published in 2009. Most early childhood professionals express general agreement with the basic principles and guidelines of developmentally appropriate practice that NAEYC has articulated in these editions. Since a lot has happened in the early childhood field since the first publication in 1997, each edition reflects the growing complexities and changes affecting the profession of early childhood education. Figure 5–1 briefly outlines the differences between the prior/second and current/third editions. A similar chart comparing developmentally appropriate practice for infants and toddlers in these two editions can be found on the website. It is not possible to gain a thorough understanding of DAP and how to use it effectively in the classroom with only the information in this chapter. References at the end of this chapter are a good starting place for a deeper understanding of DAP. For our purposes, we will discuss some very basic concepts of DAP.

Developmentally appropriate practice means teaching young children in ways that

- Meet children where they are, as individuals and as a group. This means taking into account their physical, emotional, social, and cognitive development characteristics.
- Help each child reach challenging and achievable goals that contribute to his or her ongoing development—a stretch, but not an impossible leap.
- Recognize that what makes something challenging and achievable will vary depending on the individual learner's development in all areas; her store of experiences, knowledge, and skills; and the context within which the learning opportunity takes place (Copple & Bredekamp, 2009).

PUBLICATION YEAR	1996	2009
STATEMENT	28 pages	31 pages
BOOK	181 pages	352 pages (Plus DVD with video clips and resources in PDF)
DEFINITION	DAP = Knowledge of: Age-Related development and learning + Individual Strengths, interest, and needs + Social and cultural contexts of children's lives	DAP = Knowledge of: Age-related development and learning + Individual strengths, interests, and needs + Social and cultural contexts of children's lives + Meet children where they are and help meet challenging, achievable goals + Base practices on knowledge, not assumptions
THEORETICAL AND RESEARCH BASE	12 Principles stated as prologue	12 Principles stated as prologue
RECOMMENDED PRACTICES	37 guidelines Creating a caring community of learners (5) Teaching to enhance development and learning (7) Constructing appropriate curriculum (9) Assessing children's learning and development (8) Establishing reciprocal relationships with families (8)	37 Guidelines Creating a caring community of learners (5) Teaching to enhance development and learning (10) Planning curriculum to achieve important goals (6) Assessing children's development and learning (9) Establishing reciprocal relationships with families (7)
POLICY	7 Essential Policies 1. Professional preparation 2. Adequate funding 3. Resources 4. Systems for regulation and monitoring 5. Community resources 6. Individual intervention 7. Appropriate assessment	6 Considerations (plus reference to NAEYC website for details) 1. Early learning standards for children and related aligned curriculum 2. Comprehensive system of professional development and compensation. 3. Program quality rating and improvement system 4. Comprehensive, coordinated services for children 5. Program evaluation 6. Public fund to support affordability and quality

FIGURE 5-1 • Summary of DAP Revisions

A cornerstone of DAP is *intentionality*. Teaching that meets learners where they are and that helps them to reach challenging and achievable goals does not happen by chance. In everything good teachers do—from setting up the classroom to assessing children to planning the curriculum—they are intentional (Copple & Bredekamp, 2009).

In classrooms that reflect developmentally appropriate practices, teachers are in charge, but the environment is organized so that children can choose among numerous hands-on learning experiences. A balance is sought between child-choice and teacher-directed experiences.

Every developmentally appropriate practice classroom is structured; however, this is not as readily

FIGURE 5-2 • The teacher's role is one of encouraging, questioning, and experimenting.

FIGURE 5-3 • Using differentiated instruction strategies, a teacher learns how to spot what works for each child.

apparent as the structure of the teacher-directed classroom. Teachers orchestrate the classroom. The classroom is organized around the elements of time, space, and the conceptual framework of the curriculum. Early childhood teachers organize the schedule, the space of the classroom, and the curriculum with the child's physical, social, emotional, and cognitive needs in mind while seeking a balance of child-choice and teacher-led activities.

A teacher in a DAP classroom plans for children to construct knowledge based on what they already know and what they want to find out. The teacher's perspective is a developmental one in which children are expected to develop over time and move from gross approximations to refinement of skills and concepts. For example, in an early childhood classroom, children would be encouraged to write using whatever letters they know. At first, children may know only the letters of their names. As they learn more about sound/symbol relationships and how to produce letters, they will incorporate these symbols into their writing. In traditional classrooms, children are not encouraged to use the information they presently know

but are expected to wait until they know all the letters and all sound/symbol relationships before they write.

Developmentally appropriate early childhood classrooms are those that demonstrate, among other important characteristics, maximum interaction among children as they pursue a variety of independent and small-group tasks. The teacher prepares the environment with challenging and interesting materials and activities and then steps back to observe, encourage, and deepen children's use of them. In a developmentally appropriate environment, teachers ask thought-provoking questions and make appropriate comments (Barclay & Breheny, 2009).

The National Association for the Education of Young Children, in its position statement on developmentally appropriate practices in early childhood education, calls for a curriculum of active learning organized around learning centers for four- to eight-year-olds. These strategies include the following.

- Children select many of their own activities from among a variety of learning areas the teacher prepares, including dramatic play, blocks, science, math, games and puzzles, books, recordings, art, and music.

- Children are expected to be physically and mentally active. Children choose from among activities that the teacher has set up or that they spontaneously initiate.
- Children work individually or in small, informal groups most of the time.
- Children are provided concrete learning activities involving materials and people relevant to their own life experiences (Copple & Bredekamp, 2009).

In summary, a developmentally appropriate environment for young children is one that empowers children to be curious, to inquire, to experiment, and to think for themselves.

Developmentally appropriate practice does not mean a set curriculum. An underlying question guides the teacher's design and implementation of the curriculum: What are the significant facts, concrete examples, and basic understandings we can examine in studying this topic? Obviously, what would interest and motivate three- to five-year-olds is different from what would interest and motivate eight- to ten-year-olds. Copple and Bredekamp (2009) describe the curriculum of the DAP classroom as one that uses themes, units, and projects. These are developed around knowledge of child development, subject matter disciplines, and the individual children's needs and backgrounds.

Finally, any description of what is developmentally appropriate is really a dynamic concept. It is meant to address nothing more or less than the best thinking of the field at a particular point in time. The position statement on DAP will likely be revisited at a particular point in time to reflect changes in the knowledge and thinking of the field of early childhood education.

The Reggio Emilia Approach

In the same vein as DAP, there is a growing interest today in integrating art in the early childhood classroom, partially as a result of the widespread interest in the **Reggio Emilia approach** to early childhood education. In the preschools of Reggio Emilia, a town in northern Italy, children spend time each day expressing their ideas through art media. Activities stem from the interests and ideas of the children. They have an active part in the planning of the curriculum, and their personal input is shown in their creative art experiences. The result is that children express themselves artistically in a much more mature way than most children their age (Clyde et al., 2006).

In the Reggio Emilia approach, the arts are integrated into the school curriculum as problem-solving activities rather than as discrete subjects or disciplines taught for their own sake. Children's art making is emphasized to reinforce concepts, and their art products are considered to represent aspects of their learning. Visual arts are seen as an additional "language," one in which children's ideas and concepts are expressed in art media (Bruner, 2004).

Perhaps the most innovative activity to evolve from the Reggio Emilia approach is a unique form of documentation. American early childhood teachers are familiar with documentation in the form of note taking, videotaping, language experience, written comments, and checklists. However, in the Reggio Emilia approach, documentation in the child's own words is accompanied by artworks or photographs. Documentation panels display the child's work with great care and attention to both the content and aesthetic aspects of the display. Documentation describes in the child's own words—and some times the teacher's as well—the images, ideas, and processes represented by the child's artwork. Documentation may appear on trifolds, bulletin boards, or charts. The words of the children or teachers are in large print so that children, teachers, parents, and visitors can easily read them. This form of documentation makes visible the child's learning, as it often shows the process of the art experience from beginning to end (Clyde et al., 2006).

Working with children in Reggio ways must begin with reflective practice—looking at the ways you are working and asking questions of yourself and your colleagues. This entails taking responsibility for your own professional development, which requires constant reflection, collaboration, and questioning (Wien, 2008). An excellent resource on incorporating Reggio principles in classroom instruction is the NAEYC's *Working in the Reggio Way: A Beginner's Guide for American Teachers* (2005).

Gardner (2004) describes Reggio classrooms as the best preschools in the world, "a shining testament to human possibilities" (p. 17). Is it possible to create such shining examples of early childhood education in the United States? It seems that using the visual arts as a basis for learning across the curriculum might be a good beginning.

Differentiated Instruction

A concept that is a basic part of DAP is differentiated instruction. The term **differentiated instruction** is often associated with individualized planning and teaching strategies for young children. Quite simply, it means providing different types of learning experiences and environments to suit each child's individual needs.

A beginning teacher will soon discover that no two children learn at the same pace or in the same way. Some need lots of practice; others "get it" immediately. Some take to new materials easily; others are slower to accept them. In early elementary levels, some children can learn from reading, while others get more from listening or from visual aids. Some elementary children have trouble writing clearly, but others express complex ideas in art or music.

When using differentiated instructional strategies, a teacher learns how to spot what works for each child.

She checks to be sure that lessons contain activities and content that each child in the group can "connect with" in some way. See Figure 5–4: The Journey of Differentiated Instruction—5 Steps for further information on the essentials of differentiated instruction.

Characteristics of a Differentiated Classroom

The most obvious feature of a differentiated classroom is that it is child centered. The following are other indicators that differentiated instruction is present.

- Teachers and students accept and respect one another's similarities and differences.
- The teacher is primarily a coordinator of time, space, and activities rather than a provider of information. The aim is to help students become independent, self-reliant learners.

Every child who walks through the classroom door brings: special gifts to the learning table. Each one has some hidden strength that enables him or her to learn. In preparing to differentiate you have to find out who your learners are---what abilities, interests, and experiences have shaped them. In addition you must honor the unique developmental needs of each child. In a differentiated instruction and developmentally appropriate classroom, the teacher is the one who extends, engages, questions, affirms, and challenges children as they are constructing their own knowledge.

The following are the 5 steps to differentiated instruction

Step 1. Know the children.
What skills and abilities do they have?
What differences from cultural background, life experience and home life influence their ability to learn?

Step 2. Determine the learning goal.
What do you want the students to understand or be able to do? What learning standards and curriculum goals will you address?

Step 3. Identify proof or evidence that they understand what has been taught.
What behaviors and comments would tell you that students understand?
What products, performances, constructions and experiments would express understanding of the concepts, skills and information taught?

Step 4. Plan the learning experience.
How should the concept be introduced?
What teaching strategies should be used?
What learning activities should be used?
What resources are needed?
How will students be grouped?

Step 5. Reassess and adjust according to new need and changes.
What is the evidence for knowing that children have understood the concepts and processes involved?
What measures (e.g., observation, questioning) will give you the information you need to know if the child is on track or if he or she needs further adjustment?

FIGURE 5-4 • The Journey to Differentiated Instruction: 5 Steps

- Children and teachers work together in setting group and individual goals.
- Children work in a variety of group sizes as well as independently. Flexible grouping is evident.
- Time is used flexibly in the sense that pacing is based on student needs.
- Students have choices about topics they wish to study, ways they want to work, and how they want to demonstrate their learning.
- The teacher uses a variety of instructional strategies to help target instruction to student needs.
- Students are assessed in multiple ways, and each student's progress is measured at least in part from where that student begins.
- Assessment is an ongoing diagnostic activity that guides instruction. Learning tasks are planned and adjusted based on assessment data.

In differentiated instruction, learning, activities, and materials may be varied by difficulty to challenge children at different readiness levels. They may be varied by topics in response to children's individual interests. Activities and materials may also be varied

by students' preferred ways of learning or expressing themselves.

Differentiated instruction is a way of thinking about teaching and learning. Some further suggestions for strategies to differentiate instruction are found in Figure 5–6.

> "The great teacher is not the man (or woman) who supplies the most facts, but the one in whose presence we become different people."
> Ralph Waldo Emerson

Differentiated Instruction and Process Learning

Another term associated with differentiated instruction is **process learning**. Process learning conceives of learning in terms of its processes rather than its products. In process learning, the focus is on providing children experiences that promote thinking and problem solving without specifically identified outcomes. The early childhood classroom abounds with opportunities for children to actively engage in learning activities rather than listening unquestioningly as they receive the knowledge of others. In process learning, children not only learn by doing but also reflect on the learning process itself. By doing so, they are able to transfer the information learned in one process or learning situation to another. For example, as the child manipulates blocks, continually building up and breaking down structures, he is learning the process of balance. This process involves size, weight, and object placement. These concepts, in turn, can be applied in the science/discovery center with "sink or float" experiments.

Explaining Process Learning to Parents/Caregivers

To a casual observer, a child's process learning experiences may appear to be simply "playing" or just "messing around." Yet this type of learning is crucial in that it is self-initiated, ongoing, and transferable to other learning situations. Early childhood teachers need to explain the importance of process learning to parents and caregivers to encourage children's continued and active involvement in process learning. What may seem aimless is actually active processing, storing, and receiving information by a child's exploration. Process learning helps children develop information process-

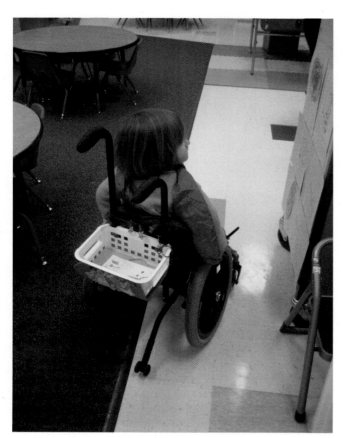

FIGURE 5-5 • Adapting a wheelchair can provide a child with a portable cubby for classroom materials.

Directions: Individualize lessons for particular children by altering lesson and classroom *structure,* the number and kinds of *practices,* the kind and amount of *feedback*, the amount and kind of *choice and control* given to students, the *teaching strategies* used, the nature of *examples* provided, and the kind of *motivational strategies* (i.e., encouragement strategies, such as belief statements).

Place. Change the environment or amount of space. Use carrels, centers, music, different desk arrangements, carpet squares, lower or brighter lighting.

Amount. Give more or less time (e.g., to explore materials). Use more repetition and break instruction into smaller steps. Reduce or increase the number of things to be learned. Alter the number of examples and the kind of feedback given. Provide additional practice.

Rate. This is the "oftenness." Change the pace. Give more breaks. Create more or less structure for the activity (e.g., intensity of teacher-directed lessons).

Target objectives. Make sure students are clear about goals or outcomes. Consider alternative goals or alternative means of reaching goals. Decide what a child can realistically achieve (know and be able to do). Make objectives life centered and connected to interests.

Instruction. Use more or less direct instruction (models, demonstration, examples, descriptive feedback, reassurance). Cause students to be mentally and physically active, engaged, and involved with questions. Use Gardner's multiple intelligences to plan each day and monitor the week. Use multisensory approaches: visual, auditory, kinesthetic, tactile. Use humor.

Curriculum materials. Give easier materials to read or adapt current materials (e.g., highlight, tape record, rewrite). Use hands-on materials such as games or art media.

Utensils. Use visual and auditory aids. Teach meaning-making tools and strategies (i.e., ways to learn to comprehend, such as shortcuts, cue sheets, cue cards, mnemonics). Don't just teach strategies: teach when to use them and how.

Level of difficulty. Make the lesson easier or harder to challenge appropriately. Highlight text essentials. Allow notes during tests. Change amount of structure or supervision.

Assistance (from other people). Use peer tutoring, grouping, structure changes, and prompts.

Response. Allow students to show what they know in a variety of ways. Use projects that call for a product or piece to perform. Give exemptions (e.g., from oral reading).

Cornett, Claudia E., *Creating Meaning Through Literature and the Arts,* 2nd Edition, © 2003, pp. 70–71. Reprinted by permission of Pearson Education, Inc. Upper Saddle River, NJ.

FIGURE 5-6 • PARTICULAR Strategies to Individualize or Differentiate

ing skills that can be applied across the curriculum. Most importantly, process learning emphasizes information discovered by the *learner*. This type of independent, active learning is key to acquiring knowledge all through life.

Differentiated Instruction and Multiple Intelligences

When planning early childhood activities using differentiated instructional strategies, an understanding of multiple intelligences is essential if you are to meet the individual needs of children. According to Howard **Gardner's multiple intelligence theory**, each of us possesses eight "intelligences," or ways to be smart (Gardner, 1999). Some of us are more adept at using our hands; others are good at making rhymes or singing songs. Each type of intelligence gives us something to offer the world. What makes us unique is the way each intelligence expresses itself in our lives.

By recognizing multiple intelligences, we can help children enhance their individual strengths. Yet understanding multiple intelligences means more than focusing on individual characteristics. Just imagine a grown person who could do nothing but write

FIGURE 5-7 • The teacher uses a variety of instructional strategies to help target instruction to student needs.

poetry or solve algebra problems. To do everyday things like drive a car or follow a recipe, a person needs to be smart in more than one way.

An emphasis on the multiple intelligences is also relevant in working with young children with disabilities. Although specific disabilities can affect specific parts of the brain, other parts of the brain may not be affected. "Idiot savants," for example, have an extraordinary skill or ability in a specific area despite limitations in other areas of cognitive or social development. Addressing the education of young children with disabilities through the multiple intelligences may help us to discover or "awaken" hidden talents. It is important for all young children to discover their own interests and abilities, and this is no less true for young children with disabilities. An emphasis on the multiple intelligences may help children discover what they are good at and put a focus on ability rather than disability.

Each of us is smart in all eight ways. Here's how to recognize these multiple intelligences in ourselves and in children.

Word Smart (Linguistic Intelligence)

At younger ages, children who are word smart enjoy listening and telling stories. They are effective in expressing themselves and convincing others by using language and their rich vocabulary. These children are often successful learners by listening and hearing because they sort information through their listening and repeating skills. Young children with this dominance often demand story after story around bedtime. When they enter school, they have highly developed verbal skills, enjoy developing rhymes and often puns. In short, they tend to think in words. They like oral and silent reading exercises, playing word games, and enjoying a variety of reading and writing materials at learning centers. They also favor making up poetry and stories, getting into involved discussions, debates, creative writing, and telling complicated jokes.

Older children possess strong vocabularies, and, at times, can get so lost in a book that they almost forget about their dinner. At this age, they may subscribe to their favorite magazines, or use a word processing application to keep a personal diary or secret journal.

Older children who are word smart also have a rich vocabulary and are sensitive to the meaning of words, grammar rules, and the function of language in writing and orally. Journalists, lawyers, and storytellers often demonstrate this type of intelligence.

Logic Smart (Logical/Mathematical Intelligence)

Children with high logical/mathematical intelligence are curious about how things work. They like to ask questions and investigate. They use numbers easily and enjoy solving problems. They have the ability to understand logical patterns, categories and relationships, and causes and effects. They enjoy working with manipulatives, strategy games, logical puzzles, and experiments and working on timelines. They tend to be systematic and analytical, and they always have a logical rationale or argument for what they are doing or thinking. They like to use computers.

Older children often become quite skilled at many areas of mathematics, calculus, and science, perhaps even creating a hypothesis for the development of a new invention. Students at this age also enjoy puzzles and recognize patterns in the world around them. Scientists, accountants, and computer programmers generally have this ability.

Picture Smart (Visual/Spatial Intelligence)

We often say, "A picture is worth a thousand words," or "Seeing is believing." Visual/spatial intelligence represents not only the knowing that occurs through the shapes, images, patterns, designs, and textures we see with our external eyes, but it also includes the images we are able to conjure inside our heads. People with high visual intelligence are able to visualize three-dimensional objects. They take the information and translate it into images and pictures in their minds. When they need to, they have the ability to retrieve the information through the images and pictures they made earlier.

Young children might build cities out of blocks and create impromptu murals on the kitchen and bedroom walls. They like to draw, paint, make interesting designs and patterns from fabric, colored construction paper, and clay. As well, they love putting together jigsaw puzzles.

These children enjoy mazes and jigsaw puzzles. They like to spend their free time drawing and building with Legos®. These children tend to enjoy daydreaming.

Older children tend to be good at reading maps and finding their way around new places, daydreaming, and creating accurate drawings; they may find it easier to learn information that is presented in images rather than just by words. Older children who are picture smart have the ability to understand geometry and recognize the relationships of objects in space. Children with visual intelligence in schools are successful in geometry. They also are very good in visual arts, sculpture, architecture, and photography.

Music Smart (Musical Intelligence)

Musical intelligence is that special ability to recognize tonal patterns, rhythm, and beat. In other words, it is the ability to understand and express well numerous musical forms. Such learners are most sensitive to environmental sounds, the human voice, and musical instruments. In short, they possess a strong ear for music. Unlike the average person, they are more obviously affected by rhythms, musical patterns tones, and various sounds. You can easily detect a change in their facial expressions, emotional responses, and/or specific body movements when they listen to music.

Music smart also involves the capacity to understand and express oneself musically. Children with this ability can keep time with music, sing in tune, and tell the difference between types of music. They can appreciate melodies and enjoy listening to music and singing to themselves.

Young children can often be heard banging on pots and/or singing nonsense songs to themselves. Children with a dominant musical intelligence may enjoy a hum and easily turn sounds into rhythms; they retain melodies and lyrics well.

Older children acquire good memories for lyrics, perhaps emitting the odd wince here and there when their friends sing "Happy Birthday" off key. They are often quite skilled at mimicking language accents, sounds, the speech patterns of others, and recognizing different musical instruments in a composition.

Musical children often play a musical instrument. They participate in the school choir or school band. They like to sing or drum to themselves. They can remember and repeat a melody after listening to it only once. They learn through rhythm and melody. They need music to study or learn. They learn new things more easily if the ideas are sung, tapped out, or whistled.

Body Smart (Bodily/Kinesthetic Intelligence)

Bodily/kinesthetic intelligence is related to physical movement and the knowledge of the body and how it functions. It includes the ability to use many parts of the body to express emotion, to play a game, and to interpret and invoke effective body language. Children with this ability enjoy and learn best from activities that use the body and involve movement, such as dance, crafts, mime, sports, acting, and using manipulatives.

People with bodily intelligence use their physical selves to communicate and solve problems. They are good with objects and activities involving their bodies, hands, and fingers.

People with bodily intelligence prefer to learn through their body or feelings. These people are more successful in learning if they can touch, manipulate, and move or feel whatever they are learning.

Young children who demonstrate a strong bodily/kinesthetic intelligence are highly coordinated. They enjoy all sorts of athletics and would rather be a participant than a spectator. Also, this way of understanding the world is most evident in young children who have a hard time sitting still and are well coordinated.

Children with high kinesthetic intelligence learn best with activities such as games, acting, hands-on tasks, and building. These children process information by applying it and through bodily sensation (e.g., in a classroom where people from history are acted out or an assignment that allows them to build something such as Lego® towers, etc.).

Children with bodily intelligence like being physically active, playing sports, dancing, and acting. They like doing crafts and working on mechanical projects.

Older children who demonstrate this type of intelligence may be good dancers or athletes—or particularly good at mimicking the classroom teacher!

Person Smart (Interpersonal Intelligence)

Person smart is the ability to understand people and relationships. People with interpersonal intelligence understand and care about people and their feelings and interact effectively with them. They approach people with empathy, recognize differences among people, and value their points of view with sensitivity to their motives, moods, and intentions. These people are sensitive to facial expressions, gestures, and voice. They get along with others and they are able to maintain good relationships with one or more people among family and friends.

Young children with interpersonal intelligence enjoy playing with other children and often have more than one friend. They care about their friends and like to help to solve their problems. They love team activities of all kinds and are very good team members, pulling their own weight and often much more. These children like to teach other children and take part in school organizations and clubs. They have the ability to influence people and are natural leaders.

Older children tend to become natural leaders, picking up on subtle social cues and knowing how to put others at ease. In short, they work well within groups and often end up in leadership roles.

Self Smart (Intrapersonal Intelligence)

Being self smart is having the ability to think about and understand oneself. People with intrapersonal intelligence are aware of their strengths, weaknesses, moods, and motivations. They effectively use self-discipline to achieve personal goals. They often enjoy working alone, sometimes even shying away from others and going off quietly by themselves. They are often strong willed and self-confident and possess definite, well-thought-out opinions on various issues.

These children are self-motivated. They can monitor their thoughts and feelings and control them effectively. Intrapersonal children need their own quiet space most of the time. They prefer to study individually and learn best through observing and listening. They like to play by themselves. They use self-knowledge to make decisions and to set goals. They are sensitive to their own feelings and moods.

Older children may keep journals or logs, express strong emotions and well-developed opinions, and seem blithely unconcerned by other kids' notions of what's "in" and what's "out."

Nature Smart (Naturalistic Intelligence)

This intelligence involves understanding the natural world of plants and animals, noticing their characteristics, and categorizing them. It generally involves keen observation and the ability to classify other things as well. It may be exercised by exploring nature, making collections of objects, studying them, and grouping them. Children with this type of intelligence may like working on activities related to nature such as fishing, hiking, or camping.

Children with naturalistic intelligence enjoy outdoor activities and have a strong connection to the outside world or to animals. They easily notice patterns and objects from nature. They love collecting flowers, rocks, and leaves. They may enjoy stories, shows, or any subjects that deal with animals or natural happenings. They are interested in the care of animals and zoology. These children also show an interest

FIGURE 5-8 • The child with a naturalistic intelligence enjoys outdoor activities.

in endangered species. They easily learn the characteristics, names, and any information about species found in the world. Older children love to learn the names of trees and flowers and have a good eye for the differences between them. They can spend hours compiling science reports on their favorite animals and exotic plants.

By exploring all of the intelligences, children become well-rounded individuals who are successful in many aspects of life. Early childhood teachers need to recognize these different strengths in children as they emerge. Some children may respond more to words, others to music, and still others to visual stimuli. The point is to plan activities that allow children to express themselves in the way that suits them best. If children have the opportunity to learn in ways that align with their particular intelligence(s) and to improve in those intellectual capacities that are not as strong, they will grow to become intelligent in more ways than one. See the Online Companion for observation sheets to help you in understanding your own intelligences and how to use them in your teaching.

In summary, the multiple intelligence theory can be a useful way to help children learn and truly understand what they are learning. Although the multiple intelligence theory has powerful implications for teachers, it is not an educational prescription (Nicholson-Nelson, 1998). You must decide how best to use it in your own classroom setting.

Bloom's Taxonomy

Another concept that fits into our discussion of effective teaching strategies is **Bloom's taxonomy.** Benjamin Bloom and his colleagues developed a classification system that has served educators since 1956. This system is a common structure for categorizing questions and designing instruction. The taxonomy is divided into six levels:

- Knowledge—Exhibit recollection of data
- Comprehension—State a problem in one's own words
- Application—Use knowledge in a new way
- Analysis—Distinguish between facts and inferences
- Synthesis—Put parts together to form a whole
- Evaluation—Make judgments about the value of ideas, things

In the 1950s, Bloom found that 95% of test questions developed to assess student learning required them only to think at the lowest level of learning, the recall of information. Information and/or knowledge alone are not enough. Back then and today, knowledge without the ability to know how, when, and where to apply it is ineffective.

In the early childhood classroom, then, the teacher must help students move up the ladder to higher-level thought. In order to foster children's creativity, higher-level thinking (above the first two levels of knowledge and comprehension) is crucial. As we have learned, the focus of creative activities is not to do things in the "right" way. Rather, the goal is to develop different ways of thinking and learning while being creative, exploring materials, and having fun. As discussed in earlier chapters, creative thinking involves creating something new or original. The aim of creative thinking is to stimulate curiosity and promote divergence. Figure 5–9 presents each level of thinking in Bloom's taxonomy with suggestions on useful verbs, sample question stems, and related potential activities and products for each level.

Differentiated Instruction and Children with Special Needs

Adapting a classroom to accommodate children with special needs is a process similar to differentiating instruction. In both cases, the teacher provides activities and content that are appropriate for each student. For this reason, it is essential to know the actual capabilities of each student. The following are some specific ways to adapt (or differentiate) instruction in the early childhood classroom for children with special needs.

- Meet each child at his or her own level of development, foster that stage, and enable the child to move on to the next level. For example, children have individual differences when it comes to motor development. Some children will be able to carry out complex actions such as tying their shoes or doing a complicated drawing, while others may barely be able to draw a line. A child with special needs in the motor area may barely be able to communicate preverbally with pointing, while other children without special needs may have lots of words but differ in the complexity of their thinking. Each needs to be worked with at his or her own level and then helped to advance.

KNOWLEDGE		
USEFUL VERBS	SAMPLE QUESTION STEMS	POTENTIAL ACTIVITIES/ PRODUCTS
Tell	What happened after . . . ?	Make a list of the main events.
List	How many . . . ?	Make a timeline of events.
Describe	Who was it that . . . ?	Make a facts chart.
Relate	Can you name the . . . ?	List all the . . . in the story.
Locate	Describe what happened at . . .	Make a chart showing . . .
Write	Who spoke to . . . ?	Recite a poem.
Find	Can you tell why . . . ?	
State	Find the meaning of . . .	
Name	What is . . . ?	
	Which is true or false?	
COMPREHENSION		
USEFUL VERBS	SAMPLE QUESTION STEMS	POTENTIAL ACTIVITIES/ PRODUCTS
Explain	Can you write in your own words?	Cut out or draw pictures to show a particular event.
Interpret	Can you write a brief outline?	Illustrate what you think the main idea was.
Outline	What do you think happened next?	Make a cartoon strip showing the sequence of events.
Discuss	What do you think?	Paint a picture of some aspect you like.
Distinguish	What was the main idea?	Make your own book about the story.

FIGURE 5-9 • Bloom's Taxonomy.

(Continues)

COMPREHENSION		
USEFUL VERBS	SAMPLE QUESTION STEMS	POTENTIAL ACTIVITIES/ PRODUCTS
Predict	Who was the key character?	
Restate	Can you distinguish between?	
Translate	What are the differences between . . . ?	
Compare	Can you give me an example of . . . ?	
Describe	Can you give me a definition of . . . ?	

APPLICATION		
USEFUL VERBS	SAMPLE QUESTION STEMS	POTENTIAL ACTIVITIES/ PRODUCTS
Solve	Do you know another instance where . . . ?	Make a model to demonstrate how it will work.
Show	Could this have happened in . . . ?	Make a scrapbook about the areas of study.
Use	Can you group by characteristics such as . . . ?	Make a papier-mâché map.
Illustrate	What things would you change if . . . ?	Take a collection of photos to demonstrate a point.
Construct	Can you apply what you learned to some experience of your own?	Make a clay model of . . .
Complete	What questions would you ask of . . . ?	Paint a mural of . . .
Examine	From the information given, can you develop a set of instructions about . . . ?	
Classify	Would this information be useful if you had to . . . ?	

FIGURE 5-9 • Bloom's Taxonomy. *(Continued)*

ANALYSIS		
USEFUL VERBS	SAMPLE QUESTION STEMS	POTENTIAL ACTIVITIES/ PRODUCTS
Analyze	Which events could have happened . . . ?	Make a family tree showing relationships.
Distinguish	How was this similar to . . . ?	Put on a play about the topic.
Examine	What was the underlying theme of . . . ?	Design a questionnaire to gather information.
Compare	Can you compare your . . . with that presented in . . . ?	Conduct an investigation to produce information to support a view.
Contrast	What do you see as other possible outcomes . . . ?	Make a jigsaw puzzle.
Investigate	Can you distinguish between . . . ?	Construct a graph to illustrate selected information.
Categorize	What was the turning point in . . . ?	Write a commercial to sell a product.
Identify	What was the problem with . . . ?	
Explain	Can you explain what must have happened where . . . ?	
Separate		
Advertise		
SYNTHESIS		
USEFUL VERBS	SAMPLE QUESTION STEMS	POTENTIAL ACTIVITIES/ PRODUCTS
Create	Can you design a . . . to . . . ?	Invent a machine to do a specific task.
Invent	Why not compose a song about . . . ?	Create a new product.
Compose	Can you see a possible solution to . . . ?	Give it a name and plan a marketing campaign.

FIGURE 5-9 • Bloom's Taxonomy. *(Continued)*

(Continues)

SYNTHESIS		
USEFUL VERBS	SAMPLE QUESTION STEMS	POTENTIAL ACTIVITIES/ PRODUCTS
Predict	If you had access to all resources, how would you deal with . . . ?	Write about your feelings in relation to . . .
Plan	Why don't you devise your own way to deal with . . .	Design a CD, book, or magazine cover for . . .
Construct	What would happen if . . . ?	Write a TV show, play, puppet show, role-play, song, or pantomime about . . .
Design	How many ways can you . . . ?	Devise a way to . . .
Imagine	Can you create new and unusual uses for . . . ?	
Propose	Can you create a new recipe for a tasty dish?	
Devise		
Formulate		
EVALUATION		
USEFUL VERBS	SAMPLE QUESTION STEMS	POTENTIAL ACTIVITIES/ PRODUCTS
Judge	Is there a better solution to . . . ?	Prepare a list of criteria to judge a . . . show.
Select	Judge the value of . . .	Make a booklet about five rules you see as important.
Choose	Can you defend your position about . . . ?	Convince others that . . .
Decide	Do you think . . . is a good or bad thing?	Conduct a debate about an issue of special interest.
Justify	How would you have handled . . . ?	Write a half-yearly report.

FIGURE 5-9 • Bloom's Taxonomy. *(Continued)*

Debate	What changes to . . . would you recommend?	Prepare a case to present your view about . . .
Verify	Do you believe?	
Argue	What do you think about . . . ?	
Recommend		
Assess		
Discuss		
Rate		
Prioritize		
Determine		

FIGURE 5-9 • Bloom's Taxonomy. *(Continued)*

FIGURE 5-10 • After the children have started an activity, circulate among them to offer suggestions or answer questions as needed.

- Tailor the environment to each child's strengths and weaknesses and help all children, special needs or not, to build greater competency.
- Interact with children in ways that help them to think and solve problems at their own levels. These interactions need to be a part of an ongoing, trusting relationship that children have with you and with each other. Having dynamic relationships is essential while climbing up the developmental ladder (Greenspan, 2001).
- Make sure that the child is gradually using most of his or her senses. For example, if a child has a visual-processing difficulty, begin by offering activities that draw on other senses, including hearing, smell, or touch, as a way to engage him or her. Gradually introduce simple visual-processing experiences. As the child comes to recognize that he or she can succeed, the child will feel more competent and be more inclined to participate in activities he or she finds challenging.
- Increase challenges in manageable, easy steps so children are successful 70% to 75% of the time. Again, keep in mind that it is important to use warm and caring words of encouragement and lively praise as children attempt to meet each new challenge (Greenspan, 2001).

FIGURE 5-11 • Adapting instruction for children with special needs often involves creating an appropriate and comfortable learning environment.

FIGURE 5-12 • The teacher must help the student move up toward higher-level thought.

Adapting Instruction for Older Children with Special Needs

Some suggestions for differentiating instruction and adapting a classroom for older children with special needs follow.

- Adapt the number of items that the learner is expected to learn or complete. For example, if typical learners are to know the 50 states, have students with special needs only be responsible for remembering a certain number at a time. This would be dependent on the student's level of disability.
- Adapt the time allotted and allowed for learning, task completion, or testing. For example, allow the student with a special need additional time to complete timed assignments. If the total project is due by a particular time, have the student complete each portion of the project over various intervals with the required finished project due at a later time.
- Increase the amount of personal assistance you provide with a special-needs learner. For

example, allow for peer teaching. Pair the special learner with more advanced student to provide support.
- Adapt the way instruction is delivered to the learner. For example, provide students with an audiotape and/or videotape of the lesson. Allow for field trips, guest speakers, peer teaching, computer support, or video productions performed by students.
- Adapt the skill level, problem type, or rules about how the learner may approach the work. For example, allow the student to be creative, providing that the task is completed according to the teacher's specifications. The student may draw a picture of the assignment or conduct an interview, depending on the subject. Allow the student to come up with the idea.
- Adapt how the student may respond to instruction. For example, allow students to draw pictures, write an essay, or complete specific computer software programs relating to the lesson.

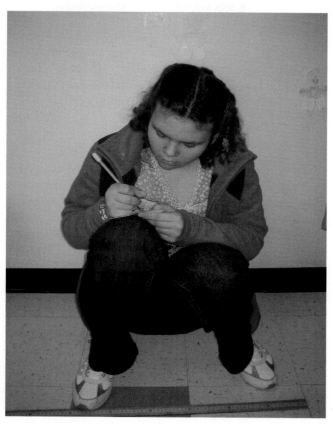

FIGURE 5-13 • The child with an interpersonal intelligence learning style often prefers to work alone.

- Adapt the extent to which a learner is actively involved in the task. Tailor the student's participation in a task to his or her abilities, whether intellectual or physical.
- Adapt the goals or outcome expectations while using the same materials. For example, in a writing assignment, alter the expectations for a student with disabilities who takes longer to write a paragraph.
- Provide different instruction and materials to meet a student's individual goals. For example, instead of requiring the student with special needs to memorize the names of the 50 states, allow her or him to work on a puzzle of the United States.

Attention Span and Children's Physical Needs

One must also consider a child's attention span and activity patterns when planning creative activities; it may mean the difference between successful creative learning experiences and creative activities that dissolve into chaos.

Attention span. A general rule to remember on the length of a child's interests (**attention span**) is this: The younger the child, the shorter the attention span. It is not unusual for toddlers and two-year-olds to have a maximum attention span of two to three minutes on average. Attention span gradually increases as a child gets older, and a child of six years of age can be expected to attend for an average of 15 minutes maximum. A teacher may come to expect a longer attention span than is really possible simply because the child maintains the appearance of attention. More often than not, however, young children make it quite obvious when their attention span is waning—by a yawn, a turned head, fidgeting, excess wiggling, or even by physically leaving—giving clear signs that attention to the task is "turned off."

An early childhood teacher needs to be able to read these obvious signs of lessening (or lost) attention. When they appear, it is time to move on to another topic, suggest a new activity, ask a question, do some "body stretching," or use any other change of pace to get back the child's interest. However, if a teacher has planned developmentally appropriate activities—those that are not too easy and present just enough of a challenge—even very young children will attend longer. Noting which activities keep the children's interest longer and planning for their frequent inclusion in the program are good ways to work with children's developmental needs and interests. Including activities that appeal to the children's multiple intelligences is also part of planning developmentally appropriate activities for young children.

In direct contrast, many teachers feel compelled to "forge ahead" on their lesson plans despite children's lack of interest or involvement. Although it may be difficult to scrap one's lesson plans in midstream, it is even more difficult to try to "make" children pay attention when the activities just do not match their needs and interests. As many experienced teachers have found, it is far easier to work with children's specific needs and interests, adapting as necessary to meet their changing developmental needs. If, for instance, interest at the art center is waning and children choose to go elsewhere when allowed the option to do so, a teacher needs to reevaluate the activities in that center to see if they are, in fact, a suitable match for the developmental needs of the learners.

Children might be ready to move from tearing and pasting to trying out scissors because their fine motor skills are better developed from previous tearing experiences. Or they may be ready for colored

FIGURE 5-14 • Children with special needs enjoy music activities that are adapted to their ability levels.

markers as a change of pace from crayons. The point is that by changing activities and equipment to keep them matched to children's present developmental levels, you are helping those children attend to activities longer *on their own*. Young children will, however, never be bored using the same media over and over again if they have new, interesting, and exciting ideas, thoughts, and feelings to express. With a store of continual, meaningful experiences to think or feel something about, children's stores of ideas, feelings, and imagination will be constantly enriched.

When there is a new thought or feeling pushing to be expressed, children will continually be challenged to find new and different ways to use the same paints, clay, crayons, paper, and markers to give form to their ideas. Think about it: Adult artists use the same materials for decades. What changes is how they use the materials and what they want to communicate (Seefeldt, 2008).

Another approach to working with short attention spans is to plan around the expected attention span of the children in the group. For example, for a 10-minute circle time, a teacher of a group of three-year-olds might plan an average of four activities taking about two to three minutes each. This could be four different finger plays; two poems, one finger play, and one song; or two Simon Says games and two finger plays. The point is to work with what you know about the group of young children with whom you are working.

Another important point about attention span is its highly individual nature. Some three-year-olds may attend to a very favorite activity for longer than three minutes, while a first grader of 6 may not be able to attend to a language arts lesson for 5 minutes! In this case, you need to consider the match between the individual child and the specific activity.

Activity patterns. A young child will generally attend better to new activities that are a good match to her or his present level of development—that is, activities that are neither too difficult nor too easy. It is also important to vary activities so that the new and the old are in an interesting as well as developmentally appropriate pattern for young children. A good **activity pattern** is one that begins with the familiar (or favorite), reviews some other related activities, and then moves on to introduce the new and different. For example, in introducing the letter B, the teacher may begin with a favorite song, "Buttons, the Clown." Then she has the children identify picture cards of foods that begin with B and later introduces the phoneme /b/ and related written words. In a similar activity pattern, a teacher of four-year-olds begins with a favorite finger play about five little monkeys, has five children role play the monkeys, and then introduces a new book he plans to read about monkeys and their babies, which is part of a new animal unit.

An activity pattern for young children also must take into account their physical characteristics. Children develop large muscle skills first and enjoy practicing these skills. They also need practice to develop small-motor skills. Therefore activity patterns should include time for both large- and small-motor tasks. In the previous example, the teacher of four-year-olds included a large-motor task (jumping like monkeys) with a small-motor task (a finger play). Including both types of activities in one session also helps increase attention span because they are favorite large-motor activities.

THIS ONE'S for YOU! Research on the Effects of the No Child Left Behind Act

The No Child Left Behind Act (NCLB), which was authorized by Congress in 2001, has been studied by many researchers in the past several years to judge its effectiveness. Most recently, in August of 2009 the National Center for Analysis of Longitudinal Data in Education Research (CALDER) and the National Center for Performance Incentives at Peabody College of Vanderbilt University hosted a research conference entitled "NCLB: Emerging Findings." The conference brought together more than 20 policy analysts and prominent scholars from the education policy research field to present and debate emergent findings on the merits and the weakness of NCLB. The following are some of the research findings from this conference.

Two researchers from the University of Michigan and Swarthmore College studied the long-term effects of the NCLB on children's achievement by performing a statistical analysis of state-level test data. More specifically, they compared test score changes across states that already had school-accountability policies in place prior to NCLB and those that did not. They reported that NCLB appears to have generated some meaningful gains in important measures of student achievement, particularly with gains in 4th grade math achievement. However, there was little evidence for any positive effects in reading (Dee & Jacob, 2009).

In another study of the effects of NCLB, researchers from the University of Chicago conducted a statistical analysis of 5th grade test scores from the Chicago public schools. They found that both the introduction of NCLB in 2002 and the introduction of similar district-level reforms in 1996 generated noteworthy increases in reading and math scores among students in the middle of the achievement distribution. Yet the least academically advantaged students in Chicago did not score higher in math or in reading following the introduction of NCLB. In their analysis, the authors also found only mixed evidence of score gains among the most advantaged students (Neal & Schanzenbach, 2009). Their results support the hypothesis that:

> Accountability systems based on the number of students who achieve a proficiency standard provide relatively weak incentives to devote extra attention to either students who have no realistic chance of becoming proficient in the near term or student who are already proficient. (Neal & Schanzenbach, 2009, p. 5)

The quote that they use to begin their study very clearly reflects this effect of NCLB:

> We were told to cross off the kids who would never pass. We were told to cross off the kids who, if we handed them the test tomorrow, they would pass. And then the kids who were left over, those were the kids we were supposed to focus on. (deVise, 2007)

In another study, researchers from Vanderbilt University, Peabody College, examined the effect of NCLB using longitudinal, student-level test score data from seven states with more than 2 million students as subjects. The results were compared from the 2002–03 and 2005–06 school years. In analyzing this data, they had two research questions: (1) Has NCLB increased achievement among lower-performing students?; and (2) Have these gains come at the expense of students who are already proficient or who are far below the proficiency targets? In their data analysis, the authors found consistent evidence of an achievement trade-off in the predicted direction, though the effects on any given student were not large. Unlike some researchers, they found mixed evidence at best that students far below the proficient level have been harmed by NCLB. In fact, at higher grade levels, this group appears to have benefitted (Ballou & Springer, 2009).

In yet another study, researchers from Western Washington University used statewide observations of 3rd- and 4th-grade math tests to study the effects of NCLB on racial groups. Their statistical analysis demonstrated that students of successful racial groups at schools likely to be sanctioned gained less academically over the subsequent test year than comparable peers at passing schools. Taken as a whole, their evidence suggests that building administrators participate in strategic instruction. That is, administrators focus their efforts on racial groups that have trouble making adequate yearly progress (AYP). They conclude that given the limit on school resources, this redirection of resources toward one racial group causes a lessening in academic performance of students in successful racial groups (Krieg, 2009).

Besides the findings of this conference, in another study on the effects of NCLB, the Arizona State University Education Policy Research Unit (EPRU) stated in a recent release that AYP is fundamentally flawed and should be suspended until the premises underlying it can be confirmed or refuted by solid,

Continued

scientific research (EPRU, 2009). Their study concludes that NCLB's 100% proficiency goal is unattainable. They also conclude that AYP is underfunded and the system fails to provide adequate programs aimed at offsetting the impact of poverty. Therefore, schools attended by the neediest children are penalized disproportionately (Mathis, 2009).

After reading all of these research findings, what are we to learn from them that we can use as teachers of young children? At the most basic level, we need to remember that assessment of learning is an important part of accountability. However, assessment must not include merely standardized tests of that which is easy to measure. What we know about developmentally appropriate practice, Bloom's taxonomy, and differentiated instruction all tell us that the child, not state standards, is the basis of the curriculum. These principles need to be your guiding force as you face the challenges inherent in the NCLB and other curriculum standards.

Creative activities for young children must also have a good balance between active and quiet activities. All of one type activity would not be appropriate for the developmental needs of young children. A good rule to remember here follows: The younger the child, the greater the tendency to become overstimulated. Activities for toddlers and two-year-olds should be limited in number to avoid overstimulation. Activities should be added as children can handle them.

Also, in a single instructional setting (or lesson), young children of all ages need active as well as quiet activities because they have a difficult time sitting quietly for extended periods. In the previous example with first graders, the teacher could provide an appropriate balance of active and quiet activities by having children go to the board and write a *b* on it or even having them walk over to an object beginning with the letter *b*. This way, children's physical inability to sit quietly for extended amounts of time is considered in the lesson. In the example of the teacher of four-year-olds, we see similar planning for active (jumping) behavior and quiet (listening to a story) behavior. By following the more active with a more quiet activity, the teacher is working with the physical needs of young children to be active and to rest after exertion.

Transitions from group times. Transitions from group times to the next activities can be chaotic if

THINK ABOUT IT   Why Coloring Books?

Many early childhood teachers would have to admit that they use predrawn images that they have children either add to or complete by coloring in. One 4th-grade teacher I know requires an intensive book report for his class and then gives them a picture to color in for the cover! Where does creativity enter into that?

Whenever I discuss this "coloring book problem," whether with students or colleagues, many of them share their experiences with coloring books and dittos and remark that coloring was, and still is, a very relaxing activity. Why would this be bad for children?

Dittos and coloring books are adult-generated images designed to occupy children's time. There are times when occupying children's time is exactly what we want to do—for example, during long car trips.

Coloring in coloring books can be relaxing because children are not required to think to complete the work. In school, do we want children not to think? Activities such as these often reduce children's ability to think for themselves and result in dependence on the teacher at a time when children should be learning independence.

Teachers sometimes use these methods so they can accomplish work of their own, such as correcting homework and classroom papers. Children can become so accustomed to seeing adult-generated images that when asked to create drawings of their own, they become frustrated because their work resembles that of a child rather than that of an adult. If children become frustrated, they lose interest in drawing and the creative process.

group times are uninteresting, too long, or too demanding. If children in a group become wiggly and uncomfortable, you can expect a difficult transition.

Even a short, interesting group time can end with a mad exodus if precautions are not taken.

Children don't settle down immediately between activities. They need time to transition between active and more concentrated, quiet play. Getting rid of wiggles on demand is seldom an easy process. Each child has her or his own way and time to achieve quiet. A group of young children without wiggles would be cause for concern. A healthy group of children needs a patient teacher, one who can accept the various ways in which individual children respond to the request for quiet.

Another suggestion for preventing chaotic transitions from group times is to share the day's schedule with the children at the beginning of the day. This way they know what will happen. Any special rules may need to be reviewed. Then as each activity begins and ends, reminders will suffice: "Do you remember what we are going to do after our story today?" "When we get ready for our walk, we will need to get our coats. How can we do that without bumping into each other when we leave the circle?" When children help with the plans and participate in setting the limits, they are more apt to understand,

remember, and be willing to help enforce the rules. Do not forget to give positive reinforcement when things go well, not just reminders when someone fails to remember. However, positive reinforcement should not become so automatic or mechanical that children begin to doubt its sincerity. Some genuine response—a smile, pat, or word—is always more effective than a stock phrase.

Transitions to free-choice times. A key strategy for avoiding mad dashes at the beginning of free-choice times is the assurance that children will have ample time for their favorite activities. If free-choice time is too short or few activities are interesting, some children will run to grab their chosen activity. Others will flit about aimlessly and not bother to start anything because they know they will have to stop soon. It is important to have enough interesting things to do and to use a system that allows children to select a second activity if the first is not satisfactory. Children who are bored or frustrated during free-choice time are rarely cooperative when it is time to clean up. A free-choice time that is too long, however, will give you tired children who are no longer constructively busy and are ready to misbehave. It takes flexibility and a good eye for the quality of work and play to know the right amount of time for free play.

THINK ABOUT IT   Children with Special Needs—Truth or Fiction?

Many adults have had little or no experience with people who are disabled in some way because, usually, people with disabilities have been separated from the mainstream into programs especially designed for them. For teachers with little or no previous experience with people with disabilities, having children with disabilities in their classrooms may provide them with the opportunity to learn to value such children for their unique strengths as well as to better understand their disabilities. Teachers and other adults may find that as they become acquainted with children who are disabled, their beliefs about physical or mental limitations are changed. For example, they may find the following.

- Children who are blind do not use alternative sensory channels for information automatically;

they must learn to use hearing, smell, and tactile senses as well as movement to replace sight. Adults must help them develop these skills.

- Children with loss of hearing—even if the loss is severe or profound—are not necessarily quiet. They may be constantly babbling, chattering, or using jargon and other forms of unintelligible speech.

- Children with Down syndrome typically appear to be cheerful, compliant, and loving, but they are not always so. They may surprise you with anger and stubborn resistance.

- Children with severe and multiple physical handicaps such as cerebral palsy may have normal or superior cognitive ability masked by their inability to express themselves readily.

Transitions to group times: back together.
Moving into a group time is often facilitated by a little advance publicity. It builds interest to have something in a bag and as the children ask about it, say, "I'll show you at group time." Children will look forward to group times in which they have a chance to show their block building, artwork, or the book they have drawn and stapled. The morning planning time can give advance notice of exciting things to come, and reminders can keep interest alive throughout the day.

From the first arrival at group time, there should be a teacher or classroom assistant in place to be with the children. Trying to control behavior at a distance is always hazardous and never more so than during a transition.

Sometimes teachers let children look at books until all are ready for story time or music. When the last things are put away at cleanup time, the teacher walks over to the rug and says, "Time to collect the books." Some children have just arrived and have opened the cover of their favorite storybook. Some children are in the middle of reading their favorite book. Some children may resist and some might cooperate, but they will all be left with the feeling that the teacher does not value books except as a tool to keep them quiet.

You might try this different approach. When all the children are seated and looking at books, sit down with them. You may share books with some of the children or just wait for a reasonable period of time. Then you may give a warning that it will soon be time to put the books away. As children finish, collect their books and allow others to finish while you begin the discussion or possibly a finger play to occupy those who are through. When most books have been collected, then you may have your group activity. This process respects children and their interest in books.

Consider the Teacher/Caregiver

> "Be careful what you say to children. When their bones are brittle and their hair silver, they will quote you in their hearts." Rheta Grimsley Johnson

Attitude

Attitude is basic to facilitating creative activities with young children. Some teacher attitudes and ideas that help facilitate creative behavior in young children include the following.

Tolerate small mistakes. When children do not have to worry about being perfect, they have more energy to be creative.

Avoid telling the child the best way to do things. To tell a child the best way implies, first, that the teacher knows it; second, that the child does not know it; and third, that the child has to ask the teacher to know the next time.

Be concerned about what children are doing—not about the final product. In creative activities, young children are in a process—playing, drawing, painting, building. Although they are interested in mastering tasks and producing things of which they are proud, they are not like adults. The final product may not be as important as experimenting, or as using their minds and senses while doing it. That is why young children often build a complex structure with blocks and then take great joy in knocking it over. They want to see what happens!

Older children enjoy the process of creating as well as younger children. However, older children will show more concern for the product, which is natural at this developmental level. Encouraging an open, "what-if?" approach to creative activities will help the older child concentrate on the process as well as the product.

Resist the temptation to always have quiet and order. Silence may not be the spirit of joy. Cleanliness may not be the companion of discovery. Timing and flexibility are all important in these matters.

Get involved. The teacher who is painting, drawing, and working beside the children or accompanying them on a field trip or a walk is a companion and friend. To children, the activity must be worth doing if the teacher is doing it, too. This helps motivation and is a legitimate entry into the children's world. Besides, it's fun! Be careful, however, not to cause children to copy what you are doing. Be sure to "slip away" before this happens.

Strategies for Success

Teachers plan creative activities with children's needs and interests in mind. In addition to assessing whether the planned activity is developmentally appropriate for a particular group of children, there are some general planning guidelines to follow that will help ensure the success of these activities.

Preparation

Often, teachers attempt a creative activity that they have not experienced before. They may have read about it in a book, heard about it from a friend, or seen it at a workshop. They try it because they feel it should work and the children should gain something from it. Often it does succeed, but sometimes it does not. The unfortunate part is that when it does not, the teacher may not know whether it was because of the activity itself or the way it was prepared for and offered. For any activity, especially for a first-time experience, the following suggestions may be helpful.

Try the activity before presenting it to the children. Do this physically, if possible, or else mentally. Sometimes things sound better than they really are. The children should experiment, not be experimented on.

Make sure all necessary equipment is present. Too few scissors, paints without brushes, and paper without paste can cause a great deal of frustration. Creativity and frustration don't mix well.

Think through the activity. Review in your mind (and on paper) the best way to present the activity, step by step. Consider what might be the best time of the day for the activity. Think about how you will distribute the materials. Think through the activity and write down the necessary steps in sequential order.

Modify the activity, if necessary, to meet the developmental needs of the children. Few activities are right for all cultures, all situations, or every type of child. Be sure to include appropriate materials for children with special needs. All teachers must be sensitive to this.

In as little time as possible, explain the activity so that the children know how to begin and proceed. For this part, rules are not necessary but understanding is.

After the children have started, circulate among them. Offer suggestions where helpful, and answer questions as needed. Try to let the children answer their own questions as well as solve their own problems. The teacher's role remains that of facilitator.

Presentation of Creative Activities

The success of any creative activity is influenced by how it is presented, which in turn is affected by how prepared the teacher is for guiding the children in the activity. In planning for each activity, the teacher should do the following.

- Identify goals for the activity.
- Identify possible learning from the activity.
- List the materials necessary for the activity.
- Determine how to set up the activity.
- Decide how to stimulate the children and how to keep their interest alive.
- Anticipate questions the children might ask.
- Plan ways to evaluate the activity.
- Consider follow-up activities.
- Consider cleanup time and requirements.

A broad range of creative activities should be included each week. This gives children a variety of choices to suit their many interests. Not only should each curriculum area be highlighted, but certain types of behavior should also be considered. Dramatic play, creative movement, singing, outdoor activities, and small-group projects should all take place within each week.

Do not move too fast when presenting new ideas or activities for young children. As we learned earlier, when using methods of differentiated instruction, time is flexible and is based on the needs of the child. Children need time to explore and create with new materials. For the very young child, even more time may be needed. Activities should be repeated so that the children learn new ways of approaching the material and expand their understanding through repetition. Purposely leave out specific art activities in the classroom for several days so that if a child does not want to try it the first day or the second day, she has another chance.

Proper sequencing should be given close attention. Activities should build upon each other. For example, some children may want to taste, feel, and smell an apple before they draw or paint one. Once a child is involved in a creative activity, a few words of encouragement may be all that is needed to keep the child interested. It is useful to watch for children who are having problems. A little help may be needed to solve a small problem. Children need enough time to finish an activity. Be sure children are not stopped just when they are beginning to have fun.

THIS ONE'S for YOU! Fragile! Speak to with Care

The way a teacher speaks to and with a young child can mean the difference between the child's positive feelings of self and those not-so-positive feelings. The following suggestions may be helpful to you as you work with young children, helping them grow. Cherish their uniqueness.

- Before speaking to children, get their attention. Putting your hand on a child's shoulder or speaking the child's name helps. As much as possible, stoop to the child's eye level.

- The younger the child, the simpler your statement should be.

- Act as if you expect your words to be heeded. Young children are influenced by the confidence in the adult's tone and action.

- Give children time to respond—their reaction time is slower than yours. Try not to answer your own questions!

- Tell children what they *can* do rather than what they *cannot* do. Use positive rather than negative suggestions or statements.

- Give only as much help as is needed, and give simple directions. Use manual guidance to aid verbal suggestions with young children.

- Use encouraging rather than discouraging statements: "You can do it," not "Is it too hard?"

- Use specific rather than general statements: "You need to put on your socks, and now your shoes," not, "Put on your clothes."

- Use pleasant requests rather than scolding: "You will need to pick up your materials now," not, "Get those things picked up."

- Use substitute suggestions rather than negative comments: "Use that pencil from the drawer over there," not, "Don't use that."

- Give a choice between two things when possible. You might say, "Will you wash your face, or shall I help you?" This means the child will be washed in any case. Never give a choice where there is none, such as, "Do you want to wash?" when washing is necessary. Try not to say, "Would you like to?" if you do not intend to abide by the child's choice.

- Remember to show disapproval in what the child does when necessary, but never disapproval of the child. You can say, "You are a good climber, but you will need to climb on the jungle gym. This roof is not solid enough."

- Working with a child—trying to tell or show the child how to do it alone—is better for learning than doing it for the child.

- Keep your promises to children. For example, if you say you will let someone have a turn later, be sure to offer that turn as soon as you can, even though the child may have found another activity. Let the child decide whether to leave the present activity to take a turn.

- Encourage children to use language (to replace physical force, crying, whining, etc.) to communicate their problems, needs, and wishes.

- Children learn through example. Many things, such as manners, are "caught," not always necessarily "taught."

Completing a Creative Activity

At the end of each day, the teacher evaluates the day's activities. Ideas for the next day can be revised or created based on what then appears best. What were the successes of the day? How interested were the children in what they were doing? What did their conversation and play indicate? What does the teacher feel like doing? The key words are *question, think, feel,* and *decide*. A person who works with young children must always be open to new information and feedback.

Strategies for Success—The National Level

All of the information in this chapter so far has centered on the developmental approach to teaching young children. This is, and will continue to be, the most basic and direct approach to working with young children in creative activities and in all other areas. However, anyone who teaches young children in the United States today needs to be aware of the three-pronged national

FIGURE 5-15 • The child with intrapersonal intelligence learning style often prefers to work alone.

focus on (1) legislation in education, (2) content standards, and (3) standards for teachers. What follows is a brief description of each of these three areas. More in-depth information on these issues can be found in the references listed at the end of this chapter.

Legislation and Education

In 2001, the **No Child Left Behind (NCLB) Act** was authorized by Congress. This particular act has been highly publicized for its dramatic emphasis on improving U.S. schools to create more equitable educational opportunities for all children. NCLB is intended to provide all children with a fair, equal, and significant opportunity to obtain a high-quality education. One of the most significant (and controversial) provisions of NCLB is the requirement that states set standards and conduct annual assessments to gauge school districts' progress in improving students' academic achievement. This leads us directly to the second focus in our discussion of standards.

Content Standards

NCLB requires that state departments of education develop challenging academic content standards and academic assessments. The law also requires testing of all children in at least grades 3 through 8 in reading and math. These annual tests are meant to measure the adequate yearly progress (AYP) of each student.

The content standards are important for preschool teachers as well as K–5 teachers. Although most **national standards** are written for grades K–12, they are often

FIGURE 5-16 • Music smart learners enjoy learning to play simple instruments.

written in broad language, making them applicable in some cases to prekindergarten. Some national standards written for the primary grades begin with pre–K. Also, most states have developed or are developing their own content standards, and these often include pre–K content standards. Head Start has developed its own set of standards, the Head Start Child Outcomes Framework (2009). These serve as a framework of building blocks that are important for school success.

As a result of the development of content standards, many early childhood teachers have been increasingly integrating the subject matter standards into their programs for several years and have been involved in the standards movement in many states. Most teachers recognize that we must have expectations and standards for our early childhood programs. But they also know the nature of learning at this age, and they carefully define how content standards are most appropriately and effectively incorporated into preschool and kindergarten programs. Because a program uses playful ways to build children's success does not mean the curriculum is not rigorous or content based. It means that it is just right for what's best for three-, four-, and five-year-old children. (See references at the end of this chapter for websites that provide activities linked to standards.)

With regard to the emphasis on assessment that is part of the NCLB Act, observation of young children is at the heart of early childhood practice. As we have seen earlier, the early childhood curriculum grows out of an understanding of the young child. Knowing as much as possible about each child's uniqueness, strengths, and needs, educators can create an effective environment to support development and learning for all ages.

In this standards issue, once again as early childhood professionals, we must create our own definition of assessment rather than yielding to others' definition. Owning the word, we can keep its meaning from narrowing to the domain of standardized tests or high-stakes evaluation. Owning the word in our developmental sense, we can keep the conversation focused on the *uses* of assessment—not assessment as an end in itself, but as a means of helping young children and families reach valuable goals.

Early Childhood Learning Standards

Content standards are no longer the domain of elementary education. Early learning standards for preschool children are all around us. As of September 2009, 47 states were implementing early childhood standards in mathematics, science, social studies, social/emotional development, physical development and health, and the creative arts (http:www.ccsso.org).

Just what are early learning standards for preschool children? The Early Childhood Education Assessment Consortium of the Council of Chief State School Officers (CCSSO) defines early learning standards as those that "describe expectations for the learning and development of young children across the domains of: health and physical well-being; approaches to learning; language development and symbol systems; and general knowledge about the world around them" (http://www.ccsso.org).

Most of the learning standards developed are for the preschool years, ages three to five. However, some states have also developed (or are developing) standards or expectations for infants and toddlers.

All of these state early learning standards have many features in common and are based on generally accepted knowledge of child development. The differences lie in the formatting or the inclusion of

specific content or developmental areas. On the federal level, Head Start developed a Child Outcomes Framework in 2000. This framework is now an important part of the evaluation of the effectiveness of Head Start programs across the country. Standards for children younger than kindergarten age differ from those for older children because the primary tasks of young children are to acquire and refine foundational skills—skills that will help them successfully learn content in the later grades. The National Association for the Education of Young Children (NAEYC) and the National Association of Early Childhood Specialists in State Departments of Education (NAECS/SDE) in a joint policy statement suggest that early learning standards can be a valuable part of a comprehensive, high-quality system of services for young children (NAEYC, 2002).

However, throughout the field of education there is cause for concern about how these standards are used. In the same joint NAEYC and NAECS/SDE position statement, the authors warn that there are educational and developmental risks for vulnerable young children if standards are not well developed and implemented (NAEYC, 2009).

However, there are some definite benefits to standards if they are used in the proper way.

- Standards reinforce the fact that there is an incredible potential for learning and growth in the infant, toddler, and preschool years and that there is value and importance in providing high-quality early childhood programs for children's long-term success in school and in life.
- Standards help establish expectations for children at different ages and create a commonality for communication about children's accomplishments and capabilities.
- Standards provide a framework for accountability—a way for early educators to show parents, the community at large, and themselves just what children are learning in early childhood programs (NAEYC, 2009).

Just as with all other national standards, there are some definite drawbacks to early learning standards.

- They lead to teaching to the standards only in a cookie-cutter style curriculum.
- They bring a pressure of accountability with the risk of a push-down in curriculum and inappropriate expectations for younger children.

THIS ONE'S for YOU!   Getting Started with Multiple Intelligences—Try These Ideas

Here are a few classroom activity suggestions that can get you started with multiple intelligences.

- For musical or bodily/kinesthetic learners who persist in drumming, humming, and tapping during quiet work time, provide thin plastic straws for them to tap on desks. This is much less distracting to others!

- For bodily/kinesthetic students who tear paper, scribble on desks, and gouge textbooks, provide a small piece of clay for them to keep in their desks. Allow them to manipulate while working, listening—anytime.

- For musical students, provide a set of headphones with a music tape to aid concentration.

- Before reading a story to your group, take a moment to imagine how you could turn it into a participatory reading event for your children who are musical or bodily/kinesthetic. For example, before you read a story about a particular animal, instruct students that every time you read the animal's name, they are to make a noise like that animal.

- Assign a different mouth noise to represent each punctuation mark you are teaching. When you put sentences on the board that need punctuation, students will vie for the privilege of reading a sentence with the appropriate noisy punctuation, while you or a student adds the marks to the sentence. (If you can't handle the mouth noises, you might try instruments like a cymbal or rattle.)

- When practicing vocabulary words, let children who are musical make up a rap or song about the spelling (or meaning) of a word/set of facts. Have your spatial learners draw a "word picture" or "math fact picture." First write the word or math fact in the middle of the paper; then draw a picture around it that will help them remember the word. Have your linguistic learners create a crossword puzzle using vocabulary words. Both linguistic and musical learners would enjoy creating a rhyming poem using vocabulary words or math facts.

- They can result in testing and other inappropriate assessment methods being used with young children.

- Direct instruction is often assumed to be the only way to guarantee that standards are addressed. Children's learning in self-directed, exploratory ways is not trusted.

Many experienced early childhood teachers very likely could add to this list of arguments against early learning standards. Yet it is crucial for early childhood educators to take an active interest in these early learning standards to ensure that the best interests of young children are served in their use. As in all issues related to young children, educators need to be constantly vigilant that the developmental needs of our youngest citizens are acknowledged and respected in all standards and curriculum issues.

The third and final focus in our discussion directs the issue of standards for the teacher herself.

Standards for Teachers—INTASC Standards

Interstate New Teacher Assessment and Support Consortium (INTASC) standards are model standards for licensing new teachers. Drafted by representatives of the teaching profession, along with personnel from 17 state education agencies, these standards represent a common core of teaching knowledge and skills that will help all students acquire 21st-century knowledge and skills. An important attribute of these standards is that they are performance based—that is, they describe **key indicators**, or what teachers should know and be able to do, rather than listing courses that teachers should take in order to be awarded a license. You will find these standards with a brief description of each in the Online Companion.

Summary

Planning creative activities for young children begins with an awareness of the young child. There are many questions to ask about the child, the child's environment, and the teacher's own feelings in order to plan properly. The teacher's plans need to take into consideration: (1) children's needs and interests, (2) their developmental levels, and (3) available materials and resources. These are basic concepts in developmentally appropriate practice (DAP). Differentiated instruction involves providing different types of learning experiences and environments to meet children's individual needs. Gardner's Multiple intelligence theory provides further insight on how to meet children's needs by knowing how each child is "smart." Bloom's taxonomy gives us a tool to encourage children's higher-level thinking. Other considerations in planning creative activities are children's attention spans and activity patterns. A teacher should have reasonable expectations of how long young children can be attentive in certain activities and should know how to supervise these activities so that there is a good balance between active and quiet ones.

Although young children naturally compare their work with other children, competition is not necessary or helpful in creative activities. It is important that young children learn that personal feelings are normal and acceptable. Sometimes the expression of these feelings may cause problems and, therefore, may need modification. Sensitive answers to the questions, "How is the child being creative?" and "How does the child feel about it?" can help guide the teacher in facilitating creative behavior.

Teachers also need to consider their own needs, interests, skills, and abilities when planning activities for young children. Their attitude is crucial to the success of any creative activity.

In creative activities, the teacher's role is to facilitate creative expression. This generally means having a knowledge of children's developmental levels and skills, a sensitive and caring attitude toward them, and a willingness to help them interact with materials. It means guidance without interference or judgment.

To ensure the success of creative activities, careful planning is essential. Also, attention and thought must be given to the manner in which the activity is to be presented, the children's interest sustained, and the activity completed. Once the creative activity is finished, its success should be evaluated in terms of individual and program goals.

The NCLB Act, preschool learning standards, and INTASC standards are all national approaches to ensuring excellence in teaching.

Key Terms

activity pattern 100
attention span 99
Bloom's taxonomy 92
developmental level 82
differentiated instruction 86
facilitate 81
Gardner's multiple intelligence theory 88
individual differences 82
key indicators 109
national standards 107
No Child Left Behind (NCLB) Act 107
process learning 87
Reggio Emilia approach 85

Learning Activities

A. Check the list of attitudes found in this unit that facilitate creative behavior in young children.

1. Choose one example of each from your personal life in which you demonstrate the attitude.
2. Decide whether this is an attitude you already possess or one that you need to work on in order to improve.
3. Explain how you might go about modifying those attitudes in need of improvement.

B. There are strategies that teachers use to create a good climate for creative activities. There are other factors that may cause a child's creativity to be hindered by a teacher.

1. Make a list of five dos and don'ts for creative activities in the early childhood setting.

2. If possible, compare and discuss your list with those of your classmates.
3. Observe a teacher who is supervising a creative activity in an early childhood classroom. What does he or she do to facilitate children's expression of creativity?

C. Using the information in this chapter on planning and presentation of creative activities, plan a creative activity for (a) three-year-olds and third graders or (b) four-year-olds and fourth graders. In your activity plan, consider the following:

- developmental needs of the children
- attention span
- physical ability
- activity level

- appropriate materials
- appropriate motivation

D. Use the observation sheet in the Online Companion to assess your own multiple intelligences. Were you surprised by anything you learned about yourself? Can you apply this learning to your teaching? How?

E. Use the observation sheet in the Online Companion to help you reflect on your personal teaching style. Which intelligences are the strongest in you? Which are the weakest? Are you neglecting types of activities because of your own weaknesses?

F. Log onto the NCLB websites at http://www. teachersandfamilies.com/. Click on the "Parents" section, then on "Parenting Features." Click on "Your Child and No Child Left Behind." Find out what students will be included in state assessments. According to the website, what are the benefits of testing?

G. Find out the National Standards for Arts Education at the Artsedge website at http://www.artsedge. kennedy-center.org/. Click on the "Standards" line under the "Teach" section. Find curricula, lessons, and activities linked to these national standards that you can use with children in your group. Visit some of the websites listed at the end of this chapter for more activities linked to national standards.

H. Hands-On Multiple Intelligences Activities

Hands-on experience is the easiest way to explain multiple intelligences. Here's an exercise to try with your fellow students to learn more about Gardner's eight areas of intelligence.

1. Give each person an apple.
2. Ask participants to experience their apples using Gardner's eight intelligences.
   Examples: Linguistic intelligence. Have participants describe how the apple looks.
   Bodily kinesthetic/intrapersonal intelligence: How does the apple feel? Touch the apple.
   Logical/mathematical intelligence: What shape is the apple? Sort apples by color and size. Share the apples.
   Interpersonal intelligence: Compare the apple to your neighbor's apple.
   Kinesthetic Intelligence; Taste the apple.

Chapter Review

1. Discuss the ways you can plan activities to match a child's attention span.
2. List at least two ways you can plan activities to match the young child's activity level.
3. List 10 important questions that should be asked to better know and work with young children.
4. With regard to young children, discuss the difference between having feelings and expressing feelings.
5. Describe the role of facilitator as it applies to the teacher who plans and guides creative activities for children.
6. List the necessary steps in preparing a creative activity.
7. Discuss strategies for handling transition times.
8. Discuss the term *developmental level*.
9. Define the terms *differentiated instruction, process learning,* and *multiple intelligences.*
10. Discuss the national standards for elementary and preschool curriculum content, teacher certification, and the NCLB Act.
11. Describe accomplished teaching by listing the five standards associated with it.
12. Explain how using Bloom's taxonomy can help encourage a child's creative thinking.
13. List several characteristics of developmentally appropriate practice.

References

Ballou, D., & Springer, M. G. (2009). *Achievement trade-offs and No Child Left Behind.* Paper presented at Research Conference NCLB: Emergent Findings, sponsored by the National Center for Analysis of Longitudinal Data in Education Research (CALDER) and the National Center for Performance Incentives (NCPI), August 12, 2009.

Bruner, J. (2004). *The rights and potentials of children and adults.* Crossing Borders International Conference. Reggio Emilia, Italy.

Clyde, J. A., Miller, C., Sauer, S., Liebert, K., Parker, S., & Runyon, S. (2006). Teachers and children inquire into Reggio Emilia. *Language Arts, 83*(3), 215–226.

Copple, C., & Bredekamp, S. (Eds.). (2009). *Developmentally appropriate practice in early childhood programs serving children from birth through age 8* (3rd ed.). Washington, DC: NAEYC.

Dee, T. S., & Jacob, B. A. (2009). *The achievement consequences of the No Child Left Behind Act.* Research paper presented at NCLB: Emergent

Findings, sponsored by the National Center for Analysis of Longitudinal Data in Education Research (CALDER) and the National Center for Performance Incentives (NCPI), August 12, 2009.

deVise, D. (2007, March 4). Rockville schools' efforts raise questions of test-prep ethics. *Washington Post*, A4.

Education Policy Research Unit (2009). *NCLB school evaluation system is a flawed reform tool.* News release. Arizona State University: Author.

Gardner, H. (1999). *Intelligence reframed: Multiple intelligences for the 21st century.* New York, NY: Basic Books.

Gardner, H. (2004). The hundred languages of successful educational reform. *Children in Europe, 6,* 16–17.

Greenspan, S. I. (2001, September). Creating an inclusive classroom. *Scholastic Early Childhood Today,* 33–34.

Krieg, J. M. (2009). *Which students are left behind? The racial impacts of the No Child Left Behind Act.* Paper presented at Research Conference NCLB: Emergent Findings, sponsored by the National Center for Analysis of Longitudinal Data in Education Research (CALDER) and the National Center for Performance Incentives (NCPI), August 12, 2009.

Mathis, W. (2009). *NCLB school evaluation: A flawed reform tool.* News release, Arizona State University. http://epaa.asu.edu/ojs/article/view/225

NAEYC and the National Association of Early Childhood Specialists in State Departments of Education (NAECS/SDE). (2009). *Early learning standards: Creating the conditions for success.* Available at http://www.naeyc.org/positionstatements

Neal, D., & Schanzenbach, D. W. (2009). *Left behind by design: Proficiency counts and test-based accountability.* Paper presented at Research Conference NCLB: Emergent Findings, sponsored by the National Center for Analysis of Longitudinal Data in Education Research (CALDER) and the National Center for Performance Incentives (NCPI), August 12, 2009.

Nicholson-Nelson, W. (1998). *Developing student's multiple intelligences.l* New York: Scholastic.

Wien, C. A. (2008). (Ed.). *Emergent curriculum in the primary classroom: Interpreting the Reggio Emilia approach in schools.* New York, NY: Teachers College Press.

References on Developmentally Appropriate Practice

*Bredekamp, S., & Copple, C. (Eds.), 1997. *Developmentally appropriate practice in early childhood programs* (Rev. ed.). Washington, DC: NAEYC.

Bredekamp, S., & Copple, C. (2006). *Basics of developmentally appropriate practice: An introduction for teachers of children 3 to 6.* Washington, DC: NAEYC.

Bredekamp, S., & Copple, C. (2009). *Developmentally appropriate practice* (3rd ed.). Washington, DC: NAEYC

Derman-Sparks, L., & the ABC Task Force. (1989). *Anti-bias curriculum: Tools for empowering young children.* Washington, DC: NAEYC.

Helm, J. H. (2008). Got standards? Don't give up on engaged learning. *Young Child, 63*(4), 14–20.

Meisels, S. J., & Atkins-Burnett, S. (2008). *Developmental screening in early childhood: A guide* (5th ed.). Washington, DC: NAEYC.

Seefeldt, C., Galper, A., & Feeney, S. (2008). *Continuing Issues in Early Childhood Education.* Upper Saddle River, NJ: Prentice Hall.

Willis, C. (2009). *Teaching infants, toddlers, and twos with special needs.* Beltsville, MD: Gryphon House.

Wurm, J. P. (2005). Working in the Reggio way: A beginner's guide for. American teachers. St. Paul, MN: Red Leaf Press.

Additional Readings

Bakken, J., & Obiakor, F. E. (2008). *Transition planning for students with disabilities: What educators and service providers can do.* Springfield, IL: Charles C. Thomas.

Bergen, S. (2009). *Best practices for training early childhood professionals.* St. Paul, MN: Redleaf.

Gilliam, W. S. (2008). Head Start, public school prekindergarten, and a collaborative potential. *Infants and Young Children: An interdisciplinary Journal of Special Care Practices, 21*(1), 30–44.

Hodge, S. (2008). Differentiating art instruction. *SchoolArts, 108*(3), 12–14.

Ingersoll, B. (2008). The social role of imitation in autism: Implications for the treatment of imitation deficits. *Infants and Young Children: An Interdisciplinary Journal of Special Care Practices, 21*(2), 107–119.

Kennedy, M. M. (2008). Sorting out teacher quality. *Phi Delta Kappan, 90*(1), 59–63.

LeMoine, S. (2009). *Workforce designs: A policy blueprint for state early childhood professional development systems.* Washington, DC: NAEYC.

Levanger, J., & Mitchell, T. C. (2008). *I belong: Active learning for children with special needs.* Washington, DC: NAEYC.

Marks, S. U. (2008). Self-determination for students with intellectual disabilities and what I want educators to know what it means. *Phi Delta Kappan, 90*(1), 55–58.

McKinley, L. S., & Stormont, M. A. (2008). The school support checklist: Identifying support needs and barriers for children with ADHD. *Teaching Exceptional Children, 42*(2), 14–21.

Michael, M., Meese, R. L., Keith, S., & Mathews, R. (2009). Bob Bear: A strategy for improving behaviors of preschoolers identified as at risk or developmentally delayed. *Teaching Exceptional Children, 41*(5), 55–59.

Mosteller, R. (2008). When a student has Asperger's. *Instructor, 118*(2), 46–49.

NAEYC. (2008). *Standard 4: Assessment of child progress: A guide to the NSEYC Early Childhood Program Standard and Related Accreditation Criteria.* Washington, DC: Author.

NAEYC. (2008). *Standard 6: Teachers: A guide to the NAEYC early childhood program standard and related accreditation criteria.* Washington, DC: Author.

Ogu, U., & Reynard Smidt, S. (2009). Investigating rocks and sand: Addressing multiple learning styles through an inquiry-based approach. *Young Children, 64*(2), 12–19.

Schiller, P., & Willis, C. A. (2008). Of primary interest: Using brain-based teaching strategies to create supportive early childhood environments that address learning standards. *Young Children, 63*(4), 52–55.

Summers, J. A., & Wall, S. (2008). Cross referrals between programs for infants and toddlers with disabilities: Perceptions of Part C and Early Head Start Providers. *Infants and Young Children: An Interdisciplinary Journal of Special Care Practices, 21*(4), 64–70.

Tabors, P. O. (2009). *One child, two languages: A guide for early childhood educators of children learning English as a second language.* Washington, DC: NAEYC.

Towne, J. W., & Prescott, R. J. (2009). *Conversations with America's best teachers: Teacher of the Year award winners give practical advice for the classroom and beyond.* Los Angeles, CA: Inkster.

Watson, A., & McCathren, R. (2009). Including children with special needs: Are you and your early childhood program ready? *Young Children, 64*(2), 20–26.

Webb, S. J., & Jones, E. J. H. (2009). Early identification of autism: Early characteristics, onset of symptoms and diagnostic stability. *Infants and Young Children: An Interdisciplinary Journal of Special Care Practices, 22*(2), 100–118.

Willis, C. (2009). Young children with autism spectrum disorder: Strategies that work. *Young Children, 64*(1), 81–82.

Helpful Websites

Art Beyond Sight (visual impaired), http://www.artbeondsight.org

Association for Supervision and Curriculum Development, http://www.ascd.org/

Born to Explore: The Other side of ADD, http://www.borntoexplore.org

Dyslexia websites, http://www.dyslexiaparent.com and http://www.specialneeds.com

ESL Bears, http://eslbears.homestead.com/index.html

ESL Bits, http://esl-bits.net/main2.htm
Learnweb at the Harvard Graduate School of Education, http://learnweb.harvard.edu/wide/en

ESL Reading Lessons, http://5minuteenglish.com/reading.htm

ESL Teacher Lesson Plans, http://www.usingenglish.com/lesson-plans.html

LD Pride.net, http://www.ldpride.net/

New Teacher Site, http://www.teacher.scholastic.com

Telephone English, http://www.telephoningenglish.com/
Click on "Active Learning Practices for Schools (ALPS)."

The Educator's Reference Desk, http://www.eduref.org

Top Ten Tips for Working with ESL/ELL Students, http://www.teachersfirst.com/content/esl/eslhintintro.cfm

Using Humor in the Second Language Classroom, http://iteslj.org/Techniques/Chiasson-Humour

Using Humor in the ESL Classroom, http://teacherjoe.us/TeachersHumor.html

Using Games in the ESL Classroom, http://teacherjoe.us/TeachersGames.html

Websites With Standards-Related Activities

Arizona Dept. of Education—Early Childhood Education Programs, http://www.ade.state.az.us/early-childhood/

Child, Youth and Families—Education and Research Network, http://www.cyfernet.mes.umn.edu

Connect for Kids, http://www.connectforkids.org

Illinois Early Learning Project, http://www.illinoisearlylearning.org/standards/

Iowa Dept. of Education—Knowledge Base, http://www.iowa.gov/educate/

National Early Childhood Technical Assistance Center, http://www.nectac.org/topics/quality/earlylearn.asp

NYS Council on Children and Families Head Start Collaboration, http://www.earlychildhood.org

Pennsylvania Department of Education, http://www.education.state.pa.us/

PBS Teacher Source, http://www.pbs.org/teachersource/

Utah Early Childhood Professional Development Connections, http://earlychildhoodconnections.weber.edu/links.aspx

For additional creative activity resources, visit our website at www.Cengage.com/login

Creative Environments

OBJECTIVES

After studying this chapter, you should be able to:

1. Describe an appropriate physical environment for creative activities for young children.

2. Describe considerations needed to arrange appropriate environments for creative activities for children with special needs.

3. Discuss the main considerations involved in setting up activity centers.

4. List and describe interest centers that encourage children's creativity and developing skills.

5. List six factors that are important when selecting equipment to be used in creative activities for young children.

6. List five safety factors to be considered in the early childhood environment.

The setting in which a creative activity takes place is very important. Young children are very aware of negative moods and environment. A dark room or crowded space can have much more effect on them than a rainy day. The arrangement of space and the type of equipment provided have a dramatic impact on a child's creative experiences. The impact is even greater on children with special needs.

Physical Space: General Guidelines

The aesthetics of the early childhood environment were discussed earlier in Chapters 3 and 4. Here we will consider some basic guidelines for a physically appropriate early childhood environment. This is as important as the aesthetics of a room, because a positive physical environment is one of the keys to the success of the creative activities that take place within it. The following poins are some things to consider when evaluating the physical space in early childhood programs.

- Proper heat, light, and ventilation are important. Remember that children live closer to the floor than do adults and that warm air rises and is replaced by cooler air. It may be helpful to install a thermostat or thermometer at their level so you can be aware of the temperatures they are experiencing. However, it must also be remembered that children of all ages are more active than adults and that they may not feel cool at temperatures that may be uncomfortable for you.
- Consider the source of natural light in the room. Children are likely to be more comfortable if they do not face directly into strong sunlight when they work. For children with visual difficulties or limited vision, make sure the room has plenty of light.
- Chairs should be light enough for the children to handle and move without too much noise. Because

FIGURE 6-1 • Provide sufficient floor space for young children to allow them to stretch out if they wish.

the chairs are used at tables for creative activities, the kind without arms should be used. For children in wheelchairs, provide small stools for the child's feet when placing the child at a table.

- There should be some tables that accommodate from four to six children for group activities. Rectangular tables are better for art activities involving large sheets of paper. Some small tables designed to be used singly or in combinations are quite versatile. Tables with washable surfaces such as Formica are best.
- Shelves should be low and open and not too deep so that children have a chance to see, touch, and choose materials independently. Shelves that are sturdy but easy to move are more flexible in room arrangement and help create interest centers.

Safety Factors

Special consideration should be given to safety in the physical environment. Some important safety checks follow.

- Be sure that all low window areas are safe.
- Beware of and remove toxic, lead-based paints and poisonous plants, particularly berry-producing plants. (See Chapter 23 for more specific information on poisonous plants.)
- All art materials *must* be certified nontoxic. Resist the urge to keep or use any unlabeled materials. More specific information on safe art materials is found in Chapter 12.
- With all materials, ask yourself: Will the item be likely to cause splinters, pierce the skin, or cause abrasions? Will the attractive glitter stick under

fingernails? Are the fumes from a spray irritating? Will a two-year-old child's tongue-test transfer color from the object to the mouth?

- Avoid using scented felt-tip markers, which teach children bad habits about eating and sniffing art materials. A good rule of thumb: If the label on a marker says "nontoxic" or *does not* say "permanent ink," the ink is probably water based. Not only are water-based varieties safe to use, they are easier to remove from walls and clothes!
- Try out new materials yourself before creative activities to become aware of any potential safety problems. Most young children can learn to be careful workers when they understand hazards. A teacher, when discussing how to use scissors, might ask, "How can you hide the point in your fist so that you will not hurt yourself and others when you are putting them away?" Two- and three-year-old children will usually need to have adults set rules—for example, "Clay is for modeling, not for eating." Children four years of age and older can cooperatively decide on rules and regulations for safe handling of tools, materials, and equipment. However, older children may still need verbal reminders or simple signs.
- For children with visual impairments, keep the arrangement of furniture stationary until the child is familiar with the room. Be sure to warn the child when changes are made in the arrangement of the room and/or equipment.
- Regularly check to see that fire exits, fire alarms, smoke detectors, and fire extinguishers are in working order and are placed appropriately in the classroom.
- Familiarize yourself and the children with fire exits and fire drills.

Arrangement of Space and Equipment

The arrangement of the space in an early childhood program also has an effect on the safety and success of the creative activities for which it is used. Adults need to consider a number of factors in planning for the arrangement of equipment (Figure 6–2).

Children's Age and Developmental Levels

The age and developmental levels of the children using a room dictate how that room should be arranged. A group of two- and three-year-old children,

FIGURE 6-2 • Older children need more room for special projects.

walkers. Approximately 40 to 60 square feet per preschool child is recommended. Middle- and upper-level elementary students can and need to work in a much larger area than younger children. A larger working space allows for their larger physical size and provides room for various student groupings that naturally arise out of project work, which is an appropriate instructional method for this age group. See the Professional Enhancement Text for further information on developmental levels, developmental milestones by skill, and tips for success.

Supervision

Another consideration in arranging space for young children is the supervision of that space. Open play spaces should not be so large that it becomes difficult to supervise the children properly. A common technique is to divide the space up into interest centers or activity areas with limited numbers allowed at each center. (Interest or activity centers are discussed later in this chapter.) When breaking up the space in such a way as to facilitate supervision, using low, movable barriers, such as child-level bulletin boards, bookshelves, or room dividers, provides a clear view of the area and permits a more flexible use of the space itself.

In supervising a group that includes children with special needs, the teacher needs to be aware of the specific limitations of these children and to check throughout the day that their needs are being met. For example, in working with children in wheelchairs, the teacher should ensure that they are not in the same position for long periods (more than 20 to 30 minutes). The teacher also should be aware of when to move children who use wheelchairs to the proximity of ongoing activities.

Flexibility

Space should be kept as open and flexible as possible so it can be adjusted as children grow, develop, and change in their needs. Your early childhood program certainly should not look the same on the last day of the year as it did on the first day of the year! The early childhood environment must reflect the young children in it—changing and developing along with them. In response to children's growing ability to deal with more concepts, additional equipment, supplies, and interest centers should be incorporated in the room. Conversely, materials, equipment, and even whole

for example, would do quite nicely in a simple, small, enclosed space. At this age, children may be overwhelmed by too large a space or too much equipment in it. Yet as their large-motor skills are developing rapidly, the space should be big enough for active, large-motor activities. Here is where balance is very important. Also, because coordination is not well developed yet in two- and three-year-olds, the space should be as uncluttered as possible.

In contrast, a five-year-old has better coordination because of a more centralized center of gravity and doesn't fall as frequently as a two- or three-year-old child. More equipment in a room will not present a space or safety problem for the five-year-old. However, the space needs to be large enough to allow children of this age to run, jump, climb, and pretend. In organizing space for young children, then, there should be enough open space for the children to move around safely and comfortably at their level of physical coordination and to work together cooperatively and freely. Adequate room also needs to be available and easily accessible for children in wheelchairs and with

FIGURE 6-3 • In the early childhood program, there needs to be more room to work and create.

FIGURE 6-4 • Arrange space for each child's personal use.

centers need to be removed to storage when children have outgrown them. This same idea holds true for older children in middle and upper elementary grades. The classroom that never changes is boring and a less-than-stimulating learning environment for these children. In a flexible environment, space can easily be rearranged to fit these new centers without major renovations.

This same flexibility holds true when working with children with special needs. For example, at the beginning of the school year, children who are visually impaired need to be in a room where there is assigned seating. This will aid in helping them learn their classmates' voices and names. The reason for assigned seating needs to be clearly explained to the class so they can understand the importance of the seating arrangement. Another helpful suggestion is to make sure that children understand that they should identify themselves before speaking.

Traffic Flow

Even when increasing activity options in a room, space should be as free as possible to allow the traffic to flow between activities. For example, the **traffic flow** should not interfere with activities that require concentration. A language arts center is more likely to be used by children if it is away from the noise of people coming and going. The block corner, too, will be used more often if it is planned for a space that is free from interruption and traffic.

Older children will enjoy an arts center that is situated in an area where they can concentrate and work

without a lot of interruptions (i.e., away from the door or other heavy-traffic areas).

Involve children in arranging space. Sometimes children as young as four years of age, as well as older, may help determine where particular centers should be located and the reasons for such decisions. For example, a kindergarten teacher, introducing the woodworking bench, held a discussion with the children about where it should be placed. They wisely considered safety and noise factors in making their decision. Older children can actually help move desks, tables, and other equipment to carry out their own space reorganization plan. You may even tape arrows to the floor to teach the children traffic patterns for moving about the room.

Personal Space

In the early childhood years, children are growing physically and intellectually and developing their sense of self. For this reason, it is very important to plan space in such a way that each child has a place of her or his own. Having a place of one's own to keep personal belongings, extra clothes, artwork, and notes to take home helps encourage a child's developing sense of self. A snapshot of the child used to label the **personal space** is a good way, too, of assisting the growth of a sense of self. A snapshot removes all doubt that the place is private property even before a child has learned to recognize her or his name. Each child needs to be able to count on having a place belonging only to her or him.

It is only by firmly establishing an understanding of ownership that a young child learns about sharing.

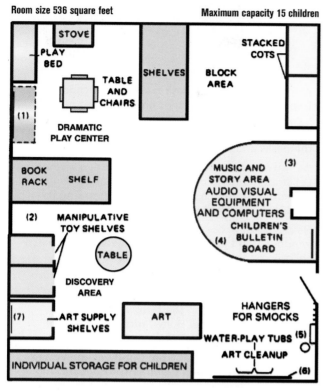

ROOM PLAN

Room size 536 square feet   Maximum capacity 15 children

1. A second bed or folding mat
2. Child-size rocking chairs
3. Adult rocking chair
4. Rug
5. Wastebasket and paper towels
6. Adult bulletin board above tubs
7. Windows

FIGURE 6-5 • Sample classroom arrangement using interest centers.

Children with attention deficit disorders (ADD) have a more intense need for concentration in a designated personal space. They tend to be most successful when they have their own materials and space in which to work. Even a cardboard box on a table can function as a study carrel for children with ADD.

Activity/Interest Centers

One approach to fostering creative activities and use of materials is to provide as part of the environment **activity** or **interest centers** and to identify activities and materials for each, based on the group of children in the class.

An activity or interest center is a defined space where materials are organized in such a way that children learn without the teacher's constant presence and direction. It is a place where children interact with materials and other children to develop certain skills and knowledge. Activities in each activity center are planned by the teacher according to the developmental needs of the children (Kostelnik & Grady, 2009).

Learning centers are places where children learn through direct interaction with other children and their environment. In centers, children learn through doing in an environment carefully prepared for their personal and active exploration.

An early childhood program organized around activity centers encourages creativity by giving children many opportunities to play, experiment, and discover as they engage in activities that help them with problem solving, learning basic skills, and understanding new concepts. In activity centers, young children can manipulate objects, engage in conversation and role playing, and learn at their own levels and paces. Materials in the interest centers also allow the children to experience various cultural and ethnic groups represented in their world.

Figure 6–6 presents the basic interest centers found in most early childhood programs. Figure 6–5 shows how interest centers can be arranged in a classroom. Again, this arrangement is a suggestion, to be adjusted to the needs of the children. For additional information on room arrangement, see Helpful websites at the end of this chapter. Several of these websites provide virtual classrooms for which you can enter actual room dimensions and arrange interest centers in that space.

Having a cubby of one's own helps the child learn about possession and care of self, which are both basic to a growing sense of independence.

If there is not enough space for individual cubbies, labeled dishpans, clear plastic shoeboxes, large round ice cream containers, or even plastic milk crates can be used. Making personal space important recognizes each child's personal needs. This says to the child, "You are important."

In developing a positive self-concept, young children also need privacy. Besides respecting a child's private cubby, the space should be arranged so that there are quiet places to be alone. Especially as a child grows intellectually, she or he needs space and time to reflect and think. Quiet places to be alone encourage this reflection where a child can enjoy her or his own thoughts and mental perceptions of the world. Older children have no less need for privacy and personal space. The classroom needs to have a designated space where a student's need to be alone is respected.

THIS ONE'S for YOU! Humor: Part of the Classroom

One necessary part of a creative environment is humor. Learning and laughter go hand in hand. You don't need to be a stand-up comedian or dress up like a clown, but a little comedy can bring a lot of joy and learning opportunities to the classroom. Try one of the ideas below. Or try them all. Do whatever feels comfortable for you. Be natural. If your students are smiling, giggling, laughing, howling, or even falling out of their chairs—you can be sure that you're on the right track.

- **Tell stories.** Share anecdotes from your own childhood.

- **Make funny noises.** Make sounds (clicks, buzzes, rings) that stand for periods, commas, and exclamation points like the late, great entertainer Victor Borge did. It will enliven any writing or grammar lesson.

- **Break the routine.** Pause for a station break in the middle of a lesson. Stand and stretch. Sit down on the floor and pretend you can't get up.

- **Use different voices.** Sing "B-I-N-G-O" operatically. Speak in a funny accent. Make sure that Charlotte's voice is different from Wilbur's.

- **Never be sarcastic.** Direct humor at *yourself*, not at your students. They'll look forward to your jokes and jests rather than dread them.

- **Surprise your students.** In the middle of a lesson say, "Pencils down. Follow me." Lead them out the door and play outside for five minutes.

- **Create hooks.** Seven times seven equals the San Francisco 49ers. "Great" has the word *eat* in it. Mnemonics are not only great memory tools but also work to liven up a lesson.

- **Act things out.** One desk is a floating iceberg. Two desks pushed together under a sheet make a covered wagon. Three desks pushed together is the ceiling of the Sistine Chapel: Tape paper under the desks and paint like Michelangelo.

- **Be outrageous.** Stand on a chair once in a while. Let students stand on their chairs when reciting a poem or singing a song. Want them to sing it louder? Let them stand on their desks!

- **Have fun at recess.** Throw your dignity out the window. Don't just stand on the sidelines and watch children on the playground—play with them!

- **Use props.** Wigs, hats, and funny glasses can turn the dullest of lessons into magic.

- **Be silly.** Fall down on the floor. Pretend the ruler is a microphone. Hula-dance. Scream "April Fool's!" in October.

- **Dress up.** One lab coat from Goodwill and you're Albert Einstein. A couple of paintbrushes sticking out of your pocket and a few bandages on your left ear and you're Vincent van Gogh.

As teachers, we want to motivate our students. We want to create an atmosphere of openness and respect. We want them to feel comfortable and happy. We want them to take risks. We want them to get along with others. We want them to be active learners. Using humor helps facilitate all of this.

What are you waiting for? Go ahead and give it a try!

Adapted from "Make 'em Laugh" by Phillip Done from *Instructor,* April 2006 issue. Copyright © 2006 by Scholastic Inc. Reprinted by permission of Scholastic Inc.

Decisions About Activity Areas: Where and When

Before setting up activity centers, you have to make a number of decisions about which centers to use, when to use them, and where they can best be placed in the classroom. Some of the questions to be addressed include the following.

- Will centers be offered all day, every day; part of the day; or only some days of the week? The ideal choice is to offer activity centers for a large block or blocks of time every day at approximately the same time. This lets children plan ahead, make choices, and get involved in activities. It allows teachers initially to structure learning centers throughout the room and gradually add, remove, or modify centers during the year.

- What room features offer potential settings for centers? You can make creative use of walls, floor, chalkboards, tables, and nooks and crannies.

- Should there be limits on the number of children using any specific center? If so, how will this be determined, and how will children know what the limits are? Activity centers need to be planned so children can work individually or in small groups of various numbers. The size of a small group

ART AREA: This is a place for painting, collage making, cutting, pasting, and chalking. It should be located near water and light and away from large-motor areas.

HOUSEKEEPING/DRAMATIC PLAY CENTER. This is a place for acting out familiar home scenes with pots, pans, and dishes and to "try out" social roles, real-life dialogues, and grown-up jobs. It includes props that are specific to a wide variety of ethnic and cultural groups represented in the class.

BLOCK-BUILDING AREA. Here children can create with both large and small blocks, Tinker Toys®, logs, Legos®, etc.

MANIPULATIVE AREA. Activity in this center enhances motor skills, eye–hand coordination, and mental, language, and social skills through the use of play materials such as puzzles, pegboards, and games.

SCIENCE/DISCOVERY CENTER. Here children can learn about nature and science. They can display what they find at home or on nature walks. It is a place to discover, explore, and ask questions.

MUSIC CENTER. This center provides a place for children to listen to CDs or iPods, to sing, to express themselves creatively in dance, and to play musical instruments. Music from many cultures and ethnic groups is included.

LANGUAGE ARTS CENTER. In this center, children can be alone with their thoughts as they explore the world of books. Books in languages other than English for bilingual and ELL/ELS students as well as books representing a multicultural approach are included.

SAND AND WATER PLAY AREA. This is a place children learn through sensory experiences with sand and water.

THE SOCIAL STUDIES CENTER; PEOPLE AND PLACES. This is a special area where children can study about families, different cultures, ethnic groups, community awareness, specific occupations, and lifestyles.

WOODWORKING CENTER. This center provides children the opportunity to develop their large and small muscles by sanding, gluing, fastening, drilling, and sawing wood.

OUTDOOR PLAY AREA. This center provides a natural learning environment where activities from indoor learning areas can be extended.

FIGURE 6-6 • Basic Interest Centers in Early Childhood Programs.

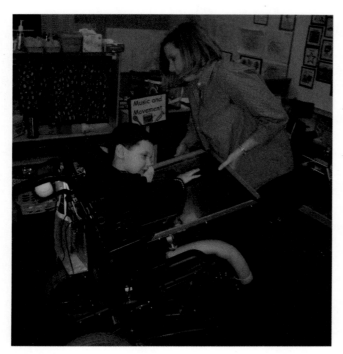

FIGURE 6-7 • The classroom area needs to be arranged to accommodate easy movement of children in wheelchairs.

of children at any center is determined by the amount of materials available, the purpose of the center, physical space considerations, and the need to avoid overstimulating confusion. Signs with stick figures and numbers can indicate the number of children who can use a specific center. For some children with ADD who may wander from center to center, make a photo display of the centers so the child can select from the photos to make an individual schedule of what she plans to do.

- What kinds of centers will provide a workable balance in terms of content? This will depend on the characteristics of the children and staff.
- How free should movement in and out of the centers be? Ideally, children should move at their own paces, guided by the teacher. This allows for more individualization within the program.
- How will children know what to do in each center? Some centers will require more direction than others. You may want to use pictures or symbols for routine directions (hands with a faucet of running water to remind children to wash; aprons on pegs

to facilitate art and cooking cleanup without having to mention it). Be sure your centers have the appropriate equipment for children with special needs. For example, children with physical disabilities may need to use art materials in different ways, such as lying on the floor over a bolster pillow to draw. For children who are auditorily impaired, be sure to provide in your centers many activities that use senses other than hearing. For the child who uses a wheelchair, which places him at a different height than the other children, it may be possible to use a beanbag chair for floor-time activities. For a child who does not have the strength to stand for long periods, a tabletop easel will let the child sit in a chair while painting.

- For elementary students, is there a place for storing ongoing projects? Milk crates or storage containers can be used for this purpose.

Condition and Organization of Materials Within the Activity Center

Activity centers with materials that are in good condition, arranged and placed far apart on open shelves, tell a child that materials are valued and important enough to be well cared for. What kind of message does a child get from crowded, open shelves with a mixture of materials and broken or missing pieces? What kind of message does he or she get from torn books?

The way you plan for and display children's artwork tells children a lot about how much you value their work. Here are some suggestions on how to manage children's artwork in a way that shows children you value their work.

Plan your artwork exhibits so they reflect children's ideas and experiences. Ask children to help select the items to be displayed. They may want to (or have you) write down why this particular work is meaningful to them. For instance, they like the medium, color, or subject.

Make interesting groupings of children's artwork. Feature a specific theme, stress a particular color, or highlight a special medium.

Display artwork outside as well as inside the classroom. Use the hallway and stairwell walls and other flat surfaces, such as doors, for your gallery.

Exhibit artwork in various stages. Include photos of the work in progress for documentation so others can enjoy the process, too.

Place artwork at children's eye level. Label the displays with large, easy-to-read letters and make up simple but catchy titles. Older children can make up these titles as well as cut out or write them out for the display.

Handle work respectfully. Let the children know that you appreciate and value their skills and creativity. Frame or mount their work attractively. (Use backgrounds with contrasting colors and interesting textures, such as burlap or corrugated cardboard.) Encourage the young artists to sign their own names. Be sure not to write on their work without permission. Take dictation on a separate strip of paper. Older children may want to write a short statement to accompany their work.

Showcase work in exciting ways. Instead of stapling work to bulletin boards, hang pictures with clothespins from clotheslines. You can use tree branches to display mobiles. Create a freestanding kiosk with four display sides from a cardboard refrigerator carton. A cardboard, folding, pattern-cutting board can be used to display art on both sides.

Arrange special areas for fragile or three-dimensional work. Supply stable shelves or low tables to display wire and clay sculptures or woodwork. Use cardboard "shadow boxes" for added emphasis and protection.

Provide individual display space. Have each child choose his or her own small area of a bulletin board that has been divided into sections. Let him or her select and change dated samples to document growth.

Organize a space where parents can collect artwork. Designate the top compartment of the child's cubby as the "art shelf" or create an art "mailbox" from a large, partitioned, cardboard beverage carton turned on its side. Use cardboard mailing tubes to send home rolled-up artwork to prevent folding, creases, and tears.

FIGURE 6-8 • Classroom planning for artwork.

Young children work best in a predictable environment where materials are organized and can be found repeatedly in the same place. Organizing materials can help children develop self-help skills and self-control, as well as help them learn to respect materials and use them well. For example, cutouts of tools or other equipment help children learn to identify materials and return them to the proper place. Organizing open storage shelves by labeling them clearly with pictures and words makes it possible for children to find materials they want to work with. When shelves are clearly labeled with few objects on them at a time, putting things back in place becomes an easier task for young children.

Labeling, too, can be done in the block area by cutting out the shapes of the blocks in colored Con-Tact® paper and pasting them on the back and shelves. Clear

THIS ONE'S for YOU!   Conquering Clutter

Many teachers struggle with the problem of "too much stuff." It's all stuff they need, but often when it's time to use it, it's hard to find. Here are some suggestions on how to conquer some basic clutter problems to help you be a bit more organized in your classroom.

Clutter Problem #1: Your Classroom is a Mess!

The colorful classroom you left in June seems like a disorganized disaster area in August. Your art center is overflowing with tissue paper from last year's projects, you can't see the wall underneath all your posters and charts, and your book area looks like a yard sale.

Solution: Start small. Choose just one space at a time to organize, such as your art center or language arts center. Close your eyes and visualize what that space might look like without clutter and how that would make your feel.

Next, look at what's *already* working. If you've been successful organizing one particular area, think about how you can apply that process in another area. For example, does your clothespin attendance system work well? Maybe you can use that same system to keep track of what group children are in or what centers they are using.

Clutter Problem #2: You Keep Everything.

Your egg carton collection is about to take over your supply closet. It's difficult to toss out something your students might need or anything special from a student you once taught.

Solution: Use the "moving test." Pretend that you are moving classrooms. Ask yourself, "Is this item worth the effort of packing it up and unpacking it at a new place?" If not, give it a new home. Another teacher's classroom might be just the place.

If you're saving something because you *might* need it someday, ask yourself, "Could I get another one easily and inexpensively if I needed it?" If the answer is yes, let it go. When it comes to sentimental items, like homemade holiday decorations, take photos, store them in an album, and then part with the original.

Clutter Problem #3: You stocked up on materials over the summer.

You love the new watercolor sets you got at a bargain price, but in between your pastels and paint, there's just no room for them in your art center. You have nowhere to put your new treasures.

Solution: Think, "Take one in, take one out." For every item you bring in the front door, send one out the back door. Chances are you have some dried-out markers taking up space. Classrooms are small spaces that often can't accommodate years of bargain hunting.

Clutter Problem #4: The Children!

After the first few days of school, the organizational systems you so lovingly created are in chaos—there are blocks in the reading area, picture books in the math area, pencils in with the markers, and paper just about everywhere. Your students need a wake-up call to their responsibility for helping to keep the classroom organized and clean.

Solution: Play Clutter Tag

Give a sheet of stickers to each child and ask them to place one on any item that's out of place. Making them aware of their clutter trails helps make them think twice about leaving things around.

FIGURE 6-9 • The age and developmental levels of the children in the group dictate the type of equipment that should be available for children's use.

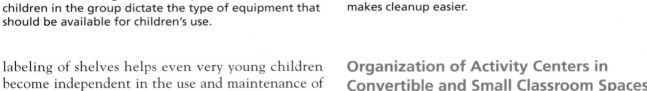

FIGURE 6-10 • Placement of the art center near a sink makes cleanup easier.

labeling of shelves helps even very young children become independent in the use and maintenance of their environment.

- For children who are visually impaired, cut out tactile shapes and attach them to shelves to assist them in finding and replacing blocks in the manipulative area. One of the challenges for the visually impaired student is maneuvering the materials. Work trays are one way for keeping track of art materials and managing and keeping materials accessible. Nonskid rubberized shelf liner is handy for keeping items from slipping away. It will also help prevent spills. A cafeteria tray with rubber shelf liner attached to the bottom provides a controllable boundary for the student's materials. For Braille readers, labels may be helpful. Ask the student what she or he prefers.
- Teachers, too, need to think about how they manage their own supplies and equipment. See "This One's for You! Conquering Clutter" for tips on this classroom issue.

Organization of Activity Centers in Convertible and Small Classroom Spaces

Many early childhood programs operate in multipurpose facilities. In family childcare homes, childcare centers in churches, and public school childcare programs, equipment must be packed up for storage after school or over the weekend. If materials are packed up and stored frequently, movable shelves that are ready for use as soon as they are rolled into place and unlocked are helpful. If shelves are not available for material storage, tables or boxes may be used. Whatever the arrangement, children should understand the system for selecting toys and replacing them in the right containers. Visual cues, such as putting red oilcloth on the storage tables and white oilcloth on the play tables, help children remember the organizational principles and keep the environment functional.

Convertible or multipurpose spaces as well as small classrooms will have to make use of portable storage. Portable storage such as a wagon, suitcase, backpack, or duffel bag can be useful. The makings of an activity can be contained in such a transportable container—a reading or writing suitcase, a block cart, a make-believe prop bag (picnic with dolls at the beach, towels), or a science backpack. The storage "vehicle" could also contain a rug, or sheet, or rope for defining the boundary of the activity. The children would use the props and other items in the box as a mini-center of sorts. The teacher would integrate the center into the program by using the questions, books, reminder cards, and other activities prepared as part of the instructional plans for that particular activity.

In small classrooms, you can double up your storage space by removing the back of shelving units so they then can serve two uses, one from either side. Also, in limited space, small shelf units and units on castors provide storage that is easily portable and allows a program to continually expand and contract spaces as the need arises.

Portable in another sense is storage that can be raised or lowered from the ceiling. Using pulleys or nets, a program can develop space to store projects. Hanging baskets and shelf units may also work for particular kinds of storage. Add-on storage may also be useful in a small space, such as under-the-shelf racks and cabinet hooks attached to shelf units. Further suggestions for dealing with small spaces can be found in the websites at the end of this chapter.

Activity boxes can be used outdoors or indoors, either in response to requests by the children or as part of the teacher-prepared activities. Activity boxes can be made up with all the materials needed for science experiences, such as a sink–float game or a cooking activity. Various objects commonly found in an early childhood center environment, such as blocks and beads, can be organized into sorting, matching, or seriation games and kept in separate boxes.

Selection of Equipment for Creative Activities

The kinds of equipment available to young children can either promote or discourage creative expression. If equipment is to encourage creative activities, it should have certain characteristics.

Characteristics of Appropriate Equipment

Simple in design. Too much detail destroys children's freedom to express themselves. Crayons, blocks, clay, sand, paints, and even empty cardboard boxes are examples of simple but useful equipment for young children.

Versatile. Equipment should be usable by both girls and boys at their developmental level for many kinds of activities.

Stimulating. Equipment should be the kind that allows children to do things and that motivates them. If adults must supervise children every minute that they are using the equipment, this may hinder creativity. Long explanations on how to use the equipment should not be necessary.

Large and easy to use. Because of the growth of muscles during this time, very small equipment can cause young children to become anxious. Big trucks and wagons are just right. Large, hollow blocks are better than small, solid ones.

Durable. Breakable equipment is soon broken by two- to five-year-old children. Equipment made of hard wood such as maple is less likely to splinter than equipment made of soft wood such as pine. Rubber-wheeled riding toys are preferred to those with wooden wheels.

For older children as well, durability of equipment is important. For example, a higher-quality brayer will last far longer through vigorous printing use by this age group.

In proper working order. Nothing impedes creativity more than things that don't work. Do a daily quick checkup on equipment to see that it's in good working order. Older students can help with this inventory and write down a to-do list of specific repairs needed. Even better, select materials that are the best quality you can afford. It's cheaper in the long run.

Available in proper amounts. Too many toys or too much equipment can decrease the effectiveness of those materials. Too many blocks can overwhelm a child and he or she may never start to build. Equally frustrating is too few blocks to complete a creation. Work for a balance in amount of equipment.

Designed to encourage children to play together. Many pieces of equipment are designed for one child to use alone. However, children need to work together and find out what others are thinking and doing. Therefore, equipment designed to get children together should also be provided.

Safe. Safety is a key consideration in selecting equipment for young children. Among the safety factors to

Word Smart
Reference books
Glue
Encyclopedias
Scissors
Computer
Desktop publishing
  software
Bulletin board
Thesaurus
Dictionary
Letter stencils
Sentence strips
Variety of paper
Newspapers
Notebooks
Magazines
Bookmaking materials
Student-made books
Writing utensils
Books on tape
Logic Smart
Pattern blocks
Protractors
Unifix cubes
Balance scales
Tape measures
Puzzles
Rulers

Strategy games
Construction sets
Objects to serve as
  counters
Dice
Cuisenaire rods
Collections for sorting/
  classifying
Science equipment
Picture Smart
Markers
Art prints
Crayons
Video equipment
Collage materials
Videotapes
Pastels
Charts
Graphic software
Colored pencils
Computer
Stencils
Puzzles
Rubber stamps
Graphs
Drafting supplies
Posters
Architectural supplies
Paints

Clay
Variety of drawing paper
Lego® sets
Music Smart
iPod
Tape recorder
Recording equipment
Headphones
Musical software
Tapes/CDs
Keyboard with headphone
Homemade instruments
Books on musicians and
  music
Instruments
Self Smart
Private, quiet place
Personal collections
Journals
Bulletin board/small
  chalkboard
Writing materials
Posters/pictures of
  individuals strong in
  this intelligence
Stories, books, and
  articles dealing with
  character development
Self-checking materials

Independent projects
Body Smart
Costumes
Puzzles
Miscellaneous props
Sand
Hats and scarves
Craft supplies
Construction sets
Tools
Stacking blocks
Building materials
Puppets
Sports books and magazines
Tactile learning materials
Scissors
Person Smart
Large table for students
  to sit around
Group games and puzzles
Autobiography and
  biography books
Conflict resolution
  materials and posters
Tutoring activities
Group projects
Board games
Comfortable chairs/rugs
Writing paper

FIGURE 6-13 • Materials for multiple intelligences—grades 1 to 5.

THIS ONE'S for YOU! Take Your Cue from Colors: Using Color Coding in Activity Centers

A tried-and-true method for helping children function independently and successfully with activity centers is the systematic use of colors and symbols. Children can quickly learn a color-coding system even if they do not yet know how to read. Colors and symbols can be used to identity activity centers, to manage children's movement in and out of centers, and to let children independently find and replace assigned materials.

Special symbol and color codes help children identify and locate each center. The symbol identifies what is learned in the center. The color code helps children easily locate the center in the classroom. For example, the art center's symbol might be a paintbrush, and its color code might be red. A card would be hung at the entrance to each center with its corresponding symbol and color code.

To manage traffic in and out of the centers, the card at the center's entrance would also indicate the number of children allowed in the center at one time. It could be a number of stick people or the actual numeral, depending on the children's knowledge of written numbers. That corresponding number of color-coded clothespins would be attached to the bottom of the card. For example, the art center might allow 10 children and thus have 10 red clothespins. The clothespins are children's "tickets" to the centers. Children must pin on the clothespin when they enter the center, wear it while using the center, and replace it on the card when they leave. When no clothespins are on the card, the center is full, and children must choose another activity until a clothespin is available.

can be contained in such a transportable container—a reading or writing suitcase, a block cart, a make-believe prop bag (picnic with dolls at the beach, towels), or a science backpack. The storage "vehicle" could also contain a rug, or sheet, or rope for defining the boundary of the activity. The children would use the props and other items in the box as a mini-center of sorts. The teacher would integrate the center into the program by using the questions, books, reminder cards, and other activities prepared as part of the instructional plans for that particular activity.

In small classrooms, you can double up your storage space by removing the back of shelving units so they then can serve two uses, one from either side. Also, in limited space, small shelf units and units on castors provide storage that is easily portable and allows a program to continually expand and contract spaces as the need arises.

Portable in another sense is storage that can be raised or lowered from the ceiling. Using pulleys or nets, a program can develop space to store projects. Hanging baskets and shelf units may also work for particular kinds of storage. Add-on storage may also be useful in a small space, such as under-the-shelf racks and cabinet hooks attached to shelf units. Further suggestions for dealing with small spaces can be found in the websites at the end of this chapter.

Activity boxes can be used outdoors or indoors, either in response to requests by the children or as part of the teacher-prepared activities. Activity boxes can be made up with all the materials needed for science experiences, such as a sink–float game or a cooking activity. Various objects commonly found in an early childhood center environment, such as blocks and beads, can be organized into sorting, matching, or seriation games and kept in separate boxes.

Selection of Equipment for Creative Activities

The kinds of equipment available to young children can either promote or discourage creative expression. If equipment is to encourage creative activities, it should have certain characteristics.

Characteristics of Appropriate Equipment

Simple in design. Too much detail destroys children's freedom to express themselves. Crayons, blocks, clay, sand, paints, and even empty cardboard boxes are examples of simple but useful equipment for young children.

Versatile. Equipment should be usable by both girls and boys at their developmental level for many kinds of activities.

Stimulating. Equipment should be the kind that allows children to do things and that motivates them. If adults must supervise children every minute that they are using the equipment, this may hinder creativity. Long explanations on how to use the equipment should not be necessary.

Large and easy to use. Because of the growth of muscles during this time, very small equipment can cause young children to become anxious. Big trucks and wagons are just right. Large, hollow blocks are better than small, solid ones.

Durable. Breakable equipment is soon broken by two- to five-year-old children. Equipment made of hard wood such as maple is less likely to splinter than equipment made of soft wood such as pine. Rubber-wheeled riding toys are preferred to those with wooden wheels.

For older children as well, durability of equipment is important. For example, a higher-quality brayer will last far longer through vigorous printing use by this age group.

In proper working order. Nothing impedes creativity more than things that don't work. Do a daily quick checkup on equipment to see that it's in good working order. Older students can help with this inventory and write down a to-do list of specific repairs needed. Even better, select materials that are the best quality you can afford. It's cheaper in the long run.

Available in proper amounts. Too many toys or too much equipment can decrease the effectiveness of those materials. Too many blocks can overwhelm a child and he or she may never start to build. Equally frustrating is too few blocks to complete a creation. Work for a balance in amount of equipment.

Designed to encourage children to play together. Many pieces of equipment are designed for one child to use alone. However, children need to work together and find out what others are thinking and doing. Therefore, equipment designed to get children together should also be provided.

Safe. Safety is a key consideration in selecting equipment for young children. Among the safety factors to

THINK ABOUT IT

Hints for a Smoother Daily Program

If you, like most teachers, are always looking for ways to improve the daily operation of your program, you may want to think about using some of the following general hints.

- Store small books easily and neatly in plastic napkin holders. These can be found at discount stores and even at garage sales.

- When odd parts of toys and games turn up around the room during the day, forget trying to return them to their proper place each time they are found. Instead, make a special container just for toy and game parts. A zipper-type plastic bag works well for this purpose. Not only will this save time during the day, but you will also always know where to look if a part is missing.

- To preserve posters, pictures, and other items you want to last from year to year, cover them with clear Con-Tact® paper. The items will be easier for children to handle, and dirt and finger marks can be wiped off easily.

- Spray new puzzles and gameboards with clear varnish (outdoors and away from the children, of course). You'll find they last much longer.

- Empty food boxes used in the housekeeping corner and for other learning games will be sturdier if you stuff them with newspaper and then tape them shut. Be sure to brush all crumbs out first.

- When sanitizing furniture and fixtures with bleach and water, put the mixture into an empty spray bottle that has been thoroughly washed and dried. The spray bottle is easy to use, and it will protect your hands from the harsh bleach.

- Instead of using tape to hang paper shapes on a wall with a hard finish, try sticking them on with dabs of toothpaste. The toothpaste can be washed off the wall when you change decorations.

- When a child paints a picture that you want to display on a wall, attach the paper to the tabletop with masking tape. The tape keeps the paper from sliding during painting, and when the child has finished, you can unpeel the ends of the tape from the table and use them to retape the painting to the wall.

---

consider are whether the equipment is developmentally appropriate (for instance, you would not select for 18-month-olds toys that are small enough to be swallowed easily), whether nontoxic and nonflammable materials were used in the manufacture of the equipment, whether the materials have any sharp edges or rough areas that could cause injury, and whether the physical environment allows for the safe use of the equipment. (Appendix F provides more complete information on appropriate toys and equipment for early childhood programs.)

Other considerations. In selecting equipment and materials for creative activities, keep these additional considerations in mind.

- Do not choose a material or piece of equipment because it looks "cute" to you. Instead, select each item with some developmental purpose in mind. For example, ask yourself, "What contribution will the item make to the growth of small- or large-motor skills of the children? How will it help a child's intellectual growth? Self-esteem? Will it encourage the growth of social skills?"

- Resist the temptation to buy inexpensive merchandise as a matter of course. Select equipment that is sturdy and durably constructed, because it will get hard use. In the long run, one high-quality, durable item will last longer and be more cost effective over time than an item that is less expensive but poorly constructed.

- Consider each new item of equipment in light of what you already have. Work toward a balanced environment, one with many sources of creative expression: working alone, in pairs, in small or large groups. In addition to equipment for large- and small-motor skills, select items that appeal to the sensorimotor explorations of young children. Equipment should be stimulating to see, interesting to touch, and satisfying to maneuver. This applies to equipment for older children as well.

- Purchase all major equipment in child size rather than doll or toy size. It is also important to have

Word Smart	Puzzles	Video camera	Reference materials
Books	Marbles/beans	Kitchen utensils for	Writing materials
Maps	Geometric shapes	making sound effects	Clay
Magazines	Straws/string/clay	Recordings of nature	Musical instruments
Pipe cleaner letters	Pattern blocks	sounds	Tape recorder
Chalkboard	**Picture Smart**	Toy microphones	**Person Smart**
Dry-erase board	Legos®/blocks	Posters of composers	Art supplies
Rice/sand/shaving cream/	Colored pencils/markers/	Tape recorders/blank	Sports equipment
finger paints	crayons/paint	tapes	Musical instruments
Texture letters	Puppet theater	**Body Smart**	Puppet theatre
Construction paper	Tongue depressors	Audiocassette tapes	Books
Laminator	Glitter	CDs and CD player	Video recorders
Pencils/pens/markers	Manipulatives	Beanbags	Seeds/gardening tools
Overhead projector	Clay	Large-motor equipment	Computer
Letter puzzles	Posters	Dress-up clothes and	Cooking supplies
Logic Smart	Puzzles	other props for	**Nature Smart**
Manipulatives	Sand/water	dramatic play	Terrarium
Counters	**Music Smart**	Manipulatives	Microscope
Abacus	iPod	**Self Smart**	Ant farm
Legos®/blocks	Musical instruments	Books	Seeds
Geo boards	Headphones	Puzzles	Soil
String art	Cassette/record/CD	Art supplies	Bird feeders
Cuisenaire rods	player	Cassettes/cassette players	Bird guides
Blocks	Keyboard	Computer	Gardening tools
Play money	Music books	Microscope	Magnifying glass

FIGURE 6-11 • Materials for multiple intelligences—preschool to kindergarten.

real-life and adult-sized equipment where appropriate. Real hammers and screwdrivers in a smaller adult size (not toy tools) work best in construction projects.

- Consider the total number of children and how many at a given time are to use the equipment. Ten two- or three-year-old children need a basic supply of equipment. Add several more children, and you may need more blocks, more cars and trucks, and so forth. Also consider the age of the children in the group. Because two- and three-year-old children spend much of their time in egocentric (solitary) play or parallel play (playing next to but not with another child), there must be enough blocks, people, animals, cars, and dishes to allow several children to engage in similar play at the same time. Yet another strategy is to have duplicate or very similar copies of favorite items on hand.

FIGURE 6-12 • The sand play area is a place children learn through sensory experiences with sand.

Interest Centers and Multiple Intelligences

As we learned in the previous chapter, young children have many ways of learning. You can incorporate what you've learned about these multiple intelligences by including appropriate materials and equipment in your activity centers that appeal to multiple intelligences. Figure 6–11 presents a list of suggested materials and activities for preschool and kindergarten children. Figure 6–13 has the same information for grades 1 through 5. You don't need to include all of these items in each center, but it is important to have a variety of materials for the multiple intelligences of children in your group.

Word Smart	Strategy games	Clay	Independent projects
Reference books	Construction sets	Variety of drawing paper	**Body Smart**
Glue	Objects to serve as	Lego® sets	Costumes
Encyclopedias	counters	**Music Smart**	Puzzles
Scissors	Dice	iPod	Miscellaneous props
Computer	Cuisenaire rods	Tape recorder	Sand
Desktop publishing	Collections for sorting/	Recording equipment	Hats and scarves
software	classifying	Headphones	Craft supplies
Bulletin board	Science equipment	Musical software	Construction sets
Thesaurus	**Picture Smart**	Tapes/CDs	Tools
Dictionary	Markers	Keyboard with headphone	Stacking blocks
Letter stencils	Art prints	Homemade instruments	Building materials
Sentence strips	Crayons	Books on musicians and	Puppets
Variety of paper	Video equipment	music	Sports books and magazines
Newspapers	Collage materials	Instruments	Tactile learning materials
Notebooks	Videotapes	**Self Smart**	Scissors
Magazines	Pastels	Private, quiet place	**Person Smart**
Bookmaking materials	Charts	Personal collections	Large table for students
Student-made books	Graphic software	Journals	to sit around
Writing utensils	Colored pencils	Bulletin board/small	Group games and puzzles
Books on tape	Computer	chalkboard	Autobiography and
Logic Smart	Stencils	Writing materials	biography books
Pattern blocks	Puzzles	Posters/pictures of	Conflict resolution
Protractors	Rubber stamps	individuals strong in	materials and posters
Unifix cubes	Graphs	this intelligence	Tutoring activities
Balance scales	Drafting supplies	Stories, books, and	Group projects
Tape measures	Posters	articles dealing with	Board games
Puzzles	Architectural supplies	character development	Comfortable chairs/rugs
Rulers	Paints	Self-checking materials	Writing paper

FIGURE 6-13 • Materials for multiple intelligences—grades 1 to 5.

THIS ONE'S for YOU! Take Your Cue from Colors: Using Color Coding in Activity Centers

A tried-and-true method for helping children function independently and successfully with activity centers is the systematic use of colors and symbols. Children can quickly learn a color-coding system even if they do not yet know how to read. Colors and symbols can be used to identity activity centers, to manage children's movement in and out of centers, and to let children independently find and replace assigned materials.

Special symbol and color codes help children identify and locate each center. The symbol identifies what is learned in the center. The color code helps children easily locate the center in the classroom. For example, the art center's symbol might be a paintbrush, and its color code might be red. A card would be hung at the entrance to each center with its corresponding symbol and color code.

To manage traffic in and out of the centers, the card at the center's entrance would also indicate the number of children allowed in the center at one time. It could be a number of stick people or the actual numeral, depending on the children's knowledge of written numbers. That corresponding number of color-coded clothespins would be attached to the bottom of the card. For example, the art center might allow 10 children and thus have 10 red clothespins. The clothespins are children's "tickets" to the centers. Children must pin on the clothespin when they enter the center, wear it while using the center, and replace it on the card when they leave. When no clothespins are on the card, the center is full, and children must choose another activity until a clothespin is available.

Summary

To ensure the proper environment for creative expression in young children, careful attention must be given to safety, amount and organization of space, light, sound, and furniture. Planning the environment in the early childhood program involves knowledge of children's needs, as well as attention to traffic flow in the room, children's developing skills, and safety. Arrangement of personal space for each child also needs to be planned.

A balance between teacher planning and children's self-direction is necessary. Interest or activity centers help children make their own choices. The placement and organization of the various activity centers have an impact on how creative materials within them are used by children, how safe the environment is, and how children's self-help skills are encouraged.

Because creative activities are so important in promoting children's development, careful attention must be directed toward the selection and care of creative materials and equipment. The best equipment is simple in design, versatile, easy to use, large, durable, working properly, available in needed amounts, designed for group play, and, above all, safe.

It is also important that equipment be stored properly so that children can reach it easily, thereby developing their self-help skills. Materials that appeal to the multiple intelligences should also be included in activity centers.

Key Terms

Activity centers 129
interest centers 119
personal space 118
traffic flow 118

Learning Activities

A. Choose one activity center from the list provided in this chapter. Design your own unique version of this activity center. Describe it in detail. List the items and activities it would include.

B. Draw an ideal room plan for creative activities. Imagine you have all the money, materials, and space necessary. Be creative. After drawing it, list what you feel is important in it, starting with the most important feature. Share this list with classmates and discuss it.

C. Using small blocks or any other similar object, show how you would arrange space in a room to ensure smooth traffic flow and noninterference among interest centers in the room.

D. Go through a school supply catalog. Find examples of furniture, shelving, and play objects that you would include in planning your ideal room in the activity preceding. Explain your choices in a developmental context.

E. Obtain a toy and equipment catalog or go to a toy store. Make a list of materials that would be useful for children's play. Imagine that you have $1,250 to spend on some additional equipment for your classroom. Make a list of items you would purchase. Assume you may not go over the $1,250 limit.

F. **Classroom Activities**

Natural Objects and Random "Calling On."
To make calling on students truly random, gather

enough any flat, smooth rocks like river rocks so that you have one for each child. Paint the children's names on them. Put them in a basket and use them for calling on children. At year's end, children take them home as a tangible reminder of their time in your classroom.

Foamy Cleanup. To help students really get into keeping their desks squeaky clean, try using shaving cream as an incentive. Spray each desk with a generous amount of shaving cream on the desktop. Then, let the children use their fingers to practice letters, numbers, their names, and so on before you wipe it away. Children will love it and it really does get the desks squeaky clean.

Bulletin Board Idea. Try using felt and fabric for your bulletin board backgrounds. Fabric doesn't fade as much as bulletin board paper and staple holes are barely noticeable. You can fold up the fabric to use again next year. Or you can change fabric backing in the middle of the year to perk up your room.

Sticky Words. To prevent word cards from landing on the floor, make them "sticky words." In a well-ventilated area, spray a light coat of spray adhesive (the kind used to mount photos, available in craft stores) on construction paper, following directions on the can to make a nonpermanent bond. Word cards can easily be repositioned on this sticky paper but won't get knocked out of place if the desk gets bumped accidentally. Also, the cards stand out on the colored construction paper background, helping children with AD/HD better focus on them. Store sheets of sticky paper in pairs with sticky sides together and then just peel them apart to use. When the paper starts losing its stick, simply respray with adhesive.

"Don't Interrupt" Reminder. If you don't want students interrupting small group or individual student conference time on a daily basis in your classroom, try this idea. To help students remember not to interrupt, wear a headband with decorative animal ears or antennae. Or if you prefer, you can wear any type of hat that you choose. This headwear serves as a visual reminder that you are busy listening to the person or group in front of you.

Help is on the way! When you are busy with a small group or an individual child, students are not expected to sit alone at their desks for an extended time pondering an assignment they do not understand. Have three students who finish their work quickly and accurately be "student helpers."

Have the helpers wear plastic visors or any special headwear. This way they are readily visible as the designated helpers. The visors also allow you to tell at a glance if the people talking and out of their seats are helpers or if they are students who are not following class rules.

Reading with Cell Phones? Students are often asked to read material silently at various times during the day. Yet some students don't comprehend what they read when they read silently. To allow for student learning differences, try using "cell phones" in your classroom. This doesn't mean that children bring cell phones from home and call their friends and families for reading help! Instead, make "cell phones" from PVC elbows. Two 90-degree PVC elbows connected to one another are just the right size for a "cell phone" for students to read into. They can read quietly into the mouthpiece of the "cell phone" and are able to hear their voices amplified in their ears. The classroom is a soft hum of students reading at their own pace and comprehending what they are reading. This is also an excellent tool for students to use to read their own writing.

Chapter Review

1. List 10 factors to consider in creating a positive physical environment for young children.
2. Discuss the considerations and requirements involved in setting up activity centers, including convertible centers.
3. List the major considerations involved in arranging space in the early childhood setting.
4. List five interest centers that early childhood experts recommend be available for the creative expression of young children. Describe what skills are developed in each.

5. Name at least five important factors to weigh when selecting proper equipment for young children's creative activities.
6. Discuss some safety precautions to consider in choosing equipment.
7. Discuss some ways to adapt the environment for children with special needs.
8. List types of materials that appeal to each of the multiple intelligences.

References

Kostelnik, M. J. & Grady, M. L. (2009). *Getting it right from the start: The Principal's Guide to Early Childhood Education.* Los Angeles, CA: SAGE/Corwin Press.

Additional Readings

Deiner, P. (2009). *Inclusive early childhood education: Development, resources, and practices.* Clifton Park, NY: Delmar Cengage Learning.

DiCarlo, C. F. (2009). Using child preferences to increase play across interest centers in inclusive early childhood classrooms. *Young Exceptional Children, 12*(4), 31–39.

Gartrell, D. (2006). *Guidance approach for the encouraging classroom.* Clifton Park, NY: Delmar Cengage Learning.

Hunter, D. (2008). What happens when a child plays at the sensory table? *Young Children, 63*(6), 77–79.

Karlen, M. (2009). *Space Planning Basics* (3rd ed.). New York, NY: John Wiley & Sons.

Kriete, R., & Bechtel, L. (2006). *The morning meeting book.* Turners Falls, MA: Northeast Foundation for Children.

Lipton, L., & Hubble, D. S. (2008). *More than 100 ways to learner-centered literacy.* Thousand Oaks, CA: SAGE.

McCombs, B. L., & Miller, L. (2006). *Learner-centered classroom practices and assessments.* Thousand Oaks, CA: SAGE.

Miles, L. R. (2009). The general store: Reflections on children at play. *Young Children, 64*(4), 36–41.

Miller, D. (2009). *Teaching with intention: Defining beliefs, aligning practice, taking action, K–5.* Washington, DC: NAEYC.

Helpful Websites

Children and Adults with Attention-Deficit Hyperactivity Disorder (CHADD), http://www.chadd.org

National Child Care Information Center Online Library, http://nccic.org

National Association for the Education of Young Children, http://www.naeyc.org

Scholastic Magazine, http://www.teacher.scholastic.com/

The ERIC Clearinghouse on Disabilities and Gifted Education, http://www.eric.ed.gov

The National Resource Center on AD/HD, http://www.help4adhd.org

The National Clearinghouse for English Language Acquisition and Language Instruction Educational Programs (NCELA), http://www.ncela.gwu.edu

The Center for Research on Education, Diversity & Excellence (CREDE), http://www.cal.org/crede

The Center for Applied Linguistics, http://www.cal.org/twi

The Northwest Regional Educational Laboratory (NWREL), http://www.nwrel.org

Room Design Websites

Classroom Design: Layout: The Art and Creative Materials Institute, http://www.emints.org/ethemes/resources/S00001368.shtml

Design Your Own Classroom, http://www.atschool.org/materials/classroom/buildaclass

Sample Classroom Floor Plans, http://www.learnnc.org/lp/pages/742

Outline Your Floor Plan, Classroom Architect, http://classroom.4teachers.org

Classroom Organization Websites

Organization Tips from Veteran Teachers, http://www.teachervision.fen.com

10 Tips for Classroom Discipline, http://www.back-toschool.about.com/od/

For additional creative activity resources, visit our website at www.Cengage.com/login

Play, Development, and Creativity

OBJECTIVES

After studying this chapter, you should be able to:

1. Name and discuss the four kinds of human growth that are influenced by play.

2. Define onlooker, solitary, parallel, associative, and cooperative play.

3. Discuss ways the environment can be adapted to encourage social play experiences for children with special needs.

4. Discuss some reasons children engage in violent play and how to deal with this type of play.

Some children are busily involved in activities in an early childhood program. One group of children is removing the wheels from the wooden trucks in the room. Now they are having races by pushing the wheelless trucks along the floor. One child notes the scraping sound being made, while another discovers that the trucks without wheels make marks on the floor.

One child is preparing a tea party for three friends. The child has baked an imaginary cake and has just finished putting on icing. Now the table is being set and the chairs arranged. Another group of children is carefully observing several small furry animals on the other side of the room.

Are these children working? Are they playing? Is there a difference between work and play for a young child? Must children be involved in games to be playing? Must toys be involved? Is play natural, or can children be taught to play?

The answers to these questions are important. They help define the meaning of the word *play*. The answers lead to an understanding of how children benefit from creative play. They give direction for the purchase and placement of creative materials that guide children's play. They help adults plan activities that help children grow through creative play.

What Is Play?

For adults, play is what they do when they have finished their work. It is a form of relaxation. For young children, play is what they do all day. Playing is living, and living is playing.

Young children do not differentiate between play, learning, and work. Children are by nature playful. They enjoy playing and will do so whenever they can. Challenges intrigue them. Why do children love to play? Because play is intrinsically motivated—that is, no one else tells them what to do or how to do it.

FIGURE 7-1 • Play is essential in the lives of young children.

An activity ceases to be play, and children's interest dwindles, if adults structure or even interfere inappropriately with play.

For older children, learning may be work. When they complete their work, then they can play. For young children, mental development results from their play. Growth of their ability to deal with the problems of life—social development—results from play. Growth of their imaginations results from play. Muscles develop in play, as well.

Play is an activity. It does not necessarily result in a product. It may involve one child or groups of children. It may be built around toys and tools or may involve nothing more than the child's imagination. A play period may last a few minutes or go on for days.

Types of Play

There are different kinds of play, different stages of play, and different purposes underlying play. The play of preschool children is different from the play of toddlers, which is different from the play of school-age children.

Generally, children under the age of three engage in exploratory play. Their objective is to explore the world through physical actions, to experiment with their movements, and discover what they can do. They poke, dump, taste, stroke, and pull whatever they encounter in order to learn about their world. From three to seven years of age, however, children's actions become more "play" than exploration, and efforts to know and understand become more important than sensory experiences. Play can also be either **free** (or **spontaneous**) play or **organized play**. In either type, children may work alone or in a group. Each type may involve materials and equipment, or it may not. Basically, free play, as its name suggests, is flexible. It is unplanned by adults. It is a self-selected, open exercise. The following scene depicts free play.

> Two teachers I know regularly take their classes to a park where there is no equipment. At first the children were disoriented, thinking there was nothing to do. The adults purposely got busy preparing food, and in time the children began to lead each other into forays of discovery. They climbed trees and fences and hills; hid from each other in the bushes; chased each other; and collected sticks and discovered pinecones, pebbles, feathers, and wonders of all sorts. They brought treasured items back and came for help when others got stuck in hard-to-get-out-of places. The adults limited them to a large, but visible, area. This was excellent teaching—nonintervention to let children find their own fun.

Organized play is also open and flexible. However, some structure is provided in terms of materials and equipment.

Teachers can promote organized play by providing representational toys and dress-up clothes. Representational toys are toys that strongly resemble real objects, such as dolls, toy vehicles, dishes, cooking utensils, stoves, telephones, and doctor kits. Dress-up clothes can include handbags, lunch boxes, briefcases, hats of various kinds, and jewelry. These representational toys prompt children to pretend to engage in the activities of others, to do the things they see adults do. (See Professional Enhancement Text section on

FIGURE 7-2 • Children are by nature playful.

FIGURE 7-3 • Outdoor play is essential for young children.

Play Materials for Children.) This is often called "dramatic" play, as children act out the roles of grownups in their lives. (More specific information about dramatic play is provided in Chapter 15.) They pretend to feed the baby, drive to work, cook dinner, talk on the telephone, and so forth. Props relevant to children's culture and community can enrich their efforts to construct and express their understanding of significant events and people in their lives.

Theories of Play

Early childhood researchers have developed a number of theories of play over the years. Parten, one of the early researchers, developed the notion of the sequence of play (Parten, 1932). According to Parten, there is a general sequential order of play activities that may be observed in young children. These types of play activities may be classified according to stages.

The earliest stage of play is **onlooker behavior** in which the child plays passively by watching or conversing with other children engaged in play activities. Also in early toddlerhood, a child at first generally plays alone. This stage is termed **solitary play**. Using all of their senses, children explore long before they use any objects in their play. They touch, smell, see, and listen. Manipulating and handling materials are important parts of play experiences. In these early play experiences, children are more involved with the manipulation of materials than they are with the uses of them. Gradually, as the toddler's social realm expands, he or she will engage in **parallel play**. Parallel play occurs when a child plays side by side with other children with some interaction, but without direct involvement.

As the number of relationships outside the home increases, the child's ability to play with other children develops further. At this point, the child may engage in **associative play**. This type of play may take the form of the child's merely being present in a group. For example, a child who participates in fingerplays during circle time or group time would be said to be engaging in associative play. Common activities occur between children. They may exchange toys and/or follow one another. Although all the children in the group are doing similar activities, specific roles are not defined, and there is no organized goal (such as building something or pretending to have a tea party). Eventually, as they grow more comfortable with their social ties, young children will begin to talk about, plan, and carry out play activities with other children. This type of play, marked by mutual involvement in a play activity, is called **cooperative play**. Children cooperate with others to construct something or act out coordinated roles.

Smilansky (1968) another researcher of play, investigated how dramatic play helps children develop socially. Generally, preschoolers' play becomes more social as they get older. Smilansky (1968) found that by engaging in socio-dramatic play (dramatic play that involves more than one player), their social skills were enhanced. She also found that participation in socio-dramatic play requires a high level of social ability, including cooperation, negotiation, sharing, problem-solving, self-regulation, and appreciation of another's play efforts. The amount and complexity of fantasy play have been found to be predictors of social skills, popularity, and positive social activity (Smilansky & Shefalya, 1990).

Importance of Play in Child Development

Children learn best in an environment that allows them to explore, discover, and play. Play is an important part of a developmentally appropriate child care program. It is also closely tied to the child's physical, mental, emotional, and social growth.

Physical Growth

Play contributes to muscle development in many ways. Throwing a ball or lifting objects helps children's muscles develop. Placing an object on top of another and grasping tools also add to a child's muscle development and hand–eye coordination. Play that requires children to look for objects, feel textures, smell various odors, hear sounds, and taste substances helps them develop their senses.

Children spend hours perfecting such abilities in play and increasing the level of difficulty to make the task ever more challenging. Anyone who has lived or worked with infants will recall the tireless way they pursue the acquisition of basic skills. Babies will repeatedly enjoy peek-a-boo long after the adult is ready to stop the game. Toddlers' falling and getting up time and time again is another example of this persistence. (For more specific examples of play for infants and toddlers, see Figure 7–4.) In older children, this repetitious physical activity is also a major characteristic of play. It is evident on playgrounds, where we see children swinging, climbing, or playing ball with fervor.

As a child gains control of her or his body, self-concept is enhanced. When a child runs, she or he feels exhilarated. When a child uses the last bit of strength to accomplish a goal, she or he gains a better sense of self. As the child discovers her or his own strength, she or he develops feelings of competency and worth. A young child is quite physical in play, playing with her or his whole being. As the child plays, she or he decides what to do and how to do it, does her or his own planning, and implements those plans in her or his own ways.

When children have a chance to be physically active, they continually gain strength. As they become more adept, they become more adventurous and learn to take reasonable risks to test their strength. When children set their own challenges, they are less likely to have accidents. Without predetermined goals, they can pace themselves and discover what they can and cannot do.

A youngster in the middle childhood years (five to eight years of age) develops physically in his or her play. At the beginning of this period of growth, the child is almost continuously active, whether standing or sitting. Toward the end of this period, however, movements of the eight-year-old child have become fluid and graceful. He or she has developed poise. In fact, he or she is continually on the go—jumping, running, chasing, or wrestling. There is an increase of speed and smoothness in fine-motor movements. The child approaches objects rapidly and smoothly, and releases them with sure abandon. Organized games with rules to follow are beginning to be popular with this age group.

During the later childhood years (in grades 4 to 5), the need for vigorous play is still important for children. A glance at children of this age group reveals one factor that stands out above all others: Children of this age vary widely. The children in the group may be about the same age, even in the same grade, but

When infants and toddlers are not sleeping, they are engaged in play and exploration, two important avenues to building understanding of their world. The following are ages and characteristics of play at each age.

Birth to 4 Months

Babies explore their new world with their eyes and ears. Some ways to play with a baby of this age are to:

Provide bright, moving objects for babies to practice focusing on.

Move your face and objects close to and away from babies. This helps the baby judge the relationship between objects and between themselves and objects.

Provide babies different views by holding them in various places, such as in your lap or on your shoulder.

Let the baby see herself in a mirror.

Talk to babies in playful ways. Smile and repeat soft sounds. Stop between sounds and watch for them to smile or move in response to your voice. If you get a playful response, repeat the sounds.

Sing to the baby. Make up songs for the baby. Dance with the baby on your shoulder.

Play with the baby's hands and feet, gently patting and rubbing.

Four to 8 Months

At this stage, infants can now also use their hands and mouths to explore their world. Some ways to play at this age are:

Choose toys that move or make sounds in response to the baby's actions. Best choices are toys that turn, honk, rattle, pop up, or play music when the baby pushes, punches, hits, or pokes them.

Check all toys for safety. Be sure toys are small enough for baby's hands to hold, but not small enough to fit entirely in the mouth.

Buy washable toys and toys made of tough, durable material. Check all toys for sharp edges or points and for small parts that could fall off.

Watch but don't interrupt when the baby is exploring new objects. Keep other children (especially older children) from interrupting play.

Entertain the baby with playing This Little Piggy Went to Market.

Sing songs to the baby when diapering, changing clothes, etc.

8 to 12 Months

By this age, babies are now fully active in exploring their world. Almost all babies crawl and creep, many walk around the room holding onto furniture, and some are already walking on their own. Babies at this age are able to drop, throw, pull, and squeeze objects. Some suggestions for play at this age are:

Provide toys that challenge the baby's skills of pulling, pushing, poking, and punching.

Provide objects to put in and dump out of containers. Some suggestions are plastic bowls, plastic storage boxes, baskets, and shoe boxes. Be sure that items to put in are small enough to fit in the containers, but too big to fit in the child's mouth. Some good items to put in containers are plastic lids, yarn balls, blocks, and rings from stack-a-ring toys.

Read to the baby.

Play pat-a-cake, peek-a-boo, and copy cat with the baby.

Play So Big with the baby. Stretch the baby's arms gently over her head, asking, "How big is baby? Soooo big!" After a while, baby will hold her arms up by herself to respond to this question.

Babies of this age enjoy the sensory feeling of moving through space in such activities as riding piggyback, swinging in a child seat, riding in a wagon or a stroller, and dancing in an adult's arms. They also enjoy bouncing on an adult's knee to the accompaniment of a song or verse.

12 to 18 Months

Children at this stage are great experimenters, trying out things to see what happens. The first pretend play occurs in this group when infants begin to act as if they are doing daily activities. They pretend to sleep, eat, or wash.

FIGURE 7-4 • Infant and toddler play.

(Continues)

Some suggestions for play are:

Provide safe places (indoors and outdoors) for walking, moving, and climbing.

Provide opportunities for going in and out, through, and under objects such as tunnels, cabinets, tables, and so forth.

Provide lifelike toys for daily activities such as cleaning, eating, bathing, and riding.

Read to the toddler, talking about the book as you go.

Participate with the child in pretend activities. Let the child "pour" you a glass of milk, and say, "Mmmm, it's delicious." Allow the child to comb your hair or pretend to wash your face. Then, extend the play to a doll and continue the actions and language.

Encourage language development by talking about play as it happens. "The baby is asleep." Or "I'm going to have such neat hair after you comb it."

Collect simple pictures of familiar items for the child to practice naming (Sluss, 2005).

FIGURE 7-4 • Infant and toddler play. *(Continued)*

there the similarities end. They vary widely in their sizes, interests, activities, and abilities, and these differences, in turn, influence every aspect of their development. The child, other children, parents, and teachers should realize that these differences are quite normal.

FIGURE 7-5 • Play is possible with technology, too!

This age group has good muscular control, has a general increase in strength, is particularly sturdy, is keenly interested in sports, and acquires the skills for games readily. Watching these children at play, one often wonders if they ever get tired. They have a lot of stamina. Arms grow longer and hands and feet grow bigger. Some children at this stage are clumsy and awkward as a result of the uneven growth of the different body parts.

Children who are eight to 12 years old select increasingly demanding physical play, which gives them a greater opportunity to develop muscle control and coordination. At this age, boundless amounts of energy and enthusiasm are hallmarks of their play. Children in this group enjoy running, tumbling, climbing on jungle gyms, and swinging. As they grow in motor skills and confidence, they begin more advanced forms of play such as roller skating, skipping rope, skateboarding, and throwing and catching. Children's increased physical abilities and improved coordination also allow participation in team sports and other organized activities in which one's physical ability affects the outcome of the game. (See the Professional Enhancement Text for physical developmental milestones by age and skills as well as lists of appropriate toys for age groups.)

Mental Growth

Play helps children develop important mental concepts. Through play activities, a child learns the meaning of such concepts as "up" and "down," "hard" and "soft," and "big" and "small." Play contributes to

THINK ABOUT IT   Traditional Childhood Games: Are They Developmentally Appropriate?

Do you remember how it felt when you were eliminated from musical chairs? It probably didn't feel good being a "loser." Children know that, to avoid being labeled a "loser," they must do whatever it takes to win. And what teacher hasn't seen this lead to children pushing, poking, and shoving while playing this game?

Games, like any other early childhood activity, are opportunities to promote children's development in one or more of the cognitive, social, emotional, and physical areas. When we select games, we need to be sure they are developmentally appropriate, just as we do when planning an activity for the rest of the curriculum (Pica, 2009).

In planning games for young children, ask yourself, "What will the children learn from the game—self-confidence, problem solving, cooperation, trust, and improved motor skills? Or rejection, competition, failure, and humiliation?" (Staley & Portman, 2000, p. 67).

Neil Williams created the Physical Education Hall of Shame, a list of children's games he considers inappropriate for physical education programs. In this list he includes dodgeball, Musical Chairs, and Red Rover (find the full list at www.auburn.edu/~brocksj/4360hastietext/hallofshame1994.pdf). These games are developmentally inappropriate because they tend (1) not to foster children's development; (2) to embarrass children in front of their classmates; (3) to focus on eliminating children, and thus, (4) to afford players limited participation time in the activity; and (5) to carry a high risk of injury of harm (Williams, 1994).

NAEYC's most current position statement on developmentally appropriate practice states that play allow children "to stretch their boundaries to the fullest in their imagination, language, interaction, and self-regulation" and offer opportunities for children "to practice their newly acquired skills" (Copple & Bredecamp, 2009, p. 18). It's really quite easy to modify a game so that it fits these guidelines. Here are some ways to do that.

Modify Musical Chairs.

Instead of playing this the traditional way, modify it so it is a cooperative game. In this game, when the music stops, the goal is for children to find ways to share the remaining chairs. This way there is no one "loser." Compared to the traditional version, in this modification, children practice problem solving and prosocial behaviors.

Modify Simon Says.

Simon Says can also be modified so it is a more cooperative game for young children. Start by dividing the class into two groups instead of one large group. Have the children arranged in either two circles or two lines. When a child moves without Simon's permission, he leaves his original circle or line to join the other group, and he continues playing. Full participation allows children to acquire the listening, direction-following, and movement skills that are the objectives of Simon Says (Pica, 2009).

Modify Duck, Duck, Goose.

Another example of changing a game to make it more cooperative is Duck, Duck, Goose. This game usually involves physical activity for only one or two players and a good deal of waiting for the rest of the children. Also, some players are repeatedly chosen to be the goose. To modify this, have the children stand in a circle and walk in place as the game is played. This way all players engage in more physical activity. Also, make it a rule that the child who is "it" can't choose someone who has already been the goose. This way, more children will have a chance to chase. When the game is modified this way, all the children benefit from a low to moderate level of physical activity as well as practice in walking in place, chasing, and fleeing (Pica, 2009).

For more developmentally appropriate game ideas to use in your classroom, check the resources for further reading at the end of this chapter.

FIGURE 7-6 • Play is possible anytime, anywhere.

FIGURE 7-7 • Free play is an important part of each child's day.

a child's knowledge of building and arranging things in sets. Children learn to sort, classify, and probe for answers. Playing outdoors, children learn to sense differences in their world as the seasons change and as they observe other subtle changes in their environment every day.

Piaget (1962) defined play as assimilation, or the child's efforts to make environmental stimuli match his or her own concepts. His theory holds that play, in and of itself, does not necessarily result in the formation of new cognitive structures. Piaget claimed that play was just for pleasure, and while it allowed children to practice things they had previously learned, it did not necessarily result in the learning of new things. In other words, play reflects what the child has already learned but does not necessarily teach the child anything new.

Piaget describes **imaginative play** as one of the purest forms of symbolic thought available to the young child. According to Piaget, play permits the child to fit the reality of the world into his or her own interest and knowledge of the world. In this sense, imaginative play contributes strongly to the child's intellectual development. Some researchers even maintain that symbolic play is a necessary part of a child's development of language (Oliver & Klugman, 2007; Porter, 2009).

In contrast, Vygotsky states that play actually facilitates cognitive development. Children not only practice what they already know, they also learn new things. Play does not so much *reflect* thought (as Piaget suggests) as it does *create* thought (Vygotsky, 1978).

Play, according to Vygotsky, offers the child opportunities to acquire information that set the foundation for additional learning. For example, through playing with blocks, a child learns the idea of equivalents (that things can be equal) by discovering that two small blocks equal one larger one; or through playing with water or sand, the child acquires knowledge of volume, which eventually leads to developing the concept of reversibility.

FIGURE 7-8 • For young children, play is what they do all day long.

Observations of children at play are full of examples to support both Piagetian and Vygotskian theories of play. A child who puts on a raincoat and a firefighter's hat and rushes to rescue his teddy bear from the pretend flames in his play house is practicing what he has previously learned about firefighters. This supports Piaget's theory. On the other hand, a child in the block center who announces to his teacher, "Look! When I put these two square blocks together, I get a rectangle!" has constructed new knowledge through her play. This supports Vygotsky's theory. Whether children are practicing what they have learned in other settings or are constructing new knowledge, it is clear that play has a valuable role in the early childhood classroom.

A child gains an understanding of his or her environment as he or she investigates stones, grass, flowers, earth, water, and anything else. Through these experiences, the child eventually begins to make his or her own generalizations: Adding water to earth makes mud. A puddle of water disappears in sand. The inner part of a milkweed pod blows away in the wind. Wet socks can be dried out in the sun.

As children play, they develop spatial concepts; as they climb in, over, and around the big box in the yard, they clarify concepts of "in," "over," and "around." They hear someone call the box "gigantic," and *gigantic* becomes a new word that attaches to a specific meaning. In the sandbox, words such as *deep*, *deeper*, and *deepest* begin to have meaning through play experiences.

Outdoor Play/Recess

Children have two classrooms—one indoors and one outdoors. The outdoor play environment should be an extension of the indoor classroom. The outdoor play area should be a learning environment as carefully planned as indoor activity centers. Outdoor play should encourage motor and social skills as well as help children refine existing cognitive structures and construct new ones. Used in this way, the outdoor play environment provides a basis for observational assessments in all areas of development.

However, with the passage of No Child Left Behind, many schools started to lessen or even eliminate time children spent outdoors or at recess. The arguments against recess involved both academic time and safety issues. Some administrators believed their schools' test scores would improve if children spent more time on schoolwork. Some feared lawsuits from playground injuries. In fact, a recent study using a national data set of 11,000 children found that 30% of third graders had fewer than 15 minutes of recess time per day (Barros, Silver, & Stein, 2009). Since the enactment of NCLB,

FIGURE 7-9 • Children learn social skills as they relate to others during play.

20% of national public school systems have decreased time for recess, averaging cuts of 50 minutes per week (Center on Education Policy, 2008).

What are children learning outdoors that they could not learn inside? There is considerable research (Jarrett, 2002; Staempfli, 2009) to suggest that outdoor play/recess has many benefits for children such as the following:

- Children are less fidgety and more on task when they have recess, and children with AD/HD are among those who benefit most.
- Research on memory and attention shows that recall is improved when learning is spaced out rather than concentrated. Recess provides breaks during which the brain can "regroup" (Jarrett & Waite-Stupiansky, 2009).
- On the playground, children exercise leadership, teach games to one another, take turns, and learn to resolve conflicts.
- In a free-choice situation, children learn negotiation skills in order to keep the play going.
- Recess before rather than after lunch leads to healthier eating.
- Children who are active during the day are more active after school. Children who are sedentary during the day tend to remain sedentary after school.
- Teachers rated children's behavior as better in classes where children had at least 15 minutes of recess (Barros, Silver, & Stein, 2009).

See End of Chapter Activities for group games to use outdoors and at recess.

Older Children's Play and Cognitive Development

Older children learn many concepts through play. They learn about such things as rules of the game and strategies in play. They begin to learn about their own skill levels in various activities and to develop preferences for specific sports and activities.

Children's increasing cognitive abilities allow them to participate in more advanced forms of organized games and team activities where rules guide actual behaviors. Although younger children often play together (actually, they may only be playing near each other), they also often play alone. Children between the ages of eight and 12 might also play alone either by choice or by necessity. However, their increasing cognitive abilities (especially in those 10 to 12 years of age) allow them to play with others in situations requiring consistent or complex rules. The cognitive abilities of 10- to 12-year-olds also allow for more advanced forms of play such as word games, riddles, and other literacy-related play.

Today's technology allows older children many new forms of play. Children can play a wide array of computer games either alone or with another child. Software, such as for chess, requires that children think and participate in active decision making, while other software requires writing and complex thinking. As technological advances become commonplace in our society, children will have even greater access to problem-solving programs, CD-ROMs, videodiscs, and simulation programs. Many eight- to 12-year-old children who have benefited from computer use in schools are sufficiently computer literate to play with the latest technologically advanced computer and video games.

Emotional Growth

One of the keys to the quality of children's emotional health is how they feel about themselves. Creative play activities help a child develop a positive self-concept. In play activities, there are no right or wrong answers. Children are not faced with the threat of failure. They learn to see themselves as capable performers. Even when things do not go well, there is little pressure built into play. Thus, young children learn to view themselves as successful and worthwhile human beings through creative play. This is an important first step in developing a positive self-concept.

Children also learn to express and understand their emotions in creative play experiences. They may be observed almost anyplace in the early childhood setting expressing their feelings about doctors by administering shots with relish or their jealousy of a new baby by reprimanding a doll, but creative play is not necessarily limited to the expression of negative feelings. The same doll that only a moment ago was being reprimanded may next be lulled and crooned to sleep in the rocking chair.

Another emotional value of creative play is that it offers the child an opportunity to achieve mastery of his or her environment. The child has control of the situation, using what props he or she chooses and in the manner he or she prefers. The child is in command. He or she establishes the conditions of the experience by using imagination and exercises his or her powers of choice and decision as the play progresses.

Play is a safe and acceptable way to test out the expression of feelings. Through play children can re-create experiences that have been important to them and elaborate on experiences that have special meaning. The child can relieve anxiety or stress through play activities and feel perfectly safe in doing so. For example, Susan gets pleasure out of hammering on a piece of wood. She feels strong as she swings the hammer and sees the deep indentations she is making in the wood. Woodworking, thus, is providing a medium through which she can release tension or aggression in an acceptable way.

Children in the middle and upper elementary grades grow emotionally when engaged in play with their peers. Playing together, children learn to accept each other's styles and personalities and learn how it feels to be accepted as part of the group. Once the child gains acceptance among his or her peers, he or she begins to have self-respect and feels confident and adequate in attempting new problems and activities.

Social Growth

Play is a characteristic behavior of children at all times and places. Nonetheless, it varies with social class and culture. Sara Smilansky (1968) initiated a new line of play research studies with her finding that sociodramatic play was more common among children of advantage than it was among those with less advantage.

At the early childhood level, however, there is likely much more similarity in children's play than difference across both culture and social class (Cote & Bernstein, 2009). This is true because young children are less socialized and more apt to create their own play than to adopt socially transmitted play activities. For the young, and to a degree all ages, play has personal meaning and value not dealt with in traditional theory and research.

Although there has been a great deal of research on play since these theories were offered (Center on Education Policy, 2008; Jarrett, 2002; Oliver & Klugman, 2007), we really have no new theories of play, according to David Elkind (2003), noted child developmentalist. Elkind asserts that all the research on play simply represents one side of the issue—the adult side. Adults, in his opinion, look at children's play as, in one way or another, facilitating healthy development. Although he does not deny the developmental value or meaning of children's play, Elkind maintains that play has a personal, experiential value of equal, if not greater, importance (2003).

As teachers of young children, we need to resist the pressure to transform play into work—into academic instruction. We encourage true play by making certain that we offer materials that leave room for the imagination—blocks, paint, paper to be cut and pasted—and that children have sufficient time to innovate with these materials.

Children learn social skills as they relate to others during play. As a child becomes proficient in his or her social relationships, he or she learns to deal with more than one person at a time. As a group participant, he or she discovers that not everyone behaves in the same way and that some forms of behavior are not acceptable. When Yuki takes a block from Manuel's building, Manuel pushes her away. Next time, she does not try that. In one situation, Yuki learns that crying will get her what she wants, while in another it does not work at all. Children establish social relationships as they sit side by side playing with clay, dough, and other manipulative materials. A child discovers that he or she can make some decisions about what he or she will or will not do. If a child does not wish to push a wagon, he or she can play somewhere else. The child cannot, however, always be the one to tell others what to do. Sometimes the child takes the role of leader and sometimes he or she finds the role of follower satisfying.

When children play together, they learn to *be* together. The development of common interests and goals takes place among children during creative play. They must learn to "give a little" as well as "take a little" when involved in creative play activities. Whether two small children are arguing over the possession of a toy or a group of children are playing together on a jungle gym, play helps children grow socially.

Ten- to 12-year-old children, in particular, develop the social skills necessary to participate in complex, cooperative forms of play. Their enhanced social skills allow them to see others' perspectives and allow them to realize the benefits of playing socially and cooperatively with other children. At this age, play that requires social skills might consist of games, team sports, and organized activities.

Children, especially 10- to 12-year-old children, shift allegiance from parents and teachers to peers. They are beginning to seek freedom and independence, which results in their playing away from home and often away from direct adult supervision. Children might visit ball fields, playgrounds, and recreation centers where others play or where special equipment is available to them.

At school, teachers can assist older children through play activities at recess, noon, or during class

Parten	Play is a measure of child's increasing social maturity.	Developmental stages of play: onlooker, solitary, parallel, associative, and cooperative
Piaget	Play is assimilation—child makes world adapt to him.	3 stages of play: sensorimotor, symbolic, and games with rules
Smilansky	Play aids child's social development.	6 criteria of dramatic play: imitative role play, make-believe, verbal make-believe, persistence in role play, interaction, and verbal communication
Vygotsky	Play directly supports the development of child's cognitive powers.	Symbolic play promotes abstract thinking.

FIGURE 7-10 • Theories of play—summary.

THINK ABOUT IT   Children's Play in Art and Literature

Throughout history, society has expressed an interest in childhood play. We have learned of adult interest in this childhood experience from early literature and works of art. Children's play was encouraged in Ancient Greece, where children were treated with gentleness and affection. Early European civilizations, however, paid relatively little attention to children's play and provided only vague information about it before the Renaissance. This does not mean that children did not play. Rather, adults made little distinction between their own activities and those of children—including their play—until modern times (after the 16th century). Also, children living during this time perhaps had less time to play than do many modern children. They worked in the fields or in their parents' homes, performing housekeeping responsibilities much as adults did. Even as late as the 19th century, children worked outside the home. At a young age, they acquired adult skills applicable to the period in which they lived. For children of the lower classes, these were work skills. Boys of the aristocracy learned hunting and swordplay, and their female counterparts needlework, the arts, and music.

We can learn about play in earlier eras by looking at how play was represented in the visual arts. Several famous classical pictures depict children's play. During the Sung Dynasty (960–1129), a number of works by various artists in China depicted One

Hundred Children at Play. Some of these paintings are displayed in the Palace Museum in Taipei, Taiwan, as well as in collections of Chinese art in museums in the United States and elsewhere. These Chinese paintings show children engaged in socio-dramatic play and the games of upperclass or aristocratic children.

Another well-known painting, *Children's Play*, by the Flemish painter Peter Bruegel (1525–1569), vividly displays more than 80 childhood games. Bruegel's painting portrays a lower socioeconomic group of children in a village. Because many of these games are still recognized and played today, the painting reveals the remarkable continuity of children's play throughout the ages.

A playground in lower Manhattan at the beginning of the 20th century is depicted in a watercolor titled *The East River* by American artist Maurice Prendergast (1859–1924). The urban scene portrayed shows both adults and children at play. Some pieces of equipment, including swings and a sandbox, are still used in children's playgrounds today.

The paintings of children at play by artists of the Sung Dynasty, by Bruegel, and by Prendergast portray children from different cultures who were separated by time as well as by space. They reflect views of childhood in different settings. All, however, have in common the view that play is a natural activity of children.

time to become more proficient in skills for ordinary games. Yet, the acquisition of physical skills needed in ordinary games involves more than physical maturation. It is a matter closely tied to social adjustment.

A child who is socially comfortable with other children will try and try until he or she can participate without ridicule from others. The teacher needs to help children feel socially comfortable in the area of games. This developmental task is actually enhanced when facilities, equipment, and play space are made available for children of this age group. Too often, the importance of vigorous play for children of this age group is overlooked because they seem so "grown up." (See Figure 7–10 for a summary of play theories.)

Adapting Environments to Encourage Social Development for Children with Special Needs

One purpose for including children with special needs in typical early childhood settings is to provide these children opportunities to interact with children who do not have disabilities (Sluss, 2005). The ultimate goal is to have these interactions lead to friendships.

Play for children with special needs may not look like what is normally viewed as play. Put a ball in front of a two-year old who is typically developing and the child will probably try to throw, hit, or kick it. A child who has a disability may or may not react to a ball placed in front of him. That is why it is essential that knowledgeable adults facilitate play for children with special needs. The adult must know how to intervene in a way that supports play.

Teachers need to work with other adults and experts to develop specific plans to create environments that facilitate play for children with special needs. In making these plans, the following points should be considered.

- Remember that children with special needs are children first.
- Use children-first language when you discuss the child. Never refer to the child by the name of the disability.
- Make appropriate adaptations for the child. Recognize that you do not know everything you need to know about how to include this child in play. Each child is unique and each disability is unique. Ask questions about how to adapt the classroom and materials to encourage the child's play.
- Children with special needs may not always initiate play. They may not engage in play on their own. Teachers must intervene to encourage

play and to use strategies that will encourage self-generated play.
- The nature of a child's special condition will affect the play. For example, a child who has cerebral palsy and is in a wheelchair may need specialized assistance in motor areas but may be willing to challenge anyone in a game of checkers.
- A child who has visual impairments may need special assistance to participate in board games but be able to move around the room with minimal assistance.

Play for children with special needs must be individualized to reflect the child's assets. Their play may not look like typical child play. Each child will have a unique way of playing. Teachers must know the child well enough to understand that child's unique play (Sluss, 2005).

Teachers should arrange the physical environment and daily schedule to facilitate opportunities for children to interact and continue to model appropriate behaviors for these children. Research indicates that selection of toy materials and their arrangement in the room is significantly related to increased frequency of positive social behaviors and decreased frequency of negative behaviors in special-needs children (Morrier, McGee, & Daily, 2009).

One way to arrange the physical environment to promote social interaction is to use specific toys. When social toys (e.g., blocks, balls, miniature cars) rather than isolate toys (e.g., crayons, modeling dough, puzzles) are used during playtimes, children engage in more interactions and less solitary play (Sluss, 2005). Balls encourage interaction between two children when they roll or toss them to each other. Wagons and toys that require two children encourage cooperation. Water play and house play are also designed to stimulate social play.

Limiting the space available to children during playtime and placing children with special needs in close proximity to peers during group time and play sessions increase social interactions (Harper & McClusky, 2003). Increasing the proximity of children and limiting the space available to children can be accomplished by creating play centers and by assigning seats during group times, ensuring that children with special needs always have peers who are typically developing on both sides of them (Harper & McClusky, 2003). These strategies can be designed around children's Individual Educational Plan (IEP) goals and can be made part of the general curricular and daily activities. When children play together, the play is greater than the sum of its parts. It may seem only to be water play, encouraging physical (gross and

THIS ONE'S for YOU!   More Information on Play

Play is the natural and best way for children to learn as they investigate for themselves and observe others at play and work. They are natural explorers who have a need and desire to investigate their world through real experiences and natural environments. There are five qualities that distinguish play for young children from other activities.

- It is a process. The outcome is not as important as the process itself.

- Play is child-initiated. The activity is done for no other reason than the child wants to do it.

- In play, everything and anything can happen; a sheet over a table becomes a castle and the little girl inside is the princess.

- Play becomes the arena for testing rules, both logical and illogical. Rules freely appear and disappear in children's play; they may be simple or complex, and they are created from children's previous knowledge. An example of rules in play is the "rule" of roles. For example, when young children play in the housekeeping center, you will often hear one of the children assigning roles to each of the other children ("You be the mommy").

- Play is very much an activity of the mind. Children may become deeply engrossed in their play and find it difficult to stop when asked. Play involves the mind in an active process as a child investigates, explores, and inquires (Hurwitz, 2003).

In the early childhood classroom, play and the curriculum should be deeply connected. A high-quality curriculum for young children should rely heavily on play. Learning to identify different types of play may give you further understanding of their importance. Types of play categories include the following.

- Practice play—play that children do repeatedly, solely for pleasure, such as playing in sand and pouring it through their fingers.

- Constructive play—play where children construct or create something, such as block building.

- Rough-and-tumble play—play that involves laughing and pretending; as the name implies, it can get a little rough. (It is not aggressive play and, when done in a safe area, is an acceptable form of play.)

- Dramatic play—play that gives children the opportunity to take on the role of another person or an animal or even an object.

- Games with rules—play governed by a set of rules, such as a game of Duck, Duck, Goose.

Understanding these categories helps teachers plan appropriate play activities to meet the developmental needs of the whole child (Hurwitz, 2003). So the next time you see children engaged in play, remember that they are practicing and developing the skills necessary to be successful students and members of the community. Let them have fun and play!

---

fine motor development), social (interactions with other children), and cognitive development (sensory stimulation, language development). But, it is more; it is enjoyable. Children are playing and they are having fun. This is the essence of play for all children (Sluss, 2005).

Toys for Children with Special Needs: Adaptation and Accessibility

Adaptation

Toys for children who have disabilities may need to be adapted. Toys can be adapted with low-tech or high-tech changes. High-tech adaptations are generally requested by an IEP and used by someone trained in assistive technology.

Yet low-tech adaptations are just as useful and can be done by adults in the classroom. Some examples are adding large knobs to puzzles, adding Velcro© to blocks, or adding grips to crayons and markers. Simple items such as muffin pans and Nerf© balls can be turned into a game. The muffin pan and soft balls is an activity generally recommended as the infant's first puzzle, but it is equally effective with children who have motor delays. Putting marbles in a hollow ball allows children with visual impairments to feel and hear the movement of the marbles inside the ball.

Accessibility

Some toys in the room should be accessible to all children. All preschoolers should be able to access blocks, dolls, books, or balls without a teacher's assistance. But be careful in that some children may become overstimulated by too many available materials. If this is creating a problem, rotate toys on a regular basis. A survey of the room can determine the level of accessibility of the toys and play materials. Consider the needs of the individual children. Materials for art should be accessible to children in wheelchairs. If a child has visual impairments, signs with large pictures or signs in Braille can be used depending on the child's degree of impairment. Being sure that the placement of the shelves and materials is stable will also help children navigate the classroom (Sluss, 2005).

Violent Play

Play, as we have discussed in this chapter, is viewed as an essential part of the early childhood program. In our world today, however, play can often be a problem because of the frequency of war and superhero play in the early childhood years. Some teachers question the importance of play when it is often focused on fighting. Some teachers resort to planning other activities that are easier to manage. Another solution some teachers use is to reduce playtime. This may seem to reduce problems in the short term, but it deprives children of the wide-ranging developmental benefits play provides. Before we consider how to deal with the problem of war and superhero play, it is important to consider some of the reasons for this type of play.

Some Reasons for Violent Play

Children are exposed to far more violence today than their teachers have experienced in their lives. Yet teachers must help today's children face and deal with this exposure to violence. Let us consider what impact the presence of violence has in a child's life.

Violence in everyday life. Many young children are exposed to some form of violence in their everyday lives. They may see violence in their homes and communities as well as in entertainment and news on the television screen. It's hardly surprising that children are bringing it into their play.

If you watch children's violent play, you will see that they often focus on the most graphic, confusing, scary, or aggressive aspects of violence. It is this context they are struggling to work out and understand in their play. Usually, the children who seem most obsessed with war play have been exposed to the most

FIGURE 7-11 • Young children enjoy playing in the home center.

violence and have the greatest need to work it out (Porter, 2009).

Feelings. Most young children look for ways to feel powerful and strong. Play can be a safe way to achieve a sense of power. From a child's point of view, play with violence is very seductive, especially when connected to the power and invincibility portrayed in entertainment. Children who use war play to help themselves feel powerful and safe are children who feel the most powerless and vulnerable (Porter, 2009).

Media, toys, and violence. Many of the action figures so popular today are highly structured toys. Just by the way they look and work, they give children powerful messages about the content and direction of play. In contrast, open-ended toys such as blocks and stuffed animals can be used in many ways that the child controls.

Many of the action and war games toys are linked to violent movies, TV shows, and video games. These toys have strong appeal because they promise

TOYS AND DOLLS: A SHORT HISTORY

The doll is probably the oldest toy in the world. Anthropologists believe most ancient dolls were probably used for religious ceremonies, but some may have been used as toys for children. Dolls often reflect the culture, lifestyle, and customs of the period during which they were made. Today, dolls are viewed mainly as toys, but for some people, dolls continue to be treasured artifacts.

Ancient dolls were made from various materials including wood, clay, shells, corncobs, feathers, animal skin, and bones. Wooden "paddle" dolls were used in Egypt nearly 4,000 years ago. Fashion dolls made of paper material became popular in Europe in the late 1300s and remained popular until the 1800s. Dolls that could say "Mama" and "Papa" were invented in the early 1800s.

The Kewpie doll was created by Rose O'Neill in the early 1900s. It was modeled after her little brother. Bye-Lo-Baby, created in the 1920s by Grace Putnam, was dubbed the "million dollar baby" because it was such a huge success. The popular Cabbage Patch Kids were created by Xavier Roberts in the mid-1970s. Raggedy Ann was created in the early 1900s by artist Johnny Gruelle, and her brother, Andy, showed up in 1920. Barbie, whose full name is Barbie Millicent Roberts, was introduced in 1959.

In 1965, G.I. Joe became the first action figure for boys. Created by Stanley Weston, G.I. Joe was based on a new television show called *The Lieutenant.* The doll proved more popular than the television show by far. Barbie's boyfriend Ken joined the doll scene in 1961. Nesting dolls are hollow wooden figures with consecutively smaller figures located inside. It is believed they originated in Japan, but they were made famous as Matryoshka dolls by Russian artists.

Toys in general have a long history, much like dolls. Just like dolls, the main purpose of a toy is fun. Toys such as yo-yos, tops, rattles, whistles, puppets, and balls were first used by children around the world thousands of years ago. In addition to fun, toys help children by teaching them about the world, stimulating their imaginations, and strengthening their muscles.

Long ago, many toys, such as rattles and bells, were believed to protect children from evil spirits. Some of the first toy-making guilds were organized in Germany during the 1400s. Before the industrial revolution, most of the toys in the world were made by parents or craftspeople.

Yo-yos were used in countries such as China and Greece more than 2,500 years ago. Pull toys on wheels were used in Egypt more than 4,000 years ago. Some of the first kites in the world were flown in China more than 2,500 years ago. Rubber balls were first used in South America more than 500 years ago. And what many consider the first video game was created 50 years ago. It consisted of a single dot of electronic light that seemed to move across a tiny oscilloscope screen (Jaffe, 2006).

dramatic power and excitement. Often, these toys cause children to replicate violent stories they see on the screen. Many young children get stuck imitating media-linked violence instead of developing creative and imaginative play.

Working with children's violent play. There are no simple or perfect solutions to children's violent play. However, here are some ways to approach the problem.

- Wherever possible, reduce the amount of violence children see. Most of young children's exposure to violence occurs in the home, so family involvement is crucial. Teachers can help families learn more about how to protect children from violence through parent workshops and family newsletters. Teachers can also help parents learn to deal with the violence that still gets in. In addition, teachers can provide parents with information on how to choose open-ended toys and toys with nonviolent themes.
- Promote imaginative and creative play. Be aware of the difference between imitative play and creative or imaginative play. Imitative play occurs when children engage in the same play with violence

day after day and bring in few new or creative ideas of their own. Piaget called this kind of behavior *imitation*, not play (Porter, 2009). In imitative play, children are less likely to work out their needs than in imaginative play.

- Take time to observe children's play and learn what children are working on and how. Use this information to help children move beyond their imitative play that focuses on violent actions. Help children learn new ways to work out the violent content of their play. For example, children can work out their feelings by pounding nails into wood, rolling and pounding out clay, and knocking down stacks of blocks.
- Encourage children to deal with issues of violence by expressing their feelings in painting, drawing, or telling stories. Older children can write down their thoughts in stories or poetry.
- Talk with children about violent play. As children struggle to feel safe and make sense of violence, they need to know adults are there to help them in the process (Porter, 2009). Talk with children to learn what confuses and scares them. When a child raises an issue about something that frightens her or him, it helps to ask an open-ended question. For example, simply ask, "What have you heard about that?" That way you can respond more exactly to what is troubling the child.
- It is important to keep in mind that children do not always understand violence as adults do. They may have misconceptions. Try to correct these misconceptions. ("The planes that go over our school do not carry bombs.") Help children sort out fantasy from reality. ("People in real life can't change back and forth like the Power Rangers do.")
- Encourage children to engage in creative play so they can transform violence into positive behavior. Provide them props, time, and a positive environment in which to act out violent ideas in more positive ways. Guide them in their approach so they might learn firsthand how to treat each other in peaceful ways. Praise them for their efforts. ("I'm glad that in real life you could solve your problem with Scott by. . .") These real-life experiences can help defuse some of the harmful lessons children learn about violence.

Given the state of our world, young children now more than ever need to find ways to work out the violence they see. For many, play helps them do this. We have a crucial role in helping meet young children's needs through play.

FIGURE 7-12 • Play is an activity that does not necessarily result in a product.

FIGURE 7-13 • Older children enjoy activities that allow them to perfect skills achieved at earlier ages.

Summary

Play is a central part of the lives of young children, not something to do when work is finished. Play may be organized (structured) or spontaneous (free). It may involve dramatics or special equipment, or it may take the form of a game. Many theorists have studied play, including Parten, Piaget, Smilansky, and Vygotsky, among others. Parten classified social play in six categories: unoccupied behavior, onlooker behavior, solitary play, parallel play, associative play, and cooperative play. Piaget defined play as assimilation, the child's efforts to make environmental stimuli match his or her own concepts. He described imaginative play as one of the purest forms of symbolic thought available to the young child. Smilansky provided six criteria of dramatic play. The first four are behaviors in which young children may engage alone, and the last two involve social dynamics in the play. Vygotsky states that play actually facilitates cognitive development. Play does not so much reflect thought as it does create thought. Play usually develops in a natural sequence that evolves from a child's level of socialization. The sequential stages of play include onlooker, solitary, parallel, associative, and cooperative play.

The needs of children are met through creative play. They learn about themselves, others, and the world around them through their play activities. Creative play has specific purposes in the early childhood program: to promote physical, mental, social, and emotional growth. Observation of children engaged in creative play will reveal some differences (stages) of play. Play is quite different for three-year-olds than it is for five-year-olds. Three-year-old children often cannot separate the real from the pretend. They prefer to be characters about whom they know something. Four-year-olds tend to be aggressive and play characters that enable them to display their aggressive feelings. Five-year-olds can separate the real world from the world of their imaginations. They are better able to control their emotions.

Teachers can adapt the environment so that it encourages the play of children with special needs. They also need to be aware of the reasons for children's violent play and how to deal with it in the early childhood program.

Older children enjoy games that allow them to perfect skills achieved at earlier ages. They enjoy games with rules. In games and other play activities, social and emotional development are as important as physical development to this age group.

Key Terms

associative play 134
cooperative play 135
free play 133
imaginative play 139
onlooker behavior 134
organized play 133
parallel play 134
solitary play 134
spontaneous play 133

Learning Activities

A. Observe children of various ages at play. Without letting them know you are watching, observe one or more children from each age group at play for periods of at least 10 minutes for each group. How are the play activities similar? How are they different? Observe children in these two groups: (1) kindergarten through grade 3 and (2) grades 4 to 5. How are their play activities similar? How are they different? What were the most prevalent forms of play observed in each group? Were you surprised by what you saw? Why or why not?

B. Select one play activity and discuss how it contributes to a child's growth in each of four areas of development discussed in this chapter (physical, mental, social, emotional). Choose an activity for each of the age groups discussed in this chapter. Compare and contrast the activities for each age group.

C. Observe the dramatic play of a group of three-year-olds and a group of five-year-olds. In what ways is their play different? How is it similar? Observe dramatic play for a group of children in each of these age groups: (1) kindergarten through grade 3 and (2) grades 4 to 5. In what ways is their dramatic play different from each other? How is it similar? Did you observe anything that surprised you? Share your observations with your fellow students.

D. Try the animal cracker game. This is a game that children enjoy and that helps them develop a better understanding of the creative possibilities of games.

1. Obtain a box of animal crackers. Stand before a full-length mirror and, without looking, take one of the crackers from the box. Look at it and then eat the cracker. With that action, you "become" the selected animal for two minutes. Observe your behavior as that animal. Do this a number of times.

2. Answer the following questions about this activity.
   a. How did you feel about doing this?
   b. How is creativity different from silliness?
   c. How do games help people develop creativity or become more creative?

E. Select an activity that children engage in for the sheer joy of doing it. List the learnings involved.

F. Record the conversations of two children playing together. Is there evidence from the discussion that one child is dominating the play? If so, on what did you base your conclusions? Compare your findings with others in class.

G. Visit a local playground. Describe the equipment available. Which pieces were most popular? Why do you believe this was so? What aspects of the arrangement and equipment are conducive to children's play? Explain.

Activities for Children

Toddler Play

- Gather up some plush animals and arrange them in a circle around the child. Ask her to make each animal's special sound, then call on each animal as if in a classroom: "Cow, you're next. Cow says . . . ."
- Toddlers love to explore, especially when there's treasure at the end! Using a ball of brightly colored yarn, mark a trail through the room and place a small treat at the end. Help the toddler follow the trail as it runs around the room and ends with his fun surprise. If the toddler gathers up the string as she goes, the path will be easier to follow.
- Box Fun. Toddlers love big boxes to play in—but don't expect complex play with them. A toddler may not be ready to rocket to the moon in the TV box, but he'll relish the cozy space, the flaps to open and close, or maybe the chance to hide away with a blanket and take a nap.
- Fun Footwork. Unroll large sheets of paper on a washable surface and put a few colors of tempera paint out on paper plates. Let the toddler step in the paint with bare feet, then hold her hands while she "paints" her foot prints all over the paper.
- Cardboard boxes offer toddlers the opportunity for a great deal of beneficial play. Take sturdy cardboard boxes of different sizes and tape them together with packing or duct tape to form long "trains." Make segments of varying heights by propping some boxes on sturdy pillows or padding. Then place the trains in a padded area or surround them with pillows. Encourage the toddlers to climb on top of the train at one end and crawl the length of the train. Moving up and down onto the different levels promotes motor planning, eye–hand coordination, and balance. You can also have them crawl through open boxes taped together in "tunnels," which will increase their body awareness.
- Stuff an empty tissue box with scarves or large pieces of nylon or similar fabric. Toddlers enjoy pulling the fabric out. Turn on some music and let the children dance with their scarves.
- Add materials to a water or sand table. A large plastic tub or box can be a portable sand table. Put in foam packing "peanuts," cotton balls, shredded paper, or even dirt. Hide some small plastic toys in the box. Give the child some scoops, funnels, or cups with which to dig for fun and to develop eye–hand coordination.

Expanding Play Experiences

One way to encourage and expand children's play is by changing the materials they normally use in activity centers. Add some of the following materials to your interest centers to expand children's play experiences.

Dramatic Play Center

- Add open-ended materials such as sheets and scarves or a large cardboard box. Ask children, "What can you do with this?"
- Have a box of unusual items (tools, beach ball, funny glasses, hats) that children can choose from when they want to add a new element to their play.
- After reading a favorite story, provide props to go with it and have children retell the story in their own way.

Block Center

- Add rope and small balls. Ask the children, "What can you do with these?"
- Add aluminum foil and flashlights to inspire new types of building.
- Have pictures of unusual buildings in the center to inspire children's building.

Shadow Play

In a group, perhaps outdoors on a bright day, encourage children to make silly movements and observe their own shadows. Introduce a quick "copy cat" (follow-the-leader) game: "Everybody jump! Everybody hop! Now, everybody dance!"

On the playground, play a shadow touch game. Have the children in the group make one connecting shadow by having their shadows touch each other's. Then play shadow tag.

Imagination Exercises

Children enjoy "being" animals or other pretend things. These activities are good for large-muscle development as well as for creative play. In these activities, encourage children to move slowly and quietly. Once they interpret the object or animal in their own way, suggest that they hold the positions while continuing to breathe slowly.

A. *Tree.* Together, close your eyes and think about different trees you've seen. Then stand up and raise your arms to look like a tree. Breathe slowly in and out and try to hold the pose for about 30 seconds.

B. *Mountain.* Sit on the floor, legs crossed or in any position that's comfortable. Slowly raise your arms to create a mountain peak. As you hold this position, have children pretend they, too, are huge, quiet mountains. You, or someone in the group, can describe the peaceful scenes you might see below.

C. *Cat.* Find a comfortable way to curl up like a cat and pretend to be sleeping in a warm, comfy place, such as near a fireplace or in a sunny place. Then wake up and stretch.

D. *Turtle.* Pretend you are a turtle by rounding your back like a shell and tucking your head, arms, and legs under the shell. Hold this pose for a bit, then very slowly stretch out your neck, arms, and legs (Church, 1993).

The following are some creative play activities that require the use of large muscles and that promote large (gross) motor skills.

Guess What I Am

Without saying a word, a child tries to act out the movements of some object. This may be an airplane making a landing, a rooster strutting around the barnyard, a cement truck dumping its load, or a clock telling the time of day. The child may think up things to do, or the teacher may whisper suggestions.

Water Play

A water table or a large tub is filled with water and used for creative water play. Children pour, mix, and stir the water. Soap may be added so they can create suds, too. They may also enjoy using water and a large paintbrush to "paint" a fence or the school building. A variety of objects can be put together to make a boat that floats. (Aluminum foil works well for this.) Creative cleanup can be developed by children as they find how water, tools, and materials can help them clean up messes.

Playing With a Hose

A child enjoys playing with a hose connected to an outlet with the water on strong. Children learn about what happens when they put their thumbs over the nozzle. They discover the push effect as water leaves the hose. They make rain by sprinkling water into the air. They create a rainbow. They hear different sounds as the water strikes different materials.

For a realistic gas pump hose to use outdoors with riding toys, fit an old piece of garden hose with a pistol grip nozzle. These nozzles are available at hardware stores.

Challenges

Look around the room to find ways to encourage children's creative play. Try some of these.

- *In the Housekeeping Corner.* How many ways can you use a scarf, pillowcase, or paper bag? What can you invent to help you carry your baby doll or your groceries? What do you need to change your house into a pet store?
- *In the Block Center.* What can you build that can be a place to park all the cars and trucks? How many ways can you build a road that is as long as the classroom? How many ways can you build a bridge, castle, apartment house, or tower?
- *In the Science Center.* How many different objects can you use to invent bubble blowers? How can you use sponges to pick up things? How many ways can you use paper to make wind?
- *At the Sand and Water Table.* What can you invent that will keep the sand (or water) from leaking out of the colander? How many different materials can you use to invent a boat that floats? What can you invent that will move sand from one container to another?
- *In the Outdoors.* How many ways can you make a shadow? What can you invent to dig with in the sand? How many ways can you balance a beach ball between you and a friend?
- *In the Art Center.* How many ways can you change a piece of paper without using a tool? What can you invent with newspaper, paperclips, and rubber bands? How can you draw with more than one crayon at a time?

Group Games

Kick the Can

Kick the Can is a little like tag. Players draw a large circle on the ground and put a can or other object in the middle. The player who is "It" guards the can. Other players try to run in and kick it out of the circle. When someone kicks the can, It must go to get it back. Meanwhile, the other players run to hide. When It gets back to the circle, he or she yells Freeze! and the others must stop. It calls out the names of the players he or she can see, and they are prisoners. Then It must find the other players. But if someone who's hidden can run and kick the can, the prisoners are free. If there are no prisoners, one of the hiding players can run into the circle and shout, "Home free!" Then everyone runs back to the circle, and the last player to get there is It for the next round.

Ghost in the Graveyard

This tag game is also called Midnight Ghost. It can be played with any number of children. One person is chosen as the ghost. While everyone else stays at a home base, the ghost runs away and hides. The groups chants, "one o'clock, two o'clock, three o'clock…" up to 12 o'clock, then shouts "Midnight! I hope I don't see the ghost tonight!" Then all the children run around. When someone sees the ghost, he or she yells, "Ghost in the graveyard!" and tries to run away. If the ghost catches you, you become a ghost, too. In the next round, all the ghosts hide and the others count again. The last person caught is the ghost for the next round.

Mother, May I?

Line up the children facing you, about 10 feet away. Give commends to one child at a time, such as, "Claire, take one hop forward." If Claire responds, "Mother, may I?" you can say either "Yes, you may" or "No, you may not." If your reply is "yes," make sure that Claire says "Thank you" before she goes. Anyone who forgets her manners or makes a move without permission is sent back to the starting line. Keep playing until one child reaches Mother. Give each child a chance to be Mother. This game helps teach children respect. To avoid frustration over misunderstood consequences ("I didn't know I had to say thank you"), make the rules of the game perfectly clear before you get started.

The Hot or Cold Game

Choose one child to be the Finder. Send him out of the room while the rest of the players hide an object, like a red ball, somewhere in the room. Ask the Finder to come back and look for the ball, while the other players call out hints: "You're getting hotter" or "you're getting colder." Play until the object is found, then give everyone a turn as the Finder. This game puts the emphasis on encouraging other players, not competing against them, so children learn to help each other out in a fun setting.

I Spy

Take turns spotting nearby objects and describing them: "I spy with my little eye something that is green . . ." The other players try to guess what the object is: "A tree!" "Jorge's shirt!" Whoever guesses right gets to be the net "spy." This game teaches patience and how to listen politely while other players have their turn.

Australian Skippyroo Kangaroo

This is a popular game played in many Australian preschools and kindergartens to help teach children their classmates' names as well as good listening skills. Children sit in a circle and an adult asks one child to go into the middle—she is the first Skippyroo, the kangaroo. Skippyroo crouches forward on the floor with her eyes closed while the kids in the circle chant: "Skippyroo, kangaroo, dozing in the midday sun, comes a hunter, run, run, run." At this point, an adult points to a child sitting in the circle, who then touches Skippyroo's shoulder and says, "Guess who's caught you just for fun?" and waits. Skippyroo tries to name the owner of the voice and if she guesses correctly, swaps places. The game begins again and continues until all the children have had a chance to be Skippyroo.

Activities for Older Children (Grades 4–5)

Marble Games

Children have been playing marble games since ancient Roman times, more than 2,000 years ago. Early marbles made of clay have been found in Egyptian tombs and in Native American burial grounds. Around 120 years ago, machines were invented to make marbles. In most marble games, players shoot their marbles. They aim for another player's marbles or for a target, such as a hole in the ground.

Ring Taw. In this marble game, players make a circle about 3 feet wide on the ground. Each player puts several marbles in the circle.

A larger circle is drawn around the first one. Players choose a starting point on the outside of the circle. They use a taw, or shooting marble, to try to hit another player's marble out of the inside of the ring.

If the shooter hits a target marble and it goes out of the ring, the person gets one point. If his shooter stays in the ring, he may shoot from the place his taw stopped.

As long as he continues to knock a target marble out of the ring, his turn continues. His turn stops if his taw does not hit a target marble or if his taw leaves the ring. The winner is the player with the most points. For more ideas for marble games, visit www.landofmarbles.com.

New Games

Invent new class games. Divide the class evenly into cooperative learning groups. Have each group brainstorm ideas for a new game to play at recess or in gym class. Groups should determine the basic rules of play and any penalties. Allow one group per day to teach its new game to the rest of the class. Use anonymous feedback cards as a way for each member of the class to offer compliments or suggestions for improvement to each group's game. Offer each group time to assess its game and make changes. Record final game rules in a class game book.

How Other Kids Play

Have students meet Lornah Kipligat, a world-class athlete who started a girls' running camp in her native Kenya. See http://www.pbs.org/frontlineworld/stories/kenya/.

What's It Like to Be a Kid in Kenya?

Explore photo albums from students in South Africa, Kenya, Ghana, and Uganda. Check out "My World" at http://www.pbskids.org/africa.

Pictograms

Have the students try their hands at Chinese pictograms with Sagwa interactive games at http://www.pbskids.org/sagwa/.

Chapter Review

1. List the four areas of development that are enhanced by play activities.
2. Explain the sequence in which play develops and the characteristics for each stage.
3. Describe and compare the characteristics of play for an infant, a toddler, a two-and-one-half-year-old, and a four-year-old.
4. Describe the characteristics of play of children in kindergarten through grade 3 and those in grades 4 and 5.
5. Discuss some adjustments teachers can make in the environment to encourage the play of children with special needs.
6. Discuss some possible causes of children's violent play and ways to deal with it in the early childhood program.

References

Barros, R. M., Silver, E. J., & Stein, R. E. K. (2009). School recess and group classroom behavior. *Pediatrics, 123*(2), 431–438.

Center on Education Policy. (2008). *Instructional time in elementary schools: A closer look at changes for specific subjects.* www.cep-dc.org/

Church, E. G. (1993, February). Moving small, moving quiet. *Scholastic Pre-K Today,* 42–45.

Copple, C., & Bredekamp, S. (2009). *Developmentally appropriate practice in early childhood programs serving children from birth through age 8* (3rd ed.). Washington, DC: NAEYC.

Cote, L. R., & Bornstein, M. H. (2009). Child and mother play in three U.S. cultural groups: Comparisons and associations. *Journal of Family Psychology, 123*(3), 355–365.

Elkind, D. (2003, May). Thanks for the memory: The lasting value of true play. *Young Children, 58,* 46–50.

Harper, L., & McCluskey, K. (2003). Teacher-child and child-child interactions in inclusive preschool settings: Do Adults inhibit peer interactions? *Phi Delta Kappan, 18*(2), 163–184.

Hurwitz, S. C. (2003). To be successful—Let them play! *Childhood Education,* Winter 2002/2003, 100–101.

Jaffe, D. (2006). *The history of toys: From spinning tops to robots.* Charleston, SC: History Press.

Jarrett, O. W. (2002). *Recess in elementary school: What does the research say?* ERIC Digest, ED466331 2002-07-00. www.ericdigests.org/2003-2/recess.html

Jarret, O. W., & Waite-Stupiansky, S. (2009). Recess—It's indispensable. *Young Children, 64*(5), 66–69.

Levin, E. D. (2003). *Teaching young children in violent times: Building a peaceable classroom* (2nd ed.). Cambridge, MA: Educators for Social Responsibility.

Morrier, J. J., McGee, G. G., & Daily, T. (2009). Effects of toy selection and arrangement on the social behaviors of an inclusive group of preschool-aged children with and without autism. *Early Childhood Services: An Interdisciplinary Journal of Effectiveness, 13*(2), 157–168.

Oliver, S. J., & Klugman, E. (2007). Building a play research agenda: What do we know about play? What new questions do we need to ask? *Exchange: The Early Childhood Leaders' Magazine, 14*(4), 14–17.

Parten, M. (1932). Social participation among preschool children. *Journal of Abnormal and Social Psychology, 27,* 243–269.

Piaget, J. (1962). *Play, dreams, and imitation in childhood.* New York, NY: W. W. Norton.

Pica, R. (2009). Learning by leaps and bounds. What makes a game developmentally appropriate? *Young Children, 64*(2), 66–69.

Porter, C. L. (2009). Predicting preschoolers' social-cognitive play behavior: Attachment, peers, temperament and physiological regulation. *Psychological Reports, 15*(6), 132–138.

Sandlund, M., McDonough, S., & Hager-Ross, C. (2009). Interactive computer play in rehabilitation of children with sensorimotor disorders: A systemic review. *Developmental Medicine and Child Neurology, 15*(3), 173–182.

Sluss, D. J. (2005). *Supporting play: Birth through age 8.* Clifton Park, NY: Thomson-Delmar Learning.

Smilansky, S. (1968). *The effects of socio-dramatic play on disadvantaged preschool children.* New York, NY: Wiley.

Smilansky, S., & Shefatya, L. (1990). *Facilitating play: A medium for promoting cognitive, socio-emotional and academic development in young children.* Gaithersburg, MD: Psychosocial & Educational Publications.

Staempfli, M. B. (2009). Reintroducing adventure into children's outdoor play environments. *Environment and Behavior, 141*(2), 268–273.

Staley, L., & Portman, P. A. (2000). Red Rover, Red Rover, It's time to move over! *Young Children, 55*(1), 67–72.

Vygotsky, L. (1978). *Mind in society: The development of higher psychological processes.* Cambridge, MA: Harvard University Press.

Williams, N. F. (1994). The Physical Education Hall of Shame, part 2. *Journal of Physical Education, Recreation & Dance, 65*(2), 17–20.

Resources for Developmentally Appropriate Games

Orlick, T. (2006). *Cooperative games and sports: Joyful activities for everyone.* Champaign, IL: Human Kinetics.

Pica, R. (2006). *Great games for young children: Over 100 games to develop self-confidence, problem-solving skills, and cooperation.* Beltsville, MD: Gryphon House.

Sanders, S. W. (2002). *Active for life: Developmentally appropriate movement programs for young children.* Washington, DC: NAEYC.

Torbert, M. (2005). Using active group games to develop basic life skills. *Young Children, 60*(4), 72–78.

Torbert, M., & Schneider, L. B. (1993). *Follow me too: A handbook of movement activities for three- to five-year-olds.* Washington, DC: NAEYC.

Additional Reading

Baines, L. A., & Slutsky, R. (2009). Developing the sixth sense: Play. *Educational Horizons, 87*(2), 13–17.

Benson, T. (2008). Dramatic play: Bring it back. *Texas Child Care, 32*(2), 24–31.

Bodrova, E. (2008). Make-believe play versus academic skills: A Vygotskian approach to today's dilemma of early childhood education. *European Early Childhood Education Research Journal, 16*(3), 357–369.

Blakley, B., Blau, R., Brady, E., Streibert, C., Zavitkovsky, A., & Zavitkovsky, D. (2009). *Activities for school-age child care: Playing and learning* (rev. ed.). Washington, DC: NAEYC.

Drew, W. F., Christie, J., Johnson, J. E., Meckley, A. M., & Nell, M. L. (2008). Constructive play: A value-added strategy for meeting early learning standards. *Young Children, 63*(3), 38–44.

Gouch, K. (2008). Understanding playful pedagogies, play narratives and play spaces. *Early Years, 28*(1), 93–102.

Hutcheson, B. (2008). Designing for play. *Schoolarts, 108*(2), 60–61.

Johnson, J., Christie, J., & Wardle, F. (2005). *Play, development and early education.* New York, NY: Allyn & Bacon.

Miller, E., & Almon, J. (2009). Crisis in the kindergarten: Why children need to play in school. *Alliance for Childhood, 16*(1), 72–75.

Mullineaux, P. Y., & DiLalla, L. F. (2009). Preschool pretend play behavior and early adolescent creativity. *Journal of Creative Behavior, 43*(1), 41–58.

Padak, N., & Rasinski, T. (2008). The games children play. *The Reading Teacher, 62*(4), 363–365.

Rivkin, M. S. (2008). *The great outdoors: Restoring children's right to play.* Washington, DC: NAEYC.

Sarama, J., & Clements, D. H. (2009). Building blocks and cognitive building block: Play to know the world mathematically. *American Journal of Play, 1*(3), 313–317.

Swann, A. C. (2009). An intriguing link between drawing and play with toys. *Childhood Education, 85*(4), 230–236.

Walsh, P. (2008). Planning for play in a playground. *The Early Childhood Leaders' Magazine, 83*(1), 88–92.

Helpful Websites

American Academy of Pediatrics, http://www.aap.org
Lists several good resources on selecting safe, appropriate toys.

The Association for the Study of Play, http://www.csuchico.edu/kine/tasp
Publishes the *Annual Volume of Play and Culture Studies*.

Block Corner, http://www.blockcorner.com
Site is an online building toy for kids of all ages. An interesting way to merge art and technology as students (grades 4–8) design block towers.

Consumer Product Safety Commission, http://www.cpsc.gov
Advises about toy selection and provides safety alerts about products on the market.

International Association for the Child's Right to Play, http://www.ncsu.edu/ipa/index.html
Offers its *Declaration of the Child's Right to Play* and publishes the quarterly newsletter *PlayRights*.

The Lion and Lamb Project, http://www.lionlamb.org
Works to stop the marketing of violence to children through guides, training, and advocacy.

National Institute for Early Education Research, http://nieer.org
Articles on the importance of child's play, particularly imaginative play and self-regulation skills.

National Lekotek Center, http://www.lekotek.org
Makes play accessible to children with disabilities. Play and learning centers for children and families are located throughout the country.

Playing for Keeps, http://www.playingforkeeps.org
Promotes healthy, constructive, nonviolent play for all children. Board members come from the toy industry and early childhood education.

Talking to Kids about War and Violence, http://www.pbs.org/parents/talkingwith kids/news/questions_1.html
PBS Parents' website; helps adults answer children's questions about violence and respond to their feelings of stress in age-appropriate ways. (Also in Spanish.)

Teachers Resisting Unhealthy Children's Entertainment (TRUCE), http://www.truceteachers.org
Prepares an annual *Toy Action Guide* and *Media Violence and Children Action Guide* for parents and teachers of young children.

Your Playground, http://www.yourplayground.org/
Design and create a park with equipment, colors, and a name. A snapshot of the park can be printed out.

Zero to Three, http://www.zerotothree.org/
Provides tips on play.

For additional creative activity resources, visit our website at www.Cengage.com/login

Using Technology to Promote Creativity

OBJECTIVES

After studying this chapter, you should be able to:

1. List at least five characteristics of developmentally appropriate computer software.

2. List the pros and cons concerning the use of technology with young children.

3. List the four basic types of children's websites.

4. Discuss several examples of technology used in the early childhood program.

5. Search for and review at least two websites for future use in early childhood classrooms.

6. Discuss the term *Web 2.0* and its difference from *Web 1.0* and the various tools and technologies in Web 2.0 and their appropriateness for the early childhood classroom.

E
lmo has e-mail. Barney and his friends use interactive CDs on their computer. Even characters on children's television are using technology as a matter-of-fact, everyday part of their lives.

It's the same scene in early childhood programs today. Computers are a part of many children's preschool experiences. You can generally find at least one computer available for children's use during learning center or free-choice time. Technology—computers, digital cameras, videos, video games, interactive CDs, DVDs—is definitely here to stay in the early childhood program.

With the growing use of technology in the early childhood program, teachers more than ever need to know the best ways to use technology with young children. This chapter provides a basic framework of information about using technology in developmentally appropriate ways in the early childhood program.

FIGURE 8-1 • Computers are a part of many children's preschool experiences.

Technology and Developmentally Appropriate Practice

Before beginning any discussion of technology in the early childhood program, it is important to consider developmental appropriateness of technology and young children.

As we have seen in Chapter 5, developmentally appropriate practice (DAP) is an underlying premise of all educational experiences for young children. Although the theories of DAP have been widely adopted in many aspects of the early childhood curriculum, developmental appropriateness is still largely absent from the methods in which the computer is used with young children. To ensure that computer technology enhances the learning experiences of young children, standards of DAP must be applied to using technology just as they are to other materials and methods in the classroom. Technology does not drive purposeful learning; teachers' intentional instructional planning does. The National Association for the Education of Young Children (NAEYC) as far back as 1996 published guidelines for the DAP use of computers in all early childhood settings (NAEYC Position Statement, 1996). This position statement is currently under revision to reflect the most recent changes in technology and young children. More current position statements on the use of technology with young children are available from the International Reading Association in its position statement, "New Literacies and 21st Century Technologies" (www.reading.org/General/AboutIRA/PositionStatements/21st CenturyLiteracies.aspx) and from the National Council for the Social Studies in its "Position Statement on Media Literacy" (www.socialstudies.org/positions/medialiteracy). When thinking of computer integration across the classroom curriculum, it is helpful to think of software as a manipulative. That is how most children see the computer—as something to manipulate or control. Any teacher who has spent a few moments with high-quality early childhood software can see that the computer is not unlike other early childhood materials such as books, playdough, and blocks. With the right kind of software, computers are open ended and discovery oriented, with three-dimensional screen manipulatives that are controlled with various devices. The child simply points the mouse, clicks, and drags the objects on the screen to the desired location. Sometimes the graphics are static, as in a picture book, and sometimes they are animated (birds fly, people walk). Therefore, computer graphics constitute manipulatives, as do blocks and puzzles. Like other manipulatives, computers can be used in many ways. They can be used wisely in a way that enhances development or in less appropriate ways that interfere with that development. No one would argue against crayons as a necessary staple in the early childhood program. But this does not mean we support having two-year-olds use crayons to color shapes on a ditto page or trace letters of the alphabet on a workbook page. Similarly, computers are advocated as an appropriate tool for use with young children, but only if they are used in a manner that supports curiosity and exploration, not as an expensive worksheet.

In working with children under the age of five, it is important to think of the computer much like a dessert instead of the main meal. Children in this age group learn best through active, physical exploration of their environments. An occasional use of the computer is appropriate with children under five years of age. But sitting down and working on a computer for long periods of time each day is not appropriate to the developmental needs of these children.

FIGURE 8-2 • An overhead projector can be a piece of useful technology in the early childhood program, especially as shown here with manipulatives.

Deciding to Use Technology

The time children spend in front of computers is time they don't have for physical activity and a host of other important activities. In making decisions regarding the use of technology in teaching and learning, teachers should carefully examine what is gained and lost when making decisions about the amount of time students spend interacting with computers and other media. For instance, when students type information, they are losing time formerly used to write—an activity that develops important handwriting and small-motor skills.

When we make the decision to have students use a computer, for example, we must think about both the gains made from using the computer (such as quick access to information) and the losses (learning to use the library, handwriting, face-to-face social skills, hands-on experiences, and understanding that simply finding mountains of information does not equate to thoughtful, accurate learning). If the computer is selected for a given activity, we need to be aware of what we are losing in the process and then make a decision about whether to provide additional time to develop the knowledge and skills that are lost when we use the technology.

Technology that Develops Creativity

Technology provides variety, interest, involvement, and reinforcement. One of the most important advantages it provides is a chance for children to develop their creativity. This occurs when they design, manipulate, and express themselves using the technology examples that follow.

Videorecordings

It is possible for children to plan and produce videorecordings of class activities. They can videorecord dramatic presentations, dancing, field trips, and other activities in and around the school.

Today, fairly inexpensive videotaping equipment is available to schools. It is lightweight, portable, and easy to use. Video can do all the things that movies and slides do, is less expensive, and can be reused. Mistakes can be erased or deleted. Children see the results of their work right away. Video can be used with dramatic play activities: A play can be videorecorded, and a children's art show can be recorded. Some children enjoy telling stories or retelling favorite events. Playtime games can be created and taped. Many portable units can be taken on field trips. Videorecordings made on field trips can be used to spark creative storytelling and the creation of new games.

Movies can be obtained by renting them or borrowing them from a library or other agency. These movies can be used to introduce engaging activities. Creative dramatics, for example, can begin with a movie that introduces a story and several characters. At a particular point, the movie can be turned off and children take the parts of the characters in acting out their own ending to the story. A video might also be used to inspire children's ideas for painting and drawing.

Photography

Young children enjoy taking pictures. Using an inexpensive camera, they can take shots of many different activities, objects, people, or whatever they find interesting.

Taking photographs is yet another way for children to experience their world. It is especially interesting and challenging for children in the elementary grades. An interesting approach to photography with upper-elementary-grade children is to focus on common themes generated by the teacher or the children. Some of these might be pictures of special people or places or pictures of people or places that make you happy or even unhappy. Children can journey around the school to document the images in their mind's eye.

Photography is an outlet for self-expression that has potential for all ages. This is due in large part to the low cost and simplicity of many cameras, which allow even the novice to take well-focused pictures. Children can share the special world of their school with others through pictures and words.

It is important, especially with younger children, to keep responsibilities simple. Explain that taking pictures is a fun activity and children can take pictures of whatever they would like to remember about their experiences at school. For example, a class of second graders came up with these ideas: happy places, happy people, special places, and special people. With older children, you may be a bit more abstract. For example, a class of fourth graders could be asked to take pictures of friendship in as many images and ways they can find. However, don't provide specific guidelines for what they photograph. Let the child be the leader.

Plan to spend some time explaining and demonstrating how to take a picture, frame the picture, activate the flash, and so forth. Leave the cameras in the art center, and let children practice with them. After they have practiced taking pictures for a while, they will be ready to really use the cameras.

When children are taking photos for the first time, a teacher or another adult needs to be on hand to help with the mechanics of looking through the viewfinder, pressing the buttons , and answering questions as they arise.

When children are out taking pictures, be sure they have notebooks and pencils with them to record where each picture was taken and its significance. So they do not forget what they have photographed, children need to write a note about each picture right after they take it. The notes can become stories later. Be certain that the students understand that their personal impressions are what you want them to describe.

Digital Cameras

Digital cameras make it possible to instantly see the picture you've just taken (and erase it if you don't like it). These cameras have incredible educational possibilities, from making labels for the classroom to showing parents their children's creations during parent–teacher conferences.

The power of a digital camera is measured in megapixels—the more a camera has, the sharper the picture. A classroom camera should have at least 5 megapixels and strong rechargeable batteries.

Of course, you'll need a computer to use with your digital camera. The computer acts as your darkroom. Once you load the pictures into your computer, it lets you alter pictures to your liking. You can also store thousands of photos for later use.

A digital camera is a great tool for teachers. You can take pictures of children's artwork throughout the year to create a portfolio of each child's work. You can take pictures of each child, print them, and post the photos on each child's cubby or personal space area.

Both regular and digital cameras can be used to photograph and document children's progress. Many times when children are working with materials, especially creating with blocks or art materials, the final

THINK ABOUT IT   Research on Photography and Young Children

Researchers have found that photographs can facilitate learning in early childhood classrooms (Einarsdottir, 2005; Good, 2005/06). Children's success in learning is significantly dependent on how engaged they are in the learning process (Mayer & Wittrock, 2006; Piaget, 1955). Einarsdottir (2005) conducted a study in which she compared two approaches to children's use of cameras. In one, the children were accompanied by an adult as they took pictures of their school. In another approach, children took pictures of their school by themselves. The results indicated that when children were with an adult, the pictures were primarily of the playground and other adults and children in their environment. All of the pictures were described as "socially expected and acceptable" photographs of children's classroom experiences. Einarsdottir (2005) suggests that the children's pictures were influenced by the adult who was with them. The children who weren't accompanied by an adult took pictures with more unique content. The pictures were frequently of other children making silly faces and engaging in entertaining activities. A majority of the pictures were of content that the author describes as private places, such as bathrooms, hallways, and cubbies where children would wander and explore. These pictures appeared to capture the children's view of and interest in their world, a view that was not filtered by an adult's perspective (Byrnes & Wasik, 2009).

In order to optimize the creative learning experiences with cameras and photos, it is important to allow the child to be actively engaged in the picture-taking process. The researchers feel that it is important to allow children to make decisions about what pictures to take and then actually use the camera to take the pictures. In this way, the activity has more meaning for the child. This is especially important when the goal is to support children's language development and increase their vocabulary.

Providing children with the opportunity to decide the content of the picture and to talk about what is in the picture reinforces children's learning of meaningful language and vocabulary (Byrnes & Wasik, 2009).

product misses the thinking and process that goes into the completed work. Documenting with photographs helps to show the progress and also gives the child opportunities to revisit her or his work.

Some other ways to use a digital camera follow.

- Experiment with time-lapse photography. Take a picture of the children in front of the same tree each month to see the seasons change.
- Preserve memories. Next time a child cleans up, snap a picture.
- Decorate bulletin boards with photos of active, happy children.
- Allow the children to become the photographers. Take pictures in the classroom, on the playground, and on walking trips. Children can view their finished photos from the camera or with a teacher on the computer, identifying what they thought was important.

Inexpensive, throwaway digital cameras are available that are well suited for children's use. You will be amazed and delighted as you see the world through children's eyes. See websites listed at the end of this chapter for general advice about purchasing digital cameras.

Editing Digital Images

Basic editing can be done on the camera or with any number of photo editing software programs. There are a number of software-/Web-based photo services that will support your photo editing and layout design. These tools make it easy to import/export photos, edit, add special effects, and organize photos into albums. Three of these sources are briefly described here.

- Picasa2—Free download from Google with one-click editing and effects. http://www.picasa.google.com
- Kodak EasyShare Gallery—This free software download is a great way to store and edit digital photos. Use one click to edit tools to enhance lighting, crop, and even create collages of four to 100 photos. http://www.kodakgallery.com
- Snapfish—This online photo service from HP facilitates camera or computer uploads—even e-mail photos from a mobile phone. Install PhotoShow for more features. http://www.snapfish.com

All of these photo tools let you e-mail photos to share with colleagues or parents to highlight special events.

"Smart" Toys

You don't have to have the most expensive computer to offer high-quality interactive learning opportunities, thanks to a new generation of **smart toys** with microprocessors as brains. Because of these microprocessors, a smart toy typically can adjust to the abilities of the player. Here are some favorites, available in most toy stores.

- Music Blocks (http://www.neurosmith.com) lets children experiment with the structure of music.
- LeapPad (http://www.Leapfrog.com) is an outstanding early language experience toy. Children can touch each letter or sound to hear it spoken in a clear voice. Multiple language options are also available.
- Pixter (http://www.fisher-price.com) is an electronic sketching device.
- Question-Air (Educational Insights, http://www.edin.com) is like a game of hot potato but with educational questions tossed in.
- GeoSafari Talking Microscope (http://www.edin.com) lets children learn about magnified bugs.

iPods and MP3 Players

The iPod is a portable digital music player that can also be used to store photos or even movies. The first iPods contained hard disks; later versions were RAM-based with more reliable performance. iPod content can only be managed by a computer running iTunes, which makes it possible to browse, store, and purchase digital content. None of these ideas was invented by Apple, but they were packaged and marketed extremely well by Apple. Today, a variety of digital music players are available for children, including the Playskool Made for Me MP3 Music Player. Another perfect player for young children is Peapod Toys' SweetPea3 with a simple operating system and built-in handle.

Compact Discs and Disc Players

If digital music is not easily accessible to your classroom, compact discs (CDs) and players are another possibility. CDs are used in computers, providing sound effects and narration on early childhood computer software. Playing recorded music on a CD is an excellent source of musical experiences for young children.

Interactive White (Smart) Boards in Elementary Classrooms

Interactive white boards (IWBs) are large screen-like boards that are placed in front of a class and connected to a computer and data projector. Any computer image can be projected onto this sturdy surface. Teachers and students can write directly on the board to make notes and highlight all sorts of amazing images.

Interactive white boards were initially developed for and used in the business world, but they eventually caught on in higher education, and by the late 1990s, K–12 schools began integrating the technology (Lacina, 2009). However, there is a lack of research on student achievement gains when IWBs are used for classroom instruction. Despite this lack of research, there is a wealth of descriptive studies in favor of their use (Cogill, 2003; Smith, Higgins, Wall, & Miller, 2005). Almost across the board, teachers report that their students are highly engaged in activities with interactive whiteboards (Curwood, 2009).

Interactive white boards appeal to children's multiple intelligences, providing opportunities for visual/spatial and bodily/kinesthetic learners than can be hard to accommodate in the print-based classroom. They also allow you to reach your students through a variety of media. For example, if you are studying Kenya, your students might use Google Earth (http://www.earth.google.com) to project the country on the whiteboard, zooming in and out to see the terrain, and clicking on photos that show details, daily life, flora, and fauna. Then, when students dive into the reading, they have a variety of background knowledge and increased motivation.

Interactive whiteboards allow users to annotate computer screen information and highlight key visual points. This technology allows presenters to make their notes directly on the whiteboard itself using either a finger or an electronic stylus. They can also use a remote device to operate the whiteboard like a mouse operates a computer.

Some teachers prefer standing at the front of the room using the interactive whiteboard. Other teachers like to circulate throughout the room while teaching, using a wireless pad that allows them to move control their computer and whiteboard while moving about. Whatever is on a computer screen can be shown on a whiteboard for an entire class to see.

Interactive whiteboard manufacturers are now packaging teaching suggestions that include lessons, activities, and clip art. Whiteboard vendor websites often have places where teachers can share and download images and lesson templates. See activities at the end of this chapter for suggestions on uses for an interactive whiteboard in the classroom.

Technology and Multiple Intelligences

Technology can help meet the needs of various learning styles. The multiple intelligences, as discussed in Chapter 5, can be enhanced with the use of technology. The list in Figure 8–3 covers the types of technology and software suitable for each of the multiple intelligences. When integrating technology into the early childhood program, teachers need to make sure to keep in mind the needs of all learners and use various methods and techniques suitable for each.

Value of Computers in Early Childhood Programs

Computers, as we have seen, have found their way into the preschool setting, taking their place beside the finger paints, playdough, books, and other media found within the early learning environment. Computer programs have been developed for young children that allow them to produce colorful graphics, music, and animations.

Children of the 21st century will use computers as integral parts of their daily lives. Yet children who are plugged into computers to do drill and practice engage in convergent thinking. In fact, these programs are just another version of convergent ditto sheet-like work. It is important to realize that using computers with young children is a process of exploration and discovery for both you and the children. How you use computers the first year in your classroom will probably be very different from how you use them five years later.

Based on recent research, some general conclusions about the value of computers with preschool and other children in early childhood programs may be made.

- *Computers can be used effectively with young children.* Researchers have consistently observed high levels of spoken communication and cooperation as young children interact at the computer. Compared with more traditional activities, such as puzzle assembly or block building, the computer elicits both more social interaction and different types of interaction. Children in comprehensive,

Following Howard Gardner's theory of multiple intelligences, teachers can encourage development by providing enrichment opportunities in each of the areas of the intellect. The following are suggestions on how to integrate technology with each of the multiple intelligences.

Linguistic Intelligence (Word Smart)
Use of word-processing programs can help teach language, writing, editing, and rewriting skills. Also, the Internet is invaluable for learning. Through e-mail, children can improve their language skills. Other technologies children may benefit from follow.

- Desktop publishing programs
- Programs that allow children to create stories, poems, and essays
- Multimedia authoring
- Videodiscs to create presentations
- Tape recorders

Logical/Mathematical (Logic Smart)
Computer programs can teach logic and critical thinking skills. These are also in game formats that can motivate children's thinking. For example, drill-and-practice math programs, while building mathematical conceptualization and functions skills, also offer engaging games that maintain young learners' interest. Database programs help explore and organize data and information.

Other technologies children may benefit from are listed here.

- Problem-solving software
- Computer-aided design programs
- Strategy game software
- Graphing calculators
- Multimedia authoring programs
- Spreadsheet programs

Visual/Spatial (Picture Smart)
Graphics programs help develop creativity and visual skills. Also, browsing the Internet and organizing files and folders will develop some spatial understanding. Other technologies children may benefit from follow.

- Drawing programs
- Image-composing programs
- Paint programs (Photopaint, Microsoft Paint)
- Reading programs with visual clues
- Web-page programs
- Three-dimensional software
- Software games
- Spreadsheet programs that allow children to see charts, maps, or diagrams
- Multimedia authoring programs

Musical Intelligence (Music Smart)
Some computer programs help write or play music. Other technologies that children may benefit from include these:

- Music-composing software
- Videodisc player
- Programs integrating stories with songs and instruments
- Reading programs that relate letter/sound with music

FIGURE 8-3 • Technology and multiple intelligences *(Continued)*.

- Programs that allow children to create their own music
- CD-ROMs about music and instruments
- Tape recorders
- Word processors to write about a movie or song

Bodily/Kinesthetic (Body Smart)
Using computers will help develop eye–hand coordination. Working with a computer will allow children to become actively involved in their learning. Other kinesthetic technologies children may benefit from are listed here.

- Software games that allow contact with the keyboard, mouse, joystick, and other devices
- Programs that allow children to move objects around the screen
- Word-processing programs
- Animation programs

Interpersonal (Person Smart)
Students can work in groups of two to four on computers. Working in groups will strengthen children's communication and cooperation skills. Technologies children may benefit from include these:

- Computer games that require two or more people
- Programs that allow children to create group presentations (PowerPoint)
- Telecommunication programs
- E-mail
- Distance education
- Helping others with any programs

Intrapersonal (Self Smart)
The computer can help children build individual skills. It allows for differences in children's learning styles and abilities. Children may work at their own pace with computers. Other technologies children may benefit from follow.

- Any programs that allow children to work independently
- Games involving only one person
- Brainstorming or problem-solving software
- Instructional games
- Word processors for journaling and recording feelings
- Developing multimedia portfolio
- Video editing

FIGURE 8-3 • Technology and multiple intelligences

technology-enhanced programs make progress in all developmental areas, including social, fine motor, gross motor, communication, cognition, and self-help skills (Ching, 2009; Lee, 2009).

- *Computers can be interactive.* The term **interactive** here means that the computer used with young children provides a vehicle for two types of interaction: child-to-computer and child-to-child. Child-to-computer interaction depends to a great extent on the software. Some software requires children to choose one response, which is then corrected. Other programs have been developed that allow children to use information on the screen to make more than one response.

Child-to-child interaction at the computer depends on the arrangement of the environment. When children work near each other by the computer, they discuss what they are doing and assist each other as they work. Some software is also designed for, or lends

FIGURE 8-4 • Interpersonal learners enjoy working with other children on computers.

itself better to, participation by more than one child. (See the end of the chapter for suggested software for children.)

The teacher and the software together also make a difference. By placing two child seats in front of the computer and one at the side for adults, the teacher is encouraging cooperation between children as well as interaction with an adult. Such an arrangement encourages children to work cooperatively and to converse as they work on the computer.

Computer work can instigate new instances and forms of collaborative work—such as helping or teaching, discussing and building on each other's ideas, cooperating, and praising. It can also increase social interaction between children with disabilities and their typically developing peers (Clements & Sarama, 2003a; Robinson, Schneider, Saytner, Johnson, & Hutinger, 2009).

Placement of computers can encourage children's learning. The ideal placement of the computer center is in a visible location. The monitors are situated so that they can be seen from throughout the classroom (Lee,

2009). Children are interested in what's happening in the computer center, although they may be working in another center. All of this stimulates peer mentoring, social interaction, language development, and cooperative play. In addition, a highly visible computer center enables you to supervise this area without leaving your current location. You need to move to the computer center only when it is necessary to assist children, or you can ask another child who is not busy if he or she is willing to help. This help encourages children's independent learning as well as peer teaching. Strive for a 10:1 ratio (or better) of children to computers to encourage computer use, cooperation, and equal access by girls and boys.

• *Age and computer use.* Age doesn't appear to be a limiting factor in computer use. Even two-year-old children can work proficiently on the computer using age-appropriate software that requires only simple keypresses or pointing with a mouse. One researcher watched children as young as three use Google to look up sites and an eight-year-old check his mom's e-mail to download a game (Buckleitner, 2008). Preschoolers can easily start the computer, load disks, type on the keyboard, and understand pictorial cues.

During the preschool years, children should have many opportunities to explore open-ended, developmentally appropriate software programs in a playful, supportive environment. These experiences will help them develop the basic skills needed to use technology equipment, such as opening and closing programs, saving and printing documents, and navigating the screen using a mouse. This will help children become confident in their ability to use a computer and will provide the foundational skills needed to use more advanced applications for purposeful work as they grow older.

As children enter the primary years, they can begin to use familiar technology tools as a part of their academic program. At the same time, adults should model the use of technology in support of the curriculum and learning experiences children are engaged in. For example, adults can model the use of technology for communication by using e-mail and word-processing programs with children to communicate with families and others important to the classroom community. There are many other ways adults can model the appropriate use of technology, such as documenting events in the classroom using digital still or video cameras and creating multimedia electronic portfolios

FIGURE 8-5 • Filming a commercial involves creativity and teamwork.

FIGURE 8-6 • Keyboard skills develop as children use a "typer" keyboard that scans directly into the computer.

that document children's learning (Ching, 2009). This way, children can see firsthand the purposeful use of technology and benefit from exposure to more advanced applications that they will eventually use independently.

- *Children prefer action.* Just as in other aspects of their play, children like action with computers, and they do not necessarily choose to follow the rules of games. They watch what happens when they press new keys, and they purposely may try to squash all the keys at one time. One of the strengths young children bring to computer use is their fearless experimentation!

A good environment for young children includes many experiences that involve the senses, adult–child and child–child conversation, and a host of other age-appropriate activities. Computers can supplement, but do not substitute for, experiences in which children can discover with all their senses. Technology is a tool, and as such it should be used because it is the best tool for the job (Parette, Blum, Boeckmann, & Watts, 2009).

Only after a sound, basic program has been developed should teachers consider buying a computer. First should come blocks, sand and water tables, art materials, books, and all other proven elements of a good program for young children.

Choosing Software for Young Children

Care must be taken to select computer software that is developmentally appropriate for the children who will use it. Research shows that different types of software have different effects (Clements & Samara, 2003b). Open-ended programs foster collaboration. Drill-and-practice programs encourage turn taking but also may encourage a competitive spirit. Violent programs can lead to aggressiveness (Clements & Samara, 2003b). The following 11 criteria distinguish software that is developmentally appropriate.

1. *Age appropriateness.* The concepts taught and their method of presentation reflect realistic expectations for young children.

THIS ONE'S for YOU! Computer Maintenance

You don't need to be a technology guru to know how to keep your computer running smoothly. Here are some maintenance steps and commonly recommended procedures for protecting your computer and prolonging its life.

- Turn on your computer when you begin each day and don't turn it off until you finish for the day. Some people turn their personal computer (PC) on and off throughout the day. This causes a computer's innards to frequently expand and contract, creating stress that can lead to premature component failure.

- **Defragment** your hard **disk** periodically. The operating systems of typical PCs and Macs scatter file fragments over the hard disk. Specific software programs combine these fragments, which reduces hard drive wear and tear and increases system performance. Some programs signal you to defragment when your hard disk reaches a specified level of fragmentation, such as 90%. Alternately, you can defragment weekly, monthly, or semiannually, depending on how often you use your PC. Don't use a program that defragments your hard disk continually. It will create more wear and tear than it prevents.

- For maximum safety, unplug your PC and any phone line leading to it during a thunderstorm unless you need to keep it on for work purposes. A nearby lightning strike will blow right past a typical surge protector and can fry a PC. Use a surge protector or uninterrupted power supply for smaller surges.

- Use a disk drive cleaning kit when you experience problems with your disk drive, or at most, once a year as preventive maintenance.

- Do not use a cleaning kit every week as some kit manufacturers suggest. This just overstresses your disk drive's read/write head.

- Your PC should be plugged into a three-pronged grounded outlet, preferably on a dedicated circuit. Don't move a PC or connect or disconnect its cables while it is on unless the cables are plugged into a universal serial bus port.

- Clean your monitor if it becomes smudged. Stay away from glass cleaners, as they can remove a monitor's antiglare finish. Use isopropyl alcohol or distilled water along with a lint-free cloth. Wet the cloth first, then the monitor.

- Keep CD-ROM discs inside a caddy or jewel case when not in use to avoid scratches. If dirt or fingerprints sully a disc, gently wipe it with a soft, lint-free cloth or use an audio CD cleaning kit.

- Remember some of these "personal maintenance" techniques to help prevent unnecessary discomfort when you or the children are working at a computer.

- Avoid chairs that are high-backed or have armrests. The idea is to ensure free mobility of the arms and shoulders so hands and lower arms won't bear all the strain.

- Don't set your wrists on a wrist rest while actively typing.

- Keep the mouse at the same level as the keyboard if possible.

- Position the monitor so you're looking slightly down at the screen and can read it without tilting your head down or back.

- Place the monitor directly in front of you so you don't twist your head or neck while typing.

- Ensure no glare from lights or windows reflects on the screen.

2. *Child control.* Children are active participants, initiating and deciding the sequence of events, rather than reactors, responding to predetermined activities. The software needs to facilitate active rather than passive involvement (Lee, 2009). The pace is set by the child, not the program.

3. *Clear instructions.* Because the majority of preschool children are nonreaders, spoken directions are essential (Bergen & Wang, 2008). If printed instructions are used, they are accompanied by spoken directions. Directions are simple and precise. Graphics accompany choices to make options clear to the children.

4. *Expanding complexity.* Entry level is low; children can easily learn to manipulate the software successfully. The learning sequence is clear; one

concept follows the next (NAEYC, 1996). The software expands as children explore, teaching the skills they are ready to learn. Through the expanding complexity of the software, children build on their knowledge.

5. *Independent exploration.* After initial exposure, children can manipulate the software without adult supervision.

6. *Process orientation.* The process of using the software is so engaging for children that the product becomes secondary. Children learn through discovery rather than being drilled in specific skills. Motivation to learn is intrinsic, not the result of praise, smiling-face stickers, or prizes.

7. *Real-world representation.* The software is a simple and reliable model of some aspect of the real world, exposing children to concrete representation of objects and their functions.

8. *Technical features.* The software has high technical quality that helps the young child pay attention. It is colorful and includes uncluttered, realistic, animated graphics. There are realistic sound effects or music that corresponds to objects on the screen. The software loads from the disks and runs fast enough to maintain the child's interest.

9. *Trial and error.* The software provides children many chances to test alternative responses. Through resolving errors or solving problems, children build structures and knowledge.

10. *Visible transformations.* Children have an impact on the software, changing objects and situations through their responses (NAEYC, 1996).

FIGURE 8-7 • The placement of computers can encourage cooperation.

11. *For bilingual students,* translation of both languages, preferably in real time, is an important feature. A program that allows the student to toggle between languages provides instant translations of each page.

In this list, it is important to note that software may have a developmental approach to learning without having all of the criteria. Some software has more developmental criteria than other software. You need to choose software that includes as many of these criteria as possible.

Choosing Developmentally Appropriate Software

Teachers basically have two options to assist them in selecting developmentally appropriate software. First, they can use a software rating scale to evaluate software themselves. Many evaluation forms, such as the **Haugland/Shade Software Developmental Scale** (Haugland & Wright, 1997), can help teachers understand the key component of quality software.

Second, several individuals and organizations have designed systems that teachers can use to evaluate software. The advantage of using an existing software evaluation system is that previewing software is unnecessary because it has already been extensively field-tested by teachers, parents, and children. Table 8–1 presents a list of online sources of educational software reviews.

Web 2.0 and Early Childhood Programs

The term **Web 2.0** has been coined to describe the Web's transition from a collection of static websites containing information to a more dynamic, interactive, social, and content-sharing environment. Web 1.0 never really left. It's just a term that refers to cyberspace before 2002. Generally, Web 1.0 sites have a commercial focus. They function more like a book or storefront in these ways:

• They are good for research and information.

• Downloads rule because information flows one way.

• Search is everything.

• They are organization centric. They own it. They design it. They write it.

TABLE 8-1 • Educational software reviews on the Internet.

SITE	INTERNET ADDRESS	INFORMATION AVAILABLE
California Instructional Technology Clearinghouse	http://www.clearinghouse. k12.ca.us	Contains the searchable California Technology in the Curriculum Evaluation database on more than 3,000 technology products.
Children's Software Review	http://www.childrenssoftware. com/	Since 1993, each issue contains 100 to 200 authoritative reviews and ratings, helpful articles, tips and spotlights on technology use in school subjects.
Educational Media Reviews Online	http://libweb.lib.buffalo.edu/ emro/search.html	An online database of video, dvd, and cd-rom reviews on materials from major educational and documentary distributors Reviews written primarily by librarians and teaching faculty in institutions across the U.S. and Canada.
Superkids Educational Software Review	http://www.superkids.com	Provides reviews and ratings of software and practical and fun tools for online and offline use.
Technology & Learning	http://www.techlearning.com	Offers a searchable database of software and websites reviews, as well as information about professional development activities and grants.
Learning Village	http://www.learning village. com/html/guide.html	Provides reviews of software, Internet content, and more.

In contrast, Web 2.0 sites enable users to:

- Create, write, and publish content.

- Share with the world by linking an article or page from one site to your online repository of favorite Web content.

- Participate. Users can post an opinion, interact with other contributors, and collaborate with a community of users who feel the way they do—or don't.

- Web 2.0 invites everyone to participate, construct, and evaluate information that is removed from the confining absolutes of documented fact and opinion that characterized Web 1.0. What is known changes with the online conversation.

Web 2.0 tools and services like blogs, wikis, podcasts, photo- and video-sharing sites, social networks, and virtual worlds are now being used daily by millions of people around the globe to connect, communicate, collaborate, create, and share with others. One of the many challenges early childhood teachers face is keeping up with all of these technologies and assessing their potential uses in their classrooms.

Many rich educational opportunities await children on Web 2.0. It provides children with a variety of learning opportunities that appear to enhance problem solving, critical thinking skills, decision making, creativity, language skills, knowledge, research skills, the ability to integrate information, social skills, and self-esteem (Nebel, Jamison, & Bennett, 2009).

Included in Web 2.0 are the four basic types of children's websites: **information, communication, interaction,** and **publication.**

Information Sites

Enhanced with sound and videos, **information sites** are rich reference resources that teachers and parents can use to model or assist children in answering questions, making new discoveries, and building knowledge. For example, a virtual trip to the zoo gives children opportunities to see pictures, hear animal sounds, and view movies of animals exploring their natural habitats. The National Zoo (http://www.si.edu/natzoo/) from the Smithsonian Institute is such a Web site. A virtual tour of a dinosaur museum (http://hooper-museum.earthsci.carleton.ca//7.html) is another possibility. Another example is taking an online tour of Italy to learn more about the children's electronic pen pals from Rome.

Communication Sites

At **communication sites**, children interact with teachers, friends, relatives, or classrooms across the street, in another city, or even across the globe. Using simple e-mail addresses, children and classroom groups write letters, compose stories, create poems, or work on a class project. For example, "The Way We Are" (http://www.epals.com/projects/info.aspx?DivID=TheWayWeAre_overview) is an e-pals project in which students learn about other people and cultures and then produce a PowerPoint show about what they learned.

Also through e-mail, children can ask "experts" questions in various disciplines. One example is Ask Dr. Math (http://mathforum.org/dr.math). This provides classrooms not only with the answers to questions, but also with the opportunity to explore a variety of math-related occupations. Another communication option is to join the Twitter community. (http://www.twitter.com). Twitter allows users to send and read messages that are limited to 140 characters. The content of these short messages, known as "tweets," offers a mixture of day-to-day chats as well as useful information. See Twitter4Teachers (http://www.twitter4teachers.pbwiki.com) for a list of teachers by grade level and subject area. The best way to regularly use Twitter is to reflect on what's happening in your classroom and to raise issues or share resources that might interest other teachers. For tips on getting started with Twitter, read "10 Easy Steps for Twitter Beginners" at www.snipurl.com/6w6o8.

Interaction Sites

Interaction sites are similar to software programs, using sound, animation, sound effects, and high-quality, realistic graphics.

An example of an interaction site is Lego Universe. Launched in 2009, this is a massive multiplayer online community building game (MMOG) designed for children and adults This is the first MMOG game involving Lego bricks in a virtual, public, shared space. Players can communicate with one another through various layers of chat and build anything they can dream up. As they build, children (and adults) can chat or team up to participate in Lego-based adventures. You can visit Lego Universe at http://universe.lego.com.

Another example of an interaction site is Club Penguin. After registering (which requires a valid e-mail address), children are asked to choose one of several penguin worlds to join. At any time, children can use a map to jump in or out of a game, or visit their own igloo, which serves as a home base. This Web experience is very easy to get into and play with no risk or downloads other than Macromedia Flash, which is becoming standard on nearly every browser. As a language experience, the program gets children busily typing with others, and there are a variety of games that require logical thinking and strategy.

Also at Club Penguin, students can learn responsible skills such as: Don't give your address, last name, password, physical description, current location, or other identifying information. Teachers can use these sites to teach students about digital citizenship within a controlled environment so they know how to conduct themselves in the uncontrolled real world.

Publication Sites

The Internet can be used as a resource for actually publishing children's work on **publication sites**. Even three-year-olds can understand that when their work is displayed on the Internet everyone in the world can see it. Imagine their pride! Motivation for learning is sparked as they create new pictures and stories. A number of Web sites post children's work, such as KidPub (http://www.kidpub.org/). Photos can be shared on an Internet Web site such as Flickr (http://www.Flickr.com), which hosts free images and videos for an online community. One of the advantages of using a publication site is that students' work is

THIS ONE'S for YOU! Assistive Technology for Children With Special Needs

For young children with disabilities, technology offers a wide range of equipment to support participation and learning called **assistive technology.** Some devices—voice synthesizers, Braille readers, switch-activated toys, and computers—are truly high tech. Yet many simple, low-tech tools are equally valuable in early childhood classrooms. For example, special handles on utensils and paintbrushes, or a handle attached to a stuffed animal, allow a child to grasp without help.

Using assistive technology to help a child with special needs may be as simple as providing a utensil with a handle. Children with special needs such as limited motor movement may have difficulty in using a mouse or pushing the button on a digital camera. Adaptation can be made through a touch-sensitive tablet or an adaptive device that takes the place of the mouse. Specially designed digital cameras allow children to take pictures by pressing an attached switch. Such devices allow children to use technology independently. Teachers may choose to learn more about customized technology options and participate in online teacher workshops. Visit the Early Childhood Technology Integrated Instructional System at http://www.wiu.edu/ectiis (NAEYC, 2008).

It is equally important to match the technology to the needs and abilities of the child. With so many options available today, it is essential that those adults most familiar with the child work closely with professionals who have special expertise in assistive technology. This type of collaborative process can ensure that the supports used will help the child achieve more independence and that technology benefits everyone.

Assistive technology options are exciting and full of promise, but not every device fits in every environment. Some might be too expensive, too cumbersome to transport between home and school, or too specialized to be used in multiple environments.

Carefully analyze each environment to determine what equipment or technology is needed to support the child's participation (Lee, 2009). Even the most advanced device won't help unless it matches the child's abilities and the demands of the environment. The challenge is to find the device that helps a young child with special needs take part in every routine and activity. The right match of assistive technology can be magical if it allows a child to be more independent and expressive.

The following websites provide more information on assistive technology.

- The Tots 'n' Tech Research Institute, http://tnt. asu.edu/. This site offers ideas for equipment and materials that can help children with special needs be more independent in caring for themselves, making friends, communicating, and doing the things that other young children do in child care and community activity settings.

- The National Early Childhood Technical Assistance Center, http://www.nectac.org/. Click on "Topics," then go to "Early Childhood Practices" and click on "Special Practices." This site provides information on various types of assistive technology, funding resources, and current legislation.

- ChildCare Plus+: The Center on Inclusion in Early Childhood, http://www.ccplus.org. This site offers a number of free and inexpensive resources, including an Adapting Toys Tool Kit that contains materials and instructions for adapting toys, adding sensory input, and promoting independent play.

---

exposed to a wider audience than typically occurs with a school-based website. For examples of art programs that post student work on Flickr, see the photo streams of Darien Public Schools' art department in Connecticut (http://www.tinyurl.com/4y3u83) and Fortismere Secondary School's art and photography department in North London (http://www.flickr.com/people/fortismereartdepartment/). If you're interested in posting student-made videos online,

TeacherTube is a safe alternative to YouTube.com See Tricia Fuglestad's TeacherTube page (http://www.tinyurl.com/4gnbz9) for an excellent example.

A Note of Caution!

Although the potential of the Internet is tremendous, some precautions must be addressed. Anyone can place anything on the Internet, some of which may be harmful to young children. A screening device is essential, such as Kid Desk: Internet Safe (1998), Net Nanny (http://www.netnanny.com), or Cyber Patrol (http://www.cyberpatrol.com). Another helpful screening device is a PG Key. The PG Key resembles a USB flash drive and plugs directly into the USB port of a child's computer. It allows adults to control when the child uses the computer. When it is unplugged, the computer can't be used. In addition, it locks in Safe Search, which allows the freedom to search the Web, but prevents most of the unwanted and dangerous content from showing up. For more information on this device, visit www.pgkey.com.

It is probably best for children to use a pen name when on the Internet—the name of their dog, cat, or favorite stuffed animal.

Blogs

A **blog** is basically an online journal. The key to the blog's popularity is how simple it is to construct and maintain. The blogger simply types in his or her thoughts and clicks "post." The blog handles the rest automatically, with the new posting appearing at the top of the blog Web page, followed by previous postings in reverse chronological order.

A blog, which requires no special software, no knowledge of html, and virtually no time, can substitute for a traditional website if your aim is to have a simple medium for communication.

Types of Blogs

Some of the most common types of blogs being used in schools today are **classroom news blogs, mirror blogs, showcase blogs,** and **literature response blogs**. Blogs often incorporate more than one of these primary functions and, given the creative minds of effective teachers and the rapidly changing nature of literacy on the Internet, many more types will probably emerge in the future.

Classroom news blogs. Many **classroom blogs** are used to share news and information with parents and students. Often this is the first type of blog a teacher will use. Teachers update classroom news blogs on a regular basis, posting homework assignments, providing updates on curriculum for parents, and sharing any other information that could benefit the home–school connection. Parents do not necessarily have to be your target audience. You may want to establish a dialogue

with students in the upper grades. With a blog, you can create a message and invite students who visit the blog to add their comments. Or the target audience could be your fellow teachers.

Mirror blogs. Mirror blogs allow bloggers to reflect on their thinking—hence the "mirror" title. A teacher may post a response about a workshop recently attended, sharing insights learned. While reading a new professional book on literacy, a blogger might post quotes or compelling new ideas found in the book to a mirror blog. Many teachers are not only posting their own reflective thinking but also include student reflections as well. Student comments of this type might include thoughts about lessons or content learned.

For example, you can write every morning before students come in or every afternoon when they leave. In a mirror blog you can reflect on the completed class day, analyzing skills met and standards addressed in preparation for the next day's lessons. Blogging becomes something like an electronic log or journal of the class's successes and identified needs for reteaching. If the blog is made public, then parents, students, and even colleagues can follow the progression to improve their support for classroom learning.

Showcase blogs. Many teachers use blogs to post student art projects, podcasts (audio clips), and writing in **showcase blogs**. Of particular interest are the ways in which second language learners can use these spaces to write and respond in their second language in more authentic ways and for more authentic audiences. *Have Fun with English! 2* (http://www.fwe2.motime.com) is an Edublogs award winner where students from Portugal practice their English. The blog is a combination of student and teacher writing, artwork, and even audio messages from students. Many of the blog posts are student podcasts describing their day with the written text just underneath.

Literature response blogs. Literature response journals are common in elementary classrooms. A **literature response blog** simply moves this idea online, where the teacher may sometimes post a prompt and invite student responses to a text. Using blogs to bridge a familiar in-school activity with this out-of-school tool provides students with a different medium for literature response.

Several resources are available to help you set up and organize a blog.

FIGURE 8-8 • Children enjoy using interactive (smart) whiteboards that are connected to a computer and a data projector.

- **Blogging? It's Elementary, My Dear Watson!** at http://www.educationworld.com/a_tech/tech/tech217.shtml—Features lesson plans and ideas for using blogging in the elementary curriculum.
- **Blogging Rubric** at http://www.masters.ab.ca/bdyck/Blog—Suggestions for how to evaluate student responses on a blog.
- **Free Blogs for Teachers** at http://www.edublogs.org

Wikis

Although blogs may be the easiest websites to maintain, they're not great for large, collaborative class projects that sort a lot of information onto separate Web pages. For that, it may be easier to have children contribute to a wiki. A **wiki** is a website that allows readers to add and edit content. It works like a communal, beyond-the-*Britannica* encyclopedia. The first wiki, WikiWikiWeb, is named after the Wiki Wiki line of Chance RT-52 buses in Honolulu International Airport, Hawaii. "Wiki-wiki" means "hurry quick" in Hawaiian.

It's a great way to make a large website without knowing HTML or Web design. The wiki format allows students to easily link to each other's work using the same collaborative method and internal linking that you see on Wikipedia.

You can set up a wiki on any topic children are studying. You can set up free accounts at http://www.pbwiki.com, http://www.seedwiki.com, and http://www.wikicities.com. Several other wiki services are:

- *PB Wiki* (http://pbwiki.com): This is quickly becoming one of the most popular wiki services for educators because it's so easy to use. For an example of PB Wiki in action, check out Stay Current at http://staycurrent.pbwiki.com.

- *Wikispaces* (http://www.wikispaces.com): This is one of the first wiki services that educators embraced. As a result, there are literally thousands of Wikispaces that you can look to for samples of what's possible.

- *Wet Paint* (http://www.wetpaint.com): This is one of the newest wiki services available to educators, but it's also one of the most intriguing. With an emphasis on tools for collaboration and professional templates, Wet Paint wikis will make you look good.

A wiki is a collaborative platform because anyone can edit or manipulate the existing text. Wikipedia is an online encyclopedia and a popular go-to source for students who are writing research papers. Wikipedia cofounder Jimmy Wales has described Wikipedia as "an effort to create and distribute a multilingual free encyclopedia of the highest possible quality to every single person on the planet in their own language" (Long, 2006).

Perhaps your instructor has a wiki as a useful way to eliminate handouts. Or you as a teacher may use a wiki to enable parents to follow along with what is happening in your class. At the upper elementary levels, it may be a useful tool for students who missed class to download work that needs to be made up. A wiki in the best sense helps students (and teachers) to work together and build upon each other's work, allowing everyone to get involved.

Personal Learning Network

The latest catchphrase to spread throughout the online educational community is **personal learning network**. This refers to a collection of people and resources you can consult to learn something or to get answers to your questions. Building learning connections is not a new practice for teachers. From the time we enter the classroom, we gather useful curriculum resources and periodically call on colleagues for advice, read educational journals, and attend professional conferences in order to improve our understanding of pedagogy and the subjects we teach. With the aid of some online tools, you can now expand your existing learning network to include people and resources from all over the world.

A good way to get started building your personal learning network is to set up a social bookmarking account. Social bookmarking is a variation of the popular practice of saving and organizing links to Web pages (sometimes called "favorites") that you want to remember and return to at a later date. In a social bookmarking system, links are usually shared with selected people through groups or networks. Since your links are stored online rather than on your computer, they are available through any computer connected to the Internet.

Social bookmarking sites encourage users to organize their collections of bookmarks with tags, which are keywords associated with the content of a linked page. Other features available through some social bookmarking services include subscription feeds that inform you when new bookmarks have been added to

your network or group, plus the ability to highlight and annotate bookmarked pages.

Two social bookmarking services popular among teachers are Delicious (http://www.delicious.com) and Diigo (http://www.diigo.com), which offers educator accounts with features intended to serve the needs to K–12 teachers. To get started with either service, you first need to register for an account and install special bookmaking buttons in your Web browser. To learn more, watch Common Craft's "Social Bookmarking in Plain English" video (www.snipurl.com/6w6pm).

Summary

Technology is definitely here to stay in the early childhood classroom. Computers are a part of many children's early childhood experiences. Early childhood teachers first and foremost must consider the developmental appropriateness of technology for young children. The concept of DAP needs to be used in all choices of technology in the early childhood classroom. However, technology can enhance the early childhood program in the following ways:

- It provides variety in the program.
- It leads to interesting learning experiences.
- It leads children to create materials or develop new ideas.
- It builds on other things children have experienced in the preschool program.

It is important to choose developmentally appropriate software that includes 10 characteristics: age-appropriateness, child control, clear instructions, expanding complexity, independent exploration, process orientation, real-world representation, technical features, trial and error, and visible transformations. The Internet has changed dramatically since 2002, when it was mostly an information source. The term Web 2.0 has been coined to describe the Web's transition from a collection of static websites containing information to a more dynamic, interactive, social, and content-sharing environment. In today's Web 2.0, early childhood teachers can utilize such tools and services as blogs, wikis, Twitter, podcasts, photo and video-sharing sites, social networks, and virtual worlds. Included in Web 2.0 are four basic types of children's websites: information, communication, interaction, and publication websites.

Each of these websites requires direct teacher involvement in order to safeguard the safety of young children's use.

FIGURE 8-9 • The teacher should be available for assistance when new software is introduced.

THIS ONE'S for YOU! Basic Technology for the Classroom

Using technology in the classroom has become an accepted practice in early childhood programs. In many teacher preparation programs, candidates must demonstrate sound knowledge and skills in using technology as a teaching and learning tool.

Listed here are some basic technologies suitable for early childhood classrooms today.

- Digital imaging is one of the most exciting technologic applications for early childhood classrooms. Photography and video have long been used to document children's learning and to help them remember and reflect on their experiences. Advances in ease of use and accessibility, along with reductions in cost of digital imaging tools, have greatly simplified the use of these tools in the classroom. Using digital images, records of children's experiences can be loaded onto the computer where children can seek them out and review them at will. The images can lead children to discuss the events with adults and peers and then perhaps use them as a basis for writing, drawing, or other forms of processing and expression.

- Word processing and writing tools (for example, WriteOn from Software Production Associates), allow children to express themselves, free from the fine-motor demands of letter formation. For many children, these tools can serve as adaptive or assistive technology to make the physical act of writing less frustrating. For others, the excitement of seeing their stories and ideas in formal print is extremely motivating and can spur them to revise and edit their work in order to see it "published."

- Computer art programs such as Kid Pix (Broderbund) are an excellent way to introduce children to open-ended exploration of the computer. Children's art programs generally provide a wide range of choices for expressing ideas, from freehand drawing to the use of stamps, text, or other special effects that can be combined to create a complex visual display. Many of these programs also provide multimedia options such as sounds, animation, and voice recording to allow children to create multimedia work. Some of these programs are simple enough for three-year-old children to use with ease and have the capability to expand and grow as children's expertise with a program increases.

- Presentation software such as HyperStudio (Robert Wagner Publishing), which is often part of art programs, can allow children to create multimedia presentations that express their ideas, experience, and understanding to others. Children can create slides in the art part of the program and then import them into a slide show to be shared with others.

- Research tools, both age-appropriate websites and software programs that provide information, such as Nature-Virtual Serengeti (http://www.disney.com) and Encarta Encyclopedia (http://www.encarta.msn.com/), can be used formally and informally to research topics in which children are interested. These applications can augment the classroom library and provide multimedia databases on a huge range of topics (Murphy, DePasquale, & McNamara, 2003).

Key Terms

assistive technology 170
Blog 171
classroom blog 171
communication sites 168
defragmenting disks 166
digital camera 159
Haugland Software Development Scale 167
information sites 168
interaction sites 169

interactive 163
literature response blog 171
mirror blog 171
personal learning network 172
publication sites 179
showcase blog 171
smart toys 160
Web 2.0 167
wiki 172

THINK ABOUT IT — Computers and Dry Eyes

Squinting at a computer screen can cut in half the number of times someone blinks each minute. And that could lead to an irritating condition called dry eye, new research suggests (Ohio State University, 2006). Results of this research appear in the journal *Optometry and Vision Science*.

"People tend to squint when they read a book or a computer display, and that squinting makes the blink rate go way down," says James Sheedy, the study's lead author and a professor of optometry at Ohio State University. "Blinking rewets the eyes. So if you work at the computer for a long time, you may be blinking far less than normal, which may cause eye strain and dry eye."

Squinting serves two purposes: It improves eyesight by helping to more clearly define objects that are out of focus. It also cuts down on the brightness from sources of glare. It may be voluntary or involuntary—a person working at a computer may not realize that he or she is squinting.

The researchers asked 10 college students to squint at different levels while looking directly at a computer screen situated about two feet in front of their eyes. All participants had 20/20 vision in both eyes. The researchers attached two tiny electrodes to the lower eyelids of each student. The electrodes were also attached to an electromyogram, a machine that records the electrical activity of muscles.

The electromyogram measured the different degrees of squint. The more the participants squinted their eyes, the less they blinked. And the less they blinked, the more their eyes ached or burned, and the more they reported sensations of dryness, irritation, and tearing. Just a slight amount of squinting reduced blink rates by half, from 15 blinks a minute to 7.5 blinks a minute.

Although dry eye is usually treated with over-the-counter eye drops and is rarely a debilitating condition, it can be irritating and painful. Sheedy says that the next step is to figure out the physiological mechanisms behind eyestrain and dry eye (Ohio State University, 2006).

Learning Activities

Taking Creative Photos

A. Obtain an inexpensive camera. Shoot a roll of color film, trying to make each picture creative.

B. Photograph the following.

1. a beautiful sunset
2. an ugly, broken-down house
3. a beautiful building
4. interesting-looking people
5. a flower in bloom
6. an animal
7. a brightly colored bird

C. Use the pictures to tell a creative story about some experience.

D. Use a digital camera for this same activity.

Digital Camera Activities

Make-a-Face Gallery

Take pictures of each child in your group with a digital camera. Turn off the flash, and zoom in close on each child's face, capturing every detail. Print each picture on an 8½" × 11-inch sheet of paper and make a "face gallery" bulletin board. If you don't have a color printer, don't worry—the pictures look great in black and white.

Bringing Home to School

Offer parents a classroom camera (or a disposable camera) to take home for the weekend. Provide a "shot list" of ideas that includes their children's bedroom, pets, favorite toys, and family members. Any 2.1-megapixel or digital camera works well. Use the photos to make a poster or bulletin board that features that child. If you don't have a digital camera, use a disposable camera. Some manufacturers produce disposable digital cameras ideally suited to this activity.

Additional Activities

A. Make tape recordings of interesting sounds. Invite the children to identify the sounds. Try any or all of the following.

1. a computer keyboard
2. a door closing
3. a car starting
4. a jet plane taking off

5. voices
6. music
7. popcorn popping

Activities for Using an Interactive Whiteboard

- **To See the Bigger Picture**—Scan the pages of a social studies or science book onto the whiteboard so the whole class can experience the book at once. The pictures and diagrams will be big enough for the whole class to see. You are also able to write on the pages and point things out.

- **To Play all Sorts of Games**—The touch-and-drag feature of the whiteboard puts sorting activities in the students' hands. Have the students touch the item on the whiteboard and drag it to its appropriate location in the sort. You can do category sorts (herbivores and carnivores) and word sorts (parts of speech, number of syllables, initial sounds). You can also do "mystery sorts" where you can begin sorting without giving away the rule. Encourage volunteers to figure out the sorting rule and then let them create their own mystery sorts.

- **To Spin a Better Story Web**—This is a second-grade activity that is related to the Magic Tree House books by Mary Pope Osborne. Use the whiteboard to create a story web spanning several of these books. By using different colors, shapes, and fonts, you can create a much-more-intricate yet easier-to-read web than would have been possible with traditional chart paper or overhead transparency. And when you want the students to have a hard copy, just print copies and they can add their own ideas or take them home to share.

- **To Keep Things Fair**—Use your interactive whiteboard to introduce all kinds of concepts, from fact families to vocabulary. The children usually want a turn. To make your choice equitable, draw "fair sticks" (which are virtual popsicle sticks programmed with students' names) to see who gets to go to the board.

- **Write a Collaborative Story**—Your students can pen a fairy tale with the classroom across the hallway or compose a haiku with students in Japan using EtherPad (http://www.etherpad.com), a program that allows real-time text editing and creation on a digital notepad with a unique URL. Just e-mail the URL to your cocreators and get to work! Contributions are color-coded and time-stamped.

- **Travel the World**—Interactive whiteboards make visiting the streets of Rome or the prairies of Kenya a reality. Programs like Google Earth allow you to choose a destination and travel there with lightning-fast speed. Use Google's Street View to go from a birds-eye angle to a straight-on perspective. Then walk past the Eiffel Tower, the Statue of Liberty, or the pyramids in Giza.

- **Build a Word Cloud**—Wordle (http://www.wordle. net) is a fantastic online tool with many possibilities on an interactive whiteboard. Students enter a piece of text and the program builds a "word cloud" based on the most frequently used words within the text. Entering the text of a favorite storybook or a chapter of a novel can reveal key vocabulary. Or you can challenge kids to create a word cloud based on the vocabulary from your latest unit of study.

- **Teach Media Literacy**—All interactive whiteboard software allows you to draw over websites, documents, and applications. Teachers use this capability to teach children critical thinking and responsible Internet use. You can pull up a website and highlight information that suggests it's a legitimate source as well as any clues or indications that it may not be the best place for valid information.

- **Play with Magnetic Poetry**—Pull up http://www. magneticpoetry.com/kidspoetry, and students can experiment with all four Magnetic Poetry Kids' Kits on a stylish digital fridge. Drag and drop adjectives, verbs, and nouns to learn about parts of speech, proper sentence construction, and poetic forms.

- **Design a Digital Robot**—Students will enjoy exploring all the tools on Sodaplay (http://www. sodaplay.com), an interactive website at which users build animated models and machines. One favorite Sodaplay application is Moovl, which lets children easily make their words and images shimmy and shake. There are some good teacher tips at http:// moovl.wordpress.com.

- **Create Customized Flashcards**—FlashcardDB (http://www.flashcarddb.com) earns raves from teachers for its ease of use, broad application, and great possibilities on the whiteboard. You can easily create a custom set of flashcards in minutes as well as access other educators' cards and teaching tools. The Study mode allows children to "flip" the cards and quiz themselves in a flash.

Activities for Children

Photo Activities

Picture Puzzles

Glue an enlarged photograph of each child to construction paper. Then use a paper cutter to cut each photo into three horizontal strips. Spread your new puzzle pieces out on the table or floor, and have the children create brand new faces by combining different features. As students play, invite them to say or write the personality traits their "people" might exhibit if they were real. For example, "She has Meg's love of sports and Drew's great math abilities." For easy storage, hole-punch the strips and put them in a binder, allowing children to mix and match during free time.

Picture Walks (Kindergarten and up)

Children take pictures while walking through the school neighborhood or the school building, or while on a field trip. During circle time, have children talk about and describe their pictures.

Matching Game

Have children take pictures of objects and other children in their class. Put the pictures in random piles and have the children work in small groups to locate the objects/people that are in the photos in the room. This can be fun and challenging when the photos show only a part of the object and the child has to figure out what object has been photographed. For example, a child may have taken a photograph of the table leg or the end of a pencil or a classmate's red sneaker. Children can search the room to find the match to their picture.

Classroom Newsletter

Create a classroom newsletter so that the children have opportunities to share their pictures. Each child should have multiple opportunities to have his/her photos included in the classroom newsletter. Let the children choose which photos to include. The newsletter can have photos of special events and class trips, but also everyday events that the children have photographed. The newsletter creates a natural opportunity for children to talk about school experiences through photographs.

Photo Storytelling

Photographs can be used to create stories, illustrate ideas in stories that the children have developed, or retell events. Through photos, children can create stories that reflect their everyday experiences. Take pictures of the events of one entire class day and write a group story about a day in the life of your classroom, accompanied by the children's photographs. As the children become more experienced using cameras, have them take pictures of activities in the classroom and "write" their own story about a typical day in their classroom. Having the children "write" means either having the children dictate their story to you or having them make approximations using scribbles or some forms of writing.

Alphabet Bodies

Give students practice in teamwork, problem solving, and communication by having them build different letters with their bodies. Then capture the results on film. First, ask children how they might build a particular letter. How many children will need to work together? How will their bodies need to be positioned? Encourage children to use listening and language skills to complete each letter-making task. Then snap away! Stand on a sturdy chair to get a better angle. Post the photographs or paste them into a scrapbook to familiarize children with the alphabet. Or make a super-simple game of Concentration by duplicating the photos to use as cards.

Music and Friends

This is a terrific getting-to-know-you activity. Play a round of musical chairs that will help students learn one another's names and interests. Place a photo of each child on the front of a chair back. (There's no need to have one less chair in this noncompetitive version of the game.) Invite children to stand in a circle around the chair and start the music. When the music stops, children sit down on the nearest chair. Ask each child to identify whose photo is on his or her chair. Older students may also share something special about that classmate. Later on, challenge children by using photos of arms and legs instead of faces.

Me Puppets

Have children cut their faces or bodies from large, close-up photographs, then mount them on heavy paper and laminate them. Attach a craft stick or glove to the back of the puppet using tape or strong glue. Children might like to change their puppet's appearance by adding cloth or paper and marker costumes. Children can use the me-puppets to tell stories and practice storytelling skills. Invite children to act out favorite stories or create new ones—starring themselves, of course. Try using the puppets during large-group time as a fun, alternative way for students to express themselves.

Twisting

Put a photographic twist on the classic game of Twister™. Make the game board by cutting out large, blown-up photos of each child and gluing them to sturdy cardboard circles. Laminate and attach the circles to a Twister board or to the floor with strong tape. Small groups can take turns playing by having one "caller" announce a name and a right or left hand/foot direction. For example, "Place your right hand on Casper." Older children can give more complex directions, such as "Place your foot on a friend who has brown hair," or "Place your hand on a friend who can play the violin."

Changing Faces

Children can "change" their faces again and again by simply laying transparency paper over their photographs. Using markers, children can add a moustache, change hair color, add a hat, or make any other change—silly or serious—that they want. Have children think and write about how they perceive themselves in these changes. Wipe off the marker as many times as desired to make new changes.

Technology Choreography Movement Activity

In this activity, children learn about technology and interpret their understandings through creative movement.

A. Prepare a tape recording (no more than three minutes) of the sounds of various machines, such as an electric can opener, microwave, coffee maker, or mixer. It is not necessary to have many sounds. Rather, juxtapose the sounds of different lengths and repeat them during the three-minute recording.

B. Play the tape. After the students identify the source of the sounds, discuss the ways in which technology (in the kitchen, garage, or other places) helps us do our work. Assign children to work in pairs or independently to prepare a choreographed interpretation of the sounds on the tape. Ask children to think about the function of the technology as they select movements.

C. Play the tape three or four times for rehearsal and preparation. Encourage students to select appropriate movement, depending on the function and "feeling" of the technology. The interpretation may take the form of finger movements, a hand jive, dance, or creative movement. Perform the choreography and critique the movements as to their connection with the function of technology.

Internet Activities—Grade 3 and Up

Your students can monitor leopards in South Africa, volcanoes in Italy, or insects in Iowa without ever leaving your classroom, thanks to webcams—permanent cameras that transmit pictures over the Internet. Here's where to find some of the best kid-friendly cams:

- **Africam**—The next best thing to taking your students on a safari. http://www.africam.com
- **JellyCam**—Your students will be fascinated by the fantastic creatures in the Oregon Coast Aquarium's moon jelly exhibit. http://www.aquarium.org
- **Monterey Bay Aquarium**—Seven different cams offer a look at marine life in the aquarium's exhibits. See penguins, otters, sharks, and more! http://www.mbayaq.org
- **Volcano Watch**—It's a known fact that kids love volcanoes. Here, satellite images let them monitor the world's most active ones. http://www.ssec.wisc.edu/data/volcano.html

Google Earth

If you're looking for a stellar example of how technology can bring abstract concepts to life, look no further than Google Earth. Google Earth turns your Windows computer into a dynamic superglobe, combining the ability to search and zoom down with enough resolution to view your own back yard. The program is an extension of Google Maps and uses satellite images taken over the past three years, combining them with local points of interest plus facts from Google.

You can zoom to a specific address or fly along a route. You can also view annotations left by other Google Earth users. Younger children can get a sense of how their neighborhood fits into their town, their county, their state, and their continent. Other educational applications are numerous, both for mapping and geography, as well as other more indirect uses, including science, history, and math.

Google Earth is free for personal use, although upgrade versions are also available. It can be downloaded at http://earth.google.com.

Try the following activities with Google Earth.

- Search for your community by using your zip code or another search method.
- List human-made structures as you view your community.
- Locate your school. Record its elevation and its latitude and longitude reading.
- Zoom in on and identify some of the smallest features you can view near your school. List what you see.
- Locate and list two or more other interesting features that you see in or near your community.
- Teach your students how to be safe on the Internet by visiting http://www.SafetyClicks.com. They can play games to become Internet savvy, visit other sites, watch a cartoon, and get tips on how to use the World Wide Web.
- Invite students to find the basics of surfing the net at http://www.albion.com/. Click on "Netiquette." After exploring this site, ask children to define the terms *netiquette, online behavior, and cyberspace.*
- Find a directory of games at http://www.surfnetkids.com/. Click on "Games." The games are listed by type (such as crossword or jigsaw) and topic (such as science or history). Play the Harry Potter games and do the word searches, quizzes, and crossword puzzles related to the Harry Potter books.
- Learn about animals at http://www.zoobooks.com, where children will find games and artwork by other students and lots of other fun activities.
- Become a wolf for a day at WolfQuest. WolfQuest is a 3D wildlife video game by the Minnesota Zoo and game developer Eduweb. WolfQuest is the first video game funded by the National Science Foundation. Download the game at http://www.wolfquest.org and you'll learn just how hard it is to live in the wild—as a wolf, anyway. You'll also learn how a real wolf thinks and what he or she eats. You'll need to register, and then download the install the file on your computer. Once you do, you can form your own pack with kids from all over the world.
- Make your own game. The best way to play a good game is to make one yourself. Try Cartoon Network's Ben Ten Alien Force Game Creator at http://gamecreator.cartoonnetwork.com, where you can drag and drop walls, ramps, and barriers into place. Then you can sprinkle your game with enemies or gems to collect. Your finished game can be saved and shared with others. There are 210 other games at Cartoon Network.

Chapter Review

1. One of your parents asks why her child has to use a computer in class. Explain why using technology is important to preschool programs, citing recent research in your answer as well as DAP.

2. Consider the several kinds of technology covered in this chapter. Choose several that you feel are appropriate for use with young children and explain how you will use them in your own work with children.

3. You are appointed chairperson of the New Technology Committee at your school. Compile a list of sources to use to evaluate software for young children. Then explain to the committee why you have chosen each, giving the pros and cons of each.

4. Many early childhood professionals question the potential value of computers for young children, especially in the preschool classroom. What is your stand on this issue? Use the information presented in this chapter to back up your answer. Discuss the various components involved in the concept of Web 2.0. Compare these components for their appropriateness in your current work with young children. Which specific technology is most appropriate for your group of children and why? What is least appropriate and why?

5. Visit one of the websites listed at the end of this chapter. Evaluate this site for potential use with young children. List its strengths and weaknesses. In what way would you use this website in your work with children?

6. Preview a computer software program designed for preschoolers. Does it allow for individual creativity? Is it developmentally appropriate? Was it easy to use?

7. Choose one of the research references from the list provided at the end of this chapter and report on its findings with regard to young children's use of computers. Apply what you have read to your own experience with children.

8. After reviewing the various safeguards on Internet use with young children, what would you recommend is the best method of safeguarding children's use of technology? Give specific websites and practices in your answer.

9. In your opinion, what is the best way for you to share class information with parents—a blog or a wiki? Explain the reasons for your choice.

References

Bergen, D., & Wang, A. (2008). The effects on children's creativity of super-realistic technologically-enhanced toys. *International Journal of Psychology, 43*(3), 16–24

Buckleitner, W. (2008). Getting the most from each click. *Children's Technology Review, 16*(4), 2.

Byrnes, J., & Wasik, B. A. (2009). Picture this: Using photography as a learning tool in early childhood classrooms. *Childhood Education, 85*(4), 243–247.

Ching, G. S. (2009). Implications of an experimental information technology curriculum for elementary students. *Computers and Education, 53*(2), 419–428.

Clements, D. H., & Samara, J. (2003a). Young children and technology: What does the research say? *Young Children, 58*(6), 34–40.

Clements, D. H., & Samara, J. (2003b). Strip mining for gold: Research and policy in educational technology—a response to "Fools Gold." *Educational Technology Review, 11*(1). Available online at http://www.aace.org/pubs/etr/issue4/clements.cfm.

Cogill, J. (2003). The use of interactive whiteboards in the primary school: Effects on pedagogy. *Research Bursary Reports* (Coventry, Becta).

Curwood, J. S. (2009). Education 2.0: Case for interactive whiteboards. *Instructor, 118*(6), 29–32.

Einarsdottir, J. (2005). Playschool in pictures: Children's photography as a research method. *Early Childhood Development and Care, 175*(5), 523–541.

Haugland, S., & Wright, J. (1997). *Young children and technology. A world of discovery*. New York: Allyn & Bacon.

Lacina, J. (2009). Interactive whiteboards: Creating higher-level, technological thinkers? *Childhood Education, 85*(4), 270–272.

Lee, Y. (2009). Pre–K children's interaction with educational software programs: An observation of capabilities and levels of engagement. *Journal of Educational Multimedia and Hypermedia, 18*(3), 289–309.

Long, C. (2006). Getting wiki with it. *NEA Today, 25*(2), 16–17.

Mayer, R., & Wittrock, M. (2006). *Brain and education*. Oxford, UK: Taylor & Francis.

NAEYC. (1996). *NAEYC Position Statement: Technology and young children—ages three through eight*. http://www.naeyc.org/positionstatements/PSTECH98.asp

NAEYC. (2008). *Meaningful technology integration in early learning environments*. www.naeyc.org/file/yc/file/200809/OnOurMinds

Nebel, M., Jamison, B., & Bennett, L. (2009). Students as digital citizens on Web 2.0. *Social Studies and the Young Learner, 21*(4), 393–401.

Ohio State University. (2006). Squinting while staring at a computer monitor can cause painful dry eye. Available online at http://researchnews.osu.edu/archive/squintrz.htm

Parette, H. P., Blum, C., Boeckmann, N. M., & Watts, E. H. (2009). Teaching word recognition to young children who are at risk using Microsoft PowerPoint coupled with direct instruction. *Early Childhood Education Journal, 36*(5), 393–401.

Piaget, J. (1955). *The child's conception of reality.* London: Routledge & Kegan.

Robinson, L., Schneider, C., Daytner, G., Johnson, J., & Hutinger, P. (2009). *Early childhood technology integrated instructional system (EC-TIIS): Phase 3. Final report.* Center for Best Practices in Early Childhood Education: Western Illinois University.

Smith, H., Higgins, S., Wall, K., & Miller, J. (2005). Interactive whiteboards: Boom or bandwagon? A critical review of the literature. *Journal of Computer Assisted Learning, 21*(9), 91–101.

Straub, E. T. (2009). Understanding technology adoption: Theory and future directions for informal learning. *Review of Educational Research, 79*(2), 625–649.

Thompson, S., & Williams, K. (2008). Using photography to tell a story. *Social Studies and the Young Learner, 20*(3), 18–21.

Additional Readings

Bausch, M. E., & Ault, M. J. (2008). Assistive technology implementation plan: A tool for improving outcomes. *Teaching Exceptional Children, 64*(4), 6–14.

Berson, I. R. (2009). Here's what we have to say! Podcasting in the early childhood classroom. *Social Studies and the Young Learner, 21*(4), 8–11.

Berson, I. R., & Berson, M. J. (2009). Panwapa: Global kids, global connections. *Social Studies and the Young Learner, 21*(4), 28–31.

Davison, S. (2009). A picture is worth a thousand words: Using digital cameras captivates second-grade learners at the zoo. *Science and Children, 46*(5), 36–39.

Epstein, A. S. (2009). *Me, you, us.* Ypsilanti, MI: HighScope Press.

Good, L. (2006). Snap it up. Using digital photography in early childhood. *Childhood Education, 82*(4), 79–85.

Gregory, D. C. (2009). Boxes with fires: Wisely integrating learning technologies into the art classroom. *Art Education, 62*(3), 47–53.

Grimes, S. M. (2008). Saturday morning cartoons go mmog. *Media International Australia, 126*(12), 120–126.

Hubbert, B. (2009). Yes, you can teach technology in the art classroom. *SchoolArts, 108*(5), 14.

Hyson, M. (2008). *Enthusiastic and engaged learners: Approaches to learning in the early childhood classroom.* Washington, DC: Teachers College Press.

Mitchell, S., Foulger, T. S., & Wetzel, K. (2009). Ten tips for involving families through internet-based communication. *Young Children, 64*(5), 46–49.

Neumann-Hinds, C. (2009). *Picture science: Using digital photography to teach young children.* St. Paul, MN: Redleaf.

Salend, S. (2009). Using technology to create and administer accessible tests. *Teaching Exceptional Children, 41*(3), 40–53.

Torrez, C. F., & Bush, G. (2009)Exploring the explorers using Internet resources. *Social Studies and the Young Learner, 21*(4), 12–16.

Zawlinski, L. (2009). HOT blogging: A framework for blogging to promote higher order thinking. *The Reading Teacher, 62*(8), 650–661.

Software for Children

Aha! I Got It! Escape Game, ages 6 and up

Alvin and the Chipmunks: The Squeakue! ages 6 and up

Blue's Kindergarten, ages 3and up

Blue Takes You to School, ages 3 and up

Curious George Turns the Town Upside Down, ages 3 and up

Elmo's World, ages 3 and up

Encleverment Experiment, ages 6 and up

Fisher-Price Little People Discovery Games, ages 3 and up

Hoyle Puzzle and Board Games 2010, ages 6 and up

Jump Start Advanced Preschool, ages 3 and up

Little Bill Thinks Big, ages 3 and up

Moomin and the Mysterious Howling, ages 6 and up

Pallurikio, ages 6 and up

PBS Kids Play! ages 3 and up

Putt-Putt Travels Through Time and Balloon O Rama, ages 3 and up

Shelly—My First Computer Game, ages 3 and up

Thomas and Friends: Building the New Line, ages 3 and up

Helpful Websites

American Library Association, http://www.ala.org
This site contains a Guide to Cyberspace for parents and kids, which includes many safety tips on children's use of the Internet.

Computer Tutor, http://ww.bbc.co.uk/computertutor/ computertutor/more_info.shtml.
This BBC site offers a basic introduction to using the computer, keyboard, and mouse. This site is excellent for students with limited computer experience.

CyberSmart! Education Company, http://www. cybersmart.org
This site provides a free K–8 curriculum, copublished with Macmillan/McGraw-Hill, that contains 65 lesson plans with student activity sheets, posters, and information for parents. The curriculum addresses such topics as Internet safety, manners, research, and advertising.

Everything Preschool, http://www.everythingpre-school.com/
Click on "Themes." This site contains more than 150 themes and activities for preschoolers. Choose from pets, dinosaurs, the grocery store, Dr. Seuss, shapes, and more. Each theme contains related songs and activities as well as ideas for art projects, snacks, bulletin boards, field trips, and the like. Recipes and articles are also included.

Girls Go Tech, http://www.girlsgotech.org/games. html
The Girl Scouts of America created this unique and educational website for grades 3 to 6. It includes four themes: Cryptic Codes, Mandala Maker, Mixed Messages, and Composing Digital Music.

Kids Click, http://www.kidsclick.com
This site lists more than 500 educational software programs for kids from babies to teens in all subject areas.

Kids Connect, http://www.kidsconnect.com
This site contains curriculum information, activities, and research by subject index or by alphabetical list. Subject categories are consistent with classroom topics and the alphabet list makes specific topics easy to find.

Kids Online.net, http://www.kids-online.net/ kidsframe.html
Check out the many educational pages at this free site. It includes a dictionary of computer terms, lessons on parts of a computer, Web building, and much more.

Kubbu, http://www.kubbu.com
This is an e-learning tool designed to facilitate teachers' work and enhance the learning process. On this site you can create games, quizzes, or crosswords, make them available to students or groups, and view and analyze the results.

National Institute on Media and the Family, http:// www.mediafamily.org
This site is designed to help families and educators maximize the benefits and minimize the harm of mass media

on children through research, education, and advocacy. It has many online tools and resources.

Northwest Educational Technology Consortium, http://www.netc.org/
This site provides generic advice on using computers in a wide variety of early childhood settings.

Scrapblog, http://www.scrapblog.com/
This site allows users to create online scrapbooks including photos, video clips, and music. This site has countless possibilities in the classroom.

Smart Kids Software, http://www.smartkidssoftware.com
On this site, which was established in 1992, you can review software by age, grade levels, and subject.

Surf Swell Island: Adventures in Internet Safety, http://www.disney.go.com/surfswell
This site provides a series of interactive games, including Disney characters, that teach children about issues of online privacy, virus awareness, and online manners. The site includes a parents' guide and a teachers' guide.

Technology and Young Children, http://www. techandyoungchildren.org
This is the NAEYC's site containing advice on how to lead discussions, share research and information, and demonstrate best practices regarding technology so it can be used to benefit children aged birth through eight years.

The Center for Digital Storytelling, http://www. storycenter.org/momquicktime.html
This Web site is dedicated to promoting the art of digital storytelling.

The Media Literacy Classroom—The Media Channel, http://www.mediachannel.org/classroom
The Media Channel is a nonprofit, international Web site focused on the media, featuring readings, resources, teaching tools, issue guides, and access to a worldwide network of organizations and publications concerned with media education.

Websites on Internet Safety

http://www.ikeepsafe.org

http://www.lsafe.org

http://www.nap.edu/netsafekids

http://www.netsmartz.com

http://www.safekids.com

http://www.wiredsafety.org

For additional creative activity resources, visit our website at www.Cengage.com/login.

Art and the Development of the Young Child

REFLECTIVE QUESTIONS

After studying this section, you should be able to answer the following questions.

1. How am I encouraging the development of self-concept in young children in my classroom management and teaching practices?

2. What are the strengths and weaknesses of my art program as it relates to the development of self-concept? What can I do to improve it so that it is more conducive to the development of a positive self-concept for young children?

3. Do I have sufficient and appropriate art materials for both large- and small-motor activities? What can I add to improve my program? What can I remove? Have I made appropriate changes for children with special needs?

4. Are the young children in my group able to fully develop their physical and mental potential in the room and the activities I have planned?

5. Does my classroom reflect the range of individual differences in social–emotional and physical–mental development present in the group? How can it be improved?

6. At what levels in the development of art-related skills are the children in my group? Have I planned activities and lessons to fit these levels?

7. Are my teaching practices based on a knowledge of social–emotional, physical–mental, and art development levels? Is this knowledge reflected in my choice of materials, supplies, and interest centers?

8. Am I aware of each child's individual schema? Can I recognize them? How do I speak with children about their art?

9. How can I assist parents in their understanding of children's development in art? Of a child's physical–mental development? Of a child's social–emotional growth?

10. Do I encourage young children to verbalize their feelings? Do I encourage this process by modeling consideration of their thoughts and actions?

11. What can I do to improve my current teaching practices in the art program?

12. Am I satisfied that the social–emotional, physical–mental, and developmental levels of art are being appropriately addressed in my teaching strategies? What can I change to better meet the individual needs of young children in all of these areas of development?

Art and Physical— Mental Growth

This chapter presents the ways in which art relates to physical and mental growth. Physical, mental, social, and emotional growth all occur together in a child, but physical and mental growth are discussed separately here for the sake of clarity.

Art and Physical (Motor) Development

The term **motor development** means "physical growth." Both terms refer to growth in the ability of children to use their bodies.

In an early childhood program, activities like dancing, drawing, painting, pasting, and other activities that exercise muscles aid a child's motor development. Exercising muscles in creative activities aids both small- and large-muscle development. Before we consider each of these types of motor development, let us look at the overall pattern of growth and development.

Pattern of Development

The process of human development follows a general pattern that includes growth in three basic directions (Figure 9–1). The first of these is called *large- to small-muscle* or **gross-motor development** to **fine-motor development**. Large- (gross) to small- (fine) motor development means that large muscles develop in the neck, trunk, arms, and legs before the small muscles in the fingers, hands, wrists, and eyes develop. This is why young children can walk long before they are able to write or even scribble.

The second direction of growth, from head to toe (or top to bottom), is called **cephalocaudal development**. This growth pattern explains why a baby is able to hold up his head long before he is able to walk: The muscles develop from the head down.

The third pattern of development is from inside to outside (or from center to outside) and is called **proxomodistal development**. This explains the ability of a

OBJECTIVES

After studying this chapter, you should be able to:

1. Explain how art aids a child's physical (motor) development.

2. Describe how art aids a child's mental development.

3. Discuss the place of art in the total early childhood program.

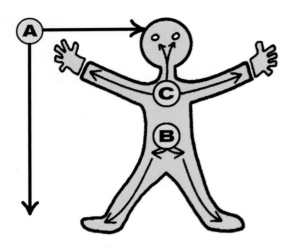

THE BODY DEVELOPS FROM

TOP (Head)	*Cephalocaudal Development*	**BOTTOM** (Toes)
INSIDE (Trunk)	*Proximodental Development*	**OUTSIDE** (Extremities)
LARGE (Trunk, Neck, Arms, Legs)	*Gross to Fine Motor Development*	**SMALL** (Fingers, Hands, Toes, Wrists, Eyes)

FIGURE 9-1 • The pattern of development.

FIGURE 9-2 • Older children are generally able to use scissors quite easily.

baby to roll over before he is able to push himself up with his arms. Because the inner muscles of the trunk develop first, rolling over comes before pulling or sitting up. Understanding these basic principles of development, especially large- to small-motor development, is important in planning appropriate art activities for young children. Let us now consider large- and small-motor development.

Large-Muscle Development

A child's proportions are constantly changing as he or she grows because different parts of the body grow at different rates. Physical disproportions are common from birth to approximately age six as the upper body is generally longer and not in proportion to the lower body. As a consequence of these body proportions in which the legs and body are not developed in proportion to the upper body region, toddlers and preschoolers have a high center of gravity and are prone to falls.

By age six, however, body proportions are more similar to those of an adult. When the child has matured to adult-like proportions, his or her center of gravity

is more centrally located so that he or she achieves a greater sense of physical balance and is able to be more purposeful in movements. (See the Professional Enhancement Text for complete listing of Developmental Milestones by Age.)

Because large muscles in the arms, legs, neck, and trunk develop first, by the time children reach preschool age, they are able to use large muscles quite well. They can walk, run, sit, and stand at will. They can use their arms and hands quite easily in large movements like clapping and climbing. Younger children enjoy large-motor play activities. Most three-year-olds and many four-year-olds are actively using their large muscles in running, wiggling, and jumping. They are not yet as developed in small motor skills (like cutting, tying, or lacing) as five-year-olds. (See the Professional Enhancement Text for a complete listing of Developmental Milestones by Skill.)

The early childhood art program gives the child a chance to exercise large-motor skills in many ways other than just in active games. Painting with a brush on a large piece of paper is as good a practice for large-muscle development as dancing. Whether it

FIGURE 9-3 • Small-motor activities are generally appropriate for older children with more developed small-motor skills.

FIGURE 9-4 • Young children learn mentally as they do things physically.

be broad arm movements made in brush strokes or to a musical beat, it is only by first developing these large muscles that a child can begin to develop small-motor skills.

Creative activities in the early childhood program provide many opportunities for exercising large-muscle skills. Activities that exercise large muscles include group murals, tracing body shapes, easel painting, clay pounding, and crayon rubbings. (See the end of this chapter for suggested activities.)

Small-Muscle Development

Small muscles in fingers, hands, and wrists are used in art activities such as painting, cutting, pasting, and clay modeling. These small-motor art activities and any other activity that involves the use of small muscles help exercise and develop a child's fine-motor control.

Small-muscle skills are different for a child at different ages. For example, many three-year-olds do not have good small-muscle development, so the muscles

in their fingers and hands are not quite developed enough to enable them to use scissors easily.

In the following report, a teacher discovered that the planned art activity was, in fact, too difficult a small-motor task for some of the children in the group. (See Professional Enhancement Text for a complete listing of developmental checklists and developmental alerts.)

Making masks out of paper bags was a good experience for many of the children. However, I found that many other children had difficulty handling the scissors and became frustrated. They were eager to have the masks, but couldn't handle the problem of not being able to manipulate the scissors [easily] enough to make a mask quickly. I tried to overcome this problem by helping them make the first holes, or cutting out part of an eye, and letting the

(continued)

child finish the job. Perhaps many theorists would say that I should have let them do it by themselves completely. But I just felt that their eagerness to make the mask and to complete the cutting once I had helped them was not to be overlooked. The children all wanted to take home their masks and ran to put them in their lockers so they wouldn't forget them. One little girl wore hers all day and had to be convinced that she couldn't eat with it on! (Author's log)

Practice in crushing and tearing paper, and later practice in using blunt scissors, all help small muscles develop. The better the small-muscle development, the easier it will be to cut with scissors. Small muscles can grow stronger only by practice and exercise. A teacher encourages a child to exercise these small muscles in small-motor artwork, such as tearing, pasting, working with clay, making and playing with puppets, and finger painting.

A teacher also encourages a child to exercise small muscles by providing the right small-motor tools. The teacher in the following report managed to use clay as the medium for helping children practice small-motor skills.

In my activities I wanted to emphasize fine-motor development, so I used clay with different-sized soda straw pieces, toothpicks, buttons, etc., to stick in the clay. The children made animals, designs, and monsters. They kept up a running commentary on how they were making a monster and could smash it if they wanted to. It seemed that the clay was a good means of having them release their fears, ideas, and emotions on many things. This clay activity went over very well. During the day, many different, as well as the same, children came back to play at the clay table. (Author's log)

Small muscles are often better developed in four- and five-year-olds. However, small-motor activities are still necessary for continued small-muscle development. Drawing with pencils, crushing paper into shapes, modeling figures with clay, and making mobiles are examples of more advanced small-motor activities.

Working with small muscles in small-motor activities helps make learning to write much easier for the child. The control over hand and finger movements used for finger painting and clay modeling is the same control the child needs to be able to write. Early childhood art activities give the child a chance to practice and develop the small-motor skills needed in schoolwork to come.

Large- and Small-Motor Activities

The early childhood art program should have a good mixture of both small- and large-motor tools and activities. A child needs to develop both large and small muscles, and artwork provides this chance.

The teacher needs to respect each child's need to develop both large and small muscles at any age. This means a teacher needs the right equipment and, more importantly, the right attitude for the level of each child. The right attitude is one that lets the child know it is all right to try many large- and small-motor activities at any age. In this type of art program, not

FIGURE 9-6 • Playing with puzzles is an excellent small-motor activity.

all four-year-olds are expected to cut well, to button a shirt successfully, or to be able to do either at all. Five-year-olds, as well as younger children, may enjoy pounding clay for no other purpose than the fun of pounding. Older children should also be allowed this same freedom of expression with both large- and small-muscle activities. Although they may appear more physically developed, middle and upper elementary children still enjoy "messing around" with clay and even finger paints.

Art activities provide both fine- and gross-motor experiences. As children create—thrusting sticks into plastic foam, forming small shapes with a marker, using a paintbrush at an easel—they move back and forth between large, sweeping motions and small, discrete movements. These movements help children develop control and coordination of both fine and gross muscles. Both types of development are important for the child's growth, not only for forming letters and numbers later in school, but also for overall physical movement. Offering children a variety of different materials, such as crayons, easel paint, scissors, recycled materials,

FIGURE 9-6 • Fine motor skills develop later than large motor skills.

and clay, helps them develop the various muscles in their arms and fingers.

Hand–Eye Coordination

In the early childhood program, as children exercise their small and large muscles, they also improve their **hand–eye coordination**. Hand–eye coordination refers to the ability to use hand(s) and eyes at the same time. Painting is a good example of an activity in which hand–eye coordination comes into play. When children paint, they use their eyes to choose the colors, their hands to hold and use the brush, and their eyes to follow the brush strokes.

Hand–eye coordination is also used in clay modeling, making a mobile, pasting, and finger painting. In all of these art activities, the child is receiving practice in coordinating (using together) the hands and eyes.

Art Activities and Reading Readiness

Hand–eye coordination is important for future schoolwork. Many reading experts believe that good hand–eye coordination helps a child learn to read. They believe that the ability to use hands and eyes together in activities like painting or playing ball helps a child learn the motor skills needed in reading. Holding a book in two hands and using the eyes to read from left to right require simple hand–eye coordination.

Reading experts believe that the growth pattern of large to small muscles affects reading ability. In other words, a child must have a chance to develop large muscles before being able to use small muscles—such as the eyes in the left-to-right movements of reading. The side-to-side or lateral movements developed in such activities as painting and printing are helpful in developing left-to-right tracking in reading. Thus, art activities are important for future reading because they exercise and develop hand–eye coordination and left-to-right tracking.

Explorations with art materials also offer opportunities to sharpen perceptions of form. Children note relationships between artistic two- and three-dimensional forms and the environment. Statements like "My clay is round like a pie," "I drew a square like that book," or "Look at the funny shape of my puppet's head; it's not like my head" indicate that children are learning about form while being involved in creative activities. **Visual acuity**—the ability to see and recognize shape and form—is implicit in all art activities. It is also an ability that needs to be developed for beginning reading.

Motor Control

All that we have discussed thus far about muscle growth and hand–eye coordination falls under the general category of motor control. As children grow, they gain progressive control over their bodies.

Children growing in small- and large-muscle skills and in hand–eye coordination are growing in total motor control. (Figure 9–8 contains suggested activities in art and other curriculum areas to enhance overall motor control for children ages two through 10. See the Professional Enhancement Text for children from six months to age two.) The child's work in various activities demonstrates this growing motor control. An observant teacher can assess an individual child's motor skills in one activity and make judgments about his or her likely skill or ability in another area. For instance, when considering art activities, a teacher recognizes that early scribbling is the beginning of motor control. Initially, children hold the crayon and scribble with very little motor control. As they grow in motor control, they can control the direction of their scribbles, then control lines to make basic forms, and finally draw pictures.

Therefore, a teacher can assess children's general motor control by knowing their artwork. For example, the teacher who knows that a certain five-year-old cannot yet cut with scissors knows how to reply to parents who ask if this child is ready for piano lessons. Observing each child's motor control in artwork helps the teacher know each child's motor control in other areas as well.

Art and Mental Development

Art and Thinking Skills

Art activities involve children mentally as well as physically. They involve both the physical ability to use art tools and the thinking processes involved in the creation itself. Let's now consider how art and thinking skills are related in art activities.

Creating art is a complex mental process. It involves mental skills such as problem solving, predicting, design, and cause and effect. For example, think about a child who wants to draw a person. First, she or he needs to remember what she or he knows about how people look, then identify the important features and represent them on paper through shapes and lines. That is no small achievement for a three- or four-year-old! Working with art materials, the child learns new concepts such as how colors can change and how paper can be used in many ways. These and similar experiences help the child develop more flexible thinking, an important mental skill that is discussed later in this chapter.

Just as art reflects children's thinking, it also enhances it. Consider an older child who wants to draw an ant and a mosquito. She or he learns about the similarities and differences between the two insects by observing; then, through drawing, the child clarifies and reinforces what she or he has learned.

Art helps children gain a great deal of knowledge in more direct ways as well. As children experiment and investigate, they learn about the physical nature of tools and materials. What will the brush do if I hit it on the paper this way—or that way? How can I make the foil plate stick to the wood? How much glue is okay to use on the tissue paper? When you offer a wide variety of materials for children to investigate freely, you broaden their opportunities for learning.

Concept of change. Change is an important concept for children to understand and it is one that develops slowly. Piaget (1955), in his writings about the growth of intelligence in young children, emphasizes the fact that mental growth is aided by a child's active exploration of the environment. The child, according to Piaget, gradually comes to understand how things can change as he or she experiences different materials in various situations in the environment. For example, by using color, mixing colors, and making colors lighter or darker, the child learns that things can change. Clay can change from hard to soft. Plaster can change from liquid to solid. (See Figure 9–7 for a more detailed explanation of Piaget's stages of mental development.)

"Learning by doing" in art helps a child grow mentally because he or she grows more flexible in his or her thinking. The child learns to think of things in the context of change, realizing that not all things are permanent. The ability to think this way is called **flexible thinking** (Figure 9–8).

Art activities with a variety of materials encourage flexibility of thought. In making a collage, the characteristics of different items are compared and relationships are discovered between new and familiar items. Flexibility of thought is encouraged as children associate particular tools with certain processes and learn

Sensorimotor Stage: Birth to two years
Uses all senses to explore the world. Nonverbal communication.

Gains object permanence—objects exist even when not seen. Example: Remove a toy from a very young child and object won't be missed because child can't see it. Once child achieves object permanence, she remembers the toy and will cry to get it back or search for it.

Moves from reflex action to directed actions toward a goal. Example: Child sees object and tries to get it by crying and crawling.

Preoperational Stage: two to seven years
Child begins to carry out mental actions (operations) that require forming and using images and symbols. Example: Uses symbols for objects and people. Likes fantasy and imaginative play, makes mental images and likes to pretend.

Rapid language growth. By age four, a 2,000-word vocabulary is average.

Has trouble reversing actions (making transformations) or understanding how objects can change shape but still be the same object. Example: Child doesn't think a tall glass of milk poured into a short fat glass is the same amount of milk.

Has inflexible thinking; does not think about something from more than one perspective. Example: Child focuses on the shape of glass of milk, thinking the taller glass has more milk even when the same milk is poured into a short fat glass.

Understanding other points of view is difficult because child is egocentric (centering on his or her own experiences). Example: Child thinks everyone thinks, feels, and sees as he does.

Concrete Operations: seven to 11 years
Develops basic concepts of objects, numbers, time, space, and causality.

Develops reversibility (two-way thinking). Example: Amount of milk is the same when poured from tall glass into short fat glass.

Can classify by different categories. Example: Child understands how a group can be a subset of another, such as animals and plants are both living things.

Uses concrete objects to learn and draw conclusions. Manipulation of objects aids the child's understanding.

Basic logic develops, but is tied to physical reality. Abstract thinking and hypothetical problem solving is not yet possible.

Formal Operations: 11 to 15 years
Child can think abstractly and hypothetically.
Can generate diverse possible solutions for problems.
Can evaluate alternatives based on many criteria.
Can form and test hypotheses, using scientific method.
Data for chart from Piaget, 1950, 1952, and 1955

FIGURE 9-7 • Summary—Piaget's States of Mental/Cognitive Development.

which tools work best with various materials. For example, a thin brush will make a thin line with paint, and a thick one creates a broader stroke. A sharp needle is needed to sew through felt, but a blunt one works well for open-weave fabrics.

Being able to think flexibly helps children become mentally prepared for later school experiences. Math, spelling, and science all require thinking that can deal with change. In science, for example, a cooking lesson involves changes that ingredients go through in the process of becoming a cake. In math activities, a child learns how numbers can change by adding and subtracting. In spelling, children learn how words change with plurals, suffixes, and prefixes. Flexibility in thought processes is, therefore, basic to most of a child's subsequent learning experiences.

Art and Sensorimotor Development

As children grow physically, they also grow mentally. This is because young children learn by doing. Jean Piaget, in his work with young children,

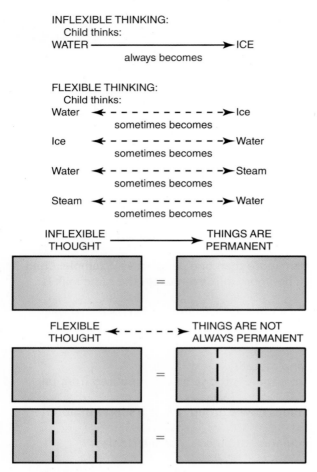

FIGURE 9-8 • Flexible and inflexible thinking.

FIGURE 9-9 • Observing a child finger painting is another way to assess a child's small motor skills.

describes a child's learning by doing as *sensorimotor development*.

The word **sensorimotor** derives from the two words *sensory* and *motor*. *Sensory* refers to the five body senses, and *motor* refers to the physical act of doing. Sensorimotor learning involves the body and its senses (sensory) as they are used in doing (motor).

For Piaget (1955), the foundation of all mental development takes place in physical knowledge, the knowledge that comes from objects. Children construct physical knowledge by acting on objects—feeling, tasting, smelling, seeing, and hearing them. They cause objects to move by throwing, banging, blowing, pushing, and pulling them. They observe changes that take place in objects when they are mixed together, heated, cooled, or changed in some other way. As physical knowledge develops, children become better able to establish relationships (comparing, classifying, ordering) between and among the objects they act upon.

Sensorimotor Learning in Art

An example of sensorimotor learning in art is modeling with clay. In using clay (the motor activity), children use their senses (sensory), such as feel and smell, to learn about clay and how to use it. A teacher can *tell* the children how clay feels and how to use it; but children truly learn about clay by physically *using* it themselves. A child needs this sensorimotor exploration with clay and many other art materials.

In the art program, children learn many things in this sensorimotor way—learning by doing. Many ideas and concepts are learned from different art activities. Just as children exercise different muscles in art activities, they also learn new concepts in many kinds of art activities. Exploring and creating with art materials encourages children to use their senses to become more aware of the environment.

CHARACTERISTICS	SKILLS AND SUGGESTED ACTIVITIES
	The Two-Year-Old
Very active, short attention span	Provide pushing and pulling toys. Encourage play with pounding bench, punching bags, and soft clay. Provide opportunities both indoors and outdoors for active free play that involves climbing, running, sliding, and tumbling.
Interest in physical manipulation; ability to stack several items; pull apart, fill, and empty containers	Provide stacking cups or blocks for stacking and unstacking. Provide pop-apart toys, such as beads, for taking apart. (Large enough not to swallow.) Provide opportunities for filling and emptying containers with sand, water, rice, beans, rocks, etc.
Increased development of fine motor skills	Provide crayons, chalk, paint, and paper for scribbling and painting. Be sure all materials are lead-free and nontoxic. Allow the child to "paint" the sidewalk, building, wheel toys, etc., with clear water and a brush large enough to handle. Provide opportunities to play with play dough, finger paint, paper for tearing, etc.
Increased development in language skills	Encourage the child to talk with you. Use pronouns such as "I," "me," "you," "they," and "we." Encourage the child to use these words. Talk with the child about pictures. Ask her to point to objects or name them. Always give the correct name for objects. Give directions to follow: "Close the door," "Pick up the doll." Be sure to make this a fun game. Teach the child the names of unusual objects such as fire extinguisher, thermometer, screwdriver, and trivet.
Likes to imitate	Encourage finger plays. Recite nursery rhymes. Encourage the child to repeat them. Play I Am a Mirror. Stand or sit facing the child and have him copy everything you do.
Shows interest in dramatic play	Provide dolls, dress-up clothes, carriage, doll bed, toy telephones for pretend conversations.
	The Three-Year-Old
Increased development of large motor skills	Provide opportunities for vigorous free play indoors and outdoors. Provide opportunities for climbing, jumping, riding wheel toys. Play Follow-the-Leader, requiring vigorous body movements.
Greater control over small muscles	Provide opportunities for free play with blocks in various sizes and shapes. Provide a variety of manipulative toys and activities such as pegboard and peg sets, Tinker Toys, puzzles with three to eight pieces. Encourage children to dress and undress themselves, serve food, set the table, water the plants.

FIGURE 9-10 • Motor skills and characteristics of children ages two through 10 years, with suggested activities to encourage physical development.

(Continues)

CHARACTERISTICS	SKILLS AND SUGGESTED ACTIVITIES
Greater motor coordination	Provide art activities. Encourage free expression with paint, crayons, chalk, colored pens, collage materials, clay, play dough. Be sure all materials are lead-free and nontoxic.
Increased development of language skills and vocabulary	Provide opportunities each day for reading stories to children in a group or individually. Encourage children to tell stories. Tape-record their stories. Encourage children to talk about anything of interest.
Beginning to understand number concepts. Usually can grasp concepts of 1, 2, and 3. Can count several numbers in a series but may leave some out.	Count objects of interest, e.g., cookies, cups, napkins, dolls. When possible, move them as you count. Allow children to count them. Display numbers in the room. Use calendars, charts, scales, and rulers.
Enjoys music and is beginning to be able to carry a tune, express rhythm	Provide music activities each day. Sing songs, create rhythms. Offer opportunities for children to move their bodies to music. Encourage children to make up songs. Record them and play them back for the children to dance to or to sing along with.
Curious about why and how things happen	Provide new experiences that arouse questions. Answer the questions simply and honestly. Use reference books with the child to find answers. Conduct simple science activities: What will the magnet pick up? Freeze water, make ice cream, plant seeds, make a terrarium, fly a kite on a windy day.
Good balance and body coordination; increased development of small and large motor skills	**The Four-Year-Old** Provide opportunities each day for vigorous free play. Provide opportunities for the child to walk on a curved line, a straight line, a balance beam. Encourage walking with a beanbag on the head. Games: "See how fast you can hop," "See how far you can hop on one foot," "See how high you can jump." Provide opportunities to throw balls (medium-sized, soft), beanbags, yarn balls.
Small motor skills are developing most rapidly now. Drawings and art express world around them.	Provide opportunity for variety of artwork. Encourage children to tell a story or talk about their finished projects. Encourage children to mix primary colors to produce secondary colors. Name the colors with them.
Increasing hand–eye coordination	Encourage children to unzip, unsnap, and unbutton clothes. Dressing self is too difficult at this point. Encourage children to tear and cut. Encourage children to lace their shoes.

FIGURE 9-10 • Motor skills and characteristics of children ages two through 10 years, with suggested activities to encourage physical development. *(Continued)*

CHARACTERISTICS	SKILLS AND SUGGESTED ACTIVITIES
Ability to group items according to similar characteristics	Play lotto games. Group buttons by color or size. Provide a mixture of seeds. Sort by kind. At cleanup time, sort blocks according to shape. Play rhyming word games.
Increased understanding of concepts related to numbers, size and weight, colors, textures, distance and position, and time	In conversation, use words related to these concepts. Play "follow direction" games. Say, "Put the pencil beside the big block," or "Crawl under the table." Provide swatches of fabric and other materials that vary in texture. Talk about differences. Blindfold the children or have them cover their eyes and ask them to match duplicate textures.
Awareness of the world around them	Build a simple bird feeder and provide feed for birds. Record the kinds of birds observed. Arrange field trips to various community locations of interest (park, fire station, police station).
Has a vivid imagination; enjoys dramatic play	Provide variety of dress-up clothes. Encourage dramatic play through props such as cash register and empty food containers, tea set, and child-sized furniture.
Good sense of balance and body coordination	**The Five- and Six-Year-Old** Encourage body movement with records, stories, rhythms. Encourage skipping to music or rhymes. Teach them simple folk dances.
A tremendous drive for physical activity	Provide free play that encourages running, jumping, balancing, and climbing. Play tug-of-war. Encourage tumbling on a mat.
Development and coordination of small muscles in hands and fingers	Encourage opportunities to paint, draw, cut, paste, mold clay. Provide small peg games and other manipulative toys. Teach sewing with large needle and thread into egg cartons or punched cards. Provide simple carpentry experiences.
Increased hand–eye coordination	Allow children to copy designs of shapes, letters, and numbers. Show a child how his name is made with letters. Encourage catching small balls.
Ability to distinguish right from left. Can discriminate between weights, colors, sizes, textures, and shapes	Play games that emphasize right from left. Games can require responses to directions such as "Put your right hand on your nose" or "Put your left foot on the green circle." Play sorting games. Sort rocks by weight; blocks by weight or shape; marbles or seeds by colors. Match fabric swatches.

FIGURE 9-10 • Motor skills and characteristics of children ages two through 10 years, with suggested activities to encourage physical development. *(Continued)*

(Continues)

CHARACTERISTICS	SKILLS AND SUGGESTED ACTIVITIES
Increased understanding of number concepts	Count anything of interest—cookies, napkins, cups, leaves, acorns, trees, children, teachers, boys, chairs, etc. Identify numbers visible on a calendar, clock, measuring containers, or other devices.
Enjoys jokes, nonsense rhymes, riddles	Read humorous stories, riddles, and nonsense rhymes.
Enjoys creative, dramatic activities	Move body to dramatize opening of a flower, falling snow, leaves, rain, wiggly worms, snakes, blowing wind. Dramatize stories as they are read. Good stories to use are: *Caps for Sale, Three Billy Goats Gruff, Three Bears.*
Good sense of balance and body coordination. More directed in their drive for physical activity. Good development and coordination of small muscles in hands and fingers	**The Six- to 10-Year-Old** Encourage movements that challenge the child such as horizontal and vertical jumps. Introduce more complex motor skills such as relay as relay runs, obstacle courses, etc. Encourage free play that allows running, jumping, balancing, throwing, and catching. Introduce basic sports such as baseball, basketball, and soccer. Provide many challenging and diverse art activities that allow for fine motor exercise. Encourage three-dimensional projects such as woodworking, papier mâché, costume-making, etc.
Improved hand–eye coordination	Continue to encourage tossing, throwing, and catching skills. Use activities that incorporate several skills such as dodge ball.
Learns to apply and refine perceptual skills developed earlier	Challenge children in art activities to see and express shape, form, color, and line in a variety of media. Provide activities that allow them to learn to identify and analyze relationships such as how light affects perception of colors, textures, and form.
Growing facility with use of numbers; can think more flexibly. Has an increasingly sophisticated sense of humor	Introduce the use of calculators for math problems. Challenge them with basic probability and estimation activities/problems. Allow them to work in small groups for problem solving. Provide joke books, humorous books, nonsense riddle and rhyme books. Encourage them to write their own humorous pieces.
Enjoys dramatic activities, but self-consciousness is becoming an issue	Encourage children to express themselves in short performances such as sketches, vignettes, "freeze-frame" scenes, and pantomime. Provide opportunities for them to see dramatic activities of other students (i.e., middle school play, dance rehearsal, etc.). Provide books, music, and artwork of great artists for children to experience. (Gallaghue & Ozmun, 2005)

FIGURE 9-10 • Motor skills and characteristics of children ages two through 10 years, with suggested activities to encourage physical development. *(Continued)*

THINK ABOUT IT

Young Children Don't Believe Everything They Hear

Childhood is a time when young minds receive a vast amount of new information. Until now, it's been thought that children believe most of what they hear. New research sheds light on children's abilities to distinguish between fantasy and reality.

Through conversation, books, and the media, young children are continually exposed to information that is new to them. Most of the information they receive is factual (e.g., the names of the planets in the solar system), but some information is not based in truth and represents nonexistent entities (e.g., the Easter Bunny). Children need to figure out which information is real and which is not. By age four, children consistently use the context in which the new information is presented to determine whether or not it is real.

That's one of the major findings in studies conducted by researchers at the Universities of Texas and Virginia and published in the journal *Child Development.*

In three studies, about 400 children ages three to six heard about something new and had to say whether they thought it was real or not. Some children heard the information defined in scientific terms ("Doctors use *sprints* to make medicine"), while others heard it defined in fantastical terms ("Fairies use *hers* to make fairy dust"). The researchers found that children's ability to use contextual cues to determine whether the information is true develops significantly between the ages of three and five.

Moreover, when new information is presented to children in a way that relates the information in a meaningful way to a familiar entity, they are more likely to use contextual cues to make a decision about whether the new information is true than if the new information is simply associated with an entity.

"These studies provide new insight into the development of children's ability to make the fantasy–reality distinction," explains Jacqueline D. Woolley, lead author of the studies and a professor at the University of Texas. "It is clear from the present studies that young children do not believe everything they hear, and that they can use the context surrounding the presentation of a new entity to make inferences about the real versus fantastical nature of that entity" (Woolley & Van Reet, 2006).

FIGURE 9-11 • Small muscles in the fingers and hands develop after the larger muscles.

Creative Activities and the Senses

Touch. Art activities that use the sense of touch teach children many important concepts. For example, working with clay helps them learn the concepts of hard and soft. Children feel the softness of clay in their hands as they work with it. When the clay is old and needs water, they feel how hard it has become. In using clay this way, children learn not only that clay is soft, but that it can be hard, too.

Increased ability to discriminate among textures develops through creative activities. Children use a variety of papers and fabrics for collages, rub crayons over different materials, and print with many objects on diverse surfaces. Opportunities to learn about texture abound at the workbench: the roughness of sandpaper, the smoothness of the dowel, and the sharpness of the wood splinter. Textured art materials help children reinforce knowledge about the physical appearance of people and animals. Yarn, cotton, and fur fabric may be used for people's hair, beards, and mustaches or for animal coats. You may want to try some of the activities suggested at the end of this chapter to help develop children's sense of touch.

Sight. Art activities involve the sense of sight as well as touch. A child sees and feels the art material being learn to use line and shape to express a certain mood or feeling in a drawing.

Color concepts. Concepts about colors are learned in the art program. While painting and drawing, children learn the names of colors, how to mix colors, and how to make colors lighter or darker. In such a sensorimotor experience, the child learns that colors are not set but can be changed if he or she chooses to do so.

When children start to perceive differences in color, they experiment with light and dark hues and tints and mixtures. Contrasts of brilliant and dull and warm and cool colors are juxtaposed for effect. Linear patterns are created with two- and three-dimensional art media. Children can make sharp lines, curved lines, coils, and squiggles with paint, crayon, string, yarn, and wire. In rural areas, children observe the slant of tall wheat and grasses, while city children notice the sharp contrasts in city skylines. Older children learn that colors can be cold or warm and use these colors to express a mood in their paintings.

FIGURE 9-12 • Tricycle play is a fun exercise for large muscles.

used. The sense of sight in artwork helps the child learn many important concepts.

The child sees the sameness and the difference in size, color, shape, and texture when working with different materials. He or she learns concepts like "big," "small," "wide," and "thin" by using many types of art materials. A child sees that different sizes of crayons make different sizes of lines. Wide brushes make paint strokes that look different from strokes made with a thin brush. He or she learns that a figure drawn with a felt-tip pen looks different from the same figure made with paint and a brush.

Ideas about basic shapes are learned by cutting with scissors, working with clay, painting, and drawing. A child also sees many basic shapes in the scrap materials used for a collage.

In artwork, the child sees that things can look alike but feel different. Sand and cornmeal may look alike, but they feel different to the child as they are glued onto paper. In this way, he or she learns that the sense of sight alone is not enough to really learn about a material.

In art activities, older children learn to see and use the elements of art in their work. For example, they

FIGURE 9-13 • Learning to dress oneself requires fine and large motor skills.

THINK ABOUT IT

Children's Brain Development and Learning a Second Language

One of the most important areas of recent research has been about the workings of the brain (Bagley, 2009; Farah, et al., 2008; Johnson, Grossman, & Kadosh, 2009). What scientists have learned has great significance for early childhood teachers.

At birth, the brain has billions of nerve cells called *neurons*. An infant is born with all the neurons he or she will have. None are added during life. Although neurons aren't added, dramatic changes do take place in the brain after birth.

In the first year of life, babies begin to develop pathways that link their neurons. These links "wire" or program the brain so that it can control different functions of the body or thinking processes. The wiring of the brain takes place very quickly. Babies just four days old respond more to their parents' language than to any other language (Partridge, 2009). Over time, the higher thinking areas of the brain are "wired," giving the growing baby greater control over his or her body and understanding of the world. In fact, a two-year-old has almost as many of these pathways as an adult (Partridge, 2009). Each child's brain becomes organized in a unique way. The organization is unique because it grows out of the child's experiences, which are unique to that child.

It is well known that, compared to adults, children tend to have a much easier time learning new languages and acquiring new skills, such as playing an instrument. A recent study of brain development in children suggests that there may be an anatomical reason for the ease with which children are able to acquire these abilities.

A group of brain imaging researchers at UCLA used magnetic resonance imaging (MRI) to obtain brain scans from children of ages 3 to 15 years. These children were all of normal health and mental function and were screened for learning or psychological disabilities. The researchers scanned the children's brains at intervals ranging from two weeks to four years, which allowed them to follow changes in their brains and construct "growth maps" of the children's brain development. Their results were published in the journal *Nature*.

Dr. Paul Thompson and his colleagues found that the children's brains develop in a specific pattern, with a spurt of growth that starts in the front of the brain from ages three to six. In subjects between the ages six and 13, the researchers found that the pattern of rapid growth moved from the front to the back, toward the areas of the brain that are specialized for language skills (Thompson, 2006).

Dr. Thompson, the lead investigator in the study, expressed surprise at the results. "The simplest model of brain development would be that all areas of the brain grow at the same rate. What we found instead was that there is a dynamic wave of growth in the brain," he said.

Thompson suggests that the ages from six to 13 might be the "most efficient" time to learn a second language, because the language systems are developing so rapidly during this time. The researchers found that there is a sharp cutoff in the growth of the language areas of the brain after age 13, so the prepubescent years may be a critical period for acquisition of a new language.

Dr. Thompson emphasizes that the results are not meant to suggest that languages cannot be learned at older ages, but that "it is simply a lot easier during those early prepubescent years."

Another finding from the imaging study is that from age 13 to 15, about 50% of the brain tissue that controls motor skills is pruned away, suggesting a "much more hardwired brain," said Thompson. Thus, activities that require motor skills, such as playing an instrument or a sport, may also have a critical period during childhood in which it is easiest to acquire the necessary abilities.

The researchers hope that their maps of brain development will enable educators to tailor programs to teach specific skills at the most biologically advantageous times (Talukder, 2006).

Vocabulary and Art

An expanding vocabulary about creative materials and processes is a natural partner to the activity itself. Children working with art materials will naturally use descriptive terms for the media and the resulting creations. The teacher's use of particular words to compare size, weight, color, texture, and shape influences children's descriptions of their artwork. Previous knowledge is combined with new information as oral language develops. "Gushy, mushy, wet paint,"

THIS ONE'S for YOU!   Your Brain: It's Greater Than You Think!

There is a huge amount of information about the brain, memory, and conscious and subconscious behavior. While you may not have time to read any of the references for further reading at the end of this chapter, here are a few fast facts about your own special brain.

1. Our Natural Filter

There exists a screening device located at the base of our brain called a **reticular activating system (RAS).** This netlike group of cells helps to decide what we are to be conscious of as it filters out other information. It allows only vital and important sensory input into our conscious awareness.

For example, you were not aware of the shirt on your back until I mentioned it, or the temperature of the room, or all the sounds in your environment. Thankfully, this filter exists or else we would go crazy having to acknowledge every color, every sensation, every blink of the eye, and so forth.

What makes understanding the RAS so interesting is that we can shift our focus such that we can become conscious of things normally blocked from our awareness. Just as mothers can hear the slightest peep from their babies over many other louder sounds, we can soon become aware of the ideas, the interesting overheard conversations, the article topics that we often block out because we're not focused and open to the possibility of receiving inspiration in a grocery store, for example.

For example, when you first started driving a new car, you thought that not many drove the same model. But soon you began to see these everywhere. People didn't rush out and buy the same car. They were always there. You just made this information important to you and thus, your RAS allowed that information through. And as an early childhood teacher, once you understand and make developmental theory important to you, you will notice it unfolding right before your eyes in your work with young children.

2. The Brain's Total Recall

When some people are hypnotized, they are able to describe episodes totally forgotten in their present memory. Under hypnosis, some people can accurately recall license plate numbers and other details of an accident they were previously unable to remember (Daugherty, 2009).

The point is, we have stored in our brain every article we've read, every experience we've had, and every image that has passed before our eyes. It is all there. The challenge—one of the keys to creative inspiration—is to retrieve this information deliberately.

3. The Great Multitasker

Another aspect of the human mind is its ability to multitask. People talk on a hands-free cellular phone while driving a car on the highway, eating a sandwich, handing a cracker to a child in the backseat, listening to music and changing stations, switching lanes, reading and following traffic signs, shifting gears, eating more sandwich, and checking in the mirror for lettuce in the teeth. The eyes blink to maintain proper moisture, the mouth chews the food, the salivary glands add moisture, and various muscles contract in precise order so that the food particles move into the stomach, which has already begun the digestive process.

The body temperature is regulated, the heart is pumping blood, the lungs inhale oxygen and expel carbon dioxide. Hair continues to grow. All the senses provide constant feedback to the brain, indicating that all the tasks associated with driving the car are being accomplished.

This is just a fraction of what's taking place every second of every day of every week. The point? The mind is a powerful machine. It is capable of many, many tasks.

It's natural for things to be done automatically if done enough times. And soon, being more creative and recognizing the ideas all around you will also just happen. The mind is constantly exploring options and possibilities. Exploring a half million of these in a matter of a few seconds is typical behavior for the subconscious mind (Daugherty, 2009). Incredibly, we don't have to be aware of this for it to happen. The key is to understand and to trust that this is how the mind works.

So, to sum up all of this:

1. We "see" things when they become important to us.

2. The mind is constantly recording information.

3. The brain is able to process and do innumerable things at once.

4. The more we practice and the more we trust, the more ideas we have.

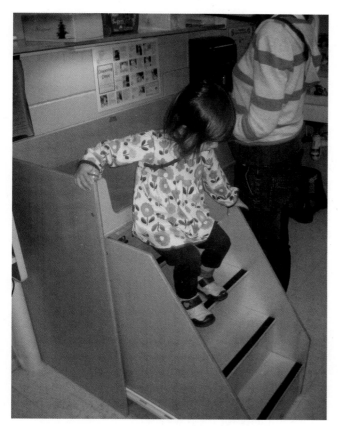

FIGURE 9-14 • Good motor control is required in order to use stairs.

chanted three-year-old Laura as she pushed the finger paint around on the tabletop. "Gushy, mushy, red paint," responded one of her tablemates.

As children grow and develop through art, they begin to use words such as *thick, thin, hard, soft, straight, curved, dark, light, smooth,* and *sticky.* Vocabulary that indicates direction is also quickly assimilated into the children's arena of understanding when they work with art materials. Five-year-old children show how much they have learned with statements like these: "I wrote my name at the top," "I put a board under the clay," and "I drew smoke coming out of the chimney."

The teacher introduces words like *soft* and *smooth* to describe the feel of velvet material. Scraps of burlap are called *rough, bumpy,* or *scratchy.* Even the word *texture* is one that can be used with young children. As they feel the different kinds of cloth, the different "feels" can easily be called "textures." Children then put together in their minds the feel of the velvet with the words *soft, smooth,* and *texture.* This is sensorimotor learning—learning through sensing as well as by association.

Learning to notice the different way things feel teaches a child about concepts that are opposite, which are important in subjects like math and science. The difference between hard and soft is similar to the difference between adding and subtracting in math; both ideas are opposites. A child learns in art that soft is not the same as hard. In math, a child learns that adding is different than or the opposite of subtracting. Mastering opposite concepts used in doing artwork thus helps the child learn the mental concepts needed later in other school subjects. (See Chapters 3 and 4 for more information on art concepts and vocabulary to use with young children.)

Art and the Total Program

The early childhood art program helps a young child grow in social, emotional, physical, and mental ways. It gives children a chance to be themselves and grow at their own individual paces.

Art should not be the only part of the early childhood program where this growth can occur. Freedom for growing at the child's own pace should be part of the whole early childhood program. The exploring, creating, and relaxing parts of artwork should be part of all the other early childhood activities. (Activities in these other program areas are included in subsequent chapters.)

Art helps a child grow through creative thinking and feeling, not only about art but also about all other things. The confidence and good feelings about themselves and their work that children develop in art apply to other things in and out of school. Seen in this way, art cannot be thought of as a separate part of the program. It is and always must be an approach to learning inseparable from all the rest.

Summary

In an early childhood program, activities like drawing, painting, pasting, and other activities that exercise muscles aid a child's overall motor development. Exercising muscles in creative activities aids both small- and large-muscle development. The process of human development follows these general patterns: gross-motor development to fine-motor development; cephalocaudal development, and proxomodistal development. According to Piaget, young children learn mentally as they do things physically. Their mental development, in his theory, falls in these stages: sensorimotor, preoperational, concrete, and formal operations. In the art program, children learn many important concepts that are used later in other learning experiences. Art activities involve children in sensorimotor learning through the use of the body, senses, and mind. Involving all the senses in art activities helps provide a complete learning experience for young children.

Young children learn important concepts such as "hard" and "soft" and "same" and "different" by doing artwork. Artwork also helps in developing their mental abilities: learning to think flexibly; being able to see fine differences; being able to hear, listen, and follow directions; and learning new words. Finally, art helps children develop a creative mental attitude that will help them succeed in all school subjects. The creative aspects of art cannot and should not be separate from the total early childhood program.

Key Terms

cephalocaudal development 183
concrete operation 189
fine-motor development 183
flexible thinking 188
formal operation 189
gross-motor development 183
hand–eye coordination 187
motor development 183
preoperational 189
proxomodistal development 183
Reticular Activating System (RAS) 198
sensorimotor 190
visual acuity 187

Learning Activities

A. Observe children in a preschool program. Include observations in the art center, the block center, and the housekeeping/dramatic play center. Describe the small- and large-motor development of children as demonstrated by their play in each of these areas.

B. Using the information in Figure 9–8, create your own activities for each of the age groups presented in this chart.

C. Listen to a group of children painting. Record or take notes on their conversations. Compare your observations to the information in this chapter on vocabulary and art. Discuss your findings with your classmates.

D. Visit an early childhood classroom. Survey and describe the equipment and materials in the room for suitability for the following:

1. small- and large-motor activities
2. hand–eye coordination activities
3. reading readiness activities
4. motor coordination activities

E. Using your observations from #4, describe the strengths and weaknesses of the supplies and equipment in the classroom you visited. What would you suggest as ways to improve it?

F. Play a game using Piaget's theory of mental development in which you say an age and students have to identify the stage in which the age belongs and act out a characteristic of thinking for that stage.

Activities for Children

The following activities are designed to help children exercise both small- and large-muscle skills and develop hand–eye coordination. Try the activities yourself, with your classmates, and with children.

Small-Motor Activities

Box Weaving

Weaving teaches children about patterns and the basic idea of how fabric is made. It also encourages small-motor skills, sequential thinking, and understanding of spatial relationships.

Materials: Lid of a box (preferably cardboard), a variety of colorful yarn, hole punch, plastic needle, scissors.

Preparation: Prepare the box lid for weaving by punching holes around the entire edge of the box approximately ½ inch apart.

Procedure: With two or three children watching, demonstrate how to put the end of the yarn through a hole and tie it securely (make the knot on the inside of the box lid). Put the yarn through a needle and let the children thread the yarn across the box lid, going back and forth into different holes. Patterns may begin to appear. Show how a second colored yarn will add more pattern and color to the weavings. A third colored yarn can be added in the middle by weaving it in with the fingers. Let children make their own patterns.

As children become more experienced at handling yarn on a plastic needle, they can be encouraged to move on to the next kind of weaving: stringing yarn from the top to bottom of box lid. Using a piece of yarn threaded on a needle, children may weave over and under, over and under, experiencing how real fabric is woven. They start at one end, leaving a tail to tie later. Children need to make sure the yarn is stretched evenly and stays taut and rigid. Children will need help threading the yarn. They can do finger weaving using thicker yarn, which is less frustrating for little fingers.

Variations: For more artistic expression, beads and feathers can be incorporated into the weaving.

Tearing, Punching, and Stapling

Children love to tear, punch, and staple. Keep a stack of old magazines and newspapers on hand for this purpose. These simple activities provide effective small-motor practice and are lots of fun for young children. If you do not have a paper punch or if a child is too young to use it, she or he can use the handle of a wooden spoon to punch large holes in the paper.

If a paper punch is used, save the circles that children punch from white waxed paper and put them in a jar full of water. After you fasten the lid on tightly, children can shake the jar and make a "snowstorm" inside.

Give children colored paper of various textures: smooth, bumpy, heavy, and tissue-thin. Challenge them to tear a tiny shape, an enormous shape, a wide shape, and so on. Children might enjoy pasting or stapling all of the interesting, ragged shapes on a long piece of paper for a big, colorful mural. Tape the mural on the wall for all to see!

Additional Small-Motor Activities

A. Decorate a Shirt

Using wax crayons, have children color a picture on a white or light-colored shirt. Press with newspaper over the picture and on the ironing board. The picture will stay indefinitely.

B. Watercolors and Salt

Children love to paint with watercolors, but sometimes the colors seem too subtle and quiet. Once a picture is done (using enough water to make it a moist picture), bring out table salt and sprinkle a little over the picture while it is still wet. The salt causes the paint to separate and gives the painting a completely new look. This is a good activity to carry out when talking about change in objects: The teacher can discuss with the children what they see as changing in the painting.

C. Printing with Feet and Hands

1. Equipment: Finger paint and finger paint paper.
2. Procedure: Children step in finger paint and print their right feet and left feet and then their hands. This work could be saved and used in social studies for a book "all about me."

D. Shaving Cream Art

An easy-to-do favorite is to take shaving cream and put a few squirts of it in an empty water table. With food coloring, dye the shaving cream the color the children choose. Watching the shaving cream turn color is half the fun; the other half is to finger paint with the colored shaving cream and save the design on paper. To save the design, put a clean sheet of white paper over the design drawn by the child, rub the paper, and lift. Hang to dry.

Shaving cream is also great to use when there are a few minutes until cleanup time and the children are restless. Squeeze a dab of shaving cream on a table in front of each child. Show how it grows and changes and how designs, mountains, and squeezy-feely shapes can be made from the cream. When time allotted is over, each child can clean up with a sponge. The children and the table will shine and smell good.

E. Creative "Found" Sculpture

On a neighborhood walk, on a field trip, or from a child's weekend trip with his or her family, collect an assortment of wood scraps such as driftwood, weathered boards, seashells, stones, twigs, dried flowers, pine cones, and leaves. Use either a flat stone or piece of wood for the base of the sculpture. The rest is up to the child's imagination; animals, designs, birds, and the like can be created. Have children simply assemble their creations and glue them together in place on the base. Markers can be used to draw in faces, make decorations, or add necessary details.

Hand–Eye Coordination Activities

A. Water Pouring

Set up a pan filled with water. Provide different-sized plastic containers, squeeze bottles, funnels, and strainers. Children enjoy pouring water from one container to another.

B. Block Bowling

Set up a long unit block on the floor. The children sit in a circle around it. Each child has a chance to knock it down by rolling a ball at it.

C. Music and Painting

Play music while the children paint.

D. Ball Rolling

Play catch with the children who are able, or roll the ball to the children who cannot catch yet. Notice which ones can catch and return the ball. Compare this ability with their motor control in art.

E. Painting With Water (Outside Activity)

Fill a bucket with water and let the children "paint" the building or sidewalk with water. Children should use large paintbrushes (1 to 2 inches wide) and buckets of water small enough to be carried around.

F. Weed Brushes

On a nice day, take the children on a walk collecting Queen Anne's lace, wild oats, goldenrod, and interesting grasses. The next day, let each child dip these items into different colors of tempera paint and use them as paintbrushes, using either one or several different colors. If the children do not want to paint with their "weed" brushes, they can simply dip their weeds in colors, leave them to dry, and take them home in a plastic bag. These dried, colored weeds make a pretty arrangement.

G. Repeated Natural Forms Collage

Another nature collage can be made using seeds, pods, and other things scattered on the ground and left by the wind.

- Children may classify the objects as large, small, round, straight, rough, smooth, hard, and soft.
- A Styrofoam egg carton is a good receptacle for small objects. (Be sure to wash it out with hot, soapy water before using it.)
- The objects may be arranged into a pattern of repeating forms, using contrasting shapes, textures, and colors. A group display tells the story of nature's materials.

H. Natural Designs

After collecting a variety of natural objects from their outdoor walks, some children may want to arrange them in bouquets. Provide children a variety of containers such as tin cans, old vases, or paper cups. They will also need sand, marbles, pebbles, clay, play dough, or salt clay to make a base to hold their natural bouquets. Children place objects randomly in the base until they are satisfied with their arrangement. The more objects available, the more interesting the arrangements will be. They are nice decorations for the housekeeping center, as well as a centerpiece for snack time.

I. Nature Walk Photographs

Take photographs during an outdoor walk. A digital camera, a regular camera, or even a disposable camera all work equally well for this activity. Try to take pictures that show a sequence of events. Back in the classroom, display the photographs in sequence. Have children think of captions for the pictures, then the story of the event, following the sequence shown in the pictures. Children who are not yet writing can dictate their captions and story to the teacher. They can also dictate their stories on a tape recorder to enjoy at a later time.

J. Favorite Collections Display

During your outdoor walks, encourage children to collect items that appeal to them. They may enjoy collecting items such as leaves, acorns, small pinecones, twigs, interesting rocks, and so on. These items can be displayed in box lids, on pieces of cardboard, or on paper plates. If children prefer, these items can be glued onto a base for a more permanent arrangement.

Activities for Checking Motor Control

A. Artwork Samples

Collect examples of artwork from children aged two to six. Categorize the examples by the degree of children's motor control as evidenced in the artwork.

B. Obstacle Course

Make an obstacle course of chairs, tables, or blocks to climb under, over, or around. Notice how easy or difficult it is for children aged three, four, and five.

C. Action Songs

Sing an action song such as, "If You're Happy and You Know It," using different directions: "Clap your hands," "Clap your hands and tap your head," "Clap your hands and shake your head." Notice which children can perform the combined actions and which can do the single actions. Note their ages.

D. Rope Games

Put a long rope on the floor in a zigzag pattern and have children walk on it. Note how many of the children can do this and how well they can do it. Put the rope in a straight line and have children pretend it is a tightrope. Have them "walk the tightrope" with a real or pretend umbrella in their hands for balance. Note the balancing ability of each child. Two children take turns holding the rope very high at first and then gradually lower and lower. The rest of the children go under the rope without touching it. Place the rope straight out on the floor. The children walk across it, hop on one foot across it, hop on two feet across it, crawl across it, jump across it, and cross it any other way they can think of. Note each child's physical control.

Large-Motor Activities

A. Blanket Statues/Shapes (suitable for kindergarten and up)

Have children make shapes using their bodies. Have them experiment with as many shapes and forms they choose. Then involve them in making "blanket statues." A child stays frozen in one position, and a blanket is placed over her or him to create a statue. Two children can create partner statues: One child rests on hands and knees and a second child rests on her or his back. Or two children stand three or four feet apart, facing one another, with their arms raised and reaching across, fingertips touching in an arch. These are just suggestions: Let children's creativity direct their movement. This activity is a good opportunity to take photographs that can later be displayed. Older children may want to write captions for their photographs, creating their own documentary of the activity.

B. Can You Guess What I Am?

Collect about 15 to 20 different animal pictures. Place these in a box on a chair over to one side. From a group of children (a small group of four or five works best) seated on the floor, the teacher chooses one child to pick out a picture from the box. The child then "acts out" the animal in the picture for the others to guess. Whoever guesses the animal is the next to pick out a picture to act out. As a variation, use transportation pictures such as a train, truck, jet, car, boat, and bus.

C. Body Creations

Invite children to create different shapes by using their bodies. For example, three children might stretch out on the floor, joining their bodies in a way that creates a triangle. Four children might position their bodies to create a square, four others can create a rectangle, and so on. Ask others in the group if they know the names of the shapes their classmates are creating. Introduce terms such as *square, triangle,* and *rectangle.* Continue the activity until all children have had an opportunity to participate. Photograph the activity and post the photos where visitors can see them.

Activities for the Senses

The following activities are designed to exercise the senses. Try the activities yourself, with your classmates, and with children.

Seeing Activities

A. Exploring With a Magnifying Glass

Provide children magnifying glasses and a tray full of different objects—stamps, coins, rocks, and leaves. Encourage young children to talk about what they are seeing. They might also want to draw or paint what they've seen.

With older children, talk about the qualities of color, line, shape, and other visual elements they see magnified in the objects. Provide opportunities for them to sketch what they see. Challenge them to draw a pattern or design using what they've seen through the magnifying glass.

Use the magnifying glass outside on a nature walk. Encourage children to talk about what they see. Provide them opportunities to express their reactions to "nature under glass" in two- and three-dimensional activities.

B. Paper Towel Telescopes

Collect paper towel rolls for telescopes. Children use the paper towel roll to see their world in a sharper focus. Looking through a tube such as this helps children focus on a single area.

Encourage children to talk about what they see. Maybe later they will want to draw or paint about what they have seen. Older children can be challenged to see if they can see specific elements of design through their telescope.

C. Examining Objects in Different Colors

Have children look at the things around them through transparent plastic or colored cellophane. They can see how the brown table looks through "yellow" or how the blue sky looks through "red." When children seem to understand how the color of different objects changes when seen through another color and have been satisfied using just a single color, they may look through two colors at once (superimpose red over blue) and see still another change.

D. See-Through Colors

Looking through color strips will help children learn how colors combine to make new colors—specifically, how the combination of two primary colors creates a secondary color. The children can relate the colors to familiar objects.

Materials: Scissors; red, yellow, and blue cellophane papers. (You can find colored cellophane paper in the wrapping paper section of a variety store. It is most readily available at Easter time when it is used to cover baskets.)

Preparation: Cut the red, blue, and yellow cellophane into strips about 4 inches long and 2 inches wide.

Procedure: Gather four children together. Give each child a color strip. Have them first look through their individual color strips by holding them up to the light. Each child names something that is the color of the strip—for example, blue is the color of water or the sky. Each child should have a turn.

Put children with different color strips into pairs. Each child in the pair looks through the two strips to see what new colors are made. The teacher then gives each pair another strip, making sure that each pair has a set of red, blue, and yellow. Allow children to explore and exchange color strips. When interest begins to wane, call the children together. Let each pair name the colors produced, and name something that is that color.

Variations: Allow children to cut up pieces of cellophane to make their own color combinations. They might tape the pieces together to make stained glass designs.

Encourage the expression of emotional and impressionistic responses of the children caused by colors. For example, "Yellow is the color of sunshine and it makes me feel happy." "Blue is the color of the ocean and I like the waves in the ocean."

E. Shadow Guessing

In this activity, children learn about the interaction of light, shadows, and distance. Shadow play also encourages creative expression.

You will need a flashlight or lamp, a sheet, and different kinds of fruit for this activity.

Hang a sheet up in the room in front of a table. Put several kinds of fruit on the table.

From behind the sheet, shine a light on the fruit one at a time. Bananas, grapes, apples, and other fruits will puzzle the children as they try to guess the type of fruit and figure out how they are appearing on the sheet.

Then, again with a small group, shine a flashlight or other light source on a wall in the dramatic play area. Have children use their fingers to produce shadow figures. They will enjoy making rabbit ears, a duck, a dog, a monster, or just abstract forms. Children can also use puppets, and the teacher can add music to allow for rhythmic movements and self-expression. Have the children move their puppets closer and farther from the light source and observe how the shadows change.

Outdoors on a bright day, encourage children to make silly movements and observe their own shadows. You can even introduce a quick "copy cat" (follow-the-leader) game: "Everybody jump! Everybody hop! Now, everybody dance!"

Hearing Activities

A. Room Noises

1. Have children close their eyes and name the different sounds they hear in the room.
2. Make up noises and sounds (birds singing, blocks dropping, sawing wood, bells, drums and other instruments, tearing paper, water splashing). Have children guess what they are.
3. A child closes both eyes while another child speaks. The first child tries to guess who is speaking.

B. Rattlesnake

You will need a small plastic bottle with beans inside. The group closes their eyes and the "leader" walks around shaking the bottle. The group then points to the direction from which they hear the sound and identifies the level of sound (i.e., "high" or "low"). This can be played with one child as well.

C. Sound Cans

Place four different substances—a small block, a piece of clay, a piece of cotton, small amount of sand—in four identical cans. When all the lids are on, shuffle the cans. The child guesses what is in each can by the noise made as the can is shaken.

D. Parrot Talk

Use a paper bag puppet of a parrot, or just use your hands and fingers to look like the mouth of a parrot talking. Discuss with the child how parrots like to repeat everything they hear. Let the child speak first while you are the parrot and repeat everything the child says. Then you speak first and the child repeats. Begin with a single word and build up to a full sentence.

Nonsensical words may also be used. Variation: Talk with the child about echoes and how they repeat the sounds two or three times. After you have echoed something the child has said or a noise the child has made, by tapping for instance, let the child be your echo.

Smelling and Tasting Activities

A. Painted Toast

Make "paint" with ¼ cup of milk and a few drops of food coloring. Paint designs or faces on white bread with a clean paintbrush. Toast the bread in a toaster. The bread can be buttered and eaten or used as part of a sandwich. This is a very popular tasting experience!

B. Community Fruit Salad

1. To further experiment with how things taste, children may help make a community fruit salad. Each child brings a different fruit: apples, peaches, pears, seedless grapes, tangerines. Have extra fruit on hand for children who don't bring theirs in.
2. Children help peel bananas and oranges, wash grapes, and cut the fruit with blunt or serrated knives.
3. Children taste each fruit separately as they are preparing the salad. Then they sample how the fruits taste together.
4. Talk about how each fruit tastes, looks, and smells different from the others.

Activities for Older Children (Grades 4–5)

A. Link Art to Dance and Physical Movement

Older children have well-developed large and small muscles as well as good overall motor coordination. Challenge them to use these skills in creative ways. Choose several artists' works that have a good deal of movement in the composition. Some suggestions are Vincent Van Gogh's *Starry Night*, Jackson Pollock's *Water Birds*, Jacob Lawrence's *Strike*, or Edgar Degas's

Ballet Scene. Review with children the elements of line and movement in art while viewing one of the prints. Have them discuss the ways the artist used lines in the painting to show movement.

Tell students that they will take turns modeling and drawing different movements. Then have volunteers pantomime individually or in small groups various kinds of movements such as those in dance, in a sport, or in a type of exercise. Have students observing the movements draw lines that represent or reflect the movements they are seeing.

Continue the activity until students have filled their sheet of drawing paper with colorful lines. Then have students exchange roles.

B. Understanding Composition by Posing a Picture

One of the most effective ways to help students understand the overall composition or structure of a work of art is to have them pose as a painting or sculpture. This requires some advance preparation on the part of the teacher. Scour your attic, basement, closets, and the local resale shop for old items of clothing and props that resemble those depicted in the artwork you have chosen to pose. Be creative. For example, in posing *Washington Crossing the Delaware* by Emanuel Leutze, you might borrow oars from a boat store. Diego Rivera's *The Flower Carrier,* Jan Van Eyck's *Arnolfini Marriage,* George Caleb Bingham's *Wood Boatmen on a River,* Pieter de Hooch's *Interior with People,* or Vincent Van Gogh's *The Bedroom of Van Gogh at Arles* are all good choices for posing.

Assign clothing, props, and their position to your students and have them really study that part of the painting to notice facial expressions, body positions, and relationship to other figures, the background, and so forth. If you have a large group, split it in half or thirds and have an audience comment on the accuracy of each group's pose. Everyone gets to participate, and students remember the artwork better by recalling their own part in it. Posing is not only great fun but also of value in increasing understanding. For example, ask students which poses were easier to hold in order to point out how some paintings create a feeling of motion or imbalance, while others give the impression of equilibrium or stability.

C. Recreating a Still Life

An activity similar to posing can be done with still life painting. This involves having children re-create with real objects one of the paintings they have been studying.

Bring in as many items as possible that are found in selected works of art. These artworks might include William J. McCloskey's *Wrapped Oranges,* Albert Dummouchel's *Still Life,* Margaret Burroughs's *Still Life,* Laura Wheeler Waring's *Still Life,* and Gustave Caillebotte's *Fruit Displayed on a Stand.*

Ask each child to identify an object and place it in its proper position so that the finished arrangement approximates the original as closely as possible. This exercise enables students to comprehend some of the basic concerns of the still life painter: the use of light, the concepts of balance and harmony, the question of focus, and the problem of rendering three-dimensional objects on a two-dimensional surface.

D. Shadowplay

Students often have difficulty determining the source of light in a painting. A simple way to demonstrate how shadows help us determine where light is coming from is to shine a flashlight on a ball from a variety of angles (behind the ball, to the left of the ball, above the ball, below the ball). Place the flashlight in the position before turning it on and ask the students if they can guess where the shadow will fall. (This exercise works best if the area around the ball is fairly plain and darkened somewhat so that the shadows can be seen clearly. Also the flashlight beam should be smaller than the ball.) One teacher did this activity near Groundhog's Day and substituted a toy stuffed animal for the ball.

E. Matching Colors Under Different Lights

To demonstrate to students that light influences the way we see color, bring in various paint chips or cloth swatches. Be sure to have multiples of the same color available. Have students view identical color samples under different light sources (fluorescent, incandescent, and natural). They will soon discover that it is almost impossible to match colors under different lighting conditions. The most accurate light for viewing colors is daylight.

F. More Telescopes

Visual perceptiveness is an important skill that comes into use not only when looking at a painting, but also when reading a book, examining a map, or even doing a math problem. To hone this ability, encourage students to look carefully for details in a painting. One way to accomplish this is to use "telescopes." These are simply four-by-six-inch index cards that students roll up into tubes and look through. The teacher can ask students to find certain things in a painting and will be able to tell by the angle of the telescopes if the child is looking in the correct place. This is a technique artists have used themselves: Frederic Church handed out a rolled up piece of cardboard to everyone who came to see his painting *Heart of the Andes* when it was exhibited in 1864.

G. Magnification—Once Again

The use of a magnifying glass can heighten the enjoyment for older children when looking at certain paintings, especially those that are extremely detailed. Allow students to use the magnifying glass one at a time and give them specific instructions as to what they should find. Explain to them that artists use very thin brushes in order to paint the tiniest details. The 16th-century Flemish master Pieter Brueghel the Elder supposedly used only a few cat's hairs as a brush for his miniscule figures. Thus, a magnifying glass enables us to appreciate the artist's creation more thoroughly. It also intrigues students to see even more than the eye alone can see.

H. Creative Color Thinking

Have children gather in small groups. Ask a recorder in each group to write down, in columns, the names of the basic colors on the color wheel. Have the students identify adjectives that are often used to describe varieties of each color, such as "sky" blue, "fire engine" red, and "grass" green. While the students work, set up columns on the board so students can compile the unique adjectives and place tally marks by those identified by more than one group. Discuss the connotations of the adjectives for yellow, red, and orange in relation to ideas or experiences of warmth. Discuss the connotations of the words listed for blue, green, and violet in relation to experiences of coolness.

I. Online Learning: Enlighten Me

Check out the website http://www.superpages.com/enlightenme, sponsored by Verizon and Fablevision. Play the Peetnik Mystery using a phone book, a Who's Who, and a map to help Penn Peetnik and his friends solve a mystery. In this activity, students make "phone calls" and find locations, which helps them practice mapping skills, research, and real-life problem solving to find clues that lead to a solution. Also on this site, children can make a book, write a book review, or print Super Thinker posters. Super Thinkers also has games, stories, and many more activities.

J. Textures

Provide students with a variety of leaves, long grasses, and other natural objects. You might want them to bring in similar natural objects as well. Have them make rubbings using white crayon or oil pastel and black paper. Suggest that students do a repeated rubbing of the item until the entire paper is covered. Discuss the results as a record of textures that can be viewed as artwork as well as a display for science. Students might want to research the types of grass and leaves they used in this activity.

K. Texture Words

Have students make and illustrate vocabulary cards for words that describe textures in nature.

Have them arrange the items by tactile sense (e.g., rough, soft, smooth). Encourage them to use these terms appropriately in storytelling and in other activities.

L. Mystery Textures

Tell students they will make a mystery texture bag. Provide small paper bags for each student. Have them secretly collect items that have varied textures associated with fall or any of the other seasons. These are the mystery items that others will be guessing. Working in pairs, students exchange bags and try to guess what the mystery objects are by feeling the textures.

M. Lines, Patterns, Textures

Have students bring in a large leaf. Have them place a magnifying glass over one part of the leaf and observe its lines, patterns, and textures. Have students create a large drawing of the small section of the leaf seen in the viewfinder.

N. Varieties of Colors

Have students look selectively for varieties of color in leaves and bring them to class. Have them describe differences using terms such as *light, dark, shiny,* or *dull.* Focus on other visual elements in the same way. For example, ask students who are wearing rough textures to stand and point them out. Develop an awareness of terms to describe textures such as *bumpy, prickly,* and *silky.*

O. Weather Diaries

Have students keep a weather diary with drawings that portray the weather as it occurs at the same time each day for five days. The time might be lunch or recess. At the end of five days, have students work in small groups to compare and contrast the different interpretations. The total group can choose drawings that best represent the weather for each day. The drawings might be put into a booklet titled "The Weather Diary of Grade Four." Present the booklet to the school library.

Chapter Review

A. Physical Development

1. Define motor development.
2. List three examples of locations of small muscles.
3. Define small-motor activities and give three examples.
4. Define large-motor activities and give three examples.
5. List three examples of locations of large muscles.

6. Tell whether each of the following activities helps a child develop a small- or a large-motor skill.
   a. tracing body forms
   b. using scissors
   c. pounding clay
   d. finger painting
   e. using finger puppets
   f. painting with a brush

g. pounding nails

h. clay modeling

7. Choose the answer that best completes each statement describing a child's motor development in art.

  a. Most three-year-olds

    i. have good small-muscle development.

    ii. do not have good small-muscle development.

    iii. have good small- and large-muscle development.

  b. One way to check small-motor skill is by having a child

    i. pound on clay.

    ii. walk a balance board.

    iii. cut paper with blunt scissors.

  c. Development of the body goes from

    i. small muscles to large muscles.

    ii. large muscles to small muscles.

    iii. arms to legs.

  d. In order to be able to use small muscles, a child must first be able to use

    i. finger muscles.

    ii. large muscles.

    iii. eye muscles.

  e. By the time children are in preschool, they can use

    i. small muscles quite well.

    ii. both large and small muscles quite well.

    iii. large muscles quite well.

  f. An art activity that exercises large motor skills is

    i. painting on large-sized paper with a wide brush.

    ii. cutting paper with scissors.

    iii. finger painting.

  g. In planning the art program, a teacher should include

    i. mostly large-motor activities for four-year-olds.

    ii. mostly small-motor activities for three-year-olds.

    iii. both large- and small-motor activities for all ages.

  h. The age group that uses mostly large-muscle activity is the

    i. three-year-old.

    ii. four-year-old.

    iii. five-year-old.

  i. A teacher in the art program should let children know that they are free to

    i. use only small-motor activity.

    ii. try all types of activities.

    iii. try only large-motor activity.

8. Define hand–eye coordination and give two examples.

9. Discuss what reading experts say about the importance of hand–eye coordination.

10. Describe how one can see motor control develop in a child's artwork.

B. Mental Development

1. Define sensorimotor learning and give one example.

2. Which of the following mental concepts does a child learn in art by the sense of touch?

  a. new words

  b. hard/soft

  c. true/false

  d. large/small

  e. smooth/rough

  f. names of colors

  g. feel of clay

  h. difference in shades of color

  i. feel of play dough

  j. sweet/sour

3. Choose the answer that best completes each of the following statements about how art helps mental development.

  a. Concepts are

    i. phrases.

    ii. songs.

    iii. ideas.

  b. The mental concept of opposites learned in art is also used in

    i. math.

    ii. finger plays.

    iii. cooking.

  c. Introducing new words in art activity

    i. often confuses children.

    ii. helps improve children's vocabulary.

    iii. has little effect on young children.

  d. An example of an activity that improves the sense of touch is

    i. a piano lesson.

    ii. work on a collage.

    iii. a seeing game.

  e. Some concepts of color a child learns in art are

    i. how to erase color errors, paint over, and choose colors.

    ii. how to choose colors, mix colors, and color over.

    iii. names of colors, how to mix colors, and how to make colors lighter or darker.

  f. An important new way of thinking that a child learns in art is

    i. flexible thinking.

    ii. inflexible thinking.

    iii. permanent thinking.

  g. Seeing and learning that clay can have many shapes and textures helps the child develop

    i. inflexible thought.

    ii. flexible thought.

    iii. permanent thinking.

  h. In artwork, very young children often use the senses of

    i. touch and sight only.

    ii. smell, taste, touch, sight, and hearing.

    iii. touch and smell only.

4. Discuss the development of a creative mental attitude as a goal in the art program for young children.
5. Identify and discuss other aspects of the school program that should be like the art program.

6. Should art be considered a separate part of the preschool program? Explain your answer.

References

Bagley, W. (2009). *A study in the correlation of mental and motor ability in school children.* Bel Air, CA: BiblioBazaar.

Daugherty, R. (2009). Understanding the mind: Five keys to a writer's creativity. www.creativityforlife.com

Farah, M. J., Betancourt, L., Shera, D. M., Savage, J. H., Giannetta, J. M., & Brodsky, N. L. (2008). Environmental stimulation, parental nurturance, and cognitive development in humans. *Developmental Science, 11*(5), 793–801.

Gallaghue, D., & Ozmun, J. (2005).6th edition. *Understanding motor development: Infants, children, Adolescents, adults* (4th ed.) New York: McGraw Hill.

Johnson, M. H., Grossman, T., & Kadosh, K. S. (2009). Mapping functional brain development: Building a social brain through interactive specialization. *Developmental Psychology, 45*(1), 151–159.

Partridge, K. (2009). *The reference shelf: The brain.* New York, NY: H. W. Wilson.

Piaget, J. (1950). *The psychology of intelligence.* New York, NY: Harcourt Brace.

Piaget, J. (1952). *The child's conception of number.* New York, NY: Humanities Press.

Piaget, J. (1955). *The child's conception of reality.* London, England: Routledge & Kegan.

Talukder, G. (2006). *Brain development study may provide some help for educators.* Online at Brain Connection, http://www.Brainconnection.com/topics/?main=new-In-rev/brain-development

Thompson, P. M. (2006). Growth patterns in the developing brain detected by using continuum mechanical tensor maps. *Nature, 204,* 190–193.

Woolley, J. D., & Van Reet, J. (2006). Effects of context on judgments concerning the reality status of novel entities. *Child Development, 77*(6), 16–23.

Additional Readings

Barbarin, O. A., & Wasik, B. H. (2009). *Handbook of child development and early education: Research to practice.* New York, NY: Guilford Press.

Bornstein, M. H. (2009). *Handbook of cross-cultural developmental science.* New York, NY: Psychology Press.

Emck, C., Bosscher, R., Beek, P., & Doreleijers, T. (2009). Gross motor performance and self-perceived motor competence in children with emotional, behavioral and pervasive developmental disorders: A review. *Developmental Medicine & Child Neurology, 51*(7), 501–517.

Essa, E. L. (2009). *Informing our practice: Useful research on young children's development.* Washington, DC: NAEYC.

Fineman, M. S., & Worthington, K. (2009). *What is right for children?* Surrey, GB: Ashgate.

Gillespie, L. G. (2009). Rocking and rolling: Supporting infants, toddlers and their families. Why do babies like boxes best? *Young Children, 64*(3), 48–49.

Harlin, R. P. (2009). Research into practice: What do we really know about learning and development? *Journal of Research in Childhood Education, 32*(1), 123–129.

Kiselv, S., Espy, K. A., & Sheffield, T. (2009). Age-related differences in reaction time performance in young children. *Journal of Experimental Child Psychology, 102*(2), 150–166.

Kovacs, C. R. (2008). Measuring motor skill learning—A practical application. *Strategies: A Journal for Physical and Sport Education, 22*(2), 25–29.

Lengen, C., Regard, M., Joller, H., Landis, T., & Lalive, P. (2009). Anomalous brain dominance and the immune system: Do left-handers have specific immunological patterns? *Brain and Cognition, 69*(1), 188–193.

Lewis, M., & Carmody, D. P. (2009). Self representation and brain development. *Developmental Psychology, 44*(5), 1329–1334.

Orr, H. B. (2009). *A theory of development and heredity.* Bel Air, CA: BiblioBazaar.

Rowe, S. H. (2009). *The physical nature of the child and how to study it.* Bel Air, CA: BiblioBazaar.

Ruth, F. (2009). The development of regulatory functions from birth to 5 years: Insights from premature infants. *Child Development, 80*(2), 544–561.

Tucker, P. (2008). The physical activity levels of pre-school children: A systematic review. *Early Childhood Research Quarterly, 23*(4), 547–558.

Helpful Websites

Brain Connection, http://www.brainconnection. positscience.com
A Web library of articles on human brain development, including infant brain development.

Brainbox Challenge, http://www.bbc.co.uk/ brainboxchalalenge/science/index.shtml
Website offers a treat for your brain, including interactive visual, spatial, coding, memory, dual tasks, and language "mind games."

Healthline, http://www.healthline.com
Source for links to dozens of child development sites.

Pediatric Health, http://yourtotalhealth.ivillage. com/pediatric-health
Learn here about the building blocks of healthy development for children.

PNN Online—The Nonprofit News and Information Source, http://www.pnnonline.org
Up-to-the-minute research on child development and many other areas such as health, arts, and the environment.

Society for Research in Child Development, http:// www.srcd.org
This organization disseminates new research information published in the journal *Child Development*.

Teach the Brain, http://www.teach-the-brain.org/
This website presents a curriculum developed as a brief intervention to help preschool children improve control of attention. The curriculum is available to download for free at this website.

The High/Scope Educational Research Foundation, http://www.highscope.org

Tufts University Child & Family Web Guide, http:// www.cfw.tufts.edu
Contains listings of trustworthy websites on topics of interest to parents and professionals. All sites have been systematically evaluated by faculty and graduate students in child development.

Zero to Three Organization, http://www. zerotothree.org
Links to the Boston University School of Medicine, the Erikson Institute.

For additional creative activity resources, visit our website at www.Cengage.com/login.

Art and Social– Emotional Growth

OBJECTIVES

After studying this chapter, you should be able to:

1. Define the terms *self-acceptance*, *self-concept*, and *social competence*.

2. Describe how the art program can add to a child's self-concept and self-acceptance.

3. Discuss how the art program helps a child in child-to-child relationships, child-to-teacher relationships, and child-to-group relationships.

The term *social–emotional growth* refers to two kinds of growth. Emotional growth is the growth of a child's feelings, and social growth is the child's growth as a member of a group.

Learning to be a member of a group involves many social skills. Young children, for example, must learn to relate to other children and adults outside the family. Often, a child's first experience of sharing an adult's attention with other children occurs in the early childhood setting. Of the social skills involved in learning to work in a group, children have to learn how to share materials, how to take turns, how to listen to others, and how and when to work on their own—to mention just a few!

This chapter covers both the social and emotional growth of the child as they occur in the early childhood art program. Although social–emotional growth occurs at the same time as physical–mental growth, the two are covered in separate chapters within this text for the sake of clarity. The developmental concepts learned and applied in this and the following two chapters are applicable to all other creative activities and materials.

We are *teaching children about art* rather than *teaching art to children*. There is a subtle but important difference in the two parts of this statement. In early childhood education, the child comes first: The emphasis is on children and how they learn, rather than on art and how it is "taught." Art plays an important role in the well-being and the education of the whole child. The objective, then, of all creative activities is to promote the development of the child in all areas, thus maximizing his or her full potential.

This chapter is divided into four main sections: (1) self-concept and self-acceptance, (2) child-to-child relationships, (3) child-to-teacher relationships, and (4) child-to-group relationships.

Self-Concept and Self-Acceptance

Self-concept can be defined as the child's growing awareness of his or her own characteristics (physical appearance as well as skills and abilities) and how these are similar to or different from those of others.

All children like to feel good about themselves. This good feeling about oneself is called *self-acceptance* or *self-esteem*. Children who feel good about themselves and believe they can do things well have a good sense of self-acceptance.

This feeling of self-acceptance was one of **Carl Rogers'**, a noted psychologist', main concepts. He felt that every human being has a single "force of life," which he calls the **actualizing tendency**, or **self-actualization**. It can be defined as the built-in motivation present in every human being to develop its potential to the fullest extent possible. Rogers believes that all creatures strive to make the very best of their existence. Among the things that humans instinctively value is **positive self-concept**, or self-esteem, self-worth, a positive self-image. Children achieve this positive self-image by experiencing the positive regard others show them over their years of growing up. Without this self-regard, children feel less positive and often helpless, and they may fail to become all they can be (Rogers, 1995).

Children who have a positive self-concept accept their strengths and limitations. The early childhood program provides an environment that nurtures the development of a positive sense of self and a good self-concept in each child. And according to Rogers, such an environment is **psychosocially safe** for young children (Thorne, 2003).

Children learn to accept themselves from birth all the way throughout life. According to Rogers, children grow in self-acceptance when they receive **unconditional positive acceptance** from the people in their lives. They learn about themselves by the way they are treated by others. The way parents hold their baby makes the baby feel accepted. A baby who is held closely and with tenderness learns to feel loved and good. The only way babies understand this is by physical touch because they do not yet understand words.

As babies grow into young children, they continue learning to accept themselves. When toddlers are encouraged and praised for messy but serious attempts to feed themselves, they learn to accept themselves and feel good about what they do. If children are accepted positively and unconditionally as they are, they learn to accept themselves.

FIGURE 10-1 • All children like to feel good about themselves.

Another psychologist whose work centered on the importance of a psychologically safe environment for children was **Erik Erikson** (Erikson, 1950). He developed a set of **stages of psychosocial development** that he felt characterized human social development. See Figure 10–2 for more information on these stages and their application in the early childhood years. Basically, his ideas centered on the influence of culture on a child's social–emotional development.

In the early childhood program, children must continue to learn to accept and feel good about themselves. The art program can be of special help in this area. When children feel they can do things well in art, they grow in both self-confidence and self-acceptance.

In the art program, young children learn more about themselves and their capabilities and affirm their sense of self. For example, a child at the easel used many bright colors and was proud of his accomplishment. "I'm Harry and I like to paint pretty colors. Write my name at the top," he calls out to his teacher. This three-year-old child's growing concept of self is evident as he views what he has painted. The good feelings about oneself, which can be fostered through art, are essential for positive development of self-concept.

The importance of a good self-concept is equally as important to middle- and upper-elementary students. They, too, need the same encouragement and emotionally safe environment in which to express themselves creatively. Just because they are physically bigger and appear more sure of themselves doesn't mean that a teacher can overlook the development of their self-concept in creative activities.

At the primary level and above, state and national standards often overpower teachers with lists of objectives, goals, and mandated learning experiences. Often in this situation with older children, teachers may impose art activities on children from a prescribed curriculum without consideration for the child's interest or concern for his or her personal experiences. This approach takes less time than it takes to listen to children, to get to know them, and to adapt the curriculum by putting the child at the center. It is far easier for adults to dictate to children.

In this adult-directed model, children learn primarily to follow directions. They are directed through one activity after another, activities that often are related to the seasons of the year or holidays. Then, children are evaluated primarily by how well they are able to follow directions.

The importance of changing such an adult focus is clearly explained by the renowned art educator, Viktor Lowenfeld:

> Because every process involves the whole child, and not only a single segment, art education may well become the catalyst for a child-centered education in which the individual and his creative potentialities are placed above subject matter, in which the child's inner equilibrium may be considered as important as scientific achievements. (Lowenfeld, 1957, p. 11)

This approach is one that obviously builds the child's self-acceptance. An early childhood teacher needs to plan the art program in such a way that it gives each child a chance to grow in self-acceptance. To do so, the program should be child centered, which

Stage 1: Trust vs. Mistrust
Birth and first year
Most fundamental stage
Trust based on dependability and quality of caregivers
Successful completion: Child feels safe and secure in the world
Unsuccessful completion: Failure to develop trust, fear, belief world is inconsistent and unpredictable

Stage 2: Autonomy vs. Shame and Doubt
Early preschool childhood/preschool years
Child develops greater sense of personal control
Child learning to control body functions leads to feeling of control and sense of independence
Child gains control over food choices, toy preferences, clothing selection
Successful completion: Child feels secure and confident
Unsuccessful completion: Sense of inadequacy and self-doubt

Stage 3: Initiative vs. Guilt
Preschool years
Child asserts power and control over the world through directing play and other social interactions
Successful completion: Child feels capable and able to lead others
Unsuccessful completion: Sense of guilt, self-doubt and lack of initiative

Stage 4: Industry vs. Inferiority
Ages 5–11 (approximately)
Through social interaction, child begins to develop a sense of pride in accomplishments and abilities
Successful completion: Children who are encouraged and commended by parents and teachers develop feelings of competence and belief in their skills
Unsuccessful completion: Child doubts ability to be successful

FIGURE 10-2 • Erickson's Stages of Psychosocial Development (1950)—Early Childhood Years.

means that it is planned for the age and ability levels of the children in it.

Naturally, if it is child centered, it is, in turn, developmentally appropriate—meeting the specific individual needs of each child. The art program is planned around the developmental needs of the child. In this way, the teacher has clear guidelines for selections of appropriate materials and activities for the level of each child in the program. (Developmental levels in art and related activities for these levels are covered in Chapter 11.)

Encouraging Self-Acceptance Through the Art Program

A climate of psychological safety is essential to the growth of a child's self-acceptance. This safe, accepting environment doesn't just happen. It is carefully planned with the following points included in the planning.

Accept children at their present developmental level. If the adult accepts the child in a positive way, the child feels this acceptance. This does not mean that the child should not be challenged. Art activities can be planned that are a slight challenge for the child's present level. But they must not be so hard that they frustrate the child. By feeling successful in art activities, children learn to feel more sure about themselves and their skills.

Self-confidence is built on a circular relationship between child and teacher. When the teacher shows confidence in a child, it helps that child develop greater self-confidence.

When four-year-old Rathnam was sweeping broad, free strokes of blue, red, and white paint across his paper, the colors inadvertently mixed at various places. Suddenly he stopped, his brush in midair, as he squinted hard at his painting. "Look, it's pink up here! And look at this," he said, pointing to a hazy lavender area.

"Yes," said his teacher, catching the excitement of the moment. "And you made them—you made those special colors."

Without hesitation Rathnam responded, "Oh, that's red and white, mixed."

"So now you can make pink whenever you want," summarized the teacher.

"Yeah," whispered Rathnam with a touch of pride and awe. "I'll mix red and white."

In this way the teacher made clear her confidence that Rathnam could repeat purposefully a technique

for changing color that he had discovered accidentally. Rathnam's response highlighted a moment of self-confidence in his ability to control this responsive art medium.

Provide an environment that is comfortable for the age level of the group. Plan the room so that it is a place where children can feel at home. It should have tables and chairs that are the right size for young children. A room for older children needs the same care in planning. This age group needs chairs and tables of the appropriate size and strength. There is often a widening difference in physical size in grades 4 to 5, so a mixture of sizes is often necessary if equipment is to be appropriate for this age group. For example, small desks and chairs often aren't the right size for fifth-grade children who have had a growth spurt. It's hard to feel good about oneself when one is too big for one's chair! If necessary, there should be covering on the floor and work areas so that children can work freely without worrying about spills. It is hard

FIGURE 10-3 • This child's obvious pride in her work reflects her positive self-concept.

for children to feel good about themselves and their work when they are always being told they are "too messy." If sponges and towels are within reach, children can clean up their own messes. A little responsibility like this is fun for them, as well as a good way to help them develop independence and confidence. By being in charge of keeping their own areas clean, children learn to feel good about how they can take care of themselves. This strengthens their self-acceptance and personal pride.

Provide an environment that is appropriate for children with special needs. Adapt the environment so that children with special needs can successfully function in the program. Figure 10–4 presents some ideas on how to make these changes for children with physical disabilities.

Provide materials and activities that are age appropriate. By giving children tools they are able to work with at their age and skill level, the teacher helps them have more success in art projects. Success helps them grow with pride and confidence and know that they can do things well. Success breeds success.

Provide creative materials and activities that the children can work on and complete by themselves. Activities that children can finish themselves help them feel more self-assured and confident about their art ability. To do this, teachers need to be good observers to know exactly what materials and activities are developmentally appropriate for each child. This match between children's developmental levels and appropriate activities and materials is an ever-changing one, as children continue to grow and develop in the early years. The creative process offers opportunities for children to gain a spirit of independence and a sense of personal autonomy when the choice of medium, process, or kind of expression is their own.

Child-to-Child Relationships

It is only after a child has developed self-acceptance that it is possible for him or her to accept other children. In the early childhood art program, there are many chances for a child to be with other children of the same age. Children who have had positive creative experiences are the ones who can honestly accept their own abilities and those of other children.

- Use plenty of verbal activities for students whose body movements are limited.
- Use a "buddy system." A partner can quietly explain points that may be confused by children with hearing impairments, help move a wheelchair, or make an area accessible for those with limited mobility. With a sighted partner, space can be explored gradually.
- Use touch to calm, direct, and assist children. Don't let a wheelchair act as a barrier; give tactile encouragement to children who use wheelchairs as often as you do other students.
- Focus on dance and pantomime activities that can be done with a child's most mobile part. Facial expressions can be a focus for those whose arms and legs are impaired, or gestures can be emphasized if hands and arms are mobile.
- Paint word pictures and give clear details. Describe art materials, tools, pictures, and props and tell stories with great detail to create mental images for those with visual impairments.
- Let children with visual impairments explore through touch as often as possible.
- Place children with hearing impairments close to the music source to feel the vibrations.
- Be sure children with hearing impairments can see your face, especially your lips, if they are lip readers. Don't stand against a window, or a shadow will be cast on your face. Don't exaggerate your speech; in fact, this distorts the sounds children are taught to observe.
- Repeat comments by children if they are too soft to be heard by those with hearing loss.
- Use visual cues, pictures, props, gestures, and directions on cards for those with hearing loss or speech/language delays.

CORNETT, CLAUDIA, E., *Creating Meaning Through Literature & the Arts,* 2nd Edition, © 2003, pp. 70–71. Reprinted by permission of Pearson Education, Inc. Upper Saddle River, NJ.

FIGURE 10-4 • Some suggestions for adapting the environment to accommodate children with physical disabilities.

The art program is a good place for child-to-child relationships, where children can work, talk, and be together. If art activities are developmentally appropriate for children, they provide a relaxed time for exploring, trying new tools, and using familiar ones. They also allow children many chances to interact with each other.

The freedom of art itself encourages children to talk about their own work or the work of other children. Working with colors, paint, paper, paste, and other materials provides children an endless supply of things to talk about.

Sharing Ideas and Opinions

Art activities also provide endless opportunities for a child to learn how other children feel about things. For example, a three-year-old boy may hear for the first time how another child his own age feels about his painting. At home, this child may hear mostly adult comments; in the early childhood setting, he can experience the ideas and feelings of an age-mate. An action as simple as putting easels side by side encourages this type of social learning. In the same way, fourth and fifth graders will learn a lot about each other's ideas and opinions as they work together planning and creating a mural for a class project.

Although this sharing can be new and exciting for a child, it can also be hard for some children to accept at first. Children may have good feelings about themselves and their work in art; likewise, they can learn to accept ideas about their work from others.

The chance to share ideas and talk about one's own work or the work of others is the beginning of a new type of relationship. It is a sharing relationship. The child begins to see that other children have different ideas and feelings. This type of sharing encourages the child to understand that people can have different feelings and ideas and still be friends. A child can learn that everyone does not have to agree all the time and can share ideas and opinions.

By the time children are in the fourth grade, they are capable of developing rather strong friendships. It is good to encourage these friendships because the social development of children is furthered as they gain feelings of inner security in having a friend. By the time

FIGURE 10-5 • In the early childhood program a child learns to share an adult's attention.

FIGURE 10-6 • Place a mirror at child level to encourage children to see themselves and others in it.

children are in the fourth or fifth grade, they are being prepared socially for peer group interaction. It is this association with a peer group that is the focus of social development of this age group. Within a peer group, the needs of the child are met in the following ways.

- The child finds models for behavior and achievement among peer group members and their activities.
- The peer group makes it possible for the child to get the attention that he or she discovers he or she needs and wants.
- The child learns to view himself or herself in different ways as he or she identifies with the group.
- The group furnishes a support in asking or doing certain things.
- The child is growing toward maturity with the help of the peer group as he or she learns to rely less on his or her parents.

Social Competence

Social competence, the ability to get along with others, is another important factor in child-to-child relationships. During the last two decades, a large body of research has accumulated that indicates that unless children achieve minimal social competence by about the age of six years, they have a high probability of being at risk throughout life. These risks are many: poor mental health, dropping out of school, low achievement, and other school difficulties (McClellan & Katz, 2003).

Peer relationships contribute a great deal to a child's social development. As one researcher states:

Indeed, the single best childhood predictor of adult adaptation is *not* IQ, *not* school grades and *not* classroom behavior, but rather the adequacy with which the child gets along with other children. Children who are generally disliked, who are aggressive and disruptive, who are unable to sustain close relationships with other children, and who cannot establish a place for themselves in the peer culture are seriously "at risk." (Hartup, 2002, p. 347)

Working together in the early childhood program, children learn how to get along with each other. Sharing materials and ideas, children learn the give and take of being in a group—the skills of social competence. See the Online Companion for a checklist of children's social competence.

Expression of Feelings

The creative art process allows children to visually translate personal feelings as well as ideas (Dewey, 1958; Lowenfeld & Brittain, 1987). Art thus becomes an emotional catharsis. The use of color and the size or placement of representations frequently reflect healthy emotions that are difficult to express in words.

It is not unusual for a teacher to notice that children vigorously pounding clay or energetically hammering nails seem to be relieving tension or frustration. Children who are afraid of the dark may paint some brown or black or purple renditions to express this feeling. Bright colors or symbols of smiling faces may express happy experiences. Art as a vent for feeling is universally acknowledged for artists of all ages (Lowenfeld & Brittain, 1987).

Expressing strong feelings through art rather than through destructive acts may provide catharsis for emotions. Teachers who accept the reality of children's feelings can understand children better and

FIGURE 10-7 • In the early childhood program, young children learn to feel good about themselves as competent individuals.

THINK ABOUT IT

Altruism at an Early Age

According to a Yiddish proverb, "If you ever need a helping hand, you'll find one at the end of your arm." A study from the Max Planck Institute for Evolutionary Anthropology in Leipzig, Germany, offers another place to find a helping hand—children and chimpanzees. Researchers developed several scenarios in which an adult was struggling with a problem and needed help. In one such scenario, an adult accidentally dropped objects on a floor and was unable to reach them.

Felix Warneken and Mike Tomasello found that children as young as 18 months willingly and spontaneously helped complete strangers in several tasks. "The results were astonishing because these children are so young—they still wear diapers and are barely able to use language," says Warneken. "But they already show helping behavior."

Going to some effort to help someone, without any benefit to yourself, is called *altruism*. So far, only humans are proven altruists, but never before has this ability been shown in children so young who have not yet developed much in the way of language skills. The study shows that even infants without much socialization are willing and able to help spontaneously.

But is altruism unique to humans? Warneken also conducted the same helping tasks with human-raised chimpanzees. Although the chimpanzees did not help with more complex tasks, they did help when their human caretaker was reaching for something. These new findings show that rudimentary forms of altruistic behaviors are present in our closest evolutionary relatives. "This is the first experiment showing altruistic helping toward goals in any nonhuman primate," says Warneken. "It has been claimed chimpanzees act mainly for their own ends, but in our experiment, there was no reward and they still helped" (Max Planck Society, 2006).

help them cope with distressing feelings. In the same way, teachers who accept children's expressions of their desires and delights can share, and thus intensify, children's joy.

Cooperation and Sharing

Working together with other children in creative activities gives a child the chance to learn about being with others. Being with others teaches a child the value of sharing and cooperation.

Working with limited amounts of crayons, paint, and paper means that a child has to share. The child soon learns that sharing is a part of being in a group. One can of red paint for two young painters is a real-life lesson in sharing. Likewise, sharing woodworking tools in the creation of three-dimensional structures teaches fourth and fifth graders how to deal with limited equipment in a cooperative way.

Cooperation among children is also part of the art program. A child learns the meaning of cooperation while helping another child glue seeds on a paper, clean a brush, or button a painting shirt. This is truly learning by doing. This is actively learning social competence.

Child-to-Teacher Relationships

The teacher in the early childhood program is a very important person in the child's eye. Children look up to their teachers and tend to take them very seriously.

A child learns new ways to be with an adult in the early childhood program. The teacher is an adult, but not the child's parent; therefore, a new type of relationship opens up. Of course, it is different in several ways from the adult–child relationship at home.

The school setting is unlike the home situation. Children learn how to be and act in a place other than the home. They learn how it is to be in a larger group than the family and how to share an adult's attention with other children.

The children learn about art as well as about themselves from the teacher. The teacher helps them feel that it is safe to be themselves and to express ideas in their own ways. The sensitive teacher lets the child know that the fun of participating in and expressing oneself in art or other creative activities is more important than the finished product. The teacher encourages older children to explore the many ways to express their ideas in the growing complexity of their work, which is characteristic of this age group.

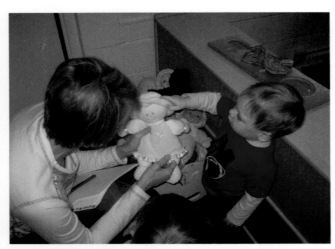

FIGURE 10-8 • Children in the early childhood program learn to be with an adult other than a parent.

A teacher opens up many new art skills and feelings for the child and is thus a very important person in the eyes of the child.

The teacher may be the first real adult friend for the child. It is, therefore, important for a good child–teacher relationship to develop during the art program. A positive feeling between teacher and child affects all of the child's school days to come.

Building Rapport

Building a warm and friendly feeling, a **rapport**, between teacher and child is not always easy; it does not happen quickly. The best learning and teaching take place, however, when the child and teacher have this feeling for each other.

THINK ABOUT IT   Research on Teachers' Nonverbal Clues

Children are quick studies when it comes to their teachers' body language, and the messages they get about their teachers' feelings toward them can have a profound effect on their classroom, a University of Florida researcher has found.

"Not only what we teach, but how we teach and the learning community we create in the classroom, are going to become the evidence for not only what you think of the students but what they think of themselves," said Vicky Zygouris-Coe, an assistant professor in the University of Florida's College of Education. Zygouris-Coe did the research for her dissertation at the University of Florida.

Zygouris-Coe found that students often interpret things such as their teachers' body language, the order in which they are called on, and the intensity with which they are listened to as signs of their teachers' feelings toward them. Many students even cast a skeptical eye on teachers' compliments, she said.

She studied 60 students in two fourth-grade classes at a local elementary school for five-and-a-half months to gather data for her dissertation. She observed the classroom environment at least twice a week and gave the children written response questions during the class "journal" time four times a month. The questions were open-ended statements such as, "My teacher thinks that I am . . . ," and the students were encouraged to write several paragraphs to explain their answers.

Each question session was followed a few days later with individual interviews in which Zygouris-Coe asked some of the children to expand on their answers.

One of the most important things teachers can do is to make an effort to know their students as well as possible. Positive nonverbal feedback from teachers—in the form of making eye contact, paying attention when students speak, and letting them know that you understand their strengths and weaknesses—can make all the difference in the world in removing barriers to the learning process.

"I hope that this will make teachers a bit more aware of how children interpret what happens in the classroom," Zygouris-Coe said. "I definitely recommend to teachers to give very specific feedback to children, not necessarily about every aspect of their behavior, but to make frequent attempts to let children know what they think about their progress, their behavior, and other specific elements of their lives."

If teachers take the time to listen to how their students feel and think about how their actions might affect students' perspectives, the classroom learning environment could be greatly improved, Zygouris-Coe said (Harmel, 1999). See Figure 10–12 for a checklist of nonverbal cues to use in your practice.

The following are some ways in which the child–teacher relationship may be enhanced.

- Welcome each child into the room. Make the child feel wanted and special.
- When speaking to children, look into their eyes.
- When speaking to children, use their names.
- Understand that children like to feel proud of themselves.
- Talk with and listen to every child as much as possible.
- Use a normal speaking voice.

Acceptance

In addition to accepting children at their individual developmental levels when planning the arts program, teachers have countless opportunities to model an accepting attitude for children. When Mirelis derisively called three-year-old Sharon's crayon picture a "scribble scrabble mess," the teacher matter-of-factly commented, "Sharon is hard at work trying out many different crayons. That's exactly how everybody begins—with big, colorful lines." Sharon smiled contentedly; Mirelis said, "Oh," and went off thinking her own thoughts but perhaps somewhat responsive to the teacher's casual yet positive acceptance of the legitimacy of scribbling in that classroom.

From such small incidents, which collectively reveal an attitude, Mirelis may realize she is accepted as a person who warrants an explanation, while Sharon may feel the teacher accepts her as she is. When children feel accepted by people who are important to them, they are better able to develop a sense of trust in those people.

FIGURE 10-9 • Sharing ideas about one's work with an adult is a social learning.

FIGURE 10-10 • Early childhood teachers need to plan the classroom environment so that it promotes children's positive social development.

When the teacher accepts and respects each child's physical and artistic abilities, the children then accept each other. By accepting each other, they learn about ideas, opinions, and feelings different from their own. These new ideas make the art program richer and more exciting for children.

Provide an Environment That Respects Individuality

As discussed earlier in Chapter 5, each individual child possesses eight "intelligences" or different learning styles. For instance, some children learn best by listening and hearing (word smart/linguistic intelligence) while others learn best by manipulating objects in their environment (body smart/kinesthetic intelligence). For this reason, teachers need to appreciate how differently children respond to new art activities just as to any other new experiences. Some children eagerly plunge into new activities, attracted perhaps to new materials or the newness of the venture, while other children temporarily hold back. Still others retreat to the safety of the familiar and are reluctant to take risks with new materials or processes.

Sensitive teachers, trying to provide a climate in which children can take risks in their own ways, will accommodate the differences they observe in children. Three-year-old Mary refused her teacher's invitation to try finger painting. She apparently had the same conflicting feelings she had expressed when clay was introduced. She wanted to play with messy materials, but was anxious about getting carried away in her play and becoming too dirty. Her response to the

THIS ONE'S for YOU!   Fostering Gratitude in Young Children

The concept of gratitude as a positive asset that can improve the quality of life is receiving increasing attention within the scientific community, particularly in the emerging field known as **positive psychology** (Seligman, Rashid, & Parks, 2006). Positive psychology has been defined as the scientific study of ordinary human strengths and virtues (Miller, 2009). It is concerned with positive traits, positive emotions, and positive institutions (Seligman, Rashid, & Parks, 2006).

Positive psychology was developed largely as a reaction to the disease model that is so prevalent in contemporary psychology in which remediating deficits and treating disorder is given greater attention than building and promoting strengths and virtues (Miller, 2009). It fits well with the positive qualities of the early childhood learning environment, which builds on children's strengths. Fostering gratitude can help promote children's strengths by making them more aware of those strengths in themselves and others.

Recent research has demonstrated that numerous benefits can be gained by experiencing and expressing gratitude. For example, those who frequently feel and express gratitude appear to enjoy their work more, to be more optimistic and energetic, to make progress toward personal goals, and to be more likely to help or support others than individuals who do not experience gratitude (Emmons & McCullough, 2004). Children who are grateful have more positive attitudes toward their families and school (Froh, Miller, & Snyder, 2008).

Fostering gratitude in children is appropriate for early childhood and elementary schools not only because it is good for students but also because schools are communities where people do things for others. Experiencing and expressing gratitude does not come naturally. It is a learned process and sometimes one that requires a certain level of inner reflection and introspection (Miller, 2006). As an early childhood educator, you need to know the capacity of the children in your group for these cognitive skills.

Although much can be done at home to foster gratitude, early childhood schools have the capacity to raise awareness of the benefits of gratitude, weave the practice of gratitude into the school day, and build on existing child-to-child and child–adult relationships. The following are some suggestions on promoting gratitude in young children.

- Parents and early childhood teachers can begin promoting gratitude in their children at an early age. For example, rather than simply teaching children to say a perfunctory thank you after receiving a gift, parents and teachers can teach children **why** they should say thank you. Because such virtues as gratitude are acquired behaviors, consistent support and encouragement from adults enable children to develop the skills necessary to experience and express gratitude.

- Encourage children to be mindful of people, events, activities, and things for which they can and should be grateful. Gently remind them, without nagging, about the many positive aspects of their lives, particularly in comparison to other children who may not be as fortunate.

- Encourage children to write thank-you notes or pictures after receiving gifts from relatives and friends and to include why they are thankful for the gifts.

- Encourage children to write thank-you notes to teachers and other school staff members who made a particular impression on them or who helped them in some way.

- Have children reflect on why they are grateful and communicate it often.

- Older children can keep gratitude journals. In them they can write down four or five particular things (e.g., people, events, or activities) that they are grateful for and why.

- Early childhood teachers and administrators and other school professionals can promote gratitude in children by modeling it themselves. For example, you could have periodic "gratitude days" during which teachers and other staff members announce what they are grateful for and ask children to do the same.

- Teachers and administrators can work together to teach behaviors associated with gratitude, such as saying thank you when someone does something for them, writing thank-you notes, and reminding children of the advantages and good fortune in their lives. This should **not** be done in a lecturing or condescending manner, but rather in a manner that encourages children to be more mindful of their blessings and the importance of acknowledging them to themselves and to others.

invitation was to run away and play with the little cars across the room.

Eventually, she drove her car toward the finger painting area while accompanying herself with a steady, persistent engine sound of rhum-rhum-rhum. She barely glanced at the children who were finger painting, then turned and raced back to the block area. Once again, Mary approached and stopped her engine sounds. She looked at the painters with side-long glances, pretending to examine the wheels on her car at the same time. The teacher, noting Mary's interest and reluctance, decided to give her more time. His only comment that day was, "When you decide you want to finger paint, you can pick the color you want." After a few days, Mary announced, "I want blue." The teacher had read Mary's nonverbal behavior correctly; her individual pattern of response had been respected.

A similar approach works with older children as well. For instance, some children may be reluctant to work with a new art technique such as printing using a brayer for the first time. A sensitive teacher accepts this and allows alternative activities for all students.

Child-to-Group Relationships

When taking part in creative activities, a child learns to be in a group. Being in a group at school is not the same as being in a family. In school, the child is a student as well as a member of the group.

As a member of a group, the child learns many things. In art, a child learns how to follow—for example, learning to use a paintbrush by following directions. When making a mural with a group of children, a five-year-old learns to follow and work with group ideas in planning the project. Learning to follow rules about cleanup is another way a child learns to follow in a group.

A child learns how to lead in a group, too. For example, a six-year-old boy who is in charge of his group's paint learns to be a leader with responsibility. Children who can go ahead with ideas on their own are learning the qualities of a leader, too. Thus, in art projects, children have many chances to learn to sometimes be leaders and sometimes be followers.

Being a member of a group is a social learning experience. A group of children engaged in a creative project is a little social group for the child. In such a group, children learn how to share and cooperate. They learn that being in a social group has advantages, such as being with other children their own age, working, sharing ideas, and having fun with them. Children also learn that it is sometimes a disadvan-

FIGURE 10-11 • Children grow in competence when the curriculum is designed to meet children's individual needs.

tage having to work with the group's rules and that it is not always easy to take turns or to play with others each day in school.

A child learns to respect the rights and ideas of others by being a member of a social group. Learning to respect others is also a part of the child's life outside the school. The things children learn about being members of a group in school help them as members of social groups outside the school.

Because young children are naturally egocentric, they face the difficult, yet necessary, task of moderating their self-interest to cope with group living. Young children must learn the self-discipline inherent in cooperating, in taking turns, and in adapting when necessary to group interests and needs. Skill in resolving interpersonal conflicts gradually develops. Creative art activities that take place in an open and flexible atmosphere provide a valuable setting for these social learnings.

How fortunate that creative experiences that give children so much pleasure should also be so effective in helping them to learn about themselves, other people, and how better to negotiate the real conditions of group living.

In your work with young children, use this checklist to assess your own use of nonverbal clues and other ways of supporting children's self-concept. Check off all items that apply to your teaching.

_____ I use eye contact when I speak to children.

_____ I pay attention when students speak.

_____ I acknowledge a child's strengths in a positive way.

_____ I use a normal speaking voice.

_____ I welcome each child into the room.

_____ I acknowledge a child's weaknesses in a positive way.

_____ I am honest in my acceptance of children's differences.

_____ I use honest compliments when they are deserved.

_____ I am honest and genuine in my assessment of children's work.

_____ I use the child's name instead of words like "honey" or "sweetie."

_____ I vary the order in which I call on children.

_____ I call on children when they don't have their hands up to answer.

_____ I speak openly about my feelings with children.

_____ I do not lie to children about how I feel about sensitive issues.

_____ I respect each child's individual differences.

_____ I am aware of certain cultural groups' dislike of direct eye contact (e.g., Native Americans).

You may want to make plans to address any of the above items you did not check.

FIGURE 10-12 • Checklist for teachers' nonverbal clues for cultivating children's self-concept.

FIGURE 10-13 • Teachers need to be honest and genuine in their assessment of children's work.

Summary

Social–emotional growth refers to two kinds of growth. Emotional growth is the growth of a child's feelings, and social growth is the child's growth as a member of a group. Self-concept and self-awareness are key social–emotional developments in the early childhood program. According to Carl Rogers, a noted psychologist, every human being is born with the drive to do his best in this life (actualizing tendency), to be positively regarded by the people in his life. A child develops a positive concept by the way he is treated by others. A psychologically safe environment is one in which the child is accepted for himself/herself with unconditional acceptance. In such an environment, a child continually grows and develops (self-actualizes). Another psychologist, Erik Erickson, developed a set of stages of psychosocial development. Basic to these stages is the way children are treated and the effect it has on the child's social–emotional development. In the early years, children develop trust, autonomy, independence, competence, and initiative.

Well-planned creative activities help children develop good feelings about themselves and their abilities. In these activities, a child learns to be with other children, to be with adults other than parents, and to be in a group. The social skills learned in the early childhood art program help children adapt to other groups outside the school.

Key Terms

actualizing tendency 211
Carl Rogers 211
Erik Erickson's stages of psychosocial development 211
positive self-concept 211

Learning Activities

A. Your first peer group may have been made up of children in your neighborhood or classmates in school. Can you remember their names? What did they look like? How did they behave toward you? How did you feel about your involvement with this group?

B. During these early years, who were the popular, amiable, rejected, or isolated children with whom you came into contact? How would you rate yourself?

C. What happened to this group? What caused it to break apart? Can you remember how you felt about this change?

D. You have a time machine. Would you go back to your childhood to give the child you were a message? Or would you go forward to the future and give your own child a message? What would those messages be? Share them with your classmates.

E. Think about a teacher who helped you feel good about yourself. Write down a list of single words describing this teacher. Make a collage using these words. Share your memory collage with fellow students.

F. Think about your childhood years. Can you remember being afraid, worried, anxious? Write down several of your unpleasant memories, including the situation that created this feeling. Now think about your work with children. Have you created similar situations for children? Share your memories and thoughts with your classmates.

G. Psychological safety requires that every child in your room feel accepted, important, and valued. Examine the images of children and adults found in your room. Consider those in textbooks, posters, calendars, and any other available materials. Think about the mixture of genders and races portrayed. Will it support psychological safety for all your students?

H. Make a slot in the top of a lidded shoebox. Decorate the box and write the words "Private Letters" on it. Then encourage students to write letters or cards (or draw pictures) to you. Be sure to answer each letter individually. Some students may use the letter box as an opportunity to write more personal notes describing their feelings, thoughts, or problems. Remember to respect the confidentiality of all letters.

I. Share your feelings with your students. If you provide a space on the board for students to write their names when they're having a hard day, remember to include your own name from time to time.

J. Allow students the chance to be heard. Set up "One Minute and Be Heard" sessions. Children need to realize that you will listen to them, but it is important that you set boundaries, too.

Activities for Children

The following activities can be used with classmates or with children in classroom settings.

"I Can" Book

Show parents of young children the specific skills their children have learned. Make an "I Can" scrapbook using samples of the child's work. Show "I Can Paint," "I Can Color," and "I Can Paste" with samples of work. Illustrate "I Know Colors," for example, with samples of the colors the child can recognize and "I Can Count" with drawings of the number of objects that the child can count.

Teachers Are People, Too

A teacher who was late one day and was explaining to the children that she'd had a flat tire was surprised to hear one four-year-old child say, "But don't you sleep here?" This teacher was obviously part of the equipment that came with the room! How much do your children know about you? Do you live in a house, an apartment? Do you come to school by car or by bus? Are you married? Do you have children of your own? Talk with children about your life. It will help broaden their understanding of the world.

Group Effort Activity

To encourage and develop children's self-esteem, cooperation, and group effort, try this activity. You will need a table, crayons, markers, paper, and tape. Cover the top of the table with paper, attaching it with tape. In the middle of the paper write the title of the picture—for example, "Our Group Art." Allow children to draw pictures on the paper during group or free choice time. When the picture is finished (to everyone's liking), take it off the table and tape it to the wall or put it on a bulletin board. As a variation, use different shapes or colors of paper. Use a round table or a rectangular table, or an animal or tree shape. Or try to have a special theme for the group artwork: nature, families, animals.

Random Moments of Good Manners

Keep a digital camera on hand to encourage children's polite behavior. Look for opportunities to "catch" children using their manners. Snap pictures of these moments and jot down the occasion and manners that were used on sticky notes. Later, print the pictures and display them on a bulletin board with a brief caption describing the situation.

Mirror Activities

Use a large, full-length or small, hand-held mirror to encourage self-awareness with toddlers, preschoolers, and children in grades kindergarten through grade three and grades four through five.

- With toddlers—Bring children to the mirror, one at a time. Encourage them to look at themselves in the mirror. Have them point to various parts of their body as you name the part: "Show me your nose." "Where is your tummy?" "Point to your mouth."
- With kindergarten through third-grade students—Ask them as they look at themselves such questions as, "Why do people look in mirrors?" "Why do people look at themselves?" "What do you like about you that you see in the mirror?" Then have two children look in the mirror together. Have each child tell the other what is special about him or her.
- With fourth and fifth graders—Have them look in the mirror. What features do they see that remind them of their parents, siblings, a famous person, other relatives? What is special about what they see? What lines and shapes do they see in their image? Have two children look into the mirror. Have them compare the lines and shapes they see in each other's face. Ask them to tell each other what is special about their images. Does either one look like a famous person?

Making a Photo Album

A. Objectives: To see oneself and others. To learn to admire oneself and others.

B. Procedure: Have each child bring in a photo of himself or herself.

1. Use large pieces of colored paper. Punch holes in the side of each sheet of paper. Tie yarn through the holes to hold the pages together.
2. Paste each child's photo on a page. Print the child's name under the photo.

C. Leave the photo album out so the children can look at and enjoy the pictures.

D. A personal picture sequence chart can be made for each child using photos taken at different times of the year (birthday, outings, holidays, etc.). Children will gain a sense of time, change, and growth in these photo charts.

E. During the year, children may want to dictate stories or short descriptive statements to accompany these photos. These "story pages" can be added to the book throughout the year.

Activities for Self-Awareness, Self-Acceptance, and Cooperation

What's Your Name?

Invite students to research the meaning of their names using a baby name book or website, such as http://www.babynames.com. Have students write the original meaning on a piece of construction paper. Then challenge them to think of a more personal meaning. For example, "The original meaning of Hannah is 'grace.' But to me, Hannah means strong runner, good friend, and cupcake lover." Encourage students to use descriptive words in writing their own meanings. Or the teacher can write them down for the student. Display students' work on the bulletin board.

Making a Web of Friends Game

Materials: Ball of thick white yarn

Gather a group of 10 children or more. Ask the children if they think people can spin webs like spiders. After the discussion, tell them that you will try to spin a web as a group. Everyone sits in a large circle. Show the children the ball of yarn. Explain that you will begin spinning the web by holding the end of the yarn ball tightly in your lap and picking a friend to toss the remaining ball to, saying something like, "I pick Claire to help spin our web." When she catches it, share something you like about her. Remind her to hold the yarn string tight in her lap as she picks the next friend to toss the yarn ball to.

Continue until the ball is completely used. The number of times a child is picked doesn't matter after everyone has had at least one turn. It's fun to see how huge your life-size web has become. Variation: See if the group can stand up together without getting tangled in the web!

Put Your Feelings in a Letter

Materials: large construction paper, any color; markers, chalk or paint, large letter stencils (for youngest children)

Start by talking with students about how art can be a way to portray your feelings. You can link this lesson to Leonardo Da Vinci or Claude Monet because of how their art changed with their feelings. Trace or sketch the first letter of the students' names (or have them do it). Have the students fill their letters in with colors and/or pictures that portray a happy feeling, a sad feeling, etc. Have the students share their letters with the class and explain their feelings.

Clothes Encounters

Gather together the spare clothes that were stored at the school for the year or packed away the previous year. Use a full-length mirror for this activity. At the end of the school year, encourage each child to try on his or her old spare clothes and examine himself or herself in the mirror. This activity provides a concrete measurement experience that is full of surprises. Talk about the "tight squeeze" of the clothes now and why this is so.

Body Shapes

A. Objectives: To encourage children's positive feelings about themselves and their bodies. To encourage cooperation among children.

B. Equipment: Large pieces of brown paper, crayons, and paints.

C. Procedure: Have a child lie down on a piece of paper. Have another child use a crayon to trace the first child's body outline on the paper. Then have the first child paint or color in his or her body shape outlined on the paper.

D. Encourage children's self-awareness by having them notice what they are wearing and the colors before they paint their outline.

Patty-Cake (for Three-Year-Olds)

A. Objectives: To learn to use body parts. To learn other children's names.

B. Procedure: Teacher begins by singing and clapping: "Patty-cake, patty-cake, baker's man. Bake me a cake as fast as you can. Roll it and pat it, mark it with a (use a child's initial). Put it in the oven for (use a child's name) and me."

1. Use all the children's names in the song. (Or each child can have a turn to sing the song and name another child in the group.)
2. Repeat it often so that children learn each other's names.

Hands On

Cover one wall with brown kraft (wrapping) paper. With bright paint (one color for each letter), write the title, "Hands On!" at the top of the paper. Children then place handprints randomly on the board by first pressing hands on a paint-coated sponge and then pressing directly on the paper. Label each print with the child's name and date.

Pattern Prints

Prepare the bulletin board by measuring off horizontal lines on backing paper to create one horizontal stripe/space for each child. At the left end of the stripes, list children's names. Then, offer children a variety of materials for printing (rubber stamps, printing letters, etc.) and an inked pad or sponge soaked in tempera paint. Allow children to create any pattern or design they would like to make.

Names

Cover a large bulletin board with a bright, solid background. Divide paper evenly into a grid design, thus providing each child with a 12-inch-square space on the board. With a marker, print each child's name in large letters at the top of the space, leaving at least 11 inches of paper exposed under each name. First, use the board as a basis for a matching game—children must match name cards to their name printed on the board. Then invite children to decorate their name with markers, crayons, or paints. As the year progresses, children can copy their names in a variety of other materials (older preschoolers may enjoy using yarn, sparkles, etc.).

Artwork

Children are always being told not to write on the walls, but now they can have the freedom and the fun to write on at least one board in the room. Once again, cover a large bulletin board with kraft (or wrapping) paper. (You may want to tack several layers at first so that you can tear off the top layer to expose a fresh piece when needed.) Then, invite children to draw to their hearts' content. If you share a special story, event, or trip, expose a fresh piece of kraft paper to create an instant mural!

Murals

A. Create a mural after a field trip. It can be made by all of the children working together on one large piece of paper, or it can be made by pasting separate paintings together on a large piece of paper.

B. Variations: Decorate some windows in the school. Plan and give a puppet show. Have children make the puppets.

I Like

You will need a tape recorder. Individually ask children to name something they like or are interested in. Record these statements and create a pause on the tape. After the short pause, ask each child to say his or her name and record it. During group meeting time, play the tape for the children, asking them to identify the child after each statement of interest. The children can check their guesses when they hear the name of the child recorded on the tape.

As a follow-up to this activity, play the tape in the art center. Some children may want to express what they heard on the tape with paint, markers, clay, or another medium. Another possible use for the tape is in the book corner. Have earphones on the tape player so children can listen quietly to their own and their friends' voices and comments. Some children might want to dictate a story about something they heard on the tape.

This Makes Me Feel Happy

A. Bring an object to a small group and say, "I would like to share something with you that makes me happy." Explain why the object makes you happy. For example, "Here is a necklace that someone I like very much gave to me. When I wear it, it reminds me of that person and I get a good feeling." Then, "I would like to give you a chance to share something with us and tell us how it makes you happy."

B. Ask children to obtain something to bring back to the group. Give each child an opportunity to share her or his object with the group. This can take place over several days as children bring sentimental objects from home. (See Chapter 7 for ideas on making a class museum to display these special objects.)

Me-Mobiles (Older Four-Year-Olds)

You will need: (1) a selection of magazines (school and department store catalogs, nature, sports, as well as any popular family magazines); (2) scissors; (3) paste; (4) construction paper; (5) wire hangers; (6) yarn (or string); and (7) name tags large enough to fit in the central triangle of the hanger.

Tie the child's name tag to the central portion of the hanger and allow at least three strings to dangle from the bar of the hanger. Have children look through magazines and cut (or tear) out three or more pictures that reflect a favorite thing or activity. Have children paste the pictures on the construction paper and then tie or staple the mounted pictures to the strings attached to the hanger. Encourage children to talk about their selections. Hangers can be hung on a "clothesline" in the classroom or in any other appropriate place.

Fill Your Talent Plate!

In this activity, you are giving children the opportunity to discover that there are many talents that people all around them possess. This activity also helps develop language and fine-motor skills.

Prior to carrying out the activity, discuss with children the meaning of the word *talent* and emphasize that everyone has special talents. Talk about personal talents of people the children know that will help them connect the meaning of the word with their own experiences.

For this activity you will need magazines, newspapers, photographs, scissors, glue, and paper plates.

Direct children to find pictures that show people doing things they are good at. Show children how to cut the pictures out and glue them on a paper talent plate. After children are finished with their talent plate, they might show it to a peer or help a partner.

Faces Charades

Start by singing songs such as "If You're Happy and You Know It" and play Simon Says to introduce the idea that facial and body expressions can convey meaning. Focus on changes in mouths, eyes, and eyebrows.

Preparation: With a small group of children in front of a wall mirror (or small, unbreakable hand mirrors) suggest that they make faces with these or other expressions: You mean *yes,* you mean *no,* you are very tired, you are very excited, you are angry, you are happy, etc. When they are able to read each other's expressions, children are ready for Faces Charades!

Procedure: Write one word or idea on an index card. Draw a picture to illustrate the feeling, or use pictures cut from magazines.

Mix up the cards. Have children choose a leader to pick the first card. The leader makes a face according to the directions on the card. The other children try to figure out what feeling the leader is expressing. The player who guesses correctly gets to pick the next card.

Variations: Cards could be of animals, favorite story characters, or any other topic that appeals to children and can be acted out.

With toddlers, you might begin with two or three very different feelings. They could tear pictures from recycled magazines to help distinguish facial expressions.

Half of Me

Materials: Pieces of lightweight cardboard, old magazines and catalogs, markers, crayons, or paint and paintbrushes, blunt-tip scissors, glue.

Procedure:

- Have children go through magazines and catalogs to find a picture of something they like. Have them cut the picture out and glue it to a piece of cardboard. Then have them cut the picture in half. An adult or older child can help the younger ones with the cutting.
- Put the halves in a box or bag.
- Pass around the box or bag of half pictures and ask each child to take out one of the pieces. Continue passing the box or bag until all the pieces have been taken.
- Ask a child to hold up one of his or her half pictures. Ask the other children to look through their pieces to see who has the other half. Invite those children to come together to fit the pieces together. Children can leave the completed piece on a table.
- Ask which child selected this picture. Then ask this child to talk about why this was a picture he or she liked. Continue the activity until all the children have had a chance to talk about their chosen pictures.

Nature Observations

Going outside and experiencing the wonders of nature can't help but enhance the child's positive sense of self. Try some of these activities.

- Find an outdoor plant that changes dramatically with the seasons—perhaps with flowers, leaves, and/or fruit. With children, observe it about once a week.

If possible, measure its growth. Record bud sizes, bark color, and other changes. Use rich words to describe the scene.

- At seasonal intervals, ask children to make their own creative representations of the plant. Save these in their portfolios to document not only the change in seasons but also their progress in drawing and writing.
- Ask children what they notice about the plant their group has adopted. With crayons, draw the plant the way it looks today. Include details and colors. Create texture with heavy layers of crayon.
- Label the drawing with the child's name and date. Ask if they can see dew on leaves or ice crystals on branches. Decorate the drawing with glitter and glue.
- On the back of the picture, write about the plant. The teacher can write this for children unable to write for themselves. What season is it? How is the plant changing? What do you think will happen next?
- For a variation, draw outdoors so children can look directly at the plant.
- Adopt a tree, plant, or shrub. How can the children help care for it?
- At the end of the year, display the four seasons as depicted by each child.

Nature Dramatizations

Dramatizations can be stimulated by phenomena in our everyday world. Encourage the children to pretend (by acting with their body movements) to be any of the following:

- leaves waving in a gentle wind, a heavy wind, and then eventually flying through the air
- snow falling softly, being made into a snowman, and then melting
- an ice cream cone or icicle melting in the sun
- rain trickling down, running into a swift stream, the sun coming out, and a rainbow appearing
- an icy hill that is hard to walk up
- a thick fog to find one's way through
- creative movements relating to jobs in winter, such as shoveling snow
- creative movements depicting a snowman as it melts
- creative movements of winter sports and activities: skating, throwing snowballs, etc.
- creative movements depicting birds flying around the bird feeder, eating seeds, flying in the air

You and the children may think of others.

Flowering Windows

Flowers can bloom as often and as long as you like if you decorate your windows with children's flower creations. And children can feel a sense of pride when they see their work on display each day. Be sure windows are securely closed and locked before decorating them. Flowers can be painted onto the window with thick tempera paint or markers. Or you may want to use Crayola Window FX Washable markers. To begin, children draw the outline of their flowers directly onto the windows using a black crayon. Then they can fill in the outlines with thick tempera paint and a paintbrush or markers. As new spring flowers bloom outdoors, they can also be added to the window display. When animals appear, they, too, can be added to the drawing for an ever-evolving window masterpiece. In the winter, children can anticipate spring's arrival by including robins or dandelions in their window displays before they appear in nature.

Activities for Older Children (Grades 4–5)

A. Older children can use cameras and take each other's pictures. They may take photos on a field trip or during a special project, or at whatever time they want. A "documentary" of their experience can be created by arranging the photos in a special order and then writing an explanatory text to go with the photos. Or have older children take pictures of each other according to a specific idea or theme, such as lines/shapes in faces; dark-haired/light-haired friends, etc.

B. Older children can sketch the body outline of another student by projecting a light onto a blank wall that has a large sheet of paper taped on it. Students can trace each other's "standing shadow" with a large dark marker. They may want to decorate the outline or fill it in with words and phrases describing that person. The point is to do another person's outline to learn more about that person. Asking questions about favorite foods, clothes, TV or movie stars, cars, etc. is a good way to learn information to fill in the outline.

C. With older children, make a mural after a field trip. Have them work as a group to decide which part of the field trip they want to feature as the topic of their mural. Encourage them to include as many art techniques as possible in their mural (i.e., collage, finger paint, tempera painting, printing, three-dimensional add-ons).

D. Give older children a chance to learn more about each other in "Talk Time." A talk time break gives them an opportunity to visit with their friends. As we know, the development of strong friendships and a peer group are characteristic of this age group. They can talk about what they did last night, their new item of clothing, what they are going to play at recess, a book they have been reading—anything they feel is important to share with their classmates. This type of experience also provides an opportunity for developing social interaction and for finding out that their friends have special interests and mutual concerns. Teachers who use this technique find that when children know they are going to have a time to visit freely, they refrain from visiting at inappropriate times. Teachers can join in the conversations, thus using this break as an information-gathering time.

E. **Family Name Crossword.** Have students write their names in large block letters in the center of a piece of paper. Then challenge them to fill in the names of their family members and pets by building off the letters in their own name, crossword-style. If students are stumped, allow them to use additional words describing what family means to them, such as *love* or *happiness.* Display the crosswords on a bulletin board for families to enjoy during an open house night. As an extra challenge, you might create a jumbo crossword that includes the names of everyone in your class.

F. **Jump-Rope Names.** Get the kinesthetic learners in your classroom off their feet and onto the playground with this active jump-rope name game. Distribute jump ropes to groups of three students and challenge them to come up with a skipping rhyme for each group member's name. Students might simply spell out their names, jumping at leach letter, or they might develop more elaborate routines. After 15 to 20 minutes of practice, have the groups perform their routines for the entire class.

G. **Celebration of Life.** Set aside a day to celebrate life. The purpose of this day is to help each child feel good about herself or himself and to recognize how precious the gift of life is. Provide each student with several blank business cards. Have them fill in their own name, address, and phone number. Then ask them to draw pictures of or list their special talents, their place in the family, or their favorite things. During group time, have them share and explain their cards.

H. **Personal Trophies.** Challenge students to make a trophy for a family member that honors something that person does well. Students might use clay, gold tempera paint, and paintbrushes.

Look at reproductions of Greek sculpture and a variety of commercial trophies featuring athletic forms. Explore different ways of modeling figures. Try working flat from clay slabs, like gingerbread men. Flattened clay balls make good bases for clay figures. Let the clay figures dry and then paint them with gold tempera paint.

I. **Personal Memories.** Motivate your students to create art and writings based on their personal memories. Share with them the following websites.

Online Resources: Two contemporary artists who make art based on their personal memories are Carmen Lomas Garza and Faith Ringgold. Both have strong online presences with their personal websites: Carmen Lomas Garza: Chicana Artist, available at http://www.carmenlomasgarza.com/ and Faith Ringgold at http://www.faithringgold.com/. Lomas Garza, a self-described Chicana narrative artist,

creates images about everyday events in the lives of Mexican Americans based on her own childhood memories and experiences in South Texas. Her website includes an artist's statement, images of her artwork, a biography, and much more.

Ringgold is an African-American artist well known for her illustrated children's books, such as *Tar Beach.* Her website offers many features, including a biography, a test about prejudice, a story to read and illustrate, frequently asked questions, and a link to send a message to the artist.

Another artist who painted from personal experience who older students could explore is the Mexican painter Frida Kahlo. Websites about this artist include Frida Kahlo & Contemporary Thoughts, http://www. fridakahlo.it/index.html; Artocyclopedia: Frida Kahlo, http://www.artcyclopedia.com/; and Frida Kahlo, National Museum of Women in the Arts, http://www. nmwa.org/.

Encourage your students to write autobiographies including artwork, photographs, and any other images they choose to include.

J. **What Is a Friend?** This activity helps build children's awareness of characteristics a friend ought to possess. Divide students into teams of three or four. Each team must decide on a list of characteristics they all agree are important in a friend. Have them list these characteristics on a piece of paper.

Have each team work together to rank the characteristics in order of importance. The characteristic they have agreed is most important should be listed as number 1, the second-most important as number 2, and so on. Once they are finished, have the students look over the paper and decide which characteristic(s) can best be applied to themselves.

Finally, explain to students that sometimes when people work in a group, positions or ideas have to be compromised so that the group can come to an agreement. Ask students to think about whether that happened to them, and whether they would have come up with the same answers if they had done the activity on their own. Remind students that if they choose not to, they need not share their list with anyone.

K. **Friendship Recipes.** As a group, discuss the characteristics of a good friend. Ask older students to list at least five important friendship attributes, such as humor, availability, kindness, loyalty, and common interests. Write the descriptions that come up on a chart to refer to again and to add to as the class thinks of new descriptions. Using these friend characteristics, have students write their own "recipes" for how to make a friend. You may compile these into a class-made book titled *Friendship Recipes.* Older students might work in teams to develop a mutually agreed-upon recipe. The team's final recipe can be written on an index card in recipe format. Use a cookbook as a guide.

L. **Caring Ropes.** For this activity, use a 20 inch leather strip or rug-yarn length for each student. Ask students to keep track of their caring deeds toward others. Each time they perform a deed, invite them to tie a knot in the rope. Keep the ropes in an accessible place, such as a desk.

M. **Georgia O'Keeffe's _The Mountain, New Mexico—Exploring Feelings._** Obtain an art print of this work. It is an excellent example of a landscape featuring varieties of warm and cool colors. If this print is not available, any other landscape with warm and cool colors will suffice.

Briefly review the concept that colors are an important way to express moods and feelings in art. Point out that many color words help people tell about feelings. Examples include feeling blue and being green with envy or red or purple with rage.

Explain that artists often refer to these color qualities as "warm" or "cool." These terms can mean that a color is used to show warm things (a fire) or cool things (a lake). The artist also remembers that colors help to express feelings.

Explain that the warm colors in this painting show the red earth of mountains in New Mexico, but they also help to express the artist's warm feelings about the land. Georgia O'Keeffe thought that forms and colors of the desert and nearby mountains were beautiful. Guide students to see the delicate shading and rhythmic curves that fill the whole painting. Discuss how the painting makes them feel about the place depicted.

As a follow-up activity, have students create a picture of a landscape on a planet no one has seen. Have them use warm or cool colors to show and express the feelings of the creatures who inhabit this planet.

Chapter Review

1. Define the terms *self-acceptance, self-concept,* and *social competence.* Describe a child with a good sense of self-acceptance and self-concept and good social competence skills.

2. Decide whether each of the following statements helps develop self-acceptance, does not help develop self-acceptance, or does not apply to the situation.
   a. holding a baby closely with tenderness
   b. giving a baby enough vitamin C each day
   c. encouraging a baby who tries to feed herself
   d. teaching a child to feed himself when the parent wants the child to do it
   e. leaving an infant alone as much as possible because too much touching spoils the baby
   f. having early dental care
   g. praising a child who dresses himself or herself
   h. discouraging the child's messy eating habits
   i. having the child's eyes examined yearly
   j. making a child ashamed of an inability to walk well

3. Choose the answer that best completes each of the following statements about an art program and a child's self-acceptance.
   a. An art program should be planned so that it is
      i. adult centered
      ii. child centered
      iii. year round
   b. With each child in the program, a teacher must
      i. encourage the child to do more advanced work
      ii. praise only successful work
      iii. accept the child's present level

   c. To challenge children, the teacher must provide activities that are
      i. a bit beyond their present level
      ii. two or three years advanced
      iii. for some children only
   d. A well-planned art room
      i. is best on the north side of the building
      ii. has child-sized chairs and tables
      iii. has mostly large chairs and tables
   e. A teacher should choose art materials on the basis of the
      i. age group using them
      ii. price of materials
      iii. type of distributor
   f. A good reason for buying high-quality art materials is
      i. the low cost of the materials
      ii. children prefer quality materials
      iii. the good results children get with quality materials
   g. In planning art activities, a teacher must consider each child's
      i. ethnic origin and sex
      ii. age
      iii. age, ability, and interest level
   h. Success in art projects
      i. depends on having high-quality materials only
      ii. helps the child's pride and self-confidence
      iii. depends on the teacher's daily attitude
   i. One good guide to help children's self-confidence is to tell children
      i. what they are doing right
      ii. to improve their drawing
      iii. to copy other children's work

j. Another good guide to help children's self-confidence is to
   i. tell them what they are doing wrong
   ii. guide their hands to help improve their drawing
   iii. encourage them to try again after mistakes

4. Complete the statement in column I about child-to-child relationships by selecting the letter of the best choice from column II.

COLUMN I	COLUMN II
1. A child can accept other children	a. see that not all people have the same ideas.
2. Sharing ideas helps children	b. affects all the other school days to come.
3. Helping another child clean a brush	c. makes the child feel good about herself.
4. Getting along with other children	d. has no effect on a child.
5. A good preschool experience	e. is an example of learning to cooperate.
	f. only after she accepts herself.

5. You have several friends that are student teachers at the upper elementary level. They believe that implementing a strong standards-based curriculum is the most important factor in a teacher's success in the classroom. Do you, as an early childhood teacher, agree or disagree with this belief? Explain your answer using information from this chapter.

6. How can you apply the concept of Carl Rogers' unconditional positive acceptance in the classroom without losing control of the classroom?

7. What are some ways you can apply the ideas of Erik Erikson in your teaching young children? Give specific examples in your answer.

8. What are the similarities and differences between the theories of Rogers and Erikson? Is one or the other (or both) more applicable to your teaching? Give real-life examples in your answer.

9. Several parents of children in your class prefer that their children not "disrespect" the teacher by looking her straight in the eye and asking too many questions. How would you answer their questions and concerns?

References

Cornett, C. E. (2003). *The arts as meaning makers.* Upper Saddle River, NJ: Merrill/Prentice Hall.

Emmons, R. A., & McCullough, M. D. (Eds.). (2004). The *psychology of gratitude.* New York, NY: Oxford University Press.

Epstein, A. S. (2009). *You, me and us: Social learning in preschool.* Ypsilanti, MI: HighScope Educational Research Foundation.

Erikson, E. (1950). *Childhood and society.* New York, NY: W. W. Norton.

Froh, J. J., Miller, D. N., & Snyder, S. F. (2008). Gratitude in children and adolescents: Development, assessment, and school-based intervention. *School Psychology Forum, 2*(1), 1–13.

Gersch, I. (2009). A positive future for educational psychology—If the profession gets it right. *Educational Psychology in Practice, 25*(1), 9–19.

Harmel, K. (1999). *UF researcher: Teachers' nonverbal clues affect student's performance.* Online at http://www.sciencedaily .com/releases/1999/01/990122130911.htm

Hartup, W. W. (2002). *Having friends, making friends, and keeping friends: Relationships as educational contexts.* Urbana, IL: ERIC Clearinghouse on Elementary and Early Childhood Education, ED345–854.

Lowenfeld, V. (1957). *Creative and mental growth* (3rd ed.). New York, NY: Macmillan.

Lowenfeld, V., & Brittain, W. L. (1987). *Creative and mental growth* (8th ed.). New York, NY: Macmillan.

Max Planck Society. (2006). http://www.mpg.de/english/portal/index.html

McClellan, D., & Katz, L. G. (2003). *Young children's social development: A checklist.* Urbana, IL: ERIC Document EDO PS–93–6.

Miller, A. (2006). A critique of positive psychology—or "The new science of happiness." *Journal of Philosophy of Education, 42*(3), 591–608.

Miller, D. N. (2009). Fostering gratitude. *Principal Leadership, 9*(6), 12–15.

Rogers, C. (1995). *On becoming a person: A therapist's view of psychotherapy.* Boston, MA: Houghton Mifflin Harcourt.

Seligman, M. E. P., Rashid, T., & Parks, A. C. (2006). Positive psychotherapy. *American Psychologist, 61*(8), 774–788.

Thorne, B. (2003). *Carl Rogers.* Thousand Oaks, CA: Sage.

Additional Readings

Benson, J. B. (Ed.). (2009). *Social and emotional development in infancy and early childhood.* Maryland Heights, MO: Elsevier Science.

Bowman, B., & Moore, E. K. (2009). *School readiness and social–emotional development: Perspectives on cultural diversity.* Washington, DC: NAEYC.

Briggs, J. L. (2008). Autonomy and aggression in the 3-year-old. *Anthropology and child development: A Cross Cultural Reader, 18*(6), 59–63.

Cooper, P. M. (2007). Teaching young children self-regulation through children's books. *Early Childhood Education Journal, 34*(5), 315–322.

Dowling, M. (2009). *Young children's personal, social and emotional development* (3rd ed.). Thousand Oaks, CA: Sage.

Epstein, A. S. (2009). *Me, you, us: Social–emotional learning in preschool.* Washington, DC: NAEYC.

Fidler, D. J., Most, D. E., Booth-LaForce, C., & Kelly, J. F. (2008). Emerging social strengths in children with Down syndrome. *Infants and Young Children: An Interdisciplinary Journal of Special Care Practices, 21*(3), 207–220.

Fields, M. V., Fields, D. M., & Perry, N. J. (2009). *Constructive guidance and discipline: Preschool and primary education.* Upper Saddle River, NJ: Prentice Hall.

Hertzog, N. B. (2008). *Ready for preschool.* Waco, TX: Prufrock Press.

Hughes, M., Thompson, H. L., & Terrell, J. B. (2009). *Handbook for developing emotional and social intelligence: Best practices, case studies and strategies.* New York, NY: John Wiley & Sons.

Kirsh, S. J. (2009). *Media and youth.* New York, NY: John Wiley & Sons.

Kohn, A. (2008). Why self-discipline is overrated: The (troubling) theory and practice of control from within. *Phi Delta Kappan, 90*(3), 167–168.

Lightfoot, C., Cole, M., & Cole, S. R. (2009). *Development of children* (6th ed.). New York, NY: Worth Publishers.

Lillvist, A., Sandberg, A., Bjorck-Akesson, E., & Granlund, M. (2009). The construct of social competence: How preschool teachers define social competence in young children. *International Journal of Early Childhood, 41*(1), 51–68.

Merrell, K. W. (2008). *Helping students overcome depression and anxiety: A practical guide.* New York, NY: Guilford Press.

Petty, K. (2009). Using guided participation to support young children's social development. *Young Children, 64*(4), 80–85.

Pianta, R. C., Cox, M. J., & Snow, K. L. (Eds.). (2007). *School readiness and the transition to kindergarten in the era of accountability.* Baltimore, MD: Brookes.

Quas, J. A., & Fivush, R. (Eds.). (2009). *Emotion in memory and development: Biological, cognitive, and social considerations.* New York, NY: Oxford University Press.

Regan, K. S. (2009). Improving the way we think about students with emotional and/or behavioral disorders. *Teaching Exceptional Children, 41*(5), 60–65.

Rubin, K. H., & Coplan, R. J. (2010). *The development of shyness and social withdrawal.* New York, NY: Guilford Press.

Schiller, P. (2009). *Seven skills for school success: Activities to develop social and emotional intelligence in young children.* Lewisville, NC: Gryphon House.

Stack, J., & Lewis, C. (2008). Steering towards a developmental account of infant social understanding. *Human Development, 15*(4), 10–21.

Taub, D. J. (2008). Exploring the impact of parental involvement on student development. *New Directions for Student Services, 122*(4), 115–128.

Timm, D. M., & Junco, R. (2008). Beyond the horizon. *New Directions for Student Services, 122*(1), 55–61.

Software for Children

Builders of Tomorrow, ages 4 and up

Creativity Express: Let's Start with Art! ages 7 and up

Dora the Explorer Lost and Found Adventure, ages 3 and up

Flip Boom, ages 5 and up

Five Little Monkeys, ages 4 and up

FLO: Return of the Water Beetles, ages 3–6

Fun Pix Mail, ages 2–9

Just Grandma and Me, ages 3–7

Kidizoon, ages 3 and up

Kid Pub, ages 3 and up

Kidspiration, Version 3, ages 4 and up

KOL Junior: A Preschool Playground, ages 2–5

Konami Kids Playground, ages 2–5

Pajama Sam in "Don't Fear the Dark," ages 3–8

Puzzle Play Software: Hidden Pictures, ages 6–8

Scratch, ages 7 and up

Super Collapse Puzzle Gallery, ages 7 and up

Toy Store Mania, ages 6–11

U Create Games, ages 6 and up

Helpful Websites

American Library Association, http://www.ala.org
Source for books to promote children's emotions and individual expression.

Child Development Institute, http://www.childdevelopmentinfo.com
Excellent website for general development information and research on social–emotional and intellectual development. It also has links to research articles on developmental issues.

Education.com, http://www.education.com
An education and child development site for parents, parenting, and educational resources. Activities in all curriculum areas. Browse by age, grade, topic.

Family Communications, http://www.fci.org
Includes information provided by elementary educators and other professionals on helping children to manage angry feelings.

NCAST-AVENUW, http://www.ncast.org
Website sponsored by the University of Washington School of Nursing and the Center on Human Development and Disability/Center on Infant Mental Health and Development. An excellent site for professionals, parents, and other caregivers providing information about nurturing environments for young children.

Preschool First, http://www.preschoolfirst.com
Online, play-based curriculum and curriculum resource for the infant/toddler and preschool years. Includes an open framework of more than 3,200 age-appropriate activities incorporating 500 behaviors children should master to be ready for kindergarten.

Teachers and Families, http://www.teachersandfamilies.com
Good source for information about child development to share with parents. The site is sponsored by the Network for Instructional Television.

The Developmental Stages of Erik Erikson, http:www.learningplaceonline.com/stages/organize/Erikson.htm
Site presents an article on Erikson's eight stages of life.

Tufts University Child & Family Web Guide, http://www.cfw.tufts.edu/
This website provides a WebGuide, a directory that evaluates, describes and provides links to hundreds of sites containing child development research and practical advice.

Zero to Three, http://www.zerotothree.org
Source for information on caring for infants and toddlers in groups.

For additional creative activity resources, visit our website at www.Cengage.com/login.

Developmental Levels and Art

As children grow older, they change in height and weight and gain new skills. They also develop different abilities in art. The artwork of a three-year-old is different from that of a four- or five-year-old. It is different in the way it looks, as well as in the way it is made.

For many years, people have been trying to explain why all children the world over draw the way they do. There are many theories of children's art, each of which offers an explanation for why children produce art and suggests strategies for teachers. Basic to all of these theories are two facts. The first is that all children go through definite stages in their development of art. The second is that the pace of each child's development in art varies with the child.

OBJECTIVES

After studying this chapter, you should be able to:

1. Describe the scribble stage, including appropriate materials for use in this stage.

2. Explain the basic forms (preschematic) stage, including appropriate materials for use in this stage.

3. Discuss the pictorial (schematic) stage, including appropriate materials for use in this stage.

4. Discuss the gang stage, including appropriate materials for use in this stage.

5. Discuss appropriate art activities and materials for toddlers, young preschoolers, older preschoolers, kindergartners, and children in grades 1 through 5.

Developmental Levels/Stages of Art

Just as young children experience various stages of physical development, they also develop art abilities in a gradual process, going through specific stages. These stages are called **developmental levels**. A developmental level is a guide to what a child can do in art at different ages, but it is not a strict guideline. Some children may be ahead of or behind the developmental level for their age. Developmental levels tell the teacher what came before and what is to come in the artwork of the young child.

There is no exact pattern for each age level. Not all three-year-olds behave alike, nor are they completely different from four-year-olds. But there is a gradual growth process, called *development*, that almost every child goes through. There is also considerable overlap between stages. Two stages may be represented in one work, and a child may regress before advancing to the next stage. An understanding of developmental levels helps an adult accept each child at the child's present level, whatever it is.

From 1830, when Ebenezer Cooke first drew attention to the successive stages of development found in children's drawings, to Rhoda Kellogg's *Analyzing Children's Art* (1970), and Viktor Lowenfeld's *Creative and Mental Growth of the Child* (1987), teachers have based their objectives for art activities on the idea that children's art is developmental. (See Figure 11–2 for a summary of several art theories.) While each art theory varies (e.g., in the number of proposed stages), they all propose a similar pattern of development—one of progressing from scribbling to more realistic representations. Ability in art develops as the child grows and matures. Each stage is a part of the natural and normal aspects of child growth and development. These stages are sequential, with each stage characterized by increasing progress. Even though stages in art have been identified and accepted, the age at which children progress through these stages is highly individual. As children's bodies and minds mature, so does their art ability. Children learn to paint, model, and build as they learn to walk—slowly, developing in their own way. They learn each new step in the process as they are ready for it. As a general guide, art development progresses from experimentation and exploration (the scribble stage in drawing), to the devising of basic forms, to the forming of symbolic figures and their naming.

Older children continue to develop and refine their abilities in art as they create more complex works of art and give greater attention to their expressive intentions. Children ages nine to eleven are in what Lowenfeld calls the **gang stage**. The title of this stage reflects the fact that children of this age are more independent of adults and more anxious to conform to their peers.

The following discussion of the development of children's drawing is intended to serve as a general guide to the overall process of development in art. The basic developmental levels, or stages, apply to all art media. For the sake of clarity, children's drawing will be the primary focus of the discussion.

FIGURE 11-1 • The way a child holds his drawing tool tells a great deal about his motor control.

Victor Lowenfeld, *Creative and Mental Growth* (1987)

Scribbling Stage—First Stage of Self-expression:
   2–4 years
Preschematic Stage—First Representational Attempts:
   4–7 years
Schematic Stage—Achievement of a Form Concept:
   7–9 years
Gang Stage—Dawning Realism:
   9–11 years
Stage of Reasoning—Pseudonaturalistic:
   11–13 years

Herbert Read, *Education Through Art* (1966)

Scribble: 2–4 years
Line: 4 years
Descriptive Symbolism: 5–6 years
Descriptive Realism: 7–8 years
Visual Realism: 9–10 years
Repression: 11–14 years
Artistic Revival: 14 years

Rhoda Kellogg, *Analyzing Children's Art* (1970)

Scribble Stage—20 basic scribbles: 2-year-olds
Combine Stage (Diagrams)—Basic shapes:
3-year-olds
Aggregate Stage—Two or more diagrams:
4-year-olds
Pictorial Stage—Representational art: 5-year-olds

FIGURE 11-2 • Summary: Theories of art development.

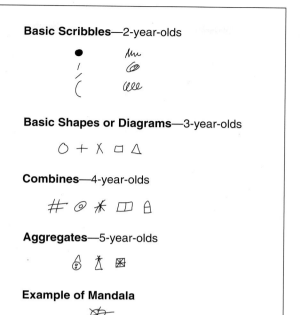

Basic Scribbles—2-year-olds

Basic Shapes or Diagrams—3-year-olds

Combines—4-year-olds

Aggregates—5-year-olds

Example of Mandala

FIGURE 11-3 • Examples of Rhoda Kellogg's stages of development in preschool.

Source: All above examples based on information in *Analyzing Children's Art*, R. Kellogg, (1970). Palo Alto, CA: National Press Books.

Children's Drawing

There are three developmental levels in drawing that are of concern to the early childhood teacher: the **scribble stage**, the **basic forms stage**, and the **pictorial** (or first drawings) **stage**. The realism stage, generally covering children ages nine years old and older, is of concern to teachers in the upper elementary levels.

The Scribble Stage

Most children begin scribbling at about one and one-half to two years of age. Children can be given a crayon or marker as soon as they no longer put everything in their mouth. They will scribble with anything at hand and on anything nearby. Their first marks are usually an aimless group of lines. Yet these first scribbles are related to later drawing and painting. They are related to art just as a baby's first babbling sounds are related to speech.

The crayon may be held upside down, sideways, with the fist, between clenched fingers, or with either hand. Children may be pleased with their scribbling and get real enjoyment from it. They enjoy the physical motions involved in scribbling. It is the act of doing—not the final product—that is important to the child. When a child gets her or his hands on materials, she or he begins to manipulate and explore randomly. This exploration delights the child and therefore leads to further manipulation and discovery.

If you watch a baby draw or a toddler scribbling, you know it is a sensorimotor activity. As a child draws or paints, every part of her or his body moves, all working to move the crayon or brush across the paper. Once the child begins the movement, it's difficult to stop! As a consequence, whatever surface the child is working on often becomes covered with paint and crayon.

> From the moment the child discovers what it looks like and feels like to put these lines down on paper, he has found something he will never lose, he has found art. This wonderful thing happens to every child when he is about two years old. (Kellogg & O'Dell, 1967)

Early Scribble Stage: Disordered or Random Scribbling

During the early scribble stage, the young child does not have control over hand movements or the marks on a page. Thus this stage is called **disordered or random scribbling**. The marks are random and go in many directions. The direction of the marks depends on whether the child is drawing on the floor or on a low table. The way the crayon is held also affects how the scribbles look. But the child is not able to make the crayon go in any one way on purpose. There is neither the desire nor the ability to control the marks. (See Figure 11–4 for some examples of random scribbles.)

Because it is the sensory experience of making marks that's important at this stage, the child doesn't even realize that she or he is producing these scribbles. The connection between herself or himself and the scribbles isn't made by the early scribbler. In fact, these children receive as much satisfaction from just handling the materials—dumping the crayons out of the box, putting them back in again, rolling them across the table or in their hands—as they do from scribbling!

Art is such a sensory experience at this age that children may use crayons in both hands as they draw, singing along in rhythm to the movements they are making. They may not even notice the crayon they're working with isn't leaving marks on the paper.

Children's drawings reflect growth in thinking (cognition) and in physical control (gross and fine motor) over materials and tools.

Note: All ages listed here are approximate. All children develop at highly individual rates.

Ages | **Characteristics of Stage**

1–2 years *Random Scribbling.* Exploration of tools and materials, showing increasing fine and gross motor control. Single and multiple dots and lines (horizontal, vertical, wavy, and diagonal) produce some twenty basic scribbles that eventually include loops, spirals, and circles. Some examples:

2–7 years *Shape Making.* Scribbles begin to used intentionally to make basic shapes or diagrams. Children combine shapes and use overlapping. Eventually, shapes form aggregates (three or more diagrams together). Some examples:

3–5 years *Symbol Making.* Lopsided geometric shapes are made. Mandalas and suns are drawn and eventually become human figures. At first, arms and legs stretch out from the head. Eventually the torso emerges and human figures appear more and more complete. Some examples:

FIGURE 11-4 • Examples of development in children's drawing.

Source: All above examples based on Kellogg (1969) and Lowenfeld and Brittain (1987).

Because it is the process that is important to children when they're toddlers, there's no need to label their scribbles with their names or ask for stories or titles to accompany the scribbles. For young children in the early scribble stage, it is appropriate for adults to comment on the process. Focusing on the process, you might say, "You covered the entire paper," "Your whole arm moved as you worked," or "You moved your crayon all around and around." These are the kinds of comments appropriate in the scribble stage. They are specific, and they are geared to the developmental level of the child. Be sure to save samples of scribbles from time to time, using portfolios to keep a visual record of the child's progress. (Portfolios are discussed in detail later in this chapter.)

A further insight into this stage of art development is provided by Rhoda Kellogg, who points out that "visual interest is an essential component of scribbling" (1970, p. 7). She divides children's scribbles into 20 basic varieties that have no specific developmental order. (See Figure 11–3 for a summary of these basic scribbles.)

Later Scribble Stage: Controlled Scribbling

At some point, children find a connection between their motions and the marks on the page. This may be about six months after the child has started to scribble, but the time will vary with each child. This very important step is called **controlled scribbling**. The child has now found it possible to control the marks. Many times, an adult cannot see any real difference in these drawings. They still look like scribbles—but they are different in a very important way.

FIGURE 11-5 • Scribble Art Bulletin Board showing various scribble examples.

FIGURE 11-6 • Example of random scribbling.

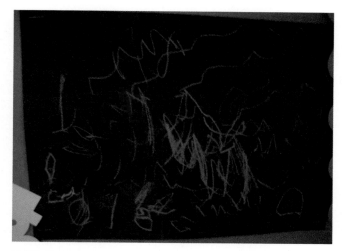

FIGURE 11-7 • Example of more controlled scribbling.

these placement patterns, however, is that unlike uncontrolled scribbles, they "require both seeing and the eye's guidance of the hand" (Kellogg, 1970, p. 23). At this point, the child's eyes have definitely begun to guide his or her hands, and he or she places the scribbles repeatedly in patterns that are visually pleasing to him or her (see Figure 11–7).

In this later scribbling stage, repeated movements among the scribbles begin to appear. At a basic level, the child is beginning to organize his or her environment. One universal form seen most often in this stage is the **mandala**—a variety of circular patterns (see Figure 11–3). During this stage, children also make sweeping, wavy, bold, and rippling lines.

The Scribble Stage and Two-Dimensional Media

The term **two-dimensional media** refers to any art form that is flat. Art in two dimensions has only two sides, front and back. Examples of two-dimensional art processes are painting, drawing, printing, and scribbling.

The child's gradual gaining of control over scribbling motion is a vital experience for the child. She or he now is able to make the marks go in the direction desired. Most children scribble at this later stage with a great deal of enthusiasm because coordination between seeing and doing is an important achievement.

Because children enjoy this newfound power, they now may scribble in lines, zigzags, or circles. When they repeat motions, they are gaining control over certain movements. They can become very involved in this type of scribbling.

Controlled scribbling is described in Kellogg's developmental theory as placement patterns of these 20 basic scribbles. Each child has one or more favorites that he or she uses repeatedly. The difference with

Children just beginning to scribble need tools that are safe and easy to hold and use. For a child between the ages of one and one-half and three years, large, nontoxic crayons are good tools for two-dimensional artwork. Pencils are dangerous for the young child and are also too difficult to hold and use. A good-quality, kindergarten-type crayon is the best tool. Crayon quality is determined by how much wax can be scratched off the paper—the more wax, the poorer the quality. The child will have to press so hard to get

FIGURE 11-8 • Example of controlled scribbling.

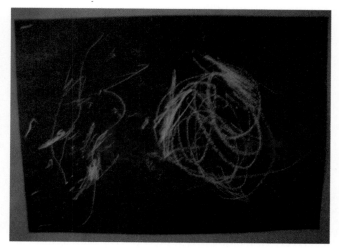

FIGURE 11-9 • Example of circular and jabbing scribbles.

a good color that his fingers (and the resulting drawings) will become cramped. The smaller the child, the better (and bigger) the crayons should be. The crayon should be large and unwrapped so it can be used on both the sides and ends. Good-quality crayons are strong enough to hold up to rough first scribbles. They also make bright, clear colors, which are pleasant for the child to use.

Because motion is the chief enjoyment in this stage, the child needs large blank paper (at least 18" × 24"). This size allows enough room for wide arm movements and large scribbles in many directions. The paper should always be large enough to give the child a big open space for undirected, random scribbles. Paper can be in a variety of shapes, such as rectangular, triangular, circular, and oval.

If possible, a child in the scribble stage should use large white paper. Crayon scribbles show up better on white paper, so the child can see more easily the results of the scribbling. The classified section of the newspaper is also appropriate paper for beginning artists. The small print of the advertisements makes a neutral, nonintrusive background for scribbling, and this section of the paper provides a generous supply of material for young scribblers, which encourages the frequency of their scribbling.

The child needs only a few crayons at a time. Because motor control is the main focus in the early period of the scribbling stage, too many different crayons may distract the child in the scribbling process. A box of 32 crayons, for example, would become an object of exploration itself and hence a distraction from the act of scribbling. This type of interruption breaks up arm movement as well as total physical involvement. New crayons may be added when a new drawing is started. The tools should mark clearly and easily.

Painting is another good two-dimensional art activity for children in the scribble stage because it offers children the most fluidity. Paintbrushes for two- and three-year-olds need to have 12-inch handles and ¾-inch to 1-inch bristles. Paint for two- and three-year-old children should be mixed with a dry soap so it is thick enough to control. The paper for painting may need to be heavier than newsprint because children will repeatedly paint the paper until it disintegrates. For these first painting activities, beginners should paint while seated at a flat table rather than while standing at an easel. It is difficult for young painters to control drips on an easel. Also, these beginning artists are likely to become distracted if they are standing at

an easel and wander off. A good deal of monitoring is required with toddlers because they are tempted to taste the materials and carry them about the room. For toddlers, the major value lies in simple experimentation with colors and textures.

Observation of the Scribble Stage

The student observer of young children (ages one and one-half to three years) should keep in mind the following points while observing scribbling. A copy of the observation sheet (Figure 11–10) may be used to record your observations.

Age. Note the age of the child. Keep in mind the average range for the scribble stage (one and one-half to three years). See how the child fits in the range. There may be an overlap between stages.

Motor control. Note how the child holds the crayon: with two fingers, clenched fingers, or a fist. If the child uses a two-finger grip, this is the start of good motor control. The other methods of holding the crayon show less motor control. See if the child can hold the crayon without dropping it during the entire drawing. This also shows good motor control. Note any other things that might show the child's degree of motor control.

Arm movements. In scribbling, a child may use one type of arm movement or a variety. Note if movements are wide, long, short, jabbing, or of other kinds. The type of arm movement used affects the basic forms the child will make in the future. For example, if circular scribbles are being made, later these scribbles become circles.

Types of scribbles. Note the kind of scribbles the child is making. They may be controlled or uncontrolled, circular, lines, or others mentioned earlier.

Use of paper. There are many ways of using paper for scribbling. Some are moving across the paper from left to right, moving across the paper from right to left, scribbling on only one part of the page, and moving the paper to make marks in the other direction. See if the child seems to know how to use the paper. Older scribblers often have more control over the paper.

Try the following activities, observing and noting what happens.

CHILD	AGE	MOTOR CONTROL	ARM MOVEMENT	TYPES OF SCRIBBLES	USE OF PAPER	EARLY PERIOD	LATER PERIOD
COMMENTS:							

FIGURE 11-10 • Scribble stage observation form.

- Provide the child with some soft, colored chalk. See if this new tool causes any differences in the way the child scribbles.
- Change to smaller paper. See if there are any differences in the child's arm movement, type of scribbles made, and use of paper.
- Place two extra colored crayons in the child's view. See if the child uses them. Then see if scribbles look different when the child uses many colors. Compare an all-one-color drawing with a many-color drawing.

The Basic Forms/Preschematic Stage

Basic forms like rectangles, squares, and circles develop from scribbles as the child finds and recognizes simple shapes in the scribbles. More importantly, they develop as the child finds the muscle control and hand–eye coordination (use of hand(s) and eyes at the same time) to repeat the shape.

In Kellogg's theory, basic forms are called **emergent diagram shapes**. These "diagrams are made with single lines forming crosses and outlines of circles, triangles, and other shapes" (Kellogg, 1970, p. 39).

At this stage, the child's drawings look more organized. This is because the child is able to make basic

FIGURE 11-11 • As the child develops muscle control and hand-eye coordination, she begins to make basic forms.

FIGURE 11-12 • The basic shape (square) emerges in this scribbling sample.

forms by controlling the lines. A child in the age range of three to four years is usually in the basic forms stage. This stage is also referred to as the **preschematic stage**. This means that in this stage, basic forms are drawn in and of themselves and not to represent a particular object. For example, the child draws a rectangular form over and over in a variety of sizes. At this point, this rectangle is not the child's schema or idea of a house. It is simply a controlled drawing of a basic form.

During this stage, children hold their tools more like adults do and have a growing control over the materials. Children can now control their scribbles, making loops, circular shapes, and lines that are distinguishable and can be repeated at will. Children at this age value their scribbles. By age three or four, children will not draw if their marker is dry. Children now ask to have their names put on their work so it can be taken home or displayed in the room.

It is important to note, again, that there may be an overlap between developmental levels in art. For example, one three-year-old child may be drawing basic forms and an occasional scribble. Another three-year-old child may still be totally in the scribble stage. Developmental levels are meant merely as guidelines, not as set limits on age and ability levels.

CHILD	AGE	MOTOR CONTROL	ARM MOVEMENT	TYPES OF SCRIBBLES	USE OF PAPER	EARLY PERIOD	LATER PERIOD

COMMENTS:

FIGURE 11-13 • Basic forms stage observation form.

Early Basic Forms Stage: Circle and Oval

Generally, the first basic form drawn is the oval or circle. This marks the **early basic forms stage**. It develops as children recognize the simple circle in their scribbles and are able to repeat it. Both the oval and the circle develop from circular scribbles. Following the discovery of the oval or circle, the child will begin to elaborate on it by adding dots and perhaps lines.

Another early basic form in this stage is the curved line or arc. This is made with the same swinging movement of an arm used in the early scribble stage. Now, however, it is in one direction only. This kind of line gradually becomes less curved, and from it come the horizontal and vertical lines. Making an intentional arc-shaped line reflects more developed motor control.

In Kellogg's full-fledged diagram stage, children begin to draw six different diagrams: the rectangle, the oval, the triangle, the Greek cross, the diagonal cross, and the odd shape.

FIGURE 11-14 • Notice how the child has placed basic forms together.

Later Basic Forms: Rectangle and Square

As muscle control of three- to four-year-olds continues to improve, more basic forms are made in their drawings. The rectangle and square forms are made when the child can purposefully draw separate lines of any length desired. The child joins the separate lines to form the rectangle or square. This indicates the **later basic forms stage**. The circle, oval, square, and rectangle are all basic forms made by the child's control of lines.

The Basic Forms Stage and Two-Dimensional Media

Children in the basic forms stage have enough motor control and hand–eye coordination to use different tools. In addition to crayons, the child may now begin to work with tempera paint. Tempera paint is the best kind for children because it flows easily from the brush onto the page. Liquid tempera in 16-ounce squeeze bottles is a convenient way to provide paint for beginning painters. Powdered tempera is also appropriate because it can be mixed with water to the desired consistency (very thick for beginners). Be sure to mix dry tempera well out of children's reach because it contains silica, which is not safe for children to breathe.

Large lead pencils are good for children in the later period of this stage; there is less danger of injury with these older children. A variety of papers can be supplied, from newsprint to construction paper. These children should be allowed plenty of time with the basic tools of drawing, painting, modeling, cutting, and pasting and should not be rushed into other media. The basic developmental goal for this age is the control of the media and tasks of drawing, painting, or modeling. (A complete list of appropriate materials is included in Chapter 12.)

Felt-tip pens or colored markers are excellent tools for this stage. They provide clear, quick, easily made, and nice-looking marks. In the basic forms stage, when the child really enjoys seeing the marks come out as desired, these pens are best. They require little pressure to make bold marks. Felt-tip pens should be nontoxic and water soluble so that most spots can be washed out of the child's clothes. (See "Think About It . . . Marker Maintenance" on page 243 for suggestions on prolonging the life of colored markers.)

The largest paper size is not as necessary in this stage as in the scribble stage. Because the child now has better motor control, it is easier to keep marks on a smaller space. Room for wide, uncontrolled movements is not as necessary. Make available paper of many sizes and shapes.

Also make available different colors and textures of paper and a variety of colored pencils and markers. Children in this stage like to make basic forms in many colors and ways as an exercise of their skill.

Student observers should realize that children of this age like to repeat forms and should not try to force them to "make something else" to fill up the paper. It is important that children practice making their own basic forms. The forms may look simple, but each drawing is a great motor achievement for them. The children may rightly be quite proud of their basic form drawings.

Observation of the Basic Forms Stage

The student observer of young children in the basic forms stage should keep in mind the following points when observing children. The points may then be recorded on a copy of the observation form, Figure 11–13. If students are observing children in both the scribbling and basic forms stages, observations of each stage may be compared to help highlight the differences in these two stages.

Age. Note the age of the child. Check Figure 11–4 for the average age range for the basic forms stage. See how the child fits in the range. See if there is an overlap between stages.

Motor control. See how the child holds the crayon. Note if it is held very tightly or if the child can draw with sureness and ease. Also note if the child draws with a lot of arm movement or uses just the hand to draw. The child who uses more hand movement and less arm movement is showing good motor control. In the basic forms stage, children use fewer unnecessary arm movements.

Types of basic forms. Write down the number and type of basic forms mentioned earlier that the child can draw. See if the shapes are well drawn or rough and unclear. Rough, less clear forms are made in the early stage. A child in the later basic forms stage draws clear, easy-to-recognize shapes.

In drawings with a variety of forms, see if one form is clearer than another. Clearer forms are the ones that the child first began to draw. The less clear forms are in the practice stage and eventually become clearer.

Use of paper. Use the same checkpoints for the use of paper that were used in the scribble stage section. In addition, see if the child fills the page with one or many basic forms. If the same shape is made over and over, it means the child is practicing a new basic form. Practice like this occurs at an early point in the stage.

THINK ABOUT IT   Marker Maintenance

Markers are wonderful for young artists. But busy artists frequently lose caps from these tools, often resulting in dried-out markers. Replacing dried-out markers can be expensive, so here are a few hints on marker maintenance to help preserve markers as long as possible.

- Solve the lost cap/dry-out problem by setting the caps with open ends up in a margarine or whipped topping container filled with plaster of Paris. Make sure the plaster does not cover the holes in the caps. When the plaster dries, the markers can be put into the caps and will stand upright until ready for use again.

- Give new life to old, dry felt markers by storing them tips down with the caps on. When the markers become dried out, remove the caps and put in a few drops of water. This usually helps "revive" them.

- Recycle dried-out markers by having children dip them in paint and use them for drawing.

- Make your own pastel markers by adding dry tempera paint (or food color) to bottles of white shoe polish that come with sponge applicator tops.

- Purchase empty plastic roller-top bottles from a school supply store. Fill them with watery tempera paint and use them as a different type of marker.

THINK ABOUT IT

Why Children Draw

The most obvious reason children draw is for the sheer pleasure of it. How many times have you witnessed a small child completely engaged in drawing and humming a joyful tune? We can probably remember our own spontaneous experiences as being pleasurable ones. Spontaneous drawing is a type of drawing that is free and without rules or limitations for the artist. Spontaneous drawings encourage children to explore and experiment with their own thoughts and ideas while leaving a record of these on paper. This type of spontaneous drawing should be nurtured at all ages.

More reasons for drawing:

- Children interact with their world and often use drawing as the medium to describe their experiences. Children's literacy skills are still developing; drawing allows them the means to communicate complex thoughts. Children's drawings tell us what they think and feel. One particular seven-year-old child drew a picture showing his mom coming home from the hospital with his new baby brother. The brother was drawn with a large smiling head and his mother was carrying him. The brother and mom were colored with bright colors and drawn with detail. Off to the side were the artist, his dad, and sister. They were drawn on a much smaller scale with little detail. It seems the message the artist was trying to convey in the drawing was that the new baby brother would become the center of attention and take much of his mother's time.

- Drawing empowers children to experiment and practice various drawing techniques and processes. This, of course, can be achieved by art activities in school. The art program teaches children to observe, create, express, and experiment with the principles and elements of drawing.

- Drawing allows the child to invent. In their drawings children create objects, characters, and worlds that erupt from their imagination. These drawings are essential and help develop a sense of self, what they like and dislike.

The Pictorial/Schematic Stage

With the two earlier stages complete, children now have the ability to draw the variety of marks that make up their first pictures. This occurs at the next developmental level in art—the **pictorial stage**. Many four-year-olds and most five-year-olds are at this level. The *schematic stage* refers to the child's ability to use his or her own special variety of marks, or *schema*. More details on schema follow later in this section.

In Kellogg's theory, children move on from the diagrams stage and enter the pictorial stage when they begin putting diagrams together to form combines or aggregates, which are basically two diagrams put together, or three or more diagrams put together (see Figure 11–17).

After children can put these shapes into combinations and aggregates, they are able to make drawings that begin to be a picture of someone or something in particular. In this way, these shapes allow for a natural transition from children's abstract to pictorial work.

Pictures or first drawings are different from scribbling in that they are not made for pure motor enjoyment.

Instead, they are made by the child for a purpose. The basic forms perfected in the preceding stage suggest images to the child that stand for ideas in the child's own mind. A new way of drawing begins. From the basic forms the child is able to draw, only particular ones are chosen. Miscellaneous scribbling is left out. In this way, children draw their first symbols. A **symbol** is a visual representation of something important to the child; it may be a human figure, animal, tree, or similar figure. Art in which symbols are used in such a way is called **representational art**. This means there has been a change from kinesthetic, or sheerly physical, activity to representational attempts. The child realizes that there is a relationship between the objects drawn and the outside world and that drawing and painting can be used to record ideas or express feelings.

The ability to draw symbols in representational art comes directly from the basic forms stage. The basic forms gradually lose more and more of their connection to body motion only. They are now put together to make symbols, which stand for real objects in the child's mind. In scribbling, the child was mainly involved in a physical activity, trying out the materials to see what she or he could do with them. Now the child is expressing in the scribble something of importance to her or him. The drawing may seem to be a scribble, but it is now a "man" or a "dog"—a definite symbol representing something in the child's life.

The human form is often the child's first symbol. A human figure is usually drawn with a circle for a head and two lines for legs or body. These are often called "tadpole" figures because of their large heads on a tiny body with extended arms. Other common symbols include trees, houses, flowers, and animals. The child can tell you what each symbol stands for in the drawing.

Further attempts to make symbols grow directly from the basic forms the child can make. Flowers and trees are combinations of spiral scribbles or circles with attached straight lines for stems or trunks. Houses, windows, doors, flags, and similar objects are simply made up of rectangles and straight lines.

It is a common adult practice to label these first drawings "children's art" because they contain recognizable objects. If children's drawings appear to be mere scribbles to an adult, they are not considered children's art because they don't look like "something." Yet being able to identify objects in a child's work does not make it children's art. Art is self-expression and has value in any form and at any stage.

Because art is now representational, children need tools that can be easily controlled and thus facilitate their ability to produce the desired symbols. Thinner crayons and paintbrushes and less fluid paints can now be made available so children can express their ideas and feelings with greater realism. Children over age five will want to be able to select representational colors, so a variety of colors of paint, crayons, and markers are necessary.

Naming and owning the art produced are also important to children in this stage. These children may ask you to record the names of their paintings or drawings as well as write stories to go with their drawings. These children recognize other children's work at this point. They will want to take their work home, as well as contribute some to display in the classroom.

Portfolios for Developmental Assessment

The pictorial stage is an excellent point at which to begin keeping a portfolio of the child's work, if you haven't started yet. Samples of the child's early, initial representational artwork will be a record of the development of the child's first symbols. As representational development proceeds, this may be forgotten without

the portfolio sample. For example, when Claire first made a scribble that she called "doggy," her teacher noted it on the sample and kept it in Claire's folder. Over the year, a collection of these various samples gave quite a graphic story of Claire's progress in art.

Keeping portfolios does not mean, however, collecting and keeping all of the child's work. Items in a child's portfolio should reflect how the child is progressing in art. Each piece in the portfolio needs to be selected with this question in mind: "What does this piece tell me about this learner?" For example, selected samples of scribbles from the early and later scribble stages tell a great deal visually how a child is progressing. In contrast, keeping all of the child's scribble work samples in the file would make it difficult to clearly see the child's development. Digital cameras are very useful in keeping portfolios of children's artwork. See Chapter 8 for details on digital portfolios and Figure 11–15 for a checklist of what to include in a child's portfolio.

A child's portfolio should contain pieces of work that are evidence of a child's development and progress. The following are suggested items to include in a child's portfolio.

_____ Work samples—These are examples of a child's work, such as drawings, photos of block buildings, finger paintings, etc. Collect a variety of samples for each type of art activity.

_____ Observations—These are written observations about a child. For example, notes on how the child handled the paintbrush, used scissors for the first time, or made basic forms with a crayon.

_____ Anecdotal records—These are factual, nonjudgmental observations of observed activities. These provide essential information about a child's progress and activities in the classroom and information on what occurs in the classroom's everyday environment.

_____ Interviews—These are notes on questions that teachers ask children so as to gain understanding about the child and the child's development in art and other areas of the curriculum.

_____ Developmental checklists—These are lists of developmental characteristics and traits arranged in a logical order. As teachers observe children, they can use these checklists to note the presence or absence of behaviors. These lists give both teachers and parents a good idea of where the child is developmentally.

FIGURE 11-15 • Checklist: What to include in a child's portfolio.

Artists generally keep a **portfolio**, or a representative collection of their work. The artist's portfolio usually has samples chosen from various periods, showing how the artist's talent has developed over time. Samples chosen from different media are also included in the portfolio to reflect the artist's versatility and range of talent. For example, you may find works done in pastels, chalk, fine line drawings, and watercolors in the portfolio.

In the early childhood art program, many teachers find the use of portfolios (or individual art files, as they are more generally called) for young children—most often children four years and older—quite helpful. There are many advantages to this practice for the young child, teacher, and parents.

The most obvious advantage of a portfolio/file is the fact that it is visible evidence of the child's development in art. From the earliest selections in the portfolio to the most recent, one can see the child's progress in art.

A portfolio/file can greatly aid the teacher during parent–teacher conferences. It is a collection of work samples that indicate how a child is developing in this area. It reduces the subjectivity of discussions by helping both teacher and parent focus objectively on the portfolio. Parents may see the obvious growth and learning evidenced in the child's artwork. But they won't know the "story" or planned learning behind each piece. To avoid this gap, be sure to include a portfolio letter when you send a child's art portfolio home for parents. In your letter, explain each piece of artwork in the portfolio. The explanation needn't be long, but merely a simple statement for each piece about the lesson taught and any cultural dimensions of the work. It also helps for a parent to know what artist's work the child had been exposed to or what elements or principles of art were discussed. You may also want to include a statement inviting families to respond to the artwork and to the art program as a whole. A portfolio letter is a great opportunity to inform children's families about all of the in-depth, creative learning that goes on in art experiences for young children.

Another excellent advantage of the portfolio is that it encourages growth of the child's aesthetic sense of choice. By involving the child in selection of pieces for the portfolio, the child learns about the process of selection. Of course, learning to be selective is a very complex skill and will take time for the child to develop. But like any other skill, given the time, opportunity, and guidance to make selections of one's own work for the portfolio (or file), the child will develop his or her own personal preferences. Be sure to date

and label and write a short comment on each piece added to the portfolio. The label should describe the media/materials used, and comments should be on some significant aspect of the piece, for example, "First time Jorge named an object in a drawing. This one he called 'Daddy.'"

For all of these reasons, then, using a portfolio in the early childhood art program has definite merits. Alongside these merits are some pitfalls one needs to keep in mind. Most important, if you plan to use portfolios for developmental assessment, stick to it for the whole year. Beginning a portfolio with good intentions and then only sporadically filling it with work reduces its importance as the year goes on—this type of portfolio is best left out of the program entirely. To be of use in developmental assessment, the portfolio needs to be as complete as possible, reflecting the process of artistic development as a whole. Many teachers find it helpful to include in their monthly planning a week set aside for portfolio selection. This way, they are sure to have it on their list of priorities. Of course, there should always be time for spontaneous inclusions whenever they occur.

Also keep in mind to include the child in portfolio development, even if it "takes longer that way." Don't forget that the development of personal preference is on a par with developmental assessment as a reason for using portfolios.

Portfolios can be made from large brown envelopes, two pieces of tag board stapled together to create a pocket, or even large pizza boxes donated by a local pizzeria. The portfolio can be personalized with the child's photo and/or a drawing or design created by the child. Children's portfolios should be kept at school and accessible to them. They may include children's completed work or works in progress. Transcriptions of the language used by children to discuss their artwork may accompany portfolios. Portfolios provide children, teachers, and parents with a picture of where children were when the collection was begun and where they are at present.

Early Pictorial (First Drawings) Stage

In the **early pictorial (first drawings) stage**, a child works on making and perfecting one or many symbols. The child practices these symbols, covering sheets of paper with many examples of the same subject. For example, a child may draw windows and doors over and over in each drawing. Also at an early point in this stage, a child's picture may be a collection of unrelated figures and objects. This type of picture is a sampling of the child's many tries at making different symbols. At this point, pictures are done very quickly.

During this early pictorial stage, the child is searching for new ideas. Symbols change constantly. A picture of a man drawn one day differs from the one drawn the day before. In this stage, there is often a great variety of forms representing the same object. Early first drawings are very flexible in appearance. Children are assigning meaning to the shapes they make. These shapes will stand for whatever the child wishes, regardless of whether they are accurate reproductions.

Later Pictorial (First Drawings) Stage: Use of Schema

In the **later pictorial (first drawings) stage**, through practice, a child draws symbols easily and more exactly. Many four-year-olds and most five-year-olds perfect to their own liking and take pride in producing a series of many symbols. A child at this point often likes to see these symbols set clearly and neatly on the page. They are now drawn one at a time with few or no other marks on the page. They are clear and well drawn. If children can draw the letters of their name

---

THIS ONE'S for YOU! Art DOs with Young Children

Knowing the stages of art development in young children is just a starting point. It is crucial that you know how to talk with young artists about their work. Here are some dos to keep in mind when you are working with young artists.

DO accept a child's work as he or she creates it. Avoid correcting or adding to a child's work. Understand that when children draw huge hands, construct unreal proportions, or leave out items that you might consider essential, they are concentrating on what is important to them at the moment. Accept their work as they create it. Observing what is emphasized or omitted will give you an important insight into a child's development.

DO understand that children's coordination and muscle development will grow as a result of creating their own artwork. Avoid using coloring books. Don't be fooled into believing that filling in pictures in a coloring book will improve a child's coordination. Children's coordination and muscle development will grow as a result of creating their own artwork.

DO offer art materials every day in the week. Children need an ongoing experience with materials so that new growth and discoveries can be made.

DO remember that children need continuity. They will not be bored if you offer them opportunities to paint, draw, build, paste, and model every day. Personal growth takes place through repeated experiences with open-ended materials.

DO avoid offering coloring books or precut patterns to the children. These are just another way of saying, "You are not capable; you do not have the ability."

DO offer children open-ended materials (paint, clay, crayons, wood, blocks) so that they may make discoveries for themselves.

DO be mindful of the words you use with young children when discussing their art work. Try to avoid asking a child, "What is that?" It's not even appropriate to try to guess. Casually saying that a painting or drawing is "great," or "terrific" does not make a child aware of his or her individuality. Avoid making models for the children, even when they protest that they "can't do it." They cannot possibly duplicate what an adult has created. Your model is a way of saying, "I know you are not able to do a good job."

DO tell children why you like their work: Comment on the red line near the blue circles or mention the two blue dots. Commenting on what you see helps children become more consciously aware of their work. Help children think about what they want to paint, draw, build, or model; for example, ask, "How does a cow eat?" or "How many legs does the animal have?"

DO see each child's work as individual and avoid comparing children's work or showing preferences. Be sure to pay attention when children are commenting about each other's work. For example, hearing something like "Oh, that's just scribble scrabble" can be responded to by saying, "That's Dustin's design" or "That's Shania's idea."

DO help the children feel confident about their work and take pride in it. Stress the individuality of each creation. Respect the many different ideas children have even though they are using the same materials.

on the page as well, they may feel this is all that belongs in the picture.

For a while, children are content to make these finished yet isolated examples of their drawing skill, but it is not long before more complex drawings are made. Children four to five years of age are able to use their symbols in drawings to tell a story or describe an event. The naming of these symbols is an important step in that the artwork becomes a clear form of visual communication. It may not look any different, but the child now calls the circle a "sun" because it represents a specific object to the child.

By five and one-half to six years of age, children generally are ready to make a picture of many things in their experience or imagination. Their drawings are made up of combinations of symbols they are familiar with and that have meaning to them. Children create new symbols as they have new experiences and ideas. However, children at this point can't be expected to make pictures of the unfamiliar or of things they have not personally experienced. Another common error made by well-intentioned teachers is a misunderstanding of this stage by expecting all children five years old and older to be able to use symbols in their art. This is not a valid expectation because the age at which children begin to use symbols is as highly individual as the age at which they learn to walk. Children use symbols when they are ready—and no sooner. Creative expression is the goal at this and all ages; a child's art does not have to include specific symbols, like a house, tree, or animals, unless the child chooses to include them.

Children need to repeat art processes over a period of time in order to become competent with and feel secure about using materials to express ideas and feelings. Four- and five-year-old children who have had many opportunities to paint will frequently move easily from manipulative scribbling to expressive symbolic or representational art.

In the later pictorial stage, each child has a special way of drawing the human form, houses, and other symbols. This individual way of drawing is called a **schema**. A schema, or individual pattern, often can be seen in drawings by the age of six. A schema comes after much practice with drawing symbols. As the child becomes more skilled in drawing, his or her drawing begins to show the child's direct experiences coming from his or her mind onto the paper. Once the child has a schema, symbols become special marks. A schema is special for each child, just as a signature is unique for each adult. One child may tell another, "That's Chad's drawing, I recognize his trees," or "I know it's Zarina's painting because she paints her skies that way." These children have developed a schema that is clearly their own, easily recognizable by others.

Importance of schema. The schema drawn by a child represents something important to the child, something that is part of the child's environment and experience. A schema is much more than an individual way of drawing, it is a mental structure that the child uses to organize and process his or her knowledge of the world. These schemas about the child's world, other people, food, and nature are created based on the child's experiences. Thus, a child's schema is highly individual and reflects things of emotional importance.

Children draw schema in a picture not according to actual size, but in a size that shows the emotional importance of the object to them. For example, people and things important to a child might be drawn large and with many details. If a tree is drawn, the limbs may be made larger because the tree is used for climbing. If it is an apple tree, the apples may be drawn very large.

Children express other responses to their environment in their drawings. A painting showing a child walking on wet grass may show the feet and toes large in size. This may show how the child felt after a walk in the early morning.

Importance of First Drawings

At about the same time children develop their own schemas, they begin to name their drawings. Naming a drawing is an important step for children. It is a sign

FIGURE 11-16 • A schema, or individual pattern, often can be seen in drawings by age six.

that their thinking has changed; they are connecting their drawings with the world around them. This is the beginning of a new form of communication—communication with the environment through art.

Soon a five-year-old may think: "My daddy is a big man; he has a head and two big legs." She then draws a head and two big legs and names her drawing "Daddy." Through drawing, the child is making a clear relationship between her father and her drawing. The symbol of a man now becomes "Daddy." Of course, a child will not verbally name all objects every time a picture is made.

In their use of schemas, children express their own personalities. They express not only what is important to them during the process of creating, but also how aware they have become in thinking, feeling, and seeing. From early drawings to the most complex, they give expression to their life experiences.

Observation of the Pictorial (First Drawings) Stage

Keep in mind the following points when observing children in the pictorial stage. You may want to use a copy of the observation form (Figure 11–18) to record your observations. (See also Figures 11–17 and 11–19.)

Age. Write down the age of the child. Check to see what the average age range is for the pictorial stage. See how the child fits in this range. There may be an overlap between stages. For example, you may see figures as well as simple, basic forms in one drawing.

Combination of basic forms. See how the child puts basic forms together to make figures. Very simple combinations mean the child is at an early point in the stage. An example would be a flower made up of a single circle and one-line stem. On the other hand, a flower of many circles with oval petals and a stem of many leaves is a more complex combination of basic forms and would show that the child is at a later point in the stage.

Size of figures. A child in both the early and later periods of this stage may use size to show importance. The large figure represents something important to the child. Note, for example, children may draw themselves or other figures such as their mother in a very large size. Extra-large heads on a small body are found mainly in the early period of this stage.

FIGURE 11-17 • Older children combine basic forms into pictorial drawings.

Notice the relative size of certain things in the picture. For a child who likes animals, a dog may be far larger than the human form. Here, too, size indicates that the object is important to the child.

Number of figures. Mark down the number of figures in each drawing. A drawing with few figures or a single figure means that the child is at an early point in the stage. The child making this type of drawing is working on developing a symbol.

At a later point, the child can draw many types of symbols and figures in one drawing. Also, drawings at a later point look as if they tell a story with the figures.

Details. Note the type and number of details a child uses in a drawing. They indicate at what point the child is in the stage.

Figures with only a few details are made in the early pictorial stage. For example, a circular head, round body, and stick arms and legs make up an early human form. A picture of a man with details such as full arms, hands, and fingers is a sign that the child is at a later point in the pictorial stage.

CHILD	AGE	COMBINATION OF BASIC FORMS	SIZE OF FIGURES	NUMBER OF FIGURES	DETAILS	USE OF FIGURES	NAMING DRAWINGS	EARLY PERIOD	LATER PERIOD
COMMENTS:									

FIGURE 11-18 • Pictorial (first drawings) stage observation form.

See if certain objects are drawn in greater detail than others. A child's experience with certain objects can cause this increase in detail. As an example, tree limbs may be unusually large in the drawings of children who love to climb trees. Special sensory experiences can also cause increase in detail. For example, a child may draw large raindrops in a drawing after a walk in the rain.

Use of figures. Note how the child uses figures. See if the paper is filled with many unrelated figures that simply fill space and look like practice forms. Lack of connection between figures can mean the child is at an early point in the stage; the child is practicing a symbol and is not yet ready to tell a story with it.

If there seems to be a connection between figures, the child is at a later point. This type of drawing is a narrative drawing, one that tells a story. It is a visual form of communication for the child.

Naming drawings. Be sure to listen to the child who wants to talk about a drawing. Note if the child names certain objects or figures, or refers to the entire drawing, but never force the child to tell you "what it is." Naming must come only through the child's own idea. It is an important step in the child's ability to communicate. Naming is only worthwhile if the child sees meaning in the work and takes the initiative in naming it.

FIGURE 11-19 • Observe the number and type of details a child uses in a drawing. What details did this young artist include?

The Gang Stage

Children ages nine through twelve fall into the gang stage of art development, according to Viktor Lowenfeld (1987). Children of this age are no longer content with symbolizing their environment. Their searching minds tells them that there is something they must know about the structure of things in order for them to be "right" in their visual statement. This is the first time that children become aware of a lack of ability to show objects the way they appear in the surrounding environment.

At this point, the child becomes more aware of how things look in her drawings. She looks at her own drawing with a critical eye and raises questions. "What is wrong with the arms? They are too short and don't seem to bend right." "Why doesn't the figure really look like it's running?" "The people are too big for the house. What can I do about it?" This awareness is often expressed with more detail in the child's schema. Drawings are still far from naturalistic. Children at this age discover space in their drawings and it is often depicted with overlapping objects in the drawings. Children of this age also begin to draw the horizon line to separate land from sky.

Because children of this age are becoming more social minded, they are beginning to compare their work with other children's. Their growing self-awareness is to the point of being extremely self-critical, often becoming critical of their own work, wanting their images to be very realistic. Children at this point often become frustrated if realism can't be achieved. The "I-can't-draw" syndrome typically starts to emerge at this stage.

Because of their awareness of lack of ability, drawing often appears less spontaneous than in previous stages (less vital and lively).

Teachers of children in this stage need to encourage the child's self-accepting attitude. The teacher must

THIS ONE'S for YOU! Stages of Art Development—Grades 1–5

With elementary students, one of the major goals of art experiences is to cultivate students' abilities to create original and expressive art. At this level, children are usually able to produce pictorial drawings at will. Art experiences for children in grades 1 through 5 need to focus on prior creative experiences and build on these.

In order to set appropriate expectations and guide artistic growth, you should be familiar with the typical stages of development in creating artwork for this level of students.

The stages of artistic growth outlined here focus on skills portraying space, proportions, and movement or action. Each stage is typical of many children at a particular grade level; however, it is not unusual to find a range of developmental levels within a class or within the work of single students during a year.

Similar variations can be expected in students' ability to respond thoughtfully to artwork. At each stage of development, some students will have greater interest and skill in responding to art than in creating art (or the reverse).

Stage 1 (usually Grades K–2). Children begin to create visual symbols to represent figures such as people, houses, and trees. The figures often seem to "float" in space. Proportions are related to the importance of a feature in the child's experience. Movement is often suggested by scribble-like lines. Three-dimensional artwork reflects the level of prior instruction and practice in using media and the physical coordination students have developed.

Stage 2 (usually Grades 1–3). In picture-making, lines or borders are often used to represent the ground below and sky above. Figures may be placed along a line or at the lower edge of the paper. Proportions are shown through relative size—a house is larger than a person. Action is implied by the general position of lines and shapes, rather than subtle shifts in direction. Children who receive instruction will show general improvement in using three-dimensional media and applying design concepts as they work.

Stage 3 (usually Grades 3–6). Students try out new ways to portray space in the pictures they draw and paint. These explorations often reflect remembered functional or logical relationships more than visual recall or observation. General proportions improve, as well as the use of diagonals to suggest action. Many students develop a strong affinity for three-dimensional work and are willing to try out new media and techniques that require several steps.

Stage 4 (usually Grades 4–6). In picture-making, students search for ways to portray recalled or observed space. Some students begin to use perspective to imply near and distant objects. Movement is suggested through more subtle angles and curves. Individual styles and preferences for two- or three-dimensional work become more evident, along with increased skill in applying design concepts to create expressive work.

FIGURE 11-20 • Older children in the gang stage become more concerned about realism in their work.

FIGURE 11-22 • Teachers can help older children in the gang stage plan their art projects.

FIGURE 11-21 • Children in the gang stage are no longer content with symbolizing their environment.

be ready with specific and direct answers to the child's questions about his work. Vague answers will not satisfy a child at this stage, but will turn the child off and eventually smother his or her desire for or interest in this valuable process of personal expression. Discuss proportions of the figure. Have a child pose, walk, jump, move his or her arms. Take the class outside to see and to sketch a tree, a house, animals—to broaden concepts of structure, form, color, relationships, texture, movement, action. Have children bring natural and man-made objects into the classroom for study. Show good examples of art that will assist the child in his or her feeling for picture organization, balance, and unity. Use the bulletin boards and other visual aids as tools for clarifying ideas and building design concepts.

While the continuous use of the crayon in the same way is satisfying in the earlier stages, it can eventually become a boring tool for the child at this stage. Encourage the child to explore new possibilities with the crayon. Introduce new techniques. Provide opportunities for the child to experiment so that he or she may discover the various effects that can be achieved with crayons when combined with different materials and used with other tools. (See Chapter 13 for these activities.)

Help children realize that they can still express themselves by exploring new uses for familiar media. For example, printing using brayers (rollers) and wood blocks is one way to encourage exploration at this stage. Group projects such as murals are also appropriate at this age because they allow children to "pool" their talents. In such a project, each child can contribute at his or her own level.

Summary

As children grow older and change in height and weight, they also develop different abilities in art. There are three developmental levels in art that are of concern to the preschool teacher: the scribble, basic forms, and pictorial stages. Teachers of children in middle and upper levels of elementary school need to build and expand on the pictorial skill that children have achieved at each level.

The scribble stage occurs in children of about one and one-half to three years of age. It covers the time from the child's first marks to more controlled scribbles. At this stage, the child enjoys the pure motion involved in scribbling.

Wide, good-quality crayons are the best tools for the scribble stage. Large paper should be given to the child to allow room for wide arm movements. Age, motor control, use of paper, and type of scribbles should be noted in scribble stage observations.

The basic forms stage covers approximately ages three to four years. The child develops more muscle control and hand–eye coordination through scribbling. Basic forms come when children can see simple forms in their scribbles and are able to repeat them. The oval or circle is usually the first basic form, followed by the rectangle or square. Children now enjoy seeing forms emerge as a result of their own will.

THINK ABOUT IT   Research on Children's Art

"Along with other data, children's drawings can be used as measures of intellectual growth, emotional maturity, and mental well-being," says Dr. Marlene Cox-Bishop, associate professor of human ecology at the University of Alberta. After collecting the artwork of more than a thousand children from around the world, Cox-Bishop knows children's pictures transcend language and cultural barriers. "We learn to communicate through drawing long before we can read or write about our ideas and our response to the world," she says.

In a cross-cultural study, Cox-Bishop compared Inuit children's drawings with those of American Midwestern children. Item by item, she examined the drawings of each child involved in her study, noting technique, line quality, use of color and space—and tried to statistically determine any gender differences. What she found surprised her: There were very few differences. A child's art is reflective of his or her culture, she says, and maybe each of the children had been similarly influenced by satellite television, common textbooks, and teachers educated in a southern culture.

What surprised her more, however, was discovering that no matter where children live, their visual consciousness develops at the same rate.

All kids learn to draw, learn to represent the world at about the same stages, which is incredible. Although the cultural information such as specific games, costumes, and houses may change, generally how kids organize space, forms, stick figures, or Mr. Potato Heads—happens at about the same age everywhere. (Cox-Bishop, 2005)

Developing visual literacy is important, Cox-Bishop says, because 80% of the messages that bombard us are visual, not written. "Visual literacy is the ability to read the images, the visual environment," she says, and children have it naturally, if briefly. "We lose those skills. They atrophy." (Cox-Bishop, 2005)

The ability to represent the world visually comes from the intuitive, emotional, right hemisphere of the brain, she says. Our culture emphasizes the more logical, linear, left hemisphere. In the process, we squelch a child's creativity.

We pin their notion of whether they're successful on good grades in reading and math and forget about the kid who could write a poem that would knock your socks off, or paint a picture—what about those kids and that part of the brain (Cox-Bishop, 2005)?

Renowned artists have had the same appreciation of children's art. Picasso was known to have collected children's art. He didn't collect it because he wanted to go back and copy the children's artistic solutions; rather, he loved its spontaneity.

Ironically, that original and personal quality cherished in a child's drawing is often scorned in an adult's.

On one hand, we appreciate children's art because it's lovely and unsophisticated. . . . Then we judge a modern artist by the fact that his art doesn't appear to be sophisticated. When we say, 'Ha! My six-year-old kid could do that,' we have forgotten something important. Perhaps that artist is yet a child, still has that child-like ability to look at the relationships of line and color and shape. (Cox-Bishop, 2005)

What's more, we forget that a child's drawing captures a wondrous and fleeting moment in time. (Johnson, 1998)

A wider variety of art materials can be used with children in the basic forms stage. Age, motor control, use of paper, and basic forms used should be noted in observations of the basic forms stage.

The pictorial stage generally occurs from ages four to six. Basic forms made in the prior stage are put together to make up symbols. The human form, birds, flowers, and animals are examples of some symbols. Naming drawings is an important part of first drawings. Children can now communicate outside themselves and with their world. A child's artwork is very individual and expresses the child's own personality.

In the pictorial stage, children make the most varied and complex drawings. Points to note in observing this stage are the age of the child and figures and details in the drawings. Children ages nine to twelve are in the gang stage of art development. This term, developed by Viktor Lowenfeld (1987), refers to the fact that peer groups assume more importance to the child than ever before.

These basic stages of art development parallel the overall development of children at particular periods. In planning the early childhood art program, the teacher must choose appropriate activities for the ability and interest levels of the age group of children in the program. Each age group has its own special considerations that must be included in a teacher's planning.

Key Terms

basic forms stage 235
controlled scribbling 236
developmental levels 233
disordered or random scribbling 235
early basic forms stage 241
early pictorial (first drawings) stage 245
emergent diagram shapes 239
gang stage 234
later basic forms stage 241
later pictorial (first drawings) stage 246
mandala 237
pictorial stage 243
portfolio 245
preschematic stage 240
representational art 243
schema 247
scribble stage 235
symbol 243
two-dimensional media 237

Learning Activities

Selecting Appropriate Materials for Art Experiences

A. Visit a preschool classroom. Examine the tools that are available for children to work with—paintbrushes, scissors, crayons, to mention a few. Inventory these in terms of how many are available, the condition of the various tools, and their suitability in terms of design and quality for young children.

B. Using toy and equipment catalogs that can be cut up, compile a catalog that pictures appropriate early childhood art materials in terms of the many areas covered in this chapter. Select and annotate each entry in each category in terms of age level, appropriateness, appearance, versatility, durability, and safety.

C. Consider the following quote:

When my daughter was about seven years old, she asked me one day what I did at work. I told her I worked at the college—that my job was to teach people how to draw. She stared back at me, incredulous, and said, "You mean they forget?" (Howard Ikemoto)

How would you answer this child? Why do you think we "forget" how to draw? What can you as a teacher do to help children continue drawing?

Scribble Stage Experiences for the Student

A. Exercise 1. Goal: To experience some of the lack of motor control of a young child in the scribble stage.

1. Use the hand opposite your writing hand to "draw" a crayon picture.

2. Discuss the following with your classmates:

   a. the clumsy feeling of the crayon in your hand
   b. your lack of control over your finger and hand movements
   c. your inability to draw exactly what you desired
   d. your difficulty in controlling the crayon, the paper, and your hand movements all at once

3. Try painting on your knees at an easel. Discuss how it felt and how it may have affected your painting. After this experience, what would you change about your approach to easels and painting for young children?

B. Exercise 2. Goal: To experience the pure motor pleasure of scribbling.

1. Close both of your eyes and do a crayon scribbling.
2. To experience feelings similar to the young child's, consider and discuss the following with your classmates:

a. your difficulty in overcoming your adult need for seeing as well as doing
b. how it feels to move your hand and fingers for movement's sake alone
c. what forms you see in your scribbles
d. your feelings about how your drawing looks

Recognizing and Evaluating the Three Art Stages

Obtain samples of drawings from children one and one-half to five years of age. Separate the samples into three groups, one for each stage. Give reasons for the stage selected for each sample, especially for the samples that are not clearly defined.

A. Note and explain the differences in scribble stage examples:

1. early or later scribbling period
2. type of scribbles (circular, jagged)
3. control of crayon

B. Note and explain the differences in basic forms examples:

1. type of basic forms used
2. how clear and exact the forms are
3. child's control of the crayon
4. early or later basic forms period

C. Note and explain the differences in pictorial examples:

1. early or later period
2. what basic forms are combined into symbols
3. observable symbols

D. Using the same drawings, see if you can determine why some people believe children draw what they feel, know, and see.

E. Make a list of children's books that feature outstanding illustrations that could be used to introduce children to the concept of the artist as well as to different techniques and a wide variety of art materials.

F. Work with a small group of children (or even one child) to try to motivate art with a firsthand experience, such as touching a tree or kitten or observing a moth. Then ask the children to draw a picture. Identify how this experience influenced the drawings.

G. Obtain samples of drawings from children in grades one through five. Separate them by grade level. Using the stages presented in the "This One's For You!" box, discuss how each sample fits (or doesn't fit) the general characteristics of that grade level/stage.

H. Collect samples of drawings from one grade level only (grades one through five). Sort them according to how they represent the grade level stage. For example, sort them out by grouping the samples most near the characteristics of the grade level stage down through those with the least characteristics of the grade level stage. Discuss the ranges of abilities represented in these samples. Share your ideas about how you would work with each of the children whose samples you have in your collection.

I. Observe a child who is making his or her first representational symbols. Keep a verbatim record of his or her comments for several different 15-minute periods. What relationship is there between the child's verbal and graphic expression?

J. From a collection of paintings by five-year-olds, list the objects that are painted with a visually established color–object relationship. List those objects that are painted with no visually established color–object relationship. What might cause some of these color choices?

K. Collect drawings of a human figure done by a second-grade class. Find how many different symbols are used for nose, mouth, body, arms, and so forth. What percentage of these children is using geometric shapes for their expression? Compare with drawings done by third graders to see if the percentages change.

L. Keep a list of the different reasons for exaggerations, omissions, or neglect of parts as shown in drawings. Illustrate each from examples of children's work.

M. Plan an art lesson that includes drawing people. Carry it out with kindergarten, second-grade, and fourth-grade children. Use the same art materials and paper size for all classes. Compare the finished products and note the differences in developmental levels.

Activities for Children

A. Display prints of famous artworks. Examples: Mondrian's *Composition with Red, Blue, and Yellow,* Pollock's *Detail of One (#31, 1950),* and Van Gogh's *Cypress Trees.* See if these examples affect the children's choice of colors, type of figures made, and amount of detail in their pictures.

B. Play music during part of the art period. Compare the drawings made with music to those done without music.

Some Variations on Easel Painting

- Use a number of shades of one color.
- Use colored paper—colored newsprint comes in pastel shades, or the backs of faded construction paper can be used.
- Use the same color of paint with same color paper.
- Use black and white paint.
- Use various sizes of brushes, or both flat and floppy ones, with the same colors of paint.

- Paint objects the children have made in carpentry, or paint dried clay objects.
- Paint large refrigerator-type boxes.
- Work on a long piece of paper to produce murals.
- Paint the fence with water and large brushes.
- Draw firmly on paper with crayons, and paint over it to produce "crayon resist" art.
- Use all pastel colors. Start with white and mix in color a bit at a time.
- Set up a table with many colors of paint and encourage children to select the colors they prefer.

Cracked Paint and Crayon Drawings

Have children draw with crayons an image or design on a piece of paper. Crumple up the picture, but don't tear it. Have them smooth out the drawings and brush over them with watery tempera paint. The paint will go into all the little cracks in the paper. After it dries, have children brush a coat of thinned white glue onto the drawing. This gives it a shiny effect.

Painting with Soft Objects

Have children dip a cotton ball in a shallow dish of wet paint and then smear it or squish it on paper or another surface. Also have them try dipping a cotton ball into dry powdered paint and rubbing it across dry paper. This creates an interesting soft effect.

Cotton Swab Painting

Have children dip cotton swabs into paint and use them as brushes.

Button Printing

Glue buttons onto small wooden dowels for children to use in printing. Vary the sizes, shapes, and designs of buttons.

Sponge Painting

Cut sponges into different shapes. Have children dip each shape in paint and then dab, press, or rub it on paper.

Paper Towel Painting

Have children wad a paper towel into a ball, dip it in paint, and dab, press, or rub it on paper.

Crayon Surfaces

Try a variety of surfaces for crayon drawings. Children may enjoy drawing with crayons on these surfaces for variety:

fabric	sticks and stones
egg cartons	spools and clothespins
paper towel rolls	cardboard
sandpaper	Styrofoam trays
wood scraps	

Finger Painting with Ice Cubes

For this variation of finger painting, use regular finger paint and glossy paper, but do not wet the paper as you normally would to prepare for finger painting. Give each child an ice cube with which to spread and dilute the paint while making designs on the paper.

Printing

A. Toy Prints

Have children dip the wheels of an old toy car, truck, or other toy in paint and then make tracks on paper.

B. Plastic Alphabet Letters and Numbers

Have children dip plastic alphabet letters and numbers in paint and print them on paper.

C. Paper Cup Printing

Have children dip the rim of a paper cup into paint and then press the rim on a piece of paper to make a design.

D. Comb Printing

Have children dip the teeth of a comb into paint and print with it by drawing it along a sheet of paper.

E. Printing With Clay

Have children pound clay into small, flat cakes about an inch thick. Then they may want to carve a design on the flat surface with a pencil or popsicle stick. If desired, the design is either brushed with paint or dipped in paint and pressed onto paper to print the design.

Fabric Painting

Wrap small pieces of burlap, nylon netting, or other textured fabrics (2½ to 3 inches square) over a sponge that has been attached to a clothespin or secured to a dowel with a piece of string or elastic. Have children dip the fabric into paint and press onto a surface.

Pinecone Printing

Roll whole or pieces of pinecones in paint. Children can dip the large ones with flat bottoms into paint and print images and designs.

Combination Painting

Thicken tempera paint with liquid starch. Divide the paint into individual portions. Have children use this paint in their paintings. While the paint is still wet, children can sprinkle the painting with any of the following for attractive combination paintings: salt, coffee grounds, eggshells, glitter, tiny Styrofoam balls, seeds, cornmeal, sequins, tiny beads. The media dry in the paint for interesting effects.

Ideas to Encourage Drawing

Try some of the following ideas to encourage children in kindergarten to grade three to use their imagination in expressing their observations through drawing.

- Draw a picture of something that can't be seen.
- Draw as many animals as you can on one page.
- Draw a map for a brain surgeon or for a heart surgeon.
- Design a special machine or device to help the President.
- Draw a picture showing how you would improve human beings.
- Draw a picture of an angry sea or a noisy city.
- Draw a picture that shows how you would make your school a better place.
- Draw a picture that shows how you would weigh an elephant.
- Design an underground city or an underwater city.
- Design a dog-exercising machine.

Drawing for Break Time

When you have several minutes to pass, encourage children to draw some of the following.

- their shoe
- their lunch
- the teacher
- a friend
- their hand holding something
- a small object big
- a car
- a dream
- a nightmare
- a leaf
- themselves

Activities for Older Children (Grades 4–5)

Scribble Art

Have each child make a scribble line on a piece of paper. The child then passes the paper to another child on the left. The child receiving the scribble is challenged to turn the scribble into an image or a design. Challenge the children to be as creative as they can be in transforming the scribbles.

Variation on a Scribble

Give each student a 6- to 8-inch-long piece of string or yarn, glue, and a piece of paper. Students glue the string or yarn into a scribble-type shape. Students pass their paper to the person sitting to their left.

Students take this piece of paper and imagine what the string brings to mind. Students use markers or crayons to create something original from the string. Have students discuss what they saw and why it became what it did.

Direction Drawing

The purpose of this activity is to help children see how, following just one set of directions, everyone will come up with his or her own unique works of abstract art. There are two basic steps in this activity: (1) teacher calls out directions for the children, and (2) children draw what they hear.

Here are some ideas on directions to call out for this activity. Of course, you can make up your own.

- Draw five circles—any size—anywhere on your paper.
- Draw four straight lines from one edge of your paper to the other.
- Draw two more straight lines from one edge of your paper to the other, only this time make the lines cross over the lines you have already drawn.
- Draw two curved lines beginning at the edge of the paper and ending up somewhere in the middle of the paper.
- Fill in three of the five circles.
- Fill in four areas of your paper however you would like.

Once the drawings are complete, have students sign their work. Display the work in the classroom. Discuss how the drawings look the same. Discuss how they are different.

Come up with more directions and try the activity again. You will be amazed at the unique qualities of all of the drawings.

Line Shape and Space: Maps from the Air

Discuss students' experiences in seeing actual or televised views of Earth from high in the sky. Have students describe any differences between extremely high views (many weather reports have satellite views) and views closer to the ground (hot air balloon or low-flying aircraft).

You may want to explain that some artists are fascinated with map-like views of Earth. They have created original artworks to suggest the special arrangements of lines and shapes that people cannot see from the ground. Good examples of artwork to use for this are Clause Herbert Breeze's *Canadian Atlas: Position of London,* Judith Wittlin's *Cincinnati,* or *Late Evening Traffic* by Yvonne Jacquette.

If you can't obtain artwork prints, have a city map available to show the grid-like structures common to many cities and rural areas where the land is flat. From the air, and on maps, you can see graceful curves made by freeways. Point out the differences between an actual map and the paintings. (A map is more complex and has labels.)

Discuss the similarities and differences between the simple map and a painting. Guide students to see how the organic lines and shapes—those with complex, irregular curves—are related to natural forms such as the rivers, borders of an island, and surrounding land. Have students identify geometric lines and shapes that suggest the human-made environment (grid lines, long lines that might be highways) in the maps.

Bring in old maps that can be cut apart and used for artwork. Have students work in small groups to identify sections of the maps where interesting organic or geometric lines and shapes occur. Ask students to offer explanations for these designs in relation to concepts from this lesson. Then have students change the map into an abstract design by adding crayon or oil pastels or by cutting along lines and creating new shapes. Compare and contrast the results.

Skeletons

Artists learn to see and sketch things in two ways. One way is to look for geometric shapes. The other is to look for lines that show the skeleton or hidden structure of an object. Bare trees in winter are perfect to study as skeletons for shape and drawing activities.

Take a few trips outside with sketchbooks and observe the barren trees for shapes and designs. Remind children to look at them as if they were skeletons. This shape is hidden when the leaves are on the tree. Help students find geometric shapes in these skeletons. Use words like *circle, oval,* and *ellipse* to describe shapes of trees. Encourage children to sketch what they see. Discuss any geometric shapes they see in terms of how the shapes all combine into one design—the tree itself.

Light Sources

Set up an environment with a light source and several geometric forms. Have students develop some experiments that will allow them to move the light source or the forms a measured distance from each other. Have them observe and draw the changes in the length and the shapes of the shadows cast when they move the light source or the objects.

Awareness in Nature

Ask students to look for examples of unusual shapes and colors in the environment (sunsets, changing colors and shapes of clouds, puddles of water with reflections). Have students use the wet-into-wet technique (painting on a wet piece of paper) to create paintings of the sky with soft, fuzzy clouds of different shapes. Note possibilities for pictures of stormy skies, sunsets, etc.

Integrated Art Activity: Science/Independent Research

Have students look through science books for illustrations of linear structures (snowflakes, bones, blood circulation, plants, geological formations, and the like). Have them select a small section of one of the illustrations and draw a similar structure on a large sheet of paper. After they have completed the drawing, have them use dark colors of crayons or oil pastels to increase the width of lines, making an abstract design. Shapes between the lines might be colored as well. Display the work and discuss relationships between the "artistic structure" and the structure shown in the scientific illustration.

Integrated Art Activity: Language Arts/Aesthetic Awareness

Explore the connotations of phrases such as "the blues," "I'm feeling blue," "green with envy," and the like. Ask students to give additional examples of the use of color-related words to describe moods or feelings. Write the phrases on the chalkboard, in two columns, so students can compare and contrast phrases for warm colors and cool colors. Have the students select one of these phrases and create an artwork that uses the phrases as a title and is dominated by variations on the color in the title.

Integrated Art Activity: Language Arts/Art Criticism

Ask students to speculate on reasons why many artists like to create paintings that portray flowers in vases. There are many reasons. Flowers in general are symbols of a cycle of life. Cut flowers are often symbolically related to the concept of enjoying moments of beauty. The colors, lines, textures, and other qualities provide a challenge for artists to interpret. The paintings are also enjoyed by many people, especially in homes where the image of a vase of flowers can add a feeling of warmth or happiness. You might want to display prints of flower paintings, such as Van Gogh's *Sunflowers* or any of Georgia O'Keeffe's flower paintings during this discussion. Provide students an opportunity to create their own flower paintings.

Aesthetic Awareness

Have students cut out, from old magazines or newspapers, some black-and-white photographs. Provide them with viewfinders. (See telescope activity in Chapter 10). Have them place the viewfinder over the photograph and look for the darkest area of the photograph. Show them how to trace around the edges of the hole of the viewfinder to mark the place on the photograph, then cut out and save the piece. Have them continue to identify and cut out four or five other pieces that differ from each other in value. Have students arrange the pieces in a light to dark sequence. Ask pairs of students to check each other's arrangements.

On the Web

Take your students to the interactive art site http://www.youdraw.com. Here they can create pictures on the Draw Pad, and even submit these drawings to be posted on the website.

Chapter Review

1. Describe a young child in the scribble stage in the following areas:

   a. age
   b. degree of motor control
   c. reason for scribbling

2. List three basic forms that a child in the basic forms stage may be able to draw.
3. Describe a schema.
4. Give four examples of symbols.
5. Discuss the importance of children naming their pictures.
6. Define the term *two-dimensional media* and give an example of a two-dimensional process.
7. List the materials that are right for children in the scribble stage and basic forms stage.

   a. For the scribble stage, what are the best (a) crayon size and type and (b) paper size and type?
   b. For the basic forms stage, what are the best (a) tools for drawing and (b) paper size and type?

8. Give an example of an early and a later combination of basic forms.
9. In the following, decide which period of the pictorial stage best shows each listed characteristic.

PERIOD	CHARACTERISTICS OF DRAWING
1. early pictorial stage 2. later pictorial stage	a. few, unrelated figures b. greater degree and amount of detail c. narrative or story drawings d. greater size to show importance e. larger head size for figures

10. Choose the answer that best completes these statements about the basic forms stage:

    a. The child with good motor control
       i. drops the crayon often.
       ii. uses a clenched grip.
       iii. uses more hand than arm movement.
    b. An early type of basic form is
       i. well drawn.
       ii. a less clear form.
       iii. combined to make a symbol.
    c. In the later period of basic forms, a child
       i. cannot draw good basic forms.
       ii. easily draws clear forms.
       iii. fills the page with practice forms.

11. Describe a child in the gang stage of art development.

References

Cox-Bishop, M. (2005). *The pictorial world of the child.* New York: Cambridge University Press.

Harris, M. E. (2009). Implementing portfolio assessment. *Young Children, 64*(3), 82–85.

Herbert Read, Read, H. (1966). *Education Through Art.* New York, NY: Pantheon Books.

Johnson, D. Folio Back Page, February 6, 1998. Online: http://www.ualberta.ca/~publicas/folio/35/11/10.htm

Kellogg, R. (1970). *Analyzing children's art.* Palo Alto, CA: National Press Books.

Kellogg, R., & O'Dell, S. (1967). *The psychology of children's art.* New York, NY: CRM, Inc.

Lowenfeld, V. (1975). *Creative and mental growth of the child* (6th ed.). New York, NY: Macmillan.

Lowenfeld, V. (1987). *Creative and mental growth of the child* (8th ed.). New York, NY: Macmillan.

Additional Readings

Colley, A., & Mulhern, G. (2009). Exploring children's stereotypes through drawings: The case of musical performance. *Social Development, 18*(2), 464–477.

Deaver, S. P. (2009). A normative study of children's drawings: Preliminary research findings. *Art Therapy: Journal of the American Art Therapy Association, 26*(1), 4–11.

Einarsdottir, J., Dockett, S., & Perry, B. (2009). Making meaning: Children's perspectives expressed through drawing. *Early Child Development and Care, 179*(2), 217–232.

Foks-Appelman, T. (2007). *Draw me a picture: The meaning of children's drawings and play from the perspective of analytical psychology.* Los Angeles, CA: BookSurge.

Garner, S. (2008). *Writing on drawing: Essays on drawing practice and research.* Bristol, UK: Intellect Ltd.

Griffiths, F. (2009). *Supporting children's communications and creativity through music, dance, drama, and art.* Abington, UK: David Fulton.

Hogge, J. E. (2008). *The butterfly's gift.* New York, NY: AuthorHouse.

House, N. Using critiques in the K–12 classroom. *Art Education, 61*(3), 48–51.

Jolley, R. P. (2009). *Children and pictures: Drawing and understanding (Understanding children's worlds).* Hoboken, NJ: Wiley-Blackwell.

Lange-Kattner, C. (2009). Habitual size and projective size: The logic of spatial systems in children's drawings. *Developmental Psychology, 45*(4), 913–927.

McNiff, S. (2009). *Art-based research.* Philadelphia, PA: Jessica Kingsley.

Milbrath, C., & Lightfoot, C. (2009). *Art and human development.* New York, NY: Psychology Press.

Moriarty, M. V. (2009). Evaluating children's use of symbol in some recent research. *International Journal of Children's Spirituality, 14*(1), 47–61.

Rubin, J. (2009). *Art therapy: An introduction.* Abingdon, UK: Routledge.

Swann, A. C. (2009). An intriguing link between drawing and play with toys. *Childhood Education, 85*(4), 230–236.

Helpful Websites

Child's Developmental Benchmarks and Stages: A Summary Guide to Appropriate Arts Activities, http://www.naeyc.org/files/yc/file/200407/ ArtsEducationPartnership.pdf
Presented by NAEYC, this site lists ages, stages, examples of what children do during stages, samples of appropriate art experiences, and what children and adults can do together in the arts.

Creativity Portal, http://www.creativity-portal.com
Click on "Newsletter," and go to February 2004 for an article on "Developmental Stages in Art."

Fresno Family, http://www.fresnofamily.com/
Click on "Parenting Articles," then on "Miscellaneous Articles," and then on "Developmental Stages of Art."

International Collection of Child Art, http://www. library.ilstu.edu/icca/
Illinois State University site contains exhibits on children's art in Japan, Jamaica, Mexico, USA, and Russia.

scribbleskidsart.com, http://www.scribbleskidsart. com
Click on "Articles" under the "References" icon.

The Web Archive of Children's Art, http://childart. indstate.edu/
This Web-accessed database presented by the Indiana State University Art Department contains digitally copied artwork by children. Each work is referenced by gender, school type, media, and subject matter.

For additional creative activity resources, visit our website at www.Cengage.com/login.

The Early Childhood Art Program

REFLECTIVE QUESTIONS

After studying this section, you should be able to answer the following questions.

1. How do my classroom art activities reflect the emphasis of process over product?

2. When I set up art activities for young children, what activities and materials do I plan to use for each different age and developmental level present in the group?

3. How do I avoid falling into a routine when planning, setting up, and using art activities with young children?

4. Am I keeping the early childhood program basic goals in mind as I plan lessons and activities?

5. Am I planning developmentally appropriate two- and three-dimensional art activities for all of the children in my group?

6. How are children using the two- and three-dimensional materials I have provided for them? Do they appear motivated and involved in exploring them?

7. How can I improve the appeal as well as range of two- and three-dimensional activities I currently use with young children?

8. What skills do the young children in my group already possess with regard to two- and three-dimensional media? Have I planned lessons and activities to match these skills?

9. What instructional strategies are best for young children's learning and enjoyment with two- and three-dimensional media?

10. How will I modify my lessons and activities as children become more proficient in their use of art materials?

11. Have I considered children with special needs in my lesson planning?

Program Basics: Goals, Setting Up, Materials, and Strategies

OBJECTIVES

After studying this chapter, you should be able to:

1. Discuss goals for the early childhood art program.

2. Describe the basic setup for the early childhood art program.

3. List and discuss the basic materials and equipment used in the early childhood art program.

Art experiences are an essential part of the early childhood curriculum. Yet creative experiences do not just happen. They are the result of careful planning. This chapter covers three major areas of concern in planning for children's creative art experiences: (1) program goals, (2) setting up for art activities, and (3) using basic art materials and equipment.

Basic Goals of the Early Childhood Art Program

The early childhood art program provides the time and place for children to express thoughts, ideas, feelings, actions, and abilities in a variety of media and activities. In the art program, children are free to actively participate in exploring art ideas and materials, discovering all the wonderful possibilities they provide. This exploration and discovery, as we learned in chapter 5, is provided by a developmentally appropriate curriculum for young children. In addition, all the principles of DAP are applicable to the early childhood art program as well as to all other parts of the curriculum.

Just as in the early childhood profession in general, there are national standards in the arts. National standards in the arts (dance, music, theater, and visual arts) were developed (National Standards for Arts Education, 1994) by experts in education and in the arts to provide a guide and resource to states and school districts that want to develop their own standards. These national standards describe what a child with a complete, sequential education in the arts from K–12 should know and be able to do at various grade levels in each artistic discipline. They are divided into three main groups: K–4, 5–8, and 9–12. Most states have standards based on the national standards in place for arts education, and other states are in the process of developing them. State-by-state summaries of art education standards are available at the

Kennedy Center Arts Edge (http://artsedge.kennedy-center.org/teach/standards.cfm). You can also access a full text of the national standard at this site. Most state standards are for dance, music, theater, and visual art and for grades K–12, but this varies from state to state and district to district.

Process, Not Product

Art programs provide young children many opportunities to work with a variety of materials and techniques to express themselves creatively.

The first and main goal in all art experiences is **process over product**, It is in the process that the child expresses experiences and feelings. The expression of one's *self* is what is important here, not what the finished product looks like. Lowenfeld and Brittain express the importance of a child's creating through art in this way:

> Art is not the same for a child as it is for an adult. For a child, art is primarily a means of expression. No two children are alike, and in fact, each child differs even from his earlier self as he constantly grows, perceives, understands, and interprets his environment. A child is a dynamic being; art becomes for him a language of thought (Lowenfeld & Brittain, p. 7, 1987).

Another reason that it is better to emphasize the process of art in early childhood programs is that young children are not yet skillful users of materials. Much of their creative effort is expended in the manipulative experience of trying materials out and becoming acquainted with them. Also, young children are more interested in *doing* than in *producing* and rarely, if ever, have a planned product in mind when they take up their paintbrushes or select collage materials. This sort of advance planning belongs to children on the verge of kindergarten age. Older children in middle and upper elementary levels will be more purposeful in their creative activities. However, this does not change the fact that the main objective of their artistic endeavors is self-expression.

Children take paints, bits of cloth, clay, wood, and stone and put them together into products that express their own ideas. In the art program, emphasis

FIGURE 12-1 • For children to work creatively in art, materials must be readily available for their use.

must be on continued satisfying experiences with many kinds of materials and a continued involvement in the process of making. Creative activities provide opportunities for self-expression by allowing children to construct something that is uniquely their own.

Needs of the Children

A second major objective of the art program is to meet the needs of children. This means that the program must be designed for their age, ability, and interest levels. Thus, a program for three-year-olds is set up to have the right materials and activities for a group with a limited interest span and limited motor control. It has materials and activities that interest them and that they can use without a lot of adult help. Two-year-olds are at the point of learning how to tear and paste and do not require scissors, whereas three- and four-year-olds are able to use scissors independently. The same applies to art activities for four-, five-, and six-year-old children. In a mixed age group, the program must be set up with a variety of materials and activities available to all children in the group. For middle and upper elementary students who are beginning to create more complex works of art, there needs to be an increased supply of materials and equipment for creative expression. The teacher's job at this level is to maximize students' use of these resources as they continue to develop their imaginations in art experiences.

Another way a teacher meets the individual needs of children is to provide art materials appropriate to the multiple intelligences of the children in the group. (See Chapter 5 for more information about multiple intelligences.)

Originality and Independence

A third important objective of the early childhood art program is to give each child the chance to think originally and to learn to work independently. In creating art, a child can use and explore all kinds of materials. This encourages original, divergent thought. Also, giving children materials that they can control at their physical level encourages independent work. Materials that appeal to a child's multiple intelligences encourage exploration. For example, providing a child who is logic smart blocks and clay encourages this child to create models and structures, which are a natural expression of his or her logical/mathematical skills. These two attributes—originality and ability to work on their own—are basic to children's creativity.

With older children, you can expect and plan for a higher degree of independence in use of materials. With ready access to a variety of materials, if allowed, children are able to be self-directed and choose the materials they need to express ideas. At this level, instead of relying on the teacher to pass out supplies and lead a lesson, self-directed, independent children are able to gather their own materials for creative work.

Most important of all, in order to encourage a child's originality and independence, be sure that you avoid using "creative fakes" with young children. These are the "cute" ideas that masquerade as creative activities. Examples of these are ditto sheets, craft kit projects, worksheets or any activity that results in identical products from each child. Another important routine to avoid is showing children an example or model of a previously made article before starting an activity. This practice limits and may even stifle a child's creativity. Viewing such a sample, the child may think, "This is what my teacher likes. I need to make something just like it."

Creative Thinking

Another goal in the early childhood art program is for children to be creative thinkers. Creative children work freely and flexibly. They attack each problem without fear of failure. Children in an art program that is right for their developmental level are able to work creatively, freely, and flexibly. They can handle the material in the setting, which helps them feel confident about their abilities. If children do not feel secure, safe, and comfortable with themselves, the teacher, and the other children, they will not be able to take the risk or meet the challenge involved in producing art.

As we have learned, all children have multiple intelligences or ways of learning. These individual learning styles will influence how each child will work in art activities. See Figure 12–2 for a summary of these learning styles and appropriate art activities for each style.

Individualized Progress

Finally, the art program must allow children to grow at their own speed. Activities may be planned to stimulate children, but true growth comes only at their own pace. Just as children learn to walk on their own, they learn to paint by painting in their own way.

In the art program, young children are given time to grow, explore, and experiment with materials at their own pace. Two- and three-year-olds, barely out of the sensorimotor stage of development, are respected for being two or three. These young children are expected to explore materials; to enjoy feeling, tasting, and playing with crayons; to scribble and mess around; to find out how paint feels on their hands and faces; and to experiment with soft clay. Children are not hurried or pressured into representing their ideas or feelings through art; similarly, they are not expected to be interested in a product, much less to produce one.

Children who have had the opportunity and time to explore and experiment with materials as toddlers are ready at three, four, or five to find out how they can gain control over the materials and use them to express themselves. In turn, preschoolers who have had the time and freedom to develop their art ability will enjoy using these skills to express themselves visually in a wide variety of media.

Individual growth rate must also be a consideration when working with children with special needs. Figure 12–4 summarizes the ways a teacher can respond to students' special needs in art activities.

A STUDENT WHO IS . . .	WILL ENJOY ART PROJECTS THAT . . .	AND WILL ENJOY HELPING OUT IN THE CLASSROOM BY . . .
Person Smart *The Socializer* • interactive • communicative • group-oriented • extroverted	• are group projects • require giving/receiving feedback • require group leaders	• distributing and collecting materials • mediating
Self Smart *The Individual* • individualistic • solitary • self-reflective • introverted	• are individual projects • focus on feelings, dreams, or self are goal-oriented	• arranging items in storage spaces • assisting teacher before or after class
Body Smart *The Mover* • physically active • hands-on • talkative	• involve physical motion such as dancing or acting • involve touching various objects, materials, and textures	• running errands • role-playing safety rules • distributing and collecting materials
Word Smart *The Word Player* • oriented toward language, words, reading, and writing	• involve spoken or written words • involve storytelling	• reading instructions aloud • labeling storage spaces • creating "rules" posters
Logic Smart *The Questioner* • inquisitive • experimental • oriented toward numbers, patterns, and relationships	• involve patterns, relationships, or symbols • require problem solving	• arranging or classifying materials for distribution • helping solve problems
Picture Smart *The Visualizer* • imaginative • creative • oriented toward colors, pictures	• involve colors and designs • involve painting, drawing, or sculpture • require active imagination	• creating displays of artworks • designing charts and posters
Music Smart *The Music Lover* • oriented toward music, rhythmic sounds, and environmental sounds	• involve rhythmic patterns, singing, humming, responding to music, keeping time, or listening for sounds	• thinking of cleanup songs • thinking of safety songs • creating displays about music or musicians

FIGURE 12-2 • Learning styles and art activities (Gardner, 1993, 1999). *(Continued)*

A STUDENT WHO IS . . .	WILL ENJOY ART PROJECTS THAT . . .	AND WILL ENJOY HELPING OUT IN THE CLASSROOM BY . . .
Nature Smart *The Outdoors Lover* • interested in the outdoors • oriented toward animals, insects, and nature in general	• involve collecting objects of nature • involve observing and recording weather • involve identifying plants and insects • involve tree rubbings • involve creating his or her own animal or insect	• working in the garden • caring for classroom pets and aquarium • arranging collections of natural objects
Acquiring English	• require limited word usage • involve terminology from their first language • involve simple name/word games	• creating labels and posters in their first language • creating images or icons for bulletin boards • sharing elements of their culture with other students

FIGURE 12-2 • Learning styles and art activities (Gardner, 1993, 1999). *(Continued)*

Respecting each child's rate of growth helps her or him feel good about herself or himself. Children who feel good about themselves will be successful in the art program and in other learning situations.

Setting Up for Art Activities

Physical Environment and Space. Whether setting up an art center or an entire room for art experiences, there are certain basic guidelines for arranging the environment. The age of the group will always be the major consideration in planning, as each age group has varying abilities and interests requiring different arrangements. Specific requirements for different age groups are covered in Chapter 6. At this point, our discussion covers basic guidelines that cross age levels. The following are considerations that are basic to setting up art activities.

General considerations. The art area should be arranged for ease in cleaning up and dispensing materials. One type of arrangement that works well is to separate wet from dry materials. For example, clay and paint centers can be placed near the room's water source.

To work creatively with art materials, children need to be free from constraints and worry related to keeping themselves and their work spaces clean. Children will need smocks to protect clothing, supplies for covering work surfaces, and tools for cleaning. Men's shirts with the arms cut off make good smocks, or children can wear an old set of clothes for art activities. These "art clothes" will be like an art journal: the various spots and splashes on them are reminders of past art projects! Children will also need to know where to place work in progress for safekeeping and where wet items can be left to dry. Providing these arrangements is part of the teacher's responsibility as a guide and facilitator.

Sharp materials such as scissors must be placed out of reach of children who have not yet mastered handling them independently and safely. Usually such materials are dispensed from a teacher-height counter placed in a location convenient to children's work tables. Easels are placed out of the way of traffic so that children can work without being jostled. Next to the easels are places for children to hang paint smocks and a rack to drape paintings to dry. The rack where children's paintings are hung is situated so that the children do not have to carry their wet paintings through areas where other children are working to hang them.

Drying racks are convenient to have in early childhood classrooms. However, the commercial type can be expensive. An inexpensive substitute can be assembled in the same manner as a bookshelf. Cardboard is placed on top of four brick or block supports (one in each corner). Several layers are built so paintings

FIGURE 12-3 • Have enough materials so children can continue with their work uninterrupted.

can be left on the shelves for drying. Two other methods for drying paintings are (1) hanging paintings on a clothesline suspended above the head of the tallest adult and (2) using a portable, folding clothes-drying rack. However, paintings can drip in both of these methods. Windowsills can also be used, especially for drying three-dimensional artwork.

Masonite boards cut in 10-inch squares are convenient for transporting wet or unfinished clay work and assemblages to a place where they can dry. Children can work directly on the boards when they start their modeling and construction. These boards can frequently be obtained from scrap piles at a lumberyard or purchased inexpensively. Foam core board or heavy corrugated cardboard can also be used. To enlarge table surfaces for drying artwork, cover the tabletop with large pieces of cardboard. You can find these at warehouse-type stores where they are used to hold large lots of merchandise on pallets. They are generally discarded every day and are available for the asking.

A place for children to wash after using wet materials must also be nearby. If you don't have the convenience of a sink in your room, a plastic kitchen tub half filled with water and placed on a low stand next to the paper towels and wastebasket works well. Include a bucket of small sponges near the art area. They are easy for children to use and can be rinsed and used again.

Set up art materials so that children have daily art experiences. The teacher should make sure every day that there are designated places, equipment, and materials for art experiences. For example, every day the teacher should prepare easels with paper and paints for children's use. This way, activity proceeds smoothly in the easel area and the teacher is free to manage the rest of the classroom.

Have a supply of paper, crayons, pencils, and clay available in a set place every day for children's use. Tearing, cutting, and pasting supplies should be ready and easily available, too. (Specific suggestions about supplies and their care are provided later in this chapter.) As part of this preparation, the teacher guides the children in learning the necessary use and care of all equipment as it is set up.

Being prepared in all these ways ensures that children will have the supplies they need, will know where to get them, and will know how to use them—which encourages them to pursue independent, creative activities on a daily basis.

Set up for weekly art activities. To enhance children's creative experiences, the teacher plans for and sets up weekly art activities in addition to the children's daily experiences. For example, a teacher might plan a unit on printing (see Chapter 13 for more information about printing), using each week to introduce a specific technique of printing. This, of course, would be in addition to and not in place of children's regular art experiences. The teacher plans in advance to set up a table or other area with printing supplies and equipment. Scurrying around for "things to print with" at the last minute can be avoided in this planned weekly approach.

Work of the previous week is evaluated before new plans are prepared. Even though plans have been carefully thought through, a teacher must be prepared to make changes resulting from unexpected events. For example, a sudden snowstorm extends the amount of time the children will play outdoors. Or one morning the road outside the building is being repaired and huge machines appear on the street. The wise teacher recognizes this event as a good learning experience and arranges time for children to observe the workers.

In weekly plans, teachers plan for a balance between the familiar and the new as they make decisions about

CHILDREN WITH SPECIAL NEEDS

All students benefit from a balanced program of creative work in two- and three-dimensional media and from the opportunity to try out different approaches to art. It is essential for you to encourage original thinking and authentically creative work for all children with special needs.

Creativity is one of the most important considerations as you conduct art activities and adapt instruction to meet the needs of individual students and groups who have special needs. Artwork that is traced, copied from adult art, or based on ditto patterns does not involve the student in significant creative activity and should not be encouraged.

Talent plays a role in students' interest and skill in art, just as it does in other subjects. During the elementary and middle school years, encourage varieties of artistic accomplishment and understanding, not just skill in representational drawing. It is unwise to identify a few students as "class artists" or to compare students' artwork in a manner that discourages further interest. Always respect each student's unique effort and insights about art.

Students with visual impairments can participant in discussions about artwork, especially with regard to themes portrayed in art that are related to the student's own experience. In art activities, provide materials to create tactile, kinesthetic artwork—clay, textured paper, cloth, small boxes, or wood blocks that student can arrange.

Students with speech and hearing impairments respond slowly to verbal communication. Use nonverbal communication: Have students point out what they see or use pantomime to express responses. Present information through diagrams, charts, and other visual aids. Nonverbal communication can be valuable for all students.

Students who have impaired mobility may need to use alternate tools and materials for some activities. Rehabilitation specialists may help you solve unique problems. A number of special tools are available for students with physical impairments (scissors, a mouthpiece that holds a pencil or brush).

Students who are mentally challenged have difficulty grasping complex ideas in art and other subjects. Even so, they often respond to art in a direct and insightful manner. They are often able to portray their ideas or feelings more successfully through art than through words. Simplify and separate into specific steps any more difficult activities. Encourage independent thinking about the ideas to be expressed.

Students who do not speak English benefit from many of the same nonverbal teaching strategies already noted. Introduce the whole class to the arts and culture of the students. This will broaden the art background of all the students and help them communicate with each other.

Respect other cultural differences. An important aspect of art is learning about the arts of cultural groups. Identify individuals and groups in your community who can help familiarize students with unique cultural traditions in the arts and crafts.

All students can benefit from learning about these examples of "living cultures" within their own community.

FIGURE 12-4 • Responding to students' special needs.

how materials and equipment are to be used. Teachers need not be concerned that children may lose interest if the same activities are offered week after week. If children have freedom to use materials in their own ways, they do not tire of working with the same ones. After children have gained success in using a material, they enjoy repeating the experience.

Because some activities require more supervision than others, a teacher needs to consider how many activities will be available for a given period. The number of activities chosen that require close supervision depends on the number of adults assigned to the room. After a teacher has made careful observations and has decided upon the activities for the week, he or she must think through what would be the best use of his or her time—for example, whether to give special attention to the block area or to the art area. If a new material or technique is being introduced, it generally requires teacher supervision. In this case, the teacher usually sits with a small group and participates in the

FIGURE 12-5 • If all materials are easily available, it is possible for young children to become deeply involved in their work.

activity with them. Unless there are several teachers in a room, it is unlikely there would be more than one group activity requiring close supervision.

In weekly and monthly planning, consideration must be given to the time of the year and to the developmental levels of the children. At the beginning of a school year, too many choices and too much open space may be upsetting to children because they are not yet familiar with the room or the school. At a time when a teacher's goal is to help children feel comfortable in the school, too many new and exciting materials can be overwhelming and distracting. The same is true for older children at the beginning of a new school year. Children will feel more comfortable as the year begins by using media and equipment they have become familiar with the previous school year. Therefore, materials offered at the beginning of the year should be those that are familiar to most children. For example, even a very shy child can feel secure at a table with crayons and paper. As children begin to know each other, feel more comfortable in the room, and become aware of the daily

routines, additional materials can be introduced and activities can be expanded.

Set up the art area so that it facilitates children's creative experiences. While specific materials and their use are discussed individually later in this chapter, there are some general ideas that apply to the use of materials by young children.

Children work better in a predictable, organized environment where art materials can always be found in the same place. For example, art materials on open storage shelves at child level make it possible for children to find the materials they want to use easily and independently. Also, when materials such as paper or paste are spaced far apart on shelves, putting things back in place becomes an easier task for young children. Using placemats or trays on child-size tables helps organize space into individual work areas.

Art activities in the early childhood program work best on child-level tables and easels. Although some children may occasionally enjoy working on the floor, it is important to have a table set up for regular art activities. It is a good idea to have a limit on the number of children for each art activity/area to ensure the proper space for children as well as sufficient materials for each child. See the Professional Enhancement Text and the Online Companion as well as the websites listed at the end of this chapter for lesson plan forms to use in planning creative activities.

Setting Up for Art Activities– Specific Ages

Ages

In addition to the general considerations discussed earlier, there are some specific, age-related considerations for setting up art activities for young children.

Planning Art Activities for Toddlers

Very young children benefit from a program divided into well-defined areas in which they have freedom to move, explore, and make decisions about activities and materials. However, when planning for this age range, special considerations must be kept in mind. **Toddler-appropriate art activities** and those for young two-year olds toddlers must involve sturdy materials that do not include tiny pieces that might be swallowed.

Put only a few materials out at a time so that young children are not overwhelmed with too many choices. Materials should be rotated often, and children should

THIS ONE'S for YOU!   Teacher Tips

The way a teacher sets up her or his own materials, supplies, and space can make or break the child's and teacher's successful experiences in art. The following are some suggestions for arranging supplies for art experiences as well as for displaying children's artwork.

- Scissors holders can be made from gallon milk or bleach containers. Simply punch holes in the container and place scissors in holes with the points to the inside. Egg cartons turned upside down with slits in each mound also make excellent scissors holders.

- Paint containers can range from muffin tins and Styrofoam egg cartons to plastic soft drink cartons with yogurt containers in them. These work well outdoors as well as indoors because they are large and not easily tipped over. Place one brush in each container; this prevents colors from getting mixed and makes cleanup easier.

- A great tool for organizing craft supplies is a large metal popcorn tin (the ones that are popular around the holidays). Fill the tin with paper towel tubes. Use the tin for sorting pipe cleaners and paper strips, placing different colors in each tube. You will save time finding the right colors and checking what colors are running low.

- Keep pencils from falling on the floor with Velcro. Attach a one-inch strip of Velcro (the rough side) to the corner of each desk. Then attach a strip of the soft side of the Velcro to a pencil, just under the eraser. In addition to keeping the pencils handy, it keeps them from being sharpened down too much. This helps make pencil stumps a thing of the past.

- When markers have dried out, pour ½ inch of nail polish remover into a paper cup and let the marker tips soak in the solution for 30 seconds. Let them dry for five minutes before using. The acetone in the remover restores moisture without diluting the color and draws ink down to the tip of the markers.

- Mr. Clean Magic Erasers are the best for cleaning dry erase boards. They even can remove permanent marker stains from dry erase boards.

- Store posters in cardboard tubes from paper towels or toilet paper. Slip the cardboard core over the outside of a rolled-up poster. Label or color code the tubes to keep them categorized for easy access. You can flatten the hardboard tubes for easy storage in small reclosable plastic bags until needed.

- Crayon containers can be made from juice and vegetable cans painted or covered with contact paper.

- Crayon pieces may be melted down in muffin trays in a warm oven. When cooled, these are nice for rubbings or drawings.

- A card file for art activities helps organize the program.

- Airtight coffee cans and plastic food containers keep clay moist and always ready for use.

- Keep two or more boxes of various sized scrap paper handy; children will be able to choose the size paper they want more easily.

- Cover a wall area with pegboard and suspend heavy shopping bags or transparent plastic bags from hooks inserted in the holes. Hang smocks in the same way on the pegboard (at child level, of course).

- Use the back of a piano or bookcase for hanging a shoe bag. Its pockets can hold many small items.

- Paint a large cardboard box to use as a three-dimensional kiosk to hang pictures on. Use shoeboxes to display children's claywork.

- For clay sharing, mold clay in the shape of a cake. Place the "cake" on a small table and use a plastic knife to slice it. Each child can work with a "slice" of clay.

- Show off young children's creative work at their eye level on classroom walls or bulletin boards. Keep bulletin boards low so children can help attach materials to them. Toddlers can safely touch displays if you slide drawings down behind clear Plexiglas frames.

- To keep artwork accessible, use press-on cork tiles to create low bulletin boards for toddlers. Use different levels of paper or cloth-covered boxes as pedestals to display clay sculptures. Display delicate clay miniatures in the partitions of a beverage six-pack carrier placed on its side.

FIGURE 12-6 • Finger painting is an appropriate art activity for toddlers.

learn to work on the floor or table area nearby and not carry materials across the room.

Art materials, such as crayons, play dough, colored markers, chalk, and paint, as well as materials such as sand and water, should be frequently available to children of this age. These materials are presented under the supervision of an adult so that appropriate use is encouraged. Also, because children of this age have difficulty sharing, duplicates of materials will help cut down on competition for the same items.

Traffic patterns and the children's distractibility also must be considered when art or any other interest areas are arranged in the room. Arrange activities requiring running water, such as play dough and painting, conveniently close to sinks. Walking babies and younger toddlers are prone to falling, grabbing, and running; therefore, they need clear, open spaces. They are also easily distracted by other activities, making task completion or cleanup difficult unless areas are visually divided. The need for occasional solitude and quiet is especially important at this age. Toddlers can easily become overstimulated if exposed to too many

activities at once. In view of all these considerations, dividing and organizing a room becomes an art in itself. Several arrangements should be tried to determine which one best fits the children's needs.

Art Activities for Young Preschoolers, Age Two to Four Years

Art activities for children ages 2–4 years must address the fact that most children of this age have a limited span of interest and attention. Many activities, even the most interesting, hold their interest for less than 10 minutes. However, it should be remembered that each child is different and interest spans may be shorter or longer depending on the individual child.

The point is that the teacher must, first of all, plan activities that appeal to the interests of the young preschooler. Simple, basic art activities are most interesting to children in this age group. Second, the teacher must be prepared to accept the fact that the activity may hold the child's interest for only a short time. It helps to remember that a period of time that seems short to an adult may be quite long to the young preschool child. Finally, alternative and extra activities should always be available for those children who may not be interested in the first activity planned or who finish the activity faster than the teacher had anticipated.

Because two- and three-year-old children require considerable supervision, many teachers prefer to introduce or arrange only one supervised art activity each day. Sometimes they will divide the whole class into small groups for simultaneous participation. Unless there are several adults, this can be a difficult undertaking. In such a setup, one-to-one interaction between teacher and child, which is so necessary in the early years, will be limited. In addition, whole-group participation in art can frequently lead to conformity of response rather than individuality of expression.

In one popular method for organizing supervised art activity, teachers have children take turns coming to an area where materials for art are arranged. The space will usually accommodate four to six children and provides opportunities for peer interaction as well as for interaction with the teacher. This arrangement allows for freedom of choice and gives children a chance to grow toward autonomous decision making about the kind of art they will do.

With the young preschool group, it is usually best to use only the basic materials at first. This helps keep the art program from being too confusing for the child.

FIGURE 12-7 • Each toddler approached finger painting in a different way.

Using only a few crayons or paints or pasting one or two kinds of things at first is a good idea. It encourages children to experiment with each new tool and medium. They learn to use the basic tools and materials first. When they have acquired the basic skills, more colors and variety can be added.

Why and when to provide a variety of materials for early childhood art deserves thoughtful consideration. After children have had opportunities to explore the basic expressive materials, varieties of the basics can be introduced, providing children do not become overwhelmed. Two- and three-year-old children and some less secure older children may still need consistency because sameness and simplicity provide a sense of security. Observant teachers will notice when a child begins to lose interest in using art materials or when a child keeps repeating the same crayon or paint symbols daily. Then it may be time to offer that child the stimulation that accompanies a change of medium or novel material. Let us now consider specific activities for the interest, ability, and skill levels of young preschool children.

Collage. (For more information about the techniques of collage, see Chapter 13.) Making a collage is a good activity for young preschoolers because it can be completed quickly and is within their interest span. It also encourages the use of small muscles as children tear and paste. Young preschoolers also benefit mentally as they learn to choose items and to arrange them in a collage. As they paste together a collage, they learn about the feel, shape, and color of many things and develop the ability to use things in unusual ways.

At times, it may seem as if young preschoolers focus more on the paste than on the items being pasted, but that is part of the fun. The teacher must be sure that the objects available are suitable for the child who is using them. For example, it is important to keep tiny, inedible objects away from children who still put things in their mouths.

With young preschoolers who are new to this activity, begin with just one thing to paste. A good idea is for them to make a tear-and-paste collage. To do this, provide the children with pieces of newspaper, colored tissue, or any colored scrap paper that tears easily. Show them, if necessary, how to tear large and small pieces. Then have them paste these torn bits of paper on colored construction paper in any way they choose. This is a good activity for young preschoolers who do not want or are not yet able to use scissors. Some scissors should be available for children who want to try cutting the pieces to paste on the collage. However, children should not be forced to practice cutting.

As children master the basic technique of pasting, more objects can be added to the collage. Some good things to add are large buttons, bits of cloth and paper (use different colors, textures, and shapes), and bottle caps. Care must be taken to ensure that the materials are not sharp, not painted with lead paint, and not small enough to swallow.

For a change of pace, different materials may be used for the backing of the collage. Children may use pieces of cardboard to paste things on, or shoebox lids, or even pieces of burlap. Teacher and children should use their imaginations to come up with ideas for new and different collage materials.

Painting. Young preschool children also get much satisfaction from working with paint and experimenting with color and form. Painting at an easel is not as easy for young preschoolers as painting on a table. It is difficult for this young artist to control drips at an easel. Also, while standing at an easel, the young child may be easily distracted and wander away.

Often, young children of this age paint one color on top of the other and enjoy the effect. But most of all, they enjoy the movement involved in painting. Finger paint is an especially good medium for this age group, as it can be manipulated over and over again. In this way, the process is stressed, not the product. This is very important for children, who at this age are learning the basic ways to use paint. This age group enjoys the feel (and sometimes the taste) of the paint. They may even use their upper arms and elbows to help them in their designs.

To save on the cost of finger paint paper and to try something new, have children finger paint on a Formica table top, an enamel-top table, a sheet of smooth Formica, or even linoleum. When this is done, a print can be made from the child's finger painting by laying a piece of newsprint paper on the finger painting and gently rubbing it with one hand. The painting is transferred in this way from the tabletop to the paper. More finger paint activities are suggested later in this chapter.

There may be some preschool children who do not like the feel of finger paint. These children should never be forced to use finger paint. Instead, another art activity should be arranged that the child will enjoy. (For more information about painting, see Chapter 13.)

Printing. **Printing** with objects is an art activity that is appropriate for the age, ability, and interest level of young preschool children. In a basic printing activity, the child learns that an object dipped in or brushed with paint makes its own mark, or print, on paper. Children use small muscles in the hand and wrist as they hold the object, dip it in paint, and print with it on paper. They learn that each object has its own unique quality because each thing makes its own imprint.

For the young preschool child, stick prints are a good place to start. In this type of printing, children dip small pieces of wood of various sizes and shapes into thick tempera paint and press them onto a piece of paper. Twigs, wooden spools, wood clothespins, and bottle caps are objects suitable for three-year-olds to use in printing.

After stick printing is mastered, printing with other objects is an appropriate activity for children in this age group. There are many printing activities with found objects presented in this book. A good way for young preschoolers to begin printing is to "walk" the inked object (e.g., a wooden spool, a pinecone, a potato masher) across the paper in even "steps." When

it gets to the other side, they walk it back again. By making three or four lines, or walks, the child has made a pattern.

After one color is used, the object can be wiped clean and another color can be used. Three-year-olds like to try many colors with the same printing object. They may even print over their first prints in a different color. More printing activities for young preschool children are found in Chapter 13 and at the end of this chapter.

Crayons. **Crayons** are the most basic, most familiar, and easiest tool for young preschoolers to use. Supply your classroom with thick ones. Large, thick crayons are easier to hold and they don't break as easily as thinner crayons. Crayons can be used to make attractive colored marks on paper.

You can test the quality of your crayons by coloring a small area, putting pressure on the crayon. If you can scratch the wax off the paper with your fingernails, the crayons are not of a good quality. There is too much wax in the crayon and it is not well intermixed with the pigment. In good crayons, pigment and wax are equally combined, and the wax cannot be scraped off the paper. Crayons of good quality can easily be combined to form new colors by putting different layers of colors one on the other.

Color an area with blue and put a layer of yellow over it. If the resulting color is not a vivid green, your crayons are of poor quality.

If thick crayons are not available in your community, buy the thin ones, but remember that they break easily. The easiest way to avoid tears and frustrations resulting from broken crayons is to break all new crayons and put them on a tray after you have peeled off the paper. The child, without hesitancy and fear that the crayon may break, can put as much pressure on it as he or she wants, and there is no competition between those who keep their crayons in "newer" condition and those who don't.

By using only pieces of crayons, the child may be encouraged to experiment with different crayon techniques, employing the broad side as well as the pointed end. Don't worry about buying a box with many colors of crayons. The more "ready-made" colors you present the child, the less will he or she use his or her imagination and creative urge to produce new colors by mixing. In general, boxes with few colors are sufficient to produce the rest by mixing, if the need for more colors arises. This need, however, depends on the age, development, and personality of the child.

Buy regular newsprint (unprinted newspaper) for crayon work. An 18 × 24-inch sheet of paper is just right. The child should have plenty of paper and should not be restricted in its use.

While most young preschoolers have crayons, they often use them only for drawing on paper. There are, however, several other ways to use crayons that the teacher might try to vary the program for young preschoolers.

- *Crayons and a variety of materials.* Crayons can be used to draw on many surfaces. Cardboard in any form (including corrugated cardboard, paper gift boxes, and food trays) provides a good surface for crayon drawings, as does Styrofoam. Crayon on sandpaper also creates an interesting effect.
- *Crayon rubbings.* Crayon rubbing is a technique that young preschool children can easily master. To make a crayon rubbing, the child puts a piece of paper over a textured surface and rubs the sides of an unpeeled crayon over the paper. The crayon picks up the texture on the paper, forming a design. Have children experiment with bumpy paper, food trays, bark, leaves, the sidewalk, bricks, and corrugated cardboard. This is a good activity for developing both small and large muscles.
- *Crayon resist.* Another way to use crayon is in crayon resist drawings. To make a resist drawing, the child first draws a picture on paper with crayons, pressing hard. She or he then paints over and around the crayon drawing with thin paint (tempera paint diluted with water). A dark-colored paint works best. The dark color fills in all the areas that the crayon has not covered. In the areas covered with crayon, the crayon "resists," or is not covered by, the paint. Crayon resist gives the feeling of a night picture. It is a thrilling experience for the child to see the changes that come when the paint crosses the paper.

See Chapter 13 for additional activities and techniques using crayons.

Art Activities for Older Preschoolers and Kindergarteners (Four to Six Years)

Just as in the case of the younger preschool child, there are preferred and suitable materials and **art activities for older preschoolers and kindergarteners (ages 4–6).** Although there may be considerable overlap, children in this age group generally differ significantly from younger preschool children.

There are some general traits of preschoolers and kindergartners four to six years old. Small-muscle development in the fingers, hands, and wrists is much improved. Whereas younger preschool children may have great difficulty buttoning their clothing or using scissors, most in this older group do not. Many are able to use crayons, colored markers, and even pencils and pens. Because these children are very interested in life beyond home and school, art activities making use of outside environments (e.g., television characters) can be stimulating. Youngsters of this age paint and draw with more purpose. Designs and pictures are within their abilities. These will probably be somewhat simple but nonetheless fun and exciting for the children to do.

If various materials are available to children five years of age and older, they can discover alternative ways of accomplishing similar tasks. For example, if glue does not hold, children may try tape or a stapler. If other fibers are available in addition to yarn, children will experiment and discover possibilities for knotting, stitching, or weaving with each. Children, finding some materials more satisfying than others, are more

FIGURE 12-8 • Pencils are appropriate tools for older children.

FIGURE 12-9 • An electric pencil sharpener is a practical yet fun tool for children to use.

apt to use them to express ideas. With variety, older children come to understand that color, line, form, and texture can be expressed through different materials.

The first cooperative or group art projects will usually take place in kindergarten. In most cases, children discuss the joint effort but work individually. Then the teacher helps arrange the individual contributions into a whole. (See Chapter 13 for a discussion of the group mural as an example of this group approach.)

Art activities for children in grades 1–5 should allow them to express their creative potential if appropriate art activities are provided for them. See the Online Companion for a Summary of Art Curriculum Goals/Activities—Grades 1–5 for a summary of appropriate curriculum goals and activities for older children.

Adapting Program Basics for Children with Special Needs

Many early childhood programs today include in their classrooms children with special needs. Although this book is not intended as a resource for teaching special

education, this section is intended to provide some very basic information on how to adapt the art program for children with special needs. References are provided at the end of this chapter and in the Online Companion for more in-depth information on this topic.

Developmental Delays

It takes many repetitions for the child with developmental delays to fully learn a new skill. For this reason, some children will appear to have mastered the task one day but then be unable to perform the same task on another day. This type of inconsistency is common for children with developmental delays (Gould & Sullivan, 1999).

Open-ended art activities are most appropriate for children with developmental delays. Some effective techniques to use are demonstration, task breakdown, and hand-over-hand assistance as needed. It also helps to demonstrate the activity by doing it first while the child watches. Another approach is to break down an activity into a series of small steps. It is most important to help the child complete one step before going on to the next. In addition, you may find that some children will need you to physically guide their hands. This would involve placing a crayon in the child's hand and then gently moving the child's hand and crayon across a sheet of paper.

Some children with developmental delays may have weak hand muscles and a poor grasp. For these children, short, stubby art instruments are frequently easier to grasp than commercially available crayons, markers, and brushes. You can adapt materials by breaking chalk and preschool crayons into small, short pieces.

Some other suggestions for working with these special needs children follow.

- Place masking tape or colored tape or draw colored lines with a permanent marker about one inch from the end of the paintbrush end to show the child where to place fingers on the brush.
- Use large pieces of paper for art activities to allow for large arm movements characteristic of children with developmental delays.
- In art activities, place the paper on a horizontal surface such as a table or the floor, or tape it to a large easel, door, or wall. Be sure to place a large sheet of plastic, such as a shower curtain or plastic tablecloth, underneath the paper to protect the surface.
- Stabilize the paper with tape, clips, clothespins, or other fasteners to prevent excess slippage.

THINK ABOUT IT — Thinking Positively About ADHD

If you enter the term *ADHD* in a popular search engine, you will find approximately 624,000 hits on the Web, highlighting the diversity and overwhelming range of information available to those seeking to learn about this condition. Most, if not all, sources describe ADHD as a "disorder" and list the various deficits and difficulties that children with ADHD experience. Parents, teachers, health care professionals, and children themselves can become discouraged as they learn about the negative aspects associated with a diagnosis of ADHD (Franklin, 2007).

ADHD occurs in 3 to 5% of school-age children (MTA Cooperative Group, 1999) making it the most common psychiatric disorder among children (Franklin, 2007).

ADHD's characteristics can be broken down into specific subtypes including predominantly hyperactive and impulsive behaviors, inattentive behaviors, or a combination of both.

Many who have studied ADHD do not believe that ADHD is a negative diagnosis at all, but that it is *society's perception* of the diagnosis that is negative (Sherman, Rasmussen, & Baydala, 2006). One researcher refers to ADHD as a *trait* rather than a *disorder* and outlines an argument in which ADHD characteristics are associated with a specific gene, which he calls the "Edison gene" after the inventor who is believed to have had ADHD (Hartmann, 2003). The trait, this researcher claims, is associated with behaviors and skills that worked to the advantage of hunter–gatherer societies and has been passed down over the course of evolution. He described how many of the symptoms of ADHD—short attention spans, poor planning skills, daydreaming, and impatience—can be viewed as adaptive characteristics. That is, these characteristics were perhaps vital to the survival of hunter–gatherer societies. For example, what might be considered "short attention span" and "poor planning" also could be described as continually monitoring the environment and being flexible, ready to change strategies and react instantly to new sights and sounds (Hartmann, 2003).

These characteristics stand in contrast to what so-called "farmer" societies possess. Farmers exhibit such characteristics as patience, being purposefully organized, and focusing on tasks until completion. Although being alert to changes in surroundings and reacting quickly may be advantageous to hunters, farmers fare better when they plan ahead, are patient, and maintain focus until goal completion (Hartmann, 2003).

Unfortunately for children with hunter-like traits, modern North American cultures typically favor farmer characteristics over hunter traits, particularly in the classroom. Children are expected to sit at their desks quietly and keep their hands still as they listen to the teacher. They must work on projects or topics for prolonged periods of time; homework must be completed after school hours; and information is typically absorbed through reading, listening, or seeing as opposed to doing. Children with farmer characteristics often perform well under these "normal" conditions. Children with ADHD characteristics, on the other hand, often find it difficult to achieve academic goals and obey classroom rules.

The suggestions discussed in this chapter are designed to help you develop a more positive approach to working with children with ADHD in the classroom. Seeing their characteristics in a more positive light is the best first step toward creating this positive environment for children with ADHD.

At the same time, encourage the child to use his or her nondominant hand to hold the paper down.

- Children with cerebral palsy will benefit greatly from consistent physical and/or verbal cues to use the less functional hand as a stabilizer while painting with the other.
- Place paper inside a sturdy shirt-size box that will provide walls to contain extraneous movements of the paintbrush or other tool.

- Use thickened paint to provide more resistance and feedback. Paint can be thickened with corn-starch, salt, sugar, flour, sawdust, or sand.

Physical Impairments

In working with children with physical impairments that affect the upper body, arms, hands, or fingers, you will need to make some modifications for art activities. For these children, you may find the following strategies helpful.

- Stabilize paper with tape, clips, clothespins, or other fasteners to prevent the slipping.
- Encourage the child to use his or her nondominant hand to hold the paper down.
- Place paper inside a sturdy shirt-size box to contain extraneous movements of the art tool.
- Mix paint to a thick consistency to provide ease of use as well as more resistance and feedback.
- Thicken paint with cornstarch, salt, sugar, flour, sawdust, or sand.

Visual Impairments

The term *visual impairment* is a general term that includes all levels of vision loss from partially sighted to complete blindness. The child with visual impairments learns about the objects and people around him or her through the senses of touch, smell, taste, and hearing. A child with a visual impairment is unable to observe and imitate others as they explore the environment. Because of this, he or she will need to learn how to investigate the world around him or her. You can help by offering verbal descriptions about what the room looks like, where furniture and playthings are located, and what other people in the room are doing.

Although some children with visual problems prefer dimmed lighting, most need bright, even lighting. To help reduce glare, use a table with a dull finish on it. If you don't have this type of table, tape light-colored construction paper on top of the table. Place the table in an area of the room where the lighting is optimal to reduce glare and shadows. Another way to reduce glare from reflection of light is to use pastel paper instead of white paper for art activities.

Some other suggestions for working with children with visual impairment follow.

- Use high-contrast materials, such as dark or bright colors on light paper. Red, yellow, and orange are the easiest colors for a child with low vision to see, especially on a dark blue background.
- Place a piece of mesh or screening under the paper the child is coloring with a crayon so that the child can feel the raised finished product.
- Show the child how to hold a crayon or marker and what to do with it if he or she has never held a crayon or marker before.
- Hang paper at eye level, either at the easel or taped to the wall. Placing the paper on a vertical surface allows the child's head and eyes to remain in a neutral position while he or she is working.

- Use markers or crayons instead of paint. When using paint, the child has to constantly change visual orientation as he or she looks from the paper to the paint and back to the paper. Markers and crayons reduce the amount of visual shifting.
- Add materials to paint such as thickeners and fragrances so the child will experience the smell as well as the paint itself. Try sand, salt, flour, cornstarch, sawdust, lemon juice, vanilla extract, and ground cinnamon.
- Allow extra time to complete projects, encourage frequent breaks, and suggest a low-key, relaxing activity to follow. Doing art activities can be extremely fatiguing for a child with visual impairments (Gould & Sullivan, 1999).

Attention Deficit/Hyperactivity Disorder and Behavioral Issues

Students with attention deficit hyperactivity disorder (ADHD) can be a challenge for any teacher. Children with ADHD display the behaviors associated with short attention span as well as those associated with hyperactivity. Children with ADD display signs of short attention span, but not hyperactivity.

Some techniques to use with these children follow.

- Plan freeform art activities such as painting, finger painting, and drawing to hold children's interest for extended periods. These activities allow them to enjoy expressing themselves in a nonverbal, nonthreatening manner.
- To transition children out of one art activity and into another, use a timer or provide another type of cue that marks the end of an activity. For example, an end-of-playtime song before the cleanup song gives children a few minutes to get used to the idea that cleanup time will follow shortly.
- Give children clear expectations before they begin an activity. For example, you might state that they will have 15 minutes to work on the activity and that you will give an advance warning when that time is almost up.
- Allow active children to either stand at the art center table or kneel on a chair. These positions are sometimes easier to maintain than sitting in a chair. If a particular child prefers to sit, however, make sure that the chair is the appropriate height, and the child's feet are flat on the floor.
- Allow children to lie on the floor while working on an art project. This position allows most of the

body to come into contact with a hard surface, providing the type of pressure touch that can be calming to the child who is active or agitated.

- Provide children with as many choices as possible to reduce noncompliant behavior. Offer choices that are acceptable to you, but give children the sense that they are in control. For example, ask the child whether he or she would like to use a fat paintbrush or a skinny one, the blue paper or the white.
- Provide an adequate work area with well-defined boundaries. If possible, move the easel next to the art table and allow the child with ADHD to work there alone. Another possibility is to place the child's paper onto a cookie sheet at the table. This provides a clear, separate area for the child to concentrate on during the activity.
- Make use of the children's excess energy by allowing them to do classroom errands. Such errands can include walking notes from the teacher down to the office, putting chairs up on desks at the end of the day, helping the teacher put supplies away, or hanging up visuals.

Establish quiet zones, create time for one-on-one interactions, listen to children's needs, and solve problems together.

Let us now consider some specific art activities and the required materials and strategies for each. More in-depth information and activities for grades 1 through 5 are found in Chapters 13 and 14.

Basic Equipment, Materials, and Use

The following section contains lists of basic art materials needed in the early childhood art program and related strategies for their use. Basic recipes for making finger paint, paste, and other related materials are found at the end of Chapter 13. In choosing from the lists, the teacher must keep in mind the motor control, coordination, and overall developmental level of children in the group.

Drawing Materials and Use

The following are basic **drawing materials and use**.

1. Sturdy sheets of paper (manila or newsprint, 8" × 12" or 12" × 18"). Spread the paper on a table or on the floor, or pin it to a wall or easel. Paper of different shapes and colors may be used for variety.
2. A basket of jumbo crayons about three quarters of an inch in width. These are a good size for

the muscle control of small fingers. Unwrap the crayons so they can be used on both the sides and the ends.
3. Watercolor markers in many colors and tip widths. (Be sure they are not permanent markers.) Colored markers come in beautiful, clear colors. Compared with paint, they have the additional advantage of staying bright and unsullied until children use them up.

Most schools set out crayons or pens jumbled together in a basket. However, you might try assembling them in separate boxes so that each user has an individual, complete set. This cuts down on arguments and means that all colors are available to each child as he or she requires them.

Another alternative is to store crayons in wide-mouth containers according to color—all red crayons in one container, all blue in another.

Crayons are an ideal medium for children: They are bold, colorful, clean, and inexpensive. They consist of an oily or waxy binder mixed with color pigments. They are of various types, some soft, some semihard, some for general use with young children (kindergarten or "fat" crayons). Crayons work well on most papers.

Chalking Materials and Use

The following are basic **chalking materials and use**:

1. A blackboard and eraser, and/or a stack of wet or dry (or both) paper.
2. A container full of colored and white chalk.

Chalk is inexpensive and comes in a variety of colors. Its most typical use is with chalkboards, but young children do not seem to use it very effectively there. They do better if they can mark on the sidewalk with it—perhaps because the rougher texture of the cement more easily pulls the color off the stick, and because children seem more able to tell what they are doing as they squat down and draw. It is, of course, necessary to explain to them that they may "write" with chalk only on special places.

Some young artists apply chalk in separate strokes, letting the color blending take place in the viewer's eye. Others are not reluctant to blend the colors and do so successfully, although the colors may get muddied. Of course, there is no need to caution children against this; they should be encouraged to explore by rubbing with fingers, a cotton swab, or other suitable implement. Most children will select and use chalks easily.

Chalk drawing is best done on a paper with a slightly coarse, abrasive surface. This texture helps the paper trap and hold the chalk particles. Many papers have this quality, including inexpensive manila paper.

Chalks are brittle and easily broken. They are also impermanent, smearing very easily. Completed works should be sprayed with a "fixative" (ordinary hairspray works well); this should be done with proper ventilation.

Chalk strokes can be strengthened by wetting the chalk or paper. Various liquids have also been used with chalks for interesting results. Chalk sticks can be dipped in buttermilk, starch, and sugar water. Liquid tends to seal the chalk, so teachers must occasionally rub a piece of old sandpaper on the end of the chalk in order to break this seal and allow the color to come off again.

Fat, soft chalk of different colors mixes with ease and provides a great beginning for small-motor, free expression. Chalk discourages tight, inhibited work and makes free expression easy. Covering each piece of chalk with a piece of aluminum foil, leaving about half an inch of the chalk exposed, prevents smearing. It also prevents the transferring of colors from one piece of chalk to another while they are stored.

If a slippery surface is desired, liquid starch may be applied to the paper before the dry chalk. There is less friction with starch, and the paper is less likely to tear.

Soaking pieces of large chalk in sugar water (one part sugar and two parts water) for about 15 minutes and then using the chalk on dry paper is another method of application. Sugar gives the chalk a shiny look when dry.

Brush Painting Materials

The following is basic information on **brush painting**.

1. Two easels (at least) with two blunt-tipped nails sticking out near each upper corner to attach the paper. (Paper can also be held on the board with spring-type clothespins.) Easels must be at the right height so that a child can paint without stretching or stooping. Children can also paint seated at a table covered with newspapers or an old shower curtain.

2. Sheets of paper (18" × 24" plain newsprint), white or in assorted colors.

3. Three or four jars of tempera paint. These may be mixed with powdered detergent for proper consistency.

4. Paint containers. These must have flat bottoms so they will not tip over easily. Quart milk cartons (cut down) are good since they can be thrown away after using. Also, plastic fruit juice cans with lids work well when unused paint must be stored.

5. Large, long-handled brushes in each jar. Those with 12-inch handles and ¾-inch bristle length are easy for young children to use. Soft, floppy, camelhair brushes allow the child to swoop about the paper most freely. When wet, the brush should have a pointed end: stiff, flat brushes make it harder to produce free movements. See Figure 13-3 Chapter 13 for more information about paintbrushes.

6. Smocks. An old shirt with the sleeves cut to the child's arm length makes a practical smock. Oilcloth or plastic aprons are also good. Extra art smocks can be made easily from either large plastic trash bags or newspaper. Cut openings for the child's head and arms at the end of a plastic trash bag. Instead of a smock, a set of old clothes can be used as "art clothes."

7. A place to dry finished paintings.

Mixing paint. Although **mixing paint** in large quantities saves teachers time, the children enjoy making it so much and this is such a good learning experience for them that mixing a fresh batch each day with one or two children helping stir is generally preferred. A surprising amount of tempera is needed in relation to the quantity of water to make rich, bright, creamy paint; thus it is best to put the tempera into the container first and then add water bit by bit. Instead of water, some teachers prefer using liquid starch because it thickens the paint mixture. However, this does increase the expense. It is also helpful to add a dash of liquid detergent, as this makes cleaning up easier. Another avenue to easier cleanup is to cut a poster board that has been laminated on both sides to fit the easel. Tape the laminated poster board over the easel so that as the students paint on the easel and get ready for the next child, the student can easily wipe off the paint with a damp cloth, rag, or paper towel. It helps the student learn how to clean up and keeps the center clean, and develops eye–hand coordination in a fun way.

At the easel, it may help children to see that if they wipe the brush on the side of the jar, the paint does not drip or run. An adult can show children that keeping each brush in its own paint jar keeps the color clear.

THIS ONE'S for YOU! Drawing Inside the Box

When working with very young children and/or students with special needs, it is helpful for teachers to think "outside the box" in order to preserve and enhance a child's natural curiosity. In an effort to teach young children to control their drawing tools, they are often presented with coloring book-type pages and instructed to "stay inside the lines." Yet, there is little, if any, real value in coloring books, including the controlled movement goal.

Instead, consider using other activities, such as a Drawing Inside the Box activity to achieve the same purpose, but in a freer and more exploratory manner. This activity involves children actually drawing inside the lids of boxes that have been attached to large paper, so the sides of the box lids provide a visual as well as a physical boundary that says, "stop" (Franklin, 2007).

The objectives of Drawing Inside the Box are:

- To control their movements while using drawing tools
- To increase attention span/focus/intention
- To develop prewriting and fine motor skills
- To build receptive and expressive language skills

Here are the specifics on how to plan and present a Drawing Inside the Box activity.

Materials:

- Large paper to cover the table top
- Glue
- Masking tape (optional)

- Box lids (e.g., shoebox lids, lids/bottoms from note cards, lids from candy boxes, etc.)
- Drawing materials
- Various sheets of white or light-colored paper cut to fit inside the different box lids (optional)

Procedure:

- Cut a large piece of paper to fit the top of a table.
- Glue several box lids around on top of the paper (inside up). Use plenty of glue and let it dry overnight.
- Provide drawing tools.
- Allow the children to draw inside, outside, and around the box lids.
- Provide language (in, out, around, etc.) and even directions, depending on a child's ability level.

As an extension or variation of this activity:

- Young children love to organize things in containers, so they may group their drawing materials inside some of the boxes.
- This could lead to a sorting, matching, or classification game—all red colors here and blue over there, all markers here and crayons there, etc.
- This activity could easily be adapted for older children and/or others with special needs by varying the sizes of the box lids (decreased or increased) and/or additional drawing materials could be used (i.e., colored pencils, oil pastels, etc.).
- Box lids could be secured onto individual desks (Franklin, 2007).

Keep several pieces of paper clipped to the easel at once. Many teachers prefer to write the child's name on the back of the paper to avoid the problem of having him or her paint over it. A developmental portfolio kept at school for each child, containing dated paintings, delights parents at conference time, enabling them to see how their child's skills have developed during the year. You can use a digital camera to take photos of selected pieces of each child's artwork for a video presentation of her or his painting experiences throughout the year.

Easel painting. With easel painting, teachers like to start with only the three primary colors (red, blue,

and yellow) in the beginning of the year and then add other colors in the second month or so. Each jar of blue tempera paint should be labeled with a strip of blue paper on which is clearly printed the word BLUE. (Label other jars in the same way.) Brushes should be thoroughly washed and kept in good condition. Teach children how to wipe up and wash the art area after its use.

At the end of each day, wash all paintbrushes thoroughly in running water, and dry them with bristles up before putting them away. Wash easels and vinyl aprons with a wet cloth and soap if necessary. Wash and put away containers. Cover leftover paint with a tight lid or aluminum foil. Hang up aprons and smocks.

Finger Painting Materials and Use

The following is basic information on **finger painting materials and use**.

1. Paper that has a shiny surface. This can be butcher paper, shelf paper, special finger paint paper, freezer wrap, or glossy gift wrap.
2. A water supply to make the paper damp. A damp sponge or rag works best. Water may also be sprinkled directly onto the paper.
3. Finger paint. This can be special finger paint or dry tempera paint mixed with liquid starch or liquid detergent to make a thick mixture.
4. Racks to dry the finished work.
5. A smock for each painter.
6. A nearby sink with running water for washing hands and cleaning up, or a bucket of soapy water, sponges, and paper towels.

For finger painting, tables should be covered with linoleum, Formica, or plastic, and children should wear smocks. Plenty of paper towels and clean rags should be provided. Smooth-surfaced paper is dipped in a pan of water and spread flat on a table.

The quickest, simplest way to make finger paint is to combine liquid starch with dry tempera. This may be done by pouring a generous dollop of starch onto the paper and then sprinkling it with dry tempera. Alternatively, some teachers like to stir the dry pigment into an entire container of starch base. No matter how the paint is originally prepared, you need to be ready to add more ingredients as children work. While mixing, strive for rich, brilliant color and sufficient paint to fill the paper completely if the child wishes. Children must be allowed to experiment with the paint as they wish, using their fingers, the palms of their hands, their wrists, and their arms.

THINK ABOUT IT — Art Displays

There are so many more ways to display children's artwork than just on the bulletin board. Here are some ideas to help get you started on new ways to display the work of young artists.

- Involve the children in selecting work for display.

- Add children's commentary, narrative, or description to the display. Be sure to write the narrative or description on a separate Post-it or paper rather than on the children's artwork.

- Personalize displays. On a large bulletin board, mark sections off for each artist. Take children's photos and invite them to draw self-portraits to hang in their own gallery. Encourage children to discuss and select the rest of the artwork they wish to display in their section of the bulletin board. See Chapter 8 for suggestions on using a digital camera for presenting children's artwork.

- Make interactive displays. Have children make and display a group collage of materials that encourage viewers to touch it when they see it. Make peephole covers for pictures. Tape the peephole cover on one side of the picture. Encourage children to guess what's under the peephole, then lift it up to see if they guessed correctly.

- Suspend wire sculptures from clear fishing line.

- Make floor display cubes out of cardboard boxes with taped-on, clear cellophane tops for peek-a-boo viewing.

- Make an elastic "clothesline" for displaying artwork. Stretch a length of ¼-inch elastic along the wall chosen for display. Staple it in place. Use miniature clothespins to hang the children's artwork. The elastic stretches slightly, and the clothespins are always in place as instant hang-ups for new artwork.

- For an interesting display method, place a huge sheet of clear, shatterproof Plexiglas over children's artwork on the classroom floor. Encourage children to take a closer look at their artwork on their tummies.

- Consider dividing your display into categories by media—watercolors, easel paintings, tabletop paintings, mixed media (collage, sand painting)—or by type, such as paintings, sculptures, or construction projects.

- Be certain to display at least one example of EVERY child's work.

- Create display panels with borrowed tri-fold screens or buy wooden lattice panels from your local garden, hardware, or lumber store. Secure them on wooden stands and use to display art work. Place heavier sculptures on tables or in safe places on the floor under one of these panels.

Prepared finger paints may be used, or the children may help mix a recipe from Chapter 13. If the recipe is used, the mixture may be separated into three or four parts and coloring added—either food color or the powdered tempera used for easel painting. Children like to add their own color; they may use salt shakers containing powdered paint and mix in the color with their fingers. Adding soap flakes (not detergents) to the paint mixture increases variety. Finger painting can also be done with interesting materials such as pudding, cold cream, and shaving cream. Be sure to check the list of ingredients on the label for any ingredients children may be allergic to.

Variations. Another method of finger painting is to cover a table with white oilcloth and let the children work on the oilcloth. The mixture can later be washed off with a hose or faucet. This activity is good for all ages.

For a change, use waxed paper instead of regular finger painting paper. Its transparent quality will lend an interesting effect. A combination of any liquid dishwashing detergent and dark-colored tempera paint (one part paint, one part soap) can be applied to waxed paper. Cover the surface evenly so the painter can make a simple design with his or her fingers.

Finger painting without paper is another variation. Children finger paint directly onto plastic trays or a table top. When each child finishes, place a piece of paper on top of the finger painting and rub across the back of the paper. Lift the paper from the tray or table top, and you will have a print of the finger painting. The trays are easily rinsed off in the sink.

Pasting Materials and Use

The following is basic information on **pasting materials and use**.

1. Small jars of paste. (Or give each child a square of waxed paper with a spoonful of paste on it. This prevents waste.) A wooden tongue depressor is a good tool for spreading the paste, or paste can be spread with the fingers. Glue sticks can also be used.
2. Sheets of plain or colored manila or construction paper in many sizes.
3. Collage materials. Some of these can be paper shapes in different colors, scraps of cloth, feathers, yarn, tinfoil, string, beans, sawdust, bottle caps, buttons, Styrofoam packing pieces, rock salt, bits of bark, and any other things that look interesting.
4. Blunt scissors, for both left- and right-handed children.

Pasting should be done away from climbing toys, building blocks, and similar large-motor activities. All the materials for pasting should be on a shelf at child level. Collage and pasting materials should be placed on a separate table and sorted into shallow containers, such as baskets or clear plastic boxes, so that children can readily see the kinds of things that are available and consider how they will look when arranged together. Some children will enjoy tearing and pasting, while others will prefer cutting and pasting. Of course, children should learn the safety rules for using scissors early in the year. The teacher must also be sure that all young children have only blunt scissors.

Keep paste in small plastic containers or jars. To help children learn to keep lids on jars, mark the bottom and top of each jar with a number or a colored X. Show children how to match up the jar with its lid by matching colored Xs or numbers. In this way, children learn to keep the lids on the jars and to recognize numbers and colors as well. Show children how to rinse out paste brushes and where to return all pasting material. Set up a place to put finished work to dry.

Using common recycled household disposables will make cleanup easier. Aluminum pie tins and frozen food trays are both excellent for holding paint, paste,

FIGURE 12-10 • The art area needs to reflect the individual needs of the children.

THIS ONE'S for YOU!

Creative Budgeting

Painting supplies can eat up a large part of your budget. The following ideas may help your budget (and maybe your creativity, too!):

1. Individual watercolor sets can be made by pouring leftover tempera paint into egg carton cups. Set them aside to dry and harden. Use the paints with water and brushes just as you would ordinary paint sets.
2. Paint containers need to be sturdy and inexpensive. Here are some ideas for different types of paint containers.

   - Cupcake or muffin tins are excellent for painting with several colors at a time.
   - Egg cartons work well when children are painting with cotton swabs. Cut cartons in thirds to make four-part containers, and pour small amounts of paint into each egg cup.

3. Store liquid tempera in recycled glue or dishwashing liquid bottles. Paint can be squirted quickly and neatly into paint cups from these bottles.
4. When using paint cups, make a nontipping cup holder from an empty half-gallon milk or juice carton. Cut holes along the length of the carton and pop in the cups.
5. Sponges can be good paint holders, too. Cut a hole the exact size of the paint jar or cup in the center of the sponge, then fit the jar/cup in the hole. Besides keeping paint containers upright, the sponges also catch drips.
6. Cotton-ball painting is more fun (and neater) when you clip spring-type clothespins to the cotton balls. Children use the clothespins like handles. The same clothespins can be used when printing with small sponge pieces.

or glue for table activities. At the end of the activity, you may want to recycle the aluminum. Another way to make cleanup easier after pasting is to fold over the top edges of a large paper bag, then tape the bag to one end of your work table. When children have finished their projects, scraps can easily be swept off the table into the bag, which can then be tossed into the trash.

Scrap Art Materials and Use

The following is basic information on **scrap art materials and use**.

1. Paste, glue, tape, and stapler
2. Colored tissue paper
3. Colored sticky tape, gummed circles, stars, and designs
4. Tempera paint, chalk, crayons, and colored markers
5. Odds and ends of scrap material—egg cartons, Styrofoam pieces, plastic containers and lids, pinecones, feathers, and buttons. For scrap art activities, all materials need to be in good order. This is because this type of activity requires a large supply of materials. A special place is needed for all supplies that is within the child's reach and at eye level.

FIGURE 12-11 • Children need smocks to protect clothing during art activities.

FIGURE 12-12 • A place for drying paintings is essential in the art room.

Scraps of cloth may be kept in one box with scrap pieces glued on the outside to show the child at a glance what is in the box. Clear plastic shoe boxes are excellent for scrap art storage, as children can easily see the contents. Buttons may be kept in a muffin tin, feathers in a plastic bag, and old bits of jewelry for puppets in a plastic shoe box. The point is to keep each material in a specific place so that it is ready for planned or spontaneous projects.

Organizing material in this simple, easy-to-find way helps children learn to work on their own. Having glue, scissors, paper, and all other materials on shelves at the child's height also encourages independent work. Cleanup time is much easier, too, when the children can see "what goes where" and can reach the places where materials are supposed to go.

Potter's Clay and Play Dough Materials and Use

The following is basic information on **potter's clay and play dough materials and use**.

1. Potter's clay or play dough (mixed from the recipes at the end of Chapter 13 and kept in an airtight container)
2. Clay or play dough table (select a table that is easy to clean, such as one with a Formica top, or spread large pieces of plastic for protection)
3. Tools for clay work (toy rolling pins, cookie cutters, spoons, and blunt plastic knives)

Working with clay and play dough requires a place away from all active centers such as building blocks, wheel toys, and climbing toys. The tables should be

FIGURE 12-13 • The way supplies are organized can make or break art activities for young children.

covered with Formica or oilcloth to make cleaning easier. Young children also enjoy working with clay on individual vinyl placemats, Masonite boards, burlap squares, or brown paper grocery bags. Newspaper does not work well because when it gets wet, bits of paper may mix with the clay. For clay projects that are meant to be hardened and possibly painted later, set up a good place for drying. Because these objects may take a few days to dry, this place must also be away from frequently used areas.

Before starting any three-dimensional projects that require several stages such as molding, drying, and then painting, the teacher must be aware of children's interest spans. Some of these projects take longer than other art activities, and some children may lose interest and not finish the project. The teacher must also consider the time needed for preparing the material, making the objects, drying them, and painting them. Then it must be decided if the children's interest is strong enough to last through the time needed for the whole project. It is an unpleasant experience for both teacher and children when a project is too rushed. This takes the joy out of the activity for all involved.

FIGURE 12-14 • Preparation of materials is an important first step in any creative activity.

Potter's clay. Potter's clay may be purchased in moist form at any art supply store. This is much easier to deal with than starting with dry powder. The clay is available in two colors—gray and terra cotta. (Terra cotta looks pretty, but stains clothing and is harder to clean up.) Clay requires careful storage in a watertight, airtight container to retain its malleable qualities. When children are through for the day, form it into large balls, press a thumb into them, and then fill the holes with water and replace the clay in the container. If oilcloth table covers are used with potter's clay, they can simply be hung up to dry, shaken well, and put away until next time.

Making play dough. Children should participate in making dough whenever possible. If allowed to help make the dough, children learn about measuring, blending, and cause and effect. They also have the chance to work together and practice cooperation.

The doughs that require no cooking are best mixed two batches at a time in separate deep dishpans. Using deep pans keeps the flour within bounds, and making two batches at a time relieves congestion and provides better participation opportunities. Tempera powder is the most effective coloring agent because it makes such intense shades of dough; adding it to the flour before pouring in the liquid works best. Dough can be kept in the refrigerator and reused several times. Removing it at the beginning of the day allows it to come to room temperature before being offered to the children—otherwise it can be discouragingly stiff and unappealing. The addition of flour or cornstarch on the second day is usually necessary to reduce stickiness.

Dough variations. All the dough recipes at the end of Chapter 13 have been carefully tested and are suitable for various purposes. In preschool centers where process, not product, is emphasized, the dough and clay are generally used again and again rather than the objects made by the children being allowed to dry and then sent home. For special occasions, however, it is nice to allow the pieces to harden and then to paint or color them. Two recipes included in Chapter 13 serve this purpose particularly well: ornamental clay and baker's dough.

For dough to be truly satisfying, children need an abundance of it rather than meager little handfuls, and they should be encouraged to use it in a manipulative, expressive way rather than in a product-oriented way.

Cleanup. For clay cleanup, sponge off tables, mats, and boards. Burlap squares can be stacked and shaken when dry, and grocery bags can be thrown away. Clay-caked hands and tools should never be washed in the sink because clay can clog the drain. Instead, have children wipe off their tools and hands with paper towels, then wash them in a basin filled with soapy water. When the clay particles settle, you can let the soapy water down the drain and throw the sediment in the trashcan. Children may rinse their hands in the sink, and the tools may be left to dry on paper towels.

The cooked cornstarch recipes are the only ones that are particularly difficult to clean up because they leave a hard, dry film on the pan during cooking. However, an hour or two of soaking in cold water converts this to a jellylike material that is easily scrubbed off with a plastic pot-scrubbing pad. If pans are soaked during nap time, children will be quite interested in the qualities of this gelatinous material when they get up. You might even have one or two of them work on scrubbing the pot clean!

Woodworking Materials and Use

The following is basic information on **woodworking materials and use**.

1. A bin of soft lumber pieces (leftover scraps of lumber)
2. Supply of nails with large heads
3. Wooden spools, corks, and twigs
4. Wooden buttons, string, and ribbons to be nailed to wood or tied to heads of nails already hammered into the wood
5. Bottle caps
6. Small-hand tools (hammer and nails are best to start with; saws, screwdrivers, a vise, and a drill may be added later)
7. Workbench
8. Sandpaper
9. A vise or C-clamp placed near the corner of the workbench, flush with the table top
10. Safety goggles

For older children:

11. Screws and screwdrivers—standard and Phillips
12. Pencils, rulers, and tape measures
13. Files, planes, levels
14. Crowbars

Carpentry needs to be done in a special area away from other activities. Provide children plenty of good wood and satisfactory tools. A sturdy workbench of the right height is helpful.

The most basic woodworking tools are hammers and saws. Hammers should be good, solid ones—not tack hammers. Supply crosscut saws that can cut with or across the grain of the wood; these should be as short as possible. A well-made vise in which to place wood securely while sawing is invaluable. Preferably there should be two of these, one at each end of the table. (Inexpensive C-clamps can also be used for this purpose, or a board can be nailed to the table while the child saws it, but this leaves the troublesome chore of removing the nails afterward.)

Very young children enjoy sawing up the large pieces of Styrofoam that come as packing for electronic equipment. Hammering into such material or into plasterboard is also quick and easy and does not require more force than two- and three-year-old children can muster. Older children need plentiful amounts of soft wood to work with.

Cabinet shops are a good source for scrap lumber. Only smooth lumber should be used. Pieces of various lengths and sizes add interest. The greater the variety of wood,

the greater the challenge for building. An old tree stump is great fun for children to pound countless nails into.

Woodworking needs careful adult supervision, since children can easily hurt themselves or each other with a hammer and saw. General guidelines for adult supervision include the following.

- Stay very close to the woodworking activity. Be within reach of each child.
- There should be no more than three or four children for one adult to supervise. Only one child at a time should use a saw.
- Show children how to saw away from their own fingers and from other children. Show them how to avoid hitting their fingers with the hammer.
- Hand out nails a few at a time.
- Never turn your back on the activity for even a few seconds.
- Make a wall-mounted tool board to store frequently used tools. Less-used tools can be stored in a cupboard. The outline of each tool can be marked on the board so children can figure out where to hang each tool. (More woodworking information is found in Chapter 14.)

Some variations for woodworking follow.

- Remember to vary the tools the children use as their skill (and self-control) increases.
- Purchase a variety of nails by the pound, not by the little box, from a hardware store. Children love an assortment of these. They can be set out in small foil pie plates to keep them from getting mixed up. These pie plates can be nailed to a long board to prevent spilling.
- Offer various kinds of trims to go with woodworking, such as wire; thick, colorful yarn; and wooden spools (with nails long enough to go through the spool).
- Have children wear safety glasses.
- Offer round things for wheels, such as bottle caps or buttons.
- Provide dowels of various sizes that will fit the holes made by the different sizes of bits.
- Younger children may use a rubber mallet with golf tees to pound into Styrofoam.

Safety

For all the activities in this chapter and in any art activities for young children, be sure that you are not using any unsafe art supplies. Potentially unsafe art supplies include the following.

- Powdered clay. It is easily inhaled and contains silica, which is harmful to the lungs. Instead, use wet clay, which cannot be inhaled.
- Paints that require solvents such as turpentine to clean brushes. Use only water-based paints.
- Cold-water or commercial dyes that contain chemical additives. Use only natural vegetable dyes made from beets, onion skins, and so on.
- Permanent markers, which may contain toxic solvents. Use only water-based markers.
- Instant papier-mâché, which may contain dust, lead, or asbestos. Use only black-and-white newspaper and library paste or liquid starch.
- Epoxy, instant glues, rubber cement, or other solvent-based glues. Use only water-based white glue.
- Aerosol spray paints. These may contain toxic solvents, and spraying makes them even more hazardous.

The teacher should:

- Read labels.
- Check for age appropriateness. The Art and Creative Materials Institute labels art materials AP (approved product) and CP (certified product) when they are safe for young children, even if ingested. These labels are round. A product bearing the square "Health Label" is safe only for children older than 12 years.
- The best way to avoid exposure to hazardous chemicals is to READ THE LABEL and follow the directions. Most hazardous consumer products are required to provide identification of hazardous chemicals on their labels. Label warnings should be taken seriously. They exist because chemicals contained in these products can be hazardous when inhaled, ingested, or absorbed though the skin. Read labels carefully and look for the following:

  DANGER—extremely flammable, corrosive and/or highly toxic
  POISON—highly toxic
  WARNING or CAUTION—less toxic

- Other key phrases to look for include HARMFUL IF SWALLOWED, AVOID SKIN CONTACT, and FLAMMABLE, all of which indicate acute, or short-term, hazards. Older products (e.g., an old bottle of rubber cement) or "professional" products (e.g., some paints and photographic solutions) may not carry a warning label. Keep children away from unlabeled products.

- Check for ventilation requirements. In most cases, one open window or door is not sufficient ventilation. You can stay safe by opening windows and turning on a fan, or, weather permitting, take your art projects outside.
- A list of materials safe for young children is available from the Art and Creative Materials Institute, Inc., P.O. Box 479 Hanson, MA 02341-0479, or visit their website at http://www.acminet.org/Safety.htm. Write to the National Art Education Association, 1916 Association Drive, Reston, VA 22091 for an updated, detailed list of safety guidelines.
- Always use products that are appropriate for the individual user. Children in grade 6 and lower and adults who may not be able to read and understand safety labeling should use only nontoxic materials.
- Do not eat or drink while using art materials. Wash up after use. Clean yourself and your supplies.
- Never use products for skin painting or food preparations unless indicated that the product is meant to be used in this way.
- Do not transfer art materials to other containers. You will lose the valuable safety information that is on the product package. Also, ingestion of these products can be avoided by keeping materials in their original containers.
- Imported art materials should be looked upon with extreme caution. Other countries have not developed the rigid safety codes adopted by the United States. Do not accept or use old art materials that may have been left in the school or donated by some well-meaning adult. If the materials do not bear the current safety codes, toss them out!
- If a marker stains the clothes or hands and does not clean up with simple soap and water, it is not appropriate or safe for young children to use.
- Use plastic containers for washing brushes; glass is dangerous in the hands of young children.
- Paper cutters should not be used by elementary children (or younger!). The paper cutter should be kept out of students' reach, and left in a locked position always with the blade turned to the wall or out of reach.
- Know your students.
- Be aware of students' allergies. Children with allergies to wheat, for example, may be irritated by wheat paste used in papier mâché. Other art materials that may cause allergic reactions include chalk or other dusty substances, water-based clay, and any material that contains petroleum products.

- Be aware of students' habits. Some students put everything in their mouths. (This can be the case at any age.) Others act out or behave aggressively. Use your knowledge of individual students' tendencies to help you plan art activities that will be safe for all students.
- A good rule of thumb about markers: If the label on a marker says "nontoxic" or does not say "permanent ink," the ink is probably water-based. Not only are water-based varieties safer to use, they are easier to remove from the wall!

Summary

The early childhood art program is a part of the early childhood curriculum in which children have the chance to work with many kinds of materials and techniques. It provides a time and place for children to put together their thoughts, ideas, feelings, actions, and abilities into their own creations.

Toddlers are very active and want to explore everything. For this reason, they need materials that are sturdy—practically indestructible—and do not include tiny pieces that might be swallowed. Only a few materials should be put out at a time so toddlers are not overwhelmed by too many choices. Art materials, like crayons, play dough, chalk, and paint, need to be frequently available to toddlers. These materials should be presented under the supervision of an adult to encourage their appropriate use. In setting up art (and all other) centers for toddlers, a teacher should arrange lots of space and clear traffic patterns because toddlers are prone to falling, grabbing, and running.

Young preschool children, two to four years of age, have a limited interest span. Even the most interesting activities hold their interest for only approximately 10 to 15 minutes. Thus, the teacher must plan several activities and alternative activities for this age group. Some appropriate art activities for children of this age are easel and finger painting, printing, collage, coloring with crayons, using play dough, making simple puppets, and sculpting.

Older preschool children and kindergartners (four to six years of age) have begun to develop better small-muscle control in the fingers, hands, and wrists. For this reason, they enjoy cutting with scissors, using smaller paintbrushes, and trying out a wide variety of colored markers. All of these activities are also appropriate for middle and upper elementary level students.

The objectives of the art program must consider the interest, age, and ability levels of the children. An important goal of the art program is the growth of a child's creativity and ability to work independently. But the main goal is to let children grow at their own individual rates.

Teachers play an important role in the success of the early childhood art program. They must choose the right materials as well as know the right way to set up and use the materials for each activity. Teachers need to adapt the early childhood program so that the program basics meet the needs of young children with special needs.

Key Terms

art activities for children ages 2–4 years 270
art activities for older preschoolers and kindergarteners (ages 4–6) 273
art activities for children in grades 1–5 274
brush painting 278
chalking materials and use 277
crayons 272
drawing materials and use 277
finger painting materials and use 280
mixing paint 278
pasting materials and use 281
printing 272
process over product 262
potter's clay and play dough materials and use 283
scrap art materials and use 282
toddler-appropriate art activities 268
woodworking materials and use 285

Learning Activities

A. It is hard to truly appreciate the individual merits of the dough recipes unless they are actually available for inspection and experimentation. As a class project, have volunteers make them up and bring them to class to try out.

B. Suppose a bad fairy has waved her wand and ruled that you can select only three basic types of creative, self-expressive activities to use for a whole year in your preschool. Which three would you select and why? Answer the same question for a group of older children, grades 1 through 5.

C. Suppose that same bad fairy has waved her wand again, and now you are allowed to purchase only paint and glue (no paper even!) for your creative activities. How limiting is this? What self-expressive activities would you actually be able to offer under these circumstances? How might you go about acquiring the necessary free materials to make them possible? Be specific.

D. Visit one or possibly several early childhood programs and observe the arts activities. Keep in mind these points in observing:

1. Are the equipment and activities right for the age, ability, and interest levels of the children?
2. Is the area well planned for each activity?
3. Are the children free to make what they want with the material?

E. Set up a classroom, real or imagined, for one or more of the following activities:

1. finger painting
2. collage
3. making puppets

Consider the following in setting up the activity:

1. location of water source
2. preparation of area
3. preparation of materials
4. preparation of children
5. teacher preparation
6. activity itself
7. cleanup
8. drying and storage space for work in progress or finished

F. Draw up a plan of a room set up for art activities for three-, four-, and five-year-old children.

1. Include the following areas:

   brush and finger painting   crayon and chalk work
   clay   woodworking
   puppetry   scrap art
   papier-mâché work

2. Show on the plan where the following areas would be found:

   storage space   water source(s)
   child-level shelves light source(s)
   drying areas

G. Ask children what they think is the hardest part about cleaning up. Record their answers. See if there is one thing that is mentioned more than others. Check on the problem to see if it is caused by room setup, supply setup, water source, or something else.

H. Go on an odds-and-ends hunt.

1. See how many different kinds of things can be found for use in art projects. Things to look for include spools, Styrofoam, feathers, buttons, and foil.
2. Sort the material and store it in the best way possible. Label each container so that children will know what is inside.

I. Choose a grade level from grades 1 through 5. Draw up a room plan for art activities for this grade level.

Include the same areas and requested information as in question F.

J. In the year 105, paper was invented by Ts'ai Lun, an official of the Chinese Imperial Court at the Han Dynasty in China. Lun's paper was made from bamboo and mulberry fibers, fishnets, and rags.

What did people use before paper? Can you name 10 uses of paper? Of what other material can paper be made? Do you know what paper is made of now? Does your school recycle its paper?

K. Try these clean-up secrets after an art activity.

For grades K–2: Have the children form a line and march around the room to fun music. When you see a piece of trash, the child in front picks it up and then goes to the end of the line. The next child in line has a turn. Children will love this.

Grades 3–5. Wander around the room and make a note of three pieces of trash. Give children one minute to clean. Reward the finders of your "secret scraps" with a small something from your "goodie box."

L. Compare a list of the various art materials used in several kindergarten classes. Rank these in order of value for the child. Are there any materials used that cannot be justified as being of value for development? Explain your answers.

Chapter Review

1. Is the product or the process more important in the art program? Explain your answer.

2. Choose the statements that describe an important purpose of art in the early childhood program.

   a. Art gives the child a chance to try new materials and techniques.
   b. Art helps the child make perfect artwork.
   c. The child has a chance to express experiences and feelings.
   d. The emphasis in art is on continued good experiences with many kinds of materials.
   e. In art, the child learns how to copy models.
   f. Learning to judge one's own work and other children's work is very important in art.
   g. Being successful in art helps develop a child's self-confidence.

3. Select the items that should be included in a list of equipment for each of the following activities.

    a. Crayoning
        i. newsprint or manila paper, 8" × 12" or 12" × 18"
        ii. lined white paper
        iii. colored tissue paper, 18" × 24"
        iv. colored markers in many colors
        v. jumbo crayons, unwrapped
        vi. jumbo crayons, all wrapped

    b. Chalk work
        i. colored chalks, white chalks
        ii. colored tissue paper
        iii. paper, wet and dry
        iv. chalkboard
        v. eraser
        vi. pencils

    c. Brush painting
        i. easels
        ii. lined 9" × 12" paper
        iii. newsprint, 18" × 24" plain or pastel
        iv. construction paper
        v. tempera paint
        vi. finger paint
        vii. glue
        viii. brushes, long (12") handles and 3/4" bristles
        ix. smocks
        x. a place to dry finished paintings

    d. Finger painting
        i. dull, porous paper
        ii. shiny-surfaced paper
        iii. water supply
        iv. crayons
        v. finger paint
        vi. colored tissue paper
        vii. smocks
        viii. racks to dry finished work

    e. Pasting
        i. glue in small jars
        ii. paste in small jars
        iii. lined 9" × 12" paper
        iv. colored tissue paper
        v. plain or manila construction paper
        vi. scissors, blunt, left and right types
        vii. collage materials
        viii. stapler and staples

    f. Puppets and scrap art
        i. paper bags
        ii. boxes
        iii. scissors, paper, paste, paints
        iv. sticks
        v. play dough
        vi. colored sticky tape
        vii. cardboard rolls
        viii. odds and ends
        ix. airtight container
        x. socks and mittens

    g. Clay and play dough
        i. Plasticine
        ii. real clay
        iii. open containers
        iv. airtight containers
        v. Formica-top tables
        vi. oilcloths
        vii. paint
        viii. scissors
        ix. tools for clay work
        x. play dough, purchased
        xi. play dough, made with help from the children

    h. Woodworking
        i. paint
        ii. workbench
        iii. supply of soft lumber pieces
        iv. bottle caps
        v. sandpaper
        vi. wooden spools, corks, twigs
        vii. clay
        viii. supply of nails

4. Choose the answer that best completes each of the following statements describing the basic objectives of the early childhood art program.

    a. The most basic objective of the art program is to
        i. produce the best artists possible.
        ii. meet the age, ability, and interest levels of the children.
        iii. fit into the total preschool program.

    b. Learning to be a creative thinker is
        i. more important in the elementary grades than for younger children.
        ii. not an objective in art.
        iii. an important objective in art.

    c. The art program must allow children the freedom to
        i. grow at their own individual paces.
        ii. do anything they please.
        iii. go against safety rules.

5. Choose the answer that best completes each of the following statements describing techniques for using material in arts and crafts.

    a. With very young children, it is best to begin with
        i. a great variety of materials.
        ii. the basic essentials.
        iii. only small-motor activities.

    b. A teacher must avoid
        i. making models for the children to copy.
        ii. helping the children with the material.
        iii. giving suggestions at cleanup time.

    c. Painting work should be done
        i. in an area near the quiet activities.
        ii. in an area away from climbing toys.
        iii. only if sunlight is available.

d. Finger painting works best with
   i. dull, porous, dry paper on wood tables.
   ii. shiny paper on the floor.
   iii. shiny paper on a table covered with Formica or oilcloth.

e. It is best to keep pasting supplies
   i. out of children's reach.
   ii. on a shelf at child-level.
   iii. in a locked cabinet.

f. Scrap art activities require
   i. a good deal of organization of supplies.
   ii. no special order in supplies.
   iii. a small amount of supplies.

g. Woodworking is an activity that
   i. needs very little supervision.
   ii. needs careful adult supervision.
   iii. is too dangerous for young children.

h. In woodworking and all art activities, it is important to encourage children to
   i. copy the teacher's models.
   ii. copy the ideas of the other children.
   iii. do what they want with the materials.

6. List some special considerations for setting up art areas for toddlers.

7. List the skills, interests, and abilities of older preschool children and kindergartners.

8. List appropriate art activities for older preschool children and kindergartners.

9. Choose the answer that best completes each of the following statements describing the skills and abilities of the young preschool child (aged two to four).

   a. The young preschool child often has
      i. better small- than large-muscle development.
      ii. better large- than small-muscle development.
      iii. good large- and small-muscle development.

   b. The interest span for a young preschool child is usually
      i. long, more than 20 minutes.
      ii. short, not more than one minute.
      iii. short, between 10 and 15 minutes.

   c. In lesson plans for young preschool children, the teacher plans
      i. only one main activity for the whole group.
      ii. alternative activities for those who have different interests.
      iii. only challenging activities to stimulate interest.

   d. Some good art materials for young preschoolers are
      i. blunt scissors, wide brushes, and large crayons.
      ii. narrow brushes, ballpoint pens, and clay.
      iii. Plasticine, play dough, and colored markers.

10. Name at least two appropriate (adapted) art activities for the following children with special needs:

    a. children with developmental delays
    b. children with visual impairments
    c. children with attention deficit disorder
    d. children with physical impairments

References

Franklin, R. (2007). Drawing inside the box. *SchoolArts*, *107*(8), 12–13.

Gardner, H. E. (1993). *Multiple intelligences*. New York, NY: Basic Books.

Gardner, H. E. (1999). *Intelligence reframed. Multiple intelligences for the 21st century*. New York, NY: Basic Books.

Greenman, J. (2008). *Caring spaces; Learning places: Children: Environments that work*. Washington, DC: NAEYC.

Gould, P., & Sullivan, J. (1999). *The inclusive early childhood classroom: Easy ways to adapt learning centers for all children*. Beltsville, MD: Gryphon House.

Hartmann, T. (2003). *The Edison gene: ADHD and the gift of the hunter child*. Rochester, VT: Park Street Press.

Lee, I. M., Balestrino, M. D., Phelps, R. A., Kurs-Lasky, M., Chaves-Genecco, D., Paradise, J. L., & Feldman, H. M. (2008). Early histories of school-aged children on-deficit-hyperactivity disorder. *Child [Development]*, *79*(6), 1853–1868.

Lougy, R. A. (2007). *Teaching young children with ADHD: Successful strategies and practical interventions for Pre-K–3*. Thousand Oaks, CA: Corwin.

Lowenfeld, V., & Brittain, W. L. (1987). *Creative and mental growth of the child* (8th ed.). New York, NY: Macmillan.

MTA Cooperative Group, 1999 A 14-month randomized clinical trial of treatment strategies for attention-deficit/hyperactivity disorder. *Archives of General Psychiatry*, *73*, 1073–1080.

Ponder, C., & Kissinger, L. (2009). Shaken and stirred: A pilot project in arts and special education. *Teaching Artist Journal*, *7*(1), 40–46.

Qualley, C. A. (2008). *Safety in the artroom*. Worcester, MA: Davis Publications.

Sherman, J., Rasmussen, C., & Baydala, L. (2006, Summer). Thinking positively: How some characteristics of ADHD can be adaptive and accepted in the classroom. *Childhood Education*, *33*(4), 196–200.

Singh, I. (2008). ADHD, culture and education. *Early Child Development and Care*, *178*(4), 347–361.

Additional Readings

Angermeir, P., Krzyzanowski, J., & Moir, K. K. (2009). *Learning in motion: 101+ sensory activities for the classroom.* (2nd ed.). Arlington, TX: Future Horizons.

Chalufour, I., & Worth, K. (2008). *Building structures with young children.* Washington, DC: NAEYC.

Curtis, D., & Carter, M. (2008). *Designs for living and learning: Transforming early childhood environments.* Washington, DC: NAEYC.

Gonzalez-Mena, J., & Stonehouse, A. (2009). *Making links: A collaborative approach to planning and practice in early childhood programs.* New York, NY: Teacher's College Press.

Lowell, C. (2008). Beyond *The Lorax*? The greening of the American curriculum. *Phi Delta Kappan, 90*(3), 218–222.

Mandel, S. M. (2009). *The new teacher toolbox: Proven tips and strategies for a great first year.* (2nd ed.). Thousand Oaks, CA: Corwin Press/SAGE.

McClard, S. T., Waters, J., Gifford, R. M., & Boyd, T. 2009 *The superior educator: A calm and assertive approach to classroom management and large group motivation.* Scotts Valley, CA: CreateSpace Publishing.

Nyman, A. L. (2006). *Instructional methods for the artroom.* Reston, VA: NAEA.

Tebbetts, C. (2007). Cooperative art education. *SchoolArts, 106*(8), 10–12.

Helpful Websites

American Art Therapy Association, http://www.arttherapy.org/

American Music Therapy Association, http://www.musictherapy.org

Arts Education Partnership, http://www.aep-arts.org

Canadian Down Syndrome Society, http://www.cdss.ca

National Art Education Association, http://www.naea-reston.org

NCRTEC Lesson Planner, http://www.ncrtec.org/tl/lp/
This site provides a concise lesson plan template. Scroll through the form boxes and enter your lesson information: Heading and Title, Goals, Curriculum Standards, Assessment, Learning Connections, Learning Activities, Teaching Strategies, Management, Materials, and Resources and Evaluation. Once the lesson is complete, a printer-friendly button formats your lesson and allows you to save it on your hard drive.

PE Central, http://www.pecentral.org
Click on Adapted Physical Education.

Scholastic, http://www.scholastic.com
This is a rich source for lesson plans, teaching strategies, and online activities.

SparkTop.org, http://www.sparktop.org/teacher
This is an award-winning website for kids ages 8–12 with learning and attention problems, including learning disabilities (LD) and attention deficit/hyperactivity disorder (ADHD).
For additional creative activity resources, visit our website at http://www.EarlyChildEd.delmar.com.

Teacher Planet, http://www.teacherplanet.com
This site features more than 330 theme-based resources arranged by calendar month or alphabetically.

The Teacher's Corner, http://www.theteacherscorner.net/
This is a great site for quick lesson plans and ideas.

4 Teachers, http://www.4teachers.org
This site offers free online tools, resources, and ready-to-use Web lessons.

VSA arts, http://www.vsarts.org/

For additional creative activity resources, visit our website at www.Cengage.com/login.

Two-Dimensional Activities

OBJECTIVES

After completing this chapter, you should be able to:

1. Discuss the various ways to motivate children in their use of the various two-dimensional media in this chapter, both inside and outside of the classroom.

2. Describe the tools, materials, techniques, and strategies involved in the two-dimensional activities of drawing/picture making, printmaking, and collage and their developmentally appropriate use in the early childhood program.

3. Define the terms *collage* and *montage* and how you would adapt each of these media to meet the developmental levels of young children.

4. Discuss specific techniques and projects most appropriate for children at the elementary level, giving developmental reasons for your choices.

5. List several two-dimensional activities appropriate for preschool children, including setup, materials, and strategies as well as several variations of the activity in order to differentiate your instruction.

Using as a framework the basic information about developmental levels, creativity, aesthetics, the principles of art and design, and planning and implementing creative activities presented thus far, let us now take a closer look at the general processes of drawing/picture making, printmaking, and collage. You will note that specific ages are not listed for many of the activities in sections of this chapter. This is because many of the activities are designed to be springboards for art experiences and are not limited to certain age groups. Use your knowledge of the developmental levels of the children in your group as a guide to choosing and using activities in this and all chapters of the book. You will, however, find the developmental information provided in the previous sections helpful in determining which activities to initiate with children. (See Chapter 3 and Appendix C for detailed information on color, line and design principles.) Children's reactions to the suggested activities will determine the appropriateness of the choice. Their interest, enthusiasm, and ability to do the activity should be your guide to each activity's appropriateness.

Picture Making/Drawing

The terms **picture making/drawing** in this chapter refer to any and all forms of purposeful visual expressions, beginning with controlled scribbling. A common error associated with picture making or drawing is to equate it with artwork that contains recognizable objects or figures. Children's pictures and drawings (artwork) may take any form, just as long as the child is expressing herself or himself visually in a nonrandom way.

To young children, the act of drawing and painting comes naturally. It is a means by which they communicate visually their ideas and feelings about themselves and their world. They may work in paint, crayon, or chalk; each material has its own distinct characteristics for the child to explore.

Sensitive teachers understand and appreciate the charm and freshness of children's early drawings and paintings. They **motivate children** by helping them recall their experiences and record these in art media. Because teachers respect the individuality of each learner, they inspire and encourage each child to express her or his own personal reactions about the world as she or he understands it. In this way, children discover and build their own unique style of expression. Each child's picture is different from the others in the class, just as her or his appearance and personality are different.

When properly motivated, the child eagerly examines materials and looks forward to proceeding with the activity. Most young children are eager to express themselves in their drawings. However, some children may need more encouragement than others to take the first step. Sometimes a few motivating ideas from the teacher can liven up a child who seems to be less motivated than usual.

Reading a familiar story or singing a song can stimulate art. For example, the artwork in children's books by artists such as Leo Lionni and Eric Carle are excellent choices to motivate a child's creativity in art activities. The colorful collage work in their children's books provides excellent examples of this medium and is sure to encourage children to create their own special collages. Such stimulation is most successful when children are able to associate themselves with the story, poem, or song. They might be asked to think about the character they liked the best, a new ending for the story, or the part that surprised them or pleased them the most and then to draw or paint what they thought.

There are many ways of motivating that awaken the child to the world of color, shape, size, texture, action, and mood. Some of the following ideas may help stimulate children's spontaneity and experimentation.

- Take a walking trip using careful observation.
- Use a digital camera to take pictures on a walking trip. Take pictures of things seen, events, products, and work being done. Then discuss these images, reflecting on them and their significance. Discuss the colors, lines, and other design principles reflected in the images.
- On the trip, gather a collection of objects for a "touch-and-see" display.
- Put up an interesting bulletin board or case display of children's and your artwork.
- Dramatize stories, animals, birds, etc.
- Encourage children to try using materials in different ways if children do not discover them on their own. For example, you might say, "I wonder if the back and side of the crayon will make the same kinds of marks as the pointed end?"
- Exhibit sincere pleasure when a discovery is announced and share it with others in the group.
- Encourage children to bring materials from home to incorporate into their art.
- Share the works of several artists that represent the same or similar theme. This will help children understand that they can draw in many different ways.
- Display the work of each child at some time during the year and call attention to the fact that everyone sees things differently (nonrealistic use of color included).
- Offer found materials that can be used as accessories or tools for artwork. Children will find a variety of ways to create with them. For example, they will use buttons for stringing, glued designs, wheels on toys, or eyes for a puppet or as shapes for print making.

FIGURE 13-1 • Two-dimensional art activities should be arranged to fit the child's developmental level.

The following online art tools are educational and fun. They also encourage collaboration among students all over the world. They are good examples of how technology can be an important part of the art program.

WORDLE (www.wordle.net). Create a pictorial "word cloud" by typing in a chunk of text (such as a student's poem or short story), spelling words your students are currently learning, or the URL of your classroom blog, then display the results to build vocabulary in a print-rich classroom.

GOOGLE SKETCHUP (http://sketchup.google.com/). SketchUp allows students to explore, explain, and present their ideas using 3-D models. Have students try it to redesign your own school building!

MR. PICASSO HEAD (www.mrpicassohead.com). Students can choose head shapes, eyes, mouths, and noses and then play with faces using this virtual Mr. Potato Head, inspired by the work of Pablo Picasso.

ROTOBALL (www.carrotrevolution.com/rotoball). Rotoball is an interactive, international animation experience. Participants are invited to create an animation that lasts exactly 15 seconds. Each animation must contain a ball entering from the left and exiting on the right to be "passed" to the next animator. You can assign student teams the challenge of creating their own animations.

REMIX (http://redstudio.moma.org/interactives/remix/index_f.html). Choose a background, add shapes, and play with opacity in this interactive collage. Layer and repeat! Red Studio also offers other tools, activities, and boards.

SCRATCH (www.scratch.mit.edu). Scratch is a new programming environment that kids can use to create and share their own animated stories, videogames, and interactive art.

FIGURE 13-2 • Art 2.0.

- Add new materials that match the group's interest at particular times. Children who live in snowy areas may need lots of white paint. Temperate spring seasons will stimulate use of pastel colors. Gold and silver papers will spark experimentation with holiday decorations. Furry fabrics may intensify interest in animals and pets.
- Make papers available in many kinds, shapes, and colors. The variety will lead to more responses and experimentation with techniques.

Children's growing awareness is gradually reflected in their pictures as the ability to interpret their environment increases. As the process continues, the teacher and children can evaluate their progress and consider how pictures might be varied, different media used, and any other changes children might suggest.

Painting with a Brush

Painting with a brush encourages the spontaneous use of color. Finger painting, covered in Chapter 12, is another form of painting that is enjoyable for children.

Materials. Basic materials for painting with brushes include the following.

- Watercolor paint sets. These are actually dehydrated tempera colors in concentrated cakes. They provide easy and convenient paint for individual use or group activity in the classroom. These watercolor sets should never be too dry and hard. Try to make an indentation with your fingernail. If the watercolor is too hard, it is not the type to buy for young children. Some watercolors come in oval button shapes. Children will enjoy using these more than the square ones because they do not have to manipulate their brush to get into the corners and because ovals are more suited to brush movements. Also, small sets are preferred to larger ones. Smaller sets encourage the child to mix her or his own colors. Many paint sets include a plastic paintbrush. Discard this: Be sure to use paint brushes with natural fiber bristles.

When buying brushes, be sure to buy those that are labeled "all media" or "for use with oils, acrylics, and watercolors." Brushes that target watercolor alone will be too soft for young children's use. Don't buy wall-painters' brushes or those where all fibers are the same length and end in a flat tip. Brushes with plastic bristles are appropriate only if the brush tapers to a point like a natural-bristled brush. (See Figure 13–3 for suggested brush sizes for various ages of children.)

Flat-tip and Round-tip Brushes—Basic Information
The best brushes are made of natural hairs from animals such as hogs.

Basic Flat Brush Sizes

Length	Width of Bristles	Ages Appropriate
8"	1"	Toddler and up
12"	½"	4 years and up
6"	½"	4 years and up
12"	¾"	3–4 years
6"	¾"	3–4 years
12"	¼"	5 years and up
8"	¼"	5 years and up

Basic Round Brush Sizes (With Pointed Tips)

8"	¾"	6 years and up
8"	½"	6 years and up

FIGURE 13-3 • Flat-tip and round-tip brushes—basic information.

Students should have the opportunity to experiment with a variety of brush sizes when painting. Thick lines can be created by gently pressing down on the brush. Thin lines can be created by lightly touching the surface of the paper with the tip of the brush. Use a wide brush for covering large areas with paint.

To use paints in cakes: Place a few drops of water on the surface of each cake of color to moisten the paint. Never grind the brush into the cake or onto the paper. Child holds the brush as they would a pencil, but farther back on the handle. Dip the brush in water and brush the surface of the moistened cake to obtain smooth, creamy paint.

To use powder paint (**tempera**): Fill a can ¼ full of dry paint. Add water slowly, stirring constantly until the paint has the consistency of thin cream. A small amount of liquid starch or liquid detergent may be added to the mixture as a binder. Use enough paint to make good, rich colors. For best results, prepare paint when needed; large amounts kept over a period of time have a tendency to sour. Containers for use with powder paint include milk cartons, juice cans, yogurt containers, coffee cans, plastic cups, and cut-down plastic bottles. A set of paints can be carried easily if containers are placed in tomato baskets, soft-drink carriers, boxes, or trays.

- Individual pieces of paper, at least 12 inches × 18 inches: roll paper, manila paper, newspaper, wallpaper, newsprint, freezer paper.
- Water containers for painting and rinsing brushes: coffee cans, milk cartons, juice cans,

FIGURE 13-4 • Painting with a brush encourages the use of colors.

and cut-down plastic bottles. Half-gallon plastic containers with handles (the kind used for milk) are light and can be filled to carry water during the painting lesson.

- Paper towels or scrap paper for blotting brushes while painting.
- Newspapers to protect painting area. Painting may be done on paper-covered tables or desks, or on paper pinned to a bulletin board or fastened to a chalkboard. Painting can also be done on the floor if it is protected with newspaper.
- A bucket of child-sized moist sponges for cleanup.

Care and Storage of Materials

- Lay paintings horizontally to dry before stacking. An unused floor space along the wall is suitable for this purpose (see Chapter 12).
- Wipe paint sets clean with paper toweling. They can be stored in a cardboard carton.
- Students should always thoroughly rinse their brush tips between colors of paint. Next, they should

gently blot the brush on a paper towel to test for missed paint. If paint appears on the towel, it should be rinsed and tested again. Sometimes paint gets deep inside the bristles and needs more rinsing.

- Rinse brushes under gently flowing water. Do not use hot water.
- Place a small amount of soap in the palm of the hands.
- Gently rub the bristles of the brush in soapy palms. This will remove stubborn paint from deep inside the bristles.
- Rinse the brush under gently running water to remove all of the soap.
- Blot, and gently reshape the bristles into a point and store brushes to dry upright in a container.
- Clean brushes after each use. Neglect will cause the brush to lose its shape. Never rest a brush vertically on its bristles.

Processes. Painting with brushes may require some demonstration of the following techniques.

- How to prepare paint trays for use. A drop or two of water is placed in each paint color to moisten it.
- How to use a variety of brush strokes. Encourage children to paint directly, using full, free strokes. Use the point, side, and flat surface of the brush. Try wide lines, thin lines, zigzag lines, and dots and dabs.
- How to mix colors on the paper as they paint. Try dipping one side of the brush in one color, the other side in a second color to blend paint in one stroke.
- How to create textures. Paint with bits of sponge, crushed paper or cloth, cardboard, string, sticks, or an old toothbrush. A stiff brush with most of the paint removed creates interesting textural effects.
- How to handle excess paint or water on a brush.
- How to clean paint trays.
- How to rinse and dry brushes.

More Painting Hints

- Thicken easel paint with liquid starch to cut down on drips.
- To help paint stick better to slick surfaces such as foil, waxed paper, Styrofoam, or plastic, mix dry tempera with liquid soap.
- To keep paints smelling fresh and sweet, add a few drops of mint extract or oil of wintergreen or cloves.
- For an added sensory experience, try adding lemon flavoring to yellow paint, mint to green, vanilla

to white, and peppermint to red paint. You might want to caution children—especially younger ones—not to taste the paint.

- Keep dated examples of each child's work in the child's portfolio to reflect her or his growth and development in creative expression. Children will enjoy seeing their progress in control and expression over the year.
- Use a digital camera to create a digital portfolio of children's artwork. One day every month, put a reminder on your calendar to carry a fully charged digital camera throughout the day. Snap the highlights of the day but especially zoom in on children's artwork. At the end of the day, empty the camera into a dated folder to keep on your hard drive. After about four months, select about 10 pictures from each folder and print them, grouped by month. This is a fun way for parents and children to see how much they've developed over the course of the year and their progress in art. See Chapter 11 for more suggestions about using portfolios with children's artwork.

More ideas on painting activities for children as well as recipes for making various types of paints are found at the end of this chapter.

Crayons

Most young children are introduced to using **crayons** before starting school. (See Chapter 12 for additional information about crayons.)

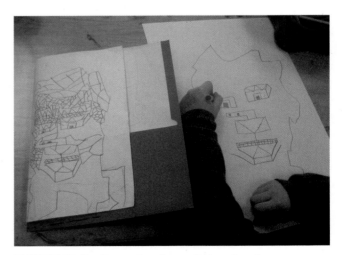

FIGURE 13-5 • Example of pencil drawing from a sketchbook.

FIGURE 13-6 • Crayon and colored marker drawing made up of geometric forms.

Materials. Crayon drawings may be done on a wide assortment of surfaces, such as newsprint, wrapping paper, newspaper, construction paper, corrugated board, cloth, and wood. This is an ideal medium for all children: it is bold, colorful, clean, and inexpensive. Crayons work well on most papers. They can be applied thinly to produce semitransparent layers of subtle color, and these layers can be coated with black crayon and scratched through for crayon etchings.

Processes. Encouraging children to experiment with crayons and to explore the use of different parts of the crayon leads to their discovery of new methods that satisfy their need for expression. The wax crayon has great versatility.

The best way to get bright, rich color from the crayon and onto the paper is by pressing hard. A cushion sheet placed underneath the drawing will assist children in creating bright colors easily.

- Make thin lines with the point of the crayon, heavy lines with the blunt end or side of the crayon.

- Vary the pressure to create subtle tints or solid, brilliant colors.
- Make rough texture by using broken lines, dots, jabs, dashes, and other strokes with the point.
- Create smooth texture by using the flat side or by drawing lines close together in the same direction with the point.
- Twist, turn, swing the crayon in arcs, and move it in various ways to achieve different effects.
- Repeat motions to create rhythm.
- Notch the side of a crayon. This creates negative lines when the crayon is used on its side, resulting in interesting designs with each stroke.
- Use crayons to make designs and patterns on finger paint paper. Then finger paint over the crayon design.
- For older children, combine the use of crayons and textiles. The child makes her or his design with wax crayons directly onto a piece of cloth. Place the cloth between two pieces of paper and press with a warm iron. This will tend to set the design somewhat permanently in the fabric. Variations in the weave and texture of the cloth will affect the design.

See the end of this chapter for crayon batik and crayon chip activities.

Avoid using coloring books or photocopied papers. Children who are frequently given such patterns to color are, in fact, being told that they and their art are inadequate. A pattern of a dog for children to color says to them—more clearly than words could—"This is what your drawing should look like; this is the RIGHT way to make a dog." Instead of dittos and coloring books, provide children a variety of art supplies, media, large blocks of time, and the freedom to work at their developmental level.

The crayon offers new areas of creative interpretation when used in combination with other materials:

- Use crayon and white chalk on colored construction paper.
- Make a crayon rubbing by placing shapes or textures under paper and rubbing over the surface.
- Make a crayon resist by first drawing in brilliant color, then covering the drawing with watercolor paint.
- Paint a colorful background, allow it to dry, and then draw directly over the painted surface with chalk or crayon.
- Use white crayon underneath a color to make a brighter color.

- Use craypas (oil pastel crayons) on colored construction paper. Apply the oil pastels thickly to get rich colors.

More crayon activities are found at the end of this chapter.

Pasting

Paste serves a useful purpose, and its properties also make it a valuable medium for creative expression. Many teachers have given up using paste in favor of glue sticks. These are easier to use and infinitely less messy than "old-fashioned" white paste. However, the stickiness, texture, odor, and changes that take place as old-fashioned white paste is used provide children with opportunities for many discoveries. When a young child picks up paste in her or his hands, the child will almost automatically spread it over her or his fingers and squeeze it or roll it to feel its stickiness. Before long, the child spreads the paste over her or his hands, sometimes even rubbing it into the palms. As paste dries, a child feels a different sensation. When the child begins to wash her or his hands, the paste is transformed from hard to sticky to slimy, a phenomenon of great interest to a child. Paste is a medium that can stimulate a child to repeated explorations of the properties of matter.

Given sufficient paste and a piece of paper, a child almost invariably smears the paste on the paper as though it were finger paint. He or she moves her or his hand across the page with sweeping motions. In some places on the paper, the child smoothes the paste until it is slick and shiny. In other places the child forms

FIGURE 13-7 • Example of thin tempera paint over a crayon drawing.

lumps of paste and then enjoys pressing down on the lumps to smooth them out. The paste-smeared paper becomes an artistic creation for the child.

Having explored paste in this manner, a child reaches for small pieces of paper and pastes piece upon piece, using large quantities of paste in the process. The child is excited by what can be accomplished with the medium. When the child attempts to lift the mound of paper that has been created, very often the paper tears. The child discovers that paste is heavy.

Adults should avoid instructing children on the uses of paste and allow them to make their own discoveries. Eventually a child will begin to create a collage, arranging random shapes of varied colors on large paper. At first the child may pay no attention to design; later she or he will learn to carefully arrange the pieces to achieve a pleasing balance. By adult standards, it may appear that the amount of paste children use is exorbitant, but their explorations are limited if they cannot have as much paste as they need.

Although most paste for children is nontoxic, a teacher should be certain that the commercial paste used in the classroom is safe because children put paste in their mouths. Paste can also be made by the child and/or the teacher. See end of Chapter for paste recipes.

Torn Paper and Pasting

Materials
- Kinds of paper: construction paper, wallpaper, gift wrap, metallic paper, tissue paper, newspaper, illustrated magazine pages
- For mounting: newsprint, construction paper, cardboard, wallpaper, newspaper (classified ad pages), cardboard box lids
- Paste, glue sticks, scissors, brushes

Process
- Demonstrate cutting and tearing paper shapes.
- Have children cut and tear paper shapes.
- Show a variety of papers different in color and texture and encourage children's suggestions about how to use them.
- Demonstrate pasting the torn pieces to the background.
- Point out how torn paper creates a textured edge, while cut edges appear smooth.
- Point out to children how, in tearing paper, greater control of the paper is achieved by tearing slowly with fingers close together.

FIGURE 13-8 • Examples of cut paper and pasting.

- Encourage children to choose light and dark colors for interesting contrast and different sizes or shapes and a variety of papers for textural effects.
- Overlap or group paper shapes to produce new shapes and new combinations of colors and textures.
- Change the texture of cut paper by wrinkling, crumpling, slitting, and folding out.

Older children are eager to use scissors in collage and other pasting activities. There are some general safety points to remember when scissors are used with children:

- Children should always cut away from their bodies.
- Children should never point scissors at anyone.
- Children should never walk with scissors or spin them on the table.
- There are scissors specially made to spring open for students who are physically challenged.
- Many scissors on the market today can be used with the right or left hand. If these are not available, keep a supply of "lefty" scissors for students who need them.

Older children who have mastered scissoring skills will enjoy cut paper activities. Some suggestions for working with cut paper follow.

- Encourage children to think about the shape of an object and its edges before cutting.
- Plan the composition. Cut the big, important shapes first. Cut details, patterns, and textures later. Glue last.
- Use a variety of shapes. Repeat shapes and change their size for variety. Repeat colors by changing their intensity or value for variety.
- Create textured areas by folding, fringing, pleating, curling, and weaving the paper.
- Overlap shapes to give depth and distance to a cut paper composition. Create distance in cut paper by working from the background forward.
- Glue small shapes, details, patterns, and textures to larger shapes before gluing them to the background.
- Glue around the outside edge of the shapes, not over the entire back of the shape.
- Create identical shapes by folding the paper once and remembering that the fold is the middle of the shape.
- Use positive and negative shapes in the composition. The positive shape is the cut shape. The remaining paper is the negative shape.
- Use the lightest colors first when creating with tissue paper. Cut and arrange all the big, important shapes before gluing. Change the arrangement of the shapes until a pleasing composition is found.

Suggested projects

- Paper collage: Use papers of various textures, colors, sizes, and shapes to create a design or picture. See the section on collage later in this chapter.
- Mosaics: These are made with small pieces of torn or cut colored paper. Making a mosaic can be a very exciting project for older children

because it combines the elements of drawing, cutting, pasting, and putting a puzzle together. It may also be used as a group project. Begin by cutting colored paper into small square pieces (one-half inch). When enough pieces have been cut, the group can try a mosaic picture. It's best to start with a simple picture, such as an animal, a tree, or a flower. After children have decided what they want to create, they select the colors that suit the idea they have in mind. Then they apply the bits of paper with glue, starting with the central figure or object and working toward the edges. Mosaics are attractive when they are pasted onto a background of colored paper or cardboard. More complex mosaics can be made by combing a variety of materials, such as gravel, pebbles, seeds, pods, and various types of grains. When using these materials, a stronger glue—like craft glue—is required.

- All-over design: Cut or tear related shapes of different sizes and colors to form a design.
- Cut-paper mural: Select a topic. Each child may cut shapes and combine them in a group mural.
- Three-dimensional picture: Paper pieces on some parts of the picture may be curled, fringed, or fastened only at the edges to allow them to protrude from the background.
- Pasting can involve anything and everything that can be stuck to paper, wood, cardboard, or together: tissues, scraps, corks, feathers, popcorn, Styrofoam pieces, yarn, paste, colored paste, and white paste. It's even possible to paste with glue on brushes or with glue on figures.
- Montage: The word **montage** literally means "putting together." Montage is an art form in which a number of smaller items have been put together. For example, a photomontage is made by cutting and joining a number of pictures into a large design. Children might make a family photomontage. After gathering some photos of important events in their family's life, they can cut or tear the photos into different sizes and glue them onto construction paper. Before gluing, encourage children to try different arrangements. Discuss such art elements as contrasting lines, colors, patterns, value (of colors), shapes, and size as children work at arranging their montages. Once the child is satisfied with her or his design, gluing can proceed.

After the glue is dry, children may use markers to outline some areas or embellish the montage. Have them think about and create details surrounding the event, not just the event itself. When the montage is complete, encourage the children to tell stories about the pictures they have chosen.

Murals

A storytelling picture or panel intended for a large wall space is called a **mural**, another form of picture making. A suitable topic for a mural may come from children's personal experiences at home, at school, or at play, or it may relate to other school subjects. In the classroom, mural making is a versatile art activity; it may involve a large group or just a few children, depending on the size of the mural. Mural-making projects are excellent for "person smart" children who enjoy activities involving other children. Of course, murals are a natural fit for children who have the picture smart (visual) learning style.

With young children, mural making should involve simple, informal, spontaneous expression with a minimum of planning. Tedious planning destroys much of the intuitive quality and reduces interest. In contrast, older children will enjoy planning a group mural almost as much as making it. Have older children think about the composition of the mural—what they could include in it. Some design elements to consider when making a mural with older children follow.

- Varied sizes and shapes
- Varied breakup of foreground and background space
- Overlapping shapes
- Shapes extending out of the picture
- Quiet areas to balance busy ones
- Large objects or figures at the bottom and smaller ones at the top to create the illusion of distance

Materials
- Kraft paper, roll paper, newspapers, wall paper, and colored construction paper
- Crayons, brushes, and paint
- Scissors, water and container, and collage materials

Processes
- Watercolor paint allows for spontaneous bold design and brilliant color, ideal for murals.
- Cut or torn paper is a flexible medium suitable for murals, permitting many changes and parts as the mural progresses. Other techniques for manipulating paper are folding, curling, pleating, twisting, fringing, and overlapping. Place

background paper on a bulletin board, then plan, pin, and move parts before attaching. Various papers such as tissue, wallpaper, illustrated magazine pages, and metallic paper add interest. Topics for group murals are limited only by the imagination of the children. Providing children a variety of experiences both in and out of the classroom will stimulate them to express their ideas visually in a mural. Sometimes an ordinary group discussion will nudge children to become interested in creating a mural.

Printmaking

Long before they enter the classroom, most children have already discovered their footprints or handprints, made as they walk or play in snow or wet sand. In a basic **printmaking activity**, the child learns that an object dipped in or brushed with paint makes its own mark or relief print on paper. This process can be repeated over and over again to create a design. Children use small muscles in the hand, wrist, and fingers as they hold the object, dip it in paint, and print with it on paper. They learn that each object has its own unique quality—that each thing makes its own print.

Techniques range from a simple fingertip printing to carving a Styrofoam plate and printing with it. Emphasis should be on the free manipulation of objects and experimentation with color, design, and techniques.

The teacher may begin by encouraging children to search for objects from the home or classroom. Household items, kitchen utensils, hardware, discarded

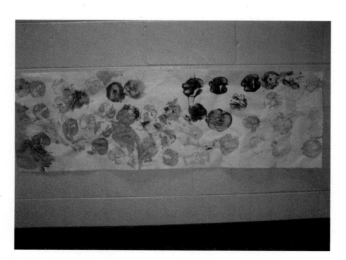

FIGURE 13-9 • A printed objects mural is displayed in a school hallway.

materials, and many objects of nature are useful in relief printing. Gradually, the child learns to look and discover textures, colors, and patterns that exist all around.

In their first attempts to organize shapes into a design, young children usually work in a random fashion. These early experiments help them develop a better understanding of the printmaking process and of the possibilities for variety of designs.

Helping Children Get Started in Printmaking

The following suggestions are some ways to introduce printmaking activities.

- Paint hands and feet and then "print" them on paper.
- Point out and discuss examples of repeated design in clothing, wrapping paper, and wallpaper in which objects appear again and again, up and down and across the whole material.
- Have children print repeat designs using found objects, such as a sponge, rubber eraser, stick, and bottle cap, or natural materials, such as leaves, twigs, stones, and bark.
- Soap is an easy material for even the younger child to handle. First, the teacher levels the surface of the soap block by shaving with a straight knife blade. Younger children might use the unleveled block, although it is always better to cut below the surface of the brand name. Using a knife or a spoon, gouge the desired design in the block of soap. The parts cut away will not print. Ink the soap with tempera paint using a paintbrush or roll paint on with a brayer. Older children are able to carve the soap themselves with a plastic knife. Challenge older pupils to experiment with arrangements and pressures to create greater variety in their prints.

The creative teacher demonstrates any necessary processes of using materials and tools without dictating what the final product will look like. He or she provides stimulation and guidance in the use of children's original ideas and encourages children to experiment with various objects and techniques.

Gradually, through their printmaking experiences, children discover for themselves the following:

- The amount of paint needed to obtain clean edges.
- The object must be painted each time it is printed. Print by pressing slowly and firmly.

THINK ABOUT IT

Pencils—Then and Now

Ancient Egyptians, Greeks, and Romans all used a variety of fine brushes to write on papyrus, an early form of paper from Egypt. The word *pencil* actually comes from the Latin *pencillus*, which means "little brush." The pencil as we know it may have started as the ancient Roman stylus, a thin metal rod that was used to scratch the papyrus, leaving a light but readable mark. Other early writing tools were made of lead and were often used to draw lines, as the ancient Egyptians did on their papyrus. Although we still call the core of a pencil the "lead," it is actually made from nontoxic graphite.

In 1564, a large deposit of graphite was discovered near Borrowdale, England. The local farmers found that it was very useful for marking their sheep. This graphite left a much darker mark than lead, which made it ideal for use by writers and artists. Pure graphite is soft and brittle, so holders were required. Sticks of graphite were cut and then wrapped in string. Later, graphite was put into wooden sticks that had been hollowed out by hand. Since the quality or purity of graphite was inconsistent around the world, the hardness or softness of pencils was difficult to control. Companies developed different methods of refining graphite and experimented with various additives.

Around 1795, Nicolas-Jacques Conte, a Frenchman, developed a process of mixing powdered graphite with finely ground clay particles. This mixture would then be shaped and baked. This technique (the Conte process) is still in use today and allows manufacturers the flexibility to produce different types of pencils. By changing the ratio of clay to graphite, manufacturers can change the hardness or softness of the pencil. This process also allows for consistent quality between batches.

By the beginning of the 20th century, two systems for identifying the grade of pencils were in use. European pencil makers were using a combination letter–number system. Most U.S. pencil makers were using a number-only system. Both systems are still in use today.

Since the 1890s, pencils have been painted yellow. American pencil makers wanted to show people that their pencils contained Chinese graphite—the best in the world at the time. In China, the color yellow is associated with respect and royalty. Today you can find pencils in every color of the rainbow (Stevens, 2006).

Here are some fun facts about pencils:

- The average pencil can be sharpened 17 times.
- Each year, more than 14 billion pencils are produced.
- Until 1876, almost all pencils were square. Then, hexagonal, round, and other shapes began to appear.
- The typical pencil can draw a line 35 miles long.
- You can write approximately 45,000 words with a pencil.

- The amount of pressure needed to get a print.
- How the shape and texture of an object determine the shape and texture of the print.
- How to repeat a print over and over to create a design.

Printmaking Materials

Materials for printmaking may include the following.

- Paint. Any of the following are suitable: tempera paint in sets of eight colors, powder paint in a thin mixture, food coloring, water-soluble printing ink.

- Stamp pad. Discarded pieces of felt or cotton cloth inside a jar lid, cut-down milk carton, frozen food tin, or similar waterproof container can be saturated with color to create a stamp pad. Another way to make a stamp pad is to fold a paper towel or similar absorbent paper in several layers. Then place it in a shallow dish such as a small foil plate and saturate it with paint.
- Paper. Absorbent papers suitable for printing include newsprint, manila paper, wallpaper, tissue, construction paper, the classified pages of the newspaper, plain wrapping paper, or paper towels. Avoid using paper with a slick finish because it does not absorb paint and ink well.

THIS ONE'S for YOU!

Did you Know…? Some Interesting Facts About Famous Artists

The following are some lesser-known facts about famous artists that you might not know.

Did you know that Georgia O'Keeffe used a special technique to mix her paints? She mixed them on a glass tray on which she also kept a separate brush for each color. In order to keep track of every color she used, she put a sample of each one on a white card with instructions of what colors were used to produce it. This enabled her to easily reproduce the color to use in another painting.

Did you know that Picasso was the first famous artist to use collage? Picasso used the collage technique when he created *Still Life With Chair Caning.*

Did you know that Helen Cordero (1915–1999) was a Native American potter best known as the

inventor of the Storyteller figure? After she raised six children, she turned to art as a way to make extra money. She first worked with beads and leather but was frustrated that the cost of the materials ate up her profits. A relative suggested she switch to clay because, "you don't have to buy anything; Mother Earth gives it all to you."

Did you know while he developed his artistic talent, Romare Bearden (1911–1988) worked as a semiprofessional baseball player, a newspaper political cartoonist, and a New York social worker? He was also a successful songwriter who had several of his songs recorded by popular artists. A song called *Seabreeze* became a hit in the 1950s and was recorded by both Billy Eckstine and Tito Puente. It was recorded again in 2003 by Branford Marsalis.

- Cloth. Absorbent pieces of discarded cloth can also be used to print on, such as pillowcases, sheets, men's handkerchiefs, old shirts, and napkins.
- Other items. Also have newspaper for covering tables, brushes for applying paint when not using a stamp pad, and cans for water.

Printmaking Techniques

The following are some common printmaking techniques suitable for young children.

Found object printing. With a few familiar objects, such as forks, spools, sticks, buttons, bottle tops, some paper, paint, and a brush, children can learn to print their own designs. Objects found in nature, such as leaves, weeds, seeds, and stones, can also be used.

Fingerprints. Children press one of their fingers onto a stamp pad or a tray filled with thickened tempera and then onto a piece of newsprint. Encourage children to experiment using different fingers, singly or in combinations. Afterward, they can add details with markers and crayons.

Texture prints. Children prepare a printing block that consists entirely of a variety of textures. This

might include natural materials such as pebbles, seeds, or other items that are glued to a stiff cardboard backing. Or children can cut and punch in cardboard to create different textures. Children then paint the block with a wide brush and then press the block onto a piece of paper.

Another texture print that involves only simple materials is a sandpaper print. The child colors on a sheet of sandpaper using wax crayons. The design is developed directly on the sandpaper and then placed face down on the paper. The teacher goes over the back of the sandpaper with a warm iron and the melted wax will transfer into a textured print onto the paper.

Monoprinting. To create a **monoprint**, apply paint to paper. Carefully place a sheet of paper over the painting and rub smoothly from the center out to the edge. If desired, children can draw in crayon on the top sheet of paper, pressing the lines into the paint on the bottom sheet. Pull the print gradually, starting from one corner.

Styrofoam prints. Children draw a picture or design using permanent markers on a flat piece of Styrofoam. These markers will dissolve the foam. They then use a brush or sponge to apply a thin layer of tempera to the surface of the tray. They place a piece of construction paper over the tempera and rub. Another way to print with Styrofoam is to make a pattern, picture, or design by squeezing glue onto the Styrofoam. After the glue has dried, tempera paint is applied to the entire surface. Place a piece of construction paper over the paint and rub. Because this is a two-step process, it is more appropriate for children in the middle and upper elementary grade levels.

Pieces of Styrofoam can also be used as printing plates after cutting them into shapes and pasting them on a background. The same applies to heavy cardboard.

Printing for older children. Older children, as we have seen in Chapter 12, continue to refine their creative skills throughout the elementary grades. In printing experiences, children in the middle and upper elementary levels are usually able to use a **brayer** (an ink roller) with a printing plate. Brayers in various sizes can be purchased at art supply stores.

The brayer is rolled in a shallow pan filled with a small amount of water-soluble ink or tempera paint. A metal or plastic tray or small cookie sheet works well for this. The child rolls the brayer over the ink to spread an even coat on the brayer. Then the ink-coated brayer is rubbed over the printing plate (e.g., a cut out design on Styrofoam) until the whole surface is covered with ink. It works best to roll the brayer in one direction, then in another at right angles.

The child then places paper on top of the inked plate and presses it down gently with the palm of the hand. She or he rubs the back of the paper with the fingertips or the back of a spoon, being sure to cover all areas including the edges. Finally, the child pulls the paper away from the block. This is called "pulling the print." Now the print is ready to dry.

Some hints for working with older children and printing with brayers follow.

- Set up three printing centers in a classroom. You may want to use a different color of ink at each center. Keep centers neat and well stocked with paper and ink.
- As students are ready to print, direct them to a center to roll the ink on their blocks with the brayer. Then have them take their inked blocks and papers to their desks and do the actual printing there. This will prevent long lines at the centers.
- For cleanup, drop a folded piece of newspaper in the pan filled with ink. Roll the brayer on the newspaper. This will remove a great deal of the

ink from both the pan and the brayer. Unfold the newspaper and refold it with the dirty side inside. Crumple and throw away the newspaper. Once most of the ink is out of the pan, it is easy to rinse both it and the brayer at the sink.

Paper stencils. The four- to five-year-old child can begin to use paper to make **stencils** in a most creative manner. Each child is given four or five pieces of drawing paper about four inches square. With scissors, the child cuts holes of various sizes and shapes in the center of each piece. It is a good idea to cut more than one hole per piece. When the holes have been cut, each child is given a tissue, small piece of cotton, or patch of cloth. This is rubbed on a piece of colored chalk to pick up enough dust to stencil. Then the child selects a shape and places it on the paper on which the design is to go. The child rubs the tissue across the hole, making strokes from the stencil paper toward the center of the opening. This is continued around the edge of the opening until the paper under the stencil has a clear print. The same shape can be continued across the paper, or other shapes and colors may be added according to the child's preference.

A child can choose the shapes and combinations desired. The same technique can be used with wax crayons and felt-tip markers instead of chalk. The crayons and markers are applied directly on the stencil. Unbleached muslin or cotton material can be used to print on as well.

The spatter technique. Simple **spatter or spray printing** is both fascinating and fun for children. It also has the advantage of allowing for a wide variety of patterns and shapes. Children can work individually or with partners on this project.

Have several children bring in old toothbrushes. Besides toothbrushes, only a small amount of watercolor paint and paper are needed. "Spray" the paint with a toothbrush. This is done by dipping the brush in paint and gently pulling a straight-edged object (ruler, emery board, or tongue depressor) across the ends of the bristles. This causes the bristles to snap forward, throwing small particles of paint onto the paper.

Children create designs by placing small, flat objects on the paper. When the bristles snap the small particles of paint forward, the object prevents the spray from striking the paper directly under the object. This leaves the shapes free of paint spray while the rest of the paper is covered with small flecks of paint.

This technique has endless possibilities. Not only can a variety of shapes be used, but colors can also be superimposed on one another. Natural forms such as twigs, leaves, and grass are excellent for this activity. Several forms can be combined, leading to interesting arrangements with unlimited variety. A field trip is a good way to find new print forms and shapes, thus encouraging children to find and learn about beauty in their own environment. Another strength of this project is that it avoids stereotyped designs and ready-cut patterns. The children create beauty for themselves.

Suggestions for Printmaking Experiments

With color
- Alternate thin watercolor with thick, opaque tempera paint.
- Use a light color to print on dark paper, or vice versa.
- Use thin tempera paint on colored paper or cloth so that the color of the background shows through.
- Combine two sizes of objects of the same shape.
- Combine objects of different sizes and shapes.
- Use one object in various positions.
- Try overlapping and grouping objects.

With texture
- Vary the amount of paint used in printing.
- Use objects that create different textures, such as sponges, corrugated paper, wadded paper or cloth, stones, vegetables, and sandpaper.

With background paper
- Use a variety of shapes and sizes of paper.
- Paint background paper and allow it to dry before printing.
- Paste pieces of tissue or colored construction paper onto background paper, allow to dry, then print.
- Print a stippled design on the background with a sponge, allow to dry, then print with a solid object.

With pattern
- Print a shape in straight rows or zigzag. Repeat design to create an all-over pattern.
- Use a different shape for each row and add a second color in alternate rows.
- Print in a border design with a single shape or group of shapes.

More ideas for printmaking are found at the end of this chapter.

FIGURE 13-10 • Scribble art project: This child begins by making pencil scribble, then outlines scribble in black marker.

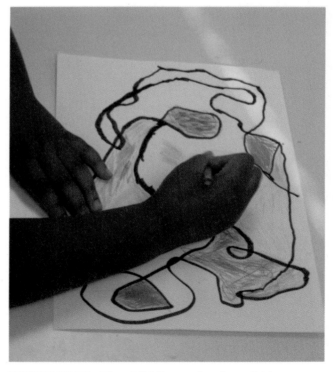

FIGURE 13-11 • The child then colors in scribble spaces.

FIGURE 13-12 • The child continues to fill in white areas with different colors.

FIGURE 13-13 • Finished scribble art example: Scribble form cut out and mounted on black construction paper.

Collage

A **collage** is a picture made by applying various materials to a flat surface. The word *collage* comes from the French word *coller,* meaning "to paste or stick." As an art expression, collage was developed in France during the early part of the 20th century by the artists Pablo Picasso and Georges Braque and in Germany by Kurt Schwitters. Collage was further developed in Germany at the Bauhaus, an experimental school of art. A collage is the product of selecting, organizing, and arranging materials of contrasting color and texture and attaching them to a flat surface.

One way children become aware of things around them is by touching. Through manipulation of everyday objects, they grow in sensitivity to shapes and textures and discover ways to use them in creating new forms and images. With added experience, the tactile sense becomes an instrument of knowledge and a tool of expression. Unlike the imitation of texture in drawing and painting, the textural materials in collage are real.

Special Needs and Matisse's Paper Cutouts

Children may be interested to know that a number of famous artists have dealt with disabilities. When the painter Henri Matisse became ill and was too infirm to paint standing in front of an easel, he changed his working process and medium. Because he was confined to his bed or a wheelchair, he began to make large collages with shapes he cut out of papers that had been painted by his studio assistants. When children begin their collage experiences, they may become very interested in knowing about how Matisse overcame his disability and continued to produce art (Thompson, S. C., 2005).

Helping Children Get Started in Collage Activities

The following suggestions are designed to help motivate children in their initial collage activities.

- Arouse children's awareness of texture by passing around various materials for them to touch and examine. Discuss the qualities of various textures by asking: "How do these materials feel? Are they smooth? Hard? Soft? Fuzzy? Sharp? How can we use these materials?"
- Arrange a "touch-and-see" display.
- Discuss sources of collage materials and encourage children to collect them.
- Demonstrate making a collage: Select and arrange materials on a background and demonstrate methods of fastening using paste, thread, and staples.
- Assess qualities of materials in relation to ideas to be expressed (e.g., gold paper is bright and "shiny like the sun" and cotton is soft and white "like snow").

THIS ONE'S for YOU!   Bits of History—Art Materials

You might like to know a little about the history behind some of the familiar art media you use with children. Here are bits of history about these everyday materials.

Chalk. The original chalks for drawing, some still in use today, were pure earth, cut and shaped into implements. The addition of a binder created a fabricated chalk that we know today as a *pastel* chalk. Chalks used by the early master painters were generally limited to reds (sanguine), black, and white.

Crayons. Of the many art materials, probably none is more familiar than wax crayons. The fact that most of us were introduced to them at a tender age may influence us to think that they are beneath the dignity of more mature artists. Such is not the case; examples abound of distinguished drawings executed in this humble medium (works by Miro and Picasso, for example). Examples of the use of crayons begin in the 19th century. Crayons consist of an oily or waxy binder impregnated with pigments of color. Records exist of a variety of prescriptions for binders involving soap, salad oil, linseed oil, spermaceti, and beeswax.

Ink. The earliest ink known, black carbon, was prepared by the early Egyptians and Chinese. This was followed by iron-gall (made from growths on trees), bistre (burnt wood), and sepia (a secretion from cuttlefish). Today, a wide variety of inks is available, but the best known is India ink, which is really a waterproof carbon black.

Pens. Those of us who take for granted our familiar metal pen points of various kinds may not realize that they are fairly new, not having been successfully developed until the 20th century. Until that time, the reed pen had been the pen of the ancients, and the quill pen was the principal instrument from the medieval period to modern times. Most of us probably remember the use of quill pens in the drawings of Rembrandt and in the historical documents drawn up by the founders of our Republic.

Brushes. Bristle is obtained from the bodies of hogs and boars found in Russia, Japan, Formosa, Korea, France, and Central and Eastern Europe. While all other animal hair has points, bristle does not: the individual bristle splits into two or three tiny forks on the end, which are called *flags*.

Materials

- Background: manila paper, construction paper, cardboard, and shirt board
- Collage materials: paper and cloth scraps, magazine pages, yarn, string, ribbon, lace, and any other items the children and teacher collect
- Natural materials: leaves, twigs, bark, seed pods, dried weeds, feathers, beans, ferns, sands, small stones, and shells
- Scissors, brushes, paste, glue sticks, stapler, and staples

Sort and keep materials of a similar nature in boxes to facilitate selection.

Processes

- When working with beginners, limit the number of collage materials. This lessens the confusion in selection.
- Encourage children to use materials in their own way. Instead of giving exact directions, suggest ways of selecting materials for variety of shape, size, color, and texture.
- Demonstrate how materials may be cut, torn, or left in their original shapes.
- As children arrange and rearrange the shapes on the background, they may form a representational picture or compose an abstract design.
- Throughout the work period, emphasize thoughtful use of space by overlapping and grouping shapes, and trying different combinations of colors and textural surfaces.
- Create three-dimensional effects by crumpling flat pieces of material and attaching them to the background in two or three places. Other techniques include overlapping, bending, folding, rolling, curling, and twisting paper.
- Include buttons, braids, tissue, or yarn for added interest and accent.
- Use glue or staples to fasten heavy materials and plastics.
- Display the collage in a shadow box, using a box lid as a frame. It can also be mounted in an old picture frame or on a sheet of colored construction paper.

THINK ABOUT IT

The History of Fingerpainting

Ruth Faison Shaw is considered by some to be the initiator of finger painting in America (Bedford, 1963). Shaw developed the technique of finger painting and a method for teaching it. Later, Shaw applied finger painting to therapeutic uses. Finger painting reached the height of its importance at the time of the Progressive Education Movement in the 1930s, and educators have since continued using it with young children.

Shaw began to experiment with finger painting in 1929, trying to foster children's expression in a visual way. In Shaw's words:

> It all began, in the most natural way in the world, with a little boy at the school who smeared the bathroom wall with iodine. All the children liked to "smear"—"smearing" with the hands is a primary impulse, a way of having fun and of learning. So, I went about the task of compounding a suitable medium with which they could smear to their hearts' content without damaging results. (1947, p. 5)

Shaw named this medium "finger painting," but finger painting was not a new technique. Fingerprints were found in Etruscan tombs in France and Pompeii. In addition, the Chinese painter Chung Isao painted with this technique in the year 750

(Betts, B. V. 1963). However, finger painting did not become well known in America until 1932 when Shaw took a position as an art teacher at the Dalton School in New York, one of the many progressive schools that supported art education (Stankiewicz, 1984). The first American exhibition of finger paintings by children was held in a Manhattan art gallery in 1933.

The materials for finger painting were an important part of the Shaw finger painting method. Shaw experimented for a long time trying to find formulas for finger paint. In the early 1930s, Shaw started to make the paint in a small factory in New York. The demand for her finger paint grew, and in 1936, she contracted with Binney & Smith to manufacture the paint. Homemade recipes for making finger paints appeared in art book activities from the 1940s and on.

This is the history of our American form of finger painting. Now, when you take out the finger paints, remember the words of Ruth Faison Shaw about creating her finger painting technique: "Finger painting belongs to the people. It is an art. It is an activity of the people" (Shaw, 1947, p. 6). And the youngest people enjoy it immensely!

- Create a nature collage using all natural materials.
- Make a paper or cloth collage, exploring a variety of one kind of material. Do the same with leaves, buttons, or one kind of material children enjoy.

Because older children enjoy creating more complex works in their art experiences, collage is an excellent medium for this age group. Here are some collage ideas for this age group.

- Keep a collection of old magazines on hand. Have students tear or cut out sections of pages with large areas of interesting colors, textures, or patterns that might be used for collages. Have them create collages with these. Allow them to trade magazine pages with one another.

FIGURE 13-14 • Example of cloth and paper collage picture.

• Collages can often send the viewer a very strong message. Have students make a collage mural about littering. Discuss how litter pollutes the school grounds and the environment. Talk about the types of items that comprise litter. Have students cut pictures from magazines of things that could litter the playground or cause environmental pollution. Students can also draw objects for the mural. Give the mural a title that reinforces the message of the artwork.

After students have completed collage activities, have them write about their artwork. More collage activities are found at the end of this chapter.

Summary

Two-dimensional media covered in this chapter include drawing/picture making, painting with a brush, using crayons, pasting, making collages, murals, and printmaking. *Picture making* and *drawing* are terms that refer to any and all forms of purposeful visual expressions, beginning with controlled scribbling. Painting is a method of picture making and can be done with a brush or with the fingers (finger painting). Collage and montage activities involve the selection, organization, and arrangement of materials and attaching them to a surface. In printing activities, the child learns that an object dipped in or brushed with paint makes its own mark or relief print on paper. This process can be repeated over and over to create a design. In all of these two-dimensional activities, the early childhood teacher encourages children's creativity by helping them recall their experiences and record these in two-dimensional media. Motivation can involve reading children's books with noteworthy art, such as that of Eric Carle and Leo Lionni, to inspire children in their own creations. This chapter covered appropriate tools, materials, techniques and strategies for all of these two-dimensional activities.

Key Terms

brayer 304
Collage 306

FIGURE 13-15 • Children's growing awareness is gradually reflected in their pictures.

crayons 296
montage 300
monoprint 303
motivate children 292
mural 300
picture making/drawing 292
pasting 298
painting with a brush 294
printing 303
Print making activity 301
spatter/spray painting 304
stencils 304
tempera 295
Torn paper and pasting 298

Learning Activities

A. Think "outside the box" and develop a list of "unlikely" two-dimensional art materials. Concentrate on using recycled materials such as newspaper, magazines, cardboard, etc.

B. Observe a preschool child painting at an easel. Describe how the child handled the brush, the application of paint, and amount of time spent painting. Then observe a first-grade child painting at an easel and describe these same things. What does your observation tell you about easel painting at various developmental levels? What would you change in either situation to enhance the painting experience for each child?

C. Make a collage, painting, or drawing that expresses one of the following:

1. How you would improve human beings
2. A special machine or device to help the President
3. How you would weigh an elephant
4. A machine that exercises a dog
5. Something that can't be seen
6. An underground city
7. After you have finished your work, see if your fellow students can guess which topic you chose. Then try the same activity with children. Compare their work with yours and that of your fellow students. Discuss the similarities and differences in each group.

D. Choose one of the children's books in the lists below by Eric Carle or Leo Lionni.

Books by Leo Lionni: *Alexander and the Wind-up Mouse* (1970), *Frederick* (1973), *Swimmy* (1973), *The Biggest House in the World* (1973), *Fish is Fish* (1974), *The Alphabet Tree* (1990), *Little Blue and Little Yellow* (1995), *Inch by Inch* (1995), *Matthew's Dream* (1995), *It's Mine!* (1996), *A Color of His Own* (1997), *Tico and the Golden Wings* (2000), *Let's Play* (2003), *Pezzettino* (2006).

Books by Eric Carle: *The Mixed-up Chameleon*, (1988), *Do You Want To Be My Friend?* (1988), *The Very Busy Spider* (1989), *Polar Bear, Polar Bear What Do You Hear?* (1997), *The Very Hungry Caterpillar* (1994), *The Grouchy Ladybug* (1996), *The Very Quiet Cricket* (1997), *From Head to Toe* (1999), *The Very Lonely Firefly* (1999) *Brown Bear, Brown Bear What Do You See?* (1996), *Papa, Please Get the Moon for Me* (1999),

Eric Carle's Very Little Library (2003), *Panda Bear, Panda Bear, What Do You See?* (2006), *Baby Bear, Baby Bear, What Do You See?* (2009), *Eric Carle's 123* (2009).

Plan a collage lesson for young children with one of these books that features collage work in your lesson introduction. Discuss the results of your lesson and the role this book played in the effectiveness of your lesson as it is reflected in the children's work.

E. Explain how you would use Garner's multiple intelligences to choose specific art activities for young children. Use at least two intelligences in your answer, giving specific examples.

F. As teachers of young children, we encourage children to be keen observers of the world around them and to reflect these observations in their artwork. This activity is designed to give you the chance to practice drawing from observation and recollection by one or more of the following activities.

Take an object apart and then draw it.

Examine an object for one minute. Put the object away. Then draw a picture of what you remember about it.

G. Show someone how to do something in a sequence of drawn pictures.

H. Draw yourself looking in a mirror.

I. Draw an object from three different views.

J. Draw a map showing your route from home to school. Include local landmarks in your map.

Activities for Children

Painting

Dip and Dye. This technique comes from the old Japanese technique of folding and dipping paper in dye. Put diluted food coloring or strong tempera paint in small bowls. Children fold paper towels or any other absorbent paper in half, quarters, thirds, and so on. They then dip the corners of the folded paper towel into the bowl of dye and allow time for the color to be absorbed. After the child has dyed the four corners of the folded paper, he or she blots the paper between several layers of paper towels or newspapers to remove the excess color and force it evenly through the layers of paper. The paper is then dipped in another color that is darker than the first. Dipping occurs on a corner or side that was not dipped before, or the paper may be redipped on the tip, a corner, or an edge that was dipped before. If paper is redipped, it should be removed before the dye completely covers the first color. After the

packet is blotted between papers again, it is carefully unfolded and placed on newspapers to dry. Children will want to make several sheets of this decorative paper because no two ever come out of the dye baths looking exactly alike. Two and three dips in the dye baths create merged and blended tones, while a pleasing repetition of colored shapes results from the way in which the paper was folded before it was dipped in the dye. The brightly patterned paper may be pressed with an iron and used for gift wraps, stationery trims, program covers, greeting cards, or for covering cartons, boxes, cans, books, and notebooks.

Bubble Wrap Painting. Lay a piece of bubble wrap on a table so that the bubbles are facing up. Have the child cover the bubbles with tempera paint. Then place a piece of construction paper on top of the bubbles. Press down on the paper so that all of the bubbles are able to make a print. Lift up the construction paper and see the design. See what happens when some of the bubbles pop when pressing down on the construction paper. How do the popped bubbles print differently than the ones with air still in them? If you use more than one color of paint, how do the paints blend?

Rainbow Painting. Use white crayons to draw simple pictures or designs on white paper. Then make a rainbow of lines over the picture, using different colors of watercolor paints. Watch as the drawings magically appear through the rainbow.

Variety Painting. For a change, try using household implements to paint or print with. Try a comb, an old toothbrush, string, an old wheel toy, sponges, a wadded bit of paper towel, alphabet letter magnets, and other safe items from the kitchen drawer. Try different motions, such as pulling the object across the paint, or quick dabbing onto the paper.

Finger Painting with Ice Cubes. For this variation of finger painting, use regular finger paint and glossy paper, but do not wet the paper as you normally would to prepare for finger painting. Give each child an ice cube with which to spread and dilute the paint while making designs on the paper.

String Painting. You will need two pieces of white drawing paper for each child, tempera paint in bowls, and 12 inch lengths of string (at least three per child). Provide several lengths of string for each bowl of tempera paint. Hold one end and dip string into paint. Lay string on paper to create a design. Redip and repeat, or use a new string and a new color. For a variety, try dropping the string onto paper. For a print design, press a second sheet of paper on top of the string design and lightly press.

Pulled String Painting. You will need yarn or string, bowls of tempera paint, construction paper or drawing paper, and a damp rag or sponge. Dip the string or yarn into a bowl of tempera paint. Do not squeeze paint out of the string. Lay the string on a sheet of paper in any design, leaving the tail end of the string off the edge of the paper. Place another piece of paper over this. Lay a hand gently over the paper and string. Pull the string from the paper, keeping the hand pressing gently on the top of the paper. Remove the top paper and see the string design! For a variation, try a folded sheet of paper and place the string inside. Try several colors, one at a time, adding each color after the first is done. Try a rope dipped in paint and place it between very large sheets of paper. Many hands can help this time!

Smash Painting. You will need white construction or drawing paper (let the children cut or tear it into interesting shapes), plastic cling-type wrap cut a bit larger than the pieces of paper, plastic eye droppers, tempera paint in three colors (white, dark blue, and light blue), and markers.

Children pick up one color of paint with an eyedropper and drip it onto the paper. Repeat with the next two colors. Then children place the plastic wrap on top of their paper and rub, causing the paints underneath to blend and swirl. Talk about the colors being created. When the child is pleased with the blended colors, remove the plastic wrap and enjoy the design. After the paintings are dry, children can add details and designs with markers and crayons.

Splotch Paintings. Mix some paint in a small cup of water. Make sure it is dark enough to show up on the paper you are using. The child "spills" some paint onto her or his paper. Watch as the puddle of paint forms an organic or free-form shape. Children can tilt the paper in different directions to spread the spill if they like. Allow the organic shape to dry. The child can use her or his imagination to turn the shape into a picture or a design.

Flashy Painting. You will need black or very dark construction paper, glitter, white glue, and newspapers. Cover the work area with newspapers. The child spreads the glue on the paper in shapes and designs. Sprinkle glitter on the paper. Slide the excess glitter off the picture and back into the glitter container. Repeat the glue and glitter process with different colors of glitter. Let the glue dry.

Homemade Paints. The following are paint recipes that are fun and different.

Face Paints

    1 tsp cornstarch
    ½ tsp water
    ½ tsp cold cream
    2 drops food coloring

Mix ingredients well. Then use different food coloring to make different colors.

Watercolors

    1 tbsp white vinegar
    1½ tbsp baking soda
    1 tbsp cornstarch
    ½ tsp glycerin
    food coloring

Mix vinegar and baking soda in small bowl and allow foaming. After foaming stops, add cornstarch and glycerin. Stir well (up to a couple of minutes). Portion the mixture into a paint palette, muffin tin, or similar container and add food coloring. Make the colors dark; drying and use will lighten them. Allow watercolors to dry in a warm place for several hours or overnight. Makes one set of watercolors.

Shiny Paint

    white glue
    tempera paint (liquid)
    dish detergent

Pour glue into small cups. Mix your choice of liquid tempera paint into each. Use to paint on wood, paper, or cardboard as you would any paint. Paint will dry shiny as if glazed. Variations: Paint pinecones, driftwood, rocks, or glass. Try painting with sponge brushes for a very smooth finish. To help paint adhere to shiny, smooth surfaces, add a few drops of dish detergent.

Salt Paint

⅛ cup liquid starch
⅛ cup water
1 tbsp tempera paint

Mix together and apply to paper with a brush. Keep stirring mixture. Paint will crystallize as it dries to a salt-like texture.

Puffy Paint

flour
salt
water
tempera paint

Mix equal parts of flour, salt, and water in a bowl. Add a small amount of tempera paint to the mixture and pour into a small plastic squeeze bottle. Repeat the procedure, making as many colors as you wish. Squeeze onto heavy paper or cardboard to make designs. Mixture will harden into puffy shapes.

Sand Paint

tempera paint (powder)
sand

Mix dry tempera paint with sand. Let children spread glue on picture and sprinkle on sand.

Cornstarch Paint

1 tbsp cold water
2 tbsp cornstarch
1 cup boiling water
food coloring

Combine cold water and cornstarch. Stir until smooth. Add boiling water and stir again until smooth. Add food coloring until paint is desired color. Let cool. Store this paint in a covered container. If it dries, add water to thin it.

Cold Cream Paint

six-sectioned muffin tin
1 tsp cornstarch
½ teaspoon cold cream
½ teaspoon water
food coloring

Mix all but the food coloring for each section of the muffin cup. Decide what food coloring color to add to each cup and mix.

Painting—It's Great Outdoors!

Break away from traditional thinking about painting inside at a table or an easel. There are many exciting painting adventures awaiting you and the children in the great outdoors. Here are a few ideas to get you started.

Water Painting. Preschoolers enjoy painting the side of a building or the sidewalk with large paintbrushes and buckets of water. The broad strokes enhance gross motor development and hand–eye coordination. This activity can also lead to a rudimentary discussion of evaporation.

Weed Painting/Printing. Go outside and collect a variety of weeds to use as paintbrushes. Queen Anne's lace is one that works especially well. Children dip the weed into a small, shallow container of paint. Then they can either print with the weed or use it as an interesting paintbrush.

Root Painting. Help children dig up dead plants and save the roots (with the stems attached). Or ask families to gather roots that children can use. Be sure that you have nontoxic roots that are bushy, with stems sturdy enough to serve as root brush handles. Mix a variety of tempera paint to a medium consistency and pour it in juice cans, paint cups, or ready-to-use frosting containers. Gather paper—any kind will do—and put it in a bag or basket to take outside. Set up easels on a grassy area, or cover a picnic table with newspapers. Put out the paper and paint. Give children lots of time to experiment and create designs and pictures with their root brushes.

Mud Finger Painting. Fill a dishpan with dirt (high clay content works best, but any "clean" soil will do). Fill another dishpan with water. Provide several large, washable trays and several plastic scoops for the soil and the water. Set up a table, preferably near a faucet with a hose. Place the trays, dishpans, and scoops on the table with smocks nearby. Children put on smocks and scoop soil and water onto their trays. Let children enjoy experimenting with this new "mud finger paint" they create by mixing water and soil together.

Outdoor Weaving. Gather long scarves, pieces of ribbon, cording, and rope in many colors, and rolls of crepe paper in as many colors as possible. Locate a nearby chain link fence. Children weave the ribbons, crepe paper, and other materials in and out of the links on the fence to create a colorful woven design on the fence. (This is not painting, but it's a fun outdoor activity!)

Sun Prints. Collect a variety of items with interesting shapes: spools, forks, cookie cutters, seashells, stray puzzle pieces. Gather several sheets of bright construction paper. Be sure not to use construction paper guaranteed not to fade. Dark blue, purple, and green construction paper work well. Attach the construction paper to one side of a large flat sheet of cardboard. Children choose shapes from the collection and place them anywhere and in any way they like on the paper. Leave everything in the sun. In a day or two, go outside and remove the objects. When the objects are removed, the sun will have bleached the paper, leaving dark silhouettes in an interesting design.

Printing

Line Printing. You will need 2 inch wide strips of various lengths of manila tag paper, one sheet of 9" × 18" white drawing paper per child, paperclips, staplers, and three plates of tempera paint per group (e.g., hot/cold colors). Children fold, curve, pleat, etc., their strips of manila tag paper and either paperclip or staple the form. They then dip each strip form into different colors of tempera paint, then print onto their drawing paper to demonstrate the element of line.

Bubble Prints. You will need 1 cup of water, food coloring, ¼ cup liquid detergent, ¼ cup liquid starch, straws, printing paper, and a 6- to 8-inch bowl. In the bowl, mix the water, drops of food coloring, liquid detergent, and liquid starch. Let children blow bubbles in the bowl using a straw. (Poke a hole in the top of the straw to prevent children accidentally sipping with the straws.) Blow until the bubbles form a structure above the rim of the bowl. Make a print by laying a sheet of white paper across the bowl rim and allowing the bubbles to pop against the paper. Talk about the lines, shapes, and patterns the bubbles make on the paper.

Pipe Cleaner Printing. Pipe cleaners can be bent into almost any shape desired and will carry paint well. These shapes glued to a heavy cardboard backing make a printing plate that is simple enough for young children but also suitable for more controlled expression by older children. Paint the pipe cleaners using thick tempera paint and press the inked plate to the paper. Or ink the block with a brayer, first having put a cardboard or pipe cleaner down either edge of the cardboard backing to keep the background clean. Press the block face down to a paint-soaked pad of paper toweling, lift by the edges, and print.

Berry Nice Prints. You will need plastic berry baskets, construction paper, tempera paint, a container large enough to dip the berry basket in, and paper. Talk about the lines children see in the plastic berry basket. Discuss how the lines cross and how they make squares. Talk about which kinds of prints the children think the baskets will make on paper.

Dip the berry basket in paint. Press the basket onto the paper. Repeat, overlapping the shapes. Continue until the pattern or design is completed. For variety, make contrasting designs by printing with white paint on black paper. Print with different colors of primary colors and watch the colors mix.

Circle Challenge. You will need paper cups of various sizes, Lifesavers candy, small round plates, and any other circular shapes to print, tempera paint, shallow container for paint, brushes, and paper.

Talk about circles. Have children identify as many circles as they can in the room. Discuss which things in a circle shape the children can think of to use in printmaking. Challenge children to bring from home as many of these items as they can.

Begin by printing with one circular printing object. Print this on the page, making a pattern or a random design. Use another circular object and print with it on the page. Try printing one line with one size circle. Do another with a different-sized circle. Alternate large and small circular shapes in one line. Print zigzag, horizontal, and vertical lines with circle shapes.

For variety, repeat the activity with another shape—square, rectangle, even triangles!

Pinecone Prints. You will need pinecones, a thin mixture of tempera paint, a container for the paint, and paper. Talk with children about pinecones, their shapes, how they feel, and how they smell.

Give each child a piece of paper. Dip a pinecone in tempera paint. Press the pinecone onto the paper. Use all sides of the pinecone to make prints.

Plunge Into It! You will need new plungers of various sizes, large sheets of butcher paper, various colors of tempera paint, and foam trays or plates.

Cover the art area with newspaper. Tape the newspaper to the floor. Lay out butcher paper, and tape it to the floor as well. Prepare paints in trays. Set plungers in paint trays.

Have children dip the plunger in paint and press the plunger onto the butcher paper to make a print. Continue printing to create a design or pattern. Add other round objects to print such as paper cups or towel rolls. Use two plungers at a time, each with a different color of paint. Use the paper as a giant class mural. Use the print as wrapping paper or book covers.

Recycled Puzzle Prints. You will need old puzzle pieces, white glue, cereal box cardboard, scissors, tempera paint, paintbrush, paper, and construction paper.

Talk about printmaking and how you can make several of the same image. Discuss what a pattern is—a repeat design. Talk about how patterns can be made of repeated lines of the same object (e.g., lines with alternating objects). Cut cereal boxes into pieces about 6" × 8".

Have children arrange several puzzle pieces on the nonprinted side of the cereal box cardboard. The pieces can be arranged to create a picture, a random design, or a pattern.

Once happy with the way the pieces look, children can glue them down. Let the glue dry. Use a paintbrush to cover the puzzle pieces with paint. Lay a sheet of paper on top of the painted puzzle pieces. Rub gently with the palm of the hand. Peel off the paper to see the print.

Tin Can Prints. Don't overlook the lowly tin can as a printing object. It can be the basis of a very versatile printing surface. Be sure the edges of the can are smooth before using it for printing. The end of the can dipped in paint makes a circular shape that can be combined in an over-all pattern, preferably using different sizes of cans.

Use the side surface of the tin can as a base for a printing plate. First, cut both ends from the can so that it will be easier to handle in the printing process. Then glue shapes cut from felt, cork, or even heavy paper and lines made from string or heavy cord around the outside of the can.

Paint the raised surfaces using thick tempera paint. Or roll the can over an inked plate so that the raised areas pick up the color. Then the can is rolled across the printing paper to make a design. The prints may be placed in rows so as to completely fill the page. Or the can may be rolled in different directions.

Bottle Top Prints. Have the children collect bottle tops ranging from soft drink bottles to larger jars. Paint these with thick color to make circular prints. Try the textures of the edge of the bottle tops. Glue felt or cork to the top to make new designs. Combine these with the tin can prints described above, thus mixing solid shapes and linear prints.

Toothpick Prints. Children create the print by pasting toothpicks to a piece of heavy cardboard in a design and then using this as a printing block.

Roller Prints. Almost any type of roller can be used to make a direct print. Collect large wooden dowels, round curtain rods, or even a rolling pin to make roller prints. Paint a design on the roller using lines and solid areas in a variety of colors. Quickly roll this across the paper and note the print made. It will fade out quickly as the paint dries on the roller. Paint the same design again and start at a different part of the paper to make the print. Continue until the child is finished with the design.

Using a wooden roller or a heavy cardboard cylinder, build up a relief surface by gluing on shapes of felt, corrugated cardboard, or cork. Or use knives and nails to cut and gouge a design in the surface of the wooden dowel. Spread some printing ink or thick tempera paint on a nonporous surface and roll the prepared roller through it and onto the paper.

What Can It Be? You will need long pieces of newsprint paper (18" × 24") or classified ad sections from the newspaper, tempera paint in a shallow pan or cookie sheet, crayons, markers, pail of soapy water, and paper towels.

Cover the floor by taping down newspapers. Tape long sheets of paper onto the newspapers. Have children step into a pan of paint; have them put their hands in the paint, too. Direct them to step out of the paint onto the paper to make foot and hand prints. Let the prints dry completely. Using crayons and markers, use the foot- and handprints to make an original design.

Yarn Prints. You will need yarn, glue, scissors, cardboard or oak tag, paper, tempera paint, and

crayons. Talk about how designs can be repeated to make patterns. Discuss how lines can be zigzag, horizontal, vertical, and so on.

Use crayons to draw a pattern, design, or picture on the cardboard. Outline parts or all of the picture with white glue. Apply glue to the yarn. Let the yarn and glue dry thoroughly. Brush tempera paint over the picture. Place another piece of paper over the picture. Press lightly with the palm of the hand. Peel off the paper to see the string print.

Crayons, Markers, and Chalk

Crayon Chips. You will need wax crayons, drawing paper, waxed paper, spoon, plastic knife, scissors, and an iron. Place a sheet of waxed paper on a pad of newspaper. Hold the crayon over the waxed paper and scrape it along the side with a spoon or plastic knife, allowing the chips to fall on the waxed paper. The crayon chips may be rearranged on the waxed paper as desired. Cover the design with another sheet of waxed paper. Place a piece of plain paper on top of this. Then apply a warm iron. Try the same technique using clear acetate instead of waxed paper. A variation would be to incorporate shapes of colored tissue into the design with the waxed crayon chips before fusing together with a warm iron. Another variation would be to substitute white drawing paper for the waxed paper. Immediately after applying the heat of the iron, pull the paper apart to reveal unusual results.

Chalk Blend Backgrounds. Rub and blend light pastel colors of chalk on a plain sheet of heavy paper. Dip a small comb in black tempera paint and use the comb with paint to make interesting repeat patterns on the paper. Spray the entire picture with hairspray to prevent smearing. Be sure to spray in a well-ventilated area.

Using Chalk in Picture Making. Don't overlook the creative possibilities of chalk as a medium for young children's drawing and picture making. Here are some creative ways to use chalk.

1. Texture: Place thin paper, such as tissue paper or tracing paper, over a surface with a unique texture like sand paper, bricks, or corrugated cardboard. Then rub over the paper with the side of the chalk so that the texture of the object appears. Numerous textures can be used for many interesting effects.
2. Chalk on wet paper: Using colored chalk on wet paper (construction paper or toweling), glide the chalk over the damp surface to give a flowing motion to the drawing. This process provides bold and colorful pictures.
3. Starch and chalk: Pour a small amount of liquid starch on a sheet of paper. Dip the colored chalk in the starch and create a unique art experience.
4. Wet chalk: Soak chalk in water for several minutes before using it on a dry surface. The wet chalk can be used on windows, paper, ceramic surfaces, and

numerous other slick areas. This chalk medium reacts much like a finger painting activity and provides a leaded glass appearance.

Texture Art

Have students touch their hair and decide whether their hair is smooth or rough, straight or curly. Then, draw a picture of their (or another child's) hair using different kinds of lines such as smooth, rough, straight, slanted, and curved.

Line Stories. Create a story using different types of lines. For example, a line is a dot that went for a walk in the snow. Each set of subsequent lines can be different things (e.g., thin parallel lines are sled tracks, thin curvy lines are bike tracks, spiral lines could be a snake, etc.).

Scribbles. Discuss scribbling, how it looks, and how much fun it is to do. Explain that this activity begins with scribbling.

The child makes a large scribble on the paper. Outline with a marker parts of the scribble. Fill the outlines with crayons. Leave some areas uncolored. Some variations: Make rules for filling the scribbles (e.g., "You can't put the same colors next to each other." "You can only use primary colors." "Use only complementary colors."). Challenge children to make scribbles using straight lines and angles. Have a group of children make a scribble picture mural. Scribble using crayon, then paint the spaces using tempera paint.

Be Like Picasso

When he was a boy, Picasso would bet his friends that he could draw anything using just one line. He always won his bets. In the book *Picasso's One-Liners* (1997), you can find a delightful assortment of his one-line drawings accompanied by his one-line quotes. Now try to be like Picasso in this activity!

1. Give students a stack of copy paper and a black fine-tip marker. Students take turns suggesting objects for the class to draw (animals work especially well), using just one line.
2. Each student gets a turn to name a subject.
3. Then everyone draws that subject using just one line, not lifting the marker until they are finished.

Students close their markers and lay them down to signal when done. When everyone is finished, students hold their drawings up for everyone to admire.

Encourage students to avoid simply drawing an outline of the object, and to let their pen explore the insides of shapes, adding texture, pattern, and detail that would not appear with just an outline. There are no such things as mistakes in this activity.

Drawings may end unexpectedly when the pen reaches a "dead end," but this is part of the fun.

Disappearing Line Drawings. You will need hard soap (the type from hotels works well), black construction paper, crayons, water, and a sink or large tub of water.

Talk with the children about lines in drawings and how they can be straight, curvy, horizontal, vertical, zigzag, and so on. This project is messy, so you may want rubber gloves and a newspaper-covered drying area.

Give each child a piece of black paper. Do a line drawing with the soap. The drawing should have lots of outlined areas in which to color. Note that the soap will not work for areas the children want white; for these areas, the children must use white crayon. Color in the drawing. Light colors work best. Rinse the drawing until the soap lines disappear. Allow to dry. Variation: Draw a design using only shapes. Repeat the process.

Crayon-Rubbing Pictures. You will need crayons, textured surfaces (e.g., sandpaper, pieces of screen, cardboard), and newsprint or another thin-type paper.

Discuss the pieces of textured surfaces with the children. Use descriptive words like *coarse, bumpy,* and *crisscross.*

Make an outline drawing with a pencil on thin paper. Hold the drawing against a surface that has a definite texture. Rub the crayon over all areas of the drawing, filling the area with an interesting texture pattern. The texture will transfer to the paper by the crayon. Place the paper against another texture and transfer this texture to another part of the drawing. Textures may be repeated or overlapped. Continue until all areas are filled with texture rubbings.

Crayon Batik. You will need crayons, paper, water, container for water, thin solution of tempera paint, brushes, and paper towels.

Discuss the fact that the term *batik* refers to a design with wrinkles. Talk about which kind of picture or design the children would like to make in this activity.

The child makes a drawing or design with crayons on paper. Soak the paper in water. Crumple the paper into a ball. Uncrumple the paper. Flatten it out. Blot off excess water with paper towels. Flow diluted tempera paint over the surface with a wet brush. Let the batik dry thoroughly. Variations: Draw with light-colored crayons and cover the drawing with dark tempera paint. Draw with dark-colored crayons and cover the drawing with light tempera paint. After the batik has dried, add more design elements or details with markers.

Tie-Dye

Materials

large pans of water (one for each color of dye used)	marbles, rocks, pebbles, wooden spools, cubes, and any other objects
rubber bands	to tie into cloth

string
liquid dye (cold-water dyes are easiest to work with)

pieces of old sheets, undershirts, or cloth squares to use as a scarf

The art of tying knots in fabric and dipping it in dye is more than 3,000 years old, so this "new" way of decorating material is actually one of the oldest. Young children enjoy the surprise achieved in creating the blurry-edged patterns resulting from a process that is actually an updated version of an ancient process called *bandhnu* in India. The designs created are determined by the manner in which the material is folded or tied. The color doesn't penetrate the tied portions.

Fill a large pot one-third full of water. Add the liquid dye and stir. The brightness of the color will depend on how much dye you add.

Circles—large and small, regular and irregular—can be tied in several ways. Tiny ones are made by pinching up bits of the fabric and winding a thread or narrow rubber band around them. Slightly larger circles can be tied over beads or marbles. A grouping of a number of small circles makes a fun arrangement, too. Large circles are created by picking up bigger loops of the material. Concentric circles are made by tying in a series or marbles or golf balls. Where the cloth is tied between the marbles, there is a very definite edge to the ring. By tying in cubes, pebbles, beans, spools, clothespins, and little sticks, an infinite variety of rings may be made. Fabric may be pleated and the pleats tied together, leaving gaps between the strings. This will produce an all-over cobweb effect.

The fabric should be dipped in water and squeezed before the child begins to tie knots. Strong white string is best for tying. Thread may be used for fine circles and narrow tape for wide bands. For very young children, rubber bands work best.

Show children how to tie-dye by placing the objects inside the cloth and fastening them with a rubber band. (Adults may need to tighten the rubber bands.) Dip the cloth in the dye. Leave it in the dye bath until the desired color is reached. Remember, colors will be lighter when the fabric dries. Remove the rubber bands and the design is revealed. When the item is removed from the dye, it should be squeezed out and rinsed thoroughly in cool water.

You will probably find it best to schedule your tie-dying for a pleasant day so you can do the work outdoors, stringing up clotheslines for finished pieces to dry on.

Stained-Glass Chalk Designs. You will need black construction paper, white glue, colored chalks, and examples of stained glass (pictures or the real thing).

Show children pictures of stained glass (or the real thing). Discuss the colors. See how the colors are in separate sections. Talk about the colors and shapes the children see in the stained glass.

Create a stained glass design and draw it on the construction paper using white glue. Experiment with different shapes and images. When the glue is dry, color between the glue lines using colored chalks. An adult sprays the design with hairspray in a well ventilated area to prevent chalk from smudging off the paper.

Torn-paper Collage. Tape a large sheet of construction paper onto an easel or wall. Explain to the children that you will pass around some construction paper and that everyone will be invited to tear up a piece. Children may tear their paper into very small pieces or big pieces—whatever they choose. Show them how to tear the paper and assist those who may need help. Invite children to glue their torn paper onto the large sheet of construction paper. When finished, engage children in a discussion about the torn-paper collage. Discuss how some may have layered paper; ask them to notice designs or shapes that were created or to find images that may be recognizable to them.

Next, invite children to create their own torn-paper collages. Suggest they choose a sheet of construction paper for their use and one or two colors for tearing. Older children may be able to work with several colors of construction paper.

Display all of the collages so that children can observe each other's work. Encourage them to talk about the things they observe.

Keep materials in a basket or tray in the art area so children can continue to experiment with torn-paper collage. Encourage collaborative work by inviting children to work in pairs or groups of four to make torn-paper collages together.

Broken-line Mosaics

Draw a solid line on the board. Demonstrate a continuous clapping for 10 seconds to represent this solid line. Have children do the same. Then draw a broken line. Model this by clapping at two-second intervals. Have students do the same. Then ask them to decide on a favorite animal. Have the children describe and tell about the animal. Then say, "Let's use broken lines to make an animal mosaic." For this activity you will need: ½ x ½-inch pieces of construction paper, 9 × 12-inch paper for background (contrasting color from scraps), white glue or glue sticks, erasers, and pencils.

The children draw an outline of their animal with a pencil and then erase parts to create a broken-line outline shape. Show students how to place one dot of glue on each of the broken lines and then place a colored-paper "tile" on each glue dot. Fill in the figure with these paper "tiles."

Matisse Cutouts. "A pair of scissors," said Matisse, "is a marvelous instrument." Your students will think so, too, as they follow the steps below to create their own paper collages.

As a group, brainstorm favorite activities. Swimming? Football? Soccer? Once children have chosen a subject, invite them to create a Matisse-like cutout. Ask children what shapes or symbols represent their favorite activities. (For example, for football, children might mention the distinctive shape of the ball, the lines of the goalposts.)

The children cut their shapes out of colored construction paper. Encourage them to use their imaginations.

Next, have them create the backgrounds for their collages, using two to four colored rectangles of paper. For example, a soccer background might include green for the field, gray for the bleachers, and blue for the sky. Then they glue their rectangles to the white paper.

Last, have the students arrange the cutout shapes on the backgrounds. They may want to add additional shapes to indicate action or energy, like bursts or squiggles. After the collages dry, show them off on a hallway bulletin board.

Chapter Review

1. Discuss how to mix, store, and use paint for picture making.
2. List some variations to include in crayon pictures.
3. Explain how to introduce children to torn-and-cut pictures.
   a. List some materials needed.
   b. List some possible demonstration strategies.
4. Discuss the importance of murals as two-dimensional art activities.
   a. List some topics for murals.
   b. List some materials for murals.
5. Discuss various printing techniques.
6. List the basic materials needed for each printing technique.
7. Define the word *collage* and give specific examples of collage activities.
8. List specific materials and techniques used in collage activities.

Paint Recipes

1. *Starch and Soap Finger Paint*

1 cup starch	1 tablespoon glycerin
1½ cups boiling water	(optional, makes it
½ cup soap flakes	smoother)
(not soap powder)	

   Method: Mix starch with enough water to make smooth paste. Add boiling water and cook until glossy. Stir in soap flakes while mixture is warm. When cool, add glycerin and coloring (powder paint, poster paint, or vegetable coloring).

2. *Flour and Salt Finger Paint, Cooked*

2 cups flour	3 cups cold water
2 teaspoons salt	2 cups hot water

   Method: Add salt to flour, then pour in cold water gradually and beat mixture with an eggbeater until it is smooth. Add hot water and boil until it becomes glossy. Beat until smooth, then mix in coloring.

3. *Flour and Salt Finger Paint, Uncooked*

1 cup flour	1 cup water
1½ teaspoons salt	

   Method: Combine flour and salt; add water. This has a grainy quality unlike the other finger paints, providing a different sensory experience.

4. *Argo Starch Finger Paint*

½ cup boiling water	6 tablespoons
2 tablespoons Argo starch	cold water

   Method: Dissolve starch in cold water in cup. Add this mixture to boiling water, stirring constantly. Heat until it becomes glossy. Add color.

5. *Wheat Flour Finger Paint*

3 parts water	1 part wheat flour

   Method: Stir flour into water; add food coloring. (Wheat flour can be bought at low cost in wallpaper stores or department stores.)

6. *Tempera Finger Paint*

dry tempera paint	½ cup liquid starch or
½ cup liquid dishwashing	detergent

   Method: Mix the tempera paint with the starch or detergent, adding starch gradually until desired thickness is reached. Paint extender can also be added to dry tempera paint.

7. *Easy Finger Painting*

clear liquid detergent	dry tempera paint

   Method: Mark off sections on a table with masking tape the size of the paper to be used (newsprint works fine). Squirt liquid detergent on this section and add about 1 teaspoon of dry paint. After the picture has been made, lay the paper on the finger paint and rub. Lift off carefully.

8. *Cold Cream Finger Paint*

   Dry tempera paint can be mixed with most brands of cold cream. This is good for a first experience with a child reluctant to use colored paint with her or his fingers.

Paste Recipes

1. *Bookmaker Paste*

1 teaspoon flour	1 heaping teaspoon
2 teaspoons salt	oil of cloves
1 pint cold water	¼ teaspoon powdered alum

Method: Mix dry ingredients with water slowly, stirring out lumps. Slow fire; cook over double boiler until it thickens.

2. *Hobby Craft Paste*

¾ cup water	½ cup Argo starch
2 tablespoons light	¾ cup water
Karo corn syrup	¼ teaspoon oil of
1 teaspoon white	wintergreen
vinegar	

Method: Combine first ¾ cup water, corn syrup, and vinegar in a medium-sized saucepan; bring to a full boil. Stir cornstarch into second ¾ cup water until smooth. Remove boiling mixture from heat. Slowly pour in cornstarch–water mixture, stirring constantly until smooth. If lumps form, smooth them out with back of spoon against side of saucepan. Stir in oil of wintergreen. May be used immediately but will set to paste consistency in 24 hours. Store in covered jar. Keeps two months. Makes about 2½ cups.

3. *Flour Paste*

Mix together ¼ cup flour and cold water—enough to make creamy mixture. Boil over low heat for 5 minutes, stirring constantly. Cool. Add cold water to thin if necessary. Add a few drops of oil of peppermint or oil of wintergreen.

4. *Co-op Paste*

1 cup sugar	1 cup flour
1 tablespoon	1 quart water
powdered alum	oil of cloves

Method: Mix and cook in double boiler until thick. Remove from heat and add 30 drops of oil of cloves. This mixture fills a juice container (8–10 oz.) about ¾ full. Needs no refrigeration.

References

Bedford, B. V. (1963). *Exploring finger paint.* Worcester, MA: Davis Publications.

Betts, B. V. (1963). *Exploring finger paint.* Worcester, MA: Davis Publications.

Picasso, P., & Galassi, S. (1997). *Picasso's one-liners.* New York, NY: Workman.

Shaw, R. G. (1947). *Finger-painting and how I do it.* New York, NY: ART for ALL.

Stankiewicz, M. A. (1984). Self-expression or teacher influence: The Shaw system of fingerpainting. *Art Education, 37*(2), 20–24.

Stevens, S. (2006, January). All about pencils. *School Arts, 108*(1) 36–37.

Thompson, S. C. (2005). *Children as illustrators: Making meaning through art and language.* Washington, DC: NAEYC.

Additional Readings

Bobick, B., & Wheeler, E. (2008). Colorful kindergarten mice. *SchoolArts, 108*(1), 44–45.

Castillo, J. (2009). *Line: Seven Elements of Art.* Glenview, IL: Crystal Productions.

Eckhoff, A., & Spearman, M. (2009). Rethink, reimagine, reinvent: The Reggio Emilia approach to including reclaimed materials in children's artwork. *Art Education, 62*(2), 10–16.

Etienne, V. (2008). *Vermeer's secret world (Adventures in Art).* New York, NY: Prestel.

Hurwitz, A., & Carroll, K. L. (2008). *Memory and experience: Thematic drawing by Qatari, Taiwanese, Malaysian and American children.* Worcester, MA: NAEA.

Kirker, S. S. (2008). A to Z with Jasper Johns. *SchoolArts, 108*(3), 26–27.

Kohl, M. A., & Solga, K. (2008). *Great American artists for kids: Hands-on art experiences in the styles of great American masters.* Bellingham, WA: Bright Ring.

Mulcahey, C. (2009). *The story in the picture: Inquiry and art making with young children.* New York, NY: Teachers College Press.

Pavlou, V. (2009). Understanding young children's three-dimensional creative potential in art. *International Journal of Art and Design Education, 28*(2), 139–150.

Ray, D. K. (2008). *Wanda Gag: The girl who lived to draw.* New York, NY: Penguin.

Temple, K. (2009). *Art for kids: Drawing in color.* Asheville, NC: Lark Books.

Watt, F. (2009) *50 things to draw and paint.* Tulsa, OK: EDC Publishing.

Software for Children

2 Simple 2 Paint a Picture, ages 4 and up

Animation-ish, ages 5 and up

ArtRage, ages 3 and up

Clicker Paint, ages 5 and up

Crayola Lights, Camera, Color! ages 3 to 8

Creativity Express: Let's Start with Art! ages 7 and up

Didi and Ditto Preschool: Mother Nature's Visit, ages 2 to 4

Digital Arts and Crafts Studio, ages 4 to 10

Disney Magic Artist, ages 4 and up

DrawPlus X2: Graphics Studio, ages 5 and up

Drawn to Life: The Next Chapter, ages 8 and up

Flip Boom, ages 5 and up

HyperStudio 5, ages 6 and up

Paint, Write, and Play, ages 4 to 7

Paper Show, ages 5 and up

TAB Kids 3.1, ages 6 to 12

UCreate Games, ages 6 and up

Wacom Bamboo Fun, ages 8 and up

Helpful Websites

Color Scheme Designer, http://colorschemedesigner.com
This site can be used to teach basic design and color wheel principles. Point and click on the portion of the color wheel to pick a central hue of your choosing from monochromatic, complementary, triad, or tetrad colors.

Crayola Crayons, http://www.crayola.com/
This website, sponsored by the Crayola Company, presents hundreds of activities for parents, educators, and "Crayola Kids."

GEM, http://www.thegateway.org/
Visit the Gateway to Educational Materials (GEM). GEM offers one-stop access to high-quality lesson plans, curriculum units, and other educational resources available on the Internet. The site includes resources from the Smithsonian American Art Museum, NASA, UNICEF, numerous universities, and other organizations.

Kathy Schrock's Guide for Educators: Art and Architecture, http://school.discoveryeducation.com/schrockguide/arts/artarch.html
(Click on Kathy Schrock's Guide for Educators.) This is part of the DiscoverySchool.com site. It provides a noteworthy gateway to sites of interest to art teachers researching and developing instructional materials.

KinderArt, http://www.kinderart.com
This site claims to have the largest collection of free art lessons on the Internet. It is addressed to teachers, parents, children, homeschoolers, and museum educators. Since 1996, it has grown into a collection of resources featuring more than 800 free lesson plans. In addition to lessons for grades K through 12, KinderArt offers printable activity pages, an interactive bulletin board, art trivia, educational links and articles, and early childhood education resources. The Lessons section lists categories from Architecture, Artists/Art History, and Crafty Ideas to Cross Curriculum, Drama, Painting, and Recycling. Users can also contribute lessons to be posted and participate in an online bulletin board.

NGA Kids, http://www.nga.gov/kids/kids.htm
Kids are able to explore color, shape, and line with interactive explorations in the National Gallery of Art.

Picasso—Maryland Electronic Fieldtrips, http://picasso.thinkport.org/
A great source for an interdisciplinary unit on Picasso in art, social studies, language arts, and math. Several of the paintings allow you to zoom in on certain features of a painting.

The Anti-Coloring Books by author Susan Striker, http://www.susanstriker.com
This site features visual image "starters" that can spur children's imaginations to create original pictures and designs. Designed to stimulate creativity and encourage problem solving and critical thinking, Striker's books help children draw their own pictures. Under the section Teacher Resources, Striker integrates art and literature by recommending a number of children's storybooks to use as motivation for art activities in the classroom.

The Pencil Pages! http://www.pencils.com/
This website, sponsored by the Incense Cedar Institute, contains information about pencil history, pencil making, kinds of pencils, renewable resources, and pencil trivia.

Viscosity, http://windowseat.ca/viscosity/index.php
A Web-based graphics program that provides brushes and special effects with which to move, smudge, and swirl a series of colors into abstract art.

 For additional creative activity resources, visit our website at www.Cengage.com/login.

Three-Dimensional Activities

OBJECTIVES

After studying this chapter, you should be able to:

1. Describe how young children work with clay.

2. Explain modeling and describe its benefits for children.

3. Discuss some guidelines to follow for successful modeling activities.

4. Define assemblage and give specific examples of assemblage activities for children, including the necessary materials and tools.

5. Discuss how cardboard may be used for three-dimensional activities and describe the materials and tools used in constructing with it.

6. Describe woodworking supplies and strategies and identify the benefits or woodworking for young children.

7. Explain how to adapt assemblage activities for children with special needs.

The term **three-dimensional art** refers to any art form that has at least three sides. Three-dimensional art is "in the round," which means that one can look at it from many sides. Modeling with clay, working with play dough, making creations with paper boxes, and creating other sculpture forms are examples of three-dimensional art activities.

Three-dimensional art projects give tactile stimulation and provide an emotional outlet through touch because of the versatility of the materials. Work in three-dimensional media also provides children the opportunity for growth in all developmental areas. Children grow physically as they use their hands, fingers, and arms creating three-dimensional objects. Their hand–eye coordination also develops as they work with clay and other three-dimensional materials in such activities as assemblage and woodworking. Growth in language occurs naturally as children work with and learn new words for three-dimensional media. Working with three-dimensional media also helps expand their use of words as they learn the words to describe three-dimensional materials and the process of using them. Self-confidence and self-concept are enhanced as children grow in their control over the forms created with three-dimensional materials.

Just as in drawing, there are basic stages of development in working with three-dimensional material, much the same as there are for two-dimensional media. While the names of stages in two-dimensional art do not apply (a child does not "scribble" with clay), the same processes of growth and basic ideas for each stage apply.

Developmental Levels and Three-Dimensional Media

When young children first learn to use a three-dimensional material like clay, they go through much the same process of growth as in the scribble stage.

Random manipulation. At first, clay is squeezed through the fingers in a very uncontrolled way. This **random manipulation** is comparable to the early scribble stage. The child at this point is exploring the media. They are interested in the qualities of the material: what it feels like and what it can do. With both clay and crayons, the child in this age range has little control over hand movements. The feel of the clay in his or her hand while squeezing—the sheer physical pleasure alone—is what the child enjoys about the clay.

Just as children make early scribbles in many directions, they also make early clay forms in many ways. A child of this age beats and pounds clay for no special purpose. The child will explore by pushing, tearing, pounding, smoothing, etc. The child does not try to make anything definite with the clay. What is made depends on whether the child pounds, flattens, or squeezes the clay. Although a child may occasionally identify a mound of clay as a house or a ball of clay as a car, he or she is usually more interested at this point in the manipulation of the material and discovering what he or she can do with it than in the object created.

Patting and rolling, making shapes. As children's muscle control develops, they begin to pat and roll the clay with purpose. This matches the controlled scribbling stage. In both scribbling and clay work, children enjoy seeing the effects of their movements. They find that they can use their hand movements to make the clay go in desired ways. At this point, a child may roll the clay into thin lengths or ropes (sometimes called "snakes"), pound it, or shape it into balls. Often, children will make whole families of coils or balls, sometimes covering their entire work surface. Lines drawn with crayon and rope lines or "snakes" made of clay are proof of the child's growing motor control.

FIGURE 14-1 • Three-dimensional objects can be created with many different materials.

FIGURE 14-2 • Play dough offers young children many opportunities to enjoy three-dimensional activities.

Circles and rectangles. An older preschool child able to draw basic forms can also make clay into similar forms. Rolling clay to make balls is an example of a basic form (circle) in clay. Boxes made of clay are examples of basic forms (rectangles) in a three-dimensional material.

In drawing and in working with clay, the circle is one of the first basic forms made. In both two- and three-dimensional media, the child is able to make this form by controlling the material.

The rectangular form usually comes after the circle. Just as in scribbling, the rectangle is made with clay when the child can shape it into whatever length desired.

Forming clay figures. Many children aged four to five can put together basic clay forms to make up figures. This is equivalent to the pictorial stage in two-dimensional media.

Most children in this age range like to make specific things with clay. They combine basic forms to build objects that are like figures in drawing by making simple things out of basic forms. The child working with clay

FIGURE 14-3 • At all ages, clay gives the child many chances for creative experiences.

puts together a round clay ball (circle) for a head and a clay stick-type line or lump for a body. This is an early combination of basic forms in clay. It is a lot like the stick figure made in early first drawings.

Later, in working with clay, children five years and older may put these forms together in more complex ways. Once they have mastered basic shapes, they may make a person with legs, arms, fingers, and feet. This parallels the later pictorial stage, when a child draws with more details.

Children at this stage do not make the same forms over and over again for practice as in the stage before. This is because a child of four or five has the motor control and hand–eye coordination to easily make any form desired. Clay is now used to make a definite object, a symbol for something important to the child. These forms are made in the child's own special way, just as in drawing.

Development of schema. This special way, or schema, of working with clay is the same for two- and three-dimensional media. It comes from much practice in making symbols and is the child's own special way of making these symbols.

In developing their personal schemas, just as in drawing, children may make things that are more important to them (symbols) larger than things that are less important. They may also use more details for an important clay figure. At this stage, these details may be made by putting other pieces on the clay, like buttons for eyes, straws for legs, and cotton for hair. Children at this point also like to create designs by sticking objects into the clay such as dried flowers, seeds, wooden sticks, feathers, beads, pipe cleaners, and wire. Creating textures by pressing various fabric and found objects into clay is another appropriate way of extending children's natural desire to design and explore with three-dimensional materials.

Children start to name their clay objects at about the same time they start to name their drawings. This is just as important with clay as with drawing. In both cases, it means children are expressing their ideas in art. They can now tell other people just what these ideas are by naming their work.

Modeling

Modeling—manipulating and shaping flexible material—has many benefits for young children. It helps them develop tactile perception, which is the understanding and appreciation of the sense of touch.

Modeling also helps develop the child's adaptability to change as he or she interacts with an ever-flexible material. In modeling three-dimensional objects, the child's concepts of form and proportion are strengthened as he or she learns to make objects with his or her hands. Older children develop an appreciation for sculpture and pottery as they appear in our environment when they create their own original sculpture and simple pottery.

Three-dimensional art is often an underexplored area of the arts in many early childhood programs. And yet, the overarching ideas of sculpture (one of the most basic of three-dimensional arts) are form, space, and material—qualities that are seen in hundreds of everyday contexts. Clay and play dough are excellent materials for developing and enhancing children's individual learning styles. Modeling with these substances has appeal for the body-smart learner because it involves tactile experiences such as squeezing, shaping, and physical manipulation. The child with an interpersonal learning style finds working with clay alongside other children a very natural learning environment. The child with a visual learning style will find clay an ideal material for making models and other similar projects involving measurement. Clay also makes a great base for a natural objects display piece for the child with a nature-smart learning style.

Materials

The soft, plastic quality of natural clay has a strong appeal for children of any age. In addition to the types of clay referred to earlier in this chapter, salt clay may be substituted for modeling; it is quite a suitable modeling material for young children. To prepare salt clay, mix together ²/₃ cup of salt, ¹/₂ cup of flour, and ¹/₃ cup of water. Add a small amount of dry powder paint or food coloring, if desired, while the mixture is moist. When the clay is left white, the dried piece has a crystalline sheen or "snow" effect caused by the salt. Finished objects dry to a durable hardness.

Paper pulp (papier-mâché), another modeling material, is easy to work with, does not crack or break readily, and is inexpensive. It can be made in either of two forms: as a pulp or in strips applied to a base. It can be molded into various three-dimensional shapes when it is wet and painted when it is dry. This medium is not appropriate for very young children because it is created in a two-step process that involves a sustained interest span. (See Figure 14–5 for papier-mâché paste recipes.)

To prepare paper pulp: Shred pieces of soft paper, such as newsprint, paper towels, newspaper, or facial tissue, into small bits or thin strips. Soak several hours in water. Then drain, squeeze out the extra water, and

FIGURE 14-4 • Modeling—manipulating and shaping flexible material—has many benefits for young children.

To make papier-mâché, mix up one of the pastes below.

Papier-Mâché Paste

3 cups water

½ cup flour

A drop or two of wintergreen

Mix the water and flour together in a large saucepan. Heat the mixture over a medium heat, stirring constantly. Add a few drops of wintergreen. **Caution:** Wintergreen is toxic. It smells like yummy gum, but don't be tempted to taste it. You use wintergreen to regtard molding. After a while, the paste will thicken. When it does, remove from the stove and let it cool.

If you are going to use your paste right away, leave it out. Make sure your project is well ventilated while drying.

Wheat Paste Method

Wheat paste or wallpaper paste

Warm water

You can get wheat paste at most hardware stores or art supply stores. Mix wheat paste and water until it is thick and creamy. Store in a container with a tight lid. Use it within 2 to 3 days.

Glue Paste

Dilute white glue (like Elmer's) 5 parts to one part.

FIGURE 14-5 • Papier-Mâché Paste Recipes.

mix the pulp with prepared wheat paste to the consistency of soft clay. Let the mixture stand for an hour before beginning to work with it. You can make a mold out of nonhardening clay and cover it with petroleum jelly. Then cover your mold with one or two layers of the paper pulp and let dry for 24 hours. Do a few more layers and let dry again. Cut the whole thing in half. Take molding clay out. Tape papier-mâché forms back together. Put three or four or even five layers of paste-soaked newspaper strips over the tape. Make sure it covers the split well. Let dry and then paint.

To prepare paper strips: The second type of papier-mâché involves the use of paper strips. Tear newspaper or newsprint into long, thin strips about ¹/₂ inch wide. Dip the strips into a wheat paste or starch and white glue mixture, and then put down a layer of wet strips over the shape to be covered. Continue putting strips on the form until there are five or six layers. This thickness is strong enough to support most papier-mâché projects.

Foundations: Good forms that can be used as foundations for papier-mâché include the following: rolled newspapers secured with string or tape, blown-up balloons, plastic bottles, paper sacks stuffed with newspapers and tied with string, and wire or wooden armatures used as skeletal forms.

Encouraging the Use of Modeling Materials

The following suggestions encourage children's modeling activities.

- Make it clear to children that in working with clay, the emphasis is on process rather than product. Clay interests and absorbs children, who will enjoy working with it because of the feelings it generates in them, the pleasure of discovery they experience, their being able to put their mark on it, and because of its change-friendly properties. Very rarely should clay be used with young children to make something permanent. Rather, clay is played with at a table with others and made back into a ball and stored away once children are finished.
- Introduce new tools for modeling to add variety to clay activities. Provide sticks, tongue depressors, a garlic press, Popsicle sticks, nails, combs, and paper clips. Of course, any tools small enough to put in the mouth should not be used with any young children, especially toddlers. All preschoolers need to be supervised in their use of modeling tools.
- Encourage children's efforts at all levels and all stages of growth. Some children find satisfaction

in manipulating a modeling material without making anything. Others, in the symbolic stage, give names to objects such as balls, pancakes, and coils. All efforts in modeling should be applauded.
- Avoid blocking children's thinking by diverting them from one method of working clay to another. One child may pull, pinch, or squeeze the material into a desired shape with head, arms, and legs extended. Another may make each part separately, then put them together into the whole figure. Some children may combine the two ways of working. No one method is better than another.
- When children are ready for other techniques, demonstrate how to:
  - moisten both parts when joining pieces of clay together, then pinch and work them together so they will not separate when the object has dried.
  - avoid delicate parts that break off.
  - smooth the material to prevent cracking.
  - create texture using fingernails or carving tools.
  - depict action by bending the head or twisting the body.
- If a child has difficulty with attaching smaller pieces of clay to a larger piece, demonstrate how to "pull" a smaller piece of clay out of the larger mass. Just be sure your suggestion helps the child accomplish his or her own goal for the clay.
- Sometimes the plastic accessories used with clay and play dough can slide all over the table, and they can be difficult for children to manage. A great way to keep them in place is to put a small piece of rubber shelf liner underneath. Cut up several sheets and show students how to put them down before using clay of play dough. It is simple, keeps small pieces in place, and makes grinding play "spaghetti" easier and less of a mess.

Wrap unfinished clay work in plastic bags or aluminum foil, or place it in a covered can with the child's name attached. A small lump of modeling material can be used as a magnet to pick up crumbs at cleanup time.

Encouraging Older Children's Modeling Activities

Children who are in the middle and upper elementary grades enjoy more exploration and challenge with modeling activities. This is a good age to introduce the work of potters. Having a potter visit your class

THINK ABOUT IT

Mobiles and Stabiles: A Short History

Two fascinating forms of sculpture are mobiles and stabiles. Here is a brief overview of these two art forms.

Mobiles have been in existence for centuries in many countries. The Chinese glass wind-bells are probably the best-known examples. A mobile produces movement with changing patterns. Making a mobile involves decisions about balance, design, sculpture, form, space, and color.

In America, mobiles were first created by artist Alexander Calder (1898–1976) in the early 1930s. Raised in a creative family and trained as an engineer, Calder was one of the most versatile artists of the 20th century. While he created sculpture in bronze, wood, and wire, he is best known for his mobiles and stabiles. After graduating from the Stevens Institute of Technology in Hoboken, New Jersey, Calder studied art in New York City. Later, while working as an illustrator, he was given a two-week assignment to cover the Ringling Brothers Circus. Fascinated by the acrobats and their athletic abilities, Calder developed a lifelong interest in the physics of balance. He created his earliest mobiles, *Calder's Circus,* as a result of this experience. One fine example of his circus mobiles is now housed at the Whitney Museum of Art in New York.

When Calder began making mobiles, he used motors to provide the energy to move his sculptures, combining his artistic and engineering gifts. But he disliked the regularity of motion caused by the method. Calder wanted his sculptures to move more spontaneously, so he later created mobiles that moved with the breeze. He wanted his mobiles to balance and move freely, suspended in the air.

Calder started creating stabiles in the mid-1930s. These were recognized as variations of his mobiles.

Stabiles are stationary, abstract creations made on a base that is freestanding and immobile. The viewer moves around a stabile to observe it.

While young children are not able to make complex moving structures, they are quite able to create something hanging in the air. Making a mobile can be an adventure in invention and a source of delight. Young children can put to work and develop a feeling for structure when creating in three-dimensional media, such as mobiles and stabiles.

Most children have built with blocks. This is building with weight and balance without permanent joints. In making a mobile or stabile, other kinds of structural problems can be added; for example, how a slender material like a wire can support weight and how paper or metal can be bent to support itself or other materials. Through working in the air, children become more aware of the principle of balance. Often, by about the age of nine or ten, children increase the complexity of their constructions by suspending small parts that move within the whole. Creating a mobile helps children develop an appreciation of sculpture in motion and helps them grow in their ability to select, arrange, design, and create in space.

Calder was a serious artist, but as his whimsical mobiles show, he was a fun-loving man as well. He truly enjoyed the adventure and process of making art. You and your children can have fun experimenting with shapes, balance, and movement by creating simple mobiles and stabiles. If you recycle scrap materials to make these sculptures, you'll help save natural resources. Try the mobile and stabile activities at the end of this chapter as a start to this fascinating art form.

---

to demonstrate how pottery or clay sculptures are made can motivate children's work in clay. As an alternative, a teacher or parent can arrange a field trip to a potter's studio so that children can see a potter's wheel, kiln, and other special tools and ways of working with clay.

Bring in beautiful earthenware serving pieces to show children these "common" dishes, bowls, and cups are made from clay. Explain that for thousands of years,

people have used clay to make utensils for eating. For members of the earliest cultures, clay was important for more than its artistic potential. Objects used in everyday life, such as vessels utilized as containers for a variety of materials from water to grain, were made from this substance taken from the earth. Bits and pieces of such vessels, called *shards,* help archeologists determine the age as well as the social, artistic, and religious aspects of particular cultures. Many of the clay

FIGURE 14-6 • Children who are in the middle elementary grades enjoy more challenging art activities.

pieces and other ceramic works now in museums had a functional importance long before museum curators gathered them as works of art for display.

Children of this age can also begin to learn about and appreciate the work of sculptors. Art prints of the sculpture work of Henry Moore are a good place to begin discussing the qualities of form, subject, and theme in sculpture. Obtain samples of sculpture pieces from a museum gift shop or from local art stores. Encourage children to view these pieces from all sides. Have them identify basic geometric forms they see in sculpture examples. Encourage children to create sculpture pieces of their own. Suggestions for more activities involving clay and play dough are at the end of this chapter.

The Value of Clay

Too little attention is given to the use of clay in the early childhood program. Many ideas can be carried out better in clay than in paint. If a child has not de-

veloped enough confidence to express himself or herself freely in painting, he or she can do so with greater ease in modeling. In modeling with clay, the child can change his or her artistic concept at will because clay is pliable. If a painting does not turn out as anticipated, it cannot be changed and the child may become discouraged. A clay object, on the other hand, can be altered multiple times.

At all ages, work with clay gives the child many chances for creative experiences. Most children like the damp feel of clay. They like to pound it, roll it, poke holes in it, and pull it apart. Just as in drawing, it is the fun of working with the clay that counts. The end product is not as important as using it; a child becomes really involved in the process.

Children should not be restricted in the size of their modelings. If they do not have enough clay, their modeling may be so small that they have difficulty in handling it. Have at least a five-pound bag of clay available for children's use.

Potter's clay is a very good three-dimensional material for young children. Clay is an exciting manipulative experience. It is pliable and thus provides a very different experience than working with paint. Preschoolers and children in all grade levels enjoy working with potter's clay. It is easy to use because it is soft and elastic. It is best bought in moist form, because the dry powder is difficult to prepare and the silica dust is unhealthy for children to inhale. Plasticene, a plastic-type clay, is more expensive and is much harder for the young child to use because it is not as soft and elastic as real clay. To make it easier for young children to use, warm and soften cold or hard Plasticene by rolling it between your hands.

To make the play dough and clay area satisfying for toddlers in their first experiences with modeling clay, use a small, low table. While many different props can be used (animals, cookie cutters, play dishes), most of the activity with this medium comes from the use of hands and fingers. Squeezing, patting, pulling apart, and rolling all help develop small muscles and make the experience relaxing and successful for toddlers. Many young children like to watch and vocalize to their friends while they use dough. If the housekeeping area is nearby, toddlers may even initiate simple imaginative games around themes of cooking, eating, and family celebrations.

Play dough can be made from water, flour, and salt; the colors can be varied each time. (Recipes for various doughs for three-dimensional activities can be

THIS ONE'S for YOU!   50 Years of Fun with Play-Doh®

In 1956, a new type of modeling clay for children was invented and began popping up in schools and stores everywhere. Originally, Play-Doh came in only one color—off-white—and came in a 1.5-pound cardboard can. Play-Doh continues to be one of the most well-known and popular children's "toys" with more than 2 billion cans sold since its invention.

In 1991, Play-Doh was sold to Hasbro and added to its Playskool Division. In 2000, Hasbro let people vote on their favorite Play-Doh colors. More than 100,000 people voted, and the winners were rose red, purple paradise, blue lagoon, and garden green.

As Play-Doh marks 50 years of malleable fun, an online search shows that the multicolored play clay appeals to more than just kids—and that many people misspell the brand name as "play dough."

At Hasbro's brightly designed website for Play-Doh, children can see examples of what can be created with Play-Doh in the Fresh Ideas Gallery, and parents and teachers can read tips on how to use Play-Doh in home and school activities. Click on "About Play-Doh" to find a history of the product. To learn about the product's origins as a failed wallpaper cleaner, check out "Failed Successes" write-up and links at: **http://www.failedsuccess.com/index.php?/weblog/comments/playdoh_history.**

Parents and teachers have long known that you can make a substance much like Play-Doh using common kitchen ingredients. Recipe Goldmine (http://www.recipegoldmine.com/childclay/childclay.html) presents more than 50 such recipes. The one listed under "Play-Doh" is closest to the store-bought product. But don't stop there. Try Kool-Aid Play Dough, Glitter Play Dough, and Dryer Lint Clay. There are even edible variations that use pumpkin pie, peanut butter, and cinnamon!

---

found at the end of this chapter.) Toddlers enjoy helping mix the dough, which can be refrigerated when not in use.

The following scene from an early childhood program emphasizes this value of clay experiences.

In my activities I wanted to emphasize fine-motor development, so I used clay with different sizes of soda straw pieces, toothpicks, buttons, etc., to stick in the clay. The children made animals, designs, and monsters. They kept up a running commentary on how they were making a monster and could SMASH it if they wanted to. It seemed that the clay was a good means of having them release their fears, ideas, and emotions on many things. This clay activity went over very well. During the day many different children, as well as the same children, came back to play at the clay table. (Author's log)

Children who perceive clay as "messy" or "slimy" may not want to work with it. Never force the issue! Be patient and give these children lots of time and plenty of opportunities to see the fun others have with clay. Some teachers find that involving timid children first in a "cleaner" aspect of clay work, such as mixing up play dough, helps involve them on a gradual basis. Hesitant children might feel more comfortable sitting near you as you pat the dough and describe how it feels. Acknowledge these simple participations. As children feel more comfortable, they may eventually try patting clay gently with you or a friend.

Strategies for Working with Clay

Working with clay requires planning and forethought. A lack of planning can result in a teacher's constantly having to remind the children about the right use of clay. Proper setup will make this unnecessary. Some tips for clay setup follow.

- The tables used for working with clay should be placed away from wheel and climbing toys. They should be covered with linoleum or Formica to make cleaning easier. If the tables in the room are Formica-topped, additional covering is not usually needed.

- The number of children at a table at one time should be limited, allowing each child enough room to spread out and use as much arm and hand movement as he or she needs.
- Each child should be given a lump of clay at least the size of a large apple or a small grapefruit. The clay may be worked with in any way the child wants. Two basic guidelines are helpful: The clay may not be thrown on the floor, and no child may interfere with another child's work.
- The teacher may sit at the table and play with clay, too; this adds to the social feeling of the modeling experience. But the teacher should avoid making objects for the child to copy. This discourages the child's creative use of the clay.
- When children are finished modeling, clay needs to be stored until its next use. It is best to form it into balls, each about the size of an apple. A hole filled with water in each ball helps keep the clay just right for use the next time. Keep the clay in a container with a wet cloth or sponge on top of the clay. The container should be covered with a tight-fitting lid. (Margarine tubs with plastic lids work well.) Clay becomes moldy if it is too wet and hard to handle if it becomes very dry. If clay should dry out, it can be restored to a proper consistency by placing the dried-out clay in a cloth bag and pounding it with a hammer until it is broken into small pieces. After the clay soaks in water, it can be kneaded until it is the proper consistency again. If clay does become moldy, there is no need to throw it away. Simply scrape off the moldy area and drain off any water collected in the bottom of the container.

Assemblage

As an art form, **assemblage** refers to placing a number of three-dimensional objects, natural or manmade, in juxtaposition to create a unified composition. Materials are combined in a new context to express an abstract, poetic, or representational theme. Assemblage makes use of three-dimensional space, resembling a still-life arrangement as objects are first selected, then grouped and regrouped. Assemblage art can also involve the creation of new and innovative artworks from what were once considered objects of waste. Through their use in assemblage pieces, reclaimed objects are endowed with a new meaning. The transformation of the objects used in assemblage pieces asks viewers to reconsider the notion of "valuable" as they are challenged to look at everyday objects with a new perspective (Taylor, 2006).

There are many ways to make an assemblage. One way is to put things together. Matchboxes, a paper cup, a cardboard roll, and an egg carton can be glued together. Another way to make an assemblage is to build up a form, using materials you can shape yourselves. For older children, cardboard is a good material for shaping an assemblage with building up a form. Cardboard can be found anywhere and it is easy to work with. All children need are scissors and glue to cut and stick the cardboard shapes together. They can bend, twist, fold, cut, or glue shapes to make a sculpture. As the Think About It . . . box on page 327 explains, stabiles are another form of an assemblage made by adding objects onto a base.

Encouraging Assemblage Activities

Try some of the following suggestions to introduce children to assemblage.

- Encourage children to bring objects from their environment and containers for assemblages. Display and discuss collected items. Explore ways of arranging the various objects, emphasizing variety of shapes, sizes, colors, textures, and methods of fastening the objects.

FIGURE 14-7 • Dioramas or scenery boxes are another form of three-dimensional activity.

THINK ABOUT IT

Research on Young Children and Three-Dimensional Media

Researchers at the University of Massachusetts at Boston have conducted several extensive studies of children's three-dimensional modeling of clay figures (Golomb, 2004; Golomb & McCormick, 1995). They also studied children's approach to two- and three-dimensional tasks that had a specific theme, while the material and conditions were varied. In one study, the two-dimensional media consisted of drawing on paper and representing themes with felt cutouts; the same themes were also made with three-dimensional items on a Plexiglas board (Gallo, Golomb, & Barroso, 2003). The results from these studies highlight the role of the medium and the significance of experience with the art form.

One of the most striking findings of these studies concerns **dimensionality.** Instead of flattening the human and animal figures as they are in children's drawings, the great majority of the children while modeling paid some attention to the different sides of the figure, at times working on all six sides: front, back, long sides, top, and bottom. This finding applied to the youngest children (four-year-olds) as well as the oldest (13-year-olds).

Also noteworthy was the use of different models on diverse tasks. For example, the children used a very specific, easily recognizable model for the human figure (upright with torso and limbs) and an upright standing three-dimensional model for an animal. Other differences between children's representation in two- and three-dimensional media were also found in the representation of facial features. In drawing, facial features are rarely omitted in children's drawings, but in modeling there was a high incidence of faceless human and animal figures. In contrast to the facial omission, the body was represented in most three-dimensional models of the youngest children.

With age and practice, they report a growing interest in size differences and in attempts to enliven the figure by action and gesture and by the addition of such details as clothing and accessories in the case of the human, spots on the turtle, and a collar on the dog. In general, they found differentiation of form was mostly age related, with older children being more skillful and able to model better-balanced sculpture. However, they found that age per se does not guarantee skill. Although technical skill improved with age, many sculptures continued to be modeled crudely at the higher age levels. Often, the technique of the older children was not better than that of the youngest.

In summary, their research supports the idea that when children become representational in the three-dimensional medium of clay, approximately during their fourth or fifth year, they exhibit some basic three-dimensional understanding. Evidence for this was seen in their modeling of multiple sides, their attention to the volume of the figure, and its upright stance. The researchers conclude that the common notion that the child's attention to frontal aspects of the figure is a sign of a lack of seeing things in dimension (dimensionality) is no longer tenable. From the very beginning of their work with clay, children develop representational concepts that are three-dimensional in nature and they refine them with continued practice. They found little support for the view that the early and primitive children's drawings are merely an expression of cognitive immaturity. Instead, they found much evidence that the young artist struggles with problems older children must also confront: how to create a satisfying representation in a medium (clay) that requires balance, uprightness, and the modeling of multiple sides, all of which require great skill and practice. Once again, we must acknowledge the great challenges young children face in their creative development. We too must acknowledge the important role early childhood teachers play in supporting this development.

- Explore ways of making items for an assemblage. Some materials for an assemblage follow.
  - Containers: Wooden boxes, cardboard boxes, cigar boxes, matchboxes, suitcases, egg cartons and crates, packing cartons. These may be painted or decorated if children desire.
  - Mounting boards: Pasteboard, corrugated cardboard, wood, crates, picture frames.
  - Objects: Wooden forms or scrap lumber, driftwood, screening, corks, cardboard boxes, discarded toys, household items, articles of nature (such as seeds, weeds, stones, twigs), and any other interesting items.
  - Adhesives: Paste, glue, staples, tape.
  - Tools: Scissors, stapler, hammer, nails, pliers.

- Encourage children to collect objects that are meaningful to them. Almost any area of interest or everyday experience is a possible theme for assemblage.
- Show children how to select objects for an assemblage according to an idea, topic, size of container, or variation in line, form, color, and texture. Demonstrate how to use multiple items for repetition of shapes.
- Encourage children to alter or transform three-dimensional forms so that they lose their original identity and take on a new meaning. They can be bent, twisted, stretched, crumpled, or painted.
- Extend possibilities for assemblage by cutting out pictures or illustrations and pasting them over cardboard, wood, or other substantial material.
- Glue, staple, or even nail objects together or onto a mounting board.
- Encourage children to arrange and rearrange objects until the desired effect is achieved. Distribute paste and other fastening materials after the arrangement has met with the child's satisfaction.

Cardboard Construction

Cardboard, an indispensable material for construction projects, stimulates and challenges the imagination of children on all levels. It is readily available in various forms. Such commonplace objects as milk and egg cartons, apple-crate dividers, towel tubes, and assorted sizes of boxes offer unlimited possibilities for creative art projects.

Encouraging Cardboard Construction Activities

Gather together an assortment of cardboard materials. Some suggestions follow.

- Assorted cardboard boxes, cartons, corrugated cardboard, paper cups, and plates of all sizes
- Recycled materials: paper bags, yarn, string, buttons, feathers, cloth, tissue paper, scraps of construction paper, and wrapping paper
- Paste, glue, tape, crayons, colored markers, paint, brushes, scissors, stapler, and staples

Most topics of interest to young children can be adapted to cardboard construction projects. Creations are as endless as the imaginations of young children. Some possibilities for creative construction projects include using boxes for making various buildings, houses, cities, and even neighborhoods. Young children also enjoy making such things as imaginary animals, people, and favorite characters from a story out of various cardboard rolls and containers. Some children have even made costumes out of boxes large enough to fit over the child's body. Cars, trucks, and trains are some other favorite construction projects with young children. Cardboard construction provides a wealth of possibilities for creative expression in arts and crafts projects as well.

Some suggestions for facilitating cardboard construction follow.

- Have the cardboard construction materials out and available for children to explore on their own. Encourage children to stack materials or combine them in different ways. Encourage children to explore the possibilities for creating they may discover while playing with the materials.
- Discuss with children and demonstrate (if needed) ways of fastening boxes together, covering them with paint or paper, and adding other parts or features.
- Encourage children to select as many objects as they need for their construction.
- Cover boxes with waxed surfaces with a layer of newspaper and wheat paste that is allowed to dry before painting. Tempera paint mixed with liquid starch adheres well to box surfaces.
- Create textured surfaces by using corrugated cardboard, shredded packing tissue, or crinkled newspaper.
- Allow the shapes and sizes of cardboard objects to suggest ideas for a project. An oatmeal box can become the body of an elephant; a milk carton will transform into a tall building.
- Use a variety of materials to complete a design, such as pieces of ribbon, buttons, sequins, spools, etc.

Older children are able to appreciate lessons combining three-dimensional assemblage projects with architectural ideas. For example, after drawing their plans for a building or structure, students might like to use boxes, cardboard, or cut-and-fold paper techniques to make three-dimensional models of their buildings. Students who are particularly excited by such projects may wish to create realistic settings for their structures as well, using sand, pebbles, dried moss, and the like to create their own miniature scene.

FIGURE 14-8 • Cut paper and cardboard construction are popular three-dimensional activities.

More assemblage activities are found at the end of this chapter.

Woodworking

Woodworking involves a range of activities from hammering nails to sanding, gluing, and painting wood. As with other three-dimensional activities, woodworking can be an excellent medium for fostering a child's creativity if the process, and not the product, is emphasized.

Planning for the Woodworking Experience

Planning for the woodworking area and related experiences is the key to success. Thought must be given to time allotment, location of the woodworking area, limits, number of children working at one time, and the role of the teacher. The following criteria need to be considered.

- Enough time should be allotted for children to explore materials without feeling rushed. If the woodworking area is a popular one, the teacher may find it necessary to set up time allotments to give all children a chance to participate.
- The workbench should be situated so that several children can move around and work without bumping into one another. It should be located out of major traffic patterns to avoid interruptions and accidents, and away from quiet areas so the noise will not disturb others. Weather permitting, and with adequate supervision, woodworking can be done outdoors.
- A specific limit should be set in advance regarding the number of children working at one time. Usually, one teacher can comfortably supervise three or four children. No more children than the set limit should be allowed in the woodworking area at one time. Teachers can enforce this number by requiring all children who are woodworking to wear an apron and safety goggles and then supplying only that number of aprons and goggles in the center.
- Tools and materials should be geared to the ability level of the children using them.
- The teacher needs to familiarize him- or herself with the use of woodworking tools and materials in order to give effective guidance and set reasonable limits. To create enthusiasm for woodworking, it is important that the teacher be excited about its possibilities. The carpentry area must be constantly supervised to avoid accidents.

Guidance for Woodworking Activities

In guiding children in woodworking activities, the teacher must first help them become familiar with the tools. In introducing the saw, for example, show the children how to hold the saw at a 45-degree angle and gently move it back and forth rhythmically. Children do not have to use a great deal of force or power for sawing; the saw will do the work on its own. Demonstrate how to fasten the wood in a vise and hold the wood with the left hand while sawing with the right hand, or vice versa for left-handers.

The rules of saw safety must be emphasized, including where to keep the hands, how to carry the saw, and where to lay it down.

In introducing the hammer, show children how to set a nail by gently tapping it into the wood. It can be driven using more vigorous strokes while holding the hammer near the end of the handle. Make a series of holes in various pieces of wood, showing how to set nails into these premade holes. Avoid too many detailed instructions or providing models or patterns. These things limit the children's initiative, independence, and creativity.

To prevent children from becoming frustrated, show them how to make handling wood easier by laying it flat and securing it with a vise. Allow children to try out their own ideas, but guide them in choosing the proper tools to use for carrying out those ideas.

Selecting Tools for Woodworking Experiences

When buying tools and equipment for woodworking, choose adult-type tools of good quality that withstand hard use. Tools should also be able to be resharpened, be reconditioned, and have broken parts replaced.

- Saws. Three types of saws are generally sold for woodworking purposes: the rip saw, the crosscut saw, and the coping saw. The rip saw has coarse teeth for cutting wood in the direction of the grain. The crosscut saw is designed to cut across the grain, while the coping saw is designed for use on thin wood and for cutting curves. Of the three saws available, the crosscut saw is the easiest for young children to manage. An 8- or 10-point saw (teeth per inch) is the most satisfactory size for children's use.
- Hammers. A 10- to 13-ounce claw hammer, with a broad head, is the most satisfactory for use by young children.
- Plane. A plane may be provided for children's use. If it is available, the blade should be adjusted to make small cuts, and children should be cautioned to use it only on surfaces free from nails, screws, or knots.
- Workbench. The workbench used must be strong, sturdy, and stable. An old door or heavy wooden packing box is ideal for a homemade workbench. Or a pair of sawhorses connected with a heavy board can be easily set up. All workbenches should be about 16 to 18 inches high, just under a child's waist height, for the most convenient work.

Optional tools

- pliers for holding nails as children are setting them
- scissors for cutting sandpaper and string
- screwdriver
- rasp for smoothing a rough or splintered edge against the grain and for rounding corners on wood
- 1-foot rule, yardstick
- pencil
- C-clamp

Storage and Care of Tools

A special wall-mounted tool board is essential for storing frequently used tools, while infrequently used tools can be stored in a cupboard. Paint the outline of each tool on the board so children can see where to put them away.

Saws should be professionally sharpened and oiled once or twice a year and wrapped in newspaper for long-term storage. Tools should be kept free from dust and rust; lightweight machine oil will remove any rust that forms.

Choosing and Using Woodworking Materials

Woods. The wood provided for young children in the woodworking area should be unfinished, smooth, and porous enough for children to pound or saw. Pine, balsa, poplar, and basswood are good, soft woods for children's use. Children work best with small pieces of wood of varying sizes, shapes, and thicknesses. Lumberyard scraps of doweling, molding, and mill ends offer endless possibilities when provided along with basic wood pieces.

Store wood in a container that allows visibility and accessibility to the child. Plastic vegetable bins work well for this.

Nails. Nails are supplied in pennyweights (dwt), which refers to the length of the nail. Common nail sizes are 2 dwt or 10; 4 dwt or $1^1/_{20}$; 6 dwt or 20; 8 dwt or $2^1/_{20}$; and 10 dwt or 30. At first, most children have trouble pounding nails without bending them, so $1^1/_{20}$ nails with large heads are best. Store nails in small jars according to size to allow children to select them easily.

Glue. Glue can be used by children who have not mastered the skill of pounding nails well enough to fasten wood pieces together. A quick-drying, all-purpose glue can be used for this purpose. Glue can also be used to make wood sculptures, attach accessories, and strengthen joints.

Screws. Screws may be provided in the woodworking area but are often difficult for young children to handle. They can be made more manageable by making a guide hole with a nail first. Older children can work more easily with screws and a screwdriver than young children. Provide both standard and Phillips-head screwdrivers with a variety of screw sizes.

Additional Materials for Woodworking

- sandpaper in four weights: coarse, medium, fine, extra fine (mount sandpaper on wooden blocks and use in a back-and-forth motion)
- brushes of medium and narrow widths
- tempera paint for painting completed creations
- accessories such as string, rubber bands, small pieces of rubber, scraps of leather, pieces of cloth and carpeting, bottle caps, pieces of Styrofoam, and metal gadgets like cup hooks, staples, and paper clips

Adaptations for Children with Special Needs

Many of the assemblage activities in this chapter and in the collage activities in Chapter 13 involve a child's working with glue and paste. This type of activity may be challenging for certain children with special needs. The following are some suggestions for modifying the gluing and pasting processes for those children who find this type of activity challenging.

Developmental Delays

If the multistep process of gluing is too complicated for the child, make a collage or assemblage without glue by using contact paper or another type of sticky base. Turn the paper sticky side up and tape it into a cookie sheet or shirt box. The child only needs to place selected items onto the sticky surface to complete the activity. No glue or tape is needed.

The following are some additional suggestions on working with children with special needs:

- Try not to overwhelm the child with too many choices. Offer only one or two materials at a time.
- Help the child organize his or her space by providing containers for each type of collage/assemblage material.
- Provide the child with a large collage/assemblage base to compensate for less mature hand–eye coordination.
- Provide a glue stick instead of white glue for children who have difficulty controlling the amount of glue needed.

Physical Impairments

For children with arm, hand, and finger control limitations, some of the following ideas may be useful.

- Stabilize the base of the collage/assemblage by taping it to the work surface to prevent slipping. A piece of nonskid shelving material or a placemat can also be used to stabilize the base of the assemblage.
- Use a 6-inch-long, 1- to 2-inch-wide dowel piece with a sponge attached to spread glue. It may be easier for a child with a weak or poor grasp to hold onto this dowel. Another alternative is to provide a wide paintbrush for applying glue.
- Place glue in an aluminum pie plate that has been taped to the work surface. The pie plate is easier for a child with limited motor control to reach and use.
- Make certain all necessary materials are placed within the child's reaching distance.
- Minimize fatigue by reducing the number of steps of the collage/assemblage process.

Attention Deficit/Hyperactivity Disorder

Children with attention deficit/hyperactivity disorder (ADHD) frequently exhibit poor organizational skills. The following are some suggestions to assist a child with ADHD in collage/assemblage activities.

- Have an adult available to sit with the child and guide him or her through the activity, providing ample praise and frequent feedback at each step of the process.
- Do not place all the project materials out on the table. Too many materials will distract and confuse children who are impulsive and easily distracted. Set out only the particular material needed for the next step of the activity. When that step is completed, set out the material for the next step, and so on.
- Place each collage material in a separate container and place the child's collage/assemblage base in a shirt box or on a cookie sheet to help define his or her workspace.

Visual Impairments

Both children who are blind and children with low vision enjoy assemblages and collages. These children are able to use their heightened sense of touch to guide them through the process and then feel their finished product at the end. Here are some suggestions on facilitating their work with collage/assemblage.

- Add yellow food coloring or yellow tempera paint to the glue so it is more easily visible on the collage surface. Use a contrasting dark blue paper for the collage base.

THIS ONE'S for YOU!

Using Recycled Materials in Three-Dimensional Activities

Recycled materials are perfect for three-dimensional art activities. They are free, readily available, and full of artistic possibilities. Here are some possibilities to start you thinking about (and using) recycled materials for three-dimensional art activities.

Paper Bags

- Collect large paper bags with attached paper or plastic handles (at least one for each child); additional paper shopping bags to use as masks; a variety of materials such as juice cans, egg cartons, plastic-foam pieces, empty boxes, fabric scraps, and straws; and scissors, glue, tape, crayons, and paint. Cut off the bottoms of the bags that have attached handles. Children can wear the bags as costumes by stepping into them and using the paper or plastic handles as shoulder straps. Arrange the collage and scrap materials on a table nearby so children can decorate their costumes with them.

- **Make a class mascot.** Provide children with two large paper shopping bags, colored yarn, and scrap materials that can be easily crumpled, including clean rags, newspaper, and pieces of cotton fabric. Invite children to choose pieces of scrap materials, crumple them, and stuff them into the paper bags. To make the mascot's head, have children stuff the first bag halfway full, and then tape it closed. Children use markers, paint, or decorative materials to make a face. Invite them to decide together on special characteristics, such as what color yarn to glue on for hair. Encourage them to work together to make a mascot that represents the whole class.

Boxes

- **Moving things.** Collect several medium-size appliance boxes that will hold one or two children. Invite children to use the boxes to make a vehicle. Provide them with smocks, paintbrushes, and tempera paint and invite them to paint their vehicle. If they want to make a train, attach the boxes to one another with twine and place the train in your dramatic-play or outdoor area.

- **Measuring.** Invite children to use the boxes for measuring, asking them to find out things like how many shoeboxes tall they are. Record their answers. Now, ask them to lie down on the floor and measure the length of their bodies using the smallest boxes. Encourage them to estimate how many boxes long they will be. Afterward, compare their estimation with the actual answer. How many boxes long or wide is the classroom?

Paper Tubes

- **Tube puppets.** Invite children to make tube puppets to use in dramatic play. Provide children with sturdy paper tubes similar to the length and weight of tubes used to hold foil or cellophane wrap. Set out a variety of materials including googly eyes, glue, yarn, felt, markers, scissors, oak tag paper, and small paper plates. Children might base their puppets on favorite storybook characters.

- **Tube bird binoculars.** Tape together two toilet tissue rolls. Let children decorate these with crayons, markers, and any other exciting "extras." Punch a hole on the outside of each of the tubes and string a ribbon or piece of yarn to make a strap for the binoculars. Go outside and start bird watching!

- **Music makers.** Use small paper tubes to make shakers for children to use during music and group-singing time. Invite children to decorate and individualize their shakers. Provide tempera paint, glue sticks, and collage materials. Enclose both ends with cardboard pieces secured with masking tape.

- **Counting the days.** Collect small paper tubes (from paper tissue rolls) to use for this counting activity. Get a large spool of twine and invite a child to string on a paper tube each day of school. Each child can take a turn decorating the tube and writing the number for each day on it. Invite the class to predict how long their "tube necklace" will be. Record their prediction and then compare on the last day of school.

Egg Cartons

- **Use your imagination.** Provide children with cardboard and Styrofoam egg cartons and a variety of construction materials including tape, glue, string, paper, scissors, feathers, buttons, markers, and paint. Invite them to use the materials to create their own works of art.

- **Sand experimenting.** Invite children to investigate the different ways they can use the cartons to manipulate sand. Give them a spray bottle filled with water so that they can moisten the sand. Can they use the egg cartons as a mold to create interesting shapes?

- **Floating experiments.** Give children cardboard and Styrofoam egg cartons and invite them to make boats to use at the water table. Have them predict which type of egg carton will work best in water. Record their responses. Now have them conduct their experiment. Does the size of the carton affect how it floats? Can they cut up the cartons to make smaller boats? Will the cartons sink if they are filled with water?

- Add sand, sawdust, or other textures to the glue to enhance tactile feedback.
- Use a small squeeze bottle or a commercial glue stick for ease of use instead of the dip-and-spread method.
- Place glue in an aluminum pie plate to provide a larger target for dipping the gluing utensil. Place colored tape around the edge of the pie plate to emphasize its boundaries.
- Mark the edges of the collage paper with a bright color paint, marker, or tape to help indicate the boundaries.
- Line a shallow baking pan with a piece of nonskid shelving material and place the collage materials in the pan.
- Guide the child's arm and show him or her where each material is located. Be sure to also say what you are doing and describe the position of each item. For example, you might say, "I am moving your hand to the right side of the pan, almost to the edge, to find the buttons."

Summary

Three-dimensional art refers to any art that has at least three sides. It is "in the round," which means one can look at it from many sides. Examples of three-dimensional art are modeling with clay and play dough, assemblage, cardboard construction, and other forms of sculpture.

Just as children have different drawing abilities at each age, they work with clay in different ways at each age. When young children first learn to use a three-dimensional material like clay, they go through much the same process as a child using crayons in the scribble stage. In work with both crayons and clay, children at this age have little control over their hands or the material. They enjoy the feel of the clay but do not have good control in working with it.

Older preschool children who can draw basic forms like circles or rectangles can also make clay into similar forms. Balls and boxes are examples of basic forms in clay. Children's muscle (motor) control helps them make these forms. Children in this age group can also put together basic forms in clay to make up figures. This is similar to making figures in the pictorial stage of two-dimensional media.

Children name their clay objects at about the same time that they name their drawings. Naming is an important form of communication in both two- and three-dimensional media.

FIGURE 14-9 • In using clay, some children may make each part separately, then put them together into the whole figure.

FIGURE 14-10 • Encourage children to create three-dimensional objects that have meaning for them.

A teacher needs to set up the room for the enjoyable use of three-dimensional materials by children. Proper tables, number of children, and care of materials are all points to keep in mind when planning for clay work.

Modeling refers to the manipulation and shaping of flexible materials. Modeling activities help children develop their sense of touch, their adaptation to change, their concepts of form and proportion, and, especially in older children, their sense of aesthetics.

Assemblage is a creative activity that involves placing a number of three-dimensional objects together to create a unified composition. Stabiles and mobiles are also examples of three-dimensional artworks. Everyday materials found in the school or home environment are media for this type of activity. Cardboard is also a suitable material for construction activities for young children.

Woodworking, another three-dimensional activity, involves a range of activities from hammering nails to sanding, gluing, and painting. Woodworking experiences for young children contribute to their total development. These experiences must be planned so that appropriate, good-quality tools are provided for the children's use. Close supervision is required in woodworking.

Assemblage activities may need to be adapted to meet the needs of children with special needs. Most of these adaptations are easily implemented.

Key Terms

assemblage 328
mobile 325
modeling 322
paper pulp (papier-mâché) 323
random manipulation 321
stabile 325
three-dimensional art 320

Learning Activities

Exercise 1

Goal: To experience how a child aged one and one-half to three years works with clay.

A. Use the hand opposite the writing hand.

B. Use a piece of real clay about the size of a large apple.

C. Squeeze the clay in one hand only.

D. Keep these points in mind:

1. how it feels to lack good muscle (motor) control
2. how hard it is to make an exact object
3. how the clay feels in the hand

Exercise 2

Goal: To feel the differences in clay.

A. Prepare large balls of real clay, Plasticene (oil-based) clay, and play dough.

B. Use the hand opposite the writing hand to squeeze and feel each of the three clay balls. (This should help you experience both the child's lack of muscle control and different materials.)

C. Consider the following points while working with each of the three balls of clay.

1. Which is the easiest to squeeze?
2. Which feels the best?
3. Which is the most fun to use?
4. Is the type most fun to use also the easiest to use?

D. Try the previous activity with children aged one and one-half to three years. Ask them the same questions. Compare answers.

Exercise 3

Goal: To help you understand how children feel when they are given a model to copy.

A. Collect several small glass or porcelain figures. These could be decorative birds, glass dolls, or any other finished figure from a variety store or other source.

B. Using clay, create a copy of one of the figures, including its intricacies.

C. Examine and discuss your finished object.

1. How did it feel to copy such a difficult model?
2. Was it a pleasant or frustrating experience?
3. Did this copying exercise make you feel happy about working with clay? Did it make you like to copy?
4. How do you think children feel about trying to copy models the teacher sets up?
5. Why is it undesirable for a teacher to have children copy a model?

Exercise 4

Obtain some pictures of modern sculpture. (Henry Moore's are good examples.)

A. Show the pictures to the children before they work with clay.

B. See if there are any effects on their work in relation to the following:

1. kinds of objects made
2. new shapes made
3. more or less clay work done

4. change in the way objects are made
5. change in the way child works with clay

Exercise 5

Read an exciting story to children before they work with clay. For example, try Maurice Sendak's *Where the Wild Things Are* or Dr. Seuss's *And To Think That I Saw It on Mulberry Street*.

A. Do not tell the children what to make.

B. See if their work with clay shows any influence from the story regarding the following:

1. type of figures made
2. size of figures made
3. details of figures made

Exercise 6

To add variety to play dough activities, try one of these variations.

A. Work a drop of food flavoring and a drop of food coloring into your play dough recipe. Match scents with colors, such as mint flavoring with green and lemon flavoring with yellow.

B. Use a tasty mixture of peanut butter and powdered milk as play dough for another three-dimensional taste treat.

C. Make your play dough recipe slippery by adding a little vegetable oil.

Activities for Children

Wooden Friends

You will need wooden clothespins, pipe cleaners, markers, popsicle sticks, felt scraps, glue, scissors, ribbon, sequins, beads, buttons, and yarn in various colors. The child uses the wooden clothespin for the body. Attach arms by twisting a pipe cleaner around the clothespin. When satisfied with the positioning of the pipe cleaner arms, glue them in place. Children may use markers to create the face. Discuss possibilities for using found materials for details, for example, popsicle sticks for skis, yarn for hair, ribbon for belts, etc. The little wooden friends come alive as children add clothes and other found materials for accessories.

Have children share thoughts and feelings about their wooden sculptures and the sculptures made by others. Ask them to comment on the likenesses and personalities of the figures and how accessories and details help convey personality and identity.

Clay-Coil Pots

For this activity you will need potter's clay, a large plastic garbage bag, and tape. Split the garbage bag at the seams and tape it to the top of your work area.

Give each child a grapefruit-sized ball of potter's clay. Show children how to make snakes by rolling out pieces of clay into coils. Make several coils or one very long coil. Roll a small ball of clay and flatten it into a round shape for the bottom of the pot. Moisten the edges of the round bottom piece with water. Wrap the coils around the round bottom piece. Continue wrapping the coil around and around, putting coil upon coil. Moisten the pieces together as you coil. Let the pot dry before painting or decorating. Children can also make free-form coil sculptures.

Crepe Paper Clay

For this activity you will need crepe paper, 1 cup of flour, 1 cup of salt, a large container, and water. Place crepe paper in a large container and add enough water to cover the paper. Soak for about 1 hour until most of the water absorbs into the paper. Pour off excess water. Save this colored water for dye in other projects. Add small amounts of flour and salt until mixture is clay-like. Mold and form shapes by hand with crepe paper clay. Let the forms dry before painting.

Pipe Cleaner Sculpture

For this activity you will need a flat sheet of Styrofoam, pipe cleaners of various lengths and widths, beads in various sizes, hole sizes and colors, and any other objects with a hole in them (such as straws, pasta, etc.).

Lay out the materials on the table or work area. Show children how the pipe cleaners can be stuck into the Styrofoam. They can slide beads, straws, pasta, and other interesting items onto the pipe cleaners.

Brown Bag Surprise

For this activity you will need lunch-size brown paper bags and items such as paper tubes, sections of egg cartons, foil, cellophane, fabric, gift wrap, feathers, sequins, yarn, bubble wrap, paper plates, Styrofoam cups, stickers, glue sticks, child safety scissors, markers, and crayons.

Place different items into individual brown bags for each child. Vary the items in each child's bag to encourage different types of experiences.

Give each child a surprise bag full of art materials. Children use the materials to create their own special art project, creating whatever they want. One child might decide to create a flat collage while another opts to make a three-dimensional assemblage. When children have finished creating their artwork, ask them to write about it. They can write about how they made their work or what materials they used, or they can make up a story to accompany the work. Encourage them to use invented spelling and to be creative. Assist those who need it with their writing.

Invite children to share their work with the group. Encourage them to describe how they made their artwork. Find an area in the classroom to display children's artwork and writing.

Foil Sculpture

For this activity you will need aluminum foil, masking tape, paintbrushes, liquid detergent, and tempera paint.

Crumple the foil into individual forms, shapes, or creations that when assembled will create a piece of sculpture. Join these forms together, if desired, with tape. Color can be added to the surface by painting with a drop or two of liquid detergent mixed in the tempera paint.

Line Sculpture

Give each student a single piece of wire about a yard long and ask them to bend this "line" into an object. Students will enjoy creating these simple line sculptures. This activity can serve as a stepping-off point for an investigation of Alexander Calder and his wire innovations.

Natural Object Sculpture

For this activity you will need natural materials (seeds, twigs, pinecones, seed pods, stones, driftwood, etc.), quick-drying glue, clear quick-drying spray, paint, construction paper, and felt.

Collect a number of natural objects of various sizes and colors. Arrange several of these items to create a small piece of sculpture. When satisfied with the creation, glue it together. Paint or colored paper can be added to enhance the design. Spray with clear spray to preserve the finish. (Spray with optimum ventilation, preferably outdoors.) Glue a piece of felt to the bottom to prevent scratching.

Spool Sculpture

For this activity you will need spools (a variety of sizes), assorted fabric pieces, glue, and anything that will serve to stimulate children's imaginations as decorations.

Each of the spool sculptures is made differently according to the imagination of the artist. Basically, the procedure involves "dressing" the spool, which serves as a body. Materials are added for clothing and are glued onto the spool. If desired, a child may use the spool purely as a base; it does not have to be a figure to dress. Details can be made with drawing materials, and bits and pieces of yarn, ribbon, and other similar materials can be glued on for interest.

Box Sculptures

For this activity you will need boxes of different sizes and shapes, paste, tempera paint, brushes, construction paper, and scraps of fabric and trim.

Have children bring in an assortment of boxes. Be sure to include cereal boxes, because they make great bases for box sculptures.

Use one box as a base. Glue smaller boxes on to make a sculpture design. Glue on cut-construction-paper details. Add fabric and trim scraps for more design details. Children may want to make a city of box sculpture buildings. They may choose to paint the sculpture. Boxes can become robots, imaginary animals, and anything else children can imagine.

Variation: For toddlers and young preschoolers, another use for cardboard boxes in various sizes is to build a train. Collect several cardboard boxes large enough for a child to sit inside. Put out a variety of supplies—markers, stickers, construction paper, glue—and tell each child to turn his or her box into a train car. Once they've decorated the outside of their boxes in whatever way they can think of, help them arrange the cars one behind the other. Then, hop aboard for an imaginary train ride! Be prepared to hang onto these boxes; the children will want to get together and ride the track again and again.

Paper-Tube Sliding Things

For this activity you will need toilet tissue or paper towel tubes, crayons, yarn, construction paper, markers, tempera paint, paintbrushes, scissors, glue, and tape.

Cut the tubes into various sizes. Give each child at least five pieces. Have children paint the tubes. Children may want to color the tubes with markers or crayons instead of paint. Cut out a head and tongue. Decorate the pieces by drawing features with crayons or markers. Glue or tape the head and tongue to separate tube pieces. When decorating with paint, wait until the tube pieces are dry. Measure a piece of yarn long enough to extend through all pieces of tubes. String the yarn through the tubes, fastening it to the first and last tube pieces. String beads between the tubes for a colorful effect. Glue on such natural objects as acorns, leaves, and grasses for an interesting effect. Some children may need assistance fastening the yarn to the tubes.

Milk Carton Construction Fun

For this activity you will need milk, juice, or cream cartons (different sizes—all cleaned and dry!); white acrylic paint; gesso or white latex house paint; pencils; paintbrushes; tempera paint; and containers for water.

Discuss homes and neighborhoods with the children. Talk about the different styles of places to live: houses, apartments, condos, and so on. Talk about shapes and sizes and such details as windows, doors, roofs, and stairways.

Have children cover the carton with white acrylic, gesso, or latex house paint. Let the paint dry thoroughly. Draw windows, doors, and so forth on the carton. Paint the carton (using tempera paint) to look like a house.

Children may want to make several houses for a neighborhood. They may even create a town/village from a favorite story.

Imaginary Animals

For this activity you will need a collection of boxes of various sizes and shapes, paste, masking tape, stapler and staples, scraps of colored paper, fabric, trim, buttons, and yarn.

Talk about animals and their shapes, sizes, and colors. Give children a collection of boxes of various sizes and shapes.

Have children stack the boxes and rearrange them until they are satisfied with their arrangement. Shapes and sizes of boxes may suggest certain animals, such as an oatmeal box for an elephant or a long, narrow box for a giraffe's neck. Smaller boxes or towel rolls can be used for legs or a head. Fasten boxes together with glue, masking tape, or a stapler. Glue on details using scraps of colored paper, fabric, trim, buttons, or yarn.

Textured surfaces can be created by using corrugated paper or egg cartons for bodies of animals. Wood shavings, bark, or wrinkled-paper scraps can be glued to the boxes to create interesting textures. Exaggerated features help to create dramatic effects, such as large buttons for eyes, frayed string or rope for a mane or tail, or pieces of cloth for ears.

Egg Carton Buggy Things

For this activity you will need egg cartons cut into single cups, pipe cleaners cut into small pieces, buttons, scraps of fabric and trim, crayons, and markers.

Discuss bugs, real and imaginary, with children. Talk about colors, shapes, "feelers," legs, and textures. Talk about other creatures, real or imaginary.

Give each child one egg cup. Have them attach pieces of pipe cleaners for legs, buttons for eyes, and pipe cleaners for feelers. Details may be added with crayons or markers. Pieces of fabric or trim can be glued on for even more details.

String a thread through the top of the egg cup to hang the creations, or make a family of creatures. Tell stories about the creatures' adventures in the bug world. Make houses for the buggy creatures out of milk cartons or other recycled boxes. Decorate the houses with markers or crayons.

Egg Carton Gardens

For this activity you will need tops from Styrofoam egg cartons, scissors, pipe cleaners, toothpicks, construction paper, crayons, markers, glue, glue brushes, glitter (optional), and twigs.

Give each child a top from a Styrofoam egg carton. Talk about flower gardens, real or imagined. ("Which kind of flowers can you see in your mind?" "Which kinds of flowers do you see in a garden?" "Think of colors and shapes.")

Children cut or tear the construction paper into flower shapes, or any shapes they want. Children decorate the flower and/or shapes with crayons and/or markers. Glitter can be applied to the shapes that have been brushed with glue. Insert a toothpick or pipe cleaner into the flower. Poke the flower into the Styrofoam egg carton top. Add twigs to fill the egg carton top as desired.

For variations: Make an egg carton zoo. Fill the egg carton top with paper animals. Create an egg carton top filled with paper "people." Classmates, family members, and characters from a favorite storybook all make fun additions! Older children might enjoy creating a scene from a favorite story in the egg carton top.

Construction Paper Characters

For this activity you will need construction paper, tape, scissors, crayons, markers, tempera paint, brushes, yarn, buttons, pieces of trim, and fabric scraps.

Talk about the people who are important in the child's life. Talk about those people's sizes, shapes, and other characteristics. Think about these things when making the construction paper creations.

Form the body by rolling the paper into a tube and taping it on the ends. The tube is both the body and the head of the person. Feet cut from construction paper can be taped on the bottom of the tube. Glue on features made of pieces of construction paper. Glue on yarn or pieces of construction paper for hair. Add fabric or trim scraps for clothing details. Features can be drawn on with crayons, markers, or paint.

For variation: Make a family of construction paper characters. Older children may want to make favorite characters from storybooks. Famous characters from history make good subjects for older children.

Construction Paper Buildings

For this activity you will need construction paper, crayons, markers, tape, stapler and staples, and markers.

Discuss types of buildings with children, such as houses, barns, silos, and apartment buildings. Talk about the shapes, colors, and details on these buildings.

Give each child a supply of colored construction paper. Have them roll paper and tape the ends for round shaped buildings. Fold paper for roofs. Tape four pieces of paper to make square or rectangular buildings. Add such details as windows and doors with crayons, markers, or paint.

For variation: Have children add cut-paper windows and doors, chimneys, and balconies. Children might make several buildings to create a city, small town, or farm. Store windows can have merchandise painted on, cut out and pasted on, or made and set behind cellophane windowpanes.

Rock Sculptures

For this activity you will need rocks of various sizes, glue, markers, paint, and scraps of fabric and trim.

Go outside and collect the rocks for this activity. Talk with children about the rocks—their colors, shapes, sizes, lines, textures, and other details. Ask them to think about what they would like to make with the rocks.

Use one rock for a base. Glue on a rock for a head or simply for another part of the sculpture. Glue on other details with bits of trim and fabric. Draw on details with markers or paint.

Variations: Make a family of rock people. Make a zoo filled with rock animals. Make abstract sculptures out of rocks. Glue small pebbles to paper boxes for unusual gifts.

Pebble Painting

Gather enough pebbles so that you have three different-sized pebbles that are cleaned for each student. You will also need three primary colors of tempera paint, three spoons per student, white paper cut into a shape of a pebble, and boxes no deeper than 4 inches.

Start by reading *Sylvester and the Magic Pebble* by William Steig. After finishing the story, introduce the pebble painting activity to the children.

- Students first choose three different-sized pebbles.
- Students tape the paper to the box.
- Student dips two pebbles into the two colors they choose.
- Placing the pebbles on the paper, students start to shake or tilt the box, creating a design.
- After pebble painting with the two colors is completed, students then use all three primary colors and pebbles to paint their second painting.
- When they are finished, have a designated drying place for all pebble paintings.

Styrofoam Sculpture/Stabile Construction

For this activity you will need Styrofoam of various sizes and shapes (sheets, broken parts of packaging materials, "peanuts"), white glue, pieces of cardboard (optional), toothpicks, scraps of fabric, trim, ribbon, markers, tempera paint, and brushes.

Talk with children about the collection of Styrofoam. Discuss size and shape of the pieces. Ask children to think about what they would like to create with these pieces.

Use a piece of cardboard or sheet of Styrofoam as a base. Glue pieces of Styrofoam onto the base. Use toothpicks to add small pieces to the design. Have children continue gluing on pieces until they are satisfied with their design.

Children can use markers to draw details on the sculpture and paint it with tempera paint. They can also glue on pieces of fabric, trim, and ribbon for interesting effects.

- Variation: Suggest children make a list of things that they have in their homes that could be recycled and used for art projects. Send the list to families along with a note requesting that they collect some of the items to donate to the classroom art area.

Cornstarch

Believe it or not, a fascinating modeling medium is plain old cornstarch. Mix 2 cups warm water and 3 cups cornstarch to make a fascinating substance for children's three-dimensional play.

Put ingredients in a bowl and mix with your hands. This mixture will solidify when left alone, but turns to liquid from the heat of your hands. Magic!

Involve the children in making the cornstarch recipe. Have them feel the dry cornstarch. Encourage their reactions to it, using their senses of sight, smell, touch, and even taste. Add a little water, and let the children mix it and feel it again. It is lumpy. After this lumpy stage, you can add a little more water until it's uniformly moist. Wet cornstarch forms an unstable material, which is fun because of its unexpected behavior—it breaks, but it also melts. It doesn't behave like glue, or like milk, or like wood; it's a liquid and it's a solid, too. If you rest your fingers lightly on the surface of the cornstarch mix, it will let your fingers drift down to the bottom of the container. If you try to punch your way to the bottom, it will resist.

Cornstarch works well in a baby bathtub set on a table, with a limit of two or three children using the entire recipe. If you leave it in its tub overnight, by morning it will be dry. Add some water, and it becomes that wonderful "stuff" again. Be sure to invite children to watch this event.

This is a clean sort of play: The white, powdery mess on the floor can be picked up easily with a dustpan and brush or a vacuum cleaner.

Children will enjoy this cornstarch mixture again and again, because it feels good and behaves in such an interesting way.

Dioramas/Scenery Boxes

A diorama is a three-dimensional scene inside a box. This activity can be used with students in kindergarten through grade 5. The materials required for this activity are: shoe box for each student, scissors, construction paper, glue, thread, black marker, and tape. Optional materials: tin foil, small boxes, markers, pencils, crayons, paint, or tissue paper.

- Ask the students to bring in a shoe box for this activity.
- A few days in advance, ask the students to think of a scene they would like to create in the shoe box. Tell them they may bring in their own objects to include in the scene.
- On the day of the project, place all the materials on a table where everyone can reach them.
- Ask two to three students to come to the table at a time and choose a few of the materials.
- The student makes the background and the bottom of their scene first. Construction paper, paint, or other materials may be used for a background.
- Students need to decide what they will put in the box and what materials they will make their items out of (maybe a box for a bed in a bedroom or a kitchen cabinet, etc.).
- While the items are being constructed, the teacher walks around the room with the thread and gives each student the needed amount. (The thread will be used to hang objects in the box. For example, fish in the ocean, birds in the sky, etc.)
- All objects should be glued in the box so they will not fall off. When the items and the background are complete, the students should create some sort of texture or pattern on the objects.
- Children may choose to hang some of the items or all of them. If the items are not hung in the box, the students use paper folded back and forth to make the objects pop out. Items may also be glued anywhere in the box.
- After they are finished, students may want to explain their scene to fellow students.

Soft Sculptures

Materials: scissors, glue, socks and stockings, yarn, crumpled newspaper, tissue paper, pillow stuffing, nylon stockings, felt pieces.

Collect mismatched socks and stockings, the larger the better.

Children stuff a sock with newspaper, tissue paper balls, pillow stuffing, or nylon stockings. Tie the sock closed with a piece of yarn. Older preschoolers can use a plastic needle and yarn to sew felt or fabric scraps onto their soft sock sculpture. Younger children can glue on designs cut out of pieces of felt.

Sewing on Burlap

For this activity you will need large plastic needles, 12 × 12-inch pieces of burlap (taped around the edges with masking tape), jumbo crayons, various kinds of yarn (precut).

- Show the children how to go in and out of the fabric with the needle.
- Have children practice making stitches on a 4-inch square of burlap with a needle and some yarn before they start this project.
- Let the children brainstorm some shapes they could sew, such as shapes in the room, from nature, etc. Each child decides on a shape to sew and then draws it on the burlap with a crayon.
- Help the students thread their needles.
- Students use the running stitch (going in and out of the fabric) to follow the outlines they have drawn.

Basket Weaving

For this activity you will need plastic cups (precut with five cuts made from the lip to the base of the cup), precut yarn or ribbon or raffia.

- Show the students the paper cup with the slits. Have children think about small things they could put in it. Suggest students think of small things they use or collect. List those things on the board.
- Then say, "Let's weave a small basket for holding something special."
- Then provide each student with a precut plastic cup and let him or her choose the fiber to use for weaving.
- Show students how to put the end of a piece of yarn (or ribbon or raffia) in a slit at the bottom of the cup.
- Show the students how to weave in and out of the slits until the yarn or other fiber is used up.
- Show them how to add another piece of fiber to finish their weaving.
- Then invite students to tell what they will put in their baskets.

Making a Paper Loom

For this activity you will need construction paper, child-safe scissors, strips of construction paper, glue. To make a paper loom, instruct the students to:

- Fold a rectangular piece of construction paper in half.
- Begin cutting lines from the folded edge, but don't cut all the way to the other end.
- Students can find the stopping point by locating a point three to four finger widths from the open end of the paper.
- Another method for finding the stopping point is to use a ruler to draw lines for the students to cut along.
- Draw a thicker line across the stopping point.
- If you have access to a copy machine that accepts heavy paper, predraw one loom and make copies to distribute to students.
- Precut enough paper strips for each loom. These can be different widths, but the length should at least be the width of the loom.
- To ensure success, have students practice weaving a single strip over and under until they understand the concept.
- Next, students should practice alternating the beginning of each new strip over and under.
- When this concept has been grasped, they can continue weaving until completion.
- Use a dot of glue to fasten the ends of the strips.

Activities for Older Children (Grades 4–5)

Leaf Mobiles

Materials: twigs, leaves, string or yarn, construction paper.

On a class walk or on the walk to school, have each child collect about six leaves and a small branch, about 12 inches long. A branch with a few twigs on it makes the best kind of mobile.

The teacher presses the leaves between two sheets of waxed paper, using an iron on the "low" setting. This preserves the leaves.

When the waxed paper has cooled, children cut around the leaves to separate them for the mobile. The waxed paper may be left on the leaves. However, if it does not stay attached, the wax coating left by the heat application is enough to harden and preserve the leaves.

Children then make holes in each leaf with a needle, hairpin, or even a pencil point. Instruct children to do this carefully, and provide close supervision.

Children insert string or thin yarn into the holes in each of the leaves. The teacher may aid the children in knotting the string or yarn.

The children then attach a piece of string or yarn (about 12 inches long) to the branch. This is a good experiment in balance, as the string has to be tied to the branch in the right spot so that the branch hangs horizontally from the string.

Next, children tie the leaves onto the branch in various places. Leaf shapes cut out of red, yellow, orange, and brown construction paper can also be attached to the branch with yarn. Acorns, seeds, or even berries may also be strung and attached for added color and variety.

Mobiles may be hung on a string across a section of the room for an attractive display.

Variations: Mobiles can be made using a small tree branch, coat hanger, or embroidery hoop. Use several small objects to balance a large one. Add glitter or sequins to create lights and shadows as objects move in the air. In designing objects to hang on the mobile, children need to think of how objects look as they turn and move.

Basic Mobiles

Materials: Thread, supports (heavy stove pipe wire, strips of wood, or dowels), wire cutters, glue, materials for making objects to be suspended (paper, wire, plastics, cardboard, straws, plaster, clay, etc.).

- Decide the number of units to be used in the mobile and their method of construction. These objects can be made from paper, wire, papier-mâché, wood, or a combination of any of these materials. Remember that an effective mobile should contain objects that have some kind of relationship to each other.
- Attach a thread to each object.
- Cut a support (a piece or wire or small wood dowel) and suspend an object from each end, making sure that it hangs evenly and that the separation is great enough to prevent objects from touching.
- Place a spot of glue on the very ends of the wire or dowel to help hold the thread of each object when tied in place. The threads supporting the objects should be comparatively short, but of different lengths.
- Tie another thread to the wire or dowel supporting the mobile by the thread. Slide the thread back and forth on the wire or dowel until it finds a point of balance. Secure it with a spot of glue.
- The thread holding the section just completed should be tied to the end of another wire or dowel and held in place with glue. Suspend an object from the other end of the wire or dowel.
- Any number of sections can be added as long as balance is maintained.
- Note: A wire stretched in a seldom-used corner of the room will enable the children to hang their mobiles while working on them. There is no limit to the ways a mobile can be constructed, once the principles of movement and balance are understood.

Creating Soft Wire Sculptures

A. Have students use three pipe cleaners to create a simple "skeleton" of a person.

B. Other pipe cleaners can be wrapped around the skeleton figure to suggest the form of muscles. Encourage children to help one another.

C. After students bend their sculptures into different poses, each pose is drawn on paper. The poses can be planned to create an action picture of a group of people. The poses might be planned and drawn to show a favorite sport, game, dance, or other activity such as a family watching television or enjoying a picnic. Drawings of all the skeleton figures should be made first. Then the students can draw in the details—clothes, faces, and the like.

D. Encourage students to draw the skeleton figures so they are about the same size as the wire sculpture. If the skeleton lines are carefully observed in each pose, their final drawings should be easy to complete and have interesting poses.

Memory Boxes—Assemblage

Students in middle and upper elementary grades are often involved in collecting things that express their interests. Talk about what collecting means to them. How are the things we save and collect reflections of parts of ourselves? Introduce the idea of a memory box for presenting their personal memorabilia. Have students bring in a shoebox or any other small box.

- First, have students prepare their memory boxes. They can paint the inside and outside of their boxes. A dark color, such as black or brown, works best because the objects of the assemblage will stand out more and the composition will be more unified.
- After the boxes have dried, preferably overnight, students will be able to compose their assemblages. Have them look through their memorabilia collections and select objects they want to use. To avoid having students glue their objects in place before they have experimented with various compositions; do not pass out glue until everyone has had a chance to explore different combinations. Students should be advised to select objects with contrasting qualities in order to create interest and variety—objects with varying sizes, colors, shapes, and textures.
- Remind students that composition is the organization of parts into a unified whole. They should carefully consider the placement of each part of their assemblage to make a composition that is pleasing to them. Remind them that they should place objects so that they can be seen as the box stands upright or hangs on a wall; they should not compose the box to be viewed from above.
- Have students use white glue to attach all the parts of their assemblage. When the glue has dried overnight, set up a display of all the memory boxes.
- Students might be interested in shadow boxes. You may be able to find boxes with interior divisions, such as boxes used to package Christmas tree ornaments or various kinds of fruit, and use these interior divisions to create a shadow box display. A memory box with interior cardboard divisions (tiny interior shelves) can also be created by cutting and attaching strips of carefully measured cardboard to the inside of a box. In this way, memorabilia items need not be glued down but only set on the cardboard "shelves."

Multicultural Awareness

Discuss examples of papier-mâché sculpture that students may have seen such as piñatas (Mexico) or large modeled heads or floats used in parades, puppets, and masks (Europe, the Americas, Asia). Ask students to explain why papier-mâché is used as a medium for those art forms instead of other materials. (In many cultures, paper is inexpensive or is saved and recycled. The paste for papier-mâché can also be made easily from a variety of inexpensive "sticky" materials, such as flour and water.)

This is a good way to introduce and motivate students for a class papier-mâché project.

Community Awareness

Have students research the buildings on the block or area nearest to their homes. Have them focus on the materials that have been used and varied textures or patterns they see. Suggest they draw the materials, patterns, or textures on unlined index cards and place labels on the back of each card, naming the material. If they are unable to name the material, an adult may assist or the drawing can serve as a reference for library research. When the drawings are completed, have the class sort and display them in groups in relation to the type of materials (brick, concrete, etc.). Discuss the variety of drawing styles for each material as well as actual variations in how the materials are used (e.g., brick patterns, concrete that imitates the appearance of natural stone).

Trophy Sculptures

For this activity you will need Styrofoam or wood blocks, pipe cleaners, glue, paper, markers, and small pieces of decorations. This activity gives children the opportunity to create an original trophy and present it to someone they want to congratulate.

Have children think of someone they want to congratulate for a noteworthy accomplishment by awarding that individual a personalized trophy. Have students use pipe cleaners to form the trophy person or object. Use small pieces of decoration to make the figure more fun. When satisfied with their figures, students glue them to the pieces of Styrofoam or wood blocks. Students can attach labels to the front of the blocks bearing the awardees' names and messages of congratulations. Be sure to have children sign their work.

A trophy can be made from just about anything. Interesting things can be glued on a paper plate for one kind of a trophy. Some things to glue for a trophy are natural objects from outside or even magazine pictures and words.

Positive and Negative Space—Hand Sculpture

Discuss with children the concept of positive and negative space. The space an object takes up is positive space. The "air" around it is negative space. When we create a painting, objects are positive space and are surrounded by negative space.

Have children trace their hands on a piece of cardboard. The cutout hand is the positive space, and the cut piece of paper is the negative space. Use the cutout cardboard hand as the base for the sculpture. Have the children try to figure out how to get the negative space to stand up (bend in half, bend bottom pieces to make a stand, use the cut out hand to support it).

Cut out other hands from construction paper—use different "poses": thumbs-up, peace sign, fist, etc. Add these to the base. Stress the idea of three-dimensional sculpting.

Early American Weaving

Older children can experience the Native American and Colonial American art of weaving with this activity that uses a modern twist on a traditional craft. The simple instructions in this activity are for a woven belt or sash.

For this activity you will need five small beverage straws, four-ply yarn (solid color), four-ply yarn (variegated), thin wire, and masking tape.

To set up your loom, cut solid yarn into lengths three times the desired length of the finished product. You will need five of these, one for threading each straw.

Cut approximately 10 yards of variegated yarn and roll into a ball. Bend thin wire to form a "needle."

For each of the beverage straws, thread the wire needle with a length of solid yarn, pull the wire through the straw, and tape one end tightly to the straw.

After all straws have been threaded and taped, begin weaving. Weaving the belt:

- Hold all five straws, with the taped ends up, in one hand.
- Using the end of the ball of variegated yarn, begin weaving with an "under/over" pattern from the bottom of the straws (where you are holding them) to the top (taped edge). When you have woven to the top of the straws, carefully push the weaving down a few inches. DO NOT push all of the weaving off the straws.
- Continue until you have reached a desired length, and tie off ends.

Recipes for Dough and Other Plastic Materials

1. *Cooked Dough*

   | ½ cup flour | 2 cups boiling water |
   | ½ cup cornstarch | ½ cup salt |

   (blend with cold water)

   Method: Add salt to boiling water. Combine flour with cornstarch and water. Pour hot mixture into cold. Put over hot water and cook until glossy. Cool overnight. Knead in flour until right consistency, adding color with flour.

2. *Cooked Dough*

   | 4 tablespoons | ½ cup boiling water |
   | cornstarch | ½ cup salt |

   Method: Mix cornstarch and salt. Add color if desired. Pour on boiling water, stir until soft and smooth. Place over fire until it forms a soft ball. In using, if it sticks to fingers, dust hands with cornstarch.

3. *Sawdust and Wheat Flour Paste*

   | 4 parts sawdust | 1 part wheat flour |

   Method: Make paste of wheat flour and water. Add sawdust. Presents interesting sensory appeal.

4. *Uncooked Play Dough*

   | 3 cups flour | 1 cup water |
   | ¼ cup salt | 1 tablespoon oil |

   coloring

   Method: Mix flour with salt; add water with coloring and oil gradually. Add more water if too stiff; add more flour if too sticky. Let children help with the mixing and measuring. Keep dough stored in plastic bags or a covered container.

5. *Salt Dough*

   | 1 cup salt | ¾ cup cold water |
   | ½ cup cornstarch | |

   Method: Combine all ingredients in a double boiler placed over medium heat. Stir the mixture constantly; in about two to three minutes it should become so thick that it follows the spoon mixing it. When the consistency is similar to bread dough, place on wax paper or aluminum foil to cool. When dough is cool enough to handle, knead for several minutes. It is then ready to use. To store for up to several days, wrap in wax paper or place in plastic bags.

6. *Ornamental Clay* (suitable for dried objects)

   | 1 cup cornstarch | 1¼ cups water |
   | 2 cups baking soda | |

   Method: Cook ingredients together until thickened, either in double boiler or over direct heat—stir constantly. When it is cool enough, turn it out and let children knead dough and make it into whatever they wish. If used for ornaments, make hole for hanging ornament while dough is still moist.

7. *Baker's Dough* (suitable for dried objects)

   | 4 cups flour | 1 to 1¼ cups water |
   | 1 cup salt | |

   Method: Mix ingredients to make the dough easy to handle. Knead and shape as desired. Bake at 350°F for 50 to 60 minutes. Material will brown slightly, but baking at lower temperatures is not as successful.

Soapy Sculpture Dough

Add this soap dough mixture to your modeling materials. It is white and very pliable and easy for children to manipulate. To make the soapy mixture, pour a box of soap flakes into a large container. Add water slowly until the mixture is the consistency of paste. Invite the children to mix it with you. Then have the children form grapefruit-sized balls with a lump of the mixture. Provide enough of these balls so each child has his or her own modeling "soap." You may want to supply toothpicks, pipe cleaners, buttons, and sequins for children to decorate their soap dough creations.

Chapter Review

1. Define the term *three-dimensional art* and give two examples.
2. Choose the answer that best completes the following statements about three-dimensional activities and the child's first learning to use clay.

   a. Children first learning to use clay
      i. make basic forms with clay.
      ii. combine basic forms to make objects.
      iii. squeeze the clay in an uncontrolled way.
   b. Children using clay for the first time work with clay in a way similar to the way they draw in the
      i. scribble stage.
      ii. basic forms stage.
      iii. pictorial stage.
   c. For children first learning to use clay, the most important thing about working with clay is
      i. what they can make with it.
      ii. how it feels.
      iii. how they can control it.
   d. The best kind of clay for children first learning to use clay is
      i. potter's clay.
      ii. oil-based Plasticene.
      iii. ceramic, nonelastic clay.

3. Decide which answer best completes each statement about three-dimensional activities and the child who can draw basic forms.

   a. A child who can draw basic forms
      i. cannot make similar forms in clay.
      ii. can make clay into similar forms.
      iii. combines these forms to make clay objects.
   b. Rolling clay to make balls is an example of
      i. lack of motor control.
      ii. uncontrolled movement like scribbling.
      iii. a basic form in clay.
   c. Children can make basic forms in clay because they
      i. can name their clay objects.
      ii. now have better motor control.
      iii. do not have enough motor control.
   d. Some simple basic forms that children can make in clay are
      i. balls, boxes, and coils.
      ii. flowers, houses, and animals.
      iii. triangles, hexagons, and octagons.

4. Choose the answer that best completes each statement about three-dimensional activities and the child in the pictorial stage of drawing.

   a. Most children like to make
      i. nothing in particular with clay.
      ii. just balls and boxes with clay.
      iii. definite things with clay.
   b. When working with clay, a child in the pictorial stage can
      i. combine basic forms to make a definite object.
      ii. make only basic forms in clay.
      iii. make only uncontrolled hand movements with clay.
   c. A simple combination of basic forms in a clay object is a
      i. house with four floors of clay and a four-part chimney.
      ii. clay box.
      iii. man made of a round ball head and a stick-type body.
   d. When children in the pictorial stage name their drawings, they
      i. have no motor control.
      ii. also name their clay objects.
      iii. are not yet ready to name their clay objects.
   e. When children name clay objects, it means they are in the related two-dimensional stage, called the
      i. scribble stage.
      ii. basic forms stage.
      iii. pictorial stage.
   f. A more complex combination of basic forms in clay is a
      i. man made with feet, fingers, hands, and arms.
      ii. clay man with feet, fingers, hands, and arms.
      iii. clay ball.
   g. When a child makes a clay figure with many more details than another figure, it means
      i. nothing of any particular importance.
      ii. that it is an important figure for the child.
      iii. that it is a simple combination of basic forms.
   h. When a clay object is made large, it means the object
      i. is a basic form.
      ii. is not very important.
      iii. stands for something important.

5. Describe the right room setup for clay work in regard to each of the following.

   a. table type
   b. location of clay tables
   c. number of children at table
   d. amount of clay for each child
   e. kind of storage container for clay

6. List the types of modeling materials and tools appropriate for young children.
7. Discuss how modeling benefits young children.
8. List several suggestions to make working with modeling materials a successful experience for young children.
9. What is assemblage? Give examples of assemblage activities.

10. List the materials and tools needed for assemblage activities for young children.
11. List appropriate materials and tools for cardboard construction activities.
12. Discuss the value of woodworking in the early childhood art program.
13. List some specific equipment required for woodworking experiences for young children.
14. Describe the role a teacher must play in woodworking experiences for young children.
15. Discuss some ways to adapt assemblage/collage activities for children with special needs.

References

Gallo, F., Golomb, C., & Barroso, A. (2003). Compositional strategies in drawing: The effects of two and three-dimensional media. *Visual Arts Research, 28*(1), 2–23.

Golomb, C. (2004). Sculpture: Representational development in a three-dimensional medium. In E. Eisner & M. Day (Eds.), *Handbook of research and policy in art education* (pp. 329–358). Mahwah, NJ: Erlbaum.

Golomb, C., & McCormick, M. (1995). Sculpture: The development of three-dimensional representation in clay. *Visual Arts Research, 21*(2), 35–50.

Taylor, T. (2006). *The altered object.* New York, NY: Lark Books.

Additional Readings

Almond, D. (2008). *Clay.* New York, NY: Bantam Doubleday.

Clough, P. (2009). *Clay in the primary school.* London, UK: A & C Black.

Collins, J. (2010). *Sculpture today.* London, UK: Phaidon Press.

Eckhoff, A., & Spearman, M. (2009). Rethink, reimagine, reinvent. *Art Education, 62*(2), 10–16.

Erickson, A. R. 2008. Albert's alphabet. *SchoolArts, 108*(2), 54–55.

Golomb, C. (2004). *The child's creation of a pictorial world.* Mahwah, NJ: Erlbaum.

Johnson, G. (2009). *1000 ideas for creative reuse: Remake, restyle, recycle, renew.* Beverly, MA: Quarry Books.

Mayesky, M. (2004). *Creative arts & activities: Clay, play dough & modeling materials.* Clifton Park, NY: Delmar Cengage Learning.

Mayesky, M. (2004). *Creative arts & activities: Paper art.* Clifton Park, NY: Delmar Cengage Learning.

O'Rorke, M. (2010). *Clay, light and water.* London, UK: A & C Black.

Paelka, L. (2010). *The complete book of polymer clay.* Newtown, CT: Taunton Press.

Pavlou, V. (2009). Understanding young children's three-dimensional creative potential in art. *International Journal of Art and Design Education, 28*(2), 139–150.

Rogers, L., & Steffan, D. (2009). Teachers on teaching: Clay play. *Young Children, 64*(3), 78–81.

Sturdevant, A. (2008). Kindergarten architects. *SchoolArts, 108*(2), 40–41.

Wayne, D. (2008). Caps for sale. *SchoolArts, 108*(4), 35–36.

Wenzel, A. (2010). *13 sculptures children should know.* New York, NY: Prestel.

Software for Children

Axe & Pixe, ages 6 and up

Bob the Builder Can Do Zoo, ages 3 and up

Bricks, ages 6 to 12

City Building, ages 6 and up

Garfield Gets Real, ages 6 and up

Kid Cad: The Amazing 3D Building Kit, ages 7 and up

Learning with the Poo Yoos—Episode 1, ages 3 and up

LEGO Battles, ages 6 and up

World of Goo, ages 7 and up

Helpful Websites

Art Interactive, http://www.hmsg.si.edu/
Click on "Education." This site is presented by the Hirshhorn Museum and Sculpture Garden. Click on "Art Interactive" under the "Education" section for ideas on creating sculptures.

All Posters, http://AllPosters.com/
This is your source for more than 150,000 affordable prints and posters featuring the works of old masters to contemporary artists.

Block Corner, http://www.blockcorner.com
This site is an online building toy for kids of all ages. An interesting way to merge art and technology as students (grades 4 to 8) design block towers.

Brain Binders, http://www.teachnet.com/ brainbinders/
This is a collection of instructions for puzzles involving paper folding (grades 4 to 8). The site includes patterns you can download and print.

Paper Critters, http://www.papercritters.com/
Students (grades 3 to 8) create people, animals or robots (to name a few) using body templates, art tools, and accessories.

Smart Kids, http://smartmuseum.uchicago.edu/ smartkids/
This Flash site, presented by the University of Chicago's David & Alfred Smart Museum of Art, provides an interactive art study experience for children.

Teachers First, http://www.teachersfirst.com
This site features a rich collection of lessons, units, and Web resources carefully selected and reviewed by experienced educators. Find resources by subject and grade level by keyword search to save you time.

Yahoo! Home: Arts: Education, http://dir.yahoo. com/Arts/Education/K_12
This Yahoo! search directory contains lists of sites with K–12 art activities. Categories include curriculum standards, drama, and lesson plans.

For additional creative activity resources, visit our website at www.Cengage.com/login.

Infusing a creative approach into every area of early childhood curriculum is the focus of Part 2. Building and expanding on the theory presented in Part 1, the chapters in Part 2 cover several other areas of the early childhood curriculum in which a creative approach is appropriate. These curricular areas include dramatic play and puppetry, movement, music, language arts, science, math, food experiences, social studies, and health and safety. Also included in Part 2 are chapters on how to take a creative approach in establishing a multicultural, antibiased curriculum.

All of the activities presented in Part 2 are based in developmental theory yet are simple to reproduce and expand upon. All are presented in the hope that they will be adapted to children's individual needs, abilities, and interest levels. Information on adapting activities for children with special needs is included where appropriate throughout Part 2. Activities in Part 2 are designed to be springboards to many learning experiences limited only by the child's and teacher's imagination and creativity.

Unlike simple manipulation of media, such as pounding clay and finger painting, the activities offered in this section generally require more skill on the part of the children and more instruction (at least initially) by the teacher. They tend to have a more definite focus and direction. In using these activities, there must be considerable latitude allowed for individual ideas to be expressed. These are valuable activities that provide opportunities for purposefulness and challenges to skills that children will enjoy. They also increase the variety of experiences available to young children in full-day centers.

In all chapters in Part 2, the teacher should always consider the developmental level of a child or a group of children before initiating any activity. Activities are included for children from preschool through grade 5. Appropriate age and/or grade levels are indicated on these activities.

Finally, while guidance of a child's activities is appropriate, each child should be given the freedom to adapt these activities and the processes used to his or her own creative needs. In other words, the approach should not be "What is it?" but "Tell me about what you've made." Most important, emphasis in all activities should be on the process and not the end product.

Rather than displaying a model or sample product at the beginning of an activity, have the children talk about their own ideas and plans for the activity. The beginning, middle, and end of every activity is the child—unique and singular in his or her own way.

PART 2

Theory into Practice: Creative Activities for the Early Childhood Program

SECTION 5
Creative Activities in Other Curricular Areas

SECTION 6
Creativity: A Multicultural View

REFLECTIVE QUESTIONS

After studying this section, you should be able to answer the following questions.

1. Do I use puppets as an instructional tool for encouraging creativity and dramatic play?

2. Have I included enough materials for puppet making for all the developmental levels, special needs, and multicultural backgrounds of my children?

3. Have I provided opportunities for young children to express themselves creatively in movement and music activities?

4. How will I modify my language arts activities so that they are appropriate for the multicultural children in my group?

5. At what levels of listening skills are the young children in my group? Do my lessons and activities meet these individual levels?

6. Have I presented language arts experiences that are appropriate to the children's current level of emerging literacy?

7. How can I be sure my classroom centers and activities are conducive to the young child's active science exploration?

8. Am I aware of the different levels of mathematic thinking present in my group of children?

9. Are my teaching practices reflective of antibiased curricular principles?

10. Have I planned developmentally appropriate food and nutrition experiences for young children? Do these practices help establish lifelong positive habits?

11. Do my room arrangement and instructional strategies emphasize appropriate health and safety practices for the young children in the group?

12. In what ways can I improve the science experiences for young children in my program?

13. In considering my language arts curriculum, what are the areas I most need to improve? What positive steps can I take to implement these improvements?

14. In what ways are children verbalizing their mathematical thinking? Do I encourage this process by providing materials and activities that foster mathematical thinking?

15. As I evaluate my classroom's physical arrangement, how can I adjust it to better represent the curriculum areas of most importance to the young children who use it?

16. Does my current math and science curriculum provide an appropriate match to the developmental levels of the children in my group?

17. What are some specific ways I can be more creative (in my instructional strategies) in curricular areas outside the arts curriculum?

18. How can I integrate art and creative activities into my entire curriculum?

19. In what way can I improve the range of language arts experiences so that the language arts are related to other curriculum areas?

20. Do my teaching and classroom practices emphasize respect for individual differences in language development? Individual differences in math and science understanding? Individual cultural differences?

21. Can I verbalize the rationale for each area of my curriculum and how it helps develop the creativity of young children?

Dramatic Play and Puppetry

"I am being **magic**!" crows Miguel, dressed in a "superman" cape and a painter's cap. "I can fly anywhere I want!" As he flaps his arms and swoops around the room, he is joined by Claudia dressed in a dancer's tutu. "Wait for me. I can fly, too!" she says. The two children glide around the room for a minute or two, until they notice Jaime sitting by himself in the block corner. Moving in his direction, Miguel invites him to join them in flight. "Jaime, I can make magic, so you can fly, too." Jaime joins Miguel and Claudia for a short time, until he spots an opening at the computer where he "lands" for another activity. Claudia soon decides to land as well, deciding to be a doctor and make a house call to check on a sick baby in the home center. Miguel continues to "be magic" for a few more moments before he too "lands" and becomes the concerned daddy of the sick baby.

OBJECTIVES

After studying this chapter, you should be able to:

1. Give the objectives of dramatic play.

2. Discuss the importance of dramatic play to a young child's development.

3. Discuss the difference between dramatic play and creative dramatics.

4. Discuss appropriate ways to use puppets in the early childhood program.

5. Discuss ways to adapt dramatic activities for children with special needs.

These children are happily engaged in dramatic play, a natural and essential part of a child's development. It is spontaneous and child directed. It is fluid, changing momentarily as children's imaginations move them to explore "being" things and "trying on" many roles.

Importance of Dramatic Play

In the above scene, it is obvious that **dramatic play** is an excellent means for children to develop their creativity and imaginations. Dramatic play allows them to exercise their special, instinctive ways of dealing with reality. They need no written lines to memorize or structured behavior patterns to imitate in order to fantasize their world. What they do need is an interesting environment and freedom to experiment and be themselves.

Dramatic play provides children one of the best ways to express themselves. They are free to express their inner feelings in a safe, creative way. Often, teachers find out how children feel about themselves

FIGURE 15-1 • Children grow in self-confidence as they engage in dramatic play activities.

and others by listening to them as they carry out dramatic play. The pretending involved in such dramatic experiences, whether planned or totally spontaneous, is a necessary part of development. In the dramatic play center, children can act out feelings that often cannot be expressed directly. For example, the child who is afraid of the doctor can express this fear by giving shots to dolls or stuffed animals in the center. In like manner, a child can act out with a friend a visit to the dentist. Thus, children can learn to deal with their anxieties as well as act out their fantasies through creative dramatic play.

Through the imitation and make-believe of dramatic play, children sort out what they understand and gain a measure of mastery and control over events they have witnessed or taken part in—making breakfast, going to work, taking care of baby, and going to the doctor. Dramatic play helps children enter and begin to make sense of the world of adults.

The Beginnings of Dramatic Play

The beginning of dramatic play is visible in the actions of children as young as one year, who put a comb to their hair, for example, and pull it along the side of their face, imitating the activity that has been performed on them with the same "prop." Given the right

prop, the baby will imitate the behavior associated with that prop. For example, if offered a cup, the baby drinks; a hat, the baby puts it on his head; or a pillow, the baby puts his head on it. Adults often describe this as "pretend" play, but it is more accurately prepretend play, because it involves only actions that are known to the child.

Actual dramatic play begins when a child uses a prop for something other than the activity for which he or she has seen it used by an adult. Thus, a hairbrush becomes a sailing boat, a wooden block becomes a hairbrush, a stick becomes a bridge. This usually happens when the child is about two years old; that is the age when children seem to be capable of making an "as if" transformation of an object, a necessary prerequisite to pretend play involving objects, others, and themselves.

Development of Dramatic Play

As children grow and develop, so does their dramatic play. From simple imitative movement, children move on to more complex dramatic play.

FIGURE 15-2 • One of the best ways children have to express themselves is through creative dramatic play.

It is important for teachers of young children to be very good observers and listeners, to see what children play with, to watch what they do with the materials, and to listen to what they say about the props and materials provided to them. It is equally important that the teacher becomes part of the play of the child, but—and this is essential—at the child's present developmental level. We all remember the relative who insisted that the Fisher Price garage could only be a garage, not a part of the fortress wall, and the legendary behavior of the father who gives the young child a gift of an electric train or racing car set and proceeds to insist that it be played with in terms of adult reality. In adult play, there is no flying of cars one over the other to win and no make-believe drivers, only Grand Prix racers. No wonder the adult ends up playing by himself, while the child returns to playing with the racing car box. This way, the child is allowed to pretend without adult guidance and limitations.

Many times creative dramatics begins with one child, and others soon join in. Playing store with a storekeeper and a number of customers is a form of creative dramatic play. Speaking on a toy telephone to

FIGURE 15-3 • Dramatic play occurs daily in the lives of children.

a friend is another form. Puppet shows in which children use finger puppets and make up a story as they go along is still another form.

Dramatic play occurs daily in the lives of young children. It is one of the ways that children naturally learn. They constantly imitate the people, animals, and machines in their world. They enjoy recreating the exciting experiences of their lives. Dramatic play is their way of understanding and dealing with the world.

Dramatic play is also an important medium for language development, as it encourages fluency in language. A child who is reluctant to speak in other situations is almost compelled to speak in order to be included in dramatic play. As play becomes elaborate, a child's language becomes more complex. When children talk with each other in a nondirective setting, such as the dramatic play center, it is possible for the flow and quality of language to develop. If others are to understand his or her role, a child needs to explain what he or she is doing so that friends will respond in appropriate ways. If the child is to understand what they are doing, he or she must listen.

When children become involved in complex make-believe, they need to listen and respond to each other. A child speaks convincingly to others when he or she wants them to change the nature of the play. If they still do not understand, he or she may try to find other ways to persuade them. When he or she needs to elaborate on his or her ideas, the child is likely to use a longer sequence of words and move from two words to more complex syntax.

As children play together, they learn new words from each other. At their make-believe restaurant, Maria prepared tacos and Justin ordered fruitcake from the menu. Justin liked the sound of the new word, *tacos*. He pretended he was eating one, even though he did not know what a taco was.

As children play, they repeat words and phrases they have learned and enjoy saying them. They name objects, talk about what they are doing, and plan as they go along. They begin to recognize the importance of planning and take time to formulate more detailed plans for their dramatizations.

Dramatic Play in the Dramatic Play Center

One of the best places for children to express themselves in creative, dramatic play is the dramatic play center. Here, in a child-sized version of the

FIGURE 15-4 • In the dramatic play center, children are free and safe to try on many social roles.

world, children are free and safe to express how they feel about themselves and others. While they carry out dramatic play in this center, they can pretend to be many different kinds of people, "trying on," so to speak, many social roles.

The dramatic play center provides endless opportunities for the teacher, as a facilitator of learning, to broaden children's horizons. The center can be decorated and rearranged to represent an area that pertains to specific content. Possibilities include creating a home, hospital, post office, grocery store, and more. The change of seasons as well as certain holidays can be easily incorporated in this center. For example, during fall, a child's rake, sweaters, and pumpkins might be included in the center. During the winter months, mittens or a child's shovel may be additions to the center. For spring, the teacher may add plastic or silk flowers and a variety of hats. Supplies in the dramatic play center should reflect the activities in the classroom and extend the skills being taught elsewhere in the room as well as introduce new skills. Be sure to include clothing, dishes, and dolls that are familiar and represent each of the ethnic groups in your classroom.

Teachers of young children further encourage children's dramatic play by providing kits containing "props" for them to use. Dramatic play kits are created by assembling a variety of available everyday items into groups that have a common use or theme. Children select the props and use them in groups or alone to play roles or create dramatic play experiences. Just letting the children know about the use of these kits is often enough to get them started. Materials for these dramatic kits can be kept together in shoeboxes or other containers. Some common types of dramatic play kits are found in Figure 15–5.

Imagination can also be used to transform regular classroom items into "new materials." Chairs can become trains, cars, boats, or houses. A table covered with a blanket or bedspread becomes a cave or special hiding place. Large cardboard cartons that children can decorate become houses, forts, fire stations, and telephone booths.

It is important to emphasize a gender-neutral approach in teaching, especially in the dramatic play area. For example, boys' dramatic play must be encouraged in an early childhood program as much as girls' dramatic play. A good tactic to encourage boys' participation is to change the themes of the dramatic play corner to topics that interest some boys. Include open-ended materials in the dramatic play areas such as blocks, flashlights, a rope, and small balls. An observant teacher, sensitive to both sexes' dramatic play and developing sex-role concepts, even gives cues that encourage all children to play in all centers.

Entering into the child's dramatic play is an important point of consideration here. The teacher should not be the leader or the organizer of the dramatic play and must try not to form premature conclusions or make assumptions for the child. The teacher observes and asks questions about what the child says and helps to draw out information from the child, maintaining the conversation on the theme provided by the child, but at a pace that allows the child to feel comfortable and pleased with the conversation. Use the Observation Sheet found in the Online Companion to assist you in observing the dramatic play of young children. The teacher also encourages children's play by providing props that extend the play but do not change the theme. In doing so, teachers provide for further dramatic play and thereby create a more effective basis from which thought processes and imagination can develop. Teachers help children with their thinking by making statements about their work—not evaluative statements, such as, "I like your cake," or assumptive

Activities in the dramatic play center afford the child experiences in the following social interactions:

- clarifying adult roles
- trying out social skills
- getting along with others
- sharing responsibilities
- making group decisions
- controlling impulsive behavior
- recognizing cause and effect
- developing positive attitudes about oneself and others
- enjoying the fantasy of the grownup world
- using oral language spontaneously
- practicing the use of symbols, which are subskills in reading
- learning social ease and confidence in one's own strengths

Materials*

full-length mirror
child sized stove
child sized refrigerator
sink
closet or rack of clothes
cooking/eating utensils
table and chairs
tea set
telephone
stethoscope
props for cleaning (broom, mop, dustpan, pail, sponge, rags, duster)
play dough
doll bed, doll carriage, baby highchair

rocking chair
empty cans
empty multicultural food boxes
mirror/hand mirror
carriage
multicultural dolls and doll clothes
iron/ironing board
puppets
a variety of hats, dresses, shirts, ties, belts, scarves, shoes, pocketbooks, and jewelry
an old suitcase (for "trips")
doctor's satchel, bandages, cotton balls, play syringe, pill bottles, a play thermometer, play money

an old briefcase
dress-up gloves, rubber gloves, baseball gloves, garden gloves
open-ended materials such as large sheets, scarves, and cardboard boxes.
a "challenge box" of unusual items (tools, large beach ball, and funny glasses) to add new elements to their play. Challenge children: "What can you do with this?"
props from favorite stories to encourage retelling experiences.

Dramatic Play Kits:

Post Office and Mail Carrier: Index card file, stamp pads, stampers, crayons, pencils, stickers, envelopes, hats, badges, mail bag, supply of "resident" or other third-class mail
Firefighter: Hats, raincoats, badge, boots, short lengths of garden hose
Grocery Store: adding machine, play money, paper pads, pencils or crayons, paper bags, empty food cartons, wax fruit, cans with smooth edges
Plumber: wrenches, sections of plastic pipes, toolkit, hats, and shirts
Painter: paint cans full of water, brushes of different sizes, drop cloth, painter's hat
Mechanic: tire pump, tool kit, boxes to become "cars," shirt, hat
Entertainer: CD player, musical instruments, costumes
*Add objects as needed for special emphasis.

FIGURE 15-5 • Experiences and equipment in the home center.

ones, such as, "What a naughty cat, eating up all the meat!"—but statements of the obvious on which the child can expand, such as, "It's a bright yellow color!"

In the dramatic play center, dramatic experience often begins with one child, and others soon join in. In observing the dramatic play of children of various ages in this center, the perceptive teacher can detect definite developmental and age differences. Younger children two to four years old generally are involved in dramatic play for a much briefer period of time than children five years of age and older. Before the child is two years old, for example, he or she may say, "Nice

baby," when he or she hugs a doll and then move on. After the age of two, the child's dramatic play may begin to combine several ideas, in contrast to the single-idea dramatization of the younger child. The older child may hold a doll and pretend to feed the "baby" a cookie. He or she may decide to put the baby to bed, covering the doll with a blanket because it is time for "baby to take a nap." This process of imitating what has been observed is called **modeling behavior**.

Instances of such modeling behavior in the dramatic play center and elsewhere are even more prevalent in older children. For example, a five-year-old child will

FIGURE 15-6 • Puppets fascinate and involve children in a way that few other art forms can.

feed the baby, discussing why milk is good for him or her, telling the baby it is nap time, and instructing the baby that children must "be good" and listen to their parents. This dramatization is in marked contrast to that of the two-year-old.

Children involved in dramatic play also use materials from various parts of the room to support their play. For example, a child who needs some pretend money to put in a purse may decide to make some in the art area, or even go to the manipulative area to gather beads, chips, or small Lego® blocks to use as money.

Whether they are searching for materials or on their way to another related location, it is perfectly natural and appropriate for children involved in dramatic play to move about the entire space as part of their play. Confining role players to one area or part of the room frustrates rather than supports their intentions. When their use of space and materials conflicts with other children's use of space and materials, the opportunity for group problem solving arises.

Dramatic play is a natural avenue for participation by children from diverse language and multicultural backgrounds. Children who are bilingual can

participate easily in dramatic activities that call for nonverbal communication. The dramatic play area can also be a place where children learn the words for their play props. For example, nametags can be made for objects in the dramatic play center in both English and children's native languages.

Dramatic play also appeals to children's various learning styles or multiple intelligences. The body-smart learner gets obvious enjoyment from the active, physical movement involved in dramatic play. The child who is word smart enjoys the ongoing dialogue that is so naturally a part of the dramatic play experience. The child with a person-smart learning style thrives in dramatic activities involving constant interaction with other children. The child with a picture-smart learning style enjoys creating the visual scenes that provide the background for dramatic play scenarios.

Remember also to provide outdoor materials and equipment for pretending and role play. With more

FIGURE 15-7 • Teachers of young children encourage their dramatic play by providing props for the children to use.

THIS ONE'S for YOU!   Puppets, Puppets, Puppets—So Many Uses!

Did you ever notice what happens when children interact with puppets? They don't look at your face—they look at and talk to the puppet! The puppet becomes a character they can have a real conversation with.

Don't let your shyness or "stage fright" prevent you from taking out the puppets that may be collecting dust on the shelf. Use them! You will be amazed at how many ways you can use puppets with young children. Here are a few ideas.

Puppets for toddlers. Put a puppet on your hand or finger and a small group of toddlers will gather in front of you. The magic of puppets helps toddlers increase their attention span. Children who would normally not last long in a group activity will be fascinated enough to sit down and stay awhile. Choose puppets children can interact with—shake their paw, tickle their ears, and give a kiss. And don't forget to have a puppet sing-a-long! You can make small finger puppets for the children to use on their fingers, too. Ideas for finger puppets are found later in this chapter.

Puppets for times of the day. Use a special puppet to begin your morning meeting. Children like seeing the puppet every day, and this routine can also help them make transitions to and from the group. You can also use the puppet to welcome children, lead the hello song, or discuss the events of the day. It can also be used to share a recent experience that may be similar to one a child in the group has had. A puppet can also talk about feelings regarding a classroom situation that needs discussion. A large puppet that has an expressive face and moveable arms would be good in this situation.

Puppets for group time. Here are some ideas for using puppets at group time.

- Use a puppet for teaching alphabet letters (i.e., a lamb puppet for the letter L). If focusing on a particular color, the puppet might wear the chosen color in a paper hat and a scarf.

- Make simple stick or finger puppets (see ideas later in this unit) representing characters from a favorite book. Do this, too, for story-songs such as "This Old Man" or "I Know an Old Lady." Children can use the puppets to play the different roles in the story or song.

- Use a puppet to introduce a story. When the story is finished, the puppet can discuss it with the children.

- Designate a special puppet, such as a Riddle Puppet, for asking children "What am I thinking?" or to play an "I Spy" game. Children will know a riddle is coming whenever you bring out this puppet.

Puppets and Math

- Have a puppet that is always backward ... he adds instead of subtracts ... he multiplies instead of divides ... he even counts backward. Have the children point out his errors and correct them.

- Have a puppet that goes crazy every time he hears a certain number. Choose your work problems so that the number is in the correct answers. Whoever gets the problem right first gets the puppet for the next problem.

- Have a puppet that always has a secret number, concept, or word. He will only give the children hints. When they figure it out, he will be approached by another puppet that will tell him a new secret.

Puppets and English

- Make puppets to represent the parts of speech. Make up a list of sentences with the puppet parts of speech in them. Have the children use the puppets to read the sentences and show how the parts of speech have to work together.

- For nonreaders, have them choose a "baby book" and adapt the story into a play and present it for the lower grades. Cross-age drama is important for the nonreader as it allows him or her to learn from the beginning without having to be humiliated.

- Create a role-playing center with written assignments. Encourage children to explore roles alternative to their own through puppets. Have a puppet play the role of an Indian child, a business person, a fish in a polluted stream, an extremely shy person on a crowded street, an invisible man, or their teacher.

Puppets for transition times. Use a puppet to announce cleanup or any other change in activity. The transition puppet might have a bell it rings or a drum it plays. Set aside a special puppet just for this role so that the children do not confuse it with others in the room. The puppet can also excuse children from group time with a song, riddle, or direction. "Anybody who is wearing BLUE can go wash their hands." Later in the year, children will enjoy taking turns using this puppet and providing the directions.

Continued

Puppets as peacemakers. A puppet can be an impartial negotiator. Try a puppet when an argument arises or a problem occurs in the classroom. Children can take their case to the puppet. Children are often more willing to listen and cooperate when they problem solve with an "impartial" puppet friend. You can even use homemade sock puppets set aside solely for this purpose to help children express their feelings. See information later in this chapter on how to make sock or glove puppets for this purpose.

Puppets as school-to-home connections. Puppets, like dolls and stuffed animals, are wonderful for creating a home–school connection. Children can take the puppet—along with the puppet's overnight bag and journal—home for the weekend to visit with the family. Don't forget to pack the disposable camera so that children can record its adventures. This take-home puppet should be large enough that children can dress it up and play with it.

Puppets as classroom friends. Introduce a new classroom family member to the class—a puppet! Children will delight in telling the puppet all about the rules and even give it a tour of the room after group time. This is especially effective with shy children. You may see them chatting away to the puppet in a way you have never seen or heard them before. A full-body puppet that looks like a stuffed animal is good for this activity because children will want to carry it around to the different centers in the room and sit next to it at snack time.

space and fewer boundaries, outdoor dramatic play is often robust and highly mobile. Children will make use of anything available—wagons, tricycles, and other wheeled toys for cars, buses, trains, and boats; large packing boxes, boards, sheets, ropes, and tires for houses, stores, forts, and caves; and sand and sand utensils for cooking, eating, and building. They may also enjoy the addition of some "indoor" materials (hats, scarves, baby dolls, dishes, chalk) to their outdoor dramatic play.

FIGURE 15-8 • The dramatic play center provides the child endless opportunities for creative expression.

FIGURE 15-9 • The "store" is open for business in the dramatic play center.

FIGURE 15-10 • Child-sized equipment in the dramatic play center facilitates children's play.

Creative Dramatics in the Elementary Grades

Dramatic play is the free play of very young children in which they explore their universe, imitating the actions and traits of those around them. It is an accepted part of the preschool and kindergarten curricula. While adults rely on reason and knowledge, children use play and imagination to explore and understand their world. It makes sense, then, for teachers to use these two resources—play and imagination—as learning tools. Dramatic play is the child's earliest expression in dramatic form, but it is not the same as creative dramatics.

Dramatic play is fragmented, existing only for the moment. It may last for a few minutes or go on for some time. It even may be played repeatedly, but it is a repetition for the pure joy of doing. It has no clear beginning and no end and no development in the dramatic sense.

Creative drama refers to informal drama that is created by the participants. It goes beyond dramatic play in scope and intent. It may make use of a story with a beginning, a middle, and an end. It may, on the other hand, explore, develop, and express ideas and feelings through dramatic enactment. It is, however,

---

THIS ONE'S for YOU! Learning Self-Control in the Dramatic Play Area

Dramatic play has long been seen as an effective way for children to learn and practice social skills. Recent research shows that dramatic play is also effective at teaching self-regulation to impulsive children. This makes sense. Successful dramatic play requires cooperation, joint planning, and goal setting among children—all functions that require a great deal of self-regulation (Riley, San Juan, Klinkner, & Ramminger, 2008).

One study followed a group of three- to four-year-olds in their early childhood classrooms to see which children showed the greatest improvement in self-control. From fall to spring, self-control was measured by observing the children during cleanup time and circle time (Elias, Eisenberg, & Berk, 2002). In their study, the researchers found that a strong predictor of improved self-regulation—particularly for the children who were most impulsive in the

fall—was their degree of involvement in complex, socio-dramatic play. In this kind of play, two or more children would interact—not just play alongside each other—and the play included make-believe and verbal interaction that went on for some time. The researchers evaluated the play by observing two areas in each classroom, the playhouse and the large block area. In the study's classrooms, the playhouse and large block area were joined, allowing children to easily combine props from both areas.

The researchers also suggested that this type of room arrangement encourages more complex make-believe play.

This study provides yet another reason for early childhood teachers to encourage young children in their dramatic play. It may also give you some new ideas on room arrangement to encourage young children's more complex dramatic play.

FIGURE 15-11 • Children learn social skills as they share dress-up clothes in the dramatic play center.

always improvised drama. This makes it different from performing a play. Actors in a play read or memorize lines written by somebody else. In creative dramatics, actors create their own words to convey meaning. Dialogue is created by the players, whether the content is taken from a well-known story or is an original plot. Lines are not written down or memorized. With each playing, the story becomes more detailed and better organized, but it remains extemporaneous and is at no time designed for an audience. Participants are guided by a leader rather than a director; the leader's goal is the optimal growth and development of the players.

The term *creative drama* is generally used to describe the improvised drama of children age six and older. Creative drama offers elementary children the opportunity to develop their creativity and imagination. Few activities have greater potential for developing the imagination than creative dramatics, yet, elementary teachers of young children often neglect this important learning tool for the elementary child.

Creative drama offers an opportunity for children with special needs to participate in a performing art.

Because of its flexibility, drama can be a joyful and freeing adventure for groups of all ages. Special needs can be served by adjusting emphases and activities to fit the ability level of the children.

Through creative dramatics, the imagination can be stimulated and strengthened in elementary students.

Guidelines for Creative Dramatics with Elementary Students

The following are some specific steps you may find helpful in setting up creative dramatic experiences for elementary children.

Provide a structure. While pretending is very natural for children, improvising a short drama can be an abstract process. Children will need structure to guide their actions and dialogue during the initial stages. The teacher can provide this structure by modeling and demonstrating the basic story, as well as possible actions, dialogue, and characterizations. In story re-enactments, be sure everyone gets a turn. But try to avoid repeating the play over and over again in the same setting, as children will probably become bored. Instead, repeat it once a day over the course of a week to maintain children's interest. It is best to keep early dramas short and simple, using only two to four characters. Older students and those with experience in creative dramatics will need less structure.

Encourage open-endedness. Creative dramatics is spontaneous and changeable. Although it works best when teachers provide a beginning structure, this structure should be flexible and open-ended. As students become more comfortable with creative dramatics, they will begin to use ideas and experiences from their own lives to create unique variations on the original themes. Using a prepared script would prevent this kind of creativity and individualization. It is a good rule not to use written dialogue.

Promote a safe environment. Creativity is enhanced when the teacher creates a fun, safe environment. Closing the classroom door during the initial learning stages of creative dramatics can help to develop a sense of safety and community. A teacher who is willing to take creative risks by modeling and participating in creative dramatics encourages the children's participation. Positive, specific feedback that acknowledges actors and their efforts will put students at ease to continue acting creatively. Finally, a teacher should

Researchers from the Manchester Metropolitan University and the Institute of Education, University of London, have been studying the use of puppets as stimuli in classrooms to provide more opportunities for more productive science lessons. Their work, the PUPPETS Project (Puppets Promoting Engagement and Talk in Science), was funded by the Nuffield Foundation, which aims to promote engagement and talk in science lessons. Although puppets are frequently used in language lessons and for emotional and social education (Thorp, 2005), the researchers were the first to conduct research into the use of puppets in primary-level science education. They wanted to explore whether puppets might have a positive impact on children's engagement in primary-school science lessons.

The main research took place with 16 primary-level teachers of children aged 7 to 11 in schools in Manchester and London. The schools represented a diverse socio-economic and cultural mix. The researchers adopted a mixture of research methods, including classroom observation and teacher and child interviews. The teachers attended workshops to become familiar with the use of puppets, after which each teacher was audio- and video-recorded during a science lesson where puppets were used. In each of these lessons, sample groups of children were audio-recorded during small-group conversations. These teachers were also taped when they had typical science lessons without puppets. Throughout the school year, teachers were requested to use the puppets in typical science lessons, taken from the teacher's lesson plans, rather than setting up special "puppet lessons" that were separate from the usual curriculum. This was to ensure that the findings from the research would be readily applicable by other teachers working within their usual curriculum constraints.

Using an open-coding approach (Strauss & Corbin, 1998), transcripts of all the conversations between teachers, puppets, and children were coded. The conversation was coded to identify discourse initiated by the teacher, the children, or the puppets.

Results of the study indicated that in each class, many of the children showed high levels of engagement and motivation in response to the puppets. Evidence of engagement included children asking when the puppets were to be used; physical interaction with the puppets (for example, holding their hands); following the puppets around the room; and talking to the puppets. Video evidence from lessons using puppets showed that nearly all children were focused on the puppets, that they had high levels of concentration, and that they stayed on task, eager to contribute to the discussion.

All of the teachers noted in their diaries and/or in their interviews that puppets enhanced children's engagement. Typical comments from teachers included:

"Children were keen to tell the puppet what they knew but also listened more attentively." "The children responded brilliantly. I thought they may be cynical, especially the Year 5 boys, but they were especially motivated."

Analysis of interview transcripts with the children confirmed this high level of interest and engagement. Comments about the use of puppets included: "Lessons are more fun." "I understand better with the puppets." "Last year I didn't really find science interesting—now it's my favourite subject."

Observation and interviews showed a number of important changes when puppets were used. These included the following:

- Nearly all of the children were highly engaged and motivated when puppets were used. They listened more, they became more involved in the lesson, and more children engaged in conversation.

- Many of the children claimed to understand science better when the teacher used puppets.

- Most of the teachers had changed aspects of their practice as a result of using puppets, such as including more opportunities for talk in their planning.

- Generally when teachers used worksheets, the children were less interested.

- There was some limited evidence that children's attainment was higher, especially among low-attaining children.

In summary, the research indicated that puppets can provide a useful mechanism to enhance children's engagement and to promote talk involving reasoning in primary science lessons. There is evidence that when teachers use the puppets, children talk more readily about scientific problems, and their use of higher-order thinking (such as explanation and justification) is enhanced. They, therefore, appear to offer a valuable extension to the teaching/learning strategies typically used by primary school teachers in science. Their findings have led to further major funding for professional development in the use of puppets in the U.K. and further research into the reasons why the use of puppets is so effective (Simon, Naylor, Keogh, Maloney, & Downing, 2008). For more information on the PUPPET project, visit http://www.puppetsproject.com/research.html

FIGURE 15-12 • In creative dramatics with elementary students, the teacher can model and demonstrate the basic story as well as possible actions.

never force students to participate in creative dramatics; rather, he or she should always ask for volunteers.

Provide feedback. Students like to receive feedback, both formal and informal. Informal feedback is best when a teacher responds in a way that is appropriate to the dramatic experience (e.g., laughing at the comedic parts). Once a drama is over, the teacher can give more formal feedback by processing the experience with students, recognizing those things that were done well.

Take your time. Allow students to slowly become comfortable with creative dramatics. Remember, creative dramatics is meant to be an enjoyable learning experience. Make having fun your number one priority.

The following are some examples of creative dramatics experiences.

• In a third-grade classroom, students using creative dramatics "become" metal containers, expanding with heat and contracting with cold. These

expanding and contracting movements are put into a drama and are eventually accompanied by a dance.

• In a first-grade classroom, children become clouds releasing raindrops, shimmery rays of sunshine, and seeds that grow roots, sprout, and squeeze their faces through the dirt.

• A fourth-grade teacher introduces a dramatic activity having individuals or small groups of students repeat the same line while portraying different qualities or characters. She says in a very mysterious way, "Are you going to wear the red hat to the fair?" She says in a very angry way, "Are you going to wear the red hat to the fair?" She asks the students, "How might a mouse ask the same question? How might a clown ask the same question?" After five minutes, students are thinking creatively and are ready to move into a dramatic activity.

• In a third-grade classroom, students are performing "The Three Billy Goats Gruff" with a twist. The teacher tells the actors before they begin that they can only use dog language. That is, they will have to act out the whole drama using only barks and pants. This forces children to convey meaning and develop characterization using only their faces and bodies while watching and reacting to other actors.

In all of these examples, teachers are using creative dramatics to reinforce concepts in the curriculum. In the process, these teachers are creating an active learning experience that is fun, allowing the students to work together to achieve a common goal and allowing everyone to be successful.

This is the essence of creative dramatics. Creative dramatics is a form of imaginative play that helps elementary students learn in an active, enjoyable way.

Adaptations for Children with Special Needs

The following suggestions are designed to help teachers include children with special needs in dramatic play.

General Suggestions

• Because the child should feel free to experiment and take risks, be careful not to make too many rules for his or her play. Enforce only those rules that are really needed for the child to play safely.

• Let the child take the lead. This may involve some patient waiting for the child to choose something to do.

- To encourage children to play together, define the space where children can play and keep it small. For example, position housekeeping toys around a small area rug and remind children that they need to stay on the rug while they are playing.
- Children with attention deficits, autism, and developmental delays tend to flit from center to center. Children cannot fully benefit from the learning experiences in a center if they are there only a moment or two. Be firm and require that children initially spend at least five minutes in a center of their choice. Then gradually build on the amount of time the child can focus on dramatic play. If five minutes is impossible for the child, start with the amount of time the child can currently tolerate.
- To help children put away dramatic play props and toys, label shelves with pictures as well as words.
- Try to let the child play with other children as much as possible. The more often you interact with children, the less often children interact with their peers (Gould & Sullivan, 2004).

Developmental Delays

Adults may be tempted to intervene too much in the play of children with developmental delays. Children need an opportunity to play at their level of ability and to independently initiate play activities. If you need to intervene when the child is playing in a group, be as unobtrusive as possible. For example, you could simply sit down as part of the children's play and become a character or prop so that you could subtly make suggestions.

Other suggestions for working with children with developmental delays follow.

- Offer dramatic play materials that are familiar and part of the child's daily life experiences.
- Encourage verbalization during play by asking questions and encouraging communication with other children.
- Some children with developmental delays fatigue very easily. Make sure that the child has supportive seating.
- The child who is not yet proficient at dramatic play may be able to carry out some kind of support role in the play, such as being the patient at a doctor's office. You can make this happen by having the appropriate props nearby or by verbally suggesting the role.
- Bring out a few props at a time to avoid unnecessarily distracting the child.

- Provide some dress-up clothes that are simple to get on and off and do not have tiny buttons or snaps. Large clothes are easier to get on and off.

Attention Deficit Hyperactivity Disorder and Behavioral Issues

Two traits—high activity levels and distractibility—may prevent children from participating in dramatic activities. These children are more able to focus on dramatic play that they have chosen and that is of personal interest. Novelty is very important. Adding a single novel toy to a play setting may be enough to refocus the child's attention. For example, if the child is playing in the dramatic play center and seems to be losing interest, add a doctor's kit with stethoscope and play syringe and cue the child to return to the play with a question such as, "Is the baby sick?"

Additional suggestions for working with these children in dramatic activities follow.

- Help children learn how to work out conflicts when playing with other children. In order to circumvent a child's acting out aggressively, offer him or her help in verbalizing what is bothering him or her (Deiner, 2009).
- Make sure that there are clear behavioral consequences for inappropriate behavior. Carefully consider whether the rules you make are really necessary.
- Exciting activities that are new or offer a lot of sensory input should be preceded and followed by calming activities. Involvement in dramatic play could be followed by quiet time sitting on a beanbag chair with a favorite toy.
- If the child attempts to leave the center after a few moments of play, ask the child to stay and do one more thing. However, children should be allowed to leave play situations that are not productive.
- Hyperactivity in and of itself does not get in the way of learning. If the child is focused on the play activity while actively moving about, there is no need to intervene. This is different from the child who cannot focus on the play or the other children and is darting aimlessly around the classroom. That child needs adult intervention to settle down to play.
- Reduce distractions in the dramatic play center by hanging sheets or lengths of fabric from the ceiling to section off the center from the rest of the room. Dramatic play could also take place in a large box or under a table that has been draped with a sheet.

- Set a timer to help the child stay in a play center. The timer provides an auditory cue for when the child can move to another center and gives the child a sense that his or her involvement in the center has a definite beginning and end.

Visual Impairments

Children with vision impairment may have not had the opportunity to learn how to play by observing others. The child may also have had limited experience with exploring and manipulating objects. It is important that children with residual (limited vision) be encouraged to use their vision. Children who are blind should be encouraged to explore the sensory properties of objects.

- Help the child explore the dramatic play area and to discuss what the objects are and what they are used for. Ask the other children in the center to explain the ongoing play to the child who is visually impaired (Deiner, 2009).
- Intervene if the child is always assigned subordinate roles in play such as that of the baby or patient. Suggest another role.
- Encourage the child who is blind to develop social skills that will help interaction with other children. The child should learn to turn his or her face toward people when they are talking and to keep his or her head in midline (Gould & Sullivan, 2004).

Puppets

Puppets are very important in the lives of young children. Even the youngest of children in the early childhood program is familiar with the puppets on *Sesame Street*. And more often than not, children have been exposed to puppets on Public Broadcasting Station programs and sponsored websites such as Between the Lions (http://www.pbskids.org/lions) and It's a BIG, BIG World (http://www.pbskids.org/bigbigworld/home.html). Puppets can be used for almost any of the dramatic experiences that have been described here. They offer the child two ways to express creativity: (1) the creative experience of making the puppet, and (2) the imaginative experience of making the puppet come to life.

Puppets fascinate and involve children in a way that few other art forms can because they allow children to enter the world of fantasy and drama so easily. In this magic world, children are free to create whatever is needed right then in their lives. See the Helpful websites section at the end of this chapter for listings of websites for puppet patterns and ideas.

Using Puppets

The use of puppets usually begins in the nursery or preschool, where they are invaluable when readily available for dramatic play. Teachers can teach fingerplays with simple finger puppets; hand puppets can act out familiar nursery rhymes. Music time is enhanced by a puppet leading the singing and other puppets joining in. The shy child who is reluctant to sing often will participate through a puppet. Puppets are also excellent for concept teaching and can help clarify abstract concepts and demonstrate concrete concepts. For instance, in the preschool the concepts of "above," "below," "behind," "in front of," and so on can be clearly shown with the puppet.

Puppets allow you to say "silly" things to your class. For example, in a science class about how the position of the sun appears to change in the day and makes the

FIGURE 15-13 • The children should choose their puppets for dramatic play.

puppet's shadow shorter, one teacher used the puppet to tell children someone must have washed it to make it shrink! The children told the puppet that the shadow couldn't have shrunk, and they explained in words understandable to other children what had happened. The children talked to the puppet as if it were a person separate from the teacher.

Puppets seem to allow children freedom to talk when they are not sure about things. Also, children sometimes are aware that the teacher "knows the answer," and thus may not respond to a question or prompt. However, a puppet probably doesn't know an answer, so children's responses and explanations are more readily forthcoming and fuller.

Some of the larger puppets have hands like gloves so the teacher can make the puppet manipulate equipment and other resources. This is particularly helpful in sorting activities, as the puppet is able to join in just like another child. If, for example, children are sorting rocks on the basis of their characteristics, the teacher can make the puppet move rocks from one group to another to promote further discussion. The puppet's actions can encourage children to justify their choice of groupings if the puppet disagrees with their classification. As they explain their ideas, children can consider the validity of their claims or recognize possible flaws in their reasoning.

Another argument for using puppets in the classroom is that they can be used by the teacher to mirror desirable behaviors. The puppet can model the way claims can be justified and reasons given for a point of view. There is no right or wrong way to use a puppet, but teachers have found it valuable to give the puppet a distinct character. If the character is consistently maintained by the teacher, children can be allowed to "take over" animating the puppet: They already know what the puppet is like—they don't have to invent a new character.

Puppets are wonderful tools for demonstrating social skills with young children. You can use them to enact a scenario that represents a frequent troublesome behavior in the classroom or an issue that one or more children are experiencing in their lives. Puppets help the children see the situation from a new perspective. For instance, if children in your group are having trouble sharing toys, you might act out a similar situation during circle time using puppets.

Puppets are used most successfully when teachers have introduced them slowly to the class and have developed a strong sense of identity for the puppet. Care needs to be taken to maintain the puppet's character, even when it is not being used. Give the puppet a seat to sit in and watch the children at work; assign a child to look after the puppet each day. It is crucial that puppets talk to children; puppets that listen to children and "whisper" to the teacher aren't as effective with young children. Puppets can effectively be used to introduce a lesson or to "talk" to small groups when children are discussing their ideas.

Teachers have noticed that their classes become more animated when puppets join in the lesson. Children want to talk to the puppet and hear what the puppet has to say.

Puppetry, as a form of dramatic play, is a sure means of stimulating creative storytelling in younger children. Some teachers tape record spontaneous puppet skits and, by writing them down, show children how they have created a story.

In a room with a climate of flexibility and freedom, children are bound to come up with countless ideas for using their puppets. Some suggestions are presented here.

- Put together a puppet center—puppet materials, props, and theater—for children to use during the day.
- Consider having a specific puppet for each center area. This puppet could remind the class that it is music time, for instance, and be used to give directions and explain new concepts. If the puppet has trouble in an area, the children could teach it and straighten out its confusion. Through such dramatic experiences, self-confidence and skills are strengthened.
- Felt boards and puppets work well together. A puppet with hands can effectively help the adult or child put pieces on or take them off the felt board. One teacher who was teaching toddlers the parts of the face used a rather "stupid" puppet that kept making mistakes by putting the parts in the wrong place. The children had a lot of fun correcting it.
- In music experiences, teachers find that puppets help young children develop a feeling for rhythm and music interpretation by moving the puppets to the beat. They also encourage reluctant children to sing, since the puppet does the singing for the child. Puppets with moving mouths are most effective but not necessary.
- Social studies is a natural area for puppets; it presents countless opportunities to dramatize holiday ideas, represent particular ethnic customs, or portray the roles of various community helpers.

- Use puppets to help children voice feelings, such as fear; other activities can include using high- and low-pitched voices and making squeaking, growling, and chirping animal sounds.
- Provide opportunities for enactments of published or original stories.
- Encourage children to present original work. Young children may have difficulty manipulating puppets and saying words at the same time. Audiotape the story in advance so that the children can then focus on the puppets' actions.

These suggestions are simply intended to be idea starters. The use of puppets in the classroom is limited only by imagination—yours and the children's.

Kinds of Puppets

Some of the most common and easiest puppets to make are stick puppets, hand puppets, finger puppets, people puppets, wooden spoon puppets, mitten and sock puppets, paper plate puppets, play dough puppets, Styrofoam ball puppets, vegetable (fruit) puppets, ping-pong ball puppets, and cylinder puppets. (See Appendix G for puppet patterns.)

Stick puppets. The simplest of all puppets, stick puppets are controlled by a single stick (any slim, rigid support) that goes up inside the puppet or is attached to the back of it.

Stick puppets are fun and easy to make. The teacher can use sticks from the lumberyard, large twigs, pencils, or wooden popsicle sticks. With this type of puppet, the child puts a bag or piece of cloth over the stick and stuffs the bag or cloth with wads of newspaper or cotton. The child then ties the top of the bag to the stick, making a head. A rubber band may be used instead of string to form a head.

The child can then paint the head or make a face with crayons or colored paper and paste. Scrap yarn, wood shavings, and buttons are also good materials for the puppet's face. Scrap pieces of fabric can be used to "dress" the puppet; wallpaper samples provide inexpensive material for puppets' clothes.

With the stick, the puppet is moved around the stage or turned from side to side. It has the advantage of being a good first puppet for preschoolers, since a stick can be attached to any little doll, toy animal, or cutout figure, and the puppet is easy to operate.

Bag puppets. The common paper bag in any size makes a good **bag puppet** for young preschoolers.

The bags are stuffed with wads of newspaper and tied, stapled, or glued shut. A body is made with a second bag stapled to the first, leaving room for the child's hand to slip in and work the puppet.

A face can be made with paint, crayons, or colored paper and paste. Odds and ends are fun to use for the face, too. Buttons make eyes; crumpled tissue, a nose; and yarn, hair. The search for the right odds and ends to make the puppet is as much fun as using the finished puppet later.

Hand puppets. Frequently called "glove" or "mitten puppets," these are the most popular for young children. (See Appendix G for basic patterns for glove and mitten puppets.) There are many types of hand puppets, but most can be classified into two general groups: (1) those with moving mouths and (2) those with moving hands.

The first (with moving mouths) is any sort of hand covering—a handkerchief, sock, mitten, or paper bag—inside of which one's fingers open and shut, forming the mouth of the puppet. The second kind has a head and two hands and is operated by putting one or two fingers in the head and one in each hand. This kind of puppet can freely pick up objects and make hand motions, thus putting more realism into a performance.

Finger puppets. The three general types of **finger puppets** are the following (see Figure 15–14).

- Finger-leg. Finger puppet in which two fingers (usually the index and middle fingers) serve as the puppet's legs.
- Finger-cap. Finger puppet that slips over an individual finger.
- Finger-face. Puppet made by drawing a face on a finger with a felt pen. Usually, one can perform with quite a few puppets of this type at one time. They are great for fingerplays!

Some advantages of finger puppets include the following.

- They are easy to manipulate, even by a toddler.
- They encourage small muscle action.
- They are inexpensive to make.
- One child alone can put on a performance with an "entire cast."
- They maintain interest because they are always easy and quick to make.
- They can be made in spare moments, as materials are small and mobile.

Wooden spoon puppets. You will need wooden spoons, yarn, string, material scraps, glue, and construction paper. Draw a face on the wooden spoon. Glue on yarn or string for hair and scraps of material for clothing.

Two-faced (paper plate) puppets. Draw a face on the back of each paper plate. Add features with various types of materials. Insert a stick between the paper plates and glue it into place. Staple edges together.

Play dough puppets. Place a small amount of play dough onto a finger. Mold play dough into a face shape covering the finger. Add beads, toothpicks, and other small objects for facial features and added emphasis.

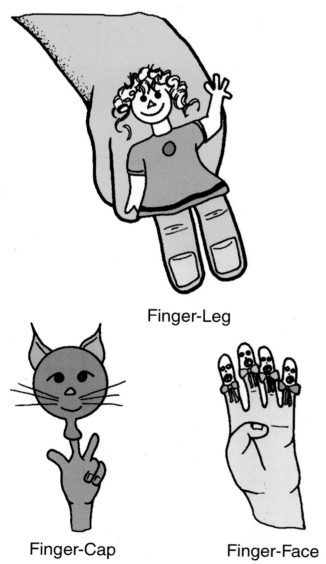

FIGURE 15-14 • There are many different kinds of finger puppets. Three examples are shown here.

Styrofoam ball puppets. Insert a stick into a Styrofoam ball. Cover the Styrofoam ball with fabric. Tie the fabric around the stick. Glue on buttons and felt scraps for facial features.

Ping-pong ball puppets. Cut an X shape out of a ball. Place a piece of lightweight fabric on your finger. Cover the area of the ball with sturdy glue. Force the ball at the X onto the fabric on your finger. While the glue is drying, draw or paste a face onto the puppet.

Sock puppet. Pull the sock over your hand. Glue or paint facial features onto the toe of the sock or decorate as desired.

Finger puppets from gloves. Recycle stray gloves and use them for finger puppets. Recycle old rubber gloves, too, by drawing features on rubber glove fingers with marking pens. Glue pompoms on each finger for the "head" and glue on bits of cloth or felt for facial or character details.

Old mitten puppets. A child can slip his or her hand into an old mitten and make the puppet "talk" by moving his or her thumb up and down against the four fingers.

Cardboard cylinder puppet. To make a **cardboard cylinder puppet**, place a cardboard cylinder from paper towels or toilet tissue over the fingers. Decorate with desired features. The cylinder could be used for the body, and a Styrofoam ball or ping-pong ball could be placed on the top for the head. Decorate as desired.

People puppets. Also called **humanettes**, these are half-person and half-puppet. The easiest **people puppet** for children is a large paper sack put over the head. Holes are cut out for the eyes, and facial features and decorations are added with paint or paper and paste. The bags can be turned up slightly above the shoulder or cut away on the sides for armholes. People puppets make a natural transition from puppetry to creative drama. Also, shy children generally feel more protected behind this kind of puppet than all the other types. Be sure not to force a child to use this type of puppet if he or she does not like his or her head covered!

More ideas for puppets are at the end of this chapter.

Summary

Dramatic play is an excellent means for developing creativity and imagination in young children when it is related to the child's personal sense of reality without imposed adult standards. Dramatic play can be adapted so it is appropriate for children with special needs. Dramatic play kits are easy to make and help develop opportunities for creative play. The use of puppets provides opportunities for creative movement, dramatics, and language development. Creative dramatics refers to informal drama that is created by the participants. It goes beyond dramatic play in scope and intent. The term creative dramatics is generally used to describe the improvised drama of children age six and older.

Other uses of puppets in the early childhood program include helping shy children express themselves, having children introduce themselves, and teaching new concepts in various areas. Types of puppets appropriate for use with young children are stick, finger, hand, people puppets (humanettes), ping-pong ball, and Styrofoam puppets.

Key Terms

bag puppet 366
cardboard cylinder puppet 367
creative dramatics 359
dramatic play 351
finger puppets 366
humanettes 367
modeling behavior 355
people puppet 367

Learning Activities

A. Create two dramatic play kits not listed or suggested in this chapter. Think divergently! Compare your kit with those of your classmates.

B. Make up a play kit of "props" children might use in one of the following activities.

   1. playing mail carrier
   2. playing dentist
   3. playing airline pilot
   4. playing waitress/waiter

C. Make one of the types of puppets discussed in this chapter. Demonstrate its use to your classmates before you use it with children. Describe how you plan to use the puppet with children in the future.

D. If you had $200 to spend for drama equipment in setting up a new room in your first year of teaching, what would you buy and why? Itemize each purchase, and give at least three uses for each item. You may use a school supply catalog for assistance in your purchasing.

   Do this for a preschool class, a class in the kindergarten to grade 3 group, and in a class in the grade 4 to 5 range. Discuss the differences in each level and how they affected your purchases.

E. Observe in two early childhood rooms. Use the observation sheet found in the Online Guide. What roles did you observe children playing in dramatic activities? How do you think these roles are related to children's real-life experiences? Explain.

   Consult the teacher in each of the two rooms you observed to learn how information obtained through observing children's dramatic play is utilized (if at all) in guiding children or in making future plans. Give examples.

   In each of the rooms you observed, what limits were placed on children during dramatic play? How do you think these limits would change in an outdoor dramatic activity?

F. Make plans for bringing in new pieces of equipment and new props to help extend children's dramatic roles in each of the situations you observed. Bring them in, and then observe how children use these materials.

G. Visit an early childhood program. Interview the director, a head teacher, and a parent. Ask each how important they feel dramatic play is to their child(ren). Ask each to share their opinions about the last (or most currently produced) school program involving the child(ren). Compare the answers you received. Discuss the similarities and differences you found in these interviews.

H. Invite some children and adults to participate in creative dramatics together. See if you notice any differences in the ways they approach the activities. Adults should all have a chance to participate! You might also try this activity with students of different ages. What do you observe in their approaches?

I. As you observe at an early childhood center, make a record of the roles taken by boys and those taken by girls as they engage in dramatic play. Discuss in class.

J. Draw a plan of what you consider to be a good dramatic play center in a classroom for young children. Draw a second plan of the same area, showing how you might rearrange it and describe what you would hope to accomplish through these changes.

K. Try your hand at planning a drama in which you would take a role. Practice on something short, like a fable or Mother Goose piece. Consider the following:

1. Examine the story for problems and themes. What is this really about? What is the conflict? Who has the problem? For example, Jack in the Beanstalk is about how goods are not equally distributed and how people are never satisfied with what they have.
2. List groups or individuals that might be affected by the problem. For example, the giant's family who now has no income; Jack's mother, wife, and friends, who see a changed Jack; neighbors who don't like have a thief around.
3. Under what circumstances might these individuals come together (e.g., some kind of meeting)? For example, a counseling session for Jack's materialistic addictions.
4. Choose a role and plan a short introduction speech about who you are and why you are there (counselor).
5. Plan the roles that the children can become. For example, children can choose to be any of the characters affected by Jack's greed.

L. Using the information in this chapter on drama, jot down ways you might use drama in an elementary classroom.

Activities for Children

Puppet Theater Ideas

Tabletop. Drape a blanket over a table. Children can crouch behind it and use the surface as a stage. Props can go beneath.

Appliance Box. Cut off the back of a large appliance box (often available free at appliance stores). Cut a hole in the front. Let children decorate with paints and markers.

Door Frame. Hang a simple curtain on a tension rod halfway up your classroom doorframe. Performers stand in the hall; the audience sits in the room.

A Quiet Puppet

Cut the bottom and top off a cereal box. Put any puppet on your hand and stick it up through the box. When children need to quiet down, bring down your hand to hide the puppet in the box, as if the puppet is frightened by the noise. When children are quiet, stick the puppet back up. Let children use the puppet in the same way.

Paper Cup Finger Puppet

Give each child a paper cup. Explain how this cup will be their puppet's head. They can paint or use felt-tip markers to draw on the features. Yarn hair can be attached with glue. Paper ears or noses can be added. Cut two paper circles in the side of the cup to place fingers in the cup to work the puppet.

Body/Box Puppet

Make a box puppet in which the child becomes the puppet. Each child will need a lightweight cardboard box (12" × 24" or 24" × 30"). Often, the first body puppets may all be ponies and horses. If the children really love these puppets, you may later want to vary the construction and produce birds, airplanes, fish, or the like.

For each puppet, remove the bottom of the cardboard box. Center a hole in the top of the box. The child's torso should comfortably fit into this space. In the middle of each side, an inch or two down from the top, cut a rectangular hole for handles. The child holds the puppet body up by the two handles. Staple a horse/pony head to the front of each body and horse tails (yarn or rope or crepe paper) to the end of each box. Have the children paint their body puppets, adding spots, saddles, blankets, manes, and faces. Once dry, the horse and pony puppets can be put into action!

Shadow Puppets

In this activity, children experiment with the effects that various light and puppet position have on shadows they make with their arms and hands. Children work in pairs to trace their shadows and create puppets with them.

Dim the lights and use flashlights to cast light on an open wall or chalkboard. Let children play, making hand puppets with their arms and hands on the open area.

Working with a partner, children trace each other's shadow puppets onto oak tag or poster board with markers.

Children (or adults) cut each traced hand shadow from the paper. Details are added to the hand shadow with crayons and markers.

Attach a craft or popsicle stick to the back of each shadow puppet with glue. Let the glue dry before using the puppet.

Pop-Up Puppets

For this activity you will need poster board, crayons, glue, paintbrushes, scissors, markers, tempera paint, a small box, and craft (or popsicle) sticks.

Cut off sides of the box to make a puppet theater. Paint the box. On poster board, draw and color people and animals. Cut them out and glue each one to the top of a craft or popsicle stick.

An adult cuts slits into the bottom of the puppet theater so the puppet characters can pop up through the floor.

Balloon Puppets

For this activity you will need balloons, markers, paste, pieces of yarn and trim, and masking tape. (Never use balloons with children under three years of age.)

Blow up the balloons, one for each child. (If children are able, let them blow up the balloons. Some children will need assistance.) Tie the ends of the balloons.

Talk about how to handle the balloons so they will not break. Have extras on hand in case they do break.

Tape the balloons to the table. Use markers to make faces on the balloons. Glue yarn on top for hair. Add other pieces of fabric for clothing. Untape the balloons when children are finished decorating them and enjoy.

Use balloons of different shapes to create fanciful animals. Make a balloon body with other balloons taped to the head.

Box Puppets

For this activity you will need small boxes (from pudding or gelatin), construction paper, paste, scissors, scrap pieces of fabric and trim, masking tape, markers, and crayons.

Give each child two small boxes. Tape the two boxes together, keeping the openings on both free. Cover the boxes with construction paper. The top box is the eye and top of the mouth. The bottom box is the bottom part of the mouth. Add bits of colored paper for eyes, a mouth, and other details. Add ears on the side of the boxes if desired. When all adhesives are dry, use and enjoy the puppet. To use the puppet, place four fingers in the top box and the thumb in the bottom box to work the mouth.

Variations: Use large boxes for big puppets. Be sure, however, that the boxes are small enough for little hands. Have fun making big tongues on the bottom box that will wag when the puppet talks. Add yarn hair that will be floppy and fun when the puppet moves.

Envelope Puppets

For this activity you will need white envelopes, markers, scissors, and crayons.

Give each child a white envelope. Seal the envelope. Holding the envelope lengthwise, draw a face on the top of the envelope. Add facial details with markers and crayons. Cut off the short bottom edge of the envelope. Slip the puppet on the hand and use as a puppet.

Pompom Puppets

For this activity you will need pompoms of varying sizes and colors, popsicle or craft sticks, paste, a hole punch, construction paper, scraps of fabric, yarn, and trim. Talk about the pompoms. Discuss what kind of puppets could be made with them. Talk about colors, details, features, and so on.

Glue a large pompom to the stick. Glue on pieces of construction paper for features and details. Use smaller pompoms for other details. Use a hole punch on colored construction paper. Glue on the colored circles from the hole punch, if desired. Add fabric strips to the stick for clothing. Glue on yarn for hair.

Variations: Make a group of pompom puppets for a group sing-along. Let children choose the songs. Make animals for the song "Farmer in the Dell" and use them as you sing the song. Use cotton balls instead of pompoms, but be aware that cotton balls are less stable decorations.

Stuffed Animal Stick Puppets

For this activity you will need popsicle sticks, twigs, pencils, small stuffed animals, yarn, or rubber bands.

Collect small stuffed animals. Attach a small stuffed animal to a stick or a pencil with a piece of string or rubber band. Dress the puppet with scraps of fabric and trim. Use this puppet like a stick puppet.

Variations: Attach small dolls to sticks to make puppets. Act out a fairy tale or a favorite story with the stuffed-animal stick puppets. Dress the stuffed animals with fabric, ribbon, and trim scraps.

Duster Puppets

Use feather or other small dusters with handles. Children use their imaginations to add eyes, nose, mouth, hats and even clothes by gluing on these details. Children make the duster puppet move by using the handle on the duster.

Lint Brush Puppets

Recycle old two-sided lint brushes for puppets. These brushes have two sides. One side can be a smiling face, and the other a frowning face. Glue on large pompoms for hair, wiggly eyes, and the other features from pieces of felt. You can even give the puppet a tie or bow with a fabric scrap.

Lonely Glove Finger Puppets

After cold weather is gone, what do you do with lonely, single gloves? Like socks, they always lose their mates. Make a finger puppet by cutting off the fingers from the glove. Use fabric glue to attach to the glove fingers small pom-poms for tails and feet, felt shapes for beaks. Add googly eyes, feathers for birds' wings and chenille stems (pipe cleaners) for claws. Slip the glove finger puppet on the finger and the fun begins!

Portable Puppet Stage

A portable puppet stage provides a special place for the children to tell stories and pretend with their puppets. While stages can be constructed, cardboard three-sided display units that you decorate make excellent stages and are easy to obtain from most craft or teacher-supply stores. One unit can be used in the story corner or children can create individual stages to use on their own.

To use the display unit as a puppet stage, cut out a good-sized opening from the middle panel for the puppet to be seen through. Decorate to suit a particular story. For example:

- Sponge paint a wild-animal or farm-animal scene.
- Stamp the child's hand print and add the child's name for use with a variety of stories.
- Paint on a flower garden.
- Use markers to make a space scene.
- Use crayons to create a circus.
- Glue on collage items.

Set the three-sided unit on a table top when a puppet tale will be told, and fold for easy storage.

Finger Puppet Playhouse

Make a playhouse that will accommodate many finger puppets. You will need a large cereal box, paint, a craft knife (for the teacher's use), and markers. Paint a wide, tall cereal box. Cut out windows and a door for the puppets to use. Cut a large hole in the back of the box for children to put their hands through. Use markers to outline where the windows and door are on the back of the box as well, so the storyteller can tell the story and move the finger puppets more easily. A town can be created with several boxes and puppets for the houses. Children can use the playhouse and finger puppets for neighborhood conversations and storytelling from one house to another. Provide several houses in the story corner and rotate the puppets to develop children's imaginations.

Activities for Older Children (Grades 4–5)

Aesthetic Awareness

Have students relate terms for movement in dance to terms that describe actual or implied motion in the visual arts. Examples include *glide, dart, slide, pivot, hop, sway,* and *twirl.* Have students create pantomimes or dances based on motions in nature such as a bird flying, a fish swimming, and a leaf falling. Have students invent vocal or instrumental sounds that seem to fit these motions, then orchestrate the sounds in different ways.

Creative Drama Exercises

The following are some exercises to get elementary children started on creative dramatics. Refer to the guidelines presented in this chapter to help you use these activities.

- Walk like the following: an elephant, a feather, a grasshopper, cooked spaghetti, uncooked spaghetti, a very quiet mouse, a very careful chicken.
- Blow a bubble, catch it in the air, and then set it down very carefully on the table.
- Walk into the kitchen, take a jar of pickles out of the refrigerator, open the jar, and eat one. It is very sour.
- Brush your teeth in the morning.
- Prepare and eat ice cream with spinach on top.
- Come into a room, look around, and hide in the closet.
- You are walking through a room when your foot gets stuck on some glue. You sit down to think and other parts of you get stuck, too.
- You are a mouse looking at some cheese on a mouse trap. Can you take it off?
- Lift something heavy, light, smelly, gooey, small, big, wiggly, or shaky.
- Tell a story without using any voice.
- Using only your face, be angry, surprised, sleepy, hurt, afraid, funny, or silly. Be someone who just heard a very loud noise.

Narrative Pantomime

Explain that in narrative pantomime, someone tells a story while others use their faces and bodies to show the story. Have everyone find a personal space in the center of the room. Be sure there is room around each child so they do not bump into one another.

Give each child a card with an animal name on it. (Arrange duplicates, but do not tell students.) Say, "When I say 'Start!' everyone is to show her or his animal in a variety of ways (e.g., shape, moves, size). Stay in your personal spot. At the 'Freeze!' signal, everyone should stop. Start."

After the activity, discuss with children their concentration, their unusual ideas, their focus, etc. Then repeat the exercise in slow motion.

Creating Costumes for Creative Dramatics

For fun and affordable costumes, use Fabric Fun® Pastel Dye Sticks. Create costumes for drama activities, flags, personal banners, ethnic costumes, quilt blocks, and much more. Students of all ages will enjoy transforming their clothing into works of art with these brilliant colors. Simply draw or stencil a design directly onto the fabric with the dye sticks, cover the design with a piece of paper or a paper towel, and then the teacher presses it with an iron to make the drawing permanent. Fabric Fun® is available in sets of seven and fifteen. For more information visit, www.pentelarts.com

Chapter Review

1. List the objectives of creative dramatics.
2. What are dramatic play kits? Give specific examples of some you would use in your classroom and what they would contain.
3. Discuss what you consider the early childhood teacher's role in children's dramatic play.
4. Do you feel that it is appropriate for the teacher to make special plans for children's dramatic play? Give examples in your explanation.
5. Discuss how to use puppets with young children.
6. Discuss the difference between dramatic play and creative dramatics.
7. If a principal or parent asked you for three good reasons to use drama as a learning tool, what reasons would you give? Why do you believe these are the most important reasons?

References

Deiner, P. (2009). *Inclusive early childhood education: Development, resources, and practice.* Clifton Park, NY: Delmar Cengage Learning.

Elias, C. L., Eisenberg, N., & Berk, L. E. (2002). Self-regulation in young children: Is there a role for socio-dramatic play? *Early Child Research Quarterly, 17*(3), 216–238.

Gould, P., & Sullivan, J. (2004). *The inclusive early childhood classroom: Easy ways to adapt learning centers for all children* (2nd ed.). Beltsville, MD: Gryphon House.

Riley, D., San Juan, R. R., Klinkner, J., & Ramminger, A. (2008). *Social and emotional development connecting science and practice in early childhood settings.* St. Paul, MN: Redleaf Press.

Simon, S., Naylor, S., Keogh, B., Maloney, J., & Downing, B. (2008). Puppets promoting engagement and talk in science. *International Journal of Science, 30*(9), 1229–1248.

Strauss, A., & Corbin, J. (1998). *Basics of qualitative research.* London, UK: Sage.

Thorp, G. (2005). *The power of puppets.* Trowbridge, UK: Positive Press.

Wright, C., Bacigalupa, C., Black, T., & Burton, M. (2008). Windows into children's thinking: A guide to storytelling and dramatization. *Early Childhood Education Journal, 35*(4), 363–369.

Additional Readings

Baker-Sennett, J., Matusov, E., & Rugoff, B. (2008). Children's planning of classroom plays with adult or child direction. *Social Development, 17*(4), 998–1018.

Deans, J., Brown, R., & Young, S. (2007). The possum story: Reflections of an early childhood drama teacher. *Australian Journal of Early Childhood, 32*(4), 1–6.

Fritz, E., Henning, E., & Swart, E. (2008). When all the school becomes a stage: Young children's enacting a community's fear and sense of loss. *International Journal of Qualitative Studies in Education, 21*(4), 375–387.

Goldstein, E. R. (2009). How we got to Sesame Street: Art on screen. *Chronicle of Higher Education, 55*(19), 13–16.

Karaolis, O. (2009). Honey bee. *Exceptional Parent, 39*(3), 38–39.

Mages, W. K. (2008). Does creative drama promote language development in early childhood? A review of the methods and measures employed in the empirical literature. *Review of Educational Research, 78*(1), 124–152.

Mayesky, M. (2004). *Creative arts & activities: Puppets.* Clifton Park, NY: Delmar Cengage Learning.

Raikes, H. H., & Edwards, C. P. (2009). *Extending the dance in infant and toddler caregiving enhancing attachment and relationships.* Washington, DC: NAEYC.

Russo, M. (2008). For the birds! Seeing, being, and creating the bird world. *Young Children, 63*(1), 26–30.

Schrandt, J. A., Townsend, D. B., & Poulson, C. L. (2009). Teaching empathy skills to children with autism. *Journal of Applied Behavior Analysis, 42*(1), 17–32.

Servizzi, K. (2008). Fixing puppets so they can talk: Puppets and puppet making in a classroom of preschoolers with special needs. *Early Childhood Research and Practice, 10*(2), 110–116.

Stephens, S. (2008). Storytelling with shadow puppets. *SchoolArts, 107*(9), 28–29.

Szecsi, T. (2008). Creative drama in preschool curriculum: Teaching strategies implemented in Hungary. *Childhood Education, 85*(2), 120–130.

Helpful Websites

Celebrate Literacy in the NWT, http://www.nwt. literacy.ca/resources/famlit/howtokit/puppets2.pdf
This site features puppet patterns including adult puppets, child's hand puppets, and basic finger puppets. It also contains tips on how to make and use puppets.

Child Drama, http://www.childdrama.com
Site includes definition and discussion of drama terms, useful books, lesson plans by age level for creative drama, and pre–K through grade 12 dramatic curriculum ideas.

Creative Drama, http://www.creativedrama.com
This site has a collection of practical teaching ideas and suggestions for teachers.

Drama Workshop: Ideas for Teaching Drama, http://www.dramateachers.co.uk/
This site provides a variety of improvisational activities for students in Grades 1–8.

Dramania, http://www.public.asu.edu/~atbrl/ dramania.html
A quick collection of drama activities for students in grades 4–8 with a collection of links for students as well as a resource for teachers.

Danielle's Place, http://daniellesplace.com/html/ puppets.html
This is an excellent source for puppet patterns and instructions on how to make and use puppets.

Legends & Lore, http://legendsandlore.com/ sockpuppets.html
This site offers instructions on how to make sock puppets.

Playing with Shadows, http://artsedge. kennedy-center.org/shadowpuppets/artsedge.html
Kennedy Center site that introduces students to the ancient Chinese art of shadow puppetry in this interactive site.

Puppets.com, http://puppets.com/

Puppet Universe.com, http://www.puppetuniverse. com
Site has numerous resources and information on all types of puppets, making and using them in activities across the curriculum. This site has numerous resources and information on all types of puppets.

Puppet Patterns, http://www.puppetpatterns.com
This is a good source for patterns for 28-inch stage-sized puppets.

Puppetools, http://www.puppetools.com/ workshop/?p=learn
Learn techniques and methods for integrating puppets into your teaching.

Teacher Help, http://www.teacherhelp.org/ puppets.htm
This site contains links to puppets, puppet patterns, paper bag puppets, and scripts.

For additional creative activity resources, visit our website at www.Cengage.com/login.

Creative Movement

OBJECTIVES

After studying this chapter, you should be able to:

1. Discuss the importance of creative movement activities for young children.

2. List creative movement activities that help children develop large and small muscles.

3. Discuss guidelines for providing creative movement activities for young children.

4. Discuss ways to adapt creative movement for children with special needs.

Movement is a powerful communicator that can fascinate or repel, delight or disgust us. And yet, unlike the use of words, movement is not a communication form often considered to be part of the basics in most schools, even in early childhood programs. Perhaps it is so basic we simply take for granted that we all know how to use it effectively. But we don't. Creative movements are frequently the part of the curriculum that teachers are most unprepared to integrate in their classrooms.

In the United States, how your body looks is very important; beautiful body images bombard us daily through the media. We have become very sensitive about our bodies. It is not surprising that teachers are sometimes uncomfortable using creative movement, especially if they're not sure exactly what that means. No one wants to appear awkward or have his or her body examined for possible ridicule.

Rather than spending time wringing our hands about the lack of value for creative movement, we can simply acknowledge the ways movement is important in our lives and move on to strategies for using kinesthetic ways of knowing in creative ways, which is the focus of this chapter. Most important is to start with some foundational truths: We all love to move. It feels good to walk, run, wiggle, and shake. It is also true we remember what we *do* more easily than what is told to us or what we only read about.

It is the same for young children—they learn by doing. They are immensely active and energetic. Movement activities are natural avenues for this energy. Reaching, jumping, balancing, and hopping are experiences that teach children how to understand and negotiate the world.

Physical movement is the young child's first means of nonverbal communication. Closing his or her eyes, crying, shaking—a nonverbal infant very clearly communicates a need for attention! Physical movements provide one of the most important avenues through which a child forms impressions about himself or herself and his or her environment.

Anyone entering a preschool classroom cannot help but be aware of children's constant activity and movement. In fact, movement is valuable at any age to combat lethargy and spark an interest in our environment. We know that children's physical and motor development influences, and is influenced by, all other aspects of development: cognitive, language, social, and emotional. Even so, early childhood teachers too often believe that children's motor skills will develop on their own. Therefore, they do not consciously plan for motor skill development as they do for other areas. This chapter addresses the importance of motor skill development and provides some guidelines for adults working with young children.

Movement activities concern the whole child and not just physical fitness and recreation. Through **creative movement activities**, a child is able to express his or her creative self in a very natural way.

The Importance of Movement Activities for Young Children

To a child, physical movement and exercise are pleasurable and fulfilling activities because the young child is busy acquiring all sorts of large and small motor skills during the early years of life. The child's main learning strategy is through physical manipulation of his or her world. Movement activities, more than any other type of activity, offer children rich opportunities for the development of their total selves.

Besides this innate human enjoyment, creative movement (physical movement coupled with novel pretend imagery) can help children's attention, speed, retention, and enjoyment of learning (Sacha & Ross, 2006). Movement and music experiences integrated within a preschool curriculum can also reinforce math and logic concepts through rhythm and patterns of beat and tempo (Shilling, 2002). In addition to cognitive learning benefits, creative movement can be a transformative experience that develops body awareness as well as personal identity and control (Graham, 2002).

There is usually no planning or forethought on the part of children in creative movement. They forget about themselves and let the music's rhythm or an idea carry their bodies away. There is no pattern of movements to be practiced or perfected. Young children are free to move about in any mood the music or rhythm suggests to them.

FIGURE 16-1 • When planning creative movement activities, teachers need to keep in mind the characteristics of each age group.

Creative Movement

Creative movement is movement that reflects the mood or inner state of a child. In creative movement, children are free to express their own personalities in their own style. They do not have an example to follow or an adult to imitate. Creative movement can occur in any situation where children feel free and want to move their bodies. It can be done to poetry, music, rhythm, or even silence. By feeling a pulse, beat, idea, or emotion, children's bodies become instruments of expression. They are musical notes running along a keyboard or wheat waving in the wind. They are anything they want to be. Their movement is an expression of that being.

Benefits of Creative Movement

Creative movement is a joyful experience for children. And in this joyful experience, children are benefiting in many ways. These benefits are sensory awareness, social development, body awareness, concentration, and personal development.

Sensory Awareness

Children perceive the world though their senses. All senses are engaged when children explore different aspects of movement. The kinesthetic sense increases as children literally feel the shapes and actions their bodies are making. Visually, children respond to the images they see as well as the images they create. The auditory sense is stimulated as children respond to sounds (and music) they make or hear. Tactile experiences such as running with bare feet, performing specific floor movements, or swirling a scarf heighten children's awareness of their sense of touch. Such full sensory awareness experiences lead to a greater understanding of themselves and their surroundings. It strengthens children's imaginative powers and increases their ability to experience life with greater meaning.

Social Development

Creative movement encourages children to interact with their environment and with each other as they share space and explore movement together. Movement activities encourage children to realize their own uniqueness, as well as recognize and appreciate the uniqueness of others. As children move creatively, they express their personal feelings and preferences. In movement activities, children learn to cooperate within a social structure and appreciate the different responses of other children.

Body Awareness

Creative movement activities help children gain a better mental picture of their own bodies. Controlling their own bodies is the first type of control children have over themselves. It is the first step toward developing internal control and self-discipline. Body awareness is an essential part of becoming aware of our feelings because they exist in our minds and bodies. When we feel angry or excited, we feel it in our whole self. Body awareness is also important in the development of spatial orientation. Children who do not perceive the space of their own bodies may frequently misjudge distances or bump into things. Movement activities also help with the development of motor skills. Creative movement activities focus on body awareness, motor fitness, rhythmic skill, strength, flexibility, coordination, endurance, and physical vitality.

Concentration

Children grow in self-control as they learn to concentrate and focus. Children must learn what it feels like to concentrate. Once children learn what focusing feels like, it can be a frame of reference for other activities where concentration is more difficult to achieve. Concentration is essential for learning in the classroom.

Personal Development

As children engage in creative movement activities, they are developing such personal traits as respect, self-esteem, and purpose. Experiences in creative movement help children respect the working space of others as they learn about "personal space" and "shared space." Children also learn to recognize, appreciate, and respect differences in the people with whom they come into contact. Children learn and respect the fact that all bodies come in various sizes and shapes. They also learn to respect these differences in their peers.

Self-esteem is the greatest benefit from incorporating creative movement into your curriculum. As children learn more and develop new skills, their self-esteem increases. When a child shouts, "I did it!" or "I know that!" she or he is showing the power she or he feels in her or his own competence. A child's self-esteem is also enhanced through participation in creative movement activities where her or his contributions are acknowledged and valued.

Creative movement can teach children to become more aware of themselves, sensitive to others, and actively conscious of the world they share. They can find meaning and exhilaration in activities that nourish rather than harm them. Creative movement provides an opportunity for all children, regardless of age, special needs, or developmental stage, to interact with each other, release energy, and have fun.

Other curricular activities can emerge from a creative movement experience. For example, reading time can involve looking at books related to dance and children making connections to their own movement experiences. Creative movement activities can also lead to children expressing emotions from their movement experience in drawings, paintings, and music activities. Children can be encouraged to explore new and creative uses of familiar objects such as dress-up costumes, balls, hoops, or free-flowing fabrics in their creative movement experiences. Creative movement also may encourage children to use familiar objects in new, creative, and imaginative ways that in turn facilitate their abstract thinking of the physical world.

Planning Creative Movement Activities to Meet Young Children's Needs

All movement activities best serve young children's needs when they address their current developmental levels. The following guidelines provide a framework to help teachers of young children be more effective in this important aspect of their work. (Appendix A presents a general measure of the average ages at which young children acquire physical skills. Also see the Professional Enhancement text, Developmental Milestones by Age.)

Guidelines for Early Childhood Teachers

When planning creative movement activities for children, teachers need to keep in mind the characteristics of each age group. Refer to Chapters 9 through 11

FIGURE 16-2 • Teachers encourage children's creative movement by moving creatively themselves.

for characteristics of preschool children. Also, see the Professional Enhancement text for Developmental Milestones by Skill. Figure 16–3 summarizes the growth and development characteristics of children from kindergarten to grade 5.

As with any age group, preschoolers need to practice skills in order to learn them. Children of this age need many opportunities for practice. Several different activities should incorporate use of a particular skill, thus allowing for extended overall practice time and preventing children from getting bored. For example, teachers may want to prepare two or three movement activities, or include several variations of an activity.

Managing Creative Movement in the Elementary Classroom. Most elementary teachers find it harder than kindergarten and preschool teachers to incorporate creative movement activities into their curriculum. The use of movement in the elementary classroom can be challenging. By their very nature, creative movements are unstructured. Too often, this type of activity can become chaotic and uncontrollable. The following suggestions may help you manage creative movement activities in the elementary classroom.

Define expectations. Let students know that you expect them to work and behave with the discipline of a dancer. Movement time is a time to focus and work with the body. Be clear that you expect the students to use and remember the "space bubble," one's personal space.

Prepare the room. Because a gym or large space may not be available, the movement activity may have to take place in the regular classroom. Establish a routine for preparing the space. For example, put all the desks to the sides of the room and back in place at the end of the activity. Have the children rehearse and memorize the procedure. Although this may take some extra effort, this is time well spent in the smooth beginnings and endings of movement activities.

Cues. The more auditory and visual cues you can provide for students, the better. Try to use a variety of visual cues and sounds. For example, you can use handclaps, a tambourine, a drum, an electronic keyboard, or any other number of percussive instruments. The command "Freeze!" is very effective in stopping a student immediately.

CHARACTERISTICS	NEEDS	TYPES OF EXPERIENCE
Kindergarten, Grades 1 and 2		
1. Spurt of growth of muscle mass	1. Vigorous exercise requiring use of large muscles	1. Running, chasing, fleeing type games; hanging, climbing, exercises
2. Gross movement skills becoming more refined	2. Exploration and variations of gross motor skills; chance to refine skills	2. Self-testing activities of all types; dance activities, movement tasks
3. Manipulative skills still unrefined but improving; will catch balls with body and arms more so than hands	3. Opportunities to manipulate large or medium-size objects; throw small balls	3. Ball-handling activities; work with beanbags, wands, hoops, progressing from large to smaller objects
4. Imaginative, imitative, curious	4. Opportunities for expression of ideas and use of body	4. Creative dance, story plays, creative stunt and floor work; exploration with all basic skills and small equipment
5. Very active, great deal of energy	5. Ample opportunities for vigorous play	5. Running, games, stunts, large apparatus like swings, jungle gym, slides
6. Short attention span	6. Activities that take short explanations and can be finished quickly	6. Simple games, simple class organization so activities can be changed quickly
7. Individualistic or egocentric	7. Experiences to learn to share or become interested in others	7. Much small group work, exploration of movement activities
Grades 3 and 4		
1. Gross motor patterns more refined and graceful	1. Use of skill for specific purposes	1. Introduce specific sport skills; expressive style skill utilized in dance; traditional dance steps
2. Hand—eye coordination improved; growth in manipulative skills	2. Opportunities to handle smaller objects; more importance placed on accuracy; throw at moving targets	2. Ball-handling activities, use of bats, paddles, target games
3. Sees need to practice skills for improvement of skill and to gain social status	3. Guided practice sessions, self-testing problem situations	3. Drills, skill drill games, self-testing practice situations; task setting
4. Increased attention span	4. Activities with continuity; more complex rules and understandings	4. Organized games with more complex rules and strategy
5. More socially mature, interested in welfare of group	5. Make a contribution to large or small group, remain with one group for a longer period of time, help make and accept decisions with a group	5. Team activities, dance compositions with small groups
6. Greater sex differences in skills; some antagonism toward opposite sex (Gr. 4)	6. Ability grouping	6. Combative type stunts, folk dance; after-school activities, clubs

FIGURE 16-3 • Summary chart of growth and development characteristics of children from kindergarten to grade 5. *(Continues)*

CHARACTERISTICS	NEEDS	TYPES OF EXPERIENCE
Grade 5		
1. Coordination highly developed, keen interest in proficiency in skills	1. Need to learn more difficult skills; more coaching on refinement of skills; use of skills in games, routines and compositions	1. Lead-up games to sports in season; instruction and practice in sport skills; more advanced dance step patterns and folk dances; track and field; apparatus routines, intramurals
2. Greater sex differences in skills and interests; most prefer to play and compete with own sex	2. Separation of sexes in classes or within classes for some activities	2. Co-educational dance; swimming, gymnastics, recreational games; sexes separate in team sports and fitness activities; intramurals for each sex
3. Good skills and physique important to social acceptance	3. Instruction and practice sessions in skills, understanding of fitness elements	3. Fitness tests; developmental exercises; work with apparatus
4. Group spirit is high, allegiance to group is strong	4. Need to belong to a group with some stability; make rules, decisions, and abide by group decisions; longer term of membership on a squad or team	4. Team games, tournaments, group dance compositions, sport squads with student leaders, track and field meets
5. Social consciousness of need for rules and abiding by rules; can assume greater responsibility	5. Participate in setting rules, opportunities for squad captains or leaders	5. Student officials; plan and conduct tournaments in class and after school; students plan own strategy, line-ups, etc.
6. Flexibility decreases	6. To maintain flexibility within structural limitations	6. Stunts, tumbling, developmental exercises

FIGURE 16-3 • Summary chart of growth and development characteristics of children from kindergarten to grade 5. *(Continued)*

Spatial arrangements. Use different patterns in class. Have students arrange themselves in various patterns such as lines, circles, dispersed patterns, groups, sitting, or standing.

Working with partners. Either pick partners for students or let them choose their own. Younger children may have more difficulty picking their own partners. Tell students that they are expected to work productively with their partners. If students are not working well together, change their partners. Review all of the rules of an activity before the students start working with their partners.

Time limits. To help keep students on task, set time limits. It is especially important to give time limits when students are working with partners or in a group.

Commenting on students' work. When you speak about a student's work, use movement vocabulary. For example, "I see Mario in a low twisted shape" or "I see Clancy in a high curved shape that reminds me of the wind." Be generous with praise and use thoughtful corrections.

Remember that creative movement is a language and a physical skill that requires practice. Be patient. With time and instruction, students will become adept at using movement to communicate ideas and concepts (Griffiths, 2009).

Using Music and Poetry to Stimulate Creative Movement Activities

Let us now consider how music and poetry can encourage children's creative movement in the classroom.

Music. Listening to music is a natural way to introduce creative movement. Distinctive types of music or rhythm should be chosen for initial movement experiences. Many resources are available that can give teachers ideas on this topic. See the suggested additional readings at the end of this chapter.

In order to provide the music or rhythm for creative movement, only a few items may be necessary. A tape or CD player some tapes or CDs, mp3 players and electronic music files on computers, sticks, and bells may be more than enough.

Some basic guidelines for using music for creative movement follow.

- Make it clear that anything the children want to do is all right, as long as it does not harm them or others.
- Ensure that children understand that they do not have to do anything anyone else does. They can do anything the music or an idea "tells" them to do.
- Allow a child to "copy" someone for a start, if she or he so desires.
- Encourage children to respect each other as different and able to move in different ways.
- Encourage children to experience freedom of movement, the relationship of movement to space, and the relationship of movement to others.
- Show children how to move in their personal space. This space can be explained by thinking of an imaginary circle or bubble around oneself.

The teacher may begin the experience by playing a CD or tape. Music that has a strong and easily recognized beat or rhythm is best. Children should not be told what to listen for: Let them listen first and then ask them to think about what the music is "telling" them.

While children are listening, the teacher may turn the music down a bit lower. The teacher might talk with each child about what the music is saying. Some children may already be moving to the music by this time, and the teacher may join in. Children may go anywhere in the room and do anything that the music "tells" them to do. For this exercise, clapping, stomping, and even shouting are all possible and helpful. When appropriate, a quieter piece of music may be played to allow children to rest and to give them a sense of contrast.

As children become involved in movement explorations, try to redirect, challenge, and stimulate their discoveries by suggestions such as, "Do what you are doing now in a slower way," "Try moving in a different

direction or at a different level," or "Try the same thing you were doing, but make it smoother or lighter."

Some creative movement activities with music can also be done with a partner. Some possibilities follow.

- Have children face a partner and do a "mirror dance" with their hands and arms. Challenge partners to do a mirror dance with their feet and legs, and then with different facial expressions.
- Have children hold hands with a partner and skip, slide, leap, and gallop until they hear a signal. Then they should find a new partner and continue to move to the music.
- Direct children to move the same way their partner moves until they hear the tambourine, then move in a different way.
- Pair children with partners. Ask: "What interesting body shapes can you and your partner make? Can the two of you create an interesting design in the space you share? Practice until you and your partner can make three different designs to music."

This general approach can be adapted to movement with dolls and puppets; movement of specific parts of the body, such as hands, feet, or toes; and movement in different kinds of space or groups. The imaginations of the children and the teacher are the only limits.

Older children may begin to be a bit self-conscious and need other suggestions to encourage their creative movements. They often enjoy working in small groups for this reason. A small-group activity involving mirror movements, copying, and shadowing is appropriate for older children. For example, working together in groups of three or more, children perform movements matching the leader of the group. The leader leads the group in a sequence of movements that the rest of the group copies as closely as possible. A second member takes over as leader, moving in a different sequence. Then, the third member leads the group in yet another sequence of movements. In this type of activity, the group's size helps students overcome the fear of the "whole class looking at me." It is also easier for children of this age to participate in a group when they know everyone else will be participating along with them in the activity. See the end of this chapter for more creative movement activities for older children.

Poetry and prose. For creative movement, poetry has rhythm as well as the power of language. It is not necessary to use rhyming verses at all times.

In the beginning, poems that rhyme may help to start a feeling of pulse and rhythm. Poems should be chosen that fit the young child's level of appreciation. By adult standards, they may be quite simple. They are often short, vivid, lively descriptions of animals or motion, but children should not be limited to these, as there are many books and collections available with a wider variety. The local library is the best resource for this. The American Library Association website (http://www.ala.org) is another good source for poetry books.

A suggested beginning may be to ask children to listen to a poem. After they have heard it, they may pick out their favorite characters in it. Discuss who these characters are and what they do. Read the poem a second time; suggest that children act out their characters as they listen to the poem. Anything goes—children may hop like bunnies, fly like planes, or do whatever they feel. More suggestions are at the end of this chapter.

Encourage each child to move in his or her own way, and encourage as many variations as you see!

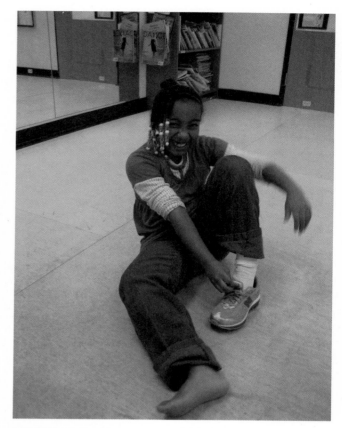

FIGURE 16-5 • Movement activities contribute to the total physical, mental, social, and emotional growth of a child.

FIGURE 16-4 • Creative movement is movement that reflects the mood or inner state of a child.

As readings continue, more complex poems may be selected, containing a series of movements or simple plots. The same general idea can also be carried through with prose.

As children become more comfortable in acting out poetry read aloud, they may become more sensitive to the less obvious actions or emotions described by the poetry. When stories or poems that have several characters and more complex interaction are read, the entire selection should first be read for listening only. Then it can be discussed to get some idea of children's understanding and appreciation. If the children are interested, several readings may be necessary.

Older children are able to sustain their interest for a longer period of time and enjoy the procedure of listening, picking out roles, and acting out what is read. They also enjoy adding costumes and props to their creative movements.

FIGURE 16-6 • Listening to music is a natural way to introduce creative movement.

Art and Creative Movement

Much of art is movement. Drawing, painting, and working with three-dimensional materials all involve movement. Lines and shapes are everywhere in art.

Creative movements can be planned so that they connect visual art with movement. The following are some suggestions to get you started.

Dance and art. Children can dance a painting or paint the dances they create. The kinesthetic pleasure of dance can motivate children to want to move, and this need to express themselves can extend to scribbles, drawing, painting, and modeling.

An example of how to help children connect dance with art is to show artwork with physical motion in it. (Degas's dancers are a natural choice.) Discuss how motion is shown in the work and why a particular step is "frozen" by the artist in the painting. Then let the children do the painting as a dance with movements and dance the painting as they think it would look before and after the artist "froze" the motions.

Creative movement and sound collages. Sounds of the body, city, nature, animals, machines, and children's names can all suggest movement. Brainstorm a category with students and then stretch it for move-

---

THINK ABOUT IT — Brain Gym

Developmental experts have known for many years that movement enhances learning. Back in the 1970s, Paul E. Dennison built on this knowledge by bringing specific movements into his learning disabilities clinics. Dr. Dennison researched these movements, simplified them, and created techniques to make them effective for everyone. He and his wife and colleague, Gail E. Dennison, developed a commercial training program, Brain Gym, which is a specific set of movements, processes, programs, materials, and educational philosophy. It is a registered trademark of the Educational Kinesiology Foundation (Brain Gym International in Ventura, California).

In its original version, it has 26 Brain Gym movements, sometimes abbreviated as the 26. These activities recall the movements naturally done during the first years of life, when the child is learning to coordinate the eyes, ears, hands, and whole body. The 26

activities are part of a program for "learning through movement" (Dennison & Dennison, 1989).

Their program is based on the premise that all learning begins with movement and that any learning challenges can be overcome by finding the right movements to subsequently create new pathways in the brain. They claim that repetition of certain movements "activates the brain for optimal storage and retrieval of information" (Brain Gym, 2009). It also claims to "promote effective communication among the nerve cells and functional centers located throughout the brain and sensory motor system" (Brain Gym, 2009).

On their website, they report that clients, teachers, and students have been reporting for more than 20 years on the effectiveness of these simple activities. Even though it is not clear yet why these movements

Continued

work so well, they often bring about dramatic improvements in areas such as:

- concentration and focus
- memory
- academics: reading, writing, math, test taking
- physical coordination
- relationships
- self-responsibility
- organizational skills
- attitude

Edu-K (short for Educational Kinesiology) is the term for the Brain Gym exercises. To explain how Edu-K works, the Dennisons describe human brain function in terms of three dimensions: laterality, focus, and centering.

The Laterality Dimension pertains to the relationship between the two sides of the brain—especially in the midfield, where the two sides must integrate. Laterality skills are fundamental to reading, writing, listening, or speaking. They are essential for the patterning of whole-body movement, and for the ability to move and think at the same time.

The Focus Dimension describes the relationship between the back and front areas of the brain. Focus affects comprehension—the ability to blend context and details into a full personal meaning and to understand new information in terms of previous experience. Attention disorders (ADD or ADHD) are related to the inability to focus.

The Centering Dimension concerns the connection between the top and bottom structures of the brain. Centering enables us to harmonize emotion with rational thought. Stress can disturb centering and equilibrium, leaving us tense and out of sorts; when we're centered, we feel more grounded and organized. (Brain Gym, http://www.braingym.org/)

Successful brain function requires efficient connections across the neural pathways located throughout the brain. Stress inhibits these connections, while the Brain Gym movements stimulate a flow of information along these networks, restoring the innate ability to learn and function with curiosity and joy.

The activities below are exercises based on the Brain Gym ideas:

- Drink Water. Water comprises more of the brain (with estimates of 90%) than of any other organ of the body. Having students drink some water before and during class can help "prime the pump." Drinking water is also very important before any stressful situation, as we tend to perspire under stress, and dehydration can affect our concentration negatively.

- Cross Marching. This exercise helps coordinate the right and left brain by exercising the information flow between the two hemispheres of the brain. It is useful for spelling, writing, listening, reading, and comprehension. Stand or sit. Put the right hand across the body to the left knee and raise it, and then do the same thing for the left hand on the right knee just as if you were marching. Do this either sitting or standing for about two minutes.

Brain Gym has been criticized as being wholly unscientific (UK Economic & Social Research Council, 2009), concluding that any exercise can improve alertness. Also, in 2007, Dr. Keith Hyatt of Western Washington University analyzed available research into the Brain Gym system as well as its theoretical base. He concluded that Brain Gym is not supported by research and that its theoretical basis does not stand up. The paper also encouraged teachers to learn how to read and understand research and to avoid teaching material that has no rational basis (Hyatt, 2007).

To learn more about this teaching method, visit the Brain Gym website at http://www.braingym.org/. For opposing views, visit the websites listed in the References section of this chapter.

---

ment possibilities. Encourage children to think of the shape, size, rhythm, energy, and vocal quality of the words. Break into small groups and ask each group to make a collage of sounds and movements. Groups can then plan a freeze-move-freeze dance and perform it. This activity could be followed by a visual art collage around the same topics danced.

Dance a painting (older students). Display a print and ask students to brainstorm all the shapes, movements, and emotions they can see in it. Direct attention to the foreground, middle ground, and background of the painting in subjects such as landscapes, seascapes, and still life. Divide children into small groups. Have each group decide a way to dance the painting, using a beginning-middle-end structure. The goal is not to merely pantomime, but to think divergently: What movements came before this moment in the art? During this moment? After this moment? What is just outside the subject matter (e.g., other people, movements)? After students prepare, they can take turns presenting. Background or mood music can be added.

FIGURE 16-7 • Teacher's active involvement in creative movement activities helps children feel free to express themselves, too.

Magic wand. Display an art print featuring a scene from history with several figures in it. Have children assume the figures' positions. Tell them that when you touch them with a magic wand, they should move in ways the figure might move. Remind children about bending and walking, using curved and straight lines, and positive and negative space. You can also add emotions: "Move as if you are in a hurry."

Artists that move. Set up a station with art books or assign students to locate art that includes movement (e.g., paintings by Matisse and Degas). Discuss how artists show movements through line, shape of body, and use of space.

Sculpture or architecture dances. Display pieces of sculpture or pictures of buildings or furniture. Ask about space, curves, and movements and how each sculpture might move if it came to life. Ask students to show the size, energy, and flow of these pieces with their bodies.

Adapting Creative Movement Activities for Children with Special Needs

Creative movement activities can benefit children with special needs because they can participate at their own level of ability. For example, children who are physically challenged can explore body parts or keep a beat by blinking their eyes. Props such as feathers, instruments, or scarves do not have to be held with the hands, but can be placed or attached to an appropriate area of the child's body or equipment. All children with special needs can feel a sense of belonging to a group and a sense of joy at being able to learn on a fundamental movement level. The necessary modifications are often simple; it is basically a matter of focusing on what the children can do, as opposed to what they cannot. Large-motor activities are important for children with special needs because they help children gain in strength, endurance, and coordination. This section uses the term *gross motor movements* in place of creative movements.

During gross movement experiences, it is important not to do too much for children with special needs. They need the chance to figure out how to get their bodies to do what they want them to do, to problem solve, and to make choices. Whenever possible, gross motor movement should take place outside or in a large indoor area where there is ample space and children can move freely.

General Suggestions

- Follow large-muscle activities with quiet activities to help children to calm and focus on other learning experiences.
- Be animated and energetic during movement activities. Children will be more motivated and focused.
- Integrate gross-motor activities into the daily schedule as part of the curriculum, during transitions, and at cleanup time.
- Modify your expectations for how long a child can do a gross-motor activity. If the child has muscle weakness or attention problems, he or she might lack the endurance to sustain activity. Children with special needs do not need to participate in gross-motor activities in the same way or as long as typically developing children. Partial participation is a valid form of involvement for some children (Petersen, 2008). Build strength and endurance from the child's current level of skill.

THINK ABOUT IT

Creative Movement for Transition Times

Whenever young children move from activity to activity (in transitional times), they often lose their focus and may even get a bit confused and disruptive. The following strategies may help children move more easily from one activity to another.

- Have children pretend they and their classmates are cars in a train, with you as the engine. Assign one child to be the caboose—to turn off the lights and close the door.

- Turn your jump rope into a dragon, worm, caterpillar, or other animal by attaching a head at one end of the rope and a tail at the other end. Have children make the body and legs by holding onto the rope with one hand and walking down the hall and out to the playground.

- Have children imagine they are tired puppies, yawning, stretching, and rolling on the floor. Direct them to lie very still. (Suggested for the beginning of rest time.)

- Construct a "feel" box or bag or a "look" box or bag. Place an item in the bag or box that will suggest the next activity or topic for each child to feel or look at.

- To help children quiet down between activities, clap a rhythm for them to copy. Start by clapping loudly, then gradually clap more softly until your hands are resting in your lap.

- Have children pretend to be a bowl of gelatin and shake all over.

- Have children pretend to lock their lips and put the key in a pocket.

- Show children how to put on "magic" ears for listening.

- Have children pretend to walk in tiptoe boots, Indian moccasins, or elf shoes.

- Have children do two things at once. Examples: tap heads and rub stomachs, clap hands and stand on one foot, snap their fingers and nod heads, etc.

- Have children march in place as they count by 2, 5, or 10, recite the ABCs, say the multiplication tables, etc.

- When children transition to their chairs, have them pretend to swim like a fish, prance like a horse, hop like bunny, move like a turtle, walk like an elephant, and the like.

- With older children, have children choose a partner. Have one student slowly print a current spelling word on his/her partner's back. The partner guesses which word was printed. Have them take turns doing this.

- Encourage parents to send children to school in sneakers so that they can participate fully in gross-motor activities.

Developmental Delays

Many children with special needs have low muscle tone and poor strength. Because of this, movement is difficult, so the child often doesn't move. This results in increased muscle weakness. It is important that the child is encouraged to have an active lifestyle in school and at home. The suggestions that follow are especially helpful to the teacher of young children.

- Use exercise videos or tapes with a child who is developmentally delayed. In these videos, the same movement and exercises are repeated, which gives the child an opportunity to practice and enables him or her to feel confident in his or her ability to keep up with the class.

- Encourage the child to participate in gross-motor activities for gradually longer periods.
- Always demonstrate the activity first.
- Allow children to watch a role model engage in the activity before attempting it themselves.
- Familiarize yourself with gross-motor developmental sequences. If the child's gross-motor skills are at the two- or three-year level, he or she may be reluctant or unable to participate in gross-motor activities that have been designed for typically developing four-year-old children.

Physical Impairments

Space in the room may be a problem if you have a child in the group who is physically impaired. The child might bring lots of equipment to school, such as a prone stander, a chair of some sort, and a wheelchair. Some children might have walkers or crutches. This child will also need space to maneuver between furniture. Keep the following recommendations in mind.

- During movement activities in the classroom, it is fine to assist the child, but slow movements are best. Quick movements might increase muscle tightness.
- Avoid always giving the child physical assistance to move, and encourage the child to do what he or she can to move independently.
- The child with physical impairments who is walking may be able to do whatever the other children are doing but for a shorter time or shorter distance.
- Occasionally, the child with physical disabilities can play the role of "time keeper" or "music director" by turning the music on and off during a musical activity, but this should not be the child's only role. It is important that the child also be part of the movement activity.

Attention Deficit/Hyperactivity Disorder and Behavioral Issues

Movement activities can be calming for children with hyperactivity and behavioral difficulties but can on occasion be overstimulating and disorganizing. Large-motor activities need to be structured with clear rules and expectations. Observe if the child is becoming overstimulated and redirect him or her to an activity where he or she can become calm and regroup (Kaufmann & Ellis, 2007). You will find the following practices helpful as you deal with children with behavioral issues.

- Teach children how to manage their behavior in gross-motor activities. Children need to be taught that there is no pushing, that indoor voices should be used, and that equipment must be shared on occasion. Instruction in these skills will have to be given frequently until the child has mastered them and can remember them even in the excitement of the activity.
- Notice and give praise when the child is following the rules during gross-motor play (Kaufmann & Ellis, 2007).
- Some children who have ADHD are highly sensitive to being touched and may perceive an innocent bump from another child as being a push. To avoid this, make sure that each child has enough space in movement activities. Define the child's personal space during movement activities with hula hoops or rug squares.

- Make sure to maintain eye contact when giving instructions.
- Structure gross-motor activities to eliminate waiting.
- Keep activities short. A child may be able to play ball activities for a few moments and then need to move on to some other kind of activity.
- If you aren't offering a choice, give clear directions rather than posing a question. Don't say, "Do you want to walk on the balance beam?" if you mean, "Walk on the balance beam" (Warren & Coaten, 2008).

Visual Impairments

Studies have shown that children with visual impairments tend to have poor levels of physical fitness (Petersen, 2008). These children will need lots of encouragement to move independently. When giving directions to the child who is visually impaired, be very clear and avoid vague words such as *this, that,* and *over there* (Warren & Coaten, 2008). Be careful not to encourage anxieties by being overprotective of the child with visual impairments.

Describe the movement experience or play equipment before involving the child. Let the child explore the equipment with his or her hands before attempting to use it.

When giving directions to the child with visual impairments, use the child's name to get his or her attention and give him or her additional time to process directions and respond (Warren & Coaten, 2008). Tell the child what will be happening next, especially before physically assisting him or her through a movement experience. Instead of just naming objects, describe them for the child (Kaufmann & Ellis, 2007).

Summary

Young children learn by doing, and movement activities are a natural avenue for children's learning. Movement activities contribute to the total development—physical, mental, social, and emotional—of young children. Movement activity is as vital for children as art and other subjects, for in movement activities, young children acquire skills, knowledge, and attitudes that help them discover and understand their bodies and their physical abilities and limitations.

Creative movement reflects the mood or inner state of an individual. Creative movement usually requires no planning or forethought on the part of children.

FIGURE 16-8 • Children can find meaning and exhilaration in creative movement activities.

They can forget about themselves and let the music's rhythm or an idea carry their bodies away. There is no exact pattern of movements to be practiced or perfected.

In planning creative movement activities for young children, the developmental level of each child is the starting point. The information provided in developmental skill charts (such as Appendix A) for young children can be used to get some idea of what to expect of children physically at different ages. The most important thing to remember is that the individual child is the measure, not any chart of developmental skills.

Poetry and music can be used to encourage children's creative movements. Listening to music is a natural way to introduce creative movement. Distinctive types of music with clear rhythmic patterns should be used for the initial creative movement experiences. Poetry also has rhythm as well as the power of language. Poems that rhyme are good to begin with, as they help children get the feel, pulse, and rhythm of the words. (There are rhythm poems in Chapter 18.) Fingerplays also provide many opportunities for creative movement activities. Whether movement activities occur with music, poetry, ropes, or hoops, they benefit young children by developing their relaxation, freedom of expression, and increased awareness of their own bodies.

Connections can be made between movement activities and art. Movement activities can be adapted for children with special needs.

Key Terms

creative movement 375
creative movement activities 375

Learning Activities

A. Choose one of the action poems at the end of this unit. Use it to conduct a creative movement activity with a group of young children (or a group of your fellow classmates). Critique your experience. Cover the following points.

  1. Was the poem appropriate for the group? Why or why not?
  2. What did you do (specifically) that worked well with the group?

  3. What did not work and why?
  4. How would you change your activity for future use? Be specific in your reply.

B. Observe a group of children involved in movement activities of any kind. Record evidence of each of the following situations.

  1. A child discovers a new way to move.
  2. A child uses small and/or large muscles in the activity.

3. A child discovers what other children are like as a result of the activity.

C. At the end of a long lesson (with children or your own classmates), try this movement activity to help you understand the importance of movement activity at all ages.

Toss around a small, soft ball for a few minutes, using these rules: You must be sitting in your seat, you cannot "whip" the ball at someone, and you may not throw it to someone who chooses not to play. The object is to see how many times you can catch the ball consecutively. This requires cooperation and encouragement. Everyone is given the chance to play, even if they aren't the world's best catchers. Encouraging one another leads to a higher count. See how high you can go with this one!

In the classroom, you can change the rule to correspond to your current lessons. For example, every student who catches the ball must name an adverb in language arts class, solve a problem in math, explain a date in history, or define a term in science. The purpose of movement is to wake up and revitalize students for their next learning experience.

D. Think about an everyday movement (e.g., washing the dishes, combing your hair). Take a minute and explore it. Go beyond "pretending" to do dishes or whatever movement you choose. Instead, explore the movement potential itself, by moving using different body parts than would normally be used. Try doing the movement fast, then very slowly. Feel the essence of the movement.

Activities for Children

Suggested Creative Movement Interpretations

Movement explorations and creative movement experiences can be used to interpret nearly every experience, creature, or phenomenon. Have children act out one of the movement interpretations listed below. (This list can be expanded with endless possibilities.) Join in the fun!

1. Life cycle of butterfly

   a. caterpillar crawling
   b. caterpillar eating grass
   c. caterpillar hanging very still from branch or twig
   d. chrysalis hanging very still
   e. butterfly emerging from chrysalis
   f. butterfly drying its wings
   g. butterfly flying

2. Piece of cellophane, lightweight plastic, or plastic wrap

   a. Teacher holds the item in his or her hands without children seeing it. Children are encouraged to guess what item might be, interpreting their guesses through movement.
   b. Teacher open hands, children watch plastic move, and then interpret what they see through movement.
   c. Piece of plastic is used for movement exploration.

3. Shaving cream

   a. spurting from aerosol can
   b. foaming up
   c. spreading on face
   d. being used for shaving

4. Airplane sequence

   a. starting motor
   b. taking off
   c. flying
   d. arriving
   e. landing safely

5. Popcorn

   a. butter melting
   b. popping
   c. everyone ending in a ball shape on the floor, all "popped"

6. Water

   a. dripping
   b. flooding
   c. flowing in a fountain
   d. freezing
   e. melting
   f. spilling
   g. spurting from a sprinkler

7. Laundry

   a. inside washing machine
   b. inside dryer
   c. being pinned to clothesline
   d. drying in a breeze

8 Fishing

   a. casting out
   b. reeling in
   c. pretending to be a fish
   d. fly fishing
   e. pretending to be a hooked line
   f. frying and eating fish

Shape and Movement Game

Cut out various shapes from construction paper. Have children scatter around the room. When you hold up a triangle, they can only move their heads. When you hold up a circle, they move only legs. For a square, they move only shoulders. For a rectangle, they move only hips. For an oval, they move their entire bodies. Change shapes rapidly. Encourage children to be creative in their movements. Playing music during this activity makes it even more fun.

Show Me Movements

Children should be scattered around the room with adequate space between them. Call out challenges like the following.

> Show me how small (tall, wide, tall, thin, etc.) you can be.
> Point to the farthest wall; touch it and return to your own place.
> Point to the nearest wall; touch it and return to your own place.
> Standing in your own place, make your feet move fast. Make them move slowly.
> Show me how slowly you can walk.
> Show me how fast you can walk.
> Be a tree (wall, ball, river, etc.).

Guide children toward looking at objects in the room and noticing where they are located. Have children close their eyes and point to objects in the room that you call out (e.g., the door, chalkboard, window, wastebasket, floor, ceiling, playhouse area, wagons, teacher's desk).

Shadow Movement Activities

On a sunny day, go outside for a "shadow hunt." Encourage children to look for shadows made by your school building, playground equipment, bushes, and their own bodies. Talk about how large shadows, such as those from trees, make the cool, shady areas people enjoy on hot days.

Inside, play a shadow game. Start by playing a cassette or CD. As the music plays, have children dance or move in any way they choose, trying to avoid stepping on one another's shadows or letting shadows "step on" them.

Encourage children to watch the patterns their shadows make as they move. After a short time, stop the music and say, "Freeze!" Children then stop moving and hold their positions until the music starts again. After you do this a few times, have a child operate the player. Let children take turns being in charge of the music.

For younger children, place a ball on the pavement of your outdoor play space on a sunny day. Invite children to take turns jumping on and off the shadow of the ball.

After older children try their own creative movements, have them move in specific ways as they try to avoid one another's shadows. For example, ask children to move like mice approaching a piece of cheese, like monkeys jumping from tree to tree, or like lively kittens running after a ball of yarn.

Variation: Change the game to number freeze. Call out a set of numbers. Tell children that they need to freeze when they hear the number seven. Continue the game by encouraging children to freeze as you call out other specified numbers.

Running Movements

Before starting this activity, go outdoors and make a mental note of landmarks such as trees, the end of a sidewalk, a large bush—anything that can serve as a marker for a running path. Make sure that there are no sharp edges or items children might run into.

Take your group outside and gather them together a short distance from one of the markers you spotted earlier. Explain that you are going to make a running path together. Say, "Let's mark our path with these streamers. Come help me tie these markers on."

Together, walk around and tie a different color streamer onto each of the markers you've chosen. Then step back and say, "Hey! Let's all run over to that tree with the blue streamer. Come on and run with me!"

Let your enthusiasm and delight fill the mood of the activity as you encourage children to participate. Catch your breath and call out, "Come on, let's run to the yellow streamer!"

Later, hand out streamers for children to carry as they run. Partners can share ends, and you can call out various ways to move—like a duck, like a robin, like a bear—as they run around the play space.

The fun in this activity is laughing and being silly together. In no way is this a race or a contest to see who can go the farthest or fastest.

"Become" One of the Following

Let children act out the features/characteristics of a bicycle, rake, hose, wheelbarrow, tire pump, beach ball, or any other familiar play objects the children come up with.

Jump Over the River

Two long sticks can serve as the banks of the river. Children jump from one bank to the other. The sticks can be moved further apart at times to make a wider river. Children can find ways to get from one side of the river to the other, like sliding, crawling, rolling, etc. Encourage any and all creative attempts to "cross."

Line Challenges

Use a tape or chalk to make a line on the floor and encourage children to see how many things they can do: jump over the line, walk on the line, hop along the line, stand on the end of the line, stretch out on the line, slide on the line, tiptoe across the line, roll over the line, lie beside the line, run around the line, or skip round and round the line. Then have children make up their own challenges.

Jet Planes

Encourage children to use creative movements in becoming a jet plane. Pretend you are a jet plane. Use your body to show the jet: on the ground, in the air, climbing up into the clouds, nose diving, coming in for a landing, on the ground again. Take off again. This time, your jet is a stunt plane. It can write in the sky. It can make loops and turn upside down. Now make a number 2. Make a 3. Now make a 5. Can you make an S? How about a P? Make the shape of a funny animal. How about a wiggly worm?

Can You Be?

Ask children to pretend their body is a huge tree. Show the tree in a big windstorm, losing its leaves in autumn, loaded with snow after a blizzard, and in the summer when the sun is so hot.

Classical Music and Movement

Selected sections of the music of Saint-Saëns' *Carnival of the Animals* are excellent for encouraging the acting out of various animal movements. These movements can include crawling, walking on all fours, jumping, and flying. Tell children the title of the music and play it for them to enjoy. Encourage them to move their bodies the way they think the animal in the music would be moving.

Another piece of music that is good for creative movements is Tchaikovsky's "Dance of the Little Swans" from *Swan Lake*. It's a natural for some fun tip-toeing!

For marching experiences, use Herbert's "March of the Toys" from *Babes in Toyland* or Grieg's "Norwegian Rustic March" from *Lyric Suite.*

For running movements, try Bizet's "The Ball" from *Children's Games.* Bizet's *Children's Games* also has a section titled "Leap Frog," which is great for creative jumping movements. In the same composition, Bizet's "Cradle Song" encourages swaying and rocking movements. "The Swan" by Saint-Saens from *Carnival of the Animals* is also good for swaying and rocking movements.

Prokofiev's "Waltz on Ice" from *Children's Suite,* Tchaikovsky's "Waltz" from *The Sleeping Beauty,* and Khachaturian's "Waltz" from *Masquerade Suite* are all excellent pieces of music for waltzing and smooth gliding creative movements.

Rope Skills

Lay out various lengths of rope in a straight line on the floor as if they were tightropes. Challenge children to try some of these skills. Can you do this while moving backward? Walk the "tightrope" with eyes shut. Jump from side to side across the rope without touching the rope. Hop from side to side without touching the rope. Lay your rope in the pattern of a circle. Get inside the circle, taking up as much space as possible, without hanging over the edges. Make up a design on your own. See if you can walk it. Can your friend? Can you walk your friend's design?

Unwinding

Children pretend they are windup toys, such as dolls, dogs, monkeys, rabbits, or clowns. The teacher winds up the toys and the children begin moving at a brisk pace, getting slower and slower until they are completely "run down" and stop or collapse to the floor. The teacher or a child rewinds the toys and the sequence is repeated.

Collapsing

The teacher explains that "collapsing" means relaxing a body part or the whole body, allowing gravity to pull it down to earth. Children stand and stretch tall, then slowly collapse (relax) one part at a time—first the fingertips, then the wrists, elbows, arms, head, and shoulders, and so on—until they are left collapsed on the floor.

Imagination and Creative Movement

Combine full-body stretching and children's creativity in these fun movement activities.
- Invite children to imagine that their foot is a paintbrush and that they need to cover the ground with a beautiful painting.
- Suggest they pretend to be zookeepers giving a giraffe a bath. Make sure they reach all the way up to wash behind his ears!
- Ask them to make believe that they are leaves on a tree. Suggest that the leaves break away from the tree and float down to the ground.
- Invite children to use their bodies to make shapes. Can they make a square? A circle? A triangle?

Creative Movement Games

Suggest a game of "Jack-in-the-box" to children. Say, "Wind yourself down and shut the door—then pop up on the count of four. Make your own music while winding yourself down." Continue the movement experience by asking children to stretch slowly like a rubber band and then snap back quickly. Say, "Quickly twist yourself into a knot; then slowly stretch your elbow to the ceiling and untie the knot."

Creative Movement—Machines

Collect pictures of machines that children are familiar with such as a computer, hand mixer, hair dryer, blender, etc. Choose one of the pictures and ask the children to think about how this machine moves. Invite the children to move their bodies and create the sounds of that particular machine. Show a picture of another machine and invite children to create movements and sounds for that machine.

Musical variation: Use rhythm sticks or a drum and play slow rhythmic beats. Invite one child to be in charge of the pictures. Explain to the children that when their classmate holds up a picture they will move like that particular machine. Children not comfortable with moving can play instruments or take turns holding up the pictures.

Magnet Movements

Pretend to have a large magnet. Ask children to imagine that this magnet can pull them toward it or push them away. Say, "The magnet is pulling you to the ceiling, higher, higher, higher. Never take your eyes away from the magnet. Now the magnet is pulling you quickly to the floor. Watch to see what the magnet does next and act it out." This movement activity is most successful when the teacher acts out the effects of the magnet along with the children.

Winter Creative Movements

If you live in an area that has a cold, snowy winter season, here are some creative movements you and your children will enjoy. Encourage children to pretend (by acting with their body movements) to be any of the following.

- leaves waving in a gentle wind, a strong wind, and then eventually flying through the air
- snow falling softly, being made into a snowman, and then melting
- an ice cream cone or icicle melting in the sun
- rain trickling down, running into a swift stream, the sun coming out, and a rainbow appearing
- an icy hill that is hard to walk up
- a thick fog to find one's way through
- creative movements relating to jobs in winter, such as shoveling snow
- creative movements depicting a snowman as it melts
- creative movements of winter sports and activities like skating, throwing snowballs, building a snowman
- creative movements depicting birds flying around the bird feeder, eating seeds, flying in the air

You and the children may think of others.

Poison Ivy Movement Activity

Discuss what poison ivy is. Ask children if any of them have had a rash from poison ivy. Talk about how it feels. This discussion leads naturally to this activity.

Designate a small area in which children can move freely. Have them move around in this space without touching anyone with any part of their bodies. If they do touch someone, they will get "poison ivy" and must move to the side and swing their arms up and down, side to side, or hop on one leg as it "heals." Call out instructions for the children to change direction, pace, and type of movement.

Falling Rain Dance

For this activity you will need long pieces of materials, such as colorful scarves, and recorded instrumental music.

Play instrumental music that changes tempo often, fast to slow and back again. Tell children they're going to pretend to be raindrops falling to the ground. Dance together, moving your bodies to the music—move slowly when the music is slow, faster as the tempo picks up. When the music stops, all dancers fall down into puddles.

Next, give children scarves. Encourage them to have fun holding the scarves and moving to the music. Try tying the scarves to children's clothing or wrists. Then continue your rain dance with added drama.

Remember to dance with the children and share your enthusiasm. Choose a variety of types of music. Don't tell children how to move, just set a mood and allow them to move as they feel like moving.

When working with younger children, be sure to have a well-defined area for their movement. This will help to keep them safe and prevent their getting "carried away with the music" and bumping into other children.

For older children, play a wide variety of music with varying tempos. Talk with them about how the different types of music make them feel. Then give children the opportunity to demonstrate these feelings by moving independently or in small groups.

For another variation, divide the children into two groups. Provide rhythm band instruments for one group and scarves for the other. Go outdoors and invite the children with instruments to play improvised music while the children with scarves dance to their tunes.

More Outdoor Activities

On a rainy day, draw children's attention to the weather. Look through the window together. Ask questions such as, "What is happening outside today?" "What is making the puddles?" Then put on your rain gear, grab umbrellas, and go for a short rainy day walk. Help children notice the rain and the wind. Together, look at rain fall onto leaves, the grass, and into puddles.

Go outdoors on a sunny day and ask children if they can move like raindrops. Can they drip-drop into puddles? Can they drop onto leaves? How would a raindrop move in the wind?

Recite this poem as they move.

> All the rain is falling down,
> Falling, falling to the ground,
> The wind goes swish right through the air,
> And blows the rain 'round everywhere.

All of these activities can also be done indoors. Just be sure you have a clear area so children can move freely about.

Bubble Gum Movements

Enjoy some "bubble gum" with children. Ask them to lie down on the floor and imagine themselves as pieces of bubble gum. Talk about things that happen to bubble gum; have children act out these actions. Say, "Bubble gum comes in lots of different shapes. What shape are you? Now someone is unwrapping you—how do you move? Now someone is chewing you up, making you into all kinds of funny shapes. Now you are being blown up into a bubble—you get bigger and bigger and bigger, and then you pop! Oh, well. You are being chewed up again, then blown up into another bubble, and now you pop. You are getting stale, so you are thrown away."

Creative Animal Dance

Introduce the activity by either reading a book that shows a variety of animals or showing children pictures of different types of animals. Ask the children to describe how the different types of animals move. Does an elephant move quickly or slowly? What about a fish or a butterfly? If they have pets at home, invite them to demonstrate how their pet moves. Play some instrumental music and invite children to move like some of the animals in the books or photographs. The next day, divide children into small groups and ask each group to make up a dance using a specific animal movement. Work with each group and assist them as they think about how the animal moves. Then invite them to choose a musical selection for their dance. Allow time for everyone to perform their animal dances for their friends. Extend the children's creative thinking and movement activities with a game of animal pantomimes. They can act out different animal movements and let their friends try to guess what they are. They can also use animal movements during transition times as they move from one area to the next.

Music and Movement—Balloons, Inside and Outside

For this activity you will need a balloon that has been blown up and a 3-foot piece of string or ribbon for each child.

Gather everyone together in a large room where children can move about freely and safely. Offer each child a blown-up balloon and let him play with it. Observe children's play and make comments to challenge and expand their movements. You might say, "Look at Jim! He taps his balloon to keep it in the air. Let's use our bodies to hit our balloons, too." Model new movements and make fun suggestions to extend children's movement explorations.

Before going outdoors, offer to tie the other end of their string or ribbon to their wrists.

Move outdoors and take time to note the effect of the wind on the movements of the balloons. Give children time to run and move with their balloons. Try to do some of the same movements you did inside and encourage children to compare their movements and the movements of their balloons with and without the wind.

Note: Young children are often frightened by the sound of a balloon bursting. If possible, use extra-thick balloons and blow them up only part of the way. If a balloon bursts, react in a calm and comforting manner. Always keep extras on hand.

Balloons let loose can be harmful to our environment because they often land in streams, rivers, and oceans where fish and wildlife swallow them and choke. Be careful that the balloons you use come back into your setting.

For younger children: Take a kite outdoors on a windy day. Give children turns flying the kite. Discuss the movements of the kite as children watch it dip and dive through the air.

For older children: Have children work in pairs or in small groups to keep a balloon in the air on a calm day. See if children in the group can use movements different from their classmates to keep the balloon in motion.

Making Friends with Movement and Music

This is a good activity early in the school year to help children get to know one another. Divide children into pairs so that each has a partner. Explain that you will turn on music and each pair will dance together at the same time. Tell the children that when you stop the music they will "freeze," holding a position. Practice freezing before you begin. Invite them to "dance and freeze" with the same partner for a few rounds. Next, call out "change partners" and suggest children choose another dance partner. Do this several times so that everyone gets to dance with a few different friends.

Extension: Find a variety of pictures in books and magazines that show people or animals moving. Create a list of words with children that describe the different movements like running, hopping, pedaling, lifting, bending, or dancing. Then, set out art materials, ask them to draw pictures that illustrate one of the movements listed, and include the "movement word" below the picture.

Yes, Let's

This is a silly, fun game. The group stands in the space waiting for someone to call out, "Let's all pretend to try on hats" (or any other similar suggestion). The group then responds with great enthusiasm "Yes, let's!" The group then pretends to try on hats until someone calls out a new request, such as "Let's all hop like a bunny!" The group then responds again, "Yes, let's!" They hop up and down until a new suggestion is made and accepted. This is a good, short, energizer and a good game for transition times.

Van Gogh, Lines, and Movement

Use an art print of van Gogh's *Starry Night*. Have the children look at the painting and name the kinds of lines they see in it. Then have the children move their bodies to show each kind of line they see. Then have the children look around the room and see how many different kinds of lines they find. Then ask them to "paint their ideas" using their bodies and motion rather than using a brush and paint.

For younger children: Children walk around doing whatever they want to with their arms and bodies. When the teacher says "Stop!" the children "freeze" and hold that position until the teacher says "Go!" Encourage children's movements of all kinds.

Activities for Older Children (Grades 4–5)

Movement, Line, and Shape

Artists use lines and shapes to send "wordless" messages or feelings to people. Show students prints of several artists' work that exemplify such use of lines and shapes. Good examples for this would be works of Mondrian (for squares and rectangles), Georgia O'Keeffe (for curvy, round shapes), and Salvador Dali (for clear lines of various shapes). Using the work of one or more of these (or other artists), have students pick out some shapes and convert themselves into the geometric figures used by the artists.

To make body sculptures, the teacher divides the class into small groups and asks them to pick a geometric shape in the artist's work and to make that shape with their bodies. Give them some rehearsal time. Children use their bodies to create the shape they see in the artist's work. Six children, for example, would be used to form a rectangle. They might do so by lying on the floor and connecting limbs so that four form the top and bottom and two form the sides. Larger versions of the shapes can be created by using more children to form each body sculpture. The groups show their body shape sculpture to the rest of the class and viewers identify the shape they see.

To build on this activity, divide the class into two groups. Each group is asked to prepare a body sculpture in which several shapes are linked. One, for example, might have a triangle, a circle, and a square linked by connecting body parts. The other group has to identify the shapes present in the sculpture.

A further challenge would be to invite the children to invent new shapes and demonstrate them for the larger group. Together, have them come up with creative titles for their original inventions.

Classical Music and Creative Activities

Play Stravinsky's ballet *Firebird*. Discuss the story of King Kastchei, the Firebird, the Prince, and the Princess. The children might enjoy making masks for the hideous ogres found in the "Infernal Dance of King Kastchei." Students could act out the parts in the story as well as narrate what happens in the ballet. Other students can be chosen to be either "low," "medium," or "high" creeping demons according to the dynamics of the music. When the theme isn't playing, the monsters can "freeze" until the theme comes back again. Children can make a class project of the performance with costumes and masks.

Creative Movements

Have children use their bodies for the following activities.

- Explore a range of movements involving body parts (i.e., bend, stretch, twist, turn, push, pull, swing, sway).
- With a partner, facing each other, one moves and the other mirrors the movements. Move a body part.

Keep that part moving as you transfer the movement to another part.

- Working with a partner, do the same movement your partner does. Now do the same movement with another body part.
- Create a dance with your partner using two different movements suggested by each person.
- Begin a movement in one body part and gradually transfer the movement to adjoining body parts. Try moving in different ways.
- Create a dance in which the movement flows from one dancer to another.
- Explore moving different body parts in unison.
- Move body parts in opposition.
- Combine a movement. Create a dance combining unison (or opposition) movements of different body parts.
- Put a piece of elastic around two body parts. Initiate a movement with one and have the attached part move with it. Initiate another movement and have the attached part resist the movement. Combine two or three movements initiated by the attached body parts moving in sequence or in resistance to the movement.
- Working with a partner, attach a piece of yarn loosely to a body part (not around the neck) and to the same body part of your partner. One begins the movement with the attached body part following the movement. Try moving in different ways.
- Create a dance with each person initiating a movement in turn, which is followed by the attached body part of the partner.

In How Many Ways?

Write the following question on a sheet of chart paper: How many ways can we move our bodies?

Show the children the question. Ask the group if they can think of 20 different ways they can move their bodies. Write the numbers 1 through 20 on the paper and write down the different ways children suggest they can move their bodies.

Use a camera to record some of the different ways the children move their bodies during this activity. Be sure to photograph each child in the class.

Then, ask the children to stand up. Ask them how many ways can they move their bodies while standing? Have they reached 20 yet? If so, can they think of more ways they can move their bodies?

How many ways can they move their heads? How about their mouths and eyes? Who can raise his eyebrows, turn his tongue, or move his nostrils?

Extension: Use the photographs to create a class book. Glue each photograph onto a sheet of paper. Have the children write information describing their photograph. Invite the class to create a title and cover for their book. Bind the pages, then read the book together and place it in the library area for everyone to enjoy.

Can You Guess?

Divide the class into small groups of four to six. Give each group the name of an object or thing written on a piece of paper. Each group must then, within a set time limit (usually 7 to 10 minutes is a good length of time) make a machine out of their bodies that makes their object or thing. Be sure to make it clear that the group is to become the machine that **makes** the object, **not** just become the object itself. In presenting their machine, children may make sounds, but may not talk in words. Bring the groups back together and have them present their machine. Once they are finished, the other groups may guess what their machine was making. Suggestions for things to make: rainbows, dreams, community, friends, monsters, solar system, a school, or other things appropriate for your group.

Linking Literacy and Movement

Can you dance your ABCs? Students work in groups to create the shapes of the letters of the alphabet with their bodies. Students can be very creative, using all different parts of their bodies to get the letters just right. This is a great activity for English-language learners to "feel" the shapes of the letters and to better recognize them when reading and writing. This activity educates the whole child—mind, body, and soul.

Scrabble and Movement

Students spell out words using letters they hop, skip, and jump to collect. Divide the class into groups of two or three. Each group should receive a set of index cards that reflects the same distribution of letters as a Scrabble set (nine As, two Bs, twelve Es, and so on). Divide a large open space in half, and send all the groups to one half and have them spread out their cards face up. (Cards should not overlap.)

Bring students back to the empty half of the playing area. On your signal, and one group member at a time, students hop, skip, or jump (you provide the directions) to their cards, pick one up, and bring it back

to the group. When a group has enough cards to spell a word, they bring their word to you for verification and record it. Students take turns collecting letters and spelling words until you call time. Award words of four letters or less one point, and words with more than four letters two points. Total the points per group and for the entire class. Celebrate success!

Movement and Math

Give students a chance to move while they add and subtract. Have partners take turns kicking large foam dice as far as they can. It doesn't matter where the dice land because they can't hurt anyone. Once the partners have their two numbers, they make as many number statements as possible. For example, if they kick a three and a six, students can calculate $3+6$, $6+3$. Have students try this activity with multiplication as well (6×3 and 3×6). Your students will get a real kick out of doing math!

Planet Hoop

Invite students to take an amazing journey to space in their very own "spaceships." First give each student a plastic hoop. Have them stand inside their hoop, holding it at waist level to make spaceships. Have them crouch with their hoops at the "launching pad" (the ground) and jump up to "blast off" at your signal. Count backward from 5 to 0, and then yell, "Blast off!" Give suggestions on how students might move (hop, skip, walk, gallop) as they "fly" their spaceships around the room to the tune of Gustov Holst's "The Planets." Fade the music out when it is time to "land" on a planet. Direct students to land by placing their hoop on the floor and sitting inside it.

Once they are seated, conduct a read-aloud to share facts about the planet each student is visiting. Volunteers might take turns reading orally. Then have students blast off again! After visiting several planets, have students travel back to Earth. This might be a good time to discuss how Earth is different from other planets.

Chapter Review

1. Compare and contrast the different requirements involved in planning creative movement activities for preschool, elementary, and fourth and fifth graders. Include in your answer at least four specific points to remember when planning and carrying out creative movement activities for each of these three groups of children.

2. Rank the objectives of creative movement for their potential to enhance young children's overall development. Give rationale for your rankings and specific examples of activities for social–emotional, physical, and cognitive development.

3. Using the developmental theories in previous chapters, develop your own criteria for selection

of music and poetry to use with young children in creative movement activities. Specify the particular age group(s) your criteria is designed to address. Then, using these criteria, give examples of specific music and poetry choices to use with these particular young children in creative movement activities.

4. Develop a lesson plan using poetry or prose in creative movement activities.

5. A parent of a visually impaired child requests that you not include her child in "unstructured" movement activities for the child's safety. Using the developmental information in previous chapters, as well as the information in this chapter, explain how you would address this parent's concerns.

References

Brain Gym—FAQ (2009). The Official Brain Gym website. Retrieved October 25, 2009, from www.braingym.org/

Dennison, P. E., & Dennison, G. E. (1989). *Brain Gym handbook: The student guide to Brain Gym, parts I and II.* Ventura, CA: Educational Kinesiology Foundation.

Graham, S. F. (2002). Dance: A transformative occupation. *Journal of Occupational Science, 9*(1), 128–134.

Griffiths, F. (2009). *Supporting children's communications and creativity through music, dance, drama and art: Creative conversations in the early years.* London, UK: David Fulton.

Hyatt, K. J. (2007). Brain Gym—Building stronger brains or wishful thinking? *Remedial and Special Education, 28*(2), 117–124.

Kaufmann, K., & Ellis, B. (2007). Preparing pre-service generalist teachers to use creative movement in K–6. *Journal of Dance Education, 7*(1), 7–13.

Petersen, D. (2008). Space, time, weight and flow: Suggestions for enhancing assessment of creative movement. *Physical Education and Sport Pedagogy, 13*(2), 191–198.

Sacha, T. J., & Ross, S. W. (2006). Effect of pretend imagery on learning dance in preschool children. *Early Childhood Education Journal, 33*(2), 341–345.

Shilling, W. A. (2002). Mathematics, music and movement: Exploring concepts and connections. *Early Childhood Education Journal, 29*(1), 179–184.

UK Economic and Social Research Council. (2007). Neuroscience & Education: Issues and Opportunities. Teaching and Learning Research Programme website. Retrieved October 26, 2009, from http://www.esrc.ac.uk/ESRCInfoCentre/index.aspx

Warren, B., & Coaten, R. (2008). *Dance: Developing self-image and self-expression through movement: Using the creative arts in therapy and healthcare: A practical introduction* (3rd ed.). London, UK: Routledge/Taylor & Francis Group.

Additional Readings

Bacon, J. (2007). *Body, movement and dance in psychotherapy.* London, UK: Taylor & Francis.

Bielenberg, K. (2008). *All active: Inclusive physical activities.* Champaign, IL: Human Kinetics.

Carlson, G. (2008). *Child of wonder: Nurturing creating and naturally curious children.* New York, NY: Common Ground Press.

Chaiklin, S., & Wengrower, H. (2009). *The art and science of dance/movement therapy: Life is dance.* London, UK: Routledge.

Compton, C. (2008). Thank you, Miss Katherine. *Phi Delta Kappan, 90*(3), 182–189.

Edwards, L. C. (2009). *The creative arts: A process approach for teachers and children.* Upper Saddle River, NJ: Prentice Hall.

Fogel, A. (2009). *The psychophysiology of self-awareness: Rediscovering the lost art of body sense.* New York, NY: W. W. Norton.

Gay, M. (2009). *Brain breaks for the classroom: Quick and easy breathing and movement activities that help students reenergize, refocus and boost brain power—anytime of the day!* New York, NY: Scholastic Teaching Resources.

Goldring, J. (2008). *Discover me: A movement education program.* Tamarac, FL: Llumina Press.

Halprin, D. (2009). *The expressive body in life, art, and therapy: Working with movement, metaphor and meaning.* London, UK: Jessica Kingsely.

Kissel, B. T. (2009). Beyond the page: Peers influence pre-kindergarten writing through image, movement and talk. *Child Education, 85*(3), 160–166.

Lengel, T., & Kuczala, M. S. (2010). *The kinesthetic classroom: Teaching and learning through movement.* Newbury Park, CA: Corwin Press.

Lorenzo-Lasa, R., Ideishi, R. I., & Ideishi, S. K. (2007). Facilitating preschool learning and movement through dance. *Early Childhood Education Journal, 35*(1), 25–29.

Logue, M. E., Robie, M., Brown, M., & Waite, K. (2009). Read my dance: Promoting early writing through dance. *Childhood Education, 85*(4), 216–221.

Pica, R. (2009). Can movement promote creativity? *Young Children, 64*(4), 60–61.

Tolrbert, M., & Schneider, L. (2008). *Follow me, too: A handbook of movement activities for three- to five-year olds.* Washington, DC: NAEYC.

White, J. (2008). *Playing and learning outdoors: Making provision for high quality experiences in the outdoor environment.* London, UK: Taylor & Francis.

Helpful Websites

CircusFit, http://www.circusfit.com
Turn your students on to fitness with CircusFit, developed by Ringling Brothers and Barnum & Bailey. The program features 21 interactive lesson plans and aerobic activities.

Dance with Snook, http://pbskids.org/bigbigworld/home.html?externalPuppet=snook
On this site, you first choose your music and then Snook will start to dance. The challenge is to get "Bob" to imitate Snook's dance moves. Students can also create a dance.

National Network for Child Care, http://www.nncc.org/
This website features movement and music activities.

The Perpetual Preschool, http://www.ecewebguide.com
More than 12,000 free ideas for parents and educators of young children are provided on this site. Click on "Music and Movement Through Your Day."

Teaching Heart, http://www.teachingheart.net/ultimate.html
This site includes free printables, lessons, lists of books, resources, and creative activity ideas.

Yahoo Home: Arts: Education, http://dir.yahoo.com/Arts/Education/K_12
This Yahoo! search directory contains a list of sites with K–12 art activities. Categories include curriculum standards, drama, and lesson plans.

For additional creative activity resources, visit our website at www.Cengage.com/login.

Creative Music

OBJECTIVES

After studying this chapter, you should be able to:

1. Outline some basic goals for music activities for young children.

2. List guidelines for planning music activities for young children.

3. List the elements of music appropriate to use with young children.

Lisa sang to herself in a sing-song way while drawing with crayons: "One purple, two purple, three purple, four purple." Next to her, William was humming the jingle for a fast-food restaurant advertisement and keeping rhythm with his coloring strokes. Out on the playground, Drew chanted, "I-am-going-to-be-a-lawn-mo-wer," and as he slid down the slide, he made a sound like a lawn mower. Picking up his cue, Inez and Christy slid down after him, each on her stomach and making motor-growling sounds.

Musical experiences like these are a common occurrence in a young child's life. Children love the sound of their own voices, and chanting is the way that they experiment with sound and rhythm. Chants are half-speaking, half-singing sounds that often accompany young children's play. Making up original chants and songs and moving rhythmically to musical beats are quite natural to a young child, for whom music is a favorite avenue for creative expression.

Music is one of our greatest inheritances as human beings. So global is the human experience of music that it has often been called the universal language of humankind. Music is all around us, a testimony to its great importance for adults. Music is equally important for children from infancy on. Children sing to communicate thoughts and feelings. They sing as they play. They grow silent and intent when they hear unusual sounds. They become quiet and relaxed when they hear soothing sounds. They move their bodies in concert with the sounds they hear.

Music is central to the human experience of children, just as it is to adults. For this reason, music should be an important part of the early childhood curriculum.

Every child begins life immersed in the most basic element of music—rhythm. The steady beat of the mother's heart introduces the baby to patterned sound. Into the safe, suspended world of the womb also come outer-world voices with unique rhythms and timbre. The unborn child responds, physically, to these external sounds, showing an innate desire to listen and learn. So, even before birth, children hear sounds in their brains. The child's world, too, is filled with music. Infants' windup musical teddy bears, crib mobiles, and go-to-sleep lullabies are just a few examples of early introductions to music. Young children respond quite naturally to music with rhythmic movement, and they also create their own musical patterns in original chants and songs as well as in unaccompanied rhythmic movements such as swinging, tapping, and even rocking in a chair. Activities that make up the natural beginnings of musical learning right in the home can be extended by the early childhood teacher to classroom music activities.

We know a foreign language is best learned when the brain is still growing rapidly, and this is also true for the language of music. So the obvious conclusion is that early years need to be musically rich. Young children are more open to types of music—from classical to country—and it is what they hear the most that becomes what they like and value. The teaching implication is to take advantage of this openness to musical

diversity by providing experiences with a wide range of styles, types, periods, and cultural music experiences.

In an early childhood program, music of all kinds is appropriate. For example, the sounds of a slow Duke Ellington tune and a fast, rhythmic portion of Stravinsky's "Rite of Spring" are equally appropriate for young children. Background music in the early childhood classroom can be as soft and soothing as Schubert's "Cradle Song" or a Brahms lullaby. For a change of pace to a livelier mood, classics such as "Tambourine" by Gretry or Bach's "Badinerie" can be used. Good music of all types has a place in all early childhood programs. The valuable place of music in the early childhood classroom is obvious in the following special education teacher's journal entry.

> I hurry into the school to get to my assigned first grade classroom. The children love music, and I look forward to working with them. I crash nose-to-nose with a teaching assistant who works with the youngest children in the school district who have severe behavioral disabilities—the children in my assigned class. Many of them come to school with concerns that would make most of us stagger.
>
> This is a particularly difficult Monday. The assistant quickly summarizes the turmoil. George has had a horrible weekend at home. Alexis has not taken her medication. Justin has spent the weekend away from the consistency of home with Mom and is in a spin as a result. Perhaps, I think, I can find a way to help.
>
> In the classroom, I find the teacher sitting in the rocking chair humming, rocking, and holding a child. Two other children are listening through headsets to Baroque music. Soft music comes from the CD player on the shelf. The music's power of relaxation fills the room. The teacher has found solutions on her own. It had been an overwhelming 90-minute beginning to the day, but now, with understanding and change of mood, the atmosphere is calm. The music speaks to the children's emotions. They can now leave their homeroom, go to their inclusive environments, and learn and play with their friends. Music has met the children's need for peace. It has elicited a sense of calm in all of them (Humpal & Wolf, 2003, p. 104).

FIGURE 17-1 • Young children respond quite naturally to music by tapping out the rhythm on drums.

You do not have to be able to play an instrument or be able to read music in order to plan appropriate music experiences for young children. It often helps to view teaching music as an *experience* to be offered, rather than a subject to be taught. It also helps to think of music experiences as ways to explore, test, and investigate ideas by connecting music to topics studied. In this way, the focus is on student participation and the process, not perfect singing or competence in playing an instrument.

As with other areas of the curriculum, **appropriate music activities** can be planned only if the teacher understands the developmental levels of the children involved. Although individual rates of development vary widely, the sequence of development follows a particular pattern. Figure 17–2 shows some important behavioral characteristics for each stage of development, along with their effect on a child's experiences with music. This material is based on the theories of Piaget (Wadsworth, 1979) and Erickson (1963). Figure 17–2 may be used as a guide for choosing from the musical activities for children listed at the end of this chapter.

Goals for Young Children's Music Experiences

Music is a common and enjoyable occurrence in a young child's life. One of the main goals of musical activities for young children is to maintain this natural appreciation of musical experiences. Focusing and then building on this natural enjoyment of music will help you produce the most successful and joyous music program for young children. As in all early childhood activities, it is the process—not the finished product—that teaches and enriches a young child.

Other goals of the early childhood music program include the following.

- numerous opportunities to sing a wide variety of songs
- frequent exposure to various forms of music with wide ranges of rhythms, tempos, and moods
- opportunities to hear and learn about music from different cultures and ethnic groups
- frequent opportunities to express feelings and emotions in song, rhythm, and movement
- opportunities to expand listening skills
- developing an increased enjoyment of music
- frequent opportunities for group participation

- opportunities to explore their own creativity in music
- experience in playing simple instruments, moving to rhythms, and expressing emotions in motion during musical activities
- learning to identify some basic musical concepts and terms, such as loud and soft, fast and slow, and high and low. (See Figure 17–3 for a summary of the elements of music and the end of the chapter for suggested activities on these elements.)

For older children, these goals also include the following:

- to have opportunities to sing in parts, in rounds, and in harmony
- to learn about a variety of major musical works such as operas, ballets, symphonies, concerts, and chamber music
- to have listening experiences with instruments and tonal qualities of strings, woodwinds, brass, and percussion
- to recognize basic meter and rhythmic notation by sound

Planning Music Activities

The two keys to success in all your musical endeavors are **flexibility** and **acceptance**. You should be able to accept more than one kind of response to a music activity and adapt the activity accordingly. If, for example, the child in a planned clapping activity chooses to pat the rug or his or her leg, accept the response and imitate it as you continue the activity. In fact, the child may interpret your imitation of his or her response as a form of praise, thus making the enjoyment of what he or she is doing even greater. Or if the child is more interested in just listening to music than in dancing to it, accept that, too. Try to catch the child for your dancing activity at another time, when he or she is in a dancing mood. In other words, take your cues from the children and build enjoyment and learning on what they already find enjoyable. Build, don't tear down, the joyful world that music naturally creates for young children.

With these guidelines in mind and with an understanding of the developmental needs of children at different ages, a teacher may plan appropriate musical activities for young children. Let us now consider some examples of specific musical experiences appropriate for young children.

AGE	BEHAVIORAL CHARACTERISTICS	MUSIC EXPERIENCES
Newborn to 1 month	Responds to stimuli by moving entire body.	Quiet singing and rocking soothe the baby. Scary sounds avoided. Sound stimuli important.
1 to 4 months	Changes from hearing to listening. Turns head toward stimulus. Follows moving objects with eyes.	Same as for newborn.
4 to 8 months	Involved in purposeful activity. Reproduces interesting events. Develops hand–eye coordination.	Hits suspended bells again and again to reproduce the sound.
8 to 12 months	Anticipates events, shows intention. Knows that objects have functions. Imitates actions.	Hits drum or xylophone with stick. Claps hands to music. Hits instrument to produce a sound. Understands purpose of instrument.
12 to 18 months	Invents new actions. Uses trial and error to solve problems.	Experiments by hitting instrument in different ways with different objects.
18 to 24 months	Creates new actions through prior thought. Imitates actions after person leaves.	Continues music activity after adult stops. Listens to radio, dances to it.
2 years	Steps in place. Pats. Runs. Increases language. Has limited attention span. Attends to spoken words a few at a time. Develops independence, is very curious. Tendency to tire easily.	Enjoys action songs and moving to music. Can learn short, simple songs. Enjoys activities with short, simple directions. Many opportunities to experiment with instruments and sound. Opportunity for frequent rest breaks in strenuous rhythmic experiences. Avoid prolonged activities.
3 years	Jumps, runs, and walks to music. Has self-control. Attentive, has longer attention span. Uses more words. Compares two objects. Participates in planning. Initiative emerges.	Special music for special movements. Can wait for a turn. Longer songs or small-group experiences can be planned. Experiments with sound comparisons. Suggests words for songs or additional activities. Can recognize several melodies and may have several favorites. Choices important along with an opportunity to try out own ideas.

FIGURE 17-2 • Developmental characteristics and music experiences.

(Continues)

4 years	Has better motor control. Interested in rules. Plans ahead with adults. Likes to imagine.	May begin skipping. Rule songs and games appropriate. Can make suggestions for music activities. Adds words to songs. Creates songs on instruments. Makes dramatic movements. Likes to experiment with the piano. Likes to play music over and over. Can identify simple melodies.
5 to 6 years	Has good motor control. Likes to have rules. Vision not yet fully developed; eye movements slow; likely to have trouble seeing small print or making fine linear distinctions when music staff is not enlarged. Heart in stage of rapid growth.	Able to sit longer. Enjoys songs and dances with rules. Can follow specific rhythm patterns. May pick out tunes on the piano. Likes musical movies but may become restless. Strenuous activity periods should be brief.
7 to 8 years	Begins to read written symbols. Concerned with rules. Cooperation and competition. Logical thought processes emerge. Can compare more than two objects after first object removed (seriation). Thoroughly enjoys group play, but groups tend to be small. Boys and girls play together.	May be able to read words to songs. Rule dances and songs especially valued. Better able to tell reality from fantasy. Can compare three or more sounds or pitches. Likes duets and doing anything musical with a friend. May want to take piano or dancing lessons. Likes group activities including singing games, playing informal instruments, phrase games.
9 to 11 years	Has more developed language arts skills. Understands rules and strategies of games. Peer group assumes greater importance. Logical thought processes are present. Has more flexible thought. Enjoys play with peer group. Boys and girls prefer same-sex play. Begins to see others' opinions and ideas as unique.	Can read words to songs, can create original lyrics. Enjoys dances with varied steps and patterns. Begins to enjoy small-group singing experiences, such as duets, trios, chorale. Can compare sounds, pitch, rhythms in music. Can understand elements of music such as tone, basic notations, styles, and forms of music. Introduce harmony and part singing for small groups. Provide duet singing experiences, all-boy, all-girl singing groups. Enjoys multicultural music and dance.

FIGURE 17-2 • Developmental characteristics and music experiences. *(Continued)*

Musical Experiences

Infants and very young toddlers experience music by hearing it, by feeling it, and by experimenting with pitch and timbre as they vocalize. Adults can provide infants and toddlers music experiences daily while giving children caring, physical contact. Singing to children during changing and feeding times is a basic way to provide music experiences for very young children.

When children enter the preschool program, music continues to be an important part of their lives. In the classroom, infants and toddlers need to hear all kinds of music. Adults need to talk about this music and how it expresses feelings. Rocking, patting, touching, and

Rhythm: Movement of sounds through time. In songs, the words usually match the rhythm.

Beat and **Accent:** Have to do with the rhythmic pulse, like the steady beat of a clock ticking. The accent is where the strongest emphasis is placed as in *one* two three, *one* two three.

Tempo: The speed, how fast or slow the music is.

Syncopation: Uneven rhythms as in jazz, yet the beat remains steady.

Melody (tune): A series (more than one) of musical tones falling into a recognizable pattern. When we sing words, they become melodies.

Pitch: The high or low tones in the sound pattern.

Timbre (Pronounced "tambur"): Tone color or unique qualities of sound (e.g., voices or sounds made by plucking, beating, rattling, or blowing various instruments).

Dynamics: Volume or relative loudness or softness of the sound; gives emotional intensity.

Texture: Layering of instruments and/or voices to create a thin or full feeling. Melodies, rhythms, and timbres can be combined to create different textures. Music made by an orchestra is an example of a full texture.

Harmony: The blending of sounds, e.g., chords; two or more pitches simultaneously.

Form: Structure, shape, or distinct pattern or a piece of music or a song. Related to *style* or *genre*.

Ostinato: Simple, rhythmic or melodic content repeated over and over to accompany a song.

FIGURE 17-3 • Summary: Basic Elements of Music.

THINK ABOUT IT   The Musical Minds of Preschoolers

What preschool teacher or childcare provider hasn't seen one of their preschoolers singing a song quietly to himself while building a block city or painting, or even just humming and tapping his feet at quiet time? That's because children seem to know intuitively that music is good for their brains!

Two recent academic studies, one at the University of Wisconsin and one at the University of California, both conducted by a team of psychologists, showed that music is essential to brain growth and development in young children (Rauscher & Shaw, 2007). These studies demonstrated that children who received early exposure to the complex multisensory stimulation inherent in learning the lyrics and melodies to new songs and singing them in a group setting scored high on intelligence tests. What particularly surprised the researchers was that early exposure to music didn't just help children artistically and emotionally, but even improved their math and science skills. Essentially, music helps hardwire a child's growing brain for the future complex thinking

and problem-solving skills they'll need every day for the rest of their lives.

According to a 2008 report from the Nemours Foundation, a nonprofit organization founded by philanthropist Alfred DuPont to improve the health of children, "Children who grow up hearing music, singing songs, and moving to the beat are enjoying what experts call a rich sensory environment" (Nemours Foundation, 2008). That's just a fancy way of saying a child is exposed to a wide variety of tastes, smells, textures, colors, and sounds. And children who enjoy such a rich environment do more than have fun. Researchers believe that in music activities, they forge more pathways between the cells in their brains (Rauscher & Shaw, 2007).

So, what are you doing to "hardwire" your students' brains for lifelong learning? The sound of a young child singing should be your cue to add music to your day and theirs.

moving with children to the beat, rhythm patterns, and melodic direction of the music are all appropriate musical experiences for infants and toddlers.

If you don't know how to begin incorporating music into your program, simply start at the opening of the day. Sing in your classroom as the children are arriving. In the mornings, to warm up your voice and the children's voices, hum a little bit. Show children all the possibilities of song. Sing high, then low. Sing softly, then loudly. Change the words of a familiar song such as "Twinkle, Twinkle, Little Star." (See end of unit for suggestions.) Change the melody. Play with your song, just as you would take a ball and dribble, roll, or twirl it. There's certainly more than one way to play with a ball. The same is true for a song.

Sing when you are doing routine tasks. Remember that making up the words is fine. Children will pick up on the joyful atmosphere you are creating and also begin spontaneous singing as they move around the classroom. Use familiar tunes as "frames" for songs describing movements. Many children know the tune to "Row, Row, Row Your Boat," "Mulberry Bush," and "Twinkle, Twinkle, Little Star," and can easily sing along with you—especially if you have lots of repetition in the words. Children will often make up verses themselves, spurring literacy learning. In such an environment, teaching songs and singing are a natural part of the early childhood program.

Playing music during periods of the day is another opportunity for a musical experience. Adults can further encourage the musical development of infants and toddlers by exposing them to a wide variety of vocal, instrumental, and environmental sounds. Simple things like talking about the sounds children hear on their walks outside—if they are loud sounds or soft, if they are near or far away—are basic beginning music experiences for very young children.

Listen to the sounds of young children playing in the dramatic play area, on the playground, in the sandbox, and in the building block area. You will often hear young children in these everyday situations singing, humming, or chanting familiar songs. Songs and singing are a common occurrence in the everyday life of a young child.

Introducing Music Elements

While musical terms alone do not create music, early childhood teachers need to understand and teach basic elements so that there is a common language to discuss music and concepts to use when exploring

---

How to Present a Song to Children
The method you choose to present a song to children will depend on the mood and the nature of the song itself.

1. **Phrase-wise method.** Introduce the song with a brief story, discussion, or question. Sing one phrase and ask children to repeat. Then sing two phrases and so on.
2. **Whole-song method.** Present the whole song in a variety of ways, rhythmic moving, dancing, playing instruments, or dramatizing to make repetition interesting and meaningful.
3. **Modeling.** The teacher or another student who knows the song models it (sings it) for the rest of the group. They join in as the song is repeated.
4. **Combination of phrase-wise and whole-song method.** The teacher sings and presents the whole song, but asks the children to respond to the easiest part of it—with voices, hands, or an instrument.

Always consider the developmental level of the children and keep songs for younger children simple—easy lyrics, limited melody (not too high or too low), and a catchy beat. The songs in the "Activities for Children" section of this chapter are good choices for presenting songs to young children. You may, of course, have many other songs of your own to teach the children in your group. The references listed in the Online Companion are sources for numerous other songs appropriate for young children.

FIGURE 17-4 • How to present a song to children.

---

music creation. In other words, to integrate music into the curriculum, teachers and students need some basic understanding of the tools of music. This is similar to the basic art concepts introduced while children are working with two- and three-dimensional media. **Spiral teaching** can be used in this instance. In spiral teaching of music elements, the teacher presents the basic facts about music without worrying about the details. For example, the teacher calls it "marching music" instead of duple time or "swinging music" instead of ¾ time. Then, as learning progresses, more and more details are introduced while at the same time they are related back to the basics. For example, the teacher now adds the word "tempo" so the song now has a "slow tempo" rather than just being "slow." The caution is for teachers not to kill the joy and spirit of music through overanalysis of music elements. There are specific suggestions on working with the basic elements of music found in the Activities for Children at the end of this chapter.

Teaching Songs

The way in which you teach songs and singing to young children reflects the same natural and enjoyable place music holds in a young child's life. The following suggestions are intended to help you present songs and singing experiences in the early childhood program in a way that maintains the young child's natural musical interest.

- Choose songs that have a natural appeal for young children. Popular topics include the children themselves, family members, animals, seasons, toys, and holidays. Be sure to include songs for all ethnic and cultural groups represented in the class, as well as in the larger community group.
- Be aware that not all children will participate in singing activities. This may be due to cultural reasons—not a lot of singing in the home, for instance—or for personal reasons, such as shyness.
- Pay attention to the songs you choose. Select one in the right key (in other words, not too low, not too high) so children can sing it. Sometimes it's not the song but the arrangement that is difficult. Be aware that some songs are not designed for the average singer (as anyone who has tried to belt out a rendition of "The Star-Spangled Banner" can tell you).
- Be aware that learning a song is really quite a complicated process for young children. It involves listening, understanding and remembering words, having correct pronunciation, and remembering and singing a tune. That is quite a number of skills to be coordinated in a short period of time. Many young children find this difficult.
- Choose songs with a clear, strong melody. If the melody is easy to follow, it will be easier to remember.
- Try out all songs yourself first.
- Once you've chosen a song, learn it yourself—and learn it well. Nothing is less inspiring to eager songsters than a teacher who has to check notes while teaching a song.
- Based on the length of a song, you may want to teach it in sections, by verses, or even in short phrases. Often, a song's wording may be a bit tricky, and you may want to practice key words a bit more. Whatever method you choose, remember

to be light on practice and heavy on praise. Don't make learning a song work; instead, give children lots of verbal encouragement during singing activities.

- Visual aids can help add to the pleasure of singing and song activities. Pictures of key characters in the song or a series of pictures of key song events add interest to song activities. For example, a flannel board with farm animals for "Farmer in the Dell" helps add interest to this old favorite song. Use puppets to accompany your teaching a song to children. If you're shy, this will help, as children can't help but focus on the puppet and not you!
- Keep on hand a list of songs you have taught the children. They really enjoy singing old favorites, and it's easy to forget which songs they know. You may want to post the list with some associated picture words so that children can choose their favorites.
- Encourage all attempts at singing. Just as with other developmental skills, each child will perform at his or her own unique level. Thus, there is never any reason to compare children's singing or encourage children to compete with one another. If you ever had the experience of hearing a group of children attempting to out-shout one another in a choral performance, you will know firsthand the results of encouraging competition between young children in singing.
- Add movements, gestures, and props when appropriate for the song and for the children. A too-heavy emphasis on gimmicks to teach a song is unnecessary if you have chosen a song that interests children and is of an appropriate level of difficulty for them to learn. Added devices need to be thought of as "spices" and used as such: A few appropriately placed hand gestures in a song are like a dash of cinnamon in the applesauce. An entire routine of cute gestures and too many props adds too much "spice" to the recipe. Let preserving the integrity of both the song and the children be your guides in the use of all "extras" in teaching songs to young children.
- Include the new song in other areas of the curriculum by playing the song softly during center time or rest periods.
- Introduce new books related to the song's topic in the language arts area.
- Include art activities related to the song's topic throughout the week's activities.
- Record children singing the song. Have the recording available in the listening center for children

THIS ONE'S for YOU!   Start the Music!

The National Association for Music Education (MENC), Texaco Foundation, National Association for the Education of Young Children, and the U.S. Department of Education developed Start the Music in 2000. This is a series of projects and events designed to help bring age-appropriate music education to every child in the United States. These organizations solicited the expertise of early childhood music educators, music therapists, education association administrators, early childhood educators, and health care providers to identify best practices for early childhood music education and to develop strategies to implement those practices.

Developmentally and individually appropriate musical experiences are guided by these beliefs (MENC, 1995).

- All children have music potential.
  - They bring their own unique interests and abilities to the music learning environment.
  - They can develop critical thinking skills through musical ideas.
  - They come to early childhood music experiences from diverse backgrounds.
  - They should experience exemplary musical sounds, activities, and materials.
- Young children should not be expected to meet performance goals.

- Their play is the work.
- They learn best in pleasant physical and social environments.
- They need diverse learning environments.
- They need effective adult models.

Start the Music recognizes the role adults play in assisting young children in their musical development. Families, caregivers, and teachers can all help children grow musically (Neely, Kenney, & Wolf, 2000, p. 1) by doing the following:

- Immersing children in musical conversations while singing, speaking rhythmically, moving expressively, and playing musical instruments. By doing these things, we stimulate children's initial awareness of the beauty and the structure of musical sound.
- Encouraging children's musical responses by smiling, nodding, and responding with expressive sounds and movements. In doing so, we show children that music making is valuable and important.
- Finding ways to encourage and motivate children's playful exploration, interpretation, and understanding of musical sound.
- Start the Music recognizes that all children are individuals and that music experiences should be a part of every child's world.

---

to enjoy (with earphones or without). Play the recording during your next musical activity session. You may want to record the next version—with rhythm instruments, with a "solo" performance by one of the children, or with any other new variation you and the children prefer.
- Refer to Appendix E and make rhythm instruments like the circle embroidery hoop, egg shaker, and small plastic bottle rattles as an activity in the arts and crafts center. Have children use these as a rhythmic accompaniment to the song.
- Use the instructions provided in Appendix E to make "flutes" out of paper towel or tissue paper rolls. Have children decorate them with crayons, colored markers, and stickers, and use their "flutes" to hum along to the song.

Varying the Rhythm of the Program

Just as variety is the spice of life, variety provides the same spark for the early childhood music program. Although young children enjoy the stability that routine provides, it is important to vary these routines to prevent lessening their, and your own, interest in music. Consider how many people can't remember the words to our national anthem, even though they've heard it innumerable times: It has become so routine that people don't really hear it anymore. The same thing can happen in your early childhood music program if you have too rigid a routine.

Varying the rhythm of the music program helps hold children's interest and makes the experience enjoyable. Variety can be provided in your choice of music, your method of presentation, and your lesson planning.

Variety in choice of music. In choosing music for young children, your own interests as well as the children's can improve variety in musical selections. Children's music need not be exclusively from music resource books. In an early childhood classroom, music selections can include classical, jazz, rap, rock, reggae, pop, and Native American, to name only a few. Young children are very interested in what's new and different and enjoy hearing popular music. In fact, most preschool children can name their favorite pop singers and their latest hits. Although music experiences should expose young children to a wide variety of musical styles, a music program including popular songs gives young children a familiar sound, a friendly starting point. Developmentally, it is appropriate to begin with the familiar, using it as a base for the introduction of new concepts to the child.

Variety in choice of music can also be provided by the families of the children. A teacher may find a rich source of musical variety by asking families to share the names of their favorite music or to share tapes, records, or CDs with the class for special activities. In preparing for special ethnic and cultural celebrations, for example, you might find families willing to share favorite holiday music with your group. Some parents may be willing to sing for the group or bring in special instruments for children to see and hear. The key is to go beyond your likes and the dictates of curriculum guides into the children's lives, their parents' lives, and the community at large, where a variety of music awaits you and your group.

Variety in presentation. We've already discussed several basic methods of presenting a song. In addition to these basics, you need to consider other ways to add variety to your presentation of songs and musical experiences for young children.

- Vary the time of day you have musical activities. Switch from afternoons to mornings and vice versa. Also, don't neglect the spontaneous inclusion of a song during the day. Mixing up a recipe together is an excellent time to vary your program by singing as you work with the children. Singing a song on a nature walk is another. Swinging and singing on the playground is fun. And who can refrain from a song ("The Wheels on the Bus" is an obvious example) on a bus trip? In essence, plan for the unexpected occasion to sing and have a mental repertoire of songs to sing with the children. Singing can make an ordinary event joyous, so start making a list of favorites for this very reason.

FIGURE 17-5 • An outdoor drum set encourages musical experiences in the open air. This is another example of variety of presentation.

- Vary your presentation by having the children choose the songs they want to sing and how they want to present them. Be sure to have available puppets, pictures, rhythm instruments, and audiovisual or other necessary equipment for their creative choices.
- Play games with music. Musical chairs is only one of these games. Games can focus on voice recognition. For example, a child is challenged to guess who is humming the song or who sang the last verse. A "name that tune" game is also a way to vary the presentation of songs. Play, sing, or hum a few bars of a song for the children to guess. Charades, or acting out a song, is an appropriate musical game for older children.

Variety in lesson planning. The key to variety in lesson planning is cross-curricular planning. More specifically, music need not be planned for only one area of the curriculum. Music should cross all curricular areas, and this can be accomplished by specifically planning for it to do just that. Here are some suggestions for this specific planning.

- When making lesson plans for the week, include music in at least two other curricular areas. For example, plan to play music during art activities, and note which selections you will use and on which day. Be sure to make a note to have the tape/CD ready and the tape/CD player set up for the days required. Then, plan to read a book at group time that relates to the new song(s) introduced that week. Plan to locate the book early.

- Use music as your cue to adding new materials and props to the dramatic play center. For example, engineer hats, trains, and railroad signs are natural additions when you've planned to teach "I've Been Working on the Railroad" to children. Putting the book *The Little Engine That Could* (Piper, 2002) in the language arts center is another example of a music-inspired topic used in another curricular area.
- Review past lesson plans to assist you in your future planning. We are creatures of habit and often tend to get in a rut when making lesson plans. Review past plans to see what kinds of music you have been introducing, the method of presentation, and curricular coverage. If a pattern is obvious, then you need a change! Make a conscious effort to find new types of music or methods of presentation, or plan a new schedule of times/days for music. If you are bored with the lessons and the planning of music lessons, the children will reflect your lack of engagement in their half-hearted participation.
- Use a variety of sources for music experiences for young children. See the Online Companion for sources of songbooks and other books on musical experiences for children.

Rhythm Activities

Rhythm is present from life's earliest moments, when a baby hears its mother's heartbeat. Infants continue to enjoy rhythms in many everyday situations, such as the soothing ticking beat of a windup swing or the soft sounds and smooth rhythms of a lullaby. One of a child's earliest musical experiences is clapping and moving to rhythmic music. Using rhythm instruments to follow the beat and feel the rhythm follows as one of the most accessible and enjoyable early childhood musical experiences. While learning a new song can be difficult for many young children, rhythm instrument activities are quite easy! With most of them, the child is simply copying one motion at a time. There is nothing to remember. Using **rhythm instruments** involves the body in keeping a beat and feeling rhythm, so children are fully participating musically. They're really creating the music themselves. And children love playing these instruments. Young children, who love movement and motion in general, are naturally drawn to the use of rhythm instruments. Listening first to the music for its rhythmic pattern and then matching the beat with rhythm instruments is the most familiar method of introducing rhythm instruments. Having young children listen to the music and

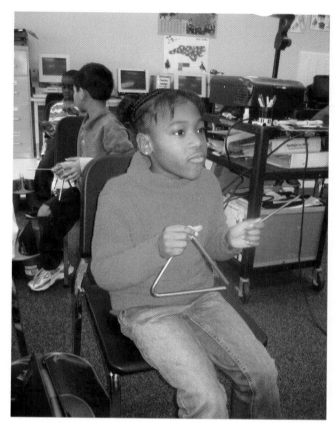

FIGURE 17-6 • Older children also enjoy the musical experience of using rhythm instruments.

clap out the beat with their hands or tap it out with their feet is another appropriate, traditional rhythm activity.

Rhythm instrument activities encourage technical exploration as well as expand movement repertoire and vocabulary. When you verbalize each movement as you do it with the children ("Now we're twirling the shakers" or "Can you click the tops of your sticks together?"), you are encouraging their exploration and learning. These activities also help children develop an awareness of rhythm, phrasing, tempo, dynamics, and other elements of music in a natural way that is suited to their developmental level and their active style of learning.

A teacher can also help a child's development of rhythm by focusing on the natural movements of the child. For example, teachers can follow a child's natural walking or running tempo by accompanying her or his steps on the drum. This can quickly become a game as the child, realizing that her or his steps dictate the beat of the drum, walks faster and slower.

THINK ABOUT IT

How Did Music Begin?

Music is a big part of our modern lives. But music in one form or another has been part of people's lives for thousands of years.

The earliest musicians were prehistoric people. Experts hypothesize that human voices were used for the first music experiences. They believe humans used different noises to express fear or joy. These sounds, along with some of the sounds they heard from animals, such as birds' chirping, might have led them to make music.

When people began to use tools, for instance to pound grains, they may have done so in a rhythm, or a regular pattern. These sounds might have led them to make other pleasing rhythms with the first percussion instruments.

Early humans probably banged rocks together to make tools. When they did, pieces might have broken off that they used for another purpose, such as scraping. Those same pieces of stone could have been used to scrape rhythms on shells, wood, or other stones. Early people probably made clapping sounds with their hands. They also might have hit sticks on a hollow tree and noticed how loud it was. This may have been the beginning of a hollow wood instrument called a slit drum.

Later, people stretched animal skins over wooden frames, then hit the drums with their hands or sticks. Such drums were used in honor of animals or plants.

Some filled gourds, shells, or other items with small stones, nut shells, or animal teeth and shook them as rattles. They were used to accompany music and dance.

One of the earliest instruments that experts have identified is the bull-roarer. It was a piece of bone with a hole in one end where a long piece of hide was attached. The bull-roarer was "played" by whirling it overhead. Music experts think the noise of the bull-roarer was intended to scare off enemies or evil spirits.

The lyre was an ancient stringed instrument made in a box or bowl shape. It had two "arms," usually made of wood or horn, with a crossbar at the end. Strings were attached at the crossbar and the body of the lyre.

Prehistoric wind instruments such as whistles were probably used in hunting and in war. These whistles might have been made of bones from birds, from shells or horns, or from phalanxes, finger, or toe bones from an animal.

In Ireland in 2004, archaeologists uncovered the remains of what they believe to be a prehistoric musical instrument. It was made of six wooden pipes that did not have holes in them, but their different lengths would have made different tones when air blew through them.

At a site in Germany in 2004, archaeologists found a flute with three finger holes carved in ivory from a mammoth. They believed the flute to be more than 30,000 years old. It was found in 31 pieces and was about 7-1/2 inches long. The flute maker probably split a mammoth tusk, hollowed it out, and then glued it back together.

Prehistoric peoples made some wind instruments from bird bones, which are hollow. Others, made from bone or horn, had to be hollowed out. People carved out the insides of the bone or horn, or they might have used fire to burn the insides away. Some Native Americans still carry on the tradition of making eagle bone flutes (Debnam, 2008).

Following children's galloping and skipping with the drum can also illustrate through sound the asymmetrical nature of those rhythms. The drum can emphasize the accent when running children leap over an object, or it can mark groups of beats (meter). Teachers can also mark the beat as children jump over a series of sticks laid out in parallel formation or pass a ball from hand to hand. Teachers provide a more fulfilling movement experience by fitting the external music source, such as a drumbeat, to the child's movement.

Some teachers feel that percussion instruments such as drums are merely noisemakers. Drums, however, can be used for musical conversations as children ask each other questions using patterns, as they drum out the rhythm of their names as they count/drum out the syllables in their names, or as they simply explore the sound of a drum. The drum can be available for children's exploratory free play, for a guided experience with an adult at circle time, or for small-group interaction in a play center.

Strategies for Using Rhythm Instruments

Whenever rhythm instruments are added, they should have a specific purpose. Instruments are not used just to make "noise," but rather to enhance an activity. Instruments should be in good condition. Be sure children know the proper use of rhythm instruments before beginning any activities. Set up rules for using rhythm instruments, but keep the rules clear and very simple. For example, "Keep the instrument away from your face" is a good, simple rule. Be sure to maintain order at the beginning and throughout all of the activity. Have children keep their hands in their laps while you pass out and collect instruments. Demonstrate the proper use of the instrument. For example, take out one pair of sticks or sand blocks and show them the correct way to play. Try using simple signals for starting and stopping that don't require your shouting over the music. Holding up rhythm sticks in a crossed formation is a good visual "stop" signal. Holding the rhythm sticks straight up can be a visual "start" signal. Have children practice picking up and playing, then stopping and putting down instruments on your signals. Using rhythm instruments, children learn to listen for a pattern of sounds in the music. In beginning rhythm activities, it's a good idea to choose music with a clear, easy-to-hear beat or rhythm. Marches and many types of ethnic music are excellent choices for this strong beat.

Some children may have difficulty hearing rhythms and/or reproducing them. This can be handled in the same way you would handle a reluctant singer. Specifically, never force the child to copy your pattern or to use a rhythm instrument or practice this activity. Your emphasis should be on the child's natural enjoyment of music. Whether he or she can reproduce a rhythm is not essential to his or her enjoyment of music. As many an adult can attest, not being able to sing on key or reproduce rhythms does not affect one's enjoyment of music.

Rhythm instruments may be made by the children as well as by the teacher. Refer to Appendix E for using recycled materials such as toweling rolls, pebbles, and spools to make rhythm instruments as yet another creative outlet for young children.

FIGURE 17-7 • This child is using large and small muscles playing his drum.

FIGURE 17-8 • Older children enjoy playing informal instruments like the recorder.

Music Experiences for Older Children

With children in the middle and upper elementary grades, teachers are able to offer a wider array of musical experiences. Children of this age need to have broad experience with a variety of forms and styles of music. They need to have an abundance of listening experiences with the world's finest music, including the classics, multicultural, folk, and composed music. By the end of fifth grade, students should have been exposed to the main periods of music history and be acquainted with composers and repertoire from each period. For these older children's listening experiences, the following are the periods of musical history and composers associated with each period:

- Baroque—Bach, Handel, Corelli
- Classic—Haydn, Mozart, Beethoven
- Romantic—Weber, Schubert, Schumann, Mendelssohn, Chopin, Wagner, Liszt, Brahms, J. Strauss, Tchaikovsky, Moussorgsky, Saint-Saëns, MacDowell, Grieg
- Post-Romantic and Impressionist—R. Strauss, Sibelius, Dukas, Debussy, Ravel, Respighi
- Modern—Stravinsky, Bartók, Kodály, Prokofiev, Hindemith, Villa-Lobos, Copland, Thomson, Menotti, Bernstein
- Light classic—Gershwin, Rodgers and Hammerstein, Gilbert and Sullivan, Irving Berlin
- Jazz and popular—Miles Davis, Marsalis, Basie, the Beatles, Elvis
- Ethnic and folk

The varied treatment that composers have given musical elements has resulted in different styles of music. The labels that are given these styles are also applicable to art and literature. For example, music experiences in the Impressionist music of Debussy can be associated with Impressionist paintings of Mary Cassatt. Art and music can both be enjoyed from the Impressionist style and time in history. The same is true for music of all periods.

Singing is an important classroom activity for children in the middle and upper elementary grades. Opportunities to sing in parts (harmony) or in rounds (like "Row, Row, Row Your Boat") are enjoyable musical experiences for children of this age. They are

---

THIS ONE'S for YOU!

Organize with Music: Songs for Interest Centers

To add a new, interesting feature to your room, try a song for each area in your room to help direct children to an area as well as to provide new ideas for play. First, list the songs you (and the children) are familiar with, then sort them according to the classroom area. For example, have children lay "miles of track" in the block areas to the tune of "I've Been Working on the Railroad." Then have them build boats with blocks to the tune "Row, Row, Row Your Boat."

Next door in the dramatic play area, as the children are "cooking" cakes, they can be encouraged to sing the "Happy Birthday Song." "The Wheels on the Bus" can be acted out with chairs arranged in rows, with a cap for the driver, and even a cardboard steering wheel.

"If You're Ready and You Know It" (a handy version of "If You're Happy and You Know It") can signal time to assemble on the rug for group time. Or start singing a familiar song like "I'm a Little Teapot" at the beginning of cleanup time and see if, after two verses, cleanup time is finished.

Your language arts center probably holds a number of nursery rhymes and storybooks already set to music. Why not use "Jack and Jill" one week, then "Hot Cross Buns" another? These nursery rhyme books will become very popular as children try to match words and pictures to the songs you sing.

Art projects are easy to organize in the art corner to songs like "Frosty the Snowman," which can inspire painting with cotton balls for fun. "Old MacDonald" is a great springboard for animal pictures, murals, designs, etc.

"Jingle Bells" can be a year-round favorite. Sing it complete with bells, triangles, drums, and xylophones. "The Ants Go Marching" is another good tune for active participation as children enjoy marching in time to the music.

Keep a song in your heart in your classroom. Use singing to help organize space and activities. Singing will draw you together at circle time, as well as help foster group cooperation. Try it for variety and fun!

becoming more familiar with vocal ranges, female (soprano, mezzo-soprano, and alto) and male (tenor, baritone, and bass). They are able to sing simple melodies while reading a musical score. They are learning more about musical notation as well. For example, they can begin to recognize and understand what a whole note, half-note, and rest notations mean.

Summary

Music is central to the human experience of both children and adults. Beginning with the rhythmic beat of the mother's heart, a child is exposed to music every day. Music is commonplace in a young child's life. Making up original chants and songs and moving rhythmically to musical beats are quite natural to a young child. Music is a natural avenue for a young child's creative expression. Appropriate musical experiences for young children must take into account the child's developmental level and need for self-expression. Careful planning is essential in providing successful learning experiences for children. Young children can be introduced to the elements of music by spiraling instruction, beginning with basic information and gradually adding information on these elements. For example, the teacher calls it "marching" music instead of duple time. The term "duple time" will be introduced at a later time after the initial learning of "marching" music is fully understood.

You do not have to be able to play an instrument or have a perfect singing voice in order to share music experiences with children. It is helpful to think of it as offering children a musical experience rather than a subject to be taught. In planning musical experiences, the teacher must consider many things. First, the teacher must plan for the developmental level of the group. Next, it is important to include activities from each area of music—singing, rhythm, instruments, movement, listening, and musical concepts such as loud and soft. It is equally important to be flexible and happy when presenting musical activities to children. You must enjoy yourself as much as the children. Using rhythm instruments involves the body in keeping a beat and feeling rhythm, so children are fully participating musically. Rhythm instruments may also be used with songs, and these instruments may be teacher- and child-made.

Children in the middle and upper elementary grades need to have broad experience with a variety of forms and styles of music. They need to have an abundance of listening experiences with the world's finest music, including the classics, multicultural, folk, and composed music. Older children can be introduced to an array of classical music styles, which can be related to art and literature of the same period. Children of this age group also enjoy singing songs of varied styles and forms.

Key Terms

acceptance in teaching music 399
appropriate music activities 399
combination of phrase-wise and whole-song method 403
flexibility in teaching music 399
music elements: rhythm, beat, accent, tempo, syncopation, melody, pitch, timbre, dynamics, texture, harmony, form, ostinato 402
phrase-wise method 403
spiral teaching 403
rhythm instruments 407
varying the rhythm of the music program 405
whole-song method 403

Learning Activities

A. Form a group of three or four children from your program, neighborhood, or local school. Spend at least 15 minutes with them singing songs they know and new ones you teach them. Following this session, write an anecdotal record for each child commenting on (a) participation in singing, (b) attitude, and (c) knowledge of songs. Compare and contrast the children and comment on the likenesses and differences you found in each anecdotal record.

B. Select from additional sources in the Online Companion an appropriate song for each of the following groups of children: four-year-olds, six-year-olds, and two-year-olds. Justify each choice using the criteria provided in this chapter. Do the same activity with a group of children in grades 4 to 5.

C. From your own childhood, recall several popular singing games and action songs that you have not found in this chapter. Tape each song along with clear directions on how to play the game or move to the song. Share the activities with your classmates.

D. Choose one of your own favorite songs (popular, rock, country). Teach it to your fellow classmates, using one of the methods discussed. Discuss your experience, including the following points: How well did your "class" learn by the method you chose? Did you feel comfortable using this method? Discuss how you would feel teaching a song you didn't especially like. Would it make any difference in your effectiveness?

E. Using a box of animal crackers and one of the suggested rhythm instruments (preferably a drum) or a hand-clapping accompaniment by your classmates, try the following creative/interpretive movement to rhythm activity.

1. Take out one animal cracker and note what animal it is.
2. "Become" that animal, acting it out by walking, hopping, sliding, etc.
3. Have one (or several) of your classmates pick up your rhythm and beat or clap, accompanying your movement.
4. See who can guess what animal you are. Whoever guesses correctly gets the next opportunity to "become" an animal.

F. Using a concept song like "Round the Mulberry Bush" (describing a daily routine), make up several verses and accompanying motions. Share your song and actions with your classmates for comments and improvements. Tape your song to use later with a group of young children. Examples of other concept songs: "Old MacDonald Had a Farm," "If You're Happy and You Know It," and "The Wheels on the Bus."

G. Make a drum (tin coffee can with plastic lid, empty oatmeal carton with lid) for the following rhythm activity.

1. Beat a rhythm on the drum for walking, running, skipping, and hopping movements.
2. Beat out a pattern of rhythm and have your peers repeat it by clapping hands (or by using their own handmade drums).
3. Imitate a pattern clapped (or made on a drum) by one of your peers in the class.

4. Sing a song (your own creation, if you like) to accompany a rhythm you make on your drum.

H. Begin a card file of songs for young children. Use your school library to locate songbooks for young children and choose at least two songs for each of the following categories.

Category	Sample Songs
Emotions	"If You're Happy and You Know It"
Actions	"Here We Go Looby Loo"
Birthdays	
Concepts	

I. Obtain a music supply catalog. Choose $150.00 worth of teaching materials. Explain why you chose each item, for what age group, and how you plan to use it.

J. Make a set of simple rhythm instruments as suggested in Appendix E. Use these instruments in a demonstration lesson on rhythm for your classmates.

K. Choose one of the composers from a particular period of music mentioned in this chapter. Obtain a CD or tape of one of the pieces referred to in this chapter. Make a lesson plan for grade 3, grade 4, or grade 5 using this piece of music. Relate the music to art and language arts activities of the same period. Share your plan with your fellow students.

L. Broadway musicals use lyrics and music to tell stories. Learn more about memorable musicals by accessing the Broadway website at http://www.pbs.org/wnet/broadway. Present to the class some of the more interesting stories you discovered in this website. Explain how you could use this information and/or website in your teaching.

M. Think of a familiar song. Take a few minutes to brainstorm all you could teach with just that one song. Write a lesson plan that uses the song in at least two curricular areas.

N. Divide a sheet of paper into two columns. List all the styles of music you can think of on one side and composers you know on the other. Take five more minutes and talk with another person to expand the list. Discuss how you both came to know the styles and composers listed.

Activities Using Music Elements

Rhythm.

Rainstorm. Sit in a circle with eyes closed. A leader begins by rubbing hand palms together. Person to the right picks it up until the whole group is participating. Then the leader switches to hand claps and that moves around the circle. Next is thigh slaps, then foot stomps, with periodical "claps" of lightning. Reverse the order to show the storm dying out.

Rhythms Circle. Stand in a circle with one person as IT. IT creates any rhythmic phrase desired and it is passed around the circle to the right until it returns to IT. The person to IT's right then becomes IT. The rhythmic phrase may be clapped, sung, or done in any way that IT chooses to use.

Follow the Leader Rhythms. Use rhythm instruments, homemade or purchased (sticks, tambourines, drums, cymbals). One child is the leader and plays different rhythms. Everyone echoes the rhythm on their instruments.

Ostinato

Repeat a Beat. Make a sound and repeat it a number of times: tap the floor, click your fingers, slap your leg, or repeat a syllable (dum dum dum). Tell children to listen carefully and to count how many times they hear the sound. Then they repeat the sound exactly. Let the children take turns making a sound while others count and repeat the patterns.

Texture

Voices Thick and Thin. Use poems or stories and assign different numbers of children to participate in solo and choral readings or parts. Ask the children how it sounds when more people are reading compared to fewer. This should produce "thicker"- and "thinner"-sounding stories. Repeat the activity using singing voices. Relate to using individual versus multiple instruments by playing recordings of the same song or music done by an orchestra and an individual instrument.

Timbre

Guess Who? In a group, tell children to close their eyes and someone will be tapped on the shoulder. Whoever is tapped says a word, like "hello." The others guess who spoke. Each time a correct response is given, ask "How did you know who spoke?" The answer will be related to the uniqueness of the person's voice. Repeat the activity. In a follow-up session, play the game again, but have the children sing "hello." Stress how each person's speaking voice is unique and so is the singing voice.

Dynamics

Dialing Dynamics. Dynamics has to do with volume. Make a volume dial out of cardboard or use an old clock. Label "soft" to "loud" on the dial with the musical symbols *pp* (very soft), *p* (soft), *f* (loud), *ff* (very loud), *mfz* (loudest). Have children sing a familiar song or talk as someone turns the dial or volume button. The children should sing or speak according to what the dial reads. For example, if the dial says "pp," children sing or talk very, very softly. Variation: Teach hand signals to show dynamics, such as a hand up high for loud, and a hand down much lower to show a softer sound.

Songs for Children

Note: These verses may be used alone or to a steady march tempo as accompaniment, such as "Turkey in the Straw." The value of these verses is in identification of body parts, counting, and creative activity.

Clap Your Hands

Clap your hands, count one, two, three;
Pull your ear, and slap your knee;
Stamp your feet, one, two, three, four;
Wiggle your fingers and touch the floor.
Raise your hands up to the skies;
Touch your nose, then touch your eyes;
Stamp your feet, one, two, three, four;
Wiggle your fingers and touch the floor.
Elbows out, now be a bird;
Touch your mouth without a word;
Softly clap and stamp your feet;
Tiptoe quietly and take your seat.

The Ants Go Marching One by One

The ants go marching one by one
Hurrah! Hurrah! (Repeat)
When the ants go marching one by one
The little one stops to suck his thumb
And they all go marching down to earth
—to get out of the rain—
Boom, boom, boom, boom, boom, boom, boom, boom!
The ants go marching two by two
Hurrah! Hurrah! (Repeat)
When the ants go marching two by two
The little one stops to tie his shoe
And they all go marching down to earth
—to get out of the rain—
Boom, boom, boom, boom, boom, boom, boom, boom!
The ants go marching three by three
Hurrah! Hurrah! (Repeat)
When the ants go marching three by three
The little one stops to climb a tree
And they all go marching down to earth
—to get out of the rain—
Boom, boom, boom, boom, boom, boom, boom, boom!
Verses:
The ants go marching four by four
The little one stops to shut the door.
The ants go marching five by five
The little one stops to kick a hive.
The ants go marching six by six
The little one stops to pick up some sticks.
Eight by eight—shut the gate.
Nine by nine—pick up a dime.
Ten by ten—shout THE END.

If You're Happy and You Know It

If you're happy and you know it
Clap your hands (Clap, clap). (Repeat)
If you're happy and you know it
Then your face will surely show it.
If you're happy and you know it
Clap your hands (Clap, clap).
If you're angry and you know it
Stamp your feet (Stamp, stamp). (Repeat)
If you're angry and you know it
Your face will surely show it.
If you're angry and you know it
Stamp your feet (Stamp, stamp).

If you're sad and you know it
Shed a tear (Sniff, sniff). (Repeat)
If you're sad and you know it
Your face will surely show it.
If you're sad and you know it
Shed a tear (Sniff, sniff).

If you're weary and you know it
Heave a sigh (Whee-you).
(Repeat refrains)
If you're joyous and you know it
Click your heels (Click, click).
(Repeat refrains)

Activities for Children

Musical Listening Activities

The following activities help young children sharpen their musical listening skills. They are most successful when used as fun "musical challenges" for young children and not as rote exercises. Space them throughout your daily and weekly activity planning, not just in the music portion of your curriculum. The auditory and listening skills they develop are used in all curriculum areas.

A. *Listening for specific sounds and being able to tell what they are* (auditory discrimination).

1. Have a child play a musical instrument such as a bell, tambourine, drum, triangle, or wood block. Another child closes his or her eyes and identifies the object played.
2. A variation of the same game is to have two sounds played with both being identified. The number can gradually be increased to see how many can be identified at once.
3. A child can go to the piano or some other instrument and hit a high or low note. Children can show with their hands, arms, or body whether the note is high or low.
4. Identifying the sound of a bell, drum, or some other musical instrument from a specific position in the room. Children close their eyes and identify where the sound came from. They might also identify the instrument and tell whether the tone was loud or soft.
5. Children identify instruments by comparing two different tones, such as large and small horns, large and small bells, wood blocks, and play blocks.

B. *Listening for sounds of nature.* The children close their eyes and listen for the rain, leaves rustling, the wind, birds, hail, snow, etc.

C. *Listening for school sounds.* Children walking, people laughing, bells ringing, etc.

D. *Listening for outdoor sounds.* Whistles, trucks, cars, train, airplane, etc. Encourage children to use descriptive words for the sounds, such as, "It is like a *bang*" (*buzz, knock, crash*).

Musical Imaginations

Ask children to think of a small animal and a large animal. Divide the class into two groups. Have one group be the small animals and the other the large animals. When you play music with high notes, have the small animals move and dance. When you play low notes, have the large animal group move and dance.

Sharing Prerecorded Music

Try using the Suzuki method when introducing children to a musical classic such as "Peter and the Wolf." Before actually introducing the classic, play the piece as background music for several weeks, during center time, for example. Then, when you tell the story of Peter and the Wolf, children already will have learned to distinguish the various melodies in the piece and will be able to anticipate what comes next. Follow up with another few weeks of just listening to the piece. Using the Suzuki method, children will never forget the music they learned.

Instrument Identification Game

Set up the music center with two chairs and tables separated by a divider. On one side of the divider, place several rhythm instruments on the table. On the other side, place pictures of the instruments. As the child on one side plays an instrument, the child on the other side holds up the picture of the identified instrument.

Listening Book

Play a piece of music with no singing. Let children draw pictures and dictate a story to go with the music. Repeat the activity several times and keep adding to the listening book.

The Blue Danube Waltz

Swinging and rocking are favorite movements of young children, and Strauss waltzes possess a compelling feeling of movement that even adults find hard to resist. Not only do children enjoy swinging their own bodies to Strauss waltzes, but they also enjoy swinging with a doll or favorite stuffed animal or puppet. Very young children may not be able to swing their arms in parallel motion because of an inability to cross the midline of the body. Thus, the teacher may need to model symmetrical arm movements. By three years of age, some children will be able to swing arms in parallel action.

Animals/Insects

Use the following classical musical selections for creative movements in acting out animals or insects. You may want to introduce the piece by giving its name and briefly discussing how this animal or insect would move.

- Griffes—"The White Peacock"
- Liadov—"Dance of the Mosquito"
- Rimsky-Korsakoff—"Flight of the Bumblebee"
- Saint-Saëns—"The Swan" from *Carnival of the Animals*
- Bizet—"Leap Frog" from *Children's Games*
- Debussy—"Golliwog's Cakewalk" from *The Children's Corner Suite*

Sesame Street

This classic children's television program is well known for great songs. Visit the website for young students to hear and sing along with Grover, Cookie Monster, and more at http://pbskids.org/music/index.html. Children may also enjoy singing along with Barney at his website http://www.pbskids.org/barney/children/music/index.html. Listen to "The Wheels on The Bus Go Round and Round," "If I Lived Under the Sea," and more!

Mr. Rogers's website

Young children love to make music. Visit Mister Rogers's website to download instructions on making a drum and other instruments for young children: http://pbskids.org/rogers/

"Twinkle, Twinkle, Little Star"—Singing and Language Skills

One of the most enjoyable ways to develop language skills in young children is to invite them to write songs with you. Take a familiar tune, add an inviting topic (such as the children themselves), mix your own words into the tune, and sing! In the process, you are encouraging young children to use descriptive vocabulary and creative thinking skills. As you sing songs about each other, you are encouraging children to appreciate each other's similarities and differences.

Start this process by helping children create songs and cheers about one another. Use the tune for "Twinkle, Twinkle, Little Star" to create a song or cheer to celebrate the unique qualities of each child. Fill in the blanks in the song with each child's name, features, or favorite things.

My Own Cheer (Tune: "Twinkle, Twinkle, Little Star")

(Child's name), (Child's name),
she's so neat!
She loves (favorite food)
when she eats.
Her hair is (hair color)
and (hair style or length) too.
She's my friend
and so are YOU!
(Child's name), (Child's name),
she's so neat!
We always smile when we meet!

This Is What I Learned to Do (Tune: "Twinkle, Twinkle, Little Star")

Try this group song/game to celebrate the special skills children have learned from family members.

This Is What I've Learned to Do
This is what I've learned to do.
(Have child pantomime skill)
See if you can do it, too.
This is what I've learned to do.
Now I pass it on to you!
This is what I've learned to do.
See if you can do it, too!

Multicultural Greeting—"Good Morning to You!" (Tune: "La Cucaracha")

Add a multicultural flavor to your group-time greeting songs. Try singing them to the tunes of different styles of music. You can start this song with the tune of "La Cucaracha" and then try it to the tune of "When the Saints Go Marching In."

Good Morning to You
Good morning to you, good morning to you.
Let's all give a great big smile.
Good morning to you,
Good morning to you,
We can sit and stay awhile, cha-cha-cha.
Personalize the song by adding each child's name to the second verse: "Let's give Cameron a big smile."

Activities for Older Children (Grades 4–5)

Sing a Picture

Display a landscape, seascape, or cityscape and ask students to brainstorm all the sounds associated with different parts of the picture. Encourage them to think creatively about what "might be." Come to an agreement on a sound for five or six parts of the picture and then discuss the pitch, dynamics (areas that are louder or softer), and how many times the sound should be repeated. Point to each area and have students make the sounds, holding them or repeating them, as decided. Next, try harmonizing sounds or doing the sounds of the picture in round form.

Variation: Use prints with several people in them and break students into groups to find songs or create songs their characters would sing. Come back together and have each group present the songs of their characters.

Finding Musical Elements in Art

Have students find musical elements in a piece of art. For example, students can compare folk art and folk music. They might also find rhythm in art, texture, tempo, style aspects, and dynamics (areas that are louder or softer).

Media Show and Sound Compositions

Have students prepare a sound and art presentation centering around a chosen topic—for example, friends, animals, feelings, weather, culture, or country. They might work in groups or pairs to find a piece of music to play as they present art on transparencies or on an easel as the song is played. Art could be student-made or "found." This also could be done as a computer slide show.

Bilingual Music

- Ask students of various cultural backgrounds to bring in CDs of their music heritage. Spend a few minutes each day listening to salsa music, steel drums, and Irish dances. Ask students: "Why do you think different cultures make different kinds of music? Can music be characterized in any way?" Connect this to your study of various countries of the world and/or to current events.
- Ask students to think of a song that's meaningful to them and have them write a paragraph explaining why. When appropriate, have students bring in their music selection and play it for the rest of the class.

Creative Percussion

At http://www.stomponline.com, your students can learn more about the creative percussion displayed in the *Stomp* stage show. Explore how everyday objects can be turned into instruments. Have students invent and name a new instrument.

Music History

Have students research the different musical styles that were popular when their parents and grandparents were growing up. Assign groups of students to a particular era and have them create a CD with representative music from their assigned era.

Technology and Music

The way we listen to music has reflected the rise of technology. Discuss with students how they listen to music today (online, on cable television, on satellite radio, on CD or MP3, and iPod players). Compare these with AM radio, tapes, vinyl records, and even wax cylinders! What did people do for music before any of those inventions came to be?

Virtual Music Tour

Create a virtual world tour of some of the great music halls and concert spaces, including spots like Lincoln Center (http://www.lincolncenter.org), the Sydney Opera House (http://www.sydneyoperahouse.com), and others. Collect images and create a brochure describing your virtual trip.

Music and Math

Have your students explore math in music. Students can create musical patterns at http://www.pbskids.org/cyberchase/games/patterns/patterns.html

Illustrate a Song

Have each child choose a favorite song to illustrate, or the whole class can do the same song to find all the ways one song could be interpreted. Students might create a group mural of a song, or songs can be cut apart, line by line, with children working on illustrating their part. By assembling all the art, the entire song is then depicted (e.g., "Home on the Range" will work nicely).

Musical Mural

While teachers frequently provide background music during art activities, rarely do children have the chance to demonstrate their musical imaginations in a complete and satisfying way. Rather than treating the music as "wallpaper music" (i.e., present but not really a point of focus), this mural activity invites children to give shape to their thoughts and feelings associated with a piece of music. Whether they have visions of sugarplums or rap jive movements dancing in their heads, the teacher's task is to guide children in developing their imagery into a story told through a mural.

Begin with a musical selection that is programmatic and concrete, such as *Peter and the Wolf.* After discussing major episodes, assign children to particular scenes of the story to illustrate on panels of the mural. Let children flesh out details of the story through visual elements (colors, shape, perspective, and line). Draw their attention to musical aspects that help tell the story (volume, speed, instrumentation).

Next, children can progress to more abstract listening exercises connected to various content areas. The class, for example, could be divided into groups with each group painting a picture based on *Pinocchio, Pocahontas, Sleeping Beauty,* or *The Nutcracker Suite* (language arts), or using other pieces of music such as *La Mer* (science), *The Blue Danube* (science), or *The Moldau* (social studies). Children can create the mural prior to learning the title and/or story of the music.

This exercise encourages active listening. Ask children what story they hear in the music. Do they all hear similar stories? How does the story they have envisioned match the actual title of the piece? What do they think the composer had in mind? These are only some of the questions that can be used to help children compare/contrast while integrating concepts from several content areas.

Art History/Aesthetic Awareness

Gather several musical selections from composers of the Impressionist era listed in this chapter. Choose one or two to play for your class. Explain that the music is from a period called "Impressionism" and that this was a movement in art as well. Obtain and display art prints of Impressionist painters such as Monet and Cassatt. Briefly discuss Impressionism in art: Impressionism developed in France during the 1860s. The artists who worked in this style wished to portray the qualities of light and color at a particular time of day. They usually took their paints outdoors so they could see and study colors. The unusually light and bright colors in Impressionist paintings shocked many critics of the 1860s. Impressionist painters rarely used black or gray. For shadows they preferred deep violets, blues, and the like. They also preferred to use patches or dot-like areas of color rather than strong outlines. They wanted the eye to "blend" colors, and developed a technique whereby they placed small dots of color next to each other, allowing the eye of the viewer to "blend" them together.

Students may want to paint in a manner to that of the Impressionists to experiment with this technique. Of course, painting outdoors is the best way to experience this style!

Music in Art

An easy way to connect music to art is to deal directly with both. Children do this when they listen to music and make pictures of what they hear or when they look at art and make music of what they see.

Many musicians have been inspired by art. Stephen Sondheim based an entire musical—*Sunday in the Park with George* (1984)—on a single painting, Georges Seurat's *Sunday Afternoon of the Island of La Grande Jatte* (1884).

Use the following works of art to help elementary children "hear" art as music: Goya's *Boy on a Ram,* Lichtenstein's *Brushstroke with Spatter,* and Picasso's *The Old Guitarist.* Of course, you may use any other selections you feel are suitable for your particular group of children. The goal is to have them see, hear, and create music and art in relationship with each other. An art museum is undoubtedly the best source for visual images, but good-quality reproductions of original art (available at art stores, museum shops, or on the Internet) can serve as effective substitutes.

Begin by leading children in an exploration of sound and movement. Ask them: "How many ways can you move your hands? How many different sounds can you make with them? What kinds of sounds can you make with your mouth and voice? What sounds can you make with the classroom percussion instruments?"

These questions—and others like them—will establish a working repertoire and create a comfortable atmosphere for experimentation. Have children describe the sounds in as much detail as they can. Let them tell you whether the sounds are loud, soft, long, short, high, low, smooth, rough, and so on. Invite them to elaborate on the things that they are reminded of by these sounds.

Such activities will invite children to interpret the sound of the trotting ram in Goya's *Boy on a Ram.* They will "hear" the tinkle of the ram's bell and the snap of the boy's riding crop. In Lichtenstein's *Brushstroke with Spatter,* they will "hear" the bold splash and strokes superimposed over the regular precise dots. In Picasso's *The Old Guitarist,* they will "hear" the mellow sounds from the old guitar.

Encourage children to note size, shape, line, texture, color, repetition, emphasis, and contrast in the art prints. Suggest ways of interpreting all of these elements as sounds. They may propose playing the dots in Lichtenstein's piece in a regular rhythm on a woodblock throughout the entire composition. They may decide to play the splatter by striking and shaking a tambourine and the brushstrokes by stroking a guitar.

Another activity. Have students look at one of the works of art mentioned previously or other prints you have available. Ask them what they see. If they name things that can move or are depicted in motion, let them show the movement(s) with their hands. If they name things that make sounds, let them try to produce these sound(s) with their hands, mouths, voices, or an instrument. Repeat this procedure for all the things they see.

Once children have finished the process of interpreting everything in art as sound, say to them, "Let's play this work of art." Find out which parts they think they should play alone, as solos, and which parts they want to play together, in chorus. Ask them in what order they think they should play the parts. Act as the composer/conductor for the first performance; then allow a series of students to take that role. Let the composer/conductor choose from the proposed sounds the ones he or she wants to use to represent each visual element. Allow him or her to conduct the piece more than once, if necessary, in order to achieve the effects he or she desires.

Chapter Review

1. Think about your own music experiences as a young child. How alike or different are they from the ones described in this chapter? Identify and discuss what you consider to be the greatest differences between what you experienced and what you plan to do in your own classroom situation.

2. Compare and contrast how preschool and elementary students approach music. How early do children become involved in musical experiences? Who initiates these activities?

3. Review the basic elements of music. Choose at least three elements and plan two music activities, one for preschool children and one for 5th graders, incorporating these elements.

4. You are asked by your principal to develop criteria for the Best Music Teacher Award at your school. List in your criteria for this award the most important teacher characteristics. List all the characteristics you feel are necessary for both preschool and elementary music teaching.

5. During your initial parent orientation meeting, the parent of one of the children in your group (who is an accomplished pianist) asks you who will teach her child music. She assumes that it will **not** be you as there is no piano in your room. How will you answer her? Include answers to the following questions in your reply: Is it necessary to accompany the singing of young children? If you can't play the piano, how would you conduct a singing activity with young children?

6. You have many different cultures represented in your group of children. How would you introduce a new song to these children? Use an example of a specific song. How could you include the families of these children in your music experiences? Give specific examples in your reply.

7. What advice would you give a teacher who is afraid to teach music because she can't play an instrument and doesn't know anything about musical notation, theory, etc.? Be specific in your reply, giving suggested activities.

8. Casper always bounces up and down to the beat instead of clapping the rhythm as directed. How would you handle this situation? Would you consider addressing it at all? Use the information in this chapter to back up your answer.

References

Debnam, B. (2008, March 10). How did music begin? *The News and Observer.*

Erickson, F. (1963). *Childhood and society.* New York, NY: W.W. Norton.

Garner, A. M. (2009). Singing and moving: Teaching strategies for audiation in children. *Music Educator Journal*, 95(4), 46–50.

Humpal, M. E., & Wolf, J. (2003, March). Music in the inclusive environment. *Young Children, 58*(3) 103–107.

MENC (National Association for Music Education). (1995). *Pre-kindergarten music standards.* Reston, VA: MENC.

Morrison, C. D. (2009). Music listening as music making. *Journal of Aesthetic Education, 43*(1), 77–91.

Neely, L., Kenney, S., & Wolf, J. (2000). *Start the music strategies.* Reston, VA: MENC.

Nemours Foundation. (2008). Music and your school-age child. http://www.education.com/reference/article/Ref_Music_Your_School/?page=4

Piper, W. (2002). *The little engine that could.* Uhrichsville, OH: Barbour.

Rauscher, F., & Shaw, G. (2007). Music training causes long-term enhancement of preschool children's spatial-temporal reasoning. *Neurological Research, 20*(2), 14–16.

Wadsworth, B. (1979). *Piaget's theory of cognitive development.* (2nd ed.). New York, NY: Longman.

Additional Readings

Aldredge-Clanton, J. (2009). *Sing and dance and play with joy!* Self-Published: Author.

Balkin, A. (2009). *Tune up to literacy.* Chicago, IL: ALA Editions.

Campbell, D. (2009). *Mozart effect for children: Awakening your child's mind, health and creativity with music.* New York, NY: HarperCollins.

Campbell, P. S. (2008). *Tunes and grooves for music education: Music for classroom use.* Upper Saddle River, NJ: Prentice Hall.

Drake, J., & Milhaud, D. (2009). *Let's have some music.* Paris, France: Editions Durand.

Harris, M. (2009). *Music and the young mind: Enhancing brain development and engaging learning.* Thousand Oaks, CA: MENC.

Kerchner, J. L. (2009). *Musical experiences in our lives: Things we learn and meanings we make.* Thousand Oaks, CA: MENC.

Kerstetter, K. (2009). Educational applications of podcasting in the music classroom. *Music Educator Journal, 95*(4), 23–26.

Marsh, K. (2009). *Musical playground: Global tradition and change in children's songs and games.* London, UK: Oxford University Press.

Mills, J. (2009). *Music in primary school.* London, UK: Oxford Press.

Nolan, K. K. (2009). *Musi-matics! Music and arts integrated math enrichment lessons.* Thousand Oaks, CA: MENC.

Peters, G. D. (2009). Music software and young children: Fun and focused instruction. *General Music Today, 22*(2), 37–40.

Reimer, B. (2009). *Seeking the significance of music education: Essays and reflections.* Thousand Oaks, CA: MENC.

Sarrazin, N. (2009). *Indian music for the classroom.* Thousand Oaks, CA: MENC.

Sobol, E. S. (2009). *An attitude and approach to teaching music to special learners.* Thousand Oaks, CA: MENC.

Woolum, K. (2009). *The effects of music in the early childhood classroom.* Saarbrucken, Germany: VDM Verlag.

Young, S. (2008). Collaboration between 3- and 4-year-olds in self-initiated play on instruments. *International Journal of Educational Research, 47*(1), 3–10.

Software for Children

Alice in Vivaldi's Four Seasons: The Music Game, ages 5 and up

Beat Drop, ages 6 and up

BIT.Trip Core, ages 6 and up

Comfy Joy of Music, ages 2–5

Didi and Diddo 1st Grade: The Wolf King, ages 5–6

Dolphin Don's Music School, ages 6 and up

Giggles: Computer Funtime for Baby, ages 0–2

Let's Tap! ages 5 and up

Magic Flute/Mozart's The Music Game, ages 4 and up

Making More Music: Create! Play! Experience! ages 8 and up

Lowey Hija and Friends, ages 2–6

Move it 2! Expressive Movement with Classical Music, ages 3–5

Morton Subotnick's Playing Music, ages 4 and up

Mozart's Musical Adventure, ages 6 and up

Music Mix Studio, ages 8 and up

My Piano: The Fun Way to Learn, ages 6 and up

Play Music Together, ages 3 and up

Rainbow Fish and the BIG Ocean Party, ages 3–7

Rockin' Pretty, ages 6 and up

Sesame Street Music Maker, ages 3 and up

Tchaikovsky's Nutcracker: The Music Game, ages 4 and up

Treasure World, ages 7 and up

Helpful Websites

Africa Focus: Sights and Sounds of a Continent, http://digicoll.library.wisc.edu/AfricaFocus/About.html
This collection from the University of Wisconsin contains more than 300 slides, 500 photos, and 50 hours of sounds from 45 different countries.

Bus Songs, http://bussongs.com/
This site has lyrics and words for children's nursery rhymes and songs, including videos and music for more than 2,000 children's songs and nursery rhymes.

Classical Music Pages, http://w3.rz-berlin.mpg.de/cmp
This site includes a short history of music, composer biographies, explanations of different musical forms, and a music dictionary, as well as links to other classical music information.

Compose a Tune! http://www.creatingmusic.com
Creating Music is a place where kids can compose music, experiment with tempo, or play with a musical sketchpad. There are games and puzzles, too.

Dallas Symphony Orchestra Kids, http://dsokids.com
This site contains a variety of resources for teachers, including lesson plans and interactive music education for kids.

KI Diddles, http://www.kididdles.com
Site contains words to 2,000 of the most popular children's songs organized alphabetically and by subject.

Listen to a Tuba! http://www.sfskids.org
What better place to learn about music than the San Francisco Symphony? At the SFS site, kids can learn about all the instruments of the orchestra and they can make their own synthesized music in the music lab.

Listen to World Music, http:// www.folkways.si.edu
From Native American ceremonial drums to Chinese folk songs, you can download and listen to traditional music from around the world on this Smithsonian site.

Listen to Your Buds, http://www.listentoyourbuds. org http://www.listentoyourbuds.org
This site highlights the dangers of listening to music (MP3 players or other devices) too loudly, with interactive links to students, parents and teachers, songs, videos and much more.

MENC, http://www.menc.org
This site contains a multitude of teacher resources as well as musical games students may enjoy.

Name that Tune! http://kids.niehs.nih.gov/ music.htm
Click on "Kids'" pages. Are you a sing-along or karaoke fan? This website has the music and lyrics to hundreds of kids' songs, and there is also a fun "Name That Tune" game.

PBS Jazz, http://www.pbs.org/jazz/kids/

Songs for Teaching, http://www.songsforteaching. com
Site offers thousands of children's songs, lyrics, sound clips, and teaching suggestions.

Song Lyrics for Teaching ESL, http://www. songsforteching.com/esleflesol.htm
This site offers words and audio clips from songs helpful in teaching ESL students. Categories include teaching conversational skills, teaching grammar, and teaching children through songs.

The Rock & Roll Hall of Fame for Teachers, http:// www.rockhall.com/
Click on "Enter," then on "Programs."

For additional creative activity resources, visit our website at www.Cengage.com/login.

Creative Language Experiences

The following scene demonstrates the power of a young child's language, both verbal and nonverbal. It also demonstrates very clearly the fact that adults often assume they know exactly what young children are saying and respond to them on this basis. Yet, communicating can be a more complicated process than this, as the scene should emphasize.

On a warm, sunny, fall afternoon, the store was filled with shoppers, many browsing the racks of women's sale-priced clothes. Among them were a grandmother and her daughter, who pushed a pretty toddler along in a stroller. The child wore a large patch over her right eye. Soon she filled the air with pleading cries, "Off, off!"

Her mother simply responded, "The doctor said you have to wear the patch, honey. We can't take it off."

When the child continued to cry "Off, off!" in a plaintive voice, the grandmother took a more direct approach, saying, "Now, I'll have no more of that. You can't take the patch off."

The little girl looked at her grandmother, then resumed her cries, "Off, off!" But this time, when she received no response from her cries, she tugged on the arm of her coat, saying, "Off, off!" She wanted her coat off, not her eye patch!

OBJECTIVES

After studying this chapter, you should be able to:

1. Discuss speaking and listening skills in young children.

2. Define the term "emerging literacy" and its various skills.

3. Explain how to choose and use children's books for teaching young children.

4. List some guidelines to follow when reading to young children.

5. Discuss the importance of poetry for young children's language development.

6. Discuss the needs of bilingual/bicultural young children.

7. Discuss the antibias curriculum.

Development of Language

Two points can be made from this scene: (1) We can never underestimate the ability of a young child to get her or his message across, and (2) we should never overestimate our understanding of a young child's message. In this chapter we will explore these points and many other facets of language development.

Language is part of a child's total development. As with physical growth, there is a definite developmental pattern to a child's use of language. There are four distinct skills involved in the development of language: speaking, listening (in the sense of comprehending or understanding speech), writing, and reading. Each of these, in turn, has its own pattern of development.

Ability in one language skill is not always directly related to competence in another. For example, many young children—like their adult counterparts—are far better speakers than listeners!

In the early childhood program, language experiences must take into consideration the developmental levels of children in each of these four distinct parts of language development. Emphasis in preschool programs, however, is not on teaching writing and reading. Developing skills that are related to reading and writing helps prepare a child for more formal instruction in these skills in later years. While this chapter focuses on the development of language skills in the early years, activities and resources are provided for older children where appropriate. The reader is referred to the reading lists in the Online Companion for sources of books on teaching reading to older children. Reading and writing skills will be handled as emerging literacy skills in this chapter. The term *reading readiness* is often used in reference to these skills as well. However, the author prefers the term *emerging literacy* because it encompasses a broader range of prereading skills development.

Development of Speech

Speech is a form of language in which words or sounds are used to convey meanings. The ability to speak is not necessarily related to the ability to understand. For example, infants make many sounds as they practice vocalizing that probably do not mean nearly what eager adults like to read into them. Three-year-old children, as another example, can sing along, not missing a single word of popular songs on the radio,

AGE	ABILITY
9 months and up	Begins to intentionally use words to communicate.
1 year	Imitates sounds. Responds to many words that are a part of experience: "Bye-bye," "Daddy," "Momma."
2 years	Should be able to follow simple commands without visual clues: "Johnny, get your hat." "Farah, bring me your ball." Uses a variety of everyday words heard in home and neighborhood: *Mommy, milk, ball, hat.* Shows developing sentence sense by the way words are put together: "Go bye bye car." "Milk all gone."
3 years	Understands and uses words other than for naming; is able to fit simple verbs, pronouns, prepositions, and adjectives such as *go, me, in,* and *big* more and more into sentences.
4 years	Should be able to give a connected account of some recent experience. Should be able to carry out a sequence of two simple directions: "Bobby, find Susie and tell her dinner's ready."
5 years	Speech should be intelligible, although some sounds may still be mispronounced. Can carry on a conversation if vocabulary is within his or her range.

Adapted from *Learning to Talk,* prepared by the U.S. National Institute of Neurological Disease and Stroke, National Institutes of Health, U.S. Department of Health, Education and Welfare. Washington, DC: U.S. Government Printing Office, 1969, pp. 22–24.

FIGURE 18-1 • Children's development of language ability.

without really knowing what the words mean. Many children can sing the alphabet song and not know what letters really mean.

In the development of speech, there are differences among children in the age at which they begin to learn to speak and the rate with which they achieve competence. The overall developmental sequence with which speech is acquired, however, generally follows the basic sequence presented in Figure 18–1. Similar to the pattern of physical development (see Chapter 9), acquisition of speech develops from general to specific.

At first, the child's speech consists of sounds that are vague and difficult to understand. Yet even in these early stages of life (from birth to 36 months), very young children can communicate quite effectively with a minimum of vocabulary. See Appendix B for a summary of the basic characteristics of these early levels of speech development and some related activities for language development at each level.

Gradually the development of speech progresses to clear and distinct words that carry specific messages, which we call *controlled verbal communication*. Generally, by the age of three years, children are rapidly building their vocabularies. They continue to increase the number of words in their speaking vocabulary for the next few years.

Development of Rules of Speech

As children learn to speak, they begin to put words together in patterns and gradually learn the grammatical rules of their language. They follow a sequence of language development from sounds without meaning to single words to two-word sentences to more complex structures. Jenny moves from saying, "Juice," to saying, "My juice," to saying, "Give Jenny apple juice." Children usually use nouns before pronouns, and *I* and *me* are often the first pronouns used.

Children usually learn the names of objects first and gradually make finer discriminations. They notice likenesses and differences. For Elise, all four-legged animals are dogs. Later she identifies dog, cat, cow, and horse, and further refines her classification to little dog and big dog.

Concepts of time and space are difficult for young children to comprehend. William cannot tell the difference between tomorrow and next week. He knows only that it is not now. After much practice and experience, children begin to recognize shades of meanings and become more precise and facile with language.

Philip talks about his warm blue coat, and Alice knows that hers is bright blue because she has heard her mother describe it that way.

Children draw generalizations about how words come together to form sentences. Then they over generalize, not realizing that there are exceptions to rules. If "I cooked the egg" is a correct grammatical construction, then "I tooked the ball" seems equally correct to Estefan. Instead of saying, "I forgot the picture," Sam is likely to tell his father that he "forgotted" the picture. When Ella says, "I runned down the hill," she demonstrates an advanced stage of language development, using a grammar rule she discovered for herself. Children learn rules about past tense as they become familiar with the language. In a similar manner, they learn the rules about plurals. If the plural of *house* is *houses*, should not the plural of *goose* be *gooses*?

A child hears sounds all around. Adults, other children, radio, and television all provide aural stimulation. As children learn to speak, adults need to accept the language they produce. Whatever the nature of the sounds they make, they should be encouraged to talk and not be restrained by criticism or corrections. If the adults around them speak well, children usually begin to use words correctly, too. A child who has many verbal interactions with adults is likely to develop greater verbal proficiency and confidence in the use of words than one who has not had such experiences.

Literacy

When we teach a child to draw, we teach him how to see. When we teach a child to play a musical instrument, we teach her how to listen. When we teach a child how to dance, we teach him how to move through life with grace. When we teach a child to read or write, we teach her how to think. Jane Alexander, chair for the National Endowment for the Arts

All the information discussed to this point falls under the general term *literacy*. **Literacy** in its most general sense is a mastery of language—speaking, listening, writing, and reading. Literacy learning, as discussed earlier, begins in infancy and continues through life. In helping children develop literacy, we must respect the language the child brings to school and use it as a base for language and literacy activities. To develop literacy, we build on what the child already knows about oral language, reading, and writing. Children's literacy grows when we encourage them to see themselves as people who can enjoy exploring oral and written language.

Enhancing Language Development

A true mastery of language requires social interaction. A classroom in which children are given many opportunities to interact with others is one in which language development is fostered. A teacher can create an environment that fosters language development of young children by creating a child-centered classroom where young children are given many opportunities to pursue their own interests and trusted to know what it is they want and need to learn.

Language experiences during self-initiated play.
When children move freely to activities of their choice in self-initiated play in a child-centered environment, more language is used with greater richness of speech than when children are in teacher-centered classrooms where formal instruction dominates the program. When children discover they can satisfy needs by speaking, they gain confidence in their abilities to speak and begin to value language.

Interaction is an important part of communication. Children speak and listen as they play with clay, play dough, paint, pegs, blocks, sand, and water. If they feel comfortable when they talk, they are more likely to experiment with language. In a housekeeping area, children talk to each other as they re-enact familiar roles. Midday snack arrangements provide natural settings for conversations. Such activities as playing with blocks, pounding and rolling clay, and experimenting with magnets all offer children rich opportunities to speak, listen, and exchange ideas with others.

FIGURE 18-2 • Reading board books with young children is part of the process of developing literacy.

Language experiences in small-group activities.
In small groups, children are more likely to talk to each other and to the teacher and have less anxiety than when they are expected to respond in large groups.

Sharing time in an early childhood program is best when it involves a small group of three to five children. In a large group, it is necessary to limit each child's conversation so that several children have an opportunity to speak, and this limitation tends to discourage children from talking. A group of three to five is a more natural situation for young children.

Formal discussion periods are neither as interesting nor as meaningful as informal conversations in a small group. A child who takes a treasured item out of her or his pocket to share with two or three friends is probably enjoying a very personal experience. But when Show and Tell time is made into a daily ritual in which many children are expected to participate, the personal excitement may disappear for the speaker. The telling supersedes the sharing, and the personal reactions of peers are not part of the experience. When incorporated into a program at an appropriate time, Show and Tell can be valued by all as a sharing experience. When it is a teacher-centered language lesson, its value is likely to be lost. Early childhood classrooms should reflect these and many other opportunities for young children's developing language skills. You may want to use the Observation Sheet titled "Classroom Literacy Environment Survey" in the Online Companion to assist you in your classroom observations.

Understanding Bilingual/Bicultural Young Children's Language Development

Our schools are blessed with an ever-growing multicultural population. This rich cultural mix is an exciting opportunity for children and teachers to learn about other cultures on a daily basis. Unfortunately, many young children from diverse developing nations are entering schools not fully prepared to receive them. The importance of including the needs of children who are bilingual/bicultural in the early childhood language program is obvious in our multicultural world.

The early childhood teacher plays a critical role in the lives of linguistically and culturally diverse young children. It is important to remember that children will not learn literacy skills in a language they do not yet speak. This is why it is so important to support the continuous development of the child's primary language while providing meaningful experiences with English. Consider using some of the following suggestions to help provide meaningful experiences in English to children from diverse language and multicultural backgrounds.

- Bilingual children can participate easily in dance, art, and drama activities that call for nonverbal communication; the arts are universal languages used to communicate when words cannot or when words are inadequate for ideas and feelings.
- Make connections to special cultural holidays, customs, people, and experiences in arts activities. Invite students to share their rich multiethnic backgrounds and use this as a basis for artistic creations. Invite parents as guests to share multicultural art forms.
- Folk literature is a universal literary form, so it is one place to begin to integrate multicultural art. Many plot lines, like that of "Cinderella," have been found in hundreds of cultures and written in dozens of languages. Include stories from students' language and cultural heritages. Encourage students to share cultural stories from home, and use these for drama, dance, art, and music activities.
- Drama, art, dance, or music based on children's literature can be a good vehicle for learning English vocabulary. Familiar songs in a language can be translated into English. Name tags or hats can be made for characters during drama (e.g., tags with *stepsister, mother, father, and prince* in both English and the child's native language).
- Give every child a small recipe box with empty index cards at the start of the year. Keep this "word box" nearby so that new words can be collected and used or referred to for children's writing activities. Make sure that each word is accompanied by a small, simple sketch representing that word.
- Look around your classroom. How many words do you see? A print-rich classroom has meaningful words taped, glued, or written on objects and equipment in each learning center. These words can be written in both English and in the child's native language. To make labels, use any word processor with a large, clear font. Type out a list (in both languages), print it on regular paper, and tape the printed words on objects. Digital cameras are great for adding pictures to these labels.

The early childhood setting becomes a home away from-home, the first contact with nonfamily members,

the first contact with culturally different people, and the first experience with nonnative speakers. A teacher's attitude and knowledge base are crucial in making the early childhood program accepting and appreciative of diversity (DeBruin-Parecki, 2007).

The possibilities are endless for teachers of young children who, as role models, are in a unique position to establish the tone or "classroom climate" through decision making, collaboration, interactions, and activities. It is possible to offer the best teaching we can to all young children who are experiencing English as an unfamiliar language. We can help these young children by following some general guidelines.

- Accept individual differences with regard to language-learning time frames. It's a myth that young children can learn a language quickly and easily. Avoid pressures to "rush" and "push out" children to join the mainstream classroom. Young children need time to acquire, explore, and experience second-language learning.
- Accept children's attempts to communicate, because trial and error are a part of the second-language learning process. Negotiating meaning and collaborating in conversations are important. Children should be given opportunities to practice both native and newly established language skills. Adults should not dominate conversations; rather, children should be listened to. Plan and incorporate opportunities for conversation within dramatic play, story time, puppetry, peer interactions, social experiences, field trips, cooking, and other enriching activities.
- Maintain an additive philosophy by recognizing that children need to acquire new language skills instead of replacing existing linguistic skills. Afford young children an opportunity to retain their native language and culture. Allow young learners ample social opportunities to practice emerging linguistic skills.
- Provide a stimulating, active, diverse linguistic environment with many opportunities for language use in meaningful social interactions. Avoid rigid or didactic grammatical approaches with young children. Children enjoy informal play experiences, dramatizations, puppetry, telephone conversations, participation in children's literature, and social interactions with peers.
- Incorporate culturally responsive experiences for all children. Valuing each child's home culture and incorporating meaningful, active participation will

help children develop interpersonal skills and contribute to eventual academic and social success.

- Use informal observations to guide the planning of activities, interactions, and other conversations for speakers of other languages.
- Provide an accepting classroom climate that values culturally and linguistically diverse young children.

See Figure 18–3 for more suggestions.

The Antibias Curriculum (ABC)

Creative teachers promote an **inclusive environment**, one that addresses both the daily life realities of cultural diversity and the potentially biased attitudes and behaviors that are part of this reality. The early childhood teacher creating an inclusive environment plans the curriculum to address the cultural differences represented by the children in the group

Here are some more strategies you can use to differentiate instruction for second-language learners.

- Start with what children know. Learn key words and sentences in the child's primary language. These words will help children feel connected to the adult, and gives the message that the adult is interested in the children's language.
- Start slowly. Allow time for children to adjust to the new surroundings before approaching them with questions and directions. Use children's names during the activities without actually directing the speech to them.
- Use on-the-spot labeling in meaningful contexts. Identify "teachable moments" to talk about object(s) a child is using or about his/her actions at that particular moment, e.g., "You picked the book" or "Yes, it is blue."
- Double the message. Use words along with plenty of gestures, body language and actions.
- Use repetition. Say the same thing many times. Emphasize the word you want them to learn, "Look at the hand. See how Mario traced his hand. Do you want to trace your hand?"
- Talk about the here and now. Remember, children (and adults) use context to understand the message. "It is cold outside. We put our jackets on to go outside."
- Expand and extend. Once children begin to use new words, add to what they say. "Yes, cookie. Is this a chocolate cookie? May I eat it?"
- Keep it short. Once the adult gets along well with the child, talk to that child for short periods in the second language. The child may not understand at first, but by hearing the second language in a variety of situations, the child will eventually begin to notice, play with, and grasp intonation patterns and sounds.
- Fine-tune your language. Simplify your messages and use short sentences. "I like your shirt." "Is it new?" "Did you get it yesterday?"
- Accept the use of any combination of a child's home language and English. Do not criticize or directly correct a child for code-switching (mixing languages).
- Recognize children's attempts to use English. Provide positive feedback when children try to use English to communicate.
- Focus on what the children are saying. Focus on the child's message rather on how well the child is using the second language. Allow children to talk or not to talk in accordance with their own paces or abilities.
- Focus on one language at a time. Avoid immediate translations. Constant translations may cause children to tune out the second language.
- Be a good language role model. Although it is common for children learning a second language to "mix" two languages in the same sentence, as a language role model, use one language at a time. Talk in ways you want children to talk.
- Use English songs and finger plays to teach simple vocabulary. Songs such as "Head, Shoulder, Knees and Toes" and "The Wheels on the Bus" teach parts of the body, directional movements, and simple nouns.
- Up the ante. Use your judgment and knowledge of the child to decide when to insist the child use verbal communication instead of gestures.

FIGURE 18-3 • Differentiating instruction for second-language learners.

and in the society in general. This inclusive curriculum reflects sensitivity to all cultural groups in all areas of the curriculum. Related inherently to the inclusive environment is the concept of an **antibias curriculum (ABC)**. This concept, developed by the NAEYC's ABC Task Force and Louise Derman-Sparks (Derman-Sparks & ABC Task Force, 1989), is an excellent starting point for planning an inclusive, antibias curriculum. The Task Force's booklet, as well as other references at the end of this chapter, contain excellent suggestions on ABC planning, working with parents, and suggested books and materials—all essential in preparing an inclusive environment for young children of all cultural groups.

The language arts curriculum is an excellent starting point for the ABC because there are hundreds of good-quality books for children representing a multitude of ethnic groups. Teachers of young children need to select literature that reflects the perspectives, experiences, and values of all ethnic and cultural groups. See Chapters 24 and 25 for more information on the ABC.

FIGURE 18-4 • Children's literacy grows when we encourage children to see themselves as people who can enjoy exploring art and written language.

Development of Listening

Just exactly how a child learns to listen to and understand language has been studied by many researchers and language experts. Some argue that language and thought grow somewhat independently, at least in the early stages of language development. This view does make sense when you consider the fact that young children are often able to learn words and phrases that have no meaning for them. (Remember how three-year-olds can sing popular songs yet do not understand the words.)

Listening is not a passive receiving of information. Good listening involves receiving and processing incoming information. Listening is more than simply hearing because good listeners filter out much of what they hear in order to concentrate on a message.

Children are not the only ones who should listen and teachers are not the only ones who should speak. Rather, children and teachers need to be good listeners, and children should listen to one another as carefully as they do to adults.

Good listeners are *active*. They get involved with what they hear, both intellectually and emotionally. Active listeners give complete attention to what they hear. They are active in that they process the information, make pertinent comments, and ask relevant questions.

Young children may act as if they understand concepts at a level that they cannot yet express in words. Because young children think in simple, basic ways, they have difficulty comprehending adult language that is abstract or too complex. Abstraction is beyond the thinking capabilities of the young child in preschool and early elementary years. The teacher or child care worker who is not aware of these language limitations of young children can easily lose their attention. For example, a visiting firefighter who described the fire hose as "a supplementary anti-incendiary device" obviously was unaware of the language level of the audience and more accustomed to addressing adults! In the same manner, a teacher who directs a child pulling another's hair to "be nice" is too general and abstract in her directions. A more appropriate, direct, and less abstract request for a young child would be, "Caleb, don't pull Jane's hair."

Physical conditions affecting the listener (deafness, hunger, fatigue, illness, and physical environment) can impair the listening process or influence the quality of listening.

The environmental climate or atmosphere in the early childhood program should motivate listening.

The atmosphere needs to be one in which children are free to express their ideas; they should feel that their contributions will be accepted and respected.

Emerging Literacy

If *reading* is defined as "the interpretation of symbols," it could be said that a child begins reading the day he or she is born. A baby gets excited when he or she sees his or her bottle. The baby stops crying when Mother enters the room and smiles. The baby gurgles with pleasure when members of the family stop to play with him or her. He or she is responding to what he or she "reads" into the actions of others. These experiences precede understanding the printed word.

Not all children should be expected to learn to read in the same way, at the same rate, or at the same age. Children begin by reading pictures, taking great delight in recognizing objects with which they are familiar. As adults read to children, thereby exposing them to words in the books they read, children begin to understand that printed words say something.

FIGURE 18-5 • Language experience stories can be combined with two-dimensional drawings.

Emergent Reading

Pretend reading of favorite books is an activity familiar to many parents and teachers of young children. During pretend reading—also called *emergent reading* (Sulzby, E. (1985)). Children practice reading-like behaviors that build their confidence in themselves as readers.

Adults interested in emergent or pretend reading have long assumed that children imitate adult reading—that is, they pick up reading-like behaviors and story language after adults read aloud to them. We can see the beginnings of independent emergent reading when children participate in adult read-alouds by "reading along" with an adult reader—mumbling, echoing phrases, and completing sentences and phrases when the adult reader pauses.

During emergent reading, children combine several information sources: the pictures and print in the book; input from adult listeners, as well as their own memory for having heard and discussed the book previously; their personal experiences; and their background knowledge about the world, language, and how stories sound. In emergent literacy programs, children enjoy and participate actively in reading experiences long before they are readers in the conventional sense of the word.

Both participation in read-aloud sessions and emergent reading give children opportunities to learn about the language and the meaning of reading in a natural setting. By giving children opportunities to interact with books through read-alouds and emergent readings, teachers help children grow as competent and confident readers (Dunst, Trivette, & Hamby, 2007).

Conventional reading involves total development—emotional, social, physical, and intellectual readiness. A child who has not yet acquired large-muscle control will not be able to develop more refined skills, such as matching shapes and recognizing patterns needed for reading. Some children are not interested or physically ready to read until they are six, seven, or even eight years of age. When children are forced to engage in reading activities before they are physically, intellectually, or emotionally ready, reading can become a burden. Vision, hearing, diet, and physical coordination are all factors to be considered. Eye-muscle development is necessary and cannot be rushed. Speaking skills are needed for success in reading. And motivation is a primary factor for success.

THINK ABOUT IT — Digital Storytelling

While Web 2.0 was covered in Chapter 8, including the use of many forms of technology in storytelling, here is some additional information on digital storytelling.

Everyone has stories to tell, and digital media offer rich, new ways to capture and share our stories with others. Digital storytelling is the art of using digital content—still images, video clips, voiceovers, sound effects, and music—to create compelling narrative movies. As an expressive medium in the classroom, digital storytelling can be used to integrate subject matter, knowledge, and skills from many areas of the curriculum. Visit the following websites to learn more about digital storytelling and how to teach it in your classroom and to see student examples.

A good place to start learning about digital storytelling is Wikipedia, which provides a brief discussion of the term, its history, and a list of links to other digital storytelling sites.

Apple has a unit plan on its website titled "Digital Storytelling: Tell Me a Story" (ali.apple.com/als/2ndmult/projects/3024.html) that provides an overview on how to transform a story into a digital story; step-by-step instructions on storyboarding, capturing images, compressing the final stories, and posting them to the Web; assessment strategies; and links to other digital storytelling resources. There is also an excellent PDF guide on using Apple's iLife suite of software to create digital stories available on the Apple Learning Interchange site (edcommunity.apple.com/ali/story.php?itemID=9552).

Mechelle De Craene offers practical classroom strategies to enable your students to get the most out of a digital storytelling project in her 2006 article titled "Digital Storytelling: A Practical Classroom Management Strategy" (terry-freedman.org.uk/artman/publish/printer_804.php).

Lastly, check out Adobe's DigKids Club section on digital storytelling (http://www.adobe.com/education/digkids/storytelling), which includes advice on teaching digital storytelling, tips on constructing digital storytelling scripts, classroom strategies, and tutorials on using Adobe products to produce digital stories.

If you are looking for examples to inspire your students take a look at the Hawaii Department of Education's annual Island Movie Contest (islandmovie.k12.hi.us), which includes a wide range of digital stories created by students at all levels. Also visit the iCan short film festival (www.sfett.com) website, which includes stories created by students from San Fernando, California over the past seven years. While on this site, check out Flickschool (flickschool.com) which includes instructional podcasts of a variety of media-related topics. Another site worth seeing is Streetside Stories (www.streedside.org/stories/digital-stories.htm), which features digital stories created by middle school students enrolled in an after school Tech Tales program. (islandmovie.k12.hi.us)

Read-Alouds and Emergent Reading

Children who participate in read-aloud sessions and do their own emergent reading of favorite books grow as readers because they are engaged in authentic, natural literacy, not in instruction-focused tasks that break up reading into separate "skills." Practice in the natural activity of emergent reading is a good preparation for later, conventional reading.

Reading with Infants and Toddlers

The way teachers use stories is as important as the stories themselves. Infants and toddlers come to a story experience with few if any preconceived notions about what that experience *should* be like. This gives the teacher plenty of room to be creative and imaginative. Within that flexibility, there are some factors to keep in mind when reading stories with infants and toddlers in order to make the story experiences we share with them as enjoyable and productive as possible.

- Allow freedom and choice. Participation in story sharing should not be compulsory for very young children. Children should be invited to join in, and if they are interested in participating, they will let you know. Try to share stories with children throughout the day, not only during a fixed period in the schedule. Initiate stories when the situation seems right, and make time when children do the initiating.
- Adjust expectations to fit children's abilities and preferences. Your understanding of child development

should, in principle, inform when you share stories and which stories you select. For example, a hungry child will not usually be interested in a story, even if that story is one of her favorites. A toddler busy pushing his doll in the stroller will probably not want to stop for a story, either. And even if it seems like the optimal time for sharing a story, when distractions seem minimal, toddlers often will wander away if they are not ready for the type of story being shared or if something else captures their attention.

- Keep story groups small and intimate. Since one of the key benefits of sharing stories with infants and toddlers is fostering close relationships among the story participants, it is best to share stories with no more than three children at a time, so everyone can nestle close. Keeping groups small also allows each child to be an active participant. One or even a very few children can join in a story's refrain without being too noisy or disruptive for the other children in the room. Small groups also make it easier to maintain children's interest through eye contact and gentle touches. Larger groups are likely to require the adult to spend more time keeping order than sharing the story, which takes away from the enjoyment.

- Show pleasure and enthusiasm. Your attitude as you share stories is critical if you want these experiences to be successful for infants and toddlers. Very young children are influenced greatly by our behavior, and they are keen observers of what we do and say. If we are enthusiastic, interested, and clearly enjoying the story, children will be more likely to feel these things, too. Pleasure is contagious—and so is boredom.

- Be expressive. Being expressive when sharing a story helps young listeners engage with what they are hearing. Being expressive might mean using a soft voice for a gentle bedtime story, or making your voice loud and growling like a tiger when telling a story about zoo animals. This also entails changing your tone of voice or accent for different characters. Another part of being expressive is using gestures, facial expressions, and body language in ways that support the story. If young children are accustomed to hearing expressive language, they will use it themselves when they begin to tell their own stories.

- Use props. Story sharing can be enriched with the careful use of props or other supplementary resources. However, props are not necessary for every story and can sometimes be distracting. For example, a teacher might introduce a large puppet to tell the story of the Little Red Hen; but if the children are more interested in the puppet than the story, then the prop might not be adding to the story experience itself.

- Follow children's cues. Children give many different cues or signs about how they like the stories we share with them. For the youngest children, those cues are likely to be conveyed through sounds and body language, such as gestures, wriggling, and facial expressions. As infants become toddlers, they can respond more explicitly by saying things such as "Again," "More," and "No," or even by getting up and simply walking away. Whenever possible, repeat a story that children express interest in hearing again. Depending on the length of the story and children's interest level, some story sessions could be quite long, while others will be much shorter. The desire for repetition, which is valuable for building vocabulary and developing language skills, shows that children are engaged. (Birckmayer, Kennedy, & Stonehouse, 2009)

By becoming aware of the benefits of linking emergent reading to read-aloud sessions and by arranging classroom space and time to promote these activities, teachers can maximize the benefits of reading aloud and emergent reading in early childhood classrooms in the following ways.

- Invite children to participate actively in read-aloud sessions. Ask questions that require children to predict what will happen next and to link the story to their own experiences. As books become more familiar to children, pause before familiar or repeated patterns and allow children to complete the reading. Give children opportunities to choose their favorite books to be read to the group.

- Provide frequent opportunities for young children to engage in book handling and emergent reading. Although for many years many classrooms have featured daily book browsing time, there are still too many classrooms in which children look at books only as a transitional or optional activity with books available to children who have finished other "required" activities or who choose to look at books during "free-choice" times. As a result, children who have had less experience with books or who work slowly have little occasion for self-directed interaction with books. Teachers should instead establish daily "serious reading time" when all children are expected to be involved with books in whatever manner is most comfortable for them—browsing through books, looking at pictures, or emergently or conventionally reading.

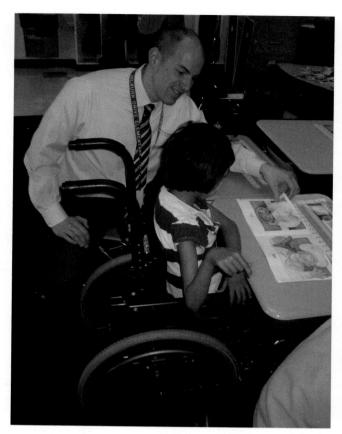

FIGURE 18-6 • A comfortable environment provides young children with a positive read-aloud experience.

FIGURE 18-7 • Provide frequent opportunities for young children to engage in book reading.

- Read favorite books repeatedly to encourage emergent reading. Follow through by making these books available for children to look at on their own or with other children and adults. Children are more likely to choose books and engage in emergent reading with books that are familiar to them. Set up the classroom so that familiar books are available and visible to children during independent time and free time. (More specific information about the language arts center is found later in this chapter.) Arrange for reading aloud to be done in or near the language arts center so that children see the connection between hearing books read and reading them on their own and that books read by the teacher can be easily put in the language arts center. Schedule time for children to independently read or look at books soon after the teacher has read to them, again highlighting the connection between the adult read-aloud and children's independent involvement with books.
- During read-aloud and independent-involvement times, teachers have opportunities to observe children's emerging literacy in real-life situations. Become more aware of how children respond during read-aloud sessions (a tape recorder might be useful). Which of the children asked and answered questions? Which ones participated in reading by chiming in on familiar parts or by making predictions? How do children's questions and comments change over several readings of the same book? What kinds of questions and comments came from you, the teacher?
- By listening to children's emergent readings (live or taped), teachers can see how much book content and book language children incorporate. Do children use the distinctive language of books? Do they use literary formulae such as "once upon a time"? What sources of information do children use when they "read"? Do they use the pictures, the print, memory of the text and discussion, and their personal experiences?
- Educate parents about the ability of their child to "pretend read" books and to participate in reading through "completion reading." Some parents worry that "pretend reading" will result in bad habits that

will prevent children from learning to "really read." Reassure all of these parents that their children's reading-like behaviors, even though they may not involve attention to print, are a source of future reading success. Parents also need to understand that allowing children to participate in read-aloud sessions through joint reading and discussion can enrich the literacy experience for parents and children.

Prewriting Skills

Another skill that is part of a child's emerging literacy is writing. In the preschool and early childhood period, a child is developing the physical skills needed to write later on in school. It is not the goal to have young children "practice" letters and words in the early childhood language arts program. Instead, the goal is to provide young children with opportunities to practice the hand–eye coordination and small-muscle skills needed to be able to write.

For preschoolers, writing is a part of the total language experience, preceded by many fine-motor-control activities. Writing begins when children first become interested in making their own marks, and it continues to be a part of their everyday experiences. When children show an interest in writing, large pieces of paper are made available along with crayons, felt-tip pens, and pencils.

For preschoolers, reading and writing are closely related. Writing can be part of the language experience of children when children dictate stories for the teacher to write down.

Use children's artwork in conjunction with reading and writing. Besides making the obvious use of

FIGURE 18-9 • "Pretend writing" is part of the process of developing literacy.

FIGURE 18-8 • Young children develop writing skills in the early childhood program.

illustrations for stories, early readers can give titles to their work. Asking children if they would like to give their work a title reflects the teacher's valuing their work. Some children may want to give their work a title; others may not. Young children can also use photographs to tell stories that the teacher writes down. Preschool children might bring their baby pictures to school and then be photographed by the teacher. Mount both pictures side by side and then have children dictate descriptions of what they could do as babies and what they can do now that they are "big." Children can share the displayed individual books. A language experience approach such as this encourages literacy. Using cartoon boards and cartoon balloons enhances writing and reading motivation. Children can dictate or write captions in the balloons, stating what different characters in the strips are saying.

Poetry Experiences

Poetry is part of the magic that motivates children to love reading. The educational benefits of including poetry in the early childhood program are many.

FIGURE 18-10 • Encourage older children in their writing skills by using appropriate word-processing software.

Exposure to poetry raises children's level of general language development and vocabulary development and whets their appetite for reading, too!

Some other benefits of including poetry on a regular basis in the early childhood program include the following.

- Poetry's often playful approach to language helps children think about language forms as well as meaning. The predictable rhythms of Mother Goose rhymes naturally segment speech sounds and expose and highlight phonetic similarities and differences in a way that normal speech does not.
- Children take pride in learning to recite short poems. Thus, poetry can be used to stimulate the development of memory, which will aid in future learning. Knowing poems enhances feelings of competence, which is important for young children. Young children who continually hear poetry read effectively and those who have the opportunity to join informally in reciting it will soon have quite a repertoire of memorized poetry without any effort. It is quite appropriate to expect

three-and four-year-old children to happily chant finger plays, Mother Goose rhymes, and short poems such as those found at the end of this unit.

- Fingerplays, or poems recited and accompanied by appropriate body movements, help develop coordination and muscle tone. Asking children to invent their own movements helps them develop problem-solving abilities. Some of these poems also help in learning to name body parts ("Hokey Pokey," for example).
- Acting out poetry can be a fun and beneficial drama and speech activity for children of all ages. By allowing children to organize and act out poems using props and costumes, the teacher encourages the development of creativity and positive self-concept as well as of language.
- Children can be encouraged to illustrate favorite poems to display in the classroom or to take home, thus stimulating artistic expression and development while aiding language development. Using colored chalks, paint, markers, and crayons, many young artists will illustrate the mood of the poem more movingly than we ever could have imagined!
- Smooth, natural transitions from one activity to another can be made through the use of carefully selected poems. The following poem, for example, is a perfect choice when the teacher wishes to move from an energetic activity to a quiet one like story time or a group discussion.

> Touch your ears.
> Touch your eyes.
> Touch your nose.
> Now bend down and touch your toes.
> Wiggle your fingers.
> Turn around.
> Now bend down and touch the ground.
> Clap your hands—1, 2, 3.
> Now see how quiet you can be.
> (Janice Hayes Andrews)

Let poetry fill your and the children's days. Why not recite a verse while lining up to go to lunch? Memorize short poems to recite when waiting for stragglers to take their seats. Start the day with a poem; end the day with one as well. Create the job of poetry selector for the job chart. Poetry can rhyme or not, speak to deep emotions, or lift us with light language and witty wordplay.

Check out the Reading is Fundamental (http://www.rif.org) website for more tips on using poetry to build literary skills. You will find many ideas for incorporating poetry into the curriculum.

Selecting Appropriate Poems

Using poetry in the classroom will, of course, be much more valuable and enjoyable if the poem selection is made carefully with the children's interests and needs in mind. Not all children have the same needs. And by no means are all children at the same developmental level. Choose poetry that meets all developmental levels in the group.

Another important criterion for selecting poetry to present in any classroom is that the teacher should like it, too. It is not possible for a teacher to read a poem well or generate much enthusiasm for it if he or she does not enjoy it.

- When selecting poems, think about what the children are likely to find appealing. From approximately three to six years of age, young children like things that seem relevant to them. In order for something to be relevant to children, it must somehow relate to the world as they know it, if not directly to them. By selecting poetry about familiar objects, events, and feelings, the teacher takes a major step toward making poetry interesting and enjoyable for young children. Older children enjoy poetry that challenges their imagination and thinking skills.
- Focus on popular topics. There are certain subjects that almost all young children enjoy. For this reason, these subjects are traditionally dealt with in most early childhood programs—self-awareness, the senses, the family, feelings, transportation, seasons, holidays, animals, plants, water, earth, sky. By selecting poems that deal with these subjects as they are being emphasized in class, you can capitalize on the interest generated by other classroom activities: science, social studies, music, and so on. Many children's poetry books classify poems according to these categories, making it easy to find appropriate poems. There are several good sources of children's poetry presented in the Online Companion for preschool, kindergarten, grade 3, and grade 4 to 5.

Children's Books

Children's books are a traditional part of the language arts program in most early childhood programs. These books must be chosen with care for young children's use. They must be right for the developmental level of the child. The pictures should be easily seen and the story easily understood by young listeners.

"ABC" or alphabet books for young children also must be chosen carefully. Very young children need simple, uncluttered alphabet books. Words should represent familiar, concrete objects, with *a* beginning *apple* rather than *atom*.

First alphabet books typically pair initial sounds with words, and these associations should depict regular sounds. Pages that proclaim "*K* is for *knife*" or "*G* is for *gnu*" bewilder rather than educate. These key words should also have unambiguous names: "*B* is for *bow-wow*," in a book filled with objects rather than sounds will confuse the child who identified the animal as a dog.

In addition, illustrations must be obvious and straightforward. Complications in naming lead to misunderstandings. One preschooler, upset because she had read an alphabet book incorrectly, sadly pointed out this problem: "I said '*R* for *rope*' but the book meant '*S* for *snake*.'" There are three additional features characteristic of good ABC books:

- Well-written ABC books focus on a central idea of concept and the alphabet sequence merely provides a story format. You should look for ABC books that follow a limited subject such as endangered species rather than a broad subject such as wild animals.
- The best ABC books provide thoughtful features such as bilevel text and addenda, with bilevel text appearing on the page in two font sizes for two reading skill levels. Younger listeners enjoy the illustrations and sometimes notice the letters of the alphabet or the larger print. Beginning readers may explore the accompanying text, which appears in smaller print size.
- Good-quality ABC publications invite the response or involvement of the children in the read-aloud experience, and they also provide teachers with a rich source of ideas for extended activities in the early childhood setting. ABC books can be starting points for group projects or individual activities.

Children interacting with their first texts are not reading in the traditional sense of relying solely on the printed word. Instead, as emergent readers, they depend on illustrations to create meaning. Consequently, in initial alphabet books, only one or two objects should appear on the page, acknowledging the young child's perceptual and spatial skills. There's

THIS ONE'S for YOU!   Comic Books…Literary Form?

Graphic novel specialist and teacher educator James Bucky Carter travels around the country sharing information on how teachers can use graphic novels (or comic books) to expand student literacy skills. In his travels, he frequently finds that some teachers believe that graphic novels are too risky to bring into the curriculum, while others resist any form of new literacy altogether, and many think they are only useful for remedial or reluctant readers. Before you make up your mind on the use of graphic novels in your teaching, consider some additional information on this media.

Sequential art narratives—broadly defined as images placed in sequence to tell a story—have been steadily gaining attention over the last couple of decades as teachers, literacy experts, and librarians have sought new means to engage reluctant readers and inspire more motivated ones. Practitioners and researchers have found these texts, usually published as graphic novels or comic books, to be of great use in increasing library circulation, creating new readers, helping English language learners, motivating male readers, and even assisting gifted and talented students (Carter, 2009).

Actually, comics are not a new phenomenon, nor are the attempts to connect them to education. Some would argue that sequential art narratives date back to the earliest cave paintings. Comic books, which grew out of the newspaper comic strips that gained popularity in the 1880s and 1890s, have existed in the United States since the 1920s. Superhero comics debuted in 1938 with *Action Comics #1*, the first appearance of Superman (Smith & Wilhelm, 2002).

There is a long history of the form being used for teaching, including hieroglyphics, tapestries, and stained glass windows (McCloud, 1999). M. Thomas Inge's *Comics as Culture* (1990), Bradford Wright's *Comic Book Nation* (2001), and Steven Krashen's *The Power of Reading* (2004) all cite studies from education and sociological journals that date back at least to the late 1930s. The term *graphic novel* has been in use in the United States since around 1964 (Carter, 2009).

Much recent attention to graphic novels results from the efforts of librarians, who noticed drastic increases in circulation once graphic novels were added to their libraries. Articles from their professional literature often proclaim that young people who never saw themselves as readers suddenly devoured books once they were exposed to graphic novels.

There is evidence that certain populations (boys, for example) prefer visual texts over those without visual elements (Smith & Wilhelm, 2002) and that allowing students to read comics may engage students who are otherwise less interested or less proficient in English (Cary, 2004). Research has also shown that comic book readers have a tendency to read more varied texts and that comic book reading often acts as a gateway to both more reading and more varied reading (Krashen, 2004).

Another concept that often goes unconsidered is that comics and graphic novels needn't only be integrated into the curriculum as additional reading material. Accepting them as books is a nice start, but writing and drawing graphic novels is an authentic creative, composing activity. By acknowledging that there is a process behind the production of comics and asking students to consider the process and even engage in it, teachers help students build crafting, composing, viewing, and visualizing skills (Carter, 2009).

Reading specialists and scholars speak again and again to the need for authentic reading and writing experiences, textual investigations that help bridge the gap between the school world and the lived world, between narrow notions of what it means to be literate and broad notions of what it means to actually succeed as an intelligent adult in contemporary society. The effective use of graphic novels and other forms of sequential art can help teachers accomplish all of these goals. When paired with other forms, old and new, this ancient type of text can be a valuable bridge between student and text, student and teacher, and the centuries themselves (Carter, 2009).

To effectively and responsibly use graphic novels in their classes, teachers must read every page and every panel of a graphic novel, weigh it against their understanding of community standards, then decide whether to bring the material into the classroom. You may find it a welcome addition to your language arts curriculum.

plenty of time later on to hunt for hidden pictures, sort out numerous nouns, or locate obscure objects after letter–sound correspondence has been mastered.

See the "Think About It" box on page 439 for guidelines on what to look for in choosing books for children.

The Language Arts Center

Create a place where children can explore the world of books. A language arts center is an important part of every early childhood as well as elementary classroom. As you use books during circle time, children will realize the magic of books—that they have good make-believe stories or are full of facts and have pretty pictures. Children will then want to explore those books on their own, so they need to have a well-organized place where they can go and read.

Think about the physical space first and be sure you find a place that is away from the more active goings-on in the room, a place where the child can quietly explore books. Gather together a table, some chairs or soft cushions, and shelves for books, tapes, CDs, and magazines. When covering some units, you might want to create an unusual seating place: For example, you might make an airplane out of a large box as you talk and read about types of transportation.

Take time to decorate nearby bulletin boards or tops of shelves with book jackets, pictures, flowers, and special collections related to the books you have in the book center. If you choose to display the letters of the alphabet, be sure you do so in a developmentally appropriate manner. These guidelines are helpful.

- Place letters where children can see them. Alphabet displays too far above children's heads are of little use. Letters need to be at eye level where children can examine them.
- Place letters where children can refer to them as they work and play. When they are writing, children are far more likely to make use of letter guides that are close at hand. Teachers can apply alphabet strips to tabletops or laminate letter-writing guides that children can take off a shelf and bring with them to wherever they are writing.
- Place letters where children can handle them. Children notice the shapes of letters when they do alphabet puzzles or use letter-shaped cookie cutters in damp sand or dough. Magnetic letters and alphabet blocks allow children to explore letter/sound connections, arrange and rearrange letters to form words, and become more aware of the sequences of sounds within words.

Place certain kinds of books on the shelves so that they are readily available at all times—Mother Goose books; poetry books; a children's simple encyclopedia (there are some two-and three-volume sets); "sense" books where children can touch, scratch, and smell as they look; some of the classic stories with which children are already familiar, such as *Goldilocks and the Three Bears*, *The Little Engine That Could*, *The Three Little Pigs*, and *The Cat in the Hat*. Books reflecting ethnic diversity should always be available for children's use. Books portraying ethnic diversity of children in the group as well as those not represented in the group need to be on the shelves.

As concepts—the alphabet, numbers, animals, families, and transportation—are introduced, provide a special bookshelf or display area where children can find books on those subjects and expand their knowledge about each concept.

You can begin to introduce the organization of a real library by color-coding the different types of books with a colored dot fastened to the bottom edge of each book. Then, use paper strips on the shelves so that children can replace the books where they belong just by matching the strip on the shelf with the mark on the book.

Help children determine what rules should be followed as they read in the language arts center; these should relate to behavior, care of books, and removal of books from the area.

FIGURE 18-11 • Organize the books in the language arts center so they are easily accessible for children's use.

THINK ABOUT IT

What to Look for in Children's Books

Children today live in an exciting media-driven time of television, video games, and computers. Yet, no medium can stir a child's imagination like the pages of a good book. There is an enormous selection of children's books available today. The following are some general guidelines on what to look for in choosing children's books from preschool through grade 5.

Baby Books. There are four basic kinds of baby books.

1. Board books feature sturdy cardboard pages that can be wiped clean.
2. Touch-and-feel books have cloth, feathers, fur, and familiar "feely" things attached to them for little ones to discover.
3. Cloth books are made of safe, washable material.
4. Bath books are constructed of soft, durable plastic and can take a lot of abuse.

What to look for:

- simple text and art
- repetition and bouncy rhymes
- bright and familiar photos or artwork (there should be a connection between baby's surroundings and the book's pictures)
- a sturdy book that can handle many spills
- rounded corners for safety
- a book the right size and shape for little hands
- a book you will enjoy as well; baby will recognize your enjoyment

Preschool. Preschool books are on a higher level than baby books but on a slightly lower level than picture books. In addition to hardcover and paperback, preschool books come in a variety of novelty formats. Among them are the following.

- Lift-the-flap books have sturdy pages and flaps to lift that reveal hidden words or pictures.
- Pop-up books have paper-engineered pages that make pictures three-dimensional.
- Pull-tab books have tabs to pull to change the pictures.

Some books combine all of these features. These kinds of books are designed to be played with as much as to be read—yet another way to show that books are fun.

What to look for in preschool books:

- a book that clearly covers the concept you are trying to teach
- a book that helps develop children's sense of humor
- an easy and fun story line
- clear and easy-to-read text
- colorful, high-quality illustrations that children can connect to their own lives and situations

Picture Books. Picture books are one of the most popular forms of children's books and are appropriate for a wide range of ages and reading levels. Picture books have varying amounts of art and text. Some are even wordless! Some story lines are simple, while others are quite complex. Subjects can be beautiful, funny, moving, scary, or just plain silly. What is important is that you find a picture book the children in your group will relate to and enjoy.

What to look for:

- art or photography children respond to
- story lines that elicit questions and discussions
- stories that develop children's sense of humor
- stories that help with children's issues—such as sibling rivalry or going to school
- stories you enjoyed as a child and would like to share with children
- titles recommended by reviewers and award committees

Early Readers. These books are designed to supplement a child's reading program at school. As with picture books, early readers cover a wide variety of subjects. They are illustrated, though the emphasis is more on text than on illustrations. Early readers are targeted toward specific reading levels or by grade. As every child is different, you may wish to judge on your own which reading level is appropriate.

What to look for:

- a reading level that will challenge but will not intimidate children
- clear text (the print size varies with reading levels)
- a topic that will stimulate further interest in reading

Continued

- favorite artists children have enjoyed at an earlier level of reading

- nonfiction subjects children enjoy, such as sports, history, fantasy, or adventure

- new subjects to introduce to children, such as fantasy and folklore

Fiction. When we enter the world of fiction, we leave behind colorful pictures and favorite characters, and subject matter becomes more complicated. The early readers are the steppingstones to these more advanced works.

What to look for:

- books with a reading level that will challenge and stimulate

- books with a subject that interests the young reader; many children want to pick out their own books at this age

- some of the more popular and enduring titles that are available in different editions (the trim size of the books may vary, and the cover art may vary as well, but almost without exception the text remains the same)

- some classic tales in abridged formats

Encourage frequent use of the language arts center. This means that you need to change the displays and what books are available so that children will want to explore continually to see what is new. It's hard to be interested in a shabby collection of books casually tossed on a table in the corner of the room!

Involve the children in decorating the language arts center. They can help you change the display or make pictures for use on the library corner bulletin board. Then the book center will be a place where they feel they belong.

Just as important as *what* you read is *how* you read it to young children. The following section gives some guidelines for reading to young children in the best possible way.

Reading to Children

Reading to young children has a few very general requirements. For instance, it is best to work with children's short attention spans by choosing books that are not too long. Young children's visual discrimination also requires books that have pictures large enough for them to see. (Remember, the small muscles of the eyes are the last to develop to maturity.) A book with a story that is simple, yet interesting in its wording, is also good for young children.

Children in the middle to upper elementary levels still enjoy illustrated books, but the story is becoming equally as important to them. These children begin to enjoy fiction in which the subject matter becomes more complex. The variety of subjects available for use with older children reflects their expanding interests and personalities. Types of books of special interest to this age group are science fiction, fantasy, mystery, and tragedy as well as books on relationships, humorous

tales, horror stories, and sports. Consider the following suggestions to help you read stories to young children more effectively.

Guidelines for Story Groups

1. Select a suitable spot—one that is quiet, away from distracting noises and activities. In the language arts center, have books displayed at children's eye level. Have books already read out for children to look at and "re-read" themselves.

2. There is no law saying that reading aloud is always a large-group activity. In fact, it is often very difficult to read to a large group of young children because interest and attention span differences multiply as the group increases in size. Ideally, a small group of six to eight children is a more manageable and comfortable size for reading effectively. With toddlers, a group of two to three children is best.

3. See that everyone is seated comfortably. Avoid crowding. Be sure that you as storyteller can see all the children's faces and that they can see yours. Rugs on the floor in a semicircle facing the teacher make a good seating arrangement. Sitting in chairs is uncomfortable for young children and causes a distraction if a child falls out of one.

4. If using a book, be sure to hold it so that all can see it. Do not hold the book in your lap. The best plan is to hold it out to one side up beside your cheek. This means that you must be able to read the story out of the side of your eye without turning the book toward you.

5. Be sure you like the story you read; otherwise you will put little enthusiasm into the telling of it.

6. Know your story well! If you do not, you will focus too much of your attention on the book. You must be free to notice the reactions of the children. Also, knowing the story well means that you will be able to tell it with appropriate enthusiasm, expression, and emphasis. Sounds are better made than read. For example, crow for *cock-a-doodle-do* and bark for *bow-wow* instead of just reading the words.

7. Read the story unhurriedly with an interesting, well-modulated voice. Read naturally—do not "talk down" to the children or have a special "storytelling" voice.

8. Do not comment so much throughout the story as you read it or point out so many things in the pictures that you break the thread of the story and spoil its effect.

9. Encourage comments and questions, but not to such a degree that it interrupts the flow of the story.

Practice reading a book to a group of children. Then go back to these guidelines to check to see if you used them effectively with children. It takes a good deal of practice to achieve mastery of the skill of story reading. If you make the experience a fun learning experience for yourself with the children, you are halfway there!

Reading to toddlers is an activity they truly enjoy. Here are a few guidelines for reading to this age group.

- While you read to toddlers, follow the lines with your fingers. This helps toddlers who are learning that pages are read from top to bottom and from left to right and that pictures and printed words are related to each other.
- Give toddlers a choice of books. Books at this age are good for memory development. As toddlers remember story lines, they begin to choose what they want to hear over and over again. Listening to preferred choices again and again increases a toddler's sense of self and security. Give toddlers several choices of books and you'll learn just which ones they love.
- Choose interactive books. Some toddlers may have difficulty sitting still. Try to find books that encourage their participation by pushing moveable parts, uncovering a hidden character, making a figure pop up, or patting the bunny.
- Use books that toddlers can carry. Toddlers like to possess books. Look for ones with handles or large plastic rings that toddlers can clutch and carry around as precious possessions.
- Show your pleasure. As you settle down to read, let children know you enjoy books and reading together. After all, toddlers are great copycats. If you are involved in a simple story, toddlers will get swept into the tale. As you encourage them to help turn pages, toddlers become truly involved with books for pleasure, for learning, and for life.

Storytelling

In today's modern world, storytelling has become a lost art. Despite a strong connection between storytelling and literacy, many teachers do not engage in storytelling to children. They may offer regular picture-book readings but neglect storytelling. Yet, the ancient art of storytelling is a vital way to inspire children's imaginations as well as language and listening skills. Storytelling is *not reading from a book to children*. In storytelling, the teacher weaves the story using his or her voice and expressions to compel the child's attention and interest.

Storytelling events that actively engage listeners in the making of the story create a shared experience that bonds the teller and the listeners. This personal interaction and active participation are very different from the story viewing that young children frequently experience in today's high-tech world (Isbell, 2003). Stories presented in a form like television, videos, or movies cannot personally involve children or invite them into the story.

Storytelling isn't limited to just one kind of story. When you develop your storytelling curriculum, be sure to include a good variety of these story types:

- Fables—Short tales that have a moral and communicate a truth about life. The main characters in fables are often animals that act and think like humans.
- Fairy tales—Stories that often feature fairies, elves, genies, pixies, leprechauns, and other make-believe characters.
- Legends—Stories that revolve around incidents that are believed to have taken place in a particular culture's history.
- Folk tales—Stories that come to us from many parts of the world. These stories reflect a particular country or people's flavor and preserve cultural traditions.

- Poetry—Rhyming poetry, in particular Mother Goose rhymes, is a source of excellent storytelling for young children.

Tips for Storytelling

Discover the right story to tell.
- Look for stories that are age appropriate.
- Find stories that you love.
- Check picture books written for different age levels.
- Collect stories from family, friends, and community.
- Create your own stories.

Learn the story.
- Read it several times.
- Break it into a beginning, middle, and end.

Speak naturally.
- Use your normal speaking voice.
- Use sound effects, such as unusual voice and story sounds, sparingly.

Use simple, natural gestures. Add gestures when they add to the story, but don't overuse them.

Polish the story. Tell it, retell it, and retell it. Once you have a story ready to tell to your satisfaction, the next step is to share it with the children.

- Make eye contact with your listeners.
- Introduce the story.
- Tell the story looking directly into your listeners' eyes.
- Encourage your listeners to interact with you.
- Enjoy and work with your audience's enthusiasm.

A puppet is a natural prop to use when storytelling. Even a shy child will relate to a puppet. Puppets are also multisensory vehicles for storytelling. They create an art and language experience that children can understand. When you find a special puppet, give it a personality and a home, and you'll be amazed how children interact with it. Use it in your story and throughout your curriculum.

Some stories include sound effects or repeated phrases that children can play with or repeat during the story. Listening to stories draws attention to the sounds of language and helps children develop sensitivity to the way language works. Children, as listeners and participants, experience the joy of the repetitive phrase, "The sky is falling" or the musical quality of the chant, "fee-fi-fo-fum." Developing auditory

FIGURE 18-12 • Read favorite books repeatedly to encourage emergent reading.

discrimination connects the sounds of words, phrases, and passages, influencing phonemic awareness in a meaningful way (Isbell, 2003). When children begin to "read" a familiar story, these sound phrases are often the first words of the story they identify and repeat.

Drawing children into the telling helps them understand how the story works, what phrases are repeated, and the sequence of action. Active participation in literacy experiences can enhance the development of comprehension, oral language, and the sense of story structure (Birckmayer, Kennedy, & Stonehouse, 2009). By providing immediate feedback to the storyteller and sharing observations, the children create the experience together.

The National Early Literacy Panel (NELP)

To this point, it can be assumed that the early years are crucial in the development of literacy in young children. In an effort to establish a more scientific basis for this belief, the National Early Literacy Panel was created. The National Early Literacy Panel (NELP) was established in 2003 to complete an in-depth analysis of scientific research on the "what" and "how" of literacy development in preschool-aged children (National Institute for Literacy, 2007). The questions that NELP wanted to answer were:

1. What are the skills preschool children need to develop in order to learn to read and write during the early elementary years?

2. What types of teaching and learning programs and/or "interventions" would be most effective to help preschool children to develop these foundational abilities?

3. What types of environments would be most beneficial to preschool children's foundational skill development?

The NELP found that preschool children need to develop their best possible abilities in the following major areas:

1. Oral language

2. Alphabet knowledge and phonological awareness

3. Print concepts

Oral language is the child's ability to receive and express thoughts, wants, needs, and feelings. In order to effectively understand and use oral language(s), a child must be exposed to enough interactive communication that he or she has developed a sense of the rules for putting sounds together to make meaningful words and an understanding of the rules to put these words into appropriate order to make meaningful phrases and sentences.

Oral language contains five components:

1. **Phonology:** The rules for putting sounds together to say and understand words. Phonology helps children later in school to learn and use phonics, the rule-based system for representing spoken sounds with letters.

2. **Morphology:** The rules for adding prefixes and suffixes to words to change their meaning. For example, by adding an "s" to a word, a child learns usually by 18 months that this means "more than one" of that person, place, or thing. The ease in the English language of making nouns plural is one of the reasons that children learn to understand and use noun labels first. Infants as young as 12 months often know 50 words that label the concepts of the people, places, and things around them.

3. **Semantics:** Knowledge and use of words in context. We most often think of semantics as a child's vocabulary. The number of words that a child knows and uses in different contexts is one of the most significant predictors of a child becoming literate. Preschool children do not learn words in isolation, or from the television. Children from birth to five learn language through interactive conversation so that they can hear and "try out" the rules for using words appropriately.

4. **Syntax:** The rules for putting words in the appropriate word order. When children can hear people use sentences and ask question and have the chance to do the same, they learn the appropriate word order that different language systems use. Researchers think that word order is another reason why in languages like English and Spanish, children tend to learn nouns first (Bornstein et al., 2004). Children are learning their language(s); that is why it is essential that they hear and have the opportunity to use and receive feedback, the appropriate words and word order in the language(s) of their home and out-of-home environments.

5. **Pragmatics:** The actual, effective use of words and sentences. Children with good pragmatic language abilities can ask and respond to a variety of types of questions, can retell stories, and can carry on conversations with other children and adults. Children with these skills are often more successful academically and socially (Massey, 2005).

As you can see, **oral language** is the key to later written language (literacy) because a child is learning the rules of how to put together sounds to make words and words to make sentences. He or she will use the same and similar rules to put together and take apart written letters to spell and read words, as well as to comprehend words in sentences. As a matter of fact, Dorothy Strickland, cochair of the NELP, states that "Oral language is the foundation for later literacy learning" (Strickland & Riley-Ayers, 2006, p. 2).

Alphabet Knowledge/Phonological Awareness

We know that in order to understand and use language across place and time, human beings invented written language. We created a set of symbols that in many languages around the globe are known as *letters*.

These letters can represent the sounds we make and hear. That is why it is necessary that children learn about the letters that are used in their language(s) to spell their names and other words that are important to them. Children during the preschool years not only must produce the sounds in their spoken languages in the combinations that their language allows but also become receptively aware of the individual sounds that make up the worlds in their spoken language(s). The more a child is "phonologically aware," the more likely he or she will be able to manipulate these and make them rhyme, realize they sound the same or different at the beginning of words, and develop other skills that will help him or her to learn to read and write.

Print Concepts

A child's print concepts help him or her to "pull it all together," to understand that we can communicate through spoken or sign-language words and sentences and that we can write the same words down for others to see and understand. Print concepts include the understanding that books, paper, crayons, pencils, and markers are very special toys that are really tools to help us understand, learn, and express ourselves in another way. By interacting with print-related materials and tools and seeing adults and older children use these tools for real purposes like creating a shopping list, preschool children learn how to use print, how to make meaningful marks, turn pages in a book—all these print concepts that we need in order to become truly literate.

FIGURE 18-13 • Children take pride in their ability to read.

NELP-Defined Effective Programs and Environments

Now that we know what the NELP has determined to be the "what" of early literacy foundations, let's look at the "how" of helping children develop these skills. The NELP, along with a secondary analysis of its original findings (Dunst, Trivette, & Hamby, 2007), determined that the most effective strategies for helping children develop oral language, alphabet knowledge and phonological awareness, and print concepts include the following types of activities. The NELP refers to these intentional literacy-teaching interactions as *interventions*.

1. Code-related interventions
2. Interactive/shared reading interventions
3. Language enhancement interventions
4. Family and home programs for improving children's literacy
5. High-quality preschool and kindergarten programs

Code-Related Interventions

Code-related interventions refer to any interactions we have with children where we intentionally help them to learn the names of letters, the sounds that make up their spoken language(s) in words, and a beginning understanding of the sounds that letters represent in different words. It is more effective to begin with letters, words, and sounds that are meaningful to children such as those that make up their names.

Interactive/Shared Reading

In addition to reading books with young children, talking about books can be a very effective strategy to build oral language, alphabet knowledge/phonological awareness, and print concepts. More effective interactive/shared reading is accomplished with smaller groups of children, usually no more than four. Children need to be able to touch and see the print and turn the pages themselves. Children are also allowed and encouraged to make comments and to ask questions during interactive/shared reading sessions (Debruin-Parecki, 2007). The emphasis is on the interaction, the adult's responsiveness and modeling of appropriate language use, and structure (Justice, 2005).

Language Enhancement

Talking with children is a strategy that we have available at all times. No expensive program to buy, no special materials to use. Just use our ears, mouths and brains. We should "strive for 5" by waiting at least 5 seconds between interchanges of comments and questions (Dickinson, D., McCabe, A., & Clark-Chiarelli, N. (2004)), with four-year-olds, conversing with them about their interests and topics related to the play and routine activities in which they are engaged. Adults tend to use longer sentences and a greater variety of words during pretend play, so talking and playing with a child in this situation can be an effective way to develop a child's language (Massey, 2005).

Family/Home Programs

Providing literacy-related resources for families to use is a nice first step in helping families to support their children's early language and literacy development. The greatest outcomes for children have been seen when family members, like early childhood professionals, talk with their children. Modeling interactive reading and conversations for families during the preschool years has been shown to have the longest-term effects on children's learning during the early elementary years (Dunst, Trivette & Hamby, 2007).

High-Quality Preschool/ Kindergarten Programs

The real measure of quality of any early childhood program is the quality of the relationships among the staff and of the staff with the children and families. Because language is learned and continuously developed through positive relationships, there are so many reasons for early childhood programs to build trust, demonstrate mutual respect, and openly and honestly communicate with and among all participants, children and adults alike.

How the NELP Can Help

Now that we know the evidence of what children need to develop and learn during the preschool years, and we know for sure that holding conversations with children every day while we are reading, playing, and helping take care of their physical needs will help develop these skills, we can make informed decisions

FIGURE 18-14 • Provide an accepting classroom climate that values culturally and linguistically diverse young children.

about how to best use the time and energy that we have with young children. Based on the information from NELP, we need to:

- Listen to children, commenting on and asking different types of questions about their changing interests;
- Wait long enough (at least 5 seconds) after making a comment or asking a question so that the child can have time to understand and respond;
- Use new words and complete sentences when we talk with children to build their vocabulary;
- Intentionally label letters by their names, especially making the connection to the letters in a child's name.

Summary

Language is a part of the child's total development. Similar to physical growth, there is a definite pattern of development related to a child's growth of language involving four distinct skills: speaking, listening, writing, and reading. Each of these four skills can develop at different rates in each individual child. This is why one child can be better at speaking than a peer who listens better than she or he speaks. A teacher of young children needs to understand each child's developmental level in each of these language skills in planning appropriate language arts experiences. For young children of non-English-language background, the early childhood teacher must create an environment that is accepting and appreciative of diversity. For non-English-speaking children, a teacher needs to accept individual differences with regard to language-learning time frames and give young children the time needed to acquire, explore, and experience second-language learning.

The ability to speak is not always directly related to the ability to understand. This is why young children can repeat words to a song without understanding what the words mean. Young children may also act as if they understand what is said when, in fact, they do not. The teacher or child care worker who is not aware of these language limitations of young children can easily lose their attention. This is because young children are really just learning how to listen.

Readiness for reading is termed *emerging literacy*. This term refers to the time immediately before a child learns to read printed symbols as well as to the continuous development of prereading skills that begins at birth.

Prewriting skills are also considered a part of a child's emerging literacy. Learning to write involves fine-motor skills and much hand–eye coordination. While actual writing practice is not appropriate in the early childhood program, activities that allow young children to practice these skills, such as painting, cutting, and working with clay, are practice writing skills.

Just as the child develops physically in a gradual process, she or he develops reading skills gradually. Early ex-

periences at home and in the early childhood program can positively influence a child's reading readiness.

The use of children's books and poetry in the early childhood program helps develop young children's reading readiness. Children's books must be appropriate for the developmental level of the child. This means that the pictures must be easily seen and the story easily understood by the young listeners.

Older children enjoy illustrations in their books, but the text is becoming equally important. Various kinds of fiction books are appropriate for middle and upper elementary children.

The way a teacher reads to young children is just as important as choosing the right books. Guidelines for reading to children as well as tips for storytelling are presented to assist teachers in these activities. The National Early Literacy Panel (NELP) analyzed scientific research on effective literacy efforts for preschool children.

Key Terms

antibias curriculum (ABC) 427
inclusive environment 427
literacy 423
pretend reading 428
National Early Literacy Panel (NELP) 440
oral language 441
phonology 441
morphology 441
semantics 441
syntax 441
pragmatics 444
alphabet knowledge/phonological awareness 441
print concepts 442
code-related interventions 442
interactive/shared reading 442
language enhancement 443

Learning Activities

A. Observe an early childhood program and describe the language development of the children. Record at least three statements from the children to share with your classmates. Discuss your findings in class.

B. Visit a library and ask a librarian to recommend two good books for each of the following age levels: two-year-olds, three- and four-year-olds, and five-year-olds. Compare the books on the following points:

1. number of pages
2. average number of sentences per page; average number of words per sentence

3. theme of the book
4. number of illustrations and size

Discuss how the books were similar and different for each age group. If possible, bring your books into class. Share your ideas about them with your classmates.

Make a second visit to the library and ask a librarian to recommend two good books for each of these levels: kindergarten to grade 3 and grades 4 to 5. Compare these books on the same points.

C. Give examples from your own experience with young children of the various language skills discussed in this chapter. For example, do you know any children who are better talkers than listeners? Better listeners than talkers?

D. Study the language development of a child three to six years of age and compare it to the information presented in Figure 18–1. What similarities do you find? What differences do you find? You may wish to make comparisons with another child of approximately the same age.

E. Based on the information given in this chapter about selecting appropriate books, begin a story file with at least five excellent books for children three to six years of age. Make a card for each book. On the card, include the title of the book, author, illustrator, publisher, copyright date, age level the story is appropriate for, and a brief summary of the story.

F. Go to a drugstore or variety store and look over the inexpensive books for children offered there. Select and purchase a desirable and undesirable one and bring them to class. Be ready to explain their weak and strong points.

G. Observe groups of children at play to collect examples of their language. Group examples according to the ages of the children. What similarities and differences do you observe?

H. Observe in a classroom where young children have free-choice activities. Select three activities and, for five minutes during each activity, record children's language as they play. During which activity was there the most talking? Why do you think this was so?

How would you change the activities to encourage more talking? Explain.

I. Use the Internet to research books for young children. (See the end of this chapter for additional websites.) Try these:

Reading Activities
http://www.storyarts.org
http://www.randomhouse.com/seussville
http://www.mythweb.com
http://www.planetozkids.com
Teacher Resources
http://www.goodcharacter.com
http://www.makingbooks.com/
http://www.reading.org (International Reading Association)
http://www.cbcbooks.org (Children's Book Council)

Find books for preschool, kindergarten to grade 3, and grades 4 to 5. Share your experience with the websites and finding books in this way.

J. Using a digital camera, snap a few photos of an early childhood classroom, school, students, and staff. Print out the photos and place them at a center where students can arrange them to tell a story. Have the students share their stories in writing or with their class.

K. Give students in an early childhood classroom disposable cameras. Send them home with the cameras and specific instructions: "Take five pictures that you can use to tell a story about yourself or your family." When the photos are printed, have children tell or write their stories. Discuss the effectiveness of this activity with your classmates. What would you do to make this activity better next time?

Poems for Young Children

Animals

My Rabbits

My two white rabbits chase each other
With humping, bumping backs.
They go hopping, hopping
And their long ears
Go flopping, flopping
And they make faces
With their noses up and down.
Today I went inside their fence
To play rabbit with them
And in one corner under a loose bush
I saw something shivering in the leaves.
And I pushed
And I looked
And I found
There in a hole in the ground,
Three baby rabbits hidden away
And they made faces
With their noses up and down.

If You Find a Little Feather

If you find a little feather,
A little white feather,
A soft and tickly feather
    It's for you.
A feather is a letter
From a bird
And it says,
"Think of me,"
"Do not forget me."
"Remember me always."
"Remember me at least until the little feather is lost."
So—if you find a little feather,
A little white feather,
A soft and tickly feather,
It's for you.
Pick it up, and put it in your pocket.

There Once Was a Puffin

Oh, there once was a puffin
Just the shape of a muffin
And he lived on an island
In the
    Bright
      Blue
        Sea!
He ate little fishes,
That were most delicious,
And he had them for supper
And he
    Had
      Them
        For tea.
But this poor little puffin,
He couldn't play nothin',
For he hadn't anybody
To
    Play
      With
        At all.
So he sat on his island,
And he cried for awhile, and
He felt very lonely,
And he felt
    Very small.
Then along came the fishes,
And they said, "If you wishes,
You can have us for playmates,
Instead
    Of
      For tea."
So they now play together
In all sorts of weather
And the puffin eats pancakes
Like you
    And
      Like me.

Caterpillar

A fuzzy, wuzzy caterpillar
On a summer day
Wriggled and wriggled and wriggled,
On his way.
He lifted up his head
To get a better view.
He wanted some nice green
Leaves to chew.
He wriggled and he wriggled
From his toes to his head
And he crawled about until
He found a comfy bed.
He curled up tight
In a warm little wrap
And settled himself
For a nice long nap.
He slept and he slept

And he slept until
One day he awoke
And broke from his shell.
He stretched and stretched
And he found he had wings!
He turned into a butterfly
Such a pretty-colored thing.
Oh, how happily
He flew away,
And he flew and he flew
In the sun all day.

Mice

I think mice
Are rather nice.
Their tails are long,
Their faces small.
They haven't any
Chins at all.
Their teeth are white,
They run about
The house at night.
They nibble things
They shouldn't touch
And no one seems
To like them much.
But I think mice
Are nice.

If I Were a Fish

I like to play in water
And if I were a fish,
I'd have water all around me
In a big glass dish.
My tail would make it splatter
'Til it splashed the sky,
And the mother fish would only say,
"No, don't get dry!"

Tiny Tim

I had a little turtle.
His name was Tiny Tim;
I put him in the bathtub
    To see if he could swim.
He drank up all the water;
He ate up all the soap;
And woke up in the morning
    With bubbles in his throat.

Seeds and Plants

Mister Carrot

Nice Mister Carrot
Makes curly hair,
His head grows underneath the ground—
And early in the morning
I find him in his bed
And give his feet a great big pull
And out comes his head!

The Apple

Within its polished universe,
The apple holds a star,
A secret constellation
To scatter near and far.
Let a knife discover
Where the five points hide.
Split the shining ruby
And find the star inside.

Seed

In the heart of a seed,
Buried deep so deep,
A dear little plant lay fast asleep.
"Wake," said the sunshine
"And creep to light."
"Wake," said the voice of raindrops bright.
The little plant heard
And rose to see
What the wonderful world
Outside might be.

Dandelions

Oh dandelions as yellow as gold,
What do you do all day?
I wait and wait in the tall green grass
Till the children come out to play.
Oh dandelion as yellow as gold,
What do you do all night?
I wait and wait in the tall green grass
Till my yellow hair turns white.
And what do the little children do
When they come out to play?
They pick me up in their hands
And blow my white hair away.

Birthdays

Five Years Old

Please, everybody look at me.
Today I'm five years old, you see.
After this, I won't be four,
Not ever, ever, anymore;
I won't be three, or two, or one,
For that was when I'd first begun.
Now I'll be five awhile, and then
I'll soon be something else again!

The Birthday Child

Everything's been different
All the day long.
Lovely things have happened,
Nothing has gone wrong.
Nobody has scolded me,
Everyone has smiled.
Isn't it delicious
To be a birthday child.

When I Was One

When I was one,
I had just begun.
When I was two,
I was nearly new.
When I was three,
I was hardly me.
When I was four,
I was not much more.
When I was five,
I was just alive.
But now I am six,
I'm as clever as clever
So I think I'll be six now
For ever and ever.

Action Poems

A Swing Song

Up, down
Up and down,
Which is the way to London Town?
Where? Where?
Up in the air,
Close your eyes, and now you are
    There.

Swinging

Hold on tightly, up we go
Swinging high and swinging low.

See-Saw

See-saw Margery Daw,
Jack shall have a new master.
He shall have but a penny a day,
Because he won't work any faster.

The Ball

Bounce the ball and catch the ball
One, and two!
Bounce the ball and catch the ball,
And I throw it back to you.
Bounce the ball and catch the ball,
One, two, three!
Bounce the ball and catch the ball,
And toss it back to me.

Blocks

Blocks will build a tower tall,
Blocks will make a long, long wall,
Blocks will build a house or plane,
A truck, a tunnel, or a train.
Get the blocks, so we can see
What they'll build for you and me.

Soap Bubbles

Fill the pipe!
Gently blow;
Now you'll see

The bubbles grow!
Strong at first,
Then they burst,
Then they go to
Nothing, oh!

All Excited

I wondered and I wondered
When I could go to school.
They said I wasn't old enough
According to the rule.
I waited and I waited
I was patient as could be.
And now—I'm all excited
It's time for school for me!

The Train

My train runs on a track
Chug-a-chug, chug-a-chug
Slow at first, then faster,
Chug-a-chug, chug-a-chug,
Chug-a-chug-chug!
Round and round the wheels go
Just listen to the whistle blow,
Toot-toot-toot!
Chug-a-chug, chug-a-chug,
Toot-toot-toot!!

Toys

See the toys on my shelf?
I can count them by myself.
One, two, three, four, five.
Here's an airplane, zoom, zoom,
And a drum, boom, boom,
A ball that bounces up and down.
A top that spins round and round.
A telephone, so I can say,
"Come and play with me today."

Raggedy Ann

Raggedy Ann is my best friend
She's so relaxed, just see her bend.
First at the waist, then at the knee
Her arms are swinging, oh so free.
Her head rolls around like a rubber ball,
She hasn't any bones at all.
Raggedy Ann is stuffed with rags,
That's why her body wigs and wags.

The Cupboard

I know a little cupboard
With a teeny tiny key.
And there's a jar of lollipops
For me, me, me.
It has a little shelf, my dears,
As dark as dark can be,
And there's a dish of Banbury Cakes
For me, me, me.
I have a small fat grandmomma

With a very slippery knee,
And she's the keeper of the cupboard
With the key, key, key.
And when I'm very good, my dears,
As good as good can be,
There's Banbury Cakes, and lollipops
For me, me, me.

If I Were

If I were an owl,
At night I'd prowl.
If I were a bear,
At night I'd growl.
If I were a sheep,
At night I'd bleat.
But since I'm a child,
At night I sleep.

Personal Hygiene

New Shoes

I have new shoes in the fall time.
And new shoes in the spring.
Whenever I wear my new shoes
I always have to sing.

Shoe Lacing

Across and across the shoe we go,
Across and across, begin at the toe.
Criss and cross us over and then,
Through the hole, and across again!

Loose Tooth

I had a little tooth that wiggled
It wiggled quite a lot;
I never could be sure if it
Was coming out or not.
I pushed it with my tongue
To see if it would drop;
But there it stayed and wiggled
Until I thought I'd pop.
My auntie tied it with a string
And slammed the kitchen door!
And now I haven't got a tooth
That wiggles anymore.

But Then

A tooth fell out
And left a space
So big my tongue
Can touch my face.
And every time
I smile, I show
A space where something
Used to grow.
I miss my tooth,
As you can guess.
But then, I have to
Brush one less!

Washing

With soap and water,
I rub my hands;
With the bubbly suds,
I scrub my hands,
Rubbity, scrubbity scrub!
Rub my hands
And scrub my hands,
Til no more dirt is seen!
Rub and scrub;
Rub and scrub
And then my hands are clean!

Naughty Soap Song

Just when I'm ready to start
    On my ears,
That is the time that my
    Soap disappears,
It jumps from my fingers, and
    Slithers and slides
Down to the end of the tub
Where it hides,
And acts in a most disobedient
    Way,
And that's why my soap's
    Growing thinner each day.

Activities for Children

Language Activities

Name Games

Playing with children's names can build sensitivity to the sounds of language and the use of words.

- The patterns and rhymes found in children's names can be explored. Begin by clapping the rhythm of children's names: Ste–pha–nie, Rich–ard, Al–li–son. Children can use rhythm sticks, drums, or triangles to follow the beat of their names and find ways to jump, step, hop, or slide to the rhythm of their names. These activities will attune children to the sound of words.

- Children's names can also be used to further understanding of the connection between the spoken and written word. Children's names are spoken and then written over cubbies, on paintings and artwork, and on other personal objects. Use lists of children's names whenever possible so the similarities and differences between names can be observed. You might list all of the children who have a birthday during each month or those voting to name the guinea pig Christina and those voting to name it Andrea. Other lists might name each child who has brown, black, or blonde hair.

Outdoor Language Experiences

Outdoor play materials can be used for language experiences. These can promote awareness of the printed word in young children. Tricycle paths can have traffic signs (commercial or teacher-made). The workbench can have rebus charts to describe something to build. Animal cages and insect containers can have rebus instructions for care. In addition, seed packages can be used to label plants in the garden, graphs of plant growth can be created, and collections of nature objects can be gathered and labeled. Charts of pictures of safety rules can be on display.

Recycled Materials for Language Experiences

- Mail-order catalogs. These are a comfortable hand size for young children and have more pictures and fewer words than regular magazines. Use them to find categories of colors, objects, beginning sounds, etc. Be sure to screen them first for any inappropriate pictures.

- Purse story. Fill old pocketbooks with assorted items such as tickets, keys, lists, make-up, combs, and so on. Have children examine the contents of the purse and tell about the owner. List their ideas. Draw pictures of how the owner of the purse might look. Tape stories about the owner.

- Original picture books. Photograph events throughout the year and have the children use these pictures to tell stories. Place photos and children's stories in a self-sticking photo album to become a permanent part of the book corner.

- For older children, use catalogs for language arts activities. Discuss words used to describe materials. For example: find synonyms for *soft usable*; explain what *preshrunk wash and wear,* or *telescoping* mean; rewrite descriptions of items to give them another meaning.

Ball Stories

This is a game that focuses on language skills as well as large and small-motor skills. Have children sit in a circle. (It may be helpful to tape masking tape on the floor to establish boundaries.) Use a medium-sized, soft, ball (spongy Nerf balls available in most discount stores work well). Begin with a story-starter line such as, "Once upon a time there lived a frog," and then toss the ball to a child in the circle. He or she says the next line to the story and tosses the ball to another child, who adds a line. The activity goes on until each child has had a chance to catch the ball and add a line to the story. The likely silliness of the story enhances the experience by adding laughter and humor to your language arts program.

Because children have different levels of development in social skills and speech and language skills, do not expect each child to add a line to the story. Some may simply attempt to catch the ball and then toss it to another child. Some may want to add a word, a phrase, a partial sentence, or an idea. Others will be willing to add many lines to the story, depending on their language skills and their level of creativity.

Feely Bag Stories

Put a few toys, small stuffed animals, and dolls into a bag. Feel around inside the bag and pull out a toy. You might start the story by saying, "Once upon a time there was a . . . (little bear). He was happily walking along until, OOPS! He bumped into a . . ." At this point in the story, pass the bag to one of the children and ask him or her to pull out another toy and continue the story. After everyone has had a chance to pull out a toy and add to the story, use your toy to create a "happily ever after" ending.

Activities for Multiple Intelligences

As we have learned earlier, all children have different learning styles or multiple intelligences. When working with young children in the language arts, try using some of the following activities to reach these various learning styles.

Body-Smart Activities

- Have children make letters with clay or paint, in sand or flour, or on the computer.
- Have children use hand movements and body formations to show letters.
- Trace letters on the child's palm, and help the child trace sandpaper letters.
- Use jump rope chants with letters for exercise breaks.
- Lead children in a game of "Simon Says" with commands such as "Simon says write a *B* in the air."
- Write each vocabulary word on a piece of paper and crumple the first one up around a small object like an eraser. Then crumple each paper over the first piece, one by one until you have a large paper ball. Have children toss the ball back and forth, but before a child throws the ball to a classmate, he or she removes one layer and reads the word.

Music-Smart Activities

- Use simple poems and rhythmic, repetitive stories.
- Use lyrics to simple songs to practice letters and reading.
- Sing the sounds.
- Use alphabet songs.
- Use tongue twisters to practice and isolate specific words.

Picture-Smart Activities

- Have children make pictures out of letters or groups of letters.
- Use different colors on bulletin boards to represent specific sounds.
- Have children draw "word pictures" to show the meaning of words. For example, *tall* would be written with tall letters, and *rain* would be written with drops of water around it.
- Have students draw a picture to represent the word and write the word inside the picture.

- Have children practice writing sight words over and over again in a rainbow of different colors. Have them write a sight word in one color, whispering the letters as they write. Next, have them trace over the top of each letter in four other colors. Make sure children write the entire word with the same color.

Number-Smart Activities

- Have children write sight words, numbered from 1 to 25, on a poster board. When children ask how to spell a word on the list, refer them to the appropriate number on the poster.
- Make dice for classroom use with letters instead of dots on them.
- Use a flannel board with cloth letters or a metal board with magnetic letters. Show students how new words are formed by changing one letter (*fine, dine, line*).
- Locate letters numerically in the alphabet by creating a poster that shows letters ordered that way (A1, B2, etc.).

Word-Smart Activities

- Provide language experiences by writing down stories as children tell them to you.
- Use word flash cards.
- Teach prereading skills—holding books, turning pages, and reading from left to right.
- Use tracing activities.
- Have students learn word families—words that are phonetically alike or sound similar.
- Use echo reading. Students repeat what is read.
- Write words you want the students to practice on slips of paper and put them into an empty water bottle. Fill the rest of the bottle with popcorn kernels, brightly colored buttons, or other small objects. Then screw on the lid, and shake it up. The students have to find the "hidden" words, read them, and cross them off the word list.

People-Smart Activities

- Make reading a social event in the classroom.
- Have students take turns reading letters, words, sentences, etc.
- Have student partners read (or look at) a book together.
- Have students teach younger children the alphabet and sight words.
- Have reading parties at which children read individually and in small groups and listen to guest readers who are visiting the class.
- Arm children with clipboards and have them seek out words in newspapers, on the classroom wall, and in the hallway at school. This is an activity that can be done alone, in groups, in pairs, in centers, and at their desks. In word hunts, children make connections between their work with words and their actual reading and writing. The goal is not to memorize a list, but to gain the tools to become a more confident contextual reader.

Self-Smart Activities

- Provide a quiet, cozy reading corner.
- Give students opportunities to read silently.
- Provide books that have a high-interest value.
- Keep special "Book Favorites" lists on a bulletin board where students can write their "All-Time Favorites."
- Have children practice reading aloud to a stuffed animal.
- Have children listen to a tape-recorded story and follow along in the book.

Word Charades

Write the sight words you are studying on index cards. Each child picks two index cards and looks up each word's meaning in the dictionary. Children take turns acting out, drawing, or expressing the meaning of their words in another creative way. The rest of the class tries to guess the meaning of the word. The first player to guess correctly wins that index card. The player who has the most cards at the end of the game gets to write the words on the chalk/white board, while the others write the words in their journals.

Mysterious Words

Discuss names with children. Ask specific questions and invite children to stand and find partners: "Who has _____ letters in his or her name?" "If your name begins with a _____, stand up." "Whose name has two vowels?" Play this game until children become familiar with the similarities between their name and their friends' names.

Then pass out 9 × 12-inch white construction paper and white crayons. Invite children to write their names on the white paper with the white crayon as many times as they like. Assure children that their magic name will appear when they complete the last step.

Pass out watercolors and paintbrushes. Have the children paint over the entire sheet of paper. Their names appear like magic!

After this activity, children most likely will want to make another mystery painting. They might make a card for someone special by writing a secret message and telling the person how to reveal that message.

Poetry Activities

Poem of the Week

Use large sheets of newsprint to print the poem of your choice. Use illustrations. Try substituting pictures for words in the poem. Have children point to the pictures when you read the poem to them.

Cluster Poems

Select a subject of interest to young children—animals, seasons, weather. Read several poems, each by a different poet. See if children like one more than another. Have them talk about why. Draw or paint pictures of their favorite.

Rhyming Nonsense

Although poetry does not have to rhyme to be effective, children do enjoy making their own rhymes. Allow them to create a poem using rhyming words of their choice. The words do not have to make sense. Write them on paper for children to see the words they have created.

Descriptive Poem

Have children select a subject that will be the title of a poem. Encourage them to give you two words that tell something about the subject, for example, cat—furry, soft; broccoli—green, yucky.

Listening Exercises

Noisy Story

The noisy story develops vocabulary and skill in sequencing of story events. It also permits pupils of varying levels to participate. Prepare a set of cards, each card having a noisy word on it: PEEP, BANG, BUZZ, ROAR. Give each child a card, considering individual reading levels. Select a leader to begin the noisy story, using the noisy word on his or her card. The other children take turns adding to the story, using the words on their cards. The leader might start the story by saying, "Bill fed the baby chick and it went *peep*." The next child might add, "The baby chick was scared when the balloon went *bang*." The story would be completed when all the children have had a turn. Other groups of words could be used: action words, animal words, people words, toy words, etc. The game could also expand to include writing the story, illustrating the story, acting the story out, and many other creative activities.

Who Is That?

Tape voices; radio and television are good sources, as well as people you know. Tape voices of people the children know: the custodian, the principal, other children. Tape singers, news announcers, political figures, comedians, cartoon characters, and movie stars. Play the voices back and have children identify them.

Where Is the Bell?

With children seated in a circle, have one child leave the room. Give one of the children in the room a bell that is small enough to hide in one hand. Ask the child who left the room to come back in. When the child has returned, have all children stand and shake their hands above their heads. You may use more than one bell when children become accustomed to the game. The player who is "it" has three chances to locate the bell.

Are You Listening?

Fill eight margarine tubs (with plastic lids) with different materials: for example, two with flour, two with buttons, two with nails, two with pins. Have children find the two that sound alike by shaking them.

Whose Voice Is It?

Form a circle of several children. Blindfold one child or have him or her cover his or her eyes. Have this child stand in the middle. Direct children to regroup so that each will be in a different place in the circle. Then have each child make a simple statement such as, "I like to play games." The child in the center then points to one child and identifies this child or asks questions (up to three) that must be answered in a sentence. If the child who is "it" guesses correctly or fails to after three times, "it" returns to the circle and another child becomes "it."

Sight Words with a Twist

Send kids to the Web and have them hunt for images to make their own sight word flashcards. Go to http://www.enchantedlearning.com or http://www.pics4learning.com, both of which offer hundreds of images that can be downloaded, printed, and pasted onto index cards. Ask students to write the words on the back so they can quiz one another. Use different colored cards to represent parts of speech (yellow cards are verbs, pink ones are adjectives), or to distinguish between themes (animal cards are green and sports are blue). Invite students to find images to make themed bingo cards and vocabulary charts (think "Food Bingo" or "Family Words").

Miscellaneous Activities

Story Plot Reporters

Discuss with children the relationship between a story's events and its plot. Then invite students to take the role of news reporters who are covering the events that make up the plot of their favorite story. First, work with children to help them condense their story into six to eight main events that include the first and last events of the story. Write their dictated versions of each event on note cards, or ask them to draw a picture of each event. Have them put their cards in order. Then, using their sequenced cards as prompts, have children present their story-plot reports. You might provide a toy microphone (or paper towel tube) for them to use in their presentation.

Comics-Style Sequence Frames

After reading aloud a story, help children determine the main events and their sequence in the story. Next, hand out six 4-inch squares of white paper to each child. Instruct children to illustrate a different main event on each square, being sure to include the first and last events of the story. Then have children sequence and glue their drawings to a 12 by 18-inch sheet of construction paper so that their story resembles a comic strip. If desired, help them write a caption for each story frame. Finally, invite children to use their sequence frames to retell the story to friends and family members.

Activities for Older Children (Grades 4–5)

The following are some suggested activities to liven up the elementary language arts program. Use your knowledge of each child's reading level to choose those activities that are most appropriate.

Book Reports

The following are some fun ways for older children to give book reports (sometimes a dreaded assignment).

- Allow students to choose a friend who has read the same book and have a debate about it.
- Give students the option of illustrating a mural explaining the sequences of the book.
- Have children simulate an interview about the book. They can ask a friend to be their interviewer or interviewee.
- Have students act out or pantomime scenes from the book.
- Encourage students to create a timeline featuring the events that occurred in the story.
- Have students develop a brochure advertising the book.
- Have students stick puppets that depict characters in the book and display them as though they were giving the report.

- Encourage students to give their report in riddle form; have the class guess what book is the subject of the riddle.
- Allow students to make up comic strips depicting story content.
- Give students the option of creating power point presentations that relate to the story. Students then present their report using the computer and the power points.
- Allow students to write the report as a newspaper article or as an advertisement for television.
- If the story content lends itself to a real-life situation, encourage students to report on the book as a happening in the present environment.
- Allow students to generate some simple sketches on the board as they are giving their report.

Recycling Phone Books

Write scavenger-hunt tasks on index cards, such as "List people whose last names are colors" (John Brown, Mary White, etc.), or "Find people whose last names are jobs" (Baker, Carpenter). This activity builds concentration, sharpens visual discrimination, and improves word recognition.

Reversibles

Explain what reversible words are with examples (*understand, stand under*). Point out that while such turnabout words differ in meaning as they are reversed, the degree of difference is not the same in each case. Players are to write or tell sentences for six pairs of reversibles, trying to use them amusingly and effectively to show their differences. Here are some reversibles to begin the activity: *understudy, study under; overcome, come over; indoors, doors in; outgoing, going out; overdone, done over; overturn, turn over; withhold, hold with; instill, still in.* This can be modified to include illustrations of the reversibles, a spelling lesson, or working as partners to develop lists.

Start With a Poem

Read the following poem together. Discuss what effect there would be on us if there were no stars. Students could make drawings of the night sky using dark-colored paper and white chalk.

The Stars

Like tiny diamond chips they shine,
Suspended in the sky,
Forever forming sparkling shapes,
Beyond the clouds so high.
But, if there were not there to view,
How lonely nights would be,
The sky would seem so empty, then,
No twinkling stars to see.

—Martin Shaw

Invisible Milk Ink Writing

Milk makes a perfect invisible ink to use on cardboard or heavyweight papers such as cardstock or construction paper. Apply milk with a small paintbrush or cotton swab and then let it dry completely. To make the message appear, rub any type of dark powdery substance over the message and the powder will stick to the milk residue. Charcoal, chalk, or graphite from a pencil lead will all work. Try making hidden messages by letting one student write the message in milk and passing it to another student to "decode."

Word Game Day

Ask students to try their luck at a new Word Game Day at http://www.m-w.com/game. Children can try different puzzle formats such as Transform Brainstorm, which lets you change a word into another word, one letter at a time, using clues to the word's meaning.

Using the Dictionary

Have your class find pictures of things and their definitions in different languages at http://www.pdictionary.com/. Children will have fun playing the games they find here with each other.

Listen to Author Podcasts

At Learn Out Loud (http://learnoutloud.com) you can watch and listen to podcasts of your favorite authors and illustrators. Find out Brian Selznick's story behind *The Invention of Hugo Cabret* and learn how Chris Van Allsburg's *Jumanji* and *The Polar Express* became blockbuster movies. Other interviews include Pam Munoz Ryan, Mark Teague, Marc Brown, Jane Yolen, and Betsy Lewin.

Group Story Writing

Visit Google Docs, where students can write and edit a story at the same time from different computers. This is a great group project tool. http://docs.google.com/

Kamishibai

Students work in groups of four, and each student is given a role: sequencer, who determines how to depict the action of the story; artist, who draws the pictures; scriptwriter, who writes a script for each picture; and performer, who acts out the scene. This technique is from Japanese culture. See the following website for more information: http://www.kamishibai.com.

Yesterday's News and Crystal Ball

Ask everyone to write a short paragraph at the start of class either telling someone what they learned yesterday or predicting what they will learn today.

Pass a Sentence

Have students in cooperative groups write a starter sentence and then pass the starter sentence around the group, asking each student to contribute to the paragraph.

Vocabulary Book

For each subject area, have students keep a vocabulary book of words they are struggling to learn. Then encourage students to use these vocabulary words across disciplines. For students who have difficulty with the writing process and definitions, have them draw a picture to help them remember a word's definition.

Poetry and Movement Activities

Theme dance. Any theme from a poem or book can be danced by first brainstorming all the ways to express the theme with body parts, movements, energy, and use of space and time. For example, the theme that courage comes out of fear can be danced in a frozen shape, movements, and frozen shape three-part dance planned and performed by small groups, who will each present a very different interpretation.

Key topic dance. Make a list of important words or topics in a poem or book. Brainstorm all the movements, shapes, levels, energy, etc., that could be used to convey the topic. Give small groups the choice of a topic or word to plan a dance or a series of creative movements to show it.

Character dance. Any character in a story or book can be explored through movement by considering all the ways a character might move. For example, how would Wilbur in *Charlotte's Web* move if he were happy? Hungry? Afraid? Tired? How is Wilbur's movement different from Charlotte's or Templeton's? How does body shape show something about a character?

Line by line. Read a poem to students first. Give each student or group a line from a poem. Then have them explore all the movement possibilities of the line (e.g., the rhythm of the words, the emotions expressed, the images). Encourage more than pantomiming. The poetry can then be danced line by line as a narrator reads, or groups can each plan to perform just one line.

Solutions

On separate paper strips, write these and other problems: lost my door key, scared to give my book report, came to school late, tore my jeans. Post one of the problems on a bulletin board. Working in small groups, children discuss how to respond to and/or solve the problem. Then the groups present and defend their responses. Guide them in considering other responses and solutions.

Reading Pictures

Have students clip magazine photos that show feelings. Show one of the pictures to a group and have them brainstorm the feelings shown in the photo. Then they write what occurred just before the photo was snapped, the dialogue when the photo was taken, and a caption for the picture. For further activities, select photos and ask the students to remark on something happening in the picture. Photos of animals from *National Geographic* work well. Have students describe the weather and location. Next, ask them to tell what happened after the picture was taken, what will happen one day later, one week later.

Pantomime in Language Arts

Prior to the pantomime activity, design a homophone word list with the children. (Homophones are words that sound alike but are spelled differently and have different meanings.) Upon completing the list, children form a circle. The teacher calls out a word and the children pantomime a meaning for that word. Then the homophone is called and the children show that meaning. Try using the following words in this exercise: *ant/aunt; bear/bare; board/bored; buy/bye; clothes/close; eight/ate; flour/flower; grate/great; hear/here; knight/night; lends/lens; marry/merry; prints/prince; ring/wring; shoe/shoo; tow/toe; we/wee; yolk/yoke.*

Activities for Multiple Intelligences

Learning sight words is an important reading skill. Planning sight word activities that are appropriate for children's multiple intelligences or learning styles can make learning sight words fun and challenging. Here are some ideas.

Body-Smart Activities

Sand letters. Fill several shallow tubs with sand. Students can work in groups, taking turns spelling each word in the sand. Once their teammates verify that a word is spelled correctly, they erase it.

Playground ball catch. Using a Sharpie marking pen, write sight words all over each of several playground balls. Have students form groups of four and stand in a close circle. One student tosses a ball to another. The student who catches the ball reads the word closest to his or her right thumb. Younger students can read any word on the ball.

Sit up/sit down. Tell students that you are going to be reading them a short story and that any time they hear one of the sight words, they should stand up. After all students are standing up, signal them to sit down. Do the same activity with the story projected on a screen as you read so that students can see the special word being read.

Body letters. Choose several students at a time to come and spell out one of the sight words by forming their bodies into the shapes of its letters as best they can. Their classmates can guess the word.

Music-Smart Activities

Singing songs. During singing time, take time to point out the sight words in song lyrics. You might also have students sing and spell the words in a familiar song.

Consonant-vowel spelling. Have students spell each word out loud to a partner. Tell them to say consonant letters out loud and to whisper the vowels. This helps students become more aware of individual letters and memorize a rhythm as they are spelling. It can lead to a discussion of the patterns of vowels and consonants as they recognize that many words start with a vowel, others have a vowel in between, and still others end with a vowel.

Teachers can have students do the following "music-smart" activities in developing language skills.

- Make up a rap or song about the spelling (or meaning) of a word/set of facts.
- Use maracas, a tambourine, or a drum to beat out the rhythm while spelling words.
- Make up a cheer with motions and words to advertise your word.
- Make up a hand-clapping rhyme or jump rope rhyme about your word.
- Use maracas, a tambourine, or other music-maker to "shake-write" the word in the air.
- Dance to music and write the word in the air with a scarf, light stick, or wand.

Person-Smart Activities

Group spelling. Ask several volunteers to come to the front of the classroom. Pronounce a sight word and have members of the group spell the word, one letter per student. Once students understand the game, divide the class into groups of two or three and tell them to whisper the spelling of the word you say. Remind them that they are whispering so that other groups have to rely on their own knowledge to spell the words.

Buddy spell. Ask students to choose partners. Give each pair one set of alphabet tiles or cubes (or index cards with one letter on each card). One student says a word, and the other arranges the letters in the correct order. Once the word is correctly spelled, the students change places and continue until they've spelled all the words.

Picture-Smart Activities

Word pictures. Have students write a sight word in large letters in the middle of a sheet of paper and then decorate the page with pictures and drawings.

Word search. Write a short story that includes sight words, and make a copy for each student. Have the students highlight or underline all of the sight words they can find.

Configuration clues. Have students write one word at a time on a sheet of paper. After each word is written, have them draw a box around it so they can see how the word looks (e.g., tall letters, short letters). Older students can draw individual boxes around each letter.

Have students implement these additional strategies in learning new words.

Draw a "word picture." First, write the word in the middle of the paper. Then draw a picture around it that will help you remember the word. Make sure that the picture surrounds the information you are trying to learn.

Create a word search using the words you are trying to learn.

Write your word in the middle of the paper. Use crayons or markers to draw around the shape of the word. Keep tracing around the shape using different colors. Finally, use black marker (or fluorescent, or whatever will stand out) to trace over the word while you spell/say it.

Self-Smart Activities

Study time. Give students a list of sight words to tape to their desk. Each day, give them a couple of minutes to study them.

Journal writing. Have students choose two words each day to copy into their personal journals. Ask them to write a sentence or illustrate a sentence that includes the word. Then relate the sentence to something they enjoy doing in their personal time.

Word-Smart Activities

Introducing words. On strips of butcher paper or word strips, write sight words, one to a strip. Introduce students to a few words each week. Explain to students that they will be learning words that are used a lot. After introducing words, hang the strips in a wall pocket so students can see them throughout the day. Any time one of the words appears in a book or someone says it out loud, have students walk to the pocket chart and point to the word.

Student writing. Have students underline the sight words each time they use them in their writing assignments. Older students can keep a Special Word Dictionary where they write these words.

Paper-plate spelling. Write one letter on each of a number of paper plates and give each student several plates. Have students stand if they have a letter that appears in a word you say. If several students stand up at the same time, acknowledge all of them as you reinforce how the word is spelled.

Logic-Smart Activities

Counting letters. To help students who need a mathematical connection to memorize sight words, have them write each word, count its letters, and write the number of letters next to it. For example, students would write *the* and place a "3" next to it. An extension of this is to have students count the consonants and vowels. Students would write *the* and next to it write "C2, V1."

Categorizing words. Give groups of students each a set of index cards with one of the sight words written on each card. Ask them to work as a group to categorize words that might go together. After they are done, have each group explain its categories. For example, students may feel that all the three-letter words or all the words with *o* in them go together. For many students, categorizing similar words will help them memorize word families. This activity helps to build and strengthen sight word vocabulary as well as to increase students' awareness of phonetic similarities.

Spelling with a fun twist. Students still need to practice their spelling words. But you can bring this review into the 21st century. Try the Puzzlemaker on the Discovery Educator Network (http://puzzlemaker. school.discovery.com). At this site, you can generate customized word searches, crossword puzzles, cryptograms, and letter tiles. By simply keying in a list of words, within seconds you have a worksheet that all of your students can complete.

Challenge students to visit Puzzlemaker themselves and create puzzles to stump their classmates.

Chapter Review

1. What do you think adults can do to foster a child's pleasure and competence in language?
2. What kinds of story experiences might encourage a child to become a storyteller himself? How will you explain to a parent of a very young child in your care the benefits of sharing stories with the child?
3. How can sharing stories strengthen relationships between adults and children? Among children? Among adults?
4. Draw a chart outlining the pattern of growth in the development of language skills. Explain your chart using the information obtained in this chapter.
5. Choose three or more fellow students to be "children." Then role play a scene of your reading to these young "children." (Let your "children" come up with some challenges: maybe they "act up," maybe they "lose interest." etc.) After your "performance," discuss the guidelines you followed in your reading activity. Discuss the problems encountered with the "children" and how they were solved.
6. Spend some time observing children speaking and listening in an early childhood classroom. Describe the differences in the way some children spoke and listened more easily than others in the group. What are the reasons for the differences you observed?
7. Your babysitter speaks to your toddler in a "baby voice." How would you explain to him why it is

important for adults to speak with children in a normal voice?
8. A friend asks you to recommend some books to purchase for her child's preschool class. What are some things you would recommend she consider when purchasing books for this group? Be sure to include in your answer why is it necessary to consider these things.
9. Much is said about being "ready" to read. What exactly does the term emerging literacy mean? Give specific examples in your answer as well as suggestions on how a teacher can help encourage this emerging literacy.
10. Your principal asks you to draft a letter to parents of your prekindergarten class explaining why teaching reading and writing is not appropriate in the early childhood program. Include in your letter exactly what is taught instead in these two areas. Read your letter aloud to your classmates.
11. Using the information in this chapter, rank from the most important to least the factors to use in working with bilingual/bicultural young children in language development.
12. Have you ever had occasions when you had to decide between appropriateness and the value of using a story, song, or book contributed by a family member of a child in your program? If so, what were the issues you considered? How did you resolve the issue, and how did you feel about your decision?

References

Birckmayer, J., Kennedy, A., & Stonehouse, A. (2009). Using stories effectively with infants and toddlers. *Young Children, 64*(1), 42–47.

Bornstein, M., Cote, L., Maital, S., Painter, K., Park, S. Pascual, L., Pecheux, M., et al. (2004). Cross-linguistic analysis of vocabulary in young children: Spanish, Dutch, French, Hebrew, Italian, Korean, and American English. *Child Development, 75*(4), 1115–1139.

Carter, J. B. (2009). Going graphic. *Educational Leadership, 66*(6), 68–72.

Cary, S. (2004). *Going graphic: Comics at work in the multilingual classroom.* Portsmouth, NH: Heinemann.

Debruin-Parecki, A. (2007). *Let's read together: Improving literacy outcomes with the adult–child interactive reading inventory.* Baltimore, MD: Brookes Publishing.

Derman-Sparks, L., & ABC Task Force. (1989). *Anti-bias curriculum: Tools for empowering young children.* Washington, DC: NAEYC.

Dickinson, D., McCabe, A., & Clark-Chiarelli, N. (2004). Preschool-based prevention of reading disability: Reality versus possibilities. In Stone, C. A., Silliman,

E. R., Herebn, B. J. & Apel, K. (Eds.) Handbook of Language and Literacy, pp. 209–177. New York: Guildford Press.

Dunst, C., Trivette, C. & Hamby, D. (2007). Predictors of and intervention associated with later literacy learning. *CELLreviews, 1*(3). Available at: http://earlyliteracylearning.org/cellreviews/cellreviews_v1_n8.pdf

Inge, M. T. (1990). *Comics as culture.* Jackson: University Press of Mississippi.

Isbell, R. T. (2003). Telling and retelling stories: Learning language and literacy. In *Spotlight on young children and language.* Washington, DC: NAEYC.

Justice, K. (2005). *Scaffolding language development through storybook interactions.* Newark, DE: International Reading Association.

Krashen, S. (2004). *The power of reading: Insights from research* (2nd ed.). Westport, CN: Libraries Unlimited.

Massey, S. (2005). Teacher–child conversations in the preschool classroom. *Early Childhood Education Journal, 31*(4), 227–231.

McCloud, S. (1999). *Understanding comics.* New York: DC Comics.

National Institute for Literacy. (2007). National early literacy panel: Synthesizing the scientific research on development of early literacy in young children. Available at: www.nifl.gov/partnershipsforreading/family/pdf

Smith, M. W., & Wilhelm, J. D. (2002). *Reading don't fix no Chevys.* Portsmouth, NH: Heinemann.

Strickland, D., & Riley-Ayers, S. (2006). *Early literacy: Policy and practice in the preschool years* (NIEER Preschool Policy Brief, issue 10). New Brunswick, NJ: National Institute for Early Education Research. Available at http://nieer.org/resources/policybriefs/10.pdf

Wright, B. (2001) *Comic book nation.* Baltimore, MD: Johns Hopkins Press.

Additional Readings

Abell, S. K. (2008). Children's literature and the science classroom. *Science and Children, 46*(3), 54–55.

Anderson, R., & Balajthy, E. (2009). Stories about struggling readers and technology. *The Reading Teacher, 62*(6), 540–542.

Atkinson, T. S., Matusevich, M. N., & Huber, L. (2009). Making science trade book choices for elementary classrooms. *The Reading Teacher, 62*(6), 484–497.

Barclay, K.(2009). Click, clack, moo: Designing effective reading instruction in preschool and early primary grades. *Child Education, 85*(3), 167–172.

Barone, D., & Wright, T. E. (2009). Literacy instruction with digital and media technologies. *The Reading Teacher, 62*(4), 292–302.

Carbo, M. (2009). Match the style of instruction to the style of reading. *Phi Delta Kappan, 90*(5), 373–378.

Carter, S. (2009). Connecting mathematics and writing workshop: It's kinda like ice skating. *The Reading Teacher, 62*(7), 606–610.

Danko-McGhee, K., & Slutsky, R. (2009). *The impact of early art experiences on literacy development.* Reston, VA: National Art Education Association.

Evers, A. J., Lang, L. F., & Smith, S. V. (2009). An ABC literacy journey: Anchoring in texts, bridging language, and creating stories. *The Reading Teacher, 62*(6), 461–470.

Faver, S. (2009). Repeated readings of poetry can enhance reading fluency. *The Reading Teacher, 62*(4), 350–352.

Fingeret, L. (2008). March of the penguins: Building knowledge in a kindergarten classroom. *The Reading Teacher, 62*(2), 96–105.

Graves, M. F., & Watts-Taffe, S. (2008). For the love of words: Fostering word consciousness in young readers. *The Reading Teacher, 62*(3), 185–193.

Helman, L. A., & Burns, M. K. (2008). What does oral language have to do with it? Helping young English-language learners acquire a sight word vocabulary. *The Reading Teacher, 62*(1), 14–19.

Jalongo, M. R. (2008). *Learning to listen, listening to learn: Building essential skills in young children.* Washington, DC: NAEYC.

Jalongo, M. R. (2009). *Young children and picture books.* Washington, DC: NAEYC.

Jones, W., & Lorenzo-Hubert, I. (2008). The relationship between language and culture. *Zero to Three, 29*(1), 11–16.

McGee, L. M., & Ukrainetz, T. A. (2009). Using scaffolding to teach phonemic awareness in preschool and kindergarten. *The Reading Teacher, 62*(7), 599–603.

Morgan, H. (2009). Gender, racial, and ethnic misrepresentation in children's books: A comparative look. *Childhood Education, 85*(3), 187–190.

Moses, A. M. (2009). What television can (and can't) do to promote early literacy development. *Young Children, 64*(3), 80–89.

Moses, A. M., & Duke, N. K. (2009). Portrayals of print literacy in children's television programming. *Journal of Literacy Research, 40*(3), 251–289.

Neier, D. (Ed.). (2009). *Here's the story: The use of narrative to promote children's language and literacy learning.* New York: Teachers College Press.

Nemeth, K. (2009). Meeting the home language mandate: Practical strategies for all classrooms. *Young Children, 64*(3), 36–42.

Neuman, S. B., & Dwyer, J. (2009). Missing in action: vocabulary instruction in pre–K. *The Reading Teacher, 62*(5), 384–392.

Ranker, J. (2009). Learning nonfiction in an ESL class: The interaction of situated practice and teacher scaffolding in a genre study. *The Reading Teacher, 62*(7), 580–589.

Ray, K. W., & Glover, M. (2009). *Already read: Nurturing writers in preschool and kindergarten.* Portsmouth, NH: Heinemann.

Shagoury, R. (2009). Nurturing writing development in multilingual classrooms. *Young Children, 64*(3), 52–58.

Shedd, M. K., & Duke, N. K. (2008). The power of planning, developing effective read-alouds. *Young Children, 63*(6), 22–27.

Tunks, K. W., & Giles, R. M. (2009). Writing their words: Strategies for supporting young authors. *Young Children, 64*(1), 22–25.

Welsh, J. G. (2008). Playing within and beyond the story: Encouraging book-related pretend play. *The Reading Teacher, 62*(2), 138–148.

Williams, C., Phillips-Birdsong, C., Hufnagel, K., Hungler, D., & Lundstrom, R. P. (2009). Word study instruction in the K–2 classroom. *The Reading Teacher, 62*(7), 570–578.

Software for Children

Adventure Workshop: Toddler, 5th ed. ages 2–6

Bailey's Book House, ages 2–5

Blue's Clues Reading Time Activities, ages 3–6

Brainversity, ages 6 and up

Cory in the House, ages 6 and up

Curious George Pre–K ABC's, pre–K–grade 2

Discover Intensive Phonics—Version 40, ages 4–9

Disney Digital Books, ages 3 and up

Free Realms, ages 9 and up

Garfield Gets Real, ages 6 and up

Harry Potter and the Half-Blood Prince, ages 7 and up

Harvest Moon Sunshine Islands, ages 8 and up

Hello Kitty: Big City Dreams, ages 5 and up

Hop! Writing, ages 9–15

Mia Reading: The Bugaboo Bugs! ages 5–9

Monsters vs. Aliens, ages 8 and up

Nitro Web Notebook, ages 5–8

PebbleGo, ages 5–7

Pokemon Ranger: Shadows of Almia, ages 6 and up

Radica Video Journal, ages 6 and up

Scribble & Write, ages 4–7

Storybook Workshop, ages 3–6

The Princess and the Frog, ages 6 and up

Where the Wild Things Are: The Video Game, ages 8 and up

Where's Waldo? The Fantastic Journey, ages 6 and up

Word Roots A1 Software, ages 9 and up

Zoboomafoo: Animal Alphabet, ages 3–6

Helpful Websites

American Speech-Language-Hearing Association, http://www.asha.org

Children's Picture Book Database, http://www.lib.muohio.edu/pictbks

Children's Book Week, http://www.bookweekonline.com/
The Children's Book Council website has dozens of resources and links to support a successful Children's Book Week.

International Reading Association, http://www.reading.org

Literacy Center, http://www.literacycenter.net

Learner.org, http://www.learner.org
Sponsored by the Annenberg Foundation, this site provides free teacher resources and teacher professional development through its satellite channel and video on demand. You can watch master reading and math teachers at work in their classroom.

Make Beliefs Comix, http://www.makebeliefs.com/

MotherGoose.com, http://www.mothergoose.com
This site includes free preschool age-appropriate games, crafts, clip art, recipes, comics, gardening ideas, and rhyming activities.

Readers Theater, http://literacyconnections.com/ReadersTheater.php

Starfall, http://www.starfall.com
This is a learn-to-read website offered as a free public service. Primarily designed for first grade, it is also useful for pre-K and K, as well as second grade.

Stories for Kids, http://podcast.denverlibrary.org

Super WHY! www.pbskids.org/superwhy/parentsteachers/index.html

Story Starter, http://www.storyit.com/Starters/ststart.htm

Teacher Planet, http://www.teacherplanet.com

Storytelling Websites

Creative Drama and Theatre Education Resource File, http://www.creativedrama.com

National Storytelling Festival, http://www.storytellingfestival.net

National Storytelling Network, http://www.storynet.org

Storytelling FAQ, http://www.timsheppard.co.uk/story/

One More Story, http://www.onemorestory.com

Fingerplays for Young Children, http://www.songsforteaching.com/fingerplays/index.htm

For additional creative activity resources, visit our website at www.Cengage.com/login.

Creative Science

When considering creative activities, it is not possible to skip the area of science. This is because true science is a highly creative activity.

There are 20 young children in a classroom. Each has just been given a small box wrapped in brightly colored gift paper. There is a big ribbon around each box. There are some objects inside each box. Each child is trying to find out what is in her or his box without taking off the ribbon and paper.

Some children are shaking their gift boxes. Some are holding them up to their ears and listening very carefully. Others are squeezing them. A few are poking the boxes. They are clearly interested in discovering the contents of what they hold in their hands.

Is this a game? It may seem so, but it is not. It is a way in which children make creative discoveries. In many ways, it is also the way that scientists make creative discoveries. The little gift box is somewhat like the world in which the children live. Children study their own little "world" by shaking the box, smelling it, squeezing it, and looking at it. Each child makes some discoveries but cannot find out everything because the box cannot be unwrapped. Children may be able to make some good guesses after studying the boxes, however. Some things are open to children's discovery; some things are not. Scientists are faced with the same problems. They, too, study the world. They, too, can observe some things and only guess about others.

Science and the Young Child

For young children, science is about trying to understand the world. Young children are natural scientists who observe the people, animals, and objects in their

OBJECTIVES

After studying this chapter, you should be able to:

1. State why science is important to the development of young children.

2. Name and describe three general kinds of science.

3. Discuss environmental education and its place in the early childhood program.

4. Discuss the discovery center and its importance in the early childhood program.

environment, conduct experiments, and report on their discoveries.

Science in early childhood is much broader than what you might at first consider it to be. Try to avoid thinking about science only in terms of activities devoted to "doing" science, such as growing plants or taking a nature walk.

Rather, view science as an ongoing part of the total curriculum, woven into daily activities and routines. Science education occurs naturally when Kenzie wonders why a cork floats and a penny sinks, when Mark questions why ice melts, when Kamal observes he can hear his heart beating as he runs, and when Madison wonders why the water she paints on the sidewalk disappears.

There are two things that both the child and the scientist do. They *investigate* (carefully study the world around them) to discover *knowledge* (find answers to questions or problems about that world). Science consists of two phases, or parts, that cannot be separated: investigation and knowledge.

Importance of Science

Science is important to young children in a number of ways. First, when children are actively involved in investigating their world, they are learning by doing—the most effective way for young children to learn. In dealing with young children, it has been found that the process of investigating is much more important than the knowledge that comes from investigating. Young children need a lot of action, not a lot of facts. This does not mean that understanding the world is put aside completely for young children. It just means that *learning how to find answers* is more important than the answers themselves. However, investigation and knowledge are a team. They cannot be completely separated from one another.

Second, science activities help young children develop skills in using their senses. Use of these skills is not limited to science. These skills can be used every day throughout a person's lifetime. Educators use the term *transfer of learning* to describe knowledge and skills that are gained in one area and used in many other areas. Science skills are particularly important because they are so highly transferable. Skills in seeing, feeling, and tasting are not limited to science even though they do represent the basic skills that are taught.

FIGURE 19-1 • Young children are naturally curious and enjoy the discovery involved in science activities.

Third, science allows children yet another chance to exercise their creative abilities. Science allows young children a chance to play with ideas and materials in an open environment where there is freedom to explore without fear of being "wrong."

Types of Science Activities

There are three types of science experiences for young children: formal, informal, and incidental.

Formal Science

Formal science experiences are planned by the teacher to develop particular skills. A formal science experience that develops young children's fine-motor skills might involve pouring and measuring with tools in the sand and water area. The teacher would plan to include a specific item such as a funnel hung low over the water table or funnels attached to each end of a length of plastic tubing that would serve a specific purpose—the

FIGURE 19-2 • Listening for sound as it travels from a spoon after it has been hit against various solid surfaces is an example of a formal science lesson.

development of fine-motor skills. While other learning might occur because of these implements' inclusion, they serve a specific developmental purpose.

Informal Science

Unlike formal science, **informal science** calls for little or no teacher involvement. Children work on their own, at their own rate, and only when they feel like it. They select the kinds of activities that interest them. They spend as much or as little time working at a given activity as they desire. It is when this sort of openness is available to children that creative potential begins to develop.

Most informal science activities occur in the discovery (science) center. The discovery center is an area in the early childhood classroom where children can participate in a variety of informal science activities that stimulate curiosity, exploration, and problem solving. In the discovery center, young children develop many skills and concepts in their active exploration of such things as sand, water, magnets, and a multitude of other real-life objects. A more specific discussion of the discovery center follows later in this chapter.

Incidental Science

Incidental science cannot be planned. It sometimes does not take place once a week or even once a month. Just what is incidental science?

A city or town may be struck by a violent windstorm. Limbs of trees are knocked down; whole trees are uprooted. Great sheets of rain fall and streets become flooded. Children are frightened by the great noise and wild lightning as the storm passes. Finally the storm is over.

Is this the time for an incidental science experience? Of course it is! This is the time for children who are interested to learn many things. They can study the roots of trees; they may have the chance to observe growth rings. They are able to examine tree bark. They can observe what happens to water as it drains from a flooded street. Some might want to talk about their feelings as the lightning flashed and the thunder crashed. Some may wish to create a painting about the experience.

A teacher cannot plan such an experience. A good teacher can, however, take advantage of such an opportunity by letting children explore and seek an-

FIGURE 19-3 • Incidental science learning can occur when a young child finger paints.

swers to questions. A teacher can encourage children to be more inquisitive and creative.

Inquiry-Based Learning

Inquiry-based learning is a term often used when discussing science experiences for young children. Inquiry refers to investigating to gather information, which is part of human behavior from birth. Infants use all of their senses—seeing, hearing, touching, tasting, and smelling—to explore and collect information.

Because inquiry is such a basic human learning strategy, it makes sense for teachers to use an inquiry-based approach in their science activities with young children.

Inquiry based learning is an approach to learning that involves a process of exploring the natural or material world that leads to asking questions and making discoveries in the search for new understandings. There are several ways to promote inquiry-based learning in the early childhood classroom:

- Ask questions that invite constructive input and validate prior knowledge. For example, instead of "Has anyone ever seen a rock before?" ask, "What do you know about rocks?" Ask open-ended questions. For example, "Tell me about what you're wondering." "What do you think might happen if…?" "What do you notice?"
- Encourage children to wait a few seconds before giving an answer to allow time for thinking. Tell the children you are going to ask a question, but you would like them all to close their eyes and think about it for a few seconds before answering.
- Repeat or paraphrase what the children say without praising or criticizing. This encourages children to think for themselves instead of seeking teacher validation. "Scott thinks that sand comes from rocks, and Claire says it is dirt from the ocean. What do you think? Where does sand come from?"

In science activities, encourage children to look closely, notice details, pose questions and reflect on what they learned. Children's wondering and reflections are essential to the learning process. Also, talking about their experiences with others allows children to articulate what they have seen or done in a way that makes sense. By listening to what others have experienced, children can understand multiple perspectives. Listening to others' insights and opinions and learning that these are of value is a key skill taught in an inquiry-based classroom.

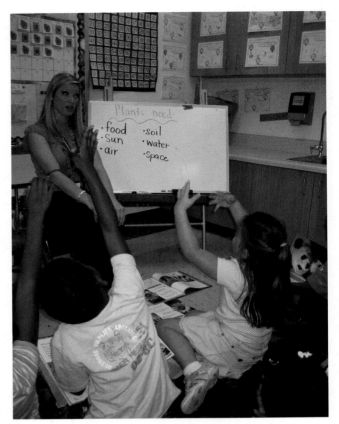

FIGURE 19-4 • The National Science Education Standards present an outline of what students in kindergarten through grade 12 need to know, understand, and do to be "scientifically literate."

National science education standards.

In 1996, the National Research Council (NRC) defined performance standards for children at each grade level, from kindergarten through high school, in its document *National Science Education Standards* (NRC, 1996). All of these standards align with what the National Association for the Education of Young People has determined to be developmentally appropriate practice (Bredekamp & Copple, 2009). These standards support the idea that children can best learn science when it is presented through hands-on, meaningful, and relevant activities.

Hundreds of people cooperated in developing the standards, including teachers, parents, school administrators, curriculum developers, college faculty and administrators, scientists, engineers, and government officials. These standards present an outline of what students in kindergarten through grade 12 need to know, understand, and be able to do to be "scientifically literate" at each grade level. For additional in formation about these standards, visit the website http://www.nsta.org/publications/nses.aspx.

The standards do not require a specific curriculum. Instead, they provide a broad outline of what science experiences students should have from kindergarten through grade 12. They promote dynamic understanding of scientific principles that is always open to review and revision. A comprehensive listing of science performance standards is not possible in this text because of their length and breadth. For our purposes, references will be made to specific activities and how they are aligned with certain science standards. The full text of the national science standards for teaching, professional development, and assessment are found in the book *National Science Education Standards* (1996).

Art and Science

Aesthetics and Science

As we have learned earlier in this text, having aesthetic awareness means being sensitive to beauty in nature and art. Such sensitivity is fostered not by talking about beauty but by experiencing it in a variety of forms—the sight of snow on evergreen boughs, the smell of the earth after a spring rain, the sound of a bird singing overhead, and the feel of a kitten's fur or the moss on the side of a tree. It is easy to forget how amazing a pebble or a pinecone can be to a young child.

For the young child, the world of nature is an especially appropriate avenue for developing aesthetic sensitivity. An early snowfall in winter may provide a child with his or her first remembered experience of snow. Seeing a rainbow in the sky may be something a three-year-old has never experienced before. Watching a butterfly move from flower to flower may provide a visual feast that a child has not yet come to take for granted.

Beauty is not just in what can be seen. It is present also in what can be touched, felt, and listened to. Because the world of nature is so full of sights, sounds, and textures, it can serve as an incredibly rich and readily available resource for the development of aesthetic sensibilities in young children.

Science and Art Materials/Activities

Children working with art materials make scientific observations, noting, for example, that water makes tempera paint thinner and that crayons become soft if they are left near the heat. Evelyn looks at her wet, drippy painting and says, "I wonder if I can blow it dry

FIGURE 19-5 • An appropriate activity for older children is preparing a report on a science experiment.

with my wind." Drew finds that his clay figure left on the windowsill overnight has "gotten all hardened up" because it is no longer wet.

Experimentation with art materials may lead to many other discoveries about cause and effect. Children notice that colors change as they are mixed and that the sponges used for printing absorb liquid. In contrast, other materials such as plastics are found to be nonabsorbent. In using many materials, children observe differences between liquids and solids and see that other items such as wax crayons and oil paints resist water. In mixing paint from powder, children learn that some materials dissolve in water. The operations of simple machines can be understood through using tools such as scissors and hammers. The potential for developing science concepts is in the art materials and in the processes—ready to be discovered and applied. These experiences are consistent with the national science standard that states that children should understand the properties of materials.

Animals link science and art. Young children's natural love of animals is a good place to begin when planning art activities that encourage science experiences.

FIGURE 19-6 • In formal science experiments, the teacher needs to organize materials in advance to ensure a successful experience for the children.

Children are intrigued by animals. Studying animals is consistent with the national science standard calling for the study of animals and their environments. Yet, animals provide more than a science experience for children: they stimulate children's artistic exploration as well. Young children, after touching, seeing, hearing, or smelling animals, will be stimulated to use art media for animal representations. Children with an emotional attachment to household or school pets will be additionally motivated to create visual images. Teachers create opportunities for guided learning about animals by providing art media and materials for children to use, by engaging children in discussions about animals, and by reading stories, showing pictures, and singing songs about animals.

Sometimes after a trip to a zoo or farm, children will be stimulated to visually express their ideas about animals. After the class trip to the zoo, four-year-old Aiden painted an elephant immediately upon returning to school. "Look! Elephants are so funny because they have a tail on both ends," he announced. The

teacher accepted his work but, realizing his confusion, clarified the differences between a trunk and a tail. This example shows how art can serve as a vehicle for direct learning by helping children express their understandings. At the same time, the art responses give the teacher clues for further planning.

Learning about animals and pets can also take place as a result of spontaneous discovery and subsequent engagement in teacher-guided art activity. One day while his kindergarten class was out playing, Edmund found a grasshopper in the field. "Can we keep him?" he begged. By asking pointed questions and providing materials, the teacher guided the children's thinking about how best to keep the insect. She offered a clear plastic cup into which the children decided to put some moist earth and grass. Edmund decided to cover the cup with a piece of paper held on with a rubber band. "I'll make some air holes for air to go in," he responded in answer to a question by the teacher.

Although the insect was set free after one day, several children spent a good deal of time observing it. The teacher suggested that the magnifying glass could be used and guided the children by asking questions: "How does the grasshopper see?" "How are its eyes different from ours?" "Which legs seem to help him jump?" "How are they different from ours?" The detailed drawings of grasshoppers made the next day showed that the questions had motivated good observation. Edmund, whose personal attachment to the insect was the greatest, created five different representations of it.

The following are some activities that expand further on the concept of animals/pets and art activities.

- Encourage older children to draw, paint, or model representations of their pets doing something characteristic.
- Suggest to children that they find pictures for collages showing animals that live in different places, move in various ways, or have different body coverings.
- Provide opportunities for children to make their drawings, paintings, or cutout animals into booklets, murals, jigsaw puzzles, or puppets.
- Offer a variety of boxes, trays, and found objects that children can use to make zoo cages or farm environments for toy animals or models they create.
- Provide scraps of furry fabrics, yarns, and spotted and striped papers in different shapes for children to paste on a background and then add appendages for real or imaginary animals.

- Make a variety of boxes, cardboard tubes, and other found objects available so children can create real or imaginary creatures.
- Provide Styrofoam trays on which children can draw simple animal forms. Pierce the outline at regular intervals for younger children to stitch. Older children can pierce through the trays themselves.
- Transfer children's animal drawings onto felt or burlap. Cut out two duplicate shapes, stitch together, and fill with beans, seeds, or shredded nylon hose for use as toys to toss.

The following sections of this chapter provide ideas that may be used as the basis for planning both formal and informal science activities. These, of course, are meant to be starting points. Teachers will think of many more activities that suit their particular groups' interests and abilities.

The Discovery/Science Center

The discovery center should have things for the children to "do." It is not a center where children just look at objects. Most teachers use a sand and water table in the discovery center. Here various materials— rice, beans, cornmeal, sawdust, mud—can be made available for children to explore, measure, and pour. Sand and water activities are usually informal science and open-ended—that is, children can freely explore and manipulate materials with no definite or specified purpose to the activity.

Another type of activity that usually is done in a discovery center is cooking. Recipes that children can prepare individually with a minimum of teacher supervision work well in the discovery center. There are many simple recipes that do not require cooking (see Chapter 21 for examples of such recipes). If heating equipment is used, an adult must always be present to supervise and assist.

The discovery center can house plants and animals for the children to observe. In addition to caring for them, children can also record information about them, such as the amount of food given to the gerbil each day, the amount of water used for the plant, or the amount the plant has grown.

"Please touch!" is the implied invitation of an interesting, ever-changing discovery center. Many teachers begin the school year with noble intentions of welcoming nature finds and other objects of scientific interest that children bring from home. Perhaps they initiate the project attractively with a bird's nest propped in a small tree branch, some special rocks, and a recently shed snake skin. If the goal of a changing display is forgotten, the old things will lose their meaning. Because there is little appeal in a dusty nest or a tattered snake skin, it is better to retire the too-familiar objects.

Discovery Walks

An easy way to keep the science discovery area new and exciting is to plan nature discovery walks as a regular part of your curriculum. The desire to collect things is a strong one in young children. A discovery walk can be a springboard to some memorable science experiences.

Give children shopping bags and take them on a mini-field trip to a nearby playground or sidewalk. Ask them to collect anything interesting to add to their bag (keeping safety in mind, of course). You'll be amazed at what your young collectors find, including flattened bottle caps, blades of grass, and even an occasional penny.

Sorting and representing. Ask children to unload their collections into a plastic tray or pan. Start sorting, comparing, classifying, and ordering. Have a sheet of paper and markers on hand so that they can trace and label their collections. If you have a computer, use a program such as Kidspiration to take this representation to another level, using the program's rich library of stickers to represent each item. (For more information about Kidspiration software, visit http://www.

FIGURE 19-7 • A leaf print made with leaves found on a discovery walk.

inspiration.com/kidspiration. This program makes it easy to break the collection into groups, sorting by attribute such as floats/sinks, paper/no paper, and so on.

A closer look. A magnifying glass is great for helping children examine their discoveries. Children can sort their collections by lines, textures, colors, or any other art element. You might add magnetic strips to the backs of rocks and place them in categories (big/little, smooth/rough, shiny/dull, etc.) on a magnetic board.

Displaying objects in the discovery center. When a child brings a collection of objects from home, provide a special place for this temporary display. For objects collected by the class, you can organize and store the displays in clear plastic boxes. This way, the displays can be easily rotated among children.

When you have popular items in your discovery center such as prisms or magnets, have duplicates on hand or use a sign-up system. Two to four children can sit on the floor and explore a collection out on a small carpet square or a bathmat. Four chairs set at a table invite four science investigators.

If you have access to a digital camera, snap a photo of each child's collection and print a large, one-page photo of each collection. Below the picture, write a short "I spy" description of a few items in the collection. For example, write, "I spy an item that is round and has lines on it." This invites children's investigation and close observation.

You can also use interesting collections as table centerpieces for special occasions. If you have access to a video camera, you can make a video about the children's collecting and investigating process and share it with parents.

Discovery Centers—Setup

Try to locate the discovery center in an area that both invites children's participation yet controls distractions. Varying the location to fit the requirements of the activity builds interest. Science is very popular on the days when it takes place under a blanket-covered table! Careful planning of space, materials, and time for science will allow children to work as safely, independently, and successfully as possible.

In preschool and kindergarten classrooms, and in elementary classrooms organized with learning centers, many science activities can be set up for independent use. Printed activity directions can be prepared to guide

reading students. Tape-recorded guides for nonreaders can also be made to reduce the amount of direct supervision needed for small-group learning activities.

Discovery Centers—Younger Preschool Children

While the activities in this text are intended for children three years of age and older, many can be adapted for younger preschool children. Two-year-olds can enjoy simple sensory explorations such as feeling air as they move it with paper fans, spinning pinwheels, or swinging streamers on a breezy day. They can feel rock textures and weights, touch ice and then the water it melts into, and watch and then move like a goldfish. They can taste raw fruits and vegetables that have grown from plants, listen to loud and soft sounds, or gaze through transparent color paddles to see their surroundings in a new light.

Three-year-olds might be expected to engage in similar activities, taking in greater detail. They will be able to direct deeper attention to such things as exploring new dimensions with a magnifying glass. This

FIGURE 19-8 • Playing at the water table, children learn many science concepts.

THIS ONE'S for YOU!   Elementary Shoe Box Science

A few simple objects in a shoebox may be all you need to interest your students in science. Unlike commercial science kits that you see in school supply catalogs, this is an inexpensive way to put together just what you need for your own particular group of students.

Collect several shoeboxes or durable corrugated cardboard boxes of similar size and shape. Each box can supplement specific areas of your science curriculum throughout the year and can be adapted to the needs of different ability levels.

Each ready-to-use box kit should create an individualized experience and should contain a set of materials and instructions for each activity. It should also relate to a current topic of study or review and reinforce children's learning on a recent topic of study. Students should be able to retrieve a box from a nearby shelf and return to their seats to complete the activity with very little assistance.

A typical science box contains the following items.

- Statement of the activity objective
- A list of materials in the box
- A list of instructions to guide children in completing the assigned task
- All materials and a worksheet (if needed) to follow instructions
- Questions children should answer upon completion of the activity

The following sample science kit can be used in grades 1–5. You may want to adapt these materials and/or directions to suit your own group of students.

Title of Kit: Blow the Can Down

Learning Objective: Students will demonstrate how air works for us.

Materials

- empty can (16 ounce)
- deflated balloon (large)
- drinking straw
- rubber band

Procedure

1. Place the empty can on a table and try to blow it over.
2. Attach the balloon to the end of a straw and secure it with a rubber band.
3. Set can on top of the deflated balloon.
4. Blow into the straw.

What Do You Think? With which method was it easier to knock the can over? Ask your students to list other ways that air works for us.

More sample shoe box science activities are found at the end of this chapter.

---

group can enjoy some of the classifying experiences on a beginning level: sorting rocks from objects that are not rocks; things that float from those that do not float; and objects that are attracted by a magnet from objects that are not attracted.

In formal science activities, younger children need easily distinguished materials and clearly defined steps. For instance, the seeds in a planting experience should be large and easy to see. A fine, dark lettuce seed is hard to distinguish from a bit of dirt, and a child may not be sure of what he or she has actually done after planting it. A large, pale bean or pumpkin seed that is obviously different from the soil would be a better choice.

Very young children can be easily sidetracked in their reasoning by what they observe. To keep the

objective of science experience evident to them, avoid using materials with irrelevant, distracting details. For instance, if size comparisons are to be made with measuring cups, use cups of the same color and shape to help children focus on size. Younger children will still be exploring materials with their mouths as well as with their fingers. Nonfood materials must not be small enough to swallow. Such foods as peanuts and popcorn should not be given to children too young to chew them well. As a matter of course, adults should closely supervise any activity for very young children.

Thoughtful questioning, careful listening to children's replies, and comments from the teacher guide formal science activities in the discovery center. Open-ended questions such as "What happens when you . . .?" help children focus their thinking.

FIGURE 19-9 • Play at the sand table provides children many opportunities for learning basic science concepts.

FIGURE 19-10 • When children work together on a science project, they learn social skills as well as scientific concepts.

A question such as "Why do you suppose . . .?" allows children to share their reasoning. Many of us use the pattern of stating the answers we hear from children in the form of a question. We may say, "So the cup of snow melted into a smaller amount of water, right? Isn't that what you found?" This style of questioning reduces children's need to discover answers for themselves, or tells them that the main discovery is to find out what the teacher wants them to say.

The discovery center is a place where many of the national science standards can be addressed. The most important aspect of the discovery center is that it is the place where children learn the creative thinking and problem-solving skills that are the foundation of the standards.

Environmental Education

Ecologists have varied estimates on how much time is left before we will have wasted natural resources and polluted the Earth to the point where we can no longer survive. Some fear the damage is already irreversible.

Others believe that there is still time—provided a profound change in attitude and behavior occurs. For adults, this change means finding new values. For children, it means growing up with an understanding of the environment and a desire to conserve and protect those things essential for continued life on this planet.

If children are to grow up in a world fit for human survival, the environment must be protected. Children should learn about nature from their earliest years. Nature is not the only part of a child's environment, however. Home, school, and neighborhood are all parts of the child's environment. In fact, everything that contributes to children's experiences—good or bad—is part of their environment. Can a child learn creativity by learning about the environment? Can a child learn to improve the environment? Can young children learn about ecology? The answer to these questions is "yes." Most of all, learning about these things can and must begin when a child is young.

Their environment is one of the most important influences in the lives of children. They need an environment full of love. They need an environment that provides for their other basic needs: water, food, clean air. Children need an environment that provides for their safety, that helps them grow intellectually, that they can understand and control.

In other words, children need to learn about their environment because their lives depend on that environment. This learning can be done in a very creative way. Activities that help children understand their environment can also help them become more creative thinkers.

THIS ONE'S for YOU!   Sand in the Discovery Center

Sand is an excellent material to include in your discovery center because sand is a material full of creative and aesthetic potential as well as science opportunities. Children love playing with it at the sand table as well as at the beach. Sand is also a medium for many other learning experiences.

For example, ask children the following questions about sand.

- What is sand? (Sand is broken-down pieces of bigger rocks.)

- How is sand made? (When a big rock is worked on by the wind, rain, and the cold, it begins to break down and little pieces fall off. These pieces get worked on by wind or water and they get smaller. The pieces of rock are now sand.)

- Where can you find sand? (You can find sand any place where rocks have been out in the weather. A good place to find sand is at a beach. There the water has beaten off pieces of rock and rubbed them back and forth, wearing them down. The wind has blown the sand pieces, making them smaller and smoother. Dry streambeds are also good places to find sand. Did you know that some big deserts are really dry sea beds?)

- Why is sand good? (Some plants, like the cactus and the watermelon, only grow in sand. Part of your house is made of sand: when you mix sand with cement and water it makes mortar, a thick paste that holds bricks and stones together. If the sand and cement and water are poured out in big spaces, you get concrete. Floors, sidewalks, bridges, and walls can all be made from concrete. The windows in your house and school are made from sand—melted sand makes glass! Sand is also used to keep our water pure, to make sandpaper, and to fill sandboxes. That's why sand is good.)

Now, try these activities for some indoor fun with sand.

Straining Sand. Use some different grades of wire mesh and screening to let children sift sand. Strain the sand through a coarse screen first. Have them examine each successive sifting. Let them use a magnifying glass to really study the sand grains. (Why do some sand grains have ragged edges, and why are other bits of sand smooth? The jagged grains of sand are made from harder rocks than the smooth sand came from.)

Dripping Sand. Fill a big coffee can with a soupy mixture of sand and water. Have children dip small frozen juice containers into the mixture and take out some of this mixture to slowly drip down into a cardboard box. Let children experiment with this procedure, holding the juice can higher, then lower, and varying the thickness of the sand–water mixture. Tall sand mountains, sand castles, and sand stalagmites can be created, and the high sides of the box should help keep the floor clean.

Shaking Sand. Put a big spoonful of mixed grains of sand into a large jar of water. Screw on the lid. Let a child shake up the contents. Then set the jar on the table so everyone can watch what happens. Ask: "Why do the biggest pieces of sand go to the bottom of the jar first?" (They are the heaviest, so they fall to the bottom the fastest.) "Why do some pieces of sand float?" (They are probably little bits of wood or plants or sand that have little air holes.) Notice how as the water clears, the last sand sorts itself out by size: The heaviest sediment falls first and tinier pieces of sand—the silt—finally float down to rest on the very top of the sand.

Sorting Sand. Obtain some sand that has a lot of black grains in it. Spread the sand out on a big sheet of paper on a table. Let the children run a magnet back and forth through the sand. The black sand grains that stick to the magnet are a black iron oxide called magnetite.

Now take all the magnetite and place it on a piece of lightweight cardboard. Tell children that they can make that black sand move around without touching or blowing on it. Can they guess how? Put the magnet up against the underside of the cardboard and move it around. The black sand follows the magnet. Let children try it. Finally, place the magnet flat under a sheet of paper. Gather up the magnetite and sprinkle it on top of the paper. Watch how the magnetite is attracted to the two ends of the magnet so that it makes an outline of the magnet on the paper.

Sand Painting. Sift clean white sand and divide it into several small bowls. Into each bowl mix a different ingredient from the following list: dry mustard, paprika, blue clothes detergent, and instant coffee. You might find other coloring agents in your kitchen. Add water and a little white glue to each bowl and then let the children make sand paintings.

Sand Printmaking. Apply white glue liberally to the veined underside of a leaf or fern. Then press the leaf onto a sheet of colored paper, and lift it off again. Sprinkle the glue leaf print on the colored paper with fine white sand and your sand print will appear.

Types of Environments

For the purposes of this chapter, the term **environment** refers to two things: man-made and natural things that children meet in their surroundings. Streets, houses, and schools are examples of man-made things in the environment. Trees, grass, and birds are parts of nature. Streetlights, cars, and buildings are man-made. Animals, clouds, and snow are natural things. Noise, light, and smells may be man-made or a part of nature.

Children have many environments in which they live. Home is one. It may be a pleasant part of a child's life or an unpleasant one. School is another environment that influences a child's life, and it, too, may be an enjoyable experience or an unpleasant one. The neighborhood environment may be friendly and safe, or it may be hostile and dangerous. There are also many people who are part of a child's environment: parents and neighbors, grocers and police officers, teachers and doctors. The people who make up the communities in which children live may make children feel very good about their lives, or they may make the children feel unhappy.

In these environments, there are also natural things and natural happenings: grass, trees, and flowers; rain, wind, and earthquakes; cats, rats, and beetles. All these things are part of a child's environment. They all affect one another. Nature influences people; people influence nature.

Ecology

Ecology is the study of all elements of an environment, both living and nonliving, and the interrelation of these elements. The term comes from two Greek words: *ecos*, meaning the "place to live" or "home," and *ology*, meaning "study of."

If we stop to consider our work with young children, we have probably touched on the subject of ecology frequently. For example, we notice the changes in the weather and discuss how these affect plants, birds, animals, and ourselves. When we plant seeds, hatch eggs, or care for a pet, we notice those things that are necessary for life and growth—nourishment, light, heat, nurturing. We like to examine and observe many organisms, but if we remove an insect from its home, we take care to restore it unharmed to its place after our observation is finished. Consequently, children learn that all life is precious, and no creature is more or less worthwhile than another.

Those of us in early childhood education are also old hands at recycling materials and using up discards. Bits of paper left over from cutting shapes find their way into the collage box instead of the wastebasket. Empty boxes evolve into constructions, large and small. The blank sides of printed sheets of paper are used for drawing. Old newspapers are used for many art projects. We all think twice before throwing anything away, and with a little encouragement, children and their parents soon catch the saving habit.

By our example, we can teach other ways of living a more ecologically sound lifestyle. For example, using durable dishes for food service rather than disposable dishes is an ecologically sound practice. When food and beverages for snacks and meals come in bottles or cans, these containers should be cleaned and the cans flattened and deposited at a recycling center. The use of personal cloth towels instead of paper towels is another good ecological practice. To encourage parents to recycle, you might consider establishing a collection site at your school, perhaps making it a cooperative project run by the parents.

To truly grasp the concept of ecology, young children need opportunities to observe the total process rather than just a portion of it or only the finished product. Help children understand the total process when you explain the need for conservation. Describing how the paper-making process begins with the cutting down of a tree in the forest and ends with the paper products that we use every day helps children understand why it is important that they use only one paper towel to dry their hands.

Incorporating the subject of ecology into the early childhood curriculum is endorsed in the National Science Education Standards. It is particularly relevant to the standard that states that children should develop an understanding of "types of resources" and "changes in environments" (National Research Council, 1996, p. 138).

These early experiences in ecology will provide students an eventual understanding and appreciation for their part in protecting the environment.

Environmental Activities in School

A child first learns about caring for the environment by caring for his or her most immediate environment, that is, home, school, playgrounds, and parks. In the early childhood years, the teacher can use everyday experiences to point out to children the importance of caring for the environment.

Getting Started

Getting young children outdoors to touch and experience nature is the starting point for learning about ecology and the environment. Unfortunately, a visit to many early childhood classrooms reveals the obvious: indoor time and space are given far more priority than outdoor. Many early childhood programs allot only a short daily period of outdoor time for children's energy release and motor development. In the elementary grades, with state-mandated curriculums, it becomes even more difficult to find time to go outdoors to study and still accommodate all the mandated subjects and time requirements.

Increased time for outdoor learning experience can be worked into the daily routine without difficulty, however, at least in good weather. Music, movement, and art acquire new dimensions outside; there is often plenty of space for construction with large blocks, boxes, tires, and boards; and snack and lunch times become picnics. Best of all, the outdoors provides a natural setting, complete with props, for dramatic play. Middle- and upper-elementary-age students enjoy reading and working on projects outdoors. Small reading groups, project work, and other academic activities can often be done just as effectively in the outdoors. Just think how much you, as a student, enjoy reading outside on a sunny, pleasant day!

Even if the outdoor space is a concrete-covered square, children experience more of nature than they would inside. They know the warmth of the sun, the power of the wind, and the coolness of shade; they find plants that spring up in cracks and insects that crawl or fly; and they experience weather in its many forms.

Obviously, the more natural an environment, the better. Slightly unkempt spaces are more interesting to investigate than blacktop or grassy lawns. In many areas, the edges of property lines where the mower does not reach hold the greatest promise for exploration.

As stated in the national standards on earth and science (Content Standard D), it is important that "all students develop an understanding of the properties of the earth" (National Research Council, 1996, p. 130). Young children are naturally interested in everything they see around them—soil, rocks, streams, rain, snow, clouds, and rainbows. During the first years of school, they should be encouraged to observe closely the objects and materials in their environment, note their properties, distinguish one from another, and develop their own explanations of how things become the way they are.

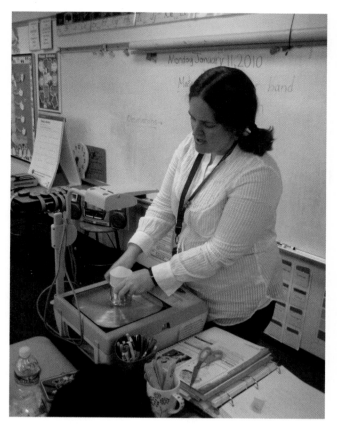

FIGURE 19-11 • In formal science experiments, a teacher often has to demonstrate some necessary steps.

Teacher's Role

To be involved with nature, all you need are curiosity, joy of exploration, and a desire to discover firsthand the wonders of nature. Young children are naturals at this. Adults take a little longer. The teacher's most important role is sharing enthusiasm, curiosity, and wonder. Adults can best do this by using their legs—stopping and getting down to see what has caught a child's attention. Just the focusing of attention, perhaps with an expression of wonderment—"Look how pretty!" or "Great, you found something amazing!"—can encourage exploration and child–adult conversation. When we share our own ideas and feelings with a child, it encourages that child to explore his or her own feelings and perceptions. In middle and upper elementary grades, as children become more familiar with their world, the teacher guides them to observe changes, including cycle changes such as cycles of the moon, predictable trends such as growth and decay, and less consistent change, such as weather.

THIS ONE'S for YOU!   How Do You Ask a Cow for Directions?

Just ask it to point. It turns out that, when they do, most cows select a south-or a north-facing view. At rest or while walking, cattle—and maybe other animals—align their spines like compass needles. When they stand up or settle down, cows tend to point one end north, their other end south.

Cows hid this sense of direction for a long time. Since people began tending cattle more than 7,000 years ago, not a single rancher or herdsman noticed that, on average, two-thirds of a herd set their heads or tails pointing north.

Recently, though, some researchers gained a new perspective by looking down on herds, rather than across them. Using satellite pictures on Google Earth, the researchers noticed that most cows (and roe deer) aligned their bodies poleward.

The researchers looked at photos of 8,500 cattle and 3,000 deer and concluded that both species have magnetic personalities. Somehow, the animals' backbones tend to fall in line with the tug of the Earth's magnetic poles.

These researchers—Dr. Hynek Burda and his colleagues—did not start out to study cows'

directional sense. Rather, the scientists wanted to see if people ever behaved like naked mole rats. Mole rats live in burrows and always put their sleeping nests facing the south side (Burda, 2008).

Dr. Burda went to Google Earth to see if people pitched their tents with a southern view. But tents show up poorly on Google Earth, so he turned to cows instead.

Cows, deer, and mole rats are not the only animals with a nose for north and south. Many long-distance migrators—especially birds—depend on the Earth's magnetic field to orient correctly for their journeys. Other migrators, including some butterflies, bats, and lobsters, lean on magnetism to find their way. Even a few nonmigrators have a magnetic sense, including honeybees, termites, and mice.

No one knows exactly how, or even if, cows and deer use their magnetic sense to some advantage. In the meantime, researchers are looking at other large mammals to see if they, too, spin their backbones north and south (Parker, 2008).

Art and Ecology

Art, music, dance, movement, and storytelling all provide opportunities for children to express their interests and discoveries developed through environmental education.

Setting up easels outdoors may inspire children to paint trees or their feelings about trees. Modeling clay outdoors may encourage children to create their own versions of natural objects in their outdoor play space. Use types of clouds to inspire soft sculptures: stratus, cumulus, etc. (See the recipes in Chapter 14 the appendices for play dough and other modeling material recipes.) In movement activities, children may reflect the wiggle of caterpillars they observed on the playground. In music, the sounds of birds and crickets can be reflected with rhythm instruments or their own voices. They may dance the story of birds, flowers, and animals awakening to the springtime sun. Children's books are also excellent for further expanding a child's understanding and appreciation of the earth. Children's sci-

ence books are an excellent way to address the national science standard that states, "It is important for students to learn how to access information from books" (National Research Council, 1996, p. 45).

The preceding are all general ideas on how to incorporate environmental education and ecology into your early childhood program. The following are some more specific activities related to environmental education and ecology for children of all ages.

- When someone in the classroom breaks a toy or piece of equipment, use the opportunity to talk with children about the consequences—that no one can play with the toy or use the equipment until it is repaired; that if it cannot be repaired, no one can ever use it again. Have children discuss ways of preventing this problem.
- Help children (and by your own example) use materials—paint, paper, crayons, and the like— conservatively by saving scraps, storing unused paint, completing a picture before starting

another, and keeping pencils and crayons off the floor.

- Encourage children to help care for and clean classroom furniture. Provide cleanup materials for washing off tables and chairs and cleaning up spills.

- Before looking at books, discuss with the children the importance of caring for them. Suggestions might include: washing hands, turning pages at the corner, and putting them in a special place away from pets and younger brothers and sisters. Remind them of their disappointment over a missing page in a story.

- Snack time offers an opportunity for children to learn to conserve. The same applies to older children at lunch time. Persuade them to take only what they will eat, to eat all they take, and to refuse what they do not want. Each child should frequently have the opportunity to clean up after snack.

- Before going on a class picnic, remind children to pick up their trash in the park and discuss with them why this is important.

- During the year, encourage appreciation for the jobs of the school custodian, the garbage collector, and others whose work is essential to maintaining a clean and pleasant environment. Invite these helpers to talk with children about what they do and how the children can help make their job easier.

- Avoid frightening children with threats about results of things they cannot control. (Example: What will happen when there is no clean air left?) Concentrate instead on the things they can do, such as keeping their own yards and school grounds neat, putting their own waste in proper receptacles, having a litter bag in the car, avoiding open burning, keeping pets clean, etc.

Pets in the Classroom

The best way for young children to learn about animals is to have them in the classroom. Through observing and caring for pets in the classroom, children can do the following.

- Grow in understanding the needs of animals for food and water, as well as safe, clean housing and attention.

- Grow in appreciation for the beauty, variety, and functional physical characteristics of animals (for example, the protective shell on a turtle, the webbed feet on a duckling, and the sharp teeth and claws on a hamster).

- Grow in compassion for and humane treatment of animals.

- Obtain inspiration for many language experiences and creative activities.

- Good classroom pets are guinea pigs, rabbits, parakeets, white mice, hamsters, turtles, salamanders, gerbils, and goldfish. Good short-time (an hour or so) classroom pet visitors are chicks, ducklings, puppies, a setting hen, kittens, and turkey poults. Of course, before purchasing or adopting any pet, be sensitive to the needs of children with allergies.

Children can help plan for the pet by building the cage or preparing the terrarium or aquarium. The necessary food and water pans can be obtained, a food supply can be stored up, bedding can be prepared, and the handling of the pet can be discussed. Arrangements must be made for pet care during all holidays and vacation periods. A trip to a pet shop would be an excellent experience.

Children should help with the care of the pet once it is obtained, but in the final analysis the teacher is responsible for seeing that the pet is treated well.

FIGURE 19-12 • Learning to care for animals is an important science activity for young children.

Children should learn that pets are not toys, that they have feelings, and that when provoked, some of them defend themselves by biting. Children should not be allowed to handle pets excessively or without supervision. It is cruel to let them wrap pets up in blankets and take them for walks in a doll buggy or to allow any other activity foreign to the pet's nature—and children should be helped to understand why. Neglected or mishandled pets give a negative message about responsibility and respect for life.

Besides learning how to care for pets, children can participate in the following activities.

- They can discuss the way pets feel, how they look, the sounds they make, the way they move, the purpose of various parts of the body, the need for food, their homes, their reproduction habits, and other attributes.
- They can create experience charts about an animal's care and characteristics.
- They can tell original stories based on the pet and tape these stories.
- They can draw, paint, or model the pet out of clay.
- They can dramatize the pet's movements.
- They can take a trip to a pet shop or zoo.
- They can show pictures of animals, telling which are tame and which are wild; which fly, hop, or swim; which live in water or on land.
- They can tell animal stories, recite animal poems, and sing animal songs.
- Older children can write journal entries about their daily observations of the classroom pet.
- They can write stories with the pet as the main character.

Outdoor Science

Many activities work well inside the school. Others are more suited to the area outside the school building. All of the following activity suggestions are consistent with national science education standards. They apply most specifically to Content Standard D in Earth Science. This standard is focused on the child's developing an understanding of: properties of earth materials, objects in the sky, and changes in earth and sky.

Beginning Activities

Children can learn many different things about nature by being outdoors. However, many young children come to school with limited direct experiences with natural environments. Thus, they may have little understanding and great fear about what may happen to them in their encounters with nature. They may fear the darkness of a wooded area. They may think that all bugs and insects bite or sting. In their minds, an earthworm may be a poisonous snake. Such children need a gradual exposure to the world of nature. They need to become familiar with the trees and bushes in the schoolyard before they feel comfortable hiking in the woods. They need to observe and care for classroom animals before they are asked to welcome a caterpillar crawling across their hand or feel the woolly head of a lamb while on a field trip to a farm.

Young children also need to realize that nature is all around them and that wildlife can be found anywhere. Some children seem to think that wildlife is somewhere very separate and far away from where they live. When asked where he might look to find wildlife, one little boy responded, "Africa." For such children, one of the most meaningful lessons would focus on becoming aware of and comfortable with wildlife in their immediate environment.

Ideas on how to begin with simple experiences include the following.

- Have students watch a bean seed sprout in the classroom and then attempt to plant and tend a vegetable garden.
- Allow children to play with snow in the texture table before making and crawling through tunnels of snow in the schoolyard.
- Have children watch birds and squirrels from a "window on nature" before suggesting that they let a goat eat from their hands.
- Have children walk barefoot in puddles, then observe their footprints made on the sidewalk.

Introduce Nature-Related Materials into the Different Learning Centers

To the language-experience center, you can add books and pictures about nature. You can also add stuffed animals, animal puppets, and a variety of plant and animal flannel-board characters. Choose pictures and other representations of animals that are as realistic as possible versus those that have a cartoonlike appearance.

To add nature-related materials to the manipulative center, you might choose simple puzzles with nature themes (animals, plants, etc.) and shells or pebbles of different colors and sizes. You might also add

THIS ONE'S for YOU! Art and Science Activities

Science is a natural springboard for art activities. Try some of the following activities to get children actively exploring the connection.

Art and Reality. Students can examine how a single object is shown realistically in many different ways by artists. For example, show five different pieces of art that feature an animal. Ask how each gives different information and feels different.

Invisible Animals. Have students examine water under a microscope or with hand lenses and sketch living organisms that reside there. Emphasize close looking to capture specifics. Sketches can be enlarged into full paintings.

Three-Dimensional Habitats. Have students use boxes to create dioramas of an animal's habitat (land or water). They might add clay sculptures, tempera paint, and found objects to their construction.

Scientific Drawings. Examine the drawings of Beatrix Potter and Robert McCloskey, both of whom studied animals and plants carefully to render their images. Students can then choose to do a careful scientific drawing, focusing on important details. Use photos or actual plants for close looking.

Color Science. Provide small groups of students a prism to investigate color. Children can paint or use crayons to record observations and discover colors.

Growing Things. Use pantyhose feet to make living heads. Fill hose with a teaspoon of grass seed and then a mixture of soil and sawdust. Tie snugly with a string. Paint on face with fabric paint. Put head in a shallow dish and pour water over it. Place in a sunny area and watch the grass "hair" grow.

Step into Painting. Have students think like scientists and tell or write their observations as they look at a piece of art (e.g., a landscape). Encourage students to focus on the painting's content and how it might have been made.

Spider Web Analysis. Slide a piece of black construction paper behind a spider web and bring it forward so that the web clings to the paper. Dust with flour or dusting powder. Spray with fixative or nonaerosol hair spray. Discuss the patterns of lines created by the web. Look closely to compare and contrast.

---

pinecones, small pieces of bark, dry wood, and other objects found in or near the yard. Similar items could be introduced into the block center as well.

FIGURE 19-13 • Science activities help young children develop skills in using their senses.

Materials from the outdoors also make wonderful additions to the art center. Dried leaves or small pieces of bark can be used for rubbings; seeds, shells, dry grasses, and feathers can be used for collages; evergreen sprigs can be used as paintbrushes.

To the music or listening center, you might add audiotapes of bird songs, ocean sounds, rainforest noises, and other sounds from nature.

The dramatic play area, too, can be enriched with materials from the outdoors. Such materials include camping equipment, garden tools, and a picnic basket filled with a variety of picnic items.

Bird Feeders

Children can design and build bird feeders with the assistance of their parents or another adult. Professionally built bird feeders can also be used outside the classroom.

Children can try to discover what food attracts various kinds of birds. Where is the best place to put a bird feeder? When is the best time of year to watch for birds? What time of day is best for bird watching at a feeder?

Older children enjoy learning the names of the birds they see at the feeders. A book with colored illustrations of local birds can be a research source for this activity. Children can keep records of which birds frequent certain feeders more than others and speculate as to why this is the case. They can make graphs representing use of each feeder.

Cloud and Sky Watching

On a mild, partly sunny or cloudy day, children can learn much about their environment. They can lie on the ground and look up at the sky. They may see distinct clouds of many shapes or clouds that join together. The sun may disappear. It may get cool very suddenly. Birds may fly past.

Children may have many different feelings as they lie still and watch the sky. Questions may arise. How do clouds seem to move? What do they look like? Are there many colors in the clouds? What do clouds look like just before a storm? The teacher might have children make up a story about clouds or suggest they paint a picture about their cloud watching.

The Sounds of Nature

Walking in the woods or along a busy street can be made exciting by listening to the sounds. In the area next to a school, there are many sounds, too. When most of the children are indoors, one or two supervised children may want to go outside and simply listen. They can take a cassette tape recorder along and record sounds, too. Play the tape and encourage children to move like the sounds make them feel.

How many different sounds can they hear? Can they hear sounds made by birds? By animals? What do the leaves in the trees sound like? How do trees without leaves sound? What other sounds can be heard? How do noises made by cars differ from noises made by trucks? How does a person feel if there is too much noise?

What Happens to Rain Water?

After a rainstorm, children can try to follow the paths taken by the water. Does all of the water flow into a sewer? Does some of it go into the ground? What happens in paved areas compared to grassy areas? What happens in dirt areas compared to grassy areas?

Older children can learn about the effects of erosion in their own parks and playgrounds. This can easily be done after a heavy rainstorm on the playground or in a nearby park. Making mud pies and mud finger painting are great follow-up activities to these observations.

Animal Hiding Places

There may be a small hole in the ground or a sand hill in a crack on the playground. Thick grass or bushes serve as hiding places for animals. Under a large rock or near the foundation of the school there may be places for living things to hide.

Children seek answers to many questions about animals. Why do animals need hiding places? Can a child create a place where an animal will choose to hide? How many natural hiding places can be found? Can children create hiding places for themselves? How do they feel when they are in their hiding places? Can they move like an animal looking for a hiding place? Can they move like that animal as it goes into its hiding place?

If creativity is to be a part of activities such as these, decisions must be left to children. Help from the teacher should not take the form of orders about what to do and what not to do. Advice is good; orders or carefully worded cookbook directions are not.

Plants in the Environment

Probably the best way to observe the magnificent color and variety to be found in plants is to visit the places where they can be seen firsthand. The school grounds are the closest source. Children can hunt with you for the tallest tree, the one with the roughest bark, and the ones with needles, pinecones, or smooth leaves. They can hunt for plants that are growing in cracks in the sidewalk, for plants that have been eaten by insects, and for seeds, berries, and roots that are exposed.

Going beyond the schoolyard, trips can be made to the grocery store, supermarket, or farmers' market to examine firsthand the potatoes, carrots, onions, eggplants, peas, cabbages, beets, and other foods. Vegetables are beautiful and occur in many colors, shapes, and sizes. One of each kind brought back to the classroom would provide a wonderful opportunity for children to make comparisons among them.

The same kind of observations can be made with fruits, or with flowers at a greenhouse, shrubs at a nursery, or plants in an arboretum or small neighborhood garden or truck farm. Plants can be looked at, cooked, taken apart, tasted, felt, counted, smelled, and weighed. They could be compared for color, texture, juiciness, shape, kind of leaf, aroma, size, and outside covering. They could be classified by the preceding characteristics as nuts, seeds, fruits, roots, leaves, stems, or vegetables, usually eaten raw or usually eaten cooked.

If trips are not possible, each child could be asked to bring one fruit, vegetable, or other plant to school, or the teacher could supply the necessary items from the school budget. Some other suggestions follow.

- Have seed catalogs available in the book center for children to browse through.
- Have children plant seeds in pots, or better yet, if a small garden plot is available, have children use it for planting and nurturing a "crop." Seed dealers can advise you on types that germinate quickly and what care they need. Press a stick such as a tongue depressor down into the soil by the seed when it sprouts. Have children mark the height of the sprout each week as it grows. The date and name of the plant can be put on the stick. If the seeds in some pots don't grow, dig them up to see what happened to them.
- Help children build a model greenhouse in the block center, using planks, large blocks, and packing boxes. They can put their plants in the greenhouse, as well as small trowels, watering cans, a bag of potting soil, and experience charts.
- Have children start plants from seeds, cuttings, bulbs, roots, and tubers. Sweet potatoes, placed in glasses so that half the potato is under water, will produce roots and a luxuriant vine. (Try to find potatoes that aren't bruised.) Bulbs of all kinds can be started. Geraniums and philodendron will produce roots from cuttings placed in water and can then be potted. Pussy willow twigs will grow roots in water.
- Show children how to make top gardens by cutting off about an inch from the top of root vegetables, such as carrots. When children place the cut end in water, new, leafy growth will shoot up.
- Have children break or cut apart seeds of various kinds to study the small plant inside. Then have a plant tasting party. Examples: Seeds—sunflowers; roots—carrots; stems—celery; leaves—lettuce; flowers—cauliflower.

- Help children sprout seeds so that their growth can be studied. A satisfactory way to do this is to cut up blotting paper or paper towels. Place a couple of layers in the bottom of a saucer, moistening the paper thoroughly. Drop six to ten radish seeds on the blotter. Smear a little Vaseline around the edge of the saucer and cover with a piece of window glass. Tiny white root hairs will develop.
- To see roots, stems, and leaves form, have children make a plastic bag greenhouse. They can place folded paper towels inside a plastic, self-locking bag, then staple a line across about two inches from the bottom. Children can fill the bags to just below the line of staples with water, then drop in seeds. Seal the bags and display them on a bulletin board for children to observe their growth and development. Children will be able to see the roots, stems, and leaves form.

Water Play Experiences

No matter in what quantity or container water is available—in a pool or basin, in a puddle or cup—there are ways to take advantage of its learning potential! A wading pool or large basin lends itself to pouring, sprinkling, and mixing with water, while a cup or a puddle is ideal for floating tiny objects like foil boats or cork stoppers and for dissolving small quantities of sugar or drink mix. Whatever facilities can be provided, water provides a marvelous science experience for young children.

Organizing the play space for water play is a matter of selecting and arranging suitable containers and appropriate equipment. A laundry tub or plastic wading pool can be placed outside with a bench or table nearby to hold objects. If water play is to take place inside, the floor covering must be water repellent, and a shelf can be used for equipment storage; a plastic tablecloth can be a weatherproof carpet and a small card table can substitute for the shelf. Plastic aprons are ideal for clothing protection, but garbage bags with neck and armholes cut serve well, too.

Objects that lead the child to science experiences might include the following:

- sponges, corks, and light pieces of wood
- funnels, strainers, colanders, plastic tubing, and siphons
- spray containers, sprinkling cans, squeeze bottles, and rubber balls
- plastic pitchers, margarine tubs, plastic cups, and yogurt containers

THINK ABOUT IT

Children's Literature and Science Learning

Two researchers have studied how children learn science from children's literature. In the first study, Mayer (1995) read a narrative account of whales individually to 16 children from kindergarten through third grade. In the book, the main character addresses and corrects a little girl's misconceptions about whales. After reading the book to each child, Mayer asked the child to retell the story and answer a set of questions. What she found was surprising. Children remembered the erroneous ideas held by the girl instead of the correct information related by the main character. Rice (2002) and her colleagues took Mayer's study a step further. They read five books about whales to two classes of second graders and one class of fourth graders, preceded and followed by a series of true/false questions. They found that students had some prior knowledge about whales from their pretest answers. In analyzing posttest results, the researchers found that children did not change their answers to most questions. However, when they did change their answers, it was to mirror the information in the book that was read to them, whether correct or incorrect. In both of these studies, the researchers found that children do remember information presented in books, whether accurate or not. This implies that teachers have a critical role to play in helping students learn science with children's literature.

So, how can teachers use children's literature in science effectively? The first step is to find the best books for your science unit. Several researchers provide examples of scientifically accurate books for teaching specific topics (Barclay, Benelli, & Schoon, 1999; Marriott, 2002; Pringle & Lamme, 2005; and Wells & Zeece, 2007). Each March, *Science and Children* publishes the list of Outstanding Trade Books for Children selected by the National Science Teachers Association (NSTA) and the Children's Book Council. Visit http://www.Nsta.org for this list.

Once you have some books to use in your unit, consider how best to use them. Try to use children's literature to motivate children for a science study. Use the books during the concept introduction phase of the learning cycle (Brown & Abell, 2007) after students have engaged in firsthand experiences with a science phenomenon. Some researchers have suggested that books with scientific errors can actually provide fruitful avenues of study. For example, Trundle and Troland (2005) suggest that, when studying the moon, teachers can have children make regular observations of the moon phases and then follow up by comparing their observations with illustrations in various books. According to Rice (2002), using children's literature in this way can help children become critical readers, questioning the accuracy of what they read.

- paintbrushes, paint rollers, and washcloths
- spoons, dippers, plastic syringes, and plastic medicine droppers

Occasionally, bubble bath, cornstarch, food coloring, or other mixables can be added to vary the appearance and physical properties of the water.

Safety tips. Always have an adult with the children in any water play situation. Never leave a child unattended. Use only unbreakable materials for water play activities: never use glass, ceramic, porcelain, pottery, china, or other breakable materials. Always gather materials ahead of time so you do not have to leave children unsupervised.

Develop water play rules with children. Discuss and generate a list of rules that are appropriate to your situation and revise them as needed. For example, you will need one set of rules when children are playing at the water table and another set for the outdoor pool.

Appropriate rules are presented here.

- No splashing is allowed.
- Keep the water in the containers.
- Mop up spills immediately.

Specific activities for water play are included at the end of this chapter.

Summary

Science activities help children acquire knowledge about the world around them through investigation of that world. In science for young children, the emphasis is on investigating; the knowledge gained is less important. Learning about science is important for all children because it gives them an opportunity to succeed. Formal science activities are planned by the teacher to develop particular skills, such as fine-motor skills or awareness of the five senses. Informal science, on the other hand, calls for little or no teacher involvement. Children work on their own and select the kind of activities that interest them. Informal science activities are less structured than formal science activities. Creativity is, therefore, better served by informal than by formal science. Incidental science activities cannot be planned because they are based on events that occur randomly. An effective early childhood teacher makes use of these events to enhance and extend students' learning.

The National Science Education Standards present an outline of what students in grades K through 12 need to know, understand, and be able to do to be "scientifically literate." They provide a broad outline of what science experiences students should have from kindergarten through grade 12.

Ecology is the study of all elements in the environment, both living and nonliving, and how these elements are interrelated. The term comes from two Greek words: *ecos*, meaning "place to live" or "home," and *ology*, meaning "study of."

Children should begin to understand that all forces in the environment affect one another. Animals influence other animals. Plants affect animals. The climate has an effect on the environment. People can make the environment pleasant or very unpleasant.

Children should have experiences with both the natural and man-made environments. These experiences take place in the school building and in the play area around the school. They also take place in the community in which the children live. Playing with sand and water allows young children to experience the natural environment.

Key Terms

ecology 470
environment 470
formal science 460
incidental science 461
informal science 461
inquiry-based learning 462

Learning Activities

Science Activities

1. Take a field trip. Walk within one square block of your home or school. Identify all of the plant life in this area. How many trees, plants, shrubs, and weeds can you observe?

2. Create a file of resources in the community that could be used to foster children's concepts of their environment and the world around them.

3. Observe in a classroom where there is a living pet or pets. Record children's conversations as they interact with the pet. Discuss how much they have learned about the animal from direct observation. What did their questions/conversations tell you about their experiences with the pet? Be specific in your answers.

4. Using a pail of water, create a puddle on a playground in order to observe children's reactions as they approach it. Describe the ways in which they play.

5. Plan a science table where children can be involved in making discoveries. List the objects you might include and describe the types of involvement each object might stimulate. Discuss your list with others in your class.

6. Visit a playground. List natural phenomena that seem to be of interest to children. As you observe children at play, describe behavior that indicates they do take an interest in these phenomena. Compare what interested you at the playground to what interested the children. Discuss the differences between your interests and those of the children.

7. Visit one (or more) of the websites listed in the Helpful websites section of this chapter. Choose a science activity from the website and use it with children. Report on the success of the activity. Rate the website on the following: (1) ease of use, (2) quality of activities, and (3) developmental appropriateness.

Making Observations

The ability to make many accurate observations is an important skill for both children and adults. The following activity is designed to test your ability to make observations using all of your senses (seeing, hearing, smelling, tasting, and touching).

A. Materials: A package of peppermint Life Savers, ruler, book of matches, small nail, sheet of sandpaper, glass of water, and waxed paper.

B. How many observations can you make about the package of peppermint Life Savers? Can you make as many as 40 observations? Try doing this with one or two partners, if possible. Do it for each of the items listed in letter A.

C. List all your observations and write down the sense or senses that you used to make each observation (seeing, hearing, etc.).

Finding Objects for Making Observations

A. Find 10 objects that can be used for making observations. Each object should provide opportunities for an observer to use all five senses. An ice cube is one such object.

B. After finding the 10 objects, try the following.

1. Decide what other materials would be helpful in making observations of this object (e.g., a ruler or magnifying glass). Make a list of these materials.
2. Collect all materials needed for observing each item and place them in small packages or boxes.
3. Choose a partner. Make observations of three of your partner's objects using materials provided by your partner. Then let your partner do the same with your objects and materials.

Describing Shapes

A. Draw three shapes on a piece of paper. The shapes should not be easily recognizable.

B. Choose a partner. Try to describe each of the shapes in such a way that the partner can draw pictures of them without seeing them. This task is more difficult than it sounds.

Finding Materials

A. Visit rummage sales, farm auctions, store sales, and secondhand stores. Look for materials that could be used by children in science activities.

B. Make a list of things that can be bought, how much they cost, and where they can be purchased. Compare your list with the lists of several other students.

C. Prepare a master list of materials for science activities.

Activities for Children

Water Play Activities

In all of the following activities, be sure that an adult is always present when children are playing with water.

Rainbow in a Bowl

This activity shows children that light is made up of color. Place a clear bowl of water away from direct sunlight. Put one drop of clear nail polish in the water. Have children look at the water and nail polish from different angles to see a rainbow of colors. Then ask them to share other times they have seen rainbows, such as in water from a sprinkler on a sunny day.

Miscellaneous Water Play Ideas

- Straws are great for blowing bubbles during water play. To prevent children from sucking up the soapy water by mistake, poke holes near the tops of the straws first.
- Make soap bubbles last longer by adding a few tablespoons of sugar to the soapy water.
- Add variety to the water play area by adding these items and activities:
  - Fill the water table with ice cubes and provide shakers of salt and lengths of string.
  - Punch a row of holes from the bottom to the top of a two-liter plastic soda bottle.
  - Put salt in the water, then let children try to float and sink objects.

- Substitute snow for water.
- Put a large chunk of ice in the water table. Provide safety goggles, rubber mallets, and rock salt.
- Provide lengths of plastic pipe, whole and also in sections cut in half lengthwise, to use as canals and ramps for rolling marbles, small toy cars, or blocks. Have children use the piping dry, then wet, and compare results.
- Punch holes in the bottom of milk cartons to make sieves. Use a variety of sizes of cartons and vary the size of the holes.
- Add foam or rubber alphabet letters and small fishnets to the water play center. Have students name the letter they catch or catch the letters that make up their name.
- Encourage children to experiment with varying the amounts of water and air inside zippered sandwich storage bags in floating experiments.
- Give children heavy aluminum foil to shape into boats.
- Challenge children to create a boat from found objects, then move it from one end of the water to the other without using their hands.
- Challenge children to make a bridge over a portion of the water using scrap materials.

Observing the Moon

Read the book *Wait Till the Moon Is Full* by Margaret Wise Brown (HarperCollins, 1989). Moon facts are woven into this story about a young raccoon that must wait for the full moon before he can go out at night.

Read this story aloud on the first day of a new moon. Explain that the time between new moons marks the time it takes the moon to make one revolution around the earth. Have students make a calendar grid on a sheet of large chart paper and mark the current date with "New Moon." Tell children that each day one person will take the moon calendar home in a poster tube. The child whose turn it is to take the calendar home should go outside that evening with an adult to observe the moon and then make a drawing on the calendar of how the moon looks. (In inclement weather, children can observe the moon from a window.) Save a brief moment in your morning routine for the moon report. You can show children daily images of the moon on the Internet at http://www.kidsastronomy.com/astroskymap/lunar. htm. Click on "Current Night Sky."

Shadow Hunting

On a sunny day, gather children in a circle outside. Bring a small object such as a book or a doll with you to demonstrate a shadow. Talk about shadows. Does everyone know what a shadow is? Has everyone seen his own shadow? What other kinds of shadows have children seen? As children are sitting in the circle, can they see their shadows and those of their neighbors? What do the shadows look like?

Next, take a shadow walk with children around the school neighborhood. Look for all sorts of shadows—birds, trees, houses, clotheslines, cars, signs, people, animals, etc. Do the shadows of things look the same as the actual objects? How are they alike? How are they different?

If possible, take a morning and an afternoon walk and observe the same shadows. Do the shadows look different at different times of the day? On your hunt, walk on both sides of the street. Art there places where there are no shadows?

During the walk, have children stand in the shade. Can they see their shadows? (Explain that shade is a shadow.) Look for shadows of moving cars, people and animals. Do the shadows change as these things move?

After you've finished the shadow walk, have some more shadow fun outdoors. Put on some music and invite children to dance. What happens to their shadows? As your children move, can they make their shadows longer? Shorter? What happens when they move their arms and legs in different directions?

As the children are moving, encourage them to step on each other's shadows. Every so often, say, "Freeze!" as you stop the music. As the children stand frozen, have them look at their shadows. Do any shadows look the same?

Build a Bird Feeder

Treat a bird to lunch. Cut windows and doors into an empty milk carton or plastic soda bottle. Have children decorate this container in such a way that birds will want to visit. They might paste on colored pictures of big juicy worms, or glue on twigs, leaves, seeds, and other outdoor things with nontoxic glue. (Keep decorations to a minimum so as not to frighten the birds.) Fill the feeder with bird seed and hang it up near windows where children are able to observe the birds enjoying their food.

Pinecones can be used for another type of bird feeder. Help children spread sugarless peanut butter on pinecones and roll them in wild birdseed. Birds love peanut butter, and it provides protein and oil for healthy feathers and bodies. Children can fasten the pinecones to the branches of a tree using floral wire.

Young children are keen observers of nature and will enjoy the variety of birds their feeders attract. See how many birds and what kinds of birds use the feeder. Encourage children to make pictures or paintings of birds that come to the feeder.

More bird-feeding ideas follow.

- Under supervision, even young children can manage to thread peanuts in shells onto a string with a large, dull-tipped rug needle. Hang up these "necklaces" for the birds. Be aware of children who may be allergic to peanuts when using this activity.

- Children can make "bird pudding" from stale bits of bread, raisins, bird seed, and bacon bits, moistened with water and put out for the birds. Put the pudding out as is or put it into half a coconut shell. A small hole drilled into the coconut shell will enable you to hang it up where it can swing freely as birds land to feed.

Rocky Road to Knowledge

Rocks, stones, and pebbles are not only interesting, abundant, and free for the taking, but they also provide a rich source of knowledge about matter and are a means of sharpening powers of observation, description, and classification.

A. Have children do the following:

1. Sort rocks by size, color, texture, and surface.
2. Identify rocks by name.
3. Take a walk to see the many ways stone is used in buildings.
4. Look for fossils in limestone.
5. Take a field trip to hunt for interesting rocks.

B. Equipment that is useful in carrying out such a study includes scales of various types, magnifying glasses, and boxes (or egg cartons) for sorting.

Explore the Powers of the Sun

Explore the power of sunlight—what it will pass through and what blocks it. Using different materials (clear glass, soda bottles of various colors, thin paper, construction paper), have children sort items by their ability to allow sunlight to pass through. Talk about shadows, too.

Plant Press

Collect nonpoisonous fallen leaves and flowers such as dandelions or clover. Pick flowers from gardens only with permission.

To make a plant press: On top of a piece of corrugated cardboard, layer two or three paper towels. Spread out leaves or flowers flat on the paper towels. Place several sheets of newspaper on top of this stack. Write the child's name with markers on the top.

Put heavy books or bricks on top of the plant press. Dry overnight. Change the newspaper each day until the plant is dry.

Use the dried leaves and flowers to make a collage by arranging the dried plants on colorful construction paper in a design. Cut pieces of construction paper may be glued on for added designs. Add more decorative details with markers or crayons.

Variations: Let children predict what they think will happen to the color and shape of plants as they dry. Measure sizes. Draw before and after pictures.

Feast on dried foods. Make fruit leather, dried fruit, or jerky. Taste raisins, dried plums, and apricots. Mix up dried milk. Make gelatin or pudding.

Study plants such as milkweed and dandelions. Make dazzling bouquets with dried flowers.

Dandelions

In spring dandelions are everywhere, and children not only notice them but touch them, note their color, count them, and pick them.

Dandelions seed early, rapidly, and in great quantity. They grow fast and recover from damage quickly and powerfully! So children may pick them, dig them up, and tear them apart. Respect for nature is an important aspect of learning about the environment, but exceptions to rules exist in every field of study. Weeds are exceptions because of their hands-on study value for young children.

Ask children if they ever noticed that dandelions let out a milky juice when picked? Or that the stem is hollow? Rub the flower on paper to obtain a yellow pigment, or create a "duplicate" dandelion by rubbing flower, stem, leaves, and soil on the paper. How fast do the dandelions in a lawn grow after being cut? Have children try watching and measuring. How deep do the roots of a dandelion go? Why not dig up some dandelions and determine which is the longest?

Early French explorers named this weed *dent-de-lion,* mispronounced by the English as "dandelion." The original means "tooth of the lion" and refers to the leaves. Can children see and feel "teeth" on the leaves? If you cut several leaves from the plant and superimpose one upon another, you will recognize the diversity of shapes.

Insect Cage

Cut openings in small plastic or cardboard cartons. Cover the opening with fine netting, taping it into place. Fine netting can also be taped over the top of any plastic container to provide a temporary home for insects. The children can observe insect life more easily if the insect cages are made from clear plastic containers.

A clean, empty, half-gallon milk carton also makes a good insect-viewer. Simply cut rectangular holes on two sides of the milk carton. Slip a nylon stocking over the carton and fasten at the top with a rubber band. Insects can be held inside for temporary viewing.

Be sure to release the insect back into its natural habitat after children view it.

Examining Windowsill Dust

Give pairs of students two index cards and have them mount them on a piece of tagboard, date them, and smear them with petroleum jelly. Partners then place one of the cards on the windowsill inside the classroom, then attach the other with masking tape to the windowsill outside. Each day for a week, have students check their dust—collecting cards, look at them under a microscope, and record their observations. Afterward, discuss what the many particles they see may be, how they got carried through the air, etc. They may want to illustrate some of the many interesting things they saw under the microscope.

Backpack Ideas

Children enjoy backpacks. You can incorporate them throughout the day in the following activities.

- Create a Writing Backpack filled with pads of paper on clipboards and colored pencils for children to carry off to a private place to write.

- Pack a Snack Backpack for taking snacks outdoors. Fill the bag with napkins, a tablecloth, finger foods, and a bottle of water.

- Fill a backpack with puzzles and quiet games for children to take to a private place for a quiet get-together.

- Put together a Take-Home Backpack filled with this week's favorite toys, games, and books for children to share with their family.

- Create an Exploring Nature Backpack. Pack this bag with some of the exploration items listed below to inspire children to explore nature all around them. Start by inviting children to look around the area and describe what they see, smell, feel, and hear. Then pass out materials for free exploration. Blow a whistle when you want to bring children back to a gathering place and share their findings. Exploration items: unbreakable magnifiers, paper towel tube "spy glasses," and pads of paper and crayons.

- Put together an Outdoor Art Backpack. There is much excitement when art materials are taken outdoors. Introduce a material (see the following list) and a technique on a table or blanket and then give children time to explore the area. Materials: drawing paper and flat crayons for nature rubbings; chalk for sidewalk and wall drawings; a collection of boxes with fasteners, rope, and glue for making a group sculpture; and paintbrushes and containers of water to paint everything in sight!

Observing Worms

Make an earthworm observatory with a large glass jar (a large peanut butter jar is good), worms, garden soil, and black construction paper.

Place a layer of small rocks or sand in the bottom of the jar so water will drain. Place two inches of moist soil and sand in the jar. Have children pick up worms and place them in the jar. Cover them with more soil. Keep the soil moist. Seal, using a lid with holes punched in it.

Wrap black construction paper around the jar. After 24 hours, remove the paper. The children should be able to see the worms tunneling through the soil.

Encourage children to talk about what interests them about worms.

Sky Gazer

Save the cardboard tubes from paper towel rolls. Punch two holes at one end of each tube and loop an 18-inch piece of yarn through them (make one for each child). Have children hang their telescope around their neck. Go outside on a nice, warm day and have children lie down on the grass. Direct them to use their telescope to look up into the sky. What do they see? Have children look some more. What else do they see?

Bugs are Fun!

For this activity you will need magnifying glasses, play dough or self-hardening clay, art materials, including construction paper, tissue paper, markers, glue, scissors, yarn, and pipe cleaners, chart paper.

In advance, read many books about insects. Have pictures for children to look at in your learning centers. Discuss the fact that scientists that study insects are called entomologists. Explain to the children that all insects go by the "3 + 3 rule"; three parts of the body (head, thorax, and abdomen) and three pairs of legs. Show the children this rule using a picture or specimen.

Explain to the children that they will be entomologists for the morning. They are going on an insect hunt together. Ask where they think they would find insects. Where would they hide if they were insects? Tell them that they will observe insects in their natural habitats. Stress to the children that they should not harm the insects, that they are scientists observing them in the field. Ask them to watch the way the insects move. What colors are they? How big are they? Look for the 3 + 3 rule.

Take children outdoors to search for insects. Give each child a magnifying glass, which will help narrow their field of vision and focus their attention on a small area. Encourage children to share what they find with one other. Be sure to repeatedly use the scientific names for the body parts in order to build vocabulary. Ask them to specifically look for the head, thorax, and abdomen.

Once back inside, have a group discussion about the insects. Make a chart with a list of insects the children found and the information they collected. Did the 3 + 3 rule help them identify insects?

Invite the children to create an insect of their choice. Have a variety of art materials available so children can choose which medium they would like to use. Encourage them to try to show the 3 + 3 rule in the insect they create. If they want, children can label the parts of their insect or dictate the labels to you.

Remember: Some children may be afraid of bugs. Be respectful and let them observe with you or a friend. Also, young children may become so absorbed in creating their own bug that they make more legs or body parts than is accurate. This is completely acceptable. Talk with the child about the various body parts and legs, and reinforce the vocabulary you are teaching.

Bubble Experiments

For this activity you will need a plastic dishpan, ingredients for bubble-blowing solution (½ cup water, ¼ cup liquid detergent, 1 teaspoon sugar, food coloring [optional]), a commercial bubble pipe and solution (optional), toilet paper tubes, sieves, straws, and pipe cleaners.

Take the children outside and talk about blowing bubbles. Try sparking children's curiosity by blowing some bubbles from a commercial bubble pipe. Explain that each child will get a chance to experiment with different ways to blow bubbles.

Put out the dishpan of bubble solution along with a variety of bubble-blowing objects such as toilet paper tubes and sieves. Invite children to experiment with these objects.

Using straws, help children construct their own bubble blowers. For each child, make slits in one end of a straw and help the child bend the slits back. Invite each child to dip that end of the straw into the solution and blow bubbles.

Pass out the pipe cleaners and help children create wands to dip in the solution. Encourage them to create different shapes with their pipe cleaners and to wave the wands through the air.

While children blow bubbles with the straws and pipe cleaners, ask, "What size bubbles does each one of the blowers make? How many bubbles come out at a time? One? More than one?" Talk about which blowers children thought worked best.

For younger children, you may want to offer several commercial bubble blowers, which tend to be sturdier and easier for small hands to manage.

For older children, encourage experimenting with ways to strengthen the bubbles they make. Ask, "Which bubbles seem stronger, the big or small bubbles? Which seem to last longer?"

Be sure to have extra bubble solution on hand in case of accidental spills. You can store any leftover solution in a jar for the next day.

As a follow-up to this activity, invite children to move as if pretending to be bubbles floating through the air. When you say, "Pop!" encourage children to jump up to represent popping bubbles.

Rock Hounds

Young children love rocks! Encourage these "rock hounds" with the following activities.

- Go on a collecting walk with the children. Give each child a paper bag and encourage everyone to look for rocks and pebbles of different sizes, shapes, and colors. Gather children in a circle outside and look over the rock collection together. Have them work in small groups to study and experiment with the rocks.

- Divide children into groups outdoors. Give each group a mound of rocks and pebbles. Encourage children to use magnifying glasses to make close observations. Ask, "How are the rocks the same or different?"

- Invite children to sort the rocks in any way they choose—by size, texture, shape, color, and so forth—onto paper plates. Once they are finished sorting, ask them to describe the rocks on each plate.

- Make a chart describing the different ways children classified the rocks. Then invite them to count the rocks on each plate. Together, discuss which plate has the most and the least amount.

- Ask children to arrange the pebbles from smallest to largest in an egg carton. Give out sheets of white paper and pencils; let children trace the smallest and largest pebbles, and then compare their differences.

- Let children use a pan balance to compare the weights of various rocks. Have them predict which rocks will be the heaviest or the lightest. Then have them test their predictions.

- After studying and experimenting with the rocks, help children create a rock museum. Display the rocks in your discovery center with signs describing the biggest, smallest, roughest, smoothest, heaviest, lightest, and so on.

- Older children may use reference books to try to identify the different rocks in their collections.

- Have a "rock 'n roll" party! Take children to a grassy area outside. Ask them to curl their bodies in a ball as if they were rocks randomly strewn on the ground. Then, invite them to roll their bodies as if they were rocks rolling down a hill.

Activities for Older Children (Grades 4–5)

Aesthetic Awareness—Light

On a sunny day, direct a beam of light through a prism onto a white piece of paper. Have students take turns describing the colors. With white paper and crayons, have them record the colors using yellow and green to achieve a yellow-green, red and purple to achieve a red-purple, and so on. Guide them to see that these colors are similar to a color wheel.

Stained Glass—Awareness of Light

Find a book illustrating stained-glass windows in medieval cathedrals in Europe such as Chartres and Notre Dame. Discuss how the windows were made, their purposes (teaching people and inspiring them to pray), and what meanings they may have for people today. Then tie this in to a more modern-day glassmaker, Louis Comfort Tiffany. Tiffany was the son of the founder of Tiffany and Co., a New York company specializing in jewelry and metal crafts. Louis was trained as a painter but is best known as the developer of stained-glass windows, lamps, and vases. He experimented with new ways to color glass and shape it into sculptural forms. Imitations of his work are often seen in restaurants and stores. Students may enjoy drawing or painting their own versions of summer-inspired stained-glass creations.

Aesthetic Awareness—Van Gogh's "Irises"

Obtain an art print of this work by Van Gogh. Discuss with children the repetition of the triangular shapes of the iris leaves and the shapes of flowers. Ask if the shapes are exactly alike (they aren't). Discuss how Van Gogh changed the shapes a little each time.

These variations help us see differences in each plant. They also add more interest to a work of art. Have students identify comparable variations in the colors of the flowers and leaves. Some children may enjoy creating their own summer flowers using these subtle variations to add interest to their work.

Optical Illusions—A Different Way of Seeing

Ask students to find library books that have optical illusions. These books are usually in the science or art section of a library. Have students look for examples of optical illusions based on positive and negative shapes or "hidden figures." Have students select one of their favorite examples and try to create an original artwork based on the illusion.

Research Inventions

Create a list of all the inventions that make your home or school more comfortable. Pick one invention and research its inventor. Also check out the invention timeline at this same website http://www.cbc.ca/kids/general/the-lab/history-of-invention/default.html.

Solar System—Science Activities for Multiple Intelligences

The following activities are designed to give children the chance to use their multiple intelligences to learn concepts involved in a study of the solar system. After students have a foundation of knowledge about the solar system from classroom readings and discussions, the following activities can enrich and strengthen their learning.

Solar system model. Have students build a three-dimensional scale model of the solar system (picture/logic smart).

Role-play activity. Have students choose a group of classmates with whom to participate in a role-playing activity. One student is the sun and each of the other students is a planet. Have students write a script, with the "planets" each saying something about themselves. Students should perform their skit for the class, with all members of the solar system standing in the correct order holding signs to identify themselves (word/picture/person smart).

Solar system tableau. Have students write a several-scene tableau that includes facts and information about the solar system. Choose a group of students to practice and perform the tableau (word/body/picture/person smart).

Solar system song. Have students create a song to teach younger students the order of the planets. The song should have a recurring rhythm and a chorus. Have students perform it for their class and a class of younger students (music/word smart).

Solar system report. Have students write a two-to three-page report about the solar system. They can include three different references and one picture (word/picture smart).

Imaginary journal. Have students write an imaginary journal for a 10-day mission into space. Tell them: "You have been selected as the first student to go into space. Decide where within the solar system your mission goes and keep a daily log explaining what you are seeing and learning. You'll need to research space missions and spacecraft before writing." Students can find facts about space travel at the Smithsonian National Air and Space Museum website: http://www.nasm.si.edu/apollo/. Direct students to use their last entry to evaluate the entire mission. How successful was it? What would they do differently? How did it make them feel? (word/person smart)

Solar system math. Have students make a chart or graph to show the distance of each planet from the sun. Have them translate the actual distance into a smaller scale and draw the solar system to this scale (logic/picture smart).

Famous astronauts play. Have students research famous astronauts who have played a major role in the exploration of space. They might write a short skit that tells interesting facts and information about these astronauts and their missions and then perform it for the class (word/person/body smart).

Weather Unit Activities for Multiple Intelligences

Verbal/linguistic. Have students read a book about weather and write a short summary of what they learned.

Logical/mathematical. Have students draw a diagram of the water cycle. Alternatively, have them create a monthly weather calendar and a graph showing weather patterns during the month. They might also analyze collected weather data.

Visual/spatial. Have students create a collage of pictures showing different types of weather. They can display data in graphs and charts.

Bodily/kinesthetic. Have students create a weather dance to perform for the "weather spirits." These students might also build weather instruments.

Musical. Have students research and build different types of percussion instruments. They might create a rhythm and teach it to others, or write a song using weather words and concepts.

Interpersonal. Have students work together in groups to build instruments, collect data, or perform songs about weather.

Intrapersonal. Have students keep a journal of weather-related activities. They might list their favorite things to do on a day when a particular kind of weather predominates.

Interviewing Inventors

Combine learning to use the library and making oral book reports with learning about inventions that have changed our lives. Before doing this activity, children should select one of the following inventors and read about that person and his or her invention.

Marie Curie—chemical processes, Geiger counter
Alexander Graham Bell—the telephone
Alice Chatham—the astronaut's helmet
Henry Ford—the automobile
The Wright Brothers—the airplane
Thomas Alva Edison—the electric light bulb, phonograph
Jonas Salk—polio vaccine
Rose O'Neill—the Kewpie doll
Rear Admiral Grace Murray Hopper—computer program compiler

Once children know the inventor and the invention well enough to discuss them with classmates, pair the students. One child assumes the role of the inventor, and the other child assumes the role of the interviewer. Together, they develop and rehearse questions and responses for a radio or television talk show. These are then performed for the class. If the children are interested in switching roles, replay the activity, giving both students an opportunity to become the inventor that they studied.

During the next phase, children imagine that they are inventors. They are to develop a fictitious individual. They then create an autobiography for the inventor they imagine themselves to be and think of an invention for which they are famous. What have they invented? What does it do? After children have had enough time to develop the character and to become familiar with the invention, use the interview format previously described.

Combine the two exercises by having students perform a television news show in which Bell, Ford, and other real inventors are interviewed. Between the interview segments, have children perform commercials for the new devices their imaginary inventors have developed.

Turtles Are Special

World Turtle Day has been established on May 23 around the world to protect turtles and tortoises as well as their habitats. Students can research these animals locally, through online zoos, or at http://www.tortoise.com. They can make dioramas of these animals' habitats or art projects showing the designs of their shells.

Letters from the Garbage Heap

To liven up lessons on recycling and decomposition, give small groups of students each a bag with clothespins, a diaper, an aluminum can, a cigarette butt, a rubber eraser, a banana peel, some wood, a plastic jug, a cotton sock, and an apple core. (Photographs or cut-out magazine pictures of the items also work well.) On a clothesline marked in increments with 2 through 4 weeks, 1 through 5 months, 1 year, 10 years, 25 years, 100 years, 500

years, and 1,000 years, ask each group to hang its trash, indicating how long they think each item will take to decompose. When groups have finished, reveal the actual times: apple, 2 through 4 weeks; banana and sock, 1 through 5 months; cigarette butt, 2 through 5 years; wood, 10 years; diaper, 25 years; plastic, 25 through 30 years; eraser, 50 through 80 years; can, 200 through 400 years. (A glass bottle takes 1,000 years to decompose!) After talking about how crowded a dump will get if we fill it with so many items that take years to decay, have students write down ways they can recycle to reduce waste.

Make a "Green Map"

Send students on an Internet exploration to make their own "earth friendly" maps. At http://www.greenmap.com, students will learn that a Green Map is a map of a neighborhood, town, or city that focuses on "green," or ecologically oriented, sites. Green Maps also mark "toxic hot spots" and other polluted areas that need help. On this interactive website, students can view Green Maps of cities around the world such as New York and Copenhagen. Step-by-step instructions guide students in designing their own Green Maps, and a large collection of map icons is provided to mark sites such as gardens, recycling centers, and wildlife areas. Questions on the site ask students to draw conclusions about their mapmaking research and work.

Artists' Flowers

Have art prints of flowers from at least two artists. Two good prints for this activity would be Van Gogh's *Sunflowers* and Georgia O'Keeffe's *Poppy*. Other floral works by these artists are also good. Of course, you may find many other artists whose paintings of flowers are appropriate for this activity.

The purpose of this activity is to see how two artists express their flowers in two contrasting ways. Each artist has his or her own vision of representing them in art. Be sure to use art terms such as color, line, and shape when discussing these works.

Explain that the artist Georgia O'Keeffe created many paintings of flowers. She once said that she made the flowers large so people would really see the beauty of the colors, shapes, and edges. Explain that the poppy, like other flowers in O'Keeffe's paintings, seems to glow with life and energy. It is a close-up view of a flower in full bloom. Encourage students to make other observations about the painting.

Then lead them in a discussion of Van Gogh's *Sunflowers,* especially their texture. Guide them to describe the mood qualities in Van Gogh's painting. For example, the flowers are on the ground, no longer growing. Many of the seeds are gone, the stems are withered, the petals look shriveled and dry. Encourage other observations. Contrast and compare the two works, using the scientific analogy of a life cycle.

Emphasize the concept that artists in many times and places have created artworks about the same subject, such as flowers. Each artist creates his or her own picture in a special way—in a different, original style. Ask students to express opinions about which of these artworks they like to see, and discuss reasons for their preferences. Stress that students may like more than one kind of art and that everyone may not like the same work.

Animals

Language Arts Experiences

- Have students write a story in which the main character is an endangered animal who is trying to teach his or her family why the species is endangered.

- Arrange for students to debate in small groups the issue of wild animals being captured and put in a zoo. Are zoos actually a form of cruelty to animals?

- Have students write a short speech (2 to 4 minutes) about an animal topic that they feel strongly about. Topics might include how to take care of pets, endangered animals, or the similarities between animals and humans.

- Have students write a story in which they become an endangered animal lost in a large city. They might write about how they feel being lost and endangered and what they would do in this situation.

- Have students choose an animal to observe for 15 minutes. The allotted time might be broken down into smaller segments if the animal is hard to observe. Encourage them to write their observations and what they learned about the animal.

Art Experiences

- Have students make a clay model of an endangered carnivore and write a short paragraph telling key facts about the animal.

- Have students work with a partner in designing an advertisement that could be published in a newspaper to promote the preservation of an endangered animal.

- Have students build a three-dimensional habitat model for an animal of their choice.

Movement Experiences

- Have students pretend they are different animals, then role-play how each animal might react to meeting the other.

- Have students perform a skit in which all of the characters are animals—some endangered and some not. The animals discuss the problems that arise from being endangered.

- Encourage students to invent a game called The Animal Game. They can make up the rules for the game, describe how it is played, and then play it!

Music Experiences

- Have students work in small groups to make up an animal song and record it on a tape recorder.

- Have students write a poem or story about an animal and add animal sounds as they read it to other students.

How Does Water Disappear?

This is an initial experience with evaporation. You will need a sponge, chalkboard, water, and a heavy piece of cardboard.

1. Moisten the sponge.
2. Make a wide, damp streak on the blackboard.
3. Observe for several minutes. What happened?
4. Make two streaks about one yard apart.
5. Use the cardboard to fan one of the streaks.
6. Compare the time it took for each to disappear.

Students should learn from this activity that water is absorbed into the air by a process called *evaporation.* Increasing the amount of air moving over the water (fanning) increases the rate of evaporation. The amount of moisture the air already contains (humidity) will be a factor. Hint: If the sponge is just moist the results will be faster than if it is soaking wet.

An alternate activity is to put a small amount of water (1⁄2 inch) in two small jars. Seal the lid of one and leave the other open. Observe for 24 hours. Discuss the differences in water remaining in each jar.

Science: A Different View of Things

Discuss the importance of imagination and observation in science. Imagining that people might walk on the moon was the first and most important step in discovering how it might be done.

Have students collect unusual rocks, shells, dried seed pods, and other small objects. Glue several objects to the bottom of a clear plastic box. Challenge students to draw the objects inside the box from each of the points they can see when looking straight through one side of the box. Provide square paper for the drawings.

Have students create drawings from unusual or imagined vantage points, such as being in a hot air balloon, flying in an airplane, being inside of a mine or a cave, looking at things under water, or looking out the window of a rocket while it is being launched or is nearing a planet.

Insects

Contrast the way an artist and a scientist might study insects. Point out that scientists and artists are both very keen observers of nature. The artist is more likely to study insects to discover the beauty or the special lines, shapes, textures, and colors. The scientist may look for the same features, but is more likely to want to explain their purpose—protection, reproduction, food gathering. Encourage students to draw their own versions of insects, using either the artistic or scientific perspective.

Challenge: Bugs or Us?

Ask the students which weighs more, all the bugs in America, or all the people in America? Have them visit http://coolbugstuff.com/facts.php to learn that if you weighed all the people in America, they would weigh less than 1/50 of the total weight of all the insects, earthworms, and spiders in the United States! But that's not all. Have them research fossilized scorpions on this same site. They will learn that fossilized scorpions still glow under ultraviolet light after 300 million years and that a cockroach head will live and respond for at least 12 hours after it has been cut off. Encourage them to research other fascinating "bug" facts on this site and report back to their fellow students. They may want to make illustrations of some of the insects they found to accompany their reports.

World's Smallest Insect

Have the students visit the North Carolina State University website at http://www.cals.ncsu.edu/ course/ent425/text01/smallest.html to find out which is the world's smallest insect. They will learn that Fairyflies are the smallest flying insect. They are actually tiny wasps that are just 0.139 mm in length, smaller than a single-celled paramecium or a grain of sand. Encourage students to draw a Fairyfly if they are interested.

Chocolate-covered Crickets

Have students visit http://wilderdom.com/games/ descriptions/EatingBugs.html. Ask them to learn from this site the definition of the word "entomophagy" (the practice of eating bugs for nutrition). Ask them to find out how to make insect flour, chocolate-covered crickets, ant-brood tacos, and mealworm chocolate chip cookies. Also ask them to find out which is lower in fat and higher in protein—bugs or beef, lamb, pork, or chicken. After learning these interesting facts, students might want to make their own recipe for an insect delight of their own!

Aesthetic Awareness

Discuss texture as a property that we experience by sight as well as touch. Stress that scientists who wish to describe and classify living and nonliving things carefully observe and often measure subtle differences in textures (as well as other properties) of objects. Provide magnifying glasses and a variety of textured materials for students to observe, touch, and describe: fine white sand, salt, sugar, flour, baby powder, or varieties of rocks or paper.

Science Outdoors

Take students outside to study the branching structures of trees. Guide them to see relationships between the branching structures in a leaf, among twigs that support leaves, larger branches, and the trunk. Have them identify other natural forms in which linear qualities are evident such as hair and fur, or shells with radial or spiraling edges. Have them draw representations of their observations.

Making Crystals

Making crystals is an amazing and fun science activity. To begin, carefully add 1 cup of very hot water to a mason jar for each child. Then have students help measure and add up to 2 cups of sugar to their water jars, ½ cup at a time, until no more dissolves. By doing this, students will be creating a saturated solution.

Have each student tie a string to a craft stick (or pencil) and a rust-proof paper clip, then suspend his or her clip just above the bottom of the jar. Cover jars with paper towels to keep dust out. As water evaporates, sugar crystals will form.

In a week or two, remove and dry the strings of crystals. Challenge students to find the edges, angles, and faces of the crystals.

Set up a crystal observation station with salt and sugar on sheets of black paper, a magnifying glass, and a flashlight. Students may notice some of the following characteristics of crystals:

- Crystals have geometric shapes, such as cubes (salt), rectangles (sugar), diamonds, or pyramids.
- Crystals have sharp, straight edges that meet to form angles.
- Crystals are solids.
- Crystal shapes range from simple to very complex.
- Crystals break smoothly and cleanly at their weakest point.
- Crystals' smooth sides are called *faces*.

Shoe Box Science Activities

Balloon in a bottle. Students will observe that air takes up space. They'll learn that pressure from the air closed in a bottle prevents a balloon from being inflated until air is allowed to escape through a straw.

Materials: medium-sized balloons, drinking straws, two-liter soda bottle with a small mouth.

Procedure:
1. Place a balloon into the bottle, but stretch its nozzle onto the threading of the bottle's opening.
2. Try to blow up the balloon.
3. Now place a straw between the balloon and the inside of the bottle.
4. Again, try to blow up the balloon.

Ask students to describe what happened the first time they tried to inflate the balloon. What happened when they placed a straw inside the bottle and tried to inflate the balloon? What do they think happened to the air in the bottle when they placed a straw inside?

How fast does it fall? Students will determine whether the weight of an object affects how fast it falls.

Materials: two pennies, two quarters, two sheets of notebook paper (one flat, one crushed into a ball), other heavy and light objects in the classroom (a baseball and a softball, a small and a large marble, small and large erasers, a short and a long pencil, etc.)

Procedure:

1. Hold two coins, one in each hand, at the same height and simultaneously drop them. Do three trials. Did they reach the ground at the same time?
2. Simultaneously drop two coins of different sizes from the same height. Do three trials. Did they reach the ground at the same time?
3. Simultaneously drop the flat sheet of paper and a coin from the same height. Do three trials. Did they reach the ground at the same time?
4. Simultaneously drop the sheet of paper that was crushed into a ball and a coin from the same height. Do three trials. Did they reach the ground at the same time?
5. Do the same with the crushed sheet and the flat sheet of paper. Do three trials. Did they reach the ground at the same time?
6. Make a chart from your data collecting record sheet and examine the results.

Weather Science

People often say, "This is a cold April" or "It seems wetter than normal." Challenge students to see if it is true or not. Contact the local weather bureau for last year's daily figures. Have students collect daily data and make comparisons between this year and last in temperature and moisture. Include more years if you want to look at trends.

Inventions

Inventors design new products because there is a strong need for them. Students can practice being inventors with these activities.

Robots. Have students design a robot that performs a needed service, such as one that fights fires or helps people with physical disabilities. Robot design challenges stimulate children to imagine all sorts of incredible inventions. Using a team-based approach builds collaborative skills. Students can create their models using construction paper or recycled household items.

Home sweet home inventions. Challenge students to design a home that uses alternate energy sources. Challenge students to design homes that withstand catastrophic weather events such as floods, hurricanes, and tornados.

Futuristic thinking. Have students create a story about how robots will be used in the future. This exercise combines science and technology with social studies and language skills to engender a look into the future. Encourage students to illustrate their stories.

Web Activities for Science Learning

- Curious how everyday technology will evolve in the future? Check out predictions from past decades and share your own ideas about what's coming with "The Future" at http://www.pbskids.org/wayback/future.
- Ready for a virtual "big dig"? Check out the American Museum of Natural History's "Ology" site at http://www.amnh.org/ology/ for dozens of great games in archaeology and paleontology.
- Learn about weather and the tools meteorologists use to make accurate predictions at the National Oceanic and Atmospheric Administration's website for students: http://www.education.noaa.gov/sweather.html.
- Ask your students: What is a hurricane? What causes it to form? What are the main parts of a hurricane? Students can visit http://www.comet.ucar.edu/nsflab/web/hurricane/311.htm to find the answers.
- Explore animals and habitats with *Nature* searchable streaming video at http://www.pbs.org/nature. Afterward, make a classroom book describing creatures and their habitats.
- Make a balloon-powered milk carton car in class to learn about air pressure. Details and materials you'll need can be found at http://www.pbskids.org/zoom/activities/sci/ballooncar.html.
- DNA is the blueprint of our bodies, and there is a copy of that blueprint in each of our body cells. Just how is that possible? Start to learn more about DNA at http://www.pbs.org/wnet/dna.
- Visit the Planet Protectors Club at http://www.epa.gov/epawaste/index.htm. There are activities in English and Spanish for all ages. Click on the age groups to find games and activities for recycling.
- Kids can visit NOVA's Fingerprinting Lab site (http://www.pbs.org/wgbh/nova/sheppard/analyze.html) and use DNA to solve the interactive mystery of who opened Jimmy Sweet's lollipop.
- Visit http://www.hqpapermaker.com/paper-history/ to learn all about paper. For just one day, record the amount of paper used in your school. Ask the office to keep track. Collect the copy number from every copy machine. Gather paper in the lunch room and from recycle bins and weigh it. Count the paper you use in your classroom. See how your paper use compares to daily paper use across the United States.
- Put the data from the above paper activity in a spreadsheet to share with your school principal and administration, the PTA, and your community. Use data to write word problems about the use of paper in our world. Make a list of ways to reduce, reuse, and recycle the paper in your school. A ton of paper prints about 7,000 newspapers. How many local newspapers are delivered each day? How many tons of paper are consumed in a year?

Chapter Review

1. What are the two phases of science? Which phase is more important for young children?

2. Choose the answer that best completes each statement about science.

   a. The teacher is most involved in planning for
   (a) formal science.
   (b) informal science.
   (c) incidental science.

   b. The teacher cannot plan for
   (a) formal science.
   (b) informal science.
   (c) incidental science.

   c. Observing skills are taught to children in
   (a) formal science.
   (b) informal science.
   (c) incidental science.

   d. Free investigation is used most often in
   (a) formal science.
   (b) informal science.
   (c) incidental science.

3. Define the term *ecology* and discuss its place in the early childhood program.

4. Discuss the discovery center and its importance in the early childhood program.

References

Barclay, D., Benelli, C., & Schoon, S. (1999). Marking the connection! Science and literacy. *Childhood Education, 75*(3), 146–152.

Bredekamp, S., & Copple, C. E. (2009). *Developmentally appropriate practice in early childhood programs serving children from birth through age 8* (2nd ed.). Washington, DC: National Association for the Education of Young Children.

Brown, P. L., & Abell, S. K. (2007). Examining the learning cycle. *Science and Children, 44*(5), 58–59.

Burda, H. (2008). Study: Herd animals detect Earth's magnetic field. *Wikinews,* August 26, 2008. Available at: http://en.wikinews.org/wiki/Study_Herd_animals_detect_Earth's_magnetic_field

Marriott, S. (2002). Red in tooth and claw? Images of nature in modern picture books. *Children's Literature in Education, 33*(3), 175–183.

Mayer, D. A. (1995). How can we best use children's literature in teaching science concepts? *Science and Children, 32*(6), 16–19, 43.

National Research Council. (1996). *National science education standards.* Washington, DC: National Academy Press.

Parker, J. W. (2008, October 8). *The Zoo.* Raleigh, NC: North Carolina Zoological Society. Available at www.nczoo.com

Pringle, R. M., & Lamme, L. L. (2005). Using picture storybooks to support young children's science learning. *Reading Horizons, 46*(1), 1–15.

Rice, D. C. (2002). Using trade books in teaching elementary science: Facts and fallacies. *The Reading Teacher, 55*(6), 552–565.

Trundle, K. C., & Troland, T. H. (2005). The moon in children's literature. *Science and Children, 43*(2), 40–43.

Wells, R., & Zeece, P. D. (2007). My place in my world: Literature for place-based environmental education. *Early Childhood Education Journal, 35*(3), 285–291.

Additional Readings

Abell, S. K. (2008). Children's literature and the science classroom. *Science and Children, 46*(3), 54–55.

Atkinson, T. S., Matusevich, N., & Huber, L. (2009). Making science trade book choices for elementary classrooms. *The Reading Teacher, 62*(6), 484–497.

Beck, C. (2008). Juggling makes physics fun: Elementary students learn the physical science behind juggling. *Science and Children, 45*(7), 28–32.

Beckstead, L. (2008). Scientific journals: A creative assessment tool. *Science and Children, 46*(3), 22–26.

Benson, J., & Miller, J. L. (2008). Experiences in nature: A pathway to standards. *Young Children, 63*(4), 22–27.

Betteley, P., & Lee, R. E., Jr. (2009). Inspiring future scientists. *Science and Children, 46*(8), 48–52.

Bake, S. (2009). Engage, investigate, and report: Enhancing the curriculum with scientific inquiry. *Young Children, 64*(6), 49–53.

Bosse, S., Jacobs, L., & Anderson, T. L. (2009). Science in the air. *Young Children, 64*(6), 10–15.

Brenneman, K. (2009). Preschoolers as scientific explorers. *Young Children, 64*(6), 54–60.

Brunsell, E. (Ed.) *Readings in science methods, K–8.* Arlington, VA: National Science Teachers Association Press.

Cartier, J. L., & Pellathy, S. L. (2009). Integration with big ideas in mind: Using big ideas to guide choices about integrating science across the curriculum. *Science and Children, 46*(8), 44–47.

Chatman, L., Nielsen, K., Strauss, E. J., & Tanner, K. D. (2008). *Girls in science: A framework for action.* Arlington, VA: NSTA Press.

Cowan, K. W., & Cipriani, S. (2009). Of water troughs and the sun: Developing inquiry through analogy. *Young Children, 64*(6), 62–67.

Crawford, E. O., Heaton, E. T., Heslop, K., & Kixmiller, K. (2009). Science learning at home involving families. *Young Children, 64*(6), 39–41.

Dexter, K. V. (2008). Designing school gardens. *School Arts, 108*(2), 32–33.

Eberbah, C., & Crowley, K. (2009). From everyday to scientific observation: How children learn to observe the biologist's world. *Review of Educational Research, 79*(1), 39–49.

Froschauer, L. (2008). *Science beyond the classroom.* Arlington, VA: NSTA Press.

Garcia-Ruiz, F. (2009). Creating a schoolyard mini garden. *Science and Children, 46*(6), 34–37.

Gelman, R., MacDonald, G., Roman, M., & Brenneman, J. (2009). *Preschool pathways to science: Facilitating scientific ways of thinking, talking, doing, and understanding.* Baltimore, MD: Brookes.

Gradle, S. A. (2008). When vines talk: Community, art, and ecology. *Art Education, 61*(6), 6–11.

Hachey, A. C., & Butler, D. L. (2009). Seeds in the window, soil in the sensory table: Science education through gardening and nature-based play. *Young Children, 64*(6), 42–48.

Keeley, P. (2008). *Science formative assessment: 75 practical strategies for linking assessment, instruction, and learning.* Arlington, VA: NSTA Press.

Klentschy, M. P. (2008). *Using science notebooks in elementary classrooms.* Arlington, VA: NSTA Press.

Konicek-Moran, R. (2008). *Everyday science mysteries: Stories for inquiry-based science teaching.* Arlington, VA: NSTA Press.

Murray, M., & Valentine-Anand, L. (2008). Dinosaur extinction, early childhood style. *Science and Children, 46*(4), 36–39.

Norton-Meier, L., Hand, B., Hockenberry, L., & Wise, K. (2008). *Questions, claims, and evidence: The important place of argument in children's science writing.* Arlington, VA: NSTA Press.

Novakowski, J. (2009). Classifying classification: Teachers examine their practices to help first grade students build a deeper understanding of how to categorize things. *Science and Children, 45*(7), 25–29.

Olson, J. K. (2008). Making time for science: Strategies to increase instructional time for science. *Science and Children, 46*(3), 50–53.

Olson, J. K., & Clough, M. P. (2009). Keeping it real: Don't forget the importance of outdoor experiences in nature. *Science and Children, 46*(7), 53–55.

Olson, J. K., Levis, J. M., Vann, R., & Bruna, K. R. (2009). Enhancing science for ELL's: Science strategies for English language learners that benefit all students. *Science and Children, 46*(5), 46–48.

Patrick, H., Mantziocopoulos, P., & Samarapungavan, A. (2009). Reading, writing, and conducting inquiry about science in kindergarten. *Young Children, 64*(6), 32–38.

Patrick, P., & Getz, A. (2008). Becoming a spider scientist. *Science and Children, 46*(3), 32–35.

Rosebery, A. S., & Warren, B. (Eds.). (2008). *Teaching science to English language learners: Building on students' strengths.* Arlington, VA: NSTA Press.

Sackes, M., Trundle, K. C., & Flevares, L. M. (2009). Using children's books to teach inquiry skills. *Young Children, 64*(6), 24–31.

Sander, J., & Nelson, S. (2009). Science conversations for young learners: Tips on guiding kindergarteners to participate in large-group discussions in science. *Science and Children, 46*(6), 43–45.

Shaffe, L. F., Hall, E., & Lynch, M. (2009). Toddlers' scientific explorations: Encounters with insects. *Young Children, 64*(6), 18–23.

Spangler, S. (2009). Beyond the fizz: Getting children excited about doing real science. *Young Children, 64*(4), 62–64.

Trefil, J. (2008). *Why science?* Arlington, VA: NSTA Press.

Yager, R. E., & Falk, J. (Eds.). (2008). *Exemplary science in informal education settings: Standards-based success stories.* Arlington, VA: NSTA Press.

Software for Children

Amazing Animals, ages 6–9

Doggie Daycare, ages 6 and up

Eye Pet, ages 3 and up

Farm Vet, ages 6 and up

GoPets: Vacation Island, ages 6 and up

Happy Trails: Animal Shelter, ages 8 and up

Harvest Moon Animal Parade, ages 7 and up

Jump Start Pet Rescue, ages 5 and up

Kitten Corner, ages 6–13

Kidspiration, ages 5 and up

LEGO Education: We Do Robotics, ages 7 and up

Madagascar: Escape 2 Africa Video Game, ages 5 and up

More bugs in boxes, ages 3–6

Penguins!, ages 6 and up

Pet Pals: New Leash on Life, ages 8 and up

Pony Paradise, ages 6–13

Puppy Playtime, ages 6–12

Putt-Putt Saves the Zoo, ages 3–7

Sammy's Science House, ages 3–6

Save the Dinosaurs, ages 6 and up

Saving Planet Earth, ages 5–8

Spectrobes: Beyond the Portals, ages 8 and up

Wonder Pets! Save the Animals!, ages 4 and up

World of Zoo, ages 6 and up

Helpful Websites

Ask Dr. Science, http://www.drscience.com

San Francisco's Exploratorium, the Museum of Science, http://www.exploratorium.edu/
Site includes hundreds of activities with accompanying explanations of how the science behind them works.

Boston's Museum of Science, http://www.mos.org/

National Science Teachers Association, http://www.nsta.org/

PBS Science, http://www.pbs.org/science/
Click on "For Educators."

American Association for the Advancement of Science, http://www.project2061.org

Discovery Channel, http://yucky.kids.discovery.com/

Earth Day, http://earthday.wilderness.org/
Click on "Lessons and materials for teachers" for excellent resources on teaching about nature and the seasons.

Look Down from Space, http://www.earth.google.com
This revolutionary Web tool uses detailed satellite photographs of every corner of Earth to provide a free, searchable, digital globe. Whether you're teaching about oceans, continents, or local crosswalks, students get a bird's eye view of it all with the click of a mouse.

University of Delaware Graduate College of Marine Studies, http://www.ocean.udel.edu/

The Space Foundation, http://www.sciencestandardslessons.org
Teachers from across the country have teamed up with the Space Foundation to develop a comprehensive bank of more than 200 science lesson plans for students in pre–K to grade 12. Divided by grade level, each lesson is tied to national science standards.

Zoo Web, http://www. http://www.zoo.com
A great site to locate zoos around the world and have a peek into their zoocams.

Track Fowl Creatures, http://www.learner.org/jnorth
Join 11,000 other schools and track seasons and animal migrations with this global project.

Outer Space, http://www.hobbyspace.com
This site is packed with all things about space—satellite photographs of the planets, information on space tourism, space games, and space-related contests.

Science Lesson Library, http://education.ti.com/us/activitycd
Check out more than 200 ready-to-use science activities on a free CD from Texas Instruments.

Arbor Day, http://www.arborday.org
This site has fun online games associated with trees and National Arbor Day.

Ideas for Legos®, http://www.LEGOeducation.com
Check out LEGO Education's teacher website, featuring math and science connections as well as free activities to download.

Science Explorations, http://www.scholastic.com/scienceexplorations
This website features in-depth investigations on six major science topics: Animals, Adaptations and the Galapagos Islands, Classifying Insects, Journey into Space, Investigating Invertebrates, Beam Up with Bats, and Research with Reptiles.

Science for Kids, http://www.eurekalert.org/scienceforkids
The American Association for the Advancement of Science sponsors this science news site for kids.

Amazing Space, http://amazing-space.stsci.edu
This site contains interactive lessons and experiments for grades 3–12 that are set up to scaffold learning.

Discovery Science Center Kids, http://www.discoverycube.org/kids
On this website, you'll find science experiments, fun facts, brain teasers, and additional cool sites. Each of the science experiments lists the materials and the procedure and offers some discussion questions about the results.

National Geographic Little Kids, http://kidsblogs. nationalgeographic.com/littlekids
This site has a wealth of science resources, lessons, discussions, and a blog focusing on teaching science to young children.

Southwest Center for Education and the Natural Environment (SCENE), http://scene.asu.edu/index. html
This site presented by Arizona State University connects the community, teachers, and students to science. It also offers activities, explains scientific inquiry, and explores the scientific method.

Try Science, http://tryscience.org
This site has experiment activities, video clips, and information on various science phenomena, including pages for teachers and parents, and is available in multiple languages.

For additional creative activity resources, visit our website at www.Cengage.com/login.

CHAPTER
20

Creative Mathematics

OBJECTIVES

After studying this chapter, you should be able to:

1. Discuss the developmental pattern of learning mathematical ideas.

2. Discuss how mathematics learning occurs in learning centers in the early childhood classroom.

3. Define "rote counting" and "rational counting."

4. Discuss "classification" and "sorting."

5. Discuss "comparing" and "ordering."

6. Describe the young child's understanding of shape and form.

Early childhood teachers face the challenging responsibility of opening young children's eyes to the world of mathematics. We may provide creative, stimulating, hands-on experiences that can initiate long-term positive feelings about mathematics, or we may provide a boring stream of workbook pages and dittos. In such a situation, where children are required to sit down, quiet down, and write it down, excitement about math may never have a chance to emerge. Math in the early childhood setting is not a sit-at-your-desk-with-paper-and-pencil activity. It is a part of a young child's active life.

Everything we know about young children tells us that early math experiences must be hands-on, filled with play and exploration. Young children's understanding of mathematical ideas takes place in an action-based learning environment.

All young children need opportunities to explore their world and experience mathematics through their play. Early mathematical experiences include such basic events as placing crackers in a toddler's hands while saying, "Here are two crackers—one, two," or allowing a three-year-old to choose how she wants her sandwich cut—into triangles, rectangles, or small squares. As a child arranges stuffed animals by size, a teacher might ask, "Which animal is the smallest?" or "Which is the largest?" Such questions reveal mathematical ideas involved in simple activities and lay the foundation for children's understanding of more complex mathematical concepts as they grow older.

When children recognize a stop sign from the back, focusing on the octagonal shape rather than the red background and the word "STOP," adults have an opportunity to talk about different shapes in the environment. Teachers in any setting can help children look for mathematical connections and relationships, encourage their questions, and promote mathematical discussion about topics that interest them. The most powerful mathematics learning for a child is seldom acquired sitting down in a group lesson.

In this chapter, the emphasis is on this active exploration of mathematical concepts as a natural part of the early childhood program.

Developmental Pattern of Learning Mathematical Ideas

It is possible to look at the child's construction of mathematical concepts the same way we look at literacy development—as emergent. The idea that literacy learning begins the day that children are born is widely accepted in the early childhood field. Mathematical learning can be viewed in a similar way. Children begin to build the foundation for future mathematical concepts during the first few months of life.

Long before children formally use numbers, they are aware of them through daily experiences. For example, children become aware of sequences in events before they can talk about what is first, second, or third. At the age of two or three, they know that one block on top of another is two blocks, and they know that if they add more they will have three, even though they may not know the words *two* and *three*. When they lift objects, they experience lightness or heaviness. Cuddling up in their mother's lap, they feel themselves small and her big. They know all this by the reality of their experience—through living and doing. Thus, children are able to tell differences in sizes of people, animals, and toys before they have any idea about measurement. They recognize, too, the difference between one and many and between few and lots before they acquire real number concepts. They develop a sense of time long before they can tell time by a clock. Their ideas about time grow out of hearing statements like "It's time for lunch." "It's time to go to bed." "We're going for a walk today." "We went to the park yesterday." In such instances, parents reinforce mathematical concepts every day in life's normal routines. Thus, when the child enters an early childhood program, he or she has already experienced many basic mathematical learnings.

This pattern of early use of numbers is similar to the general-to-specific pattern of physical growth (see Part 1). In these early stages of mathematical thinking, the child has a general understanding of numbers that will gradually move toward a more specific understanding as the developmental process continues. Thus, a general understanding of time ("It's time for lunch.") develops in a gradual process to a more specific understanding of time ("Twelve o'clock is lunch time."). Children gradually associate 12 o'clock with lunchtime. They learn with their senses, with their whole bodies. Their understandings become parts of themselves. Only after this has happened can they name these experiences. By the time they learn the words *big*, *small*, *light*, *heavy*, or the names of numbers, they will know by their own senses what these words mean.

Recognizing the importance of these early experiences in mathematics, the National Council of Teachers of Mathematics (NCTM) has developed a set of Principles and Standards for Children Pre-K–12 (2000). These standards propose mathematical content and processes students should know and be able to use as they progress through school. There are 10 standards—five content standards and five process standards—that apply across the pre-K–12 grade span. (See Figure 20–1 for a summary of these standards.) Within each standard, a number of focus areas are to be emphasized at each grade level. It is beyond the scope of this text to present and discuss each standard. However, references to specific standards will be made when appropriate. The latest information on national standards in mathematics can be accessed at the National Council of Teachers of Mathematics website: http://standards.nctm.org/. Let us now take a look at mathematics in action in the early childhood program.

Parents as Partners in Mathematical Learning

Since young children begin to learn mathematics from the day they are born, parents are obviously an early childhood teacher's partner in mathematical learning. Early childhood teachers can explain to parents how infants and toddlers begin to notice relationships as they interact with their parents or primary caregivers through songs, rocking, and other verbal and nonverbal communication. They can help parents understand that as a baby crawls through a tunnel or in and out of a cardboard box, he is using his whole body to explore and learn. Encouraging parents to place infants in different positions to encourage the child to pay attention to where things and spaces are in relation to one another is another mathematical learning early childhood teachers can point out to parents. In the same way, early childhood teachers can explain to parents that physical activities introduce spatial relation and set the stage for later understandings of geometry and numbers.

Content

Five standards describe the mathematical content that students should learn.

- number and operation
- patterns, functions, and algebra
- geometry and spatial sense
- measurement
- data analysis, statistics, and probability

Process

Five standards describe the mathematical processes through which students should acquire and use their mathematical knowledge.

- problem solving
- reasoning and proof
- communication
- connections
- representation

Societal Needs for Mathematics

- Mathematical literacy. The underpinnings of everyday life are increasingly mathematical and technologic. Our students will live in a world where intelligent decisions often require quantitative understandings.
- Cultural literacy. Mathematics is a great cultural and intellectual achievement of human kind, and our citizens should develop an appreciation and understanding of that achievement.
- Mathematics for the workplace. Just as the level of mathematics needed for intelligent citizenship has increased dramatically, so too has the level of mathematical thinking and problem solving needed in the workplace increased.
- Mathematicians, scientists, engineers, and other users of mathematics. Equity and excellence both must be the object of school mathematics programs. If schools enfranchise more students while maintaining high standards, there will be a larger number available to pursue these careers.

FIGURE 20-1 • Overview of the National Council of Teachers of Mathematics National Standards for grades pre-K through 12.

Teachers need to encourage parents to allow their children freedom to explore how their bodies fit in space and to see things from different perspectives, such as "inside" and "outside," "high" and "low." The teacher may suggest activities to parents to reinforce these concepts, such as providing an expanding tunnel or making one by taping together several cardboard boxes. Also, parents may encourage children to climb on a stack of pillows for the same reasons. Encourage parents to talk about what the child is doing so they can begin to learn the words that describe mathematical concepts: "You were **on** the pillow, and then you climbed **off**. You climbed **up** on the box, then you jumped **off**."

Parents can also use sequential words to describe events or tasks in order to help children develop mathematical concepts. For example, when the parent explains the day's schedule, the use of sequential words helps children connect events with the order of time: "**First**, we will go outside. **After** we go outside,

we will go to the playground. **Next**, we will have lunch. **Later**, we will come home for a nap."

Mathematics in the Movement Center

As we observe in the movement center, we see children climbing over, ducking under, crawling through, and walking around several pieces of climbing equipment. Anthony approaches a ladder bridge suspended between two climbing frames and hesitates. He ducks under it, just clearing the ladder. He looks back to see what he did and repeats this action several times. "What would happen if you didn't duck?" asks the teacher. Anthony silently stands beside the ladder and indicates with his hand where he would hit his head (an example of measuring vertical distance by eye and comparing lengths).

At the trampoline, Christina counts as Justin jumps. "After 10 times, it's my turn," she tells Justin (an example of using a cardinal number to obtain access to classroom equipment). The rest of the children begin to count Justin's jumps. "I can jump highest because I am the tallest," comments Juliette (an example of explaining measurement between object and event).

The children in line begin to measure themselves against each other (comparing height). When the teacher asks who jumped the highest today, the children all agree that it was Amanda. "Is she the tallest?" the teacher asks.

"Well, tomorrow I'm going to jump the highest because it's my birthday," says Justin.

"Amanda jumps in the middle of the trampoline," observes Juliette (showing she is thinking about location). "I'm going to try that tomorrow."

These specific learning experiences in the movement center fall under the three mathematics content standards of number and operation, measurement, and spatial sense. In the preceding scenes, we see how moving their own bodies through space helps children learn these specific mathematical concepts.

Playtime will allow children many chances to explore, extend, and refine their spatial discoveries. The children playing on the trampoline are learning to share power, space, things, and ideas as well as to use counting for access and comparing their jumping skills by measuring in a nonthreatening way.

Mathematics in the Language Arts Center

Very few teachers need convincing of the benefits of using children's books in the early childhood math program. Children love being read to, and books provide rich sources for learning math. Teaching math through children's books motivates children to learn math in exciting new ways. Learning math through the use of children's books encourages students to think and to reason mathematically while building students' appreciation for both math and literature.

Evaluating Children's Books for Math Learning

When evaluating which books to incorporate in a math activity, first judge the book as a worthy piece of literature. It must have an engaging story line, beautiful language, and a sense of wonder about the world (Eisenhauer & Feikes, 2009). Appropriate picture books present math concepts accurately with visual and verbal appeal. The illustrations and text must engage the reader. The reader or listener must be able to find real-world connections in the way concepts are presented. Concepts also must be presented in a way that truly engages the specific audience of young children. And finally, the book must have a "wow" factor, that special attribute that "draws the reader to new heights, stirs new ideas, and adds rich, multilayered connections to existing knowledge" (Hellwig, Monroe, & Jacobs, 2000, p. 143).

Ask yourself these questions when considering a book for a math lesson.

1. *Would I read this book to the children even if I weren't choosing it for a math lesson?* Books should be used in the classroom because they are enjoyable, not because they teach a lesson. For a book to promote interest in reading as well as be appropriate for math, it must be memorable, use natural language, have captivating images, and stand up to multiple readings.

2. *Does the book stimulate curiosity and a sense of wonder? Are children inspired to do their own investigations?* In the reading of these books, concepts that a teacher may be required to teach, such as proportion, measurement, weight, and shapes, become topics that children want to investigate on their own.

3. *Is the book meaningful to children? Can they make personal connections?* Children should be able to identify with the characters in the book as having similar life experiences, doing activities children normally do.

4. *Are the math connections natural?* When math connections are embedded in a story, the reader not only enjoys the book but also is intrigued by the math concepts. Mathematical ways of thinking are emphasized; they are not facts presented in an authoritarian tone. As such, children have opportunities to question and pursue solutions (Cesarone, 2008).

An Example of Using a Children's Book for Math Learning

You will find that children's books can be used to launch many interesting math learning activities. There are many excellent sources of children's books for math (see the Online Companion). Eric Carle's *The Very Hungry Caterpillar,* which describes the life cycle of a caterpillar through the use of vibrant, collage-like designs, is an excellent example of children's literature that can provide math experiences for a young audience.

Teaching comparisons. Size comparison is the most obvious prenumber concept that can be drawn from this book. The caterpillar changes from a tiny egg laid on a leaf to a small, hungry caterpillar to a big, brown cocoon, and finally to a large, beautiful butterfly. After reading the book to the class, the teacher might discuss with the children the size relationships depicted. Later, children can compare cutouts of phases of the caterpillar's life cycle and arrange them from largest to smallest.

Teaching ordering. The prenumber skill of ordering can be related to both the days of the week and the caterpillar's life cycle. Ask children to tell the order of the days of the week or stages of the life cycle told in the book. Ordering the days of the week in this way can promote an interest in the calendar for daily record keeping of days gone by. The life cycle can be used in a game-like situation in which children order the pictures of the cycle. This sequencing can be made self-correcting by writing the numerals 1 through 4 on the back of the pictures.

Teaching one-to-one correspondence. The fact that the caterpillar ate through a variety of foods one by one can be used to emphasize one-to-one correspondence. A learning center follow-up might require children to match pom-pom caterpillars to plastic fruits to see if there is an equal match or if there are more caterpillars than fruit.

Teaching rational counting. Children can also be asked to rationally count the number of pieces of food the caterpillar ate in the story by counting the number of fruits and then the number of other foods eaten. They might also count the number of days of the week and the life cycle changes. A later concrete learning activity would be to have children count out pieces of fruit or other similar foods eaten by the caterpillar into eat in their own particular snack time. Learning center games could involve the counting of food cutouts found in plastic containers.

Teaching cardinal numbers. The teacher might use a story to emphasize the prenumber skill of recognizing cardinal numbers. As children look at the book, the teacher might ask: "How many things did the

FIGURE 20-2 • Learning one-to-one correspondence is an essential mathematical learning.

caterpillar eat on Saturday? How many on Monday?" Later, children can work with a learning center activity that involves counting holes made by the hungry caterpillar in card stock leaves to determine how many bites the caterpillar took. A self-correcting feature can be included by simply writing the answer on the backs of the leaves.

Mathematics in the Art Center

Much incidental learning related to mathematics occurs during art activities. When materials are used for a particular process, children need to remember quantities and their order of use. Children can frequently be heard explaining a process to classmates by saying, "First you tear the strips, then you add the paste, and then you stick them on the balloon." As art projects are planned, children learn to consider the number of items needed and often the shapes that will be required. This experience relates directly to problem solving and measurement—two of the content standards in the national mathematics standards for children.

We hear, "My truck will have four wheels," and "I need a triangle shape of wood for the roof on my house." Children learn to decide "how many" as they draw and paint: how many eyes on the face, fingers on the hand, and buttons on the coat.

Differences and equivalences in number and size frequently concern children. Six-year-old Jonathan calls out, "I want 10 feathers on my peacock, and I have only nine." Bernardo, sitting next to him, responds, "I have more than you; I have 12 feathers."

Children also learn about one-to-one correspondence as materials are chosen and distributed to classmates. Four children need four scissors; five paste cups need five lumps of paste; three needles need three lengths of yarn—all direct, hands-on experiences with the standard of number and operation.

The following scenario further demonstrates how art activities can be used to provide children practice in areas related to national mathematics standards.

Two children are making headbands using shape stamps to make designs on paper strips that will fit around their heads. "This is a skinny square," says Casper, referring to his rectangle stamp. Claire laughs and looks through the shape set. She picks up an oval shape, "This is a skinny circle!" The children laugh some more as they assign names to the other shapes. (Comparing shapes provides experience with the geometry and spatial sense standard.)

Soon they are finished and Casper holds the strip while Claire measures and cuts the correct length (measurement standard). On the first try, the strip is too short, and they come to the teacher with the problem. "How could you make it longer?" she asks.

FIGURE 20-3 • Learning the concept of measurement is best done in active learning experiences.

Claire thinks they can add some paper to one end of the strip (an example of extending length to make an object longer). Eventually the children make the headbands fit. When two different children approach the center later, Casper says, "You should cut the paper first to be sure it fits." One child takes this advice, but the other ignores him and begins to make designs on the paper strips.

The children in the preceding scenario had a prolonged opportunity to explore and talk about the characteristics of shapes. This was a fun, hands-on learning experience involving the mathematical concepts of shape, measurement, and problem solving.

Mathematics at the Water Table

Some of the greatest opportunities for integrating math in children's play occur at the water table. Constant "watery" sounds are heard as children fill containers with water and pour the water back and forth. "This won't hold all the water," Grace comments (an example of measuring volume).

Elbert picks up a bottle and says, "This one is taller. It will hold the most."

Grace disagrees. "This one might hold a lot because it's very fat all the way up." (She is comparing size and capacity of containers.) She suggests that they count how many cups each holds and begins to count, but Elbert just continues to pour water from one container to another. (He is comparing capacity by direct measure.) "This one holds six cups!" says Grace (an example of measurement). "How much does yours hold?" Elbert then begins to fill his bottle with water, using the cup and a funnel. Grace counts the cups and explains, "It's four and a little bit more—not the whole thing" (a real-life use of measurement—fractions).

In the preceding scene, play reveals a progression of mathematical thought. In this situation, the children's processing of their own experiences shows the way they grow in measurement thinking. They were not concerned with a particular goal or end as much as with the means to achieve it. They did not have a clear plan in mind, and their goals and ends were self-imposed and changed as the activity proceeded.

In addition to these spontaneous mathematical experiences, you can also plan activities at the water table to build children's mathematical concepts. For example, a teacher may construct a math puzzle with three empty plastic glasses. Pour water up to the brim on the first glass. Then fill the second glass halfway, and leave the third empty. Ask children to identify which glass is empty, which is full, and which one is half-full. Children generally understand the meaning of *full* and can identify the full glass of water. Most children will also understand the concepts of *empty* and *more*, but many children have trouble with *half* and *less*.

This experience at the water table may be continued in the manipulatives area by providing measuring cups of beads, buttons, or other materials for children to further explore the concepts of *full, empty, fewer,* and *less*. Through repeated interactions and dialogue, children learn some of the vocabulary and concepts that underlie mathematics, such as equations, fractions, and the notion of zero. At the water table, these math concepts are experienced and learned by repeated activity rather than by sitting at a desk trying to do math worksheets.

Mathematics in the Dramatic Play Center

Two children are rocking their dolls and sharing a book about a hospital adventure. Suddenly, Corazon stops and says, "My doll is so sick. I have to call the doctor." She looks at a list posted near the telephone and dials (reading and using numbers). "His number is 919-555–1234" (ordering a sequence of single numbers). "Hello, doctor? My baby is so sick. What should I do? Goodbye. My doctor says I have to give my baby eleventeen pills."

"Oh, well," says Meb. "My baby was so sicker the other day before today" (time sequence). "He had eleventy-seven pills" (using numbers from the teens to the over-twenty digits). The children continue to rock their babies and share the book.

These children are using play to translate their understanding of adult activities into their own actions. Corazon understood how adults use numbers to make telephone calls. Play activity also involves intelligence. Corazon used her understanding of the pattern of telephone numbers—three digits followed by seven digits—to make her call. Her comment to Meb that her baby needed "eleventeen pills" showed her developing number sense; to Corazon, teen numbers indicate a larger quantity of an item than single digits. Meb's comeback indicated that she, too, is developing a sense of numbers because she knew that numbers ending with *-ty* are larger than numbers ending with *-teen*. Meb's verbal description of yesterday was understood by her friend and will be

replaced later with the appropriate terms after more experiences with time. This scenario can also be related directly to the national standards in math. Two of the standards—"communication" in a mathematical sense and "connections" between mathematics and everyday life—were obvious in the children's play experience.

Mathematics in the Block Center

The block center is a perfect place for math experiences. Blocks are especially good for learning math because they are real-life examples of geometric shapes and solids. The block center is usually set up in preschool rooms, but it is just as important in the early elementary classroom. Figure 20–4 lists some suggested block materials to make this center as complete a learning place as possible.

To encourage rich and varied mathematical experiences in the block center, you need to carefully plan the appropriate equipment in this center. For example, the younger the children, the larger their first blocks should be. Smaller blocks can come later, when children feel the need to supplement larger blocks. If you give too many small blocks to children early in the year and insist that they reshelve them neatly, children may come to dislike blocks, defeating your purposes in having them at all. Aside from this, block building is a tremendously satisfying activity that nourishes minds, imaginations, and the development of mathematical concepts. In fact, in a recent study, researchers reported a statistical relationship existed between the child's block play characteristics as a preschooler and their mathematics achievement at middle and high school levels (Park, Chae, & Boyd, 2008; Wolfgang, Standard, & Jones, 2001).

If your block area is popular and children must wait for turns, make a waiting list—printed neatly for children to read—and set a timer. When you use a timer, children discover that turns are coming around in a fair way. You may also want to post stick-figure pictures indicating how many children can be in the area at one time.

A child building with blocks has many experiences related to math, such as classification (grouping by the same size, for example) and order (putting blocks in order of largest to smallest). There are many other basic math ideas learned through block building, such as length, area, volume, number, and shape. Both small and large motor skills are also developed as children play with blocks.

Goals

Activities in this center afford the child experiences in

- creating real and imaginary structures.
- differentiating between sizes and shapes.
- classifying according to size and shape.
- selecting according to space.
- conceptualizing about space, size, and shape.
- defining geometric shapes.
- developing perceptive insight, hand–eye coordination, imagination, and directionality.

Materials

Set of solid wooden unit blocks (approximately 200)
Small wheel toys
Puppets (to use with puppet stage or theater)
Dolls (from housekeeping center)
Dress-up clothes, especially hats
Set of hollow blocks (varying in size)
Miscellaneous construction sets: Tinkertoys, Lego® blocks, Lincoln Logs, Bristle-blocks, Connectos, etc.
Rubber animals (zoo, farm)
Small plastic/rubber people (family, farmer, firefighter, etc.)
Planks, tiles
Old steering wheel
Packing crates, boxes, and ropes
Traffic signs
Books related to building
Pulleys and ropes
Large quantities of "junk" construction materials, egg cartons, milk cartons, rods, spools, small rectangular boxes, etc.
Measuring tapes and unusual things to measure
Pan balance for exploring weight
Playing cards or cards with dots, numerals, or both

FIGURE 20-4 • Suggestions for a block center.

Cleanup in the block center is another good chance to practice math skills. The following suggestions can help you make this cleanup a true learning experience.

- Ask children to pick up all of the blocks that are curved.
- Ask children to pick up blocks of three different lengths.
- Ask children to pick up blocks according to size.
- Ask children to pick up blocks similar to a specific block that the cleanup director names.
- Ask children to pick up blocks different from a specific block that the cleanup director names.
- Ask children to put away all of a particular shape or size block, and ask how many of that block were used.
- Ask children to stack all of the blocks that go in the lower left section of the blocks shelf. Then stack the lower middle shelf, etc.
- Ask children to put away blocks in groups of twos, threes, fours, etc.
- Ask children to put away one dozen long unit blocks.
- Ask children to put away blocks according to size, beginning with the biggest or longest and ending with the smallest or shortest.
- Select certain children to put away certain shapes, e.g., rectangles, cylinders.
- Select certain children to collect blocks according to weight.
- Have children put away a certain unit of blocks and all of the blocks that are a fraction of that unit block.
- Use an assembly line to put away blocks. This encourages cooperation.
- Ask children to pick up a number of blocks that are greater or lesser than the number of blocks the cleanup director is holding (Hirsch, 2000; Sarama & Clements, 2009).

Mathematical Concepts: Definitions and Related Activities

In our preceding discussion, many references were made to various mathematical concepts young children develop through everyday experiences in early childhood learning centers. This section provides a brief description of these basic mathematical concepts and suggests some related activities for development of these specific concepts.

Numbers

Children learn numbers by rote. A child often has no comprehension of what these abstract terms mean, but as a result of relevant experiences, he or she begins to attach meaning to numbers. Children talk about monetary values in their play, usually without any comprehension of what a dime or a quarter is. While playing store, Irene glibly sold the apple for a dollar and later sold the coat and hat for 10 cents.

Before the child is three years old, he or she often can count to 10 in proper order. Such counting (called **rote counting**), however, may have little specific meaning for the child. The words may be only sounds to him or her—sounds repeated in a particular sequence, like a familiar song. This rote counting is similar to the stage in the development of speech (see Chapter 18) when a child can repeat words without really understanding their meaning.

Quite different from and much more difficult than rote counting is understanding the numerals as they apply to a sequence of objects: that each numeral represents the position of an object in the sequence (button 1, button 2, button 3, and so on). Equally or more difficult to understand is the idea that the last number counted in a sequence of objects represents all the objects in the sequence, the total number of objects counted. This is called **rational counting**. For example, in counting six buttons, the child must grasp the idea that six, the last number counted, tells him or her how many buttons he or she has—that he or she has six buttons in all.

Rational counting, a higher-level number understanding, develops slowly for most children. However, carefully structured activities that take one idea and present it to children one step at a time help them grow from a general to a more specific understanding of numbers.

Young children frequently hear counting—as steps are being climbed, objects are being stacked, foods are being distributed, fingerplays are being played, familiar nursery rhymes and songs are being enjoyed, and during many other activities. This repetition helps the child memorize the sequence and sounds of numbers, even before the meanings of these numbers are understood. Songs, fingerplays, and nursery rhymes using the fingers as counting objects should be common practice in early childhood programs to help young children practice the sounds and sequence of numbers.

True counting ability (rational counting) is not possible until the child understands one-to-one correspondence. In other words, to rote count (to say the number sequence) is one thing, but to count items correctly—one number per item—is more difficult. Very often when a young child is given a series of things to count, the child counts two numbers for one item or two items while saying only one number. Thus, as rote counting develops, teachers should also encourage the skills of one-to-one correspondence.

Having children touch each object as they count is one way to encourage their grasp of one-to-one correspondence. Repeating this exercise in various experiences throughout the day reinforces the concept of **one-to-one correspondence**.

FIGURE 20-5 • Learning to count one's fingers is fun!

Young children should be asked to count only with number names that are meaningful to them, i.e., **cardinal numbers** (the numbers one, two, three, etc.). Young children just learning numbers often have difficulty in understanding the relationship between counting and number. For example, Beatrix may count, "One, two books." Later, when asked to bring two books to the table, she may count, "one, two" and bring only the second book. **Ordinal number** refers to the place of an object in a series of numbers. The second book in the preceding example is an ordinal number. (The cardinal number is two.)

Classification and Sorting

Classification and sorting activities are the beginnings that help children perceive a variety of relationships among things in their world.

Classification. Putting together things that are alike or that belong together is one of the processes necessary for developing the concept of numbers. In order to classify, children must be able to observe an object for likenesses and differences, as well as for attributes associated with purpose, position, location, or some other factor. Children progress through the following stages as they develop the skill of classifying.

- Sorting into graphic collections without a plan in mind. Children may put all of the blocks with a letter on them together and then, ending with a blue letter, continue by putting all blue blocks with the group. When the grouping is complete, they won't be able to tell you why the blocks belong together, only that they do.
- Grouping with no apparent plan. When asked why all the things go together, children respond with some reason, but one not immediately clear to the adult: "Well, all these are like Kimiko's."
- Sorting on the basis of some criterion. Children proceed to being able to sort a group of objects on the basis of one criterion. All of the green things or all of the round things go together, but not all of the green and round objects go together in a group.
- Creating groupings on the basis of two or more properties, putting all of the green and round objects together in a group.
- Sorting objects or events according to function, use, or on the basis of a negative concept, such as all of the things that are not used in the kitchen.

Before children can classify and sort, they need to understand concepts such as "belongingness," "put together," "alike," and "belong together." These concepts are acquired over time as children have varied hands-on experiences in the early childhood program.

Your role as teacher is to help children gain these ideas through a variety of experiences with a wide variety of materials selected specifically for classifying and sorting activities. Activity suggestions for classifying and sorting are found at the end of this chapter.

Materials for children's classifying and sorting may be kept together on a shelf in the manipulative toy or game area of your room. Boxes or sorting trays (common plastic dishpans and muffin tins work well) are kept with the materials. Sorting trays can be constructed by either attaching a series of metal jar lids to a board or piece of cardboard; mounting a number of clear plastic cups on a board; dividing a board or tray into sections with colored pieces of tape; or by mounting small, clear plastic boxes on a board. Egg cartons, plastic sewing boxes, tool boxes (such as those for storing nuts and bolts), and fishing boxes are also useful for sorting trays and stimulate children to use materials mathematically.

FIGURE 20-6 • Manipulatives and games are excellent for math activities.

THINK ABOUT IT

Virtual Manipulatives

Early childhood teachers around the world guide children's mathematical learning through the use of manipulatives—such as blocks, geoboards, Unifix cubes, Cuisenaire rods, coins, clocks, and so on. Manipulatives allow concrete, hands-on exploration and representation of mathematical concepts. In the past few years, virtual versions of these common manipulatives have become available.

Virtual manipulatives are interactive, Web-based, computer-generated images of objects that children can manipulate on the computer screen. Similar to the ways they slide, flip, rotate, and turn a concrete manipulative by hand, children can use a computer mouse to slip, flip, rotate, and turn a visual representation as if it were a three-dimensional object (Rosen & Hoffman, 2009). Using virtual manipulatives, children can apply mathematical concepts and explore processes for representing the concepts (Moyer-Packenham, Salkind, & Bolyar, 2007).

Many websites offer virtual manipulatives. One popular site, the Utah State University National Library of Virtual Manipulatives (NLVM, http://nlvm.usu.edu/en/nav/vlibrary.html), offers virtual manipulatives in five areas—number and operations, algebra, geometry, measurement, and data analysis and probability—for grades pre–K through 12, in English and Spanish. (Find more websites listed in "Virtual Manipulatives-Related websites" at the end of this chapter.)

A variety of virtual manipulatives are useful in expanding young children's experiences and supporting their learning of key skills and conceptual understanding of mathematics. Virtual manipulatives offer teachers new ways to meet the changing needs of the young children they teach. Children love using manipulatives—concrete and virtual—because they are game-like and engage their senses (Rosen & Hoffman, 2009). Many virtual manipulatives are available free on the Internet and are accessible by schools, child care programs, and in homes across the United States.

In research done in 2005, the Kaiser Foundation found that technology access is increasing for young children both at home and at school, and that by first grade, 91% of students are using computers in school. In home settings, almost half of young children have access to high-speed Internet, and children as young as four years are online several times a week (Kaiser Family Foundation, 2005).

NCTM's 2008 Position statement, *The Use of Technology in the Teaching and Learning of Mathematics,* states that technology "is an essential tool for learning mathematics in the twenty-first century." According to a joint position statement by NAEYC and NCTM (2002), "technology enhances students' learning," often by increasing the scope of the mathematical content and the range of problem situations that are within the children's reach. Studies show that a combination of physical and on-screen virtual manipulatives is more effective than either alone (Clements & Sarama, 2003).

Young children need a variety of methods to build new understandings of mathematical ideas, such as building from counting on fingers to taking tallies to offering timelines, graphs, pictures, and symbols. Teachers who make appropriate and ongoing use of virtual manipulatives add to the range of mathematical representations available, supporting the development of young learners' understandings of mathematical concepts and processes. In addition, virtual manipulatives foster mathematical communication by encouraging children to talk and write about mathematical relationships, and they encourage children to test their own rules during independent investigation (Moyer-Packenham, 2005).

Today's children live in a technology-rich world. For classrooms equipped with computers and Internet access, virtual manipulatives are an exciting and motivating, no-cost option. Virtual manipulatives, used in combination with concrete manipulatives and other real-world exploration and in ways that encourage discussion and critical thinking, can make a unique and significant contribution to young children's mathematics education (Rosen & Hoffman, 2009).

A good way to begin is to check out the National Library of Virtual Manipulatives website to see the range of activities available in the Web Resources section at the end of this chapter.

Comparing

The skill of **comparing** seems to come easily and naturally, especially when it is a personal comparison: "My shoes are newer than yours." "I've got the biggest." "My sister is little." "You've got more." When children build with blocks, they may be asked to make additional comparisons: "Which tower is the tallest?" "Pick up the heaviest blocks first." "Build something as tall as this." Have children identify parts of their buildings using the vocabulary of comparison.

When different size and shape containers are used in sand and water play, children can make comparisons based on volume. In the early childhood program, these are informal and related to children's actual experiences. "How many blue cups of water will it take to fill this bucket?" "How many red?" "Which is the heaviest?" "This doesn't hold as much."

Stories and poems, often the folk tales children are already familiar with, offer other opportunities for informal comparisons. *The Three Billy Goats Gruff*, *Goldilocks and the Three Bears*, and others offer comparisons on the basis of differing attributes.

FIGURE 20-8 • Appropriate math picture books present math concepts with visual and verbal appeal.

FIGURE 20-7 • Math problems don't have to be solved at a desk!

Throughout the preschool years, ask children to observe and note differences in the objects of their environment, to name them, and to discuss them with one another.

Ordering (Seriation)

Another mathematical idea that is a vital part of a complete number concept formation is the idea of **ordering (seriation).**

Ordering the environment into series begins when children are very young and continues throughout adult life. The child begins by perceiving opposite ends of a series:

big————————little
heavy————————light
cold————————hot
long————————short

The intervention of an adult, suitable materials, and appropriate language lead to refinement of these early basic concepts. The comparison of the height of two children is the beginning of ordering, as is the comparison of two sets of things as *more* or *less*. Ordering sticks, blocks, or nesting cups in a sequence that leads gradually from the smallest to the biggest helps children see ordered size relations.

When children line up to go outdoors, they meet another idea of order: Juan stands in front of Ne'Andrea and Yvonne stands in back of Drew. They may use their understanding of sequence when they say, "I want to be first," or "Jimmy is last."

After listening to the story of Goldilocks and the three bears, their observations may become more refined as they discuss the story. The story contains big–little and one-to-one relationships in addition to its many other enjoyable qualities.

The idea of ordering in size also appears naturally in other classroom areas. The teacher can make ordering a part of natural discussions in relation to the children's play and activities: sets of cans, bottles, and books can also be used for practicing ordering of size. With younger children, only two objects are compared at first; this will be extended to three or more objects for older children.

Children enjoy ordering and do so spontaneously. Many table toys provide ordering experiences, as do ordinary objects like measuring spoons and cups.

Your role is to provide materials and sufficient time. When children find the existing materials too easy, you can awaken their interest by encouraging them to use the toys differently, by asking them questions, and by providing additional materials.

Ordering activities can include length (sticks), height (bottles), total size (bowls and shoes), weight (stones), color (from light to dark), and other endless possibilities. Suggestions for ordering activities are found at the end of this chapter.

Shape and Form

Young children need many experiences with shapes and making comparisons between shapes before they focus on naming shapes. Usually, it is enough to introduce one new shape at a time. As the new shape is understood, other shapes may be added, thus building new learning on previous learning.

THIS ONE'S for YOU!   Money: More Than Dollars and Cents

Money is a topic that seems to be on everyone's mind. But there is a lot about money that you and your students probably don't know. The following are a few links to help you learn what all the fuss is about.

- Does the U.S. Mint use special paper to print dollar bills? In fact, they do. A very special paper is used for our dollar bills. At PBS http://www.pbs.org/wgbh/nova/moolah/anatomyprinting.html describe the intricacies in the anatomy of U.S. paper currency.

- Has our U.S. currency always looked like it does today? No, and you can find out how it has changed over the years, at http://www.friesian.com/notes.htm. You can also visit http://www.frbsf.org/federalreserve/money/funfacts.html to learn how coins and bills have changed over the years in order to stop the production of counterfeit money.

- Help! I left my $5 bill in my pants pocket and it went through the laundry! Is it still good? Yes!

Don't throw it away. Take your scraps to a bank. According to http://www.n.gov/ http://www.moneyfactory.gov/, if you have half of your bill, you can get a crisp, green replacement.

- True or false: The U.S. Mint still makes gold coins. True. At http://www.usmint.gov/kids/coinNews/coinOfTheMonth/2008/10.cfm, you'll learn that the U.S. Mint still makes commemorative and bullion versions of the $5 eagle coin.

- I want to plan some money activities for my children! At http://www.funbrain.com/cashreg/index.html, you'll find a nice collection of games to play to test money skills. Also, try the puzzle at http://www.usmint.gov/kids/games/goldenDollarPuzzle.

Money is a lot more than dollars and cents—it's a fun, interactive experience for you and the children.

In teaching young children about shape and form, it is important to include more shapes than the common geometric shapes of a circle, triangle, rectangle, and square. Since shapes aid in, or are sources of, identification, limiting instruction to the "basic shapes" excludes from the learning environment important aspects of recognition of shapes in general.

Yet familiar shapes must be taught before uncommon ones. Most of these unfamiliar shapes depend on previous shape identification and recognition. From the basis of understanding simple shapes, the child is able to build more complex structures.

Shapes of various kinds can be found throughout the child's environment. Words defining shapes should be used often. For example, everyday language should include such statements as: "That is a square box," rather than "That is square"; "The clock is round," rather than "This is round"; "Put the book on the square table," rather than "Put it over there." With these phrases, the object and its characteristic shape are made clear to the child. Later on, characteristics such as color, size, texture, and number may be added.

When unfamiliar shapes are introduced, a review of already familiar ones should precede the new introduction. Then children's thinking can be stimulated with such questions as "How is this new shape the same as . . . ?" or "How is this new shape not the same as (or different from) . . . ?" Such comparisons reinforce and review shapes already learned.

Mathematics: Grades 3–5

Mathematics is a subject most students in grades 3 through 5 like. In fact, nearly three-quarters of fourth graders report liking mathematics (Kenney & Silver, 1997). Students in grades 3 through 5 see mathematics as practical, are challenged with many new ideas, and believe that what they are learning is important. However, sometime between grades 4 and 8, students' interest in mathematics begins to wane. Although they continue to view mathematics as important, by grade 8 students are less likely to characterize it as interesting or to consider themselves good at math (Jung, Kloosterman, & McMullen, 2007). It is crucial that mathematics education in the upper elementary and early middle grades be challenging, relevant, and engaging for students.

The curriculum materials and instructional approaches a teacher uses help students connect mathematical ideas and provide a basis for making them meaningful. Because the amount of content in grades

FIGURE 20-9 • Older children enjoy measurement and prediction activities.

3 through 5 expands greatly from that of the earlier grades, students need help in building connections and managing the many new concepts and procedures they are encountering. Students in grades 3 through 5 must also understand and bear responsibility for their learning. In math, this means learning how to examine, ask questions, and consider different strategies—all with the goal of making sense of mathematical ideas and fitting them to other, related areas.

While the 10 standards of the National Council of Mathematics Teachers apply to all grade levels, the instructional emphases for grades 3 through 5 build on those outlined for grades pre–K to 2 and extend well beyond them. Although number and operation continue to be cornerstones of the curriculum in grades 3 through 5, each of the content standards (number, data, measurement, algebra, and geometry) is essential for building student knowledge at this level. Several "big ideas" or central mathematical themes for this grade band are woven through these areas, including multiplication, equivalence, and the notion of unit.

Likewise, knowledge and use of mathematical processes should be deepened and expanded in these grades. Students in grades 3 through 5 are capable of sophisticated reasoning and should be challenged and supported in their learning.

In grades 3 through 5, extending understanding from whole numbers to fractions and decimals is a key dimension of the mathematics curriculum. Students need many and varied experiences in order to understand what fractions and decimals represent, how they are related to each other, and how they are different from whole numbers. Suggestions for fraction and decimal activities are found at the end of this chapter.

Calculators: Grades 3–5

Appropriate use of calculators is an important part of a balanced mathematics education at all levels, including elementary. The National Council of Teachers of Mathematics has elaborated this position in a public statement, *Principles and Standards for School Mathematics* (NCTM, 2000). Thus, the calculator and a variety of computer software should be considered legitimate tools for learning math concepts and performing math computations and should be available to students in grades 3 through 5.

Students need access to calculators, but they also need pencil-and-paper skills. Balancing these two is an important part of an elementary teacher's work. Research has shown that students who use calculators are better at understanding mathematical concepts and solving problems (Murphy, DePasquale, & McNamara, 2003). The same studies confirm that calculator use does not interfere with students' development of computational skills, and in many of these studies, students' pencil-and-paper skills increased when they also had the opportunity to use calculators.

Calculators are tools and, as such, are only as effective as the person pushing the buttons. Just as a hammer does not build a house, a calculator does not think or solve problems. This is a job for people, and a job that students can learn early on. Also, just as a hammer does not choose where to put a nail or prevent a nail from going into the wrong board, a calculator does not know what operation to use and cannot keep a person from forgetting a decimal point. These are also jobs for people, and they involve exactly the kinds of skills that teachers can help students learn. Sometimes a calculator is the right tool for a job, and sometimes it is not. Knowing when to use a calculator and when not to use one is a skill teachers can help children develop (Jung, Kloosterman, & McMullen, 2007).

One of the most important ways in which students can use calculators is to solve problems that they would not be able to solve otherwise. With a calculator, all children can deal with problems involving numbers that are seemingly unmanageable and that arise from their everyday experience. Whenever the teacher has a class working on developing problem-solving skills and computational procedures are not the main point of the lesson, calculator use might be appropriate. Students can develop their decision-making and problem-solving skills far beyond what they would be able to do if they were limited to numbers that they could handle quickly using pencil and paper (Seeley et al., 2005).

Teachers need to create opportunities and make judgments about when and how math tools are used to support learning. They can arrange activities requiring students to use calculators and spreadsheets to solve problems. Students in grades 3 through 5 can use graphing and geometry software and calculators to explore, experiment, verify, and visualize mathematical ideas. For example, these children might explore geometric relationships using software to create, modify, and examine shapes. They might create graphs and consider how some presentations of data highlight or distort certain trends. They might use calculators to explore the relationship between decimals and whole numbers and between negative numbers and positive numbers. Students in this age group should also have the opportunity to learn how to search the Internet to gather information needed to solve mathematical problems.

The calculator is an important tool in teaching mathematics in grades 3 through 5. However, calculators do not circumvent the need for rapid recall of basic facts, a basic understanding of math concepts, or the ability to formulate and use strategies for computing. Rather, the calculator should support these goals by enhancing and stimulating student learning. As students solve problems involving many complex computations, the calculator should be used to perform calculations. The calculator serves as a tool for enabling the problem solver to focus on the big picture rather than become entangled in the calculating details. (See the end of this chapter for some suggested activities for grades 3 through 5.)

Summary

Long before a child formally uses numerals, he or she is aware of them through daily experiences. For example, a child becomes aware of sequences in events before he or she can talk about what is first, second, or third (ordinal numbers). The child recognizes, too, the difference between *one* and *many* and between *few* and *lots* before he or she acquires real number concepts. The pattern of early uses of numbers is similar to the general-to-specific pattern of physical growth. In these early stages of mathematical thinking, the child has a general understanding of numbers and will gradually move toward a more specific understanding as the developmental process continues.

It is important that adults use number terms correctly in daily experiences with children. Demonstrating their meaning in daily activities is just as important as using the right words. Mathematical concept learning is a natural part of daily activities in early childhood learning centers. In working with art, books, blocks, movement, water play, and language arts, young children are actively involved in using their emerging mathematical understandings.

Counting by rote (memory) is common for young children aged three and up. Counting with understanding (rational counting) does not occur until a child understands one-to-one correspondence.

Classification, or putting together things that are alike or that belong together, is one of the processes necessary for developing the concept of numbers. In order to classify, children must be able to observe an object for likenesses and differences, as well as for other common factors.

Comparing is another mathematical process that is appropriate in the early childhood program. Children seem to make comparisons easily and naturally, especially when the comparisons involve them personally.

Another mathematical idea that is a vital part of a complete number concept is the idea of order. Putting things in a series or in order is a process that is appropriate for early mathematical experiences.

Key Terms

cardinal numbers 503
comparing 505
ordering (seriation) 505
ordinal number 503
one-to-one correspondence 502
rational counting 502
rote counting 502

Learning Activities

A. Use one of the activities suggested in this chapter with a group of young children. Evaluate your experience. Share your evaluation with your classmates.

B. Make up some of your own activities for the mathematical concepts discussed in this chapter.

C. Choose at least two children's books from the sources listed in the Online Companion. Explain why you chose them and how you would plan to use them with young children. If possible, use them with a group of children and discuss your results.

D. Using a school supply catalog, choose three pieces of mathematical equipment appropriate for teaching seriation, geometric shapes, and size.

E. Imagine that you have $150 to spend on mathematical equipment for your classroom. Using a school supply catalog, determine how you would spend this sum. In making your selections, give the following information:

1. developmental reason for choice
2. purpose(s) for item

F. Choose one or two children from each of these age groups: three-year-olds, four-year-olds, five-year-olds. Assess each child's ability to count. Record and comment on the results of your assessment of each child. Discuss what math activities would be developmentally appropriate for these children.

G. Observe and talk with a preschool child, listening for comments and understanding related to numbers. If possible, ask the child such questions as "How old are you? What is your favorite number? How far can you count? Where do you see numbers?"

Observe and talk with a child between five and six years old, asking some of the same questions. Ask additional questions such as "Show me how you can add some things. Here are three pencils. How many will you have if you add two more pencils?" Challenge the child with number questions and problems. Assess the mathematical understanding of the two children you observed, keeping in mind the difference in their ages.

H. Log on to one of the math websites listed at the end of this chapter. Share your opinion of the merit of this site with your fellow students. What is the most useful or advantageous aspect of this resource? What is its greatest drawback? Would you use this site as a resource in the future? Why or why not?

I. Ask children in grades 3 through 5 their opinions about math. What percent of the children liked math? Ask them why they feel the way they do about math. Report your results to the class.

J. Observe in an early childhood classroom using the Math Observation sheet in the Online Companion. Discuss the results of your observation with your fellow students. Did you observe any surprises? If yes, explain what they were.

Activities for Children

Activities such as the following help children grasp the mathematical concept of counting.

- In counting activities, have the child touch each object. Count only with number names meaningful to the child. Repeat this in various settings until touching or pointing to objects is no longer necessary. Provide for many manipulative counting experiences where children use beads, buttons, cookies, napkins, children, and chairs. For example, children might match beads to boxes or children to chairs. Determine the number of places, quantity of milk, silverware, napkins, and so on needed at the table.

- Use buttons, bottle caps, or similar objects. Have children practice counting three, putting three in a box, and taking one, two, or three out of the box. After counting, children can glue the buttons or bottle caps onto a piece of paper to make a picture.

- Have children take turns trying to toss a specified number of beanbags into a large container. Allow children to choose the number of beanbags they wish to throw and count them as they throw.

Buried Treasure Count

Fill a clear plastic soda bottle two-thirds full with sand. Drop in assorted small trinkets (beads, buttons, erasers, plastic insects, charms, jewels, etc.). Cover tightly, then secure the cover with masking tape. Let children turn and shake the bottle and try to count how many treasures are buried in it. If someone counts correctly, remove the cap and add or take out some trinkets, then reseal the bottle.

Numbers and Snacks

Number concepts can be reinforced easily in everyday routines. Snack time is an excellent time for teaching about numbers. Once or twice a week, prepare snacks to reinforce mathematical concepts. Discuss the characteristic of each snack at service time. Then let children eat while they learn from the special snack you have prepared.

A. Choose a number and serve snack items in groups of that number (four raisins, four carrot sticks, four banana slices, four crackers, etc.).

B. Choose a geometric shape such as a circle, and serve round snack items (round crackers, cucumber slices, round cereal, carrot slices, banana slices, etc.).

Concept of Number and Counting

Cut face cards in half (make the cutting lines different on the separate cards so that only the two "matching" halves will fit together). Put the cards together as puzzles. Add these to the math center.

Place numerals from 1 to 10 around the room. Show children a card with objects on it and, ask them to find the numeral that tells how many objects are on the card.

Make a number book by pasting the correct number of colored squares or other shapes next to written numerals.

Set up at the math center a numeral recognition and numeration activity such as "Counting Marbles." Provide 10 paper cups and label them with the numerals 1 through 10. Provide a box with lots of marbles. Place these on a table for a mini-math center. Have children work with a partner. One child examines the numeral printed on each cup and drops in the appropriate number of marbles. The partner counts the marbles in each cup to see if the correct amount was put in it. The marbles then go back into the box.

Recycled Math Materials

To add to your supply of math manipulatives, start saving bottle caps. You will find many uses for these recyclables. Here are a few suggestions.

Bottle Cap Sizes. Give children a number of bottle caps that vary in size. Have them organize the caps from the smallest to largest and then from the largest to smallest.

Bottle Cap Groupings. Collect a variety of bottle caps that vary in size, color, and texture. Invite children to sort the caps into like groups. Notice the different ways that children sort and classify caps. They may sort by size, shape, or color or separate the plastic caps from the metal caps. Once they have completed their sorting, encourage them to describe their choice of groupings. How many more are in one group than another? Is there any other way to group them?

Bottle Cap Weights. Provide children with a pan scale and a variety of bottle caps. Have them compare the weight of plastic and metal bottle caps. Which weighs more? Have them place a large bottle cap on one side of the scale. How many small caps are equal to the weight of the large cap? Are three large caps equal to the weight of three small caps? What would happen if children put 10 more with this group? Ten less?

Bottle Cap Fill and Count. Fill a small clear plastic container with bottle caps. Ask children to estimate how many bottle caps are in the container and record each child's estimate. Have them count the number of bottle caps and compare their predictions. Then give them another container, either smaller or larger, and have them estimate how many small bottle caps will fill the container. Invite children to count the caps as they fill it up.

Bottle Cap Pairs. Collect enough bottle caps to have one pair of each. Mix them up and place them in a pile on the table. Give children time to explore the different bottle caps. Then invite one or two children to find the matching bottle caps. How many pairs of bottle caps did they find? What makes the bottle caps similar to each other? Different from the rest?

Number Roll

Position the children in a circle. Sit in the center with a ball. Pass the ball to a child while calling out a number. After the child bounces the ball the correct number of times, he or she calls out a number and passes the ball to another child. Be sure to have the child count out loud as she bounces the ball. Variation: Practice counting with young children as their classmates run, skip, or walk laps around a short indoor course. Record results on a chart to show who went the farthest.

Everyday Math

Try some of these simple, everyday math activities to increase your "math talk" with young children.

- Roll Call. Have children count how many students are present and figure out how many are absent.

- Calendar Quiz. Discuss the numbers on a calendar. How many days are left before the weekend? How many days are in a week? In a month?

- Line Up. When children are in line, have them say, "I am first," "I am second," and so on. Make a chart of the words we use to describe order.

- Twos. Ask children to think of things that come in ones, twos, threes, and so on. Make a chart and add to it throughout the year.

- Learning Time. Draw a clock on the board. Invite children to draw hands on the clock in answer to a prompt such as "When is lunch time?"

Number Books

Make a book for each child by stapling four sheets of white paper together with a colored construction paper cover. Title the cover according to a selected learning concept (Number Book, Matching Book, Shape Book, etc.). Have children look through magazines and catalogs to find pictures that illustrate that learning concept. Then have them tear out the pictures and glue them into their books.

Block Shelters

In the fall, as animals are getting ready for winter, add stuffed animals of different sizes to the block center. Encourage children to build homes for the animals. Discuss how many blocks it takes to build the animal homes. Does a bigger animal take more or fewer blocks? They can also arrange animals by size and color.

Shape Books

Choose a geometric shape, such as a circle, and have children glue pictures of circular things throughout their books. Or, label the pages of the books with different geometric shapes (circles, squares, triangles), and have children glue correspondingly shaped pictures onto the appropriate pages.

Size, Seriation, and Ordinal Numbers
Ordering/Seriation

- Challenge children with some of these activities.

- Have children find the shortest or longest block or tinker toy.

- Have children pick from three objects of differing heights the one that is the shortest. Have them describe the remaining two objects.

- Have students describe how the objects in a series, arranged from the shortest to the longest, differ from one another.

- Collect nesting materials, such as a set of measuring spoons or measuring cups. Have children arrange the objects in correct order so that they will properly "nest" together, one object fitting inside the other. Be sure to have children set the objects on the table in order from smallest to largest after they have finished "nesting" them.

- Supply three cans of different sizes and three beanbags in three sizes. Have students arrange the cans from smallest to largest in a row. Have children line the beanbags up next to the cans, putting the smallest by the smallest, etc. Shuffle the cans and the beanbags. Have children order the cans from smallest to largest this time, and then match the beanbags to the cans.

- Cut out three fish. Make each fish large enough to totally conceal the next smaller fish when placed over it. Tell children that the fish go in order, with the biggest fish first leading the others. Have them find the largest fish and then the fish that will follow. Check to see if the largest fish covers the fish that follows. For self-checking, children place each fish on top of the next to see if the next fish is smaller. Variation: Have children order from the smallest fish to the largest fish.

- Have children seriate materials such as buttons, gummed stars, lids, beads, feathers, and nails in order of size. Also have children make size comparisons between two or more of the objects.

- Have children seriate boxes or cans from smallest to largest by placing them inside one another.

- Have children roll balls of various sizes from clay or play dough, and then seriate them according to size.

- Make felt or cardboard cutouts in three or more sizes of different heights (for example, trees, houses, hats). Challenge children to arrange them in a given order beginning with shortest or tallest. (Variation: Arrange trees in order of height.)

- To reinforce the use of the ordering words *first* and *last*, have children stand in line and identify the person who is first and the person who is last. See if children can figure out who is in the middle!

- Cut out triangles whose base length is the same but whose heights are different. Select a set of triangles that varies along one dimension. Lay them in front of children in mixed order, but in such a way that the child does not have to turn them to discover size variations. Have children order them from smallest to largest (shortest to tallest) or largest to smallest.

- Show five blocks that have been ordered according to height. Arrange another set of blocks to match the first, third, and fifth blocks in the five-block pattern. Have children insert the two remaining blocks so that both sets match. Repeat, using different blocks, such as second or fourth, and so on.

Buttons and Math Activities

Ask parents to furnish buttons in all shapes and sizes. Use these for sorting by color and by size. Older children (four- and five-year-olds) can even make graphs showing how many buttons of each color have been collected.

Make at least five different designs by gluing buttons to cards. Give children the same size cards, and invite them to use buttons from the classroom supply to duplicate the designs on their cards.

Measurement

How Big Am I?

For this activity, you will need boxes, cartons, tables, chairs, barrels, unit blocks, and building blocks. Challenge children with questions such as the following: Can you build a building with blocks as high as you are tall? Can you build something as high as your arm is long? As high as to the top of your leg? Waist? Shoulder?

Telling Time

Use masking tape to make a large clock on the floor. Have children move around in the 12 hour spaces by stretching arms to a person in the middle of the clock as you call time. Explore different times (recess time, lunch time) and ways to move around (fast, slow, hop, slide, skip).

Number Shapes

Have students form the shapes of numbers with their bodies when you call out a signal. Encourage children to work together to form numbers if they need "extra strokes." Challenge them to make these shapes combining with time, space, and force.

Measuring with Our Bodies

Write the word *measure* on a sheet of chart paper. Ask children to share what they know about measuring. What does it mean to measure something? What type of things do we measure? What do we use to measure? Why do we measure things? Record their comments on the chart paper.

Have children use their bodies to measure different things. Have them estimate how many hands or arms long, tall, or wide something will be. Prepare another sheet of chart paper to record all the different things children measure. Include their estimations and actual measurements.

Have children use their hands to find out how many "hands long" the tables are. Invite a few children to one of the tables. Ask them to first estimate, or guess, how many hands long the table will be. Record their estimate on a chart paper. Then have them line up their hands lengthwise on the table. Count and record the actual hand length of the table. Next, ask them to compare their estimation with their answer. Then have them measure the width of the table. Estimate and then conduct the actual measurement. Are all of the classroom tables the same size?

Have children think of other ways to measure the tables with their bodies. How many hands high is the table from the floor? How many feet or bodies long are the tables? Encourage children to estimate and then compare their measurements.

Fun Measuring

Have students gather all the writing implements they can find in the room, and lay them out end to end. Measure the resulting length with yardsticks and rulers. How many crayons make up a yard? How many pencils make up a foot?

Measuring Shadows

Have children pair up to trace their shadows. Show them how one child in each pair can stand in the sun on a hard surface (or on a piece of paper if you're inside) while the other child uses chalk or a pencil to trace the shadow.

When children finish, have partners trade places so everyone has a shadow tracing. Suggest that children write their names on their shadows.

Encourage children to think of ways to measure the shadows, then invite them to test out their ideas. Have a variety of measuring tools handy, such as yarn, string, and ribbon.

Help each pair measure their shadows using the material they chose. One child can hold the yarn or other material at the head of the shadow tracing while the other stretches it to the bottom. Then, help the children cut it so that each child will have a length of material that represents the length of his or her shadow.

Encourage children to predict whether their shadow lengths are longer, shorter, or the same as their own bodies, others' shadows, and other objects they see.

Show them how to compare lengths of their materials against those objects to test their predictions.

For younger children: Take large sheets of Kraft paper outdoors. Have children take turns lying on the paper. Trace and cut out the outlines of children's bodies. Later, bring paint cups and brushes outdoors, and invite children to paint their paper "shadows."

For older children: Encourage children to hunt for outdoor objects (sticks, rocks, weeds) they can use as instruments to measure their shadows.

Variation: Ask children to try to change the shape of the shadows they see outdoors by moving the objects that create them. What happens to the shadow of a tricycle, a ball, or a swing when the object is moved in one way or another?

Math and Science—Honeybee Measurement

On a single flight, a honeybee can visit more than 1,000 flowers, drinking nectar with its proboscis, a tongue that resembles a drinking straw. When its "honey stomach"—which holds only one eyedropper's worth of nectar—is full, the bee deposits the nectar into hive cells.

Group children into "colonies" (small groups) for this activity. For each colony, place an eyedropper and cup of water at one end of the room and a plastic medicine cup (marked with teaspoon and tablespoon increments) across the room. To play, children take turns transferring water across the room to the medicine cups—one drop at a time! As the "bees" deposit their "honey" into the "hives," a recorder keeps count of the drops needed to produce the amounts of water, from one teaspoon to two tablespoons. When finished, explain that the drop count for each measurement equals the number of bee flights taken to produce that amount of honey. Tell children that each bee produces about half a teaspoon of honey in its lifetime.

When a bee is looking for nectar to make honey, it can travel about 1 mile in four minutes. Ask students, "How far can you travel in four minutes?" Students can time themselves while running or walking in the school gym or on your school's track. Students might use this data to determine how long it would take them to travel one mile.

Playing Numbers

This is a fast math activity that can fill up a 5-minute period. Give each child a pair of foam dice, or regular dice and a noise-absorbing surface, such as foam placemats or squares of fleece cloth. For children who can add, have them roll the dice and write the sum of the two numbers that come up. Keep rolling and adding until time is up. Who reached the highest number? Who had the lowest? Children who don't know how to add and subtract yet can count the dots that come up with each roll and record the numbers on paper. In five minutes, which number came up the most frequently? The least? Not at all?

Comparing

The following materials can be used to aid children in comparing.

- String, ribbon, pencils, rulers, clay snakes, lines, or strips of paper. Ask children which is longest, longer, shortest, and shorter.

- Buttons, dolls, cups, plastic animals, trees, boats. Have children identify the biggest one or the one bigger than another.

- Containers and coffee cans filled with various materials and sealed, or buckets or bags of items. Ask which is the heaviest or the lightest and which is heavier than another.

- Toy cars, trucks, bikes. Ask which is the fastest, the slowest, or which is faster than another.

- Paper, cardboard, books, pieces of wood, food slices, cookies. Have children make or find one that is thick, thicker, thickest, or thinnest.

Classification and Sorting

The following materials are helpful for classification and sorting activities.

Boxes of scrap materials—velvet squares, tweeds, and net cut into uniform sizes and shapes for feeling, sorting, and classifying according to texture.

- A box or shelf of bells—cow bells, Christmas bells, decorative bells, sleigh bells—all inviting children to sort and classify on any basis they decide, perhaps size, color, shape, or sound.

- A box of various textured papers, cut into uniform shapes and sizes for the younger children and into a variety of shapes for older children. Smooth papers, watercolor paper, textured papers, and others can be obtained from a local print shop.

- Collections of nuts, nails, screws, and bolts to classify and sort according to shape, size, or function.

Sorting

Make two big loops with string on a table or on the floor. Have a set of round objects of several colors and a set of red objects of different shapes and sizes. Put a round object in one loop and a red object in the other loop. Have children sort according to this rule. Then make the loops overlap.

Tell children that only objects that are round and red can go in the middle loop. Have children re-sort the objects. Provide other sets of objects that lend themselves to this type of sorting, and let children determine the sorting rules.

Shoe Sorting

You will need 10 pairs of shoes of different sizes. To begin, put all the shoes in the middle of a circle. Have children sort them into pairs (one-to-one correspondence) and then into groups of little, middle, and big. Of course, they'll need to try them on for size!

Number Quiz

Have children make up and exchange riddles about "more" and "fewer." Examples: "I'm thinking of a number that is one more than the buttons on my shirt." "I'm thinking of a number that is one fewer than the windows in our room." Have children make up and mentally solve riddles about "same" numbers. For example, "I am the same number as legs on a dog." "I am the same number as points on a triangle."

Shapes

Blocks and Shapes

Obtain spring and/or balance scales that measure in ounces or grams, such as those for weighing letters or foods. Show children how to use them carefully. Have children weigh wooden blocks. They might also combine several blocks, balance different shapes and sizes to get the same weight, and arrange blocks from lightest to heaviest.

Make a chart to record block weights. Draw pictures of blocks and leave space to record their weights.

Have children weigh blocks together. Record block weights on the chart. Compare weights of different blocks. What combinations weigh the same?

Have children find objects that weigh the same as each block. They might build a structure with blocks and predict how much it weighs. They can find out by weighing the blocks after you take the structure apart. Have students sketch block constructions, writing the weight of each block in its picture.

Have children play a shape-recognition game with Sesame Street's Zoe, matching and associating basic shapes with appropriate common objects. http://www. sesamestreet.org/muppet/-/journal_content/56_ INSTANCE_MUPP/10171/Zoe/muppet.

Shoe Print Patterns

Collect a variety of old shoes that have interesting patterns on the soles. Tape a large sheet of brown butcher paper across a table. Help children put smocks on and give them several colors of washable tempera paint and paintbrushes. Invite them to use one or several colors to paint the soles of the shoes. Then demonstrate how to place the shoes on the paper to make a print. Have children describe the different patterns or shapes created by the soles. How are they similar, and how do they differ? Rinse the soles off with a wet cloth so the shoes can be used again. Display the shoe prints in the classroom.

Shape Matching Game

For this activity you will need five or six colors of construction paper cut into shapes (circles, squares, triangles), one piece per child.

Have children sit in a circle. Direct them to place their shape marker in front of them. Call out one of the shapes. All children having that shape run around the circle in the same direction and back to their places. Different kinds of movements can be used (skipping, galloping, walking, hopping). Variation: Use colors instead of shapes. (After playing, children might make their color and shape cards into necklaces.) Use numbered flash cards or addition/subtraction problems.

Toothpick Shapes

For this activity, have children working in pairs. One child makes an arrangement of five toothpicks and shows it to his or her partner for three seconds only. The other student attempts to build a copy of the pattern. Announce "Begin!" and then "Stop!" after three seconds, then allow half a minute for students to build and discuss with their partners. Play four or six rounds, and discuss interesting patterns, shapes, or geometry concepts children used during this activity.

Shape Crawl

For this activity you will need shapes cut out of cardboard. Spread the shapes around a space. Challenge children to crawl through the shapes with questions such as the following:

- Can you crawl through without touching the sides?
- Can you crawl through using one arm and both feet?
- Can you crawl through using one foot and both hands?
- Can you crawl through with one arm and one leg?
- Can you crawl through on your back using your arms and legs?

Shape Identification Game

You will need shapes of various sizes for this activity. Explain to children that each shape has a movement that goes with it. Practice the moves with each shape. Have children in a scatter formation. When you hold up a triangle, they can only move their heads. When you hold up a circle, they can move only their legs. For a square, they can move only their shoulders; for a rectangle, only their hips. For an oval, they move their entire bodies. Change shapes rapidly. This game is fun to play with some lively music, too!

Shapes in Art

For this activity you will need colored paper shapes (circles, squares, rectangles, hexagons, ovals, etc.), crayons, markers, scissors, and glue sticks. Discuss the different shapes with children. What does half a square (half a circle, etc.) look like? Try it and see. Discuss the idea of what is and is not a half, emphasizing equal amounts.

Pass out the paper shapes and invite children to experiment with folding the shapes into equal halves. Have children cut the shapes in half.

Brainstorm where the new "half" shapes might be found in the environment. Then invite children to use their two shape halves to create a picture by pasting the shapes and adding details to illustrate their use. Children may use the shape pictures to tell a story about the halves.

As Tall as Lincoln

The Lincoln Memorial in Washington, DC, is one way the United States has honored Abraham Lincoln. The statue of Lincoln is 19 feet tall. Ask children: "How many friends do you think it would take to make a line equal to the height of the statue of Lincoln?" Have children lie on the floor head to foot to make a line that is 19 feet long. How many friends did it take to make this line? Have children compare their estimates with the actual measure.

President Lincoln was about six feet tall. Have children calculate how many Lincolns it would take to make a line 19 feet long. And the big challenge: How much taller is the statue than the president?

Activities for Older Children (Grades 4–5)

Junk Mail

Catalogs can be used in fun lessons. Have students find two items that total $11.98; have them add up the cost of all the items on a particular page. Ask: "If you had $25 to spend for your friend's birthday, what would you select?" Have students figure shipping costs on a given item.

Junk Mail Collection

Have children collect all the junk mail that their families receive in a week. At the end of the week, have them count how many pieces of junk mail each family received. How much does it weigh? Have students calculate how much junk mail each family contributes to landfills each year. Have them estimate your school's contribution of junk mail.

Cafeteria Waste

For one week, have students throw their cafeteria food waste into a container that you weigh each day. Have them determine the average weight of food waste for the week. Each day, they can observe the type of food that is thrown away. Students might create a graph to display their results. Using the data they collect, they might determine the amount of food waste generated by all the classes at your school for one year.

Math and Baseball

Older students can explore math and baseball at the same time with lessons from Ken Burns' Baseball at http://www.pbs.org/kenburns/baseball/teachers/.

Bubbling Math

Collect at least three brands of dishwashing liquid. First have students determine which brand produces the biggest bubble by blowing a straw into some solution poured onto a table. Once the bubble pops, students should measure the diameter of the liquid left on the table by the burst bubble on the table and record it. Students should conduct three trials per brand. They can then compute the average size of the bubbles. Students might also create bar graphs to compare the data they've collected.

Multiplication Activities

Memorizing the multiplication facts and understanding the concept of multiplication provide a necessary foundation for further math learning and can be particularly difficult for some students. The activities that follow help students develop this mathematical skill.

Multiplication Art

Have each student select five multiplication equations that are especially hard to remember. Then have students draw a picture of the equation and the answer. For example, a drawing for $5 \times 6 = 30$ might consist of a boy who is wearing a shirt with the number 5 on it standing in front of an apartment door with a 6 on it talking to a woman who is celebrating her thirtieth birthday with a cake that has 30 written on it.

Multiplication Building

For homework, have students choose two multiplication facts that are difficult for them. Then have them build three-dimensional creations that use those equations. For example, the equation $9 \times 6 = 54$ can be depicted by a model house with six rooms and nine objects in each room. Students should share their creations with the class without showing the equation. Students enjoy studying these models and figuring out the multiplication fact hidden within.

Multiplication Baseball

Divide the class into two teams and designate a first, second, third, and home base in the room. One group stands at the front of the room (home base) while the other group is seated. One student from Team A is "at bat," while one student from Team B "pitches" a multiplication problem. The pitcher must know the answer to their team's problem, or it's an automatic home run. After the problem is "pitched," the student at bat gives the answer and moves to first base. This continues until three students answer incorrectly, at which time the teams trade places. To make the game more challenging, divide the multiplication problems into "singles" (easy), "doubles" (moderate), "triples" (difficult), and "home runs" (extremely difficult). Students at bat can choose which type of pitch they want. You can decide how many "innings" time will allow.

Musical Multiplication

Some students who naturally learn and store information through music will enjoy memorizing their multiplication facts through songs and jingles. Don't be surprised if you hear these students singing a multiplication fact during math time. Ask students to work in pairs to create their own multiplication jingle using one multiplication pattern (5×0, 5×1, 5×2, etc.).

Multiplication Talk Show

Invite students to a multiplication talk show, where they'll participate as the guest audience and/or the featured speakers. The show is moderated by Mickey Multiplication, and the topic is "The Rough Life of a Multiplication Problem." Invite students to role-play multiplication problems after giving each number a personality. For example, Freddie Four may discuss how confused he gets when he has to play with Mr. Eight Snowman, and that the last time they played a game, he caught Mr. Snowman cheating 32 times!

Fractions and Multiple Intelligences

Some students experience a great deal of difficulty and frustration with the concept of fractions. Try some of these activities to reduce the fear of fractions and to help students understand what a fraction really is.

Fraction Order

Have students order the following fractions from largest to smallest: $\frac{1}{10}$, $\frac{2}{8}$, $\frac{3}{4}$, $\frac{1}{15}$, $\frac{7}{8}$, and $\frac{5}{12}$. Underneath each fraction, have them draw a picture to represent it (logic, word, picture smart).

Fraction Story

Have students write a story about a fractional family. For example, the Fourth family has four members: $\frac{1}{4}$, $\frac{2}{4}$, $\frac{3}{4}$, and $\frac{4}{4}$. Students should give each member of the family a unique personality relating to its fraction (word, logic smart).

Fraction Song

Invite students to make up a song to help themselves and others learn about fractions. They might want to use a familiar melody. Be sure the lyrics help students

understand that fractions are used to break down a "whole" (music, word, logic smart).

Fraction P. E. Game

Have students redesign a game they already play to include fractions. For example, in softball, every time a player scores, his team could score $\frac{2}{3}$ of a point instead of one point (body smart).

The How-to Fraction Book

What problems do students have in learning fractions? They might write a how-to book to help their peers with one of these problems. Authors should include written explanations and tips from their own experience (logic, word, picture, people smart).

Fraction Skit

Have students write and perform a short skit that teaches how to reduce fractions. They may want to use props to show that certain fractions are equal even if they look different (word, person, logic smart).

Math and the White House

The White House became home to the presidents of the United States in 1800, when President John Adams and his wife moved in. The White House is an amazing home with 132 rooms, 35 bathrooms, and 6 levels in the private-residence section of the building. The building also has 412 doors, 147 windows, 28 fireplaces, 8 staircases, and 3 elevators.

Have students use a map of the school to find the number of rooms, bathrooms, and so on. How does the school building compare with the White House? If the school is bigger, how many White Houses equal the number of rooms in it?

Art and Math

Emphasize how artists use their knowledge of measurement and geometric shapes and forms in designing architecture, in planning beautifully proportioned vases, and in many other aspects of artistic expression.

Discuss radial balance. In radial balance, shapes and lines go out from a center. We see radial designs in many flowers and wheels. Have students collect and display examples of radial balance and radial designs in human-made and natural forms. Examples might be actual objects or photos cut from old magazines and newspapers. Examples of radial balance include starfish, wheels, snowflakes, many flowers, and the like. After students develop a display, teach them to use a compass and ruler to create precisely measured radial designs.

Shape Awareness

Discuss the difference between knowing that a shape is a circle cut from paper and the process of seeing the same shape from different angles or views. Demonstrate some of the positions from which a circle (cut from paper) can look like a wide ellipse, a narrow ellipse, and a straight line. Share art prints with students that show objects or people from different angles. Discuss how shapes are changed by angle of viewing. Encourage students to draw a familiar object from an unusual view to alter its shape and appearance.

100 Days of School Activities

The 100th day of school is a good day to celebrate with some math activities. Here are a few ideas to challenge students while they're having fun.

- Have them jump rope 100 times.
- Have them build the tallest house of cards they can using 100 cards.
- Have them flip a coin 100 times, and make a graph showing the number of heads and tails.
- Have them roll a pair of dice 100 times, and create a chart showing how many times each number came up. They might construct a graph based on the chart.
- Have students interview someone who is at least 100 years old. What was life like when this person was the student's age?
- Have students find out which weighs more: 100 nickels or 100 quarters.
- Have everyone in class try to throw a tennis ball 100 yards. Have students measure each throw and calculate the length of the average throw.
- Have students count by 100s to 10,000.
- Have students recite multiplication facts up to 100 (10 × 10) with their eyes closed!
- Have students guess how much 100 jelly beans weigh. Then have them weigh the jelly beans. Give a prize to the closest guess. Warn students not to eat the jelly beans just yet.
- Have students separate the 100 jelly beans by color. What percentage of the total is the most common color? What percentage of the total is the least common color? Tell students it's still not time to eat the jelly beans!
- Have students figure out how many jelly beans each person in class would get if the 100 jelly beans were equally divided. Do not allow students to use a calculator to compute their answer, and do not allow them to eat the jelly beans yet!
- Blindfold a student, and have him or her pass out the proper number of jelly beans. What is the probability that the first jelly bean handed out will be the most common color? (Think about this one!). Give students the go-ahead to eat the jelly beans.
- Have students measure the height of the classroom ceiling. How many classrooms that size could be fit into a structure that was 100 feet tall?

- Have students measure the space required for a student's desk and the aisle around it. How big would the classroom need to be to hold 100 desks with the same spacing?
- Have the children make a collection of 100 items and display them on a posterboard.
- Make up your own trail mix using 100 of each ingredient.
- Line up 100 children.
- Say hello in 100 languages.
- Dance for 100 seconds.
- After exercising 100 times (10 jumping jacks and 10 touching toes, etc.) use a stop watch and have 100 seconds of silence.
- Children work with a buddy and trace each other's feet. Children then color and decorate one foot and then combined with other children in other groups, tape the footprints down the hall and mark off every 10 feet until you reach 100 feet. Children can see exactly how many 100 footprints are.
- Clip 100 paper clips together. With a partner, measure things in the room that are as long as, shorter than, and longer than the paper clip chain.
- Have students draw pictures of how they will look when they are 100 years old.
- Have students predict how many times they can write their name in 100 seconds. Then actually do it.
- See what you can make with 100 Legos®.

Math in Everyday Lives

This activity is based on NCTM Standard #4: Mathematical connections are made with everyday experiences, both in and out of school.

Have students brainstorm a list of ways they use math at school. Have each student choose one item from the list and illustrate it. Then have children bring in 10 ideas that demonstrate how they or their parents use math at home. Tally all the ideas of how math was used in students' homes. Have students select one idea to illustrate. Drawings could be posted on a bulletin board under two headings: "Math in School" and "Math at Home."

Line Game

Every day when lining up for lunch or going to another class, have all students except the last in line stand facing forward with hands up, palms out. Give the last student a number-line problem such as "count by 3s from 6 to 30," which he or she would solve by tapping hands by 3s with the students in line. If the student does it correctly, that student is first in line the next day.

Chapter Review

1. What is the developmental pattern in a young child's mathematical skills? Give examples and related activities in your reply.
2. What would you consider basic equipment and materials for a math center? Discuss the reasons for your choices.
3. How do learning centers assist a child's development of mathematical skills? Give examples in your reply.
4. What is rote counting? What is rational counting? How can you tell when a child is capable of either of these skills?
5. What does it mean to develop the skill of seriation? Give examples of activities that would help a child learn this skill.
6. How would you introduce shapes to a young child?
7. What are some ways to teach classification? Give specific activity examples in your reply.

References

Cesarone, B. (2008). Learning stories and children's mathematics. *Childhood Education*, *84*(3), 187–189.

Clements, D. H., & Sarama, J. (2003). Young children and technology: What does the research say? *Young Children*, *58*(6), 34–40.

Eisenhauer, J. J., & Feikes, D. (2009). Dolls, blocks, and puzzles: Playing with mathematical understandings. *Young Children*, *64*(3), 18–25.

Geist, E. (2009). Infants and toddlers exploring mathematics. *Young Children*, *64*(3), 39–41.

Hellwig, S. J., Monroe, E. E., & Jacobs, J. S. (2000). Making informed choices: Selecting children's trade books for mathematics instruction. *Teaching Children Mathematics*, *7*(3), 138–143.

Hirsch, E. S. (Ed.). (2000). *The block book* (3rd ed.). Washington, DC: NAEYC.

Jung, M., Kloosterman, P., & McMullen, M. B. (2007). Research in review: Young children's intuition for solving problems in mathematics. *Young Children*, *62*(5), 42–48.

Kaiser Family Foundation. (2005). *New report on educational media for babies, toddlers, and preschoolers*. www.kff.org/entmedia/ entmedia121405pkg.cfm

Kenney, P. A. & Silver, E. A. (Eds.). (1997). *Results from the sixth mathematics assessment of the National Assessment of Educational Progress*. Reston, VA: National Council of Teachers of Mathematics.

Moyer-Packenham, P., Salkind, G., & Bolyar, B. (2007). *Teachers' uses of virtual manipulatives in K–8 mathematics lessons*. www.allacademic.com/meta/p_ mla_apa_research_citation/1/8/5/8/0/pages185801/ p185801-1.php

Moyer-Packenham, P. (2005). Investigations: Using virtual manipulative to investigate patterns and generate rules in algebra. *Teaching Children Mathematics*, *11*(8), 437–440.

Murphy, K. L., DePasquale, R., & McNamara, E. (2003). Meaningful connections: Using technology in primary classrooms. *Young Children*, *58*(6), 12–18.

National Council of Teachers of Mathematics. (2000). *Principles and standards for school mathematics*. Reston, VA: Author. http://standards.nctm.org

National Council of Teachers of Mathematics (2008). *The use of technology in the teaching and learning of mathematics, Position Statement*. www.nctm.org/ about/content.aspx?id=6360

NAEYC & NCTM (National Council of Teachers of Mathematics). (2002). *Early childhood mathematics: Promoting good beginnings, Position statement*. www.naeyc.org/positionstatements/mathematics

Park, B., Chae, J. L., & Boyd, B. F. (2008). Young children's block play and mathematical learning. *Journal of Research in Childhood Education*, *23*(2), 157–162.

Rosen, D., & Hoffman, J. (2009). Integrating concrete and virtual manipulatives in early childhood mathematics. *Young Children*, *64*(3), 26–33.

Sarama, J., & Clements, D. H. (2009). Building blocks and cognitive building blocks: Playing to know the world. *American Journal of Play*, *1*(3), 313–337.

Seeley, C., Hagelberger, B., Schielack, J., & Krehbiel, K. (2005, September). Using calculators in elementary school. *Teaching Children Mathematics*, 52–53.

Wolfgang, J., Standard, M., & Jones, H. (2001). Block play performance among preschoolers as a predictor of later school achievement in mathematics. *Journal of Research in Childhood Education*, *15*(2), 173–180.

Additional Readings

Cai, J. (Ed.). (2009). *Effective mathematics teaching from teachers' perspectives.* Boston, MA: Sense Publishers.

Boaler, J. (2009). *What's math got to do with it? How parents and teachers can help children love their least favorite subject.* New York: Penguin.

Charner, K. (Ed.). (2009). *Learn every day about numbers.* Beltsville, MD: Gryphon House.

Evitt, M. F. (2009). *Thinking BIG, learning BIG: Connecting science, math, literacy, and language in early childhood.* Beltsville, MD: Gryphon House.

Faulkner, V. N. (2009). The components of number sense: An instructional model for teachers. *Teaching Exceptional Children, 41*(5), 16–23.

Geist, D. (2009). Infants and teachers exploring mathematics. *Young Children, 64*(3), 39–41.

Geist, D., & Geist, E. A. (2008). Do re mi, 1-2-3: That's how easy math can be—Using music to support emergent mathematics. *Young Children, 63*(2), 20–25.

Greenberg, J., & Bickart, T. S. (2008). *Math right from the start: What parents can do in the first five years.* Washington, DC: Teaching Strategies.

Hansen-Thomas, H. (2009). *English language learners and math.* Charlotte, NC: Information Age Publishing.

Lake, J. (2008). *Math memories you can count on.* Portland, MA: Stenhouse.

Lee, J., Lee, J. O., & Fox, J. (2009). Time here, time there, time everywhere: Teaching young children time through daily routines. *Childhood Education, 85*(3), 191–193.

McDonald, J. (2007). Selecting counting books: Mathematical perspectives. *Young Children, 62*(3), 38–42.

Murphy, M. S. (2009). Mathematics and social justice in Grade 1: How children understand inequality and represent it. *Young Children, 64*(3), 12–17.

Ozaki, K., Yamamoto, N., & Kamii, C. (2008). What do children learn by trying to produce the domino effect? *Young Children, 60*(5), 58–64.

Pica, R. (2008). *Jump into math: Active learning for preschool children.* Beltsville, MD: Gryphon House.

Sarama, J., & Clements, D. H. (2009). Of primary interest: Teaching math in the primary grades: The learning trajectories approach. *Young Children, 64*(2), 63–65.

Seefeldt, C., & Galper, A. (2008). *Active experiences for active children: Mathematics* (2nd ed.). Upper Saddle River, NJ: Pearson/Merrill Prentice Hall.

Saracho, O. N., & Spodek, B. (2008). *Contemporary perspectives on mathematics in early childhood education.* Charlotte, NC: Information Age Publishing.

Small, M. (2009). *Good questions: Great way to differentiate mathematics instruction.* New York: Teachers College Press.

Sriraman, B. (Ed.). (2008). *Creativity, giftedness, and talent development in mathematics.* Charlotte, NC: Information Age Publishing.

Stein, M. K., Smith, M. S., Hennigsen, M. A., & Silver, E. A. (2009). *Implementing standards-based mathematics instruction: A casebook for professional development* (2nd ed.). New York: Teachers College Press.

Wolff, A. L., & Wimer, N. (2009). Shopping for mathematics in consumer town. *Young Children, 64*(3), 34–38.

Software for Children

2 Simple Math Game 1, ages 9 and up

Callilou Counting, ages 2–6

Chutes and Ladders, ages 3–8

Curse of Montezuma, ages 6 and up

Gravitronix, ages 6 and up

Henry Hatsworth in the Puzzling Adventures, ages 7 and up

I Spy Junior, ages 3–6

Jenga, ages 8 and up

Millie's Math House, ages 2–5

Mega Man Star Force: Pegasus, ages 6 and up

Neopets: Puzzle Adventure, ages 8–10

Noddy: Playtime in Toyland, ages 4–7

Penguin Cold Cash, ages 5–11

Postman Pat: Special Delivery Service, ages 3–6

Puzzle Kingdom, ages 10 and up

Rubik's Puzzle Galaxy, ages 6 and up

Thinking Things All Around Frippletown, ages 4–8

Thomas and Friends: Special Delivery, ages 4–6

Where's Waldo? The Fantastic Journey, ages 6 and up

Helpful Websites

Math.com—The World of Math Online, http://www.math.com
This site has activities, games, homework help, practice, and teacher and parent sections.

Cool Math 4 Kids, http://www.coolmath4kids.com
This site has math games and activities for children ages 3 to 10.

Math in Daily Life, http://www.learner.org/about
Use the "Browse Teacher Resources" for topics of your choice. This site has everyday math activities with a teacher's guide from Annenberg/CPB. Explore probability, population growth, savings, and more.

National Council of Teachers of Mathematics Math Standards for Young Children, http://www.nctm.org
Check the directory of articles about the recent research on children's math learning, including this link for Standards for Grades Pre-K–2: http://standards.nctm.org/

Early Childhood Mathematics: Promoting Good Beginnings, http://www.naeyc.org/
Click on "Public Policy," then click on "NAEYC Position Statements." This is the NAEYC's position statement on Early Childhood Mathematics.

Games Central—PBS, http://pbskids.org/cyberchase/games.html
Interactive games help children learn about using measurements, mazes, angles, and shapes.

The Kaboose Family Network, http://resources.kaboose.com/games/math2.html
This site offers math games appropriate for children ages 6 and up.

Math Playground, http://www.mathplayground.com
This is an action-packed educational site for elementary students, featuring games and other activities.

Funbrain on the Rocks, http://www.funbrain.com
This site contains math games and activities correlated to national math standards.

Apples for the Teacher, http://www.apples4-theteacher.com/math.html
This site offers free preschool and elementary math activities as well as online math games and lesson plans.

AAA Math, http://www.aaamath.com
Divided into categories by topic, this website explores different mathematical themes and offers practice problems. A Spanish version of the site is available.

Math-Kitecture, http://www.math-kitecture.com
This site features real-life math from the world of architecture, showing how closely related math and architecture are.

Symmetry and Pattern, http://www.mathforum.org/geometry/rugs/index.html
A collaborative project of the Textile Museum and the Math Forum, this site explores the relationship between geometry and textile design.

National Council on Economic Education, http://www.econedlink.org
This site focuses on K–12 teaching materials and strategies. It includes model lessons and templates for creating effective lesson plans.

Jump Start: Financial Smarts for Students, http://www.jumpstart.org
This site offers free materials for teachers and students (Grades K–5) about money.

The Building Blocks, http://www.gse.buffalo.edu/org/buildingblocks
Looking to base children's mathematical skills in their current activities, the Building Blocks program offers a curriculum and resources, which support children's natural interests and experiences.

Virtual Manipulative-Related Websites

NEIRTEC, http://www.neirtec.org/activities/math_portal.htm
This is a portal to many interesting virtual manipulatives.

Shodor Interactives, http://www.shodor.org/interactivate/activities
You will find 155 interactive activities for K–12 students at this site.

Tangrams Online, http://cs.bmcc.cc.or.us/mth213/labs/online%20tangrams.htm
Click on the puzzle pieces to complete a design made of shapes.

Online Geoboard, http://www.mste.uiuc.edu/users/pavel/java/geoboard
Click on a corner, and drag the "rubber band" to any peg on the board. The length of each side is automatically shown. From there students can determine the area. With a click of the mouse, they can check their answers.

For additional creative activity resources, visit our website at www.Cengage.com/login.

Creative Food Experiences

OBJECTIVES

After studying this chapter, you should be able to:

1. Describe four ways in which food activities develop children's skills.

2. List several ways to help make food experiences more creative.

3. Give an example of a creative food experience and the necessary steps involved.

4. Discuss the problem of childhood obesity and ways to prevent or treat it.

Children learn best when they experience the world firsthand—by touch, taste, smell, sight, and hearing. If you wish to make the most of any food experience, children must be directly involved with real food and given as much responsibility as possible for growing, selecting, preparing, and eating the food.

Activities involving foods are included in most programs for young children. However, many of the food activities are under the complete direction of the teacher. Children sit and watch the teacher do the work. Sometimes children are given spoons and told to stir a mixture or are allowed to pour liquids from one container to another. Sometimes they are given the job of listening for a timer to "ding." Rarely is the child allowed to decide what foods to use, how to use them, and in what order or how long to mix ingredients. The use of foods in a classroom can be one of the most creative parts of the program. Foods are a part of each child's experience. Foods and cooking are interesting to children. All of their senses are used in food activities. They see the foods. They smell them, touch them, and taste them. Children can hear many kinds of foods boiling, popping, or frying. Other learning is enhanced by food activities, too. Art, science, and aesthetics are all related to cooking.

Importance of Food Experiences to the Total Program

Concept Building

Food activities help children develop new concepts in many areas such as language arts, science, health and safety, and mathematics.

Children learn to describe things. Children experience many shapes, sizes, and colors of food. They see that some foods start out in a round shape and become

FIGURE 21-1 • Washing hands before and after food activities is an essential learning for young children.

long and flat during the cooking process. Many foods change in size when they are heated; some change in texture and color with mixing, heating, and cooling. In food-related activities, then, the child learns to name shapes, compare sizes, and identify and describe colors.

Children learn about tastes. Children find out how heating or mixing changes taste. They learn that some things, such as salt or sugar, can change the taste of foods. They discover that some foods taste good when they are mixed together and that others do not. They also learn that a change in the outward appearance of some foods does not mean that the foods taste any different. Apple juice has the same flavor as a whole apple. Frozen orange pops taste like orange juice and a frozen banana tastes just like banana ice cream.

Children observe changes. As they did in science activities, children observe that foods change from liquids to solids and from solids to liquids. They also see steam (a gas) rising from liquids that are heated. They smell odors as foods change from solids to liquids to gases. They see how ingredients, when mixed

together, form a new substance. In baking, this same substance changes even more.

Children learn to express themselves. Language skills develop as a result of food experiences. Words like *bitter*, *sour*, *sweet*, and *salty* have real meaning. *Hot*, *cold*, *warm*, and *cool* are part of the food vocabulary. Children may learn the words *delicious* and *tasty*. They learn a more complete meaning of terms like *liquid* and *solid*, *freezing* and *boiling*, *smelly* and *odorless*. When the words relate to direct experiences, the child's vocabulary grows.

The following scene is an example of how all these skills are developed in a simple food experience.

The making of pudding went over quite well, as do all food-oriented activities. My organization ahead of time helped it to be a pleasant and not too disorganized activity! We used instant pudding and it required a specified amount of milk to be added. This fact helped us discuss the

FIGURE 21-2 • In food activities, children express their unique tastes in foods.

number of cups of milk we would need, as well as the concept of milk and nutrition, etc. They poured out the milk, measuring the amounts, and all had a chance to use the hand rotary beater to beat the pudding. This was good small motor exercise for them all. They poured out the pudding (a bit messy!). Then we had to wait for five minutes for it to set, and this helped introduce the idea of time and where the clock's hands would be when five minutes went by. All these things were discussed in making the pudding, so I feel that it was a true learning experience for all. However, I'm sure the children enjoyed eating the pudding at the end of the learning experience the best!

Many concepts can be discussed in an informal situation such as this. I hope to use many more such situations when I assume my role as a teacher of young children. Learning under such a natural and relaxed atmosphere was a pleasure for both myself and the children (Author's Log).

Children learn about others. Food activities can be used throughout the curriculum to enhance children's learning. For example, a project on different breads from around the world can be used to teach about cultural diversity and the many types of bread individuals eat. A literature table can be set up to include children's books—both fiction and nonfiction—featuring bread themes (see Online Companion for suggestions). Children can make many types of breads from different cultures. Discussion can be held on how families and cultures use bread in celebrations and traditions. Children's literature provides many examples of how people in many different lands prepare and eat a wide variety of breads. Cooking activities can include making tortillas, wontons, waffles, fry bread, challah, hoecakes, bagels, pasta, hush puppies, latkes, and fortune cookies, to name just a few multicultural foods. Each of these foods can be used in connection with other projects to make a multicultural experience. (See Chapters 24–25 for more information on multicultural curriculum and activities.)

Skill Building

There are a number of skills that children can learn from working with foods. These skills can be developed during other parts of the program also, but working with food is an excellent way to build skills in fun activities.

FIGURE 21-3 • This child is "getting eggs" to make a "very big cake."

Small-muscle coordination. Mixing foods and pouring liquids from one container to another are ways in which children develop coordination. The small muscles in the hands develop so that a child can hold a large spoon and help in the mixing process when using a recipe. The measuring, pouring, and mixing of foods all require the use of small muscles as well as hand–eye coordination. Thus, food activities provide excellent small-motor activities for young children.

Simple measuring skills. By using cups and spoons that have marks showing amounts, a child begins to understand measurements. The child is able to observe that a tablespoon is larger than a teaspoon and that a cup holds more than a tablespoon. The child can also begin to realize that if one uses too much flour, water, or salt, recipes don't turn out quite as well as when the correct amounts are used. The child begins to understand that the amount of each ingredient used makes a difference in the final product. This realization leads the child to look for ways to figure out amounts. This is when measuring tools are discovered. Older children can be challenged to make one-half of a recipe or double it. This gives them a real-life opportunity to practice multiplication, fractions, and division skills.

Social skills. Food experiences are a natural avenue for social learning. Mixing, measuring, decorating, and eating all provide many opportunities for talking with others, exchanging ideas, sharing likes and dislikes, and learning about each other. You will find that in preparing food, children many times will talk more freely about themselves and their lives in the homey, routine nature of this type of activity.

In cooking, a child may need help in holding a pan steady while pouring something into it. He or she may need help in carrying ingredients or finding certain foods. Children with special needs enjoy cooking activities as much as other children. By using some of the ideas presented in earlier chapters on adapting equipment and space, teachers can provide children with special needs the opportunity to enjoy cooking activities at their individual levels. One child may need an "expert" opinion on how much lemon to squeeze into a drink. These things call for working together. As children work together, social skills develop in the natural give-and-take of group experiences.

FIGURE 21-5 • Young children learn many basic science and mathematics concepts in food activities.

Cooking activities provide children a chance to share information with each other about family recipes and food preferences. Learning about each other's cultural differences occurs naturally in cooking experiences.

Health and Safety

As children are involved in food experiences, they learn basic information about routines and cautions about food and cooking necessary to good health and safety. This information is best learned in the process of working with food and not in a lecture-type lesson.

For example, learning that cleanliness is important in all food preparation can be taught as children work with food. Both children and adults always wash their hands with soap and water before beginning and after ending any food experience. Aprons or other cover-ups may also be necessary, especially if you are preparing foods that stain hands and fabrics easily.

Children may need encouragement to keep fingers and utensils out of their mouths while preparing food. If they do lick fingers or spoons, simply and calmly ask them to wash before proceeding. This is a good

FIGURE 21-4 • Toddlers enjoy playing in the kitchen area of the dramatic arts center.

opportunity to teach children about germs and how they are transmitted. Tasting is also a good opportunity to help children learn about how foods taste at various stages of preparation and to observe changes in texture. However, no products containing raw eggs should be eaten before being fully cooked. Raw eggs are a source of salmonella bacteria and can cause digestive problems.

Any cooking adventure involving heat, sharp knives, or operating appliances should be carefully supervised. Sharp knives are rarely needed, since plastic serrated knives will slice most produce items and are safe for even very young children. Children will need to be cautioned when observing food in the oven or on the range burner; utensil handles should be turned toward the center of the range at all times. Because electric burners don't always appear to be hot, children will need to learn how to identify when the burner is on by recognizing the position of the switch or by reading "on," "off," "high," or "low." Children must also be made aware that an electric burner remains hot for a while even after it has been turned off. All of these are important health and safety lessons for young children in food experiences.

Finally, food allergies are very common among young children, and before planning any experience, you will need to know which children are allergic to specific foods. For example, in some schools, no products with peanuts are used because of children's allergies. Some children may have ethnic food restrictions that prohibit their eating certain foods. Every adult participating in food activities, whether teacher, cook, parent, or community volunteer, must have this information. If fresh produce is to be used, adults must know what parts of plants are poisonous. Children should learn that these parts and any other wild plant must never be eaten.

Activities for Toddlers and Two- and Three-Year-Old Children

Even though food preparation activities are included in the early childhood program for children three years and up, adults are often inclined to think that children under the age of three would just make a mess. For example, many cooks in early childhood centers do not want to be bothered, and of course young children underfoot in a kitchen increase the risk of accidents and injuries. An alternative is to bring the foods and the appropriate utensils for cooking activities to the children's room. The term *cooking activities* in this instance includes all the steps necessary in the preparation and serving of foods, with or without the use of heat.

The cooking-related activities that follow are listed in progressive order, from the simple to the more involved. Many toddlers and two-year-olds are able to master many of these activities, and most three-year-olds are capable of mastering them all.

- exploring cooking utensils (banging, nesting, putting away)
- exploring cooking utensils with water (cups, bowls, beaters, spoons, funnels)
- pouring dry ingredients (corn, rice)
- pouring wet ingredients (water)
- tasting fresh fruit and vegetables
- comparing tastes, textures, and colors of fresh fruits and vegetables
- comparing tastes, textures, and colors of canned vegetables and fruits
- dipping raw fruits and vegetables in dip or sauce
- scrubbing vegetables with brushes
- breaking or tearing lettuce, breaking or snapping beans, and shelling peas
- stirring and mixing wet and dry ingredients
- measuring wet and dry ingredients (using a rubber band to mark the desired amount on container or measuring cup)
- placing toppings on pizza or snacks and decorating cookies or crackers that have been spread
- spreading on bread or crackers
- pouring milk or juices to drink
- shaking (making butter from cream or coloring sugar or coconut)
- rolling with both hands (pieces of dough for cookies)
- juicing with a hand juicer
- peeling hard-cooked eggs and fruits
- cutting with plasticl knife (fruits, vegetables, cheese)
- beating with a fork or egg beater
- grinding with a hand grinder (apples or cranberries)
- kneading bread dough
- cleaning up

Curriculum Areas

Cooking does more than build physical, health and safety, and social skills. It is an ideal project for just about all of the curriculum areas. It involves reading, math, science, creative activities, opportunities for independent learning and following directions, and drawing and writing activities. Let's look briefly at these different areas.

1.

2.

One cup water

3.

15 minutes

4.

1/4 cup sugar

5.

FIGURE 21-6 • Picture recipe for applesauce (recipe at end of chapter).

Reading. Drawings with words and numbers can be used to help prekindergarten children understand a recipe. (See picture recipes in Figures 21–6, 21–7, and 21–8.) This is a good prereading activity in kindergarten or the primary grades. Older children can read the recipe, which itself is good practice. Many books, for both preschool and elementary-age children, talk about food and cooking. (See Online Companion for sources for these books.) Display some of these books in your library area for the children to look at. If you find a book that applies to a specific cooking experience, read it to the group before beginning to cook.

In the language arts center, furnish a tape recorder for children's dictation of their real and imaginary recipes. Provide paper and art materials for later transcription into books.

Math. For most recipes, measuring instruments—cups, tablespoons, and teaspoons—are required. Measuring cups in specific colors are helpful in cooking activities for young children. For example, the blue cup is ¼ cup, the green is ½ cup, the yellow is ⅓ cup, and the red is 1 cup. The same method can be used with different colors for each measuring spoon. It's also helpful and interesting to have a food scale for measuring. Sequencing (measuring, mixing, and then baking), estimating, counting, adding, working with fractions, and discriminating size and shape are all involved in cooking experiences. Discuss each of these objects and activities as you go along, working with small groups so everyone gets a turn. Children learn better when they do than when they merely look and listen.

Older children can handle measuring and mixing ingredients on their own. You can challenge their math skills by asking them to measure the ingredients for one-half of the recipe you're going to use. Or they can figure out how to double or triple the recipe for a larger group.

Science. Cooking develops sensory skills. It involves physical and chemical changes, the use of simple machines, and predicting the outcome of a cooking experiment. For example, when making cookies, place all the ingredients on the table and give everyone a chance to smell, touch, and taste each one. Then mix the ingredients with spoons, forks, or eggbeaters. Ask children about shape and texture as you mix. Ask them to predict the outcome of your cooking experience. Then, after baking, have them compare their predictions with results.

Older children can suggest ways to alter the recipe to make it turn out in different ways. They enjoy experimenting with different spices to give their recipes a new and special flavor. It's fun to use spices from different cultural groups, too.

Science center. Provide open-ended activities for cooking explorations. For instance, try a taste test of all the different ways apples are used in cooking and eating: apple juice, cider, sauce, butter, dried, even apple cider vinegar. Or compare the appearance, taste, and texture of red, green, and yellow apples. You can also explore bananas. Brainstorm a list of how many different ways we can cook or eat them. What can you do with a frozen banana? Make ice cream! (Put chunks of frozen banana in a blender with just a hint of milk, blend until thick, and eat immediately.) How do bananas taste when they're sliced in circles? Try it and see. Try drying fruit and vegetables in the sun for tasty, healthful snacks (see recipes at chapter's end.)

Creative activities. Almost all recipes can be extended, modified, changed, or given an unexpected twist. Use your imagination, and, more important, get the children to use theirs! Use a soft pretzel recipe (recipe at end of chapter) to make animals or three-dimensional sculptures instead of the traditional pretzel shape. Add food coloring to the coating mixture (in the recipe) and paint your animals or sculptures before baking.

Drawing and writing. Have the children dictate stories, anecdotes from home, and highlights of their experiences cooking in your classroom. Involve parents and other volunteers in this activity. Those children who wish to can tell and draw about the day's cooking activity. Older children can keep personal journals of their cooking experiences. They may want to select certain favorite recipes and compile their own cookbooks.

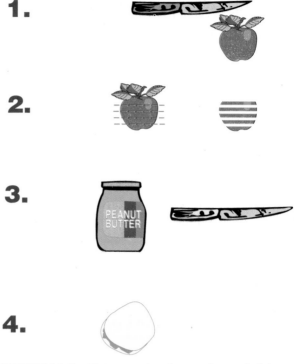

FIGURE 21-8 • Picture recipe for apple sandwiches (recipe at end of chapter).

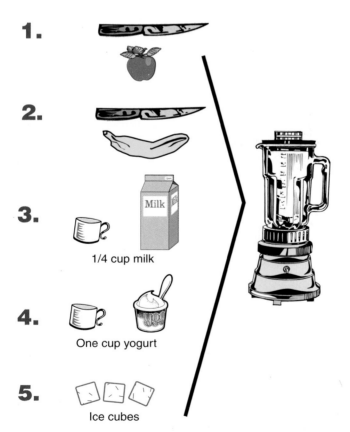

FIGURE 21-7 • Picture recipe for banana apple icy (recipe at end of chapter).

Individual Cooking Activities in Interest Centers

Food activities can also be set up as interest centers in the early childhood program. Here is an example: It's John's turn to "cook" during free-choice activity time. First, he washes his hands; second, he puts on a white paper chef's hat; and third, he begins cutting fruit into bite-sized pieces with a plastic knife. He is following a picture recipe and will eventually put the fruit on a skewer to make a fruit kabob for his snack to be eaten later with his classmates. And, he made his snack all by himself! Independent snack preparation can easily be set up in the classroom with some basic equipment and recipes designed for individual portions.

Ideas to help you set up individual cooking interest centers in your classroom and some recipe ideas follow.

Cut off one of the end flaps of a sturdy cardboard box and cut the box apart at the side seam so it will stand up using the other end flaps as supports. This will be your instruction "board." Cover the entire box with colorful contact paper. The box can be set up on a table to designate your snack and work area. Sequential picture recipes can be clipped to each section of the box/board. For example, the pictures in sequence would indicate to (1) wash hands, (2) cut fruit into pieces, (3) put fruit on skewer, and (4) place on paper plate with name on plate. Basic equipment for your snack activity center would include measuring cups, small bowls, tongue depressors, small wire whisks, five-ounce paper cups, plastic serrated knives, an electric skillet, blender, and paper chef's hats. AN ELECTRIC APPLIANCE IS OPERATED BY ADULTS ONLY.

After you've designated your snack area and gathered your equipment, you're ready to begin with the recipes that follow. Before each child actually begins the snack preparation, gather the children in a group, tell them briefly about the recipe, and remind them of any specific directions. For example, a direction might be that each child may cut up only one slice of melon. While one or two children are working in the snack area, the teacher always needs to be available for assistance as children need it.

Lettuce Wrap-Arounds. You'll need: lettuce leaves; any combination of luncheon meats or cheese slices, or spreads such as cream cheese, peanut butter, or egg salad

What to do:

1. Lay lettuce leaf flat on cutting board.
2. Place meat and/or cheese slice on lettuce leaf.
3. Add a spread or other filler and roll up the combination, securing it with a toothpick.
4. These may be eaten rolled up or cut into bite-sized pieces with a serrated knife.

Banana Shake Bag. You'll need: ¼ cup chopped peanuts; 1 banana

What to do:

1. After peeling a banana, cut it into 1-inch chunks.
2. Place peanuts in a plastic baggie.
3. Put a few banana chunks at a time in the bag and shake.
4. Serve bananas on paper plates.

Pineapple Mix-Up. You'll need: ¼ cup plus 1 tablespoon instant nonfat dry milk; ½ cup pineapple juice, chilled; ½ cup cracked ice

What to do:

1. For cracked ice, wrap some ice cubes in a towel and pound with a hammer.
2. Combine all ingredients in a blender and blend on high 30 seconds until thick and foamy.

Watch the food disappear at snack time because children love these activities. Don't forget the paper chef's hats (available at a party store) or you can make your own hats! The hats make children feel like "professional" chefs.

Guidelines for Creative Food Activities

The following are some guidelines to use to ensure that food experiences for young children are planned to enhance their creativity.

*   Activities should be open-ended. If all children must follow the same directions at the same time, they will not have a chance to be creative. In fact, just the opposite will happen: children will conform and do what the teacher tells them to do. Teachers who want to help children be creative must let them create their own directions and work at their own pace.
*   Activities should be challenging, but not too difficult for children. If food activities are too hard, children will give up. If they are too easy, children will not be challenged. It is important to start with easy things. It is also important to increase the possibilities so children will do more challenging things as they go on.
*   Activities should be varied. Children get bored if they do the same thing day after day. Variety is needed. Children should work with foods they know. They should also work with new foods they have not seen or tasted before. Some activities should be very short. Others should take a longer time to finish. In some activities, children may use just one type of food. In others, they may mix in several ingredients.
*   The process is more important than the product. Emphasis should not be placed on what the children create, but on how they have created it. If only the final product is considered, then many children will fail. Things do not always taste good—especially when children create new recipes. But if children are rewarded for the way they create, then what they have created does not seem so important.
*   Inexpensive materials and small amounts should be used. No child should feel bad if a recipe does not work. If ingredients are inexpensive, there is less chance that children will be made to feel discouraged because something they made did not taste very good.

THINK ABOUT IT

Television Viewing and Poor Diet Quality in Young Children

Researchers at Harvard Medical School and Harvard Pilgrim Health Care examined the relationship between television/video (TV) viewing and markers of diet quality among three-year-old children. They studied 613 boys and 590 girls, age three years old. Each mother/caregiver reported the number of hours her/his child watched TV on an average weekday and weekend day in the past month. From this number, the researchers calculated a weighted mean number of viewing hours.

The researchers used a validated food frequency questionnaire to determine the selected foods and nutrients reported by each mother/caregiver. The group was racially diverse with 31% non-white and 13% had a household income less than $40,000. Twenty-eight percent of the mothers/caregivers had completed less than a college degree.

The mean TV viewing for the group of children was 1.7 hours per day. For each one-hour increment of TV viewing per day, they found higher intakes of:

sugar-sweetened beverages

fast food

red and processed meats

trans-fats

They also found lower intakes of fruit and vegetables, calcium, and dietary fiber.

The researchers concluded that among three-year-olds, more TV viewing is associated with adverse dietary practices. They suggest that parents/caregivers reduce TV viewing in this age group to improve the children's diet quality (Miller, Taveras, Rifas-Shiman, & Gillman, 2008).

FIGURE 21-9 • Writing down a favorite recipe to try at home extends the learning experience.

- Activities should be carried out in a variety of places. Food activities do not have to be limited to the indoors. They can also be done outside the classroom. They work well on the school grounds or in a nearby woods. Note: An important restriction for outdoor cooking is that the teacher should inspect all food before it is used. Poison mushrooms and berries are sometimes gathered by children. These foods must be avoided.

- Be sure to plan activities for the children who are waiting to participate in the food activity. Also, be sure that these are also high-interest activities, so that children will be just as interested in these "waiting" activities as they are for the food activity. For example, this would be a good time to break out a few new puzzles, books, or computer games for children to enjoy while they are waiting.

Getting Started

Planning

Careful planning is crucial to successful food experiences. All ingredients (in sufficient quantities) need to be purchased, utensils assembled, and objectives for the activity established.

THIS ONE'S for YOU!   Keeping Produce Fresh

Fruits and vegetables should be staples of young children's diets. But how many times have you sliced an apple only to find it's bruised or mealy? Diane Barrett, Ph.D., a fruit and vegetable-products specialist at the University of California-Davis, has these tips for making your produce last.

- Get rid of bad apples. A rotten one really **can** spoil the whole bunch. Microbes in decaying fruit can travel a short distance through the air and contaminate other pieces. The same is true for other fruit, such as blueberries and strawberries.

- Put produce in its place. Most fruit and vegetables should be kept cool. But some actually do best sitting out uncovered: bananas, grapefruits, oranges, mangoes, whole pineapples, watermelons, pomegranates, winter squash, tomatoes, and potatoes.

- Consider a change of location. It's easy to forget about produce when it's hidden in the crisper drawers. Store fruits and vegetables on an eye-level shelf, where you're more likely to see them.

- Separate fruits and vegetables. Some fruits release ethylene gas, which speeds up the spoilage of vegetables.

- Only buy a week's worth. While some produce, like apples, can last longer, you'll get the best flavor and highest vitamin content if you replenish regularly. (Parents Magazine, 2009).

Children's abilities should be matched to the food experience so that the adult does not carry out the preparation while the children watch. Depending on the complexity of the recipe, the number of children, whether children with special needs are part of the group, and the time available, it may at times be necessary for the adult to complete some tasks or to use prepared foods. Keep in mind, however, that the more the adult does, the less children learn. The extra time children take learning is well spent.

Objectives for the children's learning will help focus the activity for the adults involved. Do you want children to successfully cut celery into finger-sized strips? Is your objective to have children sample a variety of food textures and discuss the differences? Will children try less familiar foods? Is your goal to facilitate cooperative work in a small group?

Common goals for food experiences for young children include strengthening their manipulative skills, expanding their knowledge about nutrition, and trying new foods. You will want to develop your own objectives for each recipe you choose based on your knowledge about the children in the group.

Goals for very young or inexperienced children will be different from those for more advanced food preparers. Initially, try to plan food preparation activities that involve only one or two skills and a limited number of ingredients. Squeezing orange juice involves one ingredient and two skills: squeezing and pouring. Washing vegetables or fruits (in a basin to conserve water, rather than under running water) and possibly then cutting them into convenient pieces is also a good beginning activity. For children who are just becoming competent in balancing, pouring, or cutting, these tasks are a real challenge. The following list will help you prepare for successful food experiences.

- Work out ahead of time a sequence of steps for the activity.
- Plan a series of activities that are gradually more complex.
- Encourage children to talk about what they are doing.
- Relate the activity to home experiences.
- Give the names for new foods, processes, and equipment used.
- When appropriate, involve children in getting supplies for the activities.
- Encourage discussion of what has been done. Allow a good amount of time for tasting and touching.
- Use follow-up activities to reinforce the learning. (See Figure 21–10.)

Using Food in Science Activities
- Plant an outdoor or indoor garden.
- Have a tasting party.
- Arrange unusual foods on a science table.
- Place carrot, beet, or pineapple tops in a shallow bowl of crushed stones or pebbles covered with water. Allow them to sprout.
- Cut off the top third of a sweet potato and put it part way in water; allow sprouts to vine at the top.
- Examine a coconut, then break it open.
- Examine and cut a fresh pineapple.
- Taste baby foods.
- Place seed catalogs on the reading shelf.
- Make a food dictionary.
- Draw pictures of favorite foods from each food group; make a meal; draw a picture of a plate and cup and fill them with foods to make a nutritious meal. Make sure to label each food.

Creative Art Activities with Food
- fruit-colored play dough
- broken eggshells on paintings
- child-made food books:
  - Foods I Like
  - Fruits I Like
  - Foods My Daddy (or Mommy, Sister, etc.) Likes
- class mural made of pictures of foods
- foods cut from flannel to arrange on a flannel or story board
- food pictures cut from newspaper or magazine advertisements to paste on colored paper
- paste pictures of foods on a chart with areas for fruits and vegetables, breads, milk, and meats
- make picture charts of favorite recipes

Table Activities—Food Experiences
- sewing cards with food pictures
- dishpans of beans with funnels, measuring cups
- food scale with beans for weighing
- balance for weighing

Field Trips—Food Experiences
- grocery store
- vegetable garden
- fruit orchard
- school kitchen
- bakery
- restaurant
- pizza restaurant
- ice cream store
- fruit and vegetable stand
- bottling company
- dairy

FIGURE 21-10 • Follow up activities to reinforce learning. *(Continued)*

- canning factory
- hatchery
- cornfield, strawberry, or melon patch
- home kitchen

Games for Cooking Experiences
- Can You Remember? (Display foods on a tray; cover. Have children try to remember where each is.)
- How Many? (Arrange different foods on a tray. Have children count items.)
- Which? (Have children identify foods that can be eaten raw, foods that are yellow, etc.)
- Grouping (Have students identify those that are yellow, those that are eaten for breakfast, etc.)
- Touch and Tell (Place food in a bag; have child feel and try to identify.)
- Smell and Tell (Have child close eyes and try to identify food by smelling.)
- Guess What? (Have children describe the characteristics of food; children try to identify items.)

FIGURE 21-10 • Follow up activities to reinforce learning. *(Continued)*

Integrated Food Units— Elementary Level

Too often in the elementary school, teachers plan food activities as "special events" or simply as add-ons to other curriculum areas. Few teachers attempt to integrate food activities into the elementary curriculum. Yet, it is quite possible to develop units based on food and food groups and to integrate learning activities from all areas of the curriculum. The following are two examples of integrated food units for the elementary school level. These units will get you started on developing many of your own integrated food units.

Potato Unit

This unit begins with the reading of Tomie de Paola's book *Jamie O'Rourke and the Big Potato* (1992). (You could also use McDonald's *The Potato Man*, 1996.) After reading the book to the group, make it available for them to read on their own for at least a week. Use the book as a basis for students' research on the history of the potato. Have children write factual reports about potatoes. These can be compiled into a class "Potato Book."

Use a 10-lb. bag of potatoes as a source of math experiences. Challenge children to estimate the number of potatoes in the bag. Help them sequence their estimations in numerical order (ascending or descending). Then have them actually count the potatoes. Discuss their estimates and compare the actual number of potatoes to these estimates. Have

them make up a summary graph showing the range of numbers between the estimates and actual number of potatoes.

Give each child a potato. Have students count the potato's eyes, estimate and then measure its circumference, and graph the results. Then, using a balance scale, have the children weigh each potato. Discuss with children the nutritional value of potatoes as you make dishes using recipes from the children's families.

Vegetable Soup

Two books that are good to read at the beginning of this unit are *Growing Vegetable Soup* by L. Ehlert (1990) and *Neighborhood Soup* by J. Nelson (1990). These books can be used as the basis for several related activities, such as a plant- and vegetable-growing activity. During the plant activity, children can plant seeds and observe their growth. Children can also keep written records of plant growth under a variety of conditions, including without light and without water.

Have children use seed catalogues and real vegetables to examine the edible parts of various plants. Then have them taste a variety of vegetables—raw and cooked—and compare the nutritional value of each.

Have children work cooperatively to make neighborhood soup. Discuss the creation of new soups. Have children brainstorm ingredients for their original soups and create labels for their soup cans. Have them work together to present a play based on *Neighborhood Soup*. Preparations can include making props and promotional posters.

Reducing Sugar in Children's Diets

Research on human infants shows that even they prefer a sweet over bitter or sour taste (Mennella & Beauchamp, 1998). This preference posed no problem when early human diets consisted of natural fruit and vegetable sources of sweetness. However, when refined **sugar** came into our diets, the total amount of sugar consumed increased dramatically. Soft drinks are the leading source of added sugar in the diet of American children (ADA(American Dental Association) 2007). A long-term research study examined soda consumption and its effect on children's body weight. The study found that for each additional daily serving of a sugar-sweetened soft drink, the incidence of obesity was significantly increased. Researchers also discovered that the odds of becoming obese increased 1.6 times for each additional glass of sugar-sweetened soft drink consumed above the daily average (HPHNow, 2009).

Although we do not know what proportion of all of this sugar is consumed by children, we do know many parents and teachers are trying to limit children's sugar consumption for two main reasons: the danger of tooth decay and a diet with too many empty calories.

Tooth decay. If teeth are not brushed frequently, sugars can cause tooth decay—dental caries, or what are more commonly called "cavities." One way to avoid dental caries is to avoid foods that are high in sugar. However, some of the foods that are most likely to cause cavities (because they are high in fruit sugar or fructose) are very nutritious. Another sugar, lactose, is contained in milk. Obviously, it would not be appropriate to eliminate all sugar-containing foods. A more preferable goal is to eliminate those foods that are high in sugars and low in nutritional value.

Childhood Obesity

The biggest risk to young children's health is both less dramatic and more sinister than the stuff of nightly news headlines. It is one that happens incrementally as children move through early childhood into elementary school and beyond. It's obesity.

Childhood obesity has reached such proportions that today's children could end up living two to five years less than they might otherwise, according to a 2005 study in the *New England Journal of Medicine* (Solomon, 2005). According to the federal Centers

---

THINK ABOUT IT   Popcorn and Its Place in American History

Even before Columbus discovered Arawak and Carib, Indians using were using popcorn for decorations and food in the West Indies in 1492. Even before Cortez found Aztecs in Mexico, they were using popcorn in necklaces and ceremonial headdresses in 1519. Even before French explorers discovered the Great Lakes region, Iroquois were popping corn in pottery crocks with heated sand. Popcorn was growing in the Americas centuries ago and providing delicious eating for its natives.

Archaeologists have uncovered proof that popcorn had been around a long time before the arrival of the Europeans in the New World. Excavations in the Bat Cave of West Central New Mexico turned up popcorn ears nearly 5,600 years old according to radio-carbon tests. An 80,000-year-old fossil pollen found 200 feet below Mexico City has been identified as corn pollen. In tombs on the east coast of Peru, researchers uncovered 1,000-year-old grains of popcorn so well preserved they still pop!

Other treasures have turned up to validate popcorn's place in the past—pottery popcorn poppers dating back to pre-Inca cultures in Peru; an old (300 A.D.) funeral urn in Mexico depicting a maize god with a popcorn-decorated headdress. In fact, research has proven that the ancestors of most Native American tribes enjoyed popcorn even before the birth of Christ. And today, popcorn is still considered one of America's favorite snacks.

Americans consume 54 quarts per man, woman, and child each year. Approximately 70 percent of that is purchased at retail stores in both raw and popped form, and eaten at home. (Popcorn, http://www.popcorn.org/index.cfm). Try some of the popcorn activities at the end of this chapter as a perfect ending to reading about popcorn!

THIS ONE'S for YOU! "Enriched"—"Fortified"—Good or Bad

Don't worry about giving young children some foods, such as white bread and sandwich buns, that say "enriched" or "fortified" on the label. Enrichment replaces some of the nutrients lost during processing and fortification adds others. Some people say that white flour and products made with white flour are not nutritious. This is not true. It's just that whole grains are a bit better because they have more of some vitamins, minerals, and fiber. All starches are valuable sources of vitamins, minerals, and calories for young children. Even the youngest child needs at least four servings from the starch group each day. It's best to offer a variety of selections from the list rather than four or more portions of the same starch.

Whole-Grain Starch Choices

barley	Oatmeal	whole-grain cereals
brown rice	Pumpernickel	whole-grain Melba toast
bulgur	rye bread	whole-grain wafers
corn tortilla	Rykrisp	whole-wheat pasta
millet	wheat germ	
oat bran	whole-grain breads	

Best Enriched/Fortified Starch Choices

bagel, bialy	cornbread or corn muffins	raisin bread
bread sticks	Matzo	rusks
cereals (ready-to-eat, not too sweet)	melba toast	spaghetti
cooked cereals (all kinds)	Noodles	
	Pasta	

Other Starch Choices

biscuits	graham crackers	pretzels
bread stuffing	hard rolls	rice cakes
English muffin	Italian bread (unenriched)	white bread (enriched)
flour tortilla	muffins (unenriched)	white rice
French bread (unenriched)	oatmeal cookies	Zwieback
fruit/nut bread	pasta salad	pretzels

for Disease Control and Prevention (CDC), the percentage of overweight children age 6 to 11 more than doubled in the past two decades. (CDC, 2009).

With obesity the problem that it is today, this generation of American children could be the first in the history of the United States to live less healthful and shorter lives than their parents (Solomon, 2005).

Fighting Obesity at the National Level

This ever-growing problem has been addressed by many professional educators and researchers. By way of example, in response to the obesity epidemic, the National Association for Sport and Physical Education (NASPE) felt that there needed to be a national focus on encouraging children to develop physically.

To answer this need, they developed in 1995 their first set of national standards that define physically healthy students. (See their website for more complete information on these standards at http://www.aahperd.org). These standards were revised in 2003 and basically define what they consider a "physically educated person" (NASPE, 2003). Participating regularly in physical activity, one of these standards, is directly related to the national obesity problem. Another NASPE standard, to achieve a health-enhancing level of physical fitness, would also help prevent obesity.

Another broad national look at obesity can be found in the Feeding Infants and Toddlers Study (FITS) conducted by Mathematics Policy Research, Inc. and sponsored by the Gerber Products Company in 2002. This study was undertaken to describe the food consumption of U.S. infants and toddlers, 4 to 24 months of age, using a national random sample of 3,022 infants and toddlers 4 to 24 months. Detailed findings were published in a supplement to the *Journal of the American Dietetic Association* (JADA) in 2003. Additional analyses of the FITS data were completed in 2005 and published in 2006.

This study found that infants as young as 7 months of age showed food patterns that have been observed in older children and adults. From 18% to 33% of infants and toddlers between the ages of 7 and 14 months consumed no discrete servings of vegetables, and 23% to 33% consumed no fruits. French fries were one of the three most common vegetables. Almost half (46%) of 7- to 8-month-olds consumed some type of dessert, sweet, or sweetened beverage, and this percentage increased as age increased.

By 19 to 24 months, 62% of toddlers consumed a baked dessert, 20% consumed candy, and 44% consumed a sweetened beverage. More than one-half of toddlers consumed too much sodium.

Based on their findings, the researchers in the FIT study had many recommendations for parents and caregivers of infants and toddlers. They were encouraged to offer a wide variety of vegetables and fruits daily, with emphasis on dark green, leafy, and deep yellow vegetables and colorful fruits. Parents and caregivers should offer desserts, sweets, sweetened beverages, and salty snacks only occasionally. They need to offer nutrient-dense, age-appropriate foods as alternatives (e.g., fruit, cheese, yogurt, and cereals). Water, milk, and 100% fruit juices should be offered as alternative beverages (PubMed, 2006).

THINK ABOUT IT   Candy, Do We Really Know You?

Here are five facts that you probably didn't know about candy.

1. The Arabs are often credited with inventing caramel. But an early use of the hot, sticky substance was not so sweet: Women in harems applied it as a hair remover.

2. Most Americans knew nothing about chocolate in 1893, when the World's Columbian Exposition in Chicago featured a display of chocolate-making equipment from Germany. Among the fairgoers was Milton Hershey, who bought every piece of equipment on display and went into the chocolate business.

3. Early American chocolate makers often touted their products' nutritional value. During the Depression, candy bars had such names as Chicken Dinner, Idaho Spud, and Big Eats. The Hershey's chocolate wrapper once carried the slogan, "More sustaining than meat."

4. The rock band Van Halen had a contract clause requiring a bowl of M&Ms backstage at its concerts—but all of the brown M&Ms had to be removed. The clause is sometimes cited as an example of ridiculous rock-star demands, but it made practical sense, singer David Lee Roth has written. If a venue got the M&Ms wrong, it was a red flag that promoters hadn't read the contract closely and were likely to mess up more important details.

5. The National Confectioners Association says 90% of parents admit sneaking Halloween goodies out of their child's trick-or-treat bags. (Brenner, 2000; Kimmerle, 2003; & Richardson, 2003).

Preventing Obesity: Empty Calories

Nutritionists and pediatricians concur that infantile and childhood obesity should be prevented. Not all overweight children are destined to become overweight adults. Conversely, not all overweight adults were overweight children. Obesity is considered the number one health risk for children in the United States. The number of children who are overweight has doubled in the last two or three decades; currently, one child in five is overweight (CDC 2009).

The best plan to prevent obesity in children is to balance their caloric intake with the number of calories they expend through exercise. Children who are overweight may also have a tendency to overeat, so they may need to reduce their consumption of empty calories as well as the size of their portions.

Another way to reduce obesity is to limit empty calories—foods high in fat or sugar but low in protein, vitamins, and/or minerals. Sugar is not the only source of empty calories. High-fat and/or high-salt snacks should also be eliminated. Good choices then for snacks and meals will include vegetables, fruits, and protein-rich items.

Because young children have a limited capacity for food intake and because for many 22% of their caloric intake comes from snacks, it is important that empty calories be avoided. Snacks, as well as meals, must center on foods that contribute to children's need for a balanced diet.

How to Limit Children's Sugar Intake

There are four primary ways to limit children's sugar intake: (1) avoid providing obvious sources of high-sugar foods, (2) avoid giving them "hidden" sugars, (3) find alternative sources of sweetness or reduce the amount of sugar in food choices, and (4) find other ways to celebrate special events without serving foods high in sugar.

Avoid high-sugar foods. The term **sugar** is generally used to refer to sucrose, which is refined sugar from sugar cane or beets. The most common form of sucrose is white, granulated table sugar. This type of sugar is an ingredient in cakes, cookies, doughnuts, pies, candy, and soft drinks. One obvious way to reduce sugar intake is to reduce the intake of these types of foods. Another method is to use one half or less of the sugar called for in a recipe.

Other common forms of sugar are fructose, dextrose, lactose, and maltose. Read the list of ingredients on prepared foods and watch for words ending with *ose*, which indicates that some form of sugar is present. These different forms of sugar have varying degrees of sweetness. For example, lactose (milk sugar) is the least sweet per unit. Fructose is nearly twice as sweet as sucrose, and invert sugar is about 30% sweeter than sucrose. All, however, provide basically empty calories.

Avoid hidden sugars. Most parents and teachers are aware that foods like candy, cake, and soft drinks contain sugar and are low in nutritional value. Very few people are aware, however, that sugar is also present in catsup, peanut butter, luncheon meats, hot dogs, pork and beans, nondairy creamer, fruit-flavored yogurt, and canned vegetables. Although these foods do contain nutrients, the addition of sugar is usually unnecessary. Use foods that contain no sugar.

Find alternative sources of sweetness. Snacks and desserts of unsweetened foods can be emphasized at home and school. Examples include unsalted popcorn, cheese, vegetables with dip, and no-sugar-added peanut butter on apples and celery.

Fresh fruits and vegetables should be given priority. When you must use canned fruits, look for fruits canned in their own juices or in the juices of other fruits. If fresh or water-packed fruits are not available, rinse fruits canned in heavy syrup with water before serving.

Activity and Obesity

Although genetics and sugar intake play a role in obesity, they alone cannot account for the huge increase in obesity rates over the past few decades. Eating too much and moving around too little are two other major causes of obesity. Most experts agree that watching excessive amounts of television is a significant risk factor associated with obesity; almost half of children ages eight to 16 years watch three to five hours of television daily (CDC, 2008). Children who are the most overweight watch the most television and eat too many snacks with a high fat content (CDC, 2009). Television viewing, playing video games, and surfing the Internet often take the place of physical activity for many children. The trancelike state associated with these activities can slow children's metabolism so much that they resemble children at complete rest (Ogden, et al., 2006).

Recommendations to Reduce the Risk of Obesity

The American Academy of Family Physicians offers the following tips on preventing childhood obesity.

- Respect the child's appetite: Children do not need to finish every drink or clean off their plates.
- Avoid prepared and sugared foods when possible.
- Keep a limited amount of high-calorie foods at home.
- Provide healthful meals, with 30% or fewer of the calories derived from fat.
- Provide ample fiber in the child's diet.
- Replace whole milk with skim milk when the child is two years of age.
- Do not provide food for comfort or as a reward.
- Do not offer sweets in exchange for a finished meal.
- Limit television viewing.
- Encourage active play.
- Establish regular family activities such as walks, ball games, and other outdoor activities (CDC 2009).

Improving Young Children's Diets

There are some very basic steps to take in order to improve a child's diet. Here are some general suggestions to accomplish this:

- Serve whole organic foods that are free from artificial additives, colors, and preservatives. (See Figure 21–11 for more information on organic foods.)
- Give children whole grains, eggs, seafood, and some dairy products.
- Eliminate canned fruits and vegetables, foods coated in sugar and syrup, and processed meats and cheeses.
- Encourage children to eat raw foods such as vegetables and fruits, which contain higher amounts of vitamins and minerals than cooked foods.
- Use whole-wheat or soy flour to completely or partially replace white flour in recipes.
- Use ground-up raisins, dates, or other dried fruit instead of sugar.

Go to http://www.mypyramid.gov/ to get the latest version of the Food Pyramid based on the child's age, height, and weight.

Some more specific suggestions concerning fruit in young children's diets are:

- Some fruits, especially dried fruits, berries, and solid fruits such as pears, are good sources of fiber. Offer children wedges of seedless oranges and apples. These fruits have fiber that's lost when they're made into juice.
- Generally, the more color a fruit (or vegetable) has, the more vitamins and minerals it contains.
- Avoid giving toddlers fruits with seeds. Pay special attention as toddlers eat dried or frozen fruits and cut firm fruits to be sure they don't choke on the hard bits.
- Bananas and avocados are favorites of young children because the fruits' textures are appealing. Both are rich in potassium and other minerals.
- Products marked "juice" must contain 100% juice. "Drinks," "ades," "punches," "cocktails," and other beverages may be little more than fruit-flavored sugar water.
- Giving a child juice made from concentrate is a good way to provide fluoride if your water supply is fluoridated.
- Encourage plain water for thirst. Juice is a food and children will fill up on it and not eat other foods. The American Academy of Pediatrics recommends four to six ounces of juice per day (AAP, 2001).
- Leave that paring knife in the drawer and keep the skin of certain fruits and vegetables on! You could be shaving off valuable nutrients. Eat these foods in their entirety: apples, cucumbers, and baked potatoes.
- Temperate fruit varieties (including apples, pears, peaches, and berries) have lots of fiber, vitamins, and antioxidants. Tropical fruits (bananas, papayas, mangos) are relatively higher in calories and lower in fiber and nutrition and so should be served in moderation.

Snacks and Obesity

It's hard for young children to go for long periods of time without feeling hungry. This is because their stomachs are small and can't hold much food at one sitting. Small meals, or snacks, can help appease the hungry child. When snacks are chosen from a wide variety of nutritious foods, they can contribute important nutrients to the child's diet.

Today, more than ever before, it's easy to have a poor diet, partly because of all the foods we have to choose from. Making wise choices regarding the food we offer young children in snacks can help prevent obesity. Selection of snacks we offer young children should be based on more than taste and appearance. Nutritional value related to calories is an important indication of whether you're getting real food values in snacks and helping keep children from becoming too heavy.

Even if you read the labels on food and signs advertising produce, you still may be misled by the various word "plays" that apply to each of the terms *organic* and *natural.* Here is some information to help you make these distinctions.

Organic
What it *means*: Items that are "**100% organic**" are certified to have been produced using only methods thought to be good for the earth. Organic food must be grown without the use of pesticides, synthetic fertilizers, sewage sludge, genetically modified organisms, or ionizing radiation. Animals used to produce meat, poultry, eggs, and dairy products cannot be given antibiotics or growth hormones.

Items that bear the *USDA* **organic** label means that the item contains at least 95% organic ingredients. Products with at least 70% organic content can be labeled *made with organic ingredients.*

Health implications: Research has yet to show that organic foods are nutritionally superior, but they are made without potentially harmful pesticides, fertilizers, antibiotics, synthetic hormones, or genetic engineering.

Remember: Organic foods can cost up to 50% more than nonorganic products. If that cost is prohibitive to you, it's better to eat healthful choices, like fruits and vegetables that are conventionally grown, rather than skipping them.

Bottom line: Going organic never hurts, especially when it comes to avoiding pesticides, which are linked to several health issues. Produce most affected by pesticides includes peaches, apples, sweet bell peppers, nectarines, strawberries, cherries, lettuce, pears, spinach, and potatoes.

Nonorganic produce lowest in pesticides are onions, avocado, sweet corn (frozen), pineapples, mango, sweet peas, asparagus, kiwi, bananas, cabbage, broccoli, and eggplant.

100% Natural
What it means: These products typically don't contain artificial colors, flavors, or preservatives and have no synthetic ingredients. But because **natural products** are not regulated, the term has little meaning beyond its descriptive value. The ingredients on the label may look similar to those found in organic foods, but they have not necessarily been produced organically.

Health implications: As with organic foods, there is no research to prove that natural products are better for you. Most food additives, while not sounding healthy, haven't been shown to be bad for you.

Remember: Just because something is *natural* does not mean it's good for you. It can still have loads of sugar, fat, or calories. The soft drink 7-Up, for example, was once marketed as "100 percent natural." The label now says, "100 percent natural flavors."

Bottom line: Always check the ingredient list and nutrition-facts panel to see what's really in an item. A healthy choice will be relatively low in sugar and saturated fat, and you won't need a chemistry degree to decipher the label. For more information, visit www.foodnews.org.

FIGURE 21-11 • Reading Labels: Organic and Natural Products.

Here are some guidelines to consider when choosing snacks.

- Judge the actual nutritional contribution the snack makes to the child's diet. A nutritious snack should supply nutrients like vitamins, calcium, and iron. Using the new Food Guide Pyramid is a good way to provide nutrients.
- Plan snacks around regular meal schedules. Snacks need not and should not interfere with or dull the child's appetite.
- Consider the number of calories a snack provides in the daily total. Snack foods should not be high in sugar or fat. Children enjoy sweet foods, but too much sugar can cause cavities. Too many foods high in sugar and fat can help cause children to become overweight. Try to set limits on the amount of sweet and fatty foods eaten.
- Make the snack easy to obtain. Snacks prepared ahead of time for children can provide important nutrients while being a neat treat.
- Choose foods that appeal in taste and appearance. If the snack does not look good, it is likely not to be eaten.

See the end of this chapter for nutritious snack ideas.

knowledge about names of shapes and colors; tastes; changes in shape, size, color, and taste; and new words. Food activities also help young children develop skills in hand–eye and small-muscle coordination, simple measuring, and socialization.

In order to ensure that food experiences for young children are planned to enhance their creativity, they must include the following basic guidelines. They must (1) be open-ended; (2) be challenging, but not too hard for three- to five-year-olds; (3) be varied, giving children choices; (4) emphasize the doing, not the end product; (5) involve inexpensive materials; and (6) not be dangerous to children.

Food activities work best in a small group. It is important that children be allowed to make decisions for themselves about what foods to use and how to use them. Adults responsible for the diets of young children must limit sugar consumption by avoiding obvious sources of sucrose and hidden sugars. Using natural sources of sweetness, reducing the focus on sweets, and finding other types of sweets for young children are all essential ways to reduce sugar in children's diets. Childhood obesity has become a major health problem in the United States. Some causes of childhood obesity are genetic, but sugar intake and lack of physical activity play large roles.

FIGURE 21-12 • Eating a balanced meal before having a dessert is one way to help fight childhood obesity.

Summary

Foods can be used in activities that help children become more creative in their approach to the world as they learn new information and skills. They develop

Key Terms

100% organic 538
Natural products 538
Organic 538
Sugar 533

Learning Activities

A. Try testing the sense of taste of some fellow students by making "creative juice."

1. Materials and ingredients: blender, common vegetables (cucumber, carrots, tomatoes, cabbage, celery, green pepper, parsley), salt, sugar, lemon juice
2. Begin with any two vegetables. Add one-half cup of cold water or crushed ice and blend. A pinch of salt and sugar and a small amount of lemon juice will improve the flavor. Taste a small amount.
3. Add a third vegetable to the mixture. Taste. Keep track of the vegetables and amounts used. Continue to add vegetables, one at a time. Make the following.

   a. a tasty vegetable juice
   b. a juice whose vegetables no one can identify
   c. a mystery juice

B. Observe a group of children experiencing a type of food for the first time—perhaps eggplant, squash, or rutabaga!

1. What kinds of expressions do they make when they taste the food?
2. How do they react when they find out what the food was that they tasted?
3. What can be said to make a child more willing to taste new foods?

C. Experiment with the sense of taste. Each person who tastes a food in this experiment must wear a blindfold or cover his or her eyes. Use small slices of baking apples or potatoes and a freshly sliced onion or garlic. Hold the onion under the blindfolded person's nose. Slip a small piece of apple or potato into the person's mouth. Have the person chew up the food and tell what it was.

D. With a group of children, try out at least one of the food experiences listed in this chapter. Evaluate the experience. Would you use this recipe again? Would you organize the experience in the same way next time? If not, what changes would you make?

E. Develop your own food-related activities. Develop an integrated unit on food for an elementary grade level. Share this unit with your fellow classmates for their input.

F. Keep a food diary for at least one week. Summarize your findings on your eating habits. Compare your eating habits with the recommended food pyramid in your summary.

G. Many educators grew up with the Food Group Wheel with four food groups. In 1992, the Food Pyramid was introduced. On April 12, 2005, the revised Food Pyramid was revealed. Go to http://www.hsph. harvard.edu/nutritionsource/pyramids.html to find a comparison of the old and new pyramids. How does your diet fit into each?

H. Go to http://www.mypyramid.gov to learn the food groups and see how much physical activity you need. Click on each color in the pyramid to learn more about the food groups, requirements and portions/serving sizes for individual foods within each group. Compare what you have learned from this website to your current diet. What changes, if any do you need to make? How would you use this website with children?

Activities for Children

Curriculum Ideas

Music/movement. Play Hot Potato! Invite children to sit in a circle. Play recorded music as the children pass a real potato around the circle. When the music stops, the child with the potato leaves the circle. Each child who leaves the circle gets a turn to start and stop the music.

Math—apple fishing game. Tie three feet of string to a wooden spoon. Attach a magnet to the end of the string. Cut and laminate many different colored and sized apples from construction paper. Attach a paper clip to each apple. Spread the apple shapes on the floor and let children try to catch the apples. Have them try to catch the red apple ... or the biggest apple. For a twist, label the apples with letters or numbers. Have children catch a specific apple or have them identify which apple they caught.

Art—Design Your Own Cereal Box

For this activity you will need: markers, crayons, empty cereal boxes, 12 × 18 colored construction paper, glue sticks

Discuss with the children different cereals they like. Encourage students to also describe the cereal boxes. Ask students to choose a favorite cereal and design a new box for it.

Students first draw around an empty cereal box to make the outline of the box. They can choose to make only the front of the cereal box or both the front and the back. Encourage students to use letters, shapes, and colors that they feel will make the cereal box special. Remind them to be sure to make their letters big enough so everyone can read them.

When they are finished, they may paste the new cover (and back) to the empty cereal box. These can be used in the home center, or in a play store.

Social studies. A trip to a local restaurant, pizzeria, or bakery can provide children with a wonderful opportunity to learn about how a favorite food is prepared. Invite children to prepare a list of questions they would like to ask during their visit. Consider taking along a portable tape recorder and camera to record the steps of the recipe the children are learning about. Children can then make the recipe at school. They can write a story about their experiences using the photos as their inspiration.

Pretend play. Wash empty yogurt containers and lids and frozen juice containers and place in the dramatic play area. Provide children with plastic spoons, bowls, and plastic fruit or small colored blocks to represent the fruits. Encourage children to use the snack props as they incorporate dolls and their classmates in dramatic play.

Math. Have children wash their hands. Then give them a bowl filled with crackers in a variety of shapes: goldfish, oyster, square, and oval. Place paper plates for each type of cracker on the table. Have children work together to sort the crackers onto each plate. Afterward children can pass the plates around and choose crackers to eat with their soup.

After a food activity, make a bar graph that lists all the recipes you've used in your class. Indicate the names of the children who liked each one. Which recipe did most children prefer? Which recipe was least preferred? Brainstorm with children how they might change the recipes to make them even better.

Literature and art. Read *Pretzel* by Margaret Rey (1997) to children. Make real pretzels with the recipe for soft pretzels found at the end of this chapter. Provide children with materials to create drawings about their pretzel-making experience. Record their dictations and encourage them to create their own pretzel book. Children can continue making pretend pretzels with play dough or clay or by twisting brown butcher paper.

Food Pyramid Activities

Help students develop an awareness of nutritious foods by creating a food pyramid on a large paper triangle. Brainstorm a list of snacks for each category. Using your paper food pyramid, have students choose food pictures from magazines, cut them out, and glue them in the appropriate categories on the pyramid. Take students online to http://www.mypyramid.gov for the latest adaptable version of the food pyramid from the FDA.

What's for Lunch?

Challenge each student to think of a favorite food that begins with the same letter as his or her first name. During morning meeting, when you ask, "What's for lunch today?" the student to your left might respond by saying, "Today for lunch we're having Megan's Meatloaf." The next student continues by saying, "Today for lunch we're having Megan's Meatloaf and Terry's Tacos," the third student says, "Today for lunch we're having Megan's Meatloaf, Terry's Tacos, and Hugh's Hamburgers," and so on. When it gets back to you, try to remember everything that's on the menu! Students will get a kick out of correcting you if you make a mistake.

Learning From Labels

Have students collect wrappers from several candy bars. Help them examine and compare the prices, nutritional components, and percentages of fat, carbohydrates, protein, and sugar in each. What conclusions can they draw?

Sun Recipes

Sun tea. The youngest of children will enjoy preparing large bottles of water with suitable herb teabags (apple cinnamon or mandarin orange spice are good choices) suspended inside and setting these out in the sunshine "to brew." From time to time have children check the color of the tea. Bring it inside when it has steeped to suit your taste. Serve your sun tea warm or ice cold and sip it together outside.

Sun-dried fruits and vegetables. Older children will be able to pare and slice apples, apricots, peaches, carrots, zucchini, and celery. Use a large, blunt-nosed needle and heavy thread to pierce and string each piece. Leave air spaces between the pieces. Do not dry in direct sunlight because it may make apricots bitter.

Fruits dried in this way will keep for months and are wonderful for snacks, either with plain yogurt or by themselves. The vegetables can also be stored until some chilly autumn day when the children toss them into chicken broth for a warming soup snack.

Apple Experiences

Count the seeds. Before you cut an apple, have children try to guess how many seeds will be inside. Cut open the apple and count them. How close were they? Write down children's guesses and the actual number of seeds that were in the apple. The next day, repeat the process. Compare your results. Were there more, less, or the same amount of seeds in the two apples?

Different apples. Next time you go to the grocery store on a field trip with children, point out all the different kinds of apples. Tell children their names. Buy a few different kinds, and when you get back to school, let children sample them. Ask them how each one tastes. Ask them how each one is different.

Apple sequencing. Gather three to five different-sized apples. Set them on a table and ask a child to arrange the apples according to size. For younger children, start with two apples and ask which is smallest.

Apple hide-and-seek. Have children cover their eyes while you "hide" an apple in the room. (It should be placed in plain view.) Tell children to find the apple but not touch it. Once they spot it they should sit back down in their place. The first one to sit down again will get to hide the apple.

Apple hide-and-seek #2. Play this game the same way as the previous game, except hide the apple. Then tell children individually whether they are "hot" or "cold" in relation to the apple. Allow other children to have a chance to hide the apple and tell their classmates whether they are "hot" or "cold." It may be a good idea to discuss the meaning of "hot" and "cold" before you play this game.

Apples in the basket. You need apples and a small laundry or bushel basket. Have children place five apples in the basket. Count with children as they place the apples in the basket. How many apples will fit in the basket? Have children guess how many will fit, and then see how many it takes to fill the basket. You can also tape numbers onto the bottom of the baskets, and have the child place the appropriate number of apples into each basket.

Apple chart. Prepare sliced red and yellow apples for lunch. Ask each child which color apple she or he ate. Allow children to mark the column on a graph that corresponds to their answer.

Fruit Game

Show children various plastic fruits you may have in your dramatic play area, or pictures cut from magazines of colorful fruits. Have children identify the fruits. Then invite them to check and see if they are wearing colors that match the different fruits. Now place the fruits (or pictures) on the floor across from children. Suggest that all those wearing red march toward the apple, those wearing yellow hop to the banana, those wearing purple gallop to the grapes, and so on. Make sure that all children have a chance to move toward the fruit.

Food Riddles

Children's listening and thinking skills will improve as they identify foods by guessing the answer to riddles.

Children sit in a small group of four to five. The adult reads the entire riddle before children respond. You can write the following riddles on index cards to read to children.

1. I'm in the dairy group. I'm white. People drink me out of a glass, cup, or carton. You put me on cereal. What am I? (milk).

2. I'm in the vegetable group. I'm long, orange, and crunchy when eaten raw. What am I? (carrot).

3. I'm in the fruit group. I'm round, shiny, and smooth to touch. I'm crunchy to bite into. I grow on a tree. What am I? (apple).

4. I'm in the meat group. I'm flat and round in shape. I often come on a bun. Sometimes people put catsup on me. What am I? (hamburger).

5. I'm in the bread and cereal group. I come in a loaf. You can slice me to make sandwiches. I smell good right after I'm baked. What am I? (bread).

6. I'm a member of the meat and poultry group. I have an oval shape. I come from a chicken. You can fry me, scramble me, or boil me. Inside I am yellow and white. What am I? (egg).

7. I'm a member of the fruit group. I'm tiny, brown, and wrinkled. I used to be a grape. You can eat me in a cereal, in cookies, or just by myself. I'm sweet but not a junk food. What am I? (raisin).

Children who are familiar with the game enjoy making up their own food riddles. Riddle games could be played concentrating on only one food group, ethnic foods, etc.

Popcorn Predictions

Materials: Paper, popped popcorn, bowl

The objective of this activity is to estimate how much popcorn will fit into various shapes. Give students a sheet of paper with different shapes on it. Then give each student one kernel of popcorn to use to estimate how many pieces it would take to fill different shapes. Give them three cups of popped popcorn each and have them put it on the shapes. Students can record their results and find out how close they were to their estimates. Then, everyone can eat the results!

Pop Goes the Student!

The objective of this activity is to dance using the word "pop."

Students start in a circle with the teacher in a visible location for all students to see. Start with

stretching exercises that incorporate stretching the upper and lower body. Thoroughly stretch large and muscle groups in the upper and lower body. Then have the students start low to the ground, while popcorn begins to "pop." As popcorn "pops" faster, the students begin to rise up from the lower-level position. As popcorn is "popping" the students move their arms and hands in front of them. As popcorn finishes "popping", the students then stand up and reach for the ceiling. Variation: Do this activity while real popcorn is popping.

Your Sense of Popcorn

Materials: Air popper, popcorn, paper, pencils

The object of this activity is to have students write about popcorn using their five senses to describe it. Start by reminding the children to be careful observers. Tell them not to speak to anyone, only to listen and look. Pop up a batch of popcorn, using an electric popcorn popper. When the popcorn is finished popping, pass out paper and pencils to the children. On the paper have students write:

1. What I see.
2. What I smell.
3. What I hear.
4. What I feel.
5. What I taste.

When students are finished writing, have them share their answers with the class.

Fruit Feast

For this activity you will need small plastic bowls, a large spoon, several plastic knives, a large knife (for an adult), paper or plastic plates, chart paper, and markers.

Send a note home to inform families that, as a way to learn about one another, children are requested to bring in their favorite fruit. On the day that the activity is planned, have several extra pieces of fruit handy just in case some children forget to bring their own.

Invite children to bring their piece of fruit to the meeting area. Write the question, "What is your favorite fruit?" on the top of a sheet of chart paper. Then go around the circle and invite children to show what they brought. Record children's responses, review their comments, and engage them in a discussion about the fruit that they brought in. How many children like the same fruit? Are there any fruits they have never seen before?

Ask children to place their fruit in the middle of the circle. How are the fruits similar? How are they different? Have them touch and smell the fruits. Create another chart to record their observations.

Explain that they will use their fruit to make a fruit salad bar for their snack. Divide them into two small groups, each led by an adult. Begin by washing hands and reviewing cooking safety rules. Invite children to help wash, peel, and cut the fruits with plastic knives. Ask an adult to cut the harder fruits first and give the pieces to children so that they can safely cut t hem and then place the different fruits into individual bowls.

Give each child a bowl and invite the group to make their own fruit salad. Before they eat, children should name the different fruits they have chosen.

Remember that many young children may not be enthusiastic about trying new foods, and some may have an aversion to specific types of food textures. Offer everyone the opportunity to participate and to touch and smell the different types of fruit. Do not require them to eat fruit if they do not want to.

Original Recipes

Ask each child to dictate a recipe to you that is made in her or his home. Write it down exactly as she or he tells you (mistakes and funny parts, too). Put the recipes together in a little booklet for parents. It will be a treasure to save and enjoy for years to come.

Sandwich Activities

Ask children about their favorite sandwich. Keep track of their answers because these can give insight into their eating habits and nutritional needs. Ask them: "Do you like mayonnaise on your sandwiches? Lettuce? Cream cheese?" "What is your favorite jelly?" (Do you know the difference between jelly and jam? Jelly is made from the juice of the fruit and it's clear. Jam has crushed fruit right in it.) "What kind of meat sandwich do you like best?" "What is your favorite bread?" (A sandwich is more bread than anything else, so it's important to have a good bread on your sandwich. A brown bread is the best because it gives your body more natural vitamins and minerals than a white bread does.)

Let their answers to these questions guide you in selecting recipes for them. Make some homemade peanut butter, homemade bread, or homemade jelly. (See recipes later in this section.)

Sandwich Collage

Materials for this activity: Small pieces of colored paper, crayons, markers, scissors, glue sticks, 12 × 18 white paper, brown paper or grocery bags

Ask children, "What is your favorite sandwich?" Have them think about different kinds of sandwiches and choose a favorite. Encourage children to describe sandwiches they like and to name the colors of the foods in them. On a large piece of paper, list the sandwiches the children named. Have children close their eyes and picture themselves eating their favorite sandwich. Then say, "Let's create a sandwich collage of your favorite sandwich."

Encourage children to be aware of the colors and shapes of the food as they create their sandwich collage. Have children draw everything they want to put on their sandwiches. Then they cut them out. Different colored bits of construction paper can be used for pickles, tomatoes, lettuce, etc.

Encourage the children to build their sandwiches from the bottom to the top. Have them use brown paper bags or brown construction paper for buns. After they are finished, have students share their collages to see if classmates can identify the ingredients.

Great Grapes

Give young children the opportunity to make choices and be creative by concocting their own snacks using only one harvest food—grapes! Set out an assortment of red, purple, and green grapes. Discuss the many grape products we eat or drink (jelly, juice, etc.). Suggest that children brainstorm new ways to prepare and eat grape snacks.

Here are a few suggestions for great grape snacks. A grape cookbook, with each recipe signed by the cook, would be a wonderful follow-up activity.

Frozen grapes. Place washed grapes on a cookie sheet with space around each one. Cut them in half to avoid the possibility of a child's choking. Freeze. When frozen, place in a plastic bag. Have children eat frozen.

Grapes to raisins. Wash and dry a large bunch of green grapes. Place in a basket in a warm sunny spot for four to seven days. You will then have raisins!

Grape fruit cocktail. Have children slice grapes in half with plastic knives. They can add sliced grapes to a can of fruit cocktail (packed in juice, not heavy syrup) along with fresh fruit chunks as desired.

Grape surprises

A. Ingredients
½ cup peanut butter
½ cup nonfat dry milk powder
2 tablespoons honey
grapes

B. Procedure
1. Mix peanut butter, milk powder, and honey until a soft, nonsticky "dough" is formed.
2. Knead dough, then press out pieces into 2-inch circles.
3. Place a grape in the center. Wrap dough around grape and seal well.
4. Variation: Place grapes inside cream cheese balls, then roll in chopped nuts.

Grapes and yogurt

A. Ingredients
small bunch of grapes
1 cup yogurt or sour cream

B. Procedure: Slice grapes with plastic knife and add to yogurt (or sour cream).

Recipes for Cooking Experiences

Soft pretzels

A. Ingredients
   1½ cups warm water
   3 cups flour
   1 pkg. yeast
   1 tablespoon sugar
   1 teaspoon salt
   1 tablespoon vegetable oil

B. Procedure
   1. Mix together all the ingredients.
   2. Add small amounts of flour until mixture does not stick to your hand.
   3. Roll out 12 small balls of dough to make snakes or worms.
   4. Loop ends together to make a pretzel knot.
   5. Coat with a mixture of one egg yolk and two tablespoons of water.
   6. Sprinkle a few pieces of salt on each pretzel.
   7. Place on a slightly greased cookie sheet.
   8. Bake at 425°F for 10–12 minutes.

Applesauce (Picture recipe in Figure 21–6)

A. Ingredients
   4 to 6 medium apples
   ¼ cup sugar
   ½ stick cinnamon (or 1–2 whole cloves, if desired)

B. Procedure (if food mill is not used)
   1. Peel and core the apples.
   2. Cut apples into quarters, and place in pot.
   3. Add a small amount of water (about 1 inch).
   4. Cover the pot and cook slowly (simmer) until apples are tender. The cooked apples can then be mashed with a fork, beaten with a beater, or put through a strainer.
   5. Add sugar to taste (about ½ cup to 4 apples) and continue cooking until sugar dissolves.
   6. Add ½ stick of cinnamon (or 1 to 2 cloves) if desired.

Note: If a food mill is used, it is not necessary to peel and core the apples. After the apples are cooked, they are put through the food mill. Children enjoy turning the handle and watching the sauce come dripping out of the holes. Variation: For fun, add a few drops of red food coloring. What happens to the color of the applesauce? Is the flavor changed? Be sure to add them while the applesauce is still hot.

Banana Apple Icy (Picture recipe in Figure 21–7)

A. Ingredients
   1 apple
   1 banana
   ¼ cup milk
   1 cup plain yogurt
   3 ice cubes

B. Procedure
   1. Peel and core 1 yellow apple.
   2. Cut it into small cubes.
   3. Peel and slice 1 banana.

   4. Put these in a blender with the milk and yogurt.
   5. Add 3 ice cubes.
   6. Blend until smooth.

Makes enough for two small glasses.

Apple sandwiches (Picture recipe in Figure 21–8)

B. Ingredients
   1 apple
   peanut butter

C. Procedure
   1. Peel and core an apple.
   2. Cut it crosswise into slices.
   3. Spread peanut butter on one apple slice and top with another apple slice.

Fruit soup

A. Ingredients
   honeydew and/or cantaloupe melon
   1 banana
   1 plum
   kiwifruit, grapes, and other fruits
   1 cup of orange juice
   1 scoop frozen yogurt

B. Procedure
   1. Scoop balls from melons with a melon baller. (Kids love doing this.) Use a honeydew melon or cantaloupe or some of each.
   2. Cut up banana with a butter knife.
   3. Add the orange juice for the base of the soup and put in a blender.
   4. Add banana pieces and whirl on high for 30 seconds.
   5. Pour soup into 3 or 4 bowls or into 8–10 small cups.
   6. Add cut-up fruit to each and then top off with a scoop of frozen yogurt.

Simple Nutritious Snacks

- Ants on a Log—Celery sticks filled with peanut butter and topped with raisins.

- Bunny Food—Combine grated carrots with raisins and a bit of honey and serve on crackers.

- Fancy Sandwiches—Cut bread into shapes with cookie cutters and spread with favorite toppings.

- Orange Delight—Mix in blender: ⅓ cup orange juice concentrate, ¼ cup powdered milk, ½ banana or other fruit, ¾ cup water, honey to taste, ice. (The more ice you add, the slushier the drink becomes.)

- Party Mix—Mix 2 cups dry cereal and 1 cup small pretzel sticks. Place on cookie sheet, sprinkle with parmesan cheese and ⅓ cup melted margarine. Bake at 250°F for 30 minutes, stirring occasionally.

- Roll-Up Salad—Spread a cabbage or lettuce leaf with peanut butter. Place a celery or carrot stick in the middle and roll up the leaf.

Super Snacks

Healthy strawberry shortcake. Cut the top off a low-fat bran muffin. Scoop out some muffin from the bottom half. Fill with sliced strawberries and low-fat plain yogurt. Put back the muffin top.

Fruit dip fondue. Stir together natural peanut butter and low-fat chocolate yogurt in equal proportions. Use as a dip for the fruit of your choice.

Asian veggie roll-ups. Soak rice paper (found at Asian markets) in water according to package directions until thickened. Cut veggies into julienne strips (carrots, zucchini, yellow squash, or peppers). Layer veggies on the rice paper (add some soy sauce if you like) and roll up.

Beautiful bagels. Use bagels as your "easel." Take ½ of a bagel, and have children spread it with low-fat cream cheese. Have available a variety of sliced vegetables such as carrots, cucumbers, bean sprouts, cherry tomatoes, green or red bell peppers, and black olives. Children can decorate their snack to their own "taste" both artistically and health-wise.

Stuffed Baked Apples

A. Ingredients
4 tart apples
¼ cup crunchy breakfast cereal
¼ cup chopped walnuts
¼ teaspoon cinnamon
1 cup raisins
2 tablespoons honey

B. Procedure

1. Core apples.
2. Combine ingredients and spoon equal amounts into each apple cavity.
3. Place apples in shallow baking dish and add ¼ cup of water.
4. Bake uncovered for 40 minutes at 300°F.

Banana Breakfast Split

A. Ingredients
1 banana, sliced lengthwise
½ cup low fat cottage cheese
1 tablespoon wheat germ
1 tablespoon raisins
1 tablespoon chopped nuts

B. Procedure

1. Place banana slices in a bowl.
2. Put scoops of cottage cheese on top.
3. Sprinkle with wheat germ, raisins, and nuts. Makes one serving.

Pear bunnies

A. Ingredients
ripe pear cut in half lengthwise
1 lettuce leaf
1 teaspoon cottage cheese
red cherry
raisins
almond slivers

B. Procedure: Place pear half on lettuce half, rounded side up. Decorate, using cottage cheese for "cottontail," cherry for nose, raisins for eyes, and almond slivers for ears.

Tropical smoothie. All you need is fruit and a blender to whip up a fresh fruit snacktime smoothie. Just put all the ingredients below in a blender and whip it on high until smooth.

1 banana
2 kiwi fruit (peeled)
½ cup peeled and diced mango
½ cup peeled and diced papaya
1 cup orange juice
3 ice cubes

Makes two to three servings.

Tortilla flats. Take a small, whole grain tortilla, top with some shredded low-fat cheese, and warm in the microwave or toaster oven.

Fruit leather. This recipe reinforces the concept that fruits like apricots, peaches, raspberries, apples, etc., can be changed and used in new ways.

A. Ingredients
1 quart or 2 pounds of fresh fruit
sugar
cinnamon
plastic wrapping paper

B. Procedure

1. Help children break open, peel, and seed or pit fruit.
2. Puree prepared fruit in blender until smooth.
3. Add 2 tablespoons sugar and ½ teaspoon cinnamon to each 2 cups of puree.
4. Pour mixture onto sheet of plastic wrap that has been placed on a large cookie sheet. Spread mixture thinly and evenly.
5. Cover mixture with a screen or a piece of cheesecloth and place in the sun until completely dry—about one or two days. It can then be eaten or rolled and stored.

Peanutty Pudding

A. Ingredients

1 package regular or sugar-free vanilla pudding
2 cups milk
peanut butter

B. Procedure

1. Prepare pudding as directed on package.
2. Pour cooked pudding into individual bowls.
3. While pudding is still warm, stir 1 tablespoon peanut butter into each bowl.

Fruit Kabobs

A. Ingredients

1 cup vanilla or lemon yogurt (low-fat, low-sugar variety)
2 cups fresh or canned fruit (chunk-style)
pretzel sticks

B. Procedure

1. Thread fruit chunks onto pretzel sticks. Talk about how colors and sizes look next to each other.
2. Dip each end piece into the yogurt before eating, or spoon yogurt over the entire kabob.

Strawberry Yogurt Shake

A. Ingredients
½ cup frozen unsweetened strawberries, thawed
2 tablespoons frozen orange juice concentrate, thawed
½ cup banana (optional)
1 cup vanilla or lemon yogurt

B. Procedure

1. Puree strawberries in blender.
2. Add remaining ingredients to blender and mix until frothy.
3. For holidays or special occasions, stick straws through colorful paper shapes and serve with shakes. Makes two servings, 3/4 cup each.

Peanut Butter Banana Smoothie

A. Ingredients
1 cup vanilla yogurt
1 to 2 tablespoons peanut butter
1 banana

B. Procedure

1. Combine all ingredients in blender.
2. Whip for 30 to 60 seconds or until smooth.
3. Serve in custard cup or small bowl to eat with a spoon, or pour into cups to drink.

Spider Cookies

A. Ingredients
round crackers
peanut butter
small pretzel sticks
raisins

B. Procedure

1. Cover 2 round crackers with a layer of peanut butter.
2. Break 4 small pretzel sticks in half to make 8 spider legs.
3. On one cracker, lay 4 legs on one side and 4 on the other, making sure pretzels stick out from each side.
4. Place another cracker on top.
5. Place 2 small dabs of peanut butter on the top of one end of the cracker.
6. Place 2 raisins in the peanut butter dabs for eyes.

Make as many as you like!

Broccoli Trees and Snow

A. Ingredients
¾ cup small curd low fat cottage cheese
½ cup plain yogurt
¼ cup fresh minced parsley
1 bunch broccoli

B. Procedure

1. Mix cottage cheese and yogurt in blender until smooth.
2. Add parsley and refrigerate until cool.
3. Cut broccoli into "dippers." (Cucumbers, zucchini, celery, carrots, radishes, and green peppers make good "dippers," too.)
4. Dip vegetables into yogurt mix and enjoy.

Fruit Sun

A. Ingredients
grapefruit sections
muskmelon balls
cherries
raisins

B. Procedure

1. Arrange grapefruit sections in a ring around muskmelon balls.
2. Cherries and raisins may be used to make a face.
3. Amounts depend on the number to be served; ½-cup servings are appropriate.

Carrot and Raisin Salad

A. Ingredients
3 cups shredded carrots (teacher to prepare)
¾ cup raisins
juice of one lemon

B. Procedure

1. Mix ingredients thoroughly.
2. Serve immediately.

Banana Bake

A. Ingredients
1 banana, peeled
butter (melted)

B. Procedure

1. Place peeled banana in shallow baking dish and brush with melted butter.
2. Bake in moderate oven (375°F) for 10–15 minutes (until tender).
3. Serve warm.
4. Yield: 1 serving.

Watermelon Ice

When watermelon is in season, try this new way to use it. In a blender, puree 6 cups of seedless watermelon with 1 tbs lemon juice. Scoop mixture into a square baking pan and smooth the top. Cover and freeze at least 3 hours. Use an ice cream scoop to serve.

Frozen Cherries

A fun way to use cherries is to freeze them. Add them to summer drinks, giving them a subtle sweet-tartness that children will love. And when the glass is empty, let them go ahead and eat this ice—it's loaded with beta carotene.

Carob-Nut Snack

A. Ingredients
1 cup dry-roasted unsalted peanuts
1 cup unsweetened carob chips
1 cup unsweetened dried banana chips
1 cup unsweetened cereal

B. Procedure: Children can take turns shaking ingredients in a plastic container with lid to mix. Serve in small cups, or carry in plastic bags on field trips. Can be stored in container for several weeks.

Peanut butter balls

A. Ingredients

½ cup fresh peanut butter
1 tablespoon jelly
½ cup dry milk powder
1 cup bran or corn flakes
⅓ cup bran or corn flakes (crushed)

B. Procedure
1. Mix the peanut butter and jelly in bowl.
2. Stir in milk powder and 1 cup bran or corn flakes. Mix well.
3. With your hands, roll the mix into small balls. Roll the balls in the crushed flakes.

Peanut Butter Apple Rolls

A. Ingredients
1 8-ounce can refrigerated crescent rolls
2 tablespoons fresh peanut butter
1 apple, peeled and finely chopped

B. Procedure

1. Separate dough into 8 triangles.
2. Spread a thick layer of peanut butter on each triangle.
3. Top with 1 tablespoon of apple.
4. Start at the shortest side of each triangle and roll to other side. Place on cookie sheet.
5. Bake at 350°F for 10–15 minutes.

Peanut Grahams

A. Ingredients
graham crackers
fresh peanut butter
one or more of the following toppings—nuts, sunflower seeds, raisins, chocolate chips, sliced bananas, sliced apples

B. Procedure

1. Break each graham cracker in half.
2. Spread some peanut butter on one half.
3. Place your favorite topping on the peanut butter.
4. Spread some peanut butter on the other graham cracker half.
5. Press the two halves together to make a sandwich.

Nutty Swiss Cheese Spread

A. Ingredients
2 cups Swiss cheese, shredded
½ cup fresh peanut butter
½ cup sour cream
¼ cup raisins

B. Procedure
1. Mix all ingredients well.
2. Use spread on bread or crackers.

Graham Cracker Bananas

A. Ingredients
4 bananas
¼ cup evaporated milk
½ cup graham cracker crumbs
¼ cup butter or margarine, melted

B. Procedure
1. Peel bananas and cut in half lengthwise.
2. Roll bananas in milk, then roll in graham cracker crumbs.
3. Place in greased baking dish. Pour melted butter over top.
4. Bake at 450°F for 10 minutes.

Broiled Bananas

A. Ingredients
1 banana (unpeeled)
1 tablespoon plain low-fat yogurt

B. Procedure
1. Make a small slit in the banana skin. Place unskinned banana slit-side up on baking sheet.
2. Broil for 5–10 minutes, until softened.
3. Open skin to expose banana. Serve with a dollop of yogurt.

Most children like bananas, so this recipe should be a hit. In this recipe, the banana is eaten with a spoon and the skin becomes the dish.

Frozen Banana Coins. An excellent use for a very ripe banana. Peel bananas. Freeze bananas on a tray. Place frozen banana in a freezer bag or freezer container. Return to freezer until ready to use. To serve, remove banana from freezer and slice into pieces. Serve immediately, or pieces will become soggy. Yield: ½ banana per serving.

Frozen Banana Pop. Cut banana in half horizontally. Carefully push one popsicle stick into each banana half. Freeze. Serve directly from freezer.

Popcorn Mix. For children older than three years of age.

A. Ingredients
2 cups plain popped popcorn
¼ cup quartered dried apricots
¼ cup raisins
¼ cup peanuts

B. Procedure: Mix all ingredients together. Store in a tightly covered container. Yield: 2¾ cups.

Fruit Designs

In the summer when fresh fruit abounds, try these fruit designs for a fun snack time.

Boat: Cut honeydew melon into the shape of a triangle for the boat. Push one end of a small straw into the melon and the other into an orange wedge for the sail.

Toadstools: Peel hard-boiled eggs; slice a piece from the bottom so theyíll stand. Top with half of a cherry tomato (remove the seeds first) and then with a bit of feta cheese.

Colored popcorn. Add several drops of food coloring to vegetable oil before staring popcorn popper. Then add popcorn kernels to the oil and food coloring. One color can be made for each batch of popcorn kernels. After popcorn cools, mix all colored popcorn together.

Have children sort the popcorn by color. They can place the different colors of popcorn in different cups. They may then want to count how many kernels are in each cup. After all this work, eat and enjoy!

Crunchy Fruit Munch

A. Ingredients
   3 quarts popped popcorn
   2 cups natural cereal with raisins
   ¾ cup dried apricots, chopped
   ¼ teaspoon salt
   1/3 cup butter or margarine
   ¼ cup honey

B. Procedure

   1. Preheat oven to 300°F. Combine first four ingredients in large baking pan; set aside.
   2. In small saucepan, combine butter or margarine and honey. Cook over low heat until butter or margarine is melted.
   3. Pour over popcorn mixture, tossing lightly until well coated.
   4. Place in oven. Bake 30 minutes, stirring occasionally.

Makes 3 quarts. Store in tightly covered container up to 2 weeks.

Popcorn With Peanut Butter

A. Ingredients
   2 quarts popped popcorn
   1 tablespoon fresh peanut butter (creamy or chunky)
   2 tablespoons butter or margarine

B. Procedure

   1. In small saucepan, melt butter or margarine and peanut butter until smooth.
   2. Pour over popped corn and mix well.

Popcorn Cheese Snacks

A. Ingredients
   2 quarts popped popcorn
   ½ cup butter or margarine
   ½ cup grated American or Parmesan cheese or both
   ½ teaspoon salt

B. Procedure

   1. Spread freshly popped popcorn in a flat pan; keep hot and crisp in oven.
   2. Melt butter and grated cheese and add salt.
   3. Pour mixture over popcorn. Stir until every kernel is cheese flavored.

Turtle Pancakes

A. Ingredients
   pancake or biscuit mix
   1/3 cup nonfat dry milk
   2 cups milk

B. Procedure

   1. Follow package directions. (For extra nutrition, add 1/3 cup nonfat milk to the standard recipe calling for 2 cups milk.)
   2. The batter should be in a bowl rather than in a pitcher; the child puts the batter on the griddle by spoonfuls, sometimes deliberately dribbling for effect.
   3. A turtle is made by adding four tiny pancakes (the legs) around the perimeter of one round pancake about 3 inches in diameter.

Homemade peanut butter. Bring to school a large bag of peanuts in the shell. Let children help you shell the peanuts. Put a cupful of peanuts into a blender. Add 1 tablespoon of peanut oil to blend the peanuts to the consistency children like.

Homemade jelly: a quick version. Defrost a 12-ounce can of frozen grape juice concentrate. Dissolve a package of unflavored gelatin into the juice. Pour this mixture into a pan and bring to a boil, stirring to dissolve the gelatin.

Remove from heat and allow to cool. Pour the mixture into a wide-mouthed jar and refrigerate.

Homemade quick whole-wheat bread. Soften 3 tablespoons of dry active yeast in 3½ to 4½ cups warm water and milk (half milk, half water) in a large bowl. Add 2 tablespoons honey, 2 teaspoons salt, ½ cup nutritional yeast (available at health food stores), and 8 cups of whole wheat flour.

Blend well. Dough should be slippery and glutinous yet stiff enough to cling to the spoon. It shouldn't flatten out and there should be no liquid showing in the bowl. Add more (or less) flour to achieve this texture.

Fill oiled bread pans 2/3 full. Let dough rise 15 minutes (while you are cleaning up) at 85 to 90°F, until it increases in height by 25%.

Bake at 400°F for 15 minutes. Turn down oven to 350°F and continue baking for 20 minutes more—or until it is golden brown.

Fruit smoothies. You'll need ½ cup plain yogurt, ½ cup orange juice, ¾ cup fresh fruit (strawberries, blueberries, raspberries, bananas, or a combination), 1 tablespoon honey, and ½ cup ice.

Place all ingredients in a blender. Blend for about 2 minutes or until mixture is smooth. Pour into cups and enjoy. Serves 2.

Fun Sandwiches

Break away from the usual peanut butter and jelly sandwiches with these fun and nutritious variations:

Veggie cream cheese and cucumber

Tuna salad and a sliced tomato

Almond butter with slivered almonds and dried cranberries

Hummus and chopped peppers

Apple butter and fresh apple slices

Whipped cream cheese and fresh blueberries

Laughing Cow Cheese light spreadable cheese with ham and grated carrot

Blueberry cream cheese and strawberry slices

Reduced-sugar jam and cream cheese

Calcium-Rich Recipes

Did you know that three out of four Americans don't get the calcium they need? Remind the children to eat three a day . . . three servings of calcium-rich milk, cheese, or yogurt every day. To make it easier, here are some calcium-rich recipes for young children.

Polka dot milk. Fill ice trays with chocolate and strawberry-flavored milk. Drop the festive frozen milk cubes into a glass of plain milk for fun, tasty "polka dots."

Lunch in a crunch. Mix the child's favorite cereal with yogurt for a creamy and crunchy lunch.

'Nilla banana ice. Create a smooth, delicious drink by blending together 1 cup of low-fat milk, banana slices, ice, and a few drops of vanilla.

Cool cuts. Cookie cutters aren't just for cookies. Use them to cut out fun shapes from cheese slices or grilled cheese sandwiches to liven up lunches.

Festive fruity flavored milk. Mix 1 cup fat-free, skim, or 1% low-fat milk and 2 tablespoons apricot, blackberry, raspberry, or strawberry fruit syrup. For each cup of milk, stir in 2 tablespoons fruit syrup. Try experimenting with different flavors of fruit syrups until you find one that provides the perfectly pleasing color to your milk. Fruit syrups are available in natural and artificially flavored varieties and are usually found in the section with pancake mixes.

Finger lickin' good yogurt. Give kids a yogurt "palette." With a plate and two to three "colors" (flavors) of yogurt—try blueberry, strawberry, and banana—kids can paint on a graham cracker canvas and eat their great-tasting masterpiece.

Perfect cheese picks. Pair cheese with other healthy foods that will satisfy even the pickiest eaters. Wrap a slice of turkey around mild Mozzarella string cheese or slices of tangy Cheddar around apple wedges.

One-Step Cookbook

These are one-process recipes. They require some preparation, but the actual recipe uses one method that demonstrates what happens when food is prepared in that manner.

Carrot curls. For this activity, you will need carrots, a vegetable peeler, and ice water. Show children how to use a vegetable peeler safely. When peeling carrots, the peeler should be pushed down and away from the body, rather than toward the body or face.

Help children peel off the outside skin of the carrot, then make additional carrot peels. Place peels in ice water in the refrigerator until they curl. Use the carrot curls for a snack.

Apples with cheese. Halve and core apples. Fill hollowed center with smooth cheese spread. Chill for 2 to 3 hours before serving.

Yogurt and cereal parfait. In a tall glass, layer lemon, vanilla, or fruit-flavored yogurt with a favorite breakfast cereal.

Banana breakfast bites. Peel bananas and cut into bite-sized pieces. Dip each piece in yogurt, then drop into a plastic bag filled with wheat germ. Shake to coat. Serve as finger food.

Fruit cubes. Make frozen cubes with fruit juice, placing a small piece of fruit in each cube before it freezes. Add a popsicle stick to each cube to make individual fruit treats on a stick.

Banana on ice. This is a tasty, low-calorie treat—only about 85 calories per banana. Simply peel a banana and wrap it in plastic wrap. Place it in the freezer for several hours or until hard. (Don't leave it in the freezer too long.) Eat frozen. It tastes exactly like banana ice cream.

Smiling sandwich. Spread peanut butter on a rice or corn cake. Use two raisins for eyes and a banana or apple slice for a smiling mouth.

Apple bake. Place a cored apple in a dish with a small amount of water. Cover with foil (for oven) or cover loosely with plastic wrap (for microwave) and bake at 350°F for 20 minutes (oven) or on high for 5 minutes (microwave). Add a sprinkle of cinnamon if desired.

Juice freeze. Fill a 6-ounce paper cup with sugar-free fruit juice, cover with plastic wrap, and push a plastic spoon through center of wrap. Freeze. Tear away cup to eat.

Dried banana chunks. Slice bananas into ¾-inch-thick slices. If desired, roll in chopped nuts. Place on baking sheet in 150°F oven with oven door open about 2 inches. Dry until shriveled, or about 12 hours.

Activities for Older Children (Grades 4–5)

Fruit Science

On a table, place three or four different varieties of apples. In front of each kind, place a label with the name of it. Children read the names and describe and compare the varieties. Give the children thin slices of the varieties to name, taste, and compare. Then, have them research facts about apples: uses and food value, growth, and environment, etc. Make a special dessert or salad using the apples. Children taste, describe, and enjoy.

Eggs

Read *Green Eggs and Ham* by Dr. Seuss (1976). Have the class try to state the moral of the story as succinctly as possible. The moral might be stated: "You never know if you'll like a new food until you try it" or "Try it, you'll like it." Make your own green eggs and ham.

Discuss with students purchasing environmentally sound egg cartons. Molded pulp cartons are generally made from 100 percent recycled paper. That makes these a better choice than polystyrene egg cartons. Polystyrene is not recycled, nor is it biodegradable.

Have students use their imaginations by drawing a picture of a food using eggs in the recipe. Encourage students to draw the picture so that the food looks interesting or fun to them. Students may wish to write a paragraph to go with their egg-recipe pictures.

National Popcorn Month

October is National Popcorn Month and a good time to examine this popular food. Visit http://www.popcorn.org for the history of popcorn, information about its nutritional value, and recipes using it. To help students practice estimation skills, pour some unpopped kernels into one glass jar and popped corn in another. How many kernels are in each? Make a Venn diagram comparing popcorn to regular kernel corn.

Food from Animals and Plants

Have students draw or cut out pictures to make a farm scene of plants and animals we eat. Have them add some plants and animals we do not eat.

Ask students to think about the grocery store. Are products from plants and animals sold together in one department or are they in separate departments? Students should distinguish produce departments from meat/deli and dairy departments. Aisles in the middle of the stores are often combinations of plant and animal products.

Polyvinyl chloride (PVC) is a huge contributor to environmental pollution. Supermarkets package their meat, fish, and poultry in polystyrene trays and then wrap them in PVC wrap. But the deli counter will cut meat and wrap it in freezer wrap or molded pulp trays, which are better. Have students offer suggestions for alternative ways to buy and package meat.

Raising Raisins

Wash a large bunch of green grapes. Remove them from the stem and weigh the grapes carefully. Record the date and weight. Place the grapes on a cooling rack and cover them with a kitchen towel. Observe and record changes in appearance and weight over time. What is the percent of weight loss after one week? Two weeks? What factors can affect the dehydration process?

Canned Food Values

Have students bring in cans of vegetables. Sort the cans by nutritional content (vitamins, proteins, calories, sodium). Compare that data with the nutritional value of fresh vegetables. When the project is completed, donate the cans to a local food collection drive.

Fast Food Actions

This game is basically a pantomime relay race. Divide the group into three or four teams, standing along a single-file line, so that there are three or four columns of children facing the leader. The first person from each line comes up to the leader and receives a word (whispered in the ear), connected to a certain, announced topic. For example, if the topic is fast food, the person may receive the words "French fries" or "pizza" as their word/s. The person must then run back to their line and act out their word. As soon as someone in their line correctly guesses the word, the "actor" moves to the end of their line and the person at the front runs up to get a new word. The game continues until all teams have rotated through completely. Suggested topics include: Things found in the kitchen, things in school, jobs, occupations, movies, books, etc.

Food and the Media

The last week of April is National Library Week. Challenge students to read a book about foods or food groups.

Provide newspapers and magazines with food advertisements. Have students cut out the ads and put them into food groups. Use food advertisements and have students "stop and think." (See the rhyme in the next paragraph.) Evaluate foods by having students respond to a series of questions related to the food groups.

Make a poster or bulletin board with the "Eating Advice" rhyme—"Eating, keep repeating, stop and think, will this help me grow?" Refer to this rhyme throughout any nutrition activities.

Food Groups

Ask students to generate a list of typical foods eaten at breakfast. Then have them write one breakfast menu. Count the number of servings from the bread, fruit, vegetable, meat, and milk groups. Knowing how many servings of each food group is recommended for a day, have the students subtract the breakfast servings to determine the food to eat the rest of the day.

After lunch, have students determine how many servings from each food group have been consumed. How many servings need to be consumed at supper in order to meet food requirements?

Internet Experiences and Cooking

Children in the middle elementary levels can explore many food ideas on the Internet. For example, they can learn when the ice cream cone was patented at http://www.abcteach.com/. Click on "Theme Units," then on "Fun/Kids," and then on "Ice Cream."

Students can learn a multitude of facts about apples and Johnny Appleseed at http://www.educationworld.com/. Type "apples" in the Search box.

Chocolate Day is another fun food concept children will learn about at http://www.theteacherscorner.net/. Under "Thematic Units," click on "Unit Index," then click on "Chocolate." In fact, you can make chocolate the topic of many more Internet experiences for children. Here are some more ideas.

- Visit http://www.aphrodite-chocolates.co.uk/history_chocolate.htm with your class to learn about Xocolatl and to unlock the secrets of this beverage once reserved for Aztec warriors and nobility.

- Discover the different kinds of chocolate candy the Mars company makes when you and your students visit http://www.mars.com/. What other products does Mars make? Why do you think they make such a variety of foods?

- Teach your students about cacao—the source of chocolate—when you visit "The Sweet Science of Chocolate" at http://www.exploratorium.edu. Type "chocolate" in the Search box. Kids can find out about chocolate's importance to early Americans.

- Find out with your class what the Ms stand for in M&Ms candy by going to http://goodbyemag.com/. Under 1999, click on "July–August," then click on "Forrest Mars, Candy Man." You can also click on "Vernon: Global M&Ms." Why did these two men create M&Ms in the first place? How has their product changed over the years?

- Take a video tour of a chocolate factory with your class and follow a chocolate bean until it becomes part of a chocolate bar when you visit Exploratorium magazine at http://www.exploratorium.edu/. Type "chocolate" in Search box.

- Visit http://virtualchocolate.com/ and have your students send virtual postcards of "chocolatey" greetings to friends. They can also read chocolate quotes, download chocolate pictures for their computer screens, and write their own chocolate quote or comment.

Chapter Review

1. Name several ways in which food activities help children learn information.

2. Name several skills that develop from activities with foods.

3. Decide which of the following statements are true.
   a. Teachers should give detailed directions to children during food activities.
   b. Children should work at their own pace.
   c. Food activities must be very easy so that no child feels challenged.
   d. Food activities should be varied.
   e. Children should work with new kinds of foods—things they have never tasted before.
   f. The end product is all that counts in food activities.
   g. Foods used in food activities should be inexpensive, if possible.
   h. Children must be warned never to throw foods away.
   i. Food activities should always be done in a kitchen.
   j. Food activities can sometimes be done in groups.

4. Decide which of the following statements are true or false.
   a. Research shows that human infants must learn to prefer sweet over sour.
   b. The average American consumes about 104 pounds of sugar per year.
   c. To avoid cavities, it is essential to eliminate all fructose from the diet.
   d. To avoid cavities, children should brush within 50 minutes after eating.
   e. The best way to reduce obesity is to limit empty calories.
   f. Empty calories are foods that are low in calories but high in protein.
   g. Hidden sugars are found in things like catsup, hotdogs, pork and beans, and canned vegetables.
   h. The most common form of sucrose is milk sugar or lactose.
   i. Approximately 12% of a young child's caloric intake comes from snacks.
   j. The major cause of childhood obesity is inherited genes.

5. Discuss some ways to prevent childhood obesity.

References

American Academy of Pediatrics. (2001). *AAP warns parents and pediatricians that fruit juice is not always the healthiest choice.* Online at http://www.aap.org/advocacy/archives/mayjuice.htm

American Dental Association (ADA). (2007). *Joint Report of the American Dental Council on Access, Prevention and Interprofessional Relations and Council on Scientific Affairs to the House of Delegates: Response to Resolution 73H-200,* October, 2001. http://www.ada.org/prof/resources/topics/topics_softdrinks.pdf

Brenner, J. G. (2000). *The emperors of chocolate,* New York: Broadway.

Center for Disease Control (CDC). (2009). *National Center for Chronic Disease Prevention and Health Promotion.* http://www.cdc.gov/healthyyouth/nutrition/facts.htm

Center for Disease Control (CDC). (2008). *Youth Risk Behavior Surveillance—U.S. 2007.* Morbidity and Mortality Atlanta, GA: Weekly Report, *57*(SS-05), 1–131.

de Paola, T. (1992). *Jamie O'Rourke and the big potato.* New York: Scholastic.

Ehlert, L. (1990). *Growing vegetable soup.* New York: Harcourt Brace.

Harvard Public Health NOW. (2009). *Nutrition experts seek to stem American addiction to sugary drinks.* http://www.hsph.harvard.edu

Hendricks, K., Briefel, R., Novak, T., & Ziegler, P. (2003). Maternal and child characteristics associated with infant and toddler feeding. Supplement to *Journal of the American Dietetic Association, 106*(Suppl. 1), S135-S148.

Kimmerle, B. (2003). *Candy: The sweet history.* Tigard, OR: Collector's Press.

Library of Medicine and National Institute of Health. (2006). *Feeding Infants and Toddlers (FITS) Study: What foods are infants and toddlers eating?* Online at http://www.pubmed.gov

McDonald, M. (1996). *The potato man.* Chicago: Children's Press.

Mennella, J. A., & Beauchamp, G. K. (1998). Early flavor experience: Research update. *Nutrition Reviews, 56*(7), 205–211.

Miller, S. A., Taveras, E. M., Rifas-Shiman, S. L., & Gillman, M. V. (2008). Association between television and poor diet quality in young children. *International Journal of Pediatric Obesity, 3*(3), 168–176.

National Association for Sport and Physical Education. (2003). *National standards for physical education* (2nd ed.). Reston, VA: Author.

National Center for Chronic Disease Prevention and Health Promotion. http://www.cdc.gov/healthyyouth/nutrition/facts.htm)

Nelson, J. (1990). *Neighborhood soup.* New York: Modern Curriculum Books.

Ogden, C. L., Carroll, M. D., Curtin, L. R., McDowell, M. A., Tabak, C. J., & Flegal, K. M. (2006). Prevalence of overweight and obesity in the U.S. 1999–2004. *Journal of the American Medical Association, 295,* 1549–1555.

Parents Magazine. (2009, March). Keep produce fresher. In *Your Child: Health,* 36.

PubMed. (2006). *Feeding Infants and Toddlers Study (FITS): What foods are infants and toddlers eating?* Online at http://www.ubmed.gov. A service of the National Library of Medicine and National Institute of Health.

Rey, M. (1997). *Pretzel.* Boston: Houghton Mifflin.

Richardson, T. (2003). *Sweets: A history of candy.* New York: Bloomsbury USA.

Seuss, D. (1976). *Green eggs and ham.* New York: Random House.

Solomon, C. G. (2005, November). Obesity and mortality: A review of the epidemiologic data. *American Journal of Clinical Nutrition,* 13–20.

Additional Readings

Appleton, N., & Jacobs. G. M. (2009). *Suicide by sugar: A startling look at our #1 national addiction.* Garden City Park, NY: Square One Publishers.

Haas, E. M., & James, P. (2009). *More vegetables, please!: Over 100 easy and delicious recipes for eating healthy foods each and every day.* Oakland, CA: New Harbinger Publications.

Holford, P. (2009). *Optimum nutrition for the mind.* Chicago, IL: ReadHowYouWant.

Karmel, A. (2010). *Top 100 finger foods: 100 recipes for a healthy, happy child.* New York: Atria.

Palmer, S. M., Salisbury-Glennon, J., Shannon, D., & Struempler, B. (2009). School gardens: An experiential learning approach for a nutrition education program to increase fruit and vegetable knowledge, preference and consumption among 2nd grade students. *Journal of Nutrition Education and Behavior, 41*(3), 212–217.

Parizkova, J. (2009). *Nutrition, physical activity, and health in early life* (2nd ed.). Danvers, MA: CRC.

Page, R., Montgomery, K., Ponder, A., & Richard, A. (2008). Targeting children in the cereal aisle: Promotional techniques and content features on ready-to-eat cereal product packaging. *American Journal of Health Education, 39*(5), 272–282.

Parker, C. G. (2009). *Diet quality of American young children.* Hauppauge, NY: Nova Science Publishers.

Sorte, J., Daeschel, I., & Amador, C. (2010). *Nutrition, health and safety for young children: Promoting wellness.* Upper Saddle River, NJ: Prentice Hall.

Whitacre, P. T., & Burns, A. C. (Eds.). (2009). *Community perspectives on obesity prevention in children: Workshop Summary.* Washington, DC: Institute of Medicine.

Software for Children

Arianna's Nutrition Expedition, grades 3–4

Arthur's Adventures With D.W., ages 3–7

Bobbin's Quest, ages 6 and up

Burger Island, ages 6 and up

Burger Shop, ages 6 and up

Chocolatier, ages 6 and up

Cloudy With a Chance of Meatballs, ages 6 and up

Diner Dash: Flo on the Go, ages 9 and up

Farm Frenzy Pizza Party, ages 6 and up

Fruit Lockers 2: The Enchanting Island, ages 6 and up

Green Valley, ages 6 and up

Harvest Moon: Frantic Farming, ages 6 and up

Harvest Moon: My Little Shop, ages 6 and up

Jessica's Cupcake Café, ages 6 and up

M & M's Adventure, ages 5 and up

M & M's Beach Party, ages 5 and up

Meriendas Saludables/Healthy Snacks, preschool–grade 2

Mr. Potatoe Saves Veggie Valley, ages 3–7

Noteniks, ages 3–8

Scoops, ages 3–6

Sponge Bob vs. The Big One: Beach Party Cook-Off, ages 6 and up

Sushi Academy, ages 6 and up

The Mammoth Food Dig, grade 4 and up

The Munchables, ages 6 and up

Helpful Websites

Nutrition and Environmental Resources, http://www.TeachFree.com
This site features current nutrition and environmental education for K through grade 12, including teaching kits, student masters for classroom instruction, and more than a dozen hot links. Sponsored by the National Cattlemen's Beef Association.

Fast Food Facts, http://www.foodfacts.info/
This website allows users to search the nutritional analysis of favorite fast foods.

Nutrition and Weight Management, http://www.caloriecontrol.org
Calorie Control Council's website provides timely information on low-calorie and reduced-fat foods and beverages, weight management, physical activity, and healthy eating including recipes.

Shape Up America, http://www.shapeup.org
This organization has a new support center on the Internet to assist consumers in individualized weight management. Developed in consultation with experts in behavior modification, nutrition, and physical activity, the center provides weight control help on a 24-hour basis.

U.S. Dept. of Agriculture, http://www.usda.gov/
U.S.D.A. has developed a Food Guide Pyramid for young children. This pyramid provides educational messages that focus on children's food preferences and nutrition requirements. The key point of the pyramid is to eat a variety of foods. An accompanying booklet, "Tips for Using the Food Guide Pyramid for Young Children 2–6 Years Old," is available for teachers and parents at their website.

National Dairy Council, http://www.dairyinfo.com
Food and Nutrition Information Education Resources Center, http://www.nalusda.gov/
Click on Education and Outreach.

Kids Health, http://www.kidshealth.org
This is an excellent source for kid-friendly, healthful snacks.

American Heart Association, http://www.americanheart.org
Visit this site for information on children and heart health.

Apples, http://www.manatee.k12.fl.us/sites/elementary/samoset/gr2appleindex.htm
This site has a great variety of information about apples, including interactive, online quizzes and lots of yummy apple fun.

Administration for Children and Families, http://www.acf.hhs.gov/
This is a Web directory specifically for teachers that offers activities, lesson plans, and snack ideas and is searchable by age group.

Popcorn!, http://www.popcorn.org/
This site offers information on popcorn, its history, games, trivia, arts and crafts, reading, math, science, and health lesson plans.

First Gov for Kids, http://www.kids.gov/
This website contains links to interactive games, news just for kids, music, and much more.

U.S. Food and Drug Administration—For Kids, Teens and Educators, http://www.cfsan.fda. gov/~dms/educate.html
This site provides a wealth of information including food safety, online games, and more.

Spatulatta: Cooking 4 Kids Online, http://www. spatulatta.com
Site includes hundreds of video recipes featuring healthy snacks, information about cooking utensils and supplies, and lessons in cooking basics.

Meals Matter, http://www.mealsmatter.org/cookingForFamily/Activities/index.aspx
This site offers activities, recipes, and a food pyramid game.

The Game Closet, http://www.kidshealth.org/kid/ closet
This site features games and activities to help children explore health and the human body.

University of Illinois Extension, Food for Thought, http://urban.ext.illinois.edu/foodforthought/
Visit this site for fun activities with food.

Zero to Three, http://www.zerotothree.com
This site features research articles on obesity in young children.

For additional creative activity resources, visit our website at www.Cengage.com/login

Creative Social Studies

OBJECTIVES

After studying this chapter, you should be able to:

1. Describe some of the first things a young child learns about him-or herself in a social sense.

2. Discuss how to use appropriate activities involving a child's name, voice, and personal appearance.

3. Discuss the importance of teaching about peace in the early childhood program.

4. Discuss personal celebrations.

5. Discuss ways to include information on community workers in social studies learning experiences.

6. Describe some points to remember in planning field trips for young children.

As we begin this chapter on social studies, consider these two examples of young children in social situations.

Situation 1

Kim is waiting at home for her son Billy, who is playing next door. When he arrives 20 minutes later than scheduled, she asks what happened. "Well, Mom," he begins in a grown-up fashion, "Dao's doll broke and I wanted to help her."

"I didn't know you knew how to fix dolls" is his mother's somewhat surprised reaction.

"Oh no, Mom. I *don't* know how. I just stayed to help her cry."

Situation 2

Greg and Marc are building together with blocks. Marc gets angry because Greg takes a block from him. They fight. The teacher intervenes and talks with Marc about using words instead of fists. She tells him to try talking to Greg: Instead of hitting him, tell Greg what was making him angry. Finally, believing she has made her point, she asks Marc, "Now, what would you like to do?"

Marc answers without hesitation, "Hit him!" And he does!

These incidents, while a bit amusing to the adults involved, both demonstrate the funny, unpredictable nature of young children in social settings. They also illustrate clearly the fact that learning to be part of a social group is not something that is natural or inborn in human beings. Young children, like those mentioned, often react in a socially unpredictable way by their very spontaneous reactions to life. Yet young children can be very sensitive to the feelings of others, even though they are direct and uninhibited in

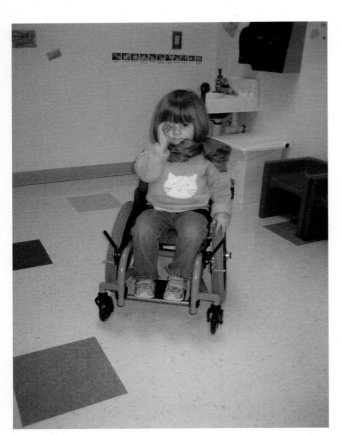

FIGURE 22-1 • Many young children in the early childhood program are dealing with emotional changes as they make the transition from home to preschool.

many situations. The fact is that learning about oneself, about others, and how to act with others is a long process.

Social studies is the study of human beings in their environment and of the concepts, skills, and attitudes that are needed in order to become social beings. Both the content and the processes of social studies can be integrated into activities in which even very young children can participate. As boys and girls reenact the roles of adults known to them, as they build houses, farms, airports, stores, and parks that they have seen or dramatize past experiences that have special meaning for them, they learn the content of social studies. As children become aware of community services such as fire and police protection or library and post office facilities, they incorporate them into their play.

Social studies are an important part of a child's education; they help the child understand the complex world in which he or she lives and enable him or her to be productive and happy within society's framework. Socially, children in the early childhood years

are just coming into touch with their own feelings. Some children are so young they are just learning the names for these feelings and barely beginning to understand their meanings. Others are dealing with emotional changes as they make the transition from preschool to elementary school. Still others are moving from early to middle childhood and experiencing the many emotional adjustments this entails. Guiding young children in their developing understanding of their own and others' emotions is a highly sensitive, challenging part of the teacher's job. Adults are most instrumental in helping young children deal with their feelings and those of others. To do this, adults must be able to deal with their own feelings, too.

Consider your own emotions for a moment and your own early childhood experiences. Think about all the changes you've come through to get you to the point you are now in your life. Change is inevitable in both your life and the lives of young children.

How do you feel about change? Do you look forward to the future, or do you hold on to the past? Do you accept or fight change? Does your view of the life cycle include both an appreciation for what has been and excitement about what might be?

Your personal approach to change has a direct effect on your relationship with young children. If you are open to change yourself, you won't shy away from their concerns about growth and development or their questions about death and aging. Your attitude toward change is conveyed in a healthy acceptance of your own life and all the changes, emotions, and challenges it brings. With this approach, teaching young children social studies concepts will be a joy for you and the children.

Preschoolers and Social Studies

Social studies have not traditionally been part of the preschool curriculum. In part, this is because the disciplines of social studies—history, geography, economics, and civics—are considered too abstract for preschoolers. But the precursors of social studies are covered in early childhood curricula in more concrete ways. Temporal awareness (history precursor; understanding the time sequence in the daily routine), spatial knowledge (geography precursor; making simple maps of familiar places), and number sense (economics precursor; playing store) are all part of the preschool curriculum. In fact, the National Association for the Education of Young Children (NAEYC) includes in its accreditation criteria socially minded traits ("understanding ourselves, our communities, and the world"; NAEYC, 2005, 2.63 to 2.75). Most preschool teachers are very aware their children are developing basic concepts about community, justice, and democracy as they learn to function as members of a social group in preschool.

Historical concepts such as "long ago" or "far in the future" have little meaning for young children, whose ideas about time do not verge far from the here and now (or the near past and immediate future). However, storytelling can introduce preschoolers to the ideas of continuity and change, similarity and difference. Young children who are beginning to sort and classify can divide time in a "binary" way ("now" and "not now") and thus comprehend that stories about history take place at a time that is "not now." Preschoolers are also interested in and capable of comparing the similarities and differences of their experiences with people in other eras. For example, four-year-olds can try to imagine how people might communicate if they didn't have telephones (Epstein, 2009).

With regard to geography, another one of the disciplines of social studies is a field of study that enables us to find answers to questions about the world around us—about where things are and how and why they got there. With young children, spatial awareness develops early and children are naturally inquisitive about the places where they live and learn. Children as young as three spontaneously draw or build maps and can understand and use them quite proficiently in the context of their personal knowledge and experience. Learning to orient oneself in space and comparing one's own location and viewpoint to that of others is a cognitive process preschoolers are able to achieve.

Social studies can thus be relevant in preschool if it is approached through such direct experiences (Epstein, 2009).

National Council for the Social Studies—National Standards

Unlike professional educator groups in literacy and mathematics, the National Council for Social Studies (NCSS) does not have early childhood standards for preschoolers. The National Social Studies standards begin at kindergarten and continue up to and including grade 12. The National Council for the Social Studies (NCSS) identified **10 thematic strands**

1. Culture
2. Time, continuity, and change
3. People, places, and environments
4. Individual development and identity
5. Individuals, groups, and institutions
6. Power, authority, and governance
7. Production, distribution, and consumption
8. Science, technology, and society
9. Global connections
10. Civic ideals and practices

FIGURE 22-2 • The 10 thematic strands of social studies.

of social studies in which all children (K–12) should have learning experiences. These 10 themes were developed from a definition that described the social studies as "the integrated study of the social studies and humanities to promote civic competence" (NCSS, 1994, p. 3).

The themes point to a fundamental knowledge drawn from many subjects and most heavily from these social sciences: anthropology, archaeology, economics, geography, history, law, philosophy, political science, psychology, religion, and sociology. The first seven thematic strands are social science discipline oriented and the remaining three are meant to be multidisciplinary.

Each of the themes derives meaning from one or more of these subjects. The 10 strands are listed in Figure 22–2. The 10 themes are meant to serve as a framework for social studies curriculum planning. This chapter will discuss several of these themes as they relate to our discussion of the social studies curriculum. The reader is referred to the Online Companion for resources with more detailed, in-depth coverage of these 10 social studies thematic strands and their application in the curriculum.

Let us now look at general social characteristics of children at various age levels in the early childhood program.

Social Characteristics

While it is impossible to predict with any certainty the developmental pattern of any individual, there are general characteristics common to age groups. It is helpful to have some general idea of what type of social characteristics to expect at various age levels. The following is a summary of age-level social characteristics.

FIGURE 22-3 • In the early childhood program, young children are learning about their world.

Preschool and kindergarten. Socially at this age level, friendships are usually limited to one or two "best" friends, but these may change frequently. Play groups are not too well organized and tend to change often. Although quarrels are frequent, they tend to be of short duration. There is great pleasure in dramatic play and beginning awareness of sex roles.

Emotional development is at a volatile stage—emotions are expressed freely and outbursts of anger are common. A vivid imagination frequently leads to grossly exaggerated fears. Competition for adult affection breeds jealousy. Mentally, students are developing rapidly in the acquisition of language. They enjoy talking to each other and in front of groups. Imagination and fantasy are at their peak.

Primary grades (6–9 years). Although friendship patterns are still likely to be characterized by "best friends," greater selectivity is now evident in the choice of friends. Games are more organized, but there is great emphasis on "rules." Quarrels are still frequent as are physical aggression, competition, and boasting. Although the difference in interests of boys and girls becomes more pronounced at this age, there is great variation in behavior from one classroom to another because of influences exerted by teachers.

Emotionally, children become very sensitive during this period. Criticism, ridicule, and failure can be devastating. Despite their own sensitivity, they are quick to hurt others. Generally, students are eager to please the teacher and want to do well in school, for which reasons they require frequent praise.

Eagerness to learn is common to this age group. Learning occurs primarily through concrete manipulation of materials. Eagerness to talk is still evident and there is much experimentation with language—including obscene language. Concepts of reciprocity, fairness, and right and wrong develop during this period.

Elementary grades (9–12 years). Peer groups begin to replace adults as sources of behavior standards and the recognition of achievement. Interests become more sharply different between the sexes—frequently resulting in "battles" between them for recognition and achievement, as well as the exchange of insults. Team games become more popular, along with class spirit. Crushes and hero worship are common.

This is the period when the conflict between adults and the group code begins to emerge. Instead of a rigid following of rules, youngsters at this age begin to understand the need for exceptions. Frequently they set very high standards for themselves—sometimes

FIGURE 22-4 • Young children form close bonds with adults outside the home in the early childhood program.

unrealistic standards—hence, feelings of frustration are common. While the desire for independence grows, the need for adult support is still strong—therefore unpredictable behavior often results. Children at this age can behave in a very "grown-up" way one minute and revert to more "childish" behavior the next. Curiosity remains strong at this age.

With these social developmental characteristics in mind, let us now look at how the early childhood program can accommodate both developmental levels and the social studies themes/standards.

Learning About One's World

A child's universe begins with himself or herself, extends to his or her family, and then to the larger community. The development of a child's self-concept—awareness of self—is the important beginning point in social studies for young children.

To know oneself in a social sense involves learning such things as one's name, one's ethnic background, one's family grouping, and occupations in one's family. In the early childhood years, learning about oneself is at a basic level—that is, young children are learning about how their lives fit into the larger social group.

Children learn about where they live—in a house, an apartment, or a condominium—and how it is like and unlike the residences of their peers. They learn the similarities and differences among families in form, style of living, and values.

Those who work with young children from preschool through the early and later elementary years can help them discover and appreciate their own uniqueness by beginning with a positive acceptance of each child.

In the early childhood years, young children need opportunities to live important experiences, to learn in an active way.

The following sections contain suggestions for including the thematic strands of social studies in the curriculum.

Individual Development and Identity (Thematic Strand #4)

Self-awareness—How Do I Look?

A positive awareness and acceptance of one's own appearance is part of the social aspect of learning "Who am I?" In the room, for example, a full-length

FIGURE 22-5 • In the early childhood program, children learn to accept their strengths and weaknesses.

mirror in a safe but clearly visible place at child level is one way for children to see themselves and each other. Some children have few opportunities to see their reflections because mirrors in their homes are too high. Providing an unbreakable hand mirror in the room is another way to encourage children to see themselves. Magnifying makeup mirrors also produce interesting reactions from children when they see their enlarged images.

The following suggested activities are designed to develop a young child's awareness and appreciation of the uniqueness of his or her physical appearance.

- Use an unbreakable mirror to bring out the idea that we are more alike than different. Discuss color, size, and shape of eyes, hair, nose, mouth, ears, etc. Have children draw pictures of their faces. Mount these on a low board and label them with children's names.
- Supply children with pictures of people with missing body parts. Have children describe what part is missing.

- Play the game "Policeman, Where Is My Child?" One child is the policeman, another the parent. The parent describes the physical appearance of the missing child (dress, hair, eyes). All children become involved as they look at themselves to see if they're being described. The policeman tries to guess which child in the room belongs to the parent.
- In the art center, keep available an array of found materials for making dress-up accessories such as jewelry, hats, or masks.
- Trace the shape of children's bodies as they lie down on large sheets of paper. Children can dress these life-sized figures with fabric, felt, yarn, buttons, beads, and any other found materials that interest them.
- Offer finger paint or water-based ink for making handprints and footprints.
- Provide plaster of Paris for making molds of hands.
- Encourage older children to draw self-portraits.
- Make shadow silhouettes of older children. In direct sunlight, have the child stand on a sheet of paper large enough to contain an outline of his shadow. Draw around his or her shadow on paper. Compare drawings of shadows made in the morning, at noon, and later in the day.

Additional activities are at the end of this chapter.

Learning Names

One of the first social learnings of a young child is the recognition of his or her own name. In the early childhood program, this recognition is further developed by

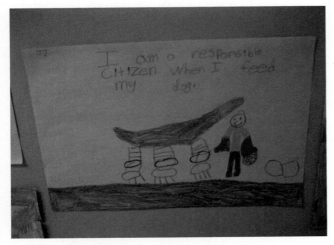

FIGURE 22-6 • A young child's drawing on the topic "When I am a responsible citizen."

teachers' and peers' recognition of this name. This basic learning is directly related to a child's individual identity.

Make it a point to concentrate on individual names of children. Avoid using endearments such as "honey," "sweetie," and "sugar." Instead, use the child's first name, and alternately use the child's first and last name. This will further develop children's self-knowledge as well as help them appreciate their own uniqueness. It also helps children learn each other's full names. The following strategies are suggested in your work with young children to help focus on the uniqueness of each child.

Strategies for Focusing on Each Child's Uniqueness

- Write a child's name on his or her work in the upper left-hand corner to teach the left-to-right sequence. While writing the child's name, say it. This provides an auditory and visual model.
- At transition times, call the child by name to go to another activity or to tell the teacher which activity he or she wants to go to. "Johnny Jones, you may ride the tricycle today. Sally Smith, you may clean off the table."
- Instruct children to go tell another child something. "Jaime, please tell Colleen it is time to come inside." Here the child is not only hearing his name, he is beginning to be able to say the other child's name and a sentence as he follows the teacher's direction.
- When children are in a group for a story, go around the group and say each child's name. Let the other children, as a group, say the child's name as you place your hand in front of the child.
- Encourage children to draw, paint, or model themselves and their families in personally meaningful ways: Me and My Best Friend; I Am Playing with My Favorite Toy; I Am Helping at My House; My Family at Dinner Time; My Family Went to . . . ; and My Wish. These renditions can be used for cooperative murals, booklets, and jigsaw puzzles.
- Provide a variety of media and found materials in the art center for children to make puppets of themselves or their families.

Additional activities are at the end of this chapter.

Concentrating on the child's voice, which is as individual as each child's name, is another good way to help develop young children's awareness of their identity. Here are some suggestions on how to actively involve young children in learning that they each have a unique voice.

- Compile a tape of all the members of the class. Discuss how each person has a different voice tone. Have children speak into the tape recorder. Afterward, play back these recordings for the group. Have children listen to the voices and guess whose they are.
- Record children telling their favorite stories (*Goldilocks and the Three Bears*, *Three Billy Goats Gruff*, *Little Red Riding Hood*), emphasizing voice inflections for the different characters.
- Play the game "Who Am I?" One child is in the center of the circle and is "it." "It" tries to guess who says, "Who Am I?" The speaker disguises his or her voice after the children have mastered the game with their natural voices.
- Have children feel objects of various textures. Another day, discuss voices using familiar comparisons. "Is your voice grating? High? Low? Soft? Hard? Scratching?" Have a box or chart of textured objects for the children to feel, such as steel wool, corrugated metal, silk, velvet, cotton puffs, wool, or a small mirror.

Additional activities are at the end of this chapter.

People, Places, and Environments: The Block Center

Learning about people, places, and environments is the third social studies theme in the national standards. The block center is an excellent place for learning about the community and neighborhood. Play models of various members of the family and people from various races, ethnic groups, industries, and professions, as well as small wheel toys with the blocks, all encourage true social play in the block center.

When children play together in the block center, they learn to share, communicate, and resolve conflicts. Children see that cleanup is easier when they cooperate with one another. Building with blocks builds friendships, too, as children create structures together and role play events from daily life or their imaginations. Dramatic play using blocks also helps young children work through important emotional issues. Because there is no right or wrong way to play, building with blocks helps boost a child self-esteem. Knocking down block structures helps children feel powerful and in control.

FIGURE 22-7 • Making friendships is an important part of growing up.

Here are some ways to encourage block play for all children.

- Locate the block and housekeeping areas side by side so children can combine activities.
- Provide props and accessories that appeal to girls as well as boys. Include tools, transportation toys, and uniformed block figures as well as accessories, like scarves, fabric pieces, and carpet samples. Be sure to include bits of colored paper, pencils, crayons, and markers. Family block and animal figures are also appealing to both boys and girls. Be sure to include family block figures of various ethnic groups, and representations of children with special needs.
- Intervene when you observe gender bias. If you hear Sam and Anthony telling Roxanna she can't play with them because they're building a firehouse and girls can't be firemen, let children know that in your room everyone can play with everything that's available. You might teach children to use the term *firefighter* as well as other terms that do not reflect gender bias. Follow up by reading books about people in careers traditionally held by the opposite sex.
- Decorate the block center walls. Hang pictures, photos, posters, and blueprints of buildings, bridges, towers, and roadways. If children enjoy drawing their own pictures of construction sites, hang those up, too. Include pictures of men, women, and children of all races doing a variety of jobs to let children know that blocks and construction are for everyone.

- Include puppets, rocks, flashlights, pulleys, string, and other interesting extras.
- Include toy vehicles of all varieties, such as cars, trucks, airplanes, helicopters, fire engines, ambulances, buses, taxis, and boats.

People in the Community (Thematic Strand #2)

Because a child does not exist in isolation, he or she is dependent on people in the community. Many people provide services for him or her—the police, the bus driver, and the baker, for example. As a child meets people in the community, he or she learns about the many roles people play and tests some of these roles in dramatic play. The child takes a tool kit and goes to fix the telephone. He or she becomes involved in relationships in which adults play varied roles and people depend on each other. He or she passes a firehouse in the neighborhood and sees where the firefighters are stationed. The child goes to the garage with his or her mother and sees the mechanic fix the family car. He

FIGURE 22-8 • Children in elementary grades (9–12 years) grow in their desire for independence yet the need for adult support is still strong.

or she goes to the post office with a family member and mails a letter to Grandmother. Children learn, through everyday experiences such as these, that others help them and they help others.

A good place to begin a discussion about understanding others in the child's world, then, is to learn about people in the child's most immediate environment. This includes the people who serve the school and community. There are many people in the child's immediate environment. It is important to emphasize the importance of all of these individuals. Each member helps to make the whole community where we live and go to school what it is; all jobs are important. The following activities are designed to help develop the idea of the importance of community workers.

Community Workers

- Find out when the garbage is collected at the school. Be there when the truck comes. Talk to the workers about their job, the service they perform, the truck and its operation and care, and possibly how citizens can help get the garbage ready for the collector. Don't overlook the fact that these helpers are also people with personal lives. Children can learn to understand that the men and women in our labor force also have spouses, children, hobbies, pets, and so on, just like the rest of us.
- Follow the preceding procedure for postal workers, grocery store clerks, mechanics, painters, laundry workers, bus drivers, cooks in the cafeteria, and custodians.
- Follow the preceding procedure for professional and semiprofessional workers—secretary, principal, nurse, music teacher, librarian, and others. Such activity should follow careful planning with the children as well as with the people you may visit. Preparing the adults beforehand for the kind of questions they can expect will give them a chance to organize their thinking. Discussing courteous and safe behavior with children is also important. If the people you talk to can be persuaded to visit the classroom informally, the experience will be all the more effective.
- Be a worker. Learn about the world of work by visiting workplaces in the neighborhood. Then children may enjoy acting out what they observed. Costumes for this can be simple, with only a hat, a mask, or an object to carry suggesting the characterization. Some children may want to bring an article of clothing to serve as a costume. Playing

the role of adults may take the form of a parade, a guessing game, pantomime, or play. Such experiences help broaden the child's understanding of life in the local community.

Excursions into the community

Every school is located in a community. You can safely assume that every community has members who care about the well-being of its children and who possess talents, hobbies, and resources that can enrich children's learning experiences.

An excursion into the community may help young children gain new information and clarify other information and can enhance and extend children's experiences. After one trip around the block, a group of five-year-old children built a block barber shop and kept up their dramatic play as barbers for several days. Even the teacher sat in a chair as the children pretended to cut hair using their fingers as scissors.

Often the comment is heard, "Why take children to a fruit and vegetable store when they shop there every week with their parents?" A visit to a store with a teacher and a group of peers is a very different experience from the same trip with mother. When a teacher takes a group to a store, the purpose of the trip is to give the children a specific experience. The event focuses on them and their purposes. When children go to a store with their families, ordinarily they are hurried along, and the child's experience is not the major consideration of the trip. Because the purposes are different on a school excursion, the experience is different.

Any planned excursion should be either an outgrowth of children's experiences or to meet a specific need. A teacher helped a group of children order carrot and radish seeds from a catalog for the school garden. Then they took a trip to the corner mailbox, a meaningful excursion because they were carrying an important letter.

Within the same group of children, needs will differ. For instance, a teacher taking four children to the zoo found that for three of them the short bus trip back and forth was the exciting part of the trip because they had never been on a bus before. For the other child, the bus ride was an everyday event, and the giraffe was the highlight of the trip. When a teacher took two children to a department store to buy burlap for a bulletin board, the ride on the escalator was the event most remembered.

Planning for trips. A teacher needs to do a good bit of planning for a trip. The purpose of a trip is to

FIGURE 22-9 • Learning to dress oneself is an important task for young children.

provide children with firsthand experiences. A child should not only be able to see, hear, and smell but also to touch and taste. A teacher also needs to know the children and their special interests and concerns.

You should not consider any trips until you are certain that you know the children well enough to anticipate any potential disruptive behavior. In many classrooms, some children may become overstimulated by the interruption of their daily routines.

You will need to familiarize yourself with the community in which the school is situated before planning excursions—become familiar with street signs and working people who come and go from the school, shops, business establishments, buildings, and service. Talk with people in the community. As you plan, try to anticipate children's reactions, remembering that you are planning for young children. This means that you will need to keep in mind these basic guidelines in planning all excursions.

- Keep it simple.
- Discuss, read about, and organize play around the places to be visited in advance.

FIGURE 22-10 • Making a topographical map of one's home state is an appropriate social studies activity for older children.

- Encourage close observations while on the outing.
- Give small amounts of information if children are interested.
- Provide time, materials, and enthusiasm for follow-up plans and projects. Visit the Online Guide for a detailed checklist for field trips.

Children are the living messages we send to a time we will not see.

Jewish proverb

Celebrations (Thematic Strand #1)

Personal celebrations. In the life of any child, there are events that deserve celebrations. When a teacher observes that a child, through his or her glee or sadness, is moved by a situation, the experience is worth emphasizing with a small but **personal celebration.** For example, a boy ties his shoes by himself for the first time. For many children, this is a very special

event. The teacher may take time to say, "Great! You did it," or "Show me how you did it!" or "How does it feel to do it all by yourself?" You might want to share a new accomplishment of your own at a time like this: "I just learned how to download my photos onto my computer all by myself!" Share good feelings with children, and a child begins to learn that feelings are important and worth celebrating. When a child ties his or her shoes, the teacher's knowing glance the next day reaffirms the child's positive feelings about himself or herself.

Teaching Young Children About Peace

Preventing conflicts is the work of politics; establishing peace is the work of education.

—Maria Montessori

This quote very simply outlines a very complicated mission for early childhood teachers—teaching about peace. Many years ago (1991), the National Association for the Education of Young Children challenged early childhood teachers to teach peace, reminding us that of all the lessons we hope to teach young children, the ability to act in peace is one of the most important. This continues to be critical in light of the increasing violence in our country, as well as in our schools. The conflicts that seem to be underway in every region of the globe demonstrate the profound need for creating paths to a peaceful and just world. Mahatma Gandhi said that if we are to have real peace in the world, we need to begin with children. Sowing the seeds for peace and justice in classrooms could nurture a new generation of world leaders and ordinary citizens who have a vision of a peaceful and just world and who have both the will and skill to bring this vision to reality (Baker, Martin & Pence, 2008).

However, this is a complicated idea—**teaching peace**—for many reasons. First, many adults define peace by describing what it is not. For now, examine peace in the eyes of a child. In the absence of war and fighting, peace is a time of safety, freedom, and celebration. Peace is the opportunity to play, to make friends, and to create (Lindsay, 2009). Peace is not the absence of conflict, but rather the evidence of resolving differences in a positive way. Another reason peace is such a difficult topic to teach is that it's obvious that most adults have not been able to maintain peace in their own world. Finally, we certainly must ask a basic question: How can we teach young children about peace in a world so filled with strife and conflict?

Many early childhood experts have written about this challenge of teaching young children about peace. To sum up the core idea of these writings, peace begins with a basic attitude made up of trust, respect, and consideration toward everyone. When the attitudes of trust, respect, and consideration are present in the environment, it is a safe place for people to be themselves. In a safe environment, people have a sense that it is acceptable to be unique, it is acceptable to disagree, and it is expected that disputes are settled without hurting one another. Every interaction in a safe environment reflects consideration and respect for individual differences (Baker et al., 2008; Lindsay, 2009).

We can choose to create an environment that teaches children how to live peacefully with one another. In every interaction we have with another person, we can cause hurt or not. It is our choice. It is the responsibility of a teacher to realize that this choice exists and to teach children about their choices. If we realize this, we will choose carefully. Teachers can be "conduits of peace" when they help children make positive and supportive connections with others. Maria Montessori taught us long ago to create peaceful environments where children can make choices within the context of clear limits and a sense of order. When she required children to walk around someone else's mat, she was teaching a simple lesson about respecting others.

If we respect one another, we will not choose to harm each other. In turn, we must help young children understand their choices. For example, an increase in rowdiness results in an increase of people getting hurt. Children must learn to make choices about their style of play, and they must learn that they share responsibility for the results of their actions. They also need to learn that they can choose to stop upsetting behavior in the future, to slow the pace before someone gets hurt.

Strategies for Teaching Peace

Teaching young children about peace begins with the implementation of two simple rules:

1. Don't hurt anybody.
2. Use words to settle problems.

Don't hurt anybody. This is a simple rule—on the surface. Yet, just think of how many ways there are to

FIGURE 22-11 • A treasure map: An activity combining art and social studies.

FIGURE 22-12 • We can choose to create an environment that teaches children how to live peacefully with one another.

hurt other people. Physical blows hurt. But so do unkind words, gestures, teasing, and exclusion. All of these are harmful and can interfere with a child's ability to learn in general, as well as learning how to act in peace.

Promoting Social Interactions Between Preschool Children with Disabilities

As early childhood teachers, we know that promoting interactions between preschool children is important because peer social interactions provide a crucial context for children's development. For example, within social interactions with peers, children develop verbal skills and learn about how to get along with others. However, many young children experience difficulty with peer relations, particularly children with disabilities (McConnell, 2002; Rogers, 2000). Children with disabilities have problems with peer interactions beyond difficulties expected based on developmental levels (Guralnick, 2001). As the field of early childhood education has become more focused on academic issues, there has been concern among early childhood education professionals that this emphasis will result in a lack of attention to other key domains of development, including social development (Kauerz & McMaken, 2004).

For children who have great difficulty interacting with peers, early educators must plan, implement, and monitor interventions to promote social interactions. Peer-related social competence is critical for the integration of children with disabilities in the classroom and community and for children's development (Hollingsworth, 2006).

Although inclusive early childhood settings are associated with increased social interaction for children with disabilities, just having typically developing children in the classroom with additional interventions may not be enough to promote peer interactions (McConnell, 2002) for improving children's social competence (Guralnick, 2001).

The following are some recommendations for setting up the environment to encourage social interactions with children with disabilities.

- Arrange playgroups involving children with and without disabilities or by pairing a child with social interaction difficulties with a child who is socially competent (though not too much above the social level of the first child).
- Keep playgroups small (two to four children).
- Make sure you have toys available that are likely to encourage social interactions (e.g., blocks, housekeeping props).
- Prepare sets of materials around play themes familiar to the children (e.g., post office).
- Have available toys/activities in which children with social interaction difficulties are particularly interested (Hollingsworth, 2006).

Through careful, systematic planning, implementation, and monitoring, early childhood teachers can improve the peer interactions of children, including children with disabilities (McConnell, 2002).

Use words. Disagreements are a natural part of life, and they will occur in the lives of young children. The key to peaceful settlement is to maintain harmony in stressful situations. It is sometimes difficult for a child to take a deep breath and clearly express the feelings of the moment. At stressful times, times of conflict or disagreements, it is important for the teacher to be with the children—but to show, not to tell. Steady the children in whatever way you can. Holding them closely in your arms or on your lap often helps a child gain focus in a stressful situation. Help the child express himself or herself. But don't put words in the child's mouth. And make sure that children in a conflict listen to one another. Asking them to repeat, or retell, what each has said to the other is one way to see if they are listening to each other.

A Teacher's Role

It is not necessary (or possible) for you to find solutions for every child's problems. You need only create an atmosphere in which children can work out their own solutions. It is the teacher's job to give children the tools they need to define and settle differences. Teaching children how to use words instead of actions to express emotions is one of the most important of these tools.

Classrooms are very special places, and they must be focused on the child. In these classrooms, there are many different personalities, different needs, different styles of behavior, and different ethnic and family backgrounds. Common to all these groups is the need to feel safe. Only on this basis can we begin to build a framework of trust and respect. It is within such a

THIS ONE'S for YOU! Google Earth, Literacy, and Geography

Google Earth is a free, 3-dimensional computer model of Earth, available at www.earth.google.com. It allows the viewer to "fly" anywhere on Earth to view satellite imagery, maps, terrain, 3-D buildings, and even explore galaxies. You can explore rich geographical content, save your toured places, and then share them with others.

The Web page Google Earth for Educators (http://www.google.com/educators/p_earth.html) suggests that teachers first practice moving freely around in the virtual environment by changing the viewing angle and position of the globe with a click of the mouse. These views may show geographical or man-made features.

With the current emphasis on literacy, children's literature has become a powerful way to integrate the curriculum in the elementary classroom. Google Earth is a tool for connecting literature from a geographic perspective. Integrating sources of literature with Google Earth is based on the simple idea that stories have settings that can be traced to a specific place. Literature is also routinely used to integrate the social studies with languages. Two examples of literature that could enrich a unit of study on geography are the books *Me on the Map* and *Geography from A to Z*.

Me on the Map by Joan Sweeny is typically used to get students interested in an exploration of maps. Access to Google Earth extends this book lesson beyond the pages of the book. When different map locations are found on Google Earth, students can see "My town, my state, my country and my world." A teacher could also get students involved in using Google Earth at a learning center to locate places in the local community.

Geography from A to Z: A Picture Glossary by Jack Knowlton is a perfect backdrop for a Google Earth lesson that makes a real world connection to a geography vocabulary. Using the conventional globe as a guide, students learn to recognize landforms. With the virtual globe, students learn to recognize the features of satellite imagery to see islands, volcanoes, forests, deserts, and bodies of water. Landform investigations could be extended in a computer lab plan with hands-on practice to locate famous landforms on earth.

The classic scavenger hunt lesson becomes an exciting computer lab activity when students are engaged in "flying" to Google Earth locations based upon clues.

Lesson plan websites provide additional opportunities for adapting lessons for Google Earth.

Geography Skills and Your Town: Go to the National Geographic website at www.nationalgeographic.com and type in the search box "Geography Skills and your Town." In this lesson plan, students use the five themes of geography to explore their town as they learn about towns across the United States. Adding Google Earth to this K–2 lesson plan from National Geographic provides a real-world aspect that makes it meaningful and fun.

Mission Geography: USA, www.nationalgeographic.com/xpeditions/lessons/matrix.html. Students in grades 3 through 5 are engaged in a research project to learn about the culture, history, and geography of the U.S. regions. Since this lesson plan already includes websites for research, adding Google Earth as one of the resources adds layers of learning to the lesson plan. In the lesson, students develop a "travel plan" to visit states in certain regions by highlighting places and characteristics that unify the region.

---

framework that each child has a chance to grow and learn. It is in the preschool class that the teaching of peace must begin. If young children do not learn it from us, will they learn it at all?

Social Studies for Older Children

The main focus of this chapter has been on social studies for children in the early years. Now let us briefly consider social studies for older children. As we have seen, children in the middle and upper elementary levels are capable of more flexible thought. Social studies activities are an excellent avenue for exploring the personal and social changes this age group is experiencing. For example, the social studies standards theme of individual development and identity can provide the basis for many learning opportunities in areas such as peer pressure, conformity, personal identity, self-concept, and social expectations, to name a few.

Art and Social Studies

Studying the work of artists who used their work for social expression and to effect social changes is an excellent social studies activity for older children. Many artists were visual recorders of their times, just as current artists reflect their own 21st-century experiences. The following artists are good examples of this kind of artists from different times in our history. By using the work of these artists, you can introduce students to the history of that period as well as to how these artists' work reflected that time. They can also learn that art as a social statement can be a powerful and effective tool.

Ben Shahn (Sept. 12, 1898–March 14, 1969)
Ben Shahn was a Lithuanian-born American artist best known for his works of social realism. He studied art at City College in New York and at the National Academy of Design. He also studied the art of Henri Matisse, Raoul Dufy, Pablo Picasso, and Paul Klee. He was dissatisfied with the work of these artists, claiming that their work was unoriginal. He eventually outgrew his pursuit of European modern art and instead redirected his efforts toward a realistic style he used to contribute to social dialogue (Kao, 2000). His work reflected social concerns of the time. His antiwar sentiment was reflected in his paintings during World War II. He was also a commercial artist for CBS, *Time, Fortune,* and *Harpers*. His well-known 1965 portrait of Martin Luther King, Jr. appeared on the cover of *Time Magazine*. Despite his growing popularity, he only accepted commissions he felt were of personal or social value. Ben Shahn's social–realist vision informed his approach to art. His examination of the status quo inspired his creative process (Kao, 2000). Although he often explored opposing themes such as modern urban life, organized labor, immigration, and injustice, he did so while maintaining a compassionate tone. He identified himself as a communicative artist. In his work, he intended to inspire social change. You might consider using one or more of the following pieces of his work to use with children:

> *Untitled,* 1932, Houston Street Playground, New York City
> *The Meaning of Social Mural,* 1940–1942, Federal Security Building, Washington, DC
> *For Full Employment after the War, Register-Vote,* 1944, The Museum of Modern Art, New York
> *Age of Anxiety,* 1953, The Joseph H. Hirschhorn Foundation, Inc.

Louise Berliawsky Nevelson (Sept. 23, 1899–April 17, 1988) Louise Berliawsky Nevelson was a Russian-born American artist known for her abstract expressionist "crates" grouped together to form a new creation. She was recognized during her lifetime as one of America's most distinguished artists, and her work continues to inspire contemporary sculptors today. In 1964, Nevelson created *Homage to 6,000,000,* a memorial to the Jews killed in the Holocaust. Once, when she was about to donate a sculpture piece to the Centre Beaubourg in Paris, the French government released a Palestinian terrorist. She compared this action to the "Hitler era." In protest she withdrew the donation of her work to the museum.

You can access the papers of Louise Nevelson (circa 1903–1979) in the Archives of American Art at http://www.aaa.si.edu/collectionsonline/neveloui/. The collection documents the life and work of the sculptor including correspondence, personal business records, writings, scrapbooks, early art work, photographs, interviews, and an extensive amount of printed material. This collection is an excellent source for students interested in the social history of this woman artist.

Romare Bearden (Sept. 11, 1911–March 12, 1988) In the summer of 1963, Romare Bearden, as a member of the New York-based African American artistic collective Spiral, suggested that the group collaborate on a collage to make a statement on the civil rights movement. The March on Washington was to be held that summer, and the group felt a need to speak to this issue. The group didn't take to his suggestion, but Bearden, a rising star in the American art world at the time, wasn't discouraged.

Over the next few months, he created a series of small-scale collages that would serve as his own personal statement on civil rights. He used clippings and snippets from magazines such as *Ebony* and *Life* and produced art that portrayed African American life as never before. These collages captured the sense of those times. When the collage-based paintings were discovered the following year and placed in an exhibition in New York, Romare Bearden, then in his early fifties, was suddenly a major artist.

This artist's social commentary can be seen in the following pieces of his work:

> *Patchwork Quilt,* 1970, Museum of Modern Art, New York
> *Return of the Prodigal Son,* 1967, Albright-Knox Gallery
> *Summertime (collage),* 1967, St. Louis Art Museum

THIS ONE'S for YOU!   Pennies for Peace

A service-learning program of the Central Asia Institute (CAI), Pennies for Peace educates American children about the world beyond their experience and shows them that they can have a positive impact on a global scale, one penny at a time. A penny in the United States is virtually worthless, but in Pakistan and Afghanistan, a penny buys a pencil and opens the door to literacy.

Originally begun by Greg Mortenson, a mountain climber who saw firsthand the need for literacy—especially among girls in Pakistan and Afghanistan—the program supports CAI's mission to provide community-based education, especially for girls.

A fifth-grade education for a girl improved not only the basic indices of health for her and her family, but also spread the value of education within her community. Literacy, for both boys and girls, provides better economic opportunities in the future and helps neutralize the power of extremist leaders.

This program is especially attractive because *only* pennies—no nickels, dimes, quarters, or dollars—are collected, making it possible for all children, including those of very limited means, to participate actively. Classrooms interested in participating should visit www.penniesforpeace.org.

The quilts of Gee's Bend. This group of internationally acclaimed Black quiltmakers creates quilts hailed as "some of the most miraculous works of modern art America has produced" by Michael Kimmelman of the *New York Times*. More than 50 quiltmakers make up the Gee's Bend Collective, owned and operated by the women of Gee's Bend, Alabama. The quiltmakers are all descended from slaves who worked on a plantation located on the Alabama River. Most of these quiltmakers have lived in indigence. Their quilts that once kept families warm inside drafty log cabins now hang inside some of the world's greatest museums. Quilts that were once thought worthless now sell for thousands of dollars. In making their quilts, a new sense of self-respect has evolved in this tightly knit, family-oriented community. You can view samples of these quilts at **http://www.auburn.edu/academic/other/geesbend/explore/catalog/slideshow/index.htm**.

The stories and graphic images of these artists are a powerful way to learn about one of the social studies—American history. Their dedication to social issues of their times is also an excellent example of civics, another part of the discipline of social studies.

Social Studies Theme of Power, Authority and Governance. The social studies theme of power, authority, and governance is an excellent base for developing learning experiences for students about their own individual rights and responsibilities in the increasingly complex social world of which they are a part. For example, students can be asked to develop hypothetical communities in which certain students play different power and authority roles. They can role play enforcing rules when someone breaks one. They can also begin to study power and authority in their local community. Children often understand more about government structure than most adults give them credit for. Teachers can begin to teach the basics of government with field trips to the mayor's and other city centers as appropriate introductions to government. Elections take place at least every other November, and they are excellent opportunities for civic education in the classroom. Rather than avoiding the voting spaces, how much more educational it would be to arrange a visit with election officials while they're in the building, then have a space in the classroom dedicated to the election process. Photographs of people around the world voting, local political campaign materials (from two or more parties), reprinted ballots to be marked or punched, and a ballot box can make up a social studies display in November. Such a display can expand on conversations with guest speakers visiting the class from the League of Women Voters and the city clerk or municipal staff charged with running elections in the local area.

Using the NCSS theme of culture and cultural diversity as a curriculum base, teachers can develop experiences to provide students an in-depth study of the specific aspects of particular cultures in similar and different places, times, conditions, and contexts. Teachers can encourage students to consider the direct and indirect connections between the assumptions, beliefs, and values of a culture. Teachers can help students analyze ways that a people's cultural ideas and actions influence its members. Through such study, students can begin to consider the impact traditions have on a person's thoughts and actions within any particular social group.

Basing learning activities on the 10 social study themes will provide students at this age level many opportunities to explore their complex and changing social world. More activity ideas are found at the end of this chapter.

Summary

Knowing how to be part of a social group is not natural or inborn in human beings. Learning about oneself and others and how to act with others is a long learning process. Social studies are an important part of a child's learning; they help the child understand the complex world in which he or she lives and enable him or her to be productive and happy within a social framework. The social studies of the preschool child must focus on the experiences of the child in his or her immediate environment. In 1994, the NCSS developed 10 thematic strands

in which all children (K–12) should have learning experiences.

Learning about oneself in a social sense includes learning one's name, one's ethnic background, and such things as family grouping and occupations in one's family. In the early childhood program, learning about oneself is at a basic level—that is, young children learn how their lives fit into the larger social group.

Those who work with young children from preschool through the entire period of early childhood can help them discover and appreciate their own uniqueness by beginning with a positive acceptance of each child.

Teaching young children about peace begins with a basic attitude of trust, respect, and consideration toward everyone. Two basic rules make up the basis of teaching about peace: (1) don't hurt anybody, and (2) use words. The United Nations General Assembly has proclaimed the decade 2000–2010 as the International Decade for a Culture of Peace and Nonviolence for the Children of the World. Studying the election process and social activist artists are appropriate social studies concepts for older children.

Key Terms

10 thematic strands of social studies 557
Personal celebration 564
teaching peace 564

Learning Activities

A. Review ways to enhance a child's understanding of self presented in this chapter and then brainstorm several additional strategies for achieving this goal.

B. There are many activities and experiences appropriate for teaching children concepts of self and other people. Think of at least three ideas other than those in this chapter.

C. Prepare a unit plan on one of the following: family, self, or a specific community worker such as a firefighter. For your unit plan, include a section titled *Children's Books* and include stories and other appropriate language arts activities.

D. Child Study
   1. Select three children of different ages (e.g., three, five, and nine years) and ask each separately to describe what fathers and mothers do, what children can or cannot do when they grow up, or what happens when they are afraid. Do not contribute your own opinions until you are sure the children have said all they would like to about the matter.

   2. What changes in ideas do you notice as you listen to children of different ages? Did any of the children have a clear misunderstanding about some aspect of the issue you discussed? If so, how did you respond? How should parents respond when this happens?

E. Observe a dispute between children in an early childhood setting. Record how it was settled. Then compare this method of settlement with the information presented in this chapter on teaching peace. How did the real-life settlement compare? Did it help the children involved learn about peace? Why or why not?

F. Interview an experienced first-, second-, or third-grade teacher. Present that teacher with each of the situations that follow. Then ask her or him to answer the questions for the situation. Write the answers down and compare them. Discuss similarities and differences in the replies.
   Situation 1: Clay ignores his fellow students most of the time. When his teacher tells the class it is time

for finger painting, he grabs as many paint jars as he can. When asked to share these paints, he refuses.

Question 1: In your years as a teacher, have you had children who have behaved like this? Why do you think they do it? What need or needs underlie their behavior?

Question 2: As a general rule, what would you say is the best way to respond to this kind of behavior? Why?

Question 3: What is the worst way to respond? Why?

Situation 2: Anton is a clown. If he's not making faces, he's telling jokes—and he's always disrupting the class. The other children laugh at him, but they don't seem to like him. In the schoolyard, he's generally alone.

Ask the same questions here as in Situation 1.

G. Brainstorm with fellow students on the causes of conflicts and then role play ways to resolve the situation. Look for more about conflict resolution and United Nations peacekeepers at http://www.pbs .org/un/classroom.

Activities for Children

Peace Puppets

Create puppets that encourage children to talk about feelings and solve problems in peaceful ways.

Ask children to think about all the different ways they feel: happy, sad, angry, cranky, excited, and so on. Talk about how the same person can feel different ways at different times. Explain that they are going to make puppets and that they can decide whether their puppet will represent one feeling (and which one) or many feelings.

Provide children with a variety of materials to design their puppets: socks, paper bags, fabric, pom-poms, yarn, felt. (See Chapter 15 for puppet-making ideas.) Ask children to name their puppets. Help them label each one with the feeling or feelings they choose.

Invite children to share their finished puppets with the group. Talk about how these puppets can be used to help people talk about and sort out feelings. For instance, if someone is feeling lonely or afraid, the appropriate puppet(s) can be brought out. If there's an argument, children might enlist the help of a puppet or two to listen to the problem and help them come up with solutions. Work together to decorate a box in which the puppets can be stored. Ask children to suggest a name for the special box—Peace Place, Puppets' Place, or the like.

Playing with Peace Puppets

Seat children in a circle. One child wears one of the newly made puppets on his or her hand. Speaking quietly, ask the child sitting closest to you to create a facial expression that shows a particular emotion. You might ask the child to show sadness, anger, or happiness. The child wearing the puppet will try to "read" the child's facial expression and talk as the puppet about that feeling. "I feel sad because I wanted to go to the store last night and my mom said we couldn't go."

Continue the activity until each child in the group has had a chance to show an emotion or express an emotion as the puppet.

Suggestions for Excursions Appropriate for Young Children

Supermarket. As eager as young children are, they have a limited attention span, so do not try to do too much. Make several trips to the supermarket, each with a different focus. Watch the goods being delivered. Watch the boxes being unpacked and merchandise being stamped. Look at all the different kinds of machines in the store.

Produce department. What are some things displayed on special cardboard or wrapped in individual papers? Why are some things displayed on crushed ice or refrigerated? See if you and the children can name the fruits and vegetables.

Dairy department. What kinds of things are sold here? Why are they kept cold? Where do the various products come from?

Meat department. Watch the butcher cut and package meat. Why is the meat kept cold? Is it cold in the back, too? See how many varieties of meat you can name.

Bakery department. Compare the ovens with ovens at home and the size of the flour sacks with the sacks that you buy. Notice the quantities of baked goods and the process of baking. What kinds of clothes do the bakers wear? Why?

Shoe repair shop. Watch the person make repairs. Try to give the person something that needs fixing. What kinds of machines do they have? What kinds of materials do they use? Try to get some scraps to take back for making collages.

Dry-cleaning shop. What kinds of smells are in the air there? What kind of machine is used for ironing? How does the cleaner know which clothes are yours?

Pet store. What kinds of pets does this store have? Are there any unusual ones? What do the various pets eat? What kinds of houses do they provide for the various pets?

Florist's shop. Visiting this shop is an especially good activity on a cold winter's day when everything outside is barren and bleak. A walk through the greenhouse may bring many questions to mind: Why are the flowers growing inside the greenhouse and not outdoors? What kinds of plants are there? What kinds of smells are there? How does the florist keep cut flowers from dying? Buy a plant and learn how to take care of it. The workroom, where bouquets, baskets of flowers, and corsages are assembled, will be of interest to children.

The police officer and crossing guard. Within walking distance of your school there is probably an intersection or a school where a police officer or crossing guard is on duty. Watch what he or she does. How does he or she tell the vehicles and pedestrians to go? To stop? The children enjoy talking to the officer and getting a good look at his or her uniform. The police station is of interest to the children, too; perhaps the desk sergeant on duty will spend a few minutes visiting with the children. (You will plan this in advance, of course.) He may show children the inside of a police car, the radio, and give them a short safety speech.

Mail delivery. Make arrangements to meet your own letter carrier at your mailbox and then at the nearest pick-up box on the corner to watch him or her gather the mail. Buy a stamp and mail a letter at the post office. Children are not usually allowed in the back of most post offices, but they can see a good deal if they look through the window of the parcel-post counter. Watch the packages being weighed and mailed.

Bus driver (conductor). Sit near the driver of the bus. Watch what he or she does. Look at the uniform.

Fire station. Some fire departments have open-house days. If yours does not, make an appointment for a visit ahead of time. Do not insist that children get on the equipment, even if invited to do so. Climbing on an engine can be a frightening experience for some young children. Usually the child is invited to try on a firefighter's hat, watch a firefighter slide down the pole, and inspect the engine. Find out how the fire alarm works, where the different firefighters stand on the truck, and what each of them does at a fire. Later, look at fire hydrants and fire escapes in buildings. Point out fire doors and fire extinguishers or sprinklers in various buildings.

Library. Take the children to the children's section of the library. Let them browse. Show them that all the books have letters or letters and numbers written on the bindings. Why? Perhaps your library has a storybook time that you can attend. How does the librarian know which book you take out? Check out some books so children can see the procedure.

Sanitation workers. Be aware of the sanitation workers, street sweepers, or snowplow drivers in action and how they are dressed. Why do they wear gloves?

Construction site. What kind of building is going up? What are the girders for? What kinds of machines can you see? What do they do? How do the workers dress? Why?

Repair site. Observe a surface or underground repair site. What is being fixed? What equipment is in use? How are the workers dressed? Why? What is under the street or sidewalk? Where did the rocks and soil come from?

Printing plant or newspaper plant. Call ahead of time and find out if tours are available and when the presses are operating. Remember to bring some paper remnants back for children's artwork.

Field Trip Hint

On any of the above field trips, try color-coding to help make the trip less stressful for chaperones. Write each student's name and number on a tab, using a specific color-coded ink. This way, chaperones only need to look for students wearing their assigned color tags. Then they can put the children in numerical order to make sure all children are accounted for—without having to call out names.

Self-Awareness Activities

Lining Up and Learning

Choose a topic, such as birth dates (with or without the year) and ask the children to line up in order of that topic. Set two points between which the lines should be made and designate which end is, in this case, January 1 and which is December 31. To make the game more challenging (and fun), prohibit speaking. Examples of other topics to line up about could be shoe size, height, favorite color, etc.

Name Toss

For this activity you will need soft balls such as Koosh, Nerf, or tennis balls and enough room for the group to stand in a circle. Start by having the group stand or sit in a circle. Before starting the activity, each child says his/her name once. Using a soft ball, call out someone's name and gently toss the ball to that person, saying "What's up, (name)?" The recipient says, "Thanks, (name of tosser)," then calls out someone else's name and tosses the ball to him/her—thanking the person who tossed the ball. This repeats until the ball gets back to the person who started the activity. Each person gets the ball and tosses it once. Then challenge the group to toss the ball through the same sequence, but faster. The names and thank you's must still happen.

All About Us

This activity centers on the children's heads and faces. Ask them to describe everything that they all have on their heads and faces. Record their responses on chart paper.

Prepare separate sheets of chart paper for each part of the head and face (nose, eyes, ears, mouth, and hair). Tell children that each day they will focus on a different part and discuss their differences and their similarities.

Invite children to begin each investigation by discussing how they all use each body part and how they are all similar: "We all use our eyes to see." Record their responses. Ask children to examine each of their classmates' specific facial features. How are their eyes similar or different? Notice how lips have different shapes. Do ears all look the same? Record children's observations on each chart.

Have children work together to summarize what they learned about their facial features. Have them reflect on why it is special to look different. What would happen if everyone looked the same?

Provide children with a variety of art materials to create a self-portrait. Include flesh-tone markers, crayons, and paper. Encourage them to use a mirror to observe their facial features and to notice the details of their faces. Ask children to describe why they are special. Record their words on a sheet of paper and attach it beneath each self-portrait.

All About Me

- From magazines, children can cut pictures that they like or that remind them of themselves.
- Make up "Guess Who" riddles describing individual children. Suggest clues that reflect the child's positive characteristics.
- Make a set of flash cards or similar cards with pictures of community workers. Children should be encouraged to bring pictures of their parents at their jobs or wearing clothing appropriate for that job. An additional activity could be to collect pictures of tools or items related to various jobs and have children sort them.
- Videotape interviews with community helpers. Children will be especially proud to hear their parents tell about their professions and jobs.
- Have children cut out or tear out pictures from magazines or brochures that show people or families of different ages or cultures having fun or working together. Children can use these to create a collage.
- Keep a supply of pictures of people available for very young children to paste into books. Older children might wish to mount the pictures as a mural on a background they have prepared with other media.

How Do I Look?

- Discuss differences in sex. Ask: "Do girls look different from boys? How? Dresses? Hair? What else? Do men look different from ladies? How? Do they sound different?" If a child brings out the difference in sex organs, accept their comments matter-of-factly.
- Take snapshots of the children, alone or in groups, and mount them on a bulletin board or in a scrapbook with the names of the children printed beneath the pictures. These pictures are an excellent starting point for a discussion about how we all

have the same body parts, even though we all look different. In this and other such activities, emphasize that we are more alike than different. Natural points in such a discussion are color, size, and shape of eyes, hair, nose, mouth, etc.

- On a more personal level, try the following self-study activity to see how you look to the children you work with.

Self-study: How children see you. Select one or two children who are at least four years old. Seat them individually at a table with paper and crayons (or felt-tip pens) and ask them to draw a picture of you. Encourage them to take their time and include as much as they want. When they are finished, give them another sheet of paper and ask them to draw a self-portrait.

When both pictures are completed, cut them out and paste them side by side. First look at each child's drawing of you. What features appear to be most important to the children? Did they overlook any important characteristics, such as a beard, long hair, or glasses? Compare the drawing of you with the self-portrait. How are they similar? How are they different? Is there more detail in your picture or in the self-portrait? Is one bigger than the other? Is there a difference in emotional expression? Do these drawings reveal anything about how these children view themselves and you?

Sharing and Learning About Each Other

Send a note home requesting a baby photograph of each child. Photocopy the baby photograph if families want it returned. Then photograph each child in the class. Cover all pictures with clear Con-Tact® paper to make them more durable.

At group time, have the children share their baby photos. Ask them to describe their picture or ask them questions to encourage discussion. Explain that they will be playing some games with their baby pictures.

Divide the children into two or three small groups, depending on the number of teachers present. Begin by placing all of their current photos face up on the table. Place their baby photos in a pile face down. Ask one child at a time to choose a baby picture and match it with the current photo on the table.

Once children have become familiar with the pairs of the photos, challenge them with a game of Concentration. Mix up all of the photos and place them face down on the table. Invite one child at a time to turn over two photos to find matching sets. If the photographs do not match, turn them over and invite the next child to try. Remove the photographs once the match is found.

Follow-up activity: Make copies of the photos you took for this activity for a class book. Glue each child's picture on the upper left corner of lined story paper. Have the child dictate information about himself or herself: age, birthday, favorite color, favorite food.

Bind all the pages together. Then take a photo of the whole class for the cover of the book. Place the book in the book corner for children to enjoy.

Shoe Game

Everyone takes off one shoe, including teachers! Place all of the shoes in a bag. While sitting in a circle, ask one child at a time to close his or her eyes and pick a shoe out of the bag. The child has to find the person in the circle wearing the matching shoe. When the child comes to the person wearing the matching shoe, he or she must say, "How do you do? Is this your shoe?" and shake hands. The child or adult with the matching shoe will be the next to pick a shoe. Repeat this until everyone has had a turn, and everyone has a matching pair of shoes.

Friendly Faces

During group time, ask children if they know what a portrait is. Tell them that they are going to make a portrait of a classmate. Share some pictures of portraits done by famous artists and discuss the various styles used in each. Portraits from artists like Van Gogh, Rembrandt, Velasquez, Picasso, and Matisse are good examples. Talk about how some portraits may look very lifelike while others may be done in very bright colors or with only a few lines.

Put the names of all children on separate slips of paper and put the slips in a hat. Draw out two slips; that will be the first pair. That pair then draws out two more names for the next pair. Continue drawing out two slips until all the children are in pairs. If you don't have an even number of children, pair a child with a teacher.

Provide children with white drawing paper, large, colored construction paper, pencils, crayons, and markers. Invite one child to sit on a chair within view of a classmate who is doing the drawing. Remind children who are drawing that they should look at their friend as they draw their portrait. The following day, have children who posed for their portraits assume the role of portrait-maker. Mount the portraits onto larger sheets of colored construction paper to create frames for the drawings. Invite children to decorate their frames. Display portraits with enough space below each portrait to add another sheet of paper.

Tell children that they will share something that they think is special about each person in the class. Focus on one or two children each day. Record the comments on one sheet of paper per child. Place these comments underneath each portrait.

Technology and Social Studies

Thanks to technology, we have some powerful new tools that can help us document and tell children's personal stories. Computers, camcorders, tape recorders, and digital cameras are steadily gaining acceptance by more teachers on a regular basis. The following activities use this technology to teach some social studies concepts.

Virtual Fieldtrips

Meet an urban beekeeper, enjoy a harpsichord concert, or witness the blessing of the bikes, all without leaving your computer. Meet Me at the Corner provides short educational tours from a child's point of view via video podcast technology. The site is geared to children ages 7–12, and each episode, from the quirky to the profound, provides suggested readings and curriculum-based follow-up activities. http://meetmeatthecorner.org.

Our Baby Book

Give each child one page or screen and invite families to send in baby pictures and information about their child as a baby. These can be scanned into the computer onto the child's page. Children's voices can be recorded as they talk about what they thought their lives were like when they were babies. Children's drawings, voices, and family photographs can be included in the project.

My Book

With the help of an adult, invite each child to create his or her own e-book about himself or herself, using software such as HyperStudio. Each page or screen can include unique family traditions. Children's drawings can be scanned and their voices recorded as they share their favorite stories. If you do not have access to a software program such as HyperStudio, have children create their drawings on white construction paper and describe their drawings and print their dictations on accompanying pages. Display children's books in the book area where they can be easily shared.

Star of the Week

Designate a special week for each child. During the special week, invite family members to visit the classroom and talk about their family's heritage. As they share special items, document the event with a digital camera. Working with each child and his or her family, create a HyperStudio project about the child or Star of the Week. If a digital camera is not available, you can take pictures with any standard camera and sequence the pictures on construction paper pages to create a Star of the Week memory book for each child.

Family Recipes

Collect family recipes on paper and then type them into any word processor or use HyperStudio or PowerPoint. The pages can be printed and sent home to each family.

Family Happenings

Take digital pictures or video of children's family dances, rituals, or songs. Using software like iMovie or PowerPoint, create a special video for any family night or parent/teacher conference.

Activities for Older Children (Grades 4–5)

Read About Artists

Encourage students to read and find out the following things about an artist of their choice.

- Life of the artist: biographical information such as birth, death marriage, children, and friends
- Who and what most influenced the artist
- Time period in which the artist lived
- Country or countries where the artist lived
- Style in which the artist worked or school of art to which the artist belonged
- Influence the artist had on the world of art (what the artist is best known for)
- Medium(s) the artist used
- A particular work of art the artist did, e.g., the most famous or controversial

Write About Art and Artists

Here is a list of possible writing and art and artist connections for language arts activities:

- Letter to the artist or someone in the picture
- Letter to the curator of a museum to request information about a work of art
- Biographical sketch of the artist
- Report on the customs of the time of the artist
- Report on the clothing styles of the time of the artist
- Story about how the work of art came to be
- Paragraph hypothesizing what the artist would do if he or she were alive today
- Play about the artist's life
- Time line of the artist's work
- TV commercial about the artist and his/her work

An American Adventure, http://www.tenement .org/immigrate

Students travel back to 1916 in "From Ellis Island to Orchard Street," an interactive game from New York's Lower East Side Tenement Museum. Players create a virtual identity and embark on a new life in New York City. Along the way, they make choices about what they will do for money, food, and fun. This video-intensive game is as absorbing as it is informative.

Social Studies Potpourri

Liven up your social studies planning with these short but challenging activities.

- Have students imagine they have just arrived in a new land and need to establish a settlement there. What laws will be necessary? What kind of government would be best? Help them draw up a plan with a list of all peoples' rights.
- The Pilgrims of Plymouth Colony came to North America in search of religious freedom, but is that why all people came? Have students research the other reasons that brought 17th-century colonists to the New World. Search for information about immigrants at http://www.pbs.org/historyofus/.

- Help students understand world populations: How many people are on our planet? Try NOVA's "Global Trends Quiz" at http://www.pbs.org/nova/ worldbalance/ to learn more.
- Have students make a collage of all the things the United States means to them or all the things it might mean to an immigrant. Is the United States a place? Or is it a set of ideas? Is it a set of institutions? Or is it the people—the many ethnic, racial, language, and other groups?
- Show students a copy of the Declaration of Independence (go to http://www.pbs.org/ktca/ liberty/chronicle_subject.html and click on "Defining Documents"). In teams, have them research the following: Who wrote the Declaration? Who signed it first? Do students recognize the names of any signers?
- Have students identify and list the ways immigrant cultures influence American culture by looking at popular elements such as food, music, film, and art. They can find more information at http://www.pbs. org/teachers/connect/resources/2014/preview/. Click on Cultural Riches.
- Go to the library to look at almanacs. Have students look up international signs and symbols. Discuss the necessity of global symbolism. Talk about your school's symbol, if there is one. If not, create a school symbol together. Set up a timeline that can be left up all year. Mark the first day of school; then have students mark significant events, such as holidays, field trips, and report card times. Ask students to write descriptive phrases on the timeline about each event. Keep the timeline updated throughout the year.

African American World for Kids

Challenge your students to participate in an online Concentration-type matching game with famous African Americans as the subject matter, http:// pbskids.org/aaworld/. Participants match drawings of famous people to descriptions of associated events. Some of the famous people included in the four levels of play are Harriet Tubman, Jesse Jackson, Jackie Robinson, Jesse Owens, Toni Morrison, Malcolm X, and Duke Ellington. The site also has an e-card section that allows students to send African American-themed postcards to their friends via e-mail. Finally, there is a question-and-answer section with commentary from students. *African American World for Kids* is a small, focused website that will be useful as a motivational and reinforcement tool for units on African-American history.

World Happenings

World Habitat Day is October 4, a good time for your students to learn how people from other countries live. Take them to http://www.un.org to help them reflect on the living conditions of others. Meet with your librarian to provide books that the children can read about other countries.

Go to the United Nations website (http://www .un.org/pubs/cyberschoolbus) to learn about flags around the world. Make a collection of flags from around the world with which to decorate your classroom.

National and International Treasures

National parks. Divide the class into groups. Have each group research a national park (there are 53 to choose from). Begin online at http://www.nps .gov/parks.html. From there, each group can link to their individual selection. Have students prepare presentations that include visuals such as maps, posters, travel brochures, and the like.

The Taj Mahal. Although not everyone has had the opportunity to visit, many people have heard about India's Taj Mahal. Have students see and read about this monument at the following websites:

http://www.taj-mahal.net
http://www.greatbuildings.com/ (type "Taj Mahal" in the "Name of Building" box)
http://www.galenfrysinger.com (click on "People and Places I Have Visited," then click on "Asia," and then "India")

What does the Taj Mahal look like? How would you describe its style? Which decorative features did you see? What is the purpose of this building?

The Roman Colosseum. People have gathered at the Roman Colosseum throughout history. Students can see what it looks like today at the following sites:

http://www.the-colosseum.net/
http://www.greatbuildings.com/ (type "Roman Colosseum" in "Name of Building" box)

What was the original function of this structure? How has it been used throughout history? Does the Colosseum look different now compared to when it was created? What shapes were used in designing it? Can you think of any modern structures that might have been influenced by the Colosseum?

Art and Social Studies

Updated art. Have students create a modern-day version of an artist's work, one that reflects the current time rather than the time in which it was created. Students can change the background or subjects' dress in their portraits.

Class flags. Have students examine the flags and symbols of countries. Discuss with them how and why these countries use the colors, shapes, designs, materials, and lines that they do. Divide the class into groups to create a class flag to represent what's important about the class. Make fabric, paper, paint, and collage materials available for the design.

Famous people sculptures. Students choose a person they wish to study who has made a significant contribution to history (explorer, president, artist, musician, activist). Have students brainstorm what facts about this person they would like to know. Have students use library and Internet sources to research their subject. They should try to discover details about how the person looked, moved, talked, and dressed, and what she or he ate, valued, achieved, etc.

After researching their subject, students might construct sculptures of that person from papier maché or make a puppet that represents that person (see Chapter 15 for papier maché and puppet making ideas). Students can use their sculptures or puppets to role play and do a presentation for the class. Allow time for questions.

History Makers—Social Studies Theme: Continuity and Change

On the classroom calendar, mark and label the birthdays of Betsy Ross (January 1) and Martin Luther King, Jr. (January 15). Have one-half of the class research Betsy Ross and the other half Dr. King. Have the Ross group present a research fact, and the King group presents a finding for a similar or the same category (e.g., birthplace). Continue the activity until no further similarities can be found.

Freedom—Social Studies Theme: Continuity and Change

Call attention to the anniversary of the Emancipation Proclamation (January 1st). Guide children in finding and considering meanings of *emancipation* and *proclamation.* Help them research the historical actions and decisions associated with the Emancipation Proclamation. Probe for and emphasize reasons the proclamation was needed.

Telephone Book Research—Social Studies Theme: Culture and Cultural Identity

The telephone book can be used as a reference tool for learning about the local community.

Have students study the telephone book. What names are predominant and what might they tell you about early settlers in the area? You might divide the class into groups to consider sources of people's last names—occupation, animal names, colors, and where they live. Encourage students to find information about local industries from the Yellow Pages. Watch for unusual advertising wording; identify state, city, and county resources. Have students seek out information on such topics as zip codes, history of the area, and location of streets.

Regional Crafts—Social Studies Theme: Culture and Continuity

Provide reference materials showing crafts created in your area in the last 100 years. Lead a discussion about how these objects are both functional and beautiful.

Have small groups of students choose one craft that they find especially appealing. Encourage each group to choose a different craft. Have them list questions about the craft. Sample questions follow:

1. How was this (basket) made?
2. How long have people been making these (wooden boxes) by hand?
3. Do people still make these (silver buttons) today?
4. What tools were needed to create the (lace on this apron)?

Then have students do research to find the answers to their questions. Suggest that they interview craftspeople in addition to using nonfiction books, encyclopedias, and multimedia sources. Have students report their findings about the craft to the class.

Tie-Dyed Squares—Social Studies Theme: Culture and Continuity

Tell students that they will create a type of fiber art called *tie-dyeing*. Explain that this art form originated in China between A.D. 617 and 906. Tie-dyed fabrics created at that time were worn mainly by the nobility and priests. You will need: art smocks, 10-inch squares of muslin (at least one per student), acrylic or tempera paint, containers for a water-paint mixture, string, safety scissors, and rubber gloves.

- Prepare several tubs of dye by mixing tempera paints or acrylic paints with water. Have students put on rubber gloves and do the following:
- Place the muslin square on a flat surface.
- Use their fingertips to gather a clump of material.
- Tie the clump by tightly wrapping string around it.
- Repeat until several clumps have been created.
- Submerge cloth in dye for about 20 minutes.
- Remove cloth and untie or cut away string.
- Dry cloth on a flat surface.

Obelisks—Egypt and Washington DC: Social Studies Theme: Culture and Continuity

Display a picture of the Washington Monument. Explain that the structure was designed by an architect named Robert Mills, and that he based his design on a type of ancient Egyptian structure called an *obelisk*.

Have students work with partners or in small groups to create a chart comparing the Washington Monument with an example of an Egyptian obelisk. (Students may want to research one of the obelisks called *Cleopatra's Needle*.) A sample chart is shown here. Students may want to use the categories listed or ones they create.

Washington Monument	Egyptian Obelisk
Height	
Weight	
Date completed	
Designer	
Today's location	
Other information	

Time Continuity and Change Standard—Activities for Multiple Intelligences

Using the theme of time, the following activities are designed for various multiple intelligences.

Time theme. Have students construct a sundial. Explain to the class how sundials were used, and give them a brief history of the sundial. (spatial/bodily–kinesthetic)

Music feelings. Play for students several pieces of music that have different rhythms and speeds. Have students write a short paper on how slow music makes them feel compared to fast music. Make sure to identify the songs and their singers or composers. (musical/intrapersonal)

Be on time! Have students prepare a five-minute oral report on the importance of being on time. (verbal–linguistic/interpersonal)

Seasonal fashions. Have students prepare and present a report to show how the seasons influence the clothes we wear. They should include as many types of media as they can in their report. (visual/spatial/linguistic)

Family research. Have students interview their parents about what their lives were like as children. Students might look through family albums for photographs of their parents as children. Have students write a brief report about their parents' lives as children, using photos as illustrations. (verbal–linguistic/intrapersonal)

Dance. Have students learn a dance such as the waltz or the jitterbug that were popular in the past and still enjoyed today. They can demonstrate the dance for the class and relate its history. (bodily–kinesthetic/interpersonal)

Timeline. Have students construct a timeline for a period of history they've recently studied, marking the important and interesting events. Add pictures and colors to make it even more interesting. (spatial/math–logic)

Family scrapbook. Have students research their family history and create a family tree. They can see how far back they can trace their family members and where they came from. Encourage students to use their family tree to start a family scrapbook. They might add funny stories or interesting facts about family members as well as pictures, letters, and drawings. (intrapersonal/interpersonal/spatial/verbal–linguistic)

Virtual Field Trips

The Internet is a powerful tool for learning about the world. Older students will enjoy the following virtual field trips and other social studies-related Web field trips.

Visit the White House. On this Web page, you can take a tour of the First Lady's garden, read current press releases, and access information about other government agencies (http://www.whitehouse.gov).

Africa. Michigan State University is the home of Exploring Africa: Africa in the Classroom (http://exploringafrica.matrix.msu.edu/). CNN's Student News Bureau provides news and discussion activities about Africa (http://cnnstudentnews.cnn.com), including a visit to the Nelson Mandela Peace Village. The Peace Corps Coverdell World Wise Schools site features lesson plans for studying Africa's water issues (http://www.peacecorps.gov/). Click on "Kids" in the "Resources for" section, then click on "Explore the World."

Latin America. The University of New Mexico's Latin American Institute offers two resources on Latin America: the Latin America Data Base (http://ladb.unm.edu) and an outreach program, Resources for Teaching about the Americas (http://laii.unm.edu/resources/), which includes resources for art, literature, social studies, and science and math units that include Latin America.

Asia. The Asia Society has a wide range of resources for K through 12 teachers and students (http://www.AskAsia.org). Asia for Educators (http://afe.easia.columbia.edu) has materials on China, Japan, Korea, and Southeast Asia, including primary source texts and multimedia modules. The Stanford Program on International and Cross-Cultural Education (http://spice.stanford.edu/catalog/) provides teaching resources and lesson plans on many cultures. Click on "SPICE Catalog."

Chapter Review

1. Discuss art activities appropriate for the following units: community helpers, self-awareness, learning one's name.
2. What areas of the curriculum (e.g., art, music, language arts) would you use to help children learn their own and others' names in various ways? Give some examples of activities you would use in each of these areas.
3. Relate incidents similar to the opening scenes in this chapter, demonstrating young children's level of social awareness. Explain why you think the children acted the way they did. Explain how an adult (or older child) would react in the same situation.
4. What community/school "helpers" would you invite to your room to aid children's understanding of their community? What would you have these visitors talk about, bring with them to class, and do with the children?
5. What are some ways the block area can be used to teach social studies ideas?
6. What are the two basic rules for beginning to teach young children about peace?
7. List the 10 themes of the National Council for the Social Studies standards for grades K through 12.

References

Baker, M., Martin, D., & Pence, H. (2008). Supporting peace education in teacher education programs. *Childhood Education, 85*(1), 20–25.

Cruzado-Guerro, J., & Kenreich, T. W. (2008). Making global connections with family book bays. *Social Studies and the Young Learner, 20*(4), P1–P4.

Epstein, A. S. (2009). *Me, you, us: Social-emotional learning in preschool.* Ypsilanti, MI: High Scope Research Foundation.

Guralnick, M. J. (2001). A framework for change in early childhood inclusion. In M. J. Guralnick (Ed.), *Early childhood inclusion: Focus on change* (pp. 3–350). Baltimore: Paul H. Brookes.

Hollingsworth, H. L. (2006). Interventions to promote peer social interactions in preschool settings. *Young Exceptional Children, 9*(1), 2–11.

Kauerz, K., & McMaken, J. (2004). *Implications for the early learning field (No Child Left Behind Policy Brief).* Denver, CO: Education Commission of the States.

Kao, D. (2000). *Ben Shahn's New York: The photography of modern times.* Cambridge, MA: Harvard University Art Museum.

Knowlton, J. (1988). *Geography from A to Z: Picture glossary.* New York: Crowell.

Lindsay, M. H. (2009). Defining peace. *SchoolArts, 108*(7), 40–41.

McConnell, S. R. (2002). Interventions to facilitate social interaction for young children with autism: Review of available research and recommendations for educational intervention and future research. *Journal of Autism and Developmental Disorders, 32*(3), 351–372.

Mille, S. (2005, Fall). Building a peaceful and just world—beginning with the children. *Childhood Education, 81*(3), 14–18.

National Association for the Education of Young Children. (1991). Guidelines for appropriate curriculum content and assessment programs serving children ages 3–8. *Young Children, 46*(3), 21–38.

National Association for the Education of Young Children. (2005). Standard 2: NAEYC accreditation criteria for curriculum: 2B: Area of development: Social emotional development. Retrieved November 22, 2009, from http://www.naeyc.org/academy/standards/standard2/standard2B.asp

National Council for the Social Studies (NCSS). (1994). *Expectations of excellence: Curriculum standards for social studies.* Washington, DC: Academy Press.

Rogers, S. J. (2000). Interventions that facilitate socialization in children with autism. *Journal of Autism and Developmental Disorders, 30*(2), 399–409.

Sweeney, J. (1996). *Me on the map.* New York: Crown.

Additional Readings

Bennett, L., & Berson, M. J. (Eds.). (2009). *Digital age: Technology-based K–12 lesson plans for social studies.* Washington, DC: National Council for the Social Studies.

Berson, I. R. (2009). Here's what we have to say! Podcasting in the early childhood classroom. *Social Studies and the Young Learner, 21*(4), 8–11.

Berson, I. E., & Berson, M. J. (2009). Panwapa: Global kids, global connections. *Social Studies and the Young Learner, 21*(3), 28–31.

Chakraborty, B., & Stone, S. (2008). The great pyramid builders: An integrated theme of ancient Egypt. *Childhood Education, 85*(1), 32P–32S.

Connolly, P., & Hayden, J. (2008). *From conflict to peace building: The power of early childhood initiatives: Lessons from around the world.* Washington, DC: NAEYC.

Essley, P. (2010). *Visual tools for differentiating content area instruction: Strategies that make concepts in math, science, and social studies accessible and support all learners across the curriculum.* New York: Scholastic Teaching Resources.

Fehr, M. C., & Fehr, D. E. (2009). *Teach boldly!: Letters to teachers about contemporary issues in education.* New York: Peter Lang Publishing.

Garbarino, J. (2009) *Children and families in the social environment.* Edison, NJ: Transaction Publishers.

McLennan, D. M. P. (2009). Ten ways to create a more democratic classroom. *Young Children, 64*(4), 100–101.

Nebel, M., Jamison, B., & Bennet, L. (2009). Students as digital citizens on Web 2.0. *Social Studies for the Young Learner, 21*(4), 5–7.

Oldendorf, S. B., & Calloway, A. (2008). Connecting children to a bigger world: Reading newspapers in the 2nd grade. *Social Studies and the Young Learner, 21*(2), 4–8.

O'Mahony, C., & Siegel, S. (2008). Designing classroom spaces to maximize social studies learning. *Social Studies and the Young Learner, 21*(2), 20–25.

Pike, K., Mumper, J., & Krieg, F. (2009). *25 totally terrific social studies activities: Step-by-step directions for a motivating project that students can do independently.* New York: Scholastic Teaching Resources.

Smutny, J. F., & vonFremd, S. E. (2009). *Differentiating for the young child: Teaching strategies across content areas, PreK3.* Thousand Oaks, CA: SAGE/Corwin Press.

Software for Children

American Girl: Mia Goes for Great, ages 6–12

Build–a–Bear Workshop: A Friend for All Seasons, ages 3 and up

Building & Co., ages 6 and up

Castle Explorer, ages 8–11

Digital Curriculum, ages 5 and up

Dog Academy, ages 6 and up

Fisher Price Wild Western Town, ages 3–7

Jakers! Let's Explore, ages 6 and up

Jungle School, ages 6 and up

MySims Kingdom, ages 6 and up

SmartGlobe, ages 5 and up

TripFlix, ages 6 and up

Trivial Pursuit, ages 8 and up

Helpful Websites

Build a Flag, http://pbskids.org/buster/games/flag/index.html
This site encourages students' creativity by having them create flags about themselves.

Committee for Children, http://www.cfchildren.org/programs/ssp/overview/
This site contains the award-winning *Second Step: A Violence Prevention Curriculum* for preschool through grade 9.

Developmental Studies Center, http://www.devstu.org
Learn how to conduct classroom meetings at this website. It also includes teacher resources on creating a safe and caring classroom.

Education for Peace, http://www.global-ed.org/e4p/resource.htm
Part of the Global Education Network, this site has classroom resources to help students learn about peaceful conflict resolution.

Field Trip, http://www.hud.gov/kids/field1.html
Students can take an interactive tour (or quick picture tour) of three community sites: a park, a library, and city hall.

Geography Zone, http://www.geographyzone.com
This site offers free geography resources including the world's largest geography quiz, Geography Challenge. Sign up your class and join nearly 1.5 million participants in 192 countries.

Google Earth, http://www.earth.google.com
Download a free 3-D map/satellite image program.

Kidspace: Culture Quest, http://www.ipl.org/div/kidspace/
Take a world tour without leaving the classroom with this excellent resource from the Internet Public Library. Travel to Africa, Australia, North, South, and Central America, Europe, and the Middle East. Many of the tours include visits to national parks, animal reserves, and museums.

Miniature Earth, http://www.miniature-earth.com/
This site shows a short but powerful video that breaks down the demographic makeup of the world.

National Association of School Psychologists, http://www.nasponline.org/resources/factsheets/bullying_fs.aspx
Find information fact sheets for schools and parents about bullying.

National Council for the Social Studies, http://www.socialstudies.org/notable.
This national organization presents" a list of notable trade books in social studies. Their annual list is compiled as a joint project of the National Council for the Social Studies and the Children's Book Council.

National Geographic Education, http://www.nationalgeographic.com/education
This site has hundreds of lessons, activities, and resources to support a study of world cultures.

National Geographic Education Network, http://www.ngsednet.org
An online service from National Geographic, this site gives teachers and students front-row seats to each issue of *National Geographic* magazine. Teachers will find magazine-related teaching resources.

Peace Games, http://www.peacefirst.org/site/
This site has links to games designed to make the players aware of and work with others.

Radio Africa, http://Africa.si.edu/Radio_Africa
Listen to the sounds of the Serengeti and the rhythms of Rwanda on Radio Africa, which streams diverse music clips from around the continent free every day.

Tiger Woods Foundation, http://twfound.org/home/default.sps
Target and the Tiger Woods Foundation have teamed up in a free online program that will help kids ages 8 to 17 to pursue their interests and reach their goals.

The 50 States, http://www.teachersfirst.com/search_action.cfm
This is an extensive elementary resource on the 50 states—a single-stop resource for state projects of various sorts.

The Safe and Responsive Schools Project, http://www.indiana.edu/~safeschl/index.html
This project, funded by the U.S. Department of Education, is dedicated to enabling schools and school districts to develop a broader perspective on school safety and violence.

Teaching Tolerance, http://www.tolerance.org
Embrace diversity in your school with the help of the inspiring magazine *Teaching Tolerance*. This publication is filled with ideas and articles on a range of cultural topics. Click on "Classroom Activities" for teaching resources.

Think Globally, http://youthink.worldbank.org
This engaging site educates kids about important world development issues like hunger, the environment, and conflict.

For additional creative activity resources, visit our website at www.Cengage.com/login.

Creative Health and Safety Experiences

H ealth is a physical state in the here and now. Safety is also a present state. Young children don't think in terms of the distant future. It's the now that interests them, not a talk on how a bad health or safety habit can hurt a person in the future.

Preaching, lecturing, and rote learning of health facts are all ineffective techniques in the early childhood classroom. What should be stressed is a positive, fun, but most of all natural approach to health and safety in the classroom. Above all else, good lifestyle habits are often *caught* rather than *taught*. Whether it's the food choices they make or the physical activities they're involved in, young children often model their behaviors after those of adults.

Health and Safety in the Early Years

Good health and safety practices need to be modeled by adults as much as they are included in actual lesson plans. Emphasis in this chapter will be on presenting basic concepts of health and safety in simple classroom activities that do not require special equipment or curriculum guides. Common sense and daily experiences form the basis of these activities.

In the area of health and safety, your actions surely speak louder than words. For example, your own shining hair, clean body, neat clothing, and fresh smell "tell" children so much more about personal hygiene and good health practices than any lesson plan. Your providing and eating healthy snacks along with children sends a clear message about the importance of eating healthful foods. Along with this emphasis on modeling behaviors, this chapter contains some basic health and safety ideas and tips on how to use them in classroom activities.

OBJECTIVES

After studying this chapter, you should be able to:

1. Discuss basic health practices in the early childhood program.

2. Discuss the appropriate way to work with young children in health and safety matters.

3. Discuss traffic safety, fire safety, and poison safety in the early childhood curriculum.

FIGURE 23-1 • Good health practices include simple ones such as washing one's hands before and after meals.

Health and Safety—National Perspective

A great deal of attention has recently been given to childhood health and safety, and for good reason. The percentage of overweight children in the United States is growing at an alarming rate, with one out of three children now considered overweight or obese (KidsHealth, 2009). Childhood injuries also remain unacceptably high (National Safe Kids Campaign, 2009). In response to these and other threats to young children's well-being, different groups and government agencies in the United States have taken steps to advance a healthier and safer environment for young children. Some of these steps include creating the National Children's Study, an index for tracking childhood health and well-being, and establishing national health objectives to promote a healthier society (Healthy People, 2010). In addition, medical organizations have issued recommendations aimed at controlling specific health threats, such as those associated with overconsumption of soft drinks and obesity (Office of the Surgeon General, 2007).

Early childhood teachers have a variety of health and safety resources to draw upon, including information about and educational programs dealing with such issues as fire safety (U.S. Fire Administration, 2009), obesity (Luttikuis, et al., 2009), and dental hygiene (American Dental Association, 2009).

THINK ABOUT IT   **What Does Fitness Mean?**

We all know that children need plenty of exercise to stay healthy. But what does "fitness" really involve for them? Alan Greene, M.D., a pediatrician, says it's best defined in two ways: (1) decreasing the amount of time children spend in sedentary pursuits each day; and (2) increasing active play.

At least two hours a day should be devoted to very active play. That means running, jumping, climbing, and similar activities. This doesn't have to be two solid hours, of course, and can be spread throughout the day. At school, Greene recommends (depending on how long the school day is) an hour or so in the morning and another hour later on devoted solely to active play. All young children

need, in terms of equipment, is plenty of space so they can run. Having some sports equipment available—balls, parachutes, and so on—gives children the opportunity to play spontaneously, as does playground equipment. It really doesn't take much. If a school only has a small outdoor space, teachers can still inspire active play. Music is a great way to encourage movement indoors, or you can bring a boom box outside to get children motivated and moving. And it's been shown that children are better listeners and exhibit more positive behaviors after they've had time for physical activity. For more information on fitness from Dr. Greene, visit http://www.drgreene.com (Greene, 2004).

THINK ABOUT IT — Physical Activity Levels of Preschool Children

A researcher from the University of Western Ontario conducted a systematic review of the research on the physical activity levels of preschool-aged children (aged 2–6 years). Thirty-nine primary studies (published from 1986–2007) representing a total of 10,316 participants (5,236 male and 5,080 female) from seven countries were examined. The physical activity behaviors of this population were considered in accordance with the National Association for Sport and Physical Education (NASPE) physical activity guidelines for preschoolers.

Upon review of the evidence, it was apparent that nearly half of preschool-aged children do not engage in sufficient physical activity. Current recommendations suggest a minimum of 60 minutes of physical activity per day. Only 54% of participants throughout the studies achieved this. Further, as with other age groups, boys participate in considerably more physical activity than girls.

The researcher felt that it was clear from the systematic review that nearly half of children studied were not meeting the recommended guidelines for physical activity. It was suggested that there was a need for effective interventions that promote and foster physical activity in children, especially for females. It was also suggested that a more objective physical activity guideline for preschoolers is necessary in order to compare and track preschoolers' activity more effectively. The simple measure of number of minutes was felt to be too general a measure of physical activity (Tucker, 2008).

Based on this review of research, it becomes apparent that early childhood teachers can play a major role in promoting preschoolers' activity levels. Keeping children actively engaged throughout the day is a simple and direct way to meet this need.

In addition, early childhood teachers can take advantage of Internet resources and fact sheets provided by such organizations as those listed at the end of this chapter.

Health Practices

Good health is often not appreciated until the later years in life, when one doesn't always have it. It is important in the early years of life, when we least appreciate health, to learn practices that will extend our health long past the early years.

Good health practices include simple ones such as brushing one's teeth and hair, bathing regularly, and having a general interest in cleanliness. Getting enough sleep and good food are also basic to good health at all ages. All these ideas and tasks are usually first taught at home and are then reinforced in the classroom. However, some young children may learn these health basics at school first because of various home situations. Teaching young children about good health practices can be done in many ways, but informal talks and simple activities work best with young children just learning to really care

for themselves physically. With older children, you can plan more in-depth activities and units to investigate various health and safety topics of interest to the children. (See chapter end for activity suggestions.)

Unlike for you and other adults, daily personal hygiene tasks are not yet routine for children. For instance, when a six-year-old boy gets up and ready for school, he often may forget to brush his teeth or comb his hair. He doesn't automatically do these tasks but has to "remember" them every morning. Often, a young child may forget to brush his or her teeth. His or her peers may forget as well. Thus, the child suffers no great social embarrassment. In this situation, an adult's gentle (confidential) reminder can help prod the memory of a forgetful child. Yet in no way should learning personal hygiene be a cause for shame or negative comments.

The health curriculum for older children in middle and upper grade levels focuses on health issues that encompass more than personal health issues. Figure 23–4 outlines some of the basic health topics generally covered in grades 3 to 5. You will probably have more topics you will want to add to this list.

FIGURE 23-2 • A balanced diet is a major part of good health.

FIGURE 23-3 • Getting enough sleep and rest are basic to good health.

Positive Approach to Health and Hygiene

In any health or personal hygiene matter, emphasis must be on the positive view of self. In all health and hygiene tasks that young children learn in the early childhood program, the teacher needs first of all to model good health and hygiene practices. There also must be planned space and time to practice these tasks.

A large mirror at children's eye level, a sink easily reached and operated by young children, and soap in a form that children can handle easily—these are but a few examples of arrangements and equipment that help children "practice" good personal hygiene. To be sure that children always have soap available for hand washing, place a bar of soap in an old knee-high nylon stocking. Tie the stocking to the faucet of the sink. This prevents the soap both from landing on the floor and leaving a soapy mess in the soap dish.

The routines of dressing, washing, eating, and resting will take up a great deal of time when working with young children. In fact, you will sometimes think of yourself as a caregiver and not a teacher. Yet these everyday activities are essential both for good health and for teaching about health. By simply talking about

FIGURE 23-4 • In any health issue, emphasis must be on the positive view of self.

these routines as you are doing them, you are teaching children about important health concepts. All of these daily routines serve as the basis for teaching children concepts of body functions and parts, as well as the habits of caring for themselves.

Each program will have routines for body care. If you're working with children under age five, it's probably mandated that child-sized toilets, sinks, and mirrors be available. If these are not, arrange for the use of platforms or small, sturdy benches or stools so children will be able to reach sinks, get their own toothbrush, and turn on faucets for themselves.

Washing hands after using the toilet and before eating, as well as brushing teeth after eating, are routines that should be established and followed at all age levels.

Another part of daily hygiene involves the quality of the classroom environment. Not only is personal hygiene important, but the learning environment itself should also be clean and attractive. Children need to be actively involved in keeping their classroom orderly. A clean and orderly room also mirrors the importance of good hygiene practices.

Figure 23–6 contains a checklist of equipment for keeping a space clean and in order. When using this checklist, remember that even the smallest child can pick up and put away a toy after playing with it.

The child's involvement in room maintenance helps his or her growing sense of responsibility, while it also helps keep the play area uncluttered and pleasant looking. It is much easier to teach children about health and hygiene when the classroom reflects a concern for cleanliness.

TOPICS	GRADE 3	GRADE 4	GRADE 5
Mental health	Thinking clearly; getting along with others; stress; healthful self-concept; criteria for responsible decisions	Being special; strengths and weaknesses, attitudes; good mental health; stress	Healthy behavior; communication-definition; expressing feelings; emotions—definition; stress management; effects of television on health; definition of health and wellness; using refusal skills
Family and social health	Getting along with family and friends; family, friends, and your health	A friend-definition; choosing friends, family and friends, peer pressure	Focus on the health of others; sharing feelings and feedback; decision making; adoption; responsible parenting
Drugs	Uses of medicine: kinds of medicine; safe use of medicine; caffeine; alcohol; tobacco; marijuana	Making decisions about drinking and smoking; a history of alcohol and tobacco; peer pressure; advertising methods; laws; marijuana; depressants, stimulants, psychedelics, and inhalants; cocaine and crack	Drugs; uses and effects; prescription and over-the-counter drugs; chemicals in cigarette smoke; effects of smoking and alcohol; illegal drugs and their chemical dependence; problem effects; of crack, marijuana
Personal health	Being in good health; proper dental care; being well-groomed; proper medical care; caring for nails; good posture	School health services; community health services; dental health products and services; care of teeth	Using seat belts for safety; using power mowers safely; health professionals; health careers; consumer protection
Safety and first aid	Safety at home; safety at play; first aid for minor injuries; bicycle safety	Joint damage and fractures; muscle injuries; fire safety; safety from animals and strangers; recreational safety; first aid for insect stings and reactions from poisonous plants; bicycle safety	Bicycle safety; poisoning and preventive action; first aid for poisoning; safety around harmful vapors

FIGURE 23-5 • Health curriculum topics, grades 3 through 5.

In your classroom check to see if you have the following:

( ) Storage shelves and cupboards in which low, open shelf space is accessible to children (most shelf space should be movable to permit rearranging the room)

( ) A peg rack or cubbies for children's coats

( ) Screen dividers or other means to create specific play areas and to provide picture display space

( ) An adequate number of wastebaskets, preferably of plastic or other washable material

( ) A dust brush, dustpan, whisk broom, sponges, small mop, and plastic pail

( ) An adequate supply of paper or cloth towels

( ) Small bars of soap for washing hands

( ) Toothbrush containers

( ) A bulletin board for emergency numbers; posted first-aid procedures

( ) File cards and box of parents' home and work telephone numbers; name and telephone number of each child's doctor and other authorized adults responsible for child

( ) A fix-it box (a carton in which to put things that need attention)

( ) Adequate space for storing items that are not being used as well as expendable items, such as paper and paints

( ) At least one drawer/cabinet with a childproof latch for storing potentially dangerous material

FIGURE 23-6 • Checklist of equipment for keeping space clean and in order.

Early Childhood Health Concerns

Prevention

While a teacher can often do very little to prevent the illnesses children bring to school, he or she is in a position to do a great deal about preventing injuries at school. Figure 23–9 presents some basic ideas about accident prevention for children from two to eleven years of age.

When it becomes necessary to deal with injury or illness, it is important to remember that a teacher is neither the child's doctor nor parent. Other than providing simple first aid and large doses of comfort, the teacher's primary responsibility is to notify the parent according to instructions on the child's emergency card. The teacher can also make the child comfortable until someone who is responsible arrives to take over. A school nurse may be available in some schools to handle a child's injury or illness.

Fortunately, real medical crises are rare, considering the number of hours and the number of children involved in routine school days. The crisis is far more likely to rest in the psychological effect on the staff, the child, and the parent.

Another area of prevention concerns poisonous plants. Knowing which plants are poisonous, a teacher can avoid an accident involving a child eating a poisonous plant. Figure 23–10 lists several common plants and which parts, if any, are toxic. It also lists treatment for a child who may have eaten part of a poisonous plant. There is a new National Poison Hotline that makes information more readily available for teachers, parents, and other caregivers. For the first time ever, people can call one national number to be connected with local poison treatment and prevention experts: 800–222–1222. This national hotline was created by Congress and is administered by the American Association of Poison Control Centers to ensure that life-saving help is available around the clock. For more information, or if you'd like to request posters and stickers for your classroom that feature the toll-free hotline, check out http://www.1-800-222-1222.info.

Safety Education

Accidents are the leading cause of death for children under age 14. Thus, the importance of providing children with an environment prepared for their experimentation and exploration cannot be understated. Accidents most frequently occur to children who have had little opportunity to explore, to find out for themselves, or to experience minor scrapes and bumps—children who feel no responsibility for their own safety.

When children do not have a safe environment in which to practice or the opportunity to face challenges, they're more likely to be involved in some type of accident. They have no idea of the consequences and no experience in making decisions or judging hazards.

A safe environment is not only free from hazards but also contains the presence of a diligent, observing, and supervising adult. Even though you have safety checked the play yard and playroom prior to the time children arrive, you should be continually alert for potential hazards. Consider some of the following playground hazards and how to avoid them:

- Grass underneath the playground equipment. Grass doesn't have enough cushioning to keep children from breaking bones or injuring their heads when they fall. Playgrounds should have wood chips, bark mulch, sand, or rubber mats underneath all equipment. The surfacing should be at last a foot deep, and it should extend at least six feet in every direction around equipment.
- Sandboxes left uncovered overnight. Animals may use it as a giant litter box, and the sandbox cold be filled with germs. It is best to keep a sandbox covered at night and remove any debris such as animal droppings and sharp twigs from the area.
- Children wearing flip-flops and hooded sweatshirts at the playground. Both of these items present a risk of both strangulation and falling. Never allow children to wear flip-flops at the playground. Sneakers have more stability and a better grip for children while climbing and they are less likely to trip while running. As harmless as that hoodie may seem, if it has drawstrings around the neck, it is a choking hazard. The strings could get caught on playground equipment and accidentally strangle a child.
- Don't allow children to attach jump ropes, clotheslines, pet leashes, or other strangulation hazards to play structures.
- Don't buy a metal play set; the slide can get incredibly hot and burn a child in seconds.
- Beware of "s" hooks with spaces between them on playground equipment. Children can catch clothing on them and injure themselves while jumping off. If you can slide a dime into the opening, it's too wide.
- Swings with seats that are made of wood or metal; the heavy material can injure children walking by. Soft rubber and canvas swings are safer for children.

As children play, you must reinforce safety rules that have been decided by you and the children. You might even post them as a reminder. But you will have to keep on reminding young children, in a positive yet firm way, as they play: "Ride your bike here." "Climb the tree with your hands free." "Remove the truck from under the swings." Be vigilant about rules such as proper play on the slide. Be sure children know to go down the slide feet first only, not to climb up the slide, and to check that there's no other child at the bottom

FIGURE 23-7 • Children learn bike safety in the early childhood program.

before they down. You will need to keep an eye on children, as lack of supervision is responsible for 40% of all playground injuries. Being prepared means looking over both your indoor and outdoor play areas for all potentially dangerous areas. For example, if swing seats are too slippery, cover them with a coat of paint to which you have added some fine sand. The sand will give just enough traction, yet it won't scratch children. Or cover swing seats with pieces of foam rubber to prevent slipping.

For any other potential emergencies, you, other adults who work with you, and the children all need to practice a prepared emergency plan. Being prepared is a must. The plan should be written and posted. Decide who will stay with children, what children will do, and what other adults will do. Teach children how to use the telephone. Have them practice dialing the emergency number, and teach those age two and up how to obtain the operator should the need arise. Even very young children can find the "0" for operator, especially if a red dot is painted over the number.

FIGURE 23-8 • Survey the playground for any possible hazards.

Think ahead. Who will transport an injured or ill child to the doctor or hospital? Have parents record the numbers of their preferred doctor and hospital, but inform them that in an emergency, you may call the health facility nearest to the school. Written permission from the parent must be on file, giving the teacher authority to take the child for any emergency medical care.

Decide about the precautions required for special-needs children. Who will stay with the child with a visual or hearing impairment, or how will you handle the child in a wheelchair if you need to evacuate the building?

Keep a first-aid kit ready, freshened periodically and within easy access in the room and the play yard. The kit should contain the following:

- a box of assorted adhesive bandages
- a box of 30 sterile gauze squares
- sterile gauze bandages, both 20 and 10 sizes
- a roll of 10-mm wide adhesive tape
- absorbent cotton
- antibacterial spray

- petroleum jelly
- cloth or absorbent sanitary pads for application of pressure

For occasional bumped foreheads and cut lips, keep on hand some form of cold pack in the freezer. An easy-to-hold, dripless cold pack can be made by half-filling a small plastic vitamin bottle with water and putting it in the freezer. Or keep a wet sponge or washcloth in the freezer to use as a cold pack—they're easier for little hands to hold than an ice cube.

At least one permanent staff person should be trained in first aid and cardiopulmonary resuscitation (CPR). Your local Red Cross or other health agency offers free courses in accident preparedness and first aid. This training should be updated annually.

All children should have a feeling of being responsible both for their own and the group's safety. Plan to include content from the guidelines of traffic, fire, and poison safety in your curriculum, as these are the three leading causes of injury and death among children.

Traffic Safety

You share in the responsibility of helping children learn to cope in traffic. Real experiences are the best way to teach young children about traffic.

The most common cause of traffic accidents involving young children is darting out in front of cars. Children, intent on their play or crossing the street to join a friend, dart into traffic midblock. Most of these accidents happen on residential streets. The goals of traffic safety, therefore, should address the midblock or "dart-out" accident and include these points.

- Stop before entering any street.
- Listen and look for traffic before crossing the street.
- Walk across residential streets cautiously.
- Be able to interpret traffic signs and signals correctly.

Stop before entering any street. For children under age five, or those who have not yet learned traffic safety, the first lesson should be on stopping before entering any street. With two-year-old children, begin by going outdoors with them and identifying the different surfaces of the school and play yard. Stop every time the surface changes and point out the change. Next, take children to a quiet, residential street or on a walk around the block. Have them identify places where the surfaces change, and stop at each place.

AGE	CHARACTERISTICS	ACCIDENT HAZARDS	MEASURES FOR PREVENTION
2–3 years	Fascinated by fire; moves about constantly; tries to do things alone; imitates	Traffic	Keep child away from streets and driveways with strong fence and firm discipline. Teach rules and dangers of traffic.
	Runs and is lightning fast; impatient with restraint	Transportation	Demonstrate safety; use seat belts, etc. Maintain vehicles including safety equipment and mechanical condition of brakes, suspension, tires, etc.
3–6 years	Explores the neighbor-hood, climbs, rides tricycles; likes and plays rough games	Tools/equipment	Store dangerous knives, sharp scissors, and garden equipment out of reach. Teach safe use of tools and kitchen equipment; careful supervision when using. Use guards on fans.
		Water	Even shallow wading pools are unsafe unless carefully supervised.
		Play areas	Guard against children involving themselves in play beyond physical capabilities (climbing up something, unable to come down).
		Toys	Large sturdy toys without sharp edges or small removable parts are safest. Provide close supervision when equipment with small parts in use. Identify safety rules for pedestrians, passengers, and cyclists.
		Burns	Use guards for radiators, hot pipes, and other hot surfaces. Temperature of water not to exceed 120°F. Minimize and properly store all combustible material.
		Poisoning	Store all medicines and poisons in locked cabinet. Store cleaning products out of reach. Store kerosene or gasoline in metal cans and out of reach. Screen windows to protect against insect bites, food contami-nation. Use proper sanitation procedures in all food preparation. Never use lead-based paint.
7–11 years	Growing independence; peer group grows in importance; can under-stand others' opinions, has a larger view of the world outside the classroom.	Cycling, pedestrian, sports accidents	Encourage use of proper safety equipment such as bike helmets, knee pads for skating; rules of the road
		Losing flexibility	Provide physical exercise and activities on a regular basis.
		Negative feelings can lead to physical fights; spending time at home alone; minor injuries as normal part of more outside and group activities	Teach ways to resolve conflicts in nonviolent ways. Provide information on ways to ensure safety when home alone. Describe first-aid procedures for treating minor in-juries. Describe ways to respond to serious injuries.

List specific policies of your center or school for prevention of accidents. It is recommended that the staff review their "minute-by-minute" accident prevention policies periodically in order to evaluate what changes are needed and to include changes in listed guidelines for substitutes and volunteers. The accident log should be consulted in such an evaluation. The same applies to the classroom teacher: Consistent accident prevention policies should be followed as well as reviewed on a regular basis.

Based on information provided by the American Academy of Pediatrics. (2006). Standards for Day Care Centers.

FIGURE 23-9 • Accident prevention.

The curb is another place to stop because the surface changes here. Learning and practicing stopping in this way establishes the habit of stopping before entering a street. Parents should also be involved in practicing this habit with their children.

Listen and look for traffic. Once children learn to stop at the curb, they must learn to look and listen for traffic before crossing the street. With adequate adult supervision, take children on a field trip to learn these precautions. Children under age five are confused as to whether traffic is traveling toward or away from them. They'll need to practice observing traffic and identifying direction as well as the speed at which cars are traveling.

Crossing a residential street. Construct a pretend street with crosswalks and corners, using masking tape or chalk on the play yard surface. Have children use their tricycles or other vehicles to role play pedestrians and drivers. Using this street, children practice crossing. They are first reminded to stop when the surface of the yard changes and the street begins and to listen and look for oncoming traffic. Additional practice can be structured using a tabletop street with toy cars and people.

With trained and adequate adult supervision, take a group of children to a corner and practice crossing the street. Emphasize to children that they should never run across the street. Running to cross is another major cause of traffic deaths. Children, who are generally less coordinated than adults, may trip and fall in front of oncoming traffic. Teach children to walk with deliberate speed as they cross. Let them know they must focus on the task of crossing, not playing, thinking about anything else, or running.

THINK ABOUT IT — Tooth Stories...The History of Dentistry

The Indus Valley Civilization in Pakistan has yielded evidence of dentistry being practices as far back as 7000 B.C. This earliest form of dentistry involved curing tooth-related disorders with bow drills operated, perhaps, by skilled bead craftsmen (Coppa, 2006).

A Sumerian text from 5000 BC describes a "tooth worm" as the cause of tooth decay (ADA, 2009). Evidence of this belief has also been found in ancient India, Egypt, Japan, and China. An Egyptian scribe called Hesy-Re is often called the first "dentist." An inscription on his tomb from around 2600 BC includes the title "the greatest of those who deal with teeth, and of physicians." This is the earliest reference to a person identified as a dental practitioner (ADA, 2009).

The legend of the worm is also found in the writings of Homer and as late as the 1300s AD when the surgeon Guy de Chauliac still promoted the belief that worms cause tooth decay.

Between 500 and 300 BC, Hippocrates and Aristotle wrote about dentistry, including the eruption of teeth, treating decayed teeth and gum disease, extracting teeth with forceps, and using wires to stabilize loose teeth and fractured jaws.

In 100 BC, Celsus, a Roman medical writer, wrote extensively in his compendium of oral hygiene, stabilization of loose teeth, and treatments for toothache, teething pain, and jaw fractures. In the period 166 to 201 AD, the Etruscans practiced dental prosthetics using gold crowns and fixed bridgework.

During the Middle Ages and throughout the 19th century, dentistry was not a profession in itself, and dental procedures were performed by barbers or general physicians. Barbers usually limited their practice to extracting teeth. Barbers and monks had an interesting association during this time period. Most doctoring was done by monks. Barbers traveled from monastery to monastery to shave the monks' heads. Since barbers knew how to use sharp instruments and became very good with these tools, they became the monks' natural choice for dental surgery.

Then, about 1,000 years ago, the church forbade monks from practicing surgery. So barbers took over the dentistry and surgery tasks. As late as the 1800s, some barbers still did dental work in remote areas. In the 1800s, anesthetics were introduced, which made dentistry much more bearable (ADA, 2009).

After this history of dentistry, aren't you glad that you are living in the 21st century? A trip to the dentist can often be pleasant and pain free, so unlike dentistry's early history.

Interpreting traffic signals and signs correctly.
Instead of easing the task, traffic signals and signs make crossing streets more difficult for children. Often children cross midblock in order to avoid the signs and signals they do not understand.

Children need to be taught the meaning of the lights and signals found at intersections. First, they need to learn that red is used to symbolize danger and means "stop." Use red on objects that may be hazardous in the room and play yard. Ask children where red flags should be placed.

Play "follow-the-leader" games, with children stopping whenever a leader holds up a red flag. Once children understand the meaning of red, play the same games using green and yellow flags. Practice crossing a pretend playground street, following the signals given by one of the children with others role-playing pedestrians and drivers.

Do not attempt to practice crossing streets at an intersection without the aid of a police officer and other well-prepared and trained adults. Police officers can take small groups of children to the intersection to explain the traffic signal lights and to practice crossing with them. Children should be at least five years of age before exposure to this activity.

Protecting children in traffic is the role and responsibility of teachers, parents, and the community alike. All adults and older children will serve as models and thus should practice traffic safety themselves at all times.

Fire Safety

Project Burn Prevention, funded by the U.S. Consumer Product Safety Commission, is a program designed to provide schools with fire prevention information. It conducts a nationwide campaign on preventing injury from burns to children. The program instructs children on what to do in case of a fire. Some goals for fire safety include the following:

- teaching children to approach fire with caution and respect
- involving children in practice fire drills
- teaching young children to "drop and roll" should they be involved in a fire
- teaching young children where the fire extinguisher is and how to use it
- teaching children how to call the fire department

THIS ONE'S for YOU!   # Children's Physical Fitness and Academic Performance

A researcher from the Department of Pediatrics, West Virginia University, and two public health workers in West Virginia Health Departments studied the relationship between increased fitness and cognitive performance in both adults and children. More specifically, they wanted to determine which aspects of children's fitness assessment are associated with their performance in four different academic areas: reading/language arts, math, science, and social studies.

To measure children's level of fitness, the researchers used a FITNESSGRAM, which measured aerobic capacity, abdominal strength, upper body strength/endurance, flexibility, and trunk life. They then compared gender and socioeconomic status with mean group performance scores across subscale scores on standardized tests in the four academic areas. The sample consisted of 965 5th-grade students (50.7% male, mean age of 10.6 years).

The researchers found that achievement test scores were significantly better for children who were in the Healthy Fitness Zone (HFZ) for aerobic capacity and abdominal strength when compared to children who were unable to achieve the healthy zone. Children in the HFZ for upper body strength performed significantly better in math. Children in the HFZ for flexibility performed significantly better in math and science. No differences were found in academic performance when children in the HFZ for trunk life were compared to children not in the healthy zone. However, when a full factorial analysis of variance was performed on the data, aerobic capacity was found to be the only fitness variable important in all four academic areas.

The results of this study indicate that aerobic training has a significant association with academic performance and that general fitness may also be involved. They suggest that this finding raises the possibility that a child's chances for academic success could be improved by increasing that child's fitness level (Wittberg, Northrup, & Cottrel, 2009).

COMMON NAME	BOTANICAL NAME	TOXIC PART	TREATMENT CODE
African Violet	Saintpaulia ionantha	Probably none**	A, B
Azalea	Rhododendron	All parts	A
Begonia	Begonia spp.*	Probably none**	A, B
Buttercup	Ranunculus spp.	All parts	A, C
Castor Bean	Rincinus communis	Chew seeds, leaves	A
Christmas Kalanchoe (or Flaming Katy)	Kalanchoe bloss Feldiana "compacta"	Probably none**	A
Christmas Pepper	Capsicum annum	Fruit—causes burns	C
Daffodil	Narcissus spp.	All parts, especially bulb	A
Dandelion	Taraxacum officinale	Probably none**	A, B
Dogwood	Cornus florida	Probably none**	A, B
Dumbcane	Dieffenbachia spp.	Leaves	A, C
English Ivy	Hedera helix	Leaves, berries	A
Hemlock	Conium maculatum	All parts, especially seed	A
Holly	Ilex	All parts, especially berries	A
Hyacinth	Hyacinthus orientalis	Bulb	A
Hydrangea	Hydrangea arborescens	Leaves and buds	A
Impatiens	Impatiens spp.	Probably none**	A
Jack-in-the-Pulpit	Arisaema triphyllum	Roots (in quantity)	A, C
Jerusalem Cherry	Solanum pseudocapsicum	Leaves, unripe berry, possibly unripe fruit	A
Jimson Weed	Datura stramonium	All parts	A
Kalanchoe Lily-of-the-Valley	Crassulaceae Convallaria majalis	Leaves All parts	A A
Mayapple	Podophyllum peltatum	All parts, except ripe fruit	A
Mistletoe	Phoradendron spp.	All parts, especially berries	A
Mockorange	Philadelphus spp.	Probably none**	A, B
Mountain Laurel	Kalmia latifolia	All parts	A
Nightshades	Solanum dulcamara, S. nigrum	All parts	A
Philodendron	Philodendron spp.	All parts	A, C
Pokeweed	Phytolacca americana	Berries, leaves if cooked improperly	A
Poinsettia	Euphorbia pulcherrima	Sap in plant	A
Pothos	Scindapsus aureus	All parts	A, C
Privet	Ligustrum vulgare	Berries, leaves	A
Pyracantha	Pyracantha coccinea lalandi	Probably none**	A, B
Rhododendron	Rhododendron maximum	All parts	A
Rose	Rosa spp.	Probably none**	A, B
Schefflera	Araliaceae	Leaves	A
Spider Plant	Liliaceae	Leaves	A
Wandering Jew	Tradescantia fluminensis	Probably none**	A, B
Water Hemlock	Cicuta masculata	All parts, especially roots	A
Wild Strawberry	Fragaria vesea	Probably none**	A, B
Yew	Taxus spp.	All parts	A

*spp. includes all species of the plant
**No known toxic reaction; individual children may have allergic reactions.
Treatment Codes:
A. Call the local poison information center to report ingestion and verify plant. Post this number near the phone.
B. No treatment necessary.
C. Give milk immediately and then call the local poison center.

Based on information provided by the American Academy of Pediatrics in *Standards for Day Care Centers,* 2006.

FIGURE 23-10 • Poisonous plants and treatment for their ingestion.

THIS ONE'S for YOU!   Bicycles

A rite of passage for many children is taking off the training wheels on their bicycle and learning how to balance on two wheels. You can probably remember that moment in your life, and even what your first bicycle looked like. Bicycles have been around for a long time, longer than you might think. Bicycles have become popular around the world as a means of transportation, recreation, and exercise. Here is a short history of this familiar vehicle.

The first documented vehicles that resemble modern bicycles were invented about 200 years ago. Comte Mede de Sivrac of France in 1791 invented the *celerifere*. The celerifere consisted of two wheels that were connected by a wooden frame. Riders on a celerifere moved by pushing their feet along the ground. In 1817, Karl von Drais of Germany improved on the celerifere by adding a steering mechanism. He called his invention a *draisienne*, but it was also known as a *hobbyhorse* or a *dandy horse*.

Both Kirkpatrick Macmillan and Gavin Dalzell added pedal-like devices to their draisienne-style bicycles about 1840. In the 1860s, the *velocipede* was invented at a French carriage shop owned by Pierre Michaux. The velocipede was the first bicycle to use pedals similar to those found on modern bicycles. His velocipede was nicknamed "the boneshaker" because its wood-and-metal construction caused a very rough and bumpy ride. Some of these early bicycles weighed more than 110 pounds!

High-wheeled bicycles called *ordinaries* first appeared about 1870. The large wheel allowed riders to travel farther with each turn of the pedals than other types of bicycles.

The first practical bicycle was the *safety bicycle*. It was first successfully produced in 1886 by James Starley. Modern bicycles have changed little since the invention of the safety bicycle (Herlihy, 2006; Oxlade, 2007).

The first mountain bikes were designed in California in the late 1970s when enthusiastic riders mounted the fat tires of a beach cruiser on a multigeared racing bike. In North America, more than 300,000 kids are injured every year while riding bikes. Always be sure that children wear a protective helmet while riding any kind of bike.

Invite a firefighter to the classroom to introduce children to fire safety practices. The firefighter can teach children the habit of dropping and rolling should they, or their clothing, catch on fire. They can also demonstrate precautions to take when using fire or heat. Follow this demonstration with a lesson on respect for fire. Even if the flame present is the seemingly harmless lit candles on a birthday cake, teach children to keep a bucket of sand and water nearby whenever handling fire. You don't have to frighten the children; just teach them the potential dangers of fire.

While the firefighter is visiting, show children where the fire extinguishers are in your classroom and how they are used. Have children practice dialing the number to reach the fire department, and hold a fire drill. Ask yourself these questions.

- Do I have a written plan for a fire drill?
- Do I conduct monthly drills based on the plan?
- Have I had the plan reviewed by the fire department?
- Have I held a meeting with the other staff to discuss the plan?
- Does everyone know where the fire extinguisher is and how to operate it?
- Have I practiced fire drills during nap and mealtimes?
- Do I have an assembly location outside of the building?
- What method do I have for accounting for the children once outside?
- Have I held fire drills with different exits blocked?

Poison Safety

Thousands of children each year are victims of accidental poisoning. The development of the poison control centers has helped to eliminate many cases of accidental poisoning. Yet children in an early childhood setting are just as susceptible to poisonings as children in a home setting. In the school, it becomes your responsibility to protect children from possible

FIGURE 23-11 • Getting outdoors on a regular basis is a good health practice in the early childhood program.

FIGURE 23-12 • Children love vigorous outdoor play, as this child notes on her drawing.

poisoning accidents. Your responsibility is to teach children two important safety measures.

1. Take medications only from adult family members, parents, physicians, or health personnel.
2. Understand that some things are to eat, while others are not.

Using food for art confuses young children on this point. Food is to eat; other substances—berries found on the playground, art materials, toys, leaves, flowers—are not for eating.

When you work with children under age five, you must supervise them carefully, preventing them from putting anything into their mouths. You can't expect babies not to put things into their mouths, as this is their way of learning about their world. However, you are responsible for observing children, for freeing the environment from poisonous substances, and for removing nonfood objects that do find their way into children's mouths. (See Figure 23–10 for a list of poisonous plants and materials. Also see Chapter 12 for a list of unsafe art supplies.)

Check your room and outdoor play area for all poisonous substances, and remove all that you find. Note which cleaning supplies and other toxic materials are stored in a place that children might encounter accidentally. If you serve meals, be certain that food items are stored separately from nonfood items. There have been tragic mistakes by hurried cooks or teachers who confused a bag of flour with a cleaning product.

Keep the number of your nearest poison control center posted by the phone, or use the National Poison Control phone number, 800–222–1222, to obtain help.

Summary

Health and safety are physical states of being in the here and now. Young children don't think in terms of the far-distant future. It's now that interests them, not a lecture on how a bad health or safety habit can hurt a person in the future. Preaching, lecturing, and rote learning of health and safety information are all ineffective techniques in the early childhood health

FIGURE 23-13 • Older children can access the Internet to research health topics.

program. Instead, a positive, fun, but most of all natural approach to health and safety in the classroom should be emphasized.

Good health practices include brushing one's teeth and hair, bathing regularly, and having a general interest in cleanliness. Getting enough sleep and good food are also basic to good health at all ages.

In all health or personal hygiene matters, emphasis should be on the positive view of the child. Even more important, the teacher must model good health and hygiene himself or herself.

Other areas that should be included in the early childhood curriculum are traffic safety, fire safety, and poison safety. When teaching concepts in these areas, young children need real, concrete experiences instead of abstract lessons.

A teacher is in a position to do a great deal about preventing injuries at school for both young children and children in grades 3 to 5. Knowing what to expect from children six years of age and younger helps a teacher prevent accidents. Knowing which plants are poisonous can also be an excellent preventive measure in the early childhood classroom.

Learning Activities

A. Interview children to find out what they know about the traffic system near the school and in their community. Ask them what traffic lights mean and where, how, and why they should cross streets. Design a lesson to promote traffic safety based on their responses.

B. Work with several children. Demonstrate their growth from birth weight to present weight by stacking hardwood blocks on a bathroom scale to equal the two weights for each child. Children may want to enter the following information in an "all-about-me" book: "When I was a baby, I weighed as much as _____ blocks. Now I weigh as much as _____ blocks." Each child can feel good about her or his present state of growth when compared with past growth.

C. Log on to one of the websites listed in the Helpful websites section on pages 604–605. Choose one of the activities posted there and incorporate it into a lesson plan. Share your plan with your fellow students for their input.

D. Design several safety-related activities of your own. Use them with a small group of children. Evaluate your experience. Share the results of your activity in class.

E. Assemble a list of local resources you could invite to your class to speak on health and safety issues. Make enough copies of your list to share with each of your classmates.

F. Choose one of the children's books from the suggested sites in the Online Companion. Plan a lesson around this book. Be sure to include the following in your plans: age/grade level, name of book, health topic to be taught, and related activities.

G. On a large sheet of paper, make a list of ways you plan to keep healthy (a nutritious and well-balanced diet, washing hands regularly, exercising). Have a group of children make a list of the ways they plan to keep healthy. Discuss with these children the similarities and differences in the lists. Then talk about things kids can do that help prevent injury. Go online to http://www.safekids.org for more information and ideas.

Activities for Children

Apple "Teeth" Snack

Cut a red apple into long thin slices. (These will be the lips.) Spread peanut butter (for gums) on one side of two apple slices. Place mini marshmallows (for teeth) onto the peanut butter of one apple slice. Place the other apple slice, peanut butter side down, on the mini marshmallows to complete the snack.

Dental Health Activities

Brushing teeth fun. Cut the tops off large plastic soda bottles and turn them upside down—they look like teeth! Secure 10 together—use a hole punch to make holes and twist ties to hold them together. Spray them with shaving cream and give the children toothbrushes to brush the teeth clean. You might consider doing this activity in your sensory table or in a large shallow tub on the floor to control the mess.

Staining teeth: A science activity. You will need two hard-boiled eggs and dark cola. To show the children how easily teeth can stain, place one egg in a jar of water and one egg in a jar of cola. The next day, remove the eggs and compare their colors. Talk about how different they look and why. Then use a toothbrush and toothpaste to brush away the stain from the cola-tinted egg. If possible, give each child a turn (you may need to soak several more eggs).

Variation: Obtain several small white ceramic tiles from construction sites, tile stores, parents who are remodeling, etc. Provide children with a variety of food products to smear on the tiles such as jelly, ketchup, syrup, and peanut butter. Have children brush the tile "tooth" with toothbrushes and real toothpaste. Which tile is stained? Talk about why.

Dental art activities. Try some of these art activities to reinforce dental health principles.

- Have children paint with toothbrushes.
- Have children finger paint with toothpaste (the gel kind works the best).
- Have children make a tooth necklace using white clay and dental floss.
- Have children design a new toothpaste brand and tube.
- Have children draw pictures of what they think the tooth fairy looks like.

Miscellaneous Dental Activities

Apple smiles. You will need apples, **miniature** marshmallows, and peanut butter for this activity. Cut apple into wedges. Give each child two apple wedges and spread peanut butter on one side. Stick mini marshmallows on the peanut butter on one of the apple wedges. Put the other apple wedge on top (peanut butter sticking to the marshmallows). The apples are lips and the marshmallows are teeth.

What brushing does. Boil an egg in water with a tea bag. Let the egg cool. The tea bag will stain the egg brown. Give **children** a toothbrush and toothpaste and let them brush the egg. The stains will disappear as they brush. Explain to them that this is what brushing does to their teeth.

How to brush your teeth. Show children how to properly brush their teeth. Obtain packets with a toothbrush, red tablets, and toothpaste from a local dentist. Have children chew the red tablets. Have them brush their teeth and then look in a mirror and see what they missed. The red spots will show the parts they missed.

Toothpaste taste test. Get as many different kinds of toothpaste as you can. Have all of the children taste them. Graph which ones are favorites.

Dental math. As children get older and start losing their baby teeth, have them investigate this event. Explain that everyone loses teeth at different rates, so their friends may have lost more or fewer teeth. Have children ask 10 friends how many teeth each of them has lost. Have the children plan: What questions will they ask? How will they record responses? How will they show the information after they have asked 10 friends? Have students make a record of the information they gathered from their friends. Find a place in the room to display the children's records. Then talk about how the records are alike and different.

Health

Hop on the Safety Train

Have the children form a circle on the floor. Engage them in singing this song (to the tune of "Where is Thumbkin?"):

Where is (child's name)?
Where is (child's name)?
Here I am!

Ask the children to wave their hands in the air when it's their turn to say, "Here I am!"

Then, ask children to form a straight line. Explain that they're going to be a pretend train and travel around the room. Suggest that children face forward and place their hands on the waist of the person in front of them. They'll enjoy chugging around in a circle, tooting their horns.

Next, invite children to travel to different parts of the room. Encourage everyone to stick together. Point out safety features, such as fire extinguishers, emergency exits, fire alarms, and first-aid kits, as children go past them. Ask children to point out any other safety items they see.

Then take the train outside to tour the play yard. While passing equipment, offer safety tips, saying things like, "I see the slide. How can we stay safe on the slide? Now we're passing the swings. What safety rules do we need to follow on our swings?"

After your trip, gather together and talk about all the places you explored.

Extensions: For younger children, provide a first-aid kit that children can explore in the dramatic play area. As children take on the role of doctor/firefighter/hospital worker, encourage them to demonstrate for their classmates the uses for the different items in the kit.

For older children, encourage them to discuss the safety practices they follow in other places, such as on a trip to the beach, at an amusement park with their families, when riding in a boat, train, taxi, or plans.

Hand-washing check. Have children wash their hands. Then take small pieces of cotton dipped in rubbing alcohol. Rub the back of each child's hand with the moistened cotton. Look at the dirt on the cotton and discuss what it means. Even when we think we've washed our hands thoroughly, there still may be dirt present. Remind children to scrub their hands with soap and warm water for as long as it takes to sing "Happy Birthday" two times (10–15 seconds) to kill germs.

Our health helpers. When children arrive at school in the morning, give them name tags that resemble little Red Cross badges. Then have them explore the different areas you have set up in the room.

- Provide a collection of books about community helpers in the book center.
- Supply the housekeeping area with bandages, small pillows, adhesive bandages, empty spray cans, gauze, syringes, and tape.
- Have materials for constructing nurses' or doctors' hats from construction paper available in the art center.
- Create a "dentist's office" in one area of the classroom, complete with magazines, reception desk, telephone, office chair, teeth models, white shirts, a drape to go over patients, and tongue depressors.

Activity in these centers will enable children to examine tools used by medical helpers and to role play health care providers.

Colds and Germs

Equipment: Atomizer from an empty perfume bottle or sprayer from window cleaning fluid.

Procedure: Discuss colds with children. Some questions to ask: "Have you ever had a bad cold? Did you go to the doctor or get medicine to take? Were you allowed to go to school or play with friends when you had a fever? Why not?" Explain that people can give someone else their cold or other sickness just by being around others. The germs they have can be carried in the air or on their hands.

Have children spray water into the air and watch how it disappears. Explain that when we cough, we can easily spray germs we cannot see onto others.

Say to children: "Sometimes we have to be by ourselves when we are sick so that others will not get sick, too." Point out that if they cough or sneeze,

they should cover their mouth and nose using a handkerchief.

Variation: Fill the spray bottle with some water and glitter and spray it around the room. Explain to children that this is how germs fly around when we don't cover our sneezes and coughs. Children will find the glitter all over the place by the time you stop "sneezing."

Another way to get the idea of spreading germs across is to put glitter in your hand and pretend to sneeze into it. Then touch a toy or a child. When children see that the glitter has transferred to whatever you have touched, they understand more clearly how germs are spread.

Another way to "spread germs." When talking about how germs are spread and the importance of hand washing, use flour to illustrate how germs get on everything. Dip your tissue in flour and pretend to sneeze. Watch the flour-germs fly. Then touch things with the tissue, leaving flour-germs on everything.

Variation: Tape together an eight-foot paper chain. Ask the children what it represents. Tell them that germs can travel eight feet in a cough or sneeze. The chain is a great visual image for them reminding them to cover their mouths when they cough and sneeze.

Is it Safe?

Equipment: Pictures cut from magazines or drawn freehand that show both safe and unsafe situations—untied shoelaces, child near stove, spilled paint, etc.

Procedure: Initiate a discussion with children, reviewing things they've learned about safety. Review safety ideas for the classroom, home, and community. Then introduce the "Is It Safe?" guessing game. Hold up a picture and have children tell if it shows a safe situation or an unsafe situation. Continue showing pictures, discussing each, and emphasizing why each situation is safe or unsafe.

It's a Circus! Gross-Motor Activities for a Healthy Body

Bring the magic of the big top into your classroom with these circus-inspired routines that keep children active and healthy.

- The Ringleader. Let the children take turns twirling a hula hoop on one arm. Then have them try spinning hula hoops on both arms. The biggest challenge: spinning them in opposite directions on both arms at the same time.
- The Tightrope Walker. Use painter's tape to create a "tightrope" on the floor. Have children walk along the tightrope, without stepping off the line, holding an opened umbrella in one hand. You might add a pirouette to make it even more challenging.
- Balancing Act. Set two stacks of five or so paperback books at opposite ends of a room. Have children take turns walking from one stack to the other, bending down to place a book on their head each time they reach a stack. See who can balance the most books.

- Through-the-Hoop Rolls. If the child can do a somersault (forward roll), you can give this a variation. Have the child pass through a hula hoop held over a carpet or a good-size rug, leading with the hands and completing the roll in a standing position.

Healthy Body Math

Have four or five children make block towers that are equal to the height of each person in the group. Use a tower of 10 blocks as a guide (benchmark) to estimate the height of each tower, and then record the estimation. Ask each group to think of ways to check their estimations. Use each of the ideas to check the predictions, and then record the actual heights. Which strategy was the best? Why? Challenge: How much of a difference is there between the tallest and the shortest people? How do you know?

Hygiene

- To clean stuffed toys, rub or shake them in a bag half filled with cornmeal. Let the toys stand for a while before brushing them off.
- When game cards get sticky from too much handling, shake them in a bag filled with talcum or baby powder.
- To remove felt marker ink from skin, try rubbing on toothpaste, then rinsing with water. Repeat the process until the ink disappears.

Helping Children Dress Themselves

- When boots won't go over a child's shoes, use a plastic bread bag (or any other plastic bag) over the shoes first. Boots slip over the shoes easily.
- When young children are learning to button up their own coats and sweaters, have them start at the bottom. They'll be more likely to get all the buttons in the right buttonholes this way.
- When zippers stick, rub them with a lead pencil to get them gliding smoothly again. Or rub the zipper with petroleum jelly or spray it with WD40 (an aerosol lubricant), being careful not to get it on the fabric.
- Use old leg warmers or old socks with the toes cut off for extra warmth for children playing in the snow. When dressing children to play in the snow, slip the legwarmers or toeless socks over their arms after pulling on their snowsuits and mittens. The legwarmers (or socks) prevent snow from getting between mittens and sleeves and keep wrists warm and toasty.

Healthy Heart Activities

Try some of the following ideas with children to increase their awareness of their wonderful, healthy hearts.

- Did you know that your heart beats more than 100,000 times a day? Get "heart smart" by checking out some amazing facts at http://www.pbs.org/wgbh/nova/heart/heartfacts.html. Share the ideas and activities with the children.
- Get into the groove with an active lifestyle by enrolling yourself and your students in the President's Challenge, sponsored by the President's Council on Physical Fitness. You can win awards for daily physical activity. Go to http://www.fitness.gov for details.
- Use a map to set a walking goal for your class. For example, find out how many miles there are from one border of your state to the other, and over the course of the year, try to log that distance as a class. Walk at school and encourage children to continue walking at home.
- Make sure children are actually playing and being active at recess and not just sitting around chatting. Encourage games and movement. Appoint a child to be the "fitness hero" for the day. Have him or her come up with fun movements on the playground.
- The heart is a muscle, and just like other muscles in the body, it gets stronger when we exercise. Have children see how long they can jump without stopping. They can either jump in place or use a jump rope. Do this every day for a week. Have them record their data. What did they notice about the length of time they were able to jump each day? What do they think would happen to the data if they did this for another week? Another month?
- Have students listen to their hearts and lungs through a stethoscope. Have them run in place for several minutes and listen to their hearts and lungs again. What has changed? Why?

Health and Safety Communications for Parents

Whenever you have important information on health and safety practices (or any other area of the program for that matter), place it on a Parent Bulletin Board by the entrance of your room to ensure greater visibility.

Important notices and letters for parents often fall off cubby shelves and are lost. To solve this problem, use a shoebag to make an attractive parent "mailbox." Label each pocket in the shoebag with a parent's name and have mothers or fathers check daily for their "mail." If you have a classroom blog, be sure to include this information on it.

Activities for Older Children (Grades 4–5)

Health and safety education serves as a place in the curriculum where students focus on personal health issues, the health issues of others, and environmental issues. A variety of exciting strategies is available to assist you in teaching health and safety to middle and upper elementary students. The more varied your approach, the more stimulating your classroom will be. The following strategies for health and safety instruction can be used to enhance your curriculum with this age group.

Taste Bud Experiment

This activity teaches about the importance of saliva in tasting food.

Have students use paper towels to dry off their tongues. Next, have them taste a variety of dry foods such as crackers, pretzels, and bagels, one at a time. Ask them to record their observations. Next, have the students take a drink or two of water. This will help stimulate saliva production. Have them try the foods again and record their findings. Chemicals in the food will dissolve in the saliva and should trigger receptors on the taste buds.

Smelly Air

This activity teaches how smells travel in the air.

Place a variety of smelly food or objects in individual containers with lids at one end of the classroom. These items might include microwave popcorn, perfume-soaked cotton balls, onions, or strong spices. Have a volunteer sit or stand at the other end of the classroom, 20 feet away. Open the containers one at a time, and use a stopwatch to find out how long it takes before the volunteer first smells the item. Between opening the different containers, run a fan for a few minutes to clear the air. Divide 20 by the number of seconds it took to smell the item to determine how many feet the smell traveled per second.

Have Germs, Will Travel

This activity teaches how germs are spread through physical contact.

Have students sit in a circle while you rub a piece of sidewalk chalk all over your hands. (Inexpensive, colored chalk works best for this experiment because it creates more dust.) The dust represents germs. Once your hands are covered in chalk, begin walking around the circle, shaking hands randomly. See how many students catch the "germs." Variation: Invite each student to cover his or her hands in chalk dust. Next, have students sit at their desks and do a simple task. After they have seen just how easily germs can be transferred, have them clean their space and wash up.

Vaccines

Explore the value of vaccination with the "Making Vaccines" interactive at http://www.pbs.org/nova/meningitis/vaccines.html. Research vaccines for humans and pets and create pamphlets with information about each one.

Cartoons

Students can draw and label their own health and safety cartoons, or they can collect cartoons that depict healthful and unhealthful practices. Share and describe these cartoons. For example, we have often heard the saying, "Laughter is the best medicine." Have students collect cartoons that make them laugh, compile those cartoons into a booklet, and then share their booklets with the class.

Teamwork—Relay Races

An excellent way to encourage teamwork is through relay races. In planning relay races, be sure that the activities center on a variety of skills such as balance, coordination, cognitive planning, and physical fitness. By including different skills in the relay race, teams will quickly realize that all teammates contribute essential skills to the group.

Some examples of relay-race stations include the spoon and hard-boiled egg pass, passing through hoops while holding a partner's hand, a maze activity, and jumping rope with a partner.

After the relay, have students respond to questions like the following:
- What station was the hardest/easiest for you and/or your team? Why?
- What beneficial skills did each classmate bring to your team?
- What do you need in place for teamwork to be effective?
- How can working as a team be more beneficial than working in isolation?

Case Histories

A case history is a short description of an event or happening. It can be used to illustrate a point. Students may also be asked to write or react to a case history to evaluate learning. Example: Nutrition: Develop a case history about someone who has poor eating habits—skips breakfast or heavily salts food. Ask students to read the case history and identify the poor eating habits.

Commercials

Students can write and act out commercials that promote positive health behaviors. For example, students might write and act out a commercial about ways a person can help improve their eating habits. These commercials could be videotaped to show to other classes.

Community Resources

Arrange field trips to community resource agencies. Community resources include the local health department, local offices of the American Lung Association and the American Heart Association, a life insurance company, a mental health center, a pharmacy, and local crisis centers. For example, you might arrange a visit to your community's water treatment facility. Discuss how this facility works to keep water safe to drink.

Current Events Newsletter

Students can research current events on a local, national, or world level and write short articles to include in a "Health Happenings" newsletter. For example, students might research the communicable diseases that are currently most prevalent in their community or in their country. Their articles might describe the cause, symptoms, transmission, and treatment of those diseases. They might also describe health habits that may reduce the incidence of the disease.

Debate

Students, individually or in organized teams, can research a health issue or topic to formulate a detailed, well-documented viewpoint to use in a debate. For example, students might research and then debate the issue "Should students who are carriers of the AIDS virus be permitted to attend school with other children?"

Diary of Events

Students can record daily happenings in a diary to learn more about their health and behaviors. For example, students might write down their daily physical activities for one week, describing their feelings after each activity. What did they learn about their behaviors? Tell students that it is not necessary to share what they have learned about themselves.

Math for Health

Incorporate running and/or brisk walking to reinforce math concepts while enjoying a healthy activity. Whether you run or walk as a class, have students set a goal at the beginning of the year of how many miles or laps around the schoolyard they will complete each week. Have students keep a calendar to record their laps or miles as they try to reach that goal. Then have them use those calendars to add their total laps, convert the laps to miles, get the class total for the week, and average their daily, weekly, and monthly totals. You can even use brisk walking or running to teach the metric system, converting meters into miles.

A Spoonful of Sugar—Math Activity

Health experts agree that most Americans eat too much sugar. Measure out 10 teaspoons of sugar and place it in a small container. This is the amount of sugar in most regular cans of soda. Many drinks and snacks contain high amounts of sugar. Food labels list the amount of sugar in grams. Have children collect the wrappers of their favorite snack foods. Check the labels and compare the amount of sugar in each snack. Which snack is lowest in sugar? Which snack is highest? Have students make graphs of their results to share with classmates.

Healthy Body Salad

This is a great activity to teach young children about how healthy eating benefits the heart and mind. You can do it to celebrate a great week of student work or as the culmination of a unit about Mr. Amazing Heart/Body. Tell students you will have a "heart-friendly party" with healthy foods that are fun to prepare and tasty to eat. Ask children to bring in a healthy ingredient to make a salad, such as green-leaf lettuce (rather than iceberg, which has low nutritional value), carrots, black olives, low-fat cheese, or fat-free dressing. As each child adds his or her ingredient into

a large bowl, describe how the ingredient is a heart-smart food. Then toss the salad and enjoy! For added fun, serve angel food cake with fresh strawberries.

Poison Prevention

Discuss poisons with your class. Contact the nearest poison control center for Mr. Yuck stickers for students to take home and put on the bottles under the sink. Also discuss dangers that exist from plants as well as those dangers inherent in taking someone else's medicine. Other ideas can be found at http://www.ppsinc.org.

Safety Signals

Plan with children how they might determine whether red traffic lights really are longer than green lights. Determine the best way to set up the study, then choose an intersection and provide stopwatches. Have students declare a hypothesis and then set out to prove it.

Reading Labels

Collect ingredient labels from several different food items. Explain to students that they must be listed in descending order of quantity in the specific item. Then provide them with a list of minimum daily requirements for various vitamins and minerals (available at http://www.fda.gov). Challenge students to check the requirements against the labels from their favorite foods. Will that cause them to make different nutritional choices?

Moving Food Chain

When students incorporate movement into a unit about the food chain, they're more likely to remember what they've learned. To help them, have students choose a plant that is a producer—either a fruit or vegetable—that they will act out during an imaginary growing period. Tell students not to reveal their choice; they must remain silent. Then have them make their bodies as low to the ground as they can, as if they were simulating the shape of a plant that has yet to grow. Tell students they will grow based on the sound and rhythms of a hand drum. Then play the drum very softly when they are seedlings in the ground, somewhat loudly when they are half way to maturation, and very loudly when they are fully mature and ready to be harvested. Walk around and gently tap each student to signal that he or she can reveal what plant he or she has grown into. You might also ask students to tell what they know about the plant or describe its nutritional value.

Interviews

Have students interview someone in the community whose career is related to health care and maintenance. Students should be prepared with a list of questions before the interview takes place. They can share their information with the class in an oral presentation.

Jingles

Students can make up jingles to describe health products or practices, or they can analyze jingles that are used on television or radio commercials. What is their favorite jingle? Why does the jingle appeal to them?

Mural

A health-related mural can be made by having students write or paste pictures on long sheets of paper. The mural can illustrate events that have happened over a long period of time. For example, students might trace the history of major epidemics of communicable diseases and make a mural that shows (1) disease outbreaks, tuberculosis, plague; (2) treatment of the disease; and (3) important people in these health issues. Place these happenings and people with their related dates on the mural.

Photography

When appropriate, encourage students to take photographs and write a description of what they see. This strategy can be used on a field trip to highlight what students have learned. For example, students might take pictures of safety hazards in their community and describe ways to remedy these hazards.

Posters

Posters are available from many health organizations as well as from local health departments. These posters, such as "Thank You for Not Smoking" from the American Cancer Society (http://www.cancer.org), can be displayed in the classroom to reinforce learning. Students can make their own posters to use in the classroom or to display in the community. Have students make a poster that discourages smoking or drug use.

Skits

Through skits, students can explore different issues that they might experience in real life. The teacher can design the roles for specific situations. For example, students might devise a skit in which a quack sells a "health food." They should use as many persuasive techniques as possible to sell the product.

Chapter Review

1. In teaching young children about health, what is the best approach and teaching strategy to use? Describe activities you would plan to use in teaching young children about health.
2. What are the basic health and other types of information you should have on hand for each child in case of emergency? Explain.
3. Discuss several ways you can prevent accidents with children six years old and younger.
4. What are some safety hazards for children ages 7 to 11?
5. What are some other areas of the curriculum in which to include health and safety ideas? Give specific examples of activities.
6. How would you teach young children about fire, traffic, and poison safety in concrete ways? Give specific examples in your reply.

References

American Academy of Pediatrics. (2006). *Standards for day care centers.* Evanston, IL: AAP.

American Dental Association. (2009). History of dentistry: Ancient origins. Accessed 11/25/09 at http://www.ada.org/public/resources/history/index.asp

Coppa, A. (2006). Early Neolithic tradition of dentistry. *Nature, 4*(6), 16–20.

Greene, A., M.D. (2004). *From first kicks to first steps.* New York: McGraw-Hill.

Herlihy, D. V. (2006). *Bicycle: The history.* New Haven, CT: Yale University Press.

KidsHealth from Nemours (2009). Overweight and Obesity. Accessed 11/26/09. http://www.kidshealth.org/parent/general/body/overweight_obesity.html

Luttikhuis, I., Baur, L., Jansen, H., Shrewsbury, V. A., O'Malley, C., Stolk, R. P., & Summerbell, C. D. (2009). *Interventions for treating obesity in children.* Washington, DC: U.S. National Library of Medicine, National Institutes of Health.

National Safe Kids Campaign. (2009). Safe Kids Worldwide, Accessed 11/26/09, from http://www.safekids.org

Office of the Surgeon General (2007, Jan. 1). Overweight in children and adolescents. Accessed 11/26/09, from http://www.surgeongeneral.gov/topics/obesity

Oxlade, C. (2007). *Bicycles (Transportation around the world)* (2nd ed.). Portsmouth, NH: Heinemann.

Peden, M., Oyebite, K., Ozanne-Smith, J., & Hyder, A. A. *World report on child injury prevention.* Geneva, Switzerland: World Health Organization.

Tucker, P. (2008). The physical activity levels of preschool-aged children: A systematic review. *Early Childhood Research Quarterly, 23*(4), 547–558.

U.S. Department of Health & Human Services. (2009). *Healthy People 2010.* Accessed 11/26/09 at http://www.healthypeople.gov/

U.S. Fire Administration. (2009). USFA Kids. Accessed 11/26/09 at http://www.usfa.dhs.gov/kids/flash.shtm

Wittberg, R. A., Northrup, K. L., & Cottrel, L. (2009). Children's physical fitness and academic performance. *American Journal of Health Education, 40*(1), 30–36.

Additional Readings

Carroll, A., & Vreeman, R. (2009). *Don't swallow your gum!: Myths, half-truths, and outright lies about your body and health.* New York: St. Martin's.

Cairns, W. (2009). *How to live dangerously: The hazards of helmets, the benefits of bacteria, and the risks of living too safe.* New York: St. Martin's.

DeMarzo, J. (2009). *Healthy breaks: Wellness activities for the classroom.* Champaign, IL: Human Kinetics.

Edlin, G., & Golanty, E. (2009). *Health and wellness* (10th ed.). Sudbury, MA: Jones & Bartlett Publishers.

Eiserman, W. D., Shisler, L., Foust, T., Buhrmann, J., Winston, R., & White, K. (2008). Updating hearing screening practices in early childhood settings. *Infants and Young Children: An Interdisciplinary Journal of Special Care Practices, 21*(3), 186–193.

Parrott, R. (2009). *Talking about health: Why communication matters.* Hoboken, NJ: Eilry-Blackwell.

Paterson, L. (2009). *How to's and what not's.* Raleigh, NC; Lulu.

Parizkova, J. (2009). *Nutrition, physical activity and health in early life* (2nd ed.). Danvers, MA: CRC.

Purdie, K. (2010). *Safety (Being healthy, feeling great).* New York: PowerKids Press.

Schaefer, A. (2009). *Staying safe (health and fitness).* Chicago, IL: Heinemann-Raintree.

Skenazy, L. (2009). *Free-range kids: Giving our children the freedom we had without going nuts with worry.* San Francisco, CA: Jossey Bass.

Sorte, J., Daeschel, I., & Amador, C. (2010). *Nutrition, health and safety for young children: Promoting wellness.* Upper Saddle River, NJ: Prentice Hall.

Webb, M. B., Dowd, K., Harden, B. J., & Landsverk, J. (2009). *Child welfare and child well-being: New perspectives from the National Survey of Child and Adolescent Well-being.* New York: Oxford University Press.

Williams, K. (2009). *Keeping kids safe, healthy, and smart: An educator's guide to child health and safety.* Lantham, MD: Rowman & Littlefield Education.

Software for Children

Adventures with the Shady Characters, preschool–grade 5

BrainPOP Jr., grades K–3

Children Fight Bac! Version 2.0, grades 1–9

D. M. Dinwiddie, Physician-in-Training, grades 2–6

Danger Rangers: Mission 547 Safety Rules! preschool–grade 2

Emergency! Disaster Rescue Squad, ages 8 and up

Health Beats Aches & Pains, grades 1–7

Health Beats Feelings & Worries, grades 2–8

Health Beats Growing and Developing, grades 1–7

Health Beats Keeping Healthy, grades 1–7

Health for Kids Series, ages 7–10

Inner Explorers: Health Beats Body Parts, grades 2–7

My Amazing Human Body, ages 6–10

Professor Garfield, preschool–grade 6

Science Is Elementary: What's Inside Your Body? grades 4–9

STARBRIGHT Asthma CD–ROM Game: Quest for the Code, grades 2–9

Ultimate 3D Skeleton, ages 9 and up

What's the Safest Thing To Do? ages 4–8

Youthealth Inner Explorers Series One, grades 1–7

Helpful Websites

American Red Cross, http://www.redcross.org
This site provides teachers with information on health promotion training programs for children 5 to 8.

Sparky's World, http://www.sparky.org
This site provides health and fire safety information and ideas. The appropriate age range is 6 years and up.

Traffic Safety Kids Page, http://www.nysgtsc.state. ny.us/kids.htm
This site provides information on traffic safety, health, and accident prevention, to name just a few topics available. Children ages 7 to 12 will enjoy this site.

Otto Club, http://www.ottoclub.org
This site, presented by the AAA Traffic Safety Department, provides health and traffic safety information and activities for preschoolers through grade 5.

Bright Futures, http://www.brightfutures.org
Bright Futures is a national initiative dedicated to promoting and improving the health of U. S. children. The Bright Futures website offers information on children's health and development in a new and practical format. There's something for everyone interested in the well-being of children. Some materials in Spanish are also available on the site, as well as links to the organizations that support Bright Futures and other useful sites for professionals and families.

National Association of the Deaf (NAD), http:// www.nad.org/
This comprehensive website offers information on education, advocacy, frequently asked questions, and recent news and research for the deaf and hearing impaired.

American Dental Association, http://www.ada.org
This website provides information for children, parents, and teachers on good dental health.

Environmental Protection Agency, Public Information, http://www.epa.gov
This website provides information and services on teaching about the environment. This information is especially designed for classroom use.

Get Up! Get Out! http://www.getupgetout.org/
This website offers information and ideas for raising awareness about the importance of healthy eating, exercise, and healthy living habits.

Smile Smarts: Oral Health Curriculum, http://www. ada.org/public/education/index.asp This American Dental Association site presents oral health topics in an attention-getting format that includes games, informative animations, and hands-on activities.

Mouth Power Online, http://www.mouthpower.org
Presented by the University of Maryland National Museum of Dentistry, this site explores several modules on oral health, cleaning teeth, story of teeth, dental time warp, and a creativity corner.

Fatburgr, http://www.fatburgr.com/
This site gives you nutritional information from your favorite restaurants. Find your food values by restaurants or categories.

The U.S. Department of Health and Human Services, http://www.hhs.gov/
Find national health objectives for 2010, with baseline statistical data and relevant publications.

All of the following sites have great ideas and information for teachers to use in health and safety activities for children.

American Academy of Pediatrics, http://www. healthychildcare.org

Discovery Education Health Connection, http:// www.discoveryhealthconnection.com

HealthLink Plus, http://www.healthlinkplus.org
Dozens of links to credible health websites are provided on this useful site.

Learn to Be Healthy, http://www.learntobehealthy. org

National Safety Council, http://www.nsc.org

Parent Resources and Information on Drug Education, http://www.pride.org

Food and Drug Administration, http://www.fda.gov

Federal Consumer Information Center, http://www. pueblo.gsa.gov

Consumer Product Safety Commission, http://www. cpsc.gov/
The following websites are good sources for information about diseases, disease prevention, and disease control.

American Academy of Allergy, Asthma, and Immunology, http://www.aaaai.org

American Cancer Society, http://www.cancer.org

American Heart Association, http://www.amhrt.org

Centers for Disease Control and Prevention, http:// www.cdc.gov

Children with Diabetes, http://www.childrenwith-diabetes.com/index_cwd.htm

Juvenile Diabetes Research Foundation International, http://www.jdf.org/

The Candlelighters Childhood Cancer Foundation, http://www.candlelighters.org

The National Association of School Nurses, http:// www.nasn.org

The following sites are good sources for information on emotional and mental health.

National Institute of Mental Health, http://www. nimh.nih.gov/

Mental Health America, http://www.nmha.org

For additional creative activity resources, visit our website at www.Cengage.com/login

Creativity: A Multicultural View

REFLECTIVE QUESTIONS

After studying this section, you should be able to answer the following questions.

1. What is my definition of the term *diversity?*
2. How important is multicultural education in early childhood settings?
3. Have I thought through my personal feelings on multicultural education and its place in the classroom?
4. How can I be sure my classroom and activities are nonbiased and reflect the culture in my school and community?
5. Have I planned to include parents and community members in my curriculum development?
6. What is the relevance of my curriculum to young children's lives?
7. What are some basic markers of a quality, multicultural, antibias program?
8. What role should young children play in planning the multicultural curriculum?
9. Am I including process-oriented, open-ended creative activities as part of my multicultural curriculum?
10. In what way am I ensuring that young children grow in their understanding and respect for each other as unique and different individuals?
11. Am I using a developmentally appropriate approach in planning my multicultural curriculum?
12. How are my own attitudes and values reflected in my classroom?
13. What groups of people and ways of life are missing from my classroom?

Section 6 continues an emphasis on creativity and developmentally appropriate activities in the early childhood program with a focus on their place in a multicultural curriculum. It is essential that early childhood programs reflect the multicultural world that exists today for our children and will continue to be a reality throughout their lives.

It is not enough to provide creative activities in a creative curriculum. Creative activities and curriculum must embrace the larger world—the multicultural world of today. That, in essence, is the rationale for Section 6.

Also, a peek into any early childhood program today will reveal a wonderfully diverse scene. It is obvious that the early childhood classroom has changed dramatically over the past 10 years and will continue to do so. Overall, young children in immigrant families account for at least 10% of children in 26 states (plus the District of Columbia), and in only eight states does the proportion fall below 5%. Thus, young children in immigrant families merit substantial attention from the federal government and states, cities, towns, and school districts spread across every region of the country.

The largest proportion of young children in immigrant families (41%) had origins in Mexico. But the remaining 59% have origins that span the globe, with 5% to 9% having origins in each of the following seven regions: the Caribbean, Central America, South America, East Asia, West Asia, Indochina (Cambodia, Laos, Thailand, Vietnam), and Europe. Another 2% to 3% had origins in the former Soviet Union or Africa. Many of these young children live in homes where languages other than English are spoken and where cultural practices differ from the American mainstream (Hernandez, Denton & Macartney, 2008; U.S. Census Reports (2006)). This diversity poses unprecedented opportunities and challenges for integrating and fostering the success of these children and their families.

From its very beginnings, our country was built on diversity, and diversity will continue to be our strength. As early childhood educators, we must recognize these cultural differences and provide children with an early educational experience that prepares them to live in a culturally diverse country.

In the following pages of this section, you will find many suggestions and ideas for addressing this crucial issue in early childhood education—the creation of a multicultural, antibias curriculum. In these chapters, while you will not find separate sections on activities for children, you will find that the chapters themselves are full of appropriate activity suggestions. You will also find in each chapter numerous references to websites, which in turn provide a multitude of suggestions for multicultural art activities, fine art from many cultures, multicultural children's books, history, and much more.

Section 6 is intended to be a beginning point in your creating a multicultural, antibias curriculum for your own individual classroom. You are encouraged to apply the ideas in these chapters in designing your own unique multicultural curriculum. It is the author's hope that in these chapters and in the references and Internet resources, you will begin to honor diversity in everything you do in working with children and their families. My goal for all early childhood teachers is that by living with differences, we gain from them, and then celebrate them each and every day.

Section 6 is divided into the following chapters:

Chapter 24: Creativity, Diversity, and the Early Childhood Program

Chapter 25: Creative Multicultural Curriculum Ideas

Creativity, Diversity, and the Early Childhood Program

6. Define "deficit" and "transformational" curricula perspectives.

7. Discuss some ways to incorporate transformational perspectives into an early childhood program.

Like learning to be a creative early childhood teacher, learning to teach in culturally diverse classrooms does not simply happen after reading this chapter or even after an early childhood course. Like creative teaching, learning to teach in a culturally diverse classroom does not happen immediately after you learn about children's learning styles or even by studying about different cultures.

OBJECTIVES

After studying this chapter, you should be able to:

1. Explain how creative teaching in a culturally diverse classroom involves process and practice.

2. Describe the role of the teacher in a creative multicultural classroom.

3. List some of the attitudes a teacher needs to have in a creative multicultural classroom.

4. Discuss how learning centers can reflect a creative multicultural curriculum.

5. Explain why creative multicultural education is important in early childhood education.

Teaching in Culturally Diverse Classrooms: Process and Practice

Learning to teach in culturally diverse classrooms is a process. It is a process a lot like learning a language. Both require a *process* and *practice for fluency*. In learning a language, you start the process by learning the sounds of the language, the culture, and history of the people who speak the language. Then you learn the rules and guidelines for speaking and writing. As you learn, you practice. Your confidence grows as you learn to think and speak and write more fluently in the new language. You make progress and you make mistakes, but you keep studying. You create opportunities to learn more about native speakers, their customs, and community rituals. And you continue to practice. You visit local communities to become familiar with the sounds and uses of your new language, all the while continuing to practice. And in the end, you must use your new language or lose it.

Becoming a creative and culturally competent teacher in the classroom is similar to learning a new language because it, too, requires a process. You must learn the vocabulary, the sounds, and the cultural perspectives of the children and their families. Understanding the history and current status of cultural groups will help you make more informed decisions about how to educate their children. Then you learn the norms and social structures of these microcultures, or neighborhoods, and how they impact the macroculture, or the general society. And you practice by meeting the individuals and families who represent the children in your schools. Meeting family members must happen for greater mutual understanding. You make progress and you make mistakes, but you keep studying and learning. You create opportunities to interact with children and their families more and more as you become fluent in negotiating across cultures. You practice, practice, practice.

Learning a language and becoming a culturally competent teacher both require a commitment to study and practice, reflection on the learning process, openness to feedback, and a willingness to collaborate with others. When you think about multicultural teaching in this way, it is obvious that planning a few holiday parties around an ethnic theme is a far cry from this type of truly creative multicultural education.

The Teacher in Multicultural Classrooms

You, as a teacher, set the tone in the creative multicultural classroom. All children have the opportunity to learn about themselves and others simply by the way you treat them and their peers. If you show respect for their worth as human beings and encourage them to respect one another, they will begin the long process of learning to celebrate human differences. Nonverbal cues, body language, and role modeling are all a part of its foundation. We may isolate ourselves from each other socially, but our classrooms become more diverse every year. Teachers confront issues of diversity in intimate ways that most adults do not. So it's crucial that teachers and administrators explore their own attitudes and beliefs regarding diversity. We cannot expect that anyone will abandon her discomfort with diversity simply because she dons the mantle of a teacher. But we can expect that all teachers develop a deeper understanding of their own diversity experiences and how they influence their interactions with children and parents. Change can be forced on you, or

change can be something that you embrace and make part of yourself. In other words, you must say, "The change I believe in begins with me."

Most important of all, the development of children's appreciation of diversity in others must be worked on by you and by the children *every day*. It must be an integral part of the early childhood curriculum of every classroom and child care center. This does not mean that you should teach a unit on Asians or Africans or Hispanics every day . . . or any day. It does not mean you should point out differences in the way the children look or dress or speak. Teepees, tomahawks, and piñatas have little to do with developing children's appreciation of one another. What counts most of all is:

- a deep *belief* in the worth of every child
- an accepting *attitude* toward each child as a unique individual
- an unqualified *support* for each child's development of emotional, social, physical, cognitive, language, and creative skills on a daily basis

FIGURE 24-1 • One of the things that counts in a multicultural curriculum is a deep belief in the worth of every child.

FIGURE 24-2 • The teacher sets the tone in the creative multicultural classroom.

A Creative Multicultural Curriculum—More Than a Piñata Party

Many preschool curricula are developed around themes such as the family, seasons, weather, holidays, animals, and community helpers. Making such programs multicultural has often meant inserting a Chinese New Year celebration or a Mexican party with a piñata. Although these activities may be fun for children, they have little to do with the immediate interpersonal concerns of children. Although such programs may seem to be teaching children to appreciate other cultures, more often than not they teach separateness instead. By focusing on a culture's differences from mainstream American culture, children from that culture may come to feel different and somehow lesser.

You are probably asking at this moment, How can this be done? It's easy to talk about integrating creative multicultural activities daily, but is it really possible or feasible in an early childhood curriculum? Given their already jam-packed schedule, how can teachers and caregivers add information about different cultures on a daily basis to every activity?

It can be done. The first step in doing it is to reconsider the concept of "curriculum." You need to think of curriculum as a *process* of helping children to grow and learn, rather than a *product* of knowledge that children must acquire.

The physical setting of the early childhood classroom supports this process-oriented approach. As we learned in Chapter 6, this means that the early childhood classroom is set up in curriculum areas or learning centers that promote children's growth and learning in each of the areas of child development: physical, cognitive, language, social, emotional, and creative. As we learned, well-organized and well-equipped learning centers make it possible for children to learn a great deal on their own through the *process* of playful interaction with materials.

But what about the various cultures themselves? How can they be integrated into curriculum areas so that children can become familiar with multicultural attitudes on a daily basis? As unlikely as it sounds, if we focus on children's likenesses—their common bonds—then they will be able to celebrate their differences with pride. The curriculum that is designed around common bonds involves children in creative multicultural activities in each of the curriculum areas on a daily basis. The common bonds curriculum is discussed later in this chapter.

What Does a Creative Multicultural Education Include?

Multicultural education includes teaching children about their own culture—their ethnic heritage. It also means exposing children to other cultures and helping them be comfortable with and respect all the ways people are different from each other. It is teaching children how to relate to one another and how to play fair. Multicultural education encourages children to notice and think about unfairness and challenges them to do something about the unfairness toward people they perceive in their world.

Creative multicultural education involves more than teaching information directly. It means providing a classroom that includes materials depicting people from many different places doing many different things. It involves creating and maintaining an environment that says, "Everyone is welcome here." It encourages children to act, think, and talk like members of their own culture. It helps children to like themselves just the way they are. It encourages children to actively explore a variety of materials and exposes them to creative experiences that might not be part of their daily home experiences.

On the other hand, multicultural education also creates an environment that allows children of different cultural backgrounds their privacy. A child may be unwilling to share insights into her or his own cultural heritage until a relationship of trust has been established with other children in the group. Children should never be pushed to participate in activities and put on the spot to validate their cultural information. Let them decide how and when they wish to express their ethnicity.

Why Is Multicultural Education Important?

We, as early childhood teachers, know that high-quality programs produce positive outcomes for children, families, and society as a whole. Yet many of us still do not understand why multicultural education is so important in the early years. The following are some basic reasons why.

- *Multicultural education encourages a sense of self.* Multicultural education is important for young children because they deserve to be in programs where it is safe for them to be who they are. Children deserve to know the truth about themselves, the real world, and the people in it. Children have the right to feel good about themselves. Children are entitled to their cultural heritage and to be proud of it.
- *Multicultural education promotes healthy cognitive and social development.* During the early years, children acquire self-concept, build their self-esteem, learn how to make friends, become aware of family and community, learn to use words to express themselves, have strong feelings and fears, use magical (and often distorted) thinking, and tend to believe everything they see and hear. These characteristics and developmental milestones result in prejudiced thinking and behavior. Consequently, this is the time to help children move ahead in their thinking and learn to function successfully and cooperatively in a culturally diverse society and world.
- *Multicultural education prepares children for the future.* Multicultural education is important because the world is changing. We will experience living in a society made up of many people from many different cultures.
- *Multicultural education discourages denial and fear of differences.* An early childhood program that doesn't provide multicultural education encourages denial and teaches children a narrow view of the world. Teaching as if there is only one perspective that really matters promotes the idea that other ways of being in the world are deficient and deviant. All children need to understand and accept that there are other perspectives and other ways of being in the world.

We Are All Alike—Common Bonds Curricula

The creative multicultural early childhood curriculum should be designed around the common bonds all of us share. Think for a moment about what most young children have in common. Your list may include some of the following.

- They live in a family.
- They live in a neighborhood.
- They live in a natural environment.
- One or both of their parents usually work for a living.
- They eat the food their family provides.
- They speak the language their family speaks.
- They play with toys and play games.
- They like to pretend.
- They like to run, jump, and move.
- They like to draw, dance, and make music.
- They want to have friends and get along well with others.

FIGURE 24-3 • In the creative multicultural early childhood program, a child feels free to be proud of her or his family and ethnic group.

- They want to be accepted and appreciated.
- They want to feel good about themselves.
- They want to succeed.

From such a list, you can begin constructing a curriculum that speaks to the common bonds of all young children. The cultural diversity of all children can be celebrated within a **common bonds curriculum.** From the list of things children have in common in all cultures, some common bonds for a creative **multicultural curriculum** might be:

- family
- self-esteem
- foods
- arts and crafts
- music and dance
- physical expression
- languages
- earth

Once the common bonds are in place, the next step is to incorporate activities related to cultural diversity. Chapter 25 contains several examples of common bonds theme units and activities that could be used in your multicultural curriculum. Of course, these ideas are only suggestions on some approaches to take to multicultural curriculum planning. Your own unique group of children will dictate what to use in your curriculum planning from the ideas in Chapter 25. These ideas and all new ideas become meaningful to young children when they relate directly to the children *in your group*. Thus, if information about other cultures is to make a difference in the lives of young children, it should relate directly to the child and her or his peers. It should involve children in learning firsthand about children like themselves from different cultures.

Creative Multicultural Learning Centers

As we learned in Chapter 6, children learn more through free-choice play than group times and structured activities. Learning centers organize children's free play and provide them with many choices. These areas are flexible and always changing to fit the children's interests and abilities or the curriculum theme.

Begin introducing multicultural curriculum by adding materials that reflect the culture of your children and the local community. Later, add a variety of materials and objects to represent diversity in the world and the many ways people live out their daily lives.

You can also teach through the interest center by adding materials to each area that support the unit theme. Here are some ideas on how to incorporate multicultural materials into some specific learning centers.

Art area. In a multicultural classroom, the art materials must include colors, patterns, and textures from other cultures. Try adding origami paper for folding, rice paper for painting, and red clay for modeling. Collage materials could also be available such as magazines with picture of people from different cultures, a file of precut pictures, or fabric scraps of imported cloth. In addition, the art area should be stocked with skin-colored crayons, markers, paint, paper, collage materials, and play dough. Consider setting out hand mirrors so that children can look at themselves or other people. Include visual display illustrating the artwork, color schemes, and visual patterns of other cultures.

In our global society, we need to help children understand that there are many ways of doing things and many ways of seeing the world. Looking at art from different cultures helps children do this. Providing open-ended experiences based on well-known artwork gives children rich exposure to art as well as cultural experiences.

Block area. Blocks adapt well to a multicultural environment because they are the most versatile piece of equipment in the early childhood classroom. If you add multicultural accessories and props to a full set of hardwood unit blocks, you will guide and expand children's play. Such props can include a variety of transportation toys such as trains, buses, double-decker buses, planes, jets, cars, horses and carts, ferries, barges, canoes, and sleds. Multiethnic, nonsexist wooden play figures as well as small dolls and paper dolls from other countries increase the variety of people. Try adding palm leaves, coconut branches, corn husks, pine branches, bark, pine needles, stones, and straw for creating roofs, houses, and fences. Display pictures of buildings from different parts of the world such as a pagoda, tree house, adobe, thatched hut, log home, sod home, tent, earth-sheltered home, apartment building, trailer, and hotel. Rubber, plastic, wooden, cloth, and carved-bone animals representing the jungle, tropical forest, desert, and forest will also enhance children's play.

Music area. Build up a broad selection of both vocal and instrumental music. Ask parents to make a cassette tape or CD of the music their family and children

THIS ONE'S for YOU!   Preschool Around the World

With the amazing diversity of cultures we find in American preschools today, it is interesting to know some facts about the preschools around the world some of your children may have come from. It may help you understand a little better the background of some of these children in your group.

China. China is such an enormous and diverse country (there are 130 million children under 7) that preschool enrollment varies widely. Almost all city kids go to school from age 3 to 5, but the national attendance rate is only 40%. The Chinese government is trying to reach children in rural areas by providing weekend and seasonal preschool classes and mobile caravans for herdsmen's children. In these preschool years, children learn about 200 Chinese characters, how to add and subtract numbers smaller than 100, and life skills like manners and hand washing. Teachers also instruct children in playacting, painting, singing, and dancing. Children spend two to three hours outside every day, playing a variety of games.

Chinese preschools have nutrition experts who plan meals for children. Children wear matching colorful uniforms on days when they have field trips or sports events. Children whose parents are very busy with work sometimes go to boarding preschools. They go home to stay with their parents midweek and on weekends.

Sweden. Tuition is subsidized in Sweden, which means no one pays more than $170 per month, and once children turn 4, they're guaranteed three hours of preschool a day for free. A typical preschool is a yellow or red one-story building with a playground, an indoor gym, a kitchen for each class, a lots of rooms with interior "windows" and doors connecting them.

The Swedes are very much concerned with the environment and conservation. So, not only do the children learn about nature, but they also play outside every day, no matter how cold or snowy. Whenever possible, playgrounds have natural surroundings—rocks to climb on and trees to hide behind.

One of the goals of Swedish preschool is to avoid gender stereotypes. You will find boys setting the table and girls shoveling the walk.

For cleanliness, everyone wears indoor shoes, slippers, or sneakers, and teachers wear clogs or Birkenstocks.

Preschoolers eat lunch at a communal table with candles. And there is no sugary cereal—a typical breakfast is caviar from a tube with butter and bread.

Kenya. Communities in this East African country usually build and support their own schools. The typical rural school is a simple structure with a dirt or cement floor and a single chalkboard, although schools in Nairobi and along the coast have more modern amenities.

Children spend most of the day watching their teacher at the blackboard and participating in call and response. Although there often isn't enough paper to go around, teachers try to teach children to read and write before they enter primary school.

In poor areas, parents must make supplies for their children, including blocks, toys, and learning charts. Bottle caps are used for counting games.

The Ministry of Health sends workers to preschools to weigh the children, examine them, give them vitamins, talk to families about AIDS prevention, and teach parents home remedies for diarrhea.

Food is in short supply in many communities, so there is not a lot of variety in the children's diets. But some schools may hire a cook to prepare the children's food.

You won't see milk cartons in a Kenyan preschool, but you may see a cow purchased by parents to provide milk for the morning chai the children drink.

Japan. Preschool is considered vital to social development, so important that nearly all three-to five-year-olds attend. Japanese preschool teachers don't use time-outs for bad behavior. If two children are fighting, a teacher might get several other children to help broker the peace. Even in the most dense urban areas, the Japanese try to give a lot of space to preschools, including a big outdoor yard.

Each child says a formal "good morning" and "goodbye" to his or her teachers and classmates every day. Japanese preschools have lots of festivals and events for the children, like market day, where the older children pretend to be merchants and the younger children are customers.

Children bring *bento* boxes for lunch—a plastic box that has compartments for rice, fish, and vegetables. Most parents like to arrange the food beautifully, sometimes into fun shapes like animals and trains. In Japanese preschools, children take turns calling the class to order, leading the morning meeting in songs, and sharing news.

Argentina. Argentina has made early childhood education a priority. Attendance is mandatory for

Continued

five-year olds, and educators are still trying to spread the word that school can be beneficial for two-, three-, and four-year olds, too. City children are much more likely to go to school before age five than rural children.

Preschool lessons can vary greatly, depending on the school. A poor rural school, for instance, might have to focus on children's basic health and nutrition needs. A teacher in the city, on the other hand, might have more time to help the children put out a class newspaper, learn English, or plant a garden.

Children start each day by raising the flag and singing a "hello" song and a special children's version of the national anthem. Public preschools require children to wear blue- or pink-checked aprons with pockets in the front and buttons in the back. Private schools require two-piece uniforms that look like jogging suits.

For lunch, children are served a three-course meal, including soup, rice and meat, and fresh fruit or Jell-O. No junk food is allowed in preschool.

Preschoolers not only do a lot of art projects—they actually study the work of great artists like Miro, Matisse, and Monet and try to draw or paint in their styles.

Sources: United Nations Educational, Scientific, and Cultural Organization (UNECSO), www.unesco.org; Organisation for Economic Co-operation and Development (OECD) www.oecd.org, www.unesco.org, 2009.

---

enjoy at home. Use music from different cultures as background music during free play and rest time. Teach children songs with simple words and melodies from other cultures and teach them songs that encourage differences, acceptance, and cooperation. Add instruments such as maracas, Tibetan bells, gongs, gourds, metal and bongo drums, woven jute rattles, wooden flutes, brass bells, conch shells, castanets, wooden xylophones, and guitars to the set of traditional rhythm instruments. Many cultures use drums and drumming as their main instrument. Though expensive, a good drum provides a wonderful sound that can serve as the basic background instrument for many music activities.

Dramatic play. The dramatic play area, like other centers, must allow children to explore a variety of lifestyles, including family systems, economic class, and culture. In this area, children try on the roles of people of different ages, skills, and occupations. Rather than teaching a particular culture, the dramatic play props should emphasize the many ways of going about our daily lives such as kinds of food to eat, types of eating utensils, and ways of dressing. Begin with items children have in their homes and expand from there.

Manipulative area (table toys). This area can be enhanced with multiethnic, nonsexist puzzles available through many common toy catalogues. Sets of graduated items from other cultures such as wooden dolls or animals make fun sequencing games. Make your own activities such as sorting foreign coins, shells, dried beans, ethnic fabric squares, and other raw materials. Make lotto, classification, and matching games such as "Which One Is Different?" "Match Ups," and "Mothers and Babies." Because of stereotyped packaging, make it a practice to take toys out of their original container and display them in plastic dish tubs or on trays.

Science center. Multicultural activities might include a collection of rocks and shells from different parts of the world. Terrariums and miniature indoor gardens model different types of soil, ground covering, and vegetation. The display might include a small cactus garden in sand, a planting of ferns in soil heavy with peat and sphagnum moss on the top, a bonsai display with smooth pebbles, a fish tank with plants that grow under the water, a Norfolk Island pine tree with bark chips, a dwarf citrus tree in sandy loam, a palm tree, bamboo shoots in water and marbles, or a tropical flowering ornamental like a hibiscus or azalea. Include pictures and photographs of gardens from around the world. Grow herbs that are used in cooking ethnic foods in a sunny window: cilantro, lemon grass, oregano, basil, mint, sage, sweet grass, and parsley are good choices. Add smells and scents from other cultures to the smelling jar kit. Create collections of different kinds of grains, beans, and soils. Examples of grains include wheat berries, rye berries, oats, millet, corn, couscous, barley, white and brown rice, red rice, and wild rice. A complete assortment of dried beans would include black-eyed peas, baby limas, black beans, pinto, kidney, great northern,

FIGURE 24-4 • Encourage children to share stories about their families and their cultures.

soybeans, and lentils. Some teachers may choose not to use food as a teaching tool. This decision is based on personal values, and each teacher must make her or his own choice.

Sensory table. You can also integrate a multicultural approach to your sand and water table areas. Try to include textures and smells that represent not only the children in the class but other cultural groups as well. Many of the grains and dried beans listed under the science area can be purchased in large quantities to use in the sensory area as children use them to learn about comparing and measuring amounts and the characteristics of the various grains. Other dry materials for the table include whole nuts in the shell, bark, dry leaves, coffee beans, soil, raw wool, raw silk, and flax. When exploring liquids with children, try adding a scent to the water. Small bottles of essential oils in various floral, wood, citrus, and herbal scents can be purchased at health food stores or international gift shops.

The sensory table can also be used for dramatic play. The addition of small people figures, transportation toys, twigs, rocks, and miniature plastic plants to a base of sand, soil, or water allows children to create environments that are unfamiliar as well as recreate environments that are common in their everyday lives. For example, children in the coastal areas of North and South Carolina could play "beach" with wet sand, shells, and small people figures. Likewise, a high-rise construction site could be created with a layer of dirt, a crane, trucks, small building blocks, and play figures.

Language arts center. Display books that emphasize diversity, ethnicity, different lifestyles, and cooperation.

Include alphabet and counting books from other cultures. A CD player and story CDs add to the interest area. Look for stories that include ethnic background music and narration by a person from that culture. You and the children can supplement your current library with homemade books. For example, take pictures of children and create your own books. Have children make books about themselves and their families. Use the resources listed at the end of this chapter to help you locate multicultural children's books appropriate for your group.

The Aesthetics of a Creative Multicultural Classroom

Designing the visual appearance of your classroom is the final touch to creating a multicultural classroom. We definitely want children to notice and interact with materials on the shelves and the displays on the tables in the room. What we don't want is children wandering around or flitting from area to area because they can't tell what their options are. The overuse of visual displays creates a form of "visual noise" that distracts children from the materials. Rather than filling every inch of wall space with bulletin boards, pictures, and posters, try using these materials as if you were decorating your own home environment. Use and create visual displays to match, reinforce, and expand the materials and learning that take place in each of the interest centers. For example, display works of art in the art area, posters of buildings and environments in the block area, and pictures of people, families, and family life scenes in the dramatic play area. Classroom entrance areas, parent sign-in tables, hallways, cubby areas, and bathrooms can become warmer, more welcoming spaces with the use of a few well-chosen and well-placed visual displays.

Classroom environments give children and parents strong messages. The classroom conveys attitudes to the children and parents by what is included in the room and what is left out. Omissions can be just as destructive as stereotypes and inaccurate information. Leaving multicultural education out of the curriculum gives children and families the message that it isn't important. It is our job as early childhood educators to make sure that the classroom includes all kinds of people doing all kinds of things and living out their daily lives in many different ways. This may be through visual images such as pictures or representations in the form of artwork and objects from daily life. Remember that displaying just one or two pictures is tokenism.

THIS ONE'S for YOU!   Gestures: Different Cultural Interpretations

It is important for early childhood teachers to understand how the gestures they use unconsciously may be misunderstood by children of different cultural backgrounds. Consider some of the following gestures and their interpretations in various cultures.

- Beckon with the index finger. This means "Come here" in the United States. To motion with the index finger to call someone is insulting or even obscene in many cultures. Expect a reaction when you beckon a student from the Middle or Far East, Portugal, Spain, Latin America, Japan, Indonesia, or Hong Kong. It is more acceptable to beckon with the palm down, with fingers or whole hand waving.

- Point at something in the room using index finger. It is impolite to point with the index finger in the Middle and Far East. Use an open hand or your thumb (in Indonesia).

- Make a "V" sign. This means "victory" in most of Europe when you make this sign with your palm facing away from you. If you face your palm, in the same gesture means "shove it."

- Smile. This gesture is universally understood. However, in various cultures there are different reasons for smiling. The Japanese may smile when they are confused or angry. In other parts of Asia, people may smile when they are embarrassed. People in other cultures may not smile at everyone to indicate a friendly greeting as we do in the United States. A smile may be reserved for friends. It is important not to judge students or their parents because they do not smile or smile at what we would consider "inappropriate" times.

- Sit with shoe soles showing. In many cultures this sends a rude message. In Thailand, Japan, and France as well as countries of the Middle or Near East, showing the soles of the feet demonstrates disrespect. You are exposing the lowest and dirtiest part of your body, so this is insulting.

- Form a circle with fingers to indicate "o.k." Although this means o.k. in the United States and in many countries around the world, there are some notable exceptions:

  In Brazil and Germany, this gesture is obscene.
  In Japan, this means "money."
  In France, it has the additional meaning of "zero" or "worthless."

- Pat a student on the head. This is very upsetting to students from Asia. The head is the repository of the soul in the Buddhist religion. Children from cultures that are influenced by Buddhism will feel uncomfortable if their head is touched.

- Pass an item to someone with one hand. In Japan this is very rude. Even a very small item such as a pencil must be passed with two hands. In many Middle and Far Eastern countries, it is rude to pass something with your left hand, which is considered unclean.

- Wave your hand with the palm facing outward to greet someone. In Europe, waving the hand back and forth can mean "no." To wave "good-bye," raise the palm outward and wag the fingers in unison. This is also a serious insult in Nigeria if the hand is too close to another person's face.

- Nod head up and down to say, "yes." In Bulgaria and Greece, this gesture means "no" (Haynes, 2009).

It gives children the message, "Yes, these people are out there in the world somewhere, but you don't have to take them seriously."

Real Life Representations

Creating an aesthetically pleasing environment that is also multicultural means avoiding the use of cartoon characters such as dolls in costumes, animal characters dressed in ethnic costumes, and stereotypical pictures of people in their traditional dress. Appropriate display materials include artwork and artifacts from existing cultures such as fabrics, paintings, beadwork, rugs, wall hangings, musical instruments, sculpture, wind chimes, and photos (actual or from magazines).

Finding Multicultural Materials

It can be a time-consuming, difficult, and expensive project to acquire a large selection of multicultural display materials for the classroom. You may find some educational catalogues that carry modern, accurate

FIGURE 24-5 • Pieces of ethnic art enhance a multicultural classroom.

FIGURE 24-6 • A shelf of interesting ethnic artifacts.

teaching posters and picture sets. NAEYC is a good source for appropriate posters and other visuals (http://www.naeyc.org/store/taxonomy/term/1454?page=1). Nationwide chain stores such as Pier I Imports and World Bazaar are other good sources for inexpensive multicultural materials. Many of the websites listed at the end of this chapter are also good sources for multicultural resources for your classroom.

Making your own materials and visual displays is perhaps the most viable way to create a multicultural classroom environment. Photographs from magazines provide pictures of people living out their daily lives in the present. Consider starting a multicultural picture file for your common bonds curriculum units.

When you have gathered enough photographs, you can mount and laminate them. Display the photographs separately or create a collage on poster board. Collages may focus on a specific theme such as boys and girls, babies, grandparents, families, homes, or workers. Create a collage of pictures of people from a specific ethnic group. This type of collage is particularly useful because it shows the diversity and individuality within an ethnic group.

In your search for photos, you will find that not all magazines are useful sources of multicultural pictures. Thumbing through popular women's magazines for appropriate photographs will prove this point, as so many images are far from real life. Be careful, too, of *National Geographic* as it can tend to highlight people in faraway places dressed in traditional costumes at special celebrations, and not in everyday life.

Multicultural/Bilingual Classrooms— Deficit and Transformational Perspectives

Recent U.S. Census survey data confirm what we know from our own observations—that there are increasingly more non-English-speaking children in our schools today. The same census data project that this will be the case far into the future in our country. There is a danger in working with non-English-speaking children of taking a deficit perspective. This type of perspective sees the child as lacking skills, a deficit caused by not speaking English. A **deficit perspective** is one that often distorts teachers' vision when interacting with children from marginalized communities: children of color, children who speak a language other than English, children whose families are poor or working class (Garcia, Jensen, & Scribner, 2009). A deficit perspective attributes many children's school failure to perceived deficits within the children, their families, and their cultures (Alvarado, 2008). For example, parents are often cited for not reading to their children, not valuing education, not using enough discipline (or disciplining their children too strictly), not speaking English at home, and/or for family "dysfunctions" that interfere with children's learning (Garcia, Jensen, & Scribner, 2009).

In direct contrast to the deficit perspective is the **transformational perspective,** which is based on the assumption that communities possess "funds of knowledge," reservoirs of knowledge and skills shared by community members (Gonzalez-Mena, 2009). On one level, this means that what families know about music or literacy can contribute to learning activities or be topics of study. At a deeper level, it means we must view families as knowledgeable and skillful as well as understand and respect teaching and learning relationships in homes and communities (Gonzalez-Mena, 2009).

These funds of knowledge are often invisible to those who are unfamiliar with lives that are different from their own. Traditional nods to multiculturalism, such as a piñata or Kwanzaa *kinara,* miss the point. Understanding others means paying close attention to ways of learning in families and communities, listening and questioning actively, and interacting in meaningful experiences (Gonzalez-Mena, 2009).

What does all of this mean for teachers? NAEYC answers this question by urging early childhood educators to accept the legitimacy of children's home language, respect and value the home culture, and promote and encourage the active involvement and support of all families (NAEYC, 1996). Similar position statements by other organizations, such as NCTE (National Council of Teachers of English) and IRA (International Reading Association) note that such an approach not only provides multiple pathways to

learning, but also has the potential to broaden the worldviews of children and teachers.

Implementing a Transformational Perspective

All of the above ideas about a transformational perspective look good on paper, but putting them into practice is yet another issue. To help you get started in developing more of a transformational perspective in your work with bilingual students, consider some of the suggestions that follow.

- *Validate children's home language.* Learn and use as many words as possible in the child's home language. Encourage other children to use these words as well.
- *Use familiar, culturally relevant literature.* Use children's rhymes from children's language to teach rhyming and letter sounds. This encourages the bilingual child's participation in oral recitations.
- *Help children share personal stories.* Write down the children's dictated stories and help them act them out. Most children want to share stories from their lives.
- *Create activities around songs from home.* Let the children share their favorite songs with classmates. They can learn each other's songs and how the songs connect to their individual worlds. You can create song books and play the songs at the listening center. Songs can be posted on charts with the children's drawings and photos.
- *Use environmental print.* With a bag from a fast-food restaurant, a movie advertisement, and a photo of a local store sign in Spanish, teachers can show children that they know and can read many words. They can then use those words to make connections to other words (Gonzalez-Mena, 2009).

Here are some suggestions to bring families into classrooms where they are valued as experts who have something to teach teachers about their children.

- Talk with families to learn how their children communicate important needs and wants (e.g., "milk," "hungry," "hurts," "diaper/potty"). Sometimes these needs, wants, and feelings may be expressed in the child's home language. Providers and teachers can be encouraged to learn this vocabulary themselves so they will recognize the words more easily when children use them (August & Shanahan, 2008).

FIGURE 24-7 • Multicultural education encourages a sense of self.

- Help parents compile booklets with rhymes and stories the parents learned as children that they can share in learning areas.
- Encourage parents to bring from home literacy materials, such as audiotapes and music CDs, videos in their home languages, calendars, and newspapers, plus paper, envelopes, and stamps that they and their children can use to write letters in the writing center (August & Shanahan, 2008).
- Involve children and family members in creating shoebox biographies—shoe boxes filled with artifacts that prompt stories about their lives—and picture books about home activities.
- Teachers and caregivers need to look for ways to incorporate aspects of children's cultures into daily routines as children become more interested in the learning process when activities look familiar to them.
- Offer written information in languages other than English as an important way to reach out to culturally diverse families.
- Teachers should always ask families how to pronounce a child's name and not assume they know. Nor should they create an "American" name for a child because they can't pronounce the child's given name.
- Be sensitive to the cultural shifts that immigrant students or other students with minority family and community cultures must make as they move between school and home. This transition may be most difficult at the beginning of the school week, after students have been immersed in their home culture over the weekend. Teachers need to be sensitive to transitional challenges and collaborate with families to develop mechanisms to ease the stress caused by them.
- Help parents gain the skills to negotiate the education system and knowledge of the norms of behavior that govern schools (Hirschler, 2005). Without this information, many minority parents, especially new immigrants, may not feel competent to negotiate the system on behalf of their child or knowledgeable enough to support their child's efforts. Teachers can help by talking with parents directly rather than using more formal written communications, such as letters or notes. This is particularly valuable to families from cultures in which personal connections and conversational language are the preferred ways of gathering information (Cruzado-Guerrero & Kenreich, 2008).

By reaching beyond taken-for-granted ways of teaching and learning in schools, we can actively challenge deficit perspectives. As you get more involved in this process of transforming teaching and learning in your classroom, you cannot help but see all children and families as skillful and knowledgeable, possessing visible and valuable resources (Gonzalez-Mena, 2009).

Summary

Learning to teach in a culturally diverse classroom involves two major factors: process and practice. It involves a deep belief in the worth of every child, an accepting attitude toward each child as a unique individual, and unqualified support for each child in all areas of that child's development. The teacher is key in a multicultural classroom as she or he sets the tone for all of the children in her or his unqualified acceptance of every child. Common bonds can be used to design a multicultural curriculum that focuses on things that all children share. Learning centers are an ideal place to begin introducing a multicultural curriculum by including everyday items that reflect cultural diversity: Children learn about other cultures in the process of using these materials. The aesthetic appearance of the multicultural classroom should include nonstereotypical representations of ethnic groups with artifacts used sparingly so they do not overwhelm children with "visual noise." In working with non-English-speaking children, it is important to avoid a deficit perspective and concentrate on a transformational one. Acknowledging a child's home language and customs and involving parents in the curriculum are ways to work toward a transformational perspective with non-English-speaking children and their families.

Key Terms

common bonds curriculum 610
multicultural curriculum 610
transformational perspective 616
deficit perspective 615

Learning Activities

1. Role play this situation with fellow students: You are a teacher in a large, multicultural, urban school. You have been asked by your center director to be in charge of the Christmas holiday program for the school. Respond to this request. Include in your dialogue with the director: (1) reasons for and/or against the program; (2) your alternate plans to a Christmas program; and (3) how you would go about initiating a multicultural curriculum in your center.

2. Visit two contrasting early childhood programs. For example, visit one small suburban center and a large, federally funded urban center. Compare and contrast the multicultural curriculum you observed in each setting. Review activity plans. Can you see in these activities the evidence of a multicultural curriculum? Why or why not? Do the activities and classroom materials you observed reflect the ethnic and cultural make-up of the group? Be specific in your reply. Are the activities developmentally appropriate? Explain why or why not.

3. Obtain an early childhood program supply catalogue. Review it for the following: supplies for holiday activities; children's multicultural books; different ethnic groups represented in toys, such as puppets, dolls, or housekeeping corner supplies. Is there an emphasis on any particular holidays? If so, which one(s) did you find? Did you find any supplies, books, toys, etc. that you would buy for your own use in your work with children? Explain which ones and why you would purchase them.

4. In your program, one of the goals of your multicultural curriculum planning is to validate children's and families' experiences and traditions. Using this goal, write a letter to parents sharing with the families what curriculum specifics you have planned for children.

5. Obtain a copy of an early childhood curriculum guide. Evaluate it for these points:
   - number of holidays included
   - number of activities included for each holiday
   - amount of time estimated to be spent on each holiday
   - developmental appropriateness of holiday activities
   - inclusion of antibias, nonstereotypical holidays, and activities

   Discuss your evaluation of the curriculum guide. Based on your evaluation, would you use this curriculum guide? Why or why not?

6. Observe the learning centers in an early childhood program. Note how much of the equipment in the centers has a multicultural focus. Select at least three pieces of equipment that are good multicultural examples and three that are not. Explain your choices.

7. Why is multicultural education important to you personally?

8. Which of the approaches to multicultural education presented in Chapter 24 fits with your own beliefs?

9. Which of the approaches presented in Chapter 24 best matches what is currently taking place in your classroom or in classrooms in which you have observed?

10. Visit and observe at least two early childhood programs. What groups of people and ways of life are missing in these programs, if any? List some specific ways you would improve these programs.

11. List five things you can do to eliminate stereotypes from your classroom.

12. List five things you can do to increase diversity in your classroom.

13. Plan a multicultural curriculum unit and list at least two items supporting the unit theme that could be added to each interest area.

Chapter Review

1. Describe how learning to teach in culturally diverse classrooms involves both process and practice.

2. List some attitudes and beliefs an early childhood teacher must have to be successful in creating a truly multicultural classroom.

3. Why isn't it enough to simply include holiday celebrations from other cultures?

4. Explain why the classroom setting is so important in developing a truly multicultural environment for young children.

5. Describe how learning centers can be equipped to more fully represent a multicultural curriculum.

6. What are some common bonds around which a multicultural curriculum can be designed?

7. Why is multicultural education important?

8. How can the early childhood education classroom be arranged so that it reflects an aesthetically pleasing multicultural curriculum?

9. What are some things to avoid when setting up your classroom for a multicultural curriculum?

10. Discuss the importance of real-life representations of different ethnic groups.

11. How would you go about gathering materials for your multicultural curriculum?

12. Define the terms *deficit perspective* and *transformational perspective*. Explain their importance in the multicultural classroom.

13. List some measures a teacher can take to encourage a transformational perspective in the early childhood classroom.

References

Alvarado, C. (Ed.). (2008). *In our own way: How anti-bias work shapes our lives.* Washington, DC: NAEYC.

August, D., & Shanahan, T. (Eds.). (2008). *Developing reading and writing in second-language learners: Lessons from the Report of the National Literacy Panel on Language-Minority Children & Youth.* New York: Routledge.

Cruzado-Guerrero, J., & Kenreich, T. W. (2008). Making global connections with family book bags. *Social Studies and the Young Learner, 20*(4), P1–P4.

Garcia, E. E., Jensen, B. T., & Scribner, K. P. (2009). The demographic imperative. *Educational Leadership, 66*(7), 8–13.

Gonzalez-Mena, J. (2009). *Diversity in early care and education* (5th ed.). Washington, DC: NAEYC.

Haynes, J. (2009). Communicating with gestures. Accessed 11/30/09 at http://www.everything.esl.net/inservices/body_language.php

Hernandez, D. J., Denton, N. A., & Macartney, S. E. (2008). The lives of children in immigrant families. *Zero to Three, 29*(2), 5–12.

Hirschler, J. A. (2005). *How teachers support English language learners in the classroom.* (Head Start Bulletin 78). Washington, DC: U.S. Department of Health and Human Services.

NAEYC. (1996). Position statement: Responding to linguistic and cultural diversity: Recommendations for effective early childhood education. *Young Children, 51*(2), 4–12.

United States Census Reports. (2006). http://www.census.gov/

Additional Readings

Berson, I. E., & Berson, M. J. (2009). Panwapa: Global kids, global connections. *Social Studies and the Young Learner, 21*(4), 28–31.

Boutte, G. S. (2008). Beyond the illusion of diversity: How early childhood teachers can promote social justice. *Social Studies and the Young Learner, 99*(4), 165–173.

Brooks, W., & McNair, J. C. (2009). But this story of mine is not unique: A review of research on African-American children's literature. *Review of Educational Research, 79*(1), 125–162.

Brown, B. B., & Carroll, A. (2008). Beyond wildlife: Teaching about Africa and stereotypes. *Social Studies and the Young Learner, 20*(4), 12–17.

Copple, C. (Ed.). *A world of difference: Readings on teaching young children in a diverse society.* Washington, DC: NAEYC.

Cullinan, B., Dove, T., Estice, R., & Lanka, J.(2008). Becoming conscious of different perspectives. *Social Studies and the Young Learner, 20*(4), 18–21.

Cohen, L. E. (2009). Exploring cultural heritage in a kindergarten classroom. *Young Children, 64*(3), 72–77.

Espinosa, L. (2010). *Getting it RIGHT for young children from diverse backgrounds.* Upper Saddle River, NJ: Pearson Education/Merrill.

Gao, J. (2008). One day with a second grade in Bejing. *Social Studies and the Young Learner, 20*(4), 4–8.

Genese, F. (2008). Early dual language learning. *Zero to Three, 29*(1), 17–23.

Gunel, E. (2008). Understanding Islam: Perspectives of a Turkish educator. *Social Studies and the Young Learner, 20*(4), 9–11.

Hernandez, D. J., Denton, N. A., & Macartney, S. E. (2008). The lives of America's youngest children in immigrant families. *Zero to Three, 29*(2), 5–12.

Jones, W., & Lorenzo-Hubert, I. (2008). The relationship between language and culture. *Zero to Three, 29*(1), 11–16.

Kirker, S. S. (2008). Where in the world art you from? *SchoolArts, 108*(4), 44–45.

Lee, R., Ramsey, P., & Sweeney, B. (2008). Engaging young children in conversations about race and social class. *Young Children, 63*(6), 68–76.

Lo, J., & Merryfield, M. M. Teaching Chinese national identity to elementary students in Hong Kong. *Social Studies and the Young Learner, 20*(4), 22–25.

Lowenstein, K. L. (2009). The work of multi-cultural teacher education: Reconceptualizing white teacher candidates as learners. *Review of Educational Research, 79*(1), 163–196.

Macrina, M., Hoover, D., & Beckey, C. (2009). The challenge of working with dual language learners—Three perspectives: Supervisor, mentor and teacher. *Young Children, 64*(2), 27–35.

McNulty, C. P., & Brown, M. S. (2009). Help wanted: Seeking the critical confluence of minorities in teaching. *Childhood Education, 85*(3), 179–181.

Morrison, K. (2009). Lessons of diversity learned the hard way. *Phi Delta Kappan, 90*(5), 360–364.

Moule, J. (2009). Understanding unconscious bias and unintentional racism. *Phi Delta Kappan, 90*(5), 321–326.

National Association for the Education of Young Children. (2009). *Books to grow on: Latino literature for young children.* Washington, DC: Author.

Nemeth, K. (2009). Meeting the home language mandate: Practical strategies for all classrooms. *Young Children, 64*(2), 36–42.

Patterson, J., & Manning, M. (2009). Quality counts 2009: Portrait of a population: How English language learners are putting schools to the test. *Childhood Education, 85*(4), 273.

Prieto, H. V. (2009). One language, two languages, three languages…more? *Young Children, 64*(1), 52–53.

Shagoury, R. (2009). Language to language: Nurturing writing development in multilingual classrooms. *Young Children, 64*(2), 52–57.

Spence, L. K. (2009). Developing multiple literacies in a website project. *The Reading Teacher, 62*(7), 592–597.

Swartz, E. (2009). Diversity: Gatekeeping knowledge and maintaining inequalities. *Review of Educational Research, 79*(2), 1044–1083.

Washington, V., & Andrews, J. G. (Eds.). (2009). *Children of 2010.* Washington, DC: NAEYC.

Zhao, Y., & Qiu, W. (2009). How good are the Asians? Refuting four myths about Asian-American academic achievement. *Phi Delta Kappan, 90*(5), 338–344.

Helpful Websites

¡Colorín Colorado!, http://www.colorincolorado.org

Cooperative Children's Book Center, http://www.education.wisc.edu/ccbc

Cyberschoolbus, http://www.cyberschoolbus.un.org

Diversity Council, http://www.diversitycouncil.org/elActivities.shtml

Educational Equity Center, http://www.edequity.org

Educators for Social Responsibility, http://www.esrnational.org

Mis Padres, Mis Maestros/My Parents, My Teachers, http://www.elvalor.org/programs/mispadres.html

National Association for Multicultural Education, http://www.nameorg.org

National Association for Bilingual Education, http://www.nabe.org

National Latino Children's Institute, http://www.nlci.org

National Council of La Raza, http://www.nclr.org

Pew Hispanic Center, http://pewhispanic.org/

Race Bridges for Schools, http://www.racebridgesforschools.com

Teach Children ESL: Games, http://teachchildrenesl.com/games.htm

Teaching for Change, http://www.teachingforchange.org

Teaching Tolerance, http://www.tolerance.org/teach/index.jsp

Walking the Walk, http://www.fpg.unc.edu/~walkingthewalk/

For additional creative activity resources, visit our website at www.Cengage.com/login

Creative Multicultural Curriculum Ideas

OBJECTIVES

After studying this chapter, you should be able to:

1. Explain how to use common bonds in planning an early childhood multicultural curriculum.

2. Discuss how art is an avenue of multicultural learning.

3. Describe how to plan multicultural activities for young children.

4. Discuss how children's books can be used in a creative multicultural curriculum.

Throughout this book, we have discussed how early childhood educators teach creatively through planned activities as well as a prepared environment. These planned activities are then grouped together to form the curriculum. All curriculum planning requires decision making. Early childhood teachers must ask themselves: What messages do I want to convey to young children? What information would be developmentally appropriate? How might I organize a multicultural curriculum?

Let us first consider briefly the multicultural curriculum at the preschool level, and then we will cover the common bonds curriculum as a good beginning to multicultural curriculum planning at all levels in the early childhood program.

Preschool Multicultural Curriculum Planning

Differences make the preschool classroom—the whole community—a vibrant and interesting place to live. This curriculum, which begins with children's own experiences, can gradually help children understand, accept, and celebrate diversity through play on a daily basis. By age three, children have an awareness of differences in language, skin color, or customs. By age four, children become aware of differences associated with handicaps. This awareness depends somewhat on how obvious the difference is. Even in the early childhood years, however, children are developing attitudes toward other racial groups.

With an understanding of the developmental sequence through which children become aware of differences, adults can better teach children about diversity. For preschoolers, the initial focus should be on increasing knowledge about similarities and differences among children. This knowledge can be revealed through awareness of different foods, family structures, celebrations, and cultural traditions. All adults need to model support and understanding of cultural diversity.

A preschooler's primary means of learning is through play. Play across cultures often involves the use of toys. Toys and other things that children play with reflect culture and provide insight into the norms and values of a society—hence, the importance of Show and Tell. Because toys and playthings have an important influence on the play of young children, adults need to make sure that the toys available are appropriate and reflect cultural diversity. Adults should evaluate toys and make sure that they are varied and span different developmental areas. Toys also should be examined to be sure that they are accessible and do not reflect a cultural bias (Gonzalez-Mena, 2009).

Now let us consider the common bonds curriculum as a strategy to planning multicultural experiences for young children.

Planning Common Bonds Curricula

By using themes that are common to children in all cultures, you will avoid activities that focus on countries, artifacts, and ceremonies. These activities teach children to be tourists (outsiders visiting an unknown culture that is totally irrelevant to their daily lives). This method of curriculum planning teaches children trivia, ignores that people of other cultures really exist today and live normal everyday lives, and does nothing to build a foundation for living in a multicultural world. In a tourist-type curriculum, children learn about the culture for a week, two weeks, or a month and then move on to other unit themes like the circus or dinosaurs. The culture they just studied may not be talked about for the rest of the year.

Common Bonds Curricula

Build your multicultural curriculum around activities that focus on common bonds for all children across cultures. In addition to those listed in Chapter 24, you might consider such concepts as the following.

Everyone is important.
Everyone has feelings.

People are similar.
People are different.
Some physical attributes stay the same.
Some physical attributes change.

In planning around these or any similar concepts, you will want to consider all of the elements of an early childhood classroom. The Multicultural Curriculum Planning form (in Figure 25–1) may help you consider such details as theme and concepts, important dates, parent newsletter articles, field trips, bulletin boards, cooking projects, and the room arrangement. It will give you a broad framework for planning a common bonds unit plan, be it a two-week period or a month. You can then use this general plan to write up specific activities for free play and group time.

Topic. Decide on the topic and the length of time the class will spend on it. Select a topic from the list in this chapter or Chapter 24 or use one of your own.

Basic concepts. Write down the basic concepts and ideas you will be exposing the children to in this unit. Remember that the early childhood years are not the time to emphasize learning facts and information. Use the topic to expose children to new experiences and invite them to explore new materials.

Special dates. Go through the calendar and write down any special dates that occur during the time the class will be focusing on this particular unit. It may be children's birthdays (if you celebrate them in your group), school breaks, and any other special events that you may incorporate into your unit or have to plan around.

Field trips/visitors. Try to take one field trip each month. If you live in an area with harsh winters, substitute a special visitor for a field trip. Use the form to list places you might take the children or visitors you might invite into the classroom to emphasize the curriculum theme.

Cooking activities/snack. Some programs offer cooking as a weekly activity. These experiences are fun for children if they can actively participate in the preparation and cooking of food. Plan cooking experiences that support the unit topic. Plan a few special snacks or meals to go along with the topic if your center or school has a food service program. Remember, parents are always a good source for recipes.

Visual displays. Often teachers change the bulletin boards to go along with the curriculum topic. Bulletin boards can be important teaching tools. Think of displays that support the concepts you are trying to teach children. Remember to include visual displays that show a variety of people in everyday situations. Use photographs and homemade displays as often as possible. Try to avoid cartoon figures that may be stereotypical and serve no purpose other than decoration.

Parent newsletter. Most programs have some form of written communication with parents. Write an article on the current topic and how you plan to incorporate multicultural concepts and activities into the daily activities. You might want to ask parents for their assistance in the newsletter as well.

Classroom. The next section of the planning form lists the interest areas or learning centers often found in early childhood classrooms. Teachers of older children may want to adjust the form to fit the subject areas in their classroom. Rotate and add materials that support the topic for each of the interest areas. In addition, use the curriculum planning form to delegate staff responsibilities for setting up or arranging interest areas to go along with the topic. For example, one person may be responsible for returning and checking out new library books. Another person takes the art area and changes the colors of the paint and construction paper and makes new play dough.

Art—Avenue to Creative Multicultural Learning

Multiculturalism is so much more than curriculum—it is a worldview. Art is an ideal means of conveying multiculturalism. Multiculturalism itself honors heritage, community, and tradition. Art objects from different cultures expand beyond their mere physical experience. A Pueblo pot, a Peruvian textile, a Celtic illumination . . . each represents centuries of culture and civilization. Works of art are valued for their artistic contribution, originality, purpose, collective identity, and universal appeal. In using art reproductions and actual art objects like pottery in the early childhood program, you are bringing the cultures of the world into children's daily lives.

In the past, roll sheets that once listed Billy, Betty, Jack, and Sue are now joined by Jamar, Okezie, Shanta,

Topic:	Weeks/Month:
Basic Concepts:	
Special Dates:	
Field Trips/Visitors:	
Cooking Activities/Snacks:	
Visual Displays:	
Parent Newsletter:	
Classroom:	
Book Area:	
Art Area:	
Block Area:	
Small-muscle/Manipulative Area:	
Dramatic Play Area:	
Music/Movement Area:	
Sand/Water Table:	
Science Table:	
Playground/Gym:	
Important Phone Numbers:	
Important E-mail Addresses:	

FIGURE 25-1 • Multicultural curriculum planning form.

Esperanza, and Thuy. Every one of the names on the roll sheet brings tradition along with hopes, fears, and dreams. Each student brings the gift of self and of culture. What a thrill to see a big smile grow on the face of a shy student who is new to the United States when the art activity is a familiar reminder of family and home! We all want to feel valued and recognized. Pride in cultural heritage helps students learn. Art is a reaffirmation of who we are.

FIGURE 25-2 • Art is an ideal means of conveying multiculturalism.

Children grow to like what is familiar and may shrink from the unusual. If they are to become accepting of differing forms of beauty, they need immersion in all its variations. For example, a classroom should contain art of many styles showing people of different ages, races, ethnic backgrounds, genders, and skin colors. It is important for children to see art from different places and time periods—images of people going about life in ways that may be unusual to them and yet show how basic needs for food, clothing, shelter, knowledge, love, and beauty are universal.

Respect for diverse peoples can be encouraged by displaying works in which individuals are portrayed in dignified contemporary situations, not just historical garb. We must take care not to demean groups; to just show Native Americans half-naked, wearing skins and feathers is inaccurate to say the least. Avoid commercial cutouts, cute cardboard pin-ups, coloring books, and patterns of ethnic groups and races *only* in historical traditional clothing, which suggests they are less advanced and still live this way. (Think how silly it would be to show Americans in Pilgrim outfits as a "typical" American image!)

Original art and a variety of types of art show children there are many possibilities. Sculpture, fine art prints, postcard prints, and art books are ways to show authentic cultural images. Most schools and public libraries have children's literature containing art in every style and media, and students can be invited to bring artifacts from home (pottery, quilts, photographs, etc.) that may be stunning sources of aesthetic stimulation and family heritage. We can cultivate the aesthetic by planning quiet times to pass around objects for closer examination.

Be sure to include posters with art images from around the world to display in your classroom. Remember that photocopy shops can enlarge paper-size images (and even postcards) to poster size. Include diverse faces and places. Children become familiar with cultural arts through displayed visual materials. Do be sure that your children also see images that reflect themselves and their own ethnic identity.

Another way to use art as an avenue to diversity is to start a multicultural treasure chest. An old toy chest or a roomy closet storage box can easily be transformed into a multicultural treasure chest. Begin with a collection of masks, sculptural crafts, dolls, fabric, banners, hats, and other objects to be incorporated into your lessons. These do not have to be expensive—flea markets, craft stands, and souvenirs are good sources. Encourage children to examine and learn from the various objects. Don't forget that children may bring in their own treasures and tell their stories. Try to coordinate specific multicultural items with lesson units. Objects speak volumes.

The Internet can be a valuable source for using art as an avenue to multicultural curriculum ideas. In addition to those mentioned below, you will find a list of websites at the end of this chapter and in the Online Companion that provide similar art sources.

Students will enjoy exploring the Metropolitan Museum's interactive site about *The Block* by Romare Bearden (http://www.metmuseum.org/explore/the_block/index_flash.html), which depicts life on a street in Harlem, New York. Jacob Lawrence and Faith Ringgold also found inspiration in the Harlem community in which they were raised. A number of Lawrence's works show scenes of everyday life in Harlem, whereas others illustrate historical themes and stories related to the cultural heritage of African American people.

The Virtual Museum of Canada's Festivities of the Living and the Dead in the Americas exhibition (http://www.virtualmuseum.ca/Exhibitions/Festival/en/wml/index.html) examines ten unique cultural celebrations held annually in diverse ethnic communities across the Americas. Perhaps the best-known of these festive events is Day of the Dead (Día de los Muertos), which is celebrated on the first and second days of November throughout Mexico, Latin America, and in many area of the United States. If you want students to compare how different cultures celebrate and honor the dead, you might have your students research the Japanese observance of Obon, which is held each year in the middle of August.

Murals and public art projects celebrate, reflect, and preserve the identity and history of communities. One of the best examples of this is the Great Wall of Los Angeles (http://www.sparcmurals.org/sparcone/), which celebrates the cultural diversity of the city and the contributions that different groups have made to its history. With more than a thousand public murals throughout the area, Los Angeles has been called the unofficial "mural capital of the world." The Mural Arts Program of Philadelphia (http://www.muralarts.org) might dispute that claim, however, having completed more than 2,000 mural projects in the city's neighborhoods.

THIS ONE'S for YOU!   Teaching Culture through Foods

Beginning in November in many schools, food becomes a special part of daily life. It's the main ingredient in family gatherings and holiday and cultural celebrations. Using food as the basis, children can learn a great deal about how different families prepare and enjoy a variety of food. And in the process, they will be learning about each other in a natural, nonstereotypical way.

Here are some suggestions on how to use food as a way to help young children learn about each other's cultures.

- Invite children to share what they know about the way food is a part of their family celebrations. Simply asking, "How does your family prepare foods for celebrations?" will start the ball rolling. You can also ask, "Who prepares the food?" or "What foods does your family make and eat that you don't see at your friends' houses?" Note children's suggestions on a large sheet of paper, comparing similarities and differences.

- This dialogue about food can then lead to investigative questions. Write children's responses to questions like these: What do you know about cooking? What would you like to find out about cooking? What would you like to learn how to cook?

- Based on children's answers to the above questions, you can develop your next steps into learning about each other through cooking. Remember to include children in devising a plan for how to explore answers to their questions and how they want to learn about cooking.

- Invite families and friends to share their favorite cultural celebration food with the class. Be sure adults let children participate in the preparation. Encourage children to ask questions and taste new things.

- A culminating event might be a major project like a class-created Cultural Foods Smorgasbord to share with families, or a less-demanding project such as writing and illustrating a class cookbook. You might even decide to have a multicultural bake sale and give the money earned to a charity of the children's choice.

Food is a natural favorite of children. Learning about each other through preparation and enjoyment of food together is natural, fun, and delicious!

Planning Multicultural Activities

As adults, we may think of countries, governments, languages, and customs when we hear the term *multicultural education*. We remember our own experiences of learning geography, making relief maps, and writing our first big report on the country of our choice. These are appropriate activities for upper elementary, middle, and high school. Because of their cognitive development, young children are not ready to learn "facts" about different cultures, and they are easily confused by events that happened long ago or that occur in faraway place. As a result, you should avoid focusing on such things as historical events, revolutions and wars, and past presidents and rulers.

Also, young children may not believe that people from other cultures are real, or they may believe that they lived long ago and are no longer living in the world today. Activities that portray characteristics of other cultures as eccentric encourage children to believe in stereotypes. Young children may not recognize real people from other cultures when they see them on the street. They may say, "No, she's not Japanese. She doesn't have a kimono or those funny shoes on." For this reason, be careful to limit the amount of multicultural activities planned around topics such as foreign foods, traditional costumes, holidays, and celebrations.

Choosing Appropriate Multicultural Activities

As early childhood educators, we know that children learn best when they are actively exploring materials, experiencing the world with their whole bodies and all of their senses, and interacting with a variety of people. An appropriate multicultural curriculum is no different from a good early childhood curriculum.

FIGURE 25-3 • In the multicultural classroom, children are encouraged to share the music of their cultures.

FIGURE 25-4 • Fill your book and/or quiet area with children's books about diverse cultures.

Rather than watering down elementary school activities and social studies lessons, try adapting proven early childhood activities. Avoid using worksheets, coloring pages, and craft projects. Go through your own activity files and curriculum books, as well as the activities in this book. Think about how they might be modified to teach multicultural concepts.

For example, use the curriculum to help all students learn about each other's families. Using the common bonds topic of "family," you might have children interview their relatives and tell the story about how and when their family first came to the United States. Students, unless they are of Native American descent, will discover that their ancestors were all once immigrants. You might also give all parents and even other relatives of your students an opportunity to visit your classroom and tell about their family traditions. Regardless of where children are from, they have much to offer each other in sharing family and cultural backgrounds. A positive incidental effect of this activity is that you will avoid unintentionally making a new student feel singled out or on display.

Another strategy in planning your multicultural activities for young children is to fill your book and/or quiet area with children's books about diverse cultures. By including many bilingual children's books, you will be helping second-language learners feel more at home in your classroom. Reading bilingual books—books that contain words in languages other than English—gives children a very good opportunity to be exposed to multiple languages. Teachers who have bilingual and multilingual books in their classrooms are sending the message that they acknowledge the importance of those languages and cultures. These teachers, by exposing their students to different alphabets and words, are also raising awareness of diversity for the English speakers in their group.

You may find that using a children's book in a child's native language can help acquaint a beginning English language learner with the topic at hand. Also, a book in the child's native language might serve well to soothe feelings of frustration and exhaustion common among second-language learners.

You will find the Association for Library Service to Children (ALCS) a great resource for bilingual and multilingual reading. Visit http://www.ala.org/ala/mgrps/divs/alsc/index.cfm for information about El Día de los Niños/El Día de los Libros: A Celebration of Children, Families, and Reading. This event, held annually on April 30, emphasizes the importance of literacy for every child regardless of linguistic and cultural background. Click on "Educators" and then on "Notable Children's Books" in the drop down menu for "a graded, annotated bibliography, and "Bilingual Books for Children," where you will find books

THIS ONE'S for YOU! Respecting Other Cultures

The values, beliefs, and behaviors of the many Spanish-speaking groups in the United States may differ from group to group and from those of the larger society. When a family or child expresses a preference that does not pose an ethical dilemma, accept and support the preference.

For example, you may notice that a child from a Hispanic culture in which children are taught to be respectful and obedient to adults does not initiate or participate in interactions with the teacher beyond giving the information the teacher requests. Allow the child to find what works best for him or her within the classroom environment. Over time, the child who is supported in the classroom will gradually adjust to classroom behaviors in ways that meet his or her needs.

Another example is assuming that students with Hispanic surnames use Spanish as their dominant language. It is important to know that although 72% of first-generation Latinos are Spanish-dominant in their speech, 78% of third and older generations are English-dominant.

Here is another example. In some cultures, children are taught that particular behaviors or activities are masculine or feminine—that is, that certain things are done only by males or by females. A child so socialized may choose not to participate (or the family may discourage the child from participating) in activities that are typically associated with the other sex, such as dramatic play with aprons and dolls or climbing on the jungle gym. If a child verbalizes or shows a desire not to participate, that desire should be respected. Of course, the child should not be allowed to express this opinion in a way that negatively affects the feelings or perceptions of other children.

THIS ONE'S for YOU! Using Dance as a Means of Understanding and Expressing Culture for Older Children

All art forms are vehicles for conveying the ideas and values of their creators; they are means of coming to understand other cultures. Dance is no exception. Multicultural units are particularly appropriate contexts for using dance to help students feel sensations created by particular dance forms (e.g., hip-hop, tap, jazz, ballroom, country line, jitterbug, and mazurka). Students can also view dances and then analyze them for the messages they give about what is important to the dancers and the culture represented. Through dance investigations, historical events can be understood from an entirely different point of view. For example, Native American ghost dancers in the 19th century created dances to celebrate the return of the lands taken by the U.S. government. The dancers tried to conjure up the powers of their ancestors and created such fervor among tribes that the government eventually forbade the dance!

Combine dance with multicultural music for another way to introduce children to other cultures. Integrate the music and dance of each culture and time period studied by analyzing how songs are historical records of how people felt, thought, and acted. Find out the significance of songs and how music even influenced history by studying France's "La Marseillaise" or the Mexican-American workers' "De Colores." Possibilities abound: Native American music, Irish jigs, music of the Civil Rights Movement, tribal mountain music, western cowboy tunes, patriotic songs, and African tribal music. Students can come to understand how music helps create identity and explore a people's values and passions expressed in song.

FIGURE 25-5 • One of the hallmarks of a multicultural classroom is an unqualified support for each child.

FIGURE 25-6 • Display artwork in your room that reflects the culture of your children and the local community.

representing many languages including Chinese, Russian, Swahili, and Hopi. You will also find translated Newberry and Caldecott titles in this section of the website.

For a collection of Web resources for professional development, see Bank Street College Library's http://streetcat.bankstreet.edu/sites/secondlang.html. These recommended links include http://www.cal.org from the Center for Applied Linguistics. This site presents a guide to online articles on topic areas such as bilingual education, language testing, and much more. Also take a look at http://www.everythingesl.net. This site for teachers contains lesson plans, activity sheets, and suggestions for books, videos, and other media in the classroom.

Picture Books and Multicultural Learning

As discussed earlier in this chapter, if information about other cultures is to make a difference in the lives of young children, it should relate directly to children and their peers. It should involve children in learning firsthand about youngsters like themselves from different cultures. But where can an early childhood teacher or caregiver find these other children—and on a daily basis? The most obvious answer is in children's multicultural picture and children's books. Good children's literature features real or imagined African Americans, Asians, Hispanics, Native Americans, Caucasians, Middle Easterners, and a whole rainbow of other children and adults. Children can come to know these multicultural characters intimately by identifying with them as you read stories about how children from different cultures play, work, and live; how they eat, dress, and go to school; how they feel, act, and even "act out." Introducing children to picture book characters in the stories and activities you provide is an especially effective way for children to get to know children from other cultures. The experience can be almost as real as having a new child from a different culture in the class.

Even if the book characters are children from a different culture, young children have no difficulty choosing them as models. Children enjoy the characters

FIGURE 25-7 • By reaching beyond for-granted ways of teaching and learning in schools, we can actively challenge deficit perspectives.

FIGURE 25-8 • Music and dance are common bonds among cultures.

in their storybooks, and if the story appeals to them, they want to hear it over and over. They come to love the characters in the stories they love. Such stories subtly let them know that multicultural children are accepted in our society because they appear in storybooks.

Even if you have different cultures represented in your group, children are exposed to even more cultural groups by adding multicultural picture books to your book corner. Be sure to read a multicultural book on a regular basis as a natural part of your daily activities. Remember, high-quality multicultural books are *first and foremost* children's literature. Let children enjoy the story first. Then you might discuss the cultural aspects of the story. If you make the reading of a multicultural story book a multicultural lesson every time you read one, children will sense that it is a "kind" of book because of the way you handle its reading. Instead, try talking about all the things that children share in common with the characters in the story. With the vast majority of multicultural books available today, this shouldn't be hard.

Resources for Children's Multicultural Books

There are many excellent educational websites that provide lists of multicultural children's books reviewed by teachers, parents, librarians, and other professionals. In these websites, children's books have been selected on the following criteria: (1) They contain accurate, sensitive, and reflective

FIGURE 25-9 • Planning a multicultural activity involves children and their families.

presentations of people from many ethnic and cultural groups; (2) they are free from stereotypes; and (3) they are good children's literature. Most of these books are set in the present. But if the story does happen some years ago, the pictures and experiences are familiar enough so that children are able to relate to them.

Internet Sources for Children's Books

The following are some websites that feature bibliographies of children's books on multicultural holidays. These are meant as starting points; you will find links to many other sites as you use these.

The International Children's Digital Library (IDCL)

The IDCL is a joint effort by the University of Maryland's Human–Computer Interaction Lab and the Internet Archive to create an extensive library of international children's literature and make it available worldwide. The site makes hundreds of children's books representing 45 different cultures freely available on the Web—fully illustrated, and in the original languages. Their address is http://www.icdlbooks.org.

The Children's Literature Web Guide

This is an excellent place to begin your search because it has links to other sites specifically devoted to children's literature. It also has discussion boards and quick reference lists of award-winning and best-selling books for children. You'll also find links to other resources for parents, teachers, and even writers and illustrators. Their address is http://www.ucalgary.ca/~dKbrown/.

"On-Lion" for Kids

This is a website put together by the New York Public Library. Its name was inspired by the two great stone lions that guard the library system's flagship building. This site offers a whole range of choices, including recommended reading lists built around different celebrations of the year (such as Hispanic Heritage Month, Thanksgiving, and Kwanzaa). You will also find information on authors, titles, and favorite characters as well as links to science and technology websites. The address is http://www.kids.nypl.org/.

Cooperative Children's Book Center (CCBC)

Sponsored by the School of Education at the University of Wisconsin–Madison, this site strives to identify authentic, reliable books by and about people of color. The CCBC presents a section listing Fifty Multicultural Books Every Child Should Know as well as links to selected sites offering critical information and perspectives on multicultural books for young children. Their address is http://www.education.wisc.edu/ccbc/books/multicultural.asp.

Notable Books for a Global Society

The Children's Literature and Reading Special Interest Group of the International Reading Association selects an annual list of multicultural books. It is a guide to multicultural literature for teachers seeking excellent selections for readers ranging from kindergarten through high school. Their journal *The Dragon Lode* (some issues available online) publishes the Notable Books for a Global Society. Included are annotations for each winning book, teaching aids for each title, and related books for each of the 25 selections. The address is: http://www.reading.ccsu.edu/TheDragonLode/.

Youth Division of the Internet Public Library

This site is organized by the Dewey decimal system, so children can use this site to start to learn how to find other books even as they explore the different resources and links on this simple but excellent site. At its heart, it's a directory of links to other websites, many of them book-related, but the descriptions are so child-friendly, youngsters will love to use this site. The address is http://www.ipl.org/youth/.

Don't forget to check with your local and national professional groups for their websites. You will find up-to-date information on developmentally appropriate materials and practice from these sites.

Children's Book Council

Go to http://www.cbcbooks.org. This is a nonprofit trade organization dedicated to encouraging literacy and the use and enjoyment of children's books. On the fifteenth of each month, they list the Hot Off the Press books that they anticipate to be best sellers.

International Reading Association

Go to http://www.reading.org/resources/tools/choices.html. This site lists teachers' and children's choices for best books for each year arranged by categories.

Multicultural Children's Literature: Celebrating Cultural Diversity Through Children's Literature

This website contains lists of annotated bibliographies of children's multicultural books appropriate for kindergarten through grade 6. Cultural groups include: African Americans, Chinese Americans, Latino/Hispanic Americans, Japanese Americans, Jewish Americans, Native Americans, and Korean Americans. Their address is: http://www.multiculturalchildrenslit.com.

Understanding Prejudice: Bibliography of Children's Books

This site contains links to children's books on diversity, multiculturalism, prejudice reduction, and other related topics. Books are recommended in categories from baby through 13 years. Their address is: http://www.understandingprejudice.org/readroom/kidsbib.htm.

Awesome Library

Go to http://www.awesomelibrary.org. This site organizes the Web with 23,000 carefully reviewed resources including the top 5% in education.

Enjoy the process of searching for just the right literature for your special group of children. The joy of seeing children's faces when they can really relate to the book you are reading to them is reward enough for the time it takes to search out appropriate literature. Only you can know which of the listed resources are appropriate for your unique situation.

Summary

Using common bonds that all cultures share in developing your multicultural curriculum, you will avoid creating a tourist curriculum. In planning curriculum, it helps to consider the theme, basic concepts, important dates, parent newsletter articles, field trips, bulletin boards, cooking projects, and room arrangement.

Art is a means of conveying multiculturalism. In using art reproductions and actual art objects like pottery in the early childhood program, you are bringing the cultures of the world into children's daily lives. Children become familiar with cultural arts through displayed visual materials. There are also various websites that can be useful in presenting diverse ethnic communities to the children.

In planning multicultural activities for young children, try not to concentrate on the eccentric portrayals of ethnic groups. Because of their cognitive developmental level, children may believe that this is the only way that cultural group appears. For the same developmental reason, don't confuse young children with facts, historical information, names of presidents, and other information not developmentally appropriate for young children.

Use bilingual and multicultural books as part of your early childhood multicultural curriculum. Bilingual books can send the message that the child's culture is important. They can also help soothe and give the non-English-speaking child relief from the frustration and exhaustion involved in learning a new language. Use multicultural books as a regular part of your classroom routine. Multicultural children's books are, above all else, literature. Allow children to enjoy the story first, and try not to make every reading of a multicultural book time for a lesson about culture. Many Internet resources are available to assist in choosing high-quality multicultural literature for children.

Learning Activities

A. Did you experience a tourist curriculum in your childhood years? If so, relate your experience to the class. What could have been done differently to prevent this? Be specific in your answer.

B. Use the Multicultural Curriculum Planning form in this chapter to design a multicultural unit plan for a group of children. If you are not working with children at this time, choose any age group for this activity. Make enough copies of the completed form to share with your classmates.

C. Use the resources provided in this chapter to locate five multicultural children's books. Make up an index card for each book, giving the title, author's name, year of publication, and publisher. Also indicate what age group/level you believe the book is most appropriate for. Write a short synopsis of the story.

Make a note on any special use that this book would be appropriate for in future curriculum planning. Make enough copies of your cards to share with your classmates. This activity is a great way to begin your own multicultural booklist collection.

D. Reply to a parent who has asked why you have all that "highbrow" artwork all over the classroom.

E. Visit an early childhood program. Observe the visual displays in the room. Did you see any stereotypical images? Were various ethnic groups represented? Were they represented in everyday images? How would you rate the visual displays that you observed? Be specific in your responses. How would you improve the visual displays in this room? Give concrete examples.

F. Review the books in the language arts center of an early childhood program. How many books did you find that were multicultural? Assess the quality of these books using the information in this chapter. Share your assessment with the class.

G. Choose one of the common bonds topics in this chapter and Chapter 24. Write a lesson plan for a group of four-year-old children using this theme. Include in your plan goals, developmentally appropriate related activities, resources, and individual/groups to be involved in your planning.

Share your plan with your colleagues for their input.

H. Using the same topic as in G, design a lesson plan for a group of fourth graders. Include the same items in your plan. Share your plan with your colleagues for their input.

I. Discuss the differences in the lesson plans in G for four-year-olds and in H for fourth graders. What are the main differences in these two lesson plans? What are the similarities (if any) in these plans?

Sample Multicultural Lesson Plans

Skin Color

Topics: "I'm Me and I'm Special," "Our Five Senses," "Colors," "Alike and Different," "Light and Dark"

Goal: To help children explore shades of skin color by making and mixing different colors of play dough

Materials: Mixing bowls, measuring cups, measuring spoons, large spoon for stirring, flour, salt, alum, oil, powdered tempera paint or cake decorator's (paste) food coloring

Method: With children, prepare five batches of play dough, one in each of the following colors: black, brown, red, yellow, white. Use this recipe or another one from this book. Give each child a small ball of play dough.

Play dough recipe

Ingredients

2 cups flour

1 cup salt

2 tablespoons alum

1-1/2 cup warm water

1 tablespoon oil

paste food coloring or powdered tempera paint

Procedure: Mix 1–3 tablespoons of powdered tempera with liquid ingredients. Stir liquids into the dry ingredients. Knead until smooth. Store in an airtight container.

Tell children there are five different colors of play dough and that they can make different colors by mixing two or three colors together. For example, combining red play dough with white play dough will make pink play dough. Have children look at the color of their skin. Encourage them to mix different colors of play dough so that their ball of play dough matches their skin color. Encourage children to experiment with combining the play

dough, talk with them about the concepts of new colors, shades of color, and lighter and darker. Make a picture recipe chart that shows how to mix colors. Display it in the art center for children's use during center time.

Variations

• Make a picture recipe chart that shows how to mix colors. Display it in the art center with the five colors of play dough available for individual children's use during center time.

• Put each child's ball of skin-colored play dough in a plastic bag and let the child take it home.

• During group time, see if children can order the balls of play dough from light to dark.

Body Learning

Topics: "Bodies," "I'm Me and I'm Special," "Alike and Different"

Goal: To help children learn about their bodies and compare their height, weight, skin color, hair, and facial features with those of their classmates

Materials: Mirrors, magnifying glasses, scale, tape measure

Method: Set above materials out on a table for children to explore. Encourage them to use the materials to find out about their bodies. Children may use the tape measure to measure each other's bodies. Talk about similarities and differences.

Variations

• Make a height and weight chart of all the children in the class. Take measurements throughout the year to help children become aware of changes in their bodies.

• Write down children's words as they describe themselves and their bodies.

• Make a poster for each child that includes his or her height, weight, and a self-description. The child may want to draw a self-portrait to add to the poster.

Let's Draw!

Topics: "I'm Me and I'm Special," "Friends," "Alike and Different," "Our Five Senses"

Goal: To help children notice facial features and the uniqueness of each person

Materials: Drawing paper, felt-tip pens, crayons

Method: Have children find a partner and ask them to sit across from each other at a table. Encourage children to draw a picture of their partner's face. Ask them to look at their partner. Then ask: "What color is his skin? What color are her eyes? Does he have freckles? What color is her hair? How long is his hair? Is her hair straight or curly?" The drawing probably won't look like the partner. That's all right because it's the looking at the features of another person that is important. Have children exchange their drawings when they are finished.

Variations

- Have children describe themselves to each other before they begin drawing.
- Have children share their drawings with the class at group time.
- Play a guessing game during group time. Have children look at each drawing and guess who it is.

Photo Masks

Topics: "I'm Me and I'm Special," "Boys and Girls," "Friends," "Changes," "Alike and Different," "Feelings"

Goal: To help children explore diversity by taking on another person's identity through role playing

Materials: Close-up photographs of people's faces (choose people in your school that exemplify a variety of differences), rubber cement, poster board, hole punch, scissors, string

Method: Have the photos enlarged to 8 x 10 inches. Cut out the photo around the hair and face. Mount the photo on poster board using rubber cement. Punch a hole on both sides above the ear. Tie a 12-inch piece of string through each hole. Introduce the masks at group time. Set them out on a "discovery table" with a mirror, or in the dramatic play area. Observe the children and notice their conversations as they try on different masks.

Variation: Record the children's voices or write down what they say as they take on other people's identities.

Face Puzzles

Topics: "I'm Me and I'm Special," "Bodies," "Alike and Different," "Friends"

Goal: To help children discover that each person's face is unique because of the color and shape of its features, but that all faces are similar because the features are in the same place on each person

Materials: Camera (digital or instant), rubber cement, poster board or foam core, mat knife or Exacto knife, pencil, ruler

Method: Take a close-up photo of each child's face. Have the photos enlarged to 8 x 10 inches. Glue the photo to the foam core or poster board and let dry. Using a ruler, mark off the photo in fourths vertically and horizontally. With a pencil, lightly draw lines for cutting out the pieces. This results in sixteen 2-inch squares. Cut out the pieces with the Exacto knife and put the child's name or initials on the back of each piece. During group time, give the pieces to each child in a plastic bag. Encourage them to try to put together their face puzzle. As they work on their own puzzle, talk about where the eyes, nose, and mouth are located on a person's face. When the children have completed their puzzles, ask them to hold up the piece that shows their mouth. Talk about how each person's mouth is different. Continue with the other facial features.

Variations: Combine three or four puzzles and see if children can unscramble them and make the correct faces. Or, set the puzzle pieces out in a tub and let children freely explore putting the pieces together to create different faces.

Puppets

Topics: "I'm Me and I'm Special," "Boys and Girls," "Friends," "Alike and Different," "Colors," "Feelings," "Folk Tales," "Books," "Bodies"

Goal: To give children an opportunity to make a three-dimensional object that represents themselves and to gain skills in verbal self-expression

Materials: Collection of tan, beige, cream, brown, peach, and other skin-colored socks, felt scraps, assorted fabric trim, yarn, buttons, glue, mirrors

Method: Explain to children, "I brought some materials so that you can make a sock puppet that looks just like you." Let children select the color of sock they want to use for their puppet. Encourage them to choose one that is like their skin color. Set out the mirror and materials on a table. Children may want to look in the mirror when deciding how to make their puppet's facial features and hair. Talk about the similarities and differences between the puppets. For example, you might say, "Each puppet is different because it looks like the person who is making it."

Variations

- Set up or make a puppet stage and encourage children to act out a story or classroom situation.
- Have children use their puppets to sing along during a favorite song.
- Have children use their puppets to act out a favorite fingerplay or poem.

Colors and Feelings

Topics: "Colors," "Feelings," "Books"

Goal: To help children express the feelings they associate with different colors

Materials: Colored construction paper, felt-tip pens, stapler

Method: Begin by asking all children wearing the color blue to stand up. Tell them to look at their blue clothes. Ask, "What do you think of" when you see the color blue?" and "How do you feel when you see the color blue?" Repeat this game with many colors. Include skin colors tan, brown, black, and peach.

Tell children they can make a color book. Work with children one at a time. Ask them what they are reminded of when they see each color and how it makes them feel. Write down their words on that particular colored sheet of construction paper. Put the sheets of paper together and staple the corner to make a simple flip book.

Variations

- Write down children's responses and add them to a bulletin board about color.
- Teach children the names of colors in another language.

What Is Your Color?

Topics: "Colors," "Bodies," "I'm Me and I'm Special," "Our Community"

Goal: To help children recognize and name skin color

Materials: Pictures of people from a variety of racial groups

Method: Hold up one picture at a time. Ask such questions as: "Who can tell me about this picture?" "Who is this person?" "What color is this person's skin?" "What color is this person's hair?" "Where do you think this person lives?" Encourage children to use descriptive color words such as *tan, ebony,* and *cream* to expand their color vocabularies. Write down children's answers. Make a bulletin board display by posting pictures along with the children's descriptions.

Variations

Mix up the pictures and lay them face down. Select a child to come up and choose a picture from the pile. Ask the child to show it to the class and describe the person in the picture.

Everyone Is Different

Topics: "I'm Me and I'm Special," "Alike and Different," "Our Five Senses," "Bodies," "Our Community"

Goal: To help children discover that all people have physical characteristics that make them unique

Materials: White paper or 3 x 5-inch cards, black ink pad, pen, magnifying glass

Method: Encourage children to make prints of their thumbs by pressing their thumb on the ink pad and then on the paper. Label each print with the child's name. At group time, show children the prints. Talk about how everyone has patterns of lines on the skin of their fingers, how each person has a different pattern, and how each person's fingerprints are different from everyone else's. No two are alike. Set out the prints and a magnifying glass on the table so children can examine the similarities and differences in the fingerprints.

Variations

Make two sets of prints for each child. Mix them up and see if children can match them.

Hair

Topics: "I'm Me and I'm Special," "Boys and Girls," "Alike and Different," "Clothes We Wear," "Bodies"

Goal: To help children notice hair as a distinguishing physical characteristic and discover that some people express their culture through hairstyle

Materials: Pictures of a variety of people with different hairstyles, a hand mirror, empty hair care containers, scarves, turbans, rubber bands, hair clips, old hair dryers, old curling irons, old crimping irons

Method: Show pictures of different hairstyles to children. Ask them to touch their hair. Talk about how hair has texture and curl; how some people have fine hair and some people have coarse hair. Some people have straight hair and some people have curly hair. Pass around the mirror so that children can look at their hair. Talk about how different people differ in the color and length of their hair. Set out hair care materials in the dramatic play area for children to use during free-choice play.

Variations

- Write down children's descriptions of their hair. Let each child draw a self-portrait to accompany the description.
- Have children make collages using pictures from a variety of magazines showing all kinds of hair and hair styles.

Photography and Self-Concept

Taking pictures of themselves and their classmates in different contexts wearing different clothing can help children understand that people remain fundamentally the same, even though they may look different from day to day. Have the children take pictures of each other on different days when they are wearing different clothing and when they are dressing up in the dramatic play area. Have them identify who is in the picture. Talk about how children and other people can look different, depending on what they are wearing. Have the children take photos of their classmates wearing different hats and talk about how they look. Have the children identify pictures of themselves and then discuss what is the same and what is different about each picture. Use points of confusion when children cannot identify themselves in a picture as a teaching moment to talk about how appearances can be different but the person inside is the same.

Story Stick

Every culture throughout history has told stories to teach, explain, preserve history, and entertain. Making up a story as a group allows each child the opportunity to share his/her own unique ideas in a creative activity. In this activity, each person will have a chance to add a part to the story. Before beginning, remind the students that the story has a beginning, middle, and an ending. It also must include who, what, when, where, and why.

You may work with the entire class or with a smaller group of students. Have students form a circle and select a stick that will be used as a cue for passing the story from person to person. The story stick is handed to the next student when it is his or her turn to tell the next part of the story.

Let the children decide who will begin the story. That person can then take the story stick and hold it while saying, "Once upon a time…" You may wish to have each student add one sentence to the story at a time.

After the story is finished, ask the children to choose one word that describes the story. Ask the children why they chose to add the part they did. And then ask them what title they would give the story.

Skin Color Matching Activity

Set out a variety of nylon knee-high stockings in various shades such as tan, black, white, yellow, red. Encourage the children to try them on their hands and arms or legs and feet. Ask questions to help children increase their awareness of skin color. For example, "Can you find a stocking that is like the color of your skin?" or "What color is that stocking on your arm?" Ask the children to try another color stocking. Then ask if it is lighter or darker than their own skin color. Be sure to tell the children that no one's skin is really white, pink, yellow, or red. Emphasize that skin color differences are interesting and desirable.

My Special Music

The object of this activity is to have children listen and dance to a variety of music that reflects the various classroom cultures.

In advance, send a note home asking families to send a favorite musical selection that reflects their culture or selection that their child enjoys at home. Remind families that the music must be appropriate for the classroom.

Materials: CD player or cassette recorder, collection of multicultural music, collection of multicultural children's instruments and rhythm instruments, favorite personal music selection, chart paper

Start by sharing a musical selection that reflects your culture or is special to you. Explain why you like the music. Tell children the name of the music, where it is from, and the names of the musicians. Invite the children to clap or dance to the music.

Then tell the children that they will each have a day to share their special music with the class. Begin each day with one child's music. Write the child's name and a short description about the featured music on a sheet of chart paper to review during morning meeting time.

Provide opportunities for the class to listen to and dance to the music during the day. Provide rhythm instruments to play along. What do they notice about the music? Is it fast or slow? Have they ever heard this type of music before? Does it remind them of other music they have heard in the classroom or at home?

Is there a special dance that is done with the music? Invite children or other family members to teach the dances. Children can also create their own dances to accompany the music.

Keep the music in the listening area so that children can have additional opportunities to listen.

Sample Lessons for Older Children

Packing Your Suitcase

This activity combines research and writing. Have students imagine that they are going to take a trip to a country of their choice, or that they are going to visit relatives in their home country. Have them make a list of clothes that they will need to pack. Then make a second list of the clothes and accessories that they might like to buy there to bring back to friends in the United States. For example, a Russian student might need to pack a warm parka, and a Guatemalan student might want to bring back an embroidered blouse for a friend. Ask students to find out how shoe and clothing sizes are determined in their target country and figure out the sizes of clothing they would need to buy.

Individual and Group Reports

Have students work independently, in pairs, or in small groups to research and present reports on one or more of the following topics.

- Where did these color names come from? Find out the origins of the words *coral, emerald green, mocha, Nile green, ruby red, saffron, salmon, terra cotta,* and *turquoise.*
- Where did these clothing names come from? Find out the origins of the words *jodhpurs, khaki, kimono, oxfords, knickers,* and *raglan sleeve.*
- Who produces the most cotton (or wool or silk)?
- Use an encyclopedia, a social studies book, or the Internet to look up current production of a certain fabric. Then make a pie chart or a line graph to illustrate your findings.

Architecture and Multicultural Learning

A country's unique architecture can be a form of art to study as well as a symbol of a cultural group's pride and unity. The Taj Mahal, the Eiffel Tower, the Leaning Tower of Pisa, the Great Pyramids of Gaza, and the Great Wall of China—all are architectural symbols of a national, proudly shared identity of a people. An architectural triumph gives a nation's citizens an identity that is unique.

The Taj Mahal is an ideal architectural subject that mixes world history and art to transport a child's mind to distant horizons and cultures.

Obtain a poster of the Taj Mahal, or download an image of it from the Internet. Introduce students to the structure while playing *Scheherazade* by Rimsky-Korsakov to command their immediate attention. The building is so different, so beautiful. Ask students what it might be. Responses may range from a castle to a wealthy person's home to a palace or religious institution.

Tell students that the Taj Mahal is actually a mausoleum for a princess, Mumtaz Mahal, who died in childbirth. *Mahal* means "chosen of the palace." Her husband, the Mogul Emperor Shah Jahan of India, was heartbroken by her death and commissioned in her memory a great mausoleum like none the world had ever seen.

The Taj Mahal took 17 years to build, from 1612 to 1629 A.D. Mumtaz sarcophagus was placed directly in the center of the perfectly symmetrical structure.

While more than 75% of the people of India are Hindu, the Mogul period of rule was Muslim. There are significant differences between these two religious groups. The Taj Mahal is clearly an example of bringing a country's people together under the common symbol that is great art.

Architecture Around the World

Ask these questions to establish a broad understanding of a particular structure researched by students.

- Name a famous architectural structure of the world and its location.
- What is the meaning of the structure's name?
- Name any distinctive building techniques and materials used.
- Define five or more new vocabulary words associated with this structure.
- Is there a musical composition that can in some way be associated with this architecture and its people?
- Write a paragraph about the most memorable aspects of this structure. If you have visited this place, let your five senses reflect your direct experience.

African Adventure

Have students read a first-person account of a classroom in Mozambique. They can also watch a video of African children playing games and e-mail the children in the video to ask what kind of music they listen to. These are the sorts of opportunities provided by Tire Tracks, a two-year research expedition across three African countries. Its corresponding education programs allow children from Akron to Zion to get in on the action. Teachers already involved with Tire Tracks have raved about its great, original ideas. See what they're excited about at http://www.tiretracks.org.

Huichol Indian Artwork

The Huichol Indians of Mexico are known for their yarn paintings. The Huichols take beeswax, which they melt in the sun, and spread it over a piece of wood. Then they push colored yarn into the wax to create images. Children can create their own yarn paintings using glue and scraps of yarn and wool.

Materials: A piece of wood or cardboard about 5 x 6 inches to 7 x 8 inches, pencils, bits of yarn or wool (all colors), white glue, books that show examples of the art of Mexico

- Children decide on an image and do a number of sketches before deciding on their final image.
- Then, they draw the final idea on the cardboard, leaving lots of space between the lines (Yarn is thicker than pencil lines.)
- Cut the yarn into manageable lengths.
- Spread a small amount of glue onto one side of the cardboard.
- Work left to right, filling in the image with yarn as they go.
- Be sure to flatten the yarn as you work and take care that no background shows through between the yarn strands.
- Let dry until the glue is completely set.

Hello in Different Languages

This can be a fun, warm-up, get-to-know-you activity with a cross-cultural theme. Ask your students to come up with the word "hello" in as many different languages as possible. Before they make suggestions, ask the group to guess how many collective languages the group will be able to come up with. After the activity, check to see if the final number of "hellos in different languages" was close to the group's guess.

Variation: Have a list of "hello" in lots of different languages from which you can read out. This is especially useful for groups who don't know many different languages as well as to learn, have fun, and illustrate the range of different languages.

Variation: Choose one of your classroom rules such as "Be Respectful" and research how to say it in another language—ideally a language that you know is spoken in a student's home. If you have an interactive whiteboard, pull up an online translator, such as http://babelfish.yahoo.com. Practice pronouncing the rule in the other language and discuss where that language is spoken. If you like, ask families to share the translation in a language that is important to them.

Chapter Review

1. Why is it important to use common bonds in planning a multicultural early childhood curriculum?
2. Discuss the importance of using art from around the world in the early childhood room.
3. Discuss some ways to present art objects to children in the multicultural curriculum.
4. Why is it inappropriate to include facts and historical information to young children in a multicultural curriculum?
5. Why is it important to avoid eccentric representations of ethnic groups with young children?
6. Discuss the importance of multicultural children's books in the early childhood program.
7. What are some resources you would use to find appropriate multicultural picture books?
8. Why is it important to use bilingual storybooks in the early childhood program?
9. How is an early childhood multicultural curriculum different from that of an upper elementary or middle school curriculum?
10. Why is it important to include multicultural children's books even if you have a single cultural group represented in your group of children?

References

Chen, D. W., Nimmo, J., & Fraser, H. (2009). Becoming a culturally responsive early childhood educator: A tool to support reflection by teachers embarking on the anti-bias journey. *Multicultural Perspectives, 11*(2), 101–106.

Derma-Sparks, L., & Edwards, J. O. (2009). *Anti-bias education for young children and ourselves.* Washington, DC: NAEYC.

Gonzalez-Mena, J. (2009). *Diversity in early care and education.* Washington, DC: NAEYC.

Lappalainen, S. (2009). Making differences and reflecting on diversities: Embodied nationality among preschool children. *International Journal of Inclusive Education, 113*(1), 63–74.

Lim, C-L., Maxwell, K. L., Able-Boone, H., & Zimmer, C. R. (2009). Cultural and linguistic diversity in early childhood teacher preparation: The impact of contextual characteristics on coursework and practica. *Early Childhood Research Quarterly, 64*(3), 124–132.

Onchwari, G., Onchwari, J. A., & Keengwe, J. (2008). Teaching the immigrant child: Application of child development theories. *Early Childhood Education Journal, 36*(3), 267–273.

Additional Readings

Bennett, C. I. (2010). *Comprehensive multicultural education: Theory and practice* (7th ed.). Boston: Allyn & Bacon.

Botelho, M. J. (2009). *Critical multicultural analysis of children's literature: Mirrors, windows, and doors.* New York: Taylor & Francis.

Campbell, D. E. (2009). *Choosing democracy: A practical guide to multicultural education.* Boston: Allyn & Bacon.

Chartock, R. K. (2009). *Strategies and lessons for culturally responsive teaching: A primer for K–12 teachers.* Boston: Allyn & Bacon.

deMelendez, W. R., & Beck, V. (2009). *Teaching young children in multicultural classrooms: Issues, concepts, and strategies* (3rd ed.). Clifton Park, NY: Delmar Cengage Learning.

DeVries, L. (2009). *Building a foundation.* Denver, CO: Outskirts Press.

Dodge, M. (2009). American picture books and Ukrainian teachers. *Young Children, 64*(4), 102–106.

Florence, N. (2009). *Multiculturalism 101.* New York: McGraw-Hill.

Gurung, R. A. G., & Prieto, L. R. (2009). *Getting culture: Incorporating diversity across the curriculum.* Sterling, VA: Stylus Publishing.

Hollingworth, L. (2009). *Complicated conversations.* Saarbrucken, Germany: LAP Lambert Academic.

May, S., & Sleeter, C. (Eds.) *Critical multiculturalism: Theory and praxis.* London: Taylor & Francis.

Moschella, M. (2010). *Culture, curriculum, and identity in education.* New York: Palgrave Macmillan.

Murphy, G., & Power, M. (2009). *A story to tell.* Sterling, VA: Stylus Publishing.

Passmore, K. (2008). Human commonalities and art. *SchoolArts, 108*(1), 46–47.

Payne, J. (2008). Sharing a world vision. *SchoolArts, 108*(1), 28–29.

Pitre, A. (2009). *Educating African American students: Foundations, curriculum, and experiences.* Lanham, MD: Rowman & Littlefield.

Steinberg, S. (2009). *Diversity and multiculturalism.* New York: Peter Lang.

Tiedt, P. L., & Tiedt, I. M. (2009). *Multicultural teaching: A handbook of activities, information, and resources.* Boston: Allyn & Bacon.

Youngquist, J., & Martinez-Griego, B. (2009). Learning in English, learning in Spanish. *Young Children, 64*(4), 92–99.

Helpful Websites

Internet Picture Dictionary, http://www. pdictionary.com

ESL Bears, http://www.eslbears.homestead.com

Illustrated Vocabulary, http://www.illustratedvocabulary.ip-providence.net

Barahona Center for the Study of Books in Spanish for Children and Adolescents, http://www2.csusm.edu/csb

A to Z Teachers Stuff, http://www.atozteacherstuff.com

Multicultural Pavilion, http://www.edchange.org/multicultural/index.html

Speakaboos, http://www.speakaboos.com/home

Visual Dictionary Online, http://visual.merriam-webster.com/

World Flag Database, http://www.flags.net

Wrapped in Pride—Kente Cloth, http://www.nmafa.si.edu/exhibits/kente/top.htm

Spanish-English Cycle Race, http://www.missmaggie.org/scholastic/cyclerace_eng_launcher.html.

Salsa, http://www.gpb.org/salsa

Myths and Legends, http://myths.e2bn.org/index.php

Multicultural Theatre in Music, http://www.yale.edu/ynhti/curriculum/units/1993/3/93.03.03.x.html

Maps: Finding Our Place in the World, http://www.fieldmuseum.lorg/maps/

Multicultural Music and Songs, http://www.songsforteaching.com/diversitymulticulturalism.htm

Mama Lisa's World, http://www.mamalisa.com/?=eh

Hello World, http://www.hello-world.com/English/EN_English.php

Global Tales, http://library.thinkquest.org/06aug/01340/index.html

KidsWrite, http://www.kalwriters.com/kidswwwrite/index.html

For additional creative activity resources, visit our website at www.Cengage.com/login

Gross- and Fine-Motor Skills[1]

By 2 Years

Gross Motor

- walks forward (average age 12 months)
- walks backward (average age 15 months)
- walks up stairs with help (average age 17 months)
- moves self from sitting to standing (average age 18 months)
- seats self in small chair (average age 18 months)
- uses rocking horse or rocking chair with aid (average age 18 months)

Fine Motor

- builds tower of two blocks (average age 15 months)
- builds tower of three or four blocks (average age 19 months)
- places pellet in bottle (average age 15 months)
- places blocks in cup (average age 15 months)
- places four rings on peg or large pegs in pegboard (average age 18 months)
- imitates vertical line stroke (average age 20 months)
- turns pages of book, two or three at a time (average age 21 months)

By 2½ Years

Gross Motor

- kicks ball forward (average age 20 months)
- jumps in place (average age 23 months)
- runs (stiffly) (average age 2 years)
- hurls small ball overhand, one hand, without direction (average age 22 months)
- pedals tricycle (average age 2 years)

Fine Motor

- builds tower of six cube blocks (average age 23 months)
- imitates circular motion with crayon, after demonstration (average age 2¼ years)
- turns pages of book, one at a time (average age 2 years)

By 3 Years

Gross Motor

- walks up and down stairs without adult help, but not alternating feet (average age 22 months)
- walks four steps on tiptoe (average age 2¼ years)
- jumps from bottom step (average age 2 years)

---

[1]Ninety percent of children at specific age level will have acquired skill.
Adapted from Gesell, A., Ilg, F. L., Ames, L. B., & Rodell, J. L. (1974). *Infant and child in the culture of today: The guidance of development in home and nursery school.* New York: Harper and Row.

- walks backward 10 feet (average age 28 months)
- broad jumps 24–34 inches (average age 2½ years)
- balances on one foot, 1 second (average age 2½ years)

Fine Motor

- imitates vertical line from demonstration (average age 22 months)
- imitates vertical or horizontal line (average age 2½ years)
- imitates V stroke from demonstration (average age 2½ years)
- strings four beads in 2 minutes (average age 2½ years)
- folds paper (average age 2½ years)
- builds tower of seven or eight cubes (average age 2½ years)

By 3½ Years

Gross Motor

- walks on tiptoe 10 feet (average age 3 years)
- balances on one foot, 5 seconds (average age 3¼ years)

Fine Motor

- imitates bridge of three blocks from demonstration (average age 3 years)
- copies circle from picture model (average age 3 years)
- imitates cross from demonstration (average age 3 years)
- closes fist, wiggles thumb (average age 35 months)
- picks longer of two lines (average age 3 years)

By 4 Years

Gross Motor

- hops, preferred foot (average age 3½ years)
- walks up stairs, one foot on each step, holding rail (average age 3½ years)
- walks down stairs, one step per tread (average age 3½ years)
- throws ball with direction (average age 3½ years)
- balances on toes (average age 3½ years)
- jumps over rope 8 inches high (average age 3½ years)

- swings on swing independently (average age 3½ years)
- jumps from height of 12 inches (average age 3½ years)
- holds standing balance, one foot advanced, eyes closed, 15 seconds (one of two tries by 4 years)

Fine Motor

- buttons up clothing (average age 3 years)
- cuts with scissors (average age 3½ years)
- touches point of nose with eyes closed (by age 4, two of three tries)
- puts 20 coins in a box, separately (by age 4, one of two tries)

By 4½ Years

Gross Motor

- balances standing on one foot, 5 seconds (average age 3¼ years)
- does forward somersault with aid (average age 3½ years)
- catches ball in arms, two of three tries (average age 4)
- catches bounced ball (average age 4 years)
- heel-to-toe walk (average age 3¾ years)
- jumps from height of 2½ feet (average age 4 years)

Fine Motor

- copies cross from picture model (average age 3¾ years)
- draws a person, three parts (average age 4 years)
- copies square from demonstration (average age 4 years)

By 5 Years

Gross Motor

- balances on one foot for 10 seconds (average age 4½ years)
- hops on nonpreferred foot (average age 4½ years)
- bounces ball two times successively with one hand (average age 4½ years)
- catches large bounced ball, two of three tries (average age 4 years)

- somersaults forward without aid (average age 4¾ years)
- balances on tiptoes for 10 seconds, one of three tries (by age 5 years)
- jumps over cord at knee height, feet together, one of three tries (average age 4½ years)
- walks heel to toe (average age 4¾ years)
- walks heel to toe, backward (average age 4¾ years)
- walks 2- by 4-inch balance beam, 3 inches off floor, without falling (average age 4½ years)

Fine Motor

- builds pyramid of six blocks after demonstration (average age 4½ years)
- clenches and bares teeth (by age 5 years)
- draws diamond after demonstration (average age 4½ years)
- copies square from picture model (average age 4¾ years)
- ties any knot that holds with lace (average age 5 years)

Language Development Objectives and Activities for Infants and Toddlers

LEVEL	OBJECTIVE	ACTIVITY
Birth to 1 month	1. To develop intimacy and awareness of communication based on personal contact. 2. To introduce the concept of oral communication. 3. To introduce verbal communication. 4. To stimulate interest in the process of talking.	1. Whisper into the child's ear. 2. Coo at the child. 3. Talk to the child. 4. Let the child explore your mouth with his or her hands as you talk.
1 to 3 months	1. To develop oral communication. 2. To develop auditory acuity. 3. To develop the concept that different people sound different. 4. To develop the concept of oral and musical communication of feelings.	1. Imitate the sounds the child makes. 2. Talk to the child in different tones. 3. Encourage others to talk and coo to the child. 4. Sing songs of different moods, rhythms, and tempos.
3 to 6 months	1. To develop the concept of positive use of verbal communication. 2. To stimulate excitement about words. 3. To develop the concept that words and music can be linked. 4. To develop the ability to name things and events.	1. Reward the child with words. 2. Talk expressively to the child. 3. Sing or chant to the child. 4. Describe daily rituals to the child as you carry them out.
6 to 9 months	1. To develop use of words. 2. To develop the concept that things have names. 3. To develop the concept that there is joy in the written word. 4. To develop the concept that language is used to describe.	1. Talk constantly to the child and reinforce intimacy. Explain processes such as feeding, bathing, and changing clothes. 2. Name toys for the child as the child plays, foods and utensils as the child eats, etc. 3. Read aloud to the child with expression and enthusiasm. 4. Describe sounds to the child as they are heard.

LEVEL	OBJECTIVE	ACTIVITY
9 to 12 months	1. To develop the concept that body parts have names. 2. To reinforce the concept that things have names. 3. To stimulate rhythm and interest in words. 4. To stimulate experimentation with sounds and words.	1. Name parts of the body and encourage the child to point to them. 2. Describe and name things seen on a walk or an automobile trip. 3. Repeat simple songs, rhymes, and finger plays. 4. Respond to sounds the child makes and encourage the child to imitate sounds.
12 to 18 months	1. To develop the ability to label things and follow directions. 2. To expand vocabulary and lay the foundation for later production of sentences. 3. To reinforce the concept of names and the ability to recognize names and sounds. 4. To encourage verbal communication. 5. To reinforce the concept of labels and increase vocabulary.	1. Link up various objects and, naming one, ask the child to get it. 2. Act out verbs (*sit, jump, run, smile,* etc.). 3. Use animal picture books and posters of animals. 4. Let the child talk on a real telephone. 5. Describe things at home or outside on a walk or an automobile trip.
18 to 24 months	1. To stimulate imitation and verbalization. 2. To improve the ability to name objects. 3. To encourage repetition, sequencing, and rhythm. 4. To develop auditory acuity, passive vocabulary, and the concept of language constancy. 5. To stimulate verbalization, selectivity, and—eventually—descriptive language. 6. To stimulate conversation.	1. Tape record the child and others familiar to the child, and play the tapes back for the child. 2. On a walk around the home or neighborhood with the child, point out and name familiar objects. 3. Play counting games, sing songs, and tell and retell familiar stories. 4. With the child, listen to the same recording of a story or song over and over. 5. Cut from magazines and mount on stiff cardboard: pictures of foods, clothing, appliances, etc. Have the child identify them as you show them. Use memorable descriptions: "orange, buttery carrots," "the shiny blue car." 6. With the child, prepare and eat a make-believe meal.
24 to 36 months	1. To practice descriptive language and build vocabulary. 2. To encourage verbalization, repetition, comprehension, and speaking in sentences. 3. To develop the concept of written symbols. 4. To encourage specific and descriptive language. 5. To increase understanding of the relation between spoken and written language, and to stimulate the use of both.	1. Keep a box of scraps of materials and small objects. Have the child select objects, using words to describe them (*fuzzy, big, red,* etc.). 2. Ask the child: "Show me the floor, the door," etc. When the child points, say, "Here's the floor," etc., and encourage the child to imitate you. 3. Label the child's possessions. Use the child's name repeatedly: "Mike's bed," "Mike's toy chest." 4. Ask "Which one?" when the child gives a single-word description, and expand on the child's language (e.g., Child: "Cookie." You: "Yes, this is a ginger cookie."). 5. Call the child's attention to familiar brand names or identifying symbols on products, buildings, and so on.

Art Talk Summary

The following are some basic art elements to keep in mind when talking with children about their art.

Color

Hue: Primary Colors	Secondary Colors
red	green
blue	violet (purple)
yellow	orange

Value

Mix black with color to make a *shade*.
Add black to a color to make it darker.
Mix white with a color to make a *tint*.
Add white to a color to make it lighter.

Line

These lines are used in artwork:
Straight
Curved
Zigzag
Horizontal
Vertical
Diagonal

Shape

These shapes are used in artwork:
Geometric
Circle
Square
Rectangle
Triangle
Oval
Diamond
Organic (natural)
Free-form

Composition

Balance in artwork can be:
Symmetrical
Radial
Asymmetrical or overall

Talk to Child About

Lines
Shapes
Colors
Content

Exhibitions and Displays

Exhibitions and Displays

It is stimulating and educational for children to see their work displayed. Whether the purpose of the exhibit is to introduce new ideas and information, to stimulate interest in a single lesson, to show children's work, or to provide an overview of their work, the subject of the exhibition should be directly related to children's interest. Exhibits should be changed often to be of educational and decorative value.

Labels

- Make large, bold letters that can be easily read.
- Keep titles brief. Descriptive material should be in smaller letters.
- Label children's work with their names as a means of creating pride through recognition of their work.
- Vary the material in making letters. In addition to paper letters, labels can be made of paint, ink, crayon, chalk, cloth, fancy papers, string, rope, yarn, and other three-dimensional materials.

Color

- Choose a basic color scheme related to the visual material displayed. Seasonal colors can be used, such as warm colors for fall (yellow, orange, red), cool colors for winter (blue, blue-green, gray), and light and cool colors for spring (colors with yellow in the mixture, such as yellow-orange).
- Use colors for mounting that are more subdued than the materials mounted. This may be accomplished by using lighter, darker, or grayer colors.
- Select a bright color for accent, as in bands or other pleasing arrangements on the larger areas of gray or lighter or darker colors.
- Create a contrast to emphasize or attract attention. Intense color makes a visual impact, such as orange against black.
- Use both light and dark color values.
- Create color patterns that lead the eye from area to area.

Balance

Balance can be achieved formally or informally. To create formal balance, the largest piece of work may be placed in the center with similar shapes on either side. Informal balance is more interesting, subtle, and compelling. Material may be grouped in blocks of different sizes, colors, or shapes and still be balanced. Margins of the bulletin board should be wider at the bottom.

Unity

Unity in design is the quality that holds the arrangement together in harmony.
- Ideas can be unified with background paper, lettering, strips of construction paper, yarn, or ribbon.
- Repetition of similar sizes, shapes, colors, or lines can help to create harmony.
- Shapes can be arranged to lead the eye from one part of the board to another.
- One large unusual background shape helps unify the design.
- Avoid cluttering the display; items placed at all angles destroy the unity.

Variety

Variety in arrangement prevents monotony. Use interesting combinations of color, form, line, and texture.

Emphasis

Emphasis is the main idea or center of interest. This can be achieved by using larger letters, a brighter color, a larger picture, an unusual shape or texture, or a three-dimensional object. Other material should be grouped into subordinate areas.

Line

Line is used to draw the eye to a specific area, to suggest direction, action, and movement, and to hold the display together. Use thick, thin, solid, dotted, or dashed lines. Diagonal lines are used to show action; zigzag lines suggest excitement; slow-moving curves are restful. Lines may be painted, cut from paper, or formed with string, yarn, ribbon, or tape.

Texture

Texture may be created with a variety of materials.
- paper and cardboard—textured wallpaper, sandpaper, foil, egg containers, corrugated cardboard
- fabrics—netting, flannel, burlap, fur, felt, carpet remnants, assorted felt scraps
- miscellaneous—chicken wire, metal screen, sheet cork

Three-Dimensional Effects

- Pull letters or objects out to the head of the pin.
- Staple a shallow box to the board as a shelf to hold lightweight three-dimensional items.
- Mount a picture on a box lid and fasten it to the board.
- Use shallow boxes as buildings, animals, and people.
- Pleat a strip of paper in an accordion fold with pictures attached.
- Use paper sculpture—strips of paper can be twisted, curled, folded, rolled, fringed, perforated, or torn. Puppets, animals, birds, flowers, people, abstract forms, and masks can also be made.
- Use three-dimensional materials in displays: Styrofoam, egg cartons, paper plates, paper cups, soda straws, cupcake cups, paper lace, toweling tubes, and other discarded materials.
- Use objects from nature—branches, shells, bark, driftwood, feathers.

Background Materials

- tissue paper, burlap, corrugated cardboard, construction paper
- blotters, textured wallpaper, shelf paper

Display Boards for Two-Dimensional Work

- standard cork boards or sheet of plywood to which cork tiles have been glued
- builder's wallboard with wood strip nailed to the top with hooks for hanging
- thick cardboard that will hold pins
- a pasteboard box open for standing on a table or the floor, depending on size
- a folding screen made from an old crate or packing box

More on Bulletin Boards— Kindergarten and Elementary Level

The most immediate evidence of an art program is the display of children's artwork. A teacher's creative approach to display is an extension of the art program in the physical environment. Bulletin boards are the most frequent form of display. Consider the following fairy tale.

Once upon a time, there was a carpenter who was building a classroom. When he was on the very top of his ladder, a hammer fell and crashed into the wall, making a very large hole. The carpenter did not know what to do since he had no materials left to repair the wall. Suddenly he had an idea! He found a 4 × 8-foot slab of cork and hung it over the hole. Then he tacked wood strips around the edges and said, "I am well pleased." He named his creation "Bulletin Board."

The dictionary defines *bulletin board* as "a board on which bulletins and other notices are posted." Teachers often have other definitions for this term: (1) a surface that must be covered before the first day of school and before parents' night; (2) a board that is always 3 inches wider than the paper just cut for it; and (3) a rectangle that has a width never sufficient for the number of letters needed to be pinned across it.

Whatever your definition, a bulletin board is much more than a board on which notices are posted. It is a visual extension of a learning experience, a visual form of motivation, and a reflection of a curriculum area. Because bulletin boards are a visual phenomenon, teachers should be concerned about their content and appearance.

Thirty spelling papers or 15 identical paper pumpkins hanging up like someone's laundry do not constitute a good bulletin board. Mimeographed pictures, commercial cardboard turkeys, and corrugated cardboard trim are not visually appealing and certainly are not reflections of the children whose interest you are trying to catch.

A display designed for the eye is also designed for the mind. Children are very much attuned to symbols. Television commercials, billboards, posters, and cereal boxes attest to the impact of images. Bulletin boards should attract constructive attention. Stereotypical smiley faces and dog-eared paper letters with a thousand pinholes will not do it. Ideas and paper fade. Stereotyped versions of an upcoming holiday do absolutely nothing for children's art development.

For an early childhood teacher, one of the best solutions is to display the children's artwork. Art is a visual extension of the child and her or his own unique ideas and expression. It is the result of the child's own experience and serves as a motivation for others and the child herself or himself. Any subject can be the theme for an effective bulletin board, but one rule of thumb is that all boards should be student-oriented and entice student participation. Boards that ask questions, have games to play, or have objects to be handled can be fun and valuable learning experiences.

Eye-catching photographs (of the children, if possible), short stories, and poems are exercises for both the eye and mind. Whatever the mode, the key is visual impact. In order for a bulletin board to be a learning experience, it first must attract children's attention. Bright colors, bold design, legible, catchy, succinct phraseology, and relevant themes are vital to bulletin boards by, for, and about children.

Try some of these suggestions for improving your bulletin boards.

- Take advantage of interest in the World Series, Olympics, or other big sports events for a variety of projects. Find bulletin board space for newspaper clippings, pictures of heroes and heroines, and posting of scores and relative standings. Have children write reports or draw pictures of games in which they are interested. Make up graphs with scores for each team. Vary these activities according to the level of children's interest and abilities.

- If you have a bulletin board too big to cope with, cut it down to size by covering it with wallpaper samples, outlining each sample with black construction paper in a kind of giant patchwork quilt effect. Each child can use one of these squares as a personal bulletin board. Or you could use each of the squares to depict a different aspect of one main theme: kinds of animals, favorite people, etc.

- Be sure all your bulletin boards and other kinds of displays are at children's eye level.

- When your classroom closet is awash with caps and mittens, why not bring their splashy colors and designs into the open with a self-portrait mural for a bulletin board? On a strip of butcher paper, draw a circle for each child. Have the students add features to turn these circles into self-portraits. Two lines looping down from each face become instant arms. Finally, have each child draw her or his own hat and mittens on the heads and hands. Encourage the young artists to copy the actual styles, colors, and designs of their own apparel as exactly as possible. This mural not only makes a colorful bulletin board, but also helps you easily identify the owners of any stray clothing.

Display Areas for Three-Dimensional Work

- Use tops of cupboards or built-in shelves.
- Build shelves with boards supported by bricks, used permanently or temporarily.
- Attach a shelf of wood or particleboard underneath a bulletin board.
- A card table can be used for temporary exhibits, then folded up when not in use.
- Small cardboard boxes fastened to bulletin boards make a display place for lightweight objects.
- Use driftwood as an interesting display for weaving and jewelry.
- Puppet display rods can be made with a board and some dowel sticks.
- Cover cardboard boxes and use them as bases for displaying art objects.
- Use a pegboard with hooks to hang objects on.

Recycled Materials

Creative teachers find that potential art materials abound everywhere and include old, discarded items. For example, in the following teaching suggestions, one kind of discarded item—the gallon milk container— presents a wealth of storage, display, and equipment possibilities.

Teaching Suggestions: Empty Containers Full of Promise

When that plastic gallon milk container is out of milk, it is full of potential for classroom implements you can make yourself. Scoops, funnels, sorting trays, display or storage containers, and carrying baskets are just waiting to be cut out.

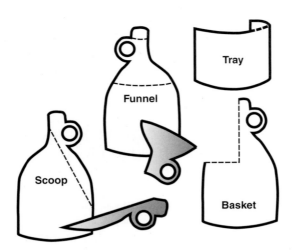

Outline the area you wish to cut with a felt-tip marker and use a sharp knife or a small pencil-type soldering iron to do the cutting. (If you use the iron,

be sure to work in a ventilated area and avoid inhaling the fumes.) Be sure that edges are not sharp and jagged. It is best to cover the cut edge with electrical tape or any other strong tape.

These containers are so readily available you can afford to experiment with a few to find just the shapes you are after. Here are directions for some basic cuts to get you started.

- Scoop—Cut away the handle and part of the side below it. The container's handle instantly becomes the scoop's handle, while the section below becomes the scoop itself.
- Sorting trays—Cut off the bottom or the entire side opposite the handle to make trays of varying depths. These are perfect for sorting small objects, such as pebbles or shells, or for examining small amounts of sand or soil.
- Funnel—Cut the handle a few centimeters from the top. Then cut around the base of the handle to make the funnel's body from the curved section of the jug. The top of the handle becomes the spout. For a larger funnel, simply cut the bottom from the container and use the top as the spout.
- Carrying basket—Cut away the upper portion of the side opposite the handle. Children then carry the jug by the handle and use it to transport all kinds of items.

Equipment for Movement Activities From Recycled Materials

A valuable addition to the movement program in the early childhood classroom is equipment made from recycled materials. For example, empty plastic gallon milk jugs can be used as safe game goals, pins for

FIGURE E-1 • Equipment using recycled material scoops.

indoor/outdoor bowling games, or cut out for scoops (see Figures E–1 and E–2) to toss yarn or other light balls in classroom movement activities.

Old pantyhose can be used to make light, child-sized rackets for great hand–eye coordination practice in racket games. These rackets are especially good for young children, as they are light enough to handle and yet sturdy enough to hit a yarn, Nerf, or plastic ball.

Using recycled materials has an obvious cost benefit in addition to demonstrating the importance of conservation to young children. Young children can possibly use these same materials at home for their own play experiences.

Even better, you can enlist parent participation and involvement in the program by asking parents to donate recycled materials to make movement equipment. Perhaps parents and children together could even get involved at home in making some of the equipment for the class's use, such as yarn balls or pantyhose rackets.

Other Ideas for Recycling Materials

Just as recycled materials were used for making movement equipment in Chapter 16, these same "discards" can be valuable art materials. Both conservation and creativity can be practiced in ways like the following.

- Be a scavenger. (But remember that the word is *scavenger*—not *beggar* or *receiver of junk goods*.)
- Begin your scavenger hunt by making a list of the equipment and supplies you think you might find in your community at little or no cost.

FIGURE E-2 • Plastic scoop and yarn ball.

- Search for your treasures in attics, basements, garages, thrift or Goodwill Industry stores, and at garage sales.
- Ask parents to help satisfy the needs of creative children, or send a "want ad" home that is specific about what you need.
- Check with wallpaper and carpet dealers. Wallpaper dealers will sometimes give you their old sample books, and carpet dealers will often sell their sample swatches for a very small sum. These carpet swatches are useful as sit-upons, as rugs for houses the children build, as colorful mats under items on display, and as working mats for use under table toys.
- Gather paper from a variety of sources:
  - Be a bag grabber. Collect plain paper bags. Cut them open and use them for painting, crayoning, etc.
  - Save old newspapers for easel painting. Bright tempera (water color) paint on a newsprint background makes a very attractive and interesting work of art.
  - Check with your community or local newspaper office. They may donate or sell newsprint or old newspapers to you at a minimal cost.

Other materials listed in Figure E–3 can be valuable in the art center.

The following materials can be valuable instructional tools in the art program as well as in other curriculum areas.

1. Empty plastic containers—detergent bottles, bleach bottles, old plastic containers. These can be used for constructing scoops, storing art materials, etc.
2. Buttons—all colors and sizes. These are excellent for collages, assemblages, as well as sorting, counting, matching, etc.
3. Egg shells. These can be washed, dried, and colored with food coloring for art projects.
4. Coffee or shortening can lids and cans themselves. These can be covered with adhesive paper and used for the storage of art supplies, games, and manipulatives.
5. Magazines with colorful pictures. These are excellent for making collages, murals, and posters.
6. Scraps of fabric—felt, silk, cotton, oil cloth, etc. These can be used to make "fabric boards" with the name of each fabric written under a small swatch attached to the board, as well as for collages, puppets, etc.
7. Yarn scraps. These can be used for separating buttons into sets; also for art activities.
8. Styrofoam scraps.
9. Scraps of lace, rickrack, or decorative trim.
10. Bottles with sprinkler tops. Excellent for water play and for mixing water as children finger paint.
11. Wallpaper books of discontinued patterns.
12. Paper doilies.
13. Discarded wrapping paper.
14. Paint color cards from paint/hardware stores.
15. Old paintbrushes.
16. Old jewelry and beads.
17. Old muffin tins. These are effective for sorting small objects and mixing paint.
18. Tongue depressors or ice cream sticks. Counters for math; good for art construction projects, stick puppets, etc.
19. Wooden clothespins. For making "people," for construction projects, for hanging up paintings to dry.

FIGURE E-3 • Beautiful junk list.

Sandbox Toys From the Kitchen

From the cupboard—Use plastic storage containers such as scoops, molds, or buckets. Foam cups are good scoops or molds. A plastic flowerpot with drainage holes can be a sifter.

Cut an egg carton into individual egg cups for molds.

Make an egg-carton sifter by cutting the lid off an egg carton and cutting the egg cup section in half the short way. In the bottom of each cup, poke a hole. The holes may be the same size or of varying sizes.

Musical Instruments From Recycled Materials

Recycling egg cartons for tambourines. Young children can make a simple tambourine from egg cartons and bottle caps. Simply put a few bottle caps in each egg carton, tape the carton closed, and you have an instrument that players can shake or hit. Children will love playing it both in rhythm and creative movement activities.

Recycling nuts and bolts for rattles. For an unusual set of musical instruments, assemble an assortment of large nuts, bolts, and washers. Young children will get excellent practice in fine finger movements when they create musical rattles out of these. All you have to do is place several washers on each bolt and loosely turn the nut onto the bolt. Place these inside empty, metal boxes, tape shut, and use as interesting sound instruments (rattles).

Making music with bottles. Gather a collection of bottles with both small and large mouths, soft drink bottles, ketchup bottles, quart canning jars, mayonnaise jars, etc.

Show children how different sounds can be made with different-sized bottles by blowing across the various openings. Have them listen for high and low sounds. Stand the bottles on a table and gently tap them with a spoon. Children can explore different sounds the bottles make by blowing across them and by tapping them with a spoon.

Rhythm instruments from recycled materials. The following are suggestions for simple rhythm instruments children can make to use in their musical experiences. Creating rhythm instruments from found objects gives young children another opportunity for self-expression. They receive satisfaction and pleasure from beating rhythmic sounds and keeping time to music with instruments they have created.

Materials

paper plates	plastic egg-shaped containers
empty spools	small plastic bottles
pebbles	sticks
nails	old Christmas bells
toweling rolls	bottle caps
embroidery hoops	dried peas, beans or corn wire
small boxes or cartons	

Bottle cap shaker. Remove plastic from inside bottle caps. Punch a hole in the center of the bottle cap. String bottle caps on a string and attach to a package handle. Paint if desired.

Spool shaker. Paint designs on a large spool. Force four pipe cleaners through the center of the spool. Attach a Christmas bell to the end of each pipe cleaner by bending the pipe cleaner to hold the bell.

Plate shaker. Decorate two paper plates with crayons or paint. Put pebbles or dried corn, peas, or beans between them and staple or sew the plates together with bright yarn or string. Bend wire to form a handle, and fit the ends inside.

Box shaker. Place small pebbles, beans, or seeds in a small box or empty, clean milk carton to make a shaker. It can be used with or without a handle. Decorate as desired.

Flute. Use a paper towel or tissue paper roll. With a pencil, punch three or four holes (about one inch apart) in the cardboard tube. Cover one end of the roll with a piece of waxed paper, as described later in the instructions for the Hummer. Children hum a tune in the open end, moving their fingers over the holes.

Sandpaper blocks. Paint two small wooden blocks. Place a strip of sandpaper on the surface, allowing an overlap on each end for fastening with thumbtacks. Children rub the blocks together to make a sound.

Clappers. Thumbtack bottle caps to a painted wooden block.

Cymbals. Cover the edges of two tin can lids with electric tape to be sure they are not sharp. Then decorate the lids. Fasten a small spool or block of wood on for a handle.

Tambourine. Punch holes in bottle caps and tie them together with thin wire, pipe cleaners, or string. Punch a hole in a paper or tinfoil plate and tie on the bottle caps.

Hummer. Decorate a tube from a waxed paper or paper towel roll. Fasten a piece of wax paper over one end of the tube. Humming through the wax paper is fun for children. Be sure to change the paper after each use.

Circle shakers. Stretch two layers of plastic cloth with uncooked rice or tapioca between them over one half of an embroidery hoop. Fasten with the other half of the hoop to make a circle shaker. (When making any shaker-type toys, be sure that the small objects used are sealed securely inside. Small objects like beans, peas, and rice can pose a serious choking risk to young children.)

Egg shakers. Fill plastic egg-shaped containers (plastic Easter eggs) with dried beans. Tape the halves together. Children use them as maracas.

Bottle shakers. Collect empty, small plastic bottles. Fill with rice, beans, or nuts until half full. Seal bottles that don't have childproof lids with tape. These are excellent shakers for tiny hands.

Drums. Glue lids on round-shaped boxes such as those containing salt, cereal, or ice cream and decorate with paint to use as drums. Older children may make drums from restaurant-size tin cans with canvas or heavy paper stretched and laced to cover the ends.

Kazoo. Use a piece of wax paper over a clean comb. Children play by pressing their lips against the paper and humming. Change the paper after each use.

Gong. Use an old license plate (the older the better). Children strike with a mallet to play. They might describe the sounds.

Jingle instrument. Use a set of metal measuring spoons. Children play by shaking or slapping them in their hand.

Wrist or ankle bells. Lace a shoestring through two or three bells. Tie to children's wrists or ankles. Children move to shake their bells.

Rubber band box. Another addition to rhythm instruments is a rubber band box. Gather together one cigar box (or similar size and weight box), five rubber bands of several lengths and thicknesses, and 10 brass fasteners.

Punch five holes 1½ inches apart in each end of the box. Attach a rubber band to a brass fastener, push through one of the holes, and open the fastener on the inside of the box to hold it down. Stretch the rubber band tight to the other end of the box and attach it in the same way. Attach the rest of the rubber bands. To use: The rubber band box can be held, placed on a table, or placed on the floor. Encourage children to pluck the rubber bands with their fingers or strum the bands with their thumbs. They can experiment with sounds and beats: high–low, fast–slow, and loud–soft.

Sound box. Another rhythm instrument is the sandpaper sound box. Gather together a box, four pieces of sandpaper (of various grades from fine to coarse), glue, scissors, and a dowel (½ × 6 inches long). Glue the top and bottom of the box closed. Allow enough time for it to dry completely. Cut the sandpaper to fit all sides of the box. Glue the sandpaper strips to the box. To use: Rub the dowel on the sandpaper. While children are using the sound boxes, you can introduce such musical concepts as loud–soft and fast–slow. The dowels can also be used alone in a rhythm band or in a parade. Extend this activity by having children make their own sound boxes if they are interested.

Clickers. Glue two baby food jar lids together (you can use a glue gun) with the tops opposite each other. Children can paint or decorate with paper or markers. When completed, children squeeze the two lids together with their fingers to make a clicking sound.

Homemade bell. You will need:
- soup can with one end removed and smoothed
- empty thread spool (wooden is best)
- 2 large buttons
- masking tape
- glue and yarn or string
- hammer and large nail
- material to decorate the outside of the bell

Punch a hole in the end of the soup can with the large nail. Cover the cut edges of the can with masking (or electric) tape. Tie two buttons to the end of a piece of yarn or string. Put masking tape on the other end of the string to make it easier to thread through the can and empty thread spool. Thread the string from inside the can to the outside. Spread glue on the bottom of the thread spool before threading the yarn or string through it. Press the thread spool tightly against the can to secure the handle. Lower the string so that the buttons hand about ⅓ of the way down the can. Tie a large knot in the string close to the top of the thread spool.

Children can decorate the can, if they so desire.

Drumsticks. Use wooden dowels with the ends wrapped in soft cloth, secured with a rubber band.

Rain sticks. Put beans, rice, or the like into a tube that can be closed tightly on both ends. Decorate with feathers, ribbon, designs, etc.

Rhythm sticks. Use wooden dowels with the ends smoothed. Paint stirrers from the local hardware store work well, too.

Shakers. Fill empty film canisters and small plastic soda bottles with rice, beans, or popping corn. Make sure to either glue the tops closed or secure them with tape.

Criteria for Selecting Play Equipment for Young Children

1. *A young child's playthings should be as free of detail as possible.* A child needs freedom to express himself or herself by creating his or her own world; too much detail hampers rather than assists. Blocks are the best example of unstructured toys. Blocks, construction sets, and other unstructured toys and equipment such as clay, sand, and paints allow the imagination free rein and are basic playthings.

2. *A good plaything should stimulate children to do things for themselves.* Equipment that makes the child a spectator, such as a mechanical toy, may entertain for the moment but has little or no play value. The equipment provided for play should encourage children to explore and create or offer the opportunity for dramatic play.

3. *Young children need large, easily manipulated playthings.* Toys that are too small can be a source of frustration because the child's muscular coordination is not yet developed enough to handle smaller forms and shapes. A child's muscles develop through play. A child needs equipment for climbing and balancing.

4. *The material from which a plaything is made has an important role in the play of the young child.* Warmth and pleasurable touch are significant to a child. The most satisfactory materials have been established as wood and cloth.

5. *The durability of the plaything is of utmost importance.* Play materials must be sturdy. Children hate to see their toys break. Axles and wheels must be strong to support a child's weight. Some materials break so readily that they prove to be very expensive.

6. *The toy must work.* What frustration when a door or drawer won't shut, wheels get stuck, or figures won't stand up! Be sure parts move correctly and that maintenance will be easy.

7. *The construction of a plaything should be simple enough for a child to comprehend.* This strengthens his or her understanding and experience of the world. The mechanics, too, should be visible and easily grasped. Small children will take them apart to see how they work.

8. *A plaything should encourage cooperative play.* As we seek to teach children to work and play together, we should provide the environment that stimulates such play.

9. *The total usefulness of the plaything must be considered in comparing price.* Will it last several children through several stages of their playing lives?

What are some good toys and play materials for young children?

All ages are approximate. Most suggestions for younger children are also appropriate for older children.

SENSORY MATERIALS	ACTIVE PLAY EQUIPMENT	CONSTRUCTION MATERIALS	MANIPULATIVE TOYS	DOLLS AND DRAMATIC PLAY	BOOKS AND MUSIC	ART MATERIALS
2-Year-Olds and Young 3-Year-Olds						
Water and sand toys: cups, shovels; Modeling dough; Sound-matching games; Bells, wood block, triangle, drum; Texture matching games, feel box	Low climber; Canvas swing; Low slide, wagon, cart, or wheelbarrow; Large rubber balls; Low 3-wheeled, steerable vehicle with pedals	Unit blocks and accessories: animals, people, simple wood cars and trucks; Interlocking construction set with large pieces; Wood train and track set; Hammer (13 oz. steel shanked), soft wood, roofing nails, nailing block	Wooden puzzles with 4–20 large pieces; Pegboards; Big beads or spools to string; Sewing cards; Stacking toys; Picture lotto, picture dominoes	Washable dolls with a few clothes; Doll bed; Child-sized table and chairs; Dishes, pots, and pans; Dress-up clothes: hats, shoes, shirts; Hand puppets; Shopping cart	Clear picture books, stories, and poems about things children know; CDs or tapes of classical music, folk music, or children's songs	Wide-tip water color markers; Large sheets of paper, easel; Finger or tempera paint, brushes; Blunt-nose scissors; White glue
Older 3- and 4-Year-Olds						
Water toys: measuring cups, egg beaters; Sand toys: muffin tins, vehicles; Xylophone, maracas, tambourine	Bicycle; Roller skates; Climbing structure; Rope or tire swing; Plastic bats and balls; Various sizes rubber balls; Balance board; Planks, boxes, old tires; Bowling pins, rings to toss, bean bags and target	More unit blocks, shapes, and accessories; Table blocks; Realistic model vehicles; Construction set with smaller pieces; Woodworking bench, saw, sandpaper, nails	Puzzles, pegboard, small beads to string; Parquetry blocks; Small objects to sort; Marbles; Magnifying glass; Simple card or board games; Flannel board with pictures, letters; Sturdy letters and numbers	Dolls and accessories; Doll carriage; Child-sized stove or sink; More dress-up clothes; Play food, cardboard cartons; Airport, doll house, or other settings with accessories; Finger or stick puppets	Simple science books; More detailed picture and story books; Sturdy CD player; Wider variety of music; Book and CD Sets	Easel, narrower brushes; Thick crayons, chalk; Paste, tape with dispenser; Collage materials; Potter's clay

5- and 6-Year-Olds

SENSORY MATERIALS	ACTIVE PLAY EQUIPMENT	CONSTRUCTION MATERIALS	MANIPULATIVE TOYS	DOLLS AND DRAMATIC PLAY	BOOKS AND MUSIC	ART MATERIALS
Water toys: food coloring, pumps, funnels Sand toys: containers, utensils Harmonica, kazoo, guitar, recorder	Outdoor games: bocce, tetherball, shuffleboard, jump rope, Frisbee, bicycle	More unit blocks, shapes, and accessories Props for roads, towns Hollow blocks Brace and bits, screwdrivers, screws, metric measure, accessories	More complex puzzles Dominoes More difficult board and card games Yarn, big needles, mesh fabric, weaving materials Magnets, balances Attribute blocks	Cash register, play money, accessories, or props for other dramatic play settings: gas station, construction, office Typewriter	Books on cultures Stories with chapters Favorite stories children can read Children's recipe books	Watercolors, smaller paper, stapler, hole punch Chalkboard Oil crayons, paint, crayons, charcoal Simple camera, film Tools for working with clay

7- to 10-Year-Olds

SENSORY MATERIALS	ACTIVE PLAY EQUIPMENT	CONSTRUCTION MATERIALS	MANIPULATIVE TOYS	DOLLS AND DRAMATIC PLAY	BOOKS AND MUSIC	ART MATERIALS
Modeling materials, papier-mâché, wire for sculpture	Jump ropes, roller skates, skateboards, equipment for team sports and ball tossing and catching	Woodworking bench; full range of tools and equipment	Computer games, puzzles, crochet and knitting supplies	Materials for skits and short dramatic activities	CDs of classical, folk, jazz, and popular music Fiction and non-fiction books	Materials for easel painting, printing, sculpting, collage, rubbings Computer programs for graphic design experiences Potter's clay

Puppet Patterns

Hand Puppet Pattern

Hand puppets can be an essential part of your curriculum and are fun for children to use. Hand puppets can be made with or without mouths, but puppets with mouths are usually preferable. The following pattern can be adapted to make people- or animal-shaped puppets (see Figure G–1). Encourage children to use their imaginations in adding faces, ears, hair, and clothes. Features can be glued, sewn, or written on the puppet.

Materials

Felt, upholstery fabric, glue, needle and thread, scissors, other decorative materials (yarn, feathers, plastic eyes, etc.)

Directions

Cut out two pattern shapes using the type of fabric you choose. Sew or glue them together, leaving the bottom open. Glue on decorative items to change a puppet's personality.

This type of puppet is fun and easy for children to use. Show them how to insert their hand the first time they use one. Keep the puppets in a puppet house in the story corner as well as in the home center for the children to use.

Mittens and Glove Patterns

For each mitten or glove: ½ yard (0.5 m) fabric, fabric glue or thread and sewing machine, scissors

Directions

Following the patterns (see Figures G–2 and G–3), cut material to the size you need. Place wrong sides together and stitch or glue. Glue on any desired features.

Child Size

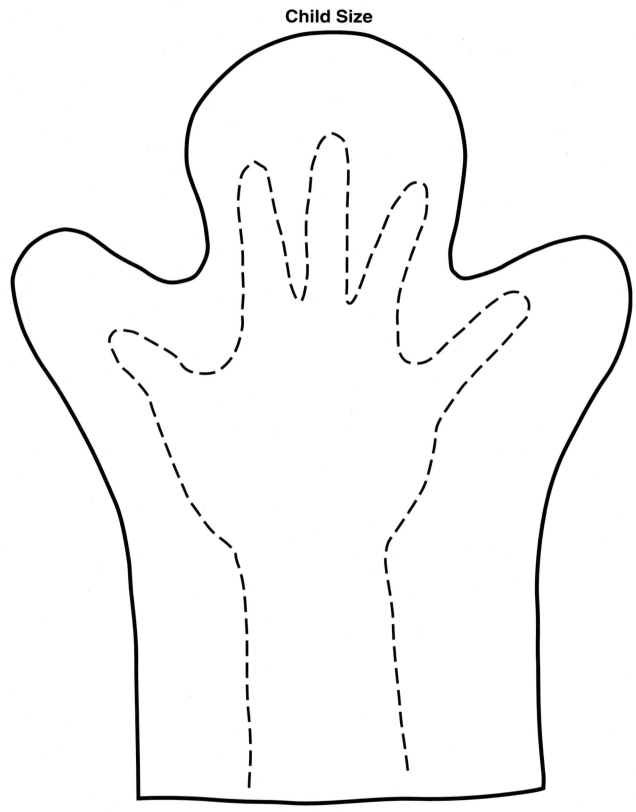

Shorten or lengthen

FIGURE G-1 • Hand puppet pattern.

FIGURE G-2 • Mitten pattern.

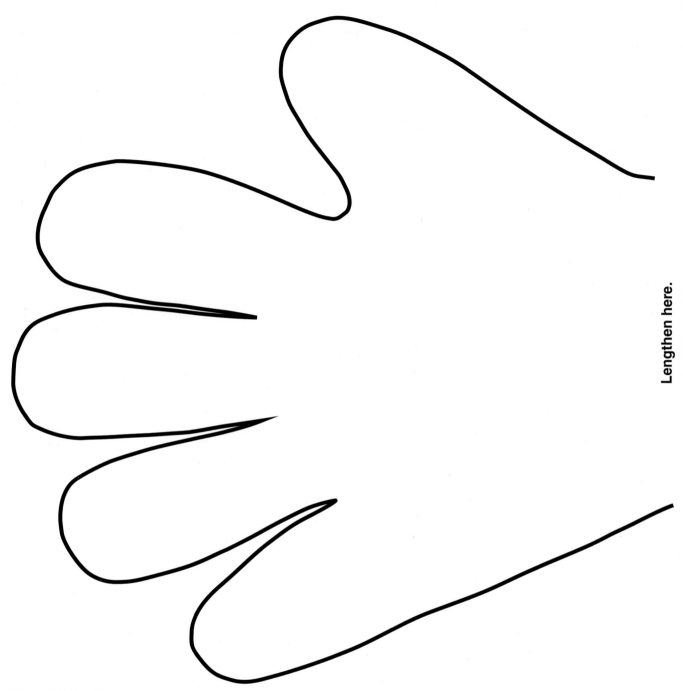

Lengthen here.

FIGURE G-3 • Glove pattern.

Software Companies

ActiVision, http://www.activision.com

Alfred Music Publishing, http://www.alfred.com

Alpha Omega Publications, http://www.aop.com

Animusic, http://www.animusic.com

Apptastic Software, Inc., http://www.apptastic.com

Atari, http://www.atari.com

Brighter Minds Media,
http://www.brightermindsmedia.com

Broderbund, http://www.broderbund.com

Crick Software, Inc., http://www.cricksoft.com

Davidson, http://www.fisher-pricestore.com

The Discovery Channel School,
http://www.discovery.com

Disney Interactive, http://www.disneystore.com

Dolphin Don's Music School,
http://www.dolphindon.com

Dorling Kindersley, http://www.dk.com

Educational Insights, http//www.educationalinsights
.com

Electronic Arts, http://www.ea.com

Encore Software, http://www.encore.com

Fisher-Price, http://www.fisher-price.com

Fun for Brains, http://www.fun4brains.com

GuruForce, Inc., http://www.gurusoftware.com

Hasbro Interactive, http://www.hasbro.com

Inspiration Software, http://www.inspiration.com

Interactive Classics, http://www.interactiveclassics
.com

Knowledge Adventure,
http://www.knowledgeadventure.com or http://
www.jumpstart.com

Konami of America, Inc., http://www.konami.com

Kutoka Interactive, http://www.kutoka.com

LeapFrog, http://www.leapfrog.com

The Learning Company/Broderbund,
http://www.broderbund.com

LEGO Media International, http://www.lego.com

Liquid Animation Pty. Ltd.,
http://www.liquidanimation.com

MagicMouse Productions, http://www.magicmouse
.com

Microsoft Multimedia, http://www.microsoft.com/
products

National Geographic Interactive,
http://www.nationalgeographic.com

Ohio Distinctive Software,
http://www.ohio-distinctive.com

PF Magic, Inc., The Learning Company/Broderbund,
http://www.broderbund.com

Scholastic, http://www.scholastic.com

School Zone Interactive, http://www.schoolzone
.com

Six Red Marbles, http://www.sixredmarbles.com/
home/

Sony Computer, http://www.us.playstation.com

Sunburst Technology, http://www.sunburst.com

TDK Mediactive, http://www.tdk-mediactive.com

THQ, http://www.thq.com

Tom Snyder Productions, http://www.tomsnyder.com

Tool Factory, http://www.toolfactory.com

Viva Media, http://www.viva-media.com

Index

D

Dance, 63, 382–84, 472, 627. *See also* Movement
Dangerous materials. *See* Health and safety
DAP. *See* Developmentally appropriate practice
Decimal activities, 507
Decision making. *See* Problem solving
Deer, 472
Deficit perspectives, 615–16
Dentistry, 587
Design concepts, 44
Developmental delays, 333, 363, 385
Developmental levels and art, 233–60
    activities for children, 254–56
    activities for older children (grades 4–5), 256–58
    art DOs with young children, 246
    basic forms/preschematic stage, 239–42
    beginning vs. end of the school year, 268
    children's drawing, 235
    developmental levels/stages of art, 233–35
    the gang stage, 234, 249–51
    grades one through five, 250
    learning activities, 253–54
    pictorial/schematic stage, 243–49
    research on children's art, 252
    the scribble stage, 235–39
    websites related to, 259
Developmentally appropriate practice (DAP)
    attention spans, 99–100
    described, 82–85
    developmental level, described, 82
    individual differences, 82
    learning activities, 110–11
    Particular Strategies to Individualize or Differentiate, 88f
    references on, 112
    technology and, 157
    websites related to, 113–14
Diagonal crosses, 241
Differentiated instruction, 22–23, 86–92, 88f
Digital cameras, 159–60, 174, 244, 279, 296
Digital storytelling, 429
Dimensionality, 329
Disabilities. *See* Children with special needs
Discovery/science centers, 465–68, 469
Discovery walks, 465–66
Disc players, 160
Disordered scribbling, 235–36
Displaying children's work, 65, 122f, 244–45, 269, 279–80, 296, 307, 466, 645–47
Display materials in multicultural classrooms, 614, 624
Distractibility, 270, 363–64. *See also* Attention deficit/Hyperactivity Disorder and behavioral issues
Ditto sheets, 263, 297
Divergent thinking, 5–6, 28, 64
Diversity. *See* Multicultural curriculum
Diversity within media strategies, 426–27
Documentation, 85
Dolls, 147, 651–53. *See also* Dramatic play and puppetry
The Dragon Lode (journal), 630
Dramatic play and puppetry, 134, 145, 351–73, 359–62
    acting out poetry, 433
    activities for children, 369–71
    activities for older children (grades 4–5), 371–72
    adaptations for children with special needs, 362–63
    beginnings of dramatic play, 352
    creative drama, 359–62
    criteria for selecting play equipment for young children, 651–53
    development of dramatic play, 352–53
    dramatic play, described, 359
    in the dramatic play center, 353–62
    experiences and equipment in the home center, 355f
    fingerplays, 433
    gender-neutral, 354
    importance of, 351–53
    learning activities, 368–69
    mathematics and, 500
    modeling behavior, 355–56
    in multicultural classrooms, 612
    nature-related materials and, 474
    puppets, 363–67, 654–57
    PUPPETS Project, 361
    websites related to, 373
Drawing, 235, 243, 277, 292–301, 475, 527. *See also* Basic forms/preschematic stage; Crayons; Markers; Pencils
Drawing Inside the Box, 279
Drums, 651
Drumsticks, 652
Dry eye condition, 175
Drying artwork, 265–66
Duck, Duck, Goose, 138
Dyes, 286

E

Early basic forms stage, 241
Early Childhood Education Assessment Consortium of the Council of Chief State School Officers (CCSSO), 108
Early childhood learning standards, 108–9
Early civilizations, 143, 147, 302
Early pictorial (first drawings) stage, 245–46
Easel painting, 279
The East River (Prendergast), 143
Ecology, 468–73. *See also* Science
Edison gene, 275
Educational software reviews on the Internet, 168t
Egg cartons, 334, 650
Egg shakers, 651
Einarsdottir, J., 159
Einstein, Albert, 82
Eisner, E. W., 49
Elements of art, 44, 46
Elkind, David, 142
Emergency plans, 586, 587–88
Emergent diagram shapes, 239–40
Emergent reading, 428–29
Emerson, Ralph Waldo, 87
Emotions, 10, 30, 91, 141–42, 146, 216–17, 558. *See also* Art and social-emotional growth
Emphasis, 646
Empty containers, 648
English as a second language, 265f, 267, 356, 424–27, 426f, 615–17, 626, 628
Enriched and fortified foods, 534
Environment, 5, 115–31
    activity/interest centers, 119–25, 163–64
    arrangement of space and equipment, 115–19, 268
    for children with special needs, 117, 122, 124, 214, 214f
    cleanliness of, 585
    clutter, 123
    color coding materials, 128
    convertible and small classroom spaces, 124–25
    for creative movement, 377
    described, 470
    for dramatic play, 356, 360, 362
    for early childhood art activities, 265–66
    to encourage peer-related social competence, 565
    general guidelines, 115–16
    helpful websites, 131
    learning activities, 129
    light, 115
    materials for multiple intelligences, 127f, 128f, 219, 221
    to motivate listening, 427–28
    portable storage, 124–25
    predictable, organized spaces, 268
    psychosocially safe environments, 211, 213–14
    safety factors, 116
    sample classroom arrangement, 119f
    selection of equipment for creative activities, 125–28, 653–55
    social studies themes, 561–62
    teacher tips, 126, 242, 265, 269
    promoting independence via, 214
    traffic flow, 118, 128, 270
    for working with clay, 327–28
Environmental education, 468–73
Epoxy, 286
Equipment, 116–19, 125–28, 355f, 651–53. *See also* Cleaning and maintenance of materials; Materials
Erikson, Erik, 211, 212f, 222, 399
Evaluation of creative activities, 106
Examples/models, 62
Exercise. *See* Movement
Exhibitions. *See* Displaying children's work
Experiences in the home center, 355f
Exploration, 20
Eye strain, 175

F

Facilitator role of teachers, 81, 105, 265, 354–55
Failure, 20
Families
    communication with, 623
    family celebrations, 625
    family/home programs, 443
    interpreting children's creative work for, 65, 67–68
    of multicultural students, 616–17
    as partners in mathematical learning, 495–96
    teaching about family histories, 626
Fantasy, 59–60, 195
Farmer societies, 275
Feedback
    art DOs with young children, 246
    for creative movement, 379
    for dramatic play, 360, 362
    for evaluation of creative activities, 106, 250–51